Contemporary Financial Management

Third Edition

Contemporary Financial Management

Third Edition

R. Charles Moyer
Texas Tech University

James R. McGuigan
JRM Investments

William J. Kretlow
University of Houston

West Publishing Company
St. Paul
New York
Los Angeles
San Francisco

Complete Teaching Package to Accompany
Contemporary Financial Management, **Third Edition**
Moyer/McGuigan/Kretlow

Authors	INSTRUCTOR'S/SOLUTIONS MANUAL
Authors	TEST BANK
R. Charles Moyer/Jesse E. Reyes/ Phillip M. Sisneros	SOFTWARE WORKSHEET TEMPLATES: *For LOTUS 1-2-3. Sets up the spreadsheet structure allowing students to solve over 60 problems from the text. Free to adopters.*
Authors	TRANSPARENCY ACETATES: *84 significant tables and graphs from the book; 124 Demonstration Problems which parallel problem examples in text.*
MICROTEST and WESTEST	MICROTEST and WESTEST *Computerized testing for microcomputers and mainframes. Available to qualified adopters.*
John D. Stowe, *University of Missouri–Columbia*	STUDY GUIDE *Outline of key ideas, True/False statements, problems, Answer Key, documentation for LOTUS 1-2-3 templates. 25 percent refactored; questions on new material.*

Composition **Science Press**
Cover photo **Courtesy of RepublicBank Corporation, Houston, Texas**

Library of Congress Cataloging-in-Publication Data

Moyer, R. Charles, 1945–
   Contemporary financial management.

   Includes bibliographies and indexes.
   1. Corporations—Finance.   2. Business
enterprises—Finance.   I. McGuigan, James R.
II. Kretlow, William.   III. Title.
HG4026.M68   1987   658.1'5   86-15945

ISBN 0-314-25863-9

R. Charles Moyer is a Professor of Finance and Chairman of the Department of Finance at Texas Tech University, where he has taught finance since 1980. Professor Moyer previously taught at the University of Houston, Lehigh University and the University of New Mexico. Born in Reading, Pennsylvania, he earned his B.A. in economics (*cum laude*) from Howard University, where he was elected to Phi Beta Kappa. He received his M.B.A. and Ph.D. in Business from the University of Pittsburgh. In addition to his teaching career, Professor Moyer has spent a year at the Federal Reserve Bank of Cleveland and a year as a Sears-AACSB Federal Faculty Fellow at the Maritime Administration, U.S. Department of Commerce, serving as a financial and economic analyst. Professor Moyer has taught extensively in executive education programs, including the Stonier Graduate School of Banking. He also is frequently called upon to provide expert testimony in public utility rate cases across the nation.

Professor Moyer has been a productive scholar. In addition to co-authoring *Contemporary Financial Management,* 3rd edition, he has also co-authored *Managerial Economics,* 4th edition (West, 1986), and *Financial Management with Lotus 1-2-3-* (West, 1986). Professor Moyer has published extensively in leading finance and economic journals including *Financial Management, Journal of Financial and Quantitative Analysis, Journal of Finance, Financial Review, Journal of Financial Research, International Journal of Forecasting, Journal of Economics and Business, Journal of Industrial Organization,* and many others. In total he has published over 60 articles. Professor Moyer serves as a member of the Program Committee of the Financial Management Association, Ombudsman for the Financial Management Association and he has served as a director of the Financial Management Association. He is an active reviewer for many finance and economic journals.

Professor Moyer serves as vice-chairman of a local hospital foundation. He enjoys athletics and is particularly active as a runner, golfer, and basketball player.

James R. McGuigan currently owns and operates his own numismatic investment firm. Prior to this activity, he was Associate Professor of Finance and Business Economics in the School of Business Administration at Wayne State University, where he taught in the undergraduate and masters programs for ten years. He has also taught at the University of Pittsburgh and Point Park College.

Dr. McGuigan received his undergraduate degree from Carnegie-Mellon University. His graduate degrees are from the Graduate Schools of Business at the University of Chicago (M.B.A.) and the University of Pittsburgh (Ph.D.).

He has published articles dealing with his research on options in the *Journal of Financial and Quantitative Analysis.* In addition to his interests in financial management, Dr. McGuigan has coauthored books in managerial economics, including *Managerial Economics,* 4th edition (West, 1986), coauthored with R. Charles Moyer.

Dr. McGuigan's other interests include running and traveling.

William J. Kretlow is an Associate Professor of Finance at the University of Houston–University Park. Born and raised in Chicago, he earned his B.S. from the University of Michigan. He received his M.B.A. from the University of Houston and his Ph.D. from Purdue University, where he was a David Ross Fellow. In addition to teaching at UH, he has been a part-time Associate Professor of Economics at Rice University. At UH, he has taught financial management and investments at all levels. He has taught large introductory sections of managerial finance at both Houston and Rice. He currently teaches in both the UH Executive M.B.A. and the Executive Development Programs. In addition, he also teaches at the Stonier Graduate School of Banking of the American Bankers Association. Professor Kretlow has chaired the UH Finance Department.

Professor Kretlow has received several teaching awards, including the University of Houston Teaching Excellence Award and the College of Business Administration Excellence in Teaching Award. He also is a recipient of Rice University's *Magna Cum Laude* Teaching Excellence Award.

In the area of academic research, Professor Kretlow has published approximately fifteen articles and given several papers at professional society meetings. His research has dealt with the capital asset pricing model, dividend policy, bond ratings and financial planning models.

Professor Kretlow's business experience includes a total of five years with Tenneco and Monsanto, and he has advised various small and medium-sized companies on a variety of financial matters. He also has served as an expert witness in a number of financial cases. He is experienced in the valuation of closely held businesses.

Contents

Preface xvii

PART ONE   **INTRODUCTION** 1

1   THE FINANCE FUNCTION: AN OVERVIEW 2

A Financial Dilemma:
Problems in Financial Management 2
Key Chapter Concepts 3
Glossary of New Terms 3
Introduction 4
Goals of the Firm 4
Organization of the Financial
Management Function 8
A Brief History of the Financial
Management Field 10

Financial Management and Other
Disciplines 11
Organization of the Text 13
Summary 15
Focus on Corporate Practice:
Takeovers and the Preservation of
Shareholder Value 16
APPENDIX 1A
Career Opportunities In Finance 19

2   THE CORPORATION AND THE INSTITUTIONAL ENVIRONMENT 30

A Financial Dilemma:
Off-Balance-Sheet Commitments of
U.S. Banks 30
Key Chapter Concepts 31
Glossary of New Terms 32
Introduction 33
Forms of Business Organization 33
The U.S. Financial System:
An Overview 35

Variability of Interest Rates 40
Relationship Between Risk and
Expected Return 43
Summary 45
APPENDIX 2A
Federal Income Taxes 48

PART TWO   **DETERMINANTS OF VALUATION** 55

3   FINANCIAL MATHEMATICS 56

A Financial Dilemma:
Prepaying Your Mortgage Loan 56
Key Chapter Concepts 56
Glossary of New Terms 57
Introduction 58
Interest 58
Compound Interest and Future
Value 61
Present Value 65
Annuities 69
Compounding Periods 77
Effective Rate Calculations 79
Present Value of Uneven Cash
Flows 80

Present Value of Deferred
Annuities 81
Determinants of Discounting and
Compounding Rates 82
Solving the Financial Dilemma 83
Using Calculators and Microcomputers
in Finance 84
Summary 86
Focus on Corporate Practice:
Compounding: Its Boring But a
Wonder 88
APPENDIX 3A
Continuous Compounding and
Discounting 96

4 THE VALUATION OF LONG-TERM SECURITIES 100

A Financial Dilemma:
  Valuation of Gulf Oil Common
  Stock 100
Key Chapter Concepts 100
Glossary of New Terms 101
Introduction 102
Valuation of Assets 102
Bond Valuation 105
Valuation of Preferred Stock 112

Valuation of Common Stock 113
Growth Models for the Valuation of
  Common Stock 118
Summary 122
Focus on Corporate Practice:
  Common Stock Evaluation Techniques
  Used by Wells Fargo Investment
  Advisors 124

5 ANALYSIS OF RISK AND RETURN 130

A Financial Dilemma:
  There Is No Free Lunch—
  J. David & Company 130
Key Chapter Concepts 131
Glossary of New Terms 132
Introduction 133
The Meaning of Risk 133
Probability Distributions 134
Risk as an Increasing Function of
  Time 139
Portfolio Risk Analysis 140
Investment Diversification and
  Risk 141

Risk Reduction Through
  Diversification 147
Security Market Line (SML) 149
Beta: A Measure of Security Risk 151
Security Market Line and Beta 154
Uses of the CAPM and Portfolio Risk
  Concepts 156
Assumptions and Limitations of the
  CAPM 157
Other Dimensions of Risk 158
Summary 159

PART THREE   **FINANCIAL ANALYSIS** 165

6 THE ANALYSIS OF FINANCIAL STATEMENTS 166

A Financial Dilemma:
  Banking on Accounting
  Gimmickry 166
Key Chapter Concepts 167
Glossary of New Terms 168
Introduction 169
Uses of Financial Analysis 169
Interpreting Financial Ratios 169
Basic Classifications of Financial
  Ratios 170
Summary of Financial Ratio
  Analysis 186
Trend Analysis 186
Return on Investment 188

Return on Stockholders' Equity 190
Sources of Comparative Financial
  Data 191
A Word of Caution about Financial
  Ratio Analysis 194
Earnings and Balance Sheet Quality
  and Financial Analysis 195
Using Financial Ratios to Forecast
  Future Financial Performance 197
Inflation and Financial Statement
  Analysis 198
Summary 202
Focus on Corporate Practice:
  Union Carbide's Paper Boom 204

7 THE ANALYSIS OF OPERATING AND FINANCIAL LEVERAGE 214

A Financial Dilemma:
  Eastern Airlines versus Delta
  Airlines 214
Key Chapter Concepts 215
Glossary of New Terms 216
Introduction 217
Leverage and the Income
  Statement 217

Breakeven Analysis 219
Operating Leverage and Business
  Risk 228
Financial Leverage and Financial
  Risk 231
Combined Leverage and Overall
  Risk 236
Summary 239

8   FINANCIAL PLANNING 246

A Financial Dilemma:
  Financial Turnaround at International
  Harvester 246
Key Chapter Concepts 247
Glossary of New Terms 247
Introduction 248
Financial Forecasting 248
An Overview of Budgeting 254
Funds Flow Analysis 259

Computerized Financial Planning
  Models 263
Summary 264
Focus on Corporate Practice:
  Long-Range Planning at Tennessee
  Gas Transmission—A Tenneco
  Company 266
An Integrative Case Problem:
  Financial Analysis and Control 271

PART FOUR   THE CAPITAL INVESTMENT DECISION 275

9   CAPITAL BUDGETING AND CASH FLOW ANALYSIS 276

A Financial Dilemma:
  Lockheed's L-1011 Tri-Star Jet
  Stalls 276
Key Chapter Concepts 277
Glossary of New Terms 278
Introduction 279
Key Terms and Concepts in Capital
  Budgeting 280
Basic Framework for Capital
  Budgeting 281
Generating Capital Investment Project
  Proposals 283
Principles of Estimating Cash
  Flows 285

Net Investment (NINV) 287
Net Cash Flows 288
Asset Expansion Projects 290
Asset Replacement Decisions 292
Problems in Cash Flow Estimation 301
Summary 302
Focus on Corporate Practice:
  The Misuse of a Sound Investment
  Tool 304
APPENDIX 9A
  Alternative Depreciation Methods 312

10   CAPITAL BUDGETING DECISION CRITERIA 316

A Financial Dilemma:
  Braniff International's Crash
  Landing 316
Key Chapter Concepts 316
Glossary of New Terms 317
Introduction 318
Evaluating Alternatives: Decision
  Models 318
Capital Rationing and the Capital
  Budgeting Decision 330
Reviewing and Postauditing an
  Accepted Project 333
A Comprehensive Example of Capital

Budgeting: Opening a New Bank
  Branch 334
Inflation and Capital Expenditures 338
Summary 339
Focus on Corporate Practice:
  Capital Budgeting Methods Used by
  Multinational Firms 341
An Integrative Case Problem:
  Capital Budgeting 348
APPENDIX 10A
  Mutually Exclusive Investments Having
  Unequal Lives 350

11   CAPITAL BUDGETING AND RISK 354

A Financial Dilemma:
  Washington Public Power Supply
  System 354
Key Chapter Concepts 355
Glossary of New Terms 355
Introduction 356
Total Project Risk Versus Portfolio
  Risk 356
Adjusting for Total Project Risk 357
Adjusting for Beta Risk in Capital
  Budgeting 367

Divisional Costs of Capital 369
Summary 370
Focus on Corporate Practice:
  Developing and Applying Risk-Adjusted
  Discount Rates in a Diversified
  Company 372
An Integrative Case Problem:
  Capital Budgeting and Risk
  Analysis 379

PART FIVE   **THE COST OF CAPITAL, CAPITAL STRUCTURE, AND DIVIDEND POLICY** 381

12   THE COST OF CAPITAL 382

A Financial Dilemma:
   Cost of Equity Capital for the Public
   Service Company of New Mexico 382
Key Chapter Concepts 383
Glossary of New Terms 383
Introduction 384
Nature of Risk Premiums 384
Relative Costs of Capital 386
Computing the Component Costs of
   Capital 387
Weighted Cost of Capital 399
Determining the Optimal Capital
   Budget 404

The Cost of Depreciation-Generated
   Funds 405
Summary 406
Focus on Corporate Practice:
   Managing Interest Rate Risk with
   Options on Eurodollar Futures 408
An Integrative Case Problem:
   Cost of Capital 415
APPENDIX 12A
   Introduction to Financial Futures 418

13   THE CAPITAL STRUCTURE DECISION 424

A Financial Dilemma:
   Coors versus Anheuser-Busch 424
Key Chapter Concepts 425
Glossary of New Terms 425
Introduction 426
Theoretical Perspectives on Capital
   Structure and Firm Valuation 427
Capital Structure Decisions Using
   EBIT-EPS Analysis 436

Financial Leverage and Stock
   Prices 438
Additional Cost of Capital and Capital
   Structure Considerations 439
Determining an Optimal Capital
   Structure: An Integrative
   Approach 441
Summary 443

14   DIVIDEND POLICY 450

A Financial Dilemma:
   Middle South Utilities Suspends its
   Dividend 450
Key Chapter Concepts 451
Glossary of New Terms 451
Introduction 452
Determinants of Dividend Policy 453
Dividend Policy and Firm Value 457
Dividend Policies 459

How Dividends are Paid 464
Stock Dividends 466
Stock Splits 468
Share Repurchases As Dividend
   Decisions 468
Summary 470
Focus on Corporate Practice:
   Stock Splits and Stock Dividends 472

PART SIX   **SOURCES OF INTERMEDIATE- AND LONG-TERM FUNDS** 481

15   TERM LOANS AND LEASES 482

A Financial Dilemma:
   Easy Money to a Hoodlum 482
Key Chapter Concepts 482
Glossary of New Terms 483
Introduction to Term Loans 484
Repayment Provisions 484
Interest Costs 486
Compensating Balances 486
Equity Participations 486
Security Provisions and Protective
   Covenants 487
Suppliers of Term Loans 489
Equipment Loans 491
Introduction to Leasing 492
Types of Leases 493

Determining the Lease Payments: The
   Lessor's Perspective 496
Tax Status of True Leases 498
Leases and Accounting Practices 499
Advantages and Disadvantages of
   Leasing 501
The Lease-Buy Analysis: The Lessee's
   Perspective 502
Summary 504
Focus on Corporate Practice:
   Leveraged Lease Financing of a
   Portion of a Nuclear Power Plant 507
An Integrative Case Problem:
   Lease and Term Loan Analysis 513

16 LONG-TERM DEBT, PREFERRED STOCK, AND COMMON STOCK 516

A Financial Dilemma:
  Corporate Restructuring Actions and
  Bond Ratings 516
Key Chapter Concepts 517
Glossary of New Terms 517
Introduction 519
Long-term Debt 519
Preferred Stock 529
Common Stock 533

Selected Capital Market Topics 540
Role of the Investment Banker 544
Summary 549
Focus on Corporate Practice:
  Standard and Poor's Bond-Rating
  Process 553
APPENDIX 16A
  Bond Refunding, Stockholder Voting
  Rights, and Rights Offerings 560

17 OPTIONS, CONVERTIBLE SECURITIES, AND WARRANTS 568

A Financial Dilemma:
  Expanded Use of Options,
  Convertibles, and Warrants in the
  1980s 568
Key Chapter Concepts 569
Glossary of New Terms 569
Introduction 570

Options 570
Convertible Securites 575
Warrants 580
Accounting for Convertible Securities
  and Warrants 584
Summary 584

PART SEVEN
THE MANAGEMENT OF WORKING CAPITAL 591

18 WORKING CAPITAL MANAGEMENT: AN OVERVIEW 592

A Financial Dilemma:
  Going Broke While Making a
  Profit 592
Key Chapter Concepts 593
Glossary of New Terms 593
Introduction 594
Importance of Working Capital 594
Levels of Working Capital
  Investment 597

Proportions of Short-term and
  Long-term Debt 600
Overall Working Capital
  Management 605
Summary 607
APPENDIX 18A
  The Term Structure of Interest
  Rates 614

19 THE MANAGEMENT OF CASH AND MARKETABLE SECURITIES 618

A Financial Dilemma:
  E.F. Hutton's Interest-Free
  "Loans" 618
Key Chapter Concepts 619
Glossary of New Terms 619
Introduction 621
Liquid Asset Balance 621

Controlling the Collection and
  Disbursement of Cash 626
Investing in Marketable Securities 633
Summary 639
Focus on Corporate Practice:
  Multilateral Netting System 640

20 THE MANAGEMENT OF ACCOUNTS RECEIVABLE 646

A Financial Dilemma:
  Examples of Credit Management
  Practices 646
Key Chapter Concepts 647
Glossary of New Terms 647
Introduction 648
Establishing Credit and Collection
  Policies 648

Evaluating Individual Credit
  Applicants 658
Summary 663
Focus on Corporate Practice:
  Trade Credit Management at
  Hiram-Walker 665

21 INVENTORY MANAGEMENT 674

A Financial Dilemma:
  **Apple Computer's Inventory
  Decisions** 674
Key Chapter Concepts 674
Glossary of New Terms 675
Introduction 676

Types and Functions of
  Inventories 676
Inventory Related Costs 677
Inventory Control Models 679
Summary 688

22 OBTAINING SHORT TERM FUNDS 694

A Financial Dilemma:
  Texaco's Financial Difficulties 694
Key Chapter Concepts 694
Glossary of New Terms 695
Introduction 696
Trade Credit 697
Accrued Expenses and Deferred
  Income 700
Short-term Bank Credit 701

Commercial Paper 706
Accounts Receivable Loans 707
Inventory Loans 710
Summary 713
Focus on Corporate Practice:
  Corporate Credit Analysis 715
An Integrative Case Problem:
  Working Capital Management 722

PART EIGHT SELECTED TOPICS IN CONTEMPORARY FINANCIAL MANAGEMENT 727

---

23 MERGERS AND ACQUISITIONS 728

A Financial Dilemma:
  The Union Carbide-GAF Affair 728
Key Chapter Concepts 729
Glossary of New Terms 729
Introduction 730
Merger Terminology 730
Types of Mergers 732
Reasons for Mergers 732

Valuation of Merger Candidates 733
Analysis of a Merger 734
Leveraged Buyouts 737
Accounting Aspects of Mergers 740
Tax Aspects of Mergers 741
Summary 742
An Integrative Case Problem:
  Mergers and Acquisitions 746

24 BUSINESS FAILURE 750

A Financial Dilemma:
  **Continental Airlines and the
  Bankruptcy Laws** 750
Key Chapter Concepts 750
Glossary of New Terms 751
Introduction 752
Definitions of Business Failure 752
Business Failure Trends 752

Causes of Business Failure 754
Alternatives for Failing
  Businesses 755
Summary 761
Focus on Corporate Practice:
  **Bankers Who Step in if Loans Go Bad
  Reveal Lenders' Other Face** 763

25 INTERNATIONAL FINANCIAL MANAGEMENT 770

A Financial Dilemma:
  **Hercules Issuance of Notes
  Denominated in European Currency
  Units** 770
Key Chapter Concepts 771
Glossary of New Terms 771

Introduction 772
Foreign Currencies and Exchange
  Rates 772
Financing Foreign Trade and
  Investments 780
Summary 781

APPENDIX A MAJOR 1986 FEDERAL INCOME TAX REFORM PROVISIONS 785

Introduction 785

Corporate Income Taxes 785

Individual Income Taxes 787

REFERENCE MATERIALS R-1

TABLES

**Table I: Compound Value Interest Factor
    (CVIF)** R-2
**Table II: Present Value Interest Factor
    (PVIF)** R-4
**Table III: Compound Sum of an Annuity
    Interest Factor (CVIFA)** R-6
**Table IV: Present Value of an Annuity
    Interest Factor (PVIFA)** R-8
Table V: Normal Distribution R-10

Index to Glossary Terms R-11
Subject Index R-15
*Check Answers to Selected
    Problems* R-23

Preface

The financial management field has witnessed a number of significant changes during the 1970s and 1980s. Widely fluctuating rates of inflation have caused the firm's cost of funds (capital) to vary substantially. This, in turn, has forced firms to be more careful in the allocation of their resources. Also, corporate and other financial practioners are increasingly employing newer financial management techniques and sophisticated computer resources to aid in their decision making. New financial instruments have been developed to help cope with this environment of uncertainty. At the same time, financial researchers have been making important theoretical strides. *Contemporary Financial Management,* 3rd edition, incorporates these changes into a text designed primarily for an introductory course in financial management. The book also will be useful for management development programs and as a reference aid to practicing finance professionals.

Although we recognize that students will enter this course with a wide variety of backgrounds in mathematics, economics, accounting, and statistics, the only presumption we make regarding prior preparation is that all students will have had at least one course in accounting.

Distinctive Features

Many financial management texts are well written and provide adequate coverage of the important topics in financial management. In writing this text, we, too, were concerned with providing a complete and well-written introduction to the field of financial management. In addition, we have created a text that is a unique improvement over current texts in three areas: organizational design, pedagogical aids to learning, and ancillary materials.

Organizational Design

Contemporary Financial Management (*CFM*) is organized around the objective of maximizing the value of the firm for its shareholders. This objective is introduced early in the book, and each major financial decision is linked to the impact it has on the value of the firm.

CFM also emphasizes the importance of risk-return tradeoffs, which must be made as a part of most financial decisions. The analysis of risk-return relationships is developed early in the book (Chapter 5) and is illustrated and emphasized throughout the text.

Other distinctive content features include the following:

1. **Extensive treatment of working capital management** For many small and medium-sized companies, the management of working capital can present more challenges than any other area of financial management. A thorough and up-to-date five-chapter section on working capital management is included.

2. **Emphasis on the impact of inflation** During the 1970s and 1980s, finance practitioners were forced to learn how to operate in an inflationary environment. Therefore, this text contains frequent discussions on the impact of inflation.

3. **Introductory coverage of investment topics** Whether they take a separate investments course or not, students are interested in and need to have an understanding of investment topics. Therefore, sections on understanding the financial pages, the operation of security markets, financial futures, and options are included.

4. **Attention to problems of international financial management** In an economy that is increasingly affected by international trade, it is important that finance students be aware of the most important dimensions of international finance. The inclusion of this material (primarily in Chapter 25) is consistent with the emphasis of the business school accrediting group (AACSB) on internationalizing the business school curriculum.

5. **Extensive development of the cash flow estimation process in capital budgeting** Perhaps the most important step in the capital budgeting process is the estimation of cash flows for potential projects. *CFM* devotes an entire chapter to this area, with a detailed discussion of the impact of recent tax law changes that affect the capital budgeting decision.

6. **Introduction to new financial instruments** Financial futures contracts, options, and options on futures contracts have become increasingly important to the contemporary financial manager. These topics are introduced to the student in an applied context which illustrates their value to the financial manager.

Pedagogical Aids

CFM has been carefully designed to assist the student in learning and to stimulate student interests. Distinctive pedagogical features include:

1. **Financial Dilemmas** Each chapter begins with an illustration of a financial management problem faced by a firm or individual. These exciting lead-ins come from real-firm situations, including Gulf Oil, J. David & Company, Eastern Airlines, Apple Computer, E. F. Hutton, Lockheed, Coors, Digital Equipment, Braniff International, and Navistar. These examples tend to focus on financial problems in the topic area of the chapter and highlight the importance of learning sound financial management principles. The Financial Dilemmas have been extensively revised and updated from the second edition, including the addition of many new examples.

2. **Focus On Corporate Practice examples** Throughout the text we have included sections detailing how specific firms approach particular financial management problems. Many of these have been written by senior financial executives. In Chapter 1, for example, T. Boone Pickens of Mesa Petroleum discusses the conflict of goals between managers and shareholders. Other equally exciting examples are included throughout the book. These examples are designed to bridge the gap between textbook theory and actual practice. They show the book's readers that the issues, tools, and techniques discussed in *CFM* are actively being discussed and used in day-to-day financial decision making. This edition updates many of the Focus on Corporate Practice examples from the second edition and adds six new examples.

3. **Integrative Case Problems** Integrative minicases are included throughout the book. These cases illustrate and apply the most important concepts of the preceding chapters. These minicases have been pretested and found to be an extremely useful tool to help the reader assimilate the material in the chapters. They have been revised from the second edition to retain their classroom integrity with some new cases added to replace older ones.

4. **Key Chapter Concepts** Each chapter opens with a detailed outline of the major points contained in the chapter. These Key Chapter Concepts outlines

greatly enhance student learning by providing a summary overview of the chapter contents before the student heads into the detailed discussion in the chapter. This is a new feature in the third edition of CFM.

5. **Chapter Glossaries** Each chapter contains a glossary of important new terms that are discussed in the chapter. The placement of the glossary at the beginning of each chapter insures that students will not be frustrated by encountering concepts before they have been defined. When studying and reviewing a chapter, a student has ready access to the definitions of important terms from the chapter. An index to the glossary is provided at the end of the text.

6. **Extensive use of examples** A large number of examples to illustrate important concepts and techniques is contained in each chapter. The majority of the examples come from actual firm situations. All examples have been revised and updated for this new edition, and will help students see how financial principles are used in everyday business practice.

7. **Part Openers** Each major section of the book opens with a brief discussion of the material contained in the following chapters. The tie of this material to the objective of shareholder wealth maximization is illustrated in a schematic diagram appearing on each part opener.

8. **Problems and Discussion Questions** Each chapter includes a complete set of problems and questions keyed to the most important issues and techniques in that chapter. Because we feel that end-of-chapter problems are an extremely important teaching and learning device, this text has one of the largest and varied end-of-chapter problem sets available. Most concepts are illustrated with more than one problem. Answers to selected end-of-chapter problems are provided at the end of the book. The end-of-chapter questions and problems have been increased in number from the second edition and many old problems have been modified in order to retain their classroom integrity.

9. **End-of-Chapter References** A list of selected references that cover major pieces of theoretical and applications-oriented literature in the area is included in each chapter. These references form a basis for extended reading or research by students. They have been updated to include the results of much recent financial research.

10. A laminated card containing abbreviated interest tables is included in each book for test purposes.

11. **Ancillary Materials** A complete set of ancillary materials is available to adopters to supplement the text, including the following:

   - An Instructor's Manual containing solutions to the end-of-chapter questions and problems and tips for teaching with the Lotus 1-2-3 templates (see below).
   - A Test Bank containing over 1,000 multiple choice questions and additional problems.
   - MicroTest diskette of the Test Bank is available in order to simplify the preparation of quizzes and exams.
   - A set of 84 Transparency Acetates of the most important tables and graphs.
   - A set of 124 Demonstration Problem Acetates. The problems parallel the major examples developed in the text.
   - Lotus 1-2-3 Templates designed to solve a wide variety of financial management problems. Problems in the text which can be solved using these

templates are indicated with a small diskette logo next to the problem. These templates are based on the most popular spreadsheet program used in business and academic institutions—Lotus 1-2-3. The templates require *absolutely no prior knowledge of Lotus 1-2-3*. All input and instructions are menu driven in a clear, concise, command menu created by the authors. All of the templates are designed so that they can be used to solve actual business financial analysis problems, not just simplified textbook examples. For example, the capital budgeting template uses the powerful macro features of Lotus 1-2-3 to "build" the correct-sized worksheet to solve any capital budgeting problem. The Study Guide contains the documentation to accompany these templates.

In addition, a Study Guide written by Professor John D. Stowe of the University of Missouri–Columbia, is available for all students. The Study Guide contains detailed chapter outlines, solved true-false questions, and a large number of solved numerical problems. Documentation to accompany the Lotus 1-2-3 templates is also included in the Study Guide.

Major Changes in this Edition

This edition has been extensively updated and revised along the lines suggested by second edition users and reviewers. The major changes in this edition are listed below.

1. Key Chapter Concepts, summary outlines of the major points covered in each chapter, have been added after the opening Financial Dilemma of every chapter.

2. A series of Lotus 1-2-3 templates which are useful for solving many financial management problems are available to adopters for use with the book.

3. The "goals of the firm" discussion in Chapter 1 has been expanded and now includes a discussion of agency problems which arise when ownership and control is separated in a firm.

4. The material dealing with the organization of the financial management function in a firm has been developed more fully to highlight the roles played by various financial management specialists in a firm.

5. A new appendix (1A) has been added which discusses 25 different career opportunities in finance.

6. The material in Chapter 2 dealing with financial intermediaries now includes a more complete discussion of the role of thrift institutions, investment companies, pension funds, insurance companies and finance companies. The impact financial deregulation has had on the practice of financial management is also discussed.

7. Appendix 2A has been updated to reflect the latest tax law changes. In addition, an appendix has been added at the end of the book summarizing the major 1986 income tax reform provisions.

8. The material dealing with annuity due calculations has been integrated with the ordinary annuity discussion in Chapter 3. A new section dealing with the valuation of perpetuities is now part of Chapter 3. Also new to Chapter 3 is a section dealing with effective rate calculations, a section dealing with the present value of deferred annuities, and a section which discusses the relative value of calculators and microcomputers as problem solving tools in finance.

9. New Appendix 3A provides a complete discussion of continuous compounding and discounting.

10. The yield-to-maturity calculations presented in Chapter 4 have been expanded and now include a discussion of deep discount and zero-coupon bonds. New graphics have been added to aid understanding of above-normal growth dividend valuation models.

11. New graphics and examples have been added to Chapter 5 to develop more fully the concept of risk in a portfolio context.

12. The financial analysis material in Chapter 6 now includes a discussion of the price-to-earnings ratio and the market-to-book ratio. An extensive new section dealing with an analysis of earnings quality and balance sheet quality has been added to this chapter.

13. Chapter 7 now includes sections dealing with risk assessment in the context of breakeven analysis and financial leverage analysis.

14. The material on financial planning in Chapter 8 has been extensively revised to place greater emphasis on pro-forma analysis and financial forecasting tools.

15. Chapter 9 has been reorganized and modified to highlight the distinction between asset replacement investments and asset expansion investments. Opportunity cost concepts and sunk cost concepts have been developed in the revised chapter.

16. Chapters 11 and 12 have been updated to reflect the results of recent research relating to project post-audits.

17. Chapter 12 contains a new section dealing with issues in implementing dividend valuation models to determine a firm's cost of equity capital. Recent research dealing with earnings growth rate forecasting is cited.

18. Chapter 13 has been reorganized to develop more clearly the concept of an optimal capital structure. Contributions in the bankruptcy cost literature and agency cost literature are recognized as having a major impact on the determination of a firm's capital structure.

19. A discussion of dividend reinvestment plans has been added to Chapter 14.

20. The section dealing with the determination of lease payments from the perspective of the lessor has been developed on an after-tax basis. The lease-buy analysis of Chapter 15 now uses a "net advantage to leasing model" which reflects the capital structure differences between the two financing alternatives.

21. Put bonds, floating rate bonds, deep discount bonds, adjustable rate preferred stock, shelf registrations, share repurchases, and interest rate swaps are now discussed in Chapter 16.

22. The determinants of the value of a financial option are discussed in a complete yet accessible manner in Chapter 17, prior to a consideration of warrants and convertible securities.

23. The use of Eurodollar deposits, money market preferred stocks, and electronic depository transfer checks are now covered in Chapter 19.

24. "ABC inventory classification and management models" and "just-in-time inventory models" have been added to Chapter 21.

25. An exchange ratio model of analyzing a potential merger has been added to Chapter 23. Leveraged buyouts are considered in detail in this chapter.

26. Recent trends in the failure and reorganization of large firms have been included in Chapter 24.

27. The concept of "interest rate parity" is now included in Chapter 25. Chapter 25 also considers the effects of exchange rate levels on business conditions and practices. A discussion of Eurobond financing has been added to this chapter.

Many of these changes, and the hundreds of other small changes and updating of material from the second edition, were based on the excellent suggestions of second edition users. We welcome comments and suggestions from users of this third edition.

Organization and Intended Use

CFM is organized into eight major parts. Part 1 defines the finance function and discusses the institutional environment facing financial decision makers. Part 2 develops the theory of valuation, risk-return analysis, and the tools of financial mathematics. Part 3 consists of three chapters that deal with financial analysis. Part 4 presents the capital investment decision, emphasizing both the theoretical and the practical aspects of capital budgeting. Part 5 deals with the determinants of an optimal capital structure, the cost of capital, and the firm's dividend policy. Part 6 describes the sources of intermediate- and long-term funds. Part 7 consists of a five-chapter sequence covering the important area of working capital management. Finally, Part 8 includes chapters dealing with mergers, bankruptcy, and international financial management.

Those instructors who wish to cover topics in an order other than that provided in the text will find it quite easy to make adjustments. For example, many instructors prefer to cover working capital management early in the course. They should find no difficulty in moving all or a portion of Chapters 18 through 22 to a position following Chapters 3, 4, or 5. Similarly, some instructors may prefer to cover the area of financial analysis later in the course. Accordingly, Chapters 6 through 8 can be moved easily to another location that is more consistent with the instructor's teaching style and objectives.

This book is designed for use in a typical 3-semester hour (or the equivalent in the quarter system) course in financial management. Typically, within the constraints of this time limit, it is often not possible to fully cover the material in Chapters 23 through 25. This material may be left for a second financial management course—often with a case orientation. Also, some instructors may wish to defer the dividend policy chapter (Chapter 14), the capital structure chapter (Chapter 13), and/or the leasing material in Chapter 15 until a later course. Finally, some schools cover inventory policy in a production (or similar) course. In these cases, Chapter 21 either can be omitted or covered only briefly.

Acknowledgments

The authors with to acknowledge the helpful comments provided by many of our first and second edition users. We are particularly grateful for the careful reviews and suggestions made by the following individuals:

Richard Bauer	Rudolph D'Souza	Richard Gendreau
Carl Beidleman	Bill Dukes	Jim Gentry
Thomas Berry	Fred Ebeid	Michael Gombola
Don Bowlin	John W. Ellis	Jim Greenleaf
Dorothy Cassetta	Keith W. Fairchild	Kamal Haddad
Robert Chatfield	Edward Farragher	Thomas Hamilton
David Cox	Mike Ferri	Charles Harper
John Crockett	Jane Finley	Delbert Hastings

Pat Hays
Shantaram P. Hedge
Robert Hehre
George Hettenhouse
L. Dean Hiebert
K. P. Hill
Shalom Hochman
Thomas Howe
Pearson Hunt
Keith B. Johnson
Charles P. Jones
Kee Kim
Thomas Klaasen
Donita Koval
Timothy Koch
Keith Laycock
Joseph J. Levitzky
David Lindsley

Charles Linke
Mike Lockett
Wayne M. Marr
Z. Lew Melynk
Richard Meyer
Edward M. Miller
Robert A. Olsen
Coleen G. Pantalone
Susan M. Phillips
Mario Picconi
Alwyn du Plessis
Ralph Pope
Dwight Porter
Robert Porter
Kelly Price
Dennis Proffitt
Ramesh Rao
William J. Regan

Jesse Reyes
Charles T. Rini
Richard Sapp
Bernard A. Shinkel
Mark Shrader
Phil Sisneros
Rolf K. Tedefalk
Richard J. Teweles
Niranjan Tripathy
Anthony M. Tuberose
George Ulseth
David Upton
Howard E. Van Anken
John M. Wachowicz, Jr.
Charlie Wade
J. Daniel Williams
Richard Zock
J. Kenton Zumwalt

In addition, we wish to acknowledge the assistance of the many business professionals who have reviewed various aspects of the text material and/or supplied us with the material for our "Financial Dilemma" and "Focus on Corporate Practice" examples:

Gordon B. Bonfield
Richard H. Brock
Roy V. Campbell
Norman Dmuchowski
Stephen H. Grace
Samuel C. Hadaway
R. Lee Haney
Raymond A. Hay
Lawrence Ingrassia

Ira G. Kawaller
Carl J. Lange
Martin H. Lange
Lewis Lehr
C. Londa
Paul MacAvoy
Frank Mastrapasqua
John H. Maxheim
Thomas R. Mongan

Robert B. Morris III
T. Boone Pickens
Jack S. Rader
M. W. Ramsey
William J. Regan
Albert J. Robison
Julie Salamon
Kenneth Schwartz
Terry J. Winders

We are also indebted to Wayne State University, the University of Houston, Lehigh University, the University of New Mexico, and Texas Tech University for the considerable support they provided. We thank Betty Heisser, Pat Burns and Margaret Williams for their typing assistance. We also owe thanks to our fellow faculty members at these universities for the encouragement and assistance they provided on a continuing basis during the preparation of the manuscript.

Finally, we wish to express our thanks to the members of the West Publishing Company staff. We are particularly appreciative of the total project support provided by Ken Zeigler and the marketing support provided by Scott Covey. Tad Bornhoft, our production edition, did a superb job of supervising the production of a most attractive and technically precise text. Tad was a pleasure to work with. Most of all we would like to thank our editor, Mary Schiller, who has provided a continual flow of excellent ideas for this project. Her high performance standards and in-depth knowledge of publishing have been invaluable in the development of this text.

Contemporary Financial Management

Third Edition

PART ONE

INTRODUCTION

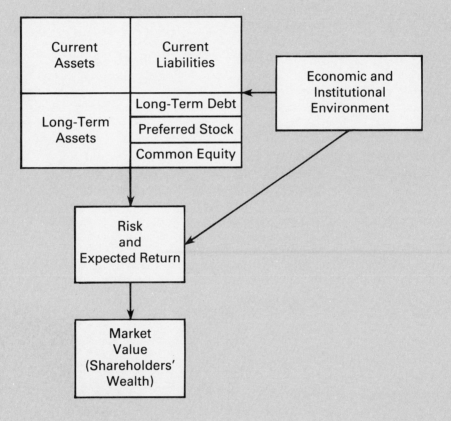

Part I of the text provides an overview introduction to the field of financial management. Chapter 1 discusses the relationship between finance and other business disciplines, the organization of the financial management function in a firm, and the history of the financial management field. This chapter also introduces the overall objective of the firm—shareholder wealth maximization. Appendix 1A details career opportunities in finance. Chapter 2 looks at the relationship between the firm and the economic/institutional environment. Economic and institutional factors have a major impact on the expected returns and the risk of these returns generated by the firm. Risk and expected return are two of the key determinants of the value of a firm and its securities. Appendix 2A highlights some aspects of Federal income tax law that are relevant to many financial management decisions.

1

THE FINANCE FUNCTION: AN OVERVIEW

A Financial Dilemma

Problems in Financial Management

- In 1983 Chevron acquired Gulf Oil for $80 a share, more than twice what the Gulf Oil stock was selling for prior to the takeover battle.
- During the early 1980s investors who committed funds to J. David & Company in hopes of earning very high returns wound up losing a total of $150 million, once again confirming the old financial adage that high returns normally can only be earned by assuming high risks.
- In 1985 Middle South Utilities, with annual revenues of $3 billion, omitted its quarterly dividend payment because of severe cash flow problems.
- During the 1970s Lockhead's stock price dropped from $73 to $3 a share partly as a result of cost overruns in some of its military projects and as a result of the costs of developing its L-1011 wide-bodied commercial jet.
- In 1985 Hercules, Inc., a U.S. chemicals manufacturer, issued debt denominated in European Currency Units instead of U.S. dollars in order to hedge its European assets.
- In 1982 Braniff Airlines crash landed in financial failure, shortly after embarking on an aggressive expansion program.
- In October 1979 underwriters of IBM's $1 billion debt issue lost an estimated $15 million on the issue of which they had earlier fought hard to get control.

Each of these situations was the direct result of financial decision making. Financial management is not an abstract field of study. Financial decisions made within various enterprises—whether large or small; international, national, or local; profit seeking or not for profit—help to determine the kinds of products and services we consume, their price, availability, and quality. In short, financial decision making has results that are felt throughout our entire economy.

The situations described above pose a number of questions in financial management which are examined in this text.

Key Chapter Concepts

1. Shareholder wealth is defined as the present value of the expected future returns to the owners of the firm. It is measured by the market value of the shareholders' common stock holdings.
2. The primary normative goal of the firm is the maximization of shareholder wealth.
3. The finance function within a large firm is usually headed by a (senior) vice-president or chief financial officer.
   a. Financial management responsibilities are often divided between the controller and treasurer.
   b. The controller normally has responsibility for all accounting related activities.
   c. The treasurer is normally concerned with the acquisition, custody, and expenditure of funds.
4. Other important topics include:
   a. Profit maximization goal
   b. Social responsibility goals
   c. Agency relationships
   d. History of the financial management field
   e. Relation of financial management to other academic disciplines
   f. Organization of the text

Glossary of New Terms

Agency relationships occur when one or more individuals (principals) hire another individual (agent) to perform a service on behalf of the principals. Agency relationships often lead to agency problems and agency costs. One of the most important agency relationships in finance is between stockholders (owners) and managers.

Present value The current value of some future payment or stream of payments, evaluated at an appropriate discount rate.

Shareholder wealth Present value of the expected future returns to the owners (that is, shareholders) of the firm. It is measured by the market value of the shareholders' common stock holdings.

Introduction

T he field of financial management is an exciting and challenging one. Students who choose to major in finance will find a wide range of rewarding job opportunities open in the fields of corporate financial management, investment analysis and management, banking, real estate, insurance, and the public sector—to name only a few broad areas of potential career opportunities. (Career opportunities in finance are examined in the appendix to this chapter.) Students who do not choose to major in finance still will be confronted with important financial decisions—both in their career and in their personal life—on a nearly daily basis.

The importance and relevance of the skills that can be learned in this finance course are apparent from the results of a recent survey of graduates of business schools. *By a wide margin, these executives indicated that the courses taken in financial management were the most useful courses in their business school curriculum.*[1]

Any business—whether large or small, profit seeking or not for profit—is a financial concern, and as such its success or failure depends in a large part on the quality of its financial decisions. Thus, financial management is an exciting area of business administration. Nearly every key decision made by a firm's managers has important financial implications, and managers daily face questions like the following:

- Will a particular investment be profitable?
- Where will the funds come from to finance the investment?
- Does the firm have adequate cash or access to cash—through bank borrowing agreements, for example—to meet its daily operating needs?
- Which customers should be offered credit and how much should they be offered?
- How much inventory should be held?
- Is a merger or acquisition advisable?
- How should profits be used or distributed? That is, what is the optimal dividend policy?
- In trying to arrive at the best financial management decisions, how should risk and return be balanced?

This text presents an introduction to the theory, institutional background, and analytical tools essential for proper decision making in these and related areas.

The remaining sections of this chapter discuss the goals of the firm, organization of the financial management function, history of the financial management field, relationship between financial management and other academic disciplines, and organization of the text.

Goals of the Firm

Financial decision making requires an understanding of the goal(s) of the firm. What objective(s) *should* guide business decision making? That is, what *should* management try to achieve for the owners of the firm? The

---

[1] John A. Pollock, J.R. Bartol, B.C. Sherony, and G.R. Carnaham, "Executives' Perceptions of Future MBA Programs." *Collegiate News and Views* (Spring 1983): 23–25.

generally accepted normative goal that management should pursue is the maximization of the value of the firm to the owners, that is, *shareholder wealth.* Before defining shareholder wealth more precisely later in this section, let us first consider the normative goal of profit maximization.

Profit Maximization

It is easy to assume that profit maximization is a primary objective of financial management. After all, it is the predominant objective of microeconomic models, and the marginal decision-making rules implied by this objective can be very useful to the financial manager in handling certain specific problems. Unfortunately, however, this objective has a number of limitations.

First, the standard microeconomic model of profit maximization is *static;* that is, it lacks a time dimension. Specifically, the profit maximization objective provides no explicit basis for comparing long-term and short-term profits. Major decisions made by financial managers, however, *must* reflect the time dimension. For example, capital expenditure decisions, which are central to the finance function, have a long-term impact on the performance of the firm. Financial managers must constantly make tradeoffs between short-run and long-run profits in conjunction with these long-term decisions.

The second limitation has to do with the definition of profits. Should a firm attempt to maximize the *dollar amount* of profits or the *rate* of profit? If the latter is chosen, what specific rate should be emphasized— profit in relation to sales, total assets, or shareholders' equity? What measure of profits should be used—the readily available measure of accounting profits or the economist's broader definition of profits, which includes (among other things) the opportunity cost of funds committed by the owners of an enterprise? (This definition is an important concept, but it is very difficult to calculate.)

The third problem associated with this objective is that it provides no real way for the financial manager to consider the risk associated with alternative decisions. For example, two projects generating identical future expected revenues and requiring identical outlays may be vastly different with respect to their *degree of risk.* The financial manager should attempt to incorporate risk analysis in resource allocation decisions where the outcomes are not known with certainty.

The profit-maximization model of firm behavior has produced a wide range of valuable insights into the efficient allocation of economic (and financial) resources. In spite of these successes, the shortcomings of this goal have lead to the development of the more comprehensive normative goal of shareholder wealth maximization.

Shareholder Wealth Maximization

The shareholder wealth maximization goal states that management *should* seek to maximize the *present value* of the *expected future returns* to the owners (that is, shareholders) of the firm. These returns can take the form of periodic dividend payments or proceeds from the sale of the stock. Present value is defined as the value today of some future payment or stream of payments, evaluated at an appropriate discount rate. It takes into account the returns that are available from alternative investment opportunities during a specific (future) time period.

Shareholder wealth is measured by the market value of the shareholders' common stock holdings. *Market value* is defined as the price at which the stock trades in the marketplace, such as on the New York Stock Exchange. Thus, total shareholder wealth equals the number of shares outstanding times the market price per share.

The objective of shareholder wealth maximization has a number of distinct advantages. First, it is conceptually possible to determine whether a particular financial decision is consistent with this objective. If a decision made by a firm has the effect of increasing the market price of the firm's stock, it is a good decision. If it appears that a certain action will not achieve this result, the action should not be taken (at least not voluntarily).

Second, shareholder wealth maximization is an *impersonal* objective. Stockholders who may be offended by a firm's policies are free to sell their shares *under more favorable terms* (that is, at a higher price) *than are available under any other strategy* and invest their funds elsewhere.

Third, this objective allows the financial manager to consider the elements of both timing and risk when making various decisions. (This advantage will become more apparent later during the discussion of capital expenditure analysis.)

For these reasons, the shareholder wealth maximization objective is the primary normative goal in financial management.

Social Responsibility Goals

The success of the firm is often linked to various constituent groups, including employees, suppliers, customers, and community neighbors. Likewise, the welfare of many of these groups is closely related to the continued growth and prosperity of the firm. Some have argued that business should (as it to some degree does) seek to balance the interests of all these constituencies, rather than be concerned with shareholder wealth maximization alone. In many cases these social responsibilities can take on almost as much importance as laws and other formal obligations.

A wide diversity of opinion exists as to what corporate social responsibility actually entails. The concept is somewhat subjective and is neither perceived uniformly nor applied uniformly by all firms. As yet no satisfactory mechanism has been suggested that specifies how these social responsibility commitments can be balanced with the interests of the owners of the firm. It can be argued, however, that a concern for the interests of all the competing constituencies of the company is justified on the basis that it is in the firm's interest to create an environment in which the goal of shareholder wealth maximization can be pursued more easily.

Other Goals of the Firm

The normative goal of shareholder wealth maximization specifies how financial decisions *should* be made. It has been observed that, in practice, not all management decisions are consistent with this objective. In other words, there is often a divergence between the shareholder wealth maximization goal and the *actual* (or *descriptive*) goals pursued by management. What is the reason for this divergency? The primary reason has been attributed to *separation of ownership and control* (management) in corporations.

Separation of ownership and control has permitted managers to pursue goals more consistent with their own self-interests, subject, of course, to the constraint that they satisfy shareholders sufficiently to maintain control of the corporation. Instead of seeking to maximize some objective (such as shareholder wealth), management is said to "satisfice" or seek acceptable levels of performance.

Maximization of their own personal welfare (or utility) may lead managers to be concerned with long-run survival (job security). The concern for long-run survival may lead management to minimize (or limit) the amount of risk incurred by the firm, since unfavorable outcomes can lead to their dismissal or possible bankruptcy for the firm. Likewise, the desire for job security is cited as one reason why management often opposes takeover offers (mergers) by other companies. Giving senior management "golden parachute" contracts to compensate them if they lose their positions as the result of a merger is one approach designed to ensure that they will act in the interests of shareholders in merger decisions, rather than in their own interests.

Agency Problems

Agency relationships occur when one or more individuals (the principals) hire another individual (the agent) to perform a service on behalf of the principals.[2] In an agency relationship, decision-making authority is often delegated to the agent from the principals. In the context of finance, one of the most important agency relationships is between stockholders (owners) and managers.

Inefficiencies that arise because of agency relationships have been called "agency problems." These problems occur because each party to a transaction is assumed to act in a manner consistent with maximizing his or her own utility (welfare). The example cited earlier of the concern by management for long-run survival (job security), rather than shareholder wealth maximization, is an example of an agency problem. Another example is the consumption of on-the-job perquisites (such as the use of company airplanes, limousines, and luxurious offices) by managers who have no (or only a partial) ownership interest in the firm. Shirking by managers is also an agency-related problem.

These agency problems give rise to a number of *agency costs,* which are incurred by shareholders to minimize agency problems. Examples of agency costs include:

1. Expenditures to structure the organization in such a way that will minimize the incentives for management to take actions contrary to shareholder interests, such as providing a portion of management's compensation in the form of stock of the corporation.

2. Expenditures to monitor management's actions, such as paying for

---

[2] See Amir Barnea, R. Haugen, and L. Senbet, *Agency Problems and Financial Contracting.* Englewood Cliffs, N.J.: Prentice-Hall, 1985, for a complete overview of the agency problem issue.

audits of managerial performance and internal audits of the firm's expenditures.

3. Bonding expenditures to protect the owners from managerial dishonesty.

4. The opportunity cost of lost profits arising from complex organizational structures that prevent management from making timely responses to opportunities.

Financial theory has shown that agency problems and their associated costs can be greatly reduced if the financial markets operate efficiently. Some agency problems can be reduced by the use of complex financial contracts. Remaining agency problems give rise to costs that show up as a reduction in the value of the firm's shares in the marketplace.

Organization of the Financial Management Function

Most large corporations divide the decision-making responsibilities of management among several different officers of the corporation, which often include manufacturing, marketing, finance, personnel, and engineering. A sample organization chart, emphasizing the finance function, is shown in Figure 1-1. The finance function is usually headed by a (senior) vice-president of finance or *chief financial officer* who reports to the president. The chief financial officer may also distribute the financial management responsibilities between the *controller* and the *treasurer*.[3]

The controller normally has responsibility for all accounting related activities. These include such functions as:

- **Financial Accounting** This function involves the preparation of the financial statements for the firm, such as the balance sheet, income statement, and the sources and uses of funds statement.

- **Cost Accounting** This department often has responsibility for preparing the firm's operating budgets and monitoring the performance of the departments and divisions within the firm.

- **Taxes** This unit prepares the reports that the company must file with the various government (local, state, and federal) agencies.

- **Data Processing** Given its responsibilities involving corporate accounting and payroll activities, the controller may also have management responsibility for the company's data processing operations.

The treasurer is normally concerned with the acquisition, custody, and expenditure of funds. These duties often include:

- **Cash and Marketable Securities Management** This group monitors the firm's short-term finances—forecasting its cash needs, obtaining funds from bankers and other sources when needed, and investing any excess funds in short-term interest-earning securities.

- **Capital Budgeting Analysis** This department is responsible for analyzing

---

[3] In smaller companies, the owner may supervise the activities of the controller and treasurer, or the chief financial officer may perform both activities under the title of controller, treasurer, or vice-president of finance.

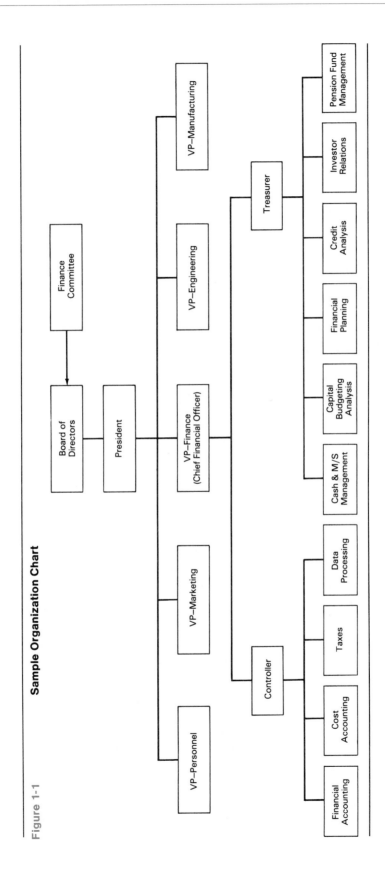

Figure 1-1 **Sample Organization Chart**

capital expenditures—that is, the purchase of long-term assets such as new facilities and equipment.

- **Financial Planning** This department is responsible for analyzing the alternative sources of long-term funds, such as the issuance of bonds or common stock, that the firm will need to maintain and expand its operations.

- **Credit Analysis** Most companies have a department that is responsible for determining the amount of credit that the firm will extend to each of its customers. While this group is responsible for performing financial analysis, it sometimes may be located in the marketing area of the firm because of its close relationship to sales.

- **Investor Relations** Many large companies have a unit that is responsible for working with institutional investors (for example, mutual funds), bond rating agencies, stockholders, and the general financial community.

- **Pension Fund Management** The treasurer may also have responsibility for the investment of employee pension fund contributions. The investment analysis and portfolio management functions may be performed either within the firm or through outside investment advisors.

It should be emphasized that *the specific functions of the controller and treasurer shown in Figure 1-1 are illustrative only and that the actual functions performed vary from company to company.* For example, in some companies, the treasurer may have responsibility for tax matters. Also, as shown in Figure 1-1, the board of directors of the company may establish a finance committee, consisting of a number of directors and officers of the firm with substantial financial expertise, to make recommendations on broad financial policy issues.

A Brief History of the Financial Management Field

Prior to the 1930s the field of financial management basically was confined to descriptive discussions of the various financial markets and the securities traded in those markets.[4] Thus, finance as a field of study traditionally focused on the liabilities and stockholders' equity side of the balance sheet and on fund raising.

The field underwent a number of significant changes during the Great Depression, when it became more involved with legal matters of bankruptcy, reorganization, and government regulation. Finance texts written during the 1930s and 1940s often devoted many chapters to bankruptcy-related matters, such as reorganization and liquidation.

Through the 1940s and into the 1950s the teaching of financial management continued to be basically qualitative and descriptive. During the 1950s, however, a number of significant changes took place in the field. First, financial management was expanded to include the asset side of the balance sheet, or the uses of a firm's funds. In addition, the application of discounted cash flow techniques to the problems of capital

---

[4] The terms *financial management, managerial finance, corporate finance,* and *business finance* are virtually equivalent and are used interchangeably. Most financial managers, however, seem to prefer either *financial management* or *managerial finance.*

expenditure analysis was being refined and perfected. Also, financial researchers were making significant breakthroughs in developing techniques for measuring the cost of capital and valuing financial assets. Progress in both the capital budgeting and the cost of capital areas has continued to the present day.

During the 1960s mathematical models using statistical and optimization techniques were applied to the allocation of current assets, such as cash, accounts receivable and inventories, and fixed assets. Throughout the 1960s and 1970s the trend continued toward a more quantitative and precise concept of financial management. Another important emphasis of the last two decades has been the integration of specific finance topics with a risk-adjusted model in an attempt to maximize the value of the firm and achieve shareholder wealth maximization.

During the decade of the 1980s there has been an increasing emphasis on applying computer (and computer-related) technology to assist in financial decision making. In addition, financial managers have become more aggressive in managing the assets of the firm in response to an environment characterized by frequently high interest rates.

Over the past 50 years financial management has developed into a more rigorous discipline, and today's employers expect business and finance graduates to possess a solid working knowledge of modern finance techniques. Table 1-1 summarizes the most significant developments in the evolution of financial management.

Financial Management and Other Disciplines

Financial management is not a totally independent area in business administration. Instead, it draws heavily on related disciplines and fields of study. The most important of these are *accounting* and *economics;* in the latter discipline, *macroeconomics* and *microeconomics* are of special significance. *Marketing, production,* and the study of *quantitative methods* also have an impact on the financial management field. Each of these is discussed in the following sections.

Table 1-1   **Evolution of Financial Management**

Period	Focus
Pre-1930	Descriptive emphasis on financial markets and securities. Little attention to asset management.
1930s and 1940s	Focus on legal matters dealing with bankruptcy and reorganization and the effects of newly emerging government regulation.
1950s	Increasing emphasis on asset management. Significant theoretical developments in valuation theory.
1960s	Application of mathematical models to allocation of current and fixed assets. Additional theoretical developments in valuation theory, cost of capital, dividend policy, and risk analysis.
1970s	Development of more precise theories and measures of risk. Application of these theories to investment analysis and valuation.
1980s	Increasing application of computer technology to assist in financial decision making.

Accounting

Financial managers often turn to accounting data to assist them in making decisions. Generally a company's accountants are responsible for developing financial reports and measures that assist its managers in assessing the past performance and future direction of the firm and in meeting certain legal obligations, such as the payment of taxes. The accountant's role includes the development of financial statements such as the *balance sheet,* the *income statement,* and the *sources and uses of funds statement* (also called the *statement of changes in financial position*).

In contrast, financial managers are primarily concerned with a firm's *cash flows,* since they often determine the feasibility of certain investment and financing decisions. The financial manager refers to accounting data when making future resource allocation decisions concerning long-term investments, when managing current investments in working capital, and when making a number of other financial decisions (for example, determining the most appropriate capital structure and identifying the best and most timely sources of funds needed to support the firm's investment programs).

In many small and medium-sized firms the accounting function and the financial management function may be handled by the same person or group of persons. In such cases the distinctions identified above may become blurred.

Economics

There are two areas of economics with which the financial manager must be familiar: *microeconomics* and *macroeconomics.* Microeconomics deals with the economic decisions of individuals, households, and firms, while macroeconomics looks at the economy as a whole.

The typical firm is heavily influenced by the overall performance of the economy and is dependent upon the money and capital markets for investment funds. Thus, financial managers should recognize and understand how monetary policies affect the cost of funds and the availability of credit. Financial managers also should be versed in fiscal policy and how it affects the economy. What the economy can be expected to do in the future is a crucial factor in generating sales forecasts as well as other types of forecasts.

The financial manager uses microeconomics when developing decision models that are likely to lead to the most efficient and successful modes of operation within the firm. Specifically, the financial manager may utilize the basic economic notion from microeconomic theory of setting marginal cost equal to marginal revenue when making long-term investment decisions (*capital budgeting*) and when managing cash, inventories, and accounts receivable (*working capital management*).

Marketing, Production, and Quantitative Methods

Figure 1-2 depicts the relationship between financial management and its primary supportive disciplines. Marketing, production, and quantitative methods are indirectly related to the key day-to-day decisions made by financial managers.

For example, financial managers should consider the impact of new product development and promotion plans made in the marketing area, since these plans will require capital outlays and have an impact on the

Figure 1-2   **Impact of Other Disciplines on Financial Management**

firm's projected cash flows. Similarly, changes in the production process may necessitate capital expenditures, which the firm's financial managers must evaluate and then finance. And, finally, the tools of analysis developed in the quantitative methods area frequently are helpful in analyzing complex financial management problems.

Organization of the Text

This text provides an introduction to both analytical tools and descriptive materials that are useful in financial management. Because this is an introductory-level text, however, it does *not* attempt to make the reader an expert in every aspect of financial decision making. Instead, it is intended to do the following:

- Acquaint the reader with the types of decisions faced by financial managers.
- Develop a framework for analyzing these decisions in a systematic manner.
- Provide the reader with the background necessary to pursue more advanced readings and courses in financial management.

Although the subject matter in this text is divided into a series of parts, it should be noted that the various types of financial decisions are interrelated and should not be considered in isolation from one another.

Part I Introduction Chapter 1 examines the financial goals of the firm and the role of the financial manager in the decision-making process. Chapter 2 provides an overview of the business environment in the United States and discusses the various forms of business organization, the role of financial institutions in the economy, and the impact of government regulations and taxes. Chapter 2 also introduces the general problem of the risk and return tradeoffs that financial managers face.

Part II Determinants of Valuation Chapter 3 develops the concepts of discounting, compounding, and present value. These concepts are used in the valuation of securities and in the evaluation of capital expenditure projects that are expected to provide benefits over a number of years. Chapter 4 considers the determinants of the valuation of a firm's shares of common stock and other long-term securities it may issue. The chapter builds explicit valuation models for each major type of security issued by a firm and relates these models to the key financial decisions made in the firm. The valuation concept is a central theme that is carried throughout the text and related to all key financial decisions. Chapter 5 provides a comprehensive introduction to the concept of risk in finance and the relationship between risk, required returns, and the shareholder wealth maximization goal of the firm.

Part III Financial Analysis Chapters 6 through 8 present some basic tools that are useful in financial analysis. Chapter 6 considers various ratios that can be used in evaluating the financial performance of a firm. Chapter 7 develops the concepts of operating and financial leverage and analyzes their effects on the firm's risk, and Chapter 8 examines the use of various types of financial planning methods, including the cash budget and the funds flow statement.

Part IV The Capital Investment Decision This portion of the text focuses on capital expenditures, that is, investments in long-term assets. Chapters 9 and 10 present the fundamentals of capital budgeting, namely, the process of investing in long-term assets. Chapter 9 deals with the measurement of the cash flows (benefits and costs) associated with long-term investment projects; Chapter 10 considers various decision-making criteria that can be used when choosing projects that will maximize the value of the firm. Chapter 11 extends the concepts developed in Chapter 10 by considering some of the decision-making techniques that attempt to deal with the problem of the risk associated with a specific project's cash flow.

Part V The Cost of Capital, Capital Structure, and Dividend Policy Chapter 12 illustrates the principles of measuring a firm's cost of capital. The cost of funds to a firm is an important input in the capital budgeting process. Chapter 13 addresses the relationship of the cost of capital to the firm's capital structure. Chapter 14 discusses the factors that influence the choice of a dividend policy and the impact of various dividend policies on the value of a firm.

Part VI Sources of Intermediate and Long-term Funds This part of the text describes the characteristics of the major sources of intermediate and long-term funds. Specifically, Chapter 15 deals with term loans and leases; Chapter 16 with long-term debt, preferred stock, and common stock; and Chapter 17 with various types of convertible securities and warrants.

Part VII The Management of Working Capital Chapters 18 through 22 examine the management of a firm's current asset and liability accounts (that is, working capital). Chapter 18 provides an overview of working capital management, with emphasis on the risk-return tradeoffs involved in working capital decision making. Chapters 19 through 21 examine the factors that must be considered in managing a firm's investments in various types of current assets. Specifically, Chapter 19 deals with cash and marketable securities, Chapter 20 with accounts receivable, and Chapter 21 with inventories. Finally, Chapter 22 discusses the various sources (and associated costs) of secured and unsecured short-term credit.

Part VIII Selected Topics in Contemporary Financial Management
Chapter 23 examines the merger and acquisition alternative, which many firms choose as a way of expanding, diversifying, or both. Chapter 24 describes the alternatives available to a failing firm. The final chapter of the text, Chapter 25, discusses international financial management.

Summary

- The primary normative goal of financial management decision making is the *maximization of shareholder wealth* as measured by the price of the firm's stock. This objective permits decision makers explicit to make the needed tradeoffs between risk and return and between long-run versus short-run profits.
- The finance function is usually headed by a (senior) vice-president or *chief financial officer*. The financial management responsibilities are often divided between the *controller* and the *treasurer*. The controller normally has responsibility for all accounting related activities. The treasurer is normally concerned with the acquisition, custody, and expenditure of funds.
- Over the past 50 years financial management has developed into a much more analytically rigorous discipline.
- Financial management is closely related to other areas of business decision making, particularly accounting and economics.

FOCUS ON CORPORATE PRACTICE

Takeovers and the Preservation of Shareholder Value

T. Boone Pickens, Jr.
General Partner, Mesa Limited Partnership
Chairman and Chief Executive Officer, Mesa Petroleum Co.

In 1956, T. Boone Pickens, Jr. formed Petroleum Exploration, Inc., a predecessor company to Mesa Limited Partnership. He began the company with $2,500 in cash and a $100,000 line of credit. During the first quarter of 1985, Mesa's assets topped $4 billion. Mesa is the largest independent oil company in the United States. Its management is strongly committed to increasing the value of the shareholders' investment. An investment of $10,000 made in Mesa in 1964 would be worth more than $250,000 today. T. Boone Pickens, Jr. has become a crusader for shareholder rights. He believes strongly that takeover activity, or the threat of takeovers, is a key ingredient in maintaining the efficiency of American industry and protecting the interests of shareholders. The following sequence of questions and answers clearly articulate this philosophy.

Q. Why are takeovers necessary?

Mr. Pickens: The competition for control created by a healthy takeover market has become a powerful engine of economic growth. Takeovers, on balance, increase corporate efficiency, productivity, and accountability. They redeploy undervalued assets and revitalize moribund operations.

Takeover activity increases the nation's aggregate wealth by translating inherent asset value into actual market value. Wealth once trapped in the equity securities of overcapitalized corporations is redirected into the hands of America's 47 million public shareholders, who tend to reinvest it in more productive areas of the economy.

Q. What factors have led to a reduction of incentives for management to maximize returns to owners of many of the largest American corporations?

Mr. Pickens: A fundamental characteristic of publicly held corporations is the separation of ownership and control. This characteristic is most apparent in many of today's Fortune 500 companies.

In the growth phase of a corporation, managers tend to respond to two powerful incentives to achieve superior returns. The first incentive is the substantial ownership interest often held by the founders and managers of a growing corporation. The direct link between corporate performance and management rewards ensures that the interests of all equity owners are well served. A second incentive for growing corporations is the performance standard imposed by equity investors who periodically provide growth capital. It is difficult for corporate managers to turn their backs on public shareholders if those shareholders recently participated in a public offering. This is particularly true if the company perceives a possibility of returning to the capital markets for more equity funds in future years. Unless the corporation demonstrates competitive or superior performance, investors will be less inclined to participate when the need for additional capital arises.

Over time, equity ownership by management tends to become less significant as corporate founders are replaced by succeeding generations of professional managers. Also, the concern for the expectations of equity owners wanes as corporations mature and enter periods of low growth or gradual decline, which do not require the firm to enter the capital markets for additional equity funds. Gradually, today's shareholders come to be perceived more as a troublesome constituency of past expansion than as a potential source of future success.

Q. How can shareholders activism and the threat of takeovers provide a performance incentive to a shirking manager?

Mr. Pickens: The rise of the activist shareholder helps to counterbalance the gradual separation of ownership and control in large corporations. It gives rise to mergers, acquisitions, divestitures, buyouts, recapitalizations, share repurchases, and other actions—known collectively as corporate restructuring. The net effect of the restructuring movement is overwhelmingly positive. A study by the New York securities firm of Goldman Sachs determined that approximately $80 billion in stock appreciation, or roughly a third of the stock gains experienced by the Standard and Poor's 500 companies during 1984 and 1985, is attributable to corporate restructuring.

Q. What can be done to assure that managers work toward the objective of maximizing the value of the firm's shares?

Mr. Pickens: I believe that conscientious executives and employees can correct much of the problem on a purely voluntary basis. At Mesa, we created a corporate culture emphasizing the interests of owners long before takeover activity became a national issue.

Mesa's commmitment to its owners is evident throughout its organizational structure. During 1985, more than 90 percent of the company's employees owned Mesa stock purchased with their own funds. Many key employees hold significant ownership interests in Mesa. We discovered long ago that workers who own stock soon begin to think like owners. Employees at all levels are told upon their arrival, and periodically reminded, that they work for shareholders.

Mesa's emphasis on maximizing value for shareholders is clearly recognized by the investing public. Mesa securities have consistently traded in the market at or near the appraised value of the underlying assets, a record few of our competitors can match.

In order to make corporate America truly competitive again, we need to rediscover our basic principles, recognize who owns our corporations, and manage our companies in the best interest of owners. Stock ownership by employees should be encouraged at all levels. Companies lacking ownership incentive programs should institute them, and managers and employees should consider making personal investments in the future of their enterprises.

Thank you, Mr. Pickens.

Questions and Topics for Discussion

1. Define "shareholder wealth." Explain how it is measured.

2. What are the differences between shareholder wealth maximization and profit maximization? If a firm chooses to pursue the objective of shareholder wealth maximization, does this preclude the use of profit maximization decision-making rules? Explain.

3. Which type of corporation is more likely to be a shareholder wealth maximizer—one with wide ownership and no owners directly involved in the firm's management, or one that is closely held?

4. Is the shareholder wealth maximization goal a short- or long-term goal? Explain your answer.

5. It has been argued that shareholder wealth maximization is not a realistic normative goal for the firm, given the social responsibility activities that the firm is "expected" to engage in (such as contributing to the arts, education, etc.). Explain why these social responsibility activities are not necessarily inconsistent with shareholder wealth maximization.

6. Shareholder wealth maximization is referred to as a "normative goal." Explain what is meant by this statement.

7. Explain why management may tend to pursue goals other than shareholder wealth maximization.

8. Explain what is meant by "agency relationships" and "agency costs."

9. In the agency relationship between the shareholders (owners) and management of a firm, give some examples of agency costs incurred by shareholders.

10. Explain the differences in the responsibilities of the treasurer and the controller in a large corporation.

11. Explain the relationship between financial management and (a) microeconomics and (b) macroeconomics.

12. How does financial management in the 1970s and 1980s differ from financial management in the 1920s and 1930s—both as a profession and as a field of study?

Selected References

Barnea, Amir, R. Haugen, and L. Senbet. *Agency Problems and Financial Contracting.* Englewood Cliffs, NJ: Prentice-Hall, 1985.

Beranek, William. "Research Directions in Finance." *Quarterly Review of Economics and Business* (Spring 1981): 6–24.

Fama, Eugene. "Agency Problems and the Theory of the Firm." *Journal of Political Economy* (April 1980): 288–307.

Findlay, M. Chapman, and G. A. Whitmore. "Beyond Shareholder Wealth Maximization." *Financial Management* (Winter 1974): 25–35.

Jensen, Michael C., and William H. Meckling. "Theory of the Firm: Managerial Behavior, Agency Costs, and Ownership Structure." *Journal of Financial Economics* (October 1976): 305–360.

Lewellen, Wilbur G. "Management and Ownership in the Large Firm." *Journal of Finance* (May 1969): 299–322.

McGuigan, James R., and R. Charles Moyer. *Managerial Economics,* 4th ed. St. Paul, MN: West, 1986, chap. 1.

Weston, J. Fred. "Developments in Financial Theory." *Financial Management* (June 1981): 5–22.

APPENDIX 1A

CAREER OPPORTUNITIES IN FINANCE[5]

The financial profession offers a number of exciting career opportunities. In this appendix we provide complete job descriptions of a selected number of career choices that are open to finance professionals. In addition to these complete job descriptions, we provide a summary description of other career opportunities in finance.

Detailed Job Descriptions

Detailed job descriptions are provided for five major finance career options. These options span the spectrum from corporate finance to banking and investment analysis, and from entry level positions to leadership roles in the financial functions of a firm.

1. Junior Analyst— Finance, Planning, and Administration

Basic Function Review the company's business plans and annual budget and analyze and summarize various financing proposals sent to the company.

Primary Responsibilities and Duties
- Assess the financial markets.
- Prepare a competitive analysis of the industry.
- Prepare and review the corporate budget and business plan.
- Provide financial research services and implement any decision taken in order to manage overall capital structure.
- Gather, analyze, and summarize pertinent treasury information in report form.
- Develop sinking fund strategy for repurchase of company bonds.
- Implement borrowing decisions.
- Participate in financings of a corporate and project financing nature.
- Prepare specific management reports regarding financial performance as well as financial market performance.
- Prepare for rating agency reviews.
- Implement approved financial plans and policies.
- Analyze, design, and implement a variety of computer-based information systems for worldwide treasury application.

[5] Source: Jack S. Rader, *Careers in Finance* (Tampa, Florida: Financial Management Association, 1983). Reprinted with permission. A complete job description for the careers which are summarized in the final section of this appendix can be found in the *Careers in Finance* publication.

Types of Decisions

- Determine company liquidity requirements.
- Evaluate externally submitted proposals and determine whether they make economic sense for the company.
- Determine whether requests from other locations meet specific guidelines of corporate policy.

Organizational Relationships

- Report directly to the manager of finance, planning, and administration.

Eduction and Experience

- MBA

Representative Skills and Knowledge

Requires:
- In-depth knowledge of short- and long-term financial markets.
- Background in quantitative analytical techniques.
- Knowledge of basic and advanced corporate finance principles, combined with mathematical and statistical analysis of finance alternatives.
- Use of quantitative methods on the interactive computer.
- Knowledge of general economic/financial interrelationships as they affect the financial markets and business plans.
- Knowledge of computer-based approaches to managing debt information requirements.
- Ability to participate on special study teams or task forces.

Other

- Interpersonal skills and the ability to communicate clearly are prime requisites.

2. Vice-President of Finance

Basic Function Plan, direct, and execute the long-term financings required to fund corporate capital requirements at the lowest cost.

Primary Responsibilities and Duties

- Plan and execute the financings required to fund corporate capital requirements while maintaining a balanced capital structure.
- Direct, support, and review the actions of the department in obtaining long-term financing and maintaining positive relations with lenders and rating agencies.
- Provide a capital budgeting and financial projection system.
- Integrate projections of capital requirements with the status of credit markets and the company's capital structure.
- Coordinate the activities of underwriters, lawyers, and accountants in order to complete financings in a timely manner.
- Maintain contact with all company lenders and keep them informed of the company's goals and progress.

- Provide financial support for various contractual arrangements.
- Monitor pension fund assets and various special projects.

Types of Decisions
- Select underwriters, lenders, and counsel to structure financings.
- Decide on the type of financing that is most appropriate to meet capital requirements and financial structure targets at the lowest cost.
- Determine the timing of the issue of new financings.
- Decisions are reviewed by the Senior Vice-President of Finance.

Organizational Relationships
- The incumbent directly supervises the Assistant Vice-President of Finance, Manager of Pension Investments, and Manager of Financial Analysis.
- Work progress is discussed with the supervisor approximately once a year.

Work Relationships
Frequently work with:
- Bankers who are lenders and provide trustee services.
- Long-term lenders (insurance companies).
- Investment bankers.
- Investment advisors who manage pension fund.
- Industry groups.
- Legal counsel.

Education and Experience
- MBA in finance or two or three years of progressively responsible experience in financial/investment analysis.
- Five to six years (including at least three years of management) of experience in investment banking, financial consulting, or a comparable job.

Representative Skills and Knowledge
Should:
- Be resourceful.
- Be a good communicator.
- Have analytical/problem solving/creative abilities.
- Have high degree of verbal, quantitative, and interpersonal skills.
- Understand business principles and practices.
- Have complete understanding of financial management.
- Be a quick, clear thinker.

Other
- This is a complex job with very high responsibility and visibility both inside and outside of the company. Feedback on success and failure is quick. Stamina is required for the long hours and travel.

3. Securities Analyst—Common Stock

Basic Function Prepare company and industry-wide analyses of common stocks, interview outside corporation management, summarize and interpret information, and recommend appropriate action by a presentation to the investment committee.

Primary Responsibilities and Duties

- Analyze companies and industries to determine suitability for common stock investments; determine prospects for future growth and assist in maintenance of portfolio.
- Review common stock presently in the portfolio to assure continued acceptability to company objectives.
- Consider and evaluate alternative investment scenarios.
- Gather necessary information from divisional records, outside sources, and financial reports.
- Compile information into summaries with recommendations and make presentations to senior officers and to the investment committee.
- Prepare statistics relating to common stock or equivalent investments.
- Participate in investment process by mastering and improving upon traditional analytical approaches.

Types of Decisions

- Determine the suitability of present or prospective investments based on company objectives.
- Establish priorities for individual research.
- Aggressively discover and pursue investment ideas in an expeditious manner.
- Determine the value of alternative investment possibilities.

Organizational Relationships

- The incumbent reports to the Investment Officer.
- Contact corporate management of outside firms.

Education and Experience

- Required to have 2–3 years experience.
- MBA is desirable.

Representative Skills and Knowledge

Must:
- Possess human relations skills, tact, and diplomacy.
- Have excellent skills in preparing oral and written reports.
- Have a high degree of judgment.
- Be able to develop ideas in a concise and meaningful conceptual framework.
- Show initiative.

Should also have:
- A comprehensive knowledge of investment analysis, economic principles, company and industry trends, market judgment, and sense of market timing.
- A knowledge of company policies, practices, and objectives.

4. Corporate Banking Officer

Basic Function To maintain and expand existing relationships with clients by marketing all of the bank's services and to develop new client relationships.

Primary Responsibilities and Duties

- Call on Fortune 500 companies headquartered near the bank's offices.
- Maintain existing clients in the face of product innovations, constant competition, and the fact that many products have specified terms.
- Identify opportunities for all of the services offered by the bank, including credit, cash management, pension management, foreign exchange and interest rate exposure management, tax questions, and merger and acquisition activities.
- Perform administrative follow-up on overdrawn deposit accounts, loan documents, rate information, memo writing for credit approvals, credit analysis, etc.
- Bring in the appropriate specialists to discuss technical products with clients.
- Stay current with the technical aspects of new products.
- Get to know customers better through personal calls.
- Review files and annual reports.

Types of Decisions

- Overdraft approval.
- Extension of credit to a client (including how much and at what pricing).
- Whether or not a specialist should be introduced.
- Determining the best approach to take in convincing the bank's management that a deal is right.
- Credit extensions require approval at higher levels.
- Often the toughest decisions are about prioritizing activities.

Consequences of Error

- A poor recommendation will either not get approved and make the person recommending it look foolish in front of superiors or be approved at the risk of losing significant funds/income for the bank and the department.
- An unsuccessful recommendation of a good deal will result in a loss for the client.
- The dollar amounts involved can be staggering.
- What is said to a customer or a superior can make or break a relationship (and a reputation).

Organizational Relationships

- Informal discussions are held with the immediate supervisor at least monthly.
- There is an annual review of performance which is written and included in the personnel file.
- Most work is performed as half of a two-person team.

Work Relationships (Contacts)

- In-house communications take place with everyone from senior vice-president to clerks.
- External communications occur with chief financial officers, treasurers, assistant treasurers, and other financial officers.

Education and Experience

- People with BAs are often successful as bankers as there is a good opportunity to learn the necessary skills on the job; however, it takes longer to develop skills that way.
- The bank has an intensive six-month training program followed by regular seminars and "product knowledge" sessions while on the job.

Representative Skills and Knowledge

Must:

- Be well versed in the bank's structure, function, capabilities, etc.
- Be knowledgeable of new products and people who have knowledge of them.
- Know how to use the telephone, a calculator, dictating equipment, and a word processor/personal computer.
- Understand present value analysis, international trade transactions, foreign exchange, swaps, and other finance techniques.
- Be familiar with tax law, FASB rulings, and maintain a general familiarity with current market conditions.
- Be able to use ratio analysis/financial analysis/credit analysis.
- Be able to read and understand financial statement footnotes.
- Be able to digest information in a credit file to get a feel for relationship.
- Understand the regulations governing lending limits relative to total exposure, reserve requirements, Federal Reserve Bank effects on float times, and documentation (as tedious as it is).

Other

- The job hours are of an 8:30 to 6:00 p.m. type with occasional late hours for specific jobs. Weekends are often used for review. This is a rare opportunity to see the workings of many different kinds of companies.

5. General Credit Manager

Basic Function Establish and administer the broad credit and collection policies of the company as they apply to domestic and export customer sales of the manufacturing divisions and specialized distribution and service units. This receivables management is carried out through all company credit and collection units on both a direct and non-direct basis as required to optimize the company's receivables turnover.

Primary Responsibilities and Duties

- Approve all extraordinary lines of credit, including those that exceed delegated field authority.
- Visit key customers to maintain good commercial relationships and determine financial liability.

- Work with appropriate division and field sales personnel to coordinate and communicate terms of payment, credit decisions, and disputed or uncollectible billings.
- Prepare monthly cash collection forecasts and monitor and report daily cash receipts.
- Coordinate all legal matters pertaining to receivables management with company and outside attorneys.
- Establish objectives for domestic and export treasury managers.
- Supervise the maintenance and safekeeping of special customer records, files, reports, and ledgers.
- Represent the company at financial professional association meetings and seminars.
- Keep informed of legislation and changes in laws and regulations which affect financing, credit, and collection policies and procedures.
- Sign documents as necessary as an authorized officer of the company.
- Direct the preparation of periodic reports on receivables and analyze customer's accounts and reserve requirements; report unusual trends in developments to management along with corrective action needed.
- Develop policy and procedures for recruiting and soliciting professional personnel to staff the credit and collection offices.
- Administer the department salary program and provide the direct and indirect training of department personnel.
- Supervise the effective utilization of funds allocated for the operations of domestic and export credit collection units.
- Supervise the booking and collection processing of domestic and export customer's notes and trade acceptances.
- Prepare and formulate, within prescribed time limits, various data and reports as may be required by the Vice-President/Treasurer.
- Develop budgets for domestic and export credit and collection units.

Types of Decisions
- Final decision-making responsibility exists in credit/collection problems and procedures, personnel decisions, reporting unit structure, budget and merit increase considerations, and establishment of department/ receivables objectives. (All major aspects of the preceding are reviewed with the Vice-President/Treasurer.)
- Recommendations concerning bad debts are submitted to the Vice-President/Treasurer for final approval.
- Objectives are established for domestic and export credit and collection units.

Organizational Relationships
- The incumbent directly supervises four zone treasury managers, three directors of treasury services, one subsidiary vice-president and treasurer, one manager of international collections, and one credit manager of international standard sales. Approximately 150 employees report through these positions.
- The incumbent reports directly to the Vice-President/Treasurer.

Work Relationships

- Work with marketing management to increase both domestic and export sales volume through financing plans designed to accomplish this goal with minimum risk.
- Supervise the counseling of both domestic and export customers as to better financing arrangements and more effective control of internal operations.
- Enhance the company's image among customers by providing appropriate credit and collection activities conducive to continuing and broadening the commercial relationships that exist.

Education and Experience

- BS or BA required with a major in accounting or finance.
- Should have five years minimum in direct handling of open account credit and secured transactions; ten years minimum of direct supervision of this type of activity in a management capacity; and five years minimum as a zone, regional manager, or director of treasury services.

Representative Skills and Knowledge

- Requires a working knowledge of corporate finance, banking, commercial finance, and international credit policies and procedures.

Must be:
- A disciplined and determined negotiator.
- A leader and motivator of people.
- Skilled in selling programs and policies to customers and company units.
- Objective in thinking and open to new ideas.
- Able to size up a situation and act decisively.
- Skilled in short- and long-range planning and reorganization.

Other Career Options and Their Basic Functions

1. **Financial Analyst—Revenue** Projects future revenues for budgetary purposes and analyzes past revenue performances. A minimum of a bachelor's degree is required.

2. **Financial Analyst—Capital Budgets** Reviews capital and lease appropriation requests that require finance concurrence, coordinates and compiles data for the annual capital budget, and compiles actual and projected capital cash flows for reports. Requires an MBA degree and a capacity to do computer-based financial analysis.

3. **Manager—Capital Budgeting** Responsible for budgeting and administering the company's capital asset expenditure program. An MBA degree with three to four years of experience in managerial accounting or financial analysis and reporting is required.

4. **Manager—Project Finance** Obtains financing as requested on facilities and a project basis as appropriate to the corporate target capital structure and financial market conditions. Requires an MBA in

finance or accounting plus five years of experience in a treasury/ finance management position.

5. **Manager of Financial Planning for Subsidiaries**   Responsible for the financial planning functions, from a corporate policy point of view, for several subsidiaries of the company. Requires an MBA or BA-Finance and significant relevant work experience.

6. **Manager—Financial Planning**   Accountable for the management of the Financial Planning Department with specific attention to the analysis, development, and recommendation of system-wide financial goals including capital structure, return on investment, and dividend policy. Requires an MBA or BA in accounting or finance with ten to twelve years of closely related experience.

7. **Securities Analyst—Private Placements**   Manages two to five industrial categories of the firm's fixed income portfolio. MBA required with strong background in investments, economics, accounting, finance, English, and math.

8. **Direct Loan Analyst**   Assesses the financial condition and performance of existing and potential borrowers; analyzes direct loan offerings made to the company to determine the acceptability of the offerings to company standards; prepares recommendations on such offerings; participates in negotiations and reviews loan agreements; and monitors the stability of firms receiving loans. Requires an MBA and two to three years of experience in securities analysis.

9. **Portfolio Analyst**   Performs administrative and information gathering functions in connection with the company's securities division and the company's securities portfolio. Requires an MBA and two to three years experience in securities analysis.

10. **Manager—Pension Fund Investments**   Responsible for the prudent management of the assets held by the employees' pension fund, the control of appropriate administration expenses (trustee and consultant fees, brokerage commissions, etc.), the allocation of assets among investment managers, and the diversification of assets by type of security. Requires an MBA or Chartered Financial Analyst designation plus three to five years of experience in investment analysis or portfolio management.

11. **Director—Investor Relations**   Works in the areas of investor relations with additional responsibility for pension fund investments and corporate financings. Requires an MBA plus five to ten years of related experience.

12. **Account Executive (Securities Broker)**   Provides advice and counsel to clients concerning potential investments; executes purchase, sell, and other trade orders on behalf of clients. Requires a BA in Finance.

13. **Assistant Treasurer—Cash Control and Risk Management**   Responsible for operations of the Treasury Department involving cash management operations with specific attention to the effective direction and control of corporate funds internally and through the company's various bank accounts. Requires a BA in Finance plus related experience.

14. **Senior Banking Analyst**   Assists the supervisor of financial services with short-term asset management and provides financial data and other services as requested by various departments.

15. **Mortgage Analyst—Production**   Handles all matters related to the production, analysis, and negotiation of applications for the acquisition of conventional mortgage loans and real estate investments. Requires two to three years of mortgage analysis experience.

16. **Mortgage Analyst—Closing**   Coordinates all business matters relating to the closing of conventional mortgage loans and real estate; analyzes requests for, negotiates, and recommends changes in commitment terms.

17. **Director of Risk Management**   Protects the company from the adverse financial impact of significant unexpected losses using self-insurance, captive insurance, loss control methods, safety techniques, and conventional or non-conventional insurance; provides guidance and assistance to other staff and operating units concerning risk management, insurance, or claim situations. Requires BS degree and minimum of eight years experience, including experience in managing an insurance company.

18. **Corporate Model Analyst**   Analyzes corporate models used in planning; develops and maintains data gathering systems for systematic correct data input for model operation; develops and maintains model systems which are consistent with corporate methods; verifies and analyzes results of model output; presents and interprets model results to project initiators or to top management; and recommends subsequent action to project initiators and others. Requires strong computer, finance, accounting, quantitative analysis, and systems design skills.

19. **Consultant—Mergers and Acquisitions**   Analyzes the clients of the firm in order to prepare an in-depth analysis for use as a blueprint for raising funds through (or for) mergers and acquisitions. Requires a minimum of a BA. MBA is essential for advancement. Education should focus on finance, accounting, and computers.

20. **Vice-President—Credit Policy**   Analyzes and evaluates the credit worthiness of one-of-a-kind projects submitted to the bank by various customers. Requires a BA or MBA plus about one year in a training program.

This listing of jobs is not exhaustive. There are many additional career opportunities for finance and accounting graduates in the corporate finance, investment, banking, insurance, real estate, tax management, and financial reporting fields. However, the listing presented above should be sufficient to provide a feeling for the breadth of career opportunities which are available to finance graduates.

Good luck in your finance career!

2

THE CORPORATION AND THE INSTITUTIONAL ENVIRONMENT

A Financial Dilemma

Off-Balance-Sheet Commitments of U.S. Banks*

Off-balance-sheet commitments of the largest twenty-five U.S. banks were estimated to be $1.5 *trillion* in 1985. These potential obligations covered a broad range of activities, including:

- Standby letters of credit guaranteeing customers' commercial paper (short-term borrowings by companies) and municipal bond issues.
- Interest rate and currency swaps. (An interest rate swap is an agreement between two parties in which one party's floating rate debt repayment obligation is traded for another party's fixed rate obligation. A currency swap involves swapping interest obligations denominated in different currencies.)
- Note issuance facilities, in which the bank agrees to buy the short-term securities of a borrower if it is unable to sell them in the securities markets.
- Options (the right to buy or sell something, such as a security, at a given price) and futures con-

* Based in part on "Off-Balance-Sheet Risk: Where Is It Leading the Banks?" *Institutional Investor* (January 1986): 75–84.

tracts (a commitment to receive or deliver something at a definite time in the future at a current agreed-upon price) on such investments as Treasury Bills, foreign currency, and gold.

The magnitude of these commitments in 1985 at the seven largest U.S. banks is shown in Table 2-1.

As can be seen, these off-balance sheet commitments are far in excess of the banks' total assets.

Unlike loans, the banks are gambling that they will not have to honor all of these potential obligations. Also unlike loans, these commitments are not funded nor are they factored into the banks' capital requirements. Many of these commitments, such as options, futures, and guarantees, are undertaken in an effort to dilute, spread, and hedge a wide range of risks. However, some analysts believe that just the opposite may be occuring. The primary concern is that, if these off-balance-sheet risks are not well managed, they could lead to sudden liquidity problems or unforeseen losses for the banks.

Such commitments are difficult to detect by looking at the balance sheets of banks. As Federal Reserve chairman Paul Volcker asked in a speech to bankers, "Has the attention paid to simple capital-asset ratios driven risks off-balance-sheet—and is off-balance-sheet also out of

---

Table 2-1   **Off-Balance-Sheet Commitments of Large U.S. Banks**

Bank	Total Assets (Billion)	Total Off-Balance-Sheet Commitments (Billion)	Off-Balance-Sheet Commitments as a Percentage of Assets
Citibank	$125.8	$296.8	236%
Bank of America	107.1	209.6	196
Chase Manhattan	79.5	149.0	187
Morgan Guaranty	64.3	126.9	197
Manufacturers Hanover	61.0	101.0	165
Chemical	57.3	114.9	201
Bankers Trust	43.4	128.5	296

mind?" Consequently, investors who are considering depositing money in a bank or purchasing its common stock cannot easily evaluate the riskiness of such decisions.

This chapter examines the relationship between businesses and the institutional environment, which includes commercial banks.

Key Chapter Concepts

1. The corporate form of business organization has significant advantages over sole proprietorships and partnerships, including:
   a. Limited liability
   b. Permanency
   c. Flexibility
2. In the U.S. financial system, funds flow from net savers (such as households) to net investors (such as businesses) through financial middlemen and financial intermediaries.
   a. Financial middlemen include securities brokers and investment bankers.
   b. Financial intermediaries include commercial banks, thrift institutions, investment companies, pension funds, insurance companies, and finance companies.
3. Financial markets are classified as money or capital markets and primary or secondary markets.
   a. Short-term securities, having maturities of one year or less, are traded in money markets, and long-term securities, having maturities of one year or more, are traded in capital markets.
   b. New securities are traded in the primary markets and existing securities are traded in the secondary markets.
4. Interest rates on securities vary because of differences in maturity, risk of default, tax status, and liquidity.
5. A positive relationship (risk-return tradeoff) exists between the expected returns and risks of various securities.
6. Other important topics include:
   a. Financial deregulation
   b. Corporate and individual income taxes (appendix)

Glossary of New Terms

Capital markets Financial markets in which long-term securities are bought and sold.

Common stock Shares in the ownership of a company. Common stock represents a residual form of ownership in that dividends are paid out only after more senior financial obligations are fulfilled, such as interest on debt.

Corporation A business organization that is created as a "legal person" separate and distinct from the individual or individuals who own the firm's stock. The primary characteristics of and advantages of incorporating include limited liability for the firm's owners, permanency, and flexibility with respect to making changes in ownership.

Expected value The average of individual possible outcomes from an event, such as an investment, weighted by the probability of each possible outcome.

Investment banker A financial institition that underwrites and sells new securities. In general, investment bankers assist firms in obtaining new financing.

Money markets Financial markets in which short-term debt securities are bought and sold.

Partnership A business organization in which two or more persons form a business with the intention of making a profit. In a *general partnership* each partner has unlimited liability for the debts of the firm. *Limited partnerships* allow one or more partners to have limited liability.

Preferred stock A form of equity that has a senior claim on earnings—in the form of a (normally) fixed periodic dividend payment—and assets of a firm. This is in contrast to the claims of common stockholders.

Primary markets Financial markets in which *new* securities are bought and sold for the first time. Investment bankers are active in the primary markets.

Risk The possibility that actual future returns will deviate from expected returns.

Risk premium The difference between the required rate of return on a risky investment and the rate of return on a risk-free asset (for example, U.S. Government Treasury Bills) having the same maturity.

Secondary markets Financial markets in which *existing* securities are offered for resale. The New York Stock Exchange is a secondary market.

Sole proprietorship A business owned by one person. The owner of a sole proprietorship has unlimited liability for debts incurred by the firm.

Term structure of interest rates The pattern of interest rate yields for debt securities that are similar in all respects except for their length of time to maturity. The term structure of interest rates is usually represented by a graphic plot called a *yield curve*.

Underwriting A process whereby a group of investment bankers agrees to purchase a new security issue at a set price and then offers it for sale to the general public.

Introduction

T he way a firm's finance function operates is strongly influenced by current conditions in the firm's industry and in the economy as a whole. This chapter provides background for understanding the finance function by looking closely at the corporation and its institutional environment.

The chapter begins by examining the three basic forms of business organization. Next, an overview of the U.S. financial system is presented. Finally, the chapter discusses interest rate variability and the risk-return tradeoff concept.

Forms of Business Organization

Most businesses are organized into either a *sole proprietorship*, a *partnership*, or a *corporation*.

Sole Proprietorship

A sole proprietorship is a business owned by one person. For example, suppose Larry Jackson decides to go into the construction and remodeling business. He acquires some tools, solicits customers, and his business is on its way. He discovers one of the major advantages to a sole proprietorship: *ease of entry*.

There is also a major disadvantage to this type of business organization, however: *unlimited liability* on the part of the owners. Suppose that Jackson's venture begins to lose money, and he incurs some business debts. In order to pay those debts, Jackson may have to dip into his personal savings. If his business continues to lose money, he even may have to sell some of his personal belongings to pay his creditors.

Sole proprietorships have another disadvantage in that their owners often have difficulty raising funds to finance growth. Thus, sole proprietorships are generally small. While approximately 80 percent of all businesses in the United States are of this type, their dollar volume of business activity amounts to only 10 percent of the total business activity in the country. Sole proprietorships are especially important in the retail trade and service industries.

Partnership

A partnership is a business organization in which two or more co-owners form a business, normally with the intention of making a profit. Each partner agrees to provide a certain percentage of the funds necessary to run the business and also agrees to do some portion of the necessary work. In return the partners share in the profit (or losses) of the business.

Partnerships may be either *general* or *limited*. In a *general partnership*, each partner has unlimited liability for all of the obligations of the business. Thus, general partnerships have the same major disadvantage as sole proprietorships. Even so, approximately 90 percent of all partnerships in the United States are of this type.

A *limited partnership* usually involves one or more general partners and one or more limited partners. While the limited partners may limit their liability, the extent of this liability can vary, and the terms should be set forth in the partnership agreement. Limited partnerships are common in real estate ventures.

Although a partnership of either type is a relatively easy way to form a business, there are disadvantages to this type of organization. If one partner leaves (or dies) or another enters, the existing partnership must be dissolved and another formed. This can be especially inconvenient in a larger business. Thus, only about 5 percent of the dollar volume of business activity in the U.S. economy is represented by partnerships. Partnerships are most common in the professional areas of law, medicine, consulting, and accounting.

Corporation

A corporation is a "legal person" composed of one or more actual individuals or legal entities. It is considered to be separate and distinct from those individuals or entities. Money contributed to start a corporation is called *capital stock* and is divided into *shares;* the owners of the corporation are called *stockholders* or *shareholders.*

The corporate form of business organization has three major advantages over both sole proprietorships and partnerships including the following:

- **Limited Liability** Once stockholders have paid for their shares, they are not liable for any obligations or debts the corporation may incur. They are liable only to the extent of their investment in the shares.
- **Permanency** The legal existence of a corporation is not affected by whether or not stockholders sell their shares. Thus, it is a more permanent form of business organization.
- **Flexibility** It is relatively easy to effect a change of ownership within a corporation; one individual can merely sell shares to another. Even when shares of stock are sold, the corporation continues to exist in its original form.

As a "legal person," a corporation can purchase and own assets, borrow money, sue, and be sued. Its officers are considered to be *agents* of the corporation and are authorized to act on the corporation's behalf. For example, only an officer, such as the treasurer, can sign an agreement to repay a bank loan for the corporation.

Corporate Organization In most corporations the stockholders elect a *board of directors,* which, in theory, is responsible for managing the corporation. In practice, however, the board of directors usually deals only with broad policy matters, leaving the day-to-day operations of the business to the *officers,* who are elected by the board. Corporate officers normally include a *president, vice-president(s), treasurer,* and *secretary.* In some corporations one person holds more than one office; many small corporations have a person who serves as secretary-treasurer. In most corporations the president and various other officers are also members of the board of directors. These officers are called "inside" board members, whereas other board members, such as the company's attorney or banker, are called "outside" board members. A corporation's board of directors usually contains at least three members.

Corporate Securities In return for the use of their funds, investors in a corporation are issued certificates, or *securities.* Corporate securities represent claims against the assets and future earnings of the firm.

There are two types of corporate securities. Investors who lend money to the corporation are issued *debt securities;* these investors expect periodic interest payments, as well as the eventual return of their principal. Owners of the corporation are issued *equity securities.* Equity securities take the form of either *common stock* or *preferred stock.* Common stock is a residual form of ownership; that is, the claims of common stockholders on the firm's earnings[1] and assets are considered only after all other claims—such as those of the government, debtholders, and preferred stockholders—have been met. Common stockholders are considered to be the true owners of the corporation. Common stockholders possess certain rights or claims, including dividend rights, asset rights, voting rights, and preemptive rights.[2]

Preferred stockholders have priority over common stockholders with regard to the firm's earnings and assets. They are paid cash dividends before common stockholders. In addition, if the corporation goes bankrupt, is reorganized, or is dissolved, preferred stockholders have priority over common stockholders in the distribution of the corporation's assets. However, preferred stockholders are second in line behind the firm's creditors.

Because of the advantages of limited liability, permanency, and flexibility, and because ownership shares in corporations tend to be more liquid (and hence relatively more valuable) than ownership interests in proprietorships and partnerships, it is easy to see why the majority of business conducted in the United States in done under the corporate form of organization. This book stresses the corporate form of organization in the analysis it presents, although most of the techniques and principles discussed are equally applicable to proprietorships and partnerships.

Since all firms must operate in the confines of the macroeconomic and financial institutional environment, the following sections provide an introductory discussion of these factors. The final section of the chapter discusses risk and return tradeoffs, which must be made by all firms in all phases of financial planning and decision making.

The U.S. Financial System: An Overview

In considering any economy as a whole, the actual savings for a given period of time must equal the actual investments. This phenomenon is called the *saving-investment cycle.*

Table 2-2 presents a summary of the saving-investment cycle in the United States for 1984. Total gross savings for that year equaled $583.0 billion—$172.5 billion from personal savings by individuals, $519.0 billion from business, and a government deficit of $108.5 billion. (This latter figure is a combination of Federal, state, and local deficits, and it may be viewed as dissavings.) Gross investment also totaled $583.0 billion—$674.0 billion in gross private domestic investments less $91.0 billion in net foreign investments. (This latter figure indicates that investments of foreign entities in the U.S. exceeded the investments of U.S. entities abroad by $91.0 billion.)

---

[1] The terms *earnings, income,* and *profits* are used interchangeably throughout this text.
[2] These rights are discussed in more detail in Chapter 16.

Table 2-2   **U.S. Gross Savings and Investment, 1984 (in billions of dollars)**

Personal savings		$172.5
Gross business savings:		
Undistributed profits	$107.0	
Inventory valuation adjustment	−5.4	
Depreciation allowances	417.4	519.0
Government surplus or deficit (−)		− 108.5
Gross savings		$583.0
Gross private domestic investment:		
Fixed investment	$607.0	
Net change in business inventories	67.0	$674.0
Net foreign investment		−91.0
Gross investment		$583.0

Source: *Federal Reserve Bulletin* (February, 1986)

The saving-investment cycle depends on net savers, or *surplus spending units,* and net investors, or *deficit spending units.* The cycle is completed when the surplus spending units transfer funds to the deficit spending units. The main purpose of the U.S. financial system—including the financial markets and all financial institutions—is to facilitate this transfer of funds. Figure 2-1 graphically depicts this continual flow.

Funds flow from surplus spending units, such as households, to deficit spending units, such as businesses, through *financial middlemen* and *financial intermediaries. Financial middlemen* include *brokers,* who buy securities for investors; *dealers,* who sell securities to investors out of an inventory they carry; and *investment bankers,*[3] who assist corporations in

Figure 2-1   **Flow-of-Funds Diagram**

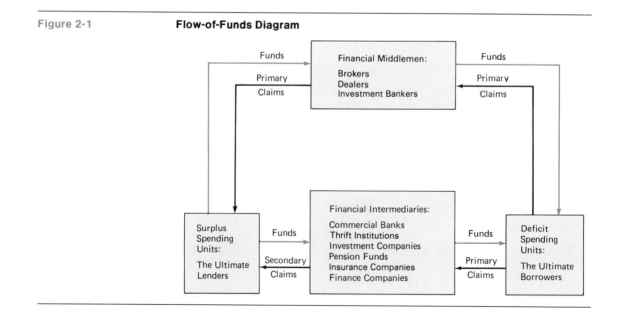

[3] The role of investment bankers in corporate finance is discussed in more detail in Chapter 16.

selling their securities. These securities are called *primary claims,* since they are sold directly by the borrower and bought directly by the saver (lender).

Financial intermediaries include commercial banks, thrift institutions, investment companies, pension funds, insurance companies, and finance companies. They differ from financial middlemen in that they issue *secondary claims* to the lender instead of primary claims. (A bank savings account is an example of a secondary claim.) A financial intermediary may lend money to a corporation even though there is a small chance that the corporation will default on its loan. In general, individuals or households are unwilling to lend funds to a corporation under these circumstances, but they will allow a commercial bank to use their funds, because the bank can guarantee them both liquidity and safety.

Thus, financial intermediaries facilitate the transfer of funds. They are compensated for their services by an *interest rate spread.* For example, a bank might loan money to a business at an average of 11 percent interest, pay depositors an average of 8 percent interest, and use the 3 percent difference to pay employee salaries and other expenses, as well as to provide a return to their stockholders. The various financial intermediaries are examined in more detail later in this section.

Financial Assets

Whereas *money* is the most obvious financial asset, there are others as well, including *debt securities* and *equity securities.* Both debt and equity securities represent claims against the assets and future earnings of the corporation. Debt and equity securities are financial *assets* of the investors who own them and, at the same time, these securities appear on the *liabilities* and stockholders' equity side of the issuing company's balance sheet.

Financial Markets

Financial markets are the vehicles through which financial assets are bought, sold, or traded. They generally are classified as *money* or *capital markets* and *primary* or *secondary markets.*

Money and Capital Markets *Money markets* deal in *short-term* securities having maturities of one year or less. *Capital markets* deal in *long-term* securities having maturities greater than one year. (In both cases the one-year breaking point is somewhat arbitrary.)

Most large corporations participate in the money markets, especially when they have more cash on hand than is needed to run their businesses. For example, Texaco, an international oil company, had over one billion dollars in short-term investments at the end of 1984—approximately 11 percent of its current assets. By participating in the money market, the company earned interest, rather than leaving its funds in a noninterest-bearing commercial bank checking account.

Corporations enter the capital markets to obtain long-term funds, either debt or equity. Most large U.S. corporations are unable to generate enough funds *internally* to satisfy their needs, so they raise additional funds *externally* in the capital markets. For example, during a recent year the El Paso Natural Gas Company, a diversified energy company, used $677 million for capital expenditures (new fixed assets), but it generated only $333 million from internal sources. The company acquired additional funds needed for capital expenditures by selling new common stock ($23 million), new preferred stock ($75 million), and long-term debt ($442 million) to investors. (The company had various other miscellaneous sources and uses of funds, which accounts for the discrepancies among the figures cited here.)

Primary and Secondary Markets   An investor who purchases *new* securities is participating in a *primary* financial market. Net proceeds from the sale of new securities go directly to the issuing company. On virtually any given business day *The Wall Street Journal* contains announcements about the issuance of new debt and equity securities. (These are called *tombstones* because of their resemblance to epitaphs.)

An investor who resells existing securities is participating in a *secondary* financial market. Secondary markets are well established in the United States, where stocks can be traded on the "floor" of a security exchange, such as the New York Stock Exchange (NYSE) or the American Stock Exchange (ASE or AMEX). (Some debt securities, such as bonds, also are traded on these exchanges.) Both the New York and the American stock exchanges are located in the Wall Street financial district of New York City. In addition, there are various regional security exchanges around the country, including the Midwest Exchange in Chicago and the Pacific Stock Exchange in San Francisco and Los Angeles.

Most individuals who invest in stocks are involved with secondary financial markets. Participation in these markets is relatively easy. Suppose, for example, that Susan Jones desires to purchase a stock that is traded, or "listed," on the NYSE. She telephones a security or brokerage firm that is a member of (that is, owns a "seat" on) that exchange. The firm wires Jones's order to its representative on the exchange floor, who purchases the stock for her.

Stocks that are not traded on security exchange floors are said to be traded "over the counter." The over-the-counter market is normally conducted by telephone and computer reporting of price quotations between brokerage firms that "make a market," that is, agree to buy and sell a particular security.

Financial Intermediaries

As indicated earlier in this section, a variety of different financial intermediaries exist to facilitate the flow of funds between surplus spending units and deficit spending units. These different financial intermediaries specialize in the types of deposits they accept (sources of funds) and the types of investments they make (uses of funds).

Commercial Banks   Commercial banks accept both demand deposits (in the form of checking accounts) and time deposits (in the form of savings accounts and certificates of deposit). These funds are loaned to individuals, businesses, and governments. They are an important source of short-term loans. Seasonal businesses, such as retailers, certain manufacturers (for example, those who deal in leisure products), some food processors, and builders often require short-term financing to help them through peak periods. Many other types of businesses have a more or less continuing need for short-term financing and make prior arrangements with their banks to borrow on short notice. Thus, banks provide significant amounts of both temporary and "permanent" short-term financing.[4]

Banks are also a major source of *term loans,* or those that have maturities greater than one year.[5] The proceeds from term loans can be used to finance current assets, such as inventory or accounts receivable, and to finance the purchase of fixed plant facilities and equipment, as well as to repay other debts.

Through their trust departments, commercial banks also invest their clients' funds in corporate securities.

Thrift Institutions Thrift institutions include savings and loan associations, mutual savings banks, and credit unions. These institutions accept both demand and time deposits. Savings and loan associations and mutual savings banks invest most of their funds in home mortgages, while credit unions are engaged primarily in consumer loans.

Investment Companies Investment companies, such as mutual funds and real estate investment trusts (REITs), pool the funds of many savers and invest these funds in various types of assets. Mutual funds invest in financial assets, such as debt and equity securities of corporations or money market instruments, depending on the objectives of the fund. Mutual funds attempt to achieve superior performance through diversification[6] and professional investment management. REITs, as the name suggests, invest their pooled funds in real estate.

Pension Funds Private pension funds pool the contributions of employees (and/or employers) and invest these funds in various types of financial assets, such as corporate securities, or real assets, such as real estate. Pension funds are often managed by bank trust departments and life insurance companies.

Insurance Companies Insurance companies receive periodic or lump-sum payments (known as premiums) from individuals or organizations in exchange for agreeing to make certain future contractual payments. Life insurance companies make payments to a beneficiary based on certain events, such as the death or disability of the insured party. Property and casualty insurance companies make payments when a financial loss occurs due to such events as fire, theft, accident, and illness. The premiums received are used to build reserves to pay future claims. These reserves are invested in various types of assets such as corporate securities.

---

[4] Short-term bank credit is discussed further in Chapter 22.
[5] Term loans are examined in Chapter 15.
[6] Diversification is the act of investing in a set of securities having different risk-return characteristics. The topic is covered in Chapter 5.

Finance Companies Finance companies obtain funds by issuing their own debt securities and through loans from commercial banks. These funds are used to make loans to individuals and businesses. Some finance companies are formed to finance the sale of the parent company's products. A well-known example is General Motors Acceptance Corporation (GMAC).

Financial Deregulation

Financial intermediaries such as commercial banks and thrift institutions have been one of the most heavily regulated areas of the economy since the collapse of the banking system in the 1930s. Various branches of the Federal (and state) government regulated entry into the business, interest rates paid on deposits, types of services offered, and types of investments (loans) permitted. These regulatory agencies included the Federal Reserve Board, Federal Deposit Insurance Corporation, and the Comptroller of the Currency.

Recent legislative action, as well as changing economic and technological (for example, information processing and telecommunications) conditions, have had a significant impact on competition within the financial services industry. The Depository Institutions Deregulation and Monetary Control Act of 1980 and the Garn-St. Germain Depository Institutions Act of 1982 specified that:

1. All commercial banks and thrift institutions are permitted to offer interest-bearing checking accounts.
2. Interest rate ceilings on savings deposits are to be phased out.
3. Reserve requirements are to be uniformly applied to commercial banks and thrift institutions.
4. Thrift institutions are permitted to offer a broader range of services and invest in additional types of financial assets.

These laws have resulted in greater competition between commercial banks and thrift institutions, as well as between these financial intermediaries and other types of financial institutions such as money market funds.

The 1980s have also witnessed the entry of new competitors into the financial services industry as well as significant mergers. For example, Sears, Roebuck & Company acquired Dean Witter, a securities broker, and Coldwell Banker, a real estate broker, to complement its Allstate Insurance Company subsidiary. Similarly, American Express and Prudential Insurance Company acquired the securities firms of Shearson and Bache, respectively. The objective of these mergers was to permit the companies to offer a full range of financial services to customers.

Finally, many states are permitting commercial banks to engage in interstate banking by expanding into neighboring states. This also should result in increased competition within the financial services industry.

Variability of Interest Rates

The interest rates that a firm pays for funds obtained in the money or capital markets are determined by supply and demand considerations.

Interest rates on different securities may vary because of differences in *maturity, risk of default, tax status,* and *liquidity.*

Term Structure of Interest Rates

The *term structure of interest rates* is the pattern of interest rate yields for debt securities that are similar in all respects except for their length of time to maturity. Graphically plotting interest rates against time to maturity results in a *yield curve.*

Table 2-3 shows the interest rates on U.S. Treasury securities of different maturities. At that particular time (October 1985), interest rates were an increasing function of the time to maturity. If the data were plotted on a graph, the yield curve would be *upward sloping.* At other times, the yield curve can be *downward sloping.* For example, in early 1980, short-term rates were about 14 percent and long-term rates were in the 12 percent range.[7]

Risk Structure of Interest Rates

The *risk structure of interest rates* is the pattern of interest rate yields for debt securities that are similar in all respects except for their default risk. As the default risk increases, so do the interest rate yields (expected returns).

In October 1985, for example, long-term corporate issues rated Aaa (the highest possible rating) by Moody's rating service were yielding approximately 11.0 percent, whereas long-term debt issues rated Baa (a lower rating) were yielding approximately 12.4 percent.[8] The 1.4 percentage point difference can be attributed to differences in the default risk.[9] High-rated companies usually employ a lower relative amount of debt to finance their assets than low-rated companies. High-rated companies also usually have a higher ratio of times interest earned, that is, operating income divided by total interest payments.

Table 2-3 **Term Structure of Interest Rates**

U.S. Treasury Notes and Bonds (Time to Maturity—Years)	Interest Rate (October 1985)
1	8.01%
2	8.86
3	9.25
5	9.69
7	10.11
10	10.24
20	10.67

Source: *Federal Reserve Bulletin* (January 1986)

[7] Appendix 18A contains an expanded discussion of the term structure of interest rates.
[8] *Federal Reserve Bulletin* (January 1986).
[9] Differences, or changes, in the interest rates often are expressed in terms of *basis points* by finance professionals. Each 1 percent difference in interest rates is divided into 100 basis points. Therefore, if the interest rate difference between two securities is 0.4 percent, this difference could be referred to as a difference of 40 basis points.

Tax and Liquidity Considerations

Differences in tax rates and liquidity also can affect interest rates. For example, the debt securities of local and state governments, commonly called "municipals," are usually exempt from Federal income taxes, and they are offered at lower interest rates than taxable debt issues.

The liquidity of an asset is the ease with which it can be bought and sold without incurring substantial losses or transactions costs. In general, the more liquid a debt security, the lower its interest rate.

Variability of Interest Rates Over Time

Whereas maturity, risk of default, tax status, and liquidity all determine interest rates at a *point in time,* interest rates also can vary substantially *over time.* Figure 2-2 shows the *prime rate* charged by banks on short-term loans during the 1977–85 period.[10] As can be seen, this interest rate has ranged from a low of 6 percent in 1977 to a high of over 21 percent during a period of high inflation in 1980.

Long-term interest rates fluctuate less sharply than short-term ones, but they nevertheless vary over a wide range with time. For example, the American Telephone and Telegraph Company (AT&T) has a number of presently outstanding long-term debt issues. One issue maturing in 1990 sold in 1956 at an interest rate of 3⅞ percent. Another issue maturing in 2007 sold in 1975 at an interest rate of 8⅝ percent, and in 1981 the company issued debt maturing in 1991 at an interest rate of 13¼ percent. This general upward trend in interest rates has affected most U.S. companies since the 1930s.

When inflation causes interest rates to rise, companies have to pay higher interest costs to acquire new capital and, as a result, have to earn higher returns on new projects in order to cover the cost of funds. Thus,

Figure 2-2   **Prime Interest Rate**

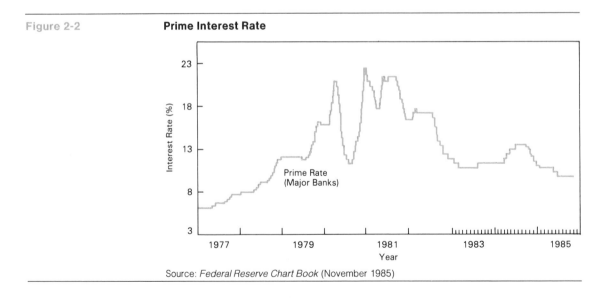

Source: *Federal Reserve Chart Book* (November 1985)

[10] The *prime rate* is the interest rate banks charge on short-term loans to their most credit-worthy customers. See Chapter 22 for a further discussion of this topic.

inflation can affect both a company's decisions about financing and its decisions about investments.

Relationship Between Risk and Expected Return

Understanding the tradeoffs that have to be made between risk and expected return is integral to financial decision making. For example, investors who purchase shares of common stock hope to receive returns that will exceed those that might be earned from some alternative investment, such as a regular savings account, U.S. Government bonds, or corporate bonds. Investors recognize that the expected return from common stocks over the long run tends to be higher than the expected return from less risky investments. To receive this higher return, however, investors must be prepared to accept a higher level of risk.

Figure 2-3 illustrates the conceptual tradeoff between risk and expected return. Note that the expected returns and risk for some common stocks overlap the expected returns and risk for some corporate bonds. Examples of low-risk common stocks include AT&T and Hershey Foods; examples of high-risk bonds include Bethlehem Steel and Pan Am.

Before continuing the dicussion of the risk-expected return tradeoff, it is necessary to define some important terms and concepts. The return from holding a security can be defined by the following equation:

$$\text{Percentage rate of return} = \frac{\text{Ending price} - \text{Beginning price} + \text{Distributions}}{\text{Beginning price}} \times 100\% \quad \textbf{(2.1)}$$

Distributions are the interest on debt or the dividends on stock.

To illustrate, suppose Tom Johnson purchased shares of Shasta Company common stock one year ago for $20 per share, sold them now for $22

Figure 2-3

Conceptual Risk-Expected Return Relationship

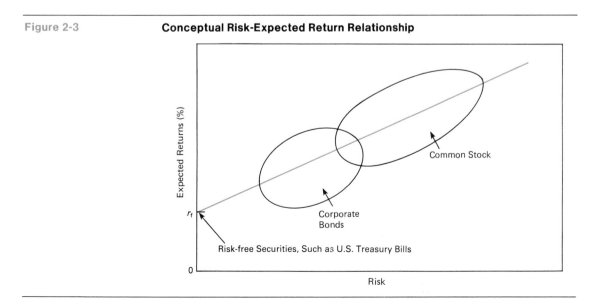

each, and received dividends of $1 per share. His return would be calculated as follows:

$$\text{Percentage rate of return} = \frac{22 - 20 + 1}{20} \times 100\%$$
$$= 15\%.$$

Returns are expressed as a percentage or fraction and usually are quoted on an annual basis.

The return Johnson received is called a *realized,* or *ex post* (after-the-fact), return. Realized returns differ from *expected,* or *ex ante* (before-the-fact), returns. Although they are calculated in the same manner, ending prices and distributions for expected returns are *estimated* values whereas ending prices and distributions for realized returns are *actual* values.

The term *risk* is used in a broad sense to refer to deviations from expectations. In finance, risk often is measured in terms of the variability of returns. Suppose, for example, that you decided to deposit a sum of money in a passbook savings account at a commercial bank, expecting to earn an annual return of 5.5 percent. Because bank failures occur infrequently and most bank deposits are insured by an agency of the government, deviations from your expected 5.5 percent return would most probably be zero. Thus, the risk associated with a passbook account is considered to be nearly zero.

Now suppose you decided to put your money into common stock. You hope or expect that the price of your stock will increase, but you also recognize that the price may decrease. Deviations from your expectation of an increased price are likely to be high. Thus, the risk associated with common stock investments is considered to be high.

The relationship between risk and expected return can be defined by the following equation:

$$\text{Expected return} = \text{Risk-free return} + \text{Risk premium.} \qquad (2.2)$$

A *risk premium* is a potential "reward" that an investor can expect to receive from making a risky investment.

To illustrate, suppose a group of investors has the opportunity to purchase stock in a new oil company that plans to drill wells in a region where no previous commercial discoveries have been made. If the risk-free return is equal to 6 percent and the forecast, or expected, return is estimated to be fairly low—say, 12 percent—it is unlikely that many investors will purchase the new stock. If the forecast return is estimated to be fairly high, however—say, 30 percent—more investors will be willing to invest in the stock. While many investors would consider a 6 percent premium insufficient compensation for the risk, they might consider a 24 percent premium enough of a reward.

The risk-return tradeoff concept is one of the most important principles in finance. It has a significant impact on the determinants of value of individual securities. It plays a major role in capital budgeting decision making, working capital management decision making, the determination of the cost of capital, and capital structure decision making. In short, there are few financial management decisions that can be made without some consideration of the risk and expected return tradeoffs involved.

Summary

- The three principal forms of business organization are the *sole proprietorship,* the *partnership,* and the *corporation.* Corporations have certain advantages over the other two forms of business organization, especially for large businesses; as a result, corporations account for about 85 percent of the dollar volume of business activity in the United States.

- A corporation is defined as a "legal person" composed of one or more actual individuals or legal entities. The owners of a corporation are called *stockholders* or *shareholders.* The stockholders elect a *board of directors* that usually deals with broad policy matters, while the day-to-day operations are supervised by the *officers.*

- Corporations issue *debt securities* to investors who lend money to the corporation and *equity securities* to investors who become owners.

- The main purpose of an economy's financial system is to facilitate the transfer of funds from *surplus spending units* to *deficit spending units.* *Financial middlemen,* such as investment bankers, bring together the surplus and deficit spending units in the capital markets so that funds can be transferred. *Financial intermediaries,* such as commercial banks, receive *primary claims* from their borrowers and issue *secondary claims* to their lenders. Secondary claims have different risk and liquidity characteristics than primary claims.

- *Financial assets* consist of *money, debt securities,* and *equity securities.*

- *Financial markets* are the vehicles through which financial assets are bought and sold. They include *money* or *capital markets* and *primary* or *secondary markets.* Money markets deal in securities with maturities of approximately one year or less, while capital markets deal in securities with maturities greater than one year. Primary markets are those in which *new* securities are issued; secondary markets are those in which *existing* securities are traded. Interest rates on securities vary at any point in time for several reasons, including maturity differences (the *term structure of interest rates*), differences in default risk (the *risk structure of interest rates*), differences in *taxability,* and differences in *liquidity.*

- Tradeoffs between *risk* and *expected return* exist in nearly all areas of financial decision making. Generally, the higher the risk associated with a security, investment project, and so on, the higher the return expected by investors.

Questions and Topics for Discussion

1. Discuss the advantages of the corporate form of ownership compared with sole proprietorships and partnerships.

2. How are corporations organized?

3. Common stock is referred to as a residual form of ownership. Explain what is meant by this statement.

4. Describe and discuss the saving-investment cycle.

5. What roles do financial middlemen and financial intermediaries play in the operation of the U.S. financial system? How do the two differ?

6. How do money and capital markets differ? How do primary and secondary markets differ? Discuss each type.

7. Describe the various types of financial intermediaries, including the sources of their funds and the types of investments they make.

8. Explain the factors that have led to increased competition within the financial services sector of the economy during the 1980s.

9. What is the term structure of interest rates?

10. What is the risk structure of interest rates?

11. How is *risk* defined in a financial sense?

12. Discuss the general relationship between risk and expected return.

Problems*

1. An investor bought 100 shares of Venus Corporation common stock 1 year ago for $40 per share. She just sold the shares for $44 each, and during the year she received four quarterly dividend checks for $40 each. Calculate the investor's percentage rate of return.

2. An investor bought ten Ellis Industries, Inc. long-term bonds 1 year ago, when they were first issued by the company. He paid $1,000 each for the bonds, and today the bonds are selling at $950 each (long-term interest rates have increased slightly over the past year). The bonds have a stated interest rate of 12 percent per year. The investor received an interest payment equaling $60 per bond 6 months ago and has just received another $60 interest payment per bond. Calculate the investor's percentage rate of return for the 1 year he has held the bonds.

3. a. Suppose a U.S. Treasury Bill, maturing in one year, can be purchased today for $92,500. Assuming that the security is held until maturity, the investor will receive $100,000 (face amount). Determine the percentage rate of return on this investment.

   b. Suppose a National Telephone and Telegraph (NTT) Company bond, maturing in 1 year, can be purchased today for $975. Assuming that the bond is held until maturity, the investor will receive $1,000 (principal) plus 7 percent interest (that is, .07 × $1000 = $70). Determine the percentage rate of return on this investment.

   c. Determine the implied risk premium on NTT bonds.

4. a. National Telephone and Telegraph (NTT) Company common stock currently sells for $60 per share. NTT is expected to pay a $4 dividend during the coming year and the price of the stock is expected to increase to $65 one year from now. Determine the *expected* (*ex ante*) percentage rate of return on NTT common stock.

   b. Suppose that 1 year later NTT's common stock is selling for $75 per share. During the 1-year period, NTT paid a $4 common stock dividend. Determine the *realized* (*ex post*) percentage rate of return on NTT common stock.

   c. Repeat Part b given that NTT's common stock is selling for $58 one year later.

   d. Repeat Part b given that NTT's common stock is selling for $50 one year later.

* Color numbers denote problems which have check answers provided at the end of the book.

Selected References

Hoffman, William H., and Eugene Willis, General Editors. *West's Federal Taxation: Corporations, Partnerships, Estates, and Trusts,* 1986 Annual Edition. St. Paul, MN: West Publishing Company, 1985.

Kaufman, George G. *The U.S. Financial System: Money, Markets, and Institutions,* 2d ed. Englewood Cliffs, NJ: Prentice-Hall, 1983.

Kidwell, David S., and Richard L. Peterson. *Financial Institutions, Markets, and Money,* 3rd ed. Hinsdale, IL: Dryden Press, 1987.

Malkiel, Burton G. *The Term Structure of Interest Rates: Theory, Empirical Evidence and Applications.* New York: McCaleb-Seiler, 1970.

Torell, John R. "U.S. Financial Deregulation: Upheaval and Promise." *Journal of Banking and Finance* (December 1983): 561–565.

Van Horne, James C. *Financial Market Rates and Flows,* 2d ed. Englewood Cliffs, NJ: Prentice-Hall, 1984.

Walker, Ernest W., and William Petty. *Financial Management of the Small Firm.* 2d ed. Englewood Cliffs, NJ: Prentice-Hall, 1986.

FEDERAL INCOME TAXES

Note

During 1986 Congress and President Reagan were considering major tax reform legislation. When this legislation eventually becomes law, many of the provisions of the current tax code discussed in this appendix may no longer be applicable. At the time this appendix was being written, it was impossible to determine the exact changes that will take place. However, because of the tax reform package agreed to by Congress in August, 1986, it is possible to identify the key features. Appendix A at the end of the book summarizes the important elements of the tax reform legislation enacted in the second half of 1986.

Glossary of New Terms

Capital gains (long term) Profits on the sale of capital assets held longer than six months.

Capital losses (long term) Losses on the sale of capital assets held longer than six months.

Investment tax credit (ITC) A credit that eligible businesses are permitted to take against their tax liabilities. It is generally equal to 6 or 10 percent of the cost of certain qualified assets the business acquires during the tax year, and it is intended to encourage business investment.

Marginal tax rate The tax rate on the last dollar of taxable income earned by an individual or firm.

S corporation A small business that takes advantage of the corporate form of organization while having its income taxed directly to the stockholders at their individual personal income tax rates. Also called a subchapter S corporation.

Tax credit A direct subtraction from the tax bill. Thus, a $100 tax credit reduces the tax bill by $100.

Tax deduction An amount subtracted from taxable income. For a corporation with a 46 percent marginal tax rate, a $100 tax deduction reduces taxable income by $100 and reduces taxes owed by $46.

Introduction

Because so many financial decisions are based on after-tax cash flows, finance and business professionals must have a basic understanding of tax matters. Tax knowledge is essential in making a wide variety of business decisions, including what form of business organization to select, what type of securities to issue, whether to lease or buy business equipment, and whether to expense or capitalize a $7,500 piece of equipment in a small business.

Corporate Income Taxes

In general, the taxable income of a corporation is calculated by subtracting business expenses from revenues. Tax-deductible business expenses normally include the cost of goods sold, selling and administrative expenses, depreciation allowances, and interest expenses.[11] Federal income taxes are computed on the resulting taxable income.

---

[11] Chapter 9 and Appendix 9A contain a detailed discussion of depreciation methods.

As of 1986, the tax rates imposed on a corporation were as follows:

Taxable Income	Rates
$1–$25,000	15%
25,001–50,000	18
50,001–75,000	30
75,001–100,000	40
Over $100,000	46
Excess over $1,000,000	For tax years beginning after 1983, an additional tax of 5% of the excess (but not to exceed $20,250)

The computation of the total tax for three companies (A, B, and C) with taxable incomes $120,000, $1,200,000, and $12,000,000, along with the average tax, is shown in Table 2A-1. The *average tax rate* of a corporation is calculated by dividing the total tax by the taxable income. The *marginal tax rate* of a corporation is defined as the tax rate on the last dollar of taxable income. All three companies in Table 2A-1 have marginal tax rates of 46 percent. The marginal tax rate is more important than the average tax rate for financial planning purposes. All but the smallest corporations (or firms operating at a loss) are taxed at the 46 percent rate on *new* income during 1986.[12]

Taxable income that is taxed at the 46 percent rate is called *operating* or

---

Table 2A-1   **Computation of Corporate Income Taxes**

Taxable Income	A—$120,000	B—$1,200,000	C—$12,000,000
	$.15 \times 25,000 = \$ 3,750$ $.18 \times 25,000 = 4,500$ $.30 \times 25,000 = 7,500$ $.40 \times 25,000 = 10,000$ $.46 \times 20,000 = 9,200$	$= \$ 25,750$ $.46 \times \$1,100,000 = \$506,000$	$= \$ 25,750$ $.46 \times \$11,900,000 = \$5,474,000$
Additional tax on amount in excess of $1,000,000	—	minimum of $\left(.05 \times \$200,000 \text{ or } \$20,250 \right) = \$10,000$	minimum of $\left(.05 \times \$11,000,000 \text{ or } \$20,250 \right) = \$ 20,250$
Total Tax	$\overline{\$34,950}$	$\overline{\$541,750}$	$\overline{\$5,520,000}$
Average Tax Rate	$\dfrac{\$ 34,950}{\$120,000} = 29.1\%$	$\dfrac{\$ 541,750}{\$1,200,000} = 45.1\%$	$\dfrac{\$ 5,520,000}{\$12,000,000} = 46\%$

---

[12] A corporation is also subject to a minimum tax (which is added to its regular tax) on income arising from what are known as "tax preferences" and include such items as excess depreciation and depletion allowances. See Hoffman, William H., and Eugene Willis, General Editors, *West's Federal Taxation: Corporations, Partnerships, Estates, and Trusts,* 1986 Annual Edition, St. Paul, MN: West Publishing Company, 1985, 2–21, for a discussion of these tax preferences and their effect on the firm's tax liability.

ordinary income. Ordinary income is often contrasted with *capital gains income* and *dividend income,*which are both taxed at lower rates.

Capital Gains Income

As a general rule, whenever a corporate asset is held for longer than six months and then sold, the resulting gain or loss is classified as a *long-term capital gain* or *loss*. The maximum capital gains tax rate for most large U.S. corporations in 1986 was 28 percent. *Short-term capital gains* on assets held for six months or less are taxed at the same marginal tax rate as ordinary income.

To illustrate the capital gains tax, suppose a large corporation purchased a factory site. The corporation later changed its plans and recently sold the land for $3 million, realizing a $1 million long-term capital gain. Assuming an effective capital gains tax rate of 28 percent, the company would owe $280,000 in Federal income taxes on the capital gain. New tax reform legislation for 1987 and beyond would eliminate this special capital gain and loss treatment. See Appendix A at the end of the book for details.

Dividend Income

Intercompany dividends, or dividends paid by one corporation to another, are normally entitled to an 85 percent exclusion from Federal income taxes. To illustrate, suppose that the Hastings Corporation owns stock in the Fremont Corporation and that Fremont pays $100,000 in dividends to Hastings during this year. Hastings has to pay taxes on only 15 percent of the $100,000, or $15,000. (The other 85 percent, or $85,000, is excluded, that is, received tax-free. However, Fremont has to pay taxes on its income before paying the $100,000 to Hastings, because dividends are *not* considered tax-deductible expenses.) The $15,000 of taxable dividend income is taxed at ordinary income tax rates.[13] Assuming that Hastings is large enough to have a marginal tax rate of 46 percent, the tax on the dividends is calculated as follows:

$$\$15,000 \times 0.46 = \$6,900.$$

For corporations having a marginal tax rate of 46 percent, intercompany dividends are taxed at an effective rate of 6.9 percent; that is, $(1 - 0.85)46\%$.

Investment Tax Credit (ITC)

As a fiscal policy measure designed to encourage economic expansion, the Federal government permits businesses to take a *credit* against their taxes amounting to either 6 percent or 10 percent of their qualifying investments (capital expenditures). The tax acts of 1981 and 1982 significantly changed the depreciation rules for Federal income tax purposes. Generally, only three different asset lives are allowed for tax purposes—three years for automobiles, light-duty trucks, and research and development equipment; five years for most other equipment; and eighteen years for

---

[13] This example assumes that the two companies are not affiliated. If they were—that is, if they had a *parent-subsidiary relationship* and the parent owned at least 80 percent of the subsidiary—100 percent of the intercompany dividends would be excluded.

real estate. The investment tax credit (ITC) is 6 percent for three-year assets and 10 percent for five-year assets. Real estate is not eligible for the ITC.[14] For tax purposes most companies take the credit in the year during which a new investment is made. However, for financial reporting purposes a company can either take the entire credit in the year of the investment (the *flow-through method*) or amortize the credit over the life of the asset (the *normalization method*).

To illustrate the ITC, suppose a corporation expands its plant in 19X1 and makes capital expenditures on new equipment totaling $10 million. Given a taxable income of $25 million, the new investment effectively reduces taxes by $1 million (see Table 2A-2).

A corporation may take ITCs up to approximately 90 percent of its taxable income in any one year. Thus, companies that are losing money or earning only small amounts cannot take full advantage of the ITC. This situation has existed in the airline industry at various times. As a result, some airlines lease their aircraft from other companies that are in a position to receive the ITC. Presumably, the airlines then benefit from lower rentals then they would be charged if the leasing companies did not receive the ITC.

The 1986 tax reform legislation abolishes the ITC effective January 1, 1986 for nearly all assets placed in service after that date. See Appendix A at the end of the book for details on the ITC and new depreciation schedules.

Loss Carrybacks and Carryforwards

Corporations that sustain net operating losses during a particular year are permitted by tax laws to apply the losses against any taxable income in other years, thereby lowering the taxes owed in those years. If such a loss is applied against a previous year, it is called a *loss carryback;* if it is applied against a succeeding year, it is called a *loss carryforward.*

The tax laws specify that a corporation's net operating loss may be carried back three years and forward fifteen years to offset taxable income in those years. For example, suppose the NOL Corporation incurs a net operating loss totaling $200,000 in 19X6. This loss may be carried back three years to 19X3. If the NOL Corporation had 19X3 taxable income of $125,000, for example, it could receive a tax refund equal to the taxes it paid for that year. The remaining $75,000 portion of the 19X6 net operating loss next could be carried back to 19X4.

Table 2A-2 **Sample Tax Computation**

Taxable income		$25.0 million
Taxes:		
Tax (assume a 46% rate)	$11.5 million	
Less Investment tax credit		
(10% × $10 million)	$ 1.0 million	10.5 million
Net income		$14.5 million

[14] The investment tax credit is discussed in detail in Chapter 9.

See Appendix A at the end of the book for details on the effect of tax reform in this area.

Deferred Federal Income Taxes

Companies may opt to *defer* payment of some portion of their Federal income taxes for a number of legal reasons. For example, many corporations use the straight-line depreciation method to calculate the income they report to their stockholders and an accelerated depreciation method to calculate taxable income. As shown in Table 2A-3, this usually results in the taxes currently owed being less than they would be if the company used straight-line depreciation methods for tax purposes. Using straight-line depreciation, the company's income before taxes is $20 million; using accelerated depreciation, its income before taxes is $18 million. Taxes of $9.2 million are calculated on the taxable income figure of $20 million, but only $8.28 million in taxes is currently owed. The result is that $0.92 million in taxes is deferred. The company effectively can continue to defer payment of these taxes as long as it continues to purchase a sufficient amount of new fixed assets. When it ceases purchasing such assets or purchases fewer of them, it will have to pay the deferred taxes.

Deferred taxes also can result from other timing differences, such as differences in the timing of the recognition of income on long-term contracts.

S Corporations

The Internal Revenue Code allows certain small businesses to take advantage of the corporate form of organization while having their

---

Table 2A-3   **Simplified Income Statements Illustrating Deferred Federal Income Taxes**

(A) Calculation of Taxes for Financial Reporting and Tax Purposes (in millions of dollars)

	Financial Reporting Purposes	Tax Purposes
Sales	$100.00	$100.00
Expenses, excluding depreciation	70.00	70.00
Depreciation:		
Straight-line	10.00	
Accelerated		12.00
Income before taxes	$ 20.00	$ 18.00
Taxes (46%)	9.20	8.28
Net income	$ 10.80	$ 9.72

(B) Partial Income Statement Reported to Stockholders (in millions of dollars)

Income before taxes	$ 20.00
Federal income taxes:	
Current	$ 8.28
Deferred	0.92
Total Federal income tax	$ 9.20
Net income	$ 10.80

business income taxed directly to their shareholders at individual income tax rates. These businesses were previously called *Subchapter S corporations* and were renamed *S corporations* in the Subchapter S Revision Act of 1982. To qualify for S corporation status, a firm may not have more than 35 shareholders.

Gains or losses of S corporations are not taxed as corporate income. Rather, they are taxed as individual income to the shareholders regardless of whether the shareholders actually receive any income. For new businesses that incur losses, the S corporation form of organization can be advantageous if the shareholders have other taxable income with which to offset the losses. In addition, S corporations avoid the *double taxation of dividends* (discussed in the following section), since the corporate income is taxed only once.

Individual Income Taxes

Individuals are required to pay Federal income taxes on earnings from wages, interest, dividends, and rents. In 1985 the first $3540 of taxable income for married taxpayers filing jointly was not taxed, while the next $2180 of taxable income was taxed at a rate of 11 percent. The marginal rate increased gradually up to 50 percent for taxable incomes over $169,020 for married couples.

For most individuals, long-term capital gains are taxed at 40 percent of their marginal tax rate. Suppose, for example, that Robert Bloomfield sold stock in 1985 for $3,000 more than its original purchase price. Assuming that he is in a 50 percent tax bracket (that is, his income is taxed at a 50 percent marginal rate) and that he had held the stock for longer than six months, the $3,000 is a long-term capital gain and is effectively taxed at a 20 percent (40 percent of the 50 percent) marginal tax rate.

Single taxpayers may exclude from their taxable income $100 in dividends received from domestic corporations. (The dividend exclusion is $200 on a joint return.) For example, if a single taxpayer in a 30 percent tax bracket receives $500 in dividends during a particular year, the tax owed is $400 × 0.30 = $120. Interest income is fully taxable.

Dividends are paid by corporations out of their after-tax earnings. Thus, dividends are in effect taxed *twice*, since individuals receiving them also pay taxes on them. This *double taxation of dividends* has been the subject of much controversy in recent years. Although many economists claim that it hinders capital formation, the government has been reluctant to relinquish this source of revenue.

Since long-term capital gains are taxed at lower rates than dividends, most individuals prefer to receive capital gains, all other things being equal. The effects of this tax treatment are evident in the types of stocks that have been traditionally held. As a *very* general rule, retired persons in lower tax brackets who need current income to live on have owned stocks that pay good dividends. Working people in higher tax brackets who have money to invest have tended to own stocks in companies that reinvest a large portion of their earnings back into the company. These "growth" companies usually pay smaller dividends, but their investors hope to receive capital gains, which will be taxed later at lower rates.

The 1986 tax reform legislation eliminates the $100 dividend exclusion for individuals (effective January 1, 1987) and eliminates the special tax treatment of capital gains. See Appendix A at the end of the book for details.

Questions and Topics for Discussion

1. What are the differences between the operating income, capital gains income, and dividend income of a corporation? At approximately what rates are these different types of income taxed?

2. What is the investment tax credit (ITC)?

3. What are deferred Federal income taxes?

4. What is an S corporation?

5. How do corporate and individual tax rates differ?

6. What is meant by the "double taxation of dividends"?

7. Imagine that a wealthy family has investments that yield dividends that put them in a 50 percent tax bracket. They would like to incorporate in order to reduce their taxes, but an aspect of the tax laws prevents them from doing this. Discuss.

8. Suppose that someone running for public office in your area has begun criticizing one of the prominent local corporations because its income tax rate is only 35 percent instead of the statutory 46 percent. What are some of the possible reasons why the corporation can operate well within the law and still have an income tax rate less than the statutory 46 percent.

Problems*

1. Last year, the Connersville Corporation had taxable ordinary income of $2 million and capital gains income of $500,000. The company also had $50,000 in dividend income and paid its stockholders $150,000 in dividends. Based on 1986 tax rates, calculate the Connersville Corporation's tax bill.

2. Last year the Muncie Corporation had earnings before interest and taxes (operating income) equal to $1 million. It paid $200,000 in dividends to its stockholders and $100,000 in interest to its creditors. During the year the company also repaid a bank loan of $150,000. In addition, it had capital expenditures of $500,000, all of which qualified for a 10 percent investment tax credit. Assuming a corporate tax rate of 46 percent on all taxable income, calculate the Muncie Corporation's tax bill.

3. Calculate the income tax that a single individual in a 30 percent tax bracket would pay during 1986 on the following items:
   a. A $600 gain on the sale of stock held for 3 months.
   b. A $600 gain on the sale of stock held for 3 years.
   c. Dividend income of $600.
   d. Interest income of $600.

---

* Color numbers denote problems which have check answers provided at the end of the book.

PART TWO

DETERMINANTS OF VALUATION

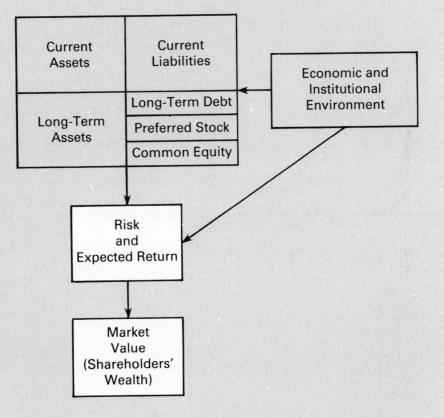

The primary objective of financial management is to maximize the value of the stock of the firm's shareholders. This section discusses the valuation process in detail. Chapter 3 develops the tools of financial mathematics essential for any serious analysis of important financial decisions that have an impact on the firm over a number of years.

Chapter 4 builds valuation models for a firm's securities. This is a most important chapter since valuation is the dominant theme that is carried throughout the text and related to all financial decisions. Chapter 5 explores the determinants of risk and relates risk to the valuation process.

3

FINANCIAL MATHEMATICS

A Financial Dilemma

Prepaying Your Mortgage Loan

In the early 1980s interest rates were near their historical highs. Home mortgage rates of 16 to 18 percent were not uncommon for conventional new home mortgages. Banks and savings and loan institutions were paying very high costs to attract and retain funds. At the same time, these institutions were burdened with many older mortgages written at low, fixed rates of interest.

In an attempt to free up some funds invested in low interest rate mortgages, a number of financial institutions offered plans designed to encourage people to pay off their low rate mortgages more rapidly. First Federal Savings and Loan Association offered Natalie Mayer the opportunity to increase her monthly principal and interest mortgage payments from $852.39 to $1,691.49. In return, First Federal agreed to reduce the interest rate on the loan from 10.875 percent per annum to 10.00 percent. With the new payment plan, the loan would be paid off in five years and ten months, compared with twenty-seven years and ten months under the original loan terms. First Federal computed the total (undiscounted) interest savings over the life of the loan to be $166,577.47. The current loan balance is $89,435.61.

If Mayer believes she will have opportunities to invest the funds needed for the early payment plan at a 15 percent annual rate of return over the life of the mortgage, should she accept the First Federal offer?

This type of problem illustrates the value of having a working knowledge of financial mathematics. As we shall see later in the chapter, the difference between the two alternatives is dramatic.

Key Chapter Concepts

1. The concept of interest
   a. Simple interest is paid on the principal sum only.
   b. Compound interest is paid on both the initial principal amount *and* on any interest earned, but not withdrawn during earlier periods.
2. Future (compound) value calculations determine the value at some point in time in the future of X dollars invested today, earning at some compound rate of interest, i, per period.
3. Present value calculations determine the value today (present value) of some amount to be received in the future.
4. An annuity is a series of equal periodic payments.
   a. Ordinary annuity payments are made at the end of each period.
   b. Annuity due payments are made at the beginning of each period.
5. Compound sum (future value) of an annuity calculations determine the future value of an annuity stream of cash flows.
6. Present value of an annuity calculations determine the present value of an annuity stream of cash flows.
7. Other important topics
   a. Compounding frequency
   b. Determining the present value of uneven cash flow streams
   c. Determining the present value of deferred annuities

Glossary of New Terms

Annuity The payment or receipt of a series of equal amounts of money per period for a specified amount of time. In an *ordinary annuity,* payments are made at the end of each period; in an *annuity due,* payments are made at the beginning.

Capital recovery problem An annuity amount necessary to recover a capital investment.

Compound interest Interest that is paid not only on the principal, but also on any interest earned but not withdrawn during earlier periods.

Discount rate The rate of interest used in the process of finding present values (discounting).

Effective interest rate The actual rate of interest paid by the borrower or earned by the lender.

Future value (or terminal value) The value at some future point in time of a present amount of money, or a series of payments, evaluated at the appropriate interest (growth) rate.

Interest The return earned by or the amount paid to an individual who foregoes current consumption or alternative investments and "rents" money to a business, bank, the government, some other form of institution, or another individual.

Nominal interest rate The periodic rate of interest that is stated in a loan agreement or security. Frequently the *effective interest rate* is greater than the nominal rate because of factors like the frequency of compounding and the deduction of interest in advance.

Perpetuity A financial instrument which agrees to pay an equal amount of money per period into the indefinite future (that is, infinity).

Present value The value today of a future amount of money or a series of future payments evaluated at the appropriate discount rate.

Principal An amount of money that has been borrowed or invested.

Sinking fund problem An annuity amount that must be invested each period (year) to produce a future value.

Introduction

Understanding the concept of compound interest is crucial to effective financial management. In fact, anyone who is involved with money should have some comprehension of compound interest. Consider the following:

- A banker who makes loans and other investments.
- A financial officer whose job includes the consideration of various alternative sources of funds in terms of their cost.
- A corporate planner who must choose among various alternative investment projects.
- A securities analyst who evaluates the securities that the firm sells to investors.
- An individual who is confronted with a host of daily financial problems ranging from personal credit account management to deciding whether to make certain purchases for the home.

Each of these individuals makes frequent use of some form of financial mathematics. However, many people fear that a working knowledge of compound interest might be too difficult to master. Instead, the availability of interest tables and calculators make the subject readily accessible.

While an understanding of compound interest factors is useful in and of itself, it is also a necessary prelude to topics including the following:

- Valuation of securities and other assets.
- Capital budgeting (the analysis of investment projects).
- The cost of capital.
- Working capital (short-term asset and liability) management.
- Lease analysis.

This chapter introduces the concepts and skills necessary to understand compound interest and its applications. The analysis in this chapter assumes that the student will use the interest tables (Tables I through IV) at the end of the book. Many students will have access to financial calculators, such as those made by Texas Instruments and Hewlett-Packard. The last section of this chapter provides a general discussion of the use of financial calculators. That section also compares the capabilities of financial calculators and microcomputers to solve financial problems.

Interest

Money can be thought of as having a time value. In other words, an amount of money received today is worth more than the same dollar amount would be if it were received a year from now. The primary reason that a dollar today is worth more than a dollar to be received sometime in the future is the fact that the current dollar can be invested to earn a rate of return. (This holds true even if risk and inflation are not considerations.) Suppose, for example, that you had $100 and decided to put it into a savings account for a year. By doing this, you would temporarily give up, or forego, spending the $100 however you wished, or you might forego the return that the $100 might earn from some alternative investment, such as U.S. Treasury bonds. Or you might forego paying an additional $100 on your mortgage. Similarly, a bank that loans money to a firm foregoes the opportunity to earn a return on some alternative investment.

Interest is the return earned by or the amount paid to someone who has foregone current consumption or alternative investment opportunities and "rented" money in a creditor relationship.[1] The *principal* is the amount of money borrowed or invested. The *term* of a loan is the length of time or number of time periods during which the borrower can use the principal. The *rate of interest* is the percentage on the principal that the borrower pays the lender per time period as compensation for foregoing other investment or consumption opportunities.

Simple Interest

Simple interest is the interest paid (in the case of borrowed money) or earned (in the case of invested money) on the principal sum only. The amount of simple interest is equal to the product of the principal times the rate per time period times the number of time periods:

$$I = PV_0 \times i \times n, \tag{3.1}$$

where I = the simple interest in dollars; PV_0 = the principal amount at time 0, or the present value; i = the interest rate per time period; and n = the number of time periods. The following problems illustrate the use of Equation 3.1.

1. *What is the simple interest on $100 at 10 percent per annum for 6 months?* Substituting $100 for PV_0, 10% (0.10) for i, and $6/12$ (0.5) for n yields the following:

$$I = \$100 \times 0.10 \times 0.5$$
$$= \$5.$$

2. *If Gene Smith bought a house and borrowed $30,000 at a 10 percent annual interest rate, what would be his first month's interest payment?* Substituting $30,000 for PV_0, 10 percent (0.10) for i, and $1/12$ for n yields the following:

$$I = \$30,000 \times 0.10 \times 1/12$$
$$= \$250.$$

3. *Mary Schiller receives $30 every 3 months from a bank account that pays a 6 percent annual interest rate. How much is invested in the account?* Because PV_0 is the unknown in this example, Equation 3.1 is rearranged:

$$PV_0 = \frac{I}{i \times n} \tag{3.2}$$

---

[1] Although there are other forms of returns, and these are dealt with throughout the text, this discussion is limited to borrowing/lending situations.

Substituting \$30 for I, 0.06 for i, and ¼ (0.25) for n yields the following:

$$PV_0 = \frac{\$30}{0.06 \times 0.25}$$
$$= \$2,000.$$

It is also useful to be able to calculate the amount of funds a person can expect to receive at some point in the future. In financial mathematics, the *terminal,* or future value of an investment is called FV_n and denotes the principal plus interest accumulated at the end of n years. It is written as follows:

$$FV_n = PV_0 + I. \tag{3.3}$$

4. *Mr. E. Z. Go borrows \$1,000 for 9 months at a rate of 8 percent per annum. How much will he have to repay at the end of the 9-month period?*
Combining Equations 3.1 and 3.3 to solve for FV_n results in the following new equation:

$$FV_n = PV_0 + (PV_0 \times i \times n),$$

or

$$FV_n = PV_0 [1 + (i \times n)]. \tag{3.4}$$

Substituting \$1,000 for PV_0, 0.08 for i, and ¾ (9 months = ¾ of 1 year) for n yields the following:

$$FV_{3/4} = \$1,000[1 + (0.08 \times ¾)]$$
$$= \$1,000(1 + 0.06)$$
$$= \$1,060.$$

This problem can be illustrated using the following time line:

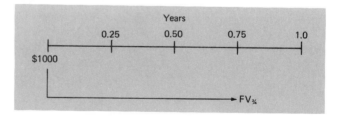

5. *Ms. E. Z. Come agrees to invest \$1,000 in a venture that promises to pay 10 percent simple interest each year for 2 years. How much money will she have at the end of the second year?* Using Equation 3.4 and assuming two 10 percent simple interest payments, the future value of Ms. E. Z. Come's investment at the end of 2 years is computed as follows:

$$FV_2 = PV_0 + (PV_0 \times i \times 2)$$
$$= \$1,000 + (\$1,000 \times 0.10 \times 2)$$
$$= \$1,000 + \$200$$
$$= \$1,200.$$

This problem can be illustrated using the following time line:

In general, in the case of *simple interest,* the future, or terminal, value (FV_n) at the end of *n* years is given by Equation 3.4.

Compound Interest and Future Value

Compound interest is interest that is paid not only on the principal, but also on any interest earned but not withdrawn during earlier periods. For example, if Jerry Jones deposits $1,000 in a savings account paying 6 percent interest compounded annually, the future (compound) value of his account at the end of 1 year (FV_1) is calculated as follows:

$$FV_1 = PV_0 (1 + i) \qquad (3.5)$$
$$= \$1,000(1 + 0.06)$$
$$= \$1,060.$$

This problem can be illustrated using the following time line:

If Jones leaves the $1,000 *plus* the accumulated interest in the account for another year, its worth at the end of the second year is calculated as follows:

$$FV_2 = FV_1(1 + i) \qquad (3.6)$$
$$= \$1,060(1 + 0.06)$$
$$= \$1,123.60.$$

This problem can be illustrated using the following time line:

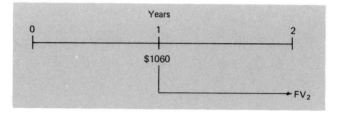

Recall that in the case of compound interest, interest in each period is earned not only on the principal, but also on any interest accumulated during previous periods and not withdrawn. Note that if Jones's account paid simple interest instead of compound interest, its value at the end of 2 years would be $1,120 instead of $1,123.60. The $3.60 difference is the interest on the first period's interest, $0.06 \times \$60$.

If Jones makes no withdrawals from the account for another year, it will total the following at the end of the third year:

$$FV_3 = FV_2(1 + i) \qquad (3.7)$$
$$= \$1,123.60(1 + 0.06)$$
$$= \$1,191.02.$$

This problem can be illustrated using the following time line:

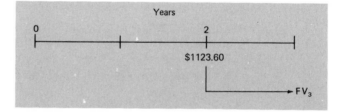

If the account paid only simple interest, it would be worth only $1,180 at the end of 3 years.

A general formula for computing compound values can be developed by combining Equations 3.5, 3.6, and 3.7. Substituting Equation 3.6 into Equation 3.7 yields the following equation:

$$FV_3 = FV_1(1 + i)(1 + i),$$

or

$$FV_3 = FV_1(1 + i)^2. \qquad (3.8)$$

Substituting Equation 3.5 into Equation 3.8 yields the following:

$$FV_3 = PV_0(1 + i)(1 + i)^2,$$

or

$$FV_3 = PV_0(1 + i)^3. \tag{3.9}$$

This equation can be further generalized to calculate the future value at the end of year n for any sum compounded at interest rate i:

$$FV_n = PV_0(1 + i)^n. \tag{3.10}$$

Although Equation 3.10 is useful for solving compound value problems involving 1, 2, 3, or even 4 years into the future, it is rather tedious to use this equation for problems involving longer time periods. For example, solving for 20 years into the future would require calculating $(1 + i)^{20}$. *Compound value interest factors* (CVIFs) are commonly used to simplify such computations. Table I at the end of the book provides a listing of compound value interest factors for various interest rates covering up to 60 years (or other time periods). Since each compound value interest factor is defined as $(1 + i)^n$, Equation 3.10 may be rewritten as follows:

$$FV_n = PV_0(CVIF_{i,n}), \tag{3.11}$$

where i = the nominal interest rate per annum and n = the number of years.

To better understand Table I, it is helpful to think of each factor as the result of investing or lending $1 for a given number of time periods, n, at

Table 3-1   **Compound (Future) Value Interest Factors (CVIFs) for $1 at Interest Rate i for n Years***

Year (n)	Interest Rate (i)				
	1%	5%	6%	8%	10%
1	1.010	1.050	1.060	1.080	1.100
2	1.020	1.102	1.124	1.166	1.210
3	1.030	1.158	1.191	1.260	1.331
4	1.041	1.216	1.262	1.360	1.464
5	1.051	1.276	1.338	1.469	1.611
8	1.083	1.477	1.594	1.851	2.144
9	1.094	1.551	1.689	1.999	2.358
10	1.105	1.629	1.791	2.159	2.594
20	1.220	2.653	3.207	4.661	6.728
25	1.282	3.386	4.292	6.848	10.835

*The values in this and similar tables in this text have been rounded off to three places. When large sums of money are involved, more accurate tables or financial calculators should be used.

interest rate i. The solution for any amount other than $1 is the product of that principal amount times the factor for a $1 principal amount.

A portion of Table I is reproduced here as Table 3-1. Table 3-1 can be used to determine the value of $1,000 compounded at 6 percent for 20 years:

$$FV_{20} = PV_0(CVIF_{0.06,20})$$
$$= \$1,000(3.207)$$
$$= \$3,207.$$

The 3.207 figure is arrived at by reading the 6 percent, or 0.06, column down and the 20 row under the "Year" heading across to where they meet.

As another example, $1,000 compounded at 10 percent for 20 years yields the following:

$$FV_{20} = PV_0(CVIF_{0.10,20})$$
$$= \$1,000(6.728)$$
$$= \$6,728.$$

The compound value interest factor tables also can be used to solve for interest rates and the number of years. For example, to determine how long it would take for $1,000 invested at 8 percent to double, search the 8 percent column to locate a compound value interest factor of 2.000. The closest value to this figure is 1.999. Reading to the left of this figure, it can be seen that the original $1,000 would be worth nearly $2,000 in 9 years. This problem also can be solved algebraically:

$$FV_n = PV_0(CVIF_{0.08,n})$$
$$CVIF_{0.08,n} = \frac{FV_n}{PV_0}$$
$$= \frac{\$2,000}{\$1,000}$$
$$= 2.000.$$

Referring to Table 3-1, the closest value to CVIF = 2.000 under the 8 percent column is 1.999, which occurs at approximately 9 years.[2]

It is also useful to be able to solve compound value problems for i. For example, the compound value interest factor for an investment requiring an initial outlay of $1,000 and promising a $1,629 return after 10 years is

[2] In a shortcut solution to this type of problem known as the "Rule of 72," the number 72 is divided by the interest rate to determine the number of years it would take for a sum of money to double. In this case, 72/8% = 9. The Rule of 72 also can be used to determine the interest rate required for a sum of money to double in a given number of years: 72/9 = 8%. The Rule of 72 does not yield exact figures, but it can be used to calculate very good approximations.

as follows:

$$CVIF_{i,10} = \frac{FV_{10}}{PV_0}$$

$$= \frac{\$1,629}{\$1,000}$$

$$= 1.629.$$

Reading across the 10-year row in Table 3-1, 1.629 is found in the 5 percent column. Thus, the investment yields a 5 percent compound rate of return. For values that fall between those found in the interest tables in this book, interpolation can be used. Examples of interpolation are provided in Chapters 4 and 10. Financial calculators can provide accurate answers to all the problems discussed in this chapter. Interpolation is not required when calculators are used.

Compounding also can be illustrated graphically. Figure 3-1 shows the effects of time, n, and interest rate, i, on the growth of a $100 investment. As the figure shows, the higher the compound interest rate, the faster the growth rate of the value of the initial principal. The notion that an interest rate may be thought of as a *growth rate* will be useful during later discussions of valuation and cost of capital.

Present Value

The compound, or future, value calculations answer the question, What will be the future value of X dollars invested today, compounded at some rate of interest, i? The financial decision maker, however, often is faced with another type of problem: Given some future value, FV_n, what is its equivalent value today? That is, what is its present value, PV_0? The solution requires *present value* calculations, which are used to determine the dollar amount today, PV_0, that is equivalent to some promised *future* dollar amount, FV_n. The equivalence depends upon the rate of interest (return) that can be earned on investments during the time period under consideration.

The relationship between compound value and present value can be shown by rewriting Equation 3.10 to solve for PV_0:

$$FV_n = PV_0(1 + i)^n, \tag{3.10}$$

or

$$PV_0 = FV_n \left[\frac{1}{(1 + i)^n} \right], \tag{3.12}$$

where $1/(1 + i)^n$ is the reciprocal of the compound value factor. The process of finding present values is frequently called *discounting*. Equation 3.12 is the basic discounting formula.

To illustrate the use of Equation 3.12, suppose your banker offers to pay

Figure 3-1 **Growth of a $100 Investment at Various Compound Interest Rates**

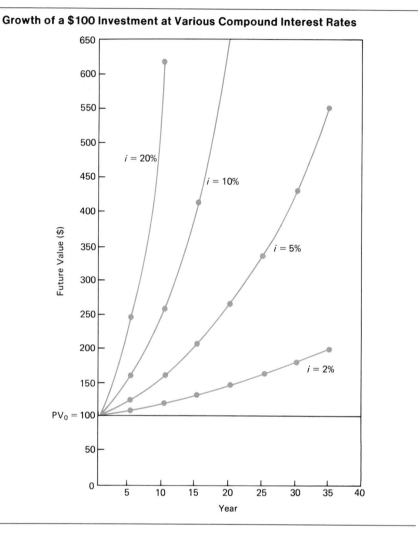

you $255.20 in 5 years if you deposit X dollars today at an annual 5 percent interest rate. Whether the investment would be worthwhile depends on how much money you must deposit, or the *present value* of the X dollars. Table 3-1 can be used to solve the problem as follows:

$$PV_0 = FV_5 \left(\frac{1}{CVIF_{0.05,5}} \right)$$

$$= \$255.20 \left(\frac{1}{1.276} \right)$$

$$= \$200.$$

This problem can be illustrated with the following time line:

Thus, an investment of $200 today would yield a return of $55.20 in 5 years.

Because determining the reciprocals of the compound value interest factors, $1/(1 + i)^n$, can be a tedious process, *present value interest factors* (PVIFs) are commonly used to simplify such computations. Accordingly, Equation 3.12 can be written in the following form:

$$PV_0 = FV_n(PVIF_{i,n}). \qquad (3.13)$$

Table II at the end of the book provides a number of present value interest factors. A portion of Table II is reproduced here as Table 3-2.

For example, Table 3-2 can be used to determine the present value of $1,000 received 20 years in the future discounted at 10 percent:

$$PV_0 = FV_{20}(PVIF_{0.10,20})$$
$$= \$1,000(0.149)$$
$$= \$149.$$

Thus, $149 invested today at 10 percent interest compounded annually for 20 years would be worth $1,000 at the end of the period. Conversely, the promise of $1,000 in 20 years is worth $149 today, given a 10 percent interest rate.

Present value interest factors also can be used to solve for interest rates. For example, suppose you wish to borrow $5,000 today from an associate.

Table 3-2   **Present Value Interest Factors (PVIFs) for $1 at Interest Rate *i* for *n* Years**

Year (n)	Interest Rate, (i)					
	1%	5%	6%	8%	10%	13%
1	0.990	0.952	0.943	0.926	0.909	0.885
2	0.980	0.907	0.890	0.857	0.826	0.783
3	0.971	0.864	0.840	0.794	0.751	0.693
4	0.961	0.823	0.792	0.735	0.683	0.613
5	0.951	0.784	0.747	0.681	0.621	0.543
8	0.923	0.677	0.627	0.540	0.467	0.376
10	0.905	0.614	0.558	0.463	0.386	0.295
20	0.820	0.377	0.312	0.215	0.149	0.087
25	0.780	0.295	0.233	0.146	0.092	0.047

The associate is willing to loan you the money if you promise to pay back $6,802 four years from today. The compound interest rate your associate is charging can be determined as follows:

$$PV_0 = FV_4(PVIF_{i,4})$$
$$\$5,000 = \$6,802(PVIF_{i,4}).$$
$$PVIF_{i,4} = \frac{5,000}{6,802}$$
$$= 0.735.$$

Reading across the 4-year row in Table 3-2, 0.735 is found in the 8 percent column. Thus, the effective interest rate on the loan is 8 percent per year, compounded annually.

Another common example of the use of present value tables is the calculation of the compound rate of growth of an earnings or dividend stream. Suppose the Gamma Machine Corporation had earnings of $3.50 per share in 19X1. These earnings grew to $6.45 at the end of 19X6. Over this 5-year period, what was the compound annual rate of growth in Gamma's earnings? The answer to this problem can be obtained by solving for the present value interest factor over the 5-year period as follows:

$$\$3.50 = \$6.45\,(PVIF_{i,5})$$
$$PVIF_{i,5} = 0.543.$$

Figure 3-2

Present Value of $100 at Various Discount Rates

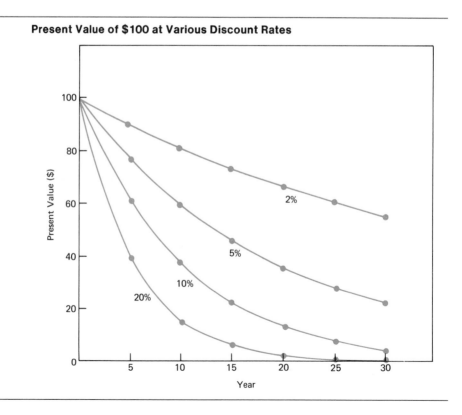

Figure 3-3

Time Line of an Ordinary Annuity of $100 per Period for 4 Periods

End of Period

0	1	2	3	4
	$100	$100	$100	$100

Receipts

From Table II or Table 3-2 we find this present value interest factor in the 5-year row under the 13 percent interest, or growth rate, column. Hence the compound annual rate of growth in Gamma's earnings per share is 13 percent.

The discounting process also can be illustrated graphically. Figure 3-2 shows the effects of time, n, and interest rate, i, on the present value of a $100 investment. As the figure shows, the higher the discount rate, the lower the present value of the $100.

Annuities

An *annuity* is the payment or receipt of equal amounts of money per period for a specified amount of time.[3] An *ordinary annuity* is one in which the payments or receipts occur at the *end* of each period, as shown in Figure 3-3. An *annuity due* is one in which payments or receipts occur at the *beginning* of each period, as shown in Figure 3-4. Most lease payments, such as apartment rentals, as well as life insurance premiums are annuities due.

In a 4-year ordinary annuity the last payment is made at the end of the fourth year. In a 4-year annuity due, the last payment is made at the end of the third year (the beginning of the fourth year).

Compound Sum (Future Value) of an Ordinary Annuity

Compound sum of annuity (CSAN) problems ask the question, If R dollars are deposited in an account at the end of each year for n years, and if the deposits earn interest rate i compounded annually, what will be the value of the account at the end of n years? To illustrate, suppose Ms. Jefferson receives a 3-year ordinary annuity of $1,000 per year and deposits the money in a savings account at the end of each year. The account earns interest at a rate of 6 percent compounded annually. How much will her account be worth at the end of the 3-year period?

The problem involves the calculation of future values. The last deposit, R_3, made at the end of year 3, will earn no interest. Thus, its future value follows:

$$FV_{3rd} = R_3(1 + 0.06)^0$$
$$= \$1,000(1)$$
$$= \$1,000.$$

---

[3] This discussion focuses primarily on periods of one year.

Figure 3-4

Time Line of an Annuity Due of $100 per Period for 4 Periods

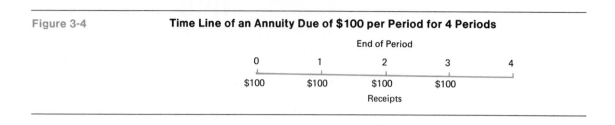

End of Period

| 0 | 1 | 2 | 3 | 4 |

$100 $100 $100 $100

Receipts

The second deposit, R_2, made at the end of year 2, will be in the account for 1 full year before the end of the 3-year period, and it will earn interest. Thus, its future value is as follows:

$$
\begin{aligned}
FV_{2nd} &= R_2(1 + 0.06)^1 \\
&= \$1,000(1.06) \\
&= \$1,060.
\end{aligned}
$$

The first deposit, R_1, made at the end of year 1, will be in the account earning interest for 2 full years before the end of the 3-year period. Thus, its future value is the following:

$$
\begin{aligned}
FV_{1st} &= R_1(1 + 0.06)^2 \\
&= \$1,000(1.124) \\
&= \$1,124.
\end{aligned}
$$

The sum of the three figures is the compound sum of the annuity:

$$
\begin{aligned}
CSAN &= FV_{3rd} + FV_{2nd} + FV_{1st} \\
&= \$1,000 + \$1,060 + \$1,124 \\
&= \$3,184.
\end{aligned}
$$

Figure 3-5

Time Line of a Compound Sum of an Ordinary Annuity (R = $1,000; i = 6%; n = 3)

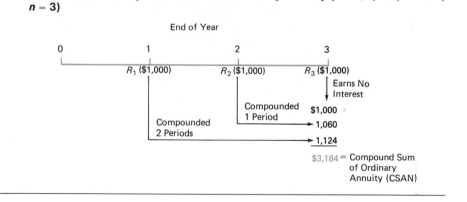

End of Year

| 0 | 1 | 2 | 3 |

R_1 ($1,000) R_2 ($1,000) R_3 ($1,000)

Earns No Interest

Compounded 1 Period $1,000

Compounded 2 Periods   1,060

1,124

$3,184 = Compound Sum of Ordinary Annuity (CSAN)

Table 3-3   **Compound Sum of an Ordinary Annuity Interest Factors (CVIFA) for $1 per Year at Interest Rate *i* for *n* Years**

	Interest Rate, (*i*)			
End of year, (*n*)	1%	5%	6%	10%
1	1.000	1.000	1.000	1.000
2	2.010	2.050	2.060	2.100
3	3.030	3.152	3.184	3.310
4	4.060	4.310	4.375	4.641
5	5.101	5.526	5.637	6.105
10	10.462	12.578	13.181	15.937
20	22.019	33.066	36.786	57.275
25	28.243	47.727	54.865	98.347

The compound sum of an annuity interest factor (CVIFA) is the sum of the compound value interest factors from Table I. In this example the compound sum of an annuity interest factor is calculated as:

$$\text{CVIFA}_{0.06,3} = \text{CVIF}_{0.06,2} + \text{CVIF}_{0.06,1} + \text{CVIF}_{0.06,0}$$
$$= 1.124 + 1.060 + 1.000$$
$$= 3.184.$$

Figure 3-5 illustrates this concept.

Tables of the compound sum of an ordinary annuity interest factors are available to simplify such computations. Table III at the end of the book provides a number of compound sum of an annuity interest factors. A portion of Table III is reproduced here as Table 3-3.

The compound sum of an ordinary annuity (CSAN) may be calculated by multiplying the annuity amount, R, by the appropriate interest factor, $\text{CVIFA}_{i,n}$:[4]

$$\text{CSAN} = R(\text{CVIFA}_{i,n}). \tag{3.14}$$

Table 3-3 can be used to solve the problem involving Ms. Jefferson's annuity. Since $R = \$1,000$, the interest factor for $n = 3$ years, and $i = 6\%$ is 3.184, the compound sum of an ordinary annuity can be calculated as follows:

$$\text{CSAN} = R(\text{CVIFA}_{0.06,3})$$
$$= \$1,000(3.184)$$
$$= \$3,184.$$

Sinking Fund Problem   Compound sum of an annuity interest factors also can be used to find the annuity amount that must be invested each year to

---

[4] The formula for computing CVIFAs other than those shown in Table III is $\text{CVIFA}_{i,n} = [(1 + i)^n - 1]/i$.

produce a future value. This is sometimes called a *sinking fund problem*. Suppose the Omega Graphics Company wishes to set aside an equal, annual, end-of-year amount in a "sinking fund account" earning 10 percent per annum over the next 5 years. The firm wants to have $5 million in the account at the end of 5 years in order to retire (pay off) $5 million in outstanding bonds. How much must be deposited in the account at the end of each year?

We know that the future value (CSAN) is $5 million, and that the appropriate interest factor (CVIFA) from Table 3-3 or Table III is 6.105 (10 percent for 5 years). Using Equation 3.14, we can solve for the annuity amount (that is, the sinking fund deposit) as follows:

$$CSAN = R(CVIFA_{0.10,5})$$
$$\$5,000,000 = R(6.105)$$
$$R = \$819,001.$$

By depositing $819,001 at the end of each of the next 5 years in the account earning 10 percent per annum, Omega will accumulate the $5 million needed to retire the bonds.

Compound Sum of an Annuity Due

Table III at the end of the book (compound sum of an annuity interest factor) assumes *ordinary* (end-of-year) annuities. For an *annuity due*, in which payments are made at the *beginning* of each year, the interest factors in Table III must be modified.

Consider the case of Ms. Jefferson cited above. If she deposits $1,000 in a savings account at the *beginning* of each year for the next 3 years and the account earns 6 percent interest, compounded annually, how much will be in the account at the end of 3 years? (Recall that when the deposits were made at the *end* of each year the account totaled $3,184 at the end of 3 years.)

Figure 3-6 illustrates this problem as an *annuity due*. R_1 is compounded for 3 periods, R_2 for 2 periods, and R_3 for 1 period. The correct *annuity*

Figure 3-6   **Time Line of a Compound Sum of an Annuity Due (R = $1,000; i = 6%; n = 3)**

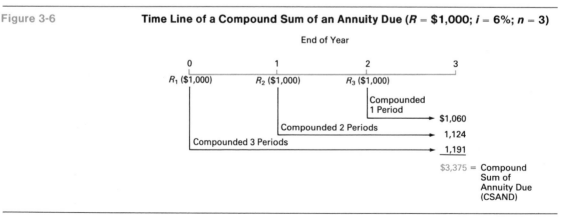

due interest factor may be obtained from Table III by multiplying the CVIFA for 3 years and 6 percent (3.184) by 1 plus the interest rate (1 + 0.06). This yields a CVIFA for an annuity due of 3.375, and the compound sum of the annuity due (CSAND) is calculated as follows:

$$\text{CSAND} = R[\text{CVIFA}_{i,n}(1 + i)], \qquad\qquad (3.15)$$

and

$$\text{CSAND} = \$1,000(3.375)$$
$$= \$3,375.$$

Note that this amount is larger than the $3,184 obtained in the ordinary annuity example given above.

Present Value of an Ordinary Annuity

The present value of an ordinary annuity (PVAN) is the sum of the present value of a series of equal periodic payments.[5] For example, to find the present value of an ordinary $1,000 annuity received at the end of each year for 5 years discounted at a 6 percent rate, the sum of the individual present values would be determined as follows:

$$\text{PVAN} = \$1,000\left[\frac{1}{(1 + 0.06)^1}\right] + \$1,000\left[\frac{1}{(1 + 0.06)^2}\right]$$
$$+ \$1,000\left[\frac{1}{(1 + 0.06)^3}\right] + \$1,000\left[\frac{1}{(1 + 0.06)^4}\right]$$
$$+ \$1,000\left[\frac{1}{(1 + 0.06)^5}\right].$$

Referring to the interest factors in Table 3-2 yields the following:

$$\text{PVAN} = \$1,000(\text{PVIF}_{0.06,1}) + \$1,000(\text{PVIF}_{0.06,2})$$
$$+ \$1,000(\text{PVIF}_{0.06,3}) + \$1,000(\text{PVIF}_{0.06,4})$$
$$+ \$1,000(\text{PVIF}_{0.06,5})$$
$$= \$1,000(0.943) + \$1,000(0.890) + \$1,000(0.840)$$
$$+ \$1,000(0.792) + \$1,000(0.747)$$
$$= \$1,000(0.943 + 0.890 + 0.840 + 0.792 + 0.747)$$
$$= \$4,212.$$

Figure 3-7 illustrates this concept.

Tables of the present value of an ordinary annuity interest factors (PVIFA) are available to simplify such computations.[6] Table IV at the

---

[5] This text focuses primarily on annual payments.
[6] The formula for computing PVIFAs other than those shown in Table IV is $\text{PVIFA}_{i,n} = [1 - 1/(1 + i)^n]/i$.

Figure 3-7

Time Line of a Present Value of an Ordinary Annuity (R = $1,000; i = 6%; n = 5)

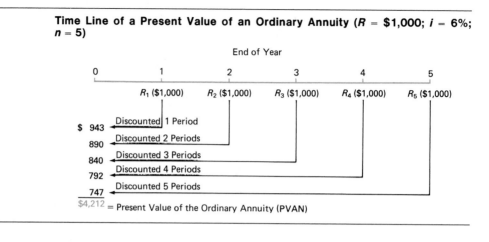

end of the book provides a number of present value of an annuity interest factors. A portion of Table IV is reproduced here as Table 3-4.

The present value of an annuity can be determined by multiplying the annuity amount by the appropriate interest factor:

$$\text{PVAN} = R(\text{PVIFA}_{i,n}). \tag{3.16}$$

Referring to Table 3-4 to determine the interest factor for i = 6% and n = 5, the present value of an annuity in the previous problem can be calculated as follows:

$$\text{PVAN} = R(\text{PVIFA}_{0.06,5})$$
$$= \$1,000(4.212)$$
$$= \$4,212.$$

Present value of an annuity interest factors also can be used to solve for the rate of return expected from an investment. Suppose the Big Spring Tool Company purchases a machine for $100,000. This machine is expected to generate annual cash flows of $23,742 to the firm over the next 5 years. What is the expected rate of return from this investment?

Table 3-4

Present Value of an Ordinary Annuity Interest Factors (PVIFA) for $1 per Year at Interest Rate i for n Years

	Interest Rate, (i)			
End of year, (n)	1%	5%	6%	10%
1	0.990	0.952	0.943	0.909
2	1.970	1.859	1.833	1.736
3	2.941	2.723	2.673	2.487
4	3.902	3.546	3.465	3.170
5	4.853	4.329	4.212	3.791
10	9.471	7.722	7.360	6.145
20	18.046	12.462	11.470	8.514
25	22.023	14.094	12.783	9.077

Using Equation 3.16, we can determine the expected rate of return in this example as follows:

$$\text{PVAN} = R(\text{PVIFA}_{i,\,5})$$
$$\$100{,}000 = \$23{,}742(\text{PVIFA}_{i,5})$$
$$\text{PVIFA}_{i,5} = 4.212.$$

From the 5-year row in Table 3-4 or Table IV, we see that a PVIFA of 4.212 occurs in the 6 percent column. Hence, this investment offers a 6 percent expected rate of return.

Capital Recovery Problem and Loan Amortization Present value of an annuity interest factors also can be used to find the annuity amount necessary to recover a capital investment, given a required rate of return on that investment. This is called a *capital recovery problem.* Similarly, present value of an annuity interest factors can be used to find the payments necessary to pay off a loan.

Suppose you borrowed $10,000 from the Whisperwood Bank. The loan is for a period of 3 years at an interest rate of 10 percent. It requires that you make three equal, annual, end-of-year payments that include both principal and interest on the outstanding balance. Equation 3.16 and either Table 3-4 or Table IV can be used to solve this problem as follows:

$$\text{PVAN} = R(\text{PVIFA}_{0.10,3})$$
$$\$10{,}000 = R(2.487)$$
$$R = \$4{,}020.91 .$$

By making three annual, end-of-year payments to the bank of $4,020.91 each, you will completely pay off your loan, plus provide the bank with its 10 percent interest return. This can be seen in the following loan amortization table:

End of Year	Payment	Interest (10%)	Principal Reduction	Remaining Balance
0	—	—	—	$10,000.00
1	$4,020.91	$1,000.00	$3,020.91	6,979.09
2	4,020.91	697.91	3,323.00	3,656.09
3	4,020.91	365.61	3,656.09*	0*

*Due to rounding, the remaining balance is not exactly zero. The use of a calculator or more accurate interest tables would eliminate this rounding error.

At the end of each year, you pay the bank $4,020.91. During the first year, $1,000 of this payment is interest (0.10 × $10,000 remaining balance), and the rest ($3,020.91) is applied against the principal balance owed at the beginning of the year. Hence, after the first payment, you owe $6,979.09 ($10,000 − $3,020.91). Similar calculations are done for years 2 and 3.

Present Value of an Annuity Due

Annuity due calculations are also important when dealing with the present value of an annuity problem. In these cases the interest factors in Table IV must be modified.

Consider the case of a 5-year annuity of $1,000 each year, discounted at 6 percent. What is the present value of this annuity if each payment is received at the *beginning* of each year? (Recall the example presented above, illustrating the concept of the present value of an ordinary annuity, in which each payment was received at the *end* of each year and the present value was $4,212.) Figure 3-8 illustrates this problem.

The first payment received at the beginning of year 1 (end of year 0) is already in its present value form and therefore requires no discounting. R_2 is discounted for 1 period, R_3 is discounted for 2 periods, R_4 is discounted for 3 periods, and R_5 is discounted for 4 periods.

The correct *annuity due* interest factor for this problem may be obtained from Table IV by multiplying the present value of an ordinary annuity interest factor for 5 years and 6 percent (4.212) by 1 plus the interest rate (1 + 0.06). This yields a PVIFA for an annuity due of 4.465, and the present value of this annuity due (PVAND) is calculated as follows:

$$PVAND = R[PVIFA_{i,n} (1 + i)], \qquad (3.17)$$

and

$$PVAND = \$1,000(4.465)$$
$$= \$4,465.$$

Note that this amount is larger than the $4,212 obtained in the ordinary annuity example presented above.

Annuity due calculations are especially important when dealing with rental or lease contracts, since it is common for these contracts to require that payments be made at the beginning of each period.

Figure 3-8   **Time Line of a Present Value of an Annuity Due ($R = \$1,000; i = 6\%; n = 5$)**

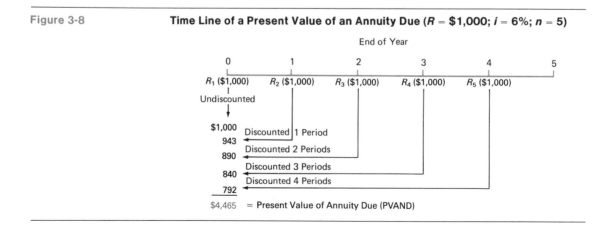

Perpetuities

A *perpetuity* is a financial instrument which agrees to pay an equal amount of money per period into the indefinite future (that is, into infinity). Thus, a perpetuity may be thought of as an infinite annuity. Some bonds (and some preferred stock) take the form of a perpetuity because these special securities never mature—that is, there is no obligation on the part of the issuer to redeem these bonds at their face value at any time in the future. A financial instrument such as this provides the holder with a series of equal, periodic payments into the indefinite future.

Consider, for example, a financial instrument which promises to pay an infinite stream of equal, annual cash flows (CF) for t = 1, 2, . . . ∞ years. If we wish to find the present value of this financial instrument, it can be represented as follows:

$$PV = \sum_{t=1}^{\infty} CF_t/(1 + i)^t \qquad (3.18)$$

where ΣCF_t equals the sum (Σ) of the cash flows promised in each period t, and i equals the rate of return required by an investor in this financial instrument. It should be apparent that Equation 3.18 represents a special type of annuity where the number of periods for the annuity equals infinity. This type of problem cannot be solved using Table IV.

For example, assume that a perpetual security promises payments of $50 per year and that an investor requires a 10 percent rate of return on this type of investment. How much would the investor be willing to pay for this security?

An examination of the PVIFA interest factors for 10 percent (in Table IV) indicates that the value in the 10% column increases as the number of years increases, but at a decreasing rate. For example, the PVIFA factor for 10% and 10 years is 6.145, while the factor for 10% and 20 years is only 8.514 (much less than twice the 10-year factor). The limiting value in any column of Table IV is 1 divided by the interest rate of that column, i. In the case of a 10 percent perpetuity, the appropriate interest factor is 1/.10, or 10. Thus Equation 3.18 can be rewritten as follows (recognizing that $CF_1 = CF_2 = CF_t = CF$):

$$PV = CF/i. \qquad (3.19)$$

In the example above, the value of a $50 perpetuity at a 10 percent required rate of return is given as:

$$PV = \$50/0.10 = \$500.$$

In Chapter 4 the concept of a perpetuity is encountered in the specific case of preferred stock and perpetual bonds. In that chapter, a proof of the relationship expressed as Equation 3.19 is also provided.

Compounding Periods

Thus far it has been assumed that compounding (and discounting) occur annually. Recall the general compound interest equation:

$$FV_n = PV_0(1 + i)^n, \qquad (3.10)$$

where PV_0 is the initial deposit, i the annual interest rate, n the number of years, and FV_n the future value that will accumulate from the annual compounding of PV_0. An interest rate of i percent per year for n years is assumed.

In some circumstances, interest on an account is compounded *semiannually* instead of annually; that is, half of the nominal annual interest rate, $i/2$, is earned at the end of 6 months. The investor earns additional interest on the interest earned *before* the end of the year, or $(i/2)PV_0$. In calculating interest compounded semiannually, Equation 3.10 is rewritten as follows:

$$FV_n = PV_0\left(1 + \frac{i}{2}\right)^{2n}.$$

The same logic applies to interest compounded *quarterly:*

$$FV_n = PV_0\left(1 + \frac{i}{4}\right)^{4n}.$$

In general, the compound interest for any number of periods during a year may be computed by means of the following equation:

$$FV_n = PV_0\left(1 + \frac{i}{m}\right)^{mn}, \tag{3.20}$$

where i is the *annual nominal interest rate,*[7] or the yearly rate of interest stated in the security or loan agreement; m is the number of times during the year the interest is compounded; and n is the number of years. (The limiting case of continuous compounding and discounting is discussed in Appendix 3A.)

Table 3-5 contains a number of future values, FV_1, for $1,000 earning a nominal interest of 10 percent with several different compounding frequencies. It can be seen that the more frequent the compounding, the greater the future value of the deposit, and the greater the *effective* interest rate. Effective interest, in contrast to *nominal* interest, is the *actual* rate of interest earned by the lender, and is generally the most economically relevant definition of interest rates.

The relationship between present values and compound values suggests that present values also will be affected by the frequency of compounding. In general, the present value of a sum to be received at the end of year n, discounted at the rate of i percent and compounded m times per year, is as follows:

$$PV_0 = \frac{FV_n}{(1 + i/m)^{mn}}. \tag{3.21}$$

Table 3-6 contains a number of present values, PV_0, for $1,000 received one year in the future discounted at a nominal interest rate of 10 percent

---

[7] Annual nominal interest rates are equivalent to effective annual rates in the case where compounding occurs only one time per year at year end.

Table 3-5   **Effects of Different Compounding Frequencies on Future Values of $1,000 at a 10 Percent Interest Rate***

Initial Amount	Compounding Frequency	Future Value, FV_1 (End of Year 1)
$1,000	Yearly	$1,100.00
1,000	Semiannually	1,102.50
1,000	Quarterly	1,103.81
1,000	Monthly	1,104.71
1,000	Daily	1,105.16
1,000	Continuously*	1,105.17

*For advanced applications, it is useful to know that continuous compounding is obtained by letting m approach infinity in $FV_n = PV_0(1 + i/m)^{mn}$. In this case, $\lim_{m \to \infty} (1 + i/m)^m = e^i$, and the compound value expression becomes $FV_n = PV_0(e)^{in}$, where e is the exponential number having the approximate value of 2.71828. See Appendix 3A for a complete discussion of continuous compounding and discounting.

with several different compounding frequencies. It can be seen that the more frequent the compounding, the smaller the present value of a future amount.

Throughout the text, much of the analysis assumes annual compounding instead of compounding for more frequent periods, because it simplifies matters and because the differences between the two are small. Similarly, unless otherwise stated, cash flows from a security or investment project are assumed to be received in a lump sum at the beginning or end of each period. More frequent compounding periods require more extensive tables or the use of a business calculator programmed to solve financial mathematics problems.

Regardless of the frequency of compounding, it is important to recognize that *effective* rates of interest are the relevant rates to use for financial and economic analysis. The next section considers the calculation of effective interest rates in more detail for those cases where compounding is done more than one time a year.

Effective Rate Calculations

The previous section illustrated the fact that the more frequently an annual *nominal* rate of interest is compounded, the greater the *effective* rate of interest which is being earned or charged. Thus, if you were given

Table 3-6   **Effects of Different Compounding Frequencies on Present Values of $1,000 at a 10 Percent Interest Rate**

Amount	Compounding Frequency	Present Value, PV_0
$1,000	Yearly	$909.09
1,000	Semiannually	907.03
1,000	Quarterly	905.95
1,000	Monthly	905.21
1,000	Daily	904.85
1,000	Continuously	904.84

the choice of receiving (1) interest on an investment, where the interest is compounded annually at a 10 percent rate, or (2) interest on an investment, where the interest is compounded semiannually at a 5 percent rate every six months, you would choose the second alternative, since it will yield a higher effective rate of interest.

There are many situations in finance where an annual effective rate of interest is given and compounding is done more frequently than annually. For example, if the annual effective rate is 20 percent and compounding is done quarterly, you may wish to know what quarterly rate of interest will result in an *effective* annual rate of interest of 20 percent.

In general, the rate of interest per period (where there is more than one compounding period per year), i_m, which will result in an effective annual rate of interest, i, if compounding occurs m times per year, can be computed as follows:

$$i_m = (1 + i)^{1/m} - 1. \qquad \textbf{(3.22)}$$

In the example above, the quarterly rate of interest which will yield an annual effective rate of interest of 20 percent is computed as follows:[8]

$$
\begin{aligned}
i_m &= (1 + 0.20)^{.25} - 1 \qquad \textbf{(3.23)} \\
&= (1.04664) - 1 \\
&= 0.04664 \text{ or } 4.664\%.
\end{aligned}
$$

Thus, if you earn 4.664 percent per period and compounding occurs 4 times per year, the effective annual rate earned will be 20 percent. This concept is encountered in Chapter 4 in the discussion of the valuation of bonds which pay interest semiannually.

Present Value of Uneven Cash Flows

Many problems in finance—particularly in the area of capital budgeting—cannot be solved according to the simplified format of the present value of an annuity because the periodic cash flows are not equal. Consider, for example, the following stream of cash flows from an investment in a piece of machinery:

End of Year	Cash Flow
0	−$1,000
1	+500
2	+1,500
3	+2,000

The present value of this or any other stream of unequal cash flows (whether positive or negative) is equal to the sum of the present values. Assuming an interest rate of 10 percent, the present value of the above

---

[8] Finding the ¼ or 0.25 root of (1 + 0.20) can be done easily with any financial or scientific calculator using the root function on the calculator.

Figure 3-9

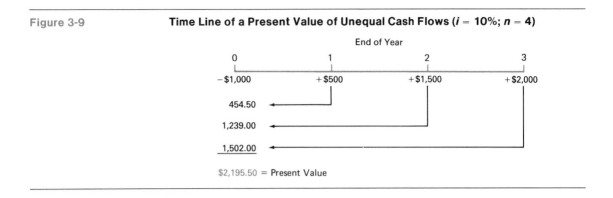

Time Line of a Present Value of Unequal Cash Flows ($i = 10\%$; $n = 4$)

investment is calculated as follows:

$$
\begin{aligned}
PV_0 &= -\$1{,}000(PVIF_{0.10,0}) + \$500(PVIF_{0.10,1}) \\
&\quad + \$1{,}500(PVIF_{0.10,2}) + \$2{,}000(PVIF_{0.10,3}) \\
&= -\$1{,}000(1.000) + \$500(0.909) + \$1{,}500(0.826) \\
&\quad + \$2{,}000(0.751) \\
&= \$2{,}195.50.
\end{aligned}
$$

An individual who invests the initial $1,000 and requires a 10 percent return will earn $2,195.50 in present value cash flows *in addition* to the required 10 percent. This is shown in Figure 3-9.

As can be seen later in the text, during the discussion of capital budgeting, calculations of this type are extremely important when making project evaluations.

Present Value of Deferred Annuities

Frequently, in finance, one encounters problems where an annuity begins beyond one year in the future. For example, suppose that you wish to provide for the college education of your daughter. She will begin college five years from now, and you wish to have $15,000 available for her at the beginning of each year in college. How much must be invested today at a 12 percent annual rate of return in order to provide the 4-year, $15,000 annuity for your daughter?

This problem can be illustrated in the time line given in Figure 3-10. Four payments of $15,000 each are required at the end of years 5, 6, 7, and 8. Of course, this problem could be solved by finding the sum of the present values of each of the payments as follows:

n	Payment Amount	$PVIF_{.12,n}$	Present Value
5	$15,000	0.567	$8,505
6	$15,000	0.507	$7,605
7	$15,000	0.452	$6,780
8	$15,000	0.404	$6,060

Sum = $28,950

Figure 3-10

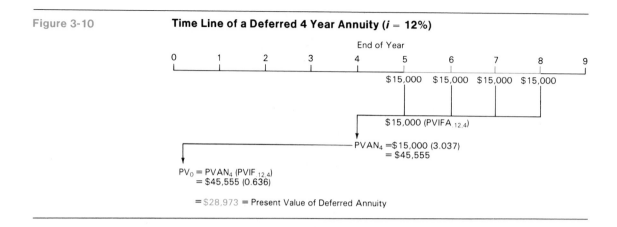

Time Line of a Deferred 4 Year Annuity ($i = 12\%$)

It should be apparent that this would be an extremely tedious method of calculation in the case of a 10-year deferred annuity, for example. Figure 3-10 illustrates one alternative means of solving this problem. First, you can calculate the present value of the 4-year annuity, evaluated at the end of year 4 (remember that this is the same as the beginning of year 5). This calculation is made by multiplying the annuity amount ($15,000) by the PVIFA for a 4-year, 12% annuity. This factor is 3.037 and can be obtained from Table IV. Next the present value of the annuity ($45,555), evaluated at the end of year 4 ($PVAN_4$), must be discounted back to the present time (PV_0). Hence we multiply $45,555 by a PVIF for 12% and 4 years. This factor, obtained from Table II, is equal to 0.636. The present value of the deferred annuity is $28,973. (This differs from the amount calculated above due to rounding in the tables. No difference will exist if this problem is solved with a calculator or tables which are carried out to more decimal places.)[9]

If you have $28,973 today and invest it in an account earning 12% per year, there will be exactly enough money in the account to permit your daughter to withdraw $15,000 at the beginning of each year in college. After the last withdrawal, the account balance will be zero.

Determinants of Discounting and Compounding Rates

This chapter has assumed values for the compounding and discounting rates that were used in the various problems. What factors determine the appropriate rate to use in a specific situation?

One important factor is the general level of interest rates in the economy. Interest rates are set by the forces of supply and demand for funds in the economy. An important factor that influences the general level of interest rates is the current and expected future level of inflation. When the inflation rate is high, interest rates also tend to be high.

[9] An alternative way to solve this problem is to multiply the annuity amount ($15,000) by the difference between ($PVIFA_{12,8}$) and ($PVIFA_{12,4}$). By subtracting ($PVIFA_{12,4}$) from ($PVIFA_{12,8}$) you are viewing this problem as an 8-year annuity which has no payments occurring during the first 4 years. In this case, the calculation yields: $PV_0 = \$15,000(4.968 - 3.037) = \$28,965$. (The slight difference from the amount calculated above is due to rounding in Table IV.)

The time frame over which an investment is being considered also influences the choice of a discounting or compounding rate. In general, interest rates tend to be higher on securities having a longer maturity than on securities having a shorter maturity.

Finally, the risk of the investment that is being considered also determines the appropriate compounding or discounting rate. At any point in time an array of interest rates are available in the market. For example, investors in low risk U.S. Government securities might require a 10 percent annual return. Investors in somewhat riskier corporate bonds might require a 13 percent annual return. Finally, investors in common stock might require a 17 percent rate of return. Generally, the higher the risk, the greater the required return on a security or investment project. The nature of risk and its impact on required returns is discussed in more detail in Chapters 5 and 12.

Solving the Financial Dilemma

Recall from the "Financial Dilemma" at the beginning of this chapter that Natalie Mayer has been offered the option of continuing her present mortgage payments of $852.39 over the next 27 years and 10 months to pay off her 10.875 percent home mortgage, or to increase the monthly payments to $1,691.49, receive a reduction in the interest rate to 10 percent, and pay off the loan in 5 years and 10 months. If Mayer has investment opportunities expected to yield a 15 percent rate of return over the life of the mortgage, should she accept the early payoff offer?

This problem can be treated as a present value of an annuity problem.[10] What Mayer wishes to determine is which alternative has the lower present value cost. For simplicity, she will ignore the effects of the tax deductibility of interest in this example. Including the tax effect does not alter the final decision. Under the original mortgage, Mayer would make 334 payments of $852.39 each month. The monthly discount rate is 1.25 percent (15%/12 months per year). The following is the present value of this annuity:

$$PVAN = \$852.39(PVIFA_{0.0125,334})$$
$$= \$67,115.$$

Under the First Federal option, Mayer would make seventy payments of $1,691.49 each month. The monthly discount rate is 1.25 percent. The present value of this annuity follows:

$$PVAN = \$1,691.49(PVIFA_{0.0125,70})$$
$$= \$78,603.$$

Thus, given a 15 percent investment opportunity rate for Mayer, the early payment plan is not worth accepting, since its present value cost is more

---

[10] The solution to this problem requires either a more complete set of tables than those provided in your text or, preferably, a financial calculator. We have simply set up the problem and indicated the final answer here. The calculations were done on a Texas Instruments Professional Business Analyst (BA-55) calculator.

than $11,000 higher than the present value cost of the original alternative.

Using Calculators and Microcomputers in Finance

The practice of financial management has been revolutionized by the development of powerful and inexpensive calculators and microcomputers. There is a temptation to think of sophisticated financial calculators as an intermediate step in the development of information processing technology which can be used by the financial manager, with the microcomputer representing the current "state of the art." In a sense this perception is correct. However, it is incorrect to conclude that the microcomputer will replace the hand-held calculator as the "tool of choice" by sophisticated financial managers. Rather, the two tools are complementary. There are certain types of problems which can be solved more efficiently with a hand-held calculator; there are other problems which are more suited to microcomputer solutions. Financial managers and students of finance should develop the skills necessary to use each of these tools.

Using Financial Calculators

There are two basic types of financial calculators available. One type, represented by the Texas Instruments (TI) family of financial calculators, uses the algebraic entry method. In contrast, the calculators produced by Hewlett-Packard use reverse polish notation (RPN) when sequencing key strokes in solving a problem. Although the algebraic entry method is probably easier to learn, the RPN method is quicker. Financial calculators are available in a price range from $20 to $125. Generally, the RPN calculators from Hewlett-Packard are more expensive (and perform more types of calculations) than the business calculators produced by TI. The choice of a calculator will depend upon your personal preference for entry methods, the functions you wish to have the calculator perform, and how much money you can afford to spend.

Calculators are generally more efficient to solve a number of problems. Generally, the easier the problem, the more likely it is that a calculator can be used to efficiently solve it. To use a calculator you only have to turn it on and enter the appropriate keystrokes. To use a microcomputer you must turn it on, load the appropriate software, and then begin the calculations. This can take more time than is necessary to completely solve many problems with a calculator. The types of problems which are most amenable to solution using a financial calculator include:

1. Making any arithmetic calculation.
2. Calculating the present value of a single future amount or the present value of an annuity (both ordinary annuity and annuity due problems).
3. Calculating the future value of a single present amount or the future value of an annuity (both ordinary annuity and annuity due problems).
4. Calculating the effective rate of interest when the present value, future value, and time period are known.
5. Calculating the effective rate of interest when the present value, annuity amount, and number of periods are known.

6. Calculating the effective rate of interest when the future value, annuity amount, and number of periods are known.

7. Solving any other problems which would normally involve calculations using Tables I through IV at the end of the book.

8. Some financial calculators (generally the more expensive ones) compute the net present value of an investment (see Chapters 9 through 11) and the internal rate of return on an investment if the investment has uneven periodic cash flows.

9. Some financial calculators compute the precise yield to maturity of a bond (see Chapter 4) or the current value of a bond. Calculators can also be used to compute the value of common stock and preferred stock under certain assumptions.

Although there are other functions that can be performed with a hand-held financial calculator, the list above is indicative of the problems which will be encountered most frequently throughout your financial management coursework.

Using Computers in Finance

Computers have revolutionized the practice of financial management in many companies. Only a decade ago the widespread use of computers in the financial management function was limited to relatively large companies that could afford large-scale computers and the costly software required to operate them. This situation has changed dramatically with the advent of powerful and low-cost micro and minicomputers.

Paralleling the availability of this hardware has been the development of flexible, inexpensive, easy to use, and very powerful software. Foremost among these developments has been the development of electronic spreadsheets. The most popular spreadsheet is *Lotus 1-2-3*. Other popular spreadsheets include *Multiplan, Excel,* and *SuperCalc.* The electronic spreadsheet incorporates the capabilities of a pencil and eraser, a calculator, and accounting and financial management techniques into an easy-to-use analysis and planning tool. An electronic spreadsheet is similar to a large electronic sheet of paper with rows and columns, like an accountant's blank accounting pad. Formulas can be set up in this worksheet just like a large sheet of paper. Unlike a sheet of paper, however, the formulas stay intact in this electronic worksheet and can be recalculated without having to redo the entire worksheet by hand. For example, if you have a 300-line income statement set up in the spreadsheet, the firm's net income can be calculated in a few seconds. Since the formulas stay intact, you can change an assumption (or correct an error) and see the impact on the bottom line in a few seconds. Imagine how long it would take to recalculate the firm's net income if all you had at your disposal was a calculator and you decided to analyze the effect of an increase in sales and variable costs by 10 percent. The spreadsheet will perform the necessary calculations in a matter of seconds. Furthermore, the analysis and formulas can be saved for future use.

Simply stated, the user of an electronic spreadsheet inputs formulas and historical data, such as the relationships found in an income statement, balance sheet, or cash budget. With these formulas and historical data, the spreadsheet has the capability to quickly generate forecasts of future financial relationships in the firm. The analyst is in a position to answer many different "what if" questions regarding the bottom line impact of changes in various assumptions.

One of the disadvantages of spreadsheet analysis is that learning to build (and then actually building) a spreadsheet to analyze a particular problem can be time consuming. If spreadsheets were already programmed to solve particular problems, the financial analyst could spend more time analyzing important financial problems rather than generating instructions for the computer. Financial analysis templates are preprogrammed spreadsheets that are set up to handle a wide variety of financial problems. Some templates are set up to handle very specific problems. Other, more sophisticated templates are flexible enough to deal with many different problems. For example, a flexible capital budgeting template would be able to analyze all types of investment projects—regardless of the expected economic life of the project, the depreciation schedule being used, or the growth rate in revenues and costs over the project life.

One of the features of *Contemporary Financial Management*, third edition, is the provision of a sophisticated, pre-programmed disk containing templates to solve a wide range of complex financial management problems. These templates are designed to be used in conjunction with the Lotus 1-2-3 electronic spreadsheet program. The templates require *no prior knowledge of Lotus 1-2-3* and are menu driven. Documentation for each of the templates is included in the *Study Guide* which accompanies this text. As part of the problem section of selected chapters we have included problems which can be solved using the financial management templates. These problems are identified by a small computer diskette logo printed next to the problem number. The computer template itself is available from your instructor.

Summary

- Financial mathematics plays an important role in many areas of financial decision making.
- An understanding of the concept of *interest* is crucial to sound financial management. *Simple interest* is interest that is either paid or earned on the principal sum only. The basic simple interest formula is as follows:

$$I = PV_0 \times i \times n.$$

- *Compound interest* is interest that is paid not only on principal, but also on any interest earned but not withdrawn during earlier periods. The basic compound (future) value formula is as follows:

$$FV_n = PV_0(1 + i)^n.$$

Compound value interest factors, like those provided in Table I at the end of the book, simplify compound value calculations.

- The *present value* of a sum of money to be received at some point of time in the future is determined by the number of years the investment extends into the future and the interest rate earned during that period. The following is the basic present value formula:

$$PV_0 = \frac{FV_n}{(1 + i)^n}.$$

Present value interest factors are found in Table II at the end of the book.

- An *annuity* is the payment or receipt of a series of equal amounts per period for a specified number of periods. In an *ordinary annuity* the payments or receipts occur at the *end* of each period. In an *annuity due* the payments or receipts occur at the *beginning* of each period. Tables III and IV at the end of the book contain interest factors for the *compound sum of an ordinary annuity* and for the *present value of an ordinary annuity*.
- *Sinking fund problems* determine the annuity amount that must be invested each year to produce a future value.
- *Capital recovery problems* determine the annuity amount necessary to recover some initial investment.
- The more frequently compounding occurs during a given period, the higher the *effective* interest rate on an investment. More frequent compounding results in higher future values and lower present values than less frequent compounding at the same interest rate.
- In solving financial mathematics problems it is necessary to answer two questions:

1. Do we need a future value or a present value?

2. Are we dealing with a single amount or an annuity?

Once these questions have been successfully answered, the following table can be used to select the appropriate table of interest factors:

	Future Value	Present Value
Single Sum	Table I	Table II
Annuity	Table III	Table IV

- The appropriate compounding or discount rate to use in a particular problem depends upon the general level of interest rates in the economy, the time frame used for analysis, and the risk of the investment being considered.
- Calculators and microcomputers can assist in solving a wide variety of complex financial management problems.

FOCUS ON CORPORATE PRACTICE

Compounding: Its Boring But a Wonder

Robert L. Rose
Staff Reporter, *The Wall Street Journal*

John Maynard Keynes supposedly called it magic. One of the Rothschilds is said to have proclaimed it the eighth wonder of the world. Today people continue to extol its wonder and its glory.

The object of their affection: compound interest, a subject that bores or confuses as many people as it impresses.

Yet understanding compound interest can help people calculate the return on savings and investments, as well as the cost of borrowing. These calculations apply to almost any financial decision, from the reinvestment of dividends to the purchase of a zero-coupon bond for an individual retirement account.

Simply stated, compound interest is "interest on interest." Interest earned after a given period, for example, a year, is added to the principal amount and included in the next period's interest calculation.

"With all the time you spend working, saving, borrowing, and investing," says Richard P. Brief, a New York University business professor, "one could argue that the calculations (of compound interest) ought to be understood by most people. And it is within reach of most people."

The power of compound interest has intrigued people for years. Early in the last century, an English astronomer, Francis Baily, figured that a British penny invested at an annual compound interest of 5% at the birth of Christ would have yielded enough gold by 1810 to fill 357 million earths. Benjamin Franklin was more practical. At his death in 1790, he left 1,000 pounds each to the cities of Boston and Philadelphia on the condition they wouldn't touch the money for 100 years. Boston's bequest, which was equivalent to about $4,600, ballooned to $332,000 by 1890.

But savers and investors don't have to live to 100 to reap its benefits.

Consider an investment with a current value of $10,000 earning annual interest of 8%. After a year the investment grows to $10,800 (1.08 times $10,000). After the second year it's worth $11,664 (1.08 times $10,800). After three more years, the investment grows to $14,693.

The same concept applies to consumer borrowing. A $10,000 loan, with an 8% interest charge compounded annually, would cost $14,693 to repay in a lump sum after five years.

More frequent compounding also results in higher annual yields. For instance, if an 8% annual interest rate is compounded quarterly, the principal would grow by 2% compounded every three months. Using the earlier example, the $10,000 investment that grew to $14,693 after five years of annual compounding would grow to $14,859 with quarterly compounding. Monthly compounding would give $14,898 and weekly compounding would result in $14,914. This helps explain why, for example, one bank can offer a savings product with a higher nominal interest rate than the competition, but a lower effective annual yield. It simply compounds less frequently.

Computers and calculators with built-in formulas make solving compound-interest problems relatively easy. Calculators without the built-in formula ought to have an exponent key (see table). People can also use compound-interest tables, which, along with explanations of interest-rate calculations, can be found in a free booklet published by Federal Reserve Bank of New York's public information department, 33 Liberty St., New York, N.Y. 10045.

Investors and savers can also take a rule-of-thumb shortcut to determine how long it would take to double a sum of money at a given interest rate with annual compounding: Divide 72 by the rate. For example, the $10,000 investment yielding 8% a year would double in about nine years (72 divided by eight).

But people should be aware that inflation compounds, too. Unless inflation disappears, that projected $20,000 investment nine years from now will be worth something less than that in today's dollars.

Figuring the Return

The formula for annual compound interest is $P \times (1 + r)^n$. P is the principal, r is the interest rate and n is the number of years.

Here are the values of $10,000 invested at 8% or 12% over various periods:

Years	8%	12%
5	$ 14,693	$ 17,623
10	21,589	31,058
20	46,610	96,463
40	217,245	930,510
100	21,997,613	835,222,660

Questions and Topics for Discussion

1. Which would you rather receive—the proceeds from a 2-year investment paying 5 percent simple interest per year, or from one paying 5 percent compound interest? Why?

2. Which is greater—the compound value interest factor (CVIF) for 10 percent and 2 years or the present value interest factor (PVIF) for 10 percent and 2 years?

3. What happens to the present value of an annuity as the interest rate increases? What happens to the compound sum of an annuity as the interest rate increases?

4. Which would you prefer to invest in—a savings account paying 6 percent compounded annually, or a savings account paying 6 percent compounded daily? Why?

5. What type of contract might require the use of annuity due computations?

6. What effect does more frequent compounding have on present values?

7. Why should each of the following be familiar with compounding and present value concepts.?
   a. A marketing manager.
   b. A personnel manager.

8. Explain what is meant by the "Rule of 72." How can it be used in finance applications? (See Footnote 2.)

9. What is the relationship between present value and future value?

10. What is the difference between an ordinary annuity and an annuity due? Give examples of each.

11. If the required rate of return increases, what is the impact on the following?
    a. A present value of an annuity.
    b. A future value (compound sum) of an annuity.

12. Explain how compound sum of an annuity interest factors can be used to solve a sinking fund problem.

13. Describe how to set up a loan amortization schedule.

14. November 21, 1980, was the day of the tragic fire in the MGM Grand Hotel in Las Vegas. At the time of the fire, the hotel had only $30 million of liability insurance. One month after the fire, the hotel bought an extra $170 million of liability coverage for a premium of $37.5 million, retroactive to November 1, 1980 (before the fire). Based on your knowledge of present value concepts, why would insurers be willing to issue insurance to MGM under these conditions?

15. A savings account advertises that "interest is compounded continuously and paid quarterly." What does this mean?

16. Give an example of a perpetuity. How does a perpetuity differ from an annuity?

17. Evaluate the following statement: "The development of powerful, inexpensive microcomputers have made the hand calculator as obsolete as the slide rule."

Problems*

1. How much will $1,000 deposited in a savings account earning a compound annual interest rate of 6 percent be worth at the end of the following number of years?
   a. 3 years.
   b. 5 years.
   c. 10 years.

* Color numbers denote problems which have check answers provided at the end of the book.

2. If you require a 9 percent return on your investments, which would you prefer?
   a. $5,000 today.
   b. $15,000 five years from today.
   b. $1,000 per year for 15 years.

3. The Lancer Leasing Company has agreed to lease a hydraulic trencher to the Chavez Excavation Company for $20,000 a year over the next 8 years. Lease payments are to be made at the beginning of each year.

   Assuming that Lancer invests these payments at an annual rate of 9 percent, how much will it have accumulated by the end of the seventh year?

4. The Mutual Assurance and Life Company is offering an insurance policy under either of the following two terms:
   a. Make a series of twelve $1,200 payments at the beginning of each of the next 12 years (the first payment being made today).
   b. Make a single lump sum payment today of $10,000 and receive coverage for the next 12 years.

   If you had investment opportunities offering an 8 percent annual return, which alternative would you prefer?

5. How much must you deposit at the end of each quarter in an account which pays a nominal rate of 20%, compounded quarterly, if at the end of 5 years you want $10,000 in the account?

6. A leading broker has advertised money multiplier certificates that will triple your money in 9 years; that is, if you buy one for $333.33 today, it will pay you $1,000 at the end of 9 years. What rate of return will you earn on these money multiplier certificates?

7. You have $10,000 to invest. Assuming annual compounding, how long will it take for the $10,000 to double if it is invested at the following rates?
   a. 8 percent.
   b. 10 percent.
   c. 14 percent.
   d. 20 percent.

8. The Tried and True Corporation had earnings of $0.20 per share in 1970. By 1987, a period of 17 years, they had grown to earnings of $1.01 per share. What has been the compound annual rate of growth in the company's earnings?

9. What is the present value of $800 to be received at the end of 8 years, assuming the following annual interest rate?
   a. 4 percent.
   b. 8 percent.
   c. 20 percent.
   d. 0 percent.

Lotus123

10. Mr. Jones bought a building for $60,000 payable on the following terms: a $10,000 down payment and twenty-five equal annual installment payments to include principal and interest of 10 percent per annum. Calculate the amount of the installment payments. How much of the first year's payment goes toward reducing the principal amount?

11. A firm purchases 100 acres of land for $200,000 and agrees to remit twenty equal annual end-of-year installments of $41,067 each. What is the true annual interest rate on this loan?

12. Thirty years ago, Jesse Jones bought ten acres of land for $1,000 per acre in what is now downtown Houston. If this land grew in value at an 8 percent per annum rate, what is it worth today?

13. Susan Robinson is planning for her retirement. She is 30 years old today and would like to have $600,000 when she turns 55. She estimates that she will be able to earn a 9 percent rate of return on her retirement investments over time; she wants to set aside a constant amount of money every year (at the end of the year) to help achieve her objective. How much money must Robinson invest at the end of each of the next 25 years to realize her goal of $600,000 at the end of that time?

14. What would you be willing to pay for a $1,000 bond paying $70 interest at the end of each year and maturing in 25 years if you wanted the bond to yield the following rates of return?

    a. 5 percent.

    b. 7 percent.

    c. 12 percent.

    (NOTE: At maturity, the bond will be retired and the holder will receive $1,000 in cash. Bonds typically are issued with $1,000 face, or par, values. The actual market value at any point in time will tend to rise as interest rates fall and fall as interest rates rise.)

15. James Street's son, Harold, is 10 years old today. Harold, a studious young fellow, is already making plans to go to college on his eighteenth birthday, and his father wants to start putting money away now for that purpose. Street estimates that Harold will need $18,000, $19,000, $20,000, and $21,000 for his freshman, sophomore, junior, and senior years, respectively. He plans on making these amounts available to Harold at the beginning of each of these years.

    Street would like to make eight annual deposits (the first of which would be made on Harold's eleventh birthday, 1 year from now, and the last on his eighteenth birthday, the day he leaves for college) in an account earning 10 percent annually. He wants the account to eventually be worth enough to *just* pay for Harold's college expenses. Any balances remaining in the account will continue to earn the 10 percent.

    How much will Street have to deposit in this "planning" account each year to provide for Harold's education?

16. There are two investment opportunities open to you: Investment 1 and Investment 2. Each has an initial cost of $10,000. Assuming that you desire a 10 percent return on your initial investment, compute the present value of the two alternatives and evaluate their relative attractiveness:

Investment 1		Investment 2	
Cash Flows	Year	Cash Flows	Year
$5,000	1	$8,000	1
6,000	2	7,000	2
7,000	3	6,000	3
8,000	4	5,000	4

17. Your great-uncle Claude is 82 years old. Over the years he has accumulated savings of $80,000. He estimates that he will live another 10 years at the most and wants to spend his savings by then. (If he lives longer than that, he figures you will be happy to take care of him.)

    Uncle Claude places his $80,000 into an account earning 10% percent annually and sets it up in such a way that he will be making ten equal annual withdrawals—the first one occurring 1 year from now—such that his account balance will be zero at the end of 10 years. How much will he be able to withdraw each year?

18. You decide to purchase a building for $30,000 by paying $5,000 down and assuming a mortgage of $25,000. The bank offers you a 15-year mortgage requiring annual end-of-year payments of $3,188 each. The bank also requires you to pay a 3 percent loan origination fee, which will reduce the effective amount the bank lends to you. Compute the annual percentage rate of interest on this loan.

19. You purchase a 5-acre vacation property for $10,000. Five years from now you expect to sell the property for $22,550. Your anticipated annual end-of-year tax payments will be $500 for each of the next 5 years. Compute the annual rate of return on this investment. Hint: Try 14 percent.

20. An investment promises to pay $6,000 at the end of each year for the next 5 years and $4,000 at the end of each year for years 6 through 10.
    a. If you require a 12 percent rate of return on an investment of this sort, what is the maximum amount you would pay for this investment?
    b. Assuming that the payments are received at the *beginning* of each year, what is the maximum amount you would pay for this investment, given a 12 percent required rate of return?

21. You are considering investing in a bond that matures 20 years from now. It pays an annual end-of-year coupon rate of interest of 8.75 percent, or $87.50 per year. The bond currently sells for $915. Your marginal income tax rate (applied to interest payments) is 50 percent. Your capital gains tax rate is 25 percent. Capital gains taxes are paid when the bond matures 20 years from now; they are computed based on the difference between the bond's current price and its maturity value of $1,000. What is your *after-tax* rate of return if you buy this bond today and hold it until maturity? Hint: Try 5 percent.

22. Your parents have discovered a $1000 bond at the bottom of their safe deposit box. The bond was given to you by your late great-aunt Hilda on your second birthday. The bond pays interest at a rate of 5 percent per annum, compounded annually. Interest accumulates and is paid at the time the bond is redeemed. You are now 27 years old. What is the present worth of the bond (principal plus interest)?

23. Suppose that a local savings and loan association advertises a 6 percent annual (nominal) rate of interest on regular accounts, compounded monthly. What is the effective annual percentage rate of interest paid by the savings and loan association?

24. Your mother is planning to retire this year. Her firm has offered her a lump sum retirement payment of $50,000 or a $6,000 lifetime annuity—whichever she chooses. Your mother is in reasonably good health and expects to live for at least 15 more years. Which option should she choose, assuming that an 8 percent interest rate is appropriate to evaluate the annuity?

25. A life insurance company has offered you a new "cash grower" policy that will be fully paid up when you turn 45. At that time it will have a cash surrender value of $18,000. When you turn 65 the policy will have a cash surrender value of $37,728. What rate of interest is the insurance company promising you on your investment?

26. Your aunt would like to help you set up your new medical practice when you complete your medical training in 6 years. She wishes to have $250,000 available for your use at that time. How much must she invest in an account at the end of each of the next 6 years in order to reach her goal, if the account offers a 12 percent annual rate of return?

27. Strikler, Inc., has issued a $10 million, 10-year bond issue. The bonds require Strikler to establish a sinking fund and make 10 equal, end-of-year deposits into the fund. These deposits will earn 8 percent annually, and the sinking

fund should have enough accumulated in it at the end of 10 years to retire the bonds. What are the annual sinking fund payments?

Lotus123

28. Construct a loan amortization schedule for a 3-year, 11 percent loan of $30,000. The loan requires 3 equal, end-of-year payments.

29. You have just had your thirtieth birthday. You have two children. One will go to college 10 years from now and require 4 beginning-of-year payments for college expenses of $10,000, $11,000, $12,000, and $13,000. The second child will go to college 15 years from now and require 4 beginning-of-year payments for college expenses of $15,000, $16,000, $17,000, and $18,000. In addition, you plan to retire in 30 years. You want to be able to withdraw $50,000 per year (at the end of each year) from an account throughout your retirement. You expect to live 20 years beyond retirement. The first withdrawal will occur on your sixty-first birthday.

What equal, annual, end-of-year amount must you save for each of the next 30 years to meet these goals, if all savings earn a 13 percent annual rate of return?

30. If you deposit $1,000 a year (at the end of each of the next 5 years) in an account paying a nominal 12 percent per year, compounded semiannually, how much will you have in the account at the end of 10 years?

31. Shyster Investments has offered you the following investment opportunity:

- $6,000 at the end of each year for the first 5 years, plus
- $3,000 at the end of each year from years 6 through 10, plus
- $2,000 at the end of each year from years 11 through 20.

a. How much would you be willing to pay for this investment if you required a 12 percent rate of return?
b. If the payments were received at the beginning of each year, what would you be willing to pay for this investment?

32. Upon retirement your goal is to spend 5 years traveling around the world. To travel in the style to which you are accustomed will require $250,000 per year at the beginning of each year. If you plan to retire in 30 years, what are the equal, annual, end-of-year payments necessary to achieve this goal? The funds in the retirement account will compound at 10 percent annually.

33. A Baldwin United agent has just presented the following offer. If you deposit $25,000 with the firm today, they will pay you $10,000 per year at the end of years 8 through 15. If you require a 15% rate of return on this type of investment, would you make this investment?

34. You deposit $4,500 per year at the end of each of the next 25 years into an account which pays 10% compounded annually. How much could you withdraw at the end of each of the 20 years following your last deposit? (The 25th and last deposit is made at the beginning of the 20-year period. The first withdrawal is made at the end of the first year in the 20-year period).

35. Upon retirement you are offered a choice between a $250,000 lump sum payment or a lifetime annuity of $51,300, with annuity payments being made at the end of each year. If you expect to live for 15 years after retirement, at what required rate of return would you be indifferent between the two alternatives (to the nearest whole percent)?

36. You deposit $10,000 at the end of each of the next 4 years into an account which pays 12% annually. What is the account balance at the end of 10 years?

37. IRA Investments develops retirement programs for individuals. You are 30 years old and plan to retire on your sixtieth birthday. You want to establish a plan with IRA that will require a series of equal, annual, end-of-year deposits into the retirement account. The first deposit will be made one year from today on your thirty-first birthday. The final payment in the account will be made on your sixtieth birthday. The retirement plan will allow you to withdraw $120,000 per year for 15 years, with the first withdrawal on your sixty-first birthday. Also at the end of the 15th year you wish to withdraw an additional $250,000. The retirement account promises to earn 12% annually.

What periodic payment must be made into the account to achieve your retirement objective?

38. A bank offers an *effective* annual interest rate of 15 percent, compounded quarterly. What rate of interest is being paid quarterly by the bank?

39. An investment requires an outlay of $100,000 today. Cash inflows from the investment are expected to be $40,000 per year at the end of years 4, 5, 6, 7, and 8. If you require a 20% rate of return on this type of investment, should the investment be undertaken?

40. An investment of $100,000 is expected to generate cash inflows of $60,000 in 1 year and $79,350 in 2 years. Calculate the expected rate of return on this investment to the nearest whole percent.

41. An investment offers the following year-end cash flows:

End of Year	Cash Flow
1	$20,000
2	$30,000
3	$15,000

Using a 15% interest rate, convert this series of irregular cash flows to an equivalent (in present value terms) 3-year annuity.

42. Congratulations! You have just won the Publishers Corporation Sweepstakes. You have been offered a lump sum of $1,000,000, or a lifetime (end of year) annuity of $100,000 per year. If you expect to live for 20 years and can earn 15 percent on your investments, which alternative should you choose (ignoring tax consequences)? If you expect to earn only 7 percent on your investments, how does your answer change?

43. Your child will go to college 12 years from now and will require $20,000, $21,000, $22,000, and $23,000 at the beginning of each year in school. In addition you and your spouse plan to retire in 20 years. You want to have $75,000 available for each of your expected 15 years of blissful retirement. These funds will need to be available at the *beginning* of each year. If you now have $15,000 which can be used to meet these obligations, how much must you invest at the end of each of the next 20 years (if all funds earn an 11 percent rate of return) in order to meet your financial objectives?

44. **a.** What payments are due on a 5-year, 10 percent loan, with an initial outstanding balance of $100,000? (At the end of 5 years, the loan will be paid off. All loan payments are equal and occur at the end of the year.)

b. What portion of the year 2 payment is principal? Interest?

45. The Nucleo-Robotics Corporation has just issued $10,000,000 of first mortgage bonds, each having a par value of $1,000 and a coupon interest rate of 15%. The bonds have a 25-year maturity and require that the firm establish a sinking fund sufficient to retire *80 percent* of the bonds by the time the bonds are scheduled to mature. Deposits into the sinking fund will begin 5 years from now and the firm will make a total of 20 end-of-year deposits into the fund. Money deposited into the sinking fund is expected to earn a 12 percent rate of return over the 20-year life of the fund. How much must the firm deposit into the fund each year in order to meet its sinking fund obligations?

Lotus123

CONTINUOUS COMPOUNDING AND DISCOUNTING

Continuous Compounding

In Chapter 3 we assumed that interest was received (or growth in a stream of payments occurred) at discrete points in time, such as at the end of each year, semiannually, quarterly, and so forth. It was shown that a nominal rate of i percent per year results in a greater than i percent effective rate per year if compounding occurs more frequently than one time at the end of the year. Specifically, the future value (FV_n) of some initial amount (PV_0) is given by Equation 3.20:

$$FV_n = PV_0(1 + i/m)^{mn}, \qquad (3.20)$$

where i is the nominal annual rate of interest or growth, m is the number of times per year that compounding occurs, and n is the number of years compounding occurs. (Recall from Footnote 7 in Chapter 3 that an annual nominal interest rate is equivalent to an effective annual rate in the case where compounding occurs one time a year at the end of the year.)

As is shown in Table 3-5, the more often the compounding takes place each year, the greater will be the future value of some present amount. Another way of looking at this is to indicate that the more often that compounding takes place each year, the greater is the *effective* rate of interest (or growth) compared to the stated, annual *nominal* rate.

At the limit, we could accrue, or compound interest *continuously*. In this limiting case, the future value equation for continuous compounding becomes:

$$FV_n = PV_0(e)^{in}, \qquad (3A.1)$$

where e is approximately equal to the value 2.71828. (This value is the base number in natural logarithms.) If you have a financial or scientific calculator, the value of e^{in} normally can be found by multiplying the nominal rate i by the number of years n and then punching the e^x key.

For example, if $1,000 is invested for 1 year at a nominal rate of 10 percent compounded continuously, the future value at the end of that year is given as follows:

$$FV_1 = \$1,000(e)^{0.10(1)} = \$1,000(2.71828)^{0.10}$$
$$= \$1,105.17.$$

In the case where the $1,000 is invested at a nominal rate of 10 percent for 3 years, the future value, assuming continuous compounding, is equal to:

$$FV_3 = \$1,000(e)^{0.10(3)} = \$1,000(2.71828)^{.3}$$
$$= \$1,349.86.$$

Continuous Discounting

Equation 3.21 can also be modified to reflect continuous discounting. At the limit where compounding takes place continuously, present values can be computed as follows:

$$PV_0 = FV_n/(e)^{in} \qquad \text{(3A.2)}$$

or equivalently:

$$PV_0 = FV_n(e)^{-in}. \qquad \text{(3A.3)}$$

For example, if \$1,349.86 is to be received 3 years from now at the continuously compounded rate of 10 percent, the present value can be computed as follows:

$$PV_0 = \$1,349.86/(2.71828)^{0.10(3)}$$
$$= \$1,000.$$

Effective Rate Calculations

When a *nominal* rate i of interest (or growth) is known and compounding occurs continuously, it is easy to compute the *effective* rate using Equation 3A.4:

$$\text{Effective (annual) rate} = e^i - 1.0 \qquad \text{(3A.4)}$$

For example, if the nominal annual rate is 20 percent and compounding occurs continuously, the effective annual rate is 22.14 percent, computed as follows:

$$\text{Effective (annual) rate} = 2.71828^{(0.2)} - 1.0$$
$$= 1.2214 - 1.0$$
$$= 0.2214 \text{ or } 22.14\%.$$

The effective rate is higher than the nominal rate because, with continuous compounding, the money is working harder; that is, interest is being accumulated more frequently (continuously) and this accumulated interest is available to earn its own interest on an ongoing (continuous) basis.

Alternatively, we may wish to calculate a continuous discount (or compounding) rate which is equivalent to an effective annual rate (when compounding is assumed to occur only one time at the end of the year). In this case, the continuous rate can be computed using Equation 3A.5 as follows:

$$\text{Continuous effective rate} = ln\,(1 + i), \qquad \text{(3A.5)}$$

where ln represents the natural logarithm (base 2.71828) and i represents the annual rate. (The natural logarithm of a number can be easily found using a financial or scientific calculator or a table of natural logarithms.)

For example, we may wish to know what continuously compounded effective rate of interest will yield the same present value of a future cash flow as an annual rate of interest of 10 percent (where compounding occurs only one time a year). This may be computed as follows:

$$\text{Continuous effective rate} = ln\ (1 + 0.10)$$
$$= 0.0953 \text{ or } 9.53\%.$$

It is logical that this continuous rate will be less than the annual rate, since the money is working harder when compounding occurs continuously (even more frequently than every second) than when it occurs only one time a year.

Problems*

1. What is the future value of $10,000 invested for 2 years at a nominal interest rate of 15 percent compounded continuously?

2. You expect to receive $5,000 in 5 years. What is the present value of this future receipt at the continuously compounded rate of 12 percent?

3. The nominal rate of interest on a bank CD is 10 percent. If compounding occurs continuously, what is the effective annual rate?

4. What continuously compounded rate of interest will yield the same present value of a $5,000 cash flow to be received 1 year in the future as an annual rate of interest of 9 percent (where compounding occurs one time a year)? Prove your answer by finding the present value of the $5,000 future cash flow under both conditions.

* Color numbers denote problems which have check answers provided at the end of the book.

4

THE VALUATION OF LONG-TERM SECURITIES

A Financial Dilemma

Valuation of Gulf Oil Common Stock*

In August 1983 Gulf Oil became the target of a takeover attempt by an investment group headed by T. Boone Pickens, Jr. and Mesa Petroleum. Prior to the takeover battle, Gulf Oil's common stock was selling for less than $40 per share, while its book value was approximately $60 per share. Gulf Oil had the reputation of being one of the weakest of the seven big international oil companies (the "Seven Sisters"). Gulf's energy reserves were showing a net decline each year, its refining and retail marketing operations (especially overseas) were losing lots of money, and its after-tax return on equity was low (approximately 9.5 percent in 1983). The low price of its common stock reflected investors' pessimistic opinions about Gulf's long-term prospects.

In order to avoid an unfriendly takeover by Pickens and his investment group, Gulf directors and officers invited various companies to submit bids for the company. On March 5, 1984, Standard Oil of California (Chevron) was the successful bidder, agreeing to purchase all the common stock of Gulf Oil for $80 per share or a total of $13.2 billion. It represented the largest corporate takeover in history.

This merger as well as many other large mergers over the past several years have raised a number of interesting valuation questions. Prior to the takeover activity, why was the market value (price) of Gulf common stock less than two-thirds its book value? Why was Chevron willing to pay more than twice the pre-takeover market value for the company? Methods used in the valuation of assets and securities are examined in this chapter.

* Adapted from articles in *The Wall Street Journal* (March 7, 1984) and *Business Week* (March 19, 1984).

Key Chapter Concepts

1. Capitalization-of-income method of valuation
   a. Value of an asset is equal to the present value of the expected future benefits discounted at the appropriate required rate of return.
   b. Required rate of return is a function of the risk or uncertainty associated with the returns from the asset.
2. Bond valuation
   a. Value of a bond with a finite maturity date is equal to the present value of the interest payments and principal payment (at maturity) discounted at the investor's required rate of return.
   b. Yield to maturity of a bond is equal to the rate of return that equates the price of the bond to the present value of the interest and principal payments.
3. Common stock valuation
   a. In the general dividend valuation model, the value of a common stock is equal to the present value of all future dividend payments discounted at the investor's required rate of return.
   b. In the constant growth dividend valuation model, the value of a common stock is equal to the next period's dividend divided by the difference between the investor's required rate of return and the dividend growth rate.
4. Other important topics include:
   a. Market value of assets and market equilibrium
   b. Valuation of perpetual bonds
   c. Valuation of preferred stock
   d. Zero-growth and above-normal growth dividend valuation models

Glossary of New Terms

Bond A long-term debt instrument that promises to pay the lender a series of periodic interest payments in addition to returning the principal at maturity. Most corporate bonds are offered in $1,000 principal amounts.

Book value The accounting value of an asset or a corporation. The book value per share of common stock is equal to the total book value of the company (that is, net worth) divided by the total number of shares of common stock outstanding.

Capital gains yield The expected percentage increase in the price of the stock.

Capitalization of income A method of determining the present value of an asset that is expected to produce a stream of future benefits. This involves *discounting* the stream of expected future benefits at an appropriate rate.

Coupon rate of interest The interest rate stated on a bond. The coupon rate of interest times the *par,* or principal, value of a bond determines the periodic dollar interest payments received by the bondholder.

Debenture A bond that is *not* secured by a mortgage on any specific asset but instead by the general credit and earning power of the issuing firm.

Dividend yield The annual dividend payment divided by the price of the stock.

Going-concern value The value of a firm, assuming that the firm's organization and assets remain intact and are used to generate future income and cash flows.

Interest rate risk The variation in the market price (and hence in the realized rate of return, or yield) of a security that arises from changes in interest rates.

Liquidation value The value of a firm, assuming that it sells all its assets and stops using them to generate future income and cash flows.

Mortgage bond A bond that is secured by a pledge of a specific asset or group of assets.

Perpetual bond A bond that has no maturity date.

Required rate of return The rate used to value a stream of future benefits from an asset (also called the *discount rate*). The riskier the return from the asset, the higher the required rate of return.

Yield to maturity The discount rate that equates the present value of all expected payments and the repayment of principal from a bond with the present bond price.

Introduction

F irms issue various types of long-term securities to help meet their needs for funds. These include long-term debt, preferred stock, and common stock. The valuation of long-term securities is important to a firm's financial managers, as well as current owners, prospective investors, and security analysts.

For example, financial managers should understand how the price or value of the firm's securities (particularly common stock) is affected by investment, financing, and dividend decisions. Similarly, both current owners and prospective investors should be able to compare their own valuations of a firm's securities with actual market prices in order to make rational security purchase and sale decisions. Likewise, security analysts use valuation techniques in evaluating long-term corporate securities when making investment recommendations.

The chapter begins with a discussion of the general concept of valuation. It continues by developing valuation models for bonds, preferred stock, and common stock.

It is assumed throughout the chapter that the firms under discussion are *going concerns;* that is, their organization and assets will remain intact and be used to generate future income and cash flows. Techniques other than the ones described here must be used to value long-term securities of firms faced with the possibility of bankruptcy. In such cases the *liquidation value* of the firm's assets is the primary determinant of the value of the various types of long-term securities.[1]

Valuation of Assets

The value of any asset is based on the *expected future benefits* the owner will receive over the life of the asset. For example, the value of a *physical asset,* such as a new piece of equipment or production plant, is based on the expected cash inflows the asset will generate for the firm over its useful life. These cash inflows take the forms of increased revenues and/or reduced costs plus any salvage value received from the sale of the asset.[2]

Similarly, the value of a *financial asset,* such as a stock or bond, is based on the expected cash returns the asset will generate for the owner during the *holding period.* These returns take the form of interest or dividend payments over the holding period plus the amount the owner receives when the asset is sold.

One way of determining the value of an asset is to calculate the present value of the stream of expected future benefits discounted at an appropriate *required rate of return.* This is known as the *capitalization-of-income* method of valuation and is represented algebraically as follows:

$$V_0 = \frac{R_1}{(1 + i)^1} + \frac{R_2}{(1 + i)^2} + \cdots + \frac{R_n}{(1 + i)^n}, \tag{4.1}$$

or, using summation notation, as follows:

$$V_0 = \sum_{t=1}^{n} \frac{R_t}{(1 + i)^t}, \tag{4.2}$$

---

[1] This topic is discussed in Chapter 24.

[2] Chapter 9 contains a more lengthy discussion of capital budgeting.

where V_0 is the value of the asset at time zero, R_t the expected cash return in period t, i the required rate of return or discount rate, and n the length of the holding period.

For example, assume that the cash returns, R_t, of an investment are expected to be an annuity of $1,000 per year for $n = 6$ years, and the required rate of return, i, is 8 percent. Using the capitalization-of-income method, the value of this investment is:

$$V_0 = \sum_{t=1}^{6} \frac{\$1,000}{(1 + 0.08)^t}$$

Recognizing this expression as the present value of an annuity (PVAN), the value of the investment is computed using Equation 3.16 of the previous chapter:

$$V_0 = \$1,000\,(\text{PVIFA}_{0.08,6})$$
$$= \$1,000(4.623)$$
$$= \$4,623.$$

The *required rate of return, i,* on an asset is a function of the uncertainty, or risk, associated with the returns from the asset.[3] As indicated in the discussion of the determinants of discount rates in the previous chapter, this function is generally upward sloping, indicating that the higher the risk, the greater is the investor's required rate of return. The measurement of risk and the development of the risk-return tradeoff function is discussed further in the next chapter.

Market Value of Assets and Market Equilibrium

From Equation 4.1 it can be seen that the value of an asset depends on both the expected cash returns, R_t, and the owner's (or prospective buyer's) required rate of return, i. However, potential buyers and sellers can have different opinions of an asset's value based on their individual assessments of the potential cash returns from the asset and individual required rates of return.

The *market price,* or *market value,* of an asset (such as shares of common stock) is determined in much the same way as the price of most goods and services in a market-oriented economy—namely, by the interaction of supply and demand. This is shown in Figure 4-1. Potential buyers are represented by a *demand* schedule showing the maximum prices they are willing to pay for given quantities of an asset, and potential sellers are represented by a *supply* schedule showing the minimum prices at which they are willing to sell given quantities of the asset. The transaction price, the price at which an asset is sold, occurs at the intersection of the demand and supply schedules. The intersection represents the *market value,* or *market price,* of the asset, P_m, in Figure 4-1.

The market price of an asset is the value placed on the asset by the *marginally satisfied buyer and seller* who exchange assets in the market-

---

[3] Recall that risk was defined in Chapter 2 as the possibility that actual future returns will deviate from expected returns.

Figure 4-1   **Market Price of an Asset**

place. A marginally satisfied buyer is one who paid his or her maximum acceptable price for the asset, and a marginally satisfied seller is one who received his or her minimum acceptable price for the asset. Clearly, many owners (potential sellers) will place a higher value on the asset than the current market price; likewise, many investors (potential buyers) will place a lower value on the asset than the current market price.

Market equilibrium exists whenever there is no tendency for the price of the asset to move higher or lower. At this point the *expected* rate of return on the asset is equal to the marginal investor's *required* rate of return. *Market disequilibrium* occurs when investors' required rates of return, i, and/or the expected returns, R_t, from the asset change. The market price adjusts over time—that is, it moves upward or downward—to reflect changing conditions, and a new market equilibrium is established.

Most financial assets are bought and sold in organized markets. The bonds, preferred stock, and common stock of many small, as well as most medium and large, firms are traded in one or more national or regional exchanges or in the over-the-counter market. Since large numbers of competing buyers and sellers operate in the markets, the market price of a security represents a *consensus* judgment as to the security's value or worth. While no such market-determined measure of value exists for securities of firms that are not publicly traded, their market values can be approximated using the market price of publicly traded securities of firms having similar operating and financial characteristics.

Book Value of an Asset

The book value of an asset represents the *accounting* value, or the historical acquisition cost minus any accumulated depreciation or other write-offs. Since market value is normally related to expected future returns, and book value is based on historical cost, the market value of an asset does not necessarily bear any relationship to the book value. In fact, the market value may be either greater or less than the book value, depending on the changes over time in the market capitalization rate and the asset's expected future returns. For example, as indicated in the Financial Dilemma at the beginning of this chapter, Gulf Oil common stock was selling for approximately two-thirds its book value prior to the takeover battle in 1983. When *new* shares of stock are sold at a price below book value, the immediate effect is a dilution in earnings and book values per share to *existing* stockholders.

Bond Valuation

The valuation of bonds is a relatively straightforward process, since future cash returns to the bondholder are always specified ahead of time in a contract. The firm issuing the bonds must meet the interest and principal payments as they come due, or the bonds will go into default. Defaulting on bond payments can have disastrous consequences for the firm and its stockholders, such as possible bankruptcy, reorganization, or both.

Due to default risk, investors normally require a higher rate of return than the risk-free rate before agreeing to hold a firm's bonds. The required rate of return varies among bond issues of different firms, depending on their relative risks of default. All other things being equal, the greater the default risk on a given bond issue, the higher the required rate of return.

Bonds Having Finite Maturity Dates

Bonds that mature within finite periods of time pay the investor two types of returns: interest payments ($I_1, I_2, \ldots, I_n$) during each of the next n periods and a principal payment (M) in period n. Period n is defined as the bond's *maturity date,* or the time at which the principal must be repaid and the bond issue retired.

The value of a bond can be computed by applying the capitalization-of-income method to the series of cash returns:

$$P_0 = \frac{I_1}{(1 + k_\mathrm{d})^1} + \frac{I_2}{(1 + k_\mathrm{d})^2} + \cdots + \frac{I_{n-1}}{(1 + k_\mathrm{d})^{n-1}} + \frac{I_n + M}{(1 + k_\mathrm{d})^n}, \quad (4.3)$$

where P_0 is the present value of the bond at time zero, or its purchase date, and k_d is the investor's required rate of return on this particular bond issue.

Since all of the interest payments on a bond are normally equal (that is, $I_1 = I_2 = \ldots = I_{n-1} = I_n = I$), Equation 4.3 can be simplified as follows:

$$P_0 = \sum_{t=1}^{n} \frac{I}{(1 + k_\mathrm{d})^t} + \frac{M}{(1 + k_\mathrm{d})^n} \quad (4.4)$$

The first term in Equation 4.4, $\sum_{t=1}^{n} I/(1 + k_\mathrm{d})^t$, represents the present value of an *annuity* of I per period for n periods; the second term, $M/(1 + k_\mathrm{d})^n$, represents the present value of a *single payment* of M in period n. Equation 4.4 can be further simplified as follows:

$$P_0 = I(\text{PVIFA}_{k_d,n}) + M(\text{PVIF}_{k_d,n}). \tag{4.5}$$

To illustrate the use of Equation 4.5, consider the following example. American Telephone and Telegraph (AT&T) in 1971 issued $500,000,000 of 7 percent *debentures* (that is, bonds that are not secured by any specific asset) maturing in 2001. The bonds were issued in $1,000 denominations (par value). For purposes of simplifying this example, assume that the bonds mature at the *end* of 2001 and that interest is paid annually at the end of each year.[4]

An investor who wishes to purchase one of these AT&T bonds at the end (December 31) of 1986 and requires an 8 percent rate of return on this particular bond issue would compute the value of the bond as shown below.[5] These calculations assume that the investor will hold the bond until maturity and receive fifteen annual interest payments of $70 each ($I = \$1,000 \times 0.07$) plus a principal payment, M, of $1,000 at the end of the fifteenth year, 2001. The cash returns from this bond are shown in Figure 4-2. Substituting these values along with $k_d = 8\%$ (0.08) into Equation 4.4 gives the following value for the bond[6]:

$$P_0 = \sum_{t=1}^{15} \frac{\$70}{(1 + 0.08)^t} + \frac{\$1,000}{(1 + 0.08)^{15}}$$
$$= \$70(\text{PVIFA}_{0.08,15}) + \$1,000(\text{PVIF}_{0.08,15})$$

---

[4] This particular bond issue actually matures on February 15, 2001, and pays interest *semiannually* on February 15 and August 15 each year.

[5] A question often arises as to why investors would require an 8 percent rate of return on bonds that pay only 7 percent interest. The answer is that the required rate of return has increased since the bonds were originally issued. At the time of issue, the prevailing rate of interest (that is, the required rate of return) on bonds of this maturity and quality was approximately 7 percent. Hence, the coupon rate was set at 7 percent. Because of such factors as tight credit market conditions, higher inflation, increased firm risk, and so on, investors now require a higher rate of return to induce them to purchase these bonds.

[6] Bond interest is normally paid *semiannually*. With semiannual interest and compounding, the value of this AT&T bond would be calculated as follows:

$$P_0 = \sum_{t=1}^{30} \frac{\$35}{(1 + 0.04)^t} + \frac{\$1,000}{(1 + 0.04)^{30}}$$
$$= \$35(\text{PVIFA}_{0.04,30}) + \$1,000(\text{PVIF}_{0.04,30})$$
$$= \$35(17.292) + \$1,000(.308)$$
$$= \$605.22 + \$308$$
$$= \$913.22 \text{ (or } \$913)$$

This value differs slightly from the value determined in the example in the text. Note that in the case of semiannual compounding, the annual interest rate is divided by 2(0.08/2 = 0.04), and the number of periods is multiplied by 2(15 × 2 = 30).

It should also be noted that the use of a semiannual discount rate of 4 percent will result in a slightly greater than 8 percent effective annual discount rate. Based on the discussion of "Effective Rate Calculations" in the previous chapter, a semiannual discount rate of (see Equation 3.22):

$$i_2 = (1 + .08)^{1/2} - 1$$
$$= .03923$$

or 3.923 percent should be used in the bond valuation calculation. However we will ignore this complication in the remainder of this chapter.

Figure 4-2

Cash Returns from an AT&T Bond

End of Year	'86	'87	'88	'89	'90	'91	'92	'93	'94	'95	'96	'97	'98	'99	'00	'01
t	0	1	2	3	4	5	6	7	8	9	10	11	12	13	14	15
Cash Return	$70	$70	$70	$70	$70	$70	$70	$70	$70	$70	$70	$70	$70	$70	$70	$70 + $1000

$$= \$70(8.559) + \$1,000(0.315)$$
$$= \$599.13 + \$315$$
$$= \$914.13 \text{ (or } \$914)$$

In other words, an investor requiring an 8 percent return on this AT&T bond would be willing to pay $914 for it at the end of 1986.

An investor who desires more than an 8 percent rate of return on this bond would value it at a price less than $914. Similarly, an investor who requires less than 8 percent rate of return would value it at a price greater than $914. This *inverse relationship* between the required rate of return and the corresponding value of a bond to the investor is illustrated for both 15-year and 3-year bonds in Table 4-1 and Figure 4-3. In other words, as the required rate of return increases, the value of the bond decreases, and vice versa.

The relationship between a bond's value and the investor's required rate of return depends on the time remaining before maturity. All other things being equal, the value of a longer-term bond is affected more by changes in required rates of return than the value of a shorter-term bond. As Table 4-1 and Figure 4-3 show, the variation in the value of the 15-year bond is considerably greater than the variation of the 3-year bond over the range of required rates of return (3 to 11 percent).

Also, as can be seen in Table 4-1, when the required rate of return (prevailing market interest rate) is less than the coupon rate, the bond is valued (sells) at a *premium* over its par value of $1,000. Conversely, when the required rate of return is greater than the coupon rate, the bond is valued at a *discount* under its par value.

Table 4-1

Value of 7 Percent Coupon Rate Bonds at Various Required Rates of Return

Required Rate of Return, k_d	Value of 15-Year Bond	Value of 3-Year Bond	Bond Value Relative to Par Value
3%	$1,478	$1,113	Premium
5	1,208	1,055	Premium
6	1,097	1,027	Premium
7	1,000	1,000	At Par
8	914	974	Discount
9	839	949	Discount
11	712	902	Discount

Figure 4-3   **Relationship Between the Value of a Bond and the Required Rate of Return**

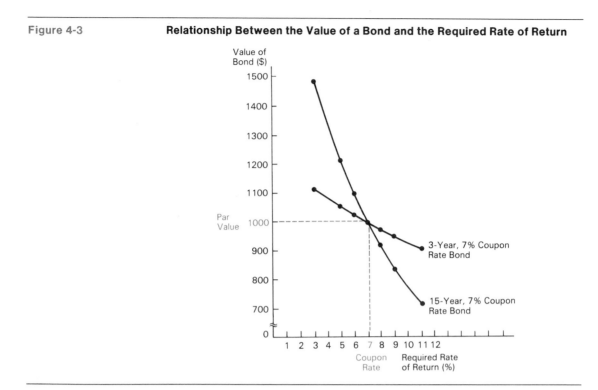

Investors who purchase a bond at the price determined by Equation 4.4 and *hold it until maturity* will realize their required rate of return, regardless of any changes in the market price of the bond.[7] However, if the market price of the bond declines due to a rise in prevailing interest rates (required rates of return), and if the bond is sold *prior to maturity,* the investors will earn less than their required rate of return and may even incur a loss on the bond. This variation in the market price (and hence in the realized rate of return) of a bond (or any fixed income security) is known as *interest rate risk.*

Perpetual Bonds

A *perpetual bond,* or perpetuity, is a bond issued without a finite maturity date.[8] Perpetual bonds promise to pay interest indefinitely, and there is no contractual obligation to repay the principal—that is, $M = 0$.

The valuation of a perpetual bond is simpler than the valuation of a bond having a finite maturity date. Assuming that the bond pays a fixed amount of interest, I, per period forever, the value is as follows:

$$P_0 = \sum_{t=1}^{\infty} \frac{I}{(1 + k_\mathrm{d})^t}, \qquad (4.6)$$

[7] This assumes that the investor reinvests all interest received from the bond at a rate equal to the required rate of return on the bond. Otherwise the realized return will differ slightly from the required return.

[8] Perpetual bonds, also referred to as "consuls," are rare. Some countries, such as Great Britain, and some railroads, such as the Canadian Pacific and the Canadian National, have issued perpetual bonds.

where k_d is the required rate of return. Equation 4.6 can be simplified to obtain the following expression[9]:

$$P_0 = \frac{I}{k_d}.$$ (4.7)

Consider, for example, the Canadian Pacific Limited Railroad's perpetual 4 percent debentures. What is the value of a $1,000 bond to an investor who requires an 8 percent rate of return on these Canadian Pacific bonds? Since $I = 0.04 \times \$1,000$, or $40, and $k_d = 8\%$, Equation 4.7 can be used to compute the answer as follows:

$$P_0 = \frac{\$40}{0.08}$$

$$= \$500.$$

Thus, the investor would be willing to pay up to $500 for this bond.

Yield to Maturity of a Bond

The *yield to maturity* of a bond is the rate of return earned on a bond purchased at a given price and held until maturity.[10] If the current price of a bond, P_0, the uniform annual interest payments, I, and the maturity value, or principal, M, are known, the yield to maturity of a bond having a finite maturity date can be calculated by solving the following equation for r:

$$P_0 = \sum_{t=1}^{n} \frac{I}{(1 + r)^t} + \frac{M}{(1 + r)^n}.$$ (4.8)

[9] Equation 4.6 is the present value of an infinite series and can be simplified to Equation 4.7 by means of the following calculations:
Rewrite Equation 4.6 as follows:

$$P_0 = I\left[\frac{1}{(1 + k_d)^1} + \frac{1}{(1 + k_d)^2} + \frac{1}{(1 + k_d)^3} + \cdots + \frac{1}{(1 + k_d)^n}\right].$$ (a)

Multiply both sides of Equation a by $(1 + k_d)$:

$$P_0(1 + k_d) = I\left[1 + \frac{1}{(1 + k_d)^1} + \frac{1}{(1 + k_d)^2} + \frac{1}{(1 + k_d)^3} + \cdots + \frac{1}{(1 + k_d)^{n-1}}\right].$$ (b)

Subtract Equation a from Equation b:

$$P_0(1 + k_d - 1) = I\left[1 - \frac{1}{(1 + k_d)^n}\right].$$ (c)

As $n \rightarrow \infty$ then $1/(1 + k_d)^n \rightarrow 0$ and Equation c approaches the following:

$$P_0(k_d) = I,$$ (d)

or

$$P_0 = \frac{I}{k_d} \qquad \text{(Equation 4.7)}.$$

[10] In contrast, *current yield* on a bond having a finite maturity date is defined as the annual interest payment, I, divided by the current price, P_0. The yield to maturity calculation assumes that cash flows from the bond occurring prior to maturity are reinvested at a rate equal to the yield to maturity.

Note that Equation 4.8 is very similar to Equation 4.4, except that k_d, the required rate of return, has been replaced by r, the yield to maturity. Equation 4.4 is used to determine the value of a bond P_0 to the investor when I, M, and k_d are known, whereas Equation 4.8 is used to determine the yield to maturity r, when I, M, and P_0 are known. The yield to maturity can be used to compare the risk of two or more bonds that are similar *in all other respects,* including time to maturity. The bond with the higher yield to maturity is the one perceived to be the riskier by investors. Also, the yield to maturity on existing bonds can be used as an estimate of the required returns of investors on any new (and similar) bonds the firm may issue.

There are a number of ways to compute the yield to maturity for a bond. First, special bond tables can be used to directly identify the yield to maturity for any particular bond. Also, many financial calculators currently available are capable of computing yields to maturity. In the absence of these aids it is necessary to use the "trial-and-error" approach in conjunction with the present value tables found at the end of the text.[11]

The steps in the trial-and-error procedure are as follows:

Step 1. Make an approximate estimate of the yield to maturity.

Step 2. Use this rate to compute the present value of the bond's cash flows (that is, purchase price, interest payments, and principal payment).

Step 3. Try a *higher* rate if a positive present value results or a *lower* rate if a negative one results.

Step 4. Repeat the process (attempting to "bracket" the yield to maturity) until a rate is found at which the present value of the cash flows is equal to zero.

In order to illustrate this procedure, consider a Chevron 7 percent debenture that matures in 1996. The par value of this bond is $1,000. As in the AT&T bond example discussed earlier, assume that the Chevron bonds mature at the end of 1996 and that interest is paid annually at the end of each year.[12] Suppose that the Chevron bonds are selling for $840 at the end of 1986 (10 years prior to maturity). Determine the bond's yield to maturity.

Table 4-2 illustrates the use of the trial-and-error procedure to calculate the yield to maturity of the Chevron bonds. Since the bond is selling at a discount—that is, less than its $1,000 par value—the yield to maturity is

---

[11] An *approximate* yield to maturity can be calculated by using the following expression:

$$\text{Approximate yield to maturity} = \frac{\text{Annual interest} + \dfrac{\text{Bond discount or premium}}{\text{Years to maturity}}}{\text{Average investment}}$$

$$= \frac{I + (M - P_0)/n}{(P_0 + M)/2}$$

If the bond is selling at a discount (premium), then the term $M - P_0$ is positive (negative). (Problems 6 and 7 at the end of the chapter contain examples of the application of this expression.)

[12] This particular bond issue actually matures on April 1, 1996, and pays interest *semiannually* on April 1 and October 1 each year.

Table 4-2   **Trial-and-Error Computation of Yield to Maturity for Chevron Bonds**

| Year (1) | Cash Flow (2) | r = 9% | | r = 10% | |
		Present Value Interest Factor (3)	Present Value (4) = (3) × (2)	Present Value Interest Factor (5)	Present Value (6) = (5) × (2)
0	$−840	1.000*	$−840	1.000*	$−840
1−10	70	6.418†	449.26	6.145†	430.15
10	1,000	.422*	422	.386*	386
Total			$ +31.26		$ −23.85

*From Table II at the back of the book.
†From Table IV at the back of the book.

greater than the 7 percent coupon rate. A trial rate of 9 percent results in a present value for the bond's cash flows of +$31.26, as shown in column 4 of Table 4-2. Since this value is positive, a higher rate must be tried. At a rate of 10 percent, as can be seen in column 6 of Table 4-2, the present value of the bond's cash flows is −$23.85. This indicates that the bond's yield to maturity is between 9 and 10 percent. A more exact yield to maturity can be computed by means of interpolation:

$$r = 9\% + \frac{31.26}{31.26 + 23.85}(10\% - 9\%)$$

$$= 9.6\%$$

Thus the yield to maturity on this bond is 9.6 percent.[13]

A number of companies, such as Allied Corporation and Cities Service, have issued zero-coupon bonds—that is, bonds that pay no interest over their life. The only payment to the holders of these bonds is the principal payment at maturity. In order to illustrate the calculation of the yield to maturity for such a bond, consider the Allied Corporation zero coupon money multiplier notes (that is, bonds) due January 15, 1996. Suppose these bonds (having a par value of $1,000) were purchased for $352 on January 15, 1986 (ten years prior to maturity). Determine the yield to maturity on these bonds.

Figure 4-4 shows the cash returns from the purchase of an Allied Corporation zero-coupon bond. Since there are no interest payments, the yield to maturity equation (Equation 4.8) can be simplified to:

$$P_0 = \frac{M}{(1 + r)^n}$$

$$= M\,(PVIF_{r,n}).$$

---

[13] The yield to maturity equation implicitly assumes that the annual interest payments are reinvested over the remaining life of the bond at the calculated rate, r.

Figure 4-4

Cash Returns from the Purchase of an Allied Corporation Zero-Coupon Bond

Jan. 15th	'86	'87	'88	'89	'90	'91	'92	'93	'94	'95	'96
t	0	1	2	3	4	5	6	7	8	9	10
Cash Return	−$352	0	0	0	0	0	0	0	0	0	+$1000

Substituting $n = 10$, $P_0 = \$352$, and $M = \$1,000$ into this expression yields:

$$352 = 1,000\ (\text{PVIF}_{r,10})$$
$$(\text{PVIF}_{r,10}) = .352.$$

From Table II at the back of the book, we find this present value interest factor in the 10-year row under the 11 percent interest rate column. Hence the yield to maturity (r) on this zero-coupon bond is 11 percent.[14]

The rate of return, or yield to maturity, on a *perpetual* bond can be found by solving the following bond valuation equation for r:

$$P_0 = \frac{I}{r}, \tag{4.9}$$

which gives

$$r = \frac{I}{P_0}. \tag{4.10}$$

It is not necessary to employ the trial-and-error method (or interpolation) to determine the yield for a perpetual bond.

For example, recall the 4 percent Canadian Pacific Limited Railroad debentures described earlier. If the current price of a bond is $640, what is the yield on the bond? Substituting $P_0 = \$640$ and $I = \$40$ (or 4 percent of $1,000) into Equation 4.10 gives the following:

$$r = \frac{\$40}{\$640}$$

$$= 0.0625\ (\text{or } 6.25 \text{ percent}).$$

Valuation of Preferred Stock

Most preferred stock pays regular, fixed dividends. Preferred dividends per share are normally not increased when the earnings of a firm increase, nor are they cut or suspended unless the firm faces serious financial problems. If preferred stock dividends are cut or suspended for a period of time for whatever reason, the firm is usually required to make up the past

---

[14] If the interest factor falls between two values in Table II one can interpolate to get a more exact answer.

due payments before paying any common stock dividends.[15] Thus, the investor's expected cash return from holding most preferred stocks can be treated as a fixed, constant amount per period.

The investor's required rate of return on a preferred stock issue is a function of the risk that the firm will be unable to meet its dividend payments. The higher the risk, the higher the required rate of return. Since bondholders have a prior claim over preferred stockholders on the income and assets of a firm, it is more risky to hold a firm's preferred stock than to hold its bonds. As a result, investors normally require a higher rate of return on preferred stock than on bonds.

Since many preferred stock issues do not have maturity dates, the cash returns (dividend payments) from holding no-maturity preferred stock can be treated as a perpetual stream of payments, or a *perpetuity*. Capitalizing the perpetual stream of dividend payments gives the following valuation expression:

$$P_0 = \sum_{t=1}^{\infty} \frac{D_p}{(1 + k_p)^t},$$ (4.11)

where D_p is the dividend per period, and k_p is the investor's required rate of return.[16]

Equation 4.11 is similar to Equation 4.6 for a perpetual bond. Like the perpetual bond valuation model, this equation can be simplified into the following valuation model:

$$P_0 = \frac{D_p}{k_p}.$$ (4.12)

To illustrate the use of Equation 4.12, assume that Gulf and Western pays annual end-of-year dividends on a $5.75 cumulative preferred stock issue. What is the value of this stock to an investor who requires a 9 percent rate of return on the investment? Substituting $5.75 for D_p and 0.09 for k_p yields the following:

$$P_0 = \frac{\$5.75}{0.09}$$

$$= \$63.89.$$

Valuation of Common Stock

In principle, the valuation of common stock is no different from the valuation of other types of securities such as bonds and preferred stock. The basic procedure involves capitalizing (that is, discounting) the expected stream of returns received from holding the common stock. This is complicated by several factors, however.

---

[15] This feature of preferred stock is called the *cumulative dividend feature.*

[16] Some preferred stock issues have a *call provision* that allows the firm to call in the stock for redemption under certain conditions that are spelled out when the preferred stock is issued. If an investor is considering purchasing a preferred stock issue that is expected to be called in the future, its value is calculated by capitalizing (that is, discounting) the call price plus the dividend payments to be received before the issue is called.

First, the returns from holding a common stock take two forms: the cash dividend payments made during the holding period and/or changes in the price of the stock (capital gains or losses) over the holding period. All the returns paid to the common stockholder are derived from the firm's earnings and can either be paid to shareholders in the current period as cash dividends or reinvested in the firm to (it is hoped) provide higher future dividends and a higher stock price.

Second, because common stock dividends are normally expected to grow rather than remain constant, the relatively simple annuity and perpetuity formulas used in the valuation of bonds and preferred stock generally are not applicable, and more complicated models must be used.

Finally, the future returns from common stock usually are much more uncertain than the returns from bonds and preferred stock. Common stock dividend payments are related to the firm's earnings in some manner, and it can be very difficult to forecast future long-term earnings and dividend payments with a high degree of accuracy.

To better understand the application of the capitalization-of-income valuation method to common stock, it is best to begin by considering the *one*-period dividend valuation model and then move on to consider multiple-period valuation models.

One-period Dividend Valuation Model

Assume that an investor plans to purchase a common stock and hold it for *one* period. At the end of that period, the investor expects to receive a cash dividend, D_1, and sell the stock for a price, P_1. What is the value of this stock to the investor *today* (time 0), given a required rate of return on the investment, k_e?

In the capitalization-of-income valuation method the discounted present value of the returns on the stock is calculated as follows:

$$P_0 = \frac{D_1}{1 + k_e} + \frac{P_1}{1 + k_e}. \qquad (4.13)$$

For example, if Ohio Engineering Company common stock is expected to pay a $1.00 dividend and sell for $27.50 at the end of one period, what is the value of this stock to an investor who requires a 14 percent rate of return? The answer is computed like this:

$$
\begin{aligned}
P_0 &= \frac{\$1.00}{(1 + 0.14)} + \frac{\$27.50}{(1 + 0.14)} \\
&= \$1.00(\text{PVIF}_{0.14,1}) + \$27.50(\text{PVIF}_{0.14,1}) \\
&= \$1.00(0.877) + \$27.50(0.877) \\
&= \$24.99 \ (\text{or } \$25).
\end{aligned}
$$

Thus, the investor who purchases the stock for $25.00, collects the $1.00 dividend, and sells the stock for $27.50 at the end of one period will receive the 14 percent required rate of return.

Two-period Dividend Valuation Model

Next, consider an investor who plans to purchase a common stock and hold it for *two* periods. The cash returns to the investor consist of cash dividends—D_1 at the end of the first period and D_2 at the end of the second period—and an amount, P_2, from the sale of the stock at the end of the second period. Capitalizing the returns at the investor's required rate of return, k_e, gives the following valuation equation:

$$P_0 = \frac{D_1}{(1 + k_e)^1} + \frac{D_2}{(1 + k_e)^2} + \frac{P_2}{(1 + k_e)^2} . \qquad (4.14)$$

Returning to the example of the Ohio Engineering Company, assume that the company is expected to pay common stock dividends of $1.00 at the end of next year and $1.00 at the end of the second year, and that the market price of the stock is expected to be $30.35 two years from now. What is the current value of the stock if the investor requires a 14 percent rate of return? Substituting $1.00 for D_1, $1.00 for D_2, $30.35 for P_2, and 14 percent, or 0.14, for k_e into Equation 4.14 gives the following value for the stock:

$$
\begin{aligned}
P_0 &= \frac{\$1.00}{(1 + 0.14)^1} + \frac{\$1.00}{(1 + 0.14)^2} + \frac{\$30.35}{(1 + 0.14)^2} \\
&= \$1.00(\text{PVIF}_{0.14,1}) + \$1.00(\text{PVIF}_{0.14,2}) + \$30.35(\text{PVIF}_{0.14,2}) \\
&= \$1.00(0.877) + \$1.00(0.769) + \$30.35(0.769) \\
&= \$24.98 \text{ (or } \$25\text{)}.
\end{aligned}
$$

n-Period Dividend Valuation Model

The dividend valuation process just described can be generalized to the n-period case. The returns to the investor who purchases a share of common stock and holds it for n periods consist of dividend payments during each of the next n periods—$D_1, D_2, \ldots, D_n$—plus an amount, P_n, from the sale of the stock at the end of the nth period. Capitalizing the returns at the investor's required rate of return, k_e, gives the following valuation equation:

$$P_0 = \frac{D_1}{(1 + k_e)^1} + \frac{D_2}{(1 + k_e)^2} + \cdots + \frac{D_n}{(1 + k_e)^n} + \frac{P_n}{(1 + k_e)^n} , \qquad (4.15)$$

which can be summarized as:

$$P_0 = \sum_{t=1}^{n} \frac{D_t}{(1 + k_e)^t} + \frac{P_n}{(1 + k_e)^n} . \qquad (4.16)$$

Consider again the Ohio Engineering Company common stock. Suppose that the investor is considering purchasing a share of this stock and holding it for 5 years. Assume that the investor's required rate of return is still 14 percent. Dividends from the stock are expected to be $1.00 in the first year, $1.00 in the second year, $1.00 in the third year, $1.25 in the fourth year, and $1.25 in the fifth year. The expected selling price of the stock at the end of 5 years is $41.00.

Using Equation 4.16, the value of the stock to the investor is computed as follows:

$$
\begin{aligned}
P_0 &= \frac{\$1.00}{(1 + 0.14)^1} + \frac{\$1.00}{(1 + 0.14)^2} + \frac{\$1.00}{(1 + 0.14)^3} \\
&\quad + \frac{\$1.25}{(1 + 0.14)^4} + \frac{\$1.25}{(1 + 0.14)^5} + \frac{\$41.00}{(1 + 0.14)^5} \\
&= \$1.00(\text{PVIF}_{0.14,1}) + \$1.00(\text{PVIF}_{0.14,2}) \\
&\quad + \$1.00(\text{PVIF}_{0.14,3}) + \$1.25(\text{PVIF}_{0.14,4}) \\
&\quad + \$1.25(\text{PVIF}_{0.14,5}) + \$41.00(\text{PVIF}_{0.14,5}) \\
&= \$1.00(0.877) + \$1.00(0.769) + \$1.00(0.675) \\
&\quad + \$1.25(0.592) + \$1.25(0.519) + \$41.00(0.519) \\
&= \$24.99 \ (\text{or } \$25).
\end{aligned}
$$

Note that the *current* value of a share of Ohio Engineering common stock is the same (that is, $P_0 = \$25.00$) regardless of whether the investor plans to hold it for 1, 2, or 5 years.[17]

A General Dividend Valuation Model

In each of the valuation models described, the current value of the stock, P_0, is dependent upon the expected price of the stock at the end of the expected holding period—P_1 in the 1-period case, P_2 in the 2-period case, and P_n in the n-period case. Although this seems straightforward, providing accurate forecasts of stock prices when applying the models to specific stocks can be difficult, if not impossible. A final generalization permits the elimination of P_n from the model while at the same time showing that the dividend valuation models that have been discussed are consistent with one another.

First, the value of the stock at the end of the nth period, P_n, must be redefined. Using the capitalization-of-income approach, it can be shown that P_n is a function of all expected *future* dividends that the investor will receive in periods $n + 1$, $n + 2$, and so on. Discounting the stream of dividends at the required rate of return, k_e, gives the value of the stock at the end of the nth period:

$$
P_n = \sum_{t=n+1}^{\infty} \frac{D_t}{(1 + k_e)^{t-n}}. \tag{4.17}
$$

Substituting Equation 4.17 into Equation 4.16 yields the following:

$$
P_0 = \sum_{t=1}^{n} \frac{D_t}{(1 + k_e)^t} + \sum_{t=n+1}^{\infty} \frac{D_t}{(1 + k_e)^t},
$$

[17] The value of a stock at *any* point in time is simply the present value of all dividends expected to be paid from that time forward. Hence, the price, P_5, of $41 reflects the present value of dividends expected in years 6 through infinity.

which can be further simplified into the following *general dividend valuation model:*

$$P_0 = \sum_{t=1}^{\infty} \frac{D_t}{(1 + k_e)^t}.$$ (4.18)

Thus, *the value of a firm's common stock to the investor is equal to the discounted present value of the expected future dividend stream.* As was shown, the valuation of a firm's common stock given by the *n*-period model (Equation 4.16) is equivalent to the valuation given by the general model (Equation 4.18). In addition, the 1- and 2-period valuation models (Equations 4.13 and 4.14) are equivalent to the general model (Equation 4.18).[18] The general dividend valuation model is applicable regardless of whether the stream of dividends over time is fluctuating or constant, increasing or decreasing.

Note that the general dividend valuation model treats the stream of dividends as a *perpetuity* having no finite termination date. Whereas this assumption is reasonable for firms that are going concerns, shorter time horizons must be used when considering firms that might be either acquired by other firms or liquidated in the foreseeable future.

There are some profitable firms (such as Digital Equipment and Teledyne) that reinvest all their earnings and do not pay current cash dividends. In fact, some profitable firms have *never* paid cash dividends for as long as they have been in existence and are not expected to do so in the near future. How can the general dividend valuation model be applied to the common stock of a firm such as this? It must be assumed that the firm will be able to start making regular, periodic cash dividend payments to its shareholders *at some time in the future.* Or, these returns could consist of the *proceeds from the sale of the firm's outstanding common stock* should the firm be acquired by another company. The value of such a firm's stock according to the general dividend valuation model (Equation 4.18) would be zero only if the firm were *never* expected to pay a cash dividend *of any type* to its shareholders.

As stated in Chapter 1, the primary goal of most firms is the *maximization of shareholder wealth.* The general dividend valuation model (Equa-

---

Figure 4-5   **Relationship between Financial Decisions and Shareholder Wealth**

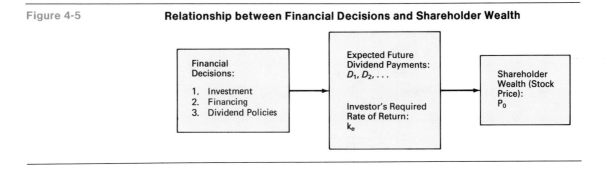

---

[18] You will be asked to demonstrate these relationships in Problem 17 at the end of this chapter.

tion 4.18) indicates that shareholder wealth, as measured by the value of the firm's common stock, P_0, is a function of the expected stream of future dividend payments and the investor's required rate of return. Thus, when making financial decisions that are consistent with the goal of maximizing shareholder wealth, management should be concerned with how these decisions affect both the expected future dividend stream and the discount rate that investors apply to the dividend stream. The relationship between financial decision making and shareholder wealth is illustrated in Figure 4-5. A primary emphasis of the financial management function is attempting to define and measure this relationship.

Growth Models for the Valuation of Common Stock

The general dividend valuation model can be simplified if a firm's dividend payments over time are expected to follow one of several fairly straightforward patterns, including *constant growth, zero growth,* and *above-normal growth.*

Constant Growth Dividend Valuation Model

If a firm's future dividend payments per share are expected to grow at a *constant* rate, g, per period forever, then the dividend at any future time period t can be forecasted as follows:

$$D_t = D_0(1 + g)^t, \tag{4.19}$$

where D_0 is the dividend in the current period ($t = 0$). The expected dividend in period 1 is $D_1 = D_0(1 + g)^1$, whereas the expected dividend in period 2 is $D_2 = D_0(1 + g)^2$, and so on. The constant-growth curve in the center of Figure 4-6 illustrates such a dividend pattern.

Figure 4-6   **Dividend Growth Patterns**

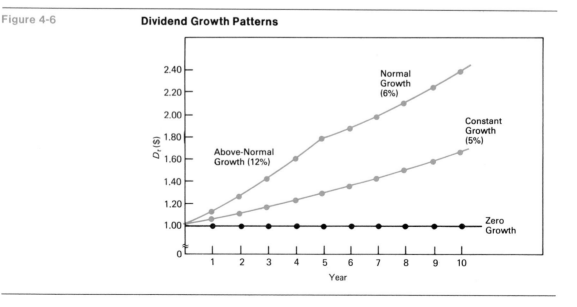

Substituting Equation 4.19 for D_t in the general dividend valuation model (Equation 4.18) yields the following:

$$P_0 = \sum_{t=1}^{\infty} \frac{D_0(1 + g)^t}{(1 + k_e)^t} . \tag{4.20}$$

Assuming that the required rate of return, k_e, is greater than the dividend growth rate, g, Equation 4.20 can be transformed algebraically to obtain the following simplified common stock valuation model[19]:

$$P_0 = \frac{D_1}{k_e - g} . \tag{4.21}$$

To apply this valuation model to a specific common stock issue, it is necessary to estimate the expected future dividend growth rate, g, per period for the firm. If the firm's historical dividend growth pattern is expected to continue into the foreseeable future, the growth rate in dividends per share for the past several years can be used to estimate the future compound annual expected dividend growth rate.

The constant growth dividend valuation model can be used to illustrate the two forms of returns an investor can expect to receive from holding a common stock. Solving Equation 4.21 for k_e yields the following:

$$k_e = \frac{D_1}{P_0} + g. \tag{4.22}$$

The investor's required rate of return is equal to the expected dividend yield, D_1/P_0, plus the capital gains yield, g—the expected increase in dividends and, ultimately, in the price of the stock.

For example, consider the Pennsylvania Manufacturing Company, which has estimated its common stock dividend for *next* year to be $0.90 per share. Earnings and dividends have been increasing at a compound annual rate of 5 percent for the past several years, and this growth rate is expected to continue into the foreseeable future. What is the value of a share of this stock to an investor who requires an 11 percent rate of return? Substituting $0.90 for D_1, 5 percent (0.05) for g, and 11 percent (0.11) for k_e in Equation 4.21 yields the following value for the Pennsylvania Manufacturing common stock:

$$P_0 = \frac{\$0.90}{0.11 - 0.05}$$

$$= \frac{\$0.90}{0.06}$$

$$= \$15.$$

[19] Equation 4.21 is often referred to in finance literature as the *Gordon model,* for Myron J. Gordon, who pioneered its use. See Myron J. Gordon. *The Investment, Financing, and Valuation of the Corporation.* Homewood, Ill.: Irwin, 1962.

Thus, the investor's 11 percent required rate of return consists of a 6 percent dividend yield (D_1/P_0 = \$0.90/\$15) plus a 5 percent capital gains yield.

Zero Growth Dividend Valuation Model

If a firm's future dividend payments per share are not expected to grow over time—that is, if they are expected to remain constant *forever*—then D_t in Equation 4.18, the general dividend valuation model, can be replaced by a constant value D to yield the following:

$$P_0 = \sum_{t=1}^{\infty} \frac{D}{(1 + k_e)^t}.$$ (4.23)

Equation 4.23 represents the value of a perpetuity and is analogous to those used for valuing a perpetual bond (Equation 4.6) and a preferred stock (Equation 4.11), and it can be simplified to obtain:

$$P_0 = \frac{D}{k_e}.$$ (4.24)

Equation 4.24 is really a special case of the constant growth model in which the dividend growth rate, g, is zero. Substituting 0 for g and D for D_1 in the constant growth dividend valuation formula gives the zero growth dividend valuation expression. Again, this model is valid only when a firm's dividend payments are expected to remain constant *forever*. Although there are few, if any, common stocks that strictly satisfy these conditions, the model still can be used to approximate the value of a stock for which dividend payments are expected to remain constant for a relatively long period into the future. Figure 4-6 also illustrates a zero growth dividend payment pattern.

To illustrate the zero growth dividend valuation model, assume that the Mountaineer Railroad common stock pays an annual dividend of \$1.50 per share, which is expected to remain constant for the foreseeable future. What is the value of the stock to an investor who requires a 12 percent rate of return? Substituting \$1.50 for D and 12 percent (0.12) for k_e in Equation 4.24 yields the following:

$$P_0 = \frac{\$1.50}{0.12}$$

$$= \$12.50.$$

Above-Normal Growth Dividend Valuation Model

Many firms experience growth rates in sales, earnings, and dividends that are *not* constant. Typically, a firm will have a period of above-normal growth as it exploits new technologies, new markets, or both; this generally occurs relatively early in the firm's life cycle. Following this period of rapid growth, earnings and dividends tend to stabilize, or grow at a more normal rate comparable to the overall average rate of growth in the economy. The reduction in the growth rate occurs as the firm reaches maturity and has fewer sizable growth opportunities. Figure 4-6 also illustrates an above-normal growth pattern.[20] A relatively simple model can be developed to determine the value of a common stock having the dividend pattern just described. If g_1 is defined as the above-normal growth rate over the first m years, and g_2 is the normal growth rate beginning in year $m + 1$ and continuing indefinitely, the current value of the common stock can be computed as follows:

$$P_0 = \sum_{t=1}^{m} \frac{D_0(1 + g_1)^t}{(1 + k_e)^t} + \frac{P_m}{(1 + k_e)^m}, \qquad (4.25)$$

or

$$P_0 = \sum_{t=1}^{m} \frac{D_0(1 + g_1)^t}{(1 + k_e)^t} + \frac{1}{(1 + k_e)^m}\left(\frac{D_{m+1}}{k_e - g_2}\right), \qquad (4.26)$$

where k_e is the investor's required rate of return and D_0 and D_{m+1} are the dividend payments in years 0 and $m + 1$, respectively. Equation 4.25 indicates that the value of a firm's common stock is equal to the discounted present value of the stream of dividends received during the above-normal growth period plus the discounted present value of the stock price at the end of the above-normal growth period.

Because dividends are expected to grow at a constant rate, g_2, beginning in year $m + 1$, the constant growth model, $D_{m+1}/(k_e - g_2)$, can be used to find the value of the stock in year m, P_m.

For example, consider the Jackson Manufacturing Company, which expects earnings and common stock dividends to grow at a rate of 12 percent per annum for the next 5 years. Following the period of above-normal growth, dividends are expected to grow at the slower rate of 6 percent for the foreseeable future. The firm currently pays a dividend D_0 of $2.00 per share. What is the value of Jackson's common stock to an investor who requires a 15 percent rate of return?

Figure 4-7

Cash Returns from Jackson Manufacturing Company Common Stock

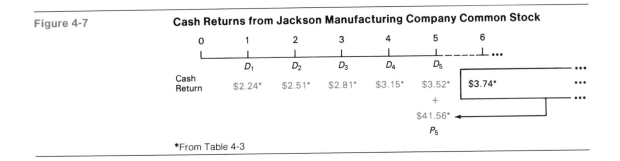

*From Table 4-3

[20] The transition between the periods of above-normal and normal, or average, growth is usually not as pronounced as Figure 4-6 indicates. Typically, a firm's growth rate *declines gradually* over time from the above-normal rate to the normal rate. Growth models similar to Equation 4.26 can be developed to handle cases like this. As an illustration, see the Focus on Corporate Practice example at the end of the chapter.

Table 4-3   **Value of the Jackson Manufacturing Company Common Stock**

Year, t	Dividend, $D_t = \$2.00(1 + 0.12)^t$	Present Value Interest Factor, $\text{PVIF}_{0.15,t}$	Present Value, D_t

Present Value of First 5 Years' Dividends, $\displaystyle\sum_{t=1}^{5} \frac{D_0(1 + g_1)^t}{(1 + k_e)^t}$

1	$\$2.00(1 + 0.12)^1 = \$2.24$	0.870	\$1.95
2	$2.00(1 + 0.12)^2 = 2.51$	0.756	1.90
3	$2.00(1 + 0.12)^3 = 2.81$	0.658	1.85
4	$2.00(1 + 0.12)^4 = 3.15$	0.572	1.80
5	$2.00(1 + 0.12)^5 = 3.53$	0.497	1.75
			$\overline{\$9.25}$

Value of Stock at End of Year 5, $P_5 = \dfrac{D_6}{k_e - g_2}$

$$P_5 = \frac{D_6}{0.15 - 0.06}$$

$$D_6 = D_5(1 + g_2)$$

$$= \$3.53(1 + 0.06)$$

$$= \$3.74.$$

$$P_5 = \frac{\$3.74}{0.15 - 0.06}$$

$$= \$41.56.$$

Present Value of P_5, $\text{PV}(P_5) = \dfrac{P_5}{(1 + k_e)^5}$

$$\text{PV}(P_5) = \frac{\$41.56}{(1 + 0.15)^5}$$

$$= \$41.56(\text{PVIF}_{0.15,5})$$

$$= \$41.56(0.497)$$

$$= \$20.66.$$

Value of Common Stock, $P_0 = \text{PV (First 5 Years' Dividends)} + \text{PV}(P_5)$

$$P_0 = \$9.25 + \$20.66$$

$$= \$29.91.$$

Figure 4-7 and Table 4-3 illustrate the solution to this problem. The present values of the dividends received during the above-normal growth period total $9.25. Based on the constant growth model, the value of the Jackson Manufacturing Company common stock at the end of year 5, P_5, is $41.56. Adding the present value of P_5, $20.66, to the present value of the dividends received during the first 5 years gives a total value of the common stock of $29.91 per share.

Summary

- The value of a long-term security is based on the *expected future returns* the owner will receive in the period during which the asset is held.

- The *capitalization-of-income* method of valuation can be used to determine the value of a security to an investor. This involves calculating the present value of the stream of expected future returns discounted at the investor's required rate of return. The required rate of return is a function of the *risk* associated with the returns from the asset.
- The *market price* of a security represents the value placed on it by marginally satisfied buyers and sellers.
- The value of a *bond having a finite maturity date* is equal to the present value of the stream of interest and principal payments discounted at the investor's required rate of return.
- The value of a *perpetual bond* is equal to the interest payment divided by the investor's required rate of return.
- The *yield to maturity* on a bond is the percentage rate of return the investor will earn if the bond is purchased at a given price and held until maturity.
- The returns from most *preferred stocks* can be treated as perpetuities. Thus, the value of a preferred stock is equal to the annual preferred dividend divided by the investor's required rate of return.
- The valuation of *common stocks* is considerably more complicated than the valuation of either bonds or preferred stocks for the following reasons:

  1. The returns can take two forms: cash dividend payments and capital gains.
  2. Common stock dividends are normally expected to grow and not remain constant.
  3. The returns from common stocks are generally more uncertain than the returns from other types of securities.

- In the *general dividend valuation model* the value of a common stock is equal to the present value of all the expected future dividends discounted at the investor's required rate of return. Simpler common stock valuation models can be derived from assumptions concerning the expected growth of future dividend payments.
- Assuming that dividends continue to grow at a *constant* rate, g, indefinitely, the value of a common stock is equal to the next year's dividend, D_1, divided by the difference between the investor's required rate of return, k_e, and the growth rate, g.

FOCUS ON CORPORATE PRACTICE

Common Stock Evaluation Techniques Used by Wells Fargo Investment Advisors

Robert B. Morris III
Vice-President, Wells Fargo Investment Advisors (WFIA),
A Division of Wells Fargo Bank, N.A.

Wells Fargo Investment Advisors (WFIA), a large investment advisory firm, is somewhat unique in that it applies, in a disciplined manner, the dividend valuation model to the problem of security valuation. The model maintains that the price of a share of stock is equal to the present value of all future dividends discounted at an appropriate rate. WFIA employs a dividend valuation model that extends into perpetuity. The time horizon requires that several factors be considered, including long-term industry and company developments regarding the industry structure, the pricing environment, and technological developments, as well as returns on equity. Given the discount rate and the risk associated with a particular stock, WFIA is able to identify overpriced or underpriced equity securities.

To effectively apply this model to a particular firm under consideration, WFIA security analysts make four distinct types of forecasts:

- Estimates of the firm's earnings and dividends for a 5-year period.
- An estimate of a fifth-year normalized earnings growth rate and dividend payout rate.
- An estimate of a maturity date and earnings growth decay rate.
- An estimate of a maturity earnings growth rate and dividend payout rate.

After having studied the latest actual earnings and dividends of the firm, the WFIA analyst estimates earnings and dividends for each of the next 5 years. Following this, the analyst estimates a normalized earnings growth rate between years 5 and 6, assuming that earning conditions are normal (that is, devoid of cyclical peaks or troughs). The analyst also estimates a normalized payout ratio based upon the same assumptions. Normalized growth and earnings projections are made within the context of "real" Gross National Product (GNP) and inflation assumptions developed within Wells Fargo Bank, which are used as a basis for evaluation by all of WFIA's security analysts.

Because a company's revenues cannot increase forever at a rate faster than the nominal GNP rate, the analyst must also estimate when earnings gains will decline *below* the nominal GNP rate: The estimate is defined as the *maturity date*. The analyst must also forecast how rapidly corporate earnings growth is expected to decay toward maturity growth. The decay rate can be either *slow, medium,* or *fast*. A slow rate implies that earnings advance in line with the fifth-year normalized rate for a number of years and then decay very quickly as the maturity date approaches. A medium rate implies that earnings growth slows by an equal amount between the sixth year and the maturity date. A fast rate implies that earnings move very quickly from the fifth-year earnings rate to the maturity rate.

The final component of the model requires the analyst to estimate the dividend payout ratio and earnings growth rate of the firm from the date of maturity into perpetuity. The maturity phase is not considered to be a period of zero rev-

Figure 4-8   **Dividend Payout Ratio and Earnings Growth Assumptions**

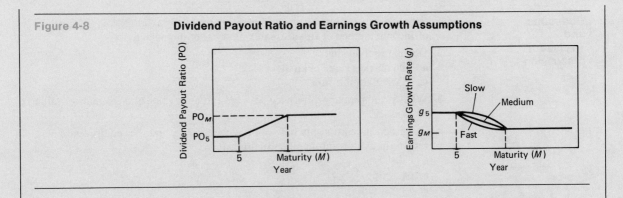

enue growth. On the contrary, it is simply a point when earnings advances are no greater than the nominal GNP rate.

Figure 4-8 illustrates the nature of the forecasts made in this valuation procedure.

Once these parameters have been specified, the expected return for the security can be solved for. Through an *iterative,* or repetitive, process the expected return can be found by solving for the discount rate that equates the present value of the forecasted future dividend stream with the current price of the stock. WFIA then compares the expected return for the security being analyzed with the expected return of other stocks having similar risk characteristics in order to identify overpriced and underpriced stocks.[21]

Based on their observations of overpriced and underpriced stocks, portfolio managers attempt to maximize the expected return of a portfolio (that is, a collection of stocks) for a given level of risk. The maximization process is accomplished through the use of a portfolio optimization program. The optimal, or best, portfolio is then selected from among the underpriced stocks.

[21] To determine the expected returns for other securities of similar risk, WFIA uses the concept of a security's *beta,* a measure of risk, and the security market line from the theory of the capital asset pricing model. This theory is explained in Chapter 5. Basically it provides a basis for assessing the tradeoffs required by investors between risk and required return.

Questions and Topics for Discussion

1. What variables must be known (or estimated) in applying the capitalization-of-income method of valuation to a physical or financial asset?
2. Define the following:
   a. The market value of an asset
   b. Market equilibrium
3. What is the primary difference between the book value and the market value of an asset?
4. Describe the relationship between the coupon rate and the required rate of return that will result in a bond selling at:
   a. a discount
   b. par value
   c. a premium
5. How does the yield to maturity on a bond differ from the coupon yield or current yield?
6. What factor or factors make the valuation of common stocks more complicated than the valuation of bonds and preferred stocks?
7. According to the general dividend valuation model, a firm that reinvests all its earnings and pays no cash dividends can still have a common stock value greater than zero. How is this possible?
8. Explain the relationship between financial decisions and shareholder wealth.
9. Explain how *each* of the following factors would affect the valuation of a firm's common stock, assuming that all other factors remain constant:
   a. The general level of interest rates shifts upward, causing investors to require a higher rate of return on securities in general.
   b. Increased foreign competition reduces the future growth potential of the firm's earnings and dividends.
   c. Investors reevaluate upward their assessment of the risk of the firm's common stock as the result of increased South American investments by the firm.
10. In the context of the constant growth dividend valuation model, explain what is meant by:
    a. dividend yield
    b. capital gains yield
11. Rank in ascending order the rates of return a typical investor would require on an investment in the following securities of a given firm:
    a. Common stock
    b. Preferred stock
    c. Bonds
    Justify your rankings.
12. Explain why the valuation models for a perpetual bond, preferred stock, and common stock with constant dividend payments (zero growth) are virtually identical.

Problems*

1. Determine the value of a $1,000 Canadian Pacific Limited perpetual 4 percent debenture (bond) at the following required rates of return:
   a. 4 percent
   b. 5 percent
   c. 6 percent
2. Canadian Pacific Limited's debentures (see Problem 1) are traded on the New York Exchange. During 1985 the high and low market prices of these

---

* Color numbers denote problems which have check answers provided at the end of the book.

bonds were $405 and $336.25 respectively. Determine the yield to maturity of one of these debentures if it was purchased under the following conditions:
a. At the high 1985 market price
b. At the low 1985 market price

3. Consider Allied Corporation's 9 percent debentures that mature on April 1, 2000. Assume that the interest on these bonds is paid and compounded annually. Determine the value of a $1,000 denomination Allied Corporation bond as of April 1, 1988 to an investor who holds the bond until maturity and whose required rate of return is:
a. 7 percent
b. 9 percent
c. 11 percent

4. Creative Financing, Inc., is planning to offer a $1,000 par value 15-year maturity bond with a coupon interest rate that changes every 5 years. The coupon rate for the first 5 years is 10 percent, 10.75 percent for the next 5 years, and 11.5 percent for the final 5 years. If you require an 11 percent rate of return on a bond of this quality and maturity, what is the maximum price you would pay for the bond? (Assume interest is paid annually at the end of each year.)

5. Public Service Electric and Gas has issued 12 percent bonds that mature at the end of 2004. Assume that interest is paid and compounded annually. Determine the *exact* yield to maturity (to the nearest tenth of 1 percent) by the trial-and-error method if an investor purchases a $1,000 denomination bond for $1,040 at the end of 1985.

6. Determine the *approximate* yield to maturity on the Public Service Electric and Gas bonds (see Problem 5) using the method described in Footnote 11 of this chapter. How does the approximate yield compare with the exact yield?

7. American Telephone & Telegraph has issued 7⅛ percent debentures that will mature on December 1, 2003. Assume that interest is paid and compounded annually. If an investor purchases a $1,000 denomination bond for $735 on December 1, 1985, determine the following:
a. The bond's *exact* yield to maturity (to the nearest tenth of 1 percent) using the trial-and-error method.
b. The bond's *approximate* yield to maturity using the method described in Footnote 11 of this chapter.

8. What would be the value of the Allied Corporation bonds (see Problem 3) at an 8 percent required rate of return if the interest were paid and compounded *semiannually*?

9. What is the value of a share of Litton Industries Series B $2.00 cumulative preferred stock to an investor who requires the following rates of return?
a. 9 percent
b. 10 percent
c. 12 percent

Lotus123

10. The Foreman Company's earnings and common stock dividends have been growing at an annual rate of 6 percent over the past 10 years and are expected to continue growing at this rate for the foreseeable future. The firm currently (that is, as of year 0) pays an annual dividend of $5.00 per share. Determine the current value of a share of Foreman common stock to investors with each of the following required rates of return:
a. 12 percent
b. 14 percent
c. 16 percent
d. 6 percent
e. 4 percent

11. General Cereal common stock dividends have been growing at an annual rate of 7 percent per year over the past 10 years. Current dividends are $1.70 per share. What is the current value of a share of this stock to an investor who requires a 12 percent rate of return if the following conditions exist?

   a. Dividends are expected to continue growing at the historical rate for the foreseeable future.

   b. The dividend growth rate is expected to *increase* to 9 percent per year.

   c. The dividend growth rate is expected to *decrease* to 6.5 percent per year.

12. The common stock of General Land Development Company (GLDC) is expected to pay a dividend of $1.25 next year and currently sells for $25. Assume that the firm's future dividend payments are expected to grow at a constant rate for the foreseeable future. Determine the implied growth rate for GLDC's dividends (and earnings) assuming that the required rate of return by investors is 12 percent.

13. The Seneca Maintenance Company currently (that is, as of year 0) pays a common stock dividend of $1.50 per share. Dividends are expected to grow at a rate of 11 percent per year for the next 4 years and then to continue growing thereafter at a rate of 5 percent per year. What is the current value of a share of Seneca common stock to an investor who requires a 14 percent rate of return?

14. During the previous 4 years Spiro Company's common dividends have grown from $1.00 (year 0) to $1.36 (year 4) per share.

   a. Determine the compound annual dividend growth rate over the 4-year period. Hint: Refer to the compound value techniques developed in Chapter 3, especially Equation 3.10.

   b. Forecast Spiro's dividends for the next 5 years, assuming that dividends continue to grow at the rate determined in Part a.

   c. Determine the current value of a share of Spiro common stock to an investor who plans to hold it for 5 years, assuming that the stock price *increases at the same rate* as the dividends. The investor's required rate of return is 12 percent.

15. Cascade Mining Company expects its earnings and dividends to increase by 7 percent per year over the next 6 years and then to remain relatively constant thereafter. The firm currently (that is, as of year 0) pays a dividend of $5.00 per share. Determine the value of a share of Cascade stock to an investor with a 12 percent required rate of return.

16. The chairman of Heller Industries told a meeting of financial analysts that he expects the firm's earnings and dividends to double over the next 6 years. The firm's current (that is, as of year 0) earnings and dividends per share are $4.00 and $2.00, respectively.

   a. Estimate the compound annual dividend growth rate over the 6-year period (to the nearest whole percent).

   b. Forecast Heller's earnings and dividends per share for each of the next 6 years, assuming that they grow at the rate determined in Part a.

   c. Based on the constant growth dividend valuation model, determine the current value of a share of Heller Industries common stock to an investor who requires an 18 percent rate of return.

   d. Why might the stock price calculated in Part c not represent an accurate valuation to an investor with an 18 percent required rate of return?

   e. Determine the current value of a share of Heller Industries common stock to an investor (with an 18 percent required rate of return) who plans to hold it for 6 years, assuming that earnings and dividends per share grow at the rate determined in Part (a) for the next 6 years and then at 6 percent thereafter.

17. Show that the 1-period and 2-period valuation models (Equations 4.13 and 4.14) are equivalent to the general dividend valuation model (Equation 4.18).

18. Ten years ago Video Toys began manufacturing and selling coin-operated arcade games. Dividends are currently $1.50 per share, having grown at a 15 percent compound annual rate over the past 5 years. The growth rate is expected to be maintained for the next 3 years, after which dividends are expected to grow at half that rate for 3 years. Beyond that time, Video Toys' dividends are expected to grow at 5 percent per year. What is the current value of a share of Video Toys common stock if your required rate of return is 18 percent?

19. Over the past 5 years the dividends of the Gamma Corporation have grown from $0.70 per share to the current level of $1.30 per share ($D_0$). This growth rate (computed to one decimal point accuracy) is expected to continue for the foreseeable future. What is the value of a share of Gamma Corporation common stock to an investor who requires a 20 percent return on her investment?

20. Bubba's Doggery currently (D_0) pays a $2.50 dividend per share. Next year's dividend is expected to be $3.00 per share. After next year dividends are expected to increase at a 9 percent annual rate for 3 years and a 6 percent annual rate thereafter.
    a. What is the current value of a share of Bubba's Doggery stock to an investor who requires a 15 percent return on his investment?
    b. If the growth rate over the next 3 years is expected to be only 7 percent and then 6 percent thereafter, what will the new stock price be?

21. The Edgar Corporation currently (D_0) pays a $2.00 per share dividend. This dividend is expected to grow at a 20% annual rate over the next 3 years and then to grow at 6% per year for the foreseeable future. What would you pay for a share of this stock if you demand a 20% rate of return?

Selected References

Copeland, Thomas E., and J. Fred Weston. *Financial Theory and Corporate Policy*. 2nd ed. Reading, Mass.: Addison-Wesley, 1983.

Elton, Edwin J., and Martin J. Gruber. "Earnings Estimates and the Accuracy of Expectational Data." *Management Science* 18 (April 1972): 409–424.

Gordon, M.J. "Dividends, Earnings and Stock Prices." *Review of Economics and Statistics* 41 (May 1959): 99–105.

Reilly, Frank K. *Investment Analysis and Portfolio Management*. 2nd ed. Hinsdale, Ill.: Dryden Press, 1985.

Williams, J. B. *The Theory of Investment Value*. Cambridge, Mass.: Harvard University Press, 1938.

5

ANALYSIS OF RISK AND RETURN

A Financial Dilemma

There Is No Free Lunch—J. David & Company

J. David & Company was established in 1979 in San Diego as a sole proprietorship by J. David Dominelli. By 1983 the firm had grown to 270 employees with offices located in Newport Beach, San Francisco, Chicago, Los Angeles, London, and the Carribean island of Montserrat. The firm operated three major divisions—J. David Municipals and Governments, J. David Securities, and J. David Intercurrency.

It is the J. David Intercurrency operation which ultimately led to the collapse of J. David Dominelli's financial empire. Dominelli employed a well-paid staff of salespersons, including former stockbrokers, lawyers, accountants, and real estate agents. These agents received 10 percent immediately for every dollar of funds they could attract to the firm's foreign currency investment operation. In addition these salespersons received non-taxable gifts, such as cars and computers, from Dominelli.

The lure to investors was extraordinarily high returns. Investors reported monthly returns of 4 to 5 percent, resulting in annual returns of 48 to 60 percent. The minimum investment was $100,000 and investors committed at least $150 million to the foreign exchange arm of J. David & Company. Monthly profits were automatically "reinvested" by the firm unless an investor explicitly withdrew the funds. J. David Intercurrency purportedly was offering these investors an opportunity to share the profits from the firm's success in trading in the highly volatile foreign currency market. The operation was apparently run much like a mutual fund. Investors had no way of knowing what their funds were invested in or how monthly profits were computed. All they received was a monthly statement indicating the profits for the month. The venture attracted many prominent and wealthy individuals.

In late 1983, the scheme began to collapse. What started out as a foreign currency trading mutual fund grew into a giant Ponzi scheme in which the early investors were paid with the capital provided by later investors. In early 1984, checks written by J. David & Company began to bounce. Dominelli soon disappeared to the Carribean island of Montserrat, only to be declared an undesirable and sent back to Miami where Federal marshalls took him into custody.

Greedy investors, seeking to earn astronomically high returns, lost some $150 million in the venture. They learned one of the most important lessons in finance—**HIGH RETURNS NORMALLY CAN ONLY BE EARNED BY ASSUMING HIGH RISKS. IN FINANCE, THERE IS NO FREE LUNCH.**

This chapter defines the concepts of risk and return and develops the relationship between these important concepts. This relationship is one of the dominant themes in finance.

Key Chapter Concepts

1. Risk refers to the possibility of achieving some outcome other than that which is expected. Risk tends to increase as one looks farther into the future.

2. Probability distributions indicate the percentage chance of various possible outcomes in a risky situation.
   a. The *expected value* of a series of possible outcomes is equal to the weighted average of the individual outcomes (payoffs) times their associated probabilities.
   b. The *standard deviation* is an important measure of the total risk of a set of possible outcomes, each having an associated probability of occurrence.
   c. The coefficient of variation is a useful total risk measure in cases when unequal-sized events are being compared, such as two investment projects of different size.

3. Portfolios are composed of two or more assets.
   a. The risk of a portfolio of assets depends on the risk of the individual assets in the portfolio and the correlation of returns between the pairs of assets in the portfolio.
   b. By combining assets which are less than perfectly, positively correlated, portfolio risk can be *reduced* below the level of the weighted average risk of the individual assets.

4. The *systematic* risk of a security or asset refers to that portion of the variability of an individual security's (asset's) returns caused by factors affecting the security market as a whole, such as interest rate changes.

5. *Beta,* measured as the slope of a regression line between market returns and a security's returns, is commonly used as a measure of systematic risk.

6. The *unsystematic* risk of a security or asset refers to that portion of the variability of a security's (asset's) returns caused by factors unique to that asset or security.

7. The *security market line* expresses the relationship between the required returns from a security (asset) and the systematic risk of that security (asset).

8. Other important risk dimensions include the risk of default on a security.

Glossary of New Terms

Beta A measure of systematic risk. It is a measure of the volatility of a security's returns relative to the returns of a broad-based market portfolio of securities.

Characteristic line A regression line relating the periodic returns for a specific security to the periodic returns on the market portfolio. The slope of this regression line is an estimate of the *beta* of the security—a measure of its systematic risk.

Coefficient of variation The ratio of the *standard deviation* to the *expected value*. It provides a *relative* measure of risk.

Correlation A relative statistical measure of the degree to which two series of numbers, such as the returns from two securities, tend to move or vary together.

Covariance An absolute statistical measure of how closely two variables (such as securities' returns) move together. It measures the degree to which increases (decreases) in the level of one variable tend to be associated with increases (decreases) in the level of another variable over time.

Diversification The act of investing in a set of securities or assets having different risk-return characteristics.

Portfolio A collection of two or more assets or securities.

Security market line (SML) The relationship between systematic risk and required rates of return for individual securities.

Standard deviation A statistical measure of the dispersion, or variability, of a set of observations around its arithmetic average, or mean. Operationally it is defined as the square root of the weighted average squared deviations of individual observations from the expected value. The standard deviation provides an *absolute* measure of risk.

Systematic risk That portion of the variability of an individual security's returns that is caused by factors affecting the market as a whole. This is also called *nondiversifiable risk*.

Unsystematic risk Risk that is unique to a firm; this is also called *diversifiable risk*.

Introduction

Chapter 4 talked about the investor's *required rate of return* on a bond, preferred stock, and common stock. These required rates of return were used to discount the expected cash flows from each of these securities to determine the value of that security. In Chapter 4 the required rate of return from a security (or other asset) was represented as an increasing function of that security's *risk;* that is, the greater the risk, the greater the required rate of return.

This chapter defines risk in more precise terms; looks at a number of alternative techniques for measuring risk; and then considers the relationships between risk, required return, and security values.

The Meaning of Risk

Risk is defined by *Webster's Dictionary* as the "possibility of loss or injury; hazard; peril; danger." Hence, risk implies that there is a chance for some unfavorable event to occur. From the perspective of security analysis or the analysis of an investment in some project (such as the development of a new product line), risk is the *possibility that actual cash flows (returns) will be less than forecasted cash flows (returns).*

An investment is said to be *risk-free* if the dollar returns from the initial investment are known with certainty. Some of the best examples of risk-free investments are United States Treasury securities. There is virtually no chance that the Treasury will fail to redeem these securities at maturity or that the Treasury will default on any interest payments owed. As a last resort, the Treasury can always print more money.[1]

In contrast, New York City bonds constitute a *risky* investment because it is possible that New York City will default on one or more interest payments and will lack sufficient funds to redeem the bonds at face value at maturity. In other words, the possible returns from this investment are *variable,* and each potential outcome can be assigned a *probability.*

If, for example, you were considering investing in New York City bonds, you might assign the following probabilities to the three possible outcomes of this investment:

Outcome	Probability
No default, bonds redeemed at maturity	0.80
Default on interest for one or more periods	0.15
No interest default, but bonds not redeemed at maturity	0.05
	1.00

These probabilities are interpreted to mean that an 80 percent chance exists that the bonds will not be in default over their life and will be redeemed at maturity, a 15 percent chance of interest default during the life of the bonds, and a 5 percent chance that the bonds will not be redeemed at maturity.

Hence, from an investment perspective, risk refers to the chance that

---

[1] Note that this discussion of risk deals with *dollar returns* and ignores other considerations, such as potential losses in purchasing power. In addition, it assumes that securities are held until maturity, which is not always the case. Sometimes a security must be sold prior to maturity for less than face value because of changes in the level of interest rates.

returns from an investment will be less than expected. We can define risk more precisely, however, by introducing some probability concepts.

Probability Distributions

The *probability* that a particular event will occur is defined as the *percentage chance* of its outcome. Probabilities may be either objectively or subjectively determined. An objective determination is based on past outcomes of similar events, whereas a subjective one is merely an opinion made by an individual about the likelihood that a given event will occur. In the case of projects that are frequently repeated—such as the drilling of developmental oil wells in an established oil field—reasonably good objective estimates can be made about the success of a new well. Similarly, good objective estimates can often be made about the expected returns of an AT&T bond. However, the expected returns from securities of new, small firms are often much more difficult to estimate objectively. Hence, highly subjective estimates regarding the likelihood of various returns are necessary. *The fact that many probability estimates in business are at least partially subjective does not diminish their usefulness.*

Let us consider the concept of probability and risk with a sample probability distribution of the returns available from an investment of $100,000 in the stock of either Consolidated Properties, Inc. (CPI), a public utility firm, or International Farm Products (IFP), a maker of farm machinery. By investing in the stock of either of these firms, an investor expects to receive dividend payments plus stock price appreciation. We will assume that the investor plans to hold the stock for one year and then sell it. Over the year, the investor feels there is a 20 percent chance for an economic *boom,* a 60 percent chance for a *normal* economic environment, and a 20 percent chance for a *recession.* Given this assessment of the economic environment *over the next year,* the investor estimates the probability distribution of returns from the investment in CPI and IFP, as Table 5-1 shows.

Expected Values

From this information the *expected value* of returns from investing in the stock of CPI and IFP can be calculated. It is the weighted average of the

---

Table 5-1   **Probability Distribution of Returns from CPI and IFP**

State of the Economy	Probability	Rate of Return Anticipated Under Each State of the Economy*	
		CPI	IFP
Recession	0.2	10%	−4%
Normal year	0.6	18	18
Boom	0.2	26	40
	1.0		

*For example, a 10 percent rate of return for CPI means that the stock value plus dividends total $110,000 at the end of one year. Working with a *discrete* probability distribution, as this example does, indicates that there is no probability of a loss by investing in CPI. This is, of course, unrealistic. In the following discussion of continuous distributions this assumption is relaxed.

possible returns from each stock, with the weights being the probability of occurrence.

Algebraically the expected value of the returns from a security or project may be defined as follows:

$$\hat{R} = \sum_{j=1}^{n} R_j P_j, \tag{5.1}$$

where $\hat{R}$ is the expected return; R_j is the outcome for the jth case, where there are n possible outcomes; and P_j is the probability that the jth outcome will occur. The expected returns for CPI and IFP are computed in Table 5-2. The expected return is 18 percent for both CPI and IFP.

Standard Deviation: An Absolute Measure of Risk

The standard deviation is a statistical measure of the dispersion of a variable about the mean. It is defined as the *square root of the weighted average squared deviations of individual observations from the mean:*

$$\sigma = \sqrt{\sum_{j=1}^{n} (R_j - \hat{R})^2 P_j}, \tag{5.2}$$

where σ is the standard deviation.

The standard deviation can be used to measure the variability of returns from an investment. As such, it gives an indication of the *risk* involved in the asset or security. The larger the standard deviation, the more variable an investment's returns and the riskier the investment. A standard deviation of zero indicates no variability and thus no risk. Table 5-3 shows the calculation of the standard deviations for the investments in CPI and IFP.

From the calculations in Table 5-3, it can be seen that IFP appears riskier than CPI, because possible returns from IFP are more variable, measured by its standard deviation of 13.91 percent, than those from CPI, which have a standard deviation of only 5.06 percent.

This example dealt with a *discrete* probability distribution of outcomes (returns) for each firm; that is, a *limited* number of possible outcomes were identified, and probabilities were assigned to them. In reality,

Table 5-2 **Expected Return Calculation for Investment in CPI and IFP**

	CPI			IFP	
R_j	P_j	$R_j \times P_j$	R_j	P_j	$R_j \times P_j$
10%	0.2	2.0%	−4%	0.2	−0.8%
18	0.6	10.8	18	0.6	10.8
26	0.2	5.2	40	0.2	8.0
Expected return = $\hat{R}$ = 18.0%			Expected return = $\hat{R}$ = 18.0%		

Table 5-3

Computation of Standard Deviations of Returns—CPI and IFP

	j	R_j	$\hat{R}$	$R_j - \hat{R}$	$(R_j - \hat{R})^2$	P_j	$(R_j - \hat{R})^2 P_j$
CPI	1 (Recession)	10%	18%	−8%	64	0.2	12.8
	2 (Normal)	18	18	0	0	0.6	0
	3 (Boom)	26	18	+8	64	0.2	12.8

$$\sum_{j=1}^{3} (R_j - \hat{R})^2 P_j = 25.6$$

$$\sigma = \sqrt{\sum_{j=1}^{n} (R_j - \hat{R})^2 P_j} = \sqrt{25.6} = 5.06\%$$

	j	R_j	$\hat{R}$	$R_j - \hat{R}$	$(R_j - \hat{R})^2$	P_j	$(R_j - \hat{R})^2 P_j$
IFP	1 (Recession)	−4%	18%	−22%	484	0.2	96.8
	2 (Normal)	18	18	0	0	0.6	0
	3 (Boom)	40	18	+22	484	0.2	96.8

$$\sum_{j=1}^{3} (R_j - \hat{R})^2 P_j = 193.6$$

$$\sigma = \sqrt{\sum_{j=1}^{n} (R_j - \hat{R})^2 P_j} = \sqrt{193.6} = 13.91\%$$

however, many different outcomes are possible for the investment in the stock of each firm—ranging from losses during the year to returns in excess of IFP's 40 percent return. To indicate the probability of *all* possible outcomes for these investments, it is necessary to construct a *continuous* probability distribution. This is done by developing a table similar to Table 5-1, except that it would have many more possible outcomes and their associated probabilities. That detailed table of outcomes and probabilities can be used to develop the expected value of returns from both IFP and CPI, and a continuous curve would be constructed to approximate the probabilities associated with each outcome. Figure 5-1 illustrates continuous probability distributions of returns for investments in the stock of IFP and CPI.

From this figure it can be seen that the CPI possible returns have a tighter probability distribution, indicating a lower variability of returns, whereas the IFP possible returns have a flatter distribution, indicating higher variability and, by extension, more risk.

The possible returns from many investments can be estimated by assuming that they follow the *normal* probability distribution. The normal probability distribution is characterized by a symmetrical, bell-like curve. If the expected continuous probability distribution of returns is approximately normal, a table of the *standard normal probability function* (Table V at the end of this text) can be used to compute the probability of occurrence of any particular outcome. From this table, for example, it is apparent that the actual outcome should be between plus or minus 1

Figure 5-1

Continuous Probability Distributions for the Expected Returns from Investments in the IFP and CPI Stocks

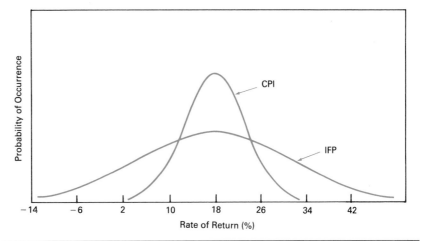

standard deviation from the expected value 68.26 percent of the time,[2] between plus or minus 2 standard deviations 95.44 percent of the time, and between plus or minus 3 standard deviations 99.74 percent of the time. This is illustrated in Figure 5-2.

The number of standard deviations, z, that a particular value of R is from the expected value, $\hat{R}$, can be computed as follows:

$$z = \frac{R - \hat{R}}{\sigma}. \qquad (5.3)$$

Table V and Equation 5.3 can be used to compute the probability of a return for an investment in IFP being less than some value R—for example, 0 percent return. First, the number of standard deviations that 0 percent is from the expected return (18 percent) must be calculated. Substituting the expected return and the standard deviation from Tables 5-2 and 5-3 into Equation 5.3 yields the following:

$$z = \frac{0\% - 18\%}{13.91\%}$$

$$= -1.29.$$

In other words, the return of 0 percent is 1.29 standard deviations *below* the mean. The nearest value in Table V is the probability associated with

[2] For example, Table V indicates that there is a probability of 0.1587 of a value occurring that is greater than $+1\sigma$ from the mean *and* a probability of 0.1587 of a value occurring that is less than -1σ from the mean. Hence, the probability of a value *between* $+1\sigma$ and -1σ is 68.26 percent—that is, $1.00 - (2 \times 0.1587)$.

Figure 5-2

Sample Illustration of Areas under the Normal Probability Distribution Curve

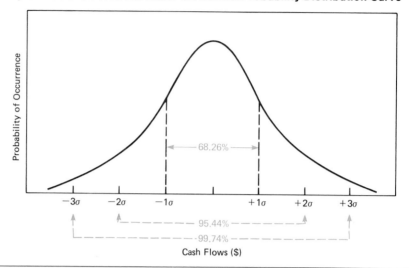

Cash Flows ($)

1.30 standard deviations, or 9.68 percent (0.0968). Thus, there is a slightly greater chance (because the actual value is 1.29 standard deviations below the mean) than 9.68 percent that IFP will have returns below 0 percent.[3] Conversely, there is nearly a 90.32 percent chance that the return will be greater than 0 percent.

Coefficient of Variation: A Relative Measure of Risk

The standard deviation is an appropriate measure of risk when the investments being compared are approximately equal in size and the returns are estimated to have symmetrical probability distributions. Because the standard deviation is an *absolute* measure of variability, it is generally *not* suitable for comparing investments with different expected returns. In these cases the *coefficient of variation* provides a better measure of risk.

Consider, for example, two assets, T and S. Asset T has expected annual returns of 25 percent and a standard deviation of 20 percent, whereas Asset S has expected annual returns of 10 percent and a standard deviation of 18 percent. Intuition tells us that Asset T is less risky, since its *relative* variation is smaller.

The coefficient of variation, v, considers relative variation and thus is well suited for use when a comparison is being made between two investments with different expected returns. It is defined as the ratio of the standard deviation, σ, to the expected value, $\hat{R}$:

$$v = \frac{\sigma}{\hat{R}}. \tag{5.4}$$

---

[3] By interpolation, the chance of having a value less than 1.29 standard deviations below the mean is 0.0986, or 0.1056 − 0.8(0.1056 − 0.0968).

As the coefficient of variation increases, so does the relative risk of an asset. The coefficients of variation for Assets T and S are computed as follows:

Asset T:

$$v = \frac{\sigma}{\hat{R}}$$

$$= \frac{20\%}{25\%}$$

$$= 0.8.$$

Asset S:

$$v = \frac{\sigma}{\hat{R}}$$

$$= \frac{18\%}{10\%}$$

$$= 1.8.$$

Asset S's returns have a larger coefficient of variation than Asset T's, and therefore Asset S is the more risky of the two investments.

In general, when comparing two equal-sized investments, the standard deviation is an appropriate measure of total risk. When comparing two investments with different expected returns, the coefficient of variation is the more appropriate measure of total risk.[4]

Risk as an Increasing Function of Time

Most investment decisions require that returns be *forecasted* several years into the future. The riskiness of these forecasted returns may be thought of as an *increasing function of time*. Returns that are generated early can generally be predicted with more certainty than those that are anticipated farther out into the future.

Consider the risk facing a firm that plans to begin producing and marketing a new home computer system. This project is expected to generate cash flows to the firm of $2 million per year over the 7-year life of the project. Even though the expected annual cash flows are equal for each year, it is reasonable to assume that the riskiness of these flows increases over time as more and more presently unknown variables have a chance to affect the project's cash flows. Figure 5-3 illustrates this situation.

The distribution is relatively tight in year 1, since the market conditions affecting that year's cash flows are reasonably well known. By year 7,

---

[4] The relationship between the coefficient of variation and several other measures of risk (including the standard deviation) is developed in John M. Wachowicz, Jr. and Ronald E. Shrieves, "An Argument for Generalized Mean-Coefficient of Variation Analysis," *Financial Management* (Winter 1980): 51–58.

Figure 5-3   **Sample Illustration of the Risk of a Project over Time**

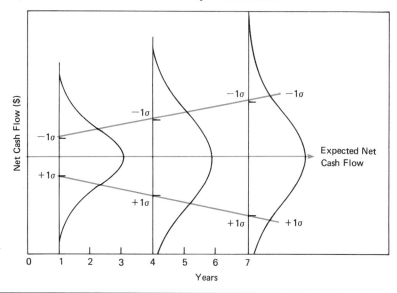

however, the distribution has become flat, indicating a considerable increase in the standard deviation, caused by increased uncertainty in market conditions.

Some types of cash flows are not subject to increasing variability. These include, for example, contractual arrangements, such as lease payments, in which the expected cash flows remain constant (or change at some predefined rate) over the life of the contract. In spite of the exceptions, it is reasonable to conclude that the riskiness of the cash flows from most investment projects gradually increases over time. Similarly, the riskiness of returns from most securities increases the farther into the future these returns are being considered. For instance, the return from the purchase of Ford Motor Company bonds is nearly guaranteed for the next year. However, projecting the returns to be received 10 years in the future is much more difficult due to the potential impact of competition, new technology, and other factors.

Portfolio Risk Analysis

Up to now the risk associated with single investments (physical assets or securities) has been considered. But firms hold portfolios of many different assets, and individuals generally hold many different securities. *Portfolio risk,* the risk associated with collections of assets or securities, is considered in the following sections. Generally we can conclude that a security or a physical asset held as part of a portfolio is *less* risky than if it were held alone.

The nature of portfolio risk will be considered. We will also develop procedures to measure the risk of assets held in a portfolio. Next, a model of the relationship between risk and return in a portfolio of assets or securities will be developed. This model, the *Capital Asset Pricing Model*

(CAPM), provides a strong analytical basis for evaluating risk-return relationships—both in the context of financial management and securities investment decisions.

Investment Diversification and Risk

Most physical assets and financial assets are held as parts of portfolios. Banks hold many different loans and many different bonds; individuals hold many different bonds and stocks; and corporations hold many different physical assets. Consequently, it is important to know how the returns from portfolios of investments behave over time—not only how the returns from any individual asset in the portfolio behave. The questions of importance are as follows:

- What return can be expected to be earned from the portfolio?
- What is the risk of the portfolio?

For example, assume that the Kreiser Aluminum Company is considering diversifying into gold mining and refining. During economic boom periods, aluminum sales tend to be brisk; gold, on the other hand, tends to be most in demand during economic downturns.[5] Thus, the returns from the aluminum business and the gold mining business are inversely, or *negatively*, related. If Kreiser expands into gold mining and refining, its overall return will tend to be less variable than individual returns from these projects. This is illustrated in Figure 5-4. Graph a shows the variation of rates of return in the aluminum industry over time, Graph b shows the corresponding variation of returns from gold mining over the same time frame, and Graph c shows the combined rate of return for both lines of business.

As can be seen from this figure, when the return from aluminum

---

Figure 5-4   **Sample Illustration of Diversification and Risk Reduction**

(a) Aluminum   (b) Gold Mining   (c) Aluminum and Gold Mining Combined

---

[5] As investors lose confidence in the economy's performance, many of them turn to gold as an investment. This drives the price of gold up and increases returns to gold mining firms, whose costs of operation are not directly related to the demand for gold.

operations is high, the return from gold mining tends to be low, and vice versa. The *combined* returns are more stable, and thus less risky.

This *portfolio effect* of reduced variability results because a *negative correlation* exists between the returns from aluminum operations and the returns from gold mining. The *correlation* between any two variables—such as rates of return or net cash flows—is a relative statistical measure of the degree to which these variables tend to move together. The *correlation coefficient* measure is the extent to which high (or low) values of one variable are associated with high (or low) values of another. Values of the correlation coefficient can range from $+1.0$ for *perfectly positively correlated* variables to -1.0 for *perfectly negatively correlated* variables. Figure 5-5 illustrates perfect positive and negative correlations for two investments, AA and BB.

For perfect positive correlation (Graph a), high rates of return from AA are always associated with high rates of return from BB; conversely, low rates of return from AA are always associated with low rates of return from BB. For perfect negative correlation (Graph b), however, the opposite is true; high rates of return from AA are associated with low rates of return from BB, and vice versa. If two variables are unrelated, the correlation coefficient between these two variables will be 0.

When two investments are perfectly negatively correlated, the maximum benefits of risk reduction are achieved by diversification. When two investments are perfectly positively correlated, adopting both of them does not result in any risk reduction. When the correlation coefficient between two projects is between $+1$ and -1, some risk reduction is achieved by diversification. The less positively correlated the returns from two investments are, the greater the portfolio effects of risk reduction will be if the firm or individual diversifies by investing in both.

In practice, the returns from most investments a firm or individual considers are positively correlated with other investments held by the firm or individual. For example, returns from projects that are closely related to the firm's primary line of business have a high positive correlation with returns from projects already being carried out, and thus provide limited opportunities to reduce risk. In the Kreiser example, if Kreiser were to build a new smelter, it would not realize the risk reduction possibilities that investing in gold mining and refining would produce. Similarly, the returns from most common stocks are positively correlated, because these

Figure 5-5

Perfect Positive and Perfect Negative Correlation for Two Projects

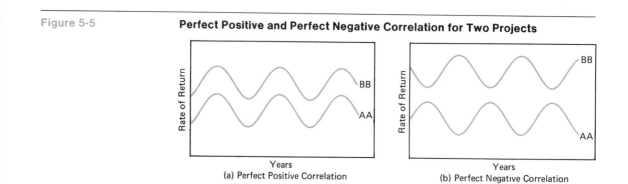

(a) Perfect Positive Correlation
(b) Perfect Negative Correlation

returns are influenced by such common factors as the general state of the economy, the level of interest rates, and so on.

Expected Returns from a Portfolio

When two or more securities are combined into a portfolio, the expected return of the portfolio is equal to the weighted average of the expected returns from the individual securities. For example, assume a portfolio contains Acme Corporation (A) securities and Babbo Corporation (B) securities, which have expected returns of 12 percent and 8 percent, respectively. If a portion W_A of the available funds (wealth) is invested in Security A, and the remaining funds W_B is invested in Security B, the expected return of the portfolio $\hat{R}_p$ is as follows:

$$\hat{R}_p = W_A \hat{R}_A + W_B \hat{R}_B, \tag{5.5}$$

where $\hat{R}_A$ and $\hat{R}_B$ are the expected returns for Securities A and B, respectively. Furthermore, $W_A + W_B = 1$, indicating that all funds are invested in either Security A or Security B.

The range of possible expected returns for a portfolio consisting of Securities A and B is 12 percent (if 100 percent of the portfolio is invested in Security A and 0 percent is invested in Security B) to 8 percent (if 100 percent is invested in Security B and 0 percent is invested in Security A). In addition, any linear weighted combination of returns for Securities A and B between 8 and 12 percent is also possible. For example, assume that 30 percent of this portfolio consists of Security A, and Security B constitutes the remaining 70 percent. In this case the expected return on the portfolio is computed as follows:

$$\hat{R}_p = 0.3\,(12\%) + 0.7\,(8\%)$$
$$= 9.2\%.$$

Figure 5-6 illustrates the relationship between the expected return for a portfolio containing securities A and B and the proportion of the total portfolio invested in each security. For example, when $W_A = 1.0$ (100%), $W_B = 0$ (since $W_A + W_B = 1.0$), and the expected portfolio return is 12 percent, the same as the return for A. When $W_A = 0.5$ (50 percent) and $W_B = 0.5$ (50 percent), the expected portfolio return is 10 percent. As shown above, when $W_A = 0.3$ and $W_B = 0.7$, the expected portfolio return is 9.2 percent. Thus it can be seen that the expected return from a portfolio of securities is simply equal to the weighted average of the individual security returns where the weights represent the proportion of the total portfolio invested in each security. This results in the linear relationship shown in Figure 5-6.

In general, the expected return from any portfolio of n securities or assets is equal to the sum of the expected returns from each security times the proportion of the total portfolio invested in that security:

$$\hat{R}_p = \sum_{i=1}^{n} W_i \hat{R}_i, \tag{5.6}$$

where $\Sigma W_i = 1$ and $0 \le W_i \le 1$.

Figure 5-6

Expected Return from a Portfolio of Assets A and B*

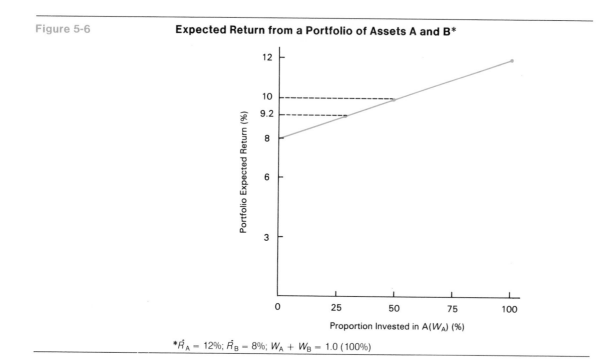

*$\hat{R}_A = 12\%; \hat{R}_B = 8\%; W_A + W_B = 1.0\,(100\%)$

Portfolio Risk

Although the expected returns from a portfolio of two or more securities can be computed as a weighted average of the expected returns from the individual securities, it is not sufficient merely to calculate a weighted average of the risk of each individual security to arrive at a measure of the portfolio's risk. Whenever the returns from the individual securities are not perfectly positively correlated, the risk of any portfolio of these securities may be reduced through the effects of diversification. Thus, diversification can be achieved by investing in a diverse set of securities that have different risk-return characteristics. The amount of risk reduction achieved through diversification depends on the degree of correlation between the returns of the individual securities in the portfolio. The lower the correlations among the individual securities, the greater the possibilities for risk reduction.

The risk for a two-security portfolio, measured by the standard deviation of portfolio returns, is computed as follows:

$$\sigma_p = \sqrt{W_A^2 \sigma_A^2 + W_B^2 \sigma_B^2 + 2W_A W_B \rho_{AB} \sigma_A \sigma_B,} \tag{5.7}$$

where W_A is the proportion of funds invested in Security A; W_B is the proportion of funds invested in Security B; $W_A + W_B = 1$; σ_A^2 is the variance of returns from Security A (or the square of the standard deviation for Security A, σ_A); σ_B^2 is the variance of returns from Security B (or the square of the standard deviation for Security B, σ_B); and ρ_{AB} is the correlation coefficient of returns between Securities A and B.

For example, consider a portfolio containing Securities A and B as described here:

	Acme (A)	Babbo (B)
Expected return	0.12	0.08
Standard deviation of returns	0.09	0.09
Proportion invested in each security	0.5	0.5

Given various values for the correlation between the securities' returns, the risk of a portfolio containing equal proportions of the two securities can be computed.

First, consider the case where $\rho_{AB} = +1.0$ (that is, perfect *positive* correlation). The portfolio's risk is calculated as follows:

$$\sigma_p = \sqrt{(0.5)^2(0.09)^2 + (0.5)^2(0.09)^2 + 2(0.5)(0.5)(+1)(0.09)(0.09)}$$

$$= \sqrt{0.002025 + 0.002025 + 0.00405}$$

$$= \sqrt{0.0081}$$

$$= 0.09.$$

When the returns from the two securities are perfectly positively correlated, the risk of the portfolio is equal to the weighted average of the risk of the individual securities (9 percent in this example). *Thus, no risk reduction is achieved when perfectly positively correlated assets are combined in a portfolio.*

The returns from most assets are not perfectly positively correlated; this allows for risk reduction through diversification. For example, consider next the case of a low positive correlation of returns, such as $\rho_{AB} = +0.1$. The portfolio risk in this example is as follows:

$$\sigma_p = \sqrt{(0.5)^2(0.09)^2 + (0.5)^2(0.09)^2 + 2(0.5)(0.5)(+0.1)(0.09)(0.09)}$$

$$= \sqrt{0.002025 + 0.002025 + 0.000405}$$

$$= \sqrt{0.004455}$$

$$= 0.067.$$

In this case diversification reduces the portfolio risk from 9 percent (the weighted average of the individual security risks) to 6.7 percent.

Finally, consider the case of a perfect *negative* correlation, $\rho_{AB} = -1.0$. In this example the portfolio risk is completely eliminated.

Table 5-4 summarizes the effects of different degrees of correlation on portfolio risk, assuming that the portfolio contains equal proportions of two securities. Figure 5-7 graphs the relationship between the correlation of returns for securities A and B and the risk (σ_p) of a portfolio containing equal proportions of securities A and B $(W_A = W_B = 0.5)$. This figure indicates that the relationship between portfolio risk and the correlation of security returns is not linear.

Table 5-4   **Portfolio Risk and Security Correlations in the Two-Security Case**

Correlation Coefficient, ρ_{AB}	Portfolio Risk, σ_p*
+1.0	0.090
+0.5	0.078
+0.1	0.067
0.0	0.064
−0.5	0.045
−1.0	0.000

*The standard deviation of returns for Securities A and B equals 0.09 and 0.09, respectively. Each possible portfolio contains equal proportions of both securities.

Figure 5-8 illustrates the relationship between portfolio risk and the proportion W invested in each of two securities, A and B, for various correlations of returns between A and B. It can be seen that in the case of perfect positive correlation ($\rho_{AB} = +1.0$) the portfolio risk is simply a weighted average of the individual security risks (in this case a constant 9 percent, since the $\sigma_A = \sigma_B = 9$ percent).

When the correlation is perfectly negative ($\rho_{AB} = -1.0$), portfolio risk is reduced to zero when $W_A = W_B = 0.5$. When a portfolio contains proportions of A and B other than $W_A = W_B = 0.5$, the portfolio risk is between 0 percent and 9 percent. (With a perfect negative correlation of returns between two securities, there will always be some proportion of A and B which will result in the complete elimination of portfolio risk. Only in the case where $\sigma_A = \sigma_B$ will this proportion be $W_A = W_B = 0.5$.)

Figure 5-7   **Portfolio Risk versus Correlation of Security Returns***

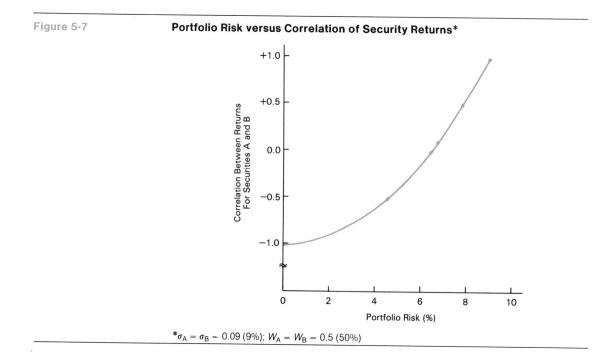

*$\sigma_A = \sigma_B = 0.09$ (9%); $W_A = W_B = 0.5$ (50%)

Figure 5-8   **Relationship Between Portfolio Risk and Portfolio Weightings***

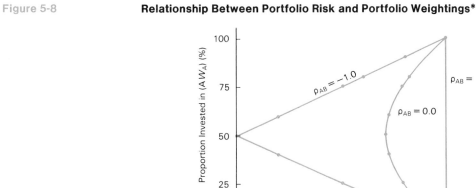

*$\sigma_A = \sigma_B = 0.09$ (9%); $W_A + W_B = 1.0$ (100%)

For a correlation of zero ($\rho_{AB} = 0.0$) risk can be reduced with various proportions of A and B but not as much as in the case of perfect negative correlation. Curves representing correlation coefficients between +1.0 and 0.0 will fall between these two curves as shown in Figure 5-8. Similarly, curves representing correlation coefficients between 0.0 and −1.0 will fall between those two curves as shown in Figure 5-8.

The preceding analysis illustrates the possibilities for portfolio risk reduction when two or more securities are combined to form a portfolio. Unfortunately, when more than two securities are involved—as is usually the case—the number of calculations required to compute the portfolio risk increases geometrically. For example, while 45 correlation coefficients are needed for a portfolio containing 10 securities, 4,950 correlation coefficients must be computed for a portfolio containing 100 securities. In other words, a 10-fold increase in securities causes a greater than 100-fold increase in the required calculations.[6] In addition, a substantial computational undertaking is required to find the particular portfolio of securities that minimizes portfolio risk for a given level of return or maximizes return for a given level of risk, even for a portfolio that contains only a few securities. Obviously a more workable method is needed to assess the effects of diversification on a portfolio of assets; this problem is discussed in the following sections.

Risk Reduction Through Diversification

Whenever the individual securities in a portfolio are less than perfectly positively correlated, diversification can reduce the portfolio's risk below the weighted average of the total risk (measured by the standard

[6] The number of correlation coefficients needed to evaluate an *n*-security portfolio is computed as $(n^2 - n)/2$.

deviation) of the individual securities. Since most securities are positively correlated with returns in the securities market in general, it is usually not possible to totally eliminate risk in a portfolio of securities. As the economic outlook improves, returns on most individual securities tend to increase; as the economic outlook deteriorates, individual security returns tend to decline. In spite of this positive "comovement" among the returns of individual securities, each security experiences some "unique" variation in its returns that is unrelated to the underlying economic factors that influence all securities. In other words, there are two types of risk inherent in all securities:

- *Systematic,* or *nondiversifiable,* risk.
- *Unsystematic,* or *diversifiable,* risk.

Systematic Risk

Systematic risk refers to that portion of the variability of an individual security's returns caused by factors affecting the market as a whole; as such, it can be thought of as being nondiversifiable. Systematic risk accounts for 25 to 50 percent of the total risk of any security. Some of the sources of systematic risk, which cause the returns from all securities to vary more or less together, include the following:

- Interest rate changes.
- Changes in purchasing power.
- Changes in investor expectations about the overall performance of the economy.

Since diversification cannot eliminate systematic risk, it is this type of risk that is the predominant determinant of individual security risk premiums.

Unsystematic Risk

Unsystematic risk is risk that is unique to the firm. It is the variability in a security's returns that is caused by factors such as the following:

- Management capabilities and decisions.
- Strikes.
- The availability of raw materials.
- The unique effects of such government regulation as pollution control.
- The effects of foreign competition.
- The particular levels of financial and operating leverage the firm employs.

Because unsystematic risk is unique to each firm, an efficiently diversified portfolio of securities can successfully eliminate most of the unsystematic risk inherent in individual securities, as is shown in Figure 5-9.

To eliminate effectively the unsystematic risk inherent in a portfolio's individual securities, it is not necessary for the portfolio to include a large number of securities. In fact, randomly constructed portfolios of as few as ten to fifteen securities on average can successfully diversify away a large

Figure 5-9   **Unsystematic Risk and Portfolio Diversification**

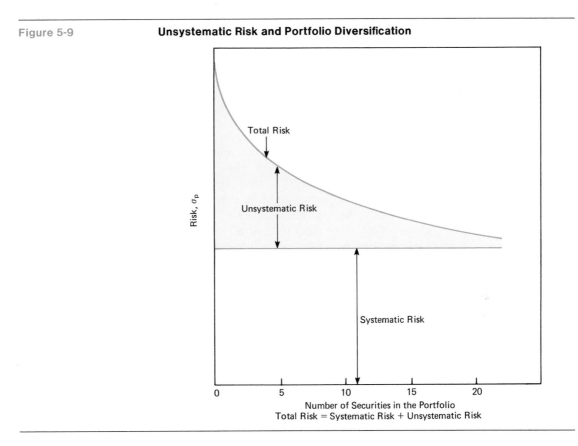

Total Risk = Systematic Risk + Unsystematic Risk

portion of the unsystematic risk of the individual securities.[7] The risk remaining *after* diversification is market-related risk, often called *systematic risk,* and it cannot be eliminated through diversification. Since unsystematic risk commonly accounts for 50 percent or more of the total risk of most individual securities, it should be obvious that the risk-reducing benefits of efficient diversification are well worth the effort.

Given the small number of securities required for efficient diversification by an individual investor, as well as the dominance of the securities markets by many large institutional investors who hold widely diversified portfolios, it is safe to conclude that the most relevant risk that must be considered for any widely traded individual security is its systematic risk. The unsystematic portion of total risk is relatively easy to diversify away.

Security Market Line (SML)

The return required of any risky asset is determined by the prevailing level of risk-free interest rates plus a risk premium. The greater the level of risk an investor perceives about a security's return, the greater the required risk premium will be. In other words, investors require returns that are

[7] W. H. Wagner and S. C. Lau. "The Effect of Diversification on Risk." *Financial Analysts Journal* (Nov.–Dec. 1971):48–53.

commensurate with the risk level they perceive. In algebraic terms, the required return, from any Security, j, k_j, is equal to the following:

$$k_j = r_f + \theta_j, \tag{5.8}$$

where r_f is the risk-free rate and θ_j is the risk premium required by investors.

The security market line (SML) indicates the "going" required rate of return in the market for a given amount of systematic risk, and it is illustrated in Figure 5-10. The SML intersects the vertical axis at the risk-free rate, r_f, indicating that any security with an expected risk premium equal to zero should be required to earn a return equal to the risk-free rate. As risk increases, so do the risk premium and the required rate of return. According to Figure 5-10, for example, a security having a risk level of a' should be required to earn a 10 percent rate of return.

Inflation and the Security Market Line

The risk-free rate of return, r_f, can be thought of as consisting of the following two components:

- A *real* rate of return that is free from the effects of any inflationary expectations.
- A *premium* that is equal to the effects of expected inflation.

Historically the real rate of return on risk-free securities, such as U.S. Government bonds, has averaged 2 to 5 percent per annum. The inflation premium is normally equal to investors' expectations about future purchasing power changes. If, for example, inflation is expected to average 2 percent over some future period, the risk-free rate of return on government securities (assuming a real rate of return of 3 percent) should be

Figure 5-10   **The Security Market Line (SML)**

Measure of Systematic Risk for Security j

approximately the following:

$$r_f = \text{Real return} + \text{Inflation premium}$$
$$= 3\% + 2\% \qquad (5.9)$$
$$= 5\%.$$

By extension, if inflation expectations suddenly increased from 2 to 4 percent, the risk-free rate should increase from 5 to 7 percent (3 percent real return plus 4 percent inflation premium).

Since the required return on any risky security, k_j, is equal to the risk-free rate plus the risk premium, an increase in inflationary expectations effectively increases the required return on all securities. This is shown in Figure 5-11. In the figure, SML_2 represents the returns required on all securities following a change in the expected future inflation rate. The required returns of all securities increase by 2 percent—the change in expected inflation. When investors increase their required returns, they become unwilling to purchase securities at existing prices, causing prices to decline. It should come as no surprise, then, that security analysts and investors take a dim view of increased inflation.

Beta: A Measure of Systematic Risk   Thus far we have not addressed the question of the appropriate risk measure to use when considering the risk-return tradeoffs illustrated by the SML. The previous discussion of risk in a portfolio context suggests that a measure of systematic risk is an appropriate starting point.

The systematic risk of a security is a function of the total risk of a security as measured by the standard deviation of the security's returns, the standard deviation of the returns from the market portfolio, and the correlation of the security's returns with those of all other securities in the

Figure 5-11   **Inflation and the Security Market Line**

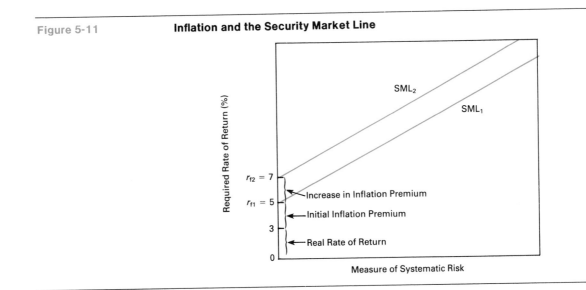

market. A broad-based security market index, such as the *Standard and Poor's 500 Market Index* or the *New York Stock Exchange Index,* is normally used as a measure of total market returns.

One useful measure of the systematic risk of a Security j is the value called *beta.* Beta is a measure of the volatility of a security's returns relative to the returns of a broad-based Market Portfolio m. It is defined as the ratio of the covariance (or comovement) of returns on Security j and Market Portfolio m to the variance of returns on the Market Portfolio:

$$\text{Beta}_j = \frac{\text{Covariance}_{j,m}}{\text{Variance}_m}.$$

$$\text{Beta}_j = \frac{\rho_{jm}\sigma_j\sigma_m}{\sigma_m^2}, \tag{5.10}$$

where beta_j is the measure of systematic risk for Security j, σ_j is the standard deviation of returns for Security j, σ_m is the standard deviation of returns for Market Portfolio m, σ_m^2 is the variance of returns for Market Portfolio m, and ρ_{jm} is the correlation coefficient between returns for Security j and Market Portfolio m.

In practice, beta may be computed as the slope of a regression line between the periodic (usually yearly, quarterly, or monthly) returns on the market portfolio (as measured by a market index, such as the *Standard and Poor's 500 Market Index*) and the periodic returns for Security j, as follows:

$$R_j = a_j + b_j R_m + e_j, \tag{5.11}$$

where R_j is the periodic return for Security j, a_j is a constant term determined by the regression, b_j is the computed historical beta for Security j, R_m is the periodic return for the market index, and e_j is a random error term.

This equation describes a line called Security j's *characteristic line.* Figure 5-12 shows the characteristic line for General Motors. The slope of this line is 0.97, indicating that the systematic returns from General Motors common stock are slightly less variable than the returns for the market as a whole. A beta of 1.0 for any security indicates that the security is of average systematic risk; that is, a security with a beta of 1.0 has the same risk characteristics as the market as a whole when only systematic risk is considered. When beta = 1.0, a 1 percent increase (decline) in market returns indicates that the *systematic* returns for the individual security should increase (decline) by 1 percent.[8] A beta of 1.5, for example, indicates that when market returns increase (decline) by 1 percent, the security's systematic returns can be expected to increase (decline) by 1.5 percent. A beta of less than 1—for example, 0.5—is indicative of a security of less than average systematic risk. In this case a 1 percent increase (decline) in market returns implies a 0.5 percent increase

---

[8] Of course, there will also be *unsystematic* components to a security's returns at any point in time. We assume these are diversified away in the portfolio.

Figure 5-12   **The Characteristic Line for General Motors**

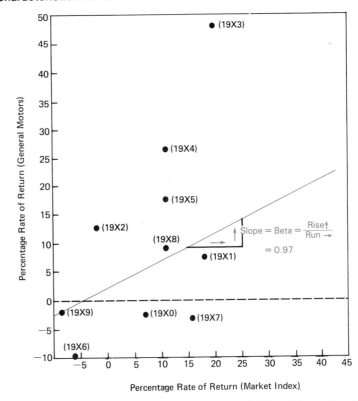

(decline) in the security's systematic returns. Table 5-5 summarizes the interpretation of betas.

The beta for the market portfolio as measured by a broad-based market index equals 1.0. This can be seen in Equation 5.10. Since the correlation of the market with itself is 1.0, the beta of the market portfolio must also be 1.0.

Table 5-5   **Interpretation of Beta Coefficients**

Beta Value	Direction of Movement in Returns	Interpretation
2.0	Same as market	Twice as risky (responsive) as market
1.0	Same as market	Risk equal to that of market
0.5	Same as market	Half as risky as market
0	Uncorrelated with market movements	No market-related risk
−0.5	Opposite of market	Half as responsive as market, but in the opposite direction

Finally, the beta of any portfolio of n securities or assets is simply the weighted average of the individual security betas:

$$\text{Beta}_p = \sum_{j=1}^{n} W_j \text{beta}_j. \tag{5.12}$$

This concept is particularly useful when evaluating the effects of capital investment projects or mergers on a firm's systematic risk.

Fortunately for financial managers, it is not necessary to compute the beta for each security every time a security's systematic risk measure is needed. Several investment advisory services, including the *Value Line Investment Survey* and Merrill Lynch, regularly compute and publish individual security beta estimates, and these are readily available. Table 5-6 lists the Value Line computed betas for selected stocks.

Security Market Line and Beta

Given the information presented thus far, it is possible to compute risk premiums, θ, that are applicable to individual securities. The SML also may be defined in terms of beta. The risk premium for any Security j is equal to the difference between the required returns of investors, k_j, and the risk-free rate, r_f:

$$\theta_j = k_j - r_f. \tag{5.13}$$

Table 5-6　　　　**Betas for Selected Stocks**

Company Name	Value Line Beta
Allied Bancshares	0.80
American Electric Power	0.75
AT&T	0.80
Apple Computer	1.70
BankAmerica	1.05
Boeing Company	1.20
Caterpillar Tractor	1.00
CBS, Inc.	1.05
Coca-Cola	0.85
Digital Equipment	1.25
Eastman Kodak	0.80
Federal Express	1.35
K Mart Corporation	1.20
Mesa Petroleum	1.15
Playboy	1.00
RCA Corporation	1.05
Supermarkets General	1.00
Texas Instruments	0.95
Weis Markets	0.65
Wisconsin Electric Power	0.75
Yellow Freight	1.15
Zenith Electric	1.35

Source: *Value Screen Plus* (New York: Arnold Bernhard and Co., Inc.) January, 1986

For example, if the expected return on the overall market portfolio, $\hat{k}_m$, is 15 percent, and the expected risk-free rate, $\hat{r}_f$, is 7 percent, the market risk premium is equal to the following:

$$\hat{\theta}_m = \hat{k}_m - \hat{r}_f$$
$$= 15\% - 7\%$$
$$= 8\%.$$

For a security with average risk (beta$_j$ = 1.0), the risk premium should be equal to the market risk premium. A security whose beta is 2.0, however, is twice as risky as the average security, so its risk premium should be twice the market risk premium:

$$\theta_j = b_j(\hat{k}_m - \hat{r}_f)$$
$$= 2.0(15\% - 7\%)$$
$$= 16\%.$$

The required return for any security may be defined in terms of its systematic risk (beta), the expected market return, $\hat{k}_m$, and the expected risk-free rate, as follows:

$$k_j = \hat{r}_f + \hat{\theta}_j,$$

or

$$k_j = \hat{r}_f + b_j(\hat{k}_m - \hat{r}_f). \qquad \textbf{(5.14)}$$

For example, if the risk-free rate is 7 percent and $\hat{k}_m$ is 12 percent, the required return for a security having a beta of 1.3 is computed as follows:

$$k_j = 7\% + 1.3\,(12\% - 7\%)$$
$$= 7\% + 6.5\%$$
$$= 13.5\%.$$

Equation 5.14 provides an explicit definition of the SML in terms of the systematic risk of individual securities. Figure 5-13 illustrates the SML from Equation 5.14. Assuming a risk-free rate of 7 percent and a market return of 12 percent, the return required on a low risk stock (for example, beta = 0.5) is 9.5 percent. The return required on a high risk stock (for example, beta = 2.0) is 17 percent, and the return required on a stock of average risk (for example, beta = 1.0) is 12 percent, the same as the market required return.

The slope of the SML is shown as being constant throughout. When measured between beta = 0 and beta = 1.0, it is equal to $(k_m - r_f)/(1 - 0)$, or simply $k_m - r_f$. This slope represents the risk premium on an average risk security.

Also, from Figure 5-13 we can determine what securities (assets) are attractive investments by comparing the *expected* return from a security

Figure 5-13   **The Security Market Line in Terms of Beta**

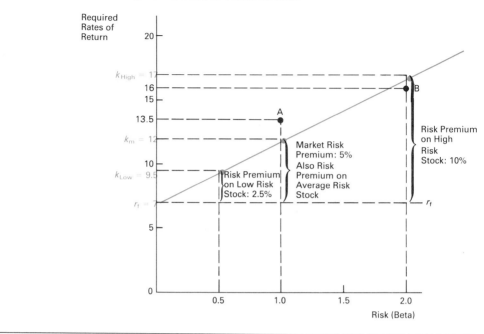

with the return *required* for that security, given its beta. For example, security A with a beta of 1.0 and an expected return of 13.5 percent would be an attractive investment since the expected return *exceeds* the 12 percent required return. In contrast, security B with a beta of 2.0 is not an acceptable investment since its expected return (16%) *is less than* its required return (17%).

If the average risk premium (measured by the slope of the SML) increases because of an increase in uncertainty regarding the future economic outlook, or because investors as a group have tended to become more averse to risk and thus require a higher rate of return for any level of risk, the slope of the SML will increase. This, in turn, will increase the risk premium on stocks with greater than average risk (beta > 1.0) more than on stocks with less than average risk (beta < 1.0). For example, if the market risk premium increases from 5 to 6 percent, the required risk premium on a security with a beta of 0.5 increases by only 0.5 percent, or $0.5 \times (6.0\% - 5.0\%)$. In contrast, the risk premium on a security with a beta of 2.0 experiences a rise in its required risk premium of 2 percent $(2.0 \times 1.0\%)$.

Uses of the CAPM and Portfolio Risk Concepts

The notion of portfolio risk and the Capital Asset Pricing Model (CAPM) which relates required returns to systematic risk (beta) are powerful pedagogical tools to explain the nature of risk and its relationship to required returns on securities and physical assets. In Chapter 12 the CAPM is discussed as one technique that can be used to estimate the cost of equity capital. That chapter considers where the necessary data may be obtained to apply the model. Also, Chapter 11 considers the use of CAPM-determined required rates of return as a technique to adjust for risk in the capital budgeting process.

Assumptions and Limitations of the CAPM

The theoretical CAPM and its applications are based upon a number of crucial assumptions about the securities markets and investors' attitudes, including the following:

- Investors hold well-diversified portfolios of securities. Hence their return requirements are primarily influenced by the systematic (rather than total) risk of each security.
- Securities are actively traded in a competitive market, where information about a given firm and its future prospects is freely available.
- Investors can borrow and lend at the risk-free rate, which remains constant over time.
- There are no brokerage charges for buying and selling securities.
- There are no taxes.
- All investors prefer the security that provides the highest return for a given level of risk, or the lowest amount of risk for a given level of return.
- All investors have common (homogeneous) expectations regarding the expected returns, variances, and correlations of returns among all securities.

Whereas these assumptions may seem fairly limiting at first glance, extensions of the basic theory presented in this chapter, which relax the assumptions, generally have yielded results consistent with the fundamental theory. In addition, statistical tests of observed behavior in securities markets tend to support the results implied by the model presented here. In spite of these restrictive assumptions, this basic model has been extensively used, both practically and conceptually, to consider the risk-return tradeoff required by investors in the securities market. For example, the CAPM (or a modification thereof) has been used in regulated public utility rate case testimony aimed at determining a reasonable allowed rate of return for the utility's investors.

However, users of this approach also should be aware of some of the major problems encountered in practical applications. These include the following:

- Estimating expected future market returns.
- Determining the most appropriate estimate of the risk-free rate.
- Determining the best estimate of an asset's *future* beta.
- Reconciling the fact that some empirical tests have shown that investors do not totally ignore unsystematic risk, as the theory suggests.
- Measures of beta have been shown to be quite unstable over time, making it difficult to confidently measure the beta *expected* by investors.

- There is an increasing body of evidence to suggest that required returns on most securities are determined by factors in addition to the risk-free rate of interest and the systematic risk of the security.

Other Dimensions of Risk

This chapter has focused on various measures of variability in returns—either total variability, measured by the *standard deviation* and the *coefficient of variation,* or systematic variability, measured by *beta.* Although variability of returns is very important, it does not adequately consider another important risk dimension—that is, the risk of failure. In the case of an individual investment project, failure is a situation in which a project generates a *negative* rate of return. In the case of a total firm, failure is the situation in which a firm loses money and is ultimately forced into bankruptcy.

For risk-averse investors, the risk of failure may play a large role in determining the types of investments undertaken. For example, the management of a firm is not likely to be eager to invest in a project that has a high risk of failure and that ultimately may cause the firm to fail if it proves to be unsuccessful. After all, the continued survival of the firm is closely tied to the economic well-being of management.

From a shareholder wealth maximization perspective, failure is a particularly undesirable occurrence. The direct and indirect costs of bankruptcy can be very high. Consequently, this failure risk is often an important determinant of investment risk. The risk and cost of failure can explain, in large part, the desire of many firms to diversify. In addition to reducing the overall risk of a firm, diversification can result in a lower probability of bankruptcy and thus lower *expected* costs incurred during bankruptcy. These costs include the following:

- The loss of funds that occurs when assets are sold at distressed prices during liquidation.
- The legal fees and selling costs incurred when a firm enters bankruptcy proceedings.
- The opportunity costs of the funds that are unavailable to investors during the bankruptcy proceedings (for example, it took over eight years to settle the Penn-Central bankruptcy).

If, through diversification, a firm can decrease the probability of bankruptcy, it can reduce its *expected* bankruptcy costs. Lower expected bankruptcy costs should increase shareholder wealth, all other things being equal.

Diversification also may reduce a firm's cost of capital. By reducing the overall risk of the firm, diversification will lower the default risk of the firm's debt securities, and the firm's bonds will receive higher ratings and require lower interest payments. In addition, the firm may be able to increase the proportion of low cost debt relative to equity in its optimal capital structure, further reducing the cost of capital and increasing shareholder wealth.[9]

[9] The concept of optimal capital structure is discussed in Chapter 13.

Although we will focus primarily on return variability as our measure of risk in this book, the risk and cost of failure also should be kept in mind.

Summary

- The *risk* of a security or an investment project is generally defined in terms of the potential *variability* of its returns. When only one return is possible—for example, as with U.S. Government securities held to maturity—there is no risk. When more than one return is possible for a particular project, it is risky.
- The *standard deviation, σ,* of the returns from an investment is an *absolute* measure of risk. It is computed as the square root of the weighted average squared deviations of individual observations from the expected value.
- When projects of unequal size (or investments with unequal expected returns) are being compared, the *coefficient of variation, v,* is a more appropriate measure of risk. The coefficient of variation is the ratio of the standard deviation to the expected value.
- Because cash flow projections and expected returns can be estimated with less certainty farther into the future, risk is generally thought to *increase over time.*
- Risk is also influenced by the possibility of investment *diversification.* For example, if a proposed project's returns are not *perfectly correlated* with the returns from the firm's other investments, the total risk of the firm may be reduced by accepting the proposed project. This is known as the *portfolio effect.*
- The *expected return from a portfolio* of two or more securities is equal to the weighted average of the expected returns from the individual securities.
- The *risk of a portfolio* is a function of both the risk of the individual securities in the portfolio and the correlation among the individual securities' returns.
- The *unsystematic* portion of the total risk in a security's return is that portion of return variability unique to the firm. Efficient diversification of a portfolio of securities can eliminate most unsystematic risk.
- *Systematic risk* refers to the portion of total risk in a security's return caused by overall market forces. This risk cannot be diversified away in a portfolio. Systematic risk forms the basis for the risk premium required by investors in any risky security.
- The *security market line* (SML) provides an algebraic or graphic representation of the risk-return tradeoff required in the marketplace for risky securities. It measures risk in terms of systematic risk.
- An index of systematic risk for a security is the security's *beta.* Beta is determined from the slope of a regression line, the *characteristic line,* between the market return and the individual security's return. It is a measure of the volatility of a security's returns relative to the returns of the market as a whole.
- The required return on common stock consists of the risk-free rate plus a risk premium. This risk premium is equal to a security's beta times the

market risk premium, and the market risk premium is equal to the difference between the expected market return and the risk-free rate.

Questions and Topics for Discussion

1. Define the following terms:
   a. Risk
   b. Probability distribution
   c. Standard deviation
   d. Required rate of return
   e. Coefficient of variation
   f. Beta coefficient
   g. CAPM
   h. Correlation coefficient
   i. Portfolio
   j. Characteristic line
   k. Security market line
   l. Covariance
   m. Systematic risk
   n. Unsystematic risk

2. If the returns from a security were known with certainty, what shape would the probability distribution of returns graph have?

3. What is the nature of the risk associated with "risk-free" U.S. Government bonds?

4. If inflation expectations increase, what would you expect to happen to the returns required by investors in bonds? What would happen to bond prices?

5. Under what circumstances will the coefficient of variation of a security's returns and the standard deviation of that security's returns give the same relative measure of risk when compared with the risk of another security?

6. Explain how diversification can reduce the risk of a portfolio of assets to below the weighted average of the risk of the individual assets.

7. What are the primary variables that influence the risk of a portfolio of assets?

8. Distinguish between unsystematic and systematic risk. Under what circumstances are investors likely to ignore the unsystematic risk characteristics of a security?

9. What effect do increasing inflation expectations have on the required returns of investors in common stock?

10. The stock of Amrep Corporation has a *beta* value estimated to be 1.4. How would you interpret this beta value? How would you evaluate the firm's systematic risk?

11. How is a security's beta value computed?

12. Under what circumstances can the beta concept be used to estimate the rate of return required by investors in a stock? What problems are encountered when using the CAPM?

13. The risk of a portfolio of two securities with a correlation of returns of -1.0 will always equal zero when the portfolio contains equal proportions of the two securities. Do you agree? Prove your answer with an example.

Problems*

1. You have estimated the following probability distributions of expected future returns for Stocks X and Y:

* Color numbers denote problems which have check answers provided at the end of the book.

Stock X		Stock Y	
Probability	Return	Probability	Return
0.1	− 10%	0.2	2%
0.2	10	0.2	7
0.4	15	0.3	12
0.2	20	0.2	15
0.1	40	0.1	16

a. What is the expected rate of return for Stock X? Stock Y?

b. What is the standard deviation of expected returns for Stock X? For Stock Y?

c. Which stock would you consider to be riskier? Why?

2. The return expected from Project number 542 is 22 percent. The standard deviation of these returns is 11 percent. If returns from the project are normally distributed, what is the chance that the project will result in a rate of return above 33 percent? What is the probability that the project will result in losses (negative rates of return)?

3. The expected rate of return for the stock of Cornhusker Enterprises is 20 percent, with a standard deviation of 15 percent. The expected rate of return for the stock of Mustang Associates is 10 percent, with a standard deviation of 9 percent.

a. Which stock would you consider to be riskier? Why?

b. If you knew that the beta coefficient of Cornhusker stock is 1.5 and the beta of Mustang is 0.9, how would your answer to Part a change?

4. The current dividend, D_0, of the stock of Sun Devil Corporation is $3 per share. Under present conditions this dividend is expected to grow at a rate of 6 percent annually for the foreseeable future. The beta of Sun Devil's stock is 1.5. The risk-free rate of return is 7 percent, and the expected market rate of return is 14 percent.

a. At what price would you expect Sun Devil's common stock to sell?

b. If the risk-free rate of return declines to 6 percent, what will happen to Sun Devil's stock price? (Assume the expected market rate of return remains at 14 percent.)

c. Sun Devil's management is considering acquisitions in the machine tool industry. They expect the firm's beta to increase to 1.6 as a result of these acquisitions. The dividend growth rate is expected to increase to 7 percent annually. Would you recommend this acquisition program to management? (Assume the same initial conditions that existed in Part a.)

5. You are considering purchasing a portfolio of securities. The securities available to you have the following expected returns:

Security	Expected Return (%)
A	14
B	9
C	15
D	11

a. If you invest 20 percent of your funds in Security A, 40 percent in B, 20 percent in C, and 20 percent in D, what is the expected return of the portfolio?

b. How does the expected return of the portfolio change if you invest 40 percent in A, 10 percent in B, 40 percent in C, and 10 percent in D?

c. In addition to the portfolio in Part b having a different expected return than the portfolio in Part a, how would you expect the two portfolios to differ with respect to risk?

6. You are considering investing in two securities, X and Y. The following data are available for the two securities:

	Security X	Security Y
Expected return	0.10	0.07
Standard deviation of returns	0.08	0.04

a. If you invest 40 percent of your funds in Security X and 60 percent in Security Y, and if the correlation of returns between X and Y is +0.5, compute the following:
   i. The expected return from the portfolio.
   ii. The standard deviation of returns from the portfolio.
b. What happens to the expected return and standard deviation of returns of the portfolio in Part a if 70 percent of your funds are invested in Security X and 30 percent of your funds are invested in Security Y?
c. What happens to the expected return and standard deviation of returns of the portfolio in Part a if the following conditions exist?
   i. The correlation of returns between Securities X and Y is +1.0.
   ii. The correlation of returns between Securities X and Y is 0.
   iii. The correlation of returns between Securities X and Y is −0.7.

7. You have the following information on two securities you have invested in:

Security	Expected Return	Standard Deviation	Beta	% Invested (w)
XEROX	15%	4.5%	1.2	35%
KODAK	12%	3.8%	0.98	65%

a. Which stock is riskier in a portfolio context? Which stock is riskier if you are considering them as individual assets (not part of a portfolio)?
b. Compute the expected return on the portfolio.
c. If the securities have a correlation of 0.60, compute the standard deviation of the portfolio.
d. Compute the beta of the portfolio.

8. Realizing the benefits of diversification you have invested in the following securities:

	United	Chubb	Chase
Expected Return	12%	14%	9%
Standard Deviation of Return	3%	5%	3%
Beta	1.65	1.2	0.89
Amount Invested in Each Security	$50,000	$125,000	$75,000

a. Compute the expected rate of return on the portfolio.
b. Compute the beta of the portfolio.

9. The SML has been estimated as follows:

$$k_j = 0.06 + 0.07 \text{ beta.}$$

This estimate assumes an expected rate of inflation of 4 percent. If inflation expectations increase from 4 to 6 percent, what will be the equation of the new SML?

10. The stock of Pizza Hot, Inc., a Mexican pizza chain, has an estimated beta of 1.5. Calculate the required rate of return on Pizza Hot's stock if the SML

in Problem 9 is appropriate, assuming the following:
a. The original inflation expectation of 4 percent.
b. The new inflation expectation of 6 percent.

11. Caledonia Minerals has an estimated beta of 1.6. The company is considering the acquisition of another firm that has a beta of 1.2. Both companies are
exactly the same size.
a. What is the expected new beta value for the combined firm?
b. The risk-free rate of return is estimated at 7 percent, and the market return is estimated as 12 percent. What is your estimate of the required return of investors in Caledonia before and after the merger?

12. Caledonia Minerals (see Problem 11) is expected to pay a $1 dividend next
year ($D_1 = \$1$). This dividend is expected to grow at a rate of 6 percent per
year for the foreseeable future if the merger is not completed. The merger is
not expected to change the current dividend rate, but future dividends are expected to grow at a 7 percent rate as a result of the merger.
a. What is the value of a share of stock in Caledonia Minerals prior to the
merger?
HINT: Use the required equity return computed in Problem 11.
b. What is the new value of a share of stock, assuming that the merger is
completed.?
c. Would you recommend that Caledonia go ahead with the merger?

13. Globe Steel has decided to diversify into the home improvement field. As a
result of this expansion, Globe's beta value drops from 1.3 to 0.9, and the expected future, long-term growth rate in the firm's dividends drops from 8 to 7
percent. The expected market return, k_m, is 14 percent; the risk-free rate, r_f,
is 7 percent; and the current dividends per share, D_0, are $3. Should Globe
undertake the planned diversification?

14. Tucker Manufacturing Company has a beta estimated at 1.0. The risk-free
rate is 6 percent, and the expected market return is 12 percent. Tucker expects to pay a $4 dividend next year ($D_1 = \$4$). This dividend is expected to
grow at 3 percent per year for the foreseeable future. The current market
price for Tucker is $40.
a. Is the current stock price an equilibrium price, based upon the SML calculation of k_e for Tucker?
b. What do you think the appropriate equilibrium price is? How will that
price be achieved?

15. Using Equation 5.14, suppose you have computed the *required* rate of return
for the stock of Bulldog Trucking to be 16.6 percent. Given the current stock
price, the current dividend rate, and analysts' projections for future dividend
growth, you *expect* to earn a rate of return of 18 percent.
a. Would you recommend buying or selling this stock? Why?
b. If your *expected* rate of return from the stock of Bulldog is 15 percent,
what would you expect to happen to Bulldog's stock price?

16. You want to construct a portfolio with a 20 percent expected return. The
portfolio is to consist of some combination of Security A and Security B:

Security	Expected Return	Beta
A	15%	0.82
B	28	1.75

a. What percentage of your portfolio should consist of Security A? Of Security B?
b. What is the beta of the portfolio?

17. Equation 5.7 can be modified to compute the risk of a three-security portfolio as follows:

$$\sigma_p = \sqrt{\begin{array}{c} W_A^2\sigma_A^2 + W_B^2\sigma_B^2 + W_C^2\sigma_C^2 + 2W_A W_B\rho_{AB}\sigma_A\sigma_B + 2W_A W_C\rho_{AC}\sigma_A\sigma_C \\ + 2W_B W_C\rho_{BC}\sigma_B\sigma_C. \end{array}}$$

You have decided to invest 40 percent of your wealth in Security A, 30 percent in Security B, and 30 percent in Security C. The following information is available about the possible returns from the three securities:

Security A		Security B		Security C	
Return (%)	Probability	Return (%)	Probability	Return (%)	Probability
10	0.25	13	0.30	14	0.40
12	0.50	16	0.35	18	0.30
14	0.25	19	0.35	22	0.30

Compute the expected return of the portfolio and the risk of the portfolio if the correlations between returns from the three securities are $\rho_{AB} = 0.70$; $\rho_{AC} = 0.60$; and $\rho_{BC} = 0.85$.

18. **a.** Koch Brickyard, Inc.'s stock is expected to return 14 percent with a standard deviation of 5 percent. Uptown Potbelly Stove Works' stock is expected to return 16 percent with a standard deviation of 9 percent. If you invest 30 percent of your funds in Koch stock and 70 percent in Uptown stock, what is the expected return on your portfolio?

   b. What is the expected risk of this portfolio if the returns for the two stocks have:

   i. A perfect positive correlation ($+1.0$).

   ii. A slightly negative correlation (-0.2).

19. Security A offers an expected return of 15 percent with a standard deviation of 7 percent. Security B offers an expected return of 9 percent with a standard deviation of 4 percent. The correlation between the returns of A and B is $+0.6$. If an investor puts one-fourth of his wealth in A and three-fourths in B, what is the expected return and risk (standard deviation) of this portfolio?

20. The beta of MacDrive is estimated to be 1.3. The beta of MacWalk is estimated to be 1.1. If these two firms merge, to form MacRun, what will be the beta of the new firm, assuming that MacWalk was two times as large as MacDrive?

Selected References

Bowman, R. G. "The Theoretical Relationship between Systematic Risk and Financial (Accounting) Variables." *Journal of Finance* (June 1979): 617–630.

Ibbotson, Roger G., and Rex A. Singuefield. *Stocks, Bonds, Bills, and Inflation: The Past and the Future.* Charlottesville, Va.: Financial Analysts Research Foundation, 1982.

Pettit, R. Richardson, and Randolph Westerfield. "Using the Capital Asset Pricing Model and the Market Model to Predict Security Returns." *Journal of Financial and Quantitative Analysis* 9 (Sept. 1974): 579–605.

Reilly, Frank K. *Investment Analysis and Portfolio Managment,* 2nd ed. Hinsdale, Ill.: Dryden, 1985.

Roll, Richard. "A Critique of the Asset Pricing Theory's Tests." *Journal of Financial Economics* (March 1977): 129–176.

Rubinstein, M. E. "A Mean-Variance Synthesis of Corporate Financial Theory." *Journal of Finance* 28 (March 1973): 167–181.

Sharpe, William F. *Portfolio Analysis and Capital Markets.* New York: McGraw-Hill, 1970.

PART THREE

FINANCIAL ANALYSIS

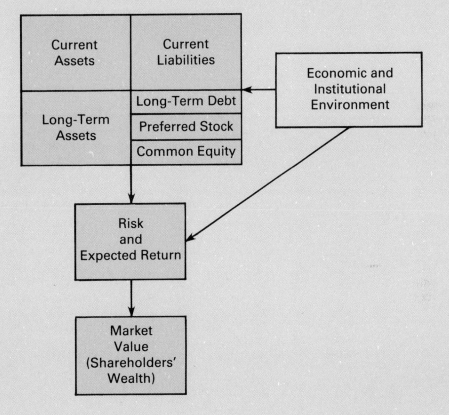

In assessing the financial condition and the risk of a firm, the tools of financial statement analysis can be very helpful. These are discussed in Chapter 6. Chapter 7 develops the concepts of operating and financial leverage and analyzes their effects on a firm's risk. Finally, Chapter 8 looks at the financial planning process for a firm. If the objective of shareholder wealth maximization is to be achieved, the firm must make long-term financial plans. Effective financial planning also can alert management to potential problem areas well in advance. By carefully evaluating current financial strengths and weaknesses and by planning for the future, risk and return can be effectively controlled to maximize the value of the firm.

6

THE ANALYSIS OF FINANCIAL STATEMENTS

A Financial Dilemma

Banking on Accounting Gimmickry*

During 1981–1982 heavy losses forced many of the nation's 3,000 savings and loan institutions (S&Ls) out of business. Many of these institutions found themselves locked in with a portfolio of relatively low yielding mortgages at a time when interest rates reached record highs. This caused the S&Ls to pay more interest on the funds they were acquiring from depositors than they were receiving in interest on the mortgages outstanding—resulting in operating losses.

Traditionally, S&L institutions have been poorly capitalized. For example, in 1984 the median ratio of equity capital to total assets for S&Ls was 3.9 percent, compared to an 8.1 percent ratio for commercial banks. This low capital ratio did not leave S&Ls with much room to absorb operating losses or unexpected losses resulting from the writeoff of bad loans.

Faced with mounting operating losses in 1981 and 1982 and increasingly large loan chargeoffs, many of these thrift institutions looked to "creative accounting" techniques to prevent them from failing. These techniques included the following:

1. In 1984 S&Ls treated as earnings a stock dividend paid to them by the Federal Home Loan Mortgage Corporation (Freddie Mac), a quasi-governmental agency which is owned by S&Ls and is involved in the secondary mortgage market. The Financial Accounting Standards Board (FASB), which establishes what are considered to be generally accepted accounting standards, initially objected to counting this stock dividend as earnings for the thrifts, since it amounted to a payment to themselves. Faced with a

heavy lobbying effort from the industry, FASB relented and the stock dividend was permitted to be counted as earnings. During 1984, this stock dividend (merely a distribution of pieces of paper) accounted for $600 million of the industry's total profits of $2.1 billion. Securities analysts claim that half of the remaining $1.5 billion was also generated by questionable accounting.

2. During 1981, many S&Ls found that by using the purchase method of accounting for mergers with other, often failing, S&Ls, they could create an intangible asset on their balance sheets called "goodwill." For some institutions, this intangible asset represents more than their total equity capital.

3. Other institutions created phantom profits by selling loans acquired in mergers. These loans, often acquired at a deep discount, were sold for more than their original cost but less than face value. Accounting principles permit the recording of a profit from this transaction even though the IRS would treat it as a loss for tax purposes.

4. Many S&Ls sell a mortgage which they originated to another institution. Commonly, the originating S&L will continue to service the mortgage and be paid a fee for providing these services. Some S&Ls have immediately recorded all of their expected fee income as a profit even though it will actually be received over a long period of time in the future.

This list of accounting abuses in the S&L industry is not exhaustive, but it does serve to highlight the extent of the problem.

Although careful financial analysis can provide excellent insights into the direction and relative strength of the firm, the financial analyst must keep in mind that generally accepted accounting principles give firms considerable latitude in reporting their financial positions. Thus the analyst must be aware of the specific accounting conventions which gave rise to the fi-

* This example is based in part, on Lee Barton, "Accounting at Thrifts Provokes Controversy as Gimmickry Mounts," *The Wall Street Journal* (March 21, 1985).

nancial statements being analyzed. As one analyst has said, *"Remember: There are only two items in a balance sheet that are for real—cash, which can be counted, and all liabilities."*[1]

Key Chapter Concepts

1. Financial analysis is a series of techniques which can be used to help identify the strengths and weaknesses of a firm.
2. Financial ratios, which use data from a firm's balance sheet, income statement, and certain market data, are often used when performing a financial analysis of a firm.
   a. *Liquidity ratios* indicate a firm's ability to meet its short-term financial obligations.
   b. *Activity ratios* indicate how efficiently a firm is using its assets to generate sales.
   c. *Financial leverage ratios* indicate a firm's capacity to meet short- and long-term debt obligations.
   d. *Profitability ratios* measure how effectively a firm's management generates profits.
   e. *Market-based ratios* reflect the financial market's assessment of a company's performance.
3. *Trend analysis* evaluates a firm's performance over time, whereas *comparative analysis* evaluates a firm's performance relative to other firms.
4. When evaluating a firm's performance based on its balance sheet, income statement, and a series of financial ratios, a good financial analyst must be aware of the accounting techniques used by the firm and must be mindful of the quality of the firm's earnings and its balance sheet.
5. Financial ratios can be very useful for forecasting events such as impending bankruptcy and the bond ratings of a firm.

[1] Heinz H. Biel, "Beware of Shibboleths." *Forbes* (May 10, 1982): 318.

Glossary of New Terms

Activity ratios Financial ratios that indicate how efficiently a firm is utilizing its assets to generate sales.

Balance sheet A financial statement that lists a firm's assets, liabilities, and owners' equity at a point in time.

Comparative analysis An examination of a firm's performance based on one or more financial ratios, which are compared with the financial ratios of competitive firms or with an industry standard.

Discriminant analysis A statistical technique designed to classify observations (firms) into two or more predetermined groups based on certain characteristics (such as financial ratios) of the observations.

EAT The abbreviation for *earnings after taxes.*

EBIT The abbreviation for *earnings before interest and taxes* (also called *operating earnings*).

EPS The abbreviation for *earnings per share.*

FIFO The abbreviation for the *first-in, first-out* inventory valuation method. The method assumes that a firm uses the oldest items in the inventory first. Thus, they are *priced out* of the inventory based on the oldest inventory acquisition costs rather than the most recent.

Financial analysis The utilization of a group of analytical techniques, including financial ratio analysis, to determine the strengths, weaknesses, and direction of a company's performance.

Financial leverage ratios Financial ratios that measure the degree to which a firm is financing its assets with fixed charge sources of funds such as debt, preferred stock, or leases.

Financial ratio A statistical yardstick that relates two numbers generally taken from a firm's income statement, balance sheet, or both at a specific point in time.

Income statement A financial statement that indicates how a firm performed during a period of time.

LIFO The abbreviation for the *last-in, first-out* inventory valuation method. The method assumes that a firm uses the most recently acquired items in the inventory first. Thus they are *priced out* of the inventory based on the most recent inventory acquisition costs rather than the oldest.

Liquidity ratios Financial ratios that indicate a firm's ability to meet short-term financial obligations.

Market-based ratios Financial ratios that measure the market's (investors') assessment of the risk and performance of a firm.

Profitability ratios Financial ratios that measure the total effectiveness of a company's management in generating profits.

Stockholders' equity The total of a firm's common stock at par, contributed capital in excess of par, and retained earnings accounts from the balance sheet. It is sometimes called the *book value* of the firm, *owners' equity,* or *net worth*.

Trend analysis An examination of a firm's performance over time. It is frequently based on one or more financial ratios.

Introduction

Chapters 6 through 8 develop the tools of financial analysis and financial forecasting. This chapter deals with the analysis of financial statements. A carefully executed financial statement analysis can assist the financial manager in assessing the current financial condition of the firm. Chapter 7 looks at the risk dimension of a firm's current financial position. The concepts of operating and financial leverage are developed as measures of a firm's risk.

Once the current financial condition of the firm and the firm's risk profile have been assessed, the financial manager is in a position to plan for the future direction of the firm, given the constraints imposed by, and the strengths of, the current financial condition. Financial managers plan for the acquisition and management of both long- and short-term assets (the capital budgeting decision and the working capital management decision). In addition, the financial manager must plan how the assets of the firm are to be funded (the capital structure decision). The impact of these plans on the future financial condition of the firm is projected by the use of pro forma financial statements and budgets. These tools are developed in Chapter 8.

Uses of Financial Analysis

A *financial analysis* assists in identifying the major strengths and weaknesses of a business enterprise. It indicates whether a firm has enough cash to meet obligations; a reasonable accounts receivable collection period; an efficient inventory management policy; sufficient plant, property, and equipment; and an adequate capital structure—all of which are necessary if the firm is to achieve the goal of maximizing shareholder wealth. Financial analysis also can be used to assess a firm's viability as an ongoing enterprise and to determine whether a satisfactory return is being earned for the risks taken.

When performing a financial analysis, the analyst may discover specific problem areas in time for remedial action. Or, the analyst may find that the firm has unused borrowing power that could finance additional income-producing assets. The results of a financial analysis can indicate certain facts and trends that can aid the financial manager in planning and implementing a course of action consistent with the goal of maximizing shareholder wealth.

Financial analyses also are used by persons other than financial managers. For example, credit managers may examine some basic financial ratios concerning a prospective customer when deciding whether or not to extend credit. Security analysts use financial analysis to assess the investment worth of different securities. Bankers use the tools of financial analysis when deciding whether to grant loans. Financial ratios have been used successfully to forecast such financial events as impending bankruptcy. Unions refer to them when evaluating the bargaining positions of certain employers. Finally, students and other job hunters may perform financial analyses of potential employers to determine career opportunities.

Interpreting Financial Ratios

A *financial ratio* is a relationship that indicates something about a firm's activities, such as the ratio between the firm's assets and liabilities, or between its accounts receivable and its annual sales. Financial ratios enable an analyst to make a comparison of a firm's financial condition over time or in relation to that of other firms. Ratios essentially standardize various elements of financial data for differences in the size of a series of financial data when making comparisons over time or between firms. For example, the total profits of IBM are many times those of Apple Computer, because IBM is a much larger firm than Apple. By computing a ratio such as net profits divided by total assets, the relative performance of the two firms can be more accurately assessed.

Successful financial ratio analysis requires that the analyst keep in mind the following key points:

- Any discussion of financial ratios is likely to include only a representative sample of possible ratios. Many other ratios can be developed to provide additional insights. In some industries, such as banking, the analyst will use special ratios unique to the activities of the firms in those industries.

- Financial ratios are only "flags" indicating potential areas of strength or weakness. A thorough analysis requires the examination of other data as well.

- Frequently a financial ratio must be dissected to discover its true meaning. For example, a low ratio may be caused by either a low numerator or a high denominator. A good financial analyst will examine both the numerator and the denominator before drawing any conclusions.

- A financial ratio is meaningful only when it is compared with some standard, such as an industry ratio trend, a ratio trend for the specific firm being analyzed, or a stated management objective.

- When financial ratios are used to compare one firm with another, it is important to remember that differences in accounting techniques may result in substantial differences in financial ratios. Failure to keep this in mind can lead to incorrect conclusions.

Basic Classifications of Financial Ratios

Because different groups in- and outside the firm have varying objectives and expectations, they approach financial analysis from different perspectives. For example, suppliers and short-term creditors are likely to be most concerned with a firm's current liquidity and near-term cash-generating capacity. Bondholders and holders of preferred stock, who have long-term claims on a firm's earnings and assets, focus on the firm's cash-generating ability over the long run and on the claims other investors have on the firm's cash flows. Common stockholders and potential investors are especially interested in measures of profitability and risk, since common stock prices are dependent on the amount and stability of a firm's future earnings and dividends. Management is concerned with all aspects of financial analysis on both a short- and a long-term basis, since it is responsible for conducting the firm's day-to-day operations and earning a competitive rate of return for risks taken.

No single financial ratio could begin to answer all these analytical needs. Thus, four different groups of ratios have been developed:

- *Liquidity ratios* indicate a firm's ability to meet short-term financial obligations.
- *Activity ratios* indicate how efficiently a firm is using its assets to generate sales.
- *Financial leverage ratios* indicate a firm's capacity to meet short- and long-term debt obligations.
- *Profitability ratios* measure how effectively a firm's management generates profits on sales, assets, and owners' investments.

In addition to these four major groups of financial ratios, there are certain "market-based" ratios which reflect the financial market's assessment of a company's stock.

Each type is discussed in detail in this chapter.[2] The financial statements of the Sandia Manufacturing Company, a medium-sized firm that produces various replacement components for the lawn equipment industry, will be examined to illustrate how ratios are used in financial analysis. Data will be used from Sandia's *balance sheet* for the years ending December 31, 19X6 and 19X5 and from its *income statement* for the year 19X6.

The balance sheet shown in Table 6-1 contains information on Sandia's *assets, liabilities,* and *owners' equity.* The figures provide a "snapshot" view of the firm's financial health on December 31, 19X6, and December 31, 19X5. Sandia's assets are recorded on the balance sheet at the price the company paid for them (that is, at historical cost). The liabilities are amounts the firm owes its creditors, and the owners' equity (also termed *net worth* or *stockholders' equity*) is the difference between total assets and total liabilities. The owners' equity accounts in Table 6-1 are (1) common stock ($10 par); (2) contributed capital in excess of par; and (3) retained earnings.

The income statement in Table 6-2 indicates Sandia's performance during the year ending December 31, 19X6. The *cost of goods sold, other operating expenses, interest expenses,* and *taxes* are deducted from the revenues generated, or *net sales,* to arrive at the firm's *net income,* or *earnings after taxes (EAT).* The statement in Table 6-2 also shows how the firm's earnings are distributed between dividend payments (payments to stockholders) and earnings retained (reinvested in the firm).

The *sources and uses of funds statement* is also useful in financial analysis. (This statement is also called the *statement of changes in financial position* or the *funds flow statement.*) It indicates how a firm obtained and invested funds during a specific time period. The sources and uses of funds statement is discussed in Chapter 8.

Liquidity Ratios

If a firm intends to remain a viable business entity, it must have enough cash on hand to pay bills on time. One way to determine whether this is the

---

[2] The ratios discussed in this chapter are only a representative sample of the total number of financial ratios that may be analyzed.

Table 6-1   **Sandia Manufacturing Company Balance Sheet (in thousands of dollars)**

	December 31, 19X6		December 31, 19X5	
Assets				
Cash		$ 2,540		$ 2,750
Marketable securities		1,800		1,625
Accounts receivable, net		18,320		16,850
Inventories		27,530		26,470
Total current assets		$50,190		$47,695
Plant and equipment	$43,100		$39,500	
Less: Accumulated depreciation	11,400		9,500	
Net plant and equipment		$31,700		$30,000
Total assets		$81,890		$77,695
Liabilities and Stockholders' Equity				
Accounts payable		$ 9,721		$ 8,340
Notes payable—bank (10%)		8,500		5,635
Accrued taxes payable		3,200		3,150
Other current liabilities		2,102		1,750
Current portion of long-term debt		2,000		2,000
Total current liabilities		$25,523		$20,875
Long-term debt (9⅝% mortgage bonds)*		$22,000		$24,000
Total liabilities		$47,523		$44,875
Common stock ($10 par)	$13,000		$13,000	
Contributed capital in excess of par	10,000		10,000	
Retained earnings	11,367		9,820	
Total stockholders' equity		$34,367		$32,820
Total liabilities and stockholders' equity		$81,890		$77,695

*Mortgage bonds require a $2,000(000) annual payment to a sinking fund.

case is to examine the relationship between a firm's current assets and approaching obligations. Liquidity ratios are quick measures of a firm's ability to provide sufficient cash to conduct business over the next few months. *Cash budgets* provide the best assessment of a firm's liquidity position. They are discussed in Chapter 8.

This section discusses two different liquidity ratios—the *current ratio* and the *quick ratio*.

Current Ratio The current ratio is defined as follows:

$$\text{Current ratio} = \frac{\text{Current assets}}{\text{Current liabilities}}. \tag{6.1}$$

Current assets include the cash a firm already has on hand and in the bank, plus any assets that can be converted into cash within a "normal" operating period of 12 months, such as marketable securities held as short-term investments, accounts receivable, inventories, and prepayments. Current liabilities include any financial obligations expected to fall due within the next year, such as accounts payable, notes payable, the

Table 6-2   **Sandia Manufacturing Company Income Statement (in thousands of dollars)**

For the Year Ending December 31, 19X6

Net sales		$112,760
Cost of goods sold		85,300
Gross margin		$ 27,460
Operating expenses:		
Selling	$6,540	
General and administrative*	9,400	
Total operating expenses		15,940
Earnings before interest and taxes (EBIT)		$ 11,520
Interest charges:		
Interest on bank notes	$ 850	
Interest on mortgage bonds	2,310	
Total interest charges		3,160
Earnings before taxes (EBT)		$ 8,360
Federal and state income taxes at a		
combined 48% rate		4,013
Earnings after taxes (EAT) and available		
for common stockholders		$ 4,347

Other information:

Dividends paid on common stock	$ 2,800
Earnings retained in the firm	$ 1,547
Shares outstanding	1,300
Market price per share	$20
Book value per share	$26.44
Earnings per share	$3.34
Dividends per share	$2.15

*Includes $150(000) in annual lease payments.

current portion of long-term debt due, other payables, and various accruals such as taxes and wages due.

Using data from Table 6-1, Sandia's current ratio at year-end 19X6 can be calculated as $50,190/$25,523 = 1.97, or about 2:1. Or, it can be said that Sandia's current assets *cover* its current liabilities about two times.

The ratio is interpreted to mean that to satisfy the claims of short-term creditors exclusively from existing current assets, Sandia must be able to convert each dollar of current assets into at least $0.51 of cash ($1.00/ 1.97 = $0.507, or $0.51). The *industry average* for the current ratio is 2.40 times,[3] meaning that the average firm in the industry must convert only $0.42 ($1.00/2.40 = $0.416, or $0.42) of each dollar of current assets into cash to meet short-term obligations.

The fact that Sandia's current ratio is below the industry average does *not* mean that the firm would consider closing its doors voluntarily to meet the demands of short-term creditors. Nor does it mean that Sandia's creditors are any less well protected than the creditors of competing firms, since no two firms—even those in the same industry—are identical. In fact, ratios that suggest the presence of a problem in one firm may be quite

[3] Industry averages are obtained from various sources. The "Sources of Comparative Financial Data" section later in this chapter discusses a number of such sources.

satisfactory for another firm.[4] Sandia's current ratio provides only *one* standard for measuring liquidity. The financial analyst must dissect, or "go behind," the ratio to discover why it differs from the industry average and determine whether a serious problem exists.

Quick Ratio The quick ratio is defined as follows:

$$\text{Quick ratio} = \frac{\text{Current assets} - \text{Inventories}}{\text{Current liabilities}}. \qquad (6.2)$$

This ratio, sometimes called the "acid test," is a more stringent measure of liquidity than the current ratio. By subtracting inventories from current assets, this ratio recognizes that a firm's inventories are often one of its least liquid current assets. Inventories, especially work in process, are very difficult to liquidate quickly at, or near, their book value. Referring to the figures on Sandia's balance sheet (Table 6-1), the firm's quick ratio at year-end 19X6 is calculated as follows:

$$\frac{\$50,190 - \$27,530}{\$25,523} = \frac{\$22,660}{\$25,523} = 0.89 \text{ times}.$$

The industry average is 0.92 times; Sandia's quick ratio is nearly equal to that.

The quick ratio is interpreted to mean that Sandia's cash and other current assets one step removed from cash—that is, marketable securities and accounts receivable—are equal to 89 percent of the current liabilities.[5] The crucial assumption behind the quick ratio is that a firm's accounts receivable may be converted into cash within the "normal" collection period (and with little "shrinkage"), or within the period of time for which credit was initially granted.

The analyst who doubts the liquidity of a firm's receivables may wish to prepare an *aging schedule*. The following one lists Sandia's accounts receivable as of December 31, 19X6:

Days Outstanding	Amount Outstanding (in Thousands of Dollars)	Percentage of Total
Less than 30	$ 9,450	51.6%
30–59	5,161	28.2
60–89	2,750	15.0
Over 90	959	5.2
Total accounts receivable	$18,320	100.0%

[4] Many practitioners view a current ratio of 1.5 times (1.5) as satisfactory for industrial firms. Public utilities, on the other hand, typically function with considerably lower ratios. However, the financial analyst must be very cautious when using any of these "rules of thumb." The safe level of a current ratio is a function of how fast the firm's current assets and liabilities turn over. In the case of a public utility, the accounts receivable turn over on a monthly basis—much faster than in the typical industrial firm. Thus, public utilities are able to safely sustain lower current ratios than industrial firms.

[5] A quick ratio of 1 times (1.0) is considered satisfactory for most industrial firms.

Unfortunately, the data required to prepare an aging schedule are normally not available to outside analysts. Hence, the aging schedule is useful primarily for internal analysis.

To evaluate the figures contained in an aging schedule, the analyst would need to consider Sandia's selling terms. If, for example, Sandia's customers are expected to pay within forty days (which, in fact, they are), then the aging schedule indicates that many accounts are past due. However, since only 5.2 percent of the firm's receivables have been outstanding over ninety days, the major problem appears to be with slow-paying rather than uncollectible accounts. Some analysts adjust the quick ratio *downward* if a significant percentage of a firm's receivables are long past due and have not been written off as losses. Adjusting Sandia's quick ratio downward involves the following calculation:

$$\frac{\text{(Current assets } - \text{ Inventories)} - \text{ Accounts outstanding over 90 days}}{\text{Current liabilities}} = \frac{\$22{,}660 - \$959}{\$25{,}523} = 0.85 \text{ times.}$$

The 0.04 difference between the quick ratio, 0.89 times, and the adjusted ratio, 0.85 times, is probably insignificant. Thus, even if Sandia's accounts over ninety days old were considered uncollectible, this alone would not indicate any real problem for the firm.

Activity Ratios

One objective of financial management is to determine how a firm's resources can best be distributed among the various asset accounts. If a proper mix of cash, receivables, inventories, plant, property, and equipment can be achieved, the firm's asset structure will be more effective in generating sales revenue.

Activity ratios indicate how much a firm has invested in a particular type of asset (or group of assets) relative to the revenue the asset is producing. By comparing activity ratios for the various asset accounts of a firm with established industry norms, the analyst can determine how efficiently the firm is allocating its resources.

This section discusses several types of activity ratios, including the *average collection period,* the *inventory turnover ratio,* the *fixed asset turnover ratio,* and the *total asset turnover ratio.*

Average Collection Period   The average collection period is the average number of days an account receivable remains outstanding. It is usually determined by dividing a firm's year-end receivables balance by the average daily credit sales (based on a 360-day year):[6]

$$\text{Average collection period} = \frac{\text{Accounts receivable}}{\text{Annual credit sales}/360}. \qquad \textbf{(6.3)}$$

---

[6] When credit sales figures are not available (which is frequently the case), total sales figures are customarily used in calculating the ratio. This results in an *overstatement* of the average daily sales and an *understatement* of the average collection period.

For firms with seasonal sales, the analyst should calculate an average of the end-of-month receivables balances. When comparing average collection period ratios with industry norms, the analyst must make sure the industry ratios have been computed in the same manner as the particular firm's ratios.

Using figures from both Sandia's balance sheet (Table 6-1) and the income statement (Table 6-2), the average collection period ratio at year-end 19X6 can be calculated as $18,320/($112,760/360) = $18,320/ $313.22 = 58.5 days. Since the industry average for this ratio is 47 days, Sandia'a ratio is substantially above the average.

Sandia's credit terms call for payment within 40 days. The ratio calculations show that 58.5 days of sales are tied up in receivables, meaning that a significant portion of Sandia's customers are not paying bills on time. (This is also indicated by the aging schedule of the firm's accounts receivable.) The analyst would interpret this ratio to mean that Sandia has allocated a greater proportion of total resources to receivables than the average firm in the industry. If Sandia implemented a more vigorous collection program and reduced the collection period to the industry norm of 47 days, some of these funds would be released for investment elsewhere. The released funds of (58.5 days − 47 days) × $313.22 per day = $3,602 could be invested in other assets that might contribute more significantly to profitability.[7]

An average collection period substantially above the industry norm is usually not desirable and may indicate too liberal a credit policy. Ultimately the firm must determine if the liberal credit policy generates enough sales and profits to justify the cost.[8] In contrast, an average collection period far *below* the industry norm may indicate that the firm's credit terms are too stringent and are hurting sales by restricting credit only to the very best customers. Although moderate-to-slow paying customers may seem troublesome individually, they can be profitable as a group, and a credit policy that is too tight may drive them to competitor firms.

Inventory Turnover Ratio The inventory turnover ratio is defined as follows:

$$\text{Inventory turnover} = \frac{\text{Costs of goods sold}}{\text{Average inventory}}. \tag{6.4}$$

Whereas the cost of goods sold is usually listed on a firm's income statement, the average inventory has to be calculated. This can be done in a number of ways. For example, if a firm has been experiencing a significant and continuing rate of growth in sales, the average inventory may be computed by adding the figures for the beginning and ending inventories for the year and dividing by two. If sales are seasonal or otherwise subject to wide fluctuations, however, it would be better to add the month-end inventory balances for the entire year and divide by twelve.

Some analysts calculate inventory turnover as simply the ratio of annual sales to ending inventory. Although the *sales-to-inventory ratio* is technically inferior and gives different results than more commonly used ratios,

---

[7] Recall that the analysis for Sandia is being done in terms of thousands of dollars. Hence, the actual released funds total $3,602,000.

[8] Chapter 20 contains an example of this type of analysis.

it may be satisfactory if used consistently when making comparisons between one firm and the industry as a whole. However, there is a problem with this ratio in that it tends to differ from one firm to another, depending on policies regarding markups on the cost of goods sold.

Since Sandia's sales are spread evenly over the year and its growth rate has been fairly moderate, the average inventory can be calculated by taking the average of the beginning and ending inventory balances, ($27,530 + $26,470)/2 = $27,000. Dividing the cost of goods sold by this figure, $85,300/$27,000, gives the inventory turnover ratio of 3.16 times. This is considerably below the industry norm of 3.9 times, indicating that Sandia has a larger investment in inventory relative to the sales being generated than the average firm.

Two factors may be responsible for Sandia's allocating an excessive amount of resources to inventory:

- The firm may be attempting to carry all possible types of replacement parts so that every order can be filled immediately. Sandia should carefully examine this policy to determine whether the cost of carrying excessive stocks is justified by the profits earned on additional sales.[9]
- Some of Sandia's inventory may be damaged, obsolete, or slow moving. Stock falling into these categories has questionable liquidity and should be recorded at a value more reflective of the realizable market value.

If a firm's inventory turnover ratio is too high, it may mean the firm is frequently running out of certain items in stock and losing sales to competitors. For inventory to contribute fully to profitability, the firm has to maintain a reasonable balance of inventory levels.

Fixed Asset Turnover Ratio The fixed asset turnover ratio is defined as follows:

$$\text{Fixed asset turnover} = \frac{\text{Sales}}{\text{Net fixed assets}}. \tag{6.5}$$

It indicates the extent to which a firm is utilizing existing property, plant, and equipment to generate sales.

The balance sheet figures that indicate how much a firm has invested in property, plant, and equipment are affected by several factors, including the following:

- The cost of the assets when acquired.
- The length of time since acquisition.
- The depreciation policies adopted by the firm.
- The extent to which fixed assets are leased rather than owned.

Because of these factors it is possible for firms with virtually identical plants to have significantly different fixed asset turnover ratios. Thus, the ratio should be used primarily for year-to-year comparisons within the same company rather than for intercompany comparisons.

---

[9] The determination of optimal inventory levels is discussed in Chapter 21.

Sandia's fixed asset turnover ratio is $112,760/$31,700 = 3.56 times—considerably below the industry average of 4.6 times. However, the financial analyst should acknowledge the shortcomings of the ratio and perform further analyses before concluding that Sandia makes inefficient use of property, plant, and equipment.

Total Asset Turnover Ratio The total asset turnover ratio is defined as follows:

$$\text{Total asset turnover} = \frac{\text{Sales}}{\text{Total assets}}. \qquad \textbf{(6.6)}$$

It indicates how effectively a firm uses total resources to generate sales and is a summary measure that is influenced by each of the activity ratios previously discussed.

Sandia's total asset turnover ratio is $112,760/$81,890 = 1.38 times, while the industry average is 1.82 times. In view of Sandia's other asset turnover ratios, the firm's relatively poor showing with regard to this ratio is not surprising. Each of Sandia's major asset investment programs—accounts receivable; inventory; and property, plant, and equipment—has been found apparently lacking. The analyst could look at these various ratios and conclude that Sandia is not generating the same level of sales from its assets relative to other firms in the industry.

Financial Leverage Ratios

Whenever a firm finances a portion of assets with any type of fixed-charge financing—such as debt, preferred stock, or leases—the firm is said to be using financial leverage. Financial leverage ratios measure the degree to which a firm is employing financial leverage, and as such are of interest to creditors and owners alike.

Both long- and short-term creditors are concerned with the amount of leverage a firm employs, since it indicates the firm's risk exposure in meeting debt service charges (that is, interest and principal repayment). A firm that is heavily debt financed offers creditors less protection in the event of bankruptcy. For example, if a firm's assets are financed with 85 percent debt, the value of the assets can decline by only 15 percent before creditors' funds are endangered. In contrast, if only 15 percent of a firm's assets are debt financed, asset values can drop by 85 percent before jeopardizing the creditors.

Owners are interested in financial leverage because it influences the rate of return they can expect to realize on investment and the degree of risk involved. For example, if a firm is able to borrow funds at 9 percent and employ them at 12 percent, the owners earn the 3 percent difference and are likely to view financial leverage favorably. On the other hand, if the firm can only earn 3 percent on the borrowed funds, the −6 percent difference (3% − 9%) will result in a lower rate of return to the owners.[10]

Either balance sheet or income statement data can be used to measure a

---

[10] The tradeoff between risk and return resulting from the use of financial leverage is discussed in Chapter 7.

firm's use of financial leverage. The balance sheet approach gives a *static* measure of financial leverage at a specific point in time and emphasizes *total* amounts of debt, whereas the income statement approach provides a more *dynamic* measure and relates required interest payments on debt to the firm's ability to pay. Both approaches are widely employed in practice.

There are several types of financial leverage ratios, including the *debt ratio,* the *debt-to-equity ratio,* the *times interest earned ratio,* and the *fixed charge coverage ratio.*

Debt Ratio   The debt ratio is defined as follows:

$$\text{Debt ratio} = \frac{\text{Total debt}}{\text{Total assets}}. \qquad (6.7)$$

It measures the proportion of a firm's total assets that is financed with creditors' funds. As used here, the term *debt* encompasses all short-term liabilities and long-term borrowings.

Bondholders and other long-term creditors are among those who are likely to be interested in a firm's debt ratio. They tend to prefer a low debt ratio, since it provides more protection in the event of liquidation or some other major financial problem. As the debt ratio increases, so do a firm's fixed interest charges. If the debt ratio becomes too high, the cash flows a firm generates during economic recessions may not be sufficient to meet interest payments. Thus, a firm's ability to market new debt obligations when it needs to raise new funds is crucially affected by the size of the debt ratio and by investors' perceptions about the risk implied by the level of the ratio.

Debt ratios are stated in terms of percentages. Sandia's debt ratio as of year-end 19X6 is ($25,523 + $22,000)/$81,890 = $47,523/$81,890 = 0.58, or 58 percent. The ratio is interpreted to mean that Sandia's creditors are financing 58 percent of the firm's total assets. This figure is considerably higher than the 47 percent industry average, indicating that Sandia has less unused borrowing capacity than the average firm in the industry.

A high debt ratio implies a low *proportionate equity base,* that is, the percentage of assets financed with equity funds. As the proportionate equity base declines, investors are more hesitant to acquire a firm's debt obligations. Whether Sandia can continue to finance its assets with 58 percent of "outsiders' " money largely depends on the growth and stability of future earnings and cash flows.

Debt-to-Equity Ratio   The debt-to-equity ratio is defined as follows:

$$\text{Debt-to-equity} = \frac{\text{Total debt}}{\text{Total equity}}. \qquad (6.8)$$

It is similar to the debt ratio and relates the amount of a firm's debt financing to the amount of owner financing.

Since most interest costs are incurred on long-term borrowed funds—that is, those having maturities greater than one year—some analysts prefer to use a *long-term debt-to-equity ratio.* Many analysts also include a firm's preferred stock with its debt when computing the debt-to-equity ratio, because preferred stock dividends, like interest requirements, are usually fixed.

The debt-to-equity ratio also is stated as a percentage. Sandia's debt-to-equity ratio at year-end 19X6 is \$47,523/\$34,367 = 1.383, or 138.3 percent. Since the industry average is 88.7 percent, Sandia's ratio indicates that the firm uses more than the usual amount of borrowed funds to finance its activities. Specifically, Sandia raises nearly \$1.38 from creditors for each dollar invested by owners. This is interpreted to mean that the firm's debt suppliers have a lower margin of safety than is common in the industry. In addition, Sandia has a greater potential for financial distress if earnings do not exceed the cost of borrowed funds.

Times Interest Earned Ratio   The times interest earned ratio is defined as follows:

$$\text{Times interest earned} = \frac{\text{Earnings before interest and taxes (EBIT)}}{\text{Interest charges}}. \qquad \textbf{(6.9)}$$

Often referred to as simply "interest coverage," this ratio employs income statement data to measure a firm's use of financial leverage. It tells the analyst the extent to which the firm's current earnings are able to meet current interest payments. The EBIT figures are used because the firm makes interest payments out of operating income, or EBIT.

Sandia's times interest earned ratio is \$11,520/\$3,160 = 3.65 times. In other words, Sandia covers annual interest payments 3.65 times; this figure is considerably below the industry norm of 6.7 times. This is further evidence that Sandia makes extensive use of creditors' funds to finance operations.

Fixed Charge Coverage Ratio   The fixed charge coverage ratio is defined as follows:

$$\text{Fixed charge coverage} = \frac{\text{EBIT} + \text{Lease payments}}{\text{Interest} + \text{Lease payments} + \text{Preferred dividends before tax} + \text{Before tax sinking fund}}. \qquad \textbf{(6.10)}$$

It measures the number of times a firm is able to cover total *fixed charges,* which include (in addition to interest payments) preferred dividends and payments required under long-term lease contracts. Many industrial corporations also are required to make *sinking fund* payments on bond issues, which are annual payments aimed at either retiring a portion of the bond obligation each year or providing for the ultimate redemption of bonds at maturity. Under most sinking fund provisions the firm either may make these payments to the bondholders' representative (the *trustee*), who determines by lot which of the outstanding bonds will be retired, or deliver to the trustee the required number of bonds purchased by the firm in the open market. Either way, the firm's outstanding indebtedness is reduced.

In calculating the fixed charge coverage ratio, the analyst must consider each of the firm's obligations on a *before-tax* basis. However, since sinking fund payments and preferred stock dividends are not tax deductible and therefore must be paid out of after-tax earnings, a mathematical adjustment has to be made. After-tax payments must be divided by $(1 - t)$, where t is the marginal tax rate. This effectively converts such payments to a before-tax basis, or one that is comparable to the EBIT.[11] And, since lease payments are deducted in arriving at the EBIT, they must be added back into the numerator of the ratio, because the fixed charges (in the denominator) also include lease payments.

The fixed charge coverage ratio is a more severe measure of a firm's ability to meet fixed financial obligations. Using figures from Sandia's income statement for 19X6,[12] the fixed charge coverage ratio can be calculated as follows:

$$\frac{\$11,520 + \$150}{\$3,160 + \$150 + \$2,000/(1 - 0.48)} = \frac{\$11,670}{\$7,156} = 1.63 \text{ times.}$$

Since the industry average is 4.5 times, it is once again apparent that Sandia provides creditors with a smaller margin of safety—that is, a higher level of risk—than the average firm in the industry. As a result, Sandia is probably straining its relations with creditors. If a "tight money" situation developed in the economy, Sandia's high debt and low coverage ratios would probably limit the firm's access to new credit sources, and Sandia might be forced to curtail operations or borrow on prohibitively expensive and restrictive terms.

Profitability Ratios

More than anything else, a firm's *profits*[13] demonstrate how well the firm is making investment and financing decisions. If a firm is unable to provide adequate returns in the form of dividends and share price appreciation to investors, it may be unable to maintain, let alone increase, its asset base. Profitability ratios measure how effectively a firm's management is generating profits on sales; total assets; and, most importantly, stockholders' investment. Thus, anyone whose economic interests are tied to the long-run survival of a firm will be interested in profitability ratios.

There are several types of profitability ratios, including the *gross profit margin ratio,* the *net profit margin ratio,* the *return on investment ratio,* and the *return on stockholders' equity ratio.*

---

[11] The rationale for this computation is as follows:

$$\text{After-tax earnings} = \text{Before-tax earnings} - \text{Tax}$$
$$= (\text{Before-tax earnings}) - (\text{Before-tax earnings}) \times t$$
$$= \text{Before-tax earnings} (1 - t).$$
$$\frac{\text{After-tax earnings}}{1 - t} = \text{Before-tax earnings.}$$

[12] Some analysts exclude preferred dividend payments when computing the fixed charge coverage ratio. In the calculation that follows, the $150 represents annual long-term lease payments, and the $2,000 represents sinking fund obligations.

[13] The terms *profits, earnings,* and *net income* are used interchangeably in this discussion.

Gross Profit Margin Ratio The gross profit margin ratio is defined as follows:

$$\text{Gross profit margin} = \frac{\text{Sales} - \text{Cost of goods sold}}{\text{Sales}}. \tag{6.11}$$

It measures the relative profitability of a firm's sales after the cost of goods sold has been deducted, thus revealing how effectively the firm's management is making decisions regarding pricing and the control of production costs.

Sandia's gross profit margin ratio is $27,460/$112,760 = 24.4%. This is just slightly below the industry average of 25.6 percent, indicating that either Sandia's pricing policies or production methods are not quite as effective as those of the average firm in the industry. Differences in inventory accounting methods (and, to a lesser extent, depreciation methods) used by Sandia and the firms included in the industry average also influence the cost of goods sold and, by extension, the gross profit margin.

Net Profit Margin Ratio The net profit margin ratio is defined as follows:

$$\text{Net profit margin} = \frac{\text{Earnings after taxes (EAT)}}{\text{Sales}}. \tag{6.12}$$

It measures how profitable a firm's sales are after all expenses, including taxes and interest, have been deducted.

Some analysts also compute an *operating profit margin ratio,* defined as EBIT/sales. It measures the profitability of a firm's operations before considering the effects of financing decisions. Since the operating profit margin is computed before considering interest charges, this ratio is often more suitable for comparing the profit performance of different firms.

Sandia's net profit margin ratio is $4,347/$112,760 = 3.85%. This is below the industry average of 4.5 percent and is interpreted to mean that Sandia is earning 0.65 percent less on each dollar of sales than the average firm in the industry. This indicates that Sandia may be having difficulty controlling either total expenses (including interest, operating expenses, and the cost of goods sold) or the prices of its products. In this case the former is probably more accurate, since Sandia's financial structure contains a greater proportion of debt, resulting in more interest charges.

Return On Investment (Total Assets) Ratio The return on investment ratio is defined as follows:

$$\text{Return on investment} = \frac{\text{Earnings after taxes (EAT)}}{\text{Total assets}}. \tag{6.13}$$

It measures a firm's net income in relation to the total asset investment.

Sandia's return on investment ratio $4,347/$81,890, is 5.31 percent—

considerably below the industry average of 8.19 percent. This is a direct result of the firm's low activity ratios and low profit margins.[14]

Return On Stockholders' Equity Ratio
The return on stockholders' equity ratio is defined as follows:

$$\text{Return on stockholders' equity} = \frac{\text{Earnings after taxes (EAT)}}{\text{Stockholders' equity}}. \quad \textbf{(6.14)}$$

It measures the rate of return that the firm's owners—that is, the common stockholders—realize on their investment. Since only the stockholders' equity appears in the denominator, the ratio is directly influenced by the amount of debt a firm is using to finance assets.

Sandia's return on stockholder's equity ratio is \$4,347/\$34,367 = 12.65%. Again, Sandia's ratio is below the industry average of 15.45 percent. The firm's low activity ratios and low profit margins result in its profitability ratios being inferior to the industry norms, even after the effects of debt financing (financial leverage) are considered.

Market-Based Ratios

The financial ratios discussed in the previous four groups are all derived from accounting income statement and balance sheet information provided by the firm. Analysts are also frequently interested in the financial market's assessment of the performance of a firm. There should be a close parallel between the accounting ratios of a firm and the market-based ratios for that firm. For example, if the accounting ratios of a firm suggest that the firm has more risk than the average firm in the industry and has lower profit prospects, this should be reflected in a lower market price of that firm's stock.

Price to Earnings (P/E) Ratio
The price to earnings ratio is defined as follows:

$$\text{P/E} = \text{Market price per share/Current earnings per share.} \quad \textbf{(6.15)}$$

(Some security analysts use projected next year's earnings per share in the denominator. There is nothing wrong with this alternative definition as long as comparisons between firms are done on the same basis.)

In general, a firm's P/E ratio should be higher the lower is the firm's risk. In addition, the better the growth prospects of its earnings, the greater the P/E multiple. For example, Long Island Lighting Company, an electric utility faced with substantial risk due to the uncertainty surrounding the construction and ultimate utilization of its Shoreham nuclear power plant, had a year-end 1985 P/E multiple of 2.0. In contrast, Wisconsin Power and Light Company, with no nuclear construction

---

[14] Some analysts also like to compute the ratio of EBIT/total assets. This measures the operating profit rate of return for a firm. An after-tax version of this ratio is earnings before interest and after tax (EBIAT) divided by total assets. These ratios are computed before interest changes. Hence they may be more suitable when comparing the operating performance of two or more firms which are financed differently.

Table 6-3   **Ratio Analysis Summary for the Sandia Manufacturing Company**

Ratio	Definition
Liquidity	
1. Current ratio	$\dfrac{\text{Current assets}}{\text{Current liabilities}}$
2. Quick ratio (acid test)	$\dfrac{\text{Current assets} - \text{Inventories}}{\text{Current liabilities}}$
Activity	
3. Average collection period	$\dfrac{\text{Accounts receivable}}{\text{Credit sales}/360}$
4. Inventory turnover	$\dfrac{\text{Cost of goods sold}}{\text{Average inventory}}$
5. Fixed asset turnover	$\dfrac{\text{Sales}}{\text{Fixed assets}}$
6. Total asset turnover	$\dfrac{\text{Sales}}{\text{Total assets}}$
Financial leverage	
7. Debt ratio	$\dfrac{\text{Total debt}}{\text{Total assets}}$
8. Debt-to-equity	$\dfrac{\text{Total debt}}{\text{Total equity}}$
9. Times interest earned	$\dfrac{\text{Earnings before interest and taxes (EBIT)}}{\text{Interest charges}}$
10. Times fixed charges earned	$\dfrac{\text{EBIT} + \text{Lease payments}}{\text{Interest} + \text{Lease payments} + \text{Before-tax sinking fund} + \text{Preferred stock dividends before tax}}$
Profitability	
11. Gross profit margin	$\dfrac{\text{Sales} - \text{Cost of goods sold}}{\text{Sales}}$
12. Net profit margin	$\dfrac{\text{Earnings after taxes (EAT)}}{\text{Sales}}$
13. Return on investment	$\dfrac{\text{Earnings after taxes (EAT)}}{\text{Total assets}}$
14. Return on stockholders' equity	$\dfrac{\text{Earnings after taxes (EAT)}}{\text{Stockholders' equity}}$
Market-Based	
15. Price to earnings ratio	$\dfrac{\text{Market price per share}}{\text{Current earnings per share}}$
16. Market to book ratio	$\dfrac{\text{Market price per share}}{\text{Book value per share}}$

worries and a very strong balance sheet, enjoyed a P/E multiple of more than 9 times at year-end 1985.

Sandia's current (19X6) earnings per share are $3.34 (earnings of $4,347 divided by 1,300 shares). If Sandia's current market price is $20 per share, its P/E ratio is 5.99 times. This is below the industry average of

Table 6-3   **(Continued)**

Calculation	Industry Average	Assessment
$\dfrac{\$50,190}{25,523} = 1.97$ times	2.40 times	Fair
$\dfrac{\$22,660}{\$25,523} = 0.89$ times	0.92 times	Satisfactory
$\dfrac{\$18,320}{\$112,760/360} = 58.5$ days	47 days	Unsatisfactory
$\dfrac{\$85,300}{(\$27,530 + \$26,470)/2} = 3.16$ times	3.9 times	Unsatisfactory
$\dfrac{\$112,760}{\$31,700} = 3.56$ times	4.6 times	Poor
$\dfrac{\$112,760}{\$81,890} = 1.38$ times	1.82 times	Poor
$\dfrac{\$47,523}{\$81,890} = 58$ percent	47 percent	Poor
$\dfrac{\$47,523}{\$34,367} = 138.3$ percent	88.7 percent	Poor
$\dfrac{\$11,520}{\$3,160} = 3.65$ times	6.7 times	Poor
$\dfrac{\$11,520 + \$150}{\$3,160 + \$150 + \$2,000/(1 - 0.48)} = 1.63$ times	4.5 times	Poor
$\dfrac{\$27,460}{\$112,760} = 24.4$ percent	25.6 percent	Fair
$\dfrac{\$4,347}{\$112,760} = 3.85$ percent	4.50 percent	Unsatisfactory
$\dfrac{\$4,347}{\$81,890} = 5.31$ percent	8.19 percent	Poor
$\dfrac{\$4,347}{\$34,367} = 12.65$ percent	15.45 percent	Poor
$\dfrac{\$20}{\$3.34} = 5.99$ times	7.8 times	Poor
$\dfrac{\$20}{26.44} = 0.76$	0.97	Poor

7.8 times, and indicates that Sandia has either higher risk than the average firm, lower growth prospects, or both.

Market (Price) to Book (Value) (P/B) Ratio   The market to book ratio is defined as follows:

$$P/B = \text{Market price per share}/\text{Book value per share} \qquad \textbf{(6.16)}$$

Generally, the higher the rate of return a firm is earning on its common equity relative to the return required by investors (the cost of common equity), the higher will be the P/B ratio.

The book value per share of common stock is determined by dividing the total common stockholders' equity for a firm by the number of shares outstanding. In the case of Sandia at year-end 19X6, the book value per share is equal to $26.44 (stockholders' equity of $34,367 divided by 1,300 shares outstanding). With a market price per share of $20, the market to book ratio for Sandia is 0.76. This compares unfavorably with the industry average of 0.97.

It should be noted that since the market to book ratio contains the book value of the common stockholders' equity in the denominator (remember that common stockholders' equity is equal to total assets minus total liabilities), it is affected by the accounting treatments used by a firm in such crucial areas as inventory valuation and depreciation. For this reason, comparisons between firms can often be misleading.

Summary of Financial Ratio Analysis

Table 6-3 on pp. 184–5 lists all the financial ratios calculated for the Sandia Manufacturing Company, summarizing the comparative financial ratio analysis undertaken for the firm.

The assessment column to the right of the table contains an evaluation of each of Sandia's ratios in comparison with the industry averages. For example, the firm's liquidity position is rated fair to satisfactory. Whereas its current ratio is somewhat below the industry norm, its quick ratio is satisfactory, indicating that Sandia probably has sufficient liquidity to meet maturing obligations. The firm's asset structure is not generating sufficient sales revenues, however. Sandia's activity ratios indicate that the firm is investing too much in receivables and inventories, as well as property, plant, and equipment, relative to the sales volume being generated. Thus, Sandia should consider implementing more stringent credit and collection policies as well as better inventory controls. The firm should also evaluate its investment in property, plant, and equipment to determine whether reductions could be made without impairing operations.

Sandia's financial leverage ratios indicate that the firm is using significantly more debt to finance operations than the average firm in the industry. Because of its poor coverage ratios, the company will likely have difficulty obtaining debt financing for further asset additions. In the event of an economic slowdown, Sandia's creditors would probably reevaluate the firm's borrowing capacity and make less funds available to it. If Sandia wants to restore its borrowing capacity, it should take steps to increase its equity base. The market-based ratios confirm the analysis performed using Sandia's financial statements.

Trend Analysis

Thus far the analysis of the Sandia Manufacturing Company has focused solely on the year 19X6. This has provided a fairly complete, if rather static, picture of the company's situation at that particular point in time in comparison with industry standards. To gain insight into the direction the company is moving, however, a trend analysis should be performed. A trend analysis indicates a firm's performance *over time* and reveals whether its position is improving or deteriorating relative to other companies in the industry.

A trend analysis requires that a number of different ratios be calculated over several years and charted to yield a graphic representation of the company's performance. Figure 6-1 depicts a trend analysis for the Sandia Company for the years 19X0 to 19X6 and indicates the direction the firm

Figure 6-1

Trend Analysis of the Financial Ratios for the Sandia Manufacturing Company from 19X0 to 19X6

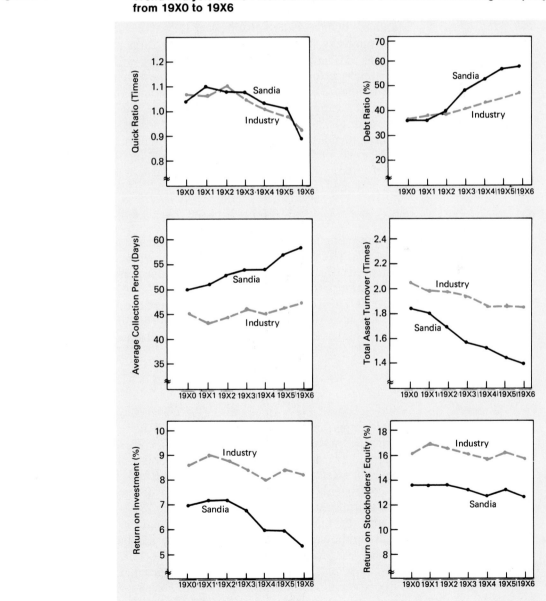

has been taking for the last several years. Each of the four different categories of financial ratios is represented in the figure. For example, it is evident that the firm's liquidity position—as measured by the quick ratio—has gradually declined over the seven-year period, falling to slightly below the industry average in 19X6. Unless this downward trend continues, however, liquidity should not be a major problem for the firm.

The trend analysis tells another story about the firm's leverage and profitability. Sandia's use of debt has exceeded the industry average since 19X2. The activity ratios—the total asset turnover ratio and the average collection period ratio—indicate that the company has used much of this new debt to finance additional assets, including a buildup in receivables. Unfortunately, the new assets have not produced offsetting increases in profits. As a result, returns on investment have dropped below the industry standards by increasing amounts over the past seven years.

In summary, the comparative financial ratio analysis and the trend analysis combined provide the financial analyst with a fairly clear picture of Sandia's performance. It is evident that the firm has employed excessive debt to finance asset additions, which have not been sufficiently productive in generating sales revenues. This has resulted in returns on investment and stockholders' equity that are significantly lower than average. If the firm intends to reverse these trends, it will have to make more effective use of assets and reduce the use of creditors' funds. This will enable the firm to improve relations with creditors and potentially increase profitability and reduce risk for its owners.

Return On Investment

The preceding discussion on ratios indicates that a firm's return on investment (ROI) is defined as the ratio of earnings after taxes (EAT) to total assets. The ROI ratio can be examined more closely to provide additional insights into its significance.

The ROI also can be viewed as a function of the net profit margin times the total asset turnover, since the net profit margin ratio = EAT/sales, and the total asset turnover ratio = sales/total assets:

$$\frac{EAT}{Total\ assets} = \frac{EAT}{Sales} \times \frac{Sales}{Total\ assets}. \tag{6.17}$$

It is important to examine a firm's ROI in terms of "margin" and "turnover," since each plays a major role in contributing to profitability. "Margin" measures the profit earned per dollar of sales but ignores the amount of assets used to generate sales. The ROI relationship brings these two components together and shows that a deficiency in either one will lower a firm's return on investment.

Using the figures from the net profit margin ratio and total asset turnover ratio calculated previously for the Sandia Company, the firm's ROI for 19X6 can be computed as 3.85% × 1.38 = 5.31%. Figure 6-2, called a *DuPont chart* because it was developed and is used by the DuPont Corporation, illustrates this relationship. For purposes of comparison, the industry average ROI = 4.50% × 1.82 = 8.19%. The ROI relationship shows Sandia to be deficient in both margin and turnover relative to the industry average. Improvement in either area would increase the firm's ROI. To improve its *margin,* for example, Sandia must either increase sales revenues more than costs or decrease costs more than sales revenues. To improve its *turnover,* the firm must either increase sales revenue or reduce the asset level required to support the current sales volume. The DuPont chart illustrates the relationship between a firm's ROI and the factors which determine it. By working back through the DuPont chart an analyst can begin to pinpoint potential areas for improvement which will enhance the firm's ROI.

The relative contributions of the net profit margin and the asset turnover ratio in the ROI relationship differ from industry to industry. Specifically, the turnover ratio is largely dependent on a firm's investment in property, plant, and equipment. Firms with large investments in fixed assets tend to have low turnover ratios; public utilities, railroads, and large industrial firms fall into this category. If these companies are to succeed, their relatively low turnover ratios must be offset by correspondingly high margins to produce competitive ROIs. For example, electric and gas utilities typically have net profit margins of 10 to 15 percent. In contrast, other industries require much lower investments in fixed assets, resulting in higher turnover ratios. A typical example is the retail grocery chain

Figure 6-2 **Determinants of Return on Investment for the Sandia Manufacturing Company, 19X6**

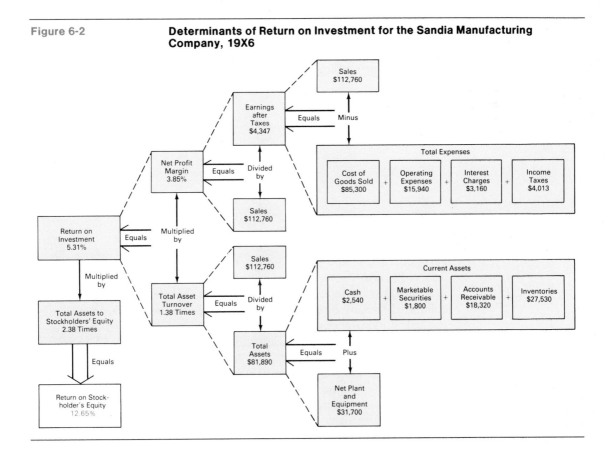

industry, which has margins of only 1 or 2 percent. Firms in this industry often achieve turnovers of 10 times or more. If a grocery chain had a lower turnover, its ROI probably would not be sufficient to attract investors.

Return On Stockholders' Equity

Figure 6-2 also shows Sandia's return on stockholders' equity, which is computed as 12.65 percent. If the firm were financed solely with common equity (stock), the return on stockholders' equity would equal the return on investment. Sandia's stockholders have only supplied about 42 percent of the firm's total capital, whereas creditors have supplied the remaining 58 percent. Since the entire 5.31 percent return on investment belongs to the stockholders (even though they only supplied 42 percent of the total capital), Sandia's return on common equity is higher than its return on investment.

To better clarify how the return on stockholders' equity is determined, a new ratio, the *equity multiplier ratio,* is defined as follows:

$$\text{Equity multiplier} = \frac{\text{Total assets}}{\text{Stockholders' equity}}. \tag{6.18}$$

Sandia's equity multiplier ratio is computed from figures found in Table 6-1 as $81,890/$34,367 = 2.38 times. The industry average for the ratio is 1.89 times. Once again it can be seen that Sandia has financed a greater proportion of assets with debt than the average firm in the industry.

The equity multiplier ratio may be used to show how a firm's use of debt to finance assets affects the return on equity, as follows:

$$\begin{aligned}
\text{Return on stockholders' equity} &= \frac{\text{Net profit}}{\text{margin}} \times \frac{\text{Total asset}}{\text{turnover}} \times \frac{\text{Equity}}{\text{multiplier}} \tag{6.19} \\
&= \frac{\text{Earnings after taxes}}{\text{Sales}} \times \frac{\text{Sales}}{\text{Total assets}} \\
&\quad \times \frac{\text{Total assets}}{\text{Stockholders' equity}}.
\end{aligned}$$

In Sandia's case the return on stockholders' equity is 3.85% × 1.38 × 2.38 = 12.65%.

Although this figure is the same as the return on equity that was computed directly by dividing earnings after tax by stockholders' equity, the calculations shown illustrate more clearly how Sandia managed to magnify a 5.31 percent return on total investment into a 12.65 percent return on stockholders' equity by making more extensive use of debt financing than did the average firm in the industry. This increased use of debt has improved Sandia's return on equity but has also increased its risk—most likely resulting in a decline in Sandia's stock price relative to other, similar firms.

**Sources of
Comparative
Financial Data**

The analyst may refer to a number of sources of financial data when preparing a comparative financial analysis, including the following:

- **Dun and Bradstreet** Dun and Bradstreet (D&B) prepares a series of fourteen key business ratios for eight hundred different lines of business. These ratios are based on the financial statements of some 400,000 companies. D&B reports three values for each ratio—the *median,* the *upper quartile,* and the *lower quartile.* Table 6-4 contains a representative sample of ratios. The median is the figure that falls in the middle when individual ratios of sampled firms are arranged by size. The figure halfway between the median and the ratio with the highest value is the upper quartile, and the figure halfway between the median and the ratio with the lowest value is the lower quartile. By reporting three values for each ratio, D&B enables the analyst to compare a particular firm with the "average" (median) firm, as well as with the "typical" firms in the top and bottom halves of the sample. The complete D&B data are reported in *Industry Norms and Key Business Ratios.*

- **Robert Morris Associates** This national association of bank loan and credit officers uses information provided by loan applications to compile sixteen ratios for over 250 lines of business. Like D&B, Robert Morris Associates reports the median, upper quartile, and lower quartile for each ratio. Data are presented for four categories of firm size. This source is especially useful to the analyst gathering information about smaller firms. The Robert Morris publication containing the data is titled *Statement Studies.*

- *Quarterly Financial Reports for Manufacturing Companies* The Federal Trade Commission (FTC) and the Securities and Exchange Commission (SEC) cooperate in jointly publishing quarterly reports on balance sheet and income statement data of various manufacturing companies. These include analyses of the firms by industry and asset size, along with presentations of financial statements in ratio form.

- **Prentice-Hall's** *Almanac of Business and Industrial Financial Ratios* This annual almanac of business and industrial financial ratios reports twenty-two ratios for 162 separate industries. It also includes the number of establishments in the sampled industry, the number without net income, and the total dollar receipts for each of the eleven size groups into which firms in each industry are classified.

- *Financial Studies of Small Business* This annual publication of Financial Research Associates is particularly valuable for the evaluation of small firms.

- **Moody's or Standard and Poor's Industrial, Financial, Transportation, and Over-the-Counter Manuals** These contain a large amount of balance sheet and income statement data, as well as other relevant background information about a firm.

- **Annual reports** Most corporations publish an annual report containing income statement and balance sheet data along with other information of interest.

Table 6-4   Dun and Bradstreet Quartile Ratios for Selected Business Lines*

Line of Business and Number of Concerns Reporting	Quick Ratio	Current Ratio	Current Liabilities to Net Worth	Current Liabilities to Inventory	Total Liabilities to Net Worth	Fixed Assets to Net Worth
	Times	Times	Percent	Percent	Percent	Percent
Mining, Agriculture, and Construction						
1211	1.7	2.4	19.3	188.6	31.3	38.7
Bituminous Coal &	**0.9**	**1.4**	**44.6**	**304.2**	**85.7**	**91.5**
Lignite (221)	0.4	0.7	112.6	526.1	183.7	151.8
1381	2.3	3.4	12.8	158.3	24.2	58.2
Drilling Oil & Gas	**1.0**	**1.5**	**33.7**	**308.9**	**79.5**	**104.7**
Wells (400)	0.5	0.7	93.7	597.2	211.1	201.2
1094	10.7	9.2	8.8	29.6	24.8	46.7
Uranium-Radium	**2.0**	**4.0**	**21.5**	**37.8**	**42.8**	**85.7**
Ore (16)	1.0	2.2	69.9	178.8	186.8	183.6
Communication, Transportation, and Utilities						
4911	1.2	2.7	14.1	175.2	119.6	155.2
Electric Services	**0.8**	**1.7**	**22.0**	**306.5**	**172.9**	**216.0**
(763)	0.5	1.1	36.2	527.1	274.2	278.9
4011	1.6	2.6	18.9	241.2	55.2	85.2
Railroads, Line-	**0.9**	**1.4**	**31.8**	**438.4**	**95.8**	**139.8**
Haul (98)	0.6	1.0	55.0	607.9	138.7	178.6
4811	3.4	5.1	10.7	182.2	91.3	109.9
Telephone Communication	**1.1**	**2.2**	**22.1**	**366.1**	**178.1**	**204.1**
(Wire or Radio)	0.6	1.0	40.6	616.3	335.9	292.0
(822)						
Manufacturing						
2911	0.9	1.8	49.3	180.4	103.8	106.4
Petroleum Refining	**0.7**	**1.2**	**80.8**	**246.5**	**184.7**	**147.3**
(71)	0.5	1.0	133.5	401.4	299.7	203.8
3573	2.1	4.1	22.5	72.3	31.4	14.7
Electric Computing	**1.2**	**2.4**	**48.9**	**117.6**	**66.9**	**32.5**
Equipment (469)	0.6	1.5	111.4	181.4	148.6	61.9
Retailing						
5141	1.5	3.3	32.1	54.7	47.3	13.6
Groceries	**0.8**	**1.8**	**82.4**	**105.7**	**118.6**	**34.2**
(1037)	0.5	1.3	175.4	165.8	237.9	75.9
5311	2.2	6.0	15.1	30.9	19.3	6.2
Department Stores	**1.2**	**3.3**	**36.6**	**54.9**	**54.1**	**18.5**
(1079)	0.5	2.1	76.9	83.6	135.5	49.4
Services						
8011	5.5	6.9	8.7	85.6	15.0	24.2
Offices of Physician	**1.6**	**2.3**	**33.2**	**310.9**	**54.7**	**53.6**
(1068)	0.6	1.0	94.7	575.3	168.4	105.8
7261	3.8	5.5	10.4	90.1	20.7	32.8
Funeral Service	**1.6**	**2.5**	**26.9**	**203.0**	**54.7**	**65.0**
(774)	0.8	1.3	63.0	383.5	131.7	114.3
Financial Institutions						

	Equity to Assets	Equity to Loans	Loans to Deposits	Loans to Assets	Net Interest Margin	Fee Income
6020	9.7	21.9	47.3	41.9	5.2	0.9
Commercial Banks	**8.1**	**16.5**	**56.8**	**50.2**	**4.5**	**0.6**
	6.9	12.7	66.0	58.3	3.9	0.4
6120	5.5	7.0	84.4	75.8	1.6	1.4
Savings and Loans	**3.9**	**4.8**	**91.5**	**82.1**	**1.0**	**0.9**
	2.8	3.4	98.7	86.5	0.4	0.6

*Ratios shown are for the upper quartile, median, and lower quartile. Boldface numbers indicate median value.

Source: Reprinted with special permission of Dun and Bradstreet Credit Services. *1984–85 Edition of Industry Norms and Key Business Ratios* (New York: Dun and Bradstreet, 1985), Murray Hill, N.J.

Table 6-4 (Continued)

Collection Period	Net Sales to Inventory	Total Assets to Net Sales	Net Sales to Net Working Capital	Accounts Payable to Net Sales	Return on Net Sales	Return on Total Assets	Return on Net Worth
Days	Times	Percent	Times	Percent	Percent	Percent	Percent
24.0	50.7	40.6	18.6	2.7	11.1	11.0	29.9
37.2	**24.0**	**68.4**	**7.7**	**4.7**	**4.5**	**4.6**	**11.6**
54.5	14.1	120.1	4.0	7.9	1.0	0.1	1.5
33.4	75.2	64.2	10.9	2.6	17.8	8.5	17.0
60.7	**29.6**	**112.1**	**5.4**	**6.2**	**3.8**	**2.1**	**3.7**
82.7	11.7	230.8	2.4	12.3	(9.4)	(7.0)	(13.9)
9.4	14.7	137.5	2.9	3.6	(0.4)	6.5	14.2
74.0	**1.7**	**199.7**	**1.8**	**11.7**	**(9.3)**	**(7.4)**	**(8.9)**
125.4	1.1	276.3	0.8	14.4	(28.9)	(25.8)	(65.3)
28.4	38.2	150.6	14.9	6.2	11.1	5.5	15.7
36.1	**23.1**	**194.3**	**7.5**	**7.6**	**7.8**	**4.3**	**11.9**
44.8	13.0	258.0	4.6	9.7	4.7	2.6	8.6
54.0	24.0	145.1	8.4	7.9	13.9	8.5	16.0
69.7	**16.5**	**192.0**	**3.6**	**14.8**	**9.7**	**4.4**	**8.3**
99.0	10.5	253.0	2.2	30.2	3.8	1.4	2.4
26.8	56.0	207.0	7.7	2.7	19.6	7.4	20.0
41.6	**31.9**	**272.5**	**3.2**	**5.3**	**13.1**	**5.1**	**15.2**
54.5	16.7	355.6	1.6	10.2	8.9	3.3	12.0
22.5	27.7	32.1	37.3	6.0	4.7	4.7	13.5
29.0	**17.4**	**46.0**	**17.4**	**8.4**	**1.3**	**2.5**	**8.4**
49.0	10.8	79.5	6.2	12.7	0.2	0.7	1.8
39.7	10.9	43.0	8.0	4.0	11.2	13.1	25.6
60.4	**5.2**	**66.8**	**3.8**	**7.0**	**5.9**	**7.9**	**12.2**
88.8	3.7	96.3	2.2	12.2	0.4	(3.8)	(2.4)
9.8	20.3	14.3	30.8	2.1	2.8	8.4	19.4
18.2	**13.9**	**19.9**	**14.4**	**3.7**	**1.1**	**4.2**	**10.7**
29.9	8.8	30.2	7.9	6.3	0.3	1.3	3.8
6.6	6.4	38.0	6.7	2.5	4.5	8.6	15.7
25.2	**4.7**	**49.5**	**4.2**	**4.7**	**2.3**	**4.6**	**8.8**
53.1	3.2	67.0	2.7	7.3	0.6	1.3	3.0
28.1	145.4	16.6	20.1	0.8	18.6	25.7	54.7
68.2	**67.1**	**33.1**	**7.1**	**1.9**	**6.0**	**8.5**	**17.7**
113.5	28.0	61.5	3.2	4.1	0.8	1.6	3.7
35.7	32.2	51.1	8.7	2.0	13.6	15.0	28.0
53.4	**19.8**	**78.9**	**4.8**	**3.4**	**6.8**	**7.8**	**13.1**
73.7	12.4	121.4	2.8	6.1	2.5	2.4	5.5

Overhead	Operating Efficiency	Net Charge-Offs to Loans	Provision for Loss to Loans	Allowance for Loss to Loans	Return on Assets	Return on Equity	Dividend Payout
2.7	56.0	0.2	0.3	1.3	1.4	15.8	16.5
3.3	**65.2**	**0.5**	**0.6**	**1.0**	**1.0**	**12.3**	**30.0**
4.1	74.8	1.0	1.1	0.8	0.7	8.3	52.2
1.4	64.9	—	0.1	0.4	0.6	13.9	3.3
1.7	**83.4**	**—**	**0.1**	**0.1**	**0.3**	**5.2**	**12.0**
2.2	114.4	—	0.3	0.1	(0.3)	(6.0)	25.4

- **10K Reports** Every widely held firm is required to annually file a 10K report with the SEC. These reports contain income statement and balance sheet data, plus a wide range of other relevant information dealing with the firm's past and current performance and expected future prospects.

- **Trade journals** These are published by trade associations and contain a great deal of financial and other types of information on member firms.

- **Commercial banks** Frequently banks compile financial reports on selected industries. One example is First Chicago's semiannual financial survey of sales finance and consumer finance companies.

- **Computerized Data Sources** There are a number of computerized data bases which are also available to assist in financial analysis. The *Compustat* data base is available from Standard and Poors. It contains complete balance sheet, income statement, stock price and dividend information for several thousand companies, covering a period of twenty years. The *Compustat* data base is available in a form for both mainframe computers and microcomputers. *Value Line* provides summary financial data and forecasts of future performance for over 1700 firms. The *Value Line* data base is available in both hard copy and in a microcomputer usable format called *Value Screen*. In addition, many of these data sources can be accessed for a small fee through computer time sharing services such as *Compuserve*.

A Word of Caution about Financial Ratio Analysis

Throughout the analysis of the Sandia Manufacturing Company performed in this chapter, it has been emphasized that the analyst must exercise caution when evaluating a firm's financial ratios. Although ratios can provide valuable information, they also can be misleading for a number of reasons.

First, ratios are only as reliable as the accounting data on which they are based. Different firms follow different accounting procedures for inventory valuation, depreciation, reporting of long-term leases, pension fund contributions, and mergers and acquisitions, to name just a few. These, in turn, affect reported earnings, assets, and owners' investments. Unless the analyst makes adjustments for accounting reporting differences, ratio comparisons between individual companies and with various industry norms can never be viewed as definitive.

Second, with the exception of disclosing upper and lower quartile values, firms that compile industry norms often do not report information about the *dispersion,* or distribution, of the individual values around the mean ratio. If the reported ratios are widely dispersed, the industry average will be of questionable value, since it may not reflect the "typical" firm in the industry. Furthermore, the standard of comparison probably should not be the "typical" firm, but rather the better performing firms in the industry. Without some measure of dispersion, however, ratios for these better performing firms cannot be determined.

Third, valid comparative analysis depends on the availability of data for appropriately defined industries. Some industry classifications are either too broad or too narrow to be reliable sources of comparative data when an analyst is evaluating a particular firm. Most firms operate in more than one industry, and this makes analysis more difficult.

Fourth, it is important to remember that financial ratios provide a *historical* record of the performance and financial condition of a firm. Further analysis is required before this historical record can be used as a basis for future projections.

Finally, comparisons of a firm's ratios with industry norms may not always be what they seem. Ratios comparing unfavorably with industry norms should be construed as "red flags" indicating the need for further investigation—not as signals of impending doom. On the other hand, even if a firm's ratios compare favorably with those of the better performing firms in the industry, it does not necessarily mean the firm is performing adequately. If, for example, the industry itself is experiencing a declining demand for its goods and services, favorable ratio comparisons may simply indicate that a firm is not decaying as rapidly as the typical firm in the industry. Thus, comparisons of selected ratios—particularly those relating to profitability—must be made with *national* industry averages in order to determine whether a particular firm in a particular industry is justified in making further investments.

In summary, ratios should not be viewed as substitutes for sound business judgment. Instead, they are simply tools that can help management make better decisions.

Earnings and Balance Sheet Quality and Financial Analysis

When performing a financial analysis of a firm, it is important to be mindful of the *quality of the earnings* reported by a firm as well as the *quality of the firm's balance sheet*. These two dimensions of financial analysis can have a critical impact on the final assessment of the firm's financial condition.

Earnings Quality

When considering the quality of a firm's earnings, there are two key factors which should be kept in mind. First, high quality earnings tend to be cash earnings. The proportion of a firm's earnings which can be viewed as cash earnings is greatly influenced by the firm's procedures with respect to sales revenue recognition. For example, a firm may recognize a sale at the time a contract is signed, a down payment is made, or when the full proceeds from the sale are actually collected as cash. Generally, the closer the recognition of a sale is to the time the full proceeds from that sale are collected, the higher the quality of the firm's reported earnings.

Some firms report a large non-cash component in their income because of special accounting practices in their industry. For example, utilities generally recognize earnings, for financial reporting purposes, on assets which are under construction but which have not yet been placed in the rate-base of the firm for ratemaking purposes. This component of earnings is frequently called "Allowance for Funds Used During Construction" (AFUDC) and it recognizes the return which the firm will ultimately earn on these assets once they are placed in service by the utility. For utilities with large construction programs, the proportion of non-cash to total earnings can be very large. For example, for the year ending March 31,

1985, El Paso Electric, which is involved in the construction of three large nuclear power plants, reported an AFUDC as a percent of net income ratio in excess of 100%, indicating that none of the firm's earnings represented cash income. In contrast, Consolidated Edison Corporation reported an AFUDC to net income ratio of only 3%, indicating that its earnings were of much higher quality than those of El Paso Electric.

In the banking industry, an analyst must look to the quality of the loans the bank has made and the adequacy of loan loss reserves, in order to determine if reported net income figures accurately reflect the earnings for the period being reviewed. If loan loss reserves are not adequate, future earnings will be adversely affected if the bank must charge off a significant portion of its bad loans. In the same context, an analyst examining any firm must consider the quality of that firm's accounts receivable. If some receivables are not likely to be collected, then the future earnings of the firm will be reduced.

Second, a firm's earnings can be viewed as being of high quality the greater the proportion of those earnings which is derived from regularly recurring transactions. To the extent that reported earnings reflect the impact of non-recurring transactions, the quality of those earnings is reduced. For example, in the fourth quarter of 1985, Texas Commerce Bancshares (TCB) sold and leased back most of its corporate headquarters building. Since this building was carried on TCB's books at an amount less than the sale price, the firm was able to recognize an eighteen million dollar after-tax gain on the transaction. This transaction is of a non-recurring nature and should not be considered when evaluating the earnings capacity of the firm. Other, similar, non-recurring gains can emerge when a firm repurchases its debt on the open market at a price lower than the face value of that debt. Also, a firm may change its accounting treatment of inventories and record a significant gain from this transaction. These are only a few examples of significant non-recurring transactions. *The important point to remember is that earnings quality is lower the greater the proportion on non-recurring items in a firm's reported earnings figures.*

Balance Sheet Quality

The quality of a firm's balance sheet should also be of concern to a financial analyst. If the assets on a firm's balance sheet have a market value equal to or greater than the book value at which they are being carried, this enhances the quality of the firm's balance sheet. In contrast, if a significant portion of the assets of a firm have a market value substantially below book value, the quality of the firm's balance sheet is reduced. Over the last decade we have seen many firms in the so-called "smokestack industries" record large losses as significant portions of their assets are abandoned and written off as losses. For example, during 1985 Union Carbide closed and revalued chemical plants for a $620 million after-tax write-off. Ideal Basic revalued its potash operations for a $125 million after-tax write-off, and Manville closed its asbestos plants, taking a $120 million after-tax write-off. These actions greatly reduce the equity ratios for the firm. Similarly, if a firm has significant amounts of inventory which cannot be moved (such as the case of the Adam computers which

Coleco once produced), the quality of the balance sheet is reduced until the firm charges off this low quality inventory.

In addition to asset quality issues, an analyst should also be aware of hidden liabilities. These hidden liabilities may take the form of such things as long-term lease obligations, which do not appear on the firm's balance sheet, or unfunded pension obligations. For example, at year-end 1984, Chrysler reported unfunded pension obligations of $947 million, which represented 69 percent of its net worth. Pan Am's unfunded pension obligations at year-end 1984 represented 115 percent of its net worth. With large potential liabilities such as these, an analyst must be quite careful before drawing conclusions about the adequacy of a firm's capital structure, based upon an analysis of its reported balance sheet.

This list of balance sheet and earnings quality issues is certainly not all inclusive, but it does give an indication of the extent to which a surface analysis of a firm's financial statements can lead to misleading conclusions about the financial condition of that firm.

Using Financial Ratios to Forecast Future Financial Performance

One of the primary limitations of traditional financial ratio analysis is that it looks at only one ratio at a time and then relies on the analyst to form a judgment about the overall financial profile of the firm. Recently, more powerful statistical techniques have been applied to assist the analyst in making judgments about the financial condition of the firm.

Discriminant analysis is a statistical technique that helps the analyst classify observations (firms) into two or more predetermined groups based on certain characteristics of the observation. In the context of financial statement analysis, the characteristics are typically financial ratios.

One early application of discriminant analysis in finance was a model developed by Edward Altman to predict bankruptcy of firms.[15] Altman identified five financial ratios that contributed significantly to the predictive accuracy of his model. The basic model was developed from a sample of sixty-six manufacturing firms—half of which went bankrupt. The following is the final discriminant function derived by Altman:

$$Z = 0.012X_1 + 0.014X_2 + 0.033X_3 + 0.006X_4 + 0.999X_5, \quad \textbf{(6.20)}$$

where

Z = The discriminant function score of a firm.

X_1 = Net working capital/Total assets (percentage).

X_2 = Retained earnings/Total assets (percentage).

X_3 = EBIT/Total assets (percentage).

X_4 = Market value of total equity (common and preferred)/ Book value of total debt (percentage).

X_5 = Sales/Total assets (number of times).

[15] Edward I. Altman, "Financial Ratios, Discriminant Analysis, and the Prediction of Corporate Bankruptcy." *Journal of Finance* (Sept. 1968): 589–609.

On the basis of his analysis, Altman established a guideline Z score, which can be used to classify firms as either financially sound (a score above 2.675) or headed toward bankruptcy (a score below 2.675). The lower the score, the greater the probability of bankruptcy; the higher the score, the lower the probability of bankruptcy.

The Altman model can be applied to the Sandia Manufacturing Company data in 19X6 to help assess its long-term financial condition (the market price of Sandia's common stock is $20 per share):

$$X_1 = \frac{\text{Current assets} - \text{Current liabilities}}{\text{Total assets}} = \frac{\$50,190 - \$25,523}{\$81,890}$$

$$= 30.12\%.$$

$$X_2 = \frac{\text{Retained earnings}}{\text{Total assets}} = \frac{\$11,367}{\$81,890} = 13.88\%.$$

$$X_3 = \frac{\text{EBIT}}{\text{Total assets}} = \frac{\$11,520}{\$81,890} = 14.07\%.$$

$$X_4 = \frac{\text{Market value of total equity}}{\text{Book value of total debt}} = \frac{\$20/\text{share} \times 1,300 \text{ shares}}{\$25,523 + \$22,000}$$

$$= 54.71\%.$$

$$X_5 = \frac{\text{Sales}}{\text{Total assets}} = \frac{\$112,760}{\$81,890} = 1.38 \text{ times.}$$

By substituting these values into the Altman Z score equation we get the following:

$$Z = 0.012(30.12) + 0.014(13.88) + 0.033(14.07)$$
$$+ 0.006(54.71) + 0.999(1.38)$$
$$= 2.73.$$

This score is slightly above the 2.675 cutoff score and indicates that even though Sandia is not in the best financial condition, failure is not expected—at least over the next year or two (the forecasting horizon used by Altman with the best predictive accuracy).

Recent refinements of Altman's bankruptcy forecasting model have broadened the spectrum of firms to which it can be applied to include retailing as well as manufacturing firms.[16] The new model is about 70 percent accurate as much as five years prior to bankruptcy.

Inflation and Financial Statement Analysis

Inflation can cause a number of problems for the financial analyst who is trying to assess the performance of a firm over time and in comparison with other firms in the industry. In particular, *inventory profits,* or

---

[16] Edward I. Altman, R. G. Haldeman, and P. Narayanan. "Zeta Analysis: A New Model to Identify Bankruptcy Risk of Corporations." *Journal of Banking and Finance* (June 1977): 29–54.

short-lived increased profits that occur as a result of the timing of price increases, can make a significant difference in a firm's reported earnings from year to year.

For example, consider a supply company that buys equipment parts wholesale from the manufacturer for $4.00 each and sells them at a retail price of $5.00 each, realizing a profit of $1.00 per unit. Suppose the manufacturer announces a price increase of $0.50 per unit to $4.50, effective on the first of next month. If the supply company passes the increase on to customers and announces a price increase of its own to $5.50, also effective on the first of next month, it will realize a gross profit of $1.50 on every unit sold, which originally cost $4.00. In other words, the company will make additional profit on the units already in inventory *prior to the price increase*. Once it begins purchasing parts from the manufacturer at the new price of $4.50 per unit, it will revert to its original $1.00 profit. In the meantime, however, the timing of the price increase will allow the company to enjoy short-lived increased profits, or inventory profits.

Most companies do not want to pay income taxes on inventory profits, preferring to use these funds to replenish inventories—especially in inflationary times. Fortunately, there is a way of avoiding or deferring the necessity of reporting these higher profits. The *last-in, first-out* (LIFO) inventory valuation method assumes that the items a firm uses from inventory are those that were acquired most recently. Thus, they can be *priced out* of the inventory based on the most recent inventory acquisition costs. In contrast, the *first-in, first-out* (FIFO) method of inventory valuation, which assumes that the items a firm uses from inventory are the oldest items in inventory, results in the firm's having to show a higher profit and therefore pay higher income taxes.

During the 1960s, most large U.S. corporations were using the FIFO method. Inflation at that time was low to moderate, and the majority of companies thought it desirable to report their net income as high as possible. By 1974, however, inflation rates had risen to about 12 percent, and companies that were experiencing increasing inventory profits began switching to the LIFO method in an attempt to conserve cash by paying less income taxes.

The accounting method used for inventory will affect a firm's profits and its balance sheet. Hence, any financial ratio that contains balance sheet inventory figures (for example, the total asset turnover ratio) or net income will vary from one firm to another, depending on the firm's accounting treatment of inventory. Another effect of inflation on financial statements is the tendency for the value of fixed assets to be understated. Also, to the extent that inflation causes a rise in interest rates, the value of long-term debt outstanding will decline. Thus, a firm will appear to be more financially levered in an inflationary period than is actually the case.

In an attempt to provide users of financial data with a better indication of the effects of inflation, the Financial Accounting Standards Board (FASB) issued *Statement of Accounting Standards No. 33,* which requires companies to supply additional information to indicate the effects of inflation on their performance over time. FASB *Statement No. 33* requires that a firm restate its "income from continuing operations" as if depreciation were based on assets all purchased with the same purchasing power. This requirement eliminates the distortion caused by a $1 million asset purchase in 1970 being treated the same as a $1 million asset purchased in 1984. Clearly, the purchasing power of a dollar was much greater in 1970 than in 1984.

FASB *Statement No. 33* also requires that a firm present a five-year comparison of such financial data as operating revenues, cash dividends, and market price per share. These financial data must be stated in terms of constant purchasing power. All inflation adjustments under FASB *Statement No. 33* are made using the Consumer Price Index for All Urban Consumers. At this point it is not clear whether the inflation reporting requirements under FASB *Statement No. 33* will be of any great value in assisting financial analysts. Nevertheless, these inflation-adjusted statements do provide a rough indication of the effects of inflation on a firm's performance over time. Table 6-5 shows the inflation adjusted financial statements provided by Pennzoil in its annual report.

Table 6-5   **Inflation Adjusted Financial Statements for Pennzoil**

Consolidated Statement of Income Adjusted for Current Cost

	Year Ended December 31, 1984	
	Historical Dollars	Adjusted for Current Cost
	(in thousands)	
Net sales	$2,348,676	$2,348,676
Costs and expenses		
Cost of goods sold and operating expenses	1,198,282	1,207,701
Depreciation, depletion, and amortization	380,619	483,964
Other expenses	339,757	339,757
Interest expense, net	80,347	80,347
Income tax	136,123	136,123
Income from continuing operations	$ 213,548	$ 100,784
Gain from decline in purchasing power of net		
amounts owed		$ 70,368
Increase in current cost of inventories and		
property, plant, and equipment during 1984*		$ 139,583
Less effect of increase in general price level		
during 1984		142,123
Excess (deficit) of increase in specific prices over		
increase in general price level		$ (2,540)

*At December 31, 1984, current cost of inventory was $292,569,000 (compared to historical cost of $151,852,000), and current cost of property, plant, and equipment, net of accumulated depreciation, depletion, and amortization, was $3,002,443,000 (compared to historical cost of $2,217,332,000).

As required by Statements of Financial Accounting Standards Nos. 33, 39, 69, and 82, supplemental "current cost" financial information has been presented employing specific price indices and other methods to measure the impact of specific price level changes in the businesses in which Pennzoil operates.

Sales and all expenses, other than depreciation, depletion, and amortization and cost of sales, are assumed to have occurred ratably throughout the years and, accordingly, have not been restated.

Table 6-5   (Continued)

Selected Financial Data Adjusted for Changing Prices	1984	1983	1982	1981	1980
	(Dollar amounts expressed in thousands except per share amounts)				
Net sales					
Historical dollars	$2,348,676	$2,064,430	$2,117,707	$2,270,325	$2,012,380
Adjusted for general inflation	$2,348,676	2,152,985	2,279,593	2,593,705	2,537,491
Income from continuing operations					
Historical dollars	$ 213,548	180,482	218,682	242,980	235,325
Current cost**	$ 100,784	86,576	104,226	130,862	143,931
Earnings per share from continuing operations					
Historical dollars	$ 3.89	3.35	4.18	4.65	4.48
Current cost**	$ 1.64	1.43	1.95	2.45	2.68
Net assets at year end					
Historical dollars	$ 955,093	1,229,045	1,180,013	1,102,978	1,023,102
Current cost	$1,909,900	2,274,980	2,294,577	2,253,366	2,344,270
Excess (deficit) of increase in specific prices over increase in general price level	$ (2,540)	(3,730)	71,774	(83,808)	78,591
Gain from decline in purchasing power of net amounts owed	$ 70,368	61,842	57,835	116,931	153,078
Cash dividends declared per common share					
Historical dollars	$ 2.20	2.20	2.20	2.20	2.00
Adjusted for general inflation	$ 2.20	2.29	2.37	2.51	2.52
Market price per share at year end					
Historical dollars	$ 44.50	34.00	35.13	48.00	50.38
Adjusted for general inflation	$ 43.78	34.86	37.39	53.07	60.68
Average consumer price index—urban consumers	311.2	298.4	289.1	272.4	246.8

**Excludes gain from decline in purchasing power of net amounts owed.
Reprinted with permission from Pennzoil Company. (1984 Annual Report)

Depreciation, depletion, and amortization expenses, as adjusted, are based on the same methods and estimated lives used in the historical financial statements. Income tax expense does not reflect any reductions for increased costs on a current cost basis, because current tax regulations do not permit a deduction for these increases. Thus, the 1984 effective tax rate (55.9% for current cost) is significantly higher than the rate in the primary statements (38.2%). During periods of persistent inflation such a tax policy effectively results in a higher tax on shareholders' investments in Pennzoil.

Pennzoil's earnings, adjusted for current cost, are significantly lower than the reported historical net income reflected in conventional historical cost financial statements. This reduction in earnings arises from the "hidden" cost of maintaining productive capacity during inflationary periods.

During periods of inflation, holders of money and other monetary assets lose purchasing power because a given amount of money will buy fewer goods and services. Conversely, debtors gain during these periods because their debts are repayable in dollars of reduced purchasing power. Because Pennzoil's monetary liabilities exceeded its monetary assets during 1984, a "holding" gain resulted. This gain arises because Pennzoil's net amounts owed will be repaid with "cheaper" inflated dollars. The gain is unrealized and does not represent funds available for distribution to shareholders.

The adjusted net assets at year-end reflect an estimate of common shareholders' equity after adjusting inventory and net property, plant, and equipment for the effects of inflation.

The changing price data included in the summarized Consolidated Statement of Income and the accompanying five-year supplemental financial data are expressed in average 1984 dollars. Because the current cost method involves the use of assumptions and estimates, the supplemental changing price data should be viewed in that context as approximations and not as precise indicators of inflation or the value of the assets of Pennzoil.

Inventory profits and inflation are only two factors that can affect a firm's reported earnings. Differences in the reporting of earnings, the recognition of sales, and other factors also can make comparisons between firms somewhat misleading. Again, the good financial analyst will always "go behind" the figures stated on a firm's income statement or balance sheet to find out what is actually occurring within a company. It should be obvious at this point that financial analysis is no simple matter. At first, it may appear as if all it involves is the evaluation of a certain number of apparently clear-cut ratios. As is evident from this chapter, however, it involves a great deal more.

Summary

- *Financial ratios* are statistical yardsticks that relate two numbers generally taken from a firm's income statements and balance sheets.
- Financial ratios fall into five categories:

  1. *Liquidity ratios,* which measure a firm's ability to meet its maturing obligations.
  2. *Activity ratios,* which measure how efficiently a firm is using resources to generate sales.
  3. *Leverage ratios,* which measure how much debt the firm is employing to finance assets.
  4. *Profitability ratios,* which measure the firm's ability to generate profits on sales, assets, and owners' investment.
  5. *Market-based ratios,* which measure the market's (investors') perceptions of a firm's performance and risk.

- *Trend analysis* introduces the element of time into financial ratio analysis. It gives the analyst a more dynamic view of a company's situation than does a pure comparative financial ratio analysis alone.
- The relationship of the return on investment (ROI) to "margin" and "turnover" can be used to determine if one or both of the two is deficient in contributing to the profitability of a firm.
- To gain further insight into the relative financial position of a firm, the analyst must compare the financial ratios with *industry averages.* The more diversified the firm, the more difficult it will be to make such a comparison. Two major sources of industry ratios are Dun and Bradstreet and Robert Morris Associates.
- The quality of a firm's earnings is higher the greater the proportion of cash earnings to total earnings and the greater the proportion of recurring income to total income.
- The quality of a firm's balance sheet is enhanced the greater the ratio of the market value of the firm's assets to the book value of those assets and the lessor the amount of "hidden liabilities" which appears on the firm's balance sheet.
- Financial ratios have been used in conjunction with sophisticated statistical techniques to forecast events such as bankruptcy of a firm.

- *Inflation* can have a significant impact on a firm's reported earnings. For example, it can influence the firm to choose a different inventory valuation method and cost accounting system. When comparing the performance of two or more firms, the financial analyst should recognize that the firms may use different accounting methods to calculate net income.

FOCUS ON CORPORATE PRACTICE

Union Carbide's Paper Boom*

If the sheer magnitude of numbers makes news, then the effect of three accounting changes announced January 24 by Union Carbide Corporation qualifies at once. Those changes will add $129 million to Carbide's regular earnings for 1980, pushing reported profits some 25% higher than analysts initially had projected. When a related, but extraordinary, one-time credit of $214 million is added in, Carbide's final net income may soar 70 percent over earlier estimates.

The impact, however, will be reflected only in the earnings the company reports to shareholders. How Carbide computes income and actual taxes for the Internal Revenue Service will not change, and thus its cash flow will not be affected by the accounting switch.

Even as analysts argue whether the accounting shift at Carbide provides more realistic or less useful numbers, or simply confuses investors, it could be a portent of similar moves by other industrial companies as they begin to wrestle with inflation accounting and changing notions of what depreciation allowances should reflect. As in other areas of change, analysts are sure to demand more data on corporate depreciation policies to help track what is afoot.

Taking Tax Credits

To be sure, not all of the accounting changes were made at Carbide's choice. The Financial Accounting Standards Board (FASB) recently mandated that certain interest costs associated with new construction projects be capitalized, thus deferring those costs to later years, after the plant goes on stream. That rule applies to all major companies. For Carbide, the change will add an extra $20 million to this year's reported earnings.

The move bringing most impact for 1980 earnings, however, was at the company's discretion. From here on, Carbide says that it will recognize on its shareholder books the full amount of any investment tax credit (ITC) allowed by the government on new plant and equipment in the year that those investments are made—just as it does for IRS purposes. Previously, for financial reporting, the company reflected those credits in book earnings year by year over the life of the asset. That shift to the flow-through method will add $17 million to Carbide's regular 1980 earnings.

But Carbide also has considerable ITC amounts on the books that it had deferred from previous years. So, in addition, during the first quarter of 1980, it will take a one-time $214 million extraordinary credit to income in order to make the balance sheet reflect the shift to flow-through accounting.

Louis G. Peloubet, Carbide's controller, argues that if the ITC is deferred, its impact on earnings is blunted by inflation. Rather than providing an immediate boost to reported profits, the ITC is taken in bit by bit over ten or more years, while costs rise and the dollar's value shrinks. With flow-through treatment, he asserts, earnings better reflect the current impact of investment decisions and are more consistent with cash flow. Studies made by Price Waterhouse & Co. and the American Institute of Certified Public Accountants conclude that more than 75% of the companies in the chemical industry and nearly 90% of all big industrial corporations now use ITC flow-through accounting. Carbide's switch,

How Union Carbide's Accounting Changes Will Boost its 1980 Earnings

	Net Income (millions of dollars)
Estimated income before changes*	$481
Additions from accounting changes	
Longer 'life' for equipment lowers depreciation charge	92
Capitalizing construction financing defers some interest cost to future	20
1980 investment tax credit flow-through cuts income tax	17
Income before extraordinary gain	610
Flow-through of unamortized prior year tax credits produces one-time gain	214
Estimated income after changes	824

*Based on mid-range of analysts' projections.
Data: Lynch, Jones & Ryan Institutional Brokers Estimate System, Union Carbide, BW estimate

Peloubet contends, now makes his company's results more comparable with most of its competitors.

A Cost Reduction

Among the five largest chemical companies, only Du Pont Co. continues to defer and amortize investment tax credits. Outside the industry, companies such as General Electric, General Motors, and AT&T follow similar policies. "It's a difference in philosophy," explains John J. Quindlen, Du Pont's controller. "We look upon the investment tax credit as a reduction in the cost of the related asset."

Along with rival Dow Chemical Co., Du Pont also differs from the other big chemical companies in the use of accelerated depreciation for both tax and investor accounting. Under that method, depreciation charges are higher during the early life of new plant and equipment; both taxes and net income are lower, and the tax break boosts cash flow.

In contrast, a majority of companies, including Union Carbide, use accelerated depreciation only for IRS purposes. That nails down the tax benefit. But for shareholder reports, these companies employ a straightline accounting method that recognizes depreciation charges in equal annual amounts over the life of the asset. Since these initial depreciation charges are lower than those using accelerated methods, reported earnings for most such companies are higher.

A Welcome Cushion

Many analysts like the conservative cushion that ITC deferral and accelerated depreciation provide. Since rapid inflation has rendered present depreciation charges woefully inadequate to cover the eventual replacement of plant and equipment, they argue that such an approach puts reported earnings more in line with current economic reality. "Accelerated depreciation gets you closer to today's world," says a Dow spokesman. "For us, it does a better job." Adds Du Pont's Quindlen: "In the chemical industry, there's a high exposure to technological obsolescence. We're satisfied that our present accounting is appropriate and prudent."

A few skeptics call such adjustments a half measure at best. And other observers argue that they may be unnecessary in light of the FASB's new inflation disclosure requirements. Beginning with 1979 annual reports, due later this spring, investors for the first time will be able to compare operating earnings based on traditional historical costs with earnings adjusted for inflation.

Up to now, Union Carbide had its own way of at least partially adjusting reported earnings for inflation. It used relatively short IRS guideline lives of machinery and equipment to calculate depreciation charges for both tax and investor reporting. Most companies in the chemical industry use somewhat longer lives for shareholder reports—lives more akin to the length of time they actually plan to use the assets. Carbide concluded that its policy gave it higher depreciation charges than many of its competitors and left it with too many assets that were fully depreciated on the books but still in use. So for future investor reporting, Carbide will lengthen by about 35% the asset lives for most machinery and equipment.

A Forerunner

Over the long term, that change is likely to bring the biggest boost to Carbide's reported earnings. For 1980, the company figures it will add $92 million. The shift to longer asset lives also will mean that Carbide will show up a bit better when historical-cost earnings are compared with inflation-adjusted earnings. Even so, the gap between those figures will remain larger than similar comparisons for Du Pont and Dow, its closest competitors.

Carbide's move to longer asset lives could be a forerunner of similar changes at other companies. For one thing, if Congress approves legislation for even shorter depreciation lives for tax purposes, such as the proposed 10/5/3 scheme, the already tenuous link between tax and actual service lives of assets will vanish. More corporations may then revamp their shareholder calculations.

As more investors compare historical cost and inflation-adjusted earnings, U.S. companies may be tempted to follow their counterparts in Britain. Martin Gibbs, partner at the British brokerage firm of Phillps Drew, notes that when companies there started to compute inflation-adjusted earnings, they found that earnings were coming out too low, so they started to spread depreciation over a longer period.

The British Experience

The experience of the British giant, Imperial Chemical Industries Ltd., is a case in point. "In the past, we had partially accounted for inflation by shortening asset lives," explains Harry E. Smith, ICI's assistant controller. In the early 1970s, for example, the company reduced the usable life for a basic petrochemical plant from 12 or 13 years to 10 years, and it still uses a 10-year life in historical-cost accounts.

But Smith adds that that policy now has been overstating inflation for several years. In calculating its current costs for inflation-adjusted earnings, he says, "we've added about 50% to the remaining asset lives."

If that trend develops in the U.S., it opens the door to wide swings in reported earnings, as the Union Carbide experience proves. And since those changes now are not always revealed, analysts are sure to demand more disclosure on corporate depreciation policies and the lives of existing assets so that they may better evaluate the overall effect.

Questions and Topics for Discussion

1. What are the primary limitations of ratio analysis as a technique of financial statement analysis?
2. What is the major limitation of the current ratio as a measure of a firm's liquidity? How may this limitation be overcome?
3. What problems may be indicated by an average collection period that is substantially above or below the industry average?
4. What problems may be indicated by an inventory turnover ratio that is substantially above or below the industry average?
5. What factors limit the use of the fixed asset turnover ratio in comparative analyses?
6. What are the three most important determinants of a firm's return on stockholders' equity?
7. What specific effects can the use of alternative accounting procedures have on the validity of comparative financial analyses?
8. How can inflation affect the comparability of financial ratios between firms?
9. What is the relationship between a firm's P/E multiple and that firm's risk and growth potential?
10. Discuss the general factors which influence the quality of a company's reported earnings and its balance sheet.
11. The electric utility industry is regulated with the goal of providing a company a fair opportunity to earn a return on common equity capital equal to that company's cost of common equity. Under these circumstances, what market to book ratio would you expect the average electric utility to experience?
12. Why would you anticipate a lower P/E ratio for a typical natural gas utility than for a computer technology firm, such as Digital Equipment?

Problems*

1. Vanity Press, Inc., has annual credit sales of $1,600,000 and a gross profit margin of 30 percent.
   a. If the firm wishes to maintain an average collection period of 50 days, what level of accounts receivable should it carry? (Assume a 360-day year.)
   b. The inventory turnover for this industry averages 6 times. If all of Vanity's sales are on credit, what level of inventory should the firm maintain in order to achieve the same inventory turnover figure as the industry?
2. Using the data in the following table for a number of firms in the same industry, do the following:
   a. Compute the total asset turnover, the net profit margin, the equity multiplier, and the return on equity for each firm.
   b. Evaluate each firm's performance by comparing the firms with one another and with the industry averages. Which firm or firms appear to be having problems? What corrective action would you suggest the submarginal firms take? Finally, what additional data would you want to have on hand when conducting your analyses?

	Firm			
	A	B	C	D
Sales (in millions of dollars)	20	10	15	25
Net income after tax (in millions of dollars)	3	0.5	2.25	3
Total assets (in millions of dollars)	15	7.5	15	24
Stockholders' equity (in millions of dollars)	10	5.0	14	10

* Color numbers denote problems which have check answers provided at the end of the book.

Industry Averages

Total asset turnover	1.4 times
Net profit margin	0.12
Equity multiplier	1.5 times
Return on equity	0.25

3. Pacific Fixtures lists the following accounts as part of its balance sheet.

Total assets	$10,000,000
Accounts payable	$ 2,000,000
Notes payable (8%)	1,000,000
Bonds (10%)	3,000,000
Common stock at par	1,000,000
Contributed capital in excess of par	500,000
Retained earnings	2,500,000
Total liabilities and stockholders' equity	$10,000,000

Compute the return on stockholders' equity if the company has sales of $20 million and the following net profit margin:

a. 3 percent.

b. 5 percent.

The following data for the Jackson Guitar Company should be used to answer Problems 4 through 10.

Jackson Guitar Company's Balance Sheet
December 31, 19X1

Cash and securities	$ 240,000	Accounts payable	$ 380,000
Accounts receivable	320,000	Notes payable (9%)	420,000
Inventory	1,040,000	Other current liabilities	50,000
Total current assets	$1,600,000	Total current liabilities	$ 850,000
Net plant and equipment	800,000	Long-term debt (10%)	800,000
Total assets	$2,400,000	Stockholders' equity	750,000
		Total liabilities and	
		stockholders' equity	$2,400,000

Income Statement
for the Year Ended December 31, 19X1

Net sales (all on credit)		$3,000,000
Cost of goods sold		1,800,000
Gross margin		$1,200,000
Operating expenses:		
Selling	$300,000	
General and administrative	560,000	
Total operating expenses		860,000
Earnings before interest and taxes		$ 340,000
Interest:		
Notes	$ 37,800	
Long-term debt	80,000	
Total interest charges		117,800
Earnings before taxes		$ 222,200
Federal income tax (40%)		88,880
Earnings after taxes		$ 133,320

Industry Averages

Current ratio	2.5 times
Quick ratio	1.1 times
Average collection period (360-day year)	35 days
Inventory turnover ratio	2.4 times
Total asset turnover ratio	1.4 times
Times interest earned ratio	3.5 times
Net profit margin ratio	4.0 percent
Return on investment ratio	5.6 percent
Total assets/stockholders' equity (equity multiplier) ratio	3.0 times
Return on stockholders' equity ratio	16.8 percent
P/E ratio	9.0 times

4. Evaluate the liquidity position of Jackson relative to that of the average firm in the industry. Consider the current ratio, the quick ratio, and the net working capital for Jackson. What problems, if any, are suggested by this analysis?

5. Evaluate Jackson's performance by looking at key activity ratios. Are any problems apparent from this analysis?

6. Evaluate the financial risk of Jackson by examining its times interest earned ratio and its equity multiplier ratio relative to the same industry average ratios.

7. Evaluate the profitability of Jackson relative to that of the average firm in its industry.

8. Give an overall evaluation of the performance of Jackson relative to other firms in its industry.

9. Construct a Du Pont chart analysis for Jackson. What areas appear to have the greatest need for improvement?

10. Jackson's current P/E ratio is 7 times. What factor(s) are most likely to account for this ratio relative to the higher industry average ratio?

11. Tarheel Furniture Company is planning to establish a wholly owned subsidiary to manufacture upholstery fabrics. Tarheel expects to earn $1 million after tax on the venture during the first year. The president of Tarheel wants to know what the subsidiary's balance sheet would look like. The president believes that it would be advisable to begin the new venture with ratios that are similar to the industry average.

Tarheel plans to make all sales on credit. All calculations assume a 360-day year. In your computations you should round all numbers to the nearest $1,000.

Based upon the industry average financial ratios presented here, complete the projected balance sheet for Tarheel's upholstery subsidiary.

	Industry Averages
Current ratio	2:1
Quick ratio	1:1
Net profit margin ratio	5 percent
Average collection period ratio	5 days
Debt ratio	50 percent
Total asset turnover ratio	4 times
Current debt/net worth ratio	20 percent

Forecasted Upholstery Subsidiary Balance Sheet

Cash	——	Accounts payable	——
Accounts receivable	——	Total current liabilities	——
Inventory	——	Long-term debt	——
Total current assets	——	Total debt	——
Fixed assets	——	Stockholders' equity	——
Total assets	——	Total liabilities and stockholders' equity	——

12. Using one (or more) of the sources of comparative financial data mentioned in this chapter, evaluate the performance of Bethlehem Steel Corporation versus the performance of Carpenter Technology. In particular, evaluate the total asset turnover, the fixed asset turnover, the net profit margin, the return on investment, and the return on stockholders' equity for each firm. Then do the following:

   a. Determine which firm seems to be performing better. What criterion did you use in reaching this conclusion?

   b. Point out some problems Bethlehem Steel seems to be having.

   c. Using the latest 5 years of data, perform a financial trend analysis on Bethlehem Steel Corporation. Consider such ratios as the current, quick, inventory turnover, average collection period, total asset turnover, net profit margin, return on investment, and return on stockholders' equity ratios. What can you say about the trend in the financial health of Bethlehem Steel?

13. The Jamesway Printing Corporation has current assets of $3.0 million. Of this total, $1.0 million is inventory, $0.5 million is cash, $1.0 million is accounts receivable, and the balance is marketable securities. Jamesway has $1.5 million in current liabilities.

   a. What are the current and the quick ratios for Jamesway?

   b. If Jamesway takes $0.25 million in cash and pays off $0.25 million of current liabilities, what happens to its current and quick ratios? What happens to its real liquidity?

   c. If Jamesway sellls $0.5 million of its accounts receivable to a bank and uses the proceeds to pay off short-term debt obligations, what happens to its current and quick ratios?

   d. If Jamesway sells $1.0 million in new stock and places the proceeds in marketable securities, what happens to its current and quick ratios?

   e. What do these examples illustrate about the current and quick ratios?

14. Red Raider Corporation had sales in 19X1 of $40 million, 30 percent of which were cash. If Red Raider normally carries 60 days of credit sales in accounts receivable, what are its average accounts receivable balances? (Assume a 360-day year.)

15. Mustang Oil Company had a return on stockholders' equity of 20 percent during 19X1. Its total asset turnover was 2 times, and its equity multiplier was 1.5 times. Calculate Mustang's net profit margin.

16. The Sooner Pigskin Company has total assets of $100 million. Of this total, $40 million was financed with common equity and $60 million with debt (both long and short term). Its average accounts receivable balance is $20 million, and this represents an 80-day average collection period. Sooner believes it can reduce its average collection period from 80 days to 60 days without affecting sales or the dollar amount of net income after tax (currently $5 million). What will be the effect of this action on Sooner's return

on investment and its return on stockholders' equity if the funds received by reducing the average collection period are used to buy back its common stock at book value? What impact will this action have on Sooner's debt ratio?

17. Hoya Enterprises has a net profit margin of 10 percent and earnings after taxes of $600,000. Its current balance sheet follows:

Current assets	$1,800,000	Current liabilities	$ 600,000
Fixed assets	3,200,000	Long-term debt	2,000,000
Total assets	$5,000,000	Common stock (at par)	500,000
		Retained earnings	1,900,000
		Total liabilities and	
		stockholders' equity	$5,000,000

a. Calculate Hoya's return on equity.
b. The industry average ratios are as follows:

Net profit margin	6 percent
Total asset turnover	2.5 times
Equity multiplier	1.4 times

Compare Hoya Enterprises with the average firm in the industry. What is the source of the major differences between Hoya and the industry average ratios?

18. Given the following data for Profiteers, Inc., and the corresponding industry averages, perform a trend analysis of the return on investment and the return on stockholders' equity. Plot the data and discuss any trends that are apparent. Also, discuss the underlying causes of these trends.

	Years				
	19X1	19X2	19X3	19X4	19X5
Profiteers, Inc.					
Net profit margin	14%	12%	11%	9%	10%
Asset turnover	1.26×	1.22×	1.20×	1.19×	1.21×
Equity multiplier	1.34×	1.40×	1.61×	1.65×	1.63×
Industry Averages					
Net profit margin	12%	11%	11%	10%	10%
Asset turnover	1.25×	1.27×	1.30×	1.31×	1.34×
Equity multiplier	1.42×	1.45×	1.47×	1.51×	1.53×

19. If a company sells additional common stock and uses the proceeds to increase its inventory level and to increase its cash balances, what is the near-term (immediate) impact (increase, decrease, no change) of this transaction on the following ratios?
   a. Current ratio
   b. Return on stockholders' equity
   c. Quick ratio
   d. Debt to total assets
   e. Total asset turnover

20. Palmer Chocolates, a maker of chocolates that specializes in Easter candy, had the following inventories over the past year:

Month	Inventory Amount
January	$25,000,000
February	60,000,000
March	90,000,000
April	30,000,000
May	20,000,000
June	22,000,000
July	25,000,000
August	38,000,000
September	50,000,000
October	60,000,000
November	70,000,000
December	30,000,000

Palmer had sales of $290,000,000 over the past year. Cost of goods sold constituted 50 percent of sales. Calculate Palmer's inventory turnover using beginning of year inventory, end of year inventory, and a monthly average inventory. Which method do you feel is most appropriate? Why?

21. The stock of Jenkins Corporation, a major steel producer, is currently selling for $50/share. The book value per share is $125. In contrast, the price per share of Dataquest's stock is $40, compared to a book value per share of $10. Dataquest is a leading software developer, and has a copyright on the best-selling database management program. Why do these two firms have such dramatically different market to book ratios?

22. Lane Enterprises had sales of $20 million and earnings after tax of $1,600,000. The firm had a total asset turnover of 2.5 times. The industry average was 2.0 times. The equity accounts for Lane are as follows:

Common stock at par	$ 600,000
Contributed capital in excess of par	2,400,000
Retained earnings	3,400,000

The following ratios represent averages for Lane's industry:

Net profit margin	6%
Total asset turnover	2 times
Equity multiplier	2.08 times

a. Use the Du Pont analysis to calculate Lane's return on equity.
b. Compare Lane's performance to the industry average.

23. Jacks Snakkz has a net profit margin of 8% and earnings after tax of $2,000,000. Its current balance sheet is as follows:

Current assets	$ 6,000,000	Current liabilities	$ 3,500,000
Fixed assets	10,000,000	Long-term debt	5,500,000
Total assets	$16,000,000	Common stock at par	2,000,000
		Retained earnings	5,000,000
		Total liabilities and capital	$16,000,000

a. Calculate Jacks' return on equity.

b. Industry average ratios are:

Net profit margin	10%
Total asset turnover	2.0 times
Equity multiplier	1.5 times

What does a comparison of Jacks Snakkz to these averages indicate about the firm's strengths and weaknesses?

c. Jacks has inventories of $3.2 million. Compute the firm's quick ratio.

Selected References

Altman, Edward I., R. G. Haldeman, and P. Narayanan. "Zeta Analysis: A New Model to Identify Bankruptcy Risk of Corporations." *Journal of Banking and Finance* (June 1977): 29–54.

Chen, Kung H., and Thomas A. Shimerda. "An Empirical Analysis of Useful Financial Ratios." *Financial Management* (Spring 1981): 51–60.

Foster, George. *Financial Statement Analysis,* 3rd edition. Englewood Cliffs, N.J.: Prentice-Hall, 1986.

Horrigan, James C. "A Short History of Financial Ratio Analysis." *Accounting Review* (April 1968): 284–294.

Lev, Baruch. *Financial Statement Analysis: A New Approach.* Englewood Cliffs, N.J.: Prentice-Hall, 1974.

Murray, Roger F. "The Penn Central Debacle: Lessons for Financial Analysis." *Journal of Finance* (May 1971): 327–332.

7

THE ANALYSIS OF OPERATING AND FINANCIAL LEVERAGE

A Financial Dilemma

Eastern Airlines versus Delta Airlines

The airline industry is subject to substantial cyclical variability. During recessions, for example, airline profits frequently decline substantially. The high level of fixed costs airlines incur is one cause of this high degree of profit variability. It costs very little less to fly a plane that is 50 percent full than to fly one that is 70 percent full. Also, with deregulation, airlines have been subject to substantial price competition from each other. Hence, when airline passenger traffic diminishes during a recession and airlines cut fares to attract more traffic from competitors, profits tend to drop at a much more rapid rate. In contrast, when passenger traffic improves, airline profits tend to expand quickly.

A firm whose production processes require the payment of substantial fixed costs relative to total costs, such as an airline, is said to use a high level of operating leverage. High operating leverage tends to increase the variability of a firm's operating income (EBIT) over the business cycle as sales levels vary. Hence, investors associate high levels of operating leverage with high levels of business (operating) risk, assuming some amount of sales variability.

When a firm is exposed to high operating risk, it often tries to offset this risk by using relatively low amounts of debt financing, that is, by using low levels of financial leverage. The use of high levels of debt financing, with the associated fixed financing charges, further increases the variability of earnings per share as sales and operating income vary.

It might be expected that firms in the airline industry would tend to employ low levels of financial leverage in order to offset their high levels of operating risk. Delta Airlines had a long-term debt to net worth ratio of about 42 percent at the end of its fiscal 1985 year (June, 1985). Delta has been a consistently profitable airline.

In contrast, Eastern Airlines has not effectively balanced its high operating risk with low levels of financial risk. Its long-term debt to net worth ratio was 439 percent at the end of 1984. Eastern has had extremely volatile profits over the past decade. During most years it has incurred substantial losses.

The impact of the high degree of financial leverage used by Eastern, coupled with its high operating leverage, can be seen in the effects of sales revenue changes on earnings per share. During a recent quarter in 1985, Eastern's sales revenues increased by nearly 9 percent while its earnings per share rose by over 380 percent. During another quarter in 1985, sales declined by almost 6 percent, while earnings per share declined by over 35 percent. In contrast, Delta experienced a 204 percent gain in earnings per share for a 9 percent increase in sales revenues. Because of its lower level of financial leverage, Delta's profits have tended to be more stable than those of Eastern and investors have considered Delta to be less risky than Eastern. Indeed, Eastern has had many close scrapes with bankruptcy over the past three years, and has recently been acquired by Texas Air Corporation.

Risk is an important factor affecting the value of a firm's securities. Accordingly, both the firm's managers and outside analysts need to develop a complete understanding of the components of risk. This chapter considers important measures of operating and financial risk that can be used to assess the total risk of a firm.

Key Chapter Concepts

1. *Leverage* involves the use of fixed operating costs or fixed capital costs by a firm.
2. *Breakeven analysis* is a technique used to study the relationships between a firm's sales, fixed operating costs, variable operating costs, and operating income (EBIT) at various levels of output.
   a. The breakeven point is that level of output where the total revenues received by the firm are just equal to total operating costs.
   b. Breakeven analysis can be performed either graphically or algebraically.
3. The *degree of operating leverage (DOL)* is defined as the percentage change in EBIT resulting from a one percent change in sales.
   a. The degree of operating leverage approaches a maximum as the firm comes closer to operating at its breakeven level of output.
   b. All other things being equal, the higher a firm's DOL, the greater is its business risk.
   c. Business risk, the inherent variability of a firm's EBIT, is also influenced by the variability of sales and operating costs over time.
4. The *degree of financial leverage (DFL)* is defined as the percentage change in earnings per share (EPS) resulting from a one percent change in EBIT.
   a. The degree of financial leverage approaches a maximum as the firm comes closer to operating at its loss level, the level where EPS = $0.
   b. All other things being equal, the higher a firm's DFL, the greater is its financial risk.
   c. Financial risk, the additional variability of a firm's EPS that results from the use of financial leverage, can also be measured by various financial ratios, such as the debt to total assets ratio, and the times interest earned ratio.
5. The *degree of combined leverage (DCL)* is defined as the percentage change in earnings per share resulting from a one percent change in sales. It is also equal to the DOL for a company times that company's DFL. The degree of combined leverage used by a firm is a measure of the overall variability of EPS, as sales levels vary, due to the use of fixed operating and capital costs.

Glossary of New Terms

Breakeven analysis A technique used to examine the relationship between a firm's sales, costs, and profits at various levels of output. It is sometimes termed *cost-volume-profit analysis*.

Business risk The inherent variability or uncertainty of a firm's operating earnings (EBIT).

Contribution margin The difference between price and variable cost per unit in breakeven analysis.

Degree of combined leverage (DCL) The percentage change in a firm's earnings per share (EPS) resulting from a 1 percent change in sales or output. This is also equal to the degree of operating leverage times the degree of financial leverage used by the firm.

Degree of financial leverage (DFL) The percentage change in a firm's EPS resulting from a 1 percent change in EBIT.

Degree of operating leverage (DOL) The percentage change in a firm's EBIT resulting from a 1 percent change in sales or output.

Financial leverage The extent to which a firm is financed by securities having fixed costs or charges, such as debt and preferred stock.

Financial risk The additional variability of a company's earnings per share that results from the use of fixed-cost sources of funds, such as debt and preferred stock. In general, the more financial leverage a firm uses, the greater its financial risk.

Fixed costs Costs that do not vary as the level of a firm's output varies.

Operating leverage The extent to which a firm uses assets having fixed costs.

Total risk The variability of returns to a firm's shareholders.

Variable costs Costs that vary in close relationship with changes in a firm's level of output.

Introduction

The concepts of operating and financial leverage are useful to financial analysis, planning, and control. In finance, *leverage* is defined as a firm's use of assets and liabilities having fixed costs in an attempt to increase potential returns to stockholders. Specifically, operating leverage involves the use of *assets* having fixed costs, whereas financial leverage involves the use of *liabilities* (and *preferred stock*) having fixed costs.

A firm utilizes operating and financial leverage in the hope of earning returns in excess of the fixed costs of the assets and liabilities (and preferred stock), thereby increasing the returns to common stockholders. Leverage is a two-edged sword, however, since it also increases the *variability* (or risk) of these returns. If, for example, a firm earns returns that are *less* than the fixed costs of assets and liabilities, then the use of leverage can actually *decrease* the returns to common stockholders. Thus, leverage magnifies shareholders' potential losses as well as potential gains. Leverage concepts are particularly revealing to the financial analyst in that they highlight the *risk-return tradeoffs* of various types of financial decisions.

This chapter begins by discussing the relationship between a firm's use of leverage and the income statement. It then moves to the concept of breakeven analysis. Next, the measurement of operating leverage and its relationship to risk is illustrated. This is followed by an examination of financial leverage and its relationship to risk. And, finally, the chapter concludes with a discussion of the combined effects of operating and financial leverage on a firm's overall level of risk and returns.

Leverage and the Income Statement

Financial statements of the Allegan Manufacturing Company are referred to throughout this chapter for purposes of illustration. Table 7-1 contains two types of income statements for the firm, a traditional format and a revised format. The traditional format shows various categories of costs as separate entries. *Operating costs* include such items as the cost of goods sold and general, administrative, and selling expenses. Interest charges and preferred dividends, which represent *capital costs,* are listed separately, as are income taxes.

The revised format is more useful in leverage analysis, since it divides the firm's operating costs into two categories, *fixed* and *variable.*

Fixed and Variable Costs

Over the short run, certain operating costs within a firm vary directly with the level of sales while other costs remain constant, regardless of changes in this level. Costs that move in close relationship to changes in sales are called *variable costs.* They are tied to the number of units produced and sold by the firm rather than to the passage of time. They include raw material and direct labor costs, as well as sales commissions.

Over the short run, certain other operating costs are independent of sales or output levels. These are termed *fixed costs* and are primarily related to the passage of time. Depreciation on property, plant, and equipment; rent; insurance; lighting and heating bills; property taxes; and the salaries of management are all usually considered fixed costs. If a firm

Table 7-1   **Traditional and Revised Income Statements**

Allegan Manufacturing Company

Year Ending December 31, 19X1

Traditional Income Statement Format

	Sales		$5,000,000
Operating leverage	*Less:* Cost of goods sold	$2,500,000	
	Selling, administrative, and general expenses	1,500,000	
	Total operating costs		4,000,000
	Earnings before interest and taxes (EBIT)		1,000,000
	Less: Interest expense		250,000
	Earnings before taxes (EBT)		750,000
Financial leverage	*Less:* Income taxes (40% rate)		300,000
	Earnings after taxes (EAT)		450,000
	Less: Preferred stock dividends		150,000
	Earnings available to common stockholders		$ 300,000
	Earnings per share (EPS)—100,000 shares		$3.00

Revised Income Statement Format

	Sales		$5,000,000
Operating leverage	*Less: Variable* operating costs	$3,000,000	
	Fixed operating costs	1,000,000	
	Total operating costs		4,000,000
	Earnings before interest and taxes (EBIT)		1,000,000
Financial leverage	*Less: Fixed* capital costs (interest)		250,000
	Earnings before taxes (EBT)		750,000
	Less: Income taxes *(variable),* 40% rate		300,000
	Earnings after taxes (EAT)		450,000
	Less: Fixed capital costs (Preferred stock dividends)		150,000
	Earnings available to common stockholders		$ 300,000
	Earnings per share (EPS)—100,000 shares		$3.00

expects to keep functioning, it must continue to pay these costs, regardless of the sales level.

A third category, *semivariable costs,* can also be considered. Semivariable costs are costs that increase in a *stepwise* manner as output is increased. One cost that sometimes behaves in a stepwise manner is management salaries. Whereas these costs are generally considered fixed, this assumption is not always strictly valid. For example, Eastern Airlines, faced with mounting losses in late 1985 and early 1986, cut the salaries of its administrative personnel by 20 percent in early 1986.

Panels a, b, and c of Figure 7-1 show the behavior of variable, fixed, and semivariable costs, respectively, over the firm's output range.

Over the *long run,* all costs are variable. In time, a firm can change the size of its physical facilities and number of management personnel in response to changes in the level of sales. Not all costs can be classified as either completely fixed or variable; some have both fixed and variable components. Costs for utilities such as water and electricity frequently fall into this category. Whereas part of a firm's utility costs (such as electricity) are fixed and must be paid regardless of the level of sales or

Figure 7-1   **Behavior of (a) Variable, (b) Fixed, and (c) Semivariable Costs**

output, another part is variable in that it is directly tied to sales or production levels. In the revised format of Allegan's income statement, these are divided into their fixed and variable components and included in their respective categories of operating costs.

Note that in the revised income statement format, both interest charges and preferred dividends represent fixed capital costs. These costs are contractual in nature and thus are independent of a firm's level of sales or earnings. Also, note that income taxes represent a variable cost that is a function of earnings before taxes.

Operating and Financial Leverage

Whenever a firm incurs either fixed operating costs or fixed capital costs, it is said to be using *leverage*. Fixed obligations allow the firm to magnify small changes into larger ones—just as a small push on one end of an actual lever results in a large "lift" at the other end.

Operating leverage has fixed operating costs for its "fulcrum." When a firm incurs fixed operating costs, a change in sales revenue is magnified into a relatively larger change in earnings before interest and taxes (EBIT). The multiplier effect resulting from the use of fixed operating costs is known as the *degree of operating leverage*.

Financial leverage has fixed capital costs for its "fulcrum." When a firm incurs fixed capital costs, a change in EBIT is magnified into a larger change in earnings per share (EPS). The multiplier effect resulting from the use of fixed capital costs is known as the *degree of financial leverage*. (Both the degree of operating leverage and the degree of financial leverage are discussed in detail later in this chapter.)

Breakeven Analysis

Many of the planning activities that take place within a firm are based on anticipated levels of output. The study of the interrelationships among a firm's sales, operating costs, and EBIT at various output levels is known as *cost-volume-profit analysis,* or *breakeven analysis.*

The term *breakeven analysis* is somewhat misleading, since this type of analysis is typically used to answer many other questions besides those dealing with the breakeven output level of a firm. For example, breakeven analysis is also used to evaluate the financial profitability of new firms and new product lines. In addition, it is a valuable analytical tool for measuring the effects of changes in selling prices, fixed costs, and variable costs on the output level that must be achieved before the firm can realize operating profits.

A breakeven analysis of a firm can be developed either graphically or algebraically (or as a combination of the two).

Graphic Method

Figure 7-2 is an example of a basic linear breakeven analysis chart. Costs and revenues (measured in dollars) are plotted on the vertical axis, while output (measured in units) is plotted on the horizontal axis. The *total revenue* function, TR, represents the total revenue the firm will realize at each output level, given that the firm charges a constant selling price, P, per unit of output. Similarly, the *total* (operating) *cost* function, TC, represents the total cost the firm will incur at each output level. Total cost is computed as the sum of the firm's fixed costs, F, which are independent of the output level, plus the variable costs, which increase at the constant rate, V, per unit of output.

The assumptions of a constant selling price per unit, P, and a constant variable cost per unit, V, yield *linear* relationships for the total revenue and total cost functions. These linear relationships are only valid, however, over some *relevant range* of output values, such as from Q_1 to Q_2 in Figure 7-2. (The concept of relevant range is discussed later in this chapter).

The breakeven point occurs at point Q_b in Figure 7-2, where the total revenue and the total cost functions intersect. If a firm's output level is below this breakeven point—that is, if TR < TC—it incurs *operating losses*, defined as a *negative EBIT*. If the firm's output level is above this breakeven point—that is, if TR > TC—it realizes *operating profits*, defined as a *positive EBIT*.

Figure 7-2   **Linear Breakeven Analysis Chart**

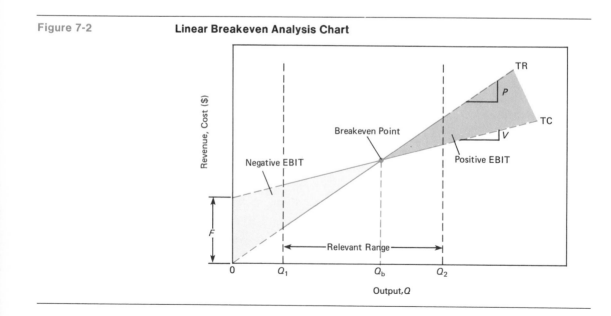

Determining a firm's breakeven point graphically involves three steps:

1. Drawing a line through the origin with a slope of P to represent the TR function.
2. Drawing a line that intersects the vertical axis at F and has a slope of V to represent the TC function.
3. Determining the point where the TR and TC lines intersect, dropping a perpendicular line to the horizontal axis, and noting the resulting value of Q_b.

Algebraic Method

To determine a firm's breakeven point algebraically, it is necessary to set the total revenue and total (operating) cost functions equal to each other and solve the resulting equation for the breakeven volume.

Total revenue is equal to the selling price per unit times the output quantity:

$$\text{TR} = P \times Q. \tag{7.1}$$

Total (operating) cost is equal to fixed plus variable costs, where the variable cost is the product of the variable cost per unit times the output quantity:

$$\text{TC} = F + (V \times Q). \tag{7.2}$$

Setting the total revenue and total cost expressions equal to each other (that is, setting EBIT = TR − TC = 0) and substituting the breakeven output Q_b for Q results in the following:

$$\text{TR} = \text{TC},$$

or

$$PQ_b = F + VQ_b. \tag{7.3}$$

Finally, solving Equation 7.3 for the breakeven output Q_b yields the following:

$$PQ_b - VQ_b = F.$$
$$(P - V)Q_b = F.$$
$$Q_b = \frac{F}{P - V}. \tag{7.4}$$

The *difference* between the selling price per unit and the variable cost per unit, $P - V$, is sometimes referred to as the *contribution margin per unit*. It measures how much each unit of output contributes to meeting fixed costs and operating profits. Thus, it can also be said that the breakeven output is equal to the fixed costs divided by the contribution margin per unit.

Breakeven analysis can also be performed in terms of dollar *sales* rather than units of output. The breakeven dollar sales volume, S_b, can be determined by the following expression:

$$S_b = \frac{F}{1 - (V/P)},$$ (7.5)

where V/P is the variable cost ratio (that is, the variable cost per dollar of sales).

Occasionally the analyst is interested in determining the output quantity at which a *target profit* (expressed in dollars) is achieved. An expression similar to Equation 7.4 can be used to find such a quantity:

$$\text{Target volume} = \frac{\text{Fixed cost} + \text{Target profit}}{\text{Contribution margin per unit}}.$$ (7.6)

Examples of Breakeven Analysis

The equations defined in the preceding section can be used to perform a breakeven analysis for the Allegan Manufacturing Company for the year ending December 31, 19X1. Assume that the firm manufactures one product, which it sells for $250 per unit. The current output, Q, is obtained by dividing total dollar sales ($5,000,000) by the selling price per unit ($250) to obtain 20,000 units per year. Its variable (operating) costs per unit, V, are determined by dividing total variable costs ($3,000,000) by current output (20,000) to obtain $150 per unit.

The firm's fixed costs, F, are given in Table 7-1 as $1,000,000. Substituting these figures into Equation 7.4 yields the following breakeven ouput:

$$Q_b = \frac{\$1,000,000}{\$250 - \$150}$$

$$= 10,000 \text{ units.}$$

Allegan's breakeven output can also be determined graphically, as shown in Figure 7-3. The breakeven level of dollar sales is also shown in Figure 7-3 to be $2,500,000.

Since a firm's breakeven output is dependent upon a number of variables—in particular, the price per unit and variable (operating) costs per unit—the firm may wish to analyze the effects of changes in any one of the variables on the breakeven output. For example, it may wish to consider either of the following: (1) changing the selling price, or (2) substituting fixed costs for variable costs.

Assume that Allegan increased the selling price per unit by $25 to $275, P'. Substituting this figure into Equation 7.4 gives a new breakeven output:

$$Q_b' = \frac{\$1,000,000}{\$275 - \$150}$$

$$= 8,000 \text{ units.}$$

Figure 7-3   **Linear Breakeven Analysis Chart for the Allegan Manufacturing Company**

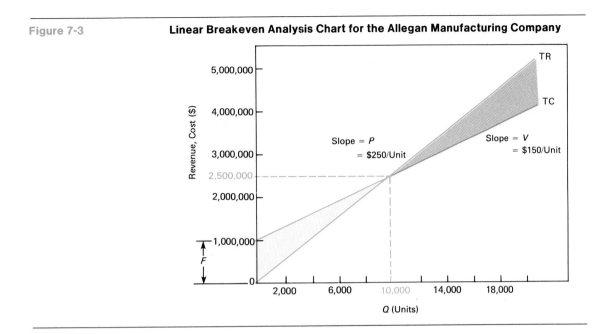

This can also be seen in Figure 7-4, in which an increase in the price per unit increases the slope of the total revenue function, TR′, and reduces the breakeven output.

Rather than increasing the selling price per unit, Allegan's management may decide to substitute fixed costs for variable costs in some aspect of the

Figure 7-4   **Linear Breakeven Analysis Chart for the Allegan Manufacturing Company Showing the Effects of a Price Increase**

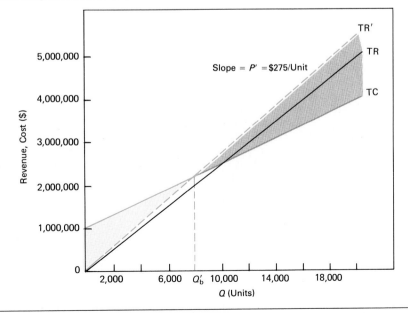

company's operations. For example, as labor wage rates increase over time, many firms seek to reduce operating costs through automation, which in effect represents the substitution of fixed-cost capital equipment for variable-cost labor. Suppose that Allegan determines it can reduce labor costs by $25 per unit by purchasing $1,000,000 in additional equipment. Assume that the new equipment is depreciated over a 10-year life using the straight line method. Under these conditions, annual depreciation of the new equipment would be $1,000,000/10 = $100,000, and the firm's new level of fixed costs, F', would be $1,000,000 + $100,000 = $1,100,000. Variable costs per unit, V', would be $150 − $25 = $125. Substituting $P = $250 per unit, $V' = $125 per unit, and $F' = $1,100,000 into Equation 7.4 yields a new breakeven output:

$$Q'_b = \frac{\$1,100,000}{\$250 - \$125}$$

$$= 8,800 \text{ units.}$$

As can be seen in Figure 7-5, the effect of this change in operations is to raise the intercept on the vertical axis; decrease the slope of the total cost function, TC'; and reduce the breakeven output.

Breakeven Analysis and Risk Assessment

The information generated from a breakeven analysis can be used to assess the operating risk to which a firm is exposed. Consider the example represented in Figure 7-3. With fixed costs of $1,000,000, a price per unit of $250 and variable costs per unit of $150, the breakeven output was

Figure 7-5

Linear Breakeven Analysis Chart for the Allegan Manufacturing Company Showing the Effects of Substituting Fixed Costs for Variable Costs

computed to be 10,000 units. If we add to this set of information the *expected* (mean) level of sales (in units) for some future period of time, the standard deviation of the distribution of sales, and the assumption that actual sales are approximately normally distributed, it is possible to compute the probability that the firm will have operating losses (that is, sell fewer units than the breakeven level) and the probability that the firm will have operating profits (that is, sell more units than the breakeven level).

For example, if expected unit sales for Allegan are 15,000 units with a standard deviation of 4,000 units, the probability of having operating losses (that is, the probability of selling fewer than 10,000 units) can be computed using Equation 5.3 and the probability values from Table V.

$$z = \frac{10,000 - 15,000}{4,000} = -1.25$$

In other words, a sales level of 10,000 units is 1.25 standard deviations *below* the mean. From Table V it can be seen that the probability associated with -1.25 standard deviations is 10.56 percent. Thus there is a 10.56 percent chance that the firm will incur operating losses and an 89.44 percent (100 percent minus 10.56 percent chance of losses) chance that the firm will record operating profits (that is, sell more than the breakeven number of units of output).

Cash Breakeven Analysis

Another concept that is sometimes useful in financial planning is *cash breakeven analysis*. Some of the firm's fixed operating costs, particularly depreciation, may represent *noncash outlays*. The cash breakeven point is calculated by deducting these noncash charges, N, from fixed costs, F, in the numerator of the breakeven equation (Equation 7.4):

$$\text{Cash breakeven output} = \frac{F - N}{P - V}. \tag{7.7}$$

It measures the volume of output (units) required to cover the firm's fixed cash operating outlays, such as management salaries, rent, and utilities.

Cash breakeven analysis also can be performed in terms of dollar sales. The cash breakeven dollar sales volume can be determined with the following expression:

$$\text{Cash breakeven sales} = \frac{F - N}{1 - (V/P)}. \tag{7.8}$$

All other things being equal, a firm with a larger proportion of its fixed costs in the form of noncash outlays will have a lower cash breakeven point and be better able to survive during a business downturn than will a firm whose fixed costs consist mainly of cash outlays.

In the Allegan Manufacturing Company example described earlier in the chapter, if $300,000 of the firm's $1,000,000 fixed costs, F, are noncash outlays, N, then Allegan's cash breakeven point can be found as follows using Equation 7.7:

$$\text{Cash breakeven output} = \frac{\$1,000,000 - \$300,000}{\$250 - \$150}$$

$$= 7,000 \text{ units.}$$

It should be emphasized that the calculation of a firm's cash breakeven output does not constitute a comprehensive method of cash flow analysis. A complete cash flow analysis, which takes account of the timing of all the firm's cash receipts and disbursements, requires the preparation of a detailed cash budget. The development and analysis of cash budgets are discussed in the following chapter.

Some Limitations of Breakeven Analysis

Breakeven analysis as it was just developed has a number of limitations. These arise from the *assumptions* that are made in constructing the model and developing the relevant data. The application of breakeven analysis is of value only to the extent that these assumptions are valid.

Constant Selling Price and Variable Cost Per Unit Recall that in the graphic breakeven analysis model, the assumptions of a constant selling price and variable cost per unit yield *linear* relationships for the total revenue and total cost functions. In practice these functions tend to be nonlinear. In many cases a firm can sell additional units of output only by lowering the price per unit. This results in a curvilinear total revenue function, as shown in Figure 7-6, instead of a straight line.

Figure 7-6   **Nonlinear Breakeven Analysis Chart**

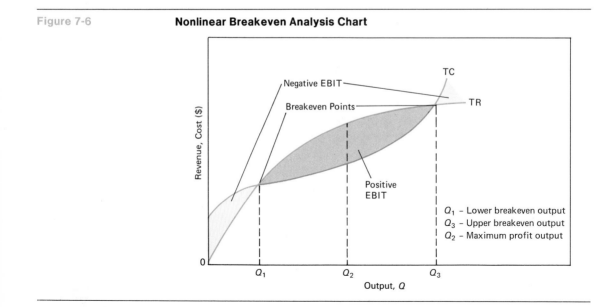

In addition, a firm's total cost function may be nonlinear as variable costs per unit initially decrease and then increase. This is also shown in Figure 7-6. Decreasing variable costs per unit can occur if, for example, labor specialization results in increased output per labor hour. Increasing variable costs per unit can occur if, for example, a firm uses more costly overtime labor as output approaches production capacity.

Nonlinear TC and TR functions can result in a firm's having more than one breakeven output point. This is shown in Figure 7-6, where a breakeven situation occurs at both Point Q_1 and Point Q_3. This is interpreted to mean that the firm will incur operating losses *below* an output level of Q_1 and *above* an output level of Q_3. The firm's total operating profits are maximized within the range of $Q_1 - Q_3$ at the point where the vertical distance between the TR and TC curves is greatest, that is, at output level Q_2.

In summary, the assumption of a constant selling price and variable cost per unit is probably valid over some "relevant range" of output levels. However, consideration of output levels outside this range will normally require modifications in the breakeven chart.

Composition of Operating Costs   Another assumption of breakeven analysis is that costs can be classified as either fixed or variable. In fact, fixed and variable costs are dependent on both the time period involved and the output range under consideration. As mentioned earlier, all costs are variable in the long run. In addition, some costs are partly fixed and partly variable. Futhermore, some costs increase in a stepwise manner as output is increased (that is, *semivariable costs*) and are constant only over relatively narrow ranges of output.

Multiple Products   The breakeven model also assumes that a firm is producing and selling either a *single* product or a *constant mix* of different products. In many cases the product mix changes over time, and problems can arise in allocating fixed costs among the various products.

Uncertainty   Still another assumption of breakeven analysis is that the selling price and variable cost per unit, as well as fixed costs, are known at each level of output. In practice these parameters are subject to uncertainty. Thus, the usefulness of the results of breakeven analysis depends on how accurate the estimates of these parameters are.

Short-Term Planning Horizon   Finally, breakeven analysis is normally performed for a planning period of one year or less. However, the benefits received from some costs may not be realized until subsequent periods. For example, research and development costs incurred during a specific period may not result in new products for several years. For breakeven analysis to be a dependable decision-making tool, a firm's operating costs must be matched with resulting revenues for the planning period under consideration.

Operating Leverage and Business Risk

As mentioned earlier in this chapter, the more operating leverage a firm uses, the greater its risk tends to be. Thus, the *degree of operating leverage* utilized by a firm can have a significant effect on the degree of risk perceived by stockholders.

Degree of Operating Leverage

A firm's degree of operating leverage (DOL) is defined as the multiplier effect resulting from the firm's use of fixed operating costs. More specifically, DOL can be computed as the *percentage change* in earnings before interest and taxes (EBIT) resulting from a given *percentage change* in sales (output):

$$\text{DOL at } X = \frac{\text{Percentage change in EBIT}}{\text{Percentage change in sales}}.$$

This can be rewritten as follows:

$$\text{DOL at } X = \frac{\dfrac{\Delta \text{EBIT}}{\text{EBIT}}}{\dfrac{\Delta \text{Sales}}{\text{Sales}}}, \tag{7.9}$$

where ΔEBIT and ΔSales are the changes in the firm's EBIT and sales, respectively. Since a firm's DOL differs at each sales (output) level, it is necessary to indicate the sales (units of output) point X, at which operating leverage is measured. The degree of operating leverage is analogous to the elasticity concept of economics (for example, price and income elasticity) in that it relates percentage changes in one variable (output) to percentage changes in another variable (EBIT).

The calculation of the DOL can be illustrated using the Allegan Manufacturing Company example discussed earlier. From Table 7-1, recall that Allegan's variable operating costs were $3,000,000 at the current sales level of $5,000,000. Thus, the firm's variable operating cost ratio is $3,000,000/$5,000,000 = 0.60, or 60 percent.

Suppose the firm increased sales by 10 percent to $5,500,000 while keeping fixed operating costs constant at $1,000,000 and the variable (operating) cost ratio at 60 percent. As can be seen in Table 7-2, this would increase the firm's earnings before interest and taxes (EBIT) to $1,200,000. Substituting the two sales figures ($5,000,000 and $5,500,000) and associated EBIT figures ($1,000,000 and $1,200,000) into Equation 7.9 yields the following:

$$\text{DOL at } \$5,000,000 = \frac{\dfrac{\$1,200,000 - \$1,000,000}{\$1,000,000}}{\dfrac{\$5,500,000 - \$5,000,000}{\$5,000,000}}$$

$$= \frac{\$200,000}{\$1,000,000} \times \frac{\$5,000,000}{\$500,000}$$

$$= 2.0.$$

Table 7-2   **Effect on Earnings per Share of a 10 Percent Increase in Sales**

Allegan Manufacturing Company
Year Ending December 31, 19X1

		(1)		(2)	% Change [(2) − (1)] ÷ (1)
Sales		$5,000,000		$5,500,000	+ 10%
Less: Variable operating costs (0.60 × Sales)	$3,000,000		$3,300,000		+ 10%
Fixed operating costs	1,000,000		1,000,000		0%
Total operating costs		4,000,000		4,300,000	+ 8%
Earnings before interest and taxes		$1,000,000		$1,200,000	+20%
Less: Interest payments (fixed capital cost)		250,000		250,000	0%
Earnings before taxes		$ 750,000		$ 950,000	+27%
Less: Income taxes (variable), 40%		300,000		380,000	+27%
Earnings after taxes		$ 450,000		$ 570,000	+27%
Less: Preferred dividends (fixed capital cost)		150,000		150,000	0%
Earnings available to common stockholders		$ 300,000		$ 420,000	+40%
Earnings per share (100,000 shares)		$3.00		$4.20	+40%

A DOL of 2.0 is interpreted to mean that each 1 percent change in sales from a base sales level of $5,000,000 results in a 2 percent change in EBIT *in the same direction as the sales change*. In other words, a sales *increase* of 10 percent results in a 10% × 2.0 = 20% *increase* in EBIT. Similarly, a 10 percent *decrease* in sales produces a 10% × 2.0 = 20% *decrease* in EBIT. The greater a firm's DOL, the greater the magnification of sales changes into EBIT changes.

Equation 7.9 requires the use of two different values of sales and EBIT. Another equation[1] that can be used to compute a firm's DOL more easily is as follows:

$$\text{DOL at } X = \frac{\text{Sales} - \text{Variable costs}}{\text{EBIT}} \qquad \textbf{(7.10)}$$

Inserting data from Table 7-1 on the Allegan Manufacutirng Company into Equation 7.10 gives the following:

$$\text{DOL at } \$5,000,000 = \frac{\$5,000,000 - \$3,000,000}{\$1,000,000}$$

$$= 2.0.$$

---

[1] Equation 7.10 is derived from Equation 7.9. Problem 13 at the end of this chapter asks for an explanation of how this is done.

This result is the same as that obtained using the more complex Equation 7.9.

A firm's DOL is a function of the nature of the production process. If the firm employs large amounts of labor-saving equipment in its operations, it tends to have relatively high fixed operating costs and relatively low variable operating costs. Such a cost structure yields a high DOL, which results in large operating profits (positive EBIT) if sales are high and large operating losses (negative EBIT) if sales are depressed.

DOL and Breakeven Analysis

The variables defined in the preceding section on breakeven analysis can also be used to develop a formula for determining a firm's DOL at any given output level. Since sales are equivalent to TR (or $P \times Q$), variable cost is equal to $V \times Q$, and EBIT is equal to total revenue (TR) less total (operating) cost, or $(P \times Q) - F - (V \times Q)$, these values can be substituted into Equation 7.10 to obtain the following:

$$\text{DOL at } Q = \frac{(P \times Q) - (V \times Q)}{(P \times Q) - F - (V \times Q)},$$

or

$$\text{DOL at } Q = \frac{(P - V)Q}{(P - V)Q - F}. \tag{7.11}$$

In the earlier discussion of breakeven analysis for the Allegan Manufacturing Company, the parameters of the breakeven model were determined as $P = \$250/\text{unit}$, $V = \$150/\text{unit}$, and $F = \$1,000,000$. Substituting these values in Equation 7.11 along with the respective output values yields the DOL values shown in Table 7-3.

Note that Allegan's DOL is largest (in absolute value terms) when the firm is operating near the breakeven point (that is, where $Q_b = 10,000$ units). Note also that the firm's DOL is negative below the breakeven

Table 7-3   **Allegan Manufacturing Company: DOL at Various Output Levels**

Output, Q	Degree of Operating Leverage, DOL	
0	0	
2,000	−0.25	
4,000	−0.67	
6,000	−1.50	
8,000	−4.00	
10,000	(Undefined)	Breakeven level
12,000	+6.00	
14,000	+3.50	
16,000	+2.67	
18,000	+2.25	
20,000	+2.00	

output level. A negative DOL indicates the percentage *reduction* in operating *losses* that occurs as a result of a 1 percent *increase* in output. For example, the DOL of -1.50 at an output level of 6,000 units indicates that, from a base output level of 6,000 units, the firm's operating *losses* are *reduced* by 1.5 percent for each 1 percent *increase* in output.

Business Risk

Business risk refers to the inherent variability or uncertainty of a firm's EBIT. It is a function of several factors, one of which is the firm's DOL. The DOL is a measure of how sensitive a firm's EBIT is to changes in sales. The greater a firm's DOL, the larger the change in EBIT will be for a given change in sales. Thus, *all other things being equal,* the higher a firm's DOL, the greater the degree of business risk.

Other factors can also affect a firm's business risk, including the variability or uncertainty of sales. A firm with high fixed costs and very stable sales will have a high DOL, but it will also have stable EBIT and, therefore, low business risk. Public utilities and pipeline transportation companies are examples of firms having these operating characteristics.

Another factor that may affect a firm's business risk is uncertainty concerning selling prices and variable costs. A firm having a low DOL can still have high business risk if selling prices and variable costs are subject to considerable variability over time.

In summary, a firm's DOL is only one of several factors that determine the firm's business risk.

Financial Leverage and Financial Risk

As mentioned earlier, financial leverage occurs whenever a firm employs funds having fixed costs. The main reason a firm employs fixed-cost funds is to increase the earnings available to common stockholders. The basic source of these funds is debt. Another source is preferred stock.[2] Fixed capital costs represent contractual obligations the company must meet regardless of EBIT.[3]

A firm's financial leverage represents the change in earnings per share (EPS) that occurs as a result of a given change in EBIT. Figure 7-7 illustrates the concept of financial leverage. Line A represents the financial leverage used by a firm financed *entirely with common stock.* A given percentage change in EBIT results in the *same* percentage change in EPS.

Line B represents a firm that uses debt (or other sources of fixed cost funds). This increases the *slope* of the EPS – EBIT line, thus increasing the responsiveness of EPS to changes in EBIT. As can be seen in Figure 7-7, a given change in EBIT yields a larger change in EPS if the firm is using debt financing (ΔEPS_B) than if the firm is financed entirely with common stock (ΔEPS_A).

It is also clear from Figure 7-7 that the use of financial leverage magnifies the returns—both positive and negative—to the shareholder.

[2] Although leases also represent a significant source of fixed cost financing for many firms, they are not discussed here in order to simplify the analysis.

[3] In financial emergencies, firms are usually able to omit preferred dividends. This can have undesirable consequences for a firm, however. Thus, the payment of preferred dividends is treated here as if it were a contractual obligation.

Figure 7-7   **Illustration of Financial Leverage**

When EBIT is at a relatively high level, such as $EBIT_2$, Firm B's use of financial leverage *increases* EPS above the level attained by Firm A, which is not using financial leverage. On the other hand, when EBIT is relatively low—for example, at $EBIT_0$—the use of financial leverage *decreases* EPS below the level that would be obtained otherwise; that is, $EPS_0' < EPS_0$. At $EBIT_0$ the use of financial leverage results in negative EPS for Firm B.

For example, the Allegan Manufacturing Company employs financial leverage, since it incurs both fixed interest and preferred stock dividend payments. Table 7-4 illustrates Allegan's EPS for various alternative levels of EBIT.

A 20 percent increase in Allegan's EBIT from $1,000,000 to $1,200,000 results in a 40 percent increase in EPS, since ($4.20 − $3.00)/ $3.00 = 0.4. Similarly, a 20 percent decrease in EBIT from $1,000,000 to $800,000 yields a 40 percent decrease in EPS. Figure 7-8 is an EPS-EBIT graph for Allegan. It can be seen in that figure that the zero EPS level occurs at an EBIT level of $500,000. This represents the $250,000 of interest payments plus the pre-tax amount of EBIT required to pay preferred dividends ($150,000/(1 − 0.4) = $250,000).

Table 7-4   **Earnings per Share for Alternative Levels of EBIT**

	Allegan Manufacturing Company				
	Year Ending December 31, 19X1				
EBIT	$400,000	$800,000	$1,000,000	$1,200,000	$1,600,000
Less: Interest expenses	250,000	250,000	250,000	250,000	250,000
Earnings before taxes	$150,000	$550,000	$ 750,000	$ 950,000	$1,350,000
Less: Income taxes	60,000	220,000	300,000	380,000	540,000
Earnings after taxes	$ 90,000	$330,000	$ 450,000	$ 570,000	$ 810,000
Less: Preferred dividends	150,000	150,000	150,000	150,000	150,000
Earnings available to common stockholders	−$60,000	$180,000	$300,000	$420,000	$660,000
Earnings per share (EPS)	−$0.60	$1.80	$3.00	$4.20	$6.60

Degree of Financial Leverage

A firm's degree of financial leverage (DFL) is computed as the *percentage change* in earnings per share (EPS) resulting from a given *percentage change* in earnings before interest and taxes (EBIT):

$$\text{DFL at } X = \frac{\text{Percentage change in EPS}}{\text{Percentage change in EBIT}}.$$

This can also be written as follows:

$$\text{DFL at } X = \frac{\dfrac{\Delta \text{EPS}}{\text{EPS}}}{\dfrac{\Delta \text{EBIT}}{\text{EBIT}}}, \qquad (7.12)$$

where ΔEPS and ΔEBIT are the changes in EPS and EBIT, respectively. Since a firm's DFL is different at each EBIT level, it is necessary to indicate the EBIT point, X, at which financial leverage is being measured.

Using the information contained in Table 7-4, the degree of financial leverage used by the Allegan Manufacturing Company can be calculated. The firm's EPS level is $3.00 at an EBIT level of $1,000,000. At an EBIT level of $1,200,000, EPS equals $4.20. Substituting these quantities into Equation 7.12 yields the following:

$$\text{DFL at } \$1,000,000 = \frac{\dfrac{\$4.20 - \$3.00}{\$3.00}}{\dfrac{\$1,200,000 - \$1,000,000}{\$1,000,000}}$$

$$= \frac{\$1.20}{\$3.00} \times \frac{\$1,000,000}{\$200,000}$$

$$= 2.0.$$

A DFL of 2.0 indicates that each 1 percent change in EBIT from a base

Figure 7-8   **EPS-EBIT Graph for the Allegan Manufacturing Company**

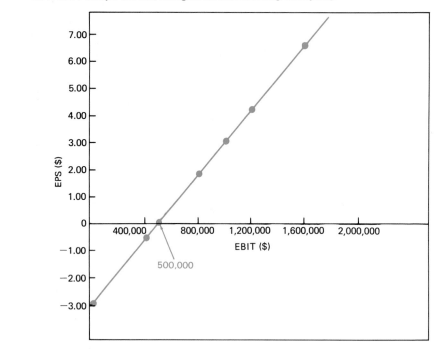

EBIT level of $1,000,000 results in a 2 percent change in EPS *in the same direction as the EBIT change.* In other words, a 10 percent *increase* in EBIT results in a $10\% \times 2.0 = 20\%$ *increase* in EPS. Similarly, a 10 percent *decrease* in EBIT produces a 20 percent *decrease* in EPS. The larger the firm's DFL, the greater the magnification of EBIT changes into EPS changes.

Measuring a firm's DFL using Equation 7.12 is somewhat cumbersome, since it necessitates using two EBIT and EPS projections. Computation is simplified when Equation 7.12 is rewritten as follows:[4]

$$\text{DFL at } X = \frac{\text{EBIT}}{\text{EBIT} - I - D_p/(1 - t)},\qquad \textbf{(7.13)}$$

where I is the firm's interest payments, D_p the firm's preferred dividend payments, t the firm's marginal income tax rate, and X the level of EBIT at which the firm's DFL is being measured.

---

[4] For the firm with no preferred stock, Equation 7.13 becomes the following:

$$\text{DFL at } X = \frac{\text{EBIT}}{\text{EBIT} - I}$$

$$= \frac{\text{EBIT}}{\text{EBT}},$$

where EBT represents earnings before taxes.

Unlike interest payments, preferred dividend payments are not tax deductible. Thus, on a comparable tax basis, a dollar of preferred dividends costs the firm more than a dollar of interest payments. Dividing preferred dividends in Equation 7.13 by $(1 - t)$ puts interest and preferred dividends on an equivalent, *pretax* basis.

Consider again the data presented in Table 7-1 on the Allegan Manufacturing Company. According to that table, EBIT = $1,000,000, I = $250,000, D_p = $150,000, and t = 40 percent, or 0.40. Substituting these values into Equation 7.13 yields the following:

$$\text{DFL at \$1,000,000} = \frac{\$1,000,000}{\$1,000,000 - \$250,000 - \$150,000/(1 - 0.40)}$$
$$= 2.0.$$

This result is the same as that obtained using Equation 7.12.

Just as a firm can change its DOL by raising or lowering fixed operating costs, it can also change its DFL by increasing or decreasing fixed capital costs. The amount of fixed capital costs incurred by a firm depends primarily on the mix between debt and common stock equity in the firm's *capital structure*. Capital structure is defined as all *permanent sources of capital* available to a firm, including permanent debt, preferred stock, and common stock equity. Thus, a firm that has a relatively large proportion of debt and preferred stock in its capital structure will have relatively large fixed capital costs and a high DFL.

Financial Risk

Financial risk refers to the additional variability of a company's earnings per share that results from the use of fixed cost sources of funds, such as debt and preferred stock. Financial leverage is one of several factors that affects financial risk. The use of increasing amounts of financial leverage raises the firm's fixed financial costs; this, in turn, increases the level of EBIT that the firm must earn in order to meet its financial obligations and remain in business. The use of financial leverage increases the variability of a firm's EPS returns to common stockholders. It also increases the firm's risk of insolvency. (Insolvency occurs when a firm is unable to meet contractual financial obligations—such as interest and principal payments, accounts payable, and income taxes—as they come due.) Thus, *all other things being equal,* the higher a firm's DFL, the greater its financial risk.

Various financial ratios can be used to measure the financial risk associated with a firm's use of leverage in its capital structure. These include the total debt-to-total assets ratio, the debt-to-equity ratio, the times interest earned ratio, and the fixed charge coverage ratio.[5] In particular, the times interest earned ratio and the fixed charge coverage ratio can help the analyst measure the extent to which a firm will be able to meet fixed capital costs out of EBIT.

In addition to using the degree of financial leverage and various financial ratios as measures of the financial risk facing a firm, it is possible

[5] Chapter 6 contains detailed explanations of these ratios.

to make more formal statements about the financial risk facing a company if the probability distribution of future operating income can be estimated. For example, consider the case of the Allegan Manufacturing Company. It was determined above that the loss level for Allegan under its current capital structure is $500,000 of EBIT. This is the level of EBIT required for earnings per share of $0. It represents the $250,000 of currently required interest payments plus the additional amount of EBIT that must be earned in order to pay the $150,000 of preferred dividends. (Remember that preferred dividends are paid out of after-tax income and that EBIT is a pre-tax figure.) At levels of EBIT above $500,000 the firm will have positive earnings per share and at levels of EBIT below $500,000 Allegan will incur losses per share of common stock.

Suppose that Allegan's managers have estimated, based upon past experience, that the expected value of EBIT over the coming year is $700,000 with a standard deviation of $200,000, and that the distribution of operating income is approximately normal. With this information it is possible to compute the probability of the firm having negative earnings per share over the coming year (or, conversely, the probability of having positive earnings per share).

Using Equation 5.3 and the probability values from Table V, the probability of Allegan having negative earnings per share is equal to the probability of having EBIT below the loss level of $500,000, or:

$$z = \frac{\$500,000 - \$700,000}{\$200,000} = -1.0$$

In other words, a level of EBIT of $500,000 is 1.0 standard deviation below the mean. From Table V it can be seen that the probability associated with -1.0 standard deviation is 15.87 percent. Thus there is a 15.87 percent chance that Allegan will have negative earnings per share with its current capital structure. Conversely, there is an 84.13 percent chance (100 percent less 15.87 percent chance of losses) of having positive earnings per share.

This type of analysis can give a financial manager a better feel for the true financial risk facing a firm. In addition when a financial manager is considering two or more alternative capital structures, this same kind of analysis can be used to help select the most desirable capital structure. This topic will be covered in detail in Chapter 13.

Combined Leverage and Overall Risk

Combined leverage occurs whenever a firm employs *both* operating leverage and financial leverage in an effort to increase the returns to common stockholders. It represents the magnification of sales increases (or decreases) into relatively larger earnings per share increases (or decreases), which result from the firm's use of both types of leverage. The joint multiplier effect is known as the *degree of combined leverage*.

Degree of Combined Leverage

A firm's degree of combined leverage (DCL) is computed as the percentage change in earnings per share resulting from a given percentage change in sales (output):

$$\text{DCL at } X = \frac{\text{Percentage change in EPS}}{\text{Percentage change in sales}}.$$

This can be rewritten as follows:

$$\text{DCL at } X = \frac{\dfrac{\Delta\text{EPS}}{\text{EPS}}}{\dfrac{\Delta\text{Sales}}{\text{Sales}}}, \tag{7.14}$$

where ΔEPS and ΔSales are the changes in a firm's EPS and sales, respectively, and X represents the level of sales at which the firm's combined leverage is measured. The degree of combined leverage is also equal to the product of the degree of operating leverage and the degree of financial leverage:[6]

$$\text{DCL at } X = \text{DOL} \times \text{DFL}. \tag{7.15}$$

To simplify matters, Equations 7.10 and 7.13 can be substituted into Equation 7.15 to obtain a new formula for determining the DCL in terms of basic income statement quantities:

$$\text{DCL at } X = \frac{\text{Sales} - \text{Variable cost}}{\text{EBIT}} \times \frac{\text{EBIT}}{\text{EBIT} - I - D_p/(1-t)},$$

or

$$\text{DCL at } X = \frac{\text{Sales} - \text{Variable costs}}{\text{EBIT} - I - D_p/(1-t)}. \tag{7.16}$$

These three formulas for calculating DCL can be illustrated using the Allegan Manufacturing Company example developed earlier in the chapter. Equation 7.14 can be used to calculate Allegan's DCL with the data from Tables 7-1 and 7-2. The EPS level was $3.00 at a sales level of $5,000,000 and $4.20 at a sales level of $5,500,000. Substituting these

---

[6] This follows logically from the definitions of DOL, DFL, and DCL:

$$\frac{\text{Percentage change in EPS}}{\text{Percentage change in sales}} = \frac{\text{Percentage change in EBIT}}{\text{Percentage change in sales}} \times \frac{\text{Percentage change in EPS}}{\text{Percentage change in EBIT}}$$

values into Equation 7.14 yields the following:

$$\text{DCL at } \$5,000,000 = \frac{\dfrac{\$4.20 - \$3.00}{\$3.00}}{\dfrac{\$5,500,000 - \$5,000,000}{\$5,000,000}}$$

$$= \frac{\$1.20}{\$3.00} \times \frac{\$5,000,000}{\$500,000}$$

$$= 4.0.$$

Substituting Sales = \$5,000,000, Variable costs = \$3,000,000, EBIT = \$1,000,000, I = \$2,500,000, D_p = \$150,000, and t = 40% (0.40) into Equation 7.16 gives the same value for Allegan's DCL:

$$\text{DCL at } \$5,000,000 = \frac{\$5,000,000 - \$3,000,000}{\$1,000,000 - \$250,000 - \$150,000/(1 - 0.40)}$$

$$= 4.0.$$

Also, recall from the earlier discussion of operating and financial leverage for Allegan that DOL = 2.0, and DFL = 2.0. Substituting these values into Equation 7.15 yields a DCL value identical to that just calculated:

$$\text{DCL at } \$5,000,000 = 2.0 \times 2.0$$

$$= 4.0.$$

This DCL is interpreted to mean that each 1 percent change in sales from a base sales level of \$5,000,000 results in a 4 percent change in Allegan's EPS.

Overall Risk

The degree of combined leverage used by a firm is a measure of the overall variability of EPS as sales levels vary due to fixed operating and capital costs. These costs can be combined in many different ways to achieve a desired DCL. In other words, there are a number of possible tradeoffs that can be made between operating and financial leverage.

Equation 7.15 shows that DCL is a function of DOL and DFL. If a firm has a relatively high DOL, for example, and wishes to achieve a certain DCL, it can offset this high DOL with a lower DFL. Or it may have a high DFL, in which case it would aim for a lower DOL. To illustrate, assume that a firm is considering purchasing assets that will increase fixed operating costs. To offset this high DOL, the firm may want to decrease the proportion of debt (and/or preferred stock) in its capital structure, thereby reducing fixed financial costs and the DFL.

The firm is limited in the amount of operating and financial leverage it can use in seeking to increase EPS. As the firm's use of leverage increases, so does its degree of risk, and investors who supply funds to the firm in the form of preferred and common equity and debt will consider this degree of risk when determining their required rates of return. The greater the firm's overall risk, the higher the rates of return investors will require. In other words, a firm that uses "excessive" amounts of leverage will have to pay higher costs for debt and preferred stock. These costs will tend to offset the returns gained from the use of leverage. Finally, "excessive" use of leverage will cause the market price of the firm's common stock to decline.

Summary

- *Leverage* refers to a firm's use of assets and liabilities having fixed costs. A firm uses leverage in an attempt to earn returns in excess of the fixed costs of these assets and liabilities, thus increasing the returns to common stockholders.
- *Breakeven analysis* is used to examine the relationship among a firm's revenues, costs, and operating profits (EBIT) at various output levels. Frequently the analyst constructs a breakeven chart based on linear cost-output and revenue-output relationships to determine the operating characteristics of a firm over a limited output range.
- *The breakeven point* is defined as the output level at which total revenues equal total (operating) costs. In the linear breakeven model, the breakeven point is found by dividing fixed (operating) costs by the difference between price and variable cost per unit.
- *Operating leverage* occurs when a firm uses assets having fixed operating costs. The *degree of operating leverage* (DOL) measures the percentage change in a firm's EBIT resulting from a 1 percent change in sales (or units of output). As a firm's fixed operating costs rise, its DOL increases.
- *Business risk* refers to the variability of a firm's EBIT. It is a function of several factors, including the firm's DOL and the variability of sales. All other things being equal, the higher a firm's DOL, the greater its business risk.
- *Financial leverage* occurs when a firm makes use of funds (primarily from debt and preferred stock) having fixed capital costs. The *degree of financial leverage* (DFL) measures the percentage change in the firm's EPS resulting from a 1 percent change in EBIT. As a firm's fixed capital costs rise, its DFL increases.
- *Financial risk* refers to the additional variability of a firm's EPS that results from the use of financial leverage.
- The *combined leverage* of a firm is equal to the *product* of the degrees of operating and financial leverage. These two types of leverage can be combined in many different ways to achieve a given degree of combined leverage (DCL). The total variability of the firm's EPS is a combination of business risk and financial risk.

Questions and Topics for Discussion

1. Define *leverage* as it is used in finance.
2. Define and give examples of the following:
   a. Fixed costs.
   b. Variable costs.
3. Explain how a linear breakeven chart is constructed when a firm's selling price, variable costs per unit, and fixed costs are known.

4. Define *contribution margin*. What is its relationship to linear breakeven analysis?

5. What are some of the limitations of breakeven analysis? How can these limitations affect actual financial decision making?

6. Define the following:
   a. Operating leverage.
   b. Business risk.

7. What other factors besides operating leverage can affect a firm's business risk?

8. Define the following:
   a. Financial leverage.
   b. Financial risk.

9. How is a firm's degree of combined leverage (DCL) related to its degrees of operating and financial leverage?

10. Assuming that all other factors remain unchanged, determine how a firm's breakeven point is affected by each of the following:
    a. The firm finds it necessary to reduce the price per unit because of competitive conditions in the market.
    b. The firm's direct labor costs increase as a result of a new labor contract.
    c. The Occupational Safety and Health Administration (OSHA) requires the firm to install new ventilating equipment in its plant. (Assume that this action has no effect on worker productivity.)

11. Is it possible for a firm to have a high degree of operating leverage and a low level of business risk? Explain.

12. Is it possible for a firm to have a high degree of combined leverage and a low level of total risk? Explain.

Problems*

Refer to the following data when working Problems 1 through 6:

The Hurricane Lamp Company forecasts that next year's sales will be $6,000,000. Fixed operating costs are estimated to be $800,000, and the variable cost ratio (that is, variable costs as a fraction of sales) is estimated to be 0.75. The firm has a $600,000 loan at 10 percent interest. It has 20,000 shares of $3 preferred stock and 60,000 shares of common stock outstanding. Hurricane Lamp is in the 40 percent corporate income tax bracket.

1. Forecast Hurricane Lamp's earnings per share (EPS) for next year. Develop a complete income statement using the revised format illustrated in Table 7-1 of this chapter. Then determine what Hurricane Lamp's EPS would be if sales were 10 percent above the projected $6,000,000 level.

2. Calculate Hurricane Lamp's degree of operating leverage (DOL) at a sales level of $6,000,000 using the following:
   a. The definitional formula (Equation 7.9).
   b. The simpler, computational formula (Equation 7.10).
   c. What is the economic interpretation of this value?

3. Calculate Hurricane Lamp's degree of financial leverage (DFL) at the EBIT level corresponding to sales of $6,000,000 using the following:
   a. The definitional formula (Equation 7.12).
   b. The simpler, computational formula (Equation 7.13).
   c. What is the economic interpretation of this value?

* Color numbers denote problems which have check answers provided at the end of the book.

Lotus123

4. Calculate Hurricane Lamp's degree of combined leverage (DCL) using the following:
   a. The definitional formula (Equation 7.14).
   b. The simpler, computational formula (Equation 7.16).
   c. The degree of operating and financial leverage calculated in Problems 2 and 3.
   d. What is the economic interpretation of this value?

Lotus123

5. Calculate Hurricane Lamp's breakeven dollar sales volume.

6. Construct an EPS-EBIT graph for the Hurricane Lamp Company.

Refer to the following data when working Problems 7 through 9:

East Publishing Company is doing an analysis of a proposed new finance text. The following data have been obtained:

Fixed costs (per edition):	
Development (reviews, class testing, and so on)	$18,000
Copyediting	5,000
Selling and promotion	7,000
Typesetting	40,000
Total	$70,000
Variable costs (per copy):	
Printing and binding	$ 4.20
Administrative costs	1.60
Salespeople's commission (2% of selling price)	.60
Author's royalties (12% of selling price)	3.60
Bookstore discounts (20% of selling price)	6.00
Total	$16.00
Projected selling price	$30.00

7. Using the above data, do the following:
   a. Determine the company's breakeven volume for this book:
      i. In units.
      ii. In dollar sales.
   b. Develop a breakeven chart for the text.
   c. Determine the number of copies East must sell in order to earn an (operating) profit of $21,000 on this text.
   d. Determine total (operating) profits at the following sales levels:
      i. 3,000 units.
      ii. 5,000 units.
      iii. 10,000 units.

8. a. Determine the degree of operating leverage (DOL) at the following sales levels:
      i. 3,000 units.
      ii. 7,000 units.
   b. What is the economic interpretation of the DOL value at 3,000 units?

9. Suppose East feels that $30.00 is too high a price to charge for the new finance text. It has examined the competitive market and determined that $24.00 would be a better selling price. What would the breakeven volume be at this new selling price?

Refer to the following data when working Problems 10 and 11:

The Alexander Company reported the following income statement for 19X1:

Sales		$15,000,000
Less: Operating expenses		
Wages, salaries, benefits	$6,000,000	
Raw materials	3,000,000	
Depreciation	1,500,000	
General, administrative, and selling expenses	1,500,000	
Total operating expenses		12,000,000
Earnings before interest and taxes (EBIT)		$ 3,000,000
Less: Interest expense		750,000
Earnings before taxes		$ 2,250,000
Less: Income taxes		1,000,000
Earnings after taxes		$ 1,250,000
Less: Preferred dividends		250,000
Earnings available to common stockholders		$ 1,000,000
Earnings per share—250,000 shares outstanding		$4.00

Assume that all depreciation and 75 percent of the firm's general, administrative, and selling expenses are *fixed costs* and that the remainder of the firm's operating expenses are *variable costs*.

Lotus123

10. a. Determine Alexander's fixed costs, variable costs, and variable cost ratio.
   b. Based on its 19X1 sales, calculate the following:
     i. The firm's DOL.
     ii. The firm's DFL.
     iii. The firm's DCL.
   c. Assuming that next year's sales increase by 15 percent, fixed operating and financial costs remain constant, and the variable cost ratio and tax rate also remain constant, use the leverage figures just calculated to forecast next year's EPS.
   d. Show the validity of this forecast by constructing Alexander's income statement for next year according to the revised format.
   e. Determine Alexander's breakeven dollar sales volume.
   f. Construct an EPS-EBIT graph based on Alexander's 19X1 income statement.

11. Recognizing that depreciation represents a *noncash* outlay,
   a. Compute Alexander's cash breakeven dollar sales volume.
   b. How does the cash breakeven sales volume compare with the ordinary breakeven sales volume computed in Problem 10?

Lotus123

12. Gibson Company sales for the year 19X1 were $3,000,000. The firm's variable operating cost ratio was 0.50, and fixed costs (that is, overhead and depreciation) were $900,000. Its average (and marginal) income tax rate is 40 percent. Currently, the firm has $2,400,000 of long-term bank loans outstanding at an average interest rate of 12.5 percent. The remainder of the firm's capital structure consists of common stock (100,000 shares outstanding at the present time).
   a. Calculate Gibson's degree of combined leverage for 19X1.
   b. Gibson is forecasting a 10 percent increase in sales for next year (19X2). Furthermore, the firm is planning to purchase additional labor-saving

equipment, which will increase fixed costs by $150,000 and reduce the variable cost ratio to 0.475. Financing this equipment with debt will require additional bank loans of $500,000 at an interest rate of 12.5 percent. Calculate Gibson's expected degree of combined leverage for 19X2.

   c. Determine how much Gibson must reduce its debt in 19X2 (for example, through the sale of common stock) to maintain its DCL at the 19X1 level.

13. Show algebraically that Equation 7.10,

$$\text{DOL at } X = \frac{\text{Sales} - \text{Variable costs}}{\text{EBIT}},$$

is equivalent to Equation 7.9,

$$\text{DOL at } X = \frac{\Delta \text{EBIT}/\text{EBIT}}{\Delta \text{Sales}/\text{Sales}}.$$

14. Albatross Airlines' fixed operating costs are $5,800,000, and its variable cost ratio is 0.20. The firm has $2,000,000 in bonds outstanding with a coupon interest rate of 8 percent. Albatross has 30,000 shares of preferred stock outstanding, which pays a $2.00 annual dividend. There are 100,000 shares of common stock outstanding. Revenues for the firm are $8,000,000, and the firm is in the 40 percent corporate income tax bracket.

   a. Compute Albatross's degree of operating leverage.

   b. Compute its degree of financial leverage.

   c. Compute its degree of combined leverage, and interpret this value.

15. Using the data on Albatross in Problem 14, compute the firm's breakeven dollar sales volume.

16. Given the following information for Computech, compute the firm's degree of combined leverage (dollars are in thousands except EPS):

	19X1	19X2
Sales	$500,000	$570,000
Fixed costs	120,000	120,000
Variable costs	300,000	342,000
Earnings before interest and taxes	80,000	108,000
Interest	30,000	30,000
Earnings per share (EPS)	$1.00	$1.56

17. McGee Corporation has fixed operating costs of $10,000,000 and a variable cost ratio of 0.65. The firm has a $20,000,000, 10 percent bank loan and a $6,000,000, 12 percent bond issue outstanding. The firm has 1,000,000 shares of $5 (dividend) preferred stock and 2,000,000 shares of common stock ($1 par). McGee's ordinary tax rate is 40% and its capital gains rate is 20 percent. Sales are expected to be $80,000,000.

   a. Compute McGee's degree of operating leverage at an $80,000,000 sales level.

   b. Compute McGee's degree of financial leverage at an $80,000,000 sales level.

   c. If sales decline to $76,000,000, forecast McGee's earnings per share.

18. A firm has earnings per share of $2.60 at a sales level of $5,000,000. If the firm has a degree of operating leverage of 3.0 and a degree of financial leverage of 5.5 (both at a sales level of $5,000,000), forecast earnings per share for a 2 percent sales decline.

19. Jenkins Appliances produces microwave ovens. Jenkins has computed its breakeven level of sales to be 60,000 units. An analysis of the market has led Jenkins to *expect* sales of 75,000 units with a standard deviation of 10,000 units.
    a. What is the probability that Jenkins will incur operating losses?
    b. What is the probability that Jenkins will operate above its breakeven point?

20. Blums, Inc. expects its operating income over the coming year to equal $1,500,000, with a standard deviation of $300,000. Blums must pay interest charges of $700,000 next year and preferred stock dividends of $240,000. Blums' marginal tax rate is 40 percent. What is the probability that Blums will have negative earnings per share next year?

21. A firm has sales of $10,000,000, variable costs of $5,000,000, EBIT of $2,000,000, and a degree of combined leverage of 3.0.
    a. If the firm has no preferred stock, what are its annual interest charges?
    b. If the firm wishes to reduce its degree of combined leverage to 2.5 by reducing interest charges, what will be the new level of annual interest charges?

Selected References

Gahlon, J. M., and James A. Gentry. "On the Relationship between Systematic Risk and the Degrees of Operating and Financial Leverage." *Financial Management* (Summer 1982): 15–23.

Gritta, Richard D. "The Effect of Leverage on Air Carrier Earnings: A Breakeven Analysis." *Financial Management* 8 (Summer 1979): 53–60.

Krainer, Robert E. "Interest Rates, Leverage, and Investor Rationality." *Journal of Financial and Quantitative Analysis* 12 (March 1977): 1–16.

Percival, John R. "Operating Leverage and Risk." *Journal of Business Research* 2 (April 1974): 223–227.

Reinhardt, U. E. "Break-Even Analysis for Lockheed's Tri Star: An Application of Financial Theory," *Journal of Finance* 28 (Sep. 1973): 821–838.

Shalit, Sol S. "On the Mathematics of Financial Leverage." *Financial Management* 4 (Spring 1975): 57–66.

8

FINANCIAL PLANNING

A Financial Dilemma

Financial Turnaround at International Harvester*

International Harvester began facing severe financial problems in 1980 when a six-month strike by employees (represented by the United Auto Workers) cost the company $579 million. Since 1980 the company has had losses of over $3 billion. Harvester's financial turnaround illustrates the types of planning and decisions that must be made in reviving a major corporation. Many of these decisions can be very painful, such as decisions to close plants, lay off employees, and sell entire divisions of the company. Some of the more significant financial decisions in Harvester's turnaround included:

- In 1981 the company sold its turbine division to its competitor, Caterpillar Tractor Company, suspended its dividends on common stock, and reached an agreement with its 225 lenders for restructuring more than $4 billion in debt. Losses for the year were $351 million.

- In 1982 Harvester sold its construction equipment division to Dresser Industries and its axle and transmission business to Dana Corporation. Losses mounted to $1.7 billion. The company's common stock, which sold in the mid-40s in 1979, fell to 2³⁄₄ during the year. At year-end its common equity was a *negative* $800 million.

- In 1983 and 1984 the company closed and consolidated a number of plants.

- In 1985 Harvester's farm equipment heritage (the company was founded by reaper inventor Cyrus McCormick in 1847) ended when it sold its agricultural business, *along with the Harvester name,* to J. I. Case Company for $488 million in cash and stock. The company planned to concentrate on making medium- and heavy-duty trucks and truck engines.

- In 1986 Harvester changed its name to Navistar International.

As a result of these decisions, the company reduced the number of plants to seven from a peak of forty-eight and its number of employees from 100,000 to 15,000. Its estimated breakeven point was reduced by 50 percent and its long-term debt to $800 million. Navistar had profits from continuing operations of $112 million in 1985 and was the industry leader in the truck business with 23 percent of the market. Despite all these drastic changes in the company, it still faces an uncertain future. Truck sales are expected to decline or remain level for the rest of the decade.

Throughout this difficult period for Harvester, the company's financial planners had to continually estimate the amount of financing the company would need and to determine the best sources to raise the needed funds. This chapter deals with the financial planning process and focuses on pro forma financial statements, which are an integral part of any financial plan.

* Based on articles in *Business Week* (January 20, 1986):28 and the *Houston Chronicle* (January 19, 1986).

Key Chapter Concepts

1. *Pro forma* financial statements show the results of some assumed event (for example, sales forecast) rather than an actual event.
2. Pro forma financial statements, including the income statement, balance sheet, and funds flow statement, are used in planning the orderly acquisition and expenditure of funds.
3. The percentage-of-sales forecasting method is used in estimating the amount of additional funds that the firm will need for a given increase in sales, based on certain assumptions about the relationship between sales and the various asset and liability accounts.
4. A cash budget is the projection of a firm's cash receipts and disbursements over a future time period and is useful in determining the amount of short-term funds the firm will need to borrow.
5. A funds flow statement compares the sources of a company's funds (that is, liquid assets) during a given period with their uses and can be used in forecasting the amount of additional financing required.
6. Other important topics include:
    a. Trend analysis
    b. Econometric forecasting
    c. Operating and capital budgets
    d. Computerized financial planning models

Glossary of New Terms

Capital budget A projection of the capital investment projects the firm plans to place in service during some future period.

Cash budget A projection of a company's cash receipts and disbursements over some future period of time.

Deterministic model A financial planning model that projects single number estimates of a financial variable or variables without specifying their probability of occurrence.

Financial forecasting The projection and estimation of a firm's future financial statements.

Financial planning model A computerized representation of some aspect of a firm's financial planning process.

Operating budget A collection of individual budgets that combine to form a part of a firm's integrated business plan, usually for the next year. It is normally composed of a *sales budget* and a *production budget*.

Optimization model A financial planning model that determines the values of financial decision variables that maximize (or minimize) some objective function such as profits (or costs).

Percentage of sales forecasting method A method of estimating the additional financing that will be needed to support a given future sales level.

Probabilistic model A financial planning model that uses probability distributions as inputs and generates a probability distribution for financial variables as output.

Pro forma financial statements Financial statements that project the results of some *assumed* event rather than an *actual* event.

Sensitivity analysis A method of analysis in which a financial planning model is rerun to determine the effect on the output variable(s) (for example, profit) of given changes in the input variable(s) (for example, sales). Sensitivity analysis is sometimes called "what if" analysis.

Trend analysis A method of analysis that estimates the future value of a financial variable on the basis of past actual values of the variable.

Introduction

Any firm that hopes to operate successfully within the competitive environment of the 1980s will have to make detailed corporate plans stating its objectives and how it intends to achieve them. A firm's financial managers normally play important roles in setting objectives and formulating plans. In addition, they are responsible for acquiring the funds necessary to run the company. Since the various types of funds available— long-term versus short-term, internal versus external, and debt versus equity—have different costs and can place different limitations and obligations on the company, it is also necessary to draw up detailed *financial plans* for the orderly acquisition and expenditure of funds.

Pro forma financial statements, which show the results of some *assumed* event rather than an *actual* event, are usually an integral part of any financial plan. For example, an operating budget that shows the level of net income that can be expected if sales and expenses are at a given assumed level next year is a pro forma income statement. Short-term plans—those that deal with one year or less—tend to be rather detailed, whereas long-term plans are more general.

This chapter presents an overview of the financial planning process, with an emphasis on the important role of pro forma financial statements. The chapter is organized as follows:

- The first section shows how financial forecasting methods can be used to estimate financing needs and develop pro forma statements.
- The next section considers the budgeting aspects of the financial planning process.
- The following section shows how pro forma funds flow statements can be used in the financial planning process.
- The final section discusses computer applications of the financial planning process and the development of pro forma statements.

Financial Forecasting

Financial forecasting involves the projection and estimation of a firm's *future* financing needs and pro forma statements. This section specifically introduces the percentage of sales forecasting method, trend analysis, and econometric techniques.

Percentage of Sales Forecasting Method

The percentage of sales forecasting method permits a company to forecast the amount of financing it will need for a given increase in sales. The use of this method is illustrated with the following example of the Industrial Supply Company (ISC).

The present ISC balance sheet and income statement are shown in Table 8-1 for 19X6. Management forecasts that sales will increase by 25 percent, or $3,750,000, next year to $18,750,000.

One of management's primary questions is the amount of funds that will be needed to finance this expected growth. Up to now, the company has financed its growth by using both *internal* and *external* funds. The company has reinvested most of its past earnings back into the company, primarily into additional inventory. The company has also used external financing in the form of short-term borrowings from its bank.

Table 8-1

Industrial Supply Company Financial Statements

Balance Sheet as of December 31, 19X6

Assets		Liabilities	
Cash	$ 500,000	Accounts payable	$1,500,000
Accounts receivable	2,000,000	Notes payable	1,000,000
Inventories	4,000,000	Total current liabilities	$2,500,000
Total current assets	$6,500,000	Long-term debt	500,000
Fixed assets, net	1,000,000	Stockholders' equity	4,500,000
Total assets	$7,500,000	Total liabilities and equity	$7,500,000

Income Statement for the Year Ending December 31, 19X6

Sales	$15,000,000
Expenses, including interest and taxes	14,250,000
Net income	$ 750,000
Dividends	250,000
Retained earnings	$ 500,000

Selected Financial Ratios

Current ratio	2.60 times
Debt ratio	40%
Rate of return on stockholders' equity	16.7%

To determine the amount of additional financing necessary to reach the expected $18,750,000 annual sales level, the ISC management has made the following observations about the company's various assets and liabilities:

1. **Cash.** Management feels the company's cash balances are generally adequate for the present sales level and would have to increase proportionately as sales increase.

2. **Accounts receivable.** The company's present average collection period is approximately forty-eight days. Management feels the company's present credit policies are appropriate for its type of business. As a result, they feel that the average collection period will remain approximately constant and that accounts receivable will increase proportionately as sales increase.

3. **Inventory.** Management feels the company's inventory is properly managed at present. Therefore, they feel inventory would have to increase proportionately for sales to increase.

4. **Fixed assets.** The company is a distributor with relatively few fixed assets (delivery trucks, forklifts, office equipment, storage racks, and so forth). Because the company's fixed assets *are being utilized at nearly full capacity,* management feels fixed assets will have to increase as sales grow. For financial planning purposes, management is willing to assume that the *net* fixed asset figure on the balance sheet will increase proportionately as sales increase.

5. **Accounts payable.** The company now maintains good relations with its suppliers. As the company purchases more inventory, its accounts payable balance will increase proportionately as sales increase.

6. **Long-term debt.** Long-term debt and notes payable do not necessarily have a direct relationship to the sales level. For example, a portion of the company's future profits may be used to pay off the present debt.

In summary, as the company's sales increase, its assets will increase proportionately to support the new sales. In addition, the current liabilities that vary directly with sales will also increase. The difference between the forecasted asset increase and the forecasted current liability increase is equal to the total financing the company will need. This relationship can be expressed in equation form as follows:

$$\begin{matrix} \text{Total} \\ \text{financing} \\ \text{needed} \end{matrix} = \begin{matrix} \text{Forecasted} \\ \text{asset} \\ \text{increase} \end{matrix} - \begin{matrix} \text{Forecasted} \\ \text{current} \\ \text{liability} \\ \text{increase} \end{matrix}$$

$$= \frac{A}{S}(\Delta S) - \frac{CL}{S}(\Delta S), \tag{8.1}$$

where A is the company's present level of assets that vary proportionately with sales, S is the company's present sales, CL is the company's present level of current liabilities that vary proportionately with sales, and ΔS is the forecasted sales increase.

A portion of the total financing needed can be generated internally. Specifically, the internal financing generated during the time period when sales increase from S to $S + \Delta S$ can be expressed in equation form as follows[1]:

$$\begin{matrix} \text{Internal} \\ \text{financing} \\ \text{provided} \end{matrix} = \begin{matrix} \text{Forecasted} \\ \text{net} \\ \text{income (NI)} \end{matrix} - \text{Dividends } (D)$$

$$= NI - D. \tag{8.2}$$

The additional financing needed can be calculated by subtracting the internal financing provided from the total financing needed:

$$\begin{matrix} \text{Additional} \\ \text{financing} \\ \text{needed} \end{matrix} = \begin{matrix} \text{Total} \\ \text{financing} \\ \text{needed} \end{matrix} - \begin{matrix} \text{Internal} \\ \text{financing} \\ \text{provided} \end{matrix}$$

$$= \left[\frac{A}{S}(\Delta S) - \frac{CL}{S}(\Delta S)\right] - [NI - D]. \tag{8.3}$$

Referring back to the ISC example, the additional financing needed to support a sales increase of $3,750,000 up to the $18,750,000 level can now be calculated. Assume that management forecasts expenses to be $17,750,000 and net income to be $1,000,000 during the coming year.

---

[1] This equation does not consider depreciation, because *net* fixed assets are assumed to increase proportionately with sales. If *gross* fixed assets are assumed to increase proportionately with sales, depreciation is treated as a source of internal financing.

Assume further that the company plans to maintain its dividend payments at the same level in 19X7 as in 19X6. Substituting this data into Equation 8.3 yields:

$$\text{Additional financing needed} = \left[\frac{7,500,000}{15,000,000}(3,750,000) - \frac{1,500,000}{15,000,000}(3,750,000) \right]$$
$$- (1,000,000 - 250,000)$$
$$= \$750,000$$

The approximate amount of additional financing that will be needed to finance ISC's forecasted growth from $15,000,000 to $18,750,000 in sales is $750,000.[2] Even though the financing will be needed gradually as sales increase, the ISC management has to decide whether to (1) borrow on a short-term basis, (2) borrow on a long-term basis, (3) sell additional common stock, or (4) cut dividends. The factors that influence the debt versus equity decision are discussed in Chapter 13; the factors that influence the short-term versus long-term debt decision are discussed in Chapter 18; and the factors that influence the dividend decision are discussed in Chapter 14. As this example illustrates, *the investment, financing, and dividend decisions of the firm are interdependent.*

Table 8-2 shows ISC's pro forma financial statements for 19X7, *assuming* that all of the additional financing needed is in the form of short-term notes payable. Examination of the selected financial ratios in

Table 8-2 **Industrial Supply Company Pro Forma Financial Statements**

Balance Sheet as of December 31, 19X7

Assets		Liabilities	
Cash	$ 625,000	Accounts payable	$1,875,000
Accounts receivable	2,500,000	Notes payable	1,750,000
Inventories	5,000,000	Total current liabilities	$3,625,000
Total current assets	$8,125,000	Long-term debt	500,000
Fixed assets, net	1,250,000	Stockholders' equity	5,250,000
Total assets	$9,375,000	Total liabilities and equity	$9,375,000

Income Statement for the Year Ending December 31, 19X7

Sales	$18,750,000
Expenses, including interest and taxes	17,750,000
Net income	$ 1,000,000
Dividends	250,000
Retained earnings	$ 750,000

Selected Financial Ratios

Current ratio	2.24 times
Debt ratio	44%
Rate of return on stockholders' equity	19.0%

[2] The $750,000 figure assumes that none of the present notes payable or long-term debt will have to be repaid during the next year.

Tables 8-1 and 8-2 shows that this financing plan will increase the rate of return on stockholders' equity from 16.7 percent in 19X6 to 19.0 percent in 19X7. However, it also reduces the firm's current ratio (measure of liquidity) from 2.60 to 2.24 and increases its debt ratio (measure of leverage) from 40 percent to 44 percent. ISC management would have to weigh these factors (as well as others) in determining how to obtain the $750,000 of additional financing needed.

The percentage of sales forecasting method for calculating financing needs is a useful and convenient financial planning technique. However, as with all analytical techniques, the application of this method should be supplemented by any additional factors that are unique to the particular situation.

One such factor is *economies of scale*. Economies of scale may result in non-linear relationships between sales and certain types of assets. In other words, the relationships may not be strictly proportional, as assumed in the model. For example, a 10 percent increase in sales may only require a 5 percent increase in fixed assets or inventories. Another factor in some industries is that capacity can only be added in *discrete* or "*lumpy*" *increments*. Once output reaches the capacity of an existing production facility, expansion requires the building of another facility. This causes fixed assets to increase in a step-wise manner as sales are increased, rather than increasing proportionately.

Trend Analysis

Trend analysis is the process of estimating the future value of some financial variable on the basis of past actual values of the variable. Both *linear* and *non-linear* trend analysis can be performed.

To illustrate a linear trend analysis, consider a company that wishes to forecast its 19X6 sales based on known sales figures since 19X0. As shown in Figure 8-1(a), a straight-line can be fitted to the data points from 19X0

Figure 8-1   **Trend Analysis**

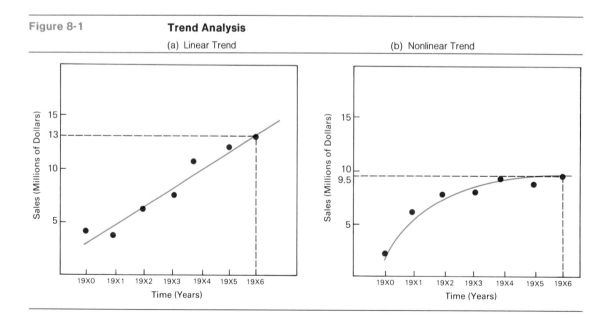

(a) Linear Trend   (b) Nonlinear Trend to 19X5 and then *extrapolated* forward to 19X6. This "best fitting" straight-line can be determined either visually or using more sophisticated *least squares* estimation procedures.[3] The visual analysis shown results in a 19X6 sales forecast of $13 million.

In some cases a nonlinear trend analysis is more representative than a linear one. This is especially true for maturing growth companies, or those whose past sales have been growing at a decreasing rate. Assume that one such company wishes to forecast 19X6 sales based on past actual sales figures since 19X0. As Figure 8-1(b) shows, this can be accomplished by plotting the past actual data and, instead of estimating the "best" straight line passing through these points, fitting a smooth curve using visual or least squares estimating techniques and then extending it until 19X6. This visual curve-fitting technique results in an estimate of $9.5 million in sales for the year.

Although trend analysis can be a useful financial forecasting technique, it has limitations. Specifically, it assumes that future trends will simply be a continuation of past trends, and this is not always the case. Thus, the analyst must exercise caution when performing a trend analysis and take into account current information about industry and economic cycles.

Econometric Techniques

Econometric techniques involve the development and empirical measurement of functional relationships between economic variables (for example, sales) and one (or more) explanatory variables.[4] For example, a company might hypothesize that its sales are a linear function of Gross National Product (GNP). A plot of the company's sales and GNP data for the last six years (19X0–19X5) is shown in Figure 8-2. A linear regression of the

Figure 8-2   **Linear Regression Model**

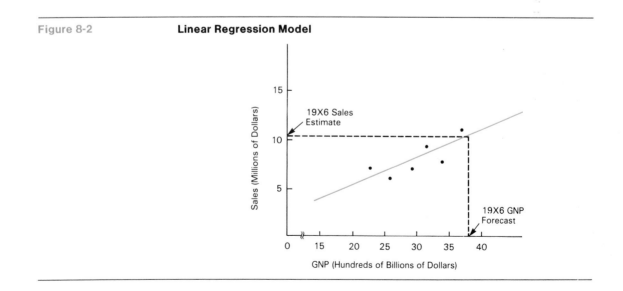

GNP (Hundreds of Billions of Dollars)

---

[3] See James R. McGuigan and R. Charles Moyer, *Managerial Economics,* 4th ed. St. Paul, MN: West Publishing, 1986, Ch. 5 for a discussion of least-squares procedures.

[4] Econometric techniques are discussed in more detail in McGuigan and Moyer, *Managerial Economics,* Chs. 5 and 8.

form

$$\text{Sales} = a + b\,\text{GNP} \qquad\qquad (8.4)$$

could be used as a model of the relationship. Once the a and b coefficients are estimated, using either visual or least-squares techniques, one can substitute a forecasted value for GNP in 19X6 into Equation 8.4 to obtain an estimate of company sales for 19X6.

More complicated relationships involving two or more explanatory variables and/or nonlinear relationships can also be employed if the simple techniques are not satisfactory.

An Overview of Budgeting

Budgets are simply pro forma financial statements that detail a firm's financial plans. They show how the company's funds will be spent on labor, materials, and capital goods and indicate how funds will be obtained.

Budgets are used to *plan, coordinate,* and *control* a firm's operations. They are essential to *planning* because they represent the company's objectives in numerical terms, such as dollars of sales, units of production, pounds of raw materials, and dollars of funds required from the capital markets. Once a firm has made financial plans, it refers to the budgets when *coordinating* its overall activities. For example, the purchasing department examines the budgets when deciding how best to integrate purchasing activities with monthly production requirements to insure the availability of sufficient raw materials. The production and marketing departments then work together to guarantee that sufficient finished goods inventories are on hand. Finally, the finance department coordinates the company's need for funds with the requirements of the purchasing, production, and marketing departments.

The projected figures in a firm's budgets are also used as a *control* device against which actual figures are compared. This insures that the various departments and divisions are functioning properly and working together toward the objectives developed in the planning phase.

A firm's budgets are based on the *assumption* of certain future sales and production levels. As pro forma financial statements, budgets predict what a company's financial statements will look like if specific plans are realized. A firm's budgets can also be combined with the current balance sheet to give a pro forma balance sheet showing what the financial status of the company will be at some point in the future if the budget forecasts prove true.

As a general rule, companies prepare and use three basic types of budgets: *operating budgets, cash budgets,* and *capital budgets.*

Operating Budgets

An operating budget, or operating plan, is basically a collection of individual budgets combined to form a part of an integrated *business plan,* usually for the next year. It is normally detailed enough to be used in coordinating a company's activities. In addition, it can function as a control device by serving as a basis for measuring performance.

The first step in the development of an operating budget involves the preparation of *sales budgets.* This is an important and difficult part of budgeting, since it requires the consideration of a large number of factors, including the overall condition of the economy and the industry, the company's plant capacity, the prices it charges and those its competitors charge, and advertising expenditures made by the company and others within the industry.

Once a firm has completed and approved the sales budgets, it can then prepare *production budgets* for its products. Normally a firm has two production goals: meeting expected sales for the budget period and providing for the desired level of ending inventory. The production budgets detail the plans for achieving these goals. In addition, the production budgets shows the firm's expected future production costs.

The final step in the development of an operating budget involves combining the sales and production budgets to calculate the expected gross profit levels for the firm's products.

Depending on how a company is organized, it can combine the operating budgets for the various products and divisions to prepare an overall corporate operating budget. Table 8-3 is an example of a corporate operating budget. Note that this is a pro forma financial statement. It assumes that the company will continue to operate successfully during the coming year at the projected sales, price, and cost levels.

Cash Budgets

A cash budget is the projection of a company's cash receipts and disbursements over some future period of time. Typically, a cash budget is prepared on an annual basis and subdivided into months. However, more detailed and refined cash budgeting is done on a weekly or even daily basis by some companies that employ good ongoing cash management procedures.

Cash budgets are useful in determining the amount of short-term funds the firm may need to borrow to cover any projected cash shortages. Short-term borrowed funds are almost always easier to obtain when the need for them is anticipated. In addition to planning for any cash shortages, the cash budget also indicates the periods when the firm may have cash surpluses. This information is helpful in managing the firm's

Table 8-3 **Corporate Operating Budget**

Midwestern Manufacturing Company
Corporate Summary Operating Budget, 19X6
Pro Forma Income Statement
(in millions of dollars)

Sales	$96.4
Expenses:	
Cost of goods sold (excluding depreciation)	$57.5
Depreciation	6.0
Selling and administrative expenses	18.8
Interest	1.6
Income before taxes	$12.5
Income taxes	6.0
Net income	$ 6.5

marketable securities investments. Thus, the cash budget is one of the most important short-range financial planning tools. And, like operating budgets, cash budgets can be useful for control and coordination purposes.

To explore actual cash budgeting procedures, the Midwestern Manufacturing Company Central Division will be examined. Table 8-4 illustrates a cash budget worksheet for that division for the first quarter of 19X6. Table 8-5 is an actual cash budget for the time period.

The first step in cash budget preparation is the estimation of cash receipts, which results directly from the sales forecast. Midwestern has found that, on the average, about 10 percent of total sales in any given month are cash sales. The remaining 90 percent are credit sales.[5]

About 30 percent of the firm's credit sales are collected during the month in which the sale is made, while all of the remaining 70 percent are collected during the following month. Thus, the total accounts receivable the firm can expect to collect during January are equal to 70 percent of the forecasted December credit sales plus 30 percent of the forecasted January sales:

$$(0.70 \times \$486,000) + (0.30 \times \$450,000) = \$340,200 + \$135,000$$
$$= \$475,200.$$

The forecasted cash receipts for February and March are calculated the same way.

The next step in cash budgeting is the scheduling of *disbursements,* or payments the firm must make to others. Many of these items remain

Table 8-4 **Cash Budget Worksheet**

Midwestern Manufacturing Company—Central Division
Cash Budget Worksheet
First Quarter, 19X6

	December	January	February	March
Budget of Receipts from Sales				
Estimated sales	$540,000	$500,000	$550,000	$620,000
Estimated credit sales	486,000	450,000	495,000	558,000
Estimated receipts:				
Cash sales		50,000	55,000	62,000
Collections of accounts receivable:				
70% of last month's credit sales		340,200	315,000	346,500
30% of current month's credit sales		135,000	148,500	167,400
Total accounts receivable collections		$475,200	$463,500	$513,900
Budget of Payments for Purchases				
Estimated purchases*	$275,000	$302,500	$341,000	
Estimated payments of accounts payable†		$275,000	$302,500	$341,000

*Purchases are estimated at 55 percent of next month's sales.
†Payments are estimated to lag purchases by one month.

[5] Estimated December credit sales are 90 percent of estimated December sales; that is, 0.90 × $540,000 = $486,000.

Table 8-5   **Cash Budget**

Midwestern Manufacturing Company—Central Division
Cash Budget*
First Quarter, 19X6

	December	January	February	March
Sales	$540,000	$500,000	$550,000	$620,000
Projected cash balance, beginning of month		$ 61,000	$ 50,700	$ 50,000
Receipts:				
Cash sales		50,000	55,000	62,000
Collection of accounts receivable		475,200	463,500	513,900
Total cash available		$586,200	$569,200	$625,900
Disbursements:				
Payment of accounts payable		$275,000	$302,500	$341,000
Wages and salaries		158,000	154,500	145,500
Rent		17,000	17,000	17,000
Other expenses		4,500	7,000	8,000
Taxes		81,000	—	—
Dividends on common stock		—	—	30,000
Purchase of new equipment				
(capital budget)		—	70,000	—
Total disbursements		$535,500	$551,000	$541,500
Excess of available cash over				
disbursements		$ 50,700	$ 18,200	$ 84,400
Cash loans needed to maintain				
balance of $50,000		—	31,800	—
Loan repayment		—	—	(31,800)
Projected cash balance, end of month		$ 50,700	$ 50,000	$ 52,600

*Prepared December 15, 19X5.

relatively constant and thus are relatively easy to budget. Others, however, such as the payment of accounts payable for purchases of merchandise, raw materials, and supplies, are more complicated. The key determinants of a firm's schedule of payables are the level of purchases per period and the terms given by suppliers.

Frequently, accounts payable become due before goods are sold and cash is received; this can lead to temporary cash shortages. In fact, many companies experience cash difficulties immediately after a good sales period. Inventories are depleted and must be replenished, but cash is low because collections from the good sales period have not yet been received. Midwestern's purchases are generally estimated to be 55 percent of next month's sales. This percentage is based on the company's past experience and can vary considerably among industries and companies. (Note that depreciation does not appear as a disbursement in the cash budget. Depreciation is a non-cash charge.)

After cash receipts and disbursements have been estimated, the next step in the cash budgeting process is the determination of a desired cash balance at the beginning of each month. This minimum cash balance figure is usually a function of several factors, including the nature of the business, tax laws, and bank requirements. Table 8-5 lists Midwestern's projected cash balances for the beginnings of January, February, and

March. In this example, $50,000 is assumed to be the most appropriate minimum cash balance for the first quarter, 19X6.[6]

It can be seen from Table 8-5 that Midwestern expects to need a short-term loan of $31,800 in February to maintain a minimum cash balance of $50,000. This is due to the fact that the company expects a decrease in the collection of accounts receivable in February, brought about by slightly lower than normal sales expected in January. In addition, the company plans to purchase new equipment in February, which will cost $70,000; this also contributes to the expected need for a short-term loan.

If the company planned to spend much more money than this on new equipment, it might decide to secure longer-term financing at this time instead of the short-term loan. The proceeds from longer-term financing could be budgeted as a separate cash receipt in February, permitting the company to separate short-term and long-term cash needs.

After projecting the need for a short-term loan in February, the cash budget in Table 8-5 shows that the loan can probably be paid at the end of March, because the available cash balance of $84,400 will still be above $50,000 after repayment of $31,800. The company has indicated the repayment on the cash budget by adding another side caption: loan repayment.[7]

Most companies follow this same general format for cash budgeting, yet few companies use *exactly* the same format. A company's actual cash budgeting system will depend on its business and its accounting proce-

Table 8-6   **Capital Budget**

Midwestern Manufacturing Company—Central Division
Capital Budget, 19X6

	Amount spent in prior years	Amount to be spent in 19X6	Amount to be spent in later years
Danville, Illinois, plant:			
Numerically controlled lathe		$ 74,000	
General office expansion and			
remodeling		117,000	$ 25,000
Pollution equipment		57,000	
Total projects under $50,000		165,000	
Total, Danville plant	$—	$ 413,000	$ 25,000
Racine, Wisconsin, plant:			
Fabrication department expansion	$58,000	$ 112,000	
Fabrication equipment		85,000	
New warehouse		575,000	$125,000
Total projects under $50,000		250,000	
Total, Racine plant	$58,000	$1,022,000	$125,000
Division total	$58,000	$1,435,000	$150,000

[6] Cash management is discussed further in Chapter 19.

[7] Note that the cash budget does not include any interest payments on this loan (or interest earned on investments of excess cash). These items generally have a relatively small impact on cash flows. However, they can be added to a cash budget if necessary.

dures. Computerized financial spreadsheet models are useful in constructing and analyzing cash budgets. (A cash budgeting spreadsheet model is discussed in the *Study Guide.* A diskette containing this model is available from your instructor.)

Capital Budgets

A company's capital budget is a listing of the capital projects it plans to place in service during some future period, usually the next year. A capital project is a planned addition to the company's fixed assets that has an economic life greater than one year. Table 8-6 shows the 19X6 capital budget for Midwestern Manufacturing Company's Central Division.

Usually only major projects having expected expenditures above some dollar amount—in this case, $50,000—are listed separately on the capital budget. Smaller projects having expenditures under that dollar amount are totaled and represented by one figure.

A firm's capital budget is a summary of the analyses conducted to determine which proposed projects the company will actually undertake.[8]

Funds Flow Analysis

Funds flow analysis is an important analytical technique used in the financial planning process. In fact, the *funds flow statement,*[9] the income statement, and the balance sheet combined constitute the major portion of a company's financial statements.

The notion of *funds* is roughly equivalent to *liquid assets;* that is, a company's liquid assets are the funds it uses to conduct business. Funds are normally defined on either a *cash basis* or a *working capital basis.* This discussion considers it on a working capital basis and considers its usefulness as a forecasting tool.

Funds flow analysis compares the *sources* of a company's funds during a particular time period—usually a year—with their *uses.* From a working capital perspective, the principal *sources* of funds are a company's operations, borrowings, proceeds from the sale of stock, and proceeds from the sale of fixed assets.

The company's operations are an *internal* source of funds, whereas the other sources are *external.* The company's operations are the most important source of funds, since the repayment of borrowings and any dividends paid to the firm's owners ultimately have to come from continuing operations, or the business cannot keep functioning.

From a working capital perspective, the principal *uses* of funds are dividends, capital expenditures, and repayment of long-term debt.

Funds Flow Statement

The funds flow statement is compiled from information gathered primarily from successive year-end balance sheets.[10] These comparative balance sheets are placed side by side so that *changes* that occurred during

---

[8] Techniques of capital budgeting, also termed *capital expenditure analysis,* are discussed in detail in Chapters 9 through 11.

[9] This is also termed the *sources and uses of funds statement.* In corporate annual reports it is referred to as the *statement of changes in financial position.*

[10] Funds flow analysis is not limited to annual financial statements. Quarterly or semiannual funds flow statements also can be developed from quarterly or semiannual balance sheet data.

the intervening year can be clearly seen. Table 8-7 shows the Midwestern Manufacturing Company's comparative balance sheets for the years ending December 31, 19X4, and December 31, 19X5. The changes, listed in the right-hand column, can be used along with the information given in the note at the bottom of Table 8-7 to construct a funds flow statement, as shown in Table 8-8.

An analysis of the funds flow statement reveals that Midwestern generated total funds of $20.1 million during 19X5. This consisted of $10.1 million from operations and $10.0 million of long-term debt. The funds from operations were calculated by adding the company's noncash expenditures, depreciation, and deferred Federal income taxes to the net income.[11] The funds generated during 19X5 were used to pay dividends on common stock ($2.5 million), make expenditures for property and equipment ($15.0 million), and repay long-term debt ($1.0 million).

Table 8-7   **Comparative Balance Sheets**

Midwestern Manufacturing Company
Comparative Balance Sheets
(in millions of dollars)*

	12/31/X4	12/31/X5	Change
Assets			
Current assets:			
Cash	$ 3.9	$ 3.3	−0.6
Accounts receivable	5.2	5.8	+0.6
Inventories	13.7	18.0	+4.3
Total current assets	$22.8	$27.1	+4.3
Property and equipment	$40.7	$55.7	+15.0
Less: Accumulated depreciation	6.3	10.8	−(+4.5)†
Net property and equipment	$34.4	$44.9	+10.5
Total assets	$57.2	$72.0	+14.8
Liabilities and Stockholders' Equity			
Current liabilities:			
Accounts payable	$ 4.0	$ 4.5	+0.5
Other current liabilities	$ 6.0	$ 8.2	+2.2
Total current liabilities	$10.0	$12.7	+2.7
Long-term debt	$ 8.8	$17.8	+9.0
Deferred Federal income taxes	$ 1.1	$ 1.4	+0.3
Stockholders' equity:			
Common stock	$ 1.0	$ 1.0	
Additional paid-in capital	19.0	19.0	
Retained earnings	17.3	20.1	+2.8
Total stockholders' equity	$37.3	$40.1	+2.8
Total liabilities and stockholders' equity	$57.2	$72.0	+14.8

*Net income for the year ending December 31, 19X5 totaled $5.3 million; dividends paid during the same period totaled $2.5 million; $1.0 million of long-term debt was retired in 19X5; and no fixed assets were sold during 19X5.
†Note that accumulated depreciation is *subtracted* when computing the column total.

[11] Many firms use accelerated depreciation methods for tax purposes and straight line depreciation for financial accounting purposes. The actual taxes currently owed are less than the total taxes calculated using straight line depreciation. The difference is a noncash adjustment to net income, appropriately termed *deferred Federal income tax*. A company's accumulated deferred Federal income taxes are listed as a liability on the balance sheet.

Table 8-8   **Funds Flow Statement**

Midwestern Manufacturing Company
Funds Flow Statement for the Year Ending December 31, 19X5
(in millions of dollars)*

Sources of Funds	
Funds provided from operations:	
Net income	$ 5.3
Plus: Depreciation	4.5
Deferred Federal income tax	0.3
Total funds provided from operations	$10.1
Common stock sold	—
Long-term debt incurred	10.0
Disposal of properties	—
Total sources of funds	$20.1
Uses of Funds	
Dividends	$ 2.5
Capital expenditures	15.0
Retirement of long-term debt	1.0
Total uses of funds	$18.5
Total increase (decrease) in funds (net working capital)	$ 1.6

*In this example the increase in funds is an increase in net working capital. Current assets increased by $4.3 million, and current liabilities increased by $2.7 million. Therefore, since net working capital is defined as current assets minus current liabilities, the increase is $4.3 million − $2.7 million = $1.6 million.

Since Midwestern's sources of funds—$20.1 million—exceeded its uses of funds—$18.5 million—during 19X5 by $1.6 million, the company's funds increased. If Midwestern were to show this increase on the comparative balance sheets, it would be described as an increase in net working capital as follows:

	12/31/X4	12/31/X5	Change
Current assets	$22.8	$27.1	+4.3
Less: Current liabilities	10.0	12.7	+2.7
Net working capital	$12.8	$14.4	+1.6

Funds Flow Analysis as a Financial Planning Technique

Funds flow analysis can also be used to determine how much additional financing a company will need in some future period. Suppose Midwestern is preparing its budgets for 19X6. In the fall of 19X5 the company's financial managers receive acceptable capital expenditure requests from the various divisions and plants totaling $20 million. Referring back to Table 8-3, it is evident that at this point in the budgeting process, net income for 19X6 is expected to be about $6.5 million, and depreciation is expected to be about $6.0 million. Deferred taxes are expected to be about $0.5 million. The firm's management plans to hold dividends constant at $2.5 million. Long-term debt retirement is expected to be $1.5 million, and the management feels that working capital should be increased by about $2.0 million. With this information at hand, the company's financial managers are in a good position to determine roughly how much additional financing Midwestern will require during 19X6. The pro forma funds flow statement shown in Table 8-9 indicates that the firm will need $13 million in additional financing during that year.

Faced with this figure, the firm's management must consider various options, such as the following[12]:

- Lowering capital expenditure requests (capital rationing).
- Securing external financing.
- Some combination of both alternatives.

Before making any final decision, Midwestern's management will want to perform an assessment of what capital market conditions are likely to be next year. It will also probably want to examine a *pro forma balance sheet,* that reflects the assumed funds flow planning illustrated in Table 8-9. An example of a pro forma balance sheet for the year ending December 31, 19X6 is shown in Table 8-10. This analysis allows the firm's management to examine the effects of different-sized capital budgets and various financing schemes on the company's balance sheet.

Table 8-9   **Pro Forma Funds Flow Statement**

Midwestern Manufacturing Company
Pro Forma Funds Flow Statement for 19X6
(in millions of dollars)

Expected Sources of Funds	
Funds expected from operations:	
Net income	$ 6.5
Plus: Depreciation	6.0
Deferred Federal income taxes	0.5
Total funds expected from operations	$13.0
Additional financing required	X
Total expected sources of funds	$13.0 + X
Expected Uses of Funds	
Dividends	$ 2.5
Capital expenditure requests	20.0
Retirement of long-term debt	1.5
Increases in working capital	2.0
Total expected uses of funds	$26.0

Since Expected Sources of Funds must equal Expected Uses of Funds:

$$\$13.0 + X = \$26.0$$
$$X = \$13.0$$

Therefore, the additional financing required is $13.0 million.

---

[12] Another option (source of funds) to consider would be to cut dividends. However, if the company is following a policy of paying stable dividends, a dividend cut could lower the price of its common stock. In this situation, the company would not find this option desirable. Dividend policy is discussed in Chapter 14.

Table 8-10   **Pro Forma Balance Sheet**

Midwestern Manufacturing Company
Pro Forma Summary Balance Sheet for the Year Ending
December 31, 19X6

	December 31, 19X5		December 31, 19X6
	Actual*	Changes†	Projected
Assets			
Current assets‡	$27.1	+2.0	$29.1
Property and equipment	$55.7	+20.0	$75.7
Less: Accumulated depreciation	10.8	6.0	16.8
Net property and equipment	$44.9	+14.0	$58.9
Total assets	$72.0	+16.0	$88.0
Liabilities and Stockholders' Equity			
Current liabilities‡	$12.7	—	$12.7
Long-term debt‖	$17.8	−1.5 + 6.5	$22.8
Deferred Federal income taxes	$ 1.4	+0.5	$ 1.9
Stockholders' equity‖			
Common stock	$ 1.0	+ 0.5	$ 1.5
Additional paid-in capital	19.0	+ 6.0	25.0
Retained earnings	20.1	+ 4.0	24.1
Total stockholders' equity	$40.1	+10.5	$50.6
Total liabilities and stockholders' equity	$72.0	+16.0	$88.0

*From Table 8-7.
†From Table 8-9.
‡This schedule assumes that the working capital increase is added to current assets.
‖This schedule assumes that one half of the projected external financing needs are raised by issuing long-term debt and the other half are raised by selling common stock.

Computerized Financial Planning Models

In the last twenty-five years or so, many companies have spent considerable amounts of time and money developing models to represent various aspects of their financial planning process. Today, these representations are usually computerized and are generally called *financial planning models*. A detailed discussion of these models is beyond the scope of this text, since it requires a familiarity with a number of quantitative techniques, such as regression analysis and linear programming—topics not covered here. A brief general introduction to the topic can be useful for informational purposes, however.

Financial planning models often are classified according to whether they are *deterministic* or *probabilistic* and whether or not they attempt to *optimize* (that is, achieve the most desirable level of) the value of some objective function, such as net income or stock price.

A *deterministic model* gives a single-number forecast of a financial variable or variables without stating anything about its probability of occurrence. An example of a deterministic model is a computerized representation of a firm's operating budget, or a *budget simulator*. Companies that employ budget simulators enter estimated future revenues and expenses into the computer and receive as output an estimate of various financial variables, such as net income and earnings per share. The model tells the company nothing about the chances of achieving these estimates, nor does it indicate whether the company will be able to manage its resources in such a way as to attain higher levels of these variables.

The main advantage of deterministic models is that they allow the user to perform *sensitivity analyses* quickly and easily. A sensitivity analysis essentially consists of rerunning the model to determine the effect on the output variables of changes in the input variables. For example, a company may want to know *what* the net income will be *if* it discontinues some product line. Thus, sensitivity analysis is also called "what if" analysis.

In recent years some companies have started preparing different budgets to reflect different assumptions about the type of year they expect to have. For instance, a company may compile three separate budgets to reflect *pessimistic, realistic,* and *optimistic* assumptions about the coming year. Whereas these scenario analysis models are essentially deterministic, they represent a first step toward the use of probabilistic models.

Probabilistic models are becoming increasingly popular, because they often provide financial decision makers with more useful information than other models. Whereas deterministic models yield single-point estimates, probabilistic models yield more general probability distributions. To illustrate, suppose a company is planning to build a new plant. Instead of estimating a single sales figure, the company's planners might estimate that there is a 25 percent chance that the firm's sales will be $2 million, a 50 percent chance that they will be $3 million, and a 25 percent chance that they will be $4 million. The use of a probabilistic planning model yields output in the form of a probability distribution, which gives the company's planners more useful information than a deterministic model would. In the case of complex probabilistic models, more input is necessary.[13]

Optimization models determine the values of financial decision variables that optimize (that is, maximize or minimize) some objective function such as profits or costs. For example, consider an oil refinery whose capacity and production costs are known. By combining these known figures with estimates of the sales prices for gasoline and heating fuel, it is possible, with the use of an optimization model, to specify what output product mix will achieve an optimal level of operating income. Optimization models are not widely used in finance, even though various applications have been proposed in the financial literature.

Summary

- A firm's financial manager plays an important role in the financial planning process. Basically, the financial planning process involves the development of a set of financial plans for the orderly acquisition and expenditure of funds. Pro forma financial statements are usually an integral part of any financial plan. *Pro forma financial statements* show the results of some *assumed* rather than *actual* events.

- *Financial forecasting* involves the projection and estimation of a company's future financial statements. The percentage of sales method, trend analysis, and econometric techniques are used for these purposes. In the

---

[13] Additional examples of probabilistic models are discussed in Chapter 11.

case of the percentage of sales method, the amount of additional financing that will be needed to support a given future sales level is estimated. In the case of trend analysis, the future value of a financial variable is estimated by extrapolating historical data. In general, the analyst should exercise caution when using either the percentage of sales method or trend analysis, since the techniques involved in these analytical methods assume that the future will simply be a continuation of the past. Econometric techniques involve the use of explanatory variables to forecast future values of financial variables.

- *Budgets* are pro forma financial statements that detail a company's future plans regarding the acquisition and spending of funds. Budgets are used for *planning, coordinating,* and *controlling* the operations of the firm. Companies generally prepare and use three types of budgets: operating budgets, cash budgets, and capital budgets.

- *Operating budgets* combine sales revenue forecasts with production cost estimates to obtain a budgeted income figure.

- *Cash budgets* are projections of cash receipts and disbursements over some future time period. The steps involved in preparing a cash budget include the following:

  1. Estimating cash receipts based on historical information about the collection of receivables.
  2. Scheduling disbursements.
  3. Determining a minimum cash balance.
  4. Calculating the amount of loans required to cover any cash shortages.

- *Capital budgets* are listings of the capital projects (planned additions to the company's fixed assets) a firm plans to place in service during some future period, usually the next year.

- The *funds flow technique* analyzes the *sources* and *uses* of a firm's funds during a particular time period (usually a year). The principal sources of funds from a working capital perspective are the company's operations, borrowings, the sale of stock, and the sale of fixed assets. The principal uses of funds are dividends, capital expenditures, and repayment of long-term debt. In addition to analyzing the actual flow of funds within a company, financial planners often prepare a pro forma funds flow statement in an attempt to determine how much external financing the firm will require.

- A *financial planning model* is a computerized representation of some aspect of a firm's financial planning process. Financial planning models are usually classified according to whether they are *deterministic* or *probabilistic* and whether or not they seek to *optimize* the value of some objective function.

FOCUS ON CORPORATE PRACTICE

Long-Range Planning at Tennessee Gas Transmission — A Tenneco Company

Gordon B. Bonfield, Senior Vice-President and Group Executive

All operating divisions of Tenneco are required to prepare a long-range plan annually. Financials are required for the first five years of the plan; beyond five years, financials are optional.

During the month of October of each year, Tenneco transmits to each of its operating divisions detailed instructions which define the general format and content of the plan. In addition, several assumptions and guidelines are provided to ensure that the various divisions are focusing on corporate goals and that divisional goals are consistent and supportive.

At this time, the planning process at Tennessee Gas Transmission (TGT) begins. At Tennessee Gas Transmission the key to successful planning is teamwork. The functional heads of all pipeline operating groups make up the Planning Committee, and hold several meetings between early November and late January. These meetings are central to TGT's planning process for two reasons. First, they are made up of people experienced in TGT's various areas of business. Second, they provide a framework for cooperation, ensuring that all functional areas work toward the same goals.

The interaction at the Planning Committee meetings leads to successful planning. At TGT the planning process is as important, or more important, than the actual numbers that are later generated. Consistent goals and action plans are developed and refined for each functional area. The Planning Committee also develops strategies that will enhance the company's position in the industry.

During the planning process, the Long-Range Planning Department gathers financial data from the relevant functional areas. This includes projected capital expenditures, O&M expenses, and rate assumptions to be used for cost-of-service projections. During the same period, TGT receives energy price forecasts from Tenneco Corporate Planning to be used for sales and transportation volume projections. As one of three major energy divisions of Tenneco, it is important that TGT use the same energy prices as the other two divisions to ensure that Tenneco's Five-Year Plan is consistent.

Periodically, the Planning Committee's progress is reviewed by the Executive Planning Committee, which is headed by the president of Tennessee Gas Transmission and composed of other senior pipeline management along with the head of the Long-Range Planning Department. The Executive Planning Committee guides the planning process and decides which direction the company will head in the next several years.

In recent years, many key issues that senior management has had to address have arisen from the planning process. For the pipeline division, these issues have been both economic and regulatory in nature. As the natural gas industry moves into an era of less regulation, outside economic forces will tend to control the pipeline division's business environment.

After final approval by the Executive Planning Committee, the Base Plan and accompanying strategies are run through the financial models. In April the financial results, along with the plan itself, are sent to Corporate Planning for review and consolidation with the other operating divisions to become Tenneco's Five-Year Plan.

Questions and Topics for Discussion

1. What are pro forma financial statements?
2. What is the percentage of sales forecasting method? What are some of the limitations financial analysts should be aware of in applying this method?
3. Explain the difference between trend analysis and econometric techniques in forecasting company sales.
4. What is an operating budget? What are the usual steps involved in preparing an operating budget?
5. What is a cash budget? What are the usual steps involved in preparing a cash budget?
6. What is a capital budget?
7. Describe funds flow analysis. What are the principal sources and uses of funds within a firm?
8. Illustrate how funds flow analysis can be used as a financial planning technique.
9. Explain the difference between deterministic and probabilistic financial planning models.
10. Explain how sensitivity analysis can be used in financial planning.

Problems*

1. Consider the Industrial Supply Company example (Table 8-1) again. Assume that the company plans to maintain its dividend payments at the same level in 19X7 as in 19X6. Also asume that all of the additional financing needed is in the form of short-term notes payable. Determine the amount of additional financing required and pro forma financial statements (that is, balance sheet, income statement, and selected financial ratios) for 19X7 under each of the following conditions:

	Increase in Sales	Increase in Expenses
a.	$3,750,000	$3,750,000
b.	$3,000,000	$2,800,000
c.	$3,000,000	$2,600,000
d.	$4,500,000	$4,200,000
e.	$4,500,000	$4,000,000

2. In the Industrial Supply Company example (Table 8-1) it was assumed that the company's fixed assets were being utilized at nearly full capacity and that net fixed assets would have to increase proportionately as sales increased. Alternatively, suppose that the company has excess fixed assets and that *no increase* in net fixed assets are required as sales are increased. Determine the amount of additional financing required for the example discussed in the chapter and the conditions in each of the parts of Problem 1.

3. Using the percentage of sales method, calculate the additional financing needed over the next year for the Baldwin Products Company if a sales level of $6.0 million is expected to be reached in 1 year. The company expects net income during the next year to equal $400,000. During the past several years the company has been paying $50,000 in dividends to its stockholders. The company expects to continue this policy for at least the next year. The actual balance sheet and income statement for Baldwin during 19X8 are provided

---

* Color numbers denote problems which have check answers printed at the end of the book.

below. Show the pro forma balance sheet for the company as of December 31, 19X9, assuming a sales level of $6.0 million is reached. Assume that the additional financing needed is obtained in the form of additional notes payable.

Baldwin Products Company
Balance Sheet
as of December 31, 19X8

Cash	$ 200,000	Accounts payable	$ 600,000
Accounts receivable	400,000	Notes payable	500,000
Inventories	1,200,000	Long-term debt	200,000
Fixed assets, net	500,000	Stockholders' equity	1,000,000
Total assets	$2,300,000	Total liabilities and equity	$2,300,000

Income Statement
for the Year Ending December 31, 19X8

Sales	$4,000,000
Expenses, including interest and taxes	$3,700,000
Net income	$ 300,000

4. Consider Problem 3 again. Suppose that the Baldwin Products' management feels that the average collection period on its additional sales—that is, sales over $4 million—will be 60 days instead of the current level. By what amount will this increase in the average collection period increase the financing needed by the company over the next year?

5. Refer to Problem 3 again. Suppose that the Baldwin Products' banker requires the company to maintain a current ratio equal to 1.6 or greater. What is the maximum amount of additional financing that can be in the form of bank borrowings (notes payable)? What other potential sources of financing are available to the company?

6. Prepare a cash budget for Atlas Products, Inc., for the first quarter of 19X2, based on the following information.

The budgeting section of the corporate finance department of Atlas Products, Inc., has received the following sales estimates from the marketing department:

	Total Sales	Credit Sales
December 19X1	$825,000	$770,000
January 19X2	730,000	690,000
February 19X2	840,000	780,000
March 19X2	920,000	855,000

The company has found that, on the average, about 25 percent of its credit sales are collected during the month when the sale is made, and the remaining 75 percent of credit sales are collected during the month following the sale. As a result, the company uses these figures for budgeting.

The company estimates its purchases at 60 percent of next month's sales, and payments for those purchases are budgeted to lag the purchases by one month.

Various disbursements have been estimated as follows:

	January	February	March
Wages and salaries	$250,000	$290,000	$290,000
Rent	27,000	27,000	27,000
Other expenses	10,000	12,000	14,000

In addition, a tax payment of $105,000 is due on January 15, and $40,000 in dividends will be declared in January and paid in March. Also, the company has ordered a $75,000 piece of equipment. Delivery is scheduled for early January, and payment will be due in February.

The company's projected cash balance at the beginning of January is $100,000, and the company desires to maintain a balance of $100,000 at the end of each month.

7. Prepare a cash budget for Elmwood Manufacturing Company for the first three months of 19X7 based on the following information.

Month	Estimated Sales	Estimated Factory Overhead	Estimated Selling & Administrative Expenses
December	$ 4,600,000	$640,000	$1,250,000
January	6,400,000	650,000	1,275,000
February	11,200,000	670,000	1,285,000
March	8,400,000	670,000	1,310,000
April	7,000,000	680,000	1,300,000

The company has found that approximately 40 percent of sales are collected during the month the sale is made and the remaining 60 percent are collected during the month following the sale. Material purchases are 30 percent of next month's estimated sales and payments lag these purchases by one month. Labor costs are 35% of next month's sales and are paid during the month incurred. Factory overhead and selling and administrative expenses are paid during the month incurred. In addition, a payment for new equipment of $1,500,000 is due in February. Also, a tax payment of $1,600,000 and a dividend payment of $650,000 are due in March.

The company's projected cash balance at the beginning of January is $1,500,000. Furthermore, Elmwood desires to maintain a $750,000 cash balance at the end of each month.

8. Prepare a funds flow statement (defined in terms of net working capital) for the Corting Manufacturing Corporation for the year ending December 19X2, based on the following comparative balance sheets.

Corting Manufacturing Corporation
Comparative Balance Sheets
(in millions of dollars)*

	December 31, 19X1	December 31, 19X2
Assets		
Current assets:		
Cash	$ 4.9	$ 0.8
Accounts receivable	7.2	7.5
Inventories	13.8	14.5
Total current assets	$25.9	$ 22.8
Property and equipment	$80.7	$115.0
Less: Accumulated depreciation	16.3	25.8
Net property and equipment	$64.4	$ 89.2
Total assets	$90.3	$112.0

Corting Manufacturing Corporation
Comparative Balance Sheets
(in millions of dollars)*
(Continued)

	December 31, 19X1	December 31, 19X2
Liabilities and Stockholders' Equity		
Current liabilities:		
Accounts payable	$ 8.0	$ 9.5
Other current liabilities	6.0	8.2
Total current liabilities	$14.0	$ 17.7
Long-term debt	$18.8	$ 31.8
Deferred Federal income taxes	$ 1.2	$ 1.4
Stockholders' equity:		
Common stock	$ 3.0	$ 3.0
Additional paid-in capital	29.0	29.0
Retained earnings	24.3	29.1
Total stockholders' equity	$56.3	$ 61.1
Total liabilities and stockholders' equity	$90.3	$112.0

*Net income for the year ended December 31, 19X2 totaled $8.3 million; dividends paid during the same period totaled $3.5 million; $2.0 million of long-term debt was retired in 19X2; and fixed assets were sold during 19X2 for $1.0 million.

9. The Norfolk Corporation is considering a $200 million expansion (capital expenditure) program next year. The company wants to know approximately how much additional financing (if any) will be required if it decides to go through with the expansion program. Next year the company expects to earn $80 million after interest and taxes. The company also expects to maintain its present level of dividends, which is $15 million. If the expansion program is accepted, the company expects its working capital requirements to increase by approximately $20 million next year to a total of $230 million. Long-term debt retirement obligations total $10 million for next year, and depreciation is expected to be $80 million. The company does not expect to sell any fixed assets next year.

10. Consider Problem 9 again. Assume that Norfolk decides to sell $30 million of existing fixed assets next year. Determine approximately how much additional financing (if any) will be required to undertake the expansion program next year.

An Integrative Case Problem

Financial Analysis and Control

Last year (19X6) Midwest Chemicals, Inc. (MCI), undertook a $20 million plant expansion and modernization program. The firm had originally planned to finance the program partially from the sale of new common stock. However, due to depressed stock prices, a stock offering was not feasible at that time. Instead, the firm financed the entire $20 million with a five-year term loan from a large insurance company. Because of tight money conditions in the economy and the relatively large amount of debt in its capital structure, MCI was required to pay 14 percent interest on the term loan. MCI also has a mortgage loan of $20 million outstanding, which is being repaid in annual installments of $2 million (due on December 30 each year) plus 10 percent interest. The balance sheet and income statement for the current year (19X7), along with some relevant industry ratios, are shown in the tables.

Midwest Chemicals, Inc.
(A) Balance Sheet as of December 31, 19X7
(in thousands of dollars)

Assets

Cash	$ 4,000	
Accounts receivable	22,000	
Inventories	22,000	
Total current assets		$ 48,000
Plant and equipment	$70,000	
Less: Accumulated depreciation	30,000	
Net plant and equipment		40,000
Total assets		$ 88,000

Liabilities and Stockholders' Equity

Accounts payable	$ 18,000
Current portion of mortgage loan ($i = 10\%$)	2,000
Total current liabilities	$ 20,000
Mortgage loan ($i = 10\%$)	16,000
Term loan	20,000
Stockholders' equity (common stock and retained earnings)	32,000
Total liabilities and stockholders' equity	$ 88,000

(B) Income Statement for the Year Ending
December 31, 19X7
(in thousands of dollars)

Sales		$148,000
Less: Raw materials	$76,000	
Labor	10,000	
Depreciation	6,000	
Cost of goods sold		92,000
Gross profit		$ 56,000
Less: Selling and administrative expenses		45,200
Earnings before interest and taxes		$ 10,800
Less: Interest expense		4,800
Net income before taxes		$ 6,000
Less: Federal and state income tax (40%)		2,400
Net income after taxes		$ 3,600
Less: Common stock dividends (1,000,000 × $2.00/share)		2,000
Net additions to retained earnings		$ 1,600

Ratio	Industry Average
Current	2.7 times
Quick	1.7 times
Debt-to-equity	86%
Times interest earned (EBIT ÷ Interest charges)	5.4 times
Net profit margin on sales	3.77%
Return on stockholders' equity	13.5%

Conditions in the capital markets have improved considerably since last year (that is, the price of MCI common stock has risen and interest rates have fallen). The treasurer of MCI has decided that this would be an opportune time to float (that is, sell) an issue of common stock and use the proceeds to reduce the amount of high-cost debt in the firm's capital structure. Specifically, the firm plans to sell 200,000 shares of new common stock at a net price of $50 per share to yield the firm $10 million. The funds would be used to repay one-half of the term loan, thus reducing its interest expenses and improving its financial position.

The MCI economists have forecast a 10 percent increase in the firm's sales for next year (19X8). Raw material, labor, and selling and administrative expenses are also expected to increase by 10 percent next year. Depreciation expenses next year are anticipated to be $4 million. The firm's (combined) Federal and state income tax rate is expected to remain at 40 percent next year. The board of directors of the firm is expected to increase the dividend rate by 10 percent to $2.20 per share.

Receivables and inventories are expected to rise by 10 percent next year as a result of the forecasted sales increase. The treasurer feels that the firm's minimum cash needs can be met with the existing $4 million balance during the coming year. New additions to plant and equipment totaling $2 million are planned during the coming year. The firm has been paying many of its trade creditors beyond the due date and would like to avoid this situation in the future. To accomplish this, the firm wants to hold its accounts payable at $18 million during the coming year, even though its raw material purchases will increase.

1. Prepare a pro forma income statement for MCI for 19X8.
2. Prepare a pro forma balance sheet for MCI as of December 31, 19X8. Use "additional short-term debt" as the balancing account to reflect the need for additional financing. (HINT: First determine MCI's assets and then determine liabilities and net worth. Total assets should equal $90,400[000].)
3. How much additional financing (beyond that generated from operations) is required to meet the needs of the firm? What are some possible sources of these funds?
4. Prepare a pro forma funds flow statement for 19X8.
5. Using a ratio analysis of the firm's pro forma statements for 19X8, evaluate the impact of the proposed financing plan on the financial condition of the firm.
6. What are the reasons why the percentage of sales forecasting method cannot be used in this case?

Selected References

Carleton, W. T., and J. M. McInnes. "Theory, Models and Implementation in Financial Management." *Management Science* (Sept. 1981):957–978.

Chambers, John C., Satinder K. Mullick, and Donald D. Smith. "How to Choose the Right Forecasting Technique." *Harvard Business Review* 49 (July–Aug. 1971):45–74.

Francis, Jack C., and Dexter R. Powell "A Simultaneous Equation Model of the Firm for Financial Analysis and Planning." *Financial Management* (Spring 1979):29–44.

Hunt, Pearson. "Funds Position: Keystone in Financial Planning." *Harvard Business Review* 53 (May–June 1975):106–115.

Judelson, David N. "Financial Controls That Work." *Financial Executive* 45 (Jan. 1977):22–27.

Maier, Steven F., and James H. Vander Weide. "A Practical Approach to Short-Run Financial Planning." *Financial Management* (Winter 1978):10–16.

Myers, Stewart C., and Gerald A. Pogue. "The Programming Approach to Corporate Financial Management." *Journal of Finance* 29 (May 1974):579–699.

Smith, Gary, and William Brainard. "The Value of A Priori Information in Estimating a Financial Model." *Journal of Finance* 31 (Dec. 1976):1299–1322.

Warren, James M., and John P. Shelton. "A Simultaneous Equation Approach to Financial Planning." *Journal of Finance* 26 (Dec. 1971):1123–1142.

Wheelwright, Steven C., and Daniel G. Clarke. "Corporate Forecasting: Promise and Reality." *Harvard Business Review* (Nov.–Dec. 1976):40–68.

PART FOUR

THE CAPITAL INVESTMENT DECISION

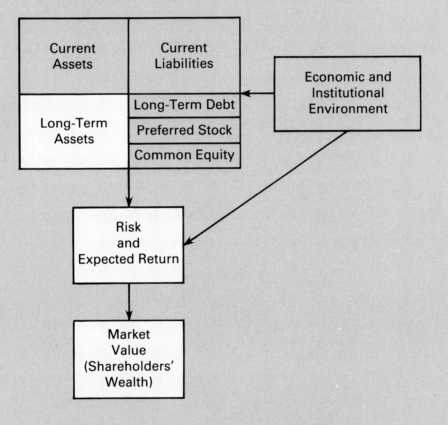

This part of the text looks at the financial management of the long-term asset portion of a firm's balance sheet. Investments in these assets (for example, property, plant, and equipment) have a major impact on a firm's future stream of earnings and the risk of those earnings. As such, the long-term investment (capital budgeting) decision has a significant effect on the value of the firm. Chapter 9 deals with the measurement of cash flows from long-term investments. Chapter 10 analyzes various investment decision criteria in light of the wealth maximization objective of the firm. Chapter 11 extends the analysis to consider techniques to account for differential levels of risk among projects.

9

CAPITAL BUDGETING AND CASH FLOW ANALYSIS

A Financial Dilemma

Lockheed's L-1011 Tri-Star Jet Stalls

During the 1970s Lockheed sought, and eventually received, a $250 million Federal loan guarantee which enabled it to complete development of its L-1011 wide-bodied commercial jet. The loan guarantee was needed because Lockheed was experiencing serious liquidity problems due to cost overruns on some of its military projects and the costs of developing the L-1011. Lockheed's stock price had dropped from $73 to $3 per share, and bankers were unwilling to lend the firm additional funds without a government guarantee.

When Lockheed analyzed the L-1011 program, the firm estimated that if it sold between 195 and 200 aircraft, the project would break even. Beyond that point substantial profits were anticipated. With firm orders for 178 aircraft in hand, Lockheed was prepared to commit 2.5 billion dollars to the project over a ten-year period.

The capital investment analysis which Lockheed did for the L-1011 program was flawed, however, because it neglected to consider the *opportunity cost* of the capital funds committed to the project. In other words, Lockheed did not consider the rate of return that could have been earned on the $2.5 billion if those funds had been invested in an alternative project. If Lockheed's analysis had considered the cost of the capital funds required, the firm would have concluded that the breakeven point was substantially above the projected 195 to 200 plane level and that the project had a negative net present value and was therefore unacceptable.

Lockheed received the requested loan guarantee. The company went forward with the L-1011 program and actually produced about 240 of the planes. Lockheed reported losses on the program well in excess of $500 million dollars. A more correct analysis of this project's cash in-

flows and required outlays might have helped Lockheed avoid this financial catastrophy.

The analysis of capital investments (that is, projects having economic lives extending beyond a year in time) is a key financial management function. Each year large and small firms spend hundreds of billions of dollars on capital investments. These investments chart the course of a company's future for many years to come. Thus it is imperative that capital investment analysis be performed correctly. This chapter develops the principles of capital investment analysis—with emphasis being placed on the estimation of cash flows from a project. Chapter 10 considers appropriate decision criteria in the capital budgeting process.

Key Chapter Concepts

1. *Capital budgeting* is the process of planning for purchases of assets whose returns (cash flows) are expected to continue beyond one year.

2. The *cost of capital* is defined as the cost of funds supplied to a firm. It represents the required rate of return that a firm must earn on its investments, and thus is an important input in the capital budgeting process.

3. There are four key steps in the capital budgeting process, including:
   a. Generating investment project proposals.
   b. Estimating cash flows.
   c. Evaluating alternatives and selecting projects to be implemented.
   d. Reviewing a project's performance after it has been implemented, and postauditing its performance after termination.

4. Investment projects can be generated by growth opportunities, generated by cost reduction opportunities, and generated in order to meet legal requirements and health and safety standards.

5. The initial outlay required to implement a project is called the *net investment*. It includes:
   a. The installed cost of the assets,
   b. Plus any net working capital requirements,
   c. Less any cash inflows from the sale of replacement assets, and
   d. Plus or minus the tax consequences associated with the sale of existing assets and/or the purchase of new assets.

6. The *net cash flow* from a project is equal to the change in net income after taxes plus the change in depreciation associated with the adoption of a project. In the last year of a project's life this net cash flow definition may have to be modified to reflect the recapture of the net working capital investment and any after-tax salvage value received.

7. The economic viability of a project can be affected by special tax considerations, such as the availability of the Investment Tax Credit and the use of accelerated depreciation methods, such as the Accelerated Cost Recovery System (ACRS) of depreciation.

Glossary of New Terms

ACRS depreciation The Accelerated Cost Recovery System of depreciation, established in 1981.

Capital budgeting The process of planning for purchases of assets whose returns (cash flows) are expected to continue beyond one year.

Capital expenditure The amount of money spent to purchase a long-term asset, such as a piece of equipment. This cash outlay is generally expected to result in a flow of future cash benefits extending beyond one year in time. (Also called *capital investment.*)

Capital rationing The process of limiting the number of capital expenditure projects because of insufficient funds to finance all projects that otherwise meet the firm's criteria for acceptability, or because of a lack of sufficient managerial resources to undertake all otherwise acceptable projects.

Contingent project A project whose acceptance depends on the adoption of one or more other projects.

Depreciation The systematic allocation of the cost of an asset over its expected economic life or some other period of time for financial reporting purposes, tax purposes, or both.

Independent project A project whose acceptance or rejection does not directly result in the elimination of other projects from consideration.

Mutually exclusive project A project whose acceptance precludes the acceptance of one or more alternative projects.

Net cash flow Cash inflow minus cash outflow. It is often measured as income after tax plus non-cash expenses associated with a particular investment project.

Net investment The net cash outlay required at the beginning of an investment project.

Normal project A project whose cash flow stream requires an initial outlay of funds followed by a series of positive net cash inflows. This is also sometimes called a *conventional project.*

Introduction

This is the first of several chapters that explicitly deal with the financial management of the assets on a firm's balance sheet. In this and the following two chapters we consider the management of long-term assets. Later in the book (Chapters 18 to 21) the emphasis shifts to the management of short-term assets, that is, the working capital decision.

Capital budgeting is the process of planning for purchases of assets whose returns are expected to continue beyond one year. A *capital expenditure* is a cash outlay that is expected to generate a flow of future cash benefits lasting longer than one year. It is distinguished from a normal operating expenditure, which is expected to result in cash benefits during the coming one-year period. (The choice of a one-year period is arbitrary, but it does serve as a useful guideline.)

There are several different types of cash outlays that may be classified as capital expenditures and evaluated using the framework of capital budgeting models, including the following:

- The purchase of a new piece of equipment, real estate, or a building in order to expand an existing product or service line or enter a new line of business.
- The replacement of an existing capital asset, such as a drill press.
- Expenditures for an advertising campaign.
- Expenditures for a research and development program.
- Investments in permanent increases of target inventory levels or levels of accounts receivable.
- Investments in employee education and training.
- The refunding of an old bond issue with a new, lower interest issue.
- Lease-versus-buy analysis.
- Merger and acquisition evaluation.

Capital expenditures are important to a firm both because they require sizable cash outlays and because they have a long-range impact on the firm's performance. Table 9-1 summarizes the capital expenditures made by U.S. firms during 1981 and 1985. Total capital expenditures of all industries in the United States during 1985 exceeded $383 *billion* dollars. During 1985 Exxon earned about $5.1 billion after taxes and made outlays for new plant facilities and equipment in excess of $8.1 billion. Bethlehem Steel had 1985 losses of $195 million, yet it made nearly $300 million in capital expenditures that year.

A firm's capital expenditures affect its future profitability and, when taken together, essentially plot the company's future direction by determining which products will be produced, which markets will be entered, where production facilities will be located, and what type of technology will be used. Capital expenditure decision making is important for another reason as well. Specifically, it is often difficult, if not impossible, to reverse a major capital expenditure without incurring considerable additional expense. For example, if a firm acquires highly specialized production facilities and equipment, it must recognize that there may be no ready used-equipment market in which to dispose of them if they do not generate the desired future cash flows. For these reasons, a firm's management

Table 9-1   **Capital Expenditures Made by Selected Groups of U.S. Firms**

Industry	(in billions of dollars)	
	1981	1985*
Manufacturing	126.79	153.44
Durable goods	61.84	73.58
Nondurable goods	64.95	79.86
Mining	16.86	16.08
Transportation	12.05	17.57
Railroad	4.24	7.24
Air	3.81	4.28
Other	4.00	6.05
Public utilities	38.40	48.08
Electric	29.74	35.53
Gas and other	8.65	12.56

*Estimated.

Source: *Survey of Current Business* (U.S. Department of Commerce), September 1985.

should establish a number of definite procedures to follow when analyzing capital expenditure projects. Choosing from among such projects is the objective of capital budgeting models.

Key Terms and Concepts in Capital Budgeting

Before proceeding with the discussion of the capital budgeting process, it is necessary to introduce a number of terms and concepts encountered in subsequent chapters.

Cost of Capital

A firm's *cost of capital* is defined as the cost of the funds supplied to it. It is also termed the *required rate of return,* since it specifies the minimum necessary rate of return required by the firm's investors. In this context, the cost of capital provides the firm with a basis for choosing among various capital investment projects. In this and the following two chapters it is assumed that the cost of capital is a known value. Chapter 12 explores the methods used to determine the cost of capital.

How Projects are Classified

A firm usually encounters several different types of projects when making capital expenditure decisions, including *independent projects, mutually exclusive projects,* and *contingent projects.* As is demonstrated in Chapter 10, project classification can influence the investment decision process.

Independent Projects   An independent project is one whose acceptance or rejection does not directly eliminate other projects from consideration. For example, a firm may want to install a new telephone communications system in its headquarters and replace a drill press during approximately the same time. In the absence of a constraint on the availability of funds, both projects could be adopted if they meet minimum investment criteria.

Mutually Exclusive Projects   A mutually exclusive project is one whose acceptance precludes the acceptance of one or more alternative proposals.

Since two mutually exclusive projects have the capacity to perform the same function for a firm, only one should be chosen. For example, Volkswagen was faced with deciding whether it should locate its U.S. assembly plant in Cleveland, Ohio, or New Stanton, Pennsylvania. It ultimately chose the New Stanton site, and this precluded the Cleveland alternative.

Contingent Projects A contingent project is one whose acceptance is dependent on the adoption of one or more other projects. For example, the installation of pollution control equipment in a new plant is contingent upon the acceptance of that new plant as a desirable investment. When a firm is considering contingent projects, it is best to consider together all projects that are dependent on one another and treat them as a single project for purposes of evaluation.

Availability of Funds

When a firm has adequate funds to invest in all projects that meet some capital budgeting selection criterion, the firm is said to be operating without a *funds constraint*. Frequently, however, the total initial cost of the acceptable projects in the absence of a funds constraint is greater than the total funds the firm has chosen to invest in capital projects. This necessitates *capital rationing,* or the setting of limits on capital expenditures, and results in some special capital budgeting problems.[1]

Basic Framework for Capital Budgeting

According to economic theory, a firm should operate at the point where the marginal cost of an additional unit of output just equals the marginal revenue derived from the output. Following this rule leads to *profit maximization*. This principle may also be applied to capital budgeting decisions. In this context, a firm's marginal revenue is the rates of return earned on succeeding investments, and marginal cost may be defined as the firm's *marginal cost of capital* (MCC), that is, the cost of successive increments of capital acquired by the firm.

Figure 9-1 illustrates a simplified capital budgeting model. This model assumes that all projects have the same risk. This assumption is relaxed in Chapter 11. The projects under consideration are indicated by lettered bars on the graph.

Project A requires an investment of $2 million and is expected to generate a 24 percent rate of return. Project B will cost $1 million ($3 million minus $2 million on the horizontal axis) and is expected to generate a 22 percent rate of return, and so on. The projects are arranged in descending order according to their expected rates of return, in recognition of the fact that no firm has an inexhaustible supply of projects offering high expected rates of return. This schedule of projects is often called the firm's investment opportunity curve (IOC). Typically, a firm will invest in its best projects first—such as Project A—before moving on to less attractive alternatives.

The MCC schedule represents the marginal cost of capital to the firm.

---

[1] These are treated in Chapter 10.

Figure 9-1   **Simplified Capital Budgeting Model**

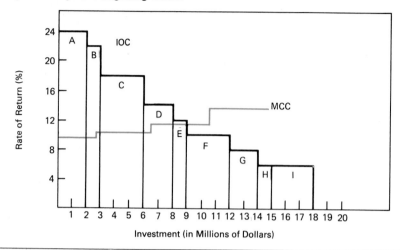

Investment (in Millions of Dollars)

Note that the schedule increases as more funds are sought in the capital markets. The reasons for this include the following:

- Investors' expectations about the firm's ability to successfully undertake a large number of new projects.
- The business risk to which the firm is exposed because of its particular line of business.
- The firm's financial risk, which is due to its capital structure.
- The supply and demand for investment capital in the capital market.
- The cost of selling new stock, which is greater than the cost of retained earnings.

The basic capital budgeting model indicates that, in principle, the firm should undertake Projects A, B, C, D, and E, since the expected returns from each project exceed the firm's marginal cost of capital. Unfortunately, however, financial decision making in practice is not this simple. Some practical problems are encountered in trying to apply this model, including the following:

- At any point in time a firm will probably not know all of the capital projects available to it. In most firms, capital expenditures are proposed continually, based on results of research and development programs, changing market conditions, new technologies, corporate planning efforts, and so on. Thus, a schedule of projects similar to Figure 9-1 will probably be incomplete at the time the firm makes its capital expenditure decisions.
- The shape of the MCC schedule itself may be difficult to determine. (The problems and techniques involved in estimating a firm's cost of capital are discussed in Chapter 12.)
- In most cases a firm can make only uncertain estimates of a project's future costs and revenues (and, consequently, its rate of return). Some

projects will be more risky than others. The riskier a project is, the greater the rate of return which is required before it will be acceptable. (This concept is considered in more detail in Chapter 11.)

In spite of these and other problems, all firms make capital investment decisions. This chapter and the following two chapters provide tools that may be applied to the capital budgeting decision-making process.

Briefly, that process consists of four important steps:

1. Generating capital investment project proposals.

2. Estimating cash flows.

3. Evaluating alternatives and selecting projects to be implemented.

4. Reviewing a project's performance after it has been implemented, and postauditing its performance after its termination.

The remainder of this chapter is devoted to a discussion of the first two steps.

Generating Capital Investment Project Proposals

Ideas for new capital investments can come from many sources, both inside and outside a firm. Proposals may originate at all levels of the organization—from factory workers up to the board of directors. Most large and medium-sized firms allocate the responsibility for identifying and analyzing capital expenditures to specific staff groups. These can include cost accounting, industrial engineering, marketing research, research and development, and corporate planning groups. In most firms, systematic procedures are established to assist in the search and analysis steps. For example, many firms provide detailed forms that the originator of a capital expenditure proposal must complete. These forms normally request information on the project's initial cost, the revenues it is expected to generate, and how it will affect the firm's overall operating expenses. These data are then channeled to a reviewer or group of reviewers at a higher level in the firm for analysis and possible acceptance or rejection.

Where a proposal goes for review often depends on how the particular project is *classified*.

Classifying Investment Projects

As noted earlier, there are several types of capital expenditures. These can be grouped into *projects generated by growth opportunities, projects generated by cost reduction opportunities,* and *projects generated in order to meet legal requirements and health and safety standards.*

Projects Generated by Growth Opportunities Assume that a firm produces a particular product that is expected to be in increasing demand during the upcoming years. If the firm's existing facilities are inadequate to handle the demand, proposals should be developed for expanding the firm's capacity. These proposals may come from the corporate planning staff group, from a divisional staff group, or from some other source.

Since most existing products eventually become obsolete, a firm's growth is also dependent on the development and marketing of new products. This involves the generation of research and development investment proposals, marketing research investments, test marketing investments, and perhaps even investments in new plant, property, and equipment. For example, in order for the mineral extraction industries to keep growing, they must continually make investments in exploration and development. Similarly, firms in high technology industries—such as electronics and computers—must undertake continuing programs of research and development to compete successfully.

Projects Generated by Cost Reduction Opportunities Just as products become obsolete over time, so do plant, property, equipment, and production processes. Normal use makes older plants more expensive to operate because of the higher cost of maintenance and down time (idle time). In addition, new technological developments may render existing equipment economically obsolete. These factors create opportunities for cost reduction investments, which include replacing old, obsolete capital equipment with newer, more efficient equipment.

Projects Generated in Order to Meet Legal Requirements and Health and Safety Standards These projects include investment proposals for such things as pollution control, ventilation, and fire protection equipment. In terms of analysis, this group of projects is best considered as contingent upon other projects.

To illustrate, suppose a firm wishes to build a new steel plant in Cleveland, Ohio. The decision will be contingent upon the investment in the amount of pollution abatement equipment required by state and local laws. Thus, the decision to invest in the new plant must be based upon the *total* cost of the plant, including the pollution abatement equipment, and not just the operating equipment alone.

In the case of existing facilities, this type of decision making is sometimes more complex. For example, suppose a firm is told it must install new pollution abatement equipment in a plant that has been in operation for some time. The firm first needs to determine the lowest cost alternative that will meet these legal requirements. "Lowest cost" is normally measured by the smallest present value of net cash outflows from the project. Then management must decide whether the remaining stream of cash flows from the plant is sufficient to justify the expenditure. If it appears as though it will not be, the firm may consider building a new facility, or it may decide to simply close down the original plant.

Project Size and the Decision-Making Process

Whereas the classification of a proposed project influences the capital investment decision-making process, there are other factors to consider—in particular, the size of the expenditure required to carry out the project.

Most firms *decentralize* the decision-making function. For example, whereas the approval of the president and the board of directors may be needed for especially large outlays, a divisional vice-president may be the final decision maker in the case of medium-sized outlays. A plant manager may have responsibility for deciding on smaller outlays, and a department head in a particular plant may be authorized to approve small outlays (of less than $2,000, for example). This "chain of command" varies with individual companies. In large firms, however, it is impossible for any one

Figure 9-2

Illustration of Estimated Cash Flows for a Normal Capital Investment Project

End of Year

0	1	2	3	4	5
$-100,000	$+50,000	$+40,000	$+30,000	$+25,000	$+5,000
(Net Investment)		(Net Cash Flows)			

person to make every decision regarding proposed capital expenditures, and a decentralized system is usually employed.

Principles of Estimating Cash Flows

The capital budgeting process is primarily concerned with the estimation of the *cash flows* associated with a project, not just the project's contribution to accounting profits. Typically, a capital expenditure requires an initial *cash outflow,* termed the *net investment.* Thus, it is important to measure a project's performance in terms of the *net cash inflows* it is expected to generate over a number of future years.

Figure 9-2 shows the estimated cash flows for a particular project. After an initial net investment of $100,000, the project is expected to generate a stream of net cash inflows over its anticipated 5-year life of $50,000 in year 1; $40,000 in year 2; $30,000 in year 3; $25,000 in year 4; and $5,000 in year 5. This type of project is called a *normal* or *conventional project.*

Nonnormal or nonconventional projects have different cash flow patterns. Table 9-2 illustrates the cash flow patterns for four nonnormal projects. Project W, for example, might be a research and development effort for a new product, or perhaps a new construction project. The company has to make cash outlays for three years before the project is expected to generate any net benefits. This type of project poses few problems for analysis. Projects X, Y, and Z, in contrast, can cause some analytical problems, as we shall see. Project X might require that certain equipment be shut down and rebuilt in year 3, and Project Y could be an investment in a mining property, with the negative cash flow in year 5 representing abandonment costs associated with closing down the mine after its mineral wealth has been depleted. Finally, Project Z might represent the investment in some pollution control equipment.

Regardless of whether a project's cash flows are expected to be normal or nonnormal, certain basic principles should be applied during their

Table 9-2

Sample Cash Flow Patterns for Nonnormal Projects

Project	Year					
	0	**1**	**2**	**3**	**4**	**5**
W	−$100,000	−$30,000	−$20,000	+$50,000	+$150,000	+$200,000
X	−100,000	+80,000	+60,000	−50,000	+75,000	+60,000
Y	−200,000	+150,000	+50,000	+40,000	+30,000	−20,000
Z	−150,000	−20,000	−20,000	−25,000	−25,000	−30,000

estimation, including the following:

- **Cash flows should be measured on an incremental basis.** In other words, the cash flow stream for a particular project should be estimated from the perspective of how the entire cash flow stream of the firm will be affected if the project is adopted as compared with how the stream will be affected if the project is not adopted. Thus, *all* changes in the firm's revenue stream, cost stream, and tax stream that would result from the acceptance of the project should be included in the analysis. In contrast, cash flows that would not be changed by the investment should be disregarded.

- **Cash flows should be measured on an after-tax basis.** Since the initial investment made on a project requires the outlay of after-tax cash dollars, the returns from the project should be measured in the same units—namely, after-tax cash flows.

- **All the indirect effects of a project should be included in the cash flow calculations.** For example, if a proposed plant expansion requires that working capital be increased for the firm as a whole—perhaps in the form of larger cash balances, inventories, or accounts receivable—the increase in working capital should be included in the *net investment* required for the project. As another example, assume that one division of a firm introduces a new product that competes directly with a product produced by another division. The first division may consider this product desirable, but when the impact on the second division's sales are considered, the project may be much less attractive.

- **Sunk costs should not be considered when evaluating a project.** A *sunk cost* is an outlay which has already been made (or committed to be made). Since sunk costs cannot be recovered, they should not be considered in the decision to accept or reject a project. For example, in 1987 the Chemtron Corporation was considering constructing a new chemical disposal facility. Two years earlier the firm had hired the R.O.E. Consulting Group to do an environmental impact analysis of the proposed site at a cost of $500,000. Since this $500,000 cost cannot be recovered whether the project is undertaken or not, it should not be considered in the accept/reject analysis which is taking place in 1987. The only costs which are relevant are the incremental outlays which will be made from this point forward if the project is undertaken.

- **The value of resources used in a project should be measured in terms of their opportunity costs.** *Opportunity costs* of resources (assets) are the cash flows which those resources could generate if they are not used in the project under consideration. For example, suppose that the site Chemtron is considering to use for its disposal facility has been owned by the firm for some time. The property originally cost $50,000, but a recent appraisal indicates that the property could be sold for $1 million. Since Chemtron must forego the receipt of $1 million from the sale of the site if the disposal facility is constructed, the appropriate opportunity cost of this piece of land is $1 million, not the original cost of $50,000.

These five principles of cash flow estimation may be applied to the specific problem of defining and calculating a project's *net investment* and *net cash flows.*

Net Investment (NINV)

The *net investment* (NINV) in a project is defined as the project's inital net cash outlay. It is calculated using the following steps:

Step 1. The new project cost plus any installation and shipping costs associated with acquiring the asset and putting it into service[2]

PLUS

Step 2. Any increases in net working capital required as a result of the new investment[3]

MINUS

Step 3. The net proceeds from the sale of existing assets when the investment is a replacement decision[4]

PLUS or MINUS

Step 4. The taxes associated with the sale of the existing asset and/or the purchase of the new one[5]

EQUALS

The net investment (NINV).

The calculation of the net investment for two example projects is illustrated below. Discussed in the following sections are some of the tax consequences which can influence the net investment of a project. These tax effects are the Investment Tax Credit (ITC) and the treatment of gains and losses from asset sales in the case of replacement decisions.

Some projects, such as project W in Table 9-2, require outlays over more than one year before positive cash inflows are generated. In these cases the NINV for that project will be equal to the present value (at time 0) of this series of outlays, discounted at the firm's cost of capital. For example, the NINV of Project W, assuming a cost of capital of 10 percent and ignoring the ITC equals $143,790, computed as follows:[6]

Year	Cash Outlay	$PVIF_{0.10,n}$	Present Value of NINV
0	$100,000	1.000	$100,000
1	30,000	0.909	27,270
2	20,000	0.826	16,520
			$143,790

[2] The asset cost plus installation and shipping costs form the basis upon which the Investment Tax Credit (ITC), if allowed, is computed. The ITC is discussed later in this chapter.

[3] The increase in working capital (such as cash, inventories, and accounts receivable) should be calculated *net* of any automatic increases in current liabilities (such as accounts payable or wages and taxes payable) that occur because the project is adopted and that have no explicit (cash) cost to the firm. For replacement-type investments there is normally no net working capital increase. For expansion (new product or additional capacity) investments, additional net working capital would normally be required.

[4] This is normally computed as the actual salvage value of the asset being replaced less any costs associated with physically removing or selling it.

[5] These taxes include the effects of the ITC, as well as any taxes associated with the disposal of the old asset. The total tax effect may be either positive or negative; this is why it is either added to or subtracted from the new project cost.

[6] For tax purposes, the installed cost of this asset would be $150,000—the actual cash outlays required to put the plant or equipment in service.

Net Cash Flows

Capital investment projects are expected to generate after-tax cash flow streams after the initial net investment has been made. The process of estimating project cash flows is an important part of the capital budgeting process.

In general, cash flows are defined as follows:

$$\text{Cash flow (CF)} = \text{Earnings after taxes (EAT)} + \text{Noncash charges.} \quad \textbf{(9.1)}$$

The most significant noncash charge normally found on a firm's income statement is depreciation.[7] Depreciation is the systematic allocation of the cost of an asset with an economic life in excess of one year. Depreciation reduces reported profits and it also reduces taxes paid by a firm.

Capital budgeting is primarily concerned with the *incremental, after-tax net cash flows* (NCF) of a particular project, or cash inflows minus cash outflows. For any year during the life of a project, these may be defined as the change in earnings after taxes, ΔEAT, plus the change in depreciation, ΔD:

$$\text{NCF} = \Delta\text{EAT} + \Delta D. \quad \textbf{(9.2)}$$

ΔEAT is equal to the change in earnings before taxes (ΔEBT) times $(1 - t)$, where t is the marginal tax rate:

$$\Delta\text{EAT} = \Delta\text{EBT}(1 - t). \quad \textbf{(9.3)}$$

ΔEBT is defined as the change in revenues, ΔR, minus the changes in cash operating costs, ΔO, and depreciation, ΔD:

$$\Delta\text{EBT} = \Delta R - \Delta O - \Delta D. \quad \textbf{(9.4)}$$

Substituting Equation 9.4 into Equation 9.3 yields the following:

$$\Delta\text{EAT} = (\Delta R - \Delta O - \Delta D)(1 - t).$$

Substituting this equation into Equation 9.2 yields the following definition of net cash flow:

$$\text{NCF} = (\Delta R - \Delta O - \Delta D)(1 - t) + \Delta D. \quad \textbf{(9.5)}$$

This equation can be further extended into an *operational* definition of NCF by defining ΔR as $R_2 - R_1$, ΔO as $O_2 - O_1$, and ΔD as $D_2 - D_1$, where

R_1 = Revenues of the firm if it *does not* adopt the project.

R_2 = Revenues of the firm if it *adopts* the project.

O_1 = Cash operating costs for the firm *without* the project.

---

[7] Depreciation *itself* is not a cash flow. Rather, it reduces earnings before taxes (EBT) and thus reduces income tax payments (a cash outflow). Equation 9.1 provides an easy procedure for reflecting the cash flow impact of depreciation.

O_2 = Cash operating costs for the firm *with* the project.

D_1 = Depreciation charges for the firm *without* the project.

D_2 = Depreciation charges for the firm *with* the project.

The definition given in Equation 9.5 can be rewritten as follows:

$$NCF = [(R_2 - R_1) - (O_2 - O_1) - (D_2 - D_1)](1 - t) + (D_2 - D_1). \quad \textbf{(9.6)}$$

In the final year of a project's economic life Equation 9.6 must be modified to reflect two additional cash flow items: (1) recovery of the after-tax salvage value of the asset(s) and (2) recovery of the net working capital investment.

Recovery of After-Tax Salvage Value

Whenever an asset is sold which has been depreciated, there are potential tax consequences which may affect the after-tax net proceeds received from the asset sale. These tax consequences are important when estimating the after-tax salvage value to be received at the end of the economic life of any project. As discussed above, the tax consequences of asset sales are also important when calculating the net investment required in a replacement investment project. There are four cases which need to be considered.

Case 1: Sale of an Asset for its Book Value If a company disposes of an asset for an amount exactly equal to the asset's tax book value, there is neither a gain nor a loss on the sale, and thus there are no tax consequences. For example, if the ABC Company sells for $50,000 an asset with a book value for tax purposes of $50,000, there are no taxes associated with this disposal. (In general the tax book value of an asset equals the installed cost of the asset less accumulated tax depreciation. Under the ACRS schedule of depreciation, discussed later in the chapter, the tax book value for assets acquired after January 1, 1983 is equal to the installed cost less one-half of any allowed Investment Tax Credit [discussed below] less accumulated ACRS depreciation.)

Case 2: Sale of an Asset for Less Than its Book Value If the ABC Company sells for $20,000 an asset having a tax book value of $50,000, the firm incurs a $30,000 pretax loss. Assuming that this asset is used in business or trade (an essential criterion for this tax treatment), this loss may be treated as an operating loss or an offset to operating income. This operating loss effectively reduces the company's taxes by an amount equal to the loss times the company's marginal tax rate.

Assume that the company's income before taxes is $100,000 (before consideration of the operating loss from the disposal of the asset). Taxes on this income are $100,000 times the company's marginal (40 percent) tax rate, or $40,000. Because of the operating loss incurred by selling the asset for $20,000, the company's taxable income is reduced to $70,000, and the taxes decline to $28,000 (40 percent of $70,000). The $12,000 difference in taxes is equal to the tax loss on the sale of the old asset times the company's marginal tax rate ($30,000 × 40%).

Case 3: Sale of an Asset for More Than its Book Value but Less Than its Original Cost   If the ABC Company sells the asset for $60,000—$10,000 more than the current tax book value—$50,000 of this amount constitutes a tax-free cash inflow, and the remaining $10,000 is taxed as operating income. As a result, the firm's taxes increase by $4,000, or the amount of the gain times the firm's marginal tax rate ($10,000 × 40%). (The IRS treats this gain as a recapture of depreciation.)

Case 4: Sale of an Asset for More Than its Original Cost   If the ABC Company sells the asset for $120,000 (assuming an original asset cost of $110,000), part of the gain from the sale is treated as ordinary income, and part is treated as a long-term *capital gain.* The gain receiving ordinary income treatment is equal to the difference between the original asset cost and the current tax book value, or $60,000 ($110,000 − $50,000). The capital gain portion is the amount in excess of the original asset cost, or $10,000. (Note: The 1986 tax reform bill abolishes this special capital gains treatment and taxes the entire gain as ordinary income. See Appendix A at the end of the book for details.)

Recovery of Working Capital

In the last year of a project that has required net working capital as part of the initial net investment, this net working capital is assumed to be liquidated and returned to the firm as cash. Hence, the net working capital must be added to the net cash flows in the last year of the project. There are, of course, no tax consequences associated with this transaction.

Interest Charges and Net Cash Flows

Often the purchase of a particular asset is closely tied to the creation of some debt obligation, such as the sale of mortgage bonds or a bank loan. Nevertheless, it is generally considered *incorrect* to deduct the interest charges associated with a particular project from the estimated cash flows. This is true for two reasons.

First, the decision about how a firm should be financed can—and should—be made independently of the decision to accept or reject one or more projects. Instead, the firm should seek some combination of debt, equity (common stock), and preferred stock capital that is consistent with management's wishes concerning the tradeoff between financial risk and the cost of capital. In many cases this will result in a capital structure with the cost of capital at or near its minimum. Because investment and financing decisions normally should be made independently of one another, each new project can be viewed as being financed with the same proportions of the various sources of capital funds that are used to finance the firm as a whole.

Second, when a discounting framework is used for project evaluation, the discount rate, or cost of capital, already incorporates the cost of funds used to finance a project. Thus, including interest charges in cash flow calculations would essentially result in a double counting of costs.

Asset Expansion Projects

A project which requires a firm to invest funds in additional assets in order to increase sales (or reduce costs) is called an *asset expansion project.* For example, suppose the TLC Yogurt Company has decided to capitalize on the tanning salon fad and plans to open a tanning salon in conjunction with its main yogurt and health foods store. In order to get the project underway the firm will rent additional space adjacent to its current store. The equipment required for the tanning salon will cost $50,000. Shipping and installation charges for the equipment is expected to total $5,000. This equipment will be depreciated on a straight line basis over its five-year economic life to an estimated salvage value of $0. (For purposes of this example we assume that no investment tax credit applies to the equipment.) In order to open the tanning salon, TLC estimates that it will have to add about $7,000 to its net working capital in the form of additional inventories of tanning supplies, cash, and accounts receivable for its tanning customers (less accounts payable).

During the first year of operations, TLC expects its total revenues (from yogurt sales and tanning services) to increase by $50,000 above the level which would have prevailed without the tanning salon addition. These incremental revenues are expected to grow to $60,000 in year 2, $75,000 in year 3, decline to $60,000 in year 4, and decline again to $45,000 during the fifth and final year of the project's life. The firm's incremental cash operating costs associated with the tanning salon, including the rental of the facility, are expected to total $25,000 during the first year and increase at a rate of 6 percent per year over the five-year project life. Depreciation will be $11,000 per year ($55,000 installed cost, assuming no salvage value, divided by five-year economic life). TLC has a marginal tax rate of 40 percent.

First, we determine the net investment required for the tanning salon expansion. TLC must make a cash outlay of $50,000 to pay for the tanning salon equipment. In addition it must pay $5,000 in cash to cover the costs of shipping and installation of the equipment. Finally, TLC must invest $7,000 in net working capital in order to get the project underway. This net working capital investment will be recovered at the termination of the project. The net investment (NINV) required at time 0 is:

Purchase price of tanning equipment	$50,000
Plus: Shipping and installation	5,000
Plus: Net working capital required	7,000
Equals: Net investment	$62,000

Next we need to calculate the annual net cash flows associated with the project. Using Equation 9.5 these cash flows can be computed as shown in Table 9-3.

The cash flows associated with the tanning salon project for TLC can be summarized as follows:

Year	Net Investment and Net Cash Flows
0	−$62,000
1	19,400
2	24,500
3	32,546
4	22,535
5	19,463

Table 9-3   **Calculation of Annual Net Cash Flows for TLC Tanning Salon**

	Year 1	Year 2	Year 3	Year 4	Year 5
Incremental revenues (ΔR)	$50,000	$60,000	$75,000	$60,000	$45,000
Minus: Incremental cash operating costs (ΔO)	25,000	26,500	28,090	29,775	31,562
Minus: Incremental depreciation (ΔD)	11,000	11,000	11,000	11,000	11,000
Equals: Earnings before tax (ΔEBT)	$14,000	$22,500	$35,910	$19,225	$ 2,438
Less: Taxes (40%) (t)	5,600	9,000	14,364	7,690	975
Equals: Earnings after tax (ΔEAT)	$ 8,400	$13,500	$21,546	$11,535	$ 1,463
Plus: Incremental depreciation (ΔD)	11,000	11,000	11,000	11,000	11,000
Plus: After-tax salvage	—	—	—	—	0
Plus: Return of net working capital	—	—	—	—	7,000
Equals: Net cash flow (NCF)	$19,400	$24,500	$32,546	$22,535	$19,463

In Chapter 10 several different capital budgeting decision models are applied to cash flows such as these to determine the desirability of capital investment projects.

Asset Replacement Decisions

The previous example of an asset expansion project illustrated the key elements of the calculation of a project's net investment and its annual net cash flows. In this section we consider an *asset replacement* decision. Asset replacements involve the retiring of one asset and the replacement of that asset with a more efficient asset.

Prior to introducing an example of an asset replacement decision, we review two important tax considerations which can have a significant impact on the economic viability of *any* investment project, whether it is an asset expansion or replacement project. These tax considerations are: (1) the Investment Tax Credit (ITC) and (2) the Accelerated Cost Recovery System (ACRS) of depreciation.

Investment Tax Credit (ITC)

The Investment Tax Credit (ITC) was initially established in 1962 as a fiscal policy tool for controlling the economy and stimulating business investment. The ITC has been modified many times since 1962. The most recent modifications have come about as a result of the Economic Recovery Tax Act (ERTA) of 1981 and the Tax Equity and Fiscal Responsibility Act (TEFRA) of 1982. Many of the changes in the ITC which were made at this time were done to conform with the Accelerated Cost Recovery System (ACRS) depreciation rules (see the section on depreciation below). During 1986 Congress enacted a major package of tax reforms. One key element of many of the reform proposals is the elimination of the ITC. The elimination of the ITC will increase the after-tax cost (net investment) of acquiring many new assets. See Appendix A at the end of the book for details on the effect of tax reform on the ITC.

The ITC allows firms to receive a credit against their Federal income taxes for qualifying new property placed in service. Qualifying property generally includes depreciable property with an Accelerated Cost Recovery System (ACRS) depreciation recovery period of three years or more. Buildings and their structural components and land are *not* eligible for the ITC. In addition to qualifying *new* property, the ITC is also available on $125,000 of *used* property. The amount of the credit is based on the ACRS recovery period as follows:[8,9]

Recovery Period (Years)	Percentage of Credit
3	6%
5, 10, and 15	10%

The ITC cannot exceed a firm's tax liability in any year. It is further limited to 100 percent of a firm's first $25,000 of tax liability plus 85 percent of its tax liability in excess of $25,000. Tax credits that cannot be used in a given year are initially carried back three years (to the earliest year first). Any remaining unused credits are then carried forward a total of fifteen years before they are lost.

If an asset is sold or disposed of prior to the end of the ACRS recovery period, all or a portion of the ITC is recaptured. The recaptured portion of the ITC is added to the taxpayer's regular tax liability for the year.[10] Table 9-4 is a schedule of the percentage recapture for various assets. As we shall see, the ITC has been an important determinant of the *net investment* portion of a project's cash flows.

Table 9-4   **Investment Tax Credit Recapture Schedule**

Property is Held for	Recapture Percentage	
	5-, 10-, 15-Year Property	3-Year Property
Less than 1 year	100%	100%
1 year or more but less than 2 years	80	66
2 years or more but less than 3 years	60	33
3 years or more but less than 4 years	40	0
4 years or more but less than 5 years	20	0
5 years or more	0	0

[8] Current tax laws give firms an alternative ITC method. Rather than taking a 6 percent ITC on three-year assets and a 10 percent ITC on five-, ten-, and fifteen-year assets, the firm can take 4 percent and 8 percent respectively. When this is done, the basis for depreciation of an asset is equal to the *full* installed cost of the asset, rather than the installed cost less one-half of the ITC. Generally, taking the full ITC and reducing the depreciable basis of an asset by one-half of the ITC is more favorable to most firms. Hence this procedure is assumed throughout the book.

[9] The maximum tax credit for passenger cars used in business and purchased after April 2, 1985 is $675.

[10] If there is a partial or full recapture of the ITC as a result of the sale of the asset before the full ITC has been earned, the basis from which a recapture of depreciation is computed is increased by 50 percent of the amount of the ITC to be recaptured.

Depreciation

Depreciation is defined as the systematic allocation of the cost of an asset over more than one year. It allows a firm to spread the costs of fixed assets over a period of years to better match costs and revenues in each accounting period. The annual depreciation expense recorded for a particular asset is simply an allocation of historical costs and does not necessarily indicate a declining market value. For example, a company that is depreciating an office building may find the building's market value *appreciating* each year.

There are a number of alternative methods of recording the depreciation of an asset for *financial reporting* purposes. These include straight line depreciation and various accelerated depreciation methods. Under the straight line depreciation method, the annual amount of an asset's depreciation is calculated as follows:

$$\text{Annual depreciation amount} = \frac{\text{Installed cost}}{\text{Number of years over which the asset is depreciated}}.$$

For *tax* purposes, the depreciation rate a firm uses has a significant impact on the cash flows of the firm. This is so because depreciation represents a *noncash* expense that is deductible for tax purposes. Hence, the greater the amount of depreciation charged in a period, the lower will be the firm's taxable income. With a lower reported taxable income, the firm's tax obligation (a cash outflow) is reduced, and the cash inflows for the firm are increased. This can be seen in the following fundamental definition of cash flows:

$$\text{Operating cash flow} = \text{Net income after tax} + \text{Noncash charges.}$$

For example, if the Longhorn Tool Company has revenues of $1,000, cash operating expenses of $500, straight line depreciation of $100, and a marginal tax rate of 40 percent, its operating cash flow will be this:

Cash revenues		$1,000
Less: Cash operating expenses	$500	
Depreciation	100	
Total		600
Net income before taxes		$ 400
Less: Taxes (40%)		160
Net income after taxes		$ 240
Plus: Depreciation		100
Operating cash flow		$ 340

Now suppose Longhorn Tool opts to use an accelerated depreciation method for tax purposes rather than the straight line method. As a result, its depreciation expense is recorded as $150 instead of $100. Its new operating cash flow will be as follows:

Cash revenues		$1,000
Less: Cash operating expenses	$500	
Depreciation	150	
Total		650
Net income before taxes		$ 350
Less: Taxes (40%)		140
Net income after taxes		$ 210
Plus: Depreciation		150
Operating cash flow		$ 360

A comparison of the two cash flow statements shows that the use of accelerated depreciation reduces net income after taxes from $240 to $210 and reduces taxes from $160 to $140, but increases operating cash flow to $360 from $340. Hence, the use of accelerated depreciation for tax purposes is desirable for the firm, because it reduces tax outlays and thereby increases cash flow.

Depreciable Life of an Asset Prior to the 1981 tax act (ERTA) and the 1982 tax act (TEFRA), there was considerable controversy between taxpayers and the IRS over what constituted the appropriate period over which to depreciate an asset. The ERTA greatly simplified the determination of a period for depreciation by creating four property classes under the ACRS and assigning all depreciable assets to one of the classes. Table 9-5

Table 9-5 **ACRS Recovery Periods***

Property Class	ACRS Normal Recovery Period	Optional Extended Straight Line Recovery Period†
Autos‡, light-duty trucks, research and development equipment, some special tools, and some race horses	3 years	3, 5, or 12 years
All other machinery and equipment except long-lived public utility property	5 years	5, 12, or 25 years
Certain public utility property, railroad tank cars, mobile homes, and theme park structures	10 years	10, 25, or 35 years
All other public utility property	15 years	15, 35, or 45 years

*The ERTA allows a firm to expense, rather than to capitalize and depreciate, up to a total of $5,000 per year. When this option is chosen, the ITC is forgone. We do not consider this alternative in our future analysis, since it has been shown to be generally disadvantageous to taxpayers.
†The optional extended straight line recovery period would only be used if a firm expected negative predepreciation net income over the near future. In this case, deferring depreciation until later years when predepreciation income is available would be advantageous.
   The estimated salvage value is not considered when using the optional extended straight line recovery period. The basis for depreciation is still the cost less one-half of the investment tax credit when the optional extended straight line method is chosen.
‡There are separate limitations on the amount of depreciation which can be claimed in any tax year for passenger automobiles.

summarizes the ACRS normal and the optional extended recovery period (depreciable life) for the four asset classes.

Under normal circumstances most firms will opt to use the ACRS normal recovery periods. Hence, we will only consider the ACRS normal recovery periods in the balance of the chapter.

(Note: The 1986 tax reform bill increases the number of asset classes and generally lengthens the depreciable life of assets. See Appendix A at the end of the book for details.

Depreciation Rate In addition to establishing the depreciable life of an asset, the ACRS depreciation system also sets the depreciation rate to be applied to the depreciable basis of each asset. Under the ACRS, the *depreciable basis of an asset is equal to the purchase price plus installation and shipping charges less 50 percent of the amount of the ITC for which an asset is eligible.*[11] The estimated salvage value of an asset is *not* considered under the ACRS. Proposed tax reforms which eliminate the ITC make the depreciable basis for all assets equal to the asset's installed cost. Estimated salvage values of an asset do not affect the depreciable basis of an asset.

For example, assume the Longhorn Tool Company acquires a $10,000 piece of machinery (including shipping and installation costs). Under ACRS guidelines, this is a five-year asset that is eligible for the full 10 percent ITC—or $1,000. The depreciable basis of this asset is as follows:[12]

Asset cost (including shipping and installation)	$10,000
Less: 50% of 10% ITC	500
Depreciable basis	$ 9,500

Table 9-6 indicates the ACRS depreciation rates that are applied to the depreciable basis of all assets except real property. A separate recovery schedule is used for eighteen-year real property (buildings). In the case of real property, the depreciation that can be claimed in the first year depends on the month the property is placed in service. Table 9-7 provides the ACRS recovery percentages for eighteen-year real property.

---

[11] As an alternative, the ACRS percentages can be applied to the full cost of the asset (including installation and shipping) without reducing this cost by 50 percent of the eligible ITC. In this case, the ITC is reduced by 2 percentage points, that is, from 6 percent to 4 percent for three-year assets and from 10 percent to 8 percent for other assets. We do not consider this alternative in our future analysis, since it was included in the law only to assist firms that were precluded from taking advantage of the ITC because of such reasons as insufficient taxable income.

[12] Even though ACRS depreciation is based on the installed cost of the asset less 50 percent of the ITC, recapture of depreciation (ordinary income) treatment is given to any amount that is more than the ACRS tax book value and less than or equal to the *full* installed cost; that is, the ITC reduction from installed cost, which determines the depreciable basis of an asset, does not affect depreciation recapture provisions.

Table 9-6   **ACRS Depreciation Rates**

Recovery Year	3-Year Property	5-Year Property	10-Year Property	15-Year Public Utility Property
1	25%	15%	8%	5%
2	38	22	14	10
3	37	21	12	9
4		21	10	8
5		21	10	7
6			10	7
7			9	6
8			9	6
9			9	6
10			9	6
11				6
12				6
13				6
14				6
15				6

Returning to the Longhorn Tool Company example, the annual ACRS depreciation would be the following:

Year	ACRS Depreciation Rate	Amount of Depreciation (ACRS Rate × $9,500)
1	15%	$1,425
2	22	2,090
3	21	1,995
4	21	1,995
5	21	1,995
	100%	$9,500

Table 9-7   **ACRS Recovery Percentages for 18-Year Real Property (Other than Low Income Housing) Placed in Service After June 22, 1984**

Year	Month Placed in Service											
	1	2	3	4	5	6	7	8	9	10	11	12
1st	9%	9%	8%	7%	6%	5%	4%	4%	3%	2%	1%	0.4%
2nd	9%	9%	9%	9%	9%	9%	9%	9%	9%	10%	10%	10%
3rd	8%	8%	8%	8%	8%	8%	8%	8%	9%	9%	9%	9%
4th	7%	7%	7%	7%	7%	8%	8%	8%	8%	8%	8%	8%
5th	7%	7%	7%	7%	7%	7%	7%	7%	7%	7%	7%	7%
6th	6%	6%	6%	6%	6%	6%	6%	6%	6%	6%	6%	6%
7th	5%	5%	5%	5%	6%	6%	6%	6%	6%	6%	6%	6%
8–12th	5%	5%	5%	5%	5%	5%	5%	5%	5%	5%	5%	5%
13th	4%	4%	4%	5%	4%	4%	5%	4%	4%	4%	5%	5%
14–17th	4%	4%	4%	4%	4%	4%	4%	4%	4%	4%	4%	4%
18th	4%	3%	4%	4%	4%	4%	4%	4%	4%	4%	4%	4%
19th		1%	1%	1%	2%	2%	2%	3%	3%	3%	3%	3.6%

ACRS Recovery Periods and Economic Life of an Asset With the adoption of the ACRS recovery periods for all assets, there is no longer any relationship between the period over which depreciation is taken on an asset and that asset's economic life. Consequently, when estimating the cash flows from a project, there normally will be several years beyond the ACRS recovery period when no depreciation expense will be recorded. It is important to remember that cash flows for all projects (assets) should be projected over the full economic life of the project, not just the ACRS recovery period.

An Example Replacement Decision

The Jones Equipment Company purchased an automated drill press five years ago that had an estimated economic life of fifteen years. The drill press originally cost $150,000 and is being depreciated at the five-year ACRS recovery rates. The current book value of the drill press is $0, since all five years' worth of depreciation have been utilized. The actual market value of this drill press is $40,000. The company is considering replacing the drill press with a new one costing $190,000. Shipping and installation charges will add an additional $10,000 to the cost. The new machine would be depreciated under the five-year ACRS schedule. The new machine is expected to have a ten-year economic life, and its actual salvage value at the end of the ten-year period is estimated to be $20,000. The purchase of the new drill press qualifies for a 10 percent ITC. Jones' current marginal tax rate is 40 percent.

Calculating the Net Investment Steps 1 and 2 of the net investment calculation are easy; the new project cost ($190,000) plus shipping and installation ($10,000) is $200,000. In this case, no new net working capital is required.

In steps 3 and 4 the net proceeds received from the sale of the old drill press have to be adjusted for taxes.

Since the old drill press is sold for $40,000, the gain from this sale is treated as a recapture of depreciation and thus taxed as ordinary income. Table 9-8 summarizes the NINV calculation for Jones Equipment. As can be seen in this table, the NINV is equal to $156,000.

Calculating Annual Net Cash Flows The Jones Equipment Company expects annual revenues to increase from $70,000 to $85,000 if the new drill press is purchased. (This might occur because the new press is faster

Table 9-8   **Net Investment Calculation for Jones Equipment Company**

Cost of new drill press	$190,000
Plus: Shipping and installation charges	10,000
Equals: Installed cost	$200,000
Plus: Increase in net working capital	0
Less: Proceeds from sale of old drill press	40,000
Equals: Net investment before taxes	$160,000
Plus: Tax on gain from sale of old drill press (40% × $40,000)	16,000
Less: ITC on new drill press (10% × $200,000)	20,000
Equals: Net investment	$156,000

than the old one and can meet the increasing demands for more work.) Assume further that while the old drill press required two operators, the new drill press is more automated and needs only one, thereby reducing annual operating costs from \$40,000 to \$20,000. The old machine is fully depreciated, whereas the new machine will be depreciated over five years under ACRS depreciation rates. The marginal tax rate of 40 percent applies.

The net cash flows resulting from the purchase of the new drill press can be computed by substituting $R_2 = \$85,000$, $R_1 = \$70,000$, $O_2 = \$20,000$, $O_1 = \$40,000$, $D_1 = \$0$, and $t = 0.40$ into Equation 9.6. The depreciation for the new machine, D_2, is according to ACRS rates as shown in Table 9-9.

Using the ACRS yearly depreciation from Table 9-8, annual net cash flows can be computed as follows:

$$NCF = [(R_2 - R_1) - (O_2 - O_1) - (D_2 - D_1)](1 - t) + (D_2 - D_1).$$

Year 1:

$$\begin{aligned} NCF_1 &= [(\$85,000 - \$70,000) - (\$20,000 - \$40,000) \\ &\quad - (\$28,500 - \$0)](1 - 0.4) + (\$28,500 - \$0) \\ &= \$32,400. \end{aligned}$$

Year 2:

$$\begin{aligned} NCF_2 &= [(\$85,000 - \$70,000) - (\$20,000 - \$40,000) \\ &\quad - (\$41,800 - \$0)](1 - 0.4) + (\$41,800 - \$0) \\ &= \$37,720. \end{aligned}$$

Years 3, 4, and 5:

$$\begin{aligned} NCF_{3-5} &= [(\$85,000 - \$70,000) - (\$20,000 - \$40,000) \\ &\quad - (\$39,900 - \$0)](1 - 0.4) + (\$39,900 - \$0) \\ &= \$36,960/\text{year}. \end{aligned}$$

In years 6 through 9 there is no depreciation under either alternative;

Table 9-9   **Computation of Annual Depreciation for Jones Equipment Company**

Depreciable cost = \$200,000 − 0.5 (0.10 ITC) (\$200,000)
= \$190,000.

Year	ACRS Rate (%)	ACRS Depreciation, D_2 (ACRS Rate × Depreciable Cost)
1	15	\$28,500
2	22	41,800
3	21	39,900
4	21	39,900
5	21	39,900
6	0	0
7	0	0
8	0	0
9	0	0
10	0	0

hence, net cash flows equal the following:

$$\text{NCF}_{6-9} = [(\$85,000 - \$70,000) - (\$20,000 - \$40,000)$$
$$- (\$0 - \$0)](1 - 0.4) + (\$0 - \$0)$$
$$= \$21,000/\text{year}.$$

Net cash flows in year 10 will be the same as in years 6 through 9 except that the $20,000 estimated salvage from the new drill press must be added,

Table 9-10　　　**Annual Net Cash Flow Worksheet for the Jones Equipment Company Drill Press Acquisition**

	Year				
	1	2	3–5	6–9	10
Change in revenues $(R_2 - R_1)$*	$15,000	$15,000	$15,000	$15,000	$15,000
Less: Change in cash operating costs $(O_2 - O_1)$†	−20,000	−20,000	−20,000	−20,000	−20,000
Less: Change in depreciation $(D_2 - D_1)$‡	28,500	41,800	39,900	0	0
Equals: Change in earnings before taxes (EBT)	$ 6,500	$−6,800	$−4,900	$35,000	$35,000
Less: Tax (40%)‖	2,600	−2,720	−1,960	14,000	14,000
Equals: Change in earnings after taxes (EAT)	$ 3,900	$−4,080	$−2,940	$21,000	$21,000
Plus: Change in depreciation $(D_2 - D_1)$	28,500	41,800	39,900	0	0
Equals: Change in net cash flow before salvage	$32,400	$37,720	$36,960	$21,000	$21,000
Plus: Salvage	0	0	0	0	20,000
Less: Tax on salvage (0.4 × salvage)	0	0	0	0	8,000
Plus: Add-back of net working capital	0	0	0	0	0
Equals: Change in net cash flow	$32,400	$37,720	$36,960	$21,000	$33,000

*The change in revenues from undertaking a project may be either positive or negative.
†The change in cash operating costs may be either positive or negative. In this case, the firm's cash operating costs *decline* by $20,000; that is, the change in cash operating costs is *negative*, indicating a cost saving. This cost saving is *added* to the change in revenues (subtracting a negative number is the same as adding a positive number). If, in another situation, operating costs were to *increase* as a result of a project, the increased costs would be *subtracted* from the change in revenues.
‡The change in depreciation may be either positive or negative. In this case, it is *positive* and has the effect of reducing the amount of taxable earnings, and thus reducing the amount of taxes paid. Hence, this *increases* the cash flow from the project. If the change in depreciation were *negative*, it would have the effect of increasing the taxable earnings, increasing taxes paid, and *reducing* the cash flows from the project.
‖In years 2 through 5 the tax figure is shown as a negative number. This is because the change in earnings before taxes is negative (indicating a reduction in taxable income). Because of this reduction in taxable income for the firm as a whole, taxes are reduced by an amount equal to the marginal tax rate (0.4) times the reduction in taxable income. This reduction in taxes is a benefit to the firm (subtracting a negative number is the same as adding a positive number).

along with its associated tax effects.[13] This $20,000 salvage is treated as ordinary income, since it represents a recapture of depreciation for tax purposes.

$$NCF_{10} = \$21,000 + \$20,000 \text{ salvage} - \text{Tax on salvage } (0.4 \times \$20,000)$$
$$= \$21,000 + \$20,000 - \$8,000$$
$$= \$33,000.$$

Table 9-10 is a summary worksheet for computing the net cash flows for the Jones Company during the ten-year estimated economic life of the new drill press.

Table 9-11 summarizes the net cash flows for the entire project. This schedule of net cash flows plus the NINV computed in the preceding section form the basis for further analysis. In Chapter 10 several different capital budgeting decision models are applied to similar cash flow streams from other projects to determine the investment desirability of these projects. The cash flows developed in this chapter are an essential input in the capital budgeting decision process.

Problems in Cash Flow Estimation

Since project cash flows occur in the future, there are varying degrees of *uncertainty* about the value of these flows. Thus, it is difficult to predict the actual cash flows of a project. The capital budgeting process assumes the decision maker is able to estimate cash flows accurately enough that these estimates can be used in project evaluation and selection. For this assumption to be realistic, a project proposal should be based on inputs from marketing managers regarding revenue estimates and on inputs from the production and engineering staffs regarding costs and achievable levels of performance. Objective inputs from these sources can help reduce the uncertainty associated with cash flow estimation.

Table 9-11   **Summary Project Cash Flows for the Jones Equipment Company**

Year	Net Investment and Net Cash Flows
0	-$156,000
1	32,400
2	37,720
3	36,960
4	36,960
5	36,960
6	21,000
7	21,000
8	21,000
9	21,000
10	33,000

[13] In this example there is no add-back of net working capital in the final year of the project, since no new net working capital was required when the project was initiated.

In addition, cash flow estimates for different projects may have varying degrees of uncertainty. For example, the returns from asset replacement projects are generally easier to forecast than the returns from new product introduction projects. Chapter 11 discusses some of the techniques used to incorporate risk analysis into capital budgeting decision models.

Another difficulty in the practical application of capital budgeting arises because of the intentional or unintentional introduction of *bias* into cash flow estimates. Specifically, someone who has a vested interest in the adoption of a specific project may find it difficult to be completely objective when estimating the project's cash flows. For this reason it is a good idea to obtain an objective outside evaluation of a proposed project before the project is implemented. In additon, an aggressive project review and postaudit should be conducted once the project is under way. These procedures can indicate areas where bias has slipped into cash flow analysis and where corrective action may be needed.

Summary

- *Capital budgeting* is the process of planning for purchases of assets whose returns are expected to continue beyond one year.
- Capital investments have a long-term impact on the performance of a firm. The proper forecasting of capital needs can help to insure that a firm's productive capacity will meet future requirements.
- Ideally a firm should invest in new projects up to the point at which the rate of return from the last project is equal to the marginal cost of capital.
- Projects may be classified as *independent, mutually exclusive,* or *contingent.* The acceptance of an independent project does not directly eliminate other projects from consideration; the acceptance of a mutually exclusive project precludes other alternatives; and the acceptance of a contingent project depends on the adoption of one or more other projects.
- The *cost of capital* is the cost of funds supplied to a firm. It is often used in conjunction with capital project evaluation techniques as a basis for choosing among various investment alternatives.
- There are four basic steps in the capital budgeting process: *the generation of proposals, the estimation of cash flows, the evaluation and selection of alternatives,* and *the postaudit/review.* The first two steps are detailed in this chapter.
- New projects may be generated by *growth opportunities, cost reduction opportunities,* or by *the need to meet legal requirements and health and safety standards.*
- Project cash flows should be measured on an *incremental after-tax* basis and should include all the indirect effects the project will have on the firm.
- Resources of a firm used in an investment project should be valued at their *opportunity cost* based upon the cash flows these resources could generate in their next best alternative use.

- *Sunk costs* represent outlays which have already been made or committed and which cannot be recovered. Sunk costs should not be considered when evaluating an investment project.

- The *net investment* (NINV) in a project is the net cash outlay required to place the project in service. It includes the project cost *plus* any necessary increases in working capital *minus* any proceeds from the sale of the old asset(s) (in the case of replacement decisions) *plus or minus* the taxes associated with the sale of the old asset(s) and/or the purchase of the new asset(s).

- The *net cash flows* (NCF) from a project are the incremental changes in a firm's cash flows that result from investing in the project. These flows include the changes in the firm's revenues, cash operating costs, and taxes with and without the project.

- An *asset expansion* project requires a firm to invest funds in additional assets in order to increase sales or reduce costs. *Asset replacements*, in contrast, involve the retiring of one asset and the replacement of that asset with a more efficient one.

- Two problems that complicate the estimation of cash flows include the element of *uncertainty* associated with cash flows and the intentional or unintentional introduction of *bias* into the estimation procedure.

FOCUS ON CORPORATE PRACTICE

The Misuse of a Sound Investment Tool*

Eileen M. Rudden
Principal, Boston Consulting Group

The next chapter takes the cash flows discussed in this chapter and uses them to analyze the feasibility of investment projects. The techniques of analysis discussed in the next chapter are mostly types of discounted cash flow analysis. This Focus example cautions users of these techniques of some potential pitfalls in implementation.

Discounted cash flow has been getting a bad name. Critics charge that the technique has contributed to America's competitive decline and that managers using DCF have systematically rejected investments critical to the livelihood of many U.S. industries.

But the problem isn't DCF itself. The problem is its frequent misapplication.

DCF is a sound conceptual model for valuing the firm. It properly focuses on cash, rather than accounting profits. High reported earnings don't help you if you get less cash out of a business than you put in. DCF also properly emphasizes the opportunity cost of the money you invest. It recognizes that the cash you get out should be greater than the cash you put in *plus* the interest you could have earned by investing the money elsewhere. So the DCF approach discounts future cash flows to current dollars, recognizing the alternative return the company could realize if it had the cash now rather than in the future.

All this is economic common sense. A firm will maximize its value by maximizing the discounted cash flows of its investments. An investment with a higher DCF is superior to one with a lower DCF.

The problem is that what works well in theory doesn't always work well in practice. It is exceedingly difficult to apply DCF correctly in evaluating single capital investments. If your company is using DCF calculations, don't be lulled by the reams of figures: Be sure to test the assumptions behind the numbers. This is especially important in large organizations, where the sensitivities in the calculation are often clouded as the investment proposal climbs through the hierarchy.

The difficulties in applying DCF correctly fall into two categories.

The first is in identifying the relevant cash flows. Far from being an exact science, this requires imprecise assumptions about market growth, price levels, and, perhaps above all, the likely actions of competitors.

In evaluating a major capacity addition, for example, most companies would consider the additional profit resulting from the incremental capacity as the relevant cash flow. But a more meaningful measure might be the difference between a project's cash flows and the cash flows associated with not investing. Giving up market share to a competitor may allow it to undercut your position in the products and volume that remain. Your cost position may deteriorate relative to that of other competitors who may invest even though you do not. Your cash flows may erode.

Too often, managers neglect to ask, "What will happen if we *don't* make this investment?" GM declined to invest in response to Toyota's challenge because small cars looked less profitable than its then-current mix. As a result, Toyota was able to expand and eventually challenge GM's base business. Many American companies that thought global expansion would be too risky today find their world-wide competitive positions eroding. They didn't evaluate carefully enough the results of *not* building a strong world-wide position.

It is impossible to quantify with any precision the impact of competitive scenarios that may or may not occur. The best that can be done is to attach a probability to each scenario—a "qualitative" and subjective judgment.

Similarly, while many companies devote considerable effort to projecting market growth, they typically assume that prices will move and market shares will behave as they have in the past. But price levels may be depressed either by too much capacity addition, or by low-cost capacity additions that displace the very high-cost facilities. Most DCF analyses do not address these possibilities. It is assumed that an individual competitor's actions do not affect market price mechanisms or other competitors' behavior.

Many incremental projects such as product line or plant additions are analyzed by DCF. Yet few companies are able to accurately predict the increases in overhead and logistics cost resulting from these investments, which increase plant complexity.

DCF is more easily applied to calculate the gains from simple cost-reducing investments, for example, the acquisition of labor-saving equipment. Yet other companies are making cost-saving investments as well. Thus, if prices reflect the changing cost structure of a competitive industry, actual earnings may be lower than anticipated. This may explain why most companies' returns fall far short of their hurdle rates for investment.

The second difficulty is the choice of discount rate. This requires a reasonable assessment of what the company can actually earn on its money if it doesn't make the investment. Many companies use a discount rate which is higher than that at which they can actually reinvest the funds. This can result in gradually liquidating a business which doesn't earn these unrealistically high returns.

This problem gains added complexity in an era of fluctuating inflation and interest rates. Reasoning that risky investments should yield more than riskless government notes, many companies have raised their discount rates in recent years. But anyone analyzing an investment proposal should ask whether the high returns that have recently been available from government securities will last over the lifetime of the proposed investment. If not, then it may be profitable to make long-term investments that yield less in the short term than prevailing interest rates. Maximizing short-term gain does not necessarily result in long-term gain if you lose your opportunity to continue reinvesting at the high hurdle rate.

As a result of such difficulties, many well-managed companies have moved away from reliance on discounted cash flow, or similar models such as the internal rate of return. Such companies still aim for high DCF, but they recognize that they can't reach that aim by applying DCF analysis to every specific project. Instead they focus on competitive quality levels, competitive cost position, share quality levels, or share of market as more reliable proxies for the longer-term value of the firm.

Even more important, many well-managed companies insist that investment projects should flow from a sound strategic plan for the business and should be analyzed within that framework. The essence of a strategic plan is that it explicitly considers the competition and charts a course to build and maintain competitive advantage. It highlights key assumptions and their sensitivities.

Line managers, financial staff, and planners who propose and review investments should explicitly question the rigid use of DCF in company capital budgeting systems. The weight of a capital proposal and the yards of figures presented as backup are unfortunately no guarantee that the assumptions used are correct. Alternative competitive assumptions may seem "qualitative" in contrast to lots of numbers. They may strain an organization's tolerance for ambiguity. And it may be uncomfortable to move away from that single number that sums it all up, the internal rate of return. But the loss of methodological tidiness is preferable to surrendering competitive position today, and tomorrow perhaps even losing your core business.

**Questions and
Topics for
Discussion**

1. Discuss how capital budgeting procedures might be used by each of the following:
   a. Personnel managers.
   b. Research and development staffs.
   c. Advertising executives.
2. What is a mutually exclusive investment project? An independent project? A contingent project? Give an example of each.
3. What effect does capital rationing have on a firm's ability to maximize shareholder wealth?
4. What are the primary types of capital investment projects? Does a project's type influence how it is analyzed?
5. Cash flows for a particular project should be measured on an incremental basis and should consider all the indirect effects of the project. What does this involve?
6. What factors should be considered when estimating a project's NINV?
7. Since depreciation is a noncash expense, why is it considered when estimating a project's net cash flows?
8. What are the potential tax consequences of selling an old asset in an asset replacement investment decision?
9. Why is it generally incorrect to consider interest charges when computing a project's net cash flows?
10. Under ACRS depreciation, does the ITC lower an asset's depreciable basis?
11. Under what conditions is the ITC recaptured when an asset is disposed of?
12. When would a firm choose to use optional extended straight line recovery periods instead of the ACRS recovery periods and rates?
13. Distinguish between asset expansion and asset replacement projects. How does this distinction affect the capital expenditure analysis process?
14. How is the opportunity cost concept used in the capital budgeting process?

Problems*

Lotus123

1. a. Calculate the annual ACRS depreciation for a machine in the 5-year ACRS recovery period group, assuming that the asset costs $20,000 and is eligible for a 10 percent ITC.
   b. If the firm uses optional extended straight line depreciation for 12 years, what is the annual depreciation?
   c. If you knew that this asset had an expected salvage value of $2,000 at the end of its 12-year economic life, would your answers to Parts a and b change?
2. The Longhorn Tube Company purchased an asset during 1985 for $100,000. The asset was being depreciated over 5 years using ACRS depreciation rates. Longhorn claimed a 10 percent ITC at the time the asset was acquired. Two and one-half years later, Longhorn has decided to sell the asset for $80,000. Longhorn's marginal tax rate is 40 percent. What are the tax consequences of selling the asset at this time?
3. The MacCauley Company has sales of $200 million and total expenses (excluding depreciation) of $130 million. Straight line depreciation on the company's assets is $15 million and the maximum accelerated depreciation allowed by law is $25 million. Assume that all taxable income is taxed at 40 percent.

* Color numbers denote problems which have check answers provided at the end of the book.

a. Calculate the MacCauley Company's cash flow from operations using both straight line and accelerated depreciation.

b. Assuming the company uses straight line depreciation for book purposes and accelerated depreciation for tax purposes, show the income statement reported to the stockholders. What is the cash flow from operations under these circumstances?

Lotus123

4. Calculate the annual depreciation of a new building acquired during July 1985. The cost of the building is $10 million.

5. Simonson Sewing Company has developed the following schedule of potential investment projects that may be undertaken during the next 6 months:

Project	Cost (in Millions of Dollars)	Expected Rate of Return (%)
A	3.0	20
B	1.5	22
C	7.0	7
D	14.0	10
E	50.0	12
F	12.0	9
G	1.0	44

a. If Simonson requires a minimum rate of return of 10 percent on all investments, which projects should be adopted?

b. In general, how would a capital budgeting constraint on the available amount of investment funds influence these decisions?

c. How would differing levels of project risk influence these decisions?

Lotus123

6. A new machine costing $100,000 is expected to save the McKaig Brick Company $15,000 per year for 12 years before depreciation and taxes. The machine will be depreciated on a straight line basis for a 12-year period to an estimated salvage value of $0. The firm's marginal tax rate is 40 percent. What are the annual net cash flows associated with the purchase of this machine? Also compute the net investment (NINV) for this project.

7. Refer back to Problem 6. How would your answer change if the firm used ACRS depreciation rates over 5 years and claimed the ITC at the time the asset was acquired?

8. The Taylor Mountain Uranium Company currently has annual cash revenues of $1,200,000 and annual cash expenses of $700,000. Depreciation amounts to $200,000 per year. These figures are expected to remain constant for the foreseeable future (at least 15 years). The firm's marginal tax rate is 40 percent.

A new high-speed processing unit costing $1,200,000 is being considered as a potential investment designed to increase the firm's output capacity. This new piece of equipment will have an estimated usable life of 10 years and a $0 estimated salvage value. If the processing unit is bought, Taylor's annual cash revenues are expected to increase to $1,600,000, and annual cash expenses will increase to $900,000. Annual depreciation will increase to $320,000.

Compute the firm's annual net cash flows for the next 10 years, assuming that the new processing unit is purchased. Also compute the net investment (NINV) for this project.

9. Refer back to Problem 8. How would your answer change if the new processing unit were depreciated over 5 years using ACRS depreciation rates and the firm claimed the ITC?

10. A firm has an opportunity to invest in a new device that will replace two of the firm's older machines. The new device costs $570,000 and requires an additional outlay of $30,000 to cover installation and shipping. The new device will cause the firm to increase its net working capital by $20,000. Both the old machines can be sold—the first for $100,000 (book value equals $95,000) and the second for $150,000 (book value equals $75,000), and the original cost of the first machine was $200,000 and the original cost of the second machine was $140,000. The new device is eligible for a 10 percent ITC. There will be no ITC recapture on either of the two machines being replaced. Capital gains are taxed at 25 percent, and the firm's marginal tax bracket for ordinary income is 40 percent. Compute the net investment of this project.

Lotus123

11. Five years ago the Mori Foods Company acquired a bean processing machine. The machine cost $30,000 and was being depreciated using the straight line method over a 10-year period to an estimated salvage value of $0.

   A new, improved processor is now available, and the firm is considering making a switch. The firm's marginal tax rate is 40 percent, and the appropriate capital gains rate is 28 percent. What are the after-tax cash flow effects of selling the old processing unit if it can be sold for the following prices?
   a. $15,000
   b. $5,000
   c. $26,000
   d. $32,000

Lotus123

12. Looking again at Problem 11, recompute the after-tax cash flow effects of selling the old processing unit, assuming that the firm was using ACRS depreciation and the old processing unit was sold for $5,000.

Lotus123

13. Looking again at Problem 11, assume that the new bean processor will cost $40,000 and will have an expected useful economic life of 10 years. The processor will be depreciated on a 5-year ACRS schedule. The new processor is eligible for the 10 percent ITC. In addition, installation and shipping costs for the new processor will be $2,000 (not included in the $40,000 purchase price). The new processor will not require any increases in working capital for the Mori Company.

   Compute the net investment for the new processor, assuming that the old processor was being depreciated on a 5-year ACRS schedule and was sold for $5,000.

Lotus123

14. Returning to Problems 11 and 13, assume that the cash operating costs for the old bean processor are $15,000 per year. The old processor could continue to function for a maximum period of 10 more years, although operating costs for years 6 through 10 are expected to be $5,000 above current levels.

   The new processor is expected to experience annual cash operating costs of $12,000 over its anticipated economic life of 10 years, and it is expected to be worth $1,000 at the end of its 10-year life. The firm's marginal tax rate is 40 percent.

   If both the new and the old processors are depreciated on a 5-year ACRS schedule, what will the net cash flows be over the next 10 years, assuming that Mori buys the new bean processor?
   Note: The cost of the old processor was $30,000 and the cost of the new processor is $42,000, including installation and shipping charges. Also assume that both the new and the old processor were acquired at a time when ACRS depreciation rates were based on the installed asset cost less one half of the 10 percent ITC.

15. Cornell, Inc., is considering the purchase a new computer system (ICX) for $130,000. The system will require an additional $30,000 for installation. If the new computer is purchased it will replace an old system which has been fully depreciated to a book value of $0. The ICX system, if purchased, will be classified as a 5-year asset and depreciated in accordance with the ACRS depreciation schedule. The new system qualifies for the investment tax credit applicable to 5-year assets. If the ICX is purchased the old system will be sold for $20,000. The ICX system, which has a useful life of 10 years, is expected to increase revenues by $32,000 per year over its useful life. Operating costs are expected to decrease by $2,000 per year over the system's useful life. The firm is taxed at a 40 percent marginal rate and capital gains are taxed at 20 percent.

  a. What net investment is required to acquire the ICX system and replace the old system?

  b. Compute the annual net cash flows associated with the purchase of the ICX system.

16. Two years Agro, Inc., purchased an ACE generator which cost $250,000. Agro had to pay an additional $50,000 for delivery and installation, and the investment in the generator required the firm to increase its net working capital position by $25,000. The generator, which is being depreciated under the ACRS guidelines for 5-year assets (the firm at the time of purchase took the 10 percent investment tax credit), has a current market value of $79,550. The firm's marginal tax rate is 40% for ordinary income. If the firm sells the asset for its current market value, compute the after-tax proceeds from the sale.

17. Benford, Inc., is planning to open a new sporting goods store in a suburban mall. Benford will lease the needed space in the mall. Equipment and fixtures for the store will cost $200,000 and be depreciated over a 5-year period under ACRS guidelines. The equipment and fixtures are eligible for a 10 percent investment tax credit. The new store will require Benford to increase its net working capital by $200,000.

  First-year sales are expected to be $1,000,000 and to increase at an annual rate of 8 percent over the expected 10-year life of the store. Cash operating expenses (including lease payments) are projected to be $700,000 during the first year and increase at a 7 percent annual rate. The salvage value of the store's equipment and fixtures is anticipated to be $10,000 at the end of 10 years.

  Benford's marginal tax rate is 40 percent for ordinary income and 28 percent for capital gains.

  a. Compute the net investment required of Benford.

  b. Compute the annual net cash flows for the 10-year projected life of the store.

Selected References

Bierman, Harold, Jr., and Seymour Smidt. *The Capital Budgeting Decision,* 6th ed. New York: Macmillan, 1984.

Clark, John J., T. J. Hindelang, and R. D. Pritchard. *Capital Budgeting: Planning and Control of Capital Expenditures.* Englewood Cliffs, N. J.: Prentice-Hall, 1979.

Herbst, Anthony F. *Capital Budgeting.* New York: Harper & Row, 1982.

Kim, S. H. and E. J. Farragher. "Current Capital Budgeting Practices." *Management Accounting* (June 1981): 26–30.

Levy, Haim, and Marshall Sarnat. *Capital Investment and Financial Decisions,* 2nd ed. Englewood Cliffs, N.J.: Prentice-Hall International, 1982.

Scott, D. F., Jr., and J. W. Petty. "Capital Budgeting Practices in Large American Firms: A Retrospective Analysis and Synthesis." *The Financial Review* (March 1984): 111–123.

ALTERNATIVE DEPRECIATION METHODS

Introduction

Prior to the ACRS depreciation method developed in the ERTA (1981) and the TEFRA (1982), a number of alternative methods of depreciation were permitted by the IRS. These methods include straight line depreciation and various accelerated methods such as the sum-of-the-years'-digits and the declining balance methods.[14] Although the recent tax law changes have rendered these techniques out of date for tax purposes, it is still useful to understand them for the following reasons:

1. Most firms will continue to carry assets acquired before 1981 on their books for many years. These assets will be depreciated under the pre-ACRS rules.

2. Some firms may continue to use these methods for financial reporting purposes.

The 1986 tax reform bill has also had a major impact on depreciation rules. See Appendix A at the end of the book for details.

Straight Line Depreciation

Under the pre-ACRS straight line depreciation method, the annual amount of an asset's depreciation is calculated as follows:[15]

$$\begin{array}{c} \text{Annual} \\ \text{depreciation} \\ \text{amount} \end{array} = \frac{\text{Cost} - \text{Estimated salvage value}}{\text{Estimated economic life (years)}}. \qquad \textbf{(9A.1)}$$

For example, if a company purchases a machine that costs $12,000 and has an estimated salvage value of $2,000 at the end of a five-year economic life, the annual depreciation amount is ($12,000 − $2,000)/5 = $2,000.

Straight line depreciation is an appropriate method to employ when an asset is being used up fairly evenly over its lifetime. Many companies use straight line depreciation for financial accounting purposes—that is, in their reports to stockholders, because it usually results in a greater reported net income—and an accelerated depreciation method for Federal income tax purposes, because accelerated depreciation can result in the deferment of tax payments.

---

[14] Occasionally an asset is depreciated according to its number of units of output or its number of hours of operation. Since these methods are not widely used, they are not discussed here.

[15] Note that under pre-ACRS depreciation rules, the annual depreciation amount was determined as the cost of the asset less its estimated salvage value divided by the estimated economic life. In comparison, under the optional extended straight line recovery periods in the ACRS system, no consideration is given to estimated salvage value in determining the annual depreciation amount.

Accelerated Depreciation Methods

Accelerated depreciation methods allow a firm to write off more of the cost of an asset during the early years of its life than would be possible with the use of straight line depreciation. The two most common pre-ACRS accelerated depreciation methods are the *declining balance method* and the *sum-of-the-years'-digits method.*

Declining Balance Method

The declining balance method allows a firm to take a percentage of the depreciation amount greater than the straight line amount during the first year of an asset's life. During subsequent years the book value, or undepreciated amount, of the asset is multiplied by this percentage to calculate annual depreciation costs.

Three commonly used variations of the declining balance method include the 200 percent declining balance, often termed *double declining balance;* the 150 percent declining balance; and the 125 percent declining balance. The pre-ACRS tax laws specified which variation could be used with different types of assets.

In the declining balance method, the annual depreciation amount of an asset is calculated by multiplying the straight line rate by the declining balance percentage figure to get an accelerated rate. The accelerated rate then is multiplied by the asset's book value at the end of each previous year. As each year's depreciation amount is subtracted from the cost of the asset, the resulting *balance* in the asset's book value *declines*. Thus, the depreciation amount *decreases* as the years pass.

Suppose the company mentioned earlier decides to depreciate its new $12,000 machine using the 200 percent declining balance method. Recall that the machine has a $2,000 salvage value and a five-year expected life. Since the straight line depreciation rate is 20 percent ($2,000/$10,000), the 200 percent declining balance method results in a 40 percent depreciation rate. Table 9A-1 shows the depreciation calculations for this example.

The tax laws permitted businesses to switch from declining balance to straight line depreciation at the time when the declining balance deprecia-

---

Table 9A-1   **Sample 200 Percent Declining Balance Depreciation Calculations**

Year (1)	Undepreciated Amount (Book Value, Beginning of Year) (2)	Depreciation Rate (3)	Depreciation Amount* (4) = (2) × (3)
1	$12,000	40%	$ 4,800
2	$12,000 − $4,800 = $7,200	40%	2,880
3	$7,200 − $2,880 = $4,320	40%	1,728
4	$4,320 − $1,728 = $2,592	40%	592
5	$2,592 − $ 592 = $2,000	—	0
			$10,000

*When using the declining balance method, the salvage value is not deducted from the cost of the asset. The asset may not be depreciated below its reasonable salvage value, however. Thus, in this example, the year 4 depreciation is only $592 (leaving a book value at the end of year 4 of $2,000—the estimated salvage value). No depreciation would be charged during year 5.

Table 9A-2   **Sample Sum-of-the-Years'-Digits Depreciation Calculations**

Year (1)	Depreciable Base (2)	Fraction (3)	Depreciation Amount (4) = (2) × (3)
1	$10,000	5/15	$ 3,333
2	10,000	4/15	2,667
3	10,000	3/15	2,000
4	10,000	2/15	1,333
5	10,000	1/15	667
			$10,000

tion became less than the straight line amount. Most businesses followed this practice, since it allowed them to write off an asset more rapidly.

Sum-of-the-Years'-Digits Method

In the sum-of-the-years'-digits method, annual depreciation charges are computed by multiplying a decreasing fraction by the asset's original cost (less salvage value). The fraction's denominator is the sum of the digits that represent each year of the asset's expected economic life. For example, the sum-of-the-years'-digits for an asset with an expected five-year lifetime is $5 + 4 + 3 + 2 + 1$, or 15.[16] The numerator of the fraction for the first year is the highest digit—in this case, 5. The second year's numerator is the next highest digit—in this case, 4—and so on.

For example, suppose the company mentioned earlier decides to depreciate its $12,000 asset according to the sum-of-the-years'-digits method. Recall that the asset has a $2,000 expected salvage value and a five-year expected useful life. The calculations are shown in Table 9A-2.

Problem

1. Using the following depreciation methods, calculate the depreciation schedule for an asset that has a $15,000 original cost, an expected useful life of 5 years, and no expected salvage value:
   a. Straight line depreciation.
   b. Sum-of-the-years'-digits depreciation.
   c. Double declining balance depreciation (200 percent).
   d. 150 percent declining balance depreciation.

[16] In general, the sum of the years' digits is equal to $n(n + 1)/2$, where n is the number of years.

10

CAPITAL BUDGETING DECISION CRITERIA

A Financial Dilemma

Braniff International's Crash Landing*

During the 1960s and the mid-1970s, Braniff International prospered. It had a reputation for providing high-quality, innovative service to its airline passengers. During this period, Braniff was well respected by travelers in its traditional service area—the Southwest and the Southeast.

In 1978 airlines were deregulated, and Braniff sought to capitalize on the new deregulated environment. It immediately applied for 624 new routes—most of them outside its traditional service area. Routes were added nationwide and to Asia, Europe, and the Middle East. Within six months, Braniff snapped up 437 of the 1,300 routes that were offered by the Civil Aeronautics Board under deregulation. In contrast, the industry leader, United Airlines, added only one new route. To service the new routes, Braniff bought forty-one new airplanes, including eight 747s, at a cost of $925 million. Braniff's long-term debt surged to $733 million.

It is widely acknowledged that Braniff's new route system was very poorly conceived. Many routes could barely justify one flight a day. Service suffered, as did maintenance on this far-flung system. In 1979 Braniff lost $44.3 million. By 1981 this loss had increased to $160.6 million. In May 1982 Braniff declared bankruptcy.

The primary reason for Braniff's failure was incomplete and inadequate capital investment decisions. Over $900 million in aircraft was purchased to service routes with poor profit potential. This chapter considers a number of techniques that can be of value when analyzing the cash flows expected to be available from capital expenditures. The techniques developed are shown to be consistent with the firm's primary objective—the maximization of shareholder wealth.

* Based on "Braniff Makes a Crash Landing." *Business Week* (May 24, 1982): 62–65.

Key Chapter Concepts

1. The *payback period* of an investment is the period of time required for the cumulative cash inflows (net cash flows) from a project to equal the initial cash outlay.
   a. Weaknesses of the payback criterion include the fact that it is not a measure of profitability; it ignores the timing of cash flows; it ignores cash flows beyond the payback period; and it has no explicit tie to the goal of shareholder wealth maximization.
   b. The payback technique can be used as a project liquidity measure and as a crude risk-screening technique.
2. The *net present value* of an investment project is defined as the present value of the stream of net cash flows from the project minus the project's net investment.
   a. A project is acceptable if it has a zero or positive net present value.
   b. By maximizing the net present value of accepted projects, a firm will also maximize shareholder wealth.
3. The *internal rate of return* (IRR) is defined as the discount rate that equates the present value of net cash flows from a project with the present value of the net investment.
   a. A project is acceptable if it has an internal rate of return that is greater than or equal to the firm's cost of capital.
   b. The net present value and internal rate of return approaches give the same accept/reject signals for independent projects, although the two may be in conflict in the case of mutually exclusive investment alternatives. In these cases, the decision indicated using the net present value technique is generally preferable.
   c. Another disadvantage of the IRR approach is the fact that it can lead to multiple internal rates of return in some cases, thus complicating the decision process. In these cases the net present value technique should be used.

4. The *profitability index* (PI) is the ratio of the present value of future net cash flows over the life of the project to the net investment.
   a. If a project has a (PI) equal to or greater than 1.0, it is acceptable.
   b. The PI can be used as a guide to resource allocation in a situation of capital rationing.
5. Project postaudits and reviews can assist management in uncovering biases in the project analysis procedure of a firm. Project reviews can also assist management in making abandonment decisions for projects which are not performing up to expectations.

Glossary of New Terms

Internal rate of return (IRR) The discount rate that equates the present value of net cash flows from a project with the present value of the net investment. It is the discount rate that gives the project a net present value equal to zero. The IRR is used to evaluate, rank, and select from among various investment projects.

Multiple rates of return Two or more internal rates of return from the same project. This situation sometimes arises when the IRR method is being used for project selection. It occurs only with nonnormal projects, or those whose cash flow patterns contain more than one sign change.

Net present value (NPV) The present value of the stream of net cash flows resulting from a project, discounted at the firm's cost of capital, minus the project's net investment. It is used to evaluate, rank, and select from among various investment projects.

Opportunity cost The rate of return that can be earned on funds if they are invested in the *next best* alternative investment.

Payback (PB) period The period of time required for the cumulative cash inflows from a project to equal the initial cash outlay. It is used to evaluate, rank, and select from among various investment projects.

Profitability index (PI) The ratio of the present value of net cash flows over the life of a project to the net investment. It is used to evaluate, rank, and select from among various investment projects. Frequently it is used in conjunction with resource allocation decisions in capital rationing situations.

Project postaudit A review of a project that assesses its progress and evaluates its performance after termination.

Reinvestment rate The rate of return at which cash flows from an investment project are assumed to be reinvested from year to year. The reinvestment rate may vary, depending on the investment opportunities available to the firm.

Introduction

T his chapter looks at some widely used capital budgeting decision models, discussing and illustrating their relative strengths and weaknesses. When combined with the cash flow procedures developed in Chapter 9 and the discounting procedures developed in Chapter 3, these models provide the basis for making capital expenditure decisions.

This chapter also examines project review and postaudit procedures and concludes by tracing a sample project through the capital budgeting analysis process.

Evaluating Alternatives: Decision Models

As mentioned in Chapter 9, there are four basic steps in the capital budgeting process—the generation of proposals, the estimation of cash flows, the evaluation and selection of alternatives, and the project postaudit and review. This chapter discusses the final two steps in that process.

There are four commonly used criteria for evaluating and selecting investment projects,[1] including the following:

- Payback (PB) period.
- Net present value (NPV).
- Internal rate of return (IRR).
- Profitability index (PI).

Payback (PB) Period

The payback (PB) period of an investment is the period of time required for the cumulative cash inflows (net cash flows) from a project to equal the initial cash outlay (net investment).

To illustrate, assume a firm is considering two projects, A and B, having costs and cash flows as shown in Table 10-1.

If, as in Project A, the expected net cash inflows are *equal* in each year, the payback period is the ratio of the net investment to the annual net cash inflows:

$$PB = \frac{\text{Net investment}}{\text{Annual net cash inflows}}. \qquad (10.1)$$

The payback (PB) period for Project A is computed as follows:

$$PB = \frac{\$50,000}{\$12,500}$$

$$= 4 \text{ years}.$$

When annual net cash inflows are *unequal,* as in Project B, the payback period is calculated by finding the point in time when cumulative net cash inflows *just equal* the net investment. As can be seen in Table 10-1, this occurs between years 4 and 5, since the cumulative net cash inflows for

---

[1] Another procedure sometimes used is the accounting rate of return (also called the average rate of return). It is computed as the ratio of average annual profits after taxes to the average investment in the project. Since this approach has been shown to be generally incorrect as a project selection criterion, it is not discussed here.

Table 10-1

Sample Project Cash Flows

	Project A		Project B	
Year	Net cash flow after taxes	Cumulative net cash flow	Net cash flow after taxes	Cumulative net cash flow
1	$12,500	$12,500	$ 5,000	$ 5,000
2	12,500	25,000	10,000	15,000
3	12,500	37,500	15,000	30,000
4	12,500	50,000	15,000	45,000
5	12,500	62,500	25,000	70,000
6	12,500	75,000	30,000	100,000

Net investment for A = $50,000.
Net investment for B = $50,000.

Project B are $45,000 after four years (less than the net investment) and $70,000 after five years (more than the net investment). The *exact* payback is computed by means of interpolation as follows:

$$PB = t + \frac{b - c}{d - c},$$ **(10.2)**

where PB equals the payback period in years; t, the last full year in which cumulative net cash inflows are less than the net investment; b, the net investment; c, the cumulative cash inflow during the last full year when it is less than the net investment (year t); and d, the cumulative cash inflow in year $t + 1$. In this case the PB for Project B is as follows:

$$PB = 4 + \frac{\$50,000 - \$45,000}{\$70,000 - \$45,000}$$

$$= 4 + \frac{\$5,000}{\$25,000}$$

$$= 4.2 \text{ years.}$$

Decision Rule The payback period method is frequently used when a company is deciding whether to accept or reject an investment project. Specifically, the payback figure is compared with a *maximum acceptable payback figure*. The project is accepted if the calculated payback is less than this standard figure and rejected if it is greater. In this case, if the firm has a 5.5-year standard, both projects would be acceptable. If Projects A and B were *mutually exclusive,* however, A would be chosen over B because of its shorter payback period.

Advantages and Disadvantages of the Payback Method The payback method is widely used both because it is simple and because very long-term commitments tend to be viewed as undesirable. In spite of its widespread industry use, however, payback has a number of serious shortcomings.

First, it generally does not measure the profitability of investment projects and essentially ignores cash flows occurring after the payback period.[2] Thus, payback figures can be misleading.

For example, assume a firm is considering two projects, C and D, each costing $10,000. It is expected that Project C will generate net cash inflows of $5,000 per year for three years, and that Project D will generate net cash inflows of $4,500 per year forever. The payback period for Project C is two years ($10,000/$5,000), whereas the payback period for Project D is 2.2 years ($10,000/$4,500). If these projects were mutually exclusive, payback would favor C, because it has the lower payback period. Yet most people would prefer an investment yielding a cash flow stream of $4,500 per year forever to one yielding a cash flow stream of $5,000 per year for only three years. The payback approach does not adequately handle these types of situations.

Second, the payback method gives equal weight to all cash inflows within the payback period, regardless of when they occur during the period. In other words, the technique ignores the *time value of money*.

Assume, for example, that a firm is considering two projects, E and F, each costing $10,000. Project E is expected to yield cash flows over a three-year period of $5,000 during the first year, $3,000 during the second year, and $2,000 during the third year. Project F is expected to yield cash flows of $2,000 during the first year, $3,000 during the second year, and $5,000 during the third year. Viewed from the payback perspective, these projects would appear to be equally attractive, yet present value concepts clearly indicate that Project E is the more desirable of the two.

In response to this problem some firms have used a present value of payback criterion. When this procedure is used, the cash flows received in each period are converted to their present value equivalent by discounting them at an appropriate rate, such as the firm's cost of capital. This procedure is not used widely in practice, however.

Third, payback provides no *objective* criterion for decision making that is consistent with shareholder wealth maximization. The choice of an acceptable payback period is largely a *subjective* one, and different people using essentially identical data may make different accept-reject decisions about a project.

The payback method is sometimes justified on the basis that it provides a measure of the *risk* associated with a project. Although it is true that there may be less risk associated with a shorter payback period than with a longer one, risk is best thought of in terms of the *variability* of project returns. Since payback ignores this dimension, it is at best a crude tool for risk analysis.

A more valid justification for the use of the payback method is that it does give some indication of a project's desirability from a *liquidity* perspective, since it measures the time required for a firm to recover its initial investment in a project. A company that is very concerned about the early recovery of investment funds—such as one investing overseas in a

---

[2] There is no reason why a good analyst needs to ignore the cash flows occurring beyond the payback period when evaluating a specific project.

politically unstable area, or one expecting a cash shortage in the future—might find this method useful.

Of course, many firms evaluate investment projects using more than one criterion. For instance, a firm might use the net present value or the internal rate of return method—both of which are discussed later in this chapter—*in addition to* payback. The combination of these methods gives some indication of both a project's profitability and its liquidity. The use of payback in conjunction with other, more technically correct methods is quite common. One survey of the capital budgeting techniques used by over one hundred of the largest firms in the United States reported that only 9 percent used payback as their primary investment criterion, whereas 44 percent used it as a secondary technique for project evaluation.[3]

In summary, payback is not a satisfactory criterion for investment decision making, because it may lead to a selection of projects that do not make the largest possible contribution to a firm's value. It can, however, be useful as a supplementary decision-making tool.

Net Present Value

The net present value (NPV) of an investment project is defined as the present value of the stream of net cash flows from the project minus the project's net investment. (The net present value method is sometimes called the discounted cash flow [DCF] technique.) The cash flows are discounted at the firm's required rate of return, that is, its *cost of capital*. A firm's cost of capital is defined as its minimum acceptable rate of return for investment projects of average risk.

The net present value of a project may be expressed as follows:

$$NPV = PVNCF - NINV, \tag{10.3}$$

where NPV is the net present value; PVNCF, the present value of net cash flows; and NINV, the net investment.

Assuming a cost of capital, k, the net present value for a project with a five-year expected life would be the following:

$$NPV = \frac{NCF_1}{(1 + k)^1} + \frac{NCF_2}{(1 + k)^2} + \frac{NCF_3}{(1 + k)^3}$$
$$+ \frac{NCF_4}{(1 + k)^4} + \frac{NCF_5}{(1 + k)^5} - NINV, \tag{10.4}$$

where $NCF_1 - NCF_5$ are the net cash flows occurring in years 1 through 5. NCF_5 may be assumed to include any salvage value remaining at the end of the project's life.

As mentioned in Chapter 9, the annual net cash flows for normal projects are usually positive after the initial net investment. Occasionally, however, one or more of the expected net cash flows over the life of a

[3] See Lawrence J. Gitman and John R. Forrester, Jr. "A Survey of Capital Budgeting Techniques Used by Major U.S. Firms." *Financial Management* (Fall 1977): 66–71.

project may be negative. When this occurs, positive numbers are used for years having positive net cash flows (net inflows), and negative numbers are used for years having negative net cash flows (net outflows).

In general, the net present value of a project may be defined as follows:

$$NPV = \sum_{t=1}^{n} \frac{NCF_t}{(1 + k)^t} - NINV$$

$$= \left(\sum_{t=1}^{n} NCF_t \times PVIF_{k,t} \right) - NINV, \qquad \textbf{(10.5)}$$

where n is the expected project life, and $\sum_{t=1}^{n} [NCF_t/(1 + k)^t]$ is the arithmetic sum of the discounted net cash flows for each year t over the life of the project (n years), that is, the present value of the net cash flows.

Table 10-2 shows the net present value computations for projects A and B introduced earlier in Table 10-1. These calculations assume a 14 percent cost of capital. The calculations in these tables also assume that cash flows are received at the end of each year rather than as a flow during the year. This assumption, although a normal one, tends to slightly understate a project's net present value or internal rate of return.

Decision Rule   In general, a project should be accepted if its net present value is greater than or equal to zero and rejected if its net present value is less than zero. This is so because a positive net present value in principle translates directly into increases in stock prices and increases in shareholders' wealth. In the previous example, Project A would be rejected because it has a negative net present value, and Project B would be accepted because it has a positive net present value.

If two or more *mutually exclusive* investments of approximately the same size all have positive net present values, the project having the largest net present value is the one selected. Assume, for example, that a firm has

---

Table 10-2   **Sample Net Present Value Calculations**

	Year	NCF	$PVIF_{0.14,t}$*	PV of NCF
Project A		**Project B**		
Present value of an annuity of $12,500 for 6 years at 14 percent:				
	1	$ 5,000	0.877	$ 4,385
PV of NCF = $12,500(PVIFA₀.₁₄,₆)	2	10,000	0.769	7,690
= $12,500(3.889)†	3	15,000	0.675	10,125
= $48,612.50	4	15,000	0.592	8,880
	5	25,000	0.519	12,975
Less: Net investment 50,000.00	6	30,000	0.456	13,680
Net present value $ − 1,387.50				$57,735
		Less: Net investment		50,000
		Net present value		$ 7,735

*From the PVIF table (Table II).
†From the PVIFA table (Table IV).

three mutually exclusive investment opportunities, G, H, and I, each requiring a net investment of about $10,000. Project G has a net present value of $2,000; H has a net present value of $4,000; and I has a net present value of $3,500. Of the three, H would be preferred to the other two, because it has the highest net present value and therefore is expected to make the largest contribution to the objective of shareholder wealth maximization.

Advantages and Disadvantages of the Net Present Value Method The net present value approach is superior to the payback method, because it considers both the magnitude and the timing of cash flows over a project's entire expected life. In a period of high inflation rates it is especially important to consider the time value of money in project analysis. Therefore, the net present value approach is favored over the payback approach, because the latter ignores the timing of cash flows.

The net present value approach also indicates whether a proposed project will yield the rate of return required by the firm's investors. The cost of capital (discount rate) represents this rate of return; when a project's net present value is greater than or equal to zero, the firm's investors can expect to earn at least their required rate of return.

The net present value criterion does have one weakness in that many people find it difficult to understand the exact meaning of the net present value dollars that are computed using this technique.[4] As a result, many firms use another present value-based method that is more easily interpreted, namely, the *internal rate of return* method.

Internal Rate of Return

The *internal rate of return* is defined as the discount rate that equates the present value of the net cash flows from a project with the present value of the net investment.[5] It is the discount rate that causes a project's net present value to equal zero.

A project's internal rate of return can be determined by means of the following equation:

$$\left(\sum_{t=1}^{n} \frac{NCF_t}{(1 + r)^t} = NINV, \right)$$ **(10.6)**

where $NCF_t/(1 + r)^t$ is the present value of net cash flows in period t discounted at the rate r, NINV is the net investment in the project, and r is the internal rate of return.

For a project having a five-year life, this basic formula can be rewritten as follows:

$$\frac{NCF_1}{(1 + r)^1} + \frac{NCF_2}{(1 + r)^2} + \frac{NCF_3}{(1 + r)^3} + \frac{NCF_4}{(1 + r)^4} + \frac{NCF_5}{(1 + r)^5} = NINV.$$ **(10.7)**

[4] The net present value of a project may be thought of as the expected number of dollars the present value of the firm (that is, shareholders' wealth) is increased by as a result of adopting the project.
[5] This is also called the *discounted cash flow* (DCF) rate of return.

Subtracting the net investment, NINV, from both sides of Equation 10.7 yields the following:

$$\frac{NCF_1}{(1 + r)^1} + \frac{NCF_2}{(1 + r)^2} + \frac{NCF_3}{(1 + r)^3} + \frac{NCF_4}{(1 + r)^4} + \frac{NCF_5}{(1 + r)^5} - NINV = 0. \quad \textbf{(10.8)}$$

This is essentially the same equation as that used in the net present value method. The only difference is that in the net present value approach a discount rate, k, is specified and the net present value is computed, whereas in the internal rate of return method the discount rate, r, which causes the project net present value to equal zero, is the unknown.

Figure 10-1 illustrates the relationship between net present value and internal rate of return. The figure plots the net present value of Project B (from Table 10-1) against the discount rate used to evaluate its cash flows. Note that at a 14 percent cost of capital, the net present value of B is $7,735—the same figure that resulted from the computations performed

Figure 10-1   **NPV Profiles: Relationship between the Net Present Value and the Internal Rate of Return for Projects A and B**

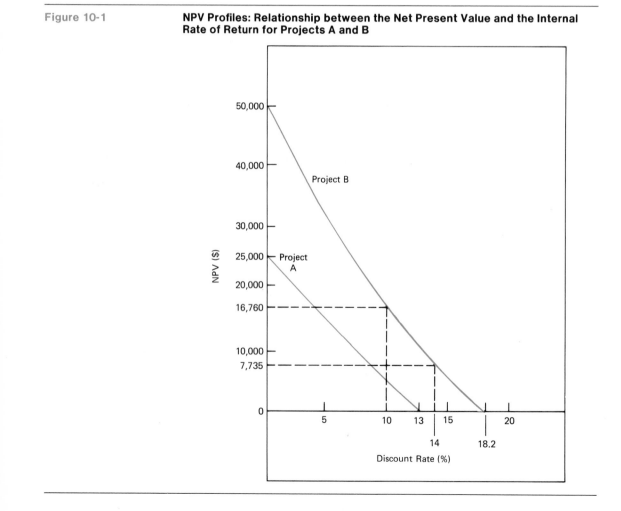

in Table 10-2. The internal rate of return of Project B is approximately equal to 18.2 percent. (The exact calculation will be illustrated algebraically.) Thus, the internal rate of return is a special case of the net present value computation.

The internal rate of return for Projects A and B now can be calculated. Since Project A is an annuity of $12,500 for six years requiring a net investment of $50,000, its internal rate of return may be computed directly with the aid of a PVIFA table such as Table IV.

In this case the present value of the annuity, PVAN, is $50,000, and the annuity, R, is $12,500 for $n = 6$ years. Equation 3.16 from Chapter 3,

$$PVAN = R(PVIFA_{i,n}),$$

can be rewritten to solve for the PVIFA as follows:

$$PVIFA_{i,n} = \frac{PVAN}{R}.$$

In this case, PVIFA = $50,000/$12,500 = 4.000. Referring to Table IV and reading across the table for $n = 6$, it can be seen that the interest factor of 4.000 occurs near 13 percent, where it is 3.998. Thus, the internal rate of return for Project A is about 13 percent.

The internal rate of return for Project B is more difficult to calculate, since the project is expected to yield uneven cash flows. In this case, the internal rate of return is computed by trial and error, with the help of a financial calculator, or by using capital budgeting spreadsheet programs such as the one provided in the *Study Guide* which accompanies this text. The steps in this procedure are as follows:

- **Step 1:** Make an approximate estimate of the internal rate of return.
- **Step 2:** Use this rate to compute the project's net present value.
- **Step 3:** Try a *higher* rate if a positive net present value results or a *lower* rate if a negative one results.
- **Step 4:** Repeat the process (attempting to "bracket" the internal rate of return) until a rate is found at which the net present value is equal to zero.

Table 10-3 illustrates this procedure. First, an r of 15 percent is tried, resulting in a net present value of $5,745. Next, a higher discount rate, 19 percent, is chosen; in this case the net present value is −$1,325. This indicates that the internal rate of return is between 15 and 19 percent. Trying 18 percent results in a net present value of $315, narrowing the range to between 18 and 19 percent.

A more exact internal rate of return can be computed by means of interpolation:

$$r = 18\% + \frac{\$315}{\$315 + \$1,325}(19\% - 18\%)$$

$$= 18\% + 0.19(1\%)$$

$$= 18.19\%.$$

Table 10-3   **Trial-and-Error Computation of the Internal Rate of Return for Project B**

Year (1)	Net Cash Flow (2)	$PVIF_{0.15,t}$ (3)	PV Cash Flows (4) = (3) × (2)	$PVIF_{0.19,t}$ (5)	PV Cash Flows (6) = (5) × (2)	$PVIF_{0.18,t}$ (7)	PV Cash Flows (8) = (7) × (2)
1	$ 5,000	0.870	$ 4,350	0.840	$ 4,200	0.847	$ 4,235
2	10,000	0.756	7,560	0.706	7,060	0.718	7,180
3	15,000	0.658	9,870	0.593	8,895	0.609	9,135
4	15,000	0.572	8,580	0.499	7,485	0.516	7,740
5	25,000	0.497	12,425	0.419	10,475	0.437	10,925
6	30,000	0.432	12,960	0.352	10,560	0.370	11,100
			$55,745		$48,675		$50,315
		Less: NINV	50,000	*Less:* NINV	50,000	*Less:* NINV	50,000
		NPV =	$ 5,745	NPV =	$−1,325	NPV =	$ 315

Decision Rule Generally the internal rate of return method indicates that a project whose internal rate of return is greater than or equal to the firm's cost of capital should be accepted, whereas a project whose internal rate of return is less than the firm's cost of capital should be rejected. In the case of Projects A and B, if the cost of capital were 14 percent B would be acceptable and A would be unacceptable.

When two independent projects are considered under conditions of no capital rationing, the net present value and internal rate of return techniques result in the same accept-reject decision. This can be seen in Figure 10-1. For example, if the firm's cost of capital is 10 percent, Project B has a positive net present value ($16,760). Its internal rate of return is 18.19 percent, exceeding the cost of capital. When two or more mutually exclusive projects are being considered, it is *generally* preferable to accept the project having the highest internal rate of return as long as it is greater than or equal to the cost of capital. In this case, if A and B were mutually exclusive, B would be chosen over A, as can be seen in Figure 10-1. Exceptions to this general rule are considered later in the chapter.

Advantages and Disadvantages of the Internal Rate of Return Method The internal rate of return method is widely used in industry by firms that employ present value–based capital budgeting techniques. In fact, in a survey of over one hundred U.S. firms, nearly 54 percent reported the use of the internal rate of return as their *primary* capital budgeting technique.[6] This popularity may be due to the fact that many people feel more comfortable dealing with the concept of a project's rate of return than with its net present value.[7] Like the net present value approach, the internal rate of return technique takes into account both the magnitude and the timing of cash flows over the entire life of a project in measuring the project's economic desirability.

---

[6] Lawrence J. Gitman and John R. Forrester, Jr. *op. cit.,* pp. 66–71.

[7] It is also easy to program a computer to perform these calculations, thus eliminating the need for trial-and-error manipulations. Some financial calculators, such as the Texas Instruments Professional Business Analyst and the Hewlett-Packard HP-12C, can also solve internal rate of return problems when the periodic cash flows are uneven.

However, there are some potential problems involved in using the internal rate of return technique. The possible existence of *multiple internal rates of return* is one such problem. Whereas equating the net present value of a project to zero will yield only one internal rate of return, *r*, for *normal* investments, there are times when two or more rates may be obtained. Recall that a normal project has an initial cash outlay or outlays (net investment) followed by a stream of positive net cash flows. If for some reason—such as large abandonment costs at the end of a project's life or a major shutdown and rebuilding of a facility sometime during its life—the initial net investment is followed by one or more positive net cash flows (inflows) that then are followed by a negative cash flow,[8] it is possible to obtain more than one internal rate of return.

Whenever a project has multiple internal rates of return, the pattern of cash flows over the project's life contains more than one sign change, for example, $- \uparrow + + \uparrow -$. In this case there are two sign changes (indicated by the arrows)—from minus to plus, and again from plus to minus.

Consider the following investment, which has three internal rates of return—0, 100, and 200 percent:

Year	Net Cash Flows
0	−$ 1,000
1	+$ 6,000
2	−$11,000
3	+$ 6,000

Unfortunately, none of these rates can be compared to the firm's cost of capital to determine the project's acceptability.

Although several techniques have been proposed for dealing with the multiple internal rate of return problem, none provides a simple, complete, and generally satisfactory solution. The best approach is to use the net present value criterion. If a project's net present value is positive, it is acceptable; if it is negative, it is not acceptable. There are many computer software packages available that compute internal rates of return, and they will usually warn the user when a potential multiple internal rate of return problem exists. Whenever this is a possibility, the use of the net present value method is preferred.

Profitability Index

The profitability index (PI), or benefit-cost ratio, is the ratio of the present value of future net cash flows over the life of a project to the net investment. It is expressed as follows:

$$PI = \frac{\sum_{t=1}^{n} NCF_t/(1 + k)^t}{NINV}$$

(10.9)

[8] Table 9-2 in Chapter 9 illustrates two such projects, X and Y.

Assuming a 14 percent cost of capital k, and using the data from Table 10-2, the profitability index for Projects A and B can be calculated as follows:

$$PI_A = \frac{\$48,612.50}{\$50,000}$$

$$= 0.97.$$

$$PI_B = \frac{\$57,735}{\$50,000}$$

$$= 1.15.$$

The profitability index is interpreted as the present value return *for each dollar of initial investment*. In comparison, the net present value approach measures the total present value dollar return.

Decision Rule   A project whose profitability index is greater than or equal to 1 is considered acceptable, while a project having a profitability index less than 1 is considered unacceptable.[9] In this case, Project B is acceptable, whereas Project A is not. When two or more *independent* projects with normal cash flows are considered, the profitability index, net present value, and internal rate of return approaches all will yield identical accept-reject signals; this is true, for example, with Projects A and B.

When dealing with mutually exclusive investments, conflicts may arise between the net present value and the profitability index criteria. This is most likely to occur if the alternative projects require significantly different net investments.

Consider, for example, the following information on Projects J and K. According to the net present value criterion, Project J would be preferred because of its larger net present value. According to the profitability index criterion, Project K would be preferred.

	Project J	Project K
Present value of net cash flows	$25,000	$ 14,000
Less: Net investment	−20,000	− 10,000
Net present value	$ 5,000	$ 4,000
$PI = \dfrac{\text{Present value of net cash flows}}{\text{Net investment}}$	1.25	1.40

When a conflict arises, the final decision must be made on the basis of other factors. For example, if a firm has no constraint on the funds available to it for capital investment—that is, no capital rationing—the net present value approach is preferred, since it will select the projects that are expected to generate the largest *total dollar* increase in the firm's wealth and, by extension, maximize shareholder wealth. If, however, the

[9] When a project has a profitability index equal to 1, the present value of the net cash flows is exactly equal to the net investment. Thus, the project has a net present value of zero, meaning that it is expected to earn the investors' required rate of return and nothing more.

firm is in a capital rationing situation, and capital budgeting is being done for only one period,[10] the profitability index approach may be preferred, since it will indicate which projects will maximize the returns *per dollar of investment*—an appropriate objective when a funds constraint exists.

Net Present Value versus Internal Rate of Return: The Reinvestment Rate Assumption

As was indicated, both the net present value and the internal rate of return methods result in identical decisions to either accept or reject an *independent* project. This is true because the net present value is greater than (less than) zero if and only if the internal rate of return is greater than (less than) the required rate of return, *k*. In the case of *mutually exclusive* projects, however, the two methods may yield contradictory results; one project may have a *higher* internal rate of return than another and, at the same time, a *lower* net present value.

Consider, for example, *mutually exclusive* Projects L and M described in the following table. Both require a net investment of $1,000. Using the internal rate of return approach, Project L is preferred, with an IRR of 21.5 percent compared with Project M's IRR of 18.3 percent. Using the net present value approach with a discount rate of 5 percent, Project M is preferred to Project L. Hence, it is necessary to determine which technique is the correct one to use in this situation.

	Project L	Project M
Net investment	$1,000	$1,000
Net cash flows:		
Year 1	$ 667	$ 0
Year 2	$ 667	$1,400
Net present value at 5%	$ 240	$ 270
Internal rate of return	21.5%	18.3%

The outcome depends on what *assumptions* the decision maker chooses to make about the *implied reinvestment rate* for the net cash flows generated from each project. This can be seen in Figure 10-2. For discount (reinvestment) rates below 10 percent, Project M has a higher net present value than Project L and is therefore preferred. For discount rates greater than 10 percent, Project L is preferred using both the net present value and internal rate of return approaches. Hence, a conflict only occurs in this case for discount (cost-of-capital) rates below 10 percent. The net present value method assumes that cash flows are *reinvested at the firm's cost of capital,* whereas the internal rate of return method assumes that these cash flows are *reinvested at the computed internal rate of return.*[11] Generally, the cost of capital is considered to be a more realistic reinvestment rate than the computed internal rate of return, because this is the rate the next (marginal) investment project can be assumed to earn.

---

[10] If the firm makes capital budgeting decisions for more than 1 period in the future, it is usually necessary to use some kind of programming model. Footnote 14 lists a number of references for some of these techniques.

[11] A more complete discussion of this problem and the underlying assumptions is found in J. Hirshleifer, "On the Theory of the Optimal Investment Decision," *Journal of Political Economy* 66 (Aug. 1958): 95–103; and James H. Lorie and Leonard J. Savage, "Three Problems in Rationing Capital," *Journal of Business* 23 (Oct. 1955): 229–239.

Figure 10-2   **NPV Profiles: Net Present Value versus Internal Rate of Return for Mutually Exclusive Alternatives**

This can be seen in Figure 9-1 in Chapter 9. The last project invested in, Project E, offers a rate of return nearly equal to the firm's marginal cost of capital.

Consequently, in the absence of capital rationing, the net present value approach is normally superior to both the profitability index and the internal rate of return when choosing among mutually exclusive investments.

Table 10-4 presents a summary of the four capital budgeting decision models discussed in the chapter.

Capital Rationing and the Capital Budgeting Decision

For each of the selection criteria previously discussed, the decision rule is to undertake *all* independent investment projects that meet the acceptance standard. This rule places no restrictions on the total amount of acceptable capital projects a company may undertake in any particular period.

However, many firms do not have unlimited funds available for investment. Rather than letting the size of their capital budget be determined by the number of profitable investment opportunities available, many companies choose to place an upper limit, or *constraint,* on the amount of funds allocated to capital investments. This constraint may be either *self-imposed*—by the firm's management—or *externally imposed*—by conditions in the capital markets.

For example, a very conservative firm may be reluctant to use debt or external equity to finance capital expenditures. Instead, it would limit capital expenditures to cash flows from continuing operations minus any dividends paid. Another firm may feel that it lacks the managerial resources to successfully undertake all acceptable projects in a given year and choose to limit capital expenditures for this reason.

Table 10-4   **Summary of the Capital Budgeting Decision Models**

Model	Project Acceptance Criterion	Strengths	Weaknesses
Payback (PB)	Accept project if PB period is less than the maximum acceptable PB.	Easy and Inexpensive to use. Provides a crude measure of project risk. Provides a measure of project liquidity.	No objective decision criterion. Not a measure of profitability. Fails to consider timing of cash flows.
Net present value (NPV)	Accept project if project has a positive or zero NPV, that is, if the present value of net cash flows, evaluated at the firm's cost of capital, equals or exceeds the net investment required.	Considers the timing of cash flows. Provides an objective, return-based criterion for acceptance or rejection. Most conceptually correct approach.	Difficulty in interpreting the meaning of the NPV computation.
Internal rate of return (IRR)	Accept project if IRR equals or exceeds the firm's cost of capital.	Same benefits as the NPV. Easy to interpret the meaning of IRR.	Multiple rates of return problem. Sometimes gives decision that conflicts with NPV.
Profitability index (PI)	Accept project if PI is greater than or equal to 1.0.	Same benefits as the NPV. Useful to guide decisions in capital rationing problems.	Sometimes gives decision that conflicts with NPV.

There are a number of externally imposed constraints that might limit a firm's capital expenditures. For example, a firm's loan agreements may contain restrictive covenants that limit future borrowing. The Ryder System, Inc., loan agreements contain a restrictive covenant that reads as follows:

> Company may not permit total consolidated debt (which includes lease obligations) to exceed 400 percent of consolidated net worth.[12]

Some of U.S. Air's loan agreements are even more restrictive:

> Company may not create any additional subordinated debt ranking on parity with the new debentures unless the total of such debt does not exceed the greater of $75,000,000 or 300 percent of the net worth of the company and all debt which it terms is subordinated to senior debt.[13]

Similarly, a weak financial position, conditions in the securities markets, or both may make the flotation of a new bond or stock issue by the firm impossible or prohibitively expensive. Examples of such market-imposed constraints include depressed stock market prices, unusually high interest rates due to a "tight money" policy on the part of the Federal Reserve, or a reluctance on the part of investors to purchase new securities if the firm has a large percentage of debt in its capital structure.

[12] *Moody's Transportation Manual.* New York: Moody's Investors Service, 1978, p. 1160.
[13] *Ibid.*, p. 1005.

Several different methods can be used in making capital budgeting decisions under capital rationing. When the initial outlays occur in two (or more) periods, the methods are quite elaborate and require the use of linear, integer, or goal programming.[14] However, when there is a single period capital budgeting constraint, a relatively simple approach employing the profitability index can be used. Briefly, the approach consists of the following steps:

- **Step 1:** Calculate the profitability index for each of a series of investment projects.

- **Step 2:** Rank the projects according to their profitability indexes (from highest to lowest).

- **Step 3:** Beginning with the project having the highest profitability index, proceed down through the list and accept projects having profitability indexes greater than or equal to 1 until the entire capital budget has been utilized.

At times a firm may not be able to utilize its entire capital budget because the next acceptable project on its list is too large, given the remaining available funds. In this case, the firm's management should choose among the following three alternatives:

- **Alternative 1:** Search for another combination of projects, perhaps including some smaller, less profitable ones that will allow for a more complete utilization of available funds *and* increase the net present value of the combination of projects.

- **Alternative 2:** Attempt to relax the funds constraint so that sufficient resources are available to accept the last project for which funds were not fully available.

- **Alternative 3:** Accept as many projects as possible and either invest any excess funds in short-term securities until the next period,[15] pay out the excess funds to shareholders as dividends, use the funds to reduce outstanding debt, or do a combination of the above.

The following example illustrates how these alternatives can be applied to an actual capital budgeting decision. Suppose that management of the Old Mexico Tile Company has decided to limit next year's capital expenditures to $550,000. Eight capital expenditure projects have been proposed—P, R, S, U, T, V, Q, and W—and ranked according to their

---

[14] The following references contain information on the use of these more advanced models: James R. McGuigan and R. Charles Moyer, *Managerial Economics,* 4th ed., St. Paul: West Publishing, 1986, pp. 96–99; or H. Martin Weingartner, *Mathematical Programming and the Analysis of Capital Budgeting Problems,* Englewood Cliffs, N.J.: Prentice-Hall, 1963. See also Sang M. Lee and A. J. Lerro, "Capital Budgeting for Multiple Objectives," *Financial Management* 3 (Spring 1974): 58–66; and Richard H. Bernhard, "Mathematical Programming Models for Capital Budgeting: A Survey, Generalization, and Critique," *Journal of Financial and Quantitative Analysis* 4 (June 1969): 111–158.

[15] If a firm does not invest a portion of its available capital resources in projects earning a rate of return at least equal to the cost of capital, an implicit opportunity cost of lost earnings is incurred. For example, suppose a firm cannot invest a portion of its capital budget because the next acceptable project requires a larger net investment than is available in remaining funds. If the firm's after-tax cost of capital is 15 percent and the unutilized funds can only be invested in short-term securities earning 5 percent after taxes, the opportunity cost of this action is a 10 percent difference, representing a loss in potential earnings. Thus, as long as profitable investment alternatives exist, the firm should seek ways to fully utilize all available capital funds.

Table 10-5   **Sample Ranking of Proposed Projects According to Their Profitability Indexes**

Project (1)	Net Investment (2)	Net Present Value (3)	Present Value of Net Cash Flows (4)	PI = (4) ÷ (2)	Cumulative Net Investment	Cumulative Net Present Value
P	$100,000	$ 25,000	$125,000	1.25	$100,000	$ 25,000
R	150,000	33,000	183,000	1.22	250,000	58,000
S	175,000	36,750	211,750	1.21	425,000	94,750
U	100,000	20,000	120,000	1.20	525,000	114,750
T	50,000	9,000	59,000	1.18	575,000	123,750
V	75,000	12,500	87,500	1.17	650,000	136,250
Q	200,000	30,000	230,000	1.15	850,000	166,250
W	50,000	− 10,000	40,000	0.80	900,000	156,250

profitability indexes, as shown in Table 10-5. Given the $550,000 ceiling, the firm's management proceeds down the list of projects, selecting P, R, S, and U, in that order. Project T cannot be accepted, since this would require a capital outlay of $25,000 in excess of the $550,000 limit. Projects P, R, S, and U together yield a net present value of $114,750 but require a total investment outlay of $525,000, leaving $25,000 from the capital budget that is not invested in projects. Management is considering the following three alternatives:

- **Alternative 1:** It could attempt to find another combination of projects, perhaps including some smaller ones, that would allow for a more complete utilization of available funds and increase the cumulative net present value. In this case, a likely combination would be Projects P, R, S, T, and V. This combination would fully utilize the $550,000 available and create a net present value of $116,250—an increase of $1,500 over the net present value of $114,750 from projects P, R, S, and U.

- **Alternative 2:** It could attempt to increase the capital budget by another $25,000 to allow Project T to be added to the list of adopted projects.

- **Alternative 3:** It could merely accept the first four projects—P, R, S, and U—and invest the remaining $25,000 in a short-term security until the next period. This alternative is not especially desirable, however, since the return on the short-term investment would surely be less than the firm's cost of capital (required rate of return). Thus, the difference between the firm's cost of capital and the return on the short-term investment would constitute an *opportunity cost*.

In this case, *Alternative 1* seems to be the most desirable of the three. In rearranging the capital budget, however, the firm should never accept a project, such as W, that does not meet the minimum acceptance criterion of a positive net present value (a profitability index greater than 1).

Reviewing and Postauditing an Accepted Project

A final important step in the capital budgeting process is the review of investment projects after they have been implemented. This can provide useful information on the effectiveness of the company's selection process. The postaudit procedure consists of comparing *actual* cash flows from an accepted project with *projected* cash flows that were estimated when the project was adopted. Because projected cash flows contain an element of uncertainty, actual values would not be expected to exactly match estimated values. Instead, a project review should be concerned with identifying systematic biases or errors in cash flow estimation on the part of individuals, departments, plants, or divisions and attempting to determine *why* these biases or errors exist. This type of analysis, when properly performed, can help a company's decision makers better evaluate investment proposals submitted in the future.

The importance of the postaudit process has been highlighted in research by Brown and Miller.[16] They observed that in the common situation where bad projects outnumber good ones, the simple procedure of making unbiased cash flow estimates and choosing projects with positive net present values will result in an upwardly biased acceptance rate for proposed projects (and returns that are, on average, below those which are expected) if there is uncertainty regarding future cash flows. In a situation such as this it is important that the firm correct for this potential bias when projects are being reviewed. The information needed to make this necessary bias-eliminating correction can be gathered from careful project postaudits.

Another objective of the project review process involves determining whether a project that has not lived up to expectations should be continued or abandoned. The decision to abandon a project requires the company to compare the cost of abandonment with any future cash flows that are expected over the project's remaining life. These estimates of future cash flows will usually be more accurate after the project has been in service for a period of time.[17]

A Comprehensive Example of Capital Budgeting: Opening a New Bank Branch

The First National Bank and Trust Company has a single banking office located in the downtown business district of a medium-sized town. As the population has moved toward the suburbs, First National has seen its share of both local banking deposits and profits decline. One of the bank's vice-presidents has proposed that First National try to reverse this trend by building a branch in a new, affluent suburban community. He has presented the bank's executive committee with the following information.

The initial cost of the bank building and equipment is $1,100,000. This facility is expected to have a useful life of twenty years. The branch building and its equipment will be depreciated over their twenty-year life using straight line depreciation to a $100,000 salvage value.[18] Conse-

---

[16] Keith C. Brown, "A Note on the Apparent Bias of Net Revenue Estimates for Capital Investment Projects," *Journal of Finance* (September 1974) pp. 1215–1216; K. C. Brown, "The Rate of Return on Selected Investment Projects," *Journal of Finance* (September 1978) pp. 1250–53; and Edward M. Miller, "Uncertainty Induced Bias in Capital Budgeting," *Financial Management* (Autumn 1978) pp. 12–18.

[17] A further discussion of the abandonment question may be found in Gordon Shillinglaw's two articles, "Profit Analysis for Abandonment Decision" and "Residual Values in Investment Analysis," reprinted in Ezra Solomon, ed., *The Management of Corporate Capital,* New York: Free Press, 1959, pp. 269–281 and 259–268, respectively. See also Alexander Robichek and James C. Van Horne, "Abandonment Value and Capital Budgeting," *Journal of Finance* 22 (Dec. 1967): 577–589.

[18] For simplicity, straight line depreciation has been assumed. As discussed in Chapter 9, the bank would most likely use an eighteen-year ACRS life on the building and a five-year ACRS life on the equipment.

quently, annual depreciation will be ($1,100,000 − $100,000)/20 = $50,000. The bank building is to be constructed on land leased for $20,000 per year. In addition to the $1,100,000 investment for the building and equipment, the parent bank's net working capital must be increased by $100,000 to accommodate the new branch.

Based upon customer surveys, population trends, the location of competitor banks, and the experience other area banks have had with their branches, it is estimated that the annual revenues from the new branch will be $400,000. Of this $400,000 in revenues, $50,000 will be drawn away from the bank's main office. (Assume that the main office will not attempt to cut its expenses because of this loss in revenues.)

In addition to the $20,000 annual expense for the land lease, the new branch will incur about $130,000 per year in other expenses, including personnel costs, utilities, and interest paid on accounts. Both expenses and revenues are expected to remain approximately constant over the branch's twenty-year life.

The bank's marginal tax rate is 40 percent. A 10 percent investment tax credit may be taken on the equipment installed in the new bank building. Of the combined building and equipment cost of $1,100,000, $200,000 represents equipment investments that are eligible for the investment tax credit.

The bank's cost of capital (required rate of return) is 9 percent after tax.

- **Step 1: Computing the Net Investment**

New project cost	$1,100,000
Plus: Increase in working capital	100,000
Gross investment	$1,200,000
Less: Investment tax credit (10% × $200,000)	20,000
Net investment	$1,180,000

The net investment equals the new project cost ($1,100,000) plus the increase in working capital ($100,000) minus the investment tax credit that may be taken on $200,000 of the investment.

- **Step 2: Computing Net Cash Flows**

Net increase in revenues ($400,000 − $50,000)	$350,000
Less: Operating costs of branch ($130,000 + $20,000)	150,000
Less: Depreciation	50,000
Net income before taxes	$150,000
Less: Tax (40%)	60,000
Net income after taxes	$ 90,000
Plus: Depreciation	50,000
Net cash flow	$140,000

Net cash flows are calculated for years 1 through 19 by subtracting branch operating costs and depreciation from the incremental revenues of $350,000. This yields net income before taxes from which taxes (at the 40 percent rate) are deducted to arrive at net income after taxes. By adding back depreciation, the net cash flow equals $140,000 for each year from 1 through 19. Net cash flows in year 20 are computed by adding the $100,000 estimated salvage and the $100,000 return of working capital[19] to the annual net cash flow of $140,000 to equal $340,000.

- **Step 3: Arraying Project Cash Flows and Evaluating Alternatives**

Net investment	$1,180,000
Net cash flows:	
Years 1–19	$ 140,000
Year 20	$ 340,000

After the project cash flows have been computed and arrayed, the desirability of the project must be determined using one or more of the four decision criteria discussed in this chapter, namely, payback, net present value, internal rate of return, or profitability index. In this example the project is evaluated using all four approaches.

- **Criterion 1: The Payback Period**

$$PB = \frac{\text{Net investment}}{\text{Annual net cash flow}}$$

$$= \frac{\$1,180,000}{\$140,000/\text{year}}$$

$$= 8.4 \text{ years}.$$

If the bank's cutoff payback period is greater than 8.4 years, the project would be accepted; if it is less than 8.4 years, the project would be rejected.

- **Criterion 2: Net Present Value**

$$NPV = PVNCF - NINV$$

$$= \sum_{t=1}^{19} \frac{\$140,000}{(1 + 0.09)^t} + \frac{\$340,000}{(1 + 0.09)^{20}} - \$1,180,000$$

$$= (\$140,000 \times PVIFA_{0.09,19})$$

$$+ (\$340,000 \times PVIF_{0.09,20}) - \$1,180,000.$$

The first term in the net present value equation is the present value of an annuity of $140,000 for 19 years at 9 percent, the bank's cost of capital. Using the present value of an annuity table (Table IV), an interest factor of 8.950 may be found. The second term is the present value of $340,000 received in 20 years at 9 percent. From the present value table (Table II), an interest factor of 0.178 is found. Thus, the net present

---

[19] The $100,000 working capital requirement is added back to the year 20 cash flows under the assumption that at the end of twenty years, when the project is terminated, there will no longer be a need for this incremental working capital, and thus the working capital of $100,000 can be liquidated and made available to the firm.

value of this project at a 9 percent cost of capital is as follows:

$$NPV = \$140,000(8.950) + \$340,000(0.178) - \$1,180,000$$
$$= \$1,253,000 + \$60,520 - \$1,180,000$$
$$= \$133,520.$$

Using the net present value criterion and a cost of capital of 9 percent, this project would be acceptable, since it has a positive net present value.

- **Criterion 3: Internal Rate of Return**

According to this method, a discount rate that makes the net present value of the project equal to zero must be found:

Present value of net cash flows − Net investment = 0,

or

$$\sum_{t=1}^{19} \frac{\$140,000}{(1 + r)^t} + \frac{\$340,000}{(1 + r)^{20}} - \$1,180,000 = 0,$$

where r is the internal rate of return.

Since the net present value was positive at an interest rate of 9 percent, only higher rates need be considered, because the higher the rate, the lower the net present value. Trying $r = 11\%$ yields the following:

$$NPV = \$140,000(7.839) + \$340,000(0.124) - \$1,180,000$$
$$= \$1,097,460 + \$42,160 - \$1,180,000$$
$$= -\$40,380.$$

Because the net present value is negative, a lower r, such as $r = 10\%$, should be tried next:

$$NPV = \$140,000(8.365) + \$340,000(0.149) - \$1,180,000$$
$$= \$1,171,100 + \$50,660 - \$1,180,000$$
$$= \$41,760.$$

Since this figure is positive, the actual internal rate of return falls somewhere between 10 and 11 percent. It is computed by interpolation as follows:

$$IRR = 10\% + \frac{\$41,760}{\$41,760 + \$40,380} (1\%)$$
$$= 10\% + 0.51(1\%)$$
$$= 10.51\%.$$

Since the internal rate of return equals 10.51 percent, which is greater than the cost of capital, the project is acceptable by this criterion.

● **Criterion 4: Profitability Index**

The profitability index is the ratio of the present value of future net cash flows to the net investment. From the previous net present value calculation, we know that the present value of net cash flows at a 9 percent cost of capital is $1,313,520 ($1,253,000 + $60,520). Thus, the profitability index is computed as follows:

$$PI = \frac{\$1,313,520}{\$1,180,000}$$

$$= 1.11.$$

Because the profitability index is greater than 1, the new branch bank project is acceptable according to this criterion.

Based on these calculations, it appears that the new branch proposal will increase shareholder wealth and therefore should be undertaken.[20] The only step remaining is to monitor the performance of the project to see if it meets, falls short of, or exceeds its projected cash flow estimates. Based upon the actual results of this project, the bank's management will be able to evaluate other new branch bank proposals in a more knowledgeable manner.

Inflation and Capital Expenditures

During inflationary periods the level of capital expenditures made by firms tends to decrease. For example, suppose the Apple Manufacturing Company has an investment opportunity that is expected to generate ten years of cash inflows of $300 per year. The original cash outflow is $2,000. If the company's cost of capital is relatively low—say, 7 percent—the net present value is positive:

$$\begin{aligned} NPV &= PV \text{ cash inflows} - PV \text{ cash outflows} \\ &= \$300(PVIFA_{0.07,10}) - \$2,000 \\ &= \$300(7.024) - \$2,000 \\ &= \$107.2. \end{aligned}$$

According to the net present value decision rule, this project is acceptable.

Suppose, however, that inflation expectations increase and the overall cost of the firm's capital rises to, say, 10 percent. The net present value of the project would then be negative:

$$\begin{aligned} NPV &= PV \text{ cash inflows} - PV \text{ cash outflows} \\ &= \$300(PVIFA_{0.10,10}) - \$2,000 \\ &= \$300(6.145) - \$2,000 \\ &= -\$156.5. \end{aligned}$$

Under these conditions, the project would not be acceptable.

---

[20] It is not normal to evaluate a project by all four criteria, as was done here. Often, however, when more than one approach is used, each is used to check a different aspect of the project. For example, the net present value might be used to check the project's profitability, and payback might be used to evaluate its risk and liquidity.

The example assumes that expected cash inflows are not affected by inflation. Admittedly, project revenues usually will increase with rising inflation, but so will expenses. As a result, it is somewhat difficult to generalize about net cash inflows. The experience of recent years, however, seems to indicate that cash flow increases are often not sufficient to offset the increased cost of capital. Thus, capital expenditure levels tend to be lower (in real terms) during periods of relatively high inflation than during low inflation times.

Fortunately, it is quite easy to adjust the capital budgeting procedure to take inflationary effects into account. The cost of capital already includes the effects of expected inflation.[21] As the expected future inflation rate increases, the cost of capital also tends to increase. Thus, the financial manager has to estimate future cash flows (revenues and expenses) that reflect the expected inflationary rate. For example, if prices are expected to increase at a rate of 5 percent per year over the life of a project, the revenue estimates made for the project should reflect this rising price trend. Cost or expense estimates also should be adjusted to reflect anticipated inflationary increases, such as labor wage rate increases and raw material price increases.

If these steps are taken, the capital budgeting procedure outlined in this and the preceding chapters will assist the financial manager even in an inflationary environment.

Summary

- The *payback period* is the number of years required for the cumulative net cash flows from a project to equal the net investment. Although the payback method is widely used, it has serious weaknesses, including the failure to account for the time value of money or to consider cash flows after the payback period.

- The *net present value* is calculated by subtracting a project's net investment from the net cash flows discounted at the firm's cost of capital. The net present value method overcomes the major flaws in the payback method.

- The *internal rate of return* of a project is the discount rate that gives the project a net present value equal to zero. This approach also solves some of the problems of the payback method.

- The *profitability index* is the ratio of the present value of net cash flows to the net investment. It gives a measure of the relative present value return per dollar of initial investment. The profitability index is useful when choosing among projects in a *capital rationing* situation.

- The net present value and internal rate of return approaches normally yield the same accept-reject decisions for a particular project. However, conflicts may arise when dealing with *mutually exclusive* projects. The reinvestment rate assumption embodied in the net present value approach—namely, that cash flows from a project are reinvested at the cost of capital—is generally more realistic than that underlying the internal rate of return method. For this reason the net present value method is generally preferred to the internal rate of return method.

[21] This is discussed in Chapter 12.

- Project postaudit reviews provide useful information regarding the effectiveness of a company's capital budgeting analysis and selection procedures. If a postaudit uncovers systematic biases in these procedures, corrective action should be taken. Project reviews may also identify whether a project should be abandoned prior to, at, or after its scheduled termination.

- In general, relatively high levels of inflation tend to reduce the level of capital expenditures in the economy. The general capital budgeting procedures discussed in this text can be applied with equal validity in an inflationary environment as long as the estimates of revenues and costs used in the capital budgeting process include expected price and cost increases.

FOCUS ON CORPORATE PRACTICE

Capital Budgeting Methods Used by Multinational Firms*

The techniques of capital budgeting described in this chapter and Chapter 9 have gained wide acceptance among major U.S. firms. Increasingly these techniques of project evaluation are being accepted by medium and smaller domestic firms as well. This Focus on Corporate Practice segment examines the capital budgeting techniques used by major multinational companies with headquarters in the U.S.

The survey results covered fifty-eight firms with a median capital budget of $200 million, and with a median of 200 major capital projects considered in the most recent year. Projects which were formally analyzed using capital budgeting techniques constituted 90 percent of all projects analyzed. Eighty-five percent of the multinational firms reported a project acceptance rate of at least 75 percent, indicating that few projects are formally analyzed unless it is anticipated that they will meet the firm's acceptance criteria.

The survey found that 76 percent of the respondents used either net present value, internal rate of return, or the profitability index as their primary capital budgeting technique. Ninety-four percent of the respondents used one of these techniques as either the primary or secondary capital budgeting technique. Some firms reported that they used different techniques to evaluate projects in foreign subsidiaries—with two firms indicating that greater weight was given to a project's payback period—in the case of foreign investments. This tends to support the role of the payback method as a supplementary risk evaluation technique.

With respect to the measurement of return from a foreign project, about 54 percent of the responses indicated that the investment's expected cash flow was the most important measure of return, with the balance using some measure of accounting profitability. About half of the firms which emphasized a project's cash flows indicated that they only considered the after-tax cash flow accruing to the parent firm; the other half also considered cash flows which were to be reinvested in the subsidiary.

The discount rate used by the majority of the firms was the after-tax weighted cost of capital. The average after-tax discount rate used by the firms in the sample was 12.5 percent. Of the forty-eight firms which used some discounted cash flow method of project analysis (NPV, IRR, or profitability index), 48 percent do not vary the discount rate used to evaluate foreign investments as compared to domestic investments. Of those twenty-five firms which reported that they do vary the discount rate used to evaluate foreign investments, the majority indicated that the rate was varied either subjectively to reflect the perceived risk differences of the foreign projects or was based upon a local (foreign) cost of capital.

Although techniques of project risk analysis are not covered until Chapter 11, it is useful to observe the risk analysis techniques used by the surveyed multinational firms. Nearly 73 percent of the firms surveyed which had large capital budgets (in excess of $500 million) reported that they experienced greater variation in foreign project returns than in the case of domestic projects. Seventy-

---

* This Focus on Corporate Practice example is based on David J. Oblak and Roy J. Helm, Jr., "Survey and Analysis of Capital Budgeting Methods Used by Multinationals," *Financial Management* (Winter 1980), pp. 37–41.

two percent of the responding companies indicated that they explicitly tried to consider the risk of investment projects. Techniques used to adjust for this risk included adjusting cash flow estimates (see the discussion of certainty equivalents in Chapter 11), adjusting the payback period, adjusting the required rate of return on the project, and borrowing funds locally (a technique designed to limit exchange rate risks).

It is clear from the discussion above that the techniques of capital budgeting which are discussed in the text have gained widespread acceptance not only in the United States, but also in companies which operate abroad.

Questions and Topics for Discussion

1. What are the primary strengths and weaknesses of the payback approach as a capital budgeting decision model?
2. How does the net present value model complement the objective of maximizing shareholder wealth?
3. When is it possible for the net present value and the internal rate of return approaches to give conflicting rankings of mutually exclusive investment projects?
4. When are multiple rates of return likely to occur in an internal rate of return computation? What should be done when a multiple rate of return problem arises?
5. Describe how the profitability index approach may be used by a firm faced with a capital rationing investment funds constraint.
6. What are the primary objectives of the investment project postaudit review?
7. What is the likely effect of inflation on the level of capital expenditures made by private firms? What must the financial manager do to insure that a firm's capital budgeting procedures will be effective in an inflationary environment?
8. What are the major problems you can foresee in applying capital budgeting techniques to investments made by public and not-for-profit sector enterprises or organizations?
9. What effect would you expect the use of ACRS depreciation rules to have on the acceptability of a project having a ten-year economic life but a five-year ACRS classification?

Problems*

1. A firm wishes to bid on a contract that is expected to yield the following after-tax net cash flows at the end of each year:

Year	Net Cash Flow
1	$ 5,000
2	8,000
3	9,000
4	8,000
5	8,000
6	5,000
7	3,000
8	− 1,500

To secure the contract, the firm must spend $30,000 to retool its plant. This retooling will have no salvage value at the end of the 8 years. Comparable investment alternatives are available to the firm that earn 12 percent compounded annually. The depreciation tax benefit from the retooling is reflected in the net cash flows in the table. Ignore the effects of the investment tax credit.

  a. Compute the project's payback period.
  b. Compute the project's net present value.
  c. Should the project be adopted?

2. A machine that costs $8,000 is expected to operate for 10 years. The estimated salvage value at the end of 10 years is $0. The machine is expected to save the company $1,554 per year before taxes and depreciation. The machine is eligible for the 10 percent investment tax credit. The company depreciates its assets on a straight line basis and has a marginal tax rate of 40 percent. What is the internal rate of return on this investment?

Lotus123

* Color numbers denote problems which have check answers provided at the end of the book.

Lotus123

3. Recalculate the internal rate of return for the machine investment in Problem 2 assuming that the firm uses 5-year ACRS depreciation rates instead of straight line depreciation over 10 years. The economic life of the machine is still 10 years, and its estimated salvage value is $0.

4. An acre planted with walnut trees is estimated to be worth $12,000 in 25 years. If you want to realize a 15 percent rate of return on your investment, how much can you afford to invest per acre? (Ignore all taxes and assume that annual cash outlays to maintain your stand of walnut trees are nil.)

5. A company is planning to invest $100,000 (before tax) in a personnel training program. The $100,000 outlay will be charged off as an expense by the firm this year (year 0). The returns from the program, in the form of greater productivity and a reduction in employee turnover, are estimated as follows (on an after-tax basis):

Years 1–10: $10,000 per year
Years 11–20: $25,000 per year

The company has estimated its cost of capital to be 12 percent. Assume that the entire $100,000 is paid at time 0 (the beginning of the project). The marginal tax rate for the firm is 40 percent.

Should the firm undertake the training program? Why or why not?

6. Two mutually exclusive investment projects have the following forecasted cash flows:

Year	A	B
0	− $20,000	− $20,000
1	+ 10,000	0
2	+ 10,000	0
3	+ 10,000	0
4	+ 10,000	+60,000

a. Compute the internal rate of return for each project.
b. Compute the net present value for each project, if the firm has a 10 percent cost of capital.
c. Which project should be adopted? Why?

7. Show that the internal rate of return of the following investment is 0, 100, and 200 percent:

Net investment	− $1,000	Year 0
Net cash flows	+ 6,000	Year 1
	− 11,000	Year 2
	+ 6,000	Year 3

Lotus123

8. ABC Hydronics is considering replacing one of its larger control devices. A new unit sells for $30,000 (delivered). An additional $3,000 will be needed to install the device. A 10 percent investment tax credit is available to the firm. The new device has an estimated 20-year service life. The estimated salvage value at the end of 20 years will be $2,000. The new control device will be depreciated over 20 years on a straight line basis to its estimated salvage value. The existing control device (original cost = $15,000) has been in use for 22 years, and it has been fully depreciated (that is, the book value equals zero). Its scrap value is estimated to be $1,000. The existing device could be used indefinitely, assuming the firm is willing to pay for its very high maintenance costs. The firm's marginal tax rate is 40 percent. The new control device re-

quires lower maintenance costs and frees up personnel who would normally have to monitor the system. Estimated annual cash savings from the new device will be $9,000. The firm's cost of capital is 12 percent.

Using this information, evaluate the relative merits of replacing the old control device using the net present value approach.

9. Recalculate the net present value of the control device investment in Problem 8, assuming that the new control device is depreciated over 5 years under the ACRS schedule. At the end of 20 years the estimated salvage value of the new device will continue to be $2,000.

Compare the answers you get to Problems 8 and 9. What effect does the use of ACRS depreciation have on the economic desirability of the project?

10. A $1,230 investment has the following expected cash returns:

Year	Net Cash Flow
1	$800
2	200
3	400

Compute the internal rate of return for this project.

11. Pinion Pot Company has $1 million available for capital investments during the current year. A list of possible investment projects, together with their net investments and net present values, is provided in the following table:

Project	Net Investment	Net Present Value
1	$200,000	$ 20,000
2	500,000	41,000
3	275,000	50,000
4	150,000	5,000
5	250,000	20,000
6	100,000	5,000
7	275,000	22,000
8	200,000	− 18,000

a. Rank the various investment projects in terms of their profitability indexes (computed to three decimal places).

b. In the order of decreasing profitability index values and considering the capital constraints, which projects should be adopted? Are all capital funds expended?

c. Is there another combination that produces a higher aggregate net present value than the one developed in Part b?

d. If less than the entire amount of available funds is invested, what is the opportunity cost of the unused funds?

12. A junior executive is fed up with the operating policies of his boss. Before leaving the office of his angered superior, the young man suggests that a well-trained monkey could handle the trivia assigned to him. Pausing a moment to consider the import of this closing statement, the boss is seized by the thought that this must have been in the back of her own mind ever since she hired the junior executive. She decides to consider seriously replacing the executive with a bright young baboon. She figures that she could argue strongly to the board that such "capital deepening" is necessary for the cost-conscious firm. Two days later, a feasibility study is completed, and the following data are presented to the president:

• It would cost $12,000 to purchase and train a reasonably alert baboon with a life expectancy of 20 years.

- Annual expenses of feeding and housing the baboon would be $4,000.
- The junior executive's annual salary is $7,000 (a potential saving if the baboon is hired).
- The baboon will be depreciated on a straight line basis over 20 years to an estimated salvage value of $400.
- The baboon purchase is eligible for a 10 percent investment tax credit.
- The firm's marginal tax rate is 40 percent.
- The firm's current cost of capital is estimated to be 11 percent.

On the basis of the net present value criterion, should the monkey be hired (and the junior executive fired)?

13. The L-S Mining Company is planning to open a new strip mine in Western Pennsylvania. The net investment required to open the mine is $10 million. Net cash flows are expected to be +$20 million at the end of year 1 and +$5 million at the end of year 2. At the end of year 3 L-S will have a net cash *outflow* of $17 million to cover the cost of closing the mine and reclaiming the land.
    a. Calculate the net present value of the strip mine if the cost of capital is 5, 10, 15, 30, 71, and 80 percent.
    b. What is unique about this project?
    c. Should the project be accepted if L-S's cost of capital is 10 percent? 20 percent?

14. Fred and Frieda have always wanted to enter the blueberry business. They locate a 50-acre piece of hillside in Maine that is covered with blueberry bushes. They figure that the annual yield from the bushes will be 200 crates. Each crate is estimated to sell for $400 for the next 10 years. This price is expected to rise to $500 per crate for all sales from years 11 through 20.

    In order to get started, Fred and Frieda must pay $150,000 for the land plus $20,000 for packing equipment. The packing equipment will be depreciated on a straight line basis to a zero estimated salvage value at the end of 20 years. The packing equipment is eligible for a 10 percent investment tax credit. Fred and Frieda believe that at the end of 20 years they will want to retire to Florida and sell their property.

    Annual cash operating expenses, including salaries to Fred and Frieda, are estimated to be $50,000 per year for the first 10 years and $60,000 thereafter. The land is expected to appreciate in value at a rate of 5 percent per year. The couple's marginal tax rate is 30 percent for ordinary income and 15 percent for capital gains and losses.
    a. If the couple requires at least a 13 percent return on their investment, should they enter the blueberry business?
    b. Assume that the land can be sold for only $50,000 at the end of 20 years (a capital loss of $100,000). Should the couple invest in the land and blueberry business? (Assume that the couple may claim the full amount of their capital loss in the year it occurs—year 20).

15. The Sisneros Company is considering building a chili processing plant in Hatch, New Mexico. The plant is expected to produce 50,000 pounds of processed chili peppers each year for the next 10 years. During the first year, Sisneros expects to sell the processed peppers for $2 per pound. The price is expected to increase at a 7 percent rate per year over the 10-year economic life of the plant. The cash costs of operating the plant, including the cost of fresh peppers, are estimated to be $50,000 during the first year. These costs are expected to increase at an 8 percent rate per year over the next 10 years.

    The plant will cost $80,000 to build. It is eligible for the 10 percent investment tax credit and will be depreciated as a 5-year ACRS asset. The estimated salvage at the end of 10 years is zero. The firm's marginal tax rate is 40 percent.

a. Calculate the net investment required to build the plant.

b. Calculate the annual net cash flows from the project.

c. If Sisneros uses a 20 percent cost of capital to evaluate projects of this type, should the plant be built? (Use the net present value criterion.)

d. Calculate the payback period for this project.

16. Note the following information on two mutually exclusive projects under consideration by J.T., Inc.

Annual Cash Flows

Year	A	B
0	$-30,000	$-60,000
1	10,000	20,000
2	10,000	20,000
3	5,000	20,000
4	5,000	20,000
5	5,000	20,000

J.T., Inc., requires a 14 percent rate of return on projects of this nature.

a. Compute the payback period on both projects.

b. Compute the internal rate of return of both projects.

c. Compute the NPV of both projects.

d. Would the firm accept either of the projects? Why?

17. Channel Tunnel, Inc., plans to build a 23-mile long tunnel under the English Channel for trains. The cost (NINV) of the tunnel is expected to be $3.3 billion. Cash inflows are expected to equal $651 million per year. How many years must the firm generate this cash inflow stream in order for investors to earn their required 19 percent rate of return?

An Integrative Case Problem

Capital Budgeting

Lotus123

Intercontinental Banking Group has had considerable success in the marketing of its franchised insurance services program to regional banking firms. Senior management has suggested that this program be expanded on a national scale to take advantage of the bank's growing expertise in this area. In order to do this the bank will have to acquire a new computer and accounting information processing system. The cost of the computer hardware to support this venture is estimated to be $4 million. In addition to this one-time capital outlay for computer equipment, the bank estimates that it will have to acquire additional equipment costing $500,000. Both the computer and the other equipment will be depreciated under ACRS rules in effect on January 1, 1985, and both are eligible equipment for the receipt of the investment tax credit. The expected economic life of the venture is ten years. Beyond that point in time the bank estimates the competition will force it to abandon this venture. The expected salvage value of all the new equipment, including the computer, is $100,000. The new venture will require the bank to invest an additional $250,000 in its net working capital.

The bank expects first year revenues from the program to be $1,400,000. These are expected to grow by $75,000 per year from year 2 through 6, and then decline by $125,000 per year from year 7 through year 10. Cash operating costs for the new venture are expected to total $225,000 during year 1 and grow at an annual rate of 6 percent per year over the 10-year life of the venture.

The firm's marginal tax rate for ordinary income is 40 percent. The capital gains rate is 30 percent. The bank requires a 10 percent after-tax rate of return on new investment projects.

1. Compute the net investment required for this insurance franchising scheme.
2. Compute the annual net cash flows associated with the investment.
3. Compute the payback period for this investment.
4. Should the bank invest in the insurance franchising system, based upon a net present value analysis?
5. Compute the internal rate of return for this investment.

Selected References

Bower, Richard S., and Jeffrey M. Jenks. "Divisional Screening Rates." *Financial Management* 4 (Autumn 1975): 42–49.

Cooley, Philip L., Rodney L. Roenfeldt, and It-Keong Chew. "Capital Budgeting Procedures under Inflation." *Financial Management* 4 (Winter 1975): 18–27.

Joy, O. Maurice. "Abandonment Values and Abandonment Decisions: A Clarification." *Journal of Finance* 31 (Sept. 1976): 1225–1228.

Lewellen, Wilbur G., Howard P. Lanser, and John J. McConnell. "Payback Substitutes for Discounted Cash Flow." *Financial Management* 2 (Summer 1973): 17–23.

Nelson, Charles R. "Inflation and Capital Budgeting." *Journal of Finance* 31 (June 1976): 923–931.

Van Horne, James C. "A Note on Biases in Capital Budgeting Introduced by Inflation." *Journal of Financial and Quantitative Analysis* 6 (Jan. 1971): 653–658.

Williams, John Daniel, and Jonathan S. Rakich. "Investment Evaluation in Hospitals." *Financial Management* 2 (Summer 1973): 30–35.

See also references in Chapter 9.

MUTUALLY EXCLUSIVE INVESTMENTS HAVING UNEQUAL LIVES

Replacement Chains

Chapter 10 discussed a number of capital budgeting decision models. When mutually exclusive investments were considered, it was implicitly assumed that the alternative projects had *equal* lives. In actual practice, however, this may not be the case. When two or more mutually exclusive alternatives have *unequal* lives, neither the net present value nor the internal rate of return method yields reliable accept-reject information unless the projects are being evaluated for an equal period of time. If, for example, a firm adopts the longer lived of two projects simply on the basis of net present value or internal rate of return data, it essentially ignores any alternative investment opportunities that might have been available at the end of the shorter-lived project.

Suppose a firm is considering two mutually exclusive investments, I and II. Project I requires an initial outlay of $2,000 and is expected to generate a five-year stream of net cash flows of $600 per year. Project II also requires an initial outlay of $2,000 but is expected to generate a ten-year stream of net cash flows of $375 per year. The firm has a 10 percent cost of capital.

Table 10A-1 shows that the net present value of Project I is $274.60 and the net present value of Project II is $304.37. Thus, the net present value criterion suggests that Project II should be chosen over Project I.

The expected life of Project II is twice as long as that of Project I.

Table 10A-1 **Cash Flows for Projects I and II**

Year	Project I Net Investment	Project I Net Cash Flow	Project II Net Investment	Project II Net Cash Flow
0	$2,000	—	$2,000	—
1		$600		$375
2		600		375
3		600		375
4		600		375
5		600		375
6		—		375
7		—		375
8		—		375
9		—		375
10		—		375

$$NPV_I = -\$2,000 + \$600(3.791) \qquad NPV_{II} = -\$2,000 + \$375(6.145)$$
$$= \$274.60. \qquad\qquad\qquad\qquad = \$304.37.$$

Therefore, the two net present values calculated in Table 10A-1 are not really comparable. At this point the firm must also consider what might happen if Project I were replaced with a similar five-year life project at the end of five years. In other words, it would create a *replacement chain* for the shorter-lived project. Suppose, for example, the firm estimates that replacing Project I with a similar project at the end of five years would cost $2,100 and, like Project I, would generate annual net cash flows of $600. This results in a new stream of cash flows for Project I, as shown in Table 10A-2. The new net present value for Project I is higher than that for Project II, thus indicating—correctly—that Project I should be chosen over Project II.

Many times it is not possible to get a series of projects (such as Project I with its replacement at the end of five years) that will have an identical time duration to that of the longer-lived project (II). For example, one project might have a life of fifteen years, whereas an alternative requires replacement every eight years. Hence, the shorter-lived project together with its replacement have a sixteen-year life, whereas the longer-lived project has a fifteen-year life. Such a comparison will normally be acceptable, since the discrepancy occurs for only one year that is fifteen years in the future. In present value terms, this will not have much impact.

The importance of time discrepancies such as these depends on the following:

- The number of years of the discrepancy. The fewer the years of the discrepancy, the less important it is.
- The number of years into the future the discrepancy occurs. The further into the future, the less important the discrepancy is.
- The relationship between the rate of return on future investments and the cost of capital. When the rate of return on future investments is equal to the cost of capital, these investments have an NPV = 0. Under these circumstances, the discrepancy can be ignored.

Table 10A-2   **Replacement Chain Cash Flows for Project I Compared with Project II**

	Project I with Replacement		Project II	
Year	Net Investment	Net Cash Flow	Net Investment	Net Cash Flow
0	$2,000	—	$2,000	—
1		$600		$375
2		600		375
3		600		375
4		600		375
5	2,100	600		375
6		600		375
7		600		375
8		600		375
9		600		375
10		600		375

$$NPV_I = -\$2,000 + \$600(6.145) - \$2,100(0.621)$$
$$= \$382.80.$$

$$NPV_{II} = -\$2,000 + \$375(6.145)$$
$$= \$304.37.$$

Equivalent Annual Annuities

An alternative approach for dealing with the problem of mutually exclusive investments having unequal lives is to use the equivalent annual annuity approach. This technique can solve the problem of time discrepancies often encountered when using the replacement chain approach.

For example, consider the case of a firm that needs to replace an aging piece of machinery. One alternative would be to buy new Machine A having a nine-year life. Another alternative would be to buy new Machine B with a five-year life. In this case, the time discrepancy between A and B is significant—four years. Commonly, this problem is dealt with by developing a string of replacement chains out to a year when both machines would need replacement. The common denominator year in this case is forty-five years—indicating nine investments in B and five investments in A.

In cases like this, the equivalent annual annuity approach is often easier to use. In our example, assume the new Machine A will require a net investment of $34,500 and generate net cash flows of $7,000 per year for nine years. Machine B will require a net investment of $25,000 and generate net cash flows of $8,000 per year for five years. The firm's cost of capital is 10 percent. In order to make our decision on the basis of the equivalent annual annuity criterion, we use the following three steps:

1. First, compute the net present value of each machine over its original expected economic life:

$$NPV_A = -\$34,500 + \$7,000(PVIFA_{0.10,9})$$
$$= -\$34,500 + \$7,000(5.759)$$
$$= \$5,813.$$
$$NPV_B = -\$25,000 + \$8,000(PVIFA_{0.10,5})$$
$$= -\$25,000 + \$8,000(3.791)$$
$$= \$5,328.$$

As these calculations indicate, if the possibility of the replacement of Machine B at the end of five years is not considered, Machine A would appear to be the best alternative because of its greater net present value.

2. Next, divide the net present value for each machine computed in Step 1 by the PVIFA factor for the project's original life. This gives the *equivalent annual annuity:*

$$\text{Equivalent annual annuity (A)} = \frac{\$5,813}{PVIFA_{0.10,9}}$$
$$= \frac{\$5,813}{5.759}$$
$$= \$1,009.38.$$

$$\text{Equivalent annual annuity (B)} = \frac{\$5,328}{PVIFA_{0.10,5}}$$
$$= \frac{\$5,328}{3.791}$$
$$= \$1,405.43.$$

3. The equivalent annual annuity method assumes that each machine will be replaced an infinite number of times into the future and will therefore provide these annual annuities in perpetuity. As perpetuities, these equivalent annual annuities can be valued (at present) by dividing the annuity amount by the cost of capital:

$$NPV_A \text{ (assuming infinite replacement)} = \frac{\$1,009.38}{0.10}$$

$$= \$10,093.80.$$

$$NPV_B \text{ (assuming infinite replacement)} = \frac{\$1,405.43}{0.10}$$

$$= \$14,054.30.$$

Machine B should be acquired, since it has the highest net present value when evaluated over an infinite replacement horizon.

In general, the equivalent annual annuity method will give the same decision as the replacement chain technique. Its advantage is that it is often computationally simpler, and it simplifies the handling of the time discrepancies that frequently arise in the replacement chain method.

Problems*

1. The Smith Pie Company is considering two mutually exclusive investments that would increase its capacity to make strawberry tarts. The firm uses a 12 percent cost of capital to evaluate potential investments. The two projects have the following costs and cash flow streams:

Year	Alternative A	Alternative B
0	− $30,000	− $30,000
1	10,500	6,500
2	10,500	6,500
3	10,500	6,500
4	10,500	6,500
5	—	6,500
6	—	6,500
7	—	6,500
8	—	6,500

a. Using this data, calculate the net present value for Projects A and B.
b. Create a replacement chain for Alternative A. Assume that the cost of replacing A will be $30,000 and that the replacement project will generate cash flows of $10,500 for years 5 through 8. Using these figures, recompute the net present value for Alternative A.
c. Which of the two alternatives should be chosen, A or B? Why?

2. Use the equivalent annual annuity method to solve Problem 1. How does your answer compare with the one obtained in Problem 1?

* Color numbers denote problems which have check answers provided at the end of the book.

11

CAPITAL BUDGETING AND RISK

A Financial Dilemma

Washington Public Power Supply System (Whoops)

The capital budgeting process discussed in the previous two chapters is, in reality, quite simple. If the present value of a project's net cash flows exceeds the outlays required (the net investment), a project is acceptable and should be undertaken. The real difficulty is developing realistic estimates of the costs and benefits from a project. The problems a firm may encounter can stem from an incomplete analysis of a project (the Lockheed case) or from a lack of sufficient concern for the profitability of the firm (Braniff's apparent preoccupation with growth and market share).

In addition to these problems, it must be recognized that nearly all projects have some element of risk—the chance that the actual cash flows will differ from the forecasted ones. This is the case for the Washington Public Power Supply System—now referred to as "Whoops" in the financial community.

In the 1970s a consortium of eighty-eight utilities in the Pacific Northwest agreed to build five nuclear power plants to meet the rapidly growing need for energy in the region. The projected cost of the five plants was $5 billion. Unfortunately, the sharp increases in energy costs in the late 1970s and early 1980s caused the growth in demand for electricity to drop rapidly. The consortium finally canceled two of the five units in the face of declining demand and postponed completion of a third unit for up to five years. The cost of these two canceled units will be over $7 billion to customers of the eighty-eight utilities over the next thirty years. In addition to their declining demand, the cost of the units rose from the initial $5 billion to over $24 billion.

This example illustrates one of the painful realities of making capital budgeting decisions—cash flows and costs from a project will rarely meet projections exactly. This is to be expected, since nearly all capital investments contain an element of risk. Although risk cannot be eliminated, a capable financial manager should try to determine at the outset what risks are being assumed when a project is undertaken. What is the worst case outcome? How likely is this outcome? What actions can be taken to reduce this risk? How will investors react to this risk? Given the answers to these questions, risky projects can be properly evaluated. This chapter examines these important questions.

Key Chapter Concepts

1. *Total project risk* refers to the chance that a project will not perform up to expectations. It is often measured by the standard deviation of cash flows from a project.

2. The *portfolio risk* of a project refers to the contribution a project makes to the risk of the firm, when the interactions between the cash flows of the project are considered in conjunction with the cash flows of the balance of the firm.

3. There are a number of techniques which can be used to analyze total project risk. These techniques include:
   a. The *subjective* or *informal approach*
   b. The *net present value/payback approach*
   c. The *risk-adjusted discount rate approach*
   d. The *hurdle rate approach*
   e. The *certainty equivalent approach*
   f. The *simulation approach*
   g. The *sensitivity analysis approach*

4. When considering the systematic risk of individual projects, the *beta* concept can be used to determine risk-adjusted discount rates for individual projects.

5. The *beta* concept can also be used to compute divisional costs of capital for firms with several operating divisions which differ substantially with respect to the risks of investments which are made.

Glossary of New Terms

Certainty equivalent The amount of cash someone would require with certainty at a point in time in order to make him or her indifferent between that certain amount and an amount expected to be received with risk at the same point in time.

Hurdle rate The minimum acceptable rate of return from an investment project. For projects of average risk, it is usually equal to the firm's cost of capital.

Risk-adjusted discount rate A discount rate that reflects the risk associated with a particular project. In capital budgeting, a higher risk-adjusted rate is used to discount cash flows for riskier projects, while a lower risk-adjusted rate is used to discount cash flows for less risky projects.

Simulation A financial planning tool that models some event, such as the cash flows from an investment project. A computerized simulation is one technique used to assess the risk associated with a particular project.

Introduction

n Chapter 5 we discussed the nature of risk and its influence on financial decision making. The greater the risk associated with an investment, the greater the return required. This basic principle applies in the capital budgeting area.

In the previous two chapters, investment projects were evaluated using the firm's weighted cost of capital (required rate of return). This approach implicitly assumes that all projects being considered are of equal risk and that this risk is the same as that for the firm as a whole. When a project has more or less than an average risk level, it is necessary to adjust the analysis to account for this risk level.

Total Project Risk Versus Portfolio Risk

When analyzing the risk associated with a capital expenditure, it is important to distinguish between the *total project risk* and the *portfolio, or beta, risk* of that investment. By total project risk we mean the chance that a project will perform below expectations—possibly resulting in losses from the project and for the firm. In the worst case, these losses could be so severe as to cause the firm to fail.

In contrast, a project that has a high level of total project risk may not affect the portfolio risk of the firm at all. Consider the case of oil and gas exploration companies. The firms know that any wildcat well they drill will cost about $2 million and have only a 10 percent chance of success. Successful wells produce profits of $24 million. Unsuccessful wells produce no profits at all, and the entire investment will be a loss. If each firm only drilled one well, there would be a 90 percent chance the firm would fail (the total project risk would be very high). In contrast, if one firm drilled one hundred wildcat wells, the risk of failure from all wells would be very low because of the portfolio risk reduction that results from drilling many wells. In this case the expected return of the firm would be as follows:

$$\text{Expected return} = \frac{\text{Expected profit per well}}{\text{Investment required per well}}$$

$$= \frac{\left(\begin{array}{c}\text{Probability of}\\\text{success}\end{array}\right)\left(\text{Profit}\right) + \left(\begin{array}{c}\text{Probability of}\\\text{failure}\end{array}\right)\left(\text{Loss}\right)}{\text{Investment required per well}}$$

$$= \frac{0.10(\$24 \text{ million}) + 0.90(-\$2 \text{ million})}{\$2 \text{ million}}$$

$$= \frac{\$2.4 \text{ million} - \$1.8 \text{ million}}{\$2 \text{ million}}$$

$$= 0.30 \text{ or } 30\%.$$

This return is achieved with very little risk relative to that facing a firm drilling a single well. As this example illustrates, the risk of drilling any individual well can be diversified away very effectively. Consequently, these risks are not market related, and they should have little, if any, impact on the beta risk of the firm. That risk remains unchanged and approximately equal to the market risk facing other oil and gas exploration companies.

This example has shown that an investment with high total project risk does not necessarily have to possess high beta risk. Of course, it is possible for a project to have both high total project risk and high beta risk. For example, a grocery store chain (which typically has low beta risk) might decide to develop and market a new line of small business computers. Because of the large number of competitors in this business and because of the grocery chain's lack of expertise, this investment can be expected to have a high level of total project risk. At the same time, the beta risk of this investment is likely to be high relative to that of the grocery chain, because business computer sales expand rapidly during boom periods and slow down dramatically during recessions.

From a capital budgeting perspective, the portfolio (beta) risk of a project is certainly important, because the beta of a firm influences the returns required by investors in that firm and hence the value of the firm's shares.

Total project risk is also important to consider in most cases for several reasons. There are a number of relatively undiversified investors, including the owners of small firms, for whom total project and total firm risk is important. Also, it is the total risk of the firm—not just the beta risk—that determines the risk of firm failure and potential bankruptcy. Stockholders, creditors, managers, and other employees are all interested in preventing the tragedy (and avoiding the costs) of total firm failure.

Consequently, in the evaluation of an investment, it is important to consider both the total project risk and the impact of the project on the beta risk of the firm. In the next section we examine a number of techniques that can be used to account for total project risk in the capital budgeting process. We conclude the chapter with a discussion of techniques to use when evaluating the beta risk of a project.

Adjusting for Total Project Risk

Several different techniques are used to analyze total project risk. These include the *subjective* or *informal approach*, the *net present value/ payback approach*, the *risk-adjusted discount rate approach (RADR)*, the *hurdle rate approach*, the *certainty equivalent approach*, the *simulation approach*, and *sensitivity analysis*.

Subjective or Informal Approach

Frequently, investment decisions are made based upon the decision maker's subjective feelings about a project's risk in relation to expected return. If a firm is evaluating two mutually exclusive investments having approximately equal net present values, the decision maker will probably choose the less risky one. This informal approach to decision making is commonly used because it is both simple and inexpensive.

If two projects under consideration have significantly different net present values as well as different levels of perceived risk, the decision becomes more complicated. In these cases the decision maker must determine—again subjectively—whether the additional risk of a project will be offset by sufficiently higher returns.

Even though subjective decision making is often useful, more precise methods yield more valuable information in many cases.

Net Present Value/Payback Approach

Many firms combine net present value (NPV) with payback (PB) when analyzing project risk. As noted in Chapter 10, the project payback period is the length of time required to recover the net investment. Since cash flow estimates tend to become more uncertain farther into the future, applying a payback cutoff point can help reduce this degree of uncertainty. For example, a firm may decide not to accept projects unless they have positive net present values *and* have paybacks of less than some stated number of years.

Like the subjective or informal approach, the net present value/payback method is both simple and inexpensive. It does suffer from some notable weaknesses, however. First, the choice of which payback criterion should be applied is purely subjective and is not directly related to the variability of returns from a project. Some investments may have relatively certain cash flows far into the future, whereas others may not. The use of a single payback cutoff point fails to allow for this. Second, some projects are more risky than others during their start-up periods; the payback criterion also fails to recognize this. Finally, this approach may cause a firm to reject some actually acceptable projects. In spite of these weaknesses, however, some firms have found this approach helpful when screening investment alternatives, particularly investments made overseas in politically unstable countries and investments in products characterized by rapid technological advances.

Risk-Adjusted Discount Rate Approach

The risk-adjusted discount rate approach (RADR) adjusts for risk by varying the rate at which expected net cash flows are discounted when determining a project's net present value. In the net present value approach, net cash flows of all projects are discounted at the firm's cost of capital. If some projects are riskier than others, however, most investors will require a higher rate of return on these projects to compensate for the increased risk.

In the risk-adjusted discount rate approach, net cash flows for each project are discounted at a risk-adjusted rate, k^*. The magnitude of k^* depends on the relationship between the risk of the individual project and the overall risk of the firm. To compute k^*, the *risk-free rate, r_f*—that is, a required rate of return associated with investment projects characterized by certain cash flow streams—is used. United States Treasury securities are good examples of risk-free investments, because there is no chance that investors will not get the dollar amount of interest and the principal repayment on schedule. Thus, the yield on U.S. Government securities, such as ninety-day Treasury Bills, is used as the risk-free rate.

Most companies are not in business to invest in risk-free securities; individual investors can do that just as well. Instead, companies assume some amount of risk, expecting to earn higher returns than those available on risk-free securities. The difference between the risk-free rate and the firm's required rate of return (cost of capital) is an *average risk premium* to compensate investors for the fact that the company's assets are risky. This relationship is expressed algebraically as follows:

$$\theta = k - r_f, \qquad\qquad (11.1)$$

where θ is the average risk premium for the firm; r_f, the risk-free rate; and k, the required rate of return for projects of average risk, that is, the firm's cost of capital.

The cash flows from a project having greater than average risk are discounted at a higher rate, k^*—that is, a risk-adjusted discount rate—to reflect the increased riskiness. Risk premiums applied to individual projects are commonly established *subjectively*. For example, some firms establish a small number of *risk classes* and then apply a different *risk premium* to each class. Average-risk projects, such as equipment replacement decisions, might be evaluated at the firm's cost of capital; medium-risk projects, such as facility expansions, might be assigned a risk premium of 3 percent *above* the firm's cost of capital; and high-risk projects, such as investments in totally new lines of business or the introduction of new products, might be assigned a risk premium of 8 percent *above* the firm's cost of capital.

Although the risk-class approach saves time in the analysis stage, it can lead to suboptimal decisions, since the risk premiums themselves are usually subjectively determined, and no explicit consideration is given to the variation in returns of the projects assigned to individual classes. In short, the risk-class approach is most useful when evaluating relatively small projects that are frequently repeated. In these cases, much is known about the projects' potential returns, and it is probably not worth the effort to try to compute more "precise" risk premiums.

Advantages of the Risk-Adjusted Discount Rate Approach The risk adjusted discount rate approach has several advantages, including the following:

- It allows the decision maker to evaluate projects more efficiently by assigning each one a definite level of risk. Projects that initially may seem undesirable because they have lower expected returns might become more attractive if they are shown to have lower risk levels that could help to offset some other high-risk investments.

- The technique provides the decision maker with a single number on which to base accept-reject decisions, thereby eliminating the problem of having to make a risk-return tradeoff at decision time.

Hurdle Rate Approach

The hurdle rate approach is similar to the risk-adjusted discount rate method except that the hurdle rate method is used with the internal rate of return decision criterion instead of the net present value criterion. If k_A^* is defined as the risk-adjusted required return for Project A instead of the risk-adjusted discount rate, the hurdle rate for Project A is k_A^*. If a project's internal rate of return is greater than the hurdle rate, the project is acceptable; if the internal rate of return is less than the hurdle rate, the project is unacceptable.

This approach has the same strengths and weaknesses as the risk-adjusted discount rate approach. However, decision makers often prefer the hurdle rate method because the accept-reject criterion is in the form of rates of return rather than net present values. As mentioned in Chapter 10, many business decision makers are more comfortable with criteria stated in the form of rates of return.

Certainty Equivalent Approach

Another approach that can be used to deal with project risk uses certainty equivalents. A certainty equivalent factor is the ratio of the amount of cash someone would require with certainty at a point in time in order to make him or her indifferent between that certain amount and an amount expected to be received with risk at the same point in time. The project is adjusted for risk by converting the expected risky cash flows to their certainty equivalents and then computing the net present value of the project. The risk-free rate, r_f—not the firm's cost of capital, k—is used as the discount rate for computing the net present value. This is done because the cost of capital is a *risky* rate, reflecting the firm's average risk, and using it would result in a double counting of risk.

Certainty equivalent factors range from 0 to 1.0. The higher the factor, the more certain the expected cash flow. For example, one project might offer expected cash flows over its five-year life as follows:

Year	Expected NCF	Certainty Equivalent Factor(α)	Certainty Equivalent Cash Flows
0	−$10,000	1.0	−$10,000
1	+5,000	0.9	+4,500
2	+6,000	0.8	+4,800
3	+7,000	0.7	+4,900
4	+4,000	0.6	+2,400
5	+3,000	0.4	+1,200

The initial outlay of $10,000 is known with certainty. It might be for the purchase price of a piece of equipment. Hence, the certainty equivalent factor for year 0 is 1.0, and the certainty equivalent cash flow is −$10,000 (−$10,000 × 1.0). The $5,000 cash inflow in year 1 is viewed as being somewhat risky. Consequently, the decision maker has assigned a certainty equivalent factor of 0.9 to the net cash flow in year 1. Multiplying $5,000 times the 0.9 certainty equivalent factor yields a certainty equivalent cash flow of $4,500. This means that the decision maker would be indifferent between receiving the promised, risky $5,000 a year from now or receiving $4,500 with certainty at the same time. A similar interpretation is given to the certainty equivalent factors and certainty equivalent cash flows for years 2 through 5.

Algebraically, the certainty equivalent factors, α, for the cash flows expected to be received during each time period, t, are expressed as follows:

$$\alpha_t = \frac{\text{Certain return}}{\text{Risky return}} .$$ **(11.2)**

For example, in period 1 the certainty equivalent factor is calculated as follows:

$$\alpha_1 = \frac{\$4,500}{\$5,000}$$

$$= 0.9.$$

The certainty equivalent factors are used to compute a certainty equivalent net present value as follows:

$$\text{NPV} = -\text{NINV}(\alpha_0) + \sum_{t=1}^{n} \frac{\text{NCF}_t \alpha_t}{(1 + r_f)^t},$$ **(11.3)**

where α_0 = Certainty equivalent factor associated with the net investment (NINV) at time 0.

n = Expected economic life of the project.

α_t = Certainty equivalent factor associated with the net cash flows (NCF) in each period, t.

r_f = Risk-free rate.

Notice in this example that the certainty equivalent factors decline into the future. This reflects the fact that *most* cash flows are viewed as being more risky the farther into the future they are projected to occur.[1] This point is discussed in more detail in Chapter 5. In Table 11-1 we have computed the certainty equivalent net present value for this project assuming an 8 percent risk-free rate. It equals $4,753, and the project is therefore acceptable.

The certainty equivalent approach of considering risk is viewed as being conceptually sound for the following reasons:

- The decision maker can adjust separately each period's cash flows to account for the specific risk of those cash flows. This is normally not done when the risk-adjusted discount rate approach is applied.[2]
- Decision makers must introduce their own risk preferences directly into the analysis. Consequently, the certainty equivalent net present value provides an unambiguous basis for making a decision. A positive net present value means the project is acceptable to that decision maker, and a negative net present value indicates it should be rejected.

---

[1] Different individuals may have different certainty equivalent factors, depending on each individual's relative risk aversion. Risk aversion is a function of many factors, including wealth, age, and the nature of a firm's reward structure.

[2] It is possible, however, to find a risk-adjusted discount rate that will provide results identical (that is, with the same risk-adjusted net present value) to those obtained from the certainty equivalent approach.

Table 11-1   **Calculation of Certainty Equivalent Net Present Value**

Year	Expected NCF	Certainty Equivalent Factor(α)	Certainty Equivalent Cash Flow	$PVIF_{0.08,t}$	Present Value of Cash Flows
0	−$10,000	1.0	−$10,000	1.000	−$10,000
1	+5,000	0.9	+4,500	0.926	+4,167
2	+6,000	0.8	+4,800	0.857	+4,114
3	+7,000	0.7	+4,900	0.794	+3,891
4	+4,000	0.6	+2,400	0.735	+1,764
5	+3,000	0.4	+1,200	0.681	+817

Certainty Equivalent NPV = +$ 4,753

Simulation Approach

Computers have made it both feasible and relatively inexpensive to apply simulation techniques to capital budgeting decisions. The simulation approach is generally more appropriate for analyzing larger projects. A simulation is a financial planning tool that models some event. When simulation is used in capital budgeting, it requires that estimates be made of the probability distribution of each cash flow element (revenues, expenses, and so on). If, for example, a firm is considering introducing a new product, the elements of a simulation might include the number of units sold, market price, unit production costs, unit selling costs, the purchase price of the machinery needed to produce the new product, and the cost of capital. These probability distributions are then entered into the simulation model to compute the project's net present value probability distribution.

Recall that net present value is defined as follows:

$$NPV = \sum_{t=1}^{n} \frac{NCF_t}{(1 + k)^t} - NINV,$$

where NCF_t is the net cash flow in period t and NINV is the net investment. In any period, NCF_t may be computed as follows:

$$NCF_t = [n(p) - n(c + s) - D](1 - t) + D, \qquad \textbf{(11.4)}$$

where n is the number of units sold; p, the price per unit; c, the unit production cost (excluding depreciation); s, the unit selling cost; D, the annual depreciation; and t, the firm's marginal tax rate. Using Equation 11.4, it is possible to simulate the net present value of the project. Based on the probability distribution of each of the elements that influence the net present value, one value for each element is selected at random.

Assume, for example, that the following values for the input variables are randomly chosen: $n = 2,000$; $p = \$10$; $c = \$2$; $s = \$1$; $D = \$2,000$ and $t = 50\%$, or 0.50. Inserting these values into Equation 11.4 gives the following calculations:

$$NCF_t = [2,000(\$10) - 2,000(\$2 + \$1) - \$2,000] (1 - 0.50) + \$2,000$$
$$= (\$20,000 - \$6,000 - \$2,000) \times 0.50 + \$2,000$$
$$= \$8,000.$$

Assuming that the net investment is equal to the purchase price of the machinery ($10,000, in this example), that the net cash flows in each year of the project's life are identical, that $k = 10\%$,[3] and that the project has a five-year life, the net present value of this particular iteration of the simulation can be computed as follows:

$$NPV = \frac{\$8,000}{(1 + 0.10)^1} + \frac{\$8,000}{(1 + 0.10)^2} + \frac{\$8,000}{(1 + 0.10)^3}$$
$$+ \frac{\$8,000}{(1 + 0.10)^4} + \frac{\$8,000}{(1 + 0.10)^5} - \$10,000$$
$$= \$8,000 \times 3.791 - \$10,000$$
$$= \$20,328.$$

In an actual simulation, the computer program is run a number of different times, using different randomly selected input variables in each instance. Thus, the program can be said to be repeated, or *iterated,* and each run is termed an *iteration.*[4] In each iteration, the net present value for the project would be computed accordingly. Figure 11-1 illustrates a typical simulation approach.

The results of these iterations are then used to plot a probability distribution of the project's net present values and to compute a mean and a standard deviation of returns.[5] This information provides the decision maker with an estimate of a project's expected returns, as well as its risk. Given this information, it is possible to compute the probability of achieving a net present value that is greater or less than any particular value.

For example, assume that the simulation for the project previously illustrated results in an expected net present value of $12,000, with a standard deviation of $6,000. The probability of the project's having a net present value of $0 or less can now be found. The value of $0 is −2.0

---

[3] A strong case can be made for using a risk-free rate to discount the cash flows generated in a simulation analysis, since the simulation technique directly considers risk by generating a probability distribution of the project's NPV or IRR. To use the cost of capital as the discount rate will result in a double-counting of risk. Although this is correct, when a risk-free rate is used as the discount rate, the NPV which results is difficult to interpret. For this reason many practitioners prefer to use the cost of capital when performing simulation analyses.

[4] Often one hundred or more iterations of a simulation model are performed.

[5] Regardless of the shape of the probability distribution for the individual variables used in the simulation, the net present value probability distribution will often be normally, or near normally, distributed.

Figure 11-1   **An Illustration of the Simulation Approach**

Steps:

Probability Distributions for:

1. Estimate probability distribution of each input variable:

   Price

   Number of Units Sold

2. Combine input variables into a mathematical model to compute the NPV of the project.

   Unit Production Cost

3. Select at random a value of each input, based upon the probability distributions specified in Step 1.

4. Compute the project's NPV.

   Unit Selling Cost

5. Repeat Steps 3 and 4 many times to arrive at the following:
   a. The project's expected (mean) NPV.
   b. The standard deviation of the project's NPV.

   Annual Depreciation

standard deviations below the mean:

$$z = \frac{\$0 - \$12,000}{\$6,000}$$

$$= -2.0$$

where z = the number of standard deviations.

It can be seen from Table V at the back of the book that the probability of a value less than -2.0 standard deviations from the mean is 2.28 percent. Thus, there is a 2.28 percent chance that the actual net present value for this project will be negative. Figure 11-2 shows the probability distribution of this project's net present value. The shaded area under the curve represents the probability that the project will have a net present value of $0 or less.

The simulation approach is a powerful one because it explicitly recognizes all of the interactions among the variables that influence a project's net present value. It provides both a mean net present value and a standard deviation that can help the decision maker analyze tradeoffs between risk and expected return.[6] Unfortunately, it can take considerable time and effort to gather the information necessary for each of the input variables and to correctly formulate the model. This limits the feasibility of simulation to very large projects. In addition, the simulation examples

---

[6] Simulation may also be applied to other decision models, such as the internal rate of return or payback approaches. In these cases the mathematical relationships involved in the simulation have to be respecified.

Figure 11-2   **A Sample Illustration of the Probability that a Project's Returns Will Be Less
                            than $0**

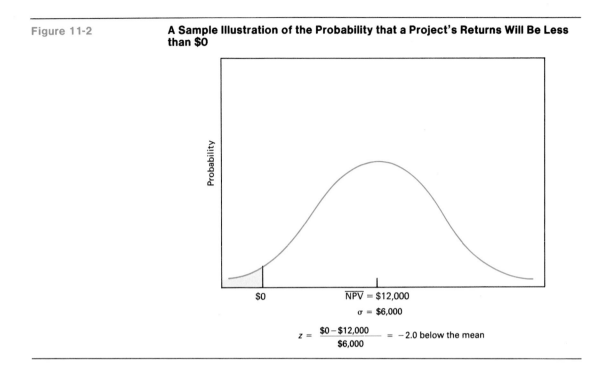

$$z = \frac{\$0 - \$12,000}{\$6,000} = -2.0 \text{ below the mean}$$

illustrated assumed that the values of the input variables were independent
of one another. If this is not true—if, for example, the price of a product
has a large influence on the number sold—then this interaction must be
incorporated into the model, introducing even more complexity.

Sensitivity Analysis   Sensitivity analysis is a procedure by means of which the change in net
present value is calculated for a given change in one of the cash flow
elements, such as product price. In other words, a decision maker can
determine *how sensitive* a project's return is to changes in a particular
variable.

Because sensitivity analysis is derived from the simulation approach, it
also requires the definition of all relevant variables that influence the net
present value of a project. The appropriate mathematical relationships
between these variables must also be defined in order that the cash flow
from the project may be estimated and the net present value computed.
Rather than dealing with the entire probability distribution for each of the
input variables, however, sensitivity analysis allows the decision maker to
use only the "best estimate" of each variable to compute the net present
value.

The decision maker can then ask various "what if" questions in which
the project's net present value is recomputed under various conditions. For
example, the best estimate of a product's price might be $10. The net
present value of the project could be computed using this input together
with best estimates of all the other variables. The next step would involve
asking a question like, What if we cannot charge more than $8 per unit?

The net present value could then be recomputed using the $8 price and the best estimates for each of the other input variables to determine the effect of the $8 price on the NPV.

Sensitivity analysis can be applied to any variable to determine the effect of changes in one or more of the inputs on a project's net present value. This process provides the decision maker with a formal mechanism for assessing the possible consequences of various scenarios.

It is often useful to construct sensitivity curves to summarize the impact of changes in different variables on the net present value of a project. A sensitivity curve has the project's net present value on the vertical axis and the variable of interest on the horizontal axis. For example, Figure 11-3 shows the sensitivity curves for two variables, sales price and cost of capital for a project.

The steep slope of the price-NPV curve indicates that the net present value is very sensitive to changes in the price for which the product can be sold. If the product price is approximately 8 percent below the base case (or initial analysis) estimate, the net present value of the project drops to $0, and the project becomes unacceptable for further price declines. In contrast, the relatively flat cost of capital-NPV curve indicates that the net present value is not very sensitive to changes in the firm's cost of capital. Similar curves could be constructed for project life, salvage value, units sold, operating costs, and other important variables.

Using Electronic Worksheets for Sensitivity Analysis The development of low-cost business and personal microcomputers has revolutionized the application of a number of financial management tools. Sensitivity analysis had been a tool used only by large firms with extensive computer capabilities. Now the availability of computer software that can be used on small business and personal computers has extended the access to these techniques to nearly everyone.

Electronic worksheets, such as the popular Lotus 1-2-3,® have made the

Figure 11-3   **Illustrative Sensitivity Curves**

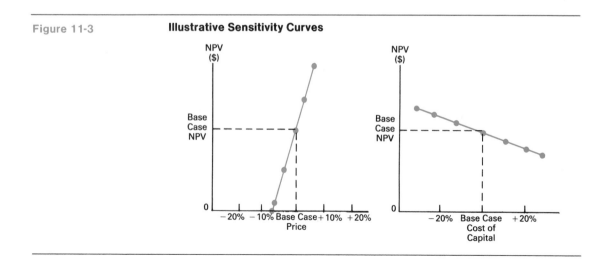

application of sensitivity analysis techniques very simple and inexpensive.[7] Once the base case has been defined and entered in the worksheet, it is very easy to ask hundreds of "what if" type of questions. For example, assume that revenues from a project were expected to be $20,000 in year 1 and to grow by 10 percent annually over the five-year life of the project. This relationship would be entered into the electronic worksheet along with similar relationships for all other factors that go into the determination of the annual net cash flows from the project. The net present value of the base case is computed by the worksheet. Now, what if the revenues will grow only by 5 percent annually, instead of 10 percent? Only one change must be made on the worksheet (redefine the growth rate to 5 percent), and the worksheet will automatically recompute each period's net cash flows and the net present value of the project. This process can be repeated very rapidly, literally hundreds of times, to develop a profile of how sensitive the project is to changes in the individual components of the project's cash flows. (The templates provided in the *Study Guide* accompanying this text can be used very effectively to illustrate the power of spreadsheets in performing sensitivity analyses.)

Adjusting for Beta Risk in Capital Budgeting

The risk adjustment procedures previously discussed are appropriate when the firm believes that a project's total risk is the relevant risk to consider in evaluating the project, and when it is assumed that the returns from the project being considered are highly positively correlated with the returns from the firm as a whole. Therefore, these methods are appropriate only when internal firm diversification benefits, which might change the firm's total risk (or the systematic portion of total risk), are not present.

The *beta* concept can also be used to determine risk-adjusted discount rates for individual projects. This approach is more appropriate for a firm whose stock is widely traded and for whom there is very little chance that bankruptcy will occur. (The probability of bankruptcy is a function of total risk, not just systematic risk.)

Just as the systematic risk (beta) of a portfolio of securities can be computed as the weighted average of the individual security betas, a firm may be considered as a portfolio of assets, each having its own measure of systematic risk (beta). From this perspective the systematic risk of the firm is simply the weighted average of the systematic risk of the individual assets.

For example, consider the security market line shown in Figure 11-4. The firm has a beta of 1.2 and uses only internally generated equity capital.[8] The market risk premium is 7 percent. When considering projects

---

[7] Lotus 1-2-3 is a registered trademark of the Lotus Development Corporation.

[8] If the firm also uses debt capital, the following procedure is used to estimate the required return on the equity-financed portion of a project. This cost of equity would have to be adjusted to account for the additional risk arising from the use of debt and would be averaged with the cost of debt, using weights for debt and equity consistent with the optimal capital structure for the firm (or a division of the firm) to arrive at an estimate of the project's systematic risk-adjusted cost of capital. For a further discussion of this point, see Thomas E. Copeland and J. Fred Weston, *Financial Theory and Corporate Practice,* 2nd ed. Reading, Mass.: Addison-Wesley, 1983, chap. 12.

Figure 11-4

Risk-adjusted Discount Rates and the SML

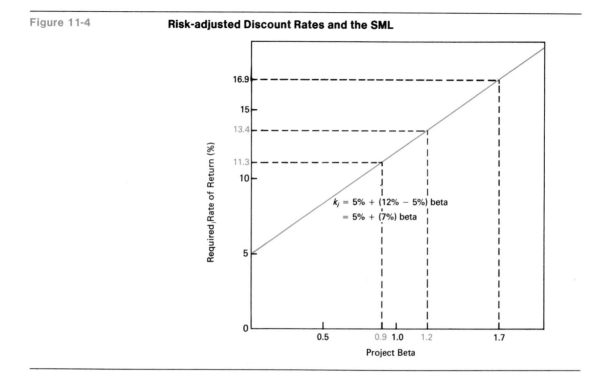

of average risk—that is, projects that are highly correlated with the firm's returns on its existing assets and that have a beta similar to the firm's beta (1.2)—the firm should use the computed 13.4 percent cost of equity from Figure 11-4. When considering projects having estimated betas greater than 1.2, it should use a higher cost of equity. For example, if a project's subjectively estimated beta is 1.7, its required return would be 16.9 percent, or $5\% + (1.7 \times 7\%)$, and this would be used as the risk-adjusted discount rate for that project.

Figure 11-5 illustrates the difference between the use of a single weighted cost of capital[9] and risk-adjusted discount rates for project evaluation. In this case, Projects 1, 2, 3, and 4 are being evaluated by the firm. Using the weighted cost of capital approach, the firm would adopt Projects 3 and 4. However, if the firm considered the differential levels of systematic risk for the four alternatives, it would accept Projects 1 and 3 and reject Projects 2 and 4. In general, *the risk-adjusted discount rate approach is considered preferable to the weighted cost of capital approach when the projects under consideration differ significantly in their risk characteristics.*

The one problem remaining with this suggested procedure involves the

---

[9] The weighted cost of capital for a firm is defined in more detail in Chapter 12. It is equal to the cost of equity times the proportion of common equity in the firm's target capital structure, plus the after-tax marginal cost of debt times the debt proportion in the firm's target capital structure, plus the after-tax marginal cost of preferred stock times its proportion in the firm's target capital structure. In general, the weighted cost of capital is the appropriate discount rate to use when evaluating projects of average risk.

Figure 11-5   **Risk-adjusted Discount Rate versus Weighted Cost of Capital**

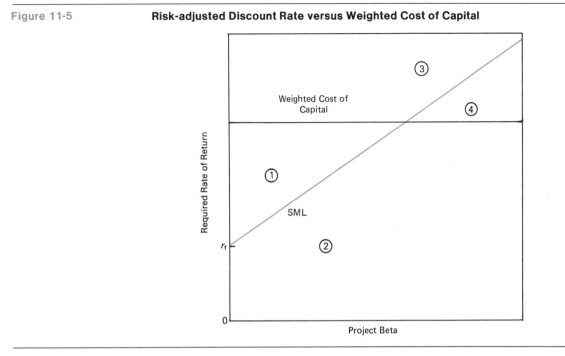

determination of beta values for individual projects. Thus far, the most workable approach available is the use of *surrogate market information.* For example, if an aluminum firm is considering investing in the leisure-time product industry, the beta for this new project could be computed using the average beta for a sample of firms engaged principally in the leisure product industry. Although the beta for the aluminum firm might be 1.3, resulting in a required equity return on projects of average risk of 14.1 percent, or $5\% + (1.3 \times 7\%)$, according to Figure 11-4, this would not be the appropriate rate for leisure product projects. Assuming a beta of 0.9 for leisure product firms, the leisure product projects would be required to earn an equity return of only 11.3 percent or $5\% + (0.9 \times 7\%)$, because of the lower average level of systematic risk associated with leisure product projects. This assumes that the leisure product projects are financed in the same manner as are the firms used to generate the surrogate betas. (See Footnote 8 for a further discussion of this point.)

Divisional Costs of Capital

The approach just outlined can also be used to compute the required rate of return (cost of capital) for investments being evaluated by a firm's various divisions. For divisions that have lower (higher) systematic risk than others, the required returns for projects adopted by these divisions should be lower (higher) than the required returns for the firm as a whole.

For example, West Coast Power is an electric utility that has a calculated beta of 0.91. The firm has three divisions: the electric power generating and distribution division, which has 70 percent of the firm's assets; an oil and gas exploration division, which has 20 percent of the assets; and a transportation and barge division, which has 10 percent of the assets. Using surrogate market information, the beta for each division is estimated as shown here:

	Estimated Divisional Beta	Proportion of Firm's Assets	Weighted Average Beta
Electric power	0.75	0.70	0.53
Exploration	1.30	0.20	0.26
Transportation	1.20	0.10	0.12

Weighted average firm beta = 0.91

Note that the weighted average of the divisional betas is equal to the firm's overall beta—in this case, 0.91.

Conglomerate firms that compete in many different product and geographical markets, such as Pacificorp, Litton or Gulf and Western Industries, often estimate separate divisional costs of capital. These divisional costs of capital reflect both the differential required returns of equity investors, estimated from the security market line, and the differential debt-carrying capacity of each division. For example, the parent company may have a debt-to-total-assets ratio of 60 percent. Individual divisions within the firm may compete against other firms that typically have higher or lower debt-to-total-assets ratios. In computing each divisional cost of capital, many firms try to reflect both the differential divisional risks and the differential normal debt ratios for each division.

Summary

- The *risk* of an investment project is defined in terms of the potential *variability* of its returns. When only one return is possible—for example, as with U.S. Government securities held to maturity—there is no risk. When more than one return is possible for a particular project, it is risky.
- Risk is also influenced by the possibility of investment *diversification*. If a proposed project's returns are not *perfectly correlated* with the returns from the firm's other investments, the total risk of the firm may be reduced by accepting the proposed project. This is known as the *portfolio effect*.
- There are several ways in which a decision maker can adjust for differential project risk in capital budgeting, including the *subjective* or *informal approach*, the *net present value/payback approach*, the *risk-adjusted discount rate approach*, the *hurdle rate approach*, the *certainty equivalent approach*, the *simulation approach*, and *sensitivity analysis*. The risk-adjusted discount rate approach is widely used by firms that attempt to consider differential project risk in their capital budgeting procedures. It requires that a *risk premium* be computed for each project or group of projects so that an appropriate risk-adjusted discount rate can be applied when evaluating a project's cash flows. The widely used hurdle rate approach is similar to the risk-adjusted discount

rate approach. The simulation approach is the most expensive of the techniques discussed in this chapter; it is normally applied only when large projects are being analyzed. The widespread availability of inexpensive and powerful computer software such as electronic worksheets has made the use of sensitivity analysis far more accessible to small- and medium-sized firms than was previously possible.

- When a project differs significantly in its *systematic risk* profile (as measured by *beta*) from the systematic risk of the total firm, a risk-adjusted discount rate appropriate for that project can be computed using the security market line relationship between risk and required return from the capital asset pricing model.

- The decision to employ some risk analysis technique to evaluate an investment project depends on the project's size and the additional cost of applying such a technique as compared with the perceived benefits. For small projects, only the simpler risk adjustment techniques should be used; for major projects that have above- or below-normal risk it is worthwhile to analyze the project's risk as precisely as possible. Failure to fully analyze the risk of a large project could result in bad investment decisions and even substantial losses.

FOCUS ON CORPORATE PRACTICE

Developing and Applying Risk-Adjusted Discount Rates in a Diversified Company

William J. Regan
Vice-President and Treasurer, American Natural Resources Co.

Norman Dmuchowski
Manager of Financial Planning, American Natural Resources Co.

American Natural Resources is an integrated natural gas operation that transports gas from major producing areas, sells gas (wholesale) to several nonaffiliated distributing companies in nine states, stores gas underground in fields in Michigan, and sells gas (retail) to over one million customers. In addition, some of the firm's subsidiaries are engaged in gas exploration and production actiities. American Natural also has a coal production and marketing subsidiary and a coal gasification subsidiary, and in 1977 it acquired Associated Truck Lines, a regional trucking firm. At the end of 1984 the firm's total assets exceeded $3.8 billion.

With its diversity of investments, American Natural is faced with the problem of evaluating investment alternatives that may differ significantly with respect to their relative risk. Should all projects be evaluated using the same discount rate, that is, the firm's cost of capital? We believe the answer to this question is no, if the projects differ in terms of their risk characteristics.

In practice, it is often difficult to estimate specific risk-adjusted discount rates to apply to each project. One way to resolve this problem is to estimate separate discount rates for each subsidiary of a diversified firm such as ours.

The approach used at American Natural Resources is based on the capital asset pricing model (CAPM). The risk-adjusted discount rate, k_j, applied in each division, is based on the security market line (SML):

$$k_j = r_f + \text{beta}_j\,(k_m - r_f).$$

The expected risk-free rate, r_f, and the expected market rate of return, k_m, are forecasted using a simulation model that considers historical returns on various asset classes and the market consensus for economic prospects that are implied by the current inflation rate and yields on U.S. Government securities of various maturities.

Next it is necessary to estimate the beta that best reflects the systematic risk of each of American Natural's subsidiaries. Since the common stock of American Natural's subsidiaries is not traded, it is not possible to estimate beta in the traditional way.

One approach we use is to identify companies with publicly traded stock that are engaged entirely (or almost entirely) in the type of operation undertaken by a subsidiary. An average of the betas for these comparative companies can be used as a surrogate measure of the beta for each subsidiary. We use sources such as *Value Line*, Merrill Lynch, and Barr Rosenberg when selecting betas of companies most similar to each of our subsidiaries to be used as surrogates.

Next, these betas are adjusted to remove the impact of the particular financial structure used in each firm. The average of these "unlevered" betas is then determined for each industry group for which American Natural Resources has a subsidiary. This surrogate unlevered beta is used to compute a risk-adjusted discount rate for each subsidiary using the security market line. These divisional risk-adjusted rates are then used to discount the tax-adjusted operating cash flows from investment proposals in each subsidiary.

We see several advantages in this approach, including the following:

- The discount rates for all the subsidiaries are comparable, since they are all based on the same assumptions and market expectations.
- The discount rates are developed for different investment life periods and reflect investor expectations of inflation and the real interest rate over the specific periods.
- The discount rates can be updated periodically to reflect changing investor expectations and industry risk.
- The procedure can also be used to estimate discount rates for potential acquisitions or atypical projects that American Natural Resources might consider.

Questions and Topics for Discussion

1. How does the basic net present value model of capital budgeting deal with the problem of project risk? What are the shortcomings of this approach?

2. How would you define *risk* as it is used in a capital budgeting analysis context?

3. Recalling the discussion in Chapter 5, when is the standard deviation of a project's cash flows an appropriate measure of project risk? When is the coefficient of variation an appropriate measure?

4. How does the basic net present value capital budgeting model deal with the phenomenon of increasing risk of project cash flows over time?

5. Describe how certainty equivalent cash flow estimates can be derived for individual project cash flows.

6. Will all individuals apply the same certainty equivalent estimates to the cash flows from a project? Why or why not?

7. When should a firm consider the portfolio effects of a new project?

8. What are the primary advantages and disadvantages of applying *simulation* to capital budgeting risk analysis?

9. On average, the expected value of returns from each $1 of premiums paid on an insurance policy is less than $1; this is due to the insurance company's administrative costs and profits. In spite of this fact, why do so many individuals and organizations purchase insurance policies?

10. Computer simulation is used to generate a large number of possible outcomes for an investment project. Most firms invest in a particular project only once, however. How can a computer simulation model be helpful to the typical decision maker who is making a one-time-only investment decision?

11. Under what circumstances do you think the use of divisional required rates of return (costs of capital) is likely to improve the capital budgeting decision process?

Problems*

1. Aunt Bessie has discovered an old lithograph of Andrew Johnson at a local flea market. The dealer is asking a price of $20. Recognizing the potential value of this item, Aunt Bessie buys the lithograph. Given the condition of the lithograph, Aunt Bessie has assigned the following probability distribution to the lithograph's ultimate selling price when she offers it to a local dealer:

Probability	Selling Price
0.05	$ 60
0.25	70
0.35	100
0.20	160
0.15	200

a. What is the expected selling price?
b. What is the standard deviation of the selling price?

* Color numbers denote problems which have check answers provided at the end of the book.

2. The Topless Auto Company, a maker of convertible cars, has estimated the probability distribution of its annual net cash flows as follows:

Probability	Cash Flows (in Thousands of Dollars)
0.10	$1,000
0.20	1,500
0.40	2,000
0.20	2,500
0.10	3,000

   a. Compute the expected annual cash flow.
   b. Compute the standard deviation of annual cash flows.
   c. Compute the coefficient of variation of annual cash flows.

3. A new project has expected annual net cash flows of $400,000 with a standard deviation of $225,000. The distribution of annual net cash flows is approximately normal.
   a. What is the probability of the project's having negative annual net cash flows?
   b. What is the probability that annual net cash flows will be greater than $550,000?

4. Two projects have the following expected net present values and standard deviations of net present values:

Project	Expected Net Present Value	Standard Deviation
A	$50,000	$25,000
B	10,000	8,000

   a. Using the standard deviation criterion, which project is riskier?
   b. Using the coefficient of variation criterion, which project is riskier?
   c. Which criterion do you think is appropriate to use in this case? Why?

5. American Steel Corporation is considering two investments. One is the purchase of a new smelter costing $100 million. The expected net present value of this project is $20 million. The other alternative is the purchase of a supermarket chain, also costing $100 million. It too has an expected net present value of $20 million. The firm's management is interested in reducing the variability of its earnings.
   a. Which project should the company invest in?
   b. What assumptions did you make to arrive at this decision?

6. Western Kodiak is a producer of home movie equipment. The firm is considering two investments having the following cash flow streams:

Year	Project A	Project B
0	−$50,000	−$30,000
1	+20,000	+15,000
2	+20,000	+5,000
3	+10,000	+5,000
4	+5,000	+5,000
5	+5,000	+40,000

Western Kodiak uses a combination of the net present value approach and the payback approach to evaluate investment alternatives. It requires that all projects have a positive net present value when cash flows are discounted at 10 percent and that all projects have a payback no longer than 3 years. Which project or projects should the firm accept? Why?

7. Tiny Tin Enterprises is the maker of small metal lighting fixtures. It is considering expanding into the growing laser copier business. Tiny Tin estimates that this expansion will cost $2.0 million and will generate a 20-year stream of expected net cash flows amounting to $400,000 per year. The weighted cost of capital for Tiny Tin is 15 percent.

   a. Compute the net present value of the laser copier project using Tiny Tin's weighted cost of capital and the expected cash flows from the project.

   b. Using the risk-adjusted discount rate approach, Tiny Tin's management has decided that this project has substantially more risk than average and has decided that it requires a 24 percent expected rate of return on projects like this. Recompute the risk-adjusted net present value of this project.

8. Apple Jacks, Inc., produces wine. The firm is considering expanding into the snack food business. This expansion will require an initial investment in new equipment of $200,000. The equipment will be depreciated on a straight line basis over a 10-year period to an estimated salvage value of $40,000. The expansion will require an increase in working capital for the firm of $40,000. The equipment is eligible for the 10 percent investment tax credit.

   Revenues from the new venture are forecasted at $200,000 per year for the first 5 years and $210,000 per year for years 6 through 10. Cash operating costs from the new venture are estimated at $90,000 for the first 5 years and $105,000 for years 6 through 10. It is assumed that at the end of year 10 the snack food equipment will be sold for its book value.

   The firm's marginal tax rate is 40 percent. The required return for projects of average risk has been estimated as 15 percent.

   a. Compute the project's net present value, assuming that it is an average risk investment.

   b. If management decides that all product line expansions have above average risk and should therefore be evaluated at a 24 percent required rate of return, what will be the risk-adjusted net present value of the project?

9. The Seminole Production Company is analyzing the investment in a new line of business machines. The initial outlay required is $35 million. The net cash flows expected from the investment are as follows:

Year	Net Cash Flow
1	$ 5 million
2	8 million
3	15 million
4	20 million
5	15 million
6	10 million
7	4 million

The firm's cost of capital (used for projects of average risk) is 15 percent.

   a. Compute the net present value of this project assuming it possesses average risk.

   b. Because of the risk inherent in this type of investment, Seminole has decided to employ the certainty equivalent approach. After considerable discussion, management has agreed to apply the following certainty equivalents to the project's cash flows:

Year	α_t
0	1.00
1	0.95
2	0.90
3	0.80
4	0.60
5	0.40
6	0.35
7	0.30

If the risk-free rate is 9 percent, compute the project's certainty equivalent net present value.

c. On the basis of this analysis, should the project be accepted?

10. A simulation model similar to the one described in this chapter has been constructed by the ZEP Corporation to evaluate the largest of its new investment proposals. After many iterations of the model, ZEP's management has arrived at an expected net present value for Project A of $1.4 million. The standard deviation of the net present value has been estimated from the simulation model results to be $0.8 million.

   a. What is the probability that the project will have a negative net present value?

   b. What is the probability that the project will have a net present value greater than $3.0 million?

11. The Buffalo Snow Shoe Company is considering manufacturing radial snow shoes, which are more durable and offer better traction. Buffalo estimates that the investment in manufacturing equipment will cost $250,000 and will have a 10-year economic life. The equipment is eligible for a 10 percent investment tax credit. Buffalo will depreciate the equipment on a straight line basis to a $0 estimated salvage value over a 10-year period. The estimated selling price of each pair of shoes will be $50. Buffalo anticipates that it can sell 5,000 pairs a year at this price. Unit production and selling costs (exclusive of depreciation) will be about $25. The firm's marginal tax rate is 40 percent. A cost of capital of 12 percent is thought to be appropriate to analyze a project of this type.

   Buffalo has decided to perform a sensitivity analysis of the project before making a decision.

   a. Compute the expected net present value of this project.

   b. Buffalo's president does not believe that 5,000 pairs of the new snow shoes can be sold at a $50 price. He estimates that a maximum of 3,000 pairs will be sold at this price. How does the change in the estimated sales volume influence the net present value of the project?

12. The Jacobs Company is financed entirely with equity. The beta for Jacobs has been estimated to be 1.0. The current risk-free rate is 10 percent, and the expected market return is 15 percent.

   a. What rate of return should Jacobs require on a project of average risk?

   b. If a new venture is expected to have a beta of 1.6, what rate of return should Jacobs demand on this project?

   c. The project in question requires an initial outlay of $10 million and is expected to generate a 10-year stream of annual net cash flows of $2.3 million. Evaluate the project using Jacob's required return for projects of average risk.

  d. Evaluate the project using the risk-adjusted rate computed in Part b.

13. Project Alpha offers the following net cash flows following an initial (year 0), certain outlay (NINV) of $75,000:

Year	Net Cash Flows	Certainty Equivalent Factor
1	$30,000	0.91
2	30,000	0.79
3	30,000	0.65
4	20,000	0.52
5	20,000	0.40
6	10,000	0.30

  a. Compute the NPV of this project at a 17 percent cost of capital.
  b. If the risk-free rate is 8 percent, what is the certainty equivalent NPV for Project Alpha?

14. A new project is expected to have a 6-year economic life. The project will have an initial cost of $100,000. This investment in equipment is eligible for the ITC. Installation and shipping charges for the equipment are estimated at $10,000. The firm uses ACRS depreciation. A working capital investment of $20,000 is required to undertake the project.

  The revenues from the project in year 1 are expected to be $60,000. These are expected to increase at a compound annual rate of 6 percent. Operating costs are $15,000. These costs are expected to increase at an 8 percent compound annual rate. The firm's marginal tax rate is 40 percent for ordinary income and 28 percent for capital gains. The expected salvage value of the equipment at the end of year 6 is $15,000.

  a. Compute the project's net investment.
  b. Compute the annual net cash flows for the project.
  c. If the firm's cost of capital is 19 percent, should the project be undertaken?
  d. The managers of the firm have decided to also evaluate this project using the certainty equivalent approach. They have established the following certainty equivalent factors for the cash flows forecasted in each year:

Year	α_t
0	1.00
1	0.95
2	0.90
3	0.80
4	0.60
5	0.50
6	0.45

The risk-free rate is 8 percent. Compute the certainty equivalent NPV for this project.

Capital Budgeting and Risk Analysis

ZeeBancorp is considering the establishment of a contract collection service subsidiary which would provide collection services to small- and medium-sized firms. Compensation would be in the form of a percentage of the amount collected. For amounts collected up to $100 the fee is 50 percent of the amount collected. For amounts collected between $100 and $500 the fee would be 40 percent of the total amount collected on the account. For amounts collected over $500 ZeeBancorp would receive 30 percent of the total amount collected on the account.

ZeeBancorp expects to generate the following amount of business during the first year of operation of the new subsidiary.

Account Class	Number of Collections	Average Amount Collected for Each Account
Up to $100	5,000	$75
Between $100 and $500	2,000	$325
Over $500	1,200	$850

Over the projected ten-year life of this collection venture, the number of accounts in each group is expected to grow at 5 percent per annum. The average amount collected from each account is expected to remain constant.

In order to establish the collection subsidiary, ZeeBancorp will have to rent office space at a cost of $220,000 for the first year. (Assume the rent is payable at the *end* of each year.) This amount is expected to grow at a rate of 8 percent per year. Other operating expenses (excluding depreciation) are expected to total $350,000 during the first year and grow at an 8 percent annual rate.

ZeeBancorp will have to invest $100,000 in net working capital if it undertakes this venture. In addition, a new computer plus other equipment will cost $250,000 to purchase and install. This equipment is eligible for a 10 percent investment tax credit and will be depreciated using the appropriate ACRS schedule. The salvage value for the computer and the other equipment is estimated to be $50,000 at the end of ten years.

The firm's *marginal* tax rate is estimated to be 40 percent over the project's life, its *average* tax rate is projected to be 35 percent over the project's life and the capital gains rate is 25 percent. The firm requires a 20 percent rate of return on projects of average risk.

1. Compute the net investment required to establish the collection subsidiary.
2. Compute the annual net cash flows over the 10-year life of the project.
3. Compute the net present value of this project assuming it is an average risk investment.
4. Should ZeeBancorp invest in the new subsidiary?
5. ZeeBancorp requires all expansion project such as this to have a payback of 4 years or less. Under these conditions should ZeeBancorp invest in the new subsidiary?
6. If management decides that this project has above-average risk and hence the required return is 25 percent, should the investment be made?
7. If collections are only 80 percent of projections and the required return is 25 percent, should the investment be made?
8. If operating (excluding depreciation) and lease expenses are expected to increase at an annual rate of 10 percent, should the collection subsidiary be established, assuming a required return of 25 percent and the original revenue projections?

Selected References

Copeland, T. E., and J. F. Weston. *Financial Theory and Corporate Policy,* 2nd ed. Reading, Mass.: Addison-Wesley, 1983.

Hertz, David B. "Risk Analysis in Capital Investment." *Harvard Business Review* 42 (Jan.–Feb. 1964): 95–106.

Lewellen, Wilbur G., and Michael S. Long. "Simulation versus Single-Value Estimates in Capital Expenditure Analysis." *Decision Sciences* 3 (1973): 19–33.

Paine, Neil R. "Uncertainty and Capital Budgeting." *Accounting Review* 39 (April 1964): 330–332.

Robichek, Alexander A. "Interpreting the Results of Risk Analysis." *Journal of Finance* 30 (Dec. 1975): 1384–1386.

Weston, J. Fred. "Investment Decisions Using the Capital Asset Pricing Model." *Financial Management* 2 (Spring 1973): 25–33.

PART FIVE

THE COST OF CAPITAL, CAPITAL STRUCTURE, AND DIVIDEND POLICY

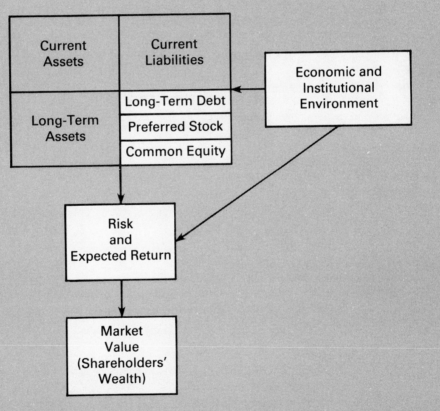

This section considers three closely related topics—the cost of capital (Chapter 12), capital structure (Chapter 13), and dividend policy (Chapter 14). The cost of capital is an important input in the capital budgeting decision process. This market-determined cost of funds also directly influences the value of a firm's securities. The cost of capital cannot be considered in isolation. The capital structure of a firm directly affects its cost of capital. A more debt-laden capital structure will at some point increase the risk of the firm's securities and increase the overall cost of capital to the firm. This results in a reduction in the value of the firm. Chapter 13 looks at the determinants of an "optimal" capital structure—one that is consistent with the objective of shareholder wealth maximization. Finally, the dividend policy of a firm can provide important information to investors that ultimately may affect the firm's risk and cost of capital as perceived by investors.

12

THE COST OF CAPITAL

A Financial Dilemma

Cost of Equity Capital for the Public Service Company of New Mexico

The Public Service Company of New Mexico (PNM) is the largest investor-owned electric utility in the state of New Mexico. As a public utility, PNM is regulated closely by the New Mexico Public Service Commission (NMPSC) and the Federal Energy Regulatory Commission (FERC). As a part of any major rate case filing, PNM must establish its cost of capital.

In a typical rate case there is little controversy about the cost of preferred stock and debt, since, for ratemaking purposes (as compared to capital budgeting purposes), these costs are based on the company's actual historical cost of raising funds from these sources. The cost of these funds is easy to identify from the books of the company. In contrast, there is normally extensive controversy regarding the cost of common equity in a utility rate case.

During the summer of 1985, PNM had a major case heard before the NMPSC. In that case four witnesses submitted cost of equity capital testimony. A listing of their recommendations follows:

Having considered volumes of conflicting testimony on the issues, the NMPSC was faced with the dilemma of making a final recommendation. The final order in the case permitted PNM to charge rates consistent with its earning a return of 15 percent on its common equity capital.

This chapter develops the principles and models that can be used to compute a firm's cost of debt, preferred stock, and common stock. All of these models require the use of some judgment by the analyst. This is particularly true in the case of the cost of common equity. The cost of common equity cannot be estimated with the precision possible in the case of debt and preferred stock. However, the analyst aware of the basic principles contained in this chapter can make reasonable estimates of the cost of equity capital for any company.

Witness	Recommended Equity Return	Methodology
George Stolnitz, U.S. Executive Agencies	14.5%	Dividend valuation
Matityahu Marcus, New Mexico Attorney General	14.1–14.9%	Dividend valuation
Dennis Gee, NMPSC Staff	14.1%	Dividend valuation
R. Charles Moyer, PNM	15.3–15.9%	Dividend valuation Risk premium on debt

The cost of equity capital was estimated from a low of 14.1 percent to a high of 15.9 percent.

Key Chapter Concepts

1. The *cost of capital* is the rate of return required by investors in the firm's securities. The cost of capital determines the rate of return which the firm must earn on its new investments in order for the firm to maximize its value.
2. The required return on any security may be thought of as consisting of a risk-free rate of return plus a premium for the risk of that security.
   a. The risk-free rate varies over time and is influenced by the expected rate of inflation and the supply and demand for funds in the overall economy.
   b. The risk premium on a specific security is influenced by the business risk of the firm, the financial risk of the firm, the marketability risk of the security, and the time to maturity of the security.
3. For capital budgeting purposes, the marginal cost of each capital source needs to be calculated.
   a. The after-tax cost of debt is equal to the pre-tax cost of new debt times one minus the firm's marginal tax rate.
   b. The after-tax cost of a perpetual preferred stock is equal to the dividend rate divided by the net proceeds to the firm from the sale of preferred stock.
   c. The cost of internal equity capital can be computed using a version of the dividend valuation model, the capital asset pricing model, or a risk-premium on debt approach.
   d. The cost of external equity capital exceeds the cost of internal equity capital by the amount of the issuance costs.
4. The weighted cost of capital is equal to the after-tax cost of debt times its proportion in the optimal capital structure, plus the after-tax cost of preferred stock times its proportion in the optimal capital structure, plus the cost of common equity times its proportion in the optimal capital structure.
5. The weighted cost of capital is appropriate for determining the return required on projects of *average* risk.
6. The optimal capital budget can be determined by comparing the expected project returns to the company's marginal cost of capital schedule.
7. The cost of depreciation-generated funds is equal to the firm's weighted (marginal) cost of capital, before considering new stock flotation costs.

Glossary of New Terms

Beta A measure of a stock's price and total return volatility relative to the volatility of prices and returns in the securities markets as a whole.

Capital Asset Pricing Model (CAPM) A theory that formally describes the nature of the risk–required return tradeoff in finance. It provides one method of computing a firm's cost of equity capital.

Investment opportunity curve A graph or listing showing a firm's investment opportunities (projects) ranked from highest to lowest expected rate of return.

Marginal cost of capital The weighted after-tax cost of the next dollars of capital the firm expects to raise to finance new investment projects.

Optimal capital budget The level of capital spending at which a firm's investment opportunity curve just intersects its marginal cost of capital curve.

Introduction

Chapters 9 through 11 considered the capital budgeting decisions of a firm. One of the key variables in capital expenditure analysis is the cost of capital. This chapter discusses the concept of the cost of capital and develops approaches that can be used to measure this important variable.

The *cost of capital* is concerned with what a firm has to pay for the capital—that is, the debt, preferred stock, retained earnings, and common stock—it uses to finance new investments. It also can be thought of as the rate of return required by investors in the firm's securities. As such, the firm's cost of capital is determined in the capital markets and is closely related to the degree of risk associated with new investments, existing assets, and capital structure. In general, the greater the risk of a firm as perceived by investors, the greater the return investors will require and the greater the cost of capital will be.

The cost of capital can also be thought of as the minimum rate of return required on new investments undertaken by the firm.[1] If a new investment earns an internal rate of return that is greater than the cost of capital, the value of the firm increases. Correspondingly, if a new investment earns a return less than the firm's cost of capital, the firm's value decreases.

This chapter discusses the nature of the tradeoff between risk and required return made by investors in a firm's securities, the measurement of the cost of individual capital components, and the weighted cost of capital and its use in the capital budgeting process. Chapter 13 continues by considering the relationship between capital structure and the cost of capital.

Nature of Risk Premiums

Throughout finance, numerous tradeoffs must be made between risk and required return. In capital budgeting, for example, companies require higher returns on projects perceived as "high risk" than on projects considered to be "low risk." This discussion focuses on the relationship between the risk and required return on a firm's securities.

The required return on any security may be thought of as consisting of a riskless, or risk-free, rate of return, r_f, plus a premium for the risk inherent in that security:

$$\text{Required return} = r_f + \text{Risk premium.} \qquad (12.1)$$

The riskless rate of return is normally measured by the rate of return on risk-free securities, such as short-term U.S. Treasury securities. This rate varies over time and is influenced by two key factors:

- The expected inflation rate.
- The supply and demand for funds in the overall economy.

When investors expect a high inflation rate and the implied loss in the purchasing power of their money, they will demand a higher rate of return

---

[1] Technically, this statement assumes that the risk of the new investments is equal to the risk of the firm's existing assets. Also, when used in this context, the cost of capital refers to a weighted cost of the various sources of capital used by the firm. The computation of the weighted cost of capital is considered later in this chapter.

on their investments—not only in risk-free securities, but in risky securities as well. Similarly, if the anticipated demand for investment funds exceeds the anticipated supply at current interest rates, the rate of return required by investors will increase to create a new, higher equilibrium rate of return. These two factors are the primary determinants of returns on risk-free securities. The returns required on all other securities also are influenced by the risk of those securities.

There are four major risk components that determine the risk premium on a specific security at any point in time:

- The business risk of the firm.
- The financial risk of the firm.
- The marketability risk of the security.
- The length of maturity of the security (interest rate risk).

The *business risk* of a firm refers to the variability in the firm's operating earnings (EBIT). It is determined by the variability in the firm's sales revenues and operating costs and by the amount of operating leverage the firm uses in producing sales.

Financial risk refers to the additional variability in a company's earnings per share that results from the use of fixed-cost sources of funds, such as debt and preferred stock. In addition, the financial risk premium includes a premium to compensate for the increased potential risk of bankruptcy that arises from the use of debt financing.

Marketability risk refers to the ability of an investor to buy and sell a company's securities quickly and easily without a significant loss of value. For example, AT&T's shares are readily marketable any time at, or very near to, the current market price. Other, less widely owned securities that are not traded on an organized exchange or traded actively in the over-the-counter market usually do not have such a ready market. This may cause time delays in the sale of the securities and necessitate price concessions. Generally the less marketable a security, the higher its required rate of return.

Interest rate risk refers to the variability in the rate of return or yield on securities (such as bonds or preferred stocks) that arises from changes in interest rates. As interest rates rise, the prices of fixed income securities fall, causing current holders of these securities to realize a lower rate of return (than was expected at the time the security was purchased), or yield, when they sell the securities.

Finally, a firm's cost of funds may increase at any point in time with increases in the amount of needed financing. For example, a company might be able to sell one million new shares of common stock at $25 per share. If the firm sought to sell an additional one million shares, however, it would probably have to offer them at a lower price in order to attract enough buyers. This would, of course, increase the cost of the funds raised by the firm. In addition, as a firm seeks increasing amounts of capital from investors, there is a point at which the investors begin to question the firm's ability to effectively manage the large number of investment projects to be financed with these funds.

Although the foregoing concepts provide a useful background for analyzing the cost of a firm's capital, they are not directly applicable to measuring the cost of capital for specific sources of funds. Before considering how the cost of capital may be estimated, it is necessary to examine the relationship between the costs of various capital sources.

Relative Costs of Capital

Figure 12-1 illustrates the general risk-return tradeoff between investors' required rates of return and various sources of funds. As was noted, the risk-free rate, r_f, is usually measured as the rate of return on short-term U.S. Treasury securities. Longer-term U.S. Government bonds normally command a higher rate than shorter-term debt, because bond prices vary more than prices of shorter-term debt securities over time, depending on changes in interest rates. Thus, if interest rates rise, the price of long-term bonds falls, resulting in losses for any investor who must sell the security. Investors normally require a premium to compensate for this *interest rate risk*.

Long-term debt securities of the U.S. government are always less risky than corporate long-term debt securities of the same maturity. The reason, of course, is that there is a finite probability, however small, that the company will default on its obligation to pay interest and principal. Since the government controls the money supply, it can always meet its financial obligations by printing more money. The actual difference in returns, or yields, between government debt and good-quality corporate debt (AAA rated) is usually less than 1 percent and sometimes less than 0.5 percent. For example, in early 1986 the average yield on AAA corporate bonds was

Figure 12-1   **General Risk-Required Return Tradeoff**

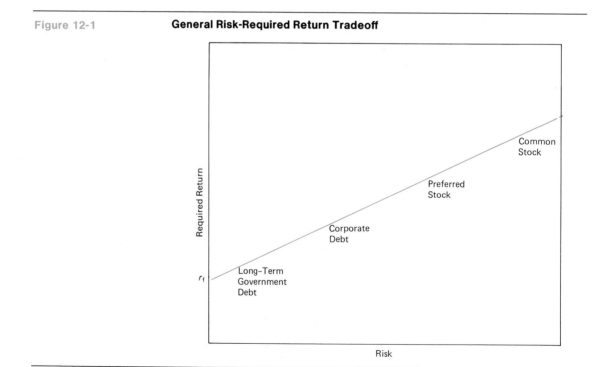

10.81 percent, and the average yield on long-term U.S. Treasury bonds was 9.9 percent. Companies with high default risk must offer high coupon interest rates to investors in order to sell their debt issues. This is because the market recognizes that these high default risk companies are more likely to have difficulty meeting their obligations than low default risk companies.

Preferred stock is normally riskier than debt. The claims of preferred stockholders on the firm's assets and earnings are junior to those of debtholders. Also, dividends on preferred stock are more likely to be cut or omitted than interest on debt. Consequently, investors in the market usually demand a higher return on preferred stock than on debt.

Finally, common stock is the most risky of the types of securities considered here, because dividends paid to common stockholders are made from cash remaining after interest and preferred dividends have been paid. Thus, the common stock dividends are the first to be cut when the firm encounters difficulties. Therefore, because there is a greater degree of uncertainty associated with common stock dividends than with the interest on debt or preferred stock dividends, common stock dividends are judged more risky. In addition, the market price fluctuations of common stocks tend to be wider than those of preferred stocks or long-term debt. As a result of this higher risk, investors' required return on common stock is higher relative to preferred stock and debt. Over the years the differences between returns realized from long-term debt and common stock investments have averaged 7.7 percent.[2]

So far this section has shown that a particular security's risk affects the return required by investors. The analysis must be taken one important step farther, however. If capital markets are to clear (that is, supply equals demand), the firm must offer returns consistent with investor expectations. Suppose, for example, that a firm offers a security for sale in the capital markets at a return that is less than investors in general expect. Obviously, not enough buyers will come forth. Unless the firm increases the return (by dropping the price, raising the interest or dividend rate, and so on), the securities will remain unsold, and the firm will not be able to raise its capital. Thus, *the cost of capital to the firm is equal to the equilibrium rate of return demanded by investors in the capital markets for securities with that degree of risk.*

Computing the Component Costs of Capital

Firms usually raise funds in "lumpy" amounts; for example, a firm may sell $50 million in bonds to finance capital expenditures at one point in time, and it may use retained earnings or proceeds from the sale of stock to finance capital expenditures later on. In spite of this tendency to raise funds in lumpy amounts from various sources at different points in time, the weighted (or composite) cost of funds, not the cost of any particular component of funds, is the cost we are interested in for capital budgeting purposes. Another way of saying this is that *it is generally incorrect to*

---

[2] See Roger C. Ibbotson and Rex A. Sinquefield, *Stocks, Bonds, Bills, and Inflation: The Past and the Future,* Charlottesville, Va.: Financial Analysts Research Foundation, 1982.

associate any particular source of financing with a particular project; that is, the investment and the financing decisions should be separate.[3]

Consider, for example, the case of a firm that is financed 50 percent with debt and 50 percent with equity. The after-tax cost of equity is 16 percent, and the after-tax cost of debt is 10 percent. The firm has two plants, A and B, which are identical in every respect. The manager of Plant A proposes to acquire a new automated packaging machine costing $10 million. A bank has offered to loan the firm the needed $10 million at a rate that will give the firm a 10 percent after-tax cost. The internal rate of return for this project has been estimated to be 12 percent. Since the rate of return exceeds the cost of funds (debt) used to finance the machine, the manager of Plant A argues that the investment should be made.

The manager of Plant B now argues that she too should be allowed to make a similar investment. Unfortunately, she is reminded that the firm has a target capital structure of 50 percent debt and 50 percent equity and that her investment will have to be financed with equity in order for the firm to maintain its target capital structure. Since the cost of equity is 16 percent and the project only offers a 12 percent return, the investment is denied for Plant B.

The point of this illustration is that two projects that are economically identical were treated very differently, simply because the method of financing the projects was tied to the accept-reject decision. To avoid problems of this type, the capital expenditure decision is usually based on a composite capital cost—that is, each project is assumed to be financed with debt and equity in the proportion in which it appears in the target capital structure. In this case, the composite cost of capital is 13 percent, computed as follows:

Source of Capital	After-tax Cost	Proportion	Composite Cost
Debt	10%	0.5	5%
Equity	16	0.5	8

Weighted cost of capital = 13%

In this example neither project should be accepted, since the cost of capital exceeds the projects' expected rates of return.

This section develops and applies methods a firm can use to compute the cost of its major component sources of capital—debt, preferred stock, retained earnings, and new common equity. These component costs are then combined into a weighted cost of capital that can be used in making capital budgeting and capital structure decisions.

Cost of Debt

The cost of debt capital to the firm is the rate of return required by investors. For a debt issue, this rate of return, k_d, equates the present value

[3] This statement is generally true. However, there are exceptions. For example, some projects may possess a higher "debt capacity" than is present for the firm as a whole. This may be due to a different level of business risk. The evaluation of mergers frequently considers the debt capacity of the to-be-acquired firm. Hence, the financing of the project may be considered along with the investment decision itself.

of all expected future receipts—interest, I, and principal repayment, M—with the offering price, P_0, of the debt security:

$$P_0 = \sum_{t=1}^{n}\frac{I}{(1 + k_d)^t} + \frac{M}{(1 + k_d)^n}. \tag{12.2}$$

Most *new* long-term debt issued by companies is sold at or close to par value (normally $1,000 per bond), and the coupon interest rate is set at the rate required by investors.[4] When debt is issued at par value, the pretax cost of debt, k_d, is equal to the coupon interest rate:

$$k_d = \text{Coupon interest rate.} \tag{12.3}$$

Interest payments made to investors, however, are deductible from the firm's taxable income. Therefore, the *after-tax* cost of debt, k_i, issued at par is computed by multiplying the coupon interest rate by one minus the firm's marginal tax rate, t:

$$k_i = k_d(1 - t). \tag{12.4}$$

To illustrate the cost of debt computation, suppose that National Telephone and Telegraph sells $100 million of 8.5 percent first mortgage bonds at par. Assuming a corporate marginal tax rate of 40 percent, the after-tax cost of debt is computed as follows:

$$k_i = k_d(1 - t) = 8.5(1 - 0.4)$$
$$= 5.1\%.$$

Equation 12.4 assumes that a firm sells the debt to yield *net proceeds,* after the cost of issuance, of $1,000 per bond. However, because of these issue costs, many bonds provide the firm with net proceeds that are less than the $1,000 par value of the bond. In addition, there have been an increasing number of bonds sold at prices considerably below par (called *deep discount bonds*). These bonds have coupon rates substantially less than prevailing market rates. They are discussed in Chapter 16.

In these cases, the computation of the pretax cost of debt is quite similar to the calculation of the yield to maturity on a bond as presented in Chapter 4. For example, suppose a firm sells a series of twenty-year, $1,000 par value bonds. The price to the public is $755, and the bonds provide a coupon rate of interest of 7 percent ($70 interest per year). (These bonds would be called *deep discount bonds.*) The issue costs per bond are $10 each. Hence, the net proceeds to the firm are as follows:

Net proceeds = $1,000 par value − $245 discount − $10 issue costs

= $745.

The pretax cost of debt to this firm is equal to the discount rate, which

---

[4] When debt is issued at par value, the coupon interest rate is equal to the yield to maturity.

equates the present value of all future interest payments ($70 per year for twenty years) plus the repayment of principal ($1,000) at the end of twenty years with the net proceeds to the firm, or

$$\$745 = \$70(\text{PVIFA}_{k_d,20}) + \$1,000(\text{PVIF}_{k_d,20}).$$

By trial and error, try 10 percent:

$$\$745 = \$70(8.514) + \$1,000(0.149)$$
$$= \$745.$$

Therefore, the pretax cost of debt is 10 percent. Assuming a 40 percent tax rate, the after-tax cost is as follows:[5,6]

$$k_i = 10\%(1 - 0.4)$$
$$= 6\%.$$

Cost of Preferred Stock

The cost of preferred stock to the firm is the rate of return required by investors on preferred stock issued by the company. Because many preferred stocks are perpetuities,[7] it is possible to use the simplified preferred stock valuation model developed in Chapter 4:

$$P_0 = \frac{D_p}{k_p}, \tag{12.5}$$

where P_0 is the preferred stock price; D_p, the annual preferred dividend; and k_p, the investors' required rate of return. The cost of preferred stock, k_p, is given by the following equation:

$$k_p = \frac{D_p}{P_{net}}. \tag{12.6}$$

In calculating preferred stock cost, the price that should be used, P_{net}, is the net proceeds to the firm, that is, the proceeds from the sale of the stock after subtracting *flotation costs*.

To illustrate, suppose Midwestern Airlines just issued 30 million shares of $2.75 cumulative preferred stock at a price to the public of $25 a share. Assuming flotation costs of $1 a share, the cost of preferred stock is

---

[5] The tax benefits of interest deductibility are only available for firms that are making profits. For a firm losing money, the tax rate in Equation 12.4 is *zero*, and the pretax cost, k_d, is the same as the after-tax cost, k_i.

[6] Whether or not a bond is sold at par or at a discount from par, the calculation of the after-tax cost of debt is the same since discounts and issue costs are amortized over the life of the issue.

[7] An increasing number of preferred stock offerings are callable, or have a fixed maturity. In these cases, the computation of the cost of the preferred is identical to that for bonds; that is, it is necessary to solve for the discount rate, k_p, which equates the present value of future promised dividends plus the present value of the retirement value (usually the par or stated value) of the preferred stock with the net proceeds to the firm.

calculated as follows:

$$k_p = \frac{\$2.75}{\$25 - \$1}$$
$$= 0.115, \text{ or } 11.5\%.$$

Since payments by the firm to preferred stockholders are in the form of dividends, they are not tax deductible so the after-tax cost of preferred stock is equal to the pretax rate.

Preferred stock is similar to long-term debt in that both types of securities normally involve fixed, uniform payments per period to the holders. In general, investors are required to pay income taxes on both interest and dividends. However, the issuing company can only deduct interest from its taxable income. As a result, in most situations in which a profitable company (with a 46 percent marginal tax rate) is choosing to leverage with either debt or preferred stock, it will prefer to issue debt, because its after-tax cost is roughly one half that of preferred stock.

Cost of Internal Equity Capital

Like the cost of debt and preferred stock, the cost of equity capital to the firm is the equilibrium rate of return required by the firm's common stock investors.

Firms raise equity capital in two ways:

- *Internally,* through retained earnings.
- *Externally,* through the sale of new common stock.

The cost of internal equity to the firm is less than the cost of new common stock, because the sale of new stock requires the payment of flotation costs.

The concept of the cost of internal equity (or simply *equity,* as it is commonly called) can be developed using several different approaches. The first considered here is based on the dividend valuation model.

Dividend Valuation Model Approach

Briefly reviewing from Chapter 4, the dividend valuation model (or the dividend capitalization model, as it is often referred to) for common stock valuation (Equation 4.18) is as follows:

$$P_0 = \sum_{t=1}^{\infty} \frac{D_t}{(1 + k_e)^t}, \qquad \textbf{(12.7)}$$

where P_0 is the stock's present value or current market price; D_t, the dividend received in period t; and k_e, the return required by investors. This equation shows that k_e, the required return and thus the cost of equity capital, equates the present value of all expected future dividends with the current market price of the stock. In principle, the cost of equity capital can be calculated by solving Equation 12.7 for k_e. In practice, however, the expected future dividends are not known and cannot be estimated with the same degree of confidence as preferred stock dividends and debt interest.

As a result, the theoretically correct general form of the dividend valuation model is generally not very useful in calculating the cost of equity capital.

If the firm's future per-share dividends are expected to grow each period perpetually at a constant rate, g, the dividend valuation model can be written as follows:

$$P_0 = \sum_{t=1}^{\infty} \frac{D_0(1 + g)^t}{(1 + k_e)^t}, \tag{12.8}$$

where D_0 is the dividend in the current period ($t = 0$). Assuming that the cost of equity, k_e, is greater than the expected dividend growth rate, g, Equation 12.8 can be transformed algebraically to the following equation:

$$P_0 = \frac{D_1}{k_e - g}, \tag{12.9}$$

where $D_1 = D_0(1 + g)$.

Equation 12.9 can be rearranged to obtain an expression for calculating the cost of equity, assuming that dividends are expected to grow perpetually at a rate g per year:[8]

$$k_e = \frac{D_1}{P_0} + g. \tag{12.10}$$

To illustrate the use of Equation 12.10, suppose the Fresno Company's common stock is currently selling at $25 a share. Its present dividend, D_0, is $2 a share, and the expected dividend growth rate is 7 percent. The investor's required return (that is, the firm's cost of equity) is calculated as follows:

$$k_e = \frac{\$2(1.07)}{\$25} + 0.07$$

$$= 0.156, \text{ or } 15.6\%.$$

In addition to being used for the constant growth case, the dividend valuation model also can be used to estimate the cost of equity capital for the no-growth case. If a stock pays a current dividend that is expected to remain constant perpetually, the appropriate valuation model follows:

$$P_0 = \frac{D}{k_e}, \tag{12.11}$$

[8] The growth rate that is relevant is the rate expected by investors. This normally is estimated by examining historical growth rates, as well as projected future growth rates provided by security analysts such as *Value Line* and Merrill Lynch. A further discussion of this issue is presented at the end of this section.

and the cost of equity capital is calculated as follows:

$$k_e = \frac{D}{P_0}. \qquad \textbf{(12.12)}$$

To illustrate, suppose the Mountaineer Railroad pays a dividend of $1.50, which is expected to remain constant forever. The firm's common stock is presently selling at $10 a share. Using these figures, the cost of equity capital is calculated as follows:

$$k_e = \frac{D}{P_0}$$
$$= \frac{\$1.50}{\$10}$$
$$= 0.15, \text{ or } 15\%.$$

The dividend valuation model also can be used to value common stocks that are expected to pay dividends that grow at variable rates in the future. For example, a young high technology company could be expected to show a period of relatively rapid growth followed by a continuing period of more normal growth. Using the dividend valuation model and defining g_1 as an above-normal growth rate expected by investors and security analysts over the first m years and g_2 as a normal, perpetual, expected growth rate beginning in year $m + 1$, the current stock price is determined as follows:

$$P_0 = \sum_{t=1}^{m} \frac{D_0(1 + g_1)^t}{(1 + k_e)^t} + \frac{P_m}{(1 + k_e)^m} \qquad \textbf{(12.13)}$$

$$= \sum_{t=1}^{m} \frac{D_0(1 + g_1)^t}{(1 + k_e)^t} + \frac{1}{(1 + k_e)^m} \times \frac{D_{m+1}}{k_e - g_2}. \qquad \textbf{(12.14)}$$

The cost of equity capital can be estimated by solving Equation 12.14 for k_e by trial and error.

For example, Avtec Corporation is a rapidly growing producer of microcircuit boards used in the aerospace industry. Its stock is currently selling for $10.95 per share. Current dividends, D_0, are $1.00 per share and are expected to grow at a rate of 10 percent per year over the next four years and 6 percent annually thereafter. Avtec's cost of internal equity, k_e, can be found by solving Equation 12.14 as follows:

$$\$10.95 = \sum_{t=1}^{4} \frac{\$1.00(1 + 0.10)^t}{(1 + k_e)^t} + \frac{1}{(1 + k_e)^4} \times \frac{D_5}{k_e - 0.06}$$

$$= \frac{\$1.10}{(1 + k_e)^1} + \frac{\$1.21}{(1 + k_e)^2} + \frac{\$1.33}{(1 + k_e)^3}$$

$$+ \frac{\$1.46}{(1 + k_e)^4} + \frac{1}{(1 + k_e)^4} \times \frac{\$1.55}{k_e - 0.06}$$

$$= \$1.10(\text{PVIF}_{k_e,1}) + \$1.21(\text{PVIF}_{k_e,2}) + \$1.33(\text{PVIF}_{k_e,3})$$

$$+ \$1.46(\text{PVIF}_{k_e,4}) + (\text{PVIF}_{k_e,4}) \frac{\$1.55}{k_e - 0.06}.$$

A trial value of 17 percent for k_e yields the following:

$$\$10.95 = \$1.10(0.855) + \$1.21(0.731) + \$1.33(0.624) + \$1.46(0.534)$$
$$+ 0.534 \left(\frac{\$1.55}{0.17 - 0.06} \right)$$
$$= \$10.95.$$

Thus, Avtec's cost of equity is 17 percent.

In principle, the general dividend valuation model approach can be used to estimate the cost of equity capital for any expected dividend pattern. In practice, there are many stocks that have not only exhibited rather constant growth rates in the past, but look as though they will continue to do so in the future. For these stocks the constant growth form of the dividend capitalization model is appropriate, and the expected growth rate often can be estimated from historical data.

Issues in Implementation

Dividend valuation models (sometimes also referred to as DCF models) are frequently used in the calculation of a firm's cost of equity capital. In implementing these models, the analyst must obtain an estimate of the growth rate(s) in earnings and dividends (and stock price) expected by investors. Where can these investor expectations be obtained?

Investors form expectations about future growth rates based upon past realized growth, current earnings and retention rates, expected future earnings rates (such as the return on equity), conditions in the markets that the firm serves, and analysts' estimates of future growth rates. Analysts' forecasts may be viewed as the best market- and investor-available summary of all of the factors which determine future growth rates. There are two reasons for this. First, there is a growing body of research which supports the conclusion that analysts' estimates of future earnings growth rates are very accurate—consistently more accurate than estimates provided from any other forecasting model.[9] Second, another body of research has confirmed the fact that analysts' forecasts outperform extrapolative forecasts in explaining share prices.[10]

Analyst forecasts are available from a number of sources. They can be obtained from individual brokerage houses and investment advisory services, such as Merrill Lynch, Salomon Brothers, E.F. Hutton, and Value Line. In addition, the New York brokerage firm of Lynch, Jones and Ryan has developed a service called the Institutional Brokers' Estimate Service (IBES). IBES summarizes the short- and long-term earnings forecasts made by over 2,400 analysts from more than 130

[9] See, for example, L. D. Brown and M. S. Rozeff, "The Superiority of Analyst Forecasts as Measures of Expectations: Evidence from Earnings," *Journal of Finance* (March, 1978), pp. 1–16; M. S. Rozeff, "Predicting Long-Term Earnings Growth: Comparisons of Expected Return Models, Submartingales and Value Line Analysts," *Journal of Forecasting* (December, 1983), pp. 425–435; and R. C. Moyer, R. E. Chatfield, and G. D. Kelley, "The Accuracy of Long-Term Earnings Forecasts in the Electric Utility Industry," *International Journal of Forecasting* (No. 3, 1985), pp. 241–252.

[10] See, for example, J. G. Cragg and B. G. Malkiel, *Expectations and the Structure of Share Prices,* (Chicago: University of Chicago Press, 1982).

brokerage firms throughout the United States. IBES covers the stocks of more than 3,400 major firms. IBES reports tell the user how many analysts follow a particular stock, the mean and median earnings per share estimates for the next quarter, the next fiscal year, and the long-term (five year) expected rate of growth in earnings for the firm. The IBES reports also show the highest and lowest estimate for each period, the number of analysts who have revised their forecasts upward and downward, and the amount of variation which exists among the forecasts provided by the different analysts. IBES reports are readily available at a low cost on computer time sharing services such as Compuserve.

Capital Asset Pricing Model (CAPM) Approach

Another technique that can be used to estimate the cost of equity capital is the *Capital Asset Pricing Model* (CAPM), as discussed in Chapter 5. The CAPM formally describes the risk-required return tradeoff for securities. Equation 12.1 illustrates that the rate of return required by investors consists of a risk-free return, r_f, plus a premium compensating the investor for bearing the risk. This risk premium varies from stock to stock.

Obviously, there is less risk associated with an investment in a stable stock, such as AT&T, than in the stock of a small wildcat oil drilling firm, W. As a result, an investor in the drilling stock requires a higher return than the AT&T investor. Figure 12-2 illustrates the difference in required rates of return (or the cost of internal equity) for the two securities. The relationship illustrated in this figure is the *security market line* (SML). The SML depicts the risk–required return relationship in the market for all securities.

Figure 12-2   **Security Market Line (SML)**

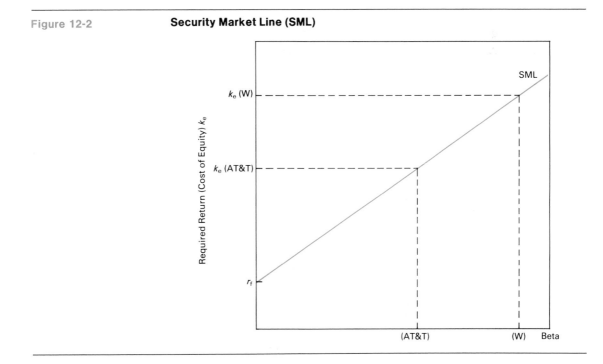

Recall from Chapter 5 that the security market line is defined in Equation 5.14 as follows:[11]

$$k_j = r_f + b_j(k_m - r_f), \qquad (12.15)$$

where k_j = the required rate of return on any Security j; r_f = the expected risk-free rate; b_j = the beta (systematic risk) measure for Security j; and k_m = the expected return on the market portfolio. Hence, the value $k_m - r_f$ equals the market risk premium, or the risk premium applicable to a stock of average (beta = 1.0) risk.

The SML concept is based upon investors' expectations regarding a security's risk and return characteristics. Required returns for any individual security are also dependent upon expected future levels of interest rates and the expected return on the market as a whole. These expected values are determined as follows:

- *The risk-free rate (r_f).* The rate for r_f that is most frequently used in computing the required return for a security is the three- or six-month U.S. Treasury Bill rate. (Some practitioners prefer to use a long-term government bond rate instead.)
- *The expected market return (k_m).* The expected market return is the return investors expect to earn in the future on an average stock— namely, one whose beta is 1.0. The average market return for stocks during the time period from 1926 to 1981 was about 11.4 percent per year.[12] These actual returns have varied substantially, depending on the holding periods assumed. Recent research indicates that the average market risk premium should be in the 5 to 7 percent range.[13]

The Firm's Beta, b_j Beta is normally estimated by using historical values of the relationship between a security's returns and the market returns. The *Value Line Investment Survey* and brokerage firms such as Merrill Lynch regularly compute and provide betas.[14]

Consider the following example. General Motors' beta has been estimated in Chapter 5 as 0.97. If 6-month U.S. Treasury Bill rates are 9.5 percent and the market return is estimated as 16 percent, the firm's cost of equity may be computed as follows:

$$\begin{aligned} k_e &= r_f + b_j(k_m - r_f) \\ &= 9.5 + 0.97(16.0 - 9.5) \\ &= 15.8\%. \end{aligned}$$

---

[11] In Equation 5.14 we used a hat ($\wedge$) over the r_f and k_m variables to indicate these are *expected* values. For simplicity, the hats are dropped here, but it should be kept in mind that we are still dealing with expected values for these variables.

[12] Ibbotson and Sinquefield, p. 71.

[13] Ibid., p. 68.

[14] Because of statistical biases inherent in the historical computation of betas, these reported betas are often adjusted to provide a better estimate of future betas.

When it seems likely that the basic risk characteristics of a firm will change significantly—perhaps because of a merger or product line expansion or contraction—the historical beta may be of little use as a forecast of the firm's future systematic risk characteristics. Under these circumstances, different methods have to be used to estimate the required future returns for the security.

The SML concept is one more tool that may be used in computing the firm's cost of equity capital, k_e. If all of the parameters required of the model are correctly estimated (r_f, k_m, and b_j), the model should give a reasonably accurate estimate of k_e. Many analysts find it useful to compute k_e in more than one way to arrive at some consensus about the rate of return investors require on a security.

It should be recalled from Chapter 5 that the beta measure of risk considers only the systematic risk or market risk of a stock. Poorly diversified investors may be more interested in total risk than in systematic risk. When this is true, the CAPM may understate required returns of those investors.

In addition, even when the beta concept can be expected to measure investment risk correctly, it is often difficult to obtain correct measures of the inputs needed to apply the model. The CAPM is an expectational model. Hence, the correct inputs must be based on market expectations about the future risk-free rate, as well as the future market risk premium. The increase in interest rate volatility has caused an increase in the volatility of bonds relative to stocks during the late 1970s and the 1980s. This has resulted in a market risk premium that tends to vary substantially and has made it more difficult to estimate. Finally, investors are faced with a whole range of risk-free rates—from thirty-day Treasury Bills to twenty-year Treasury Bonds. There is disagreement over which measure of the risk-free rate should be used.

Other Approaches for Estimating the Cost of Equity Capital

This subsection begins by considering a shortcut method of estimating the cost of equity capital based on actual historical returns and ends by discussing nondividend-paying stocks.

Studies analyzing the historical returns earned by common stock investors have found that the returns from average risk common stock investments over the years have averaged 5 to 7 percentage points higher than returns on corporate debt issues. Thus, the cost of equity capital for an average risk company (a firm with a beta of about 1.0) can be approximated by adding 5 to 7 percentage points to the company's current cost of debt. Many analysts use this shortcut method as a reference. Whenever possible, however, the other more precise methods should be used.

For stocks that do not pay dividends, the dividend capitalization model is obviously an inappropriate valuation model and therefore cannot be used directly to determine the cost of equity capital. Investors in nondividend-paying stocks expect to sell the stock in the future at a higher price than the present price, realizing a capital gain. Investors' expectations about the future price are incorporated into the following valuation model:[15]

$$P_0 = \frac{P_t}{(1 + k_e)^t},$$
(12.16)

where P_t is the expected stock price at time t. In principle, a firm could use this valuation model to determine its cost of equity capital. In practice, however, this would be difficult to do, since the company probably has no way of confidently determining the P_t expectations of investors. Instead, the cost of equity capital for nondividend-paying stocks should be determined either by using the Capital Asset Pricing Model or by estimating k_e for comparable dividend-paying stocks in their industry.

For many stocks the cost of equity capital obtained from the dividend capitalization model, the risk premium on debt approach, and the CAPM will generally be in approximate agreement with each other. If substantial differences do exist, further analysis is required. It should be emphasized that the calculation of the cost of equity capital requires the exercise of good judgment by the financial manager.

Cost of External Equity Capital

The cost of external equity is greater than the cost of internal equity for the following reasons:

- Flotation costs associated with new shares are usually high enough that they cannot realistically be ignored.
- The selling price of the new shares to the public must be less than the market price of the stock before the announcement of the new issue, or the shares cannot be expected to sell. Before any announcement, the current market price of a stock usually represents an equilibrium between supply and demand. If supply is increased (all other things being equal), the new equilibrium price will be lower.

When a firm's future dividend payments are expected to grow at a constant rate of g per period forever, the cost of external equity, k_e', is defined as follows:

$$k_e' = \frac{D_1}{P_{net}} + g,$$
(12.17)

where P_{net} is the net proceeds to the firm on a per-share basis.[16] To illustrate, consider the Fresno Company example used in the "Dividend Valuation Model Approach" section, where $P_0 = \$25$, $D_0 = \$2$, $g = 0.07$, and $k_e = 15.6$ percent.

---

[15] If investors in a nondividend-paying stock expected the company to begin paying dividends at some future date, a form of the dividend capitalization model could be constructed to reflect these expectations.

[16] An alternative approach to treat flotation costs is to allocate the dollar amount of these costs to individual projects, thus increasing the project cost. When this procedure is used, no adjustment to capital costs is required. This procedure may be superior (from a theoretical perspective) to the cost of capital adjustment procedure, but it is difficult to implement and not widely used.

Table 12-1   **Formulas for Computing Component Costs**

Cost of debt

$k_i = k_d(1 - t)$ = Coupon interest rate $\times$ (1 − Tax rate).

Cost of preferred stock

$$k_p = \frac{\text{Preferred dividend}}{\text{Net proceeds to the company}}$$

$$= \frac{D_p}{P_{net}}.$$

Cost of internal common equity

1. Dividend capitalization model approach—the case of perpetual dividends growing at a constant rate:

$$k_e = \frac{\text{Next year's expected dividend}}{\text{Common stock price}} + \text{Expected dividend growth rate}$$

$$= \frac{D_1}{P_0} + g.$$

2. Capital Asset Pricing Model Approach:

k_e = Risk-free return + Risk premium

$= r_f + b\,(k_m - r_f).$

Cost of external common equity

$$k'_e = \frac{\text{Next year's expected dividend}}{\text{Net proceeds to company, per share}} + \frac{\text{Expected dividend}}{\text{growth rate}}$$

$$= \frac{D_1}{P_{net}} + g.$$

Assuming that new common stock can be sold at $24 to net the company $23 a share after flotation costs, k'_e is calculated as follows:

$$k'_e = \frac{D_1}{P_{net}} + g$$

$$= \frac{\$2.14}{\$23} + 0.07$$

$$= 0.163, \text{ or } 16.3\%.$$

Because of the relatively high cost of newly issued equity, many companies try to avoid this means of raising capital. The question of whether or not a firm should raise capital with newly issued common stock depends on its investment opportunities.[17]

Table 12-1 summarizes the cost of capital formulas developed in the preceding sections.

Weighted Cost of Capital

Firms calculate their cost of capital in order to determine a discount rate to use for evaluating proposed capital expenditure projects. Recall that the

---

[17] This discussion is continued in the section on determining the optimal capital budget.

purpose of capital expenditure analysis is basically to determine which *proposed* projects the firm should *actually* undertake. Therefore, it is logical that *the capital whose cost is measured and compared with the expected benefits from the proposed projects should be the next or marginal capital the firm raises.* Typically, companies estimate the cost of each capital component as the cost they expect to have to pay on these funds during the coming year.[18]

In addition, as a firm evaluates proposed capital expenditure projects, it normally does not specify the proportions of debt and equity financing for each individual project. Instead, each project is presumed to be financed with the same proportion of debt and equity contained in the company's target capital structure.

Thus, the appropriate after-tax cost of capital figure to be used in capital budgeting is not only based on the next capital to be raised but is also weighted by the proportions of the capital components in the firm's long-range target capital structure. Thus, this figure is called the *weighted,* or *overall, cost of capital.*

The general expression for calculating the weighted cost of capital, k_a, follows:

$$k_a = \begin{pmatrix} \text{Equity} \\ \text{fraction} \\ \text{of} \\ \text{capital} \\ \text{structure} \end{pmatrix} \begin{pmatrix} \text{Cost} \\ \text{of} \\ \text{equity} \end{pmatrix} + \begin{pmatrix} \text{Debt} \\ \text{fraction} \\ \text{of} \\ \text{capital} \\ \text{structure} \end{pmatrix} \begin{pmatrix} \text{Cost} \\ \text{of} \\ \text{debt} \end{pmatrix}$$

$$= \left(\frac{E}{D + E}\right)(k_e) + \left(\frac{D}{D + E}\right)(k_i), \qquad \textbf{(12.18)}$$

where D is debt and E is equity in the target capital structure.[19]

To illustrate, suppose a company has a current (and target) capital structure of 75 percent equity and 25 percent debt. (The proportions of debt and equity should be the proportions in which the firm intends to raise funds in the future.) For a firm that is not planning a change in its target capital structure, these proportions should be based on the current *market value weights* of the individual components (debt, preferred stock, and common equity). The company plans to finance next year's capital budget with $75 million of retained earnings ($k_e = 15\%$) and $25 million of long-term debt ($k_d = 10\%$). Assume a 40 percent marginal tax rate. Using these figures, the weighted cost of capital being raised to finance next

[18] Stated another way, the cost of the capital acquired by the firm in earlier periods—that is, the *historical* cost of capital—is *not* used as the discount rate in determining next year's capital expenditures.

[19] If the target capital structure contains preferred stock, a preferred stock term is added to Equation 12.18. In this case Equation 12.18 becomes the following:

$$k_a = \left(\frac{E}{E + D + P}\right)(k_e) + \left(\frac{D}{E + D + P}\right)(k_i) + \left(\frac{P}{E + D + P}\right)(k_p).$$

year's capital budget is calculated as follows:

$$k_a = 0.75 \times 15.0\% + 0.25 \times 10.0\% \times (1 - 0.40)$$
$$= 12.75\%.$$

Determining the Weighted (Marginal) Cost of Capital Schedule

In the previous section the computation of the weighted (marginal) cost of capital was based on the assumption that the firm would only get equity funds from internal sources and that all debt could be acquired at a 10 percent pretax cost. This procedure for computing the weighted (marginal) cost of capital must be modified if the firm anticipates selling new common stock (having a higher component cost) or issuing additional increments of debt securities at successively higher costs in order to finance its capital budget.

To illustrate, suppose the Major Foods Corporation is developing its capital expenditure plans for the coming year. The company's schedule of potentially acceptable capital expenditure projects (defined by management as projects having an internal rate of return greater than or equal to 10 percent) for next year is as follows:

Project	Amount (in millions of dollars)	Internal Rate of Return
A	$4.0	13.8%
B	8.0	13.5
C	6.0	12.5
D	5.0	12.0
E	8.0	11.0
F	4.0	10.0

These projects are all closely related to the company's present business and have the same degree of risk as its existing assets.

The firm's current capital structure (as well as its targeted future capital structure) consists of 40 percent debt, 10 percent preferred stock, and 50 percent common equity measured on the basis of the current market value of debt and equity in the capital structure. The company can raise up to $5 million in debt funds at a pretax cost of 9 percent; debt amounts exceeding $5 million will cost 10 percent. Preferred stock can be raised at an after-tax cost of 10 percent. Major Foods' marginal tax rate is 40 percent.

Major Foods expects to generate $10 million of retained earnings over the coming year. Its present dividend rate, D_0, is $2 per share. The firm's common stock now is selling at $25 per share, and new common stock can be sold to net the firm $24 per share.[20]

Over the past several years Major Foods' earnings and dividends have grown at an average of 7 percent per year, and this growth rate is expected

[20] The net proceeds per share depend on the number of shares sold. As a very general rule, underwriters are reluctant to sell new shares in an amount that exceeds 10 to 15 percent of a company's existing shares.

to continue for the foreseeable future. The company's dividend payout ratio has been, and is expected to remain, more or less constant.

Given this information, Major Foods' weighted (marginal) cost of capital can be calculated for the coming year:

- **Step 1 Calculate the cost of capital for each individual component—the cost of debt, the cost of preferred stock, and the cost of equity.**

Cost of debt:

$$k_i = k_d(1 - t) = 9.0 \times 0.6 = 5.4\% \text{ for the first \$5 million of debt.}$$

$$k_i = k_d(1 - t) = 10.0 \times 0.6 = 6.0\% \text{ for debt exceeding \$5 million.}$$

Cost of preferred stock:

$$k_p = 10\% \text{ (given).}$$

Cost of equity:

Internal (retained earnings—$10 million):

$$k_e = \frac{D_0(1 + g)}{P_0} + g$$

$$= \frac{\$2(1.07)}{\$25} + 0.07 = 0.156, \text{ or } 15.6\%.$$

External (new common stock—amounts above $10 million):

$$k'_e = \frac{\$2(1.07)}{\$24} + 0.07 = 0.159, \text{ or } 15.9\%.$$

- **Step 2 Compute the weighted (marginal) cost of capital for each increment of capital raised.**

Major Foods should raise funds in proportion to its target capital structure from its lowest cost sources first. In this case, these sources are retained earnings (15.6 percent after-tax cost), preferred stock (10 percent after-tax cost), and the first $5 million in debt (5.4 percent after-tax cost). When these sources are exhausted, the company should consider using the higher cost sources—external equity (15.9 percent after-tax cost) and additional debt (6.0 percent after-tax cost) together with preferred stock.

How much total financing—retained earnings, preferred stock, and debt—can be done before the $5 million in low cost debt is exhausted and Major must acquire additional debt funds at the higher cost? Since we know that the target capital structure consists of 40 percent debt, the total financing, X, that this will support is equal to the amount of low cost debt available divided by the debt fraction in the capital structure:

$$X = \frac{\text{Amount of low cost debt available}}{\text{Debt fraction of capital structure}}$$

$$= \frac{\$5 \text{ million}}{0.40}$$

$$= \$12.5 \text{ million.}$$

This $12.5 million level represents a *break point* in the marginal cost of capital schedule. Beyond $12.5 million in total financing, the weighted (marginal) cost of capital will rise, because higher cost debt must now be used. Of this $12.5 million in total financing, $5 million will be debt, $1.25 million (10 percent of the total) will be preferred stock, and $6.25 million will be retained earnings.[21] The cost of this first block of funds is as follows:

$$k_a = 0.40 \times 5.4\% + 0.10 \times 10\% + 0.50 \times 15.6\%$$

$$= 10.96\%.$$

Beyond the first $12.5 million in funds, Major can use higher cost debt (6 percent after-tax cost), preferred stock (10 percent after-tax cost), and retained earnings (15.6 percent after-tax cost) until all retained earnings are exhausted. Of the total amount of retained earnings available ($10 million), $6.25 million has been used, leaving $3.75 million. The total financing that can be supported with the retained earnings is as follows:

$$X = \frac{\text{Amount of retained earnings available}}{\text{Equity fraction of capital structure}}$$

$$= \frac{\$3.75 \text{ million}}{0.5}$$

$$= \$7.5 \text{ million.}$$

This $7.5 million level represents the next break point in the weighted (marginal) cost of capital schedule. Of this $7.5 million in total financing, $3.75 million will be retained earnings, $0.75 million will be preferred stock, and $3 million will be debt. The cost of this second block of funds will be as follows:

$$k_a = 0.40 \times 6.0\% + 0.10 \times 10\% + 0.50 \times 15.6\%$$

$$= 11.20\%.$$

[21] In this case the first break point was defined by the amount of low cost debt available. It is possible that retained earnings could be exhausted before all low cost debt is used. For example, if only $5 million in retained earnings were available, the first break point would occur at $10 million, or $5 million equity/0.5. Only $4 million of low cost debt would be used in this increment, leaving $1 million for the next increment. This next increment would be $2.5 million, or $1 million debt/0.4.

Beyond the second block, all additional funds raised will be with high cost debt, new common stock, and preferred stock. The weighted cost of these funds is as follows:

$$k_a = 0.40 \times 6.0\% + 0.10 \times 10\% + 0.50 \times 15.9\%$$
$$= 11.35\%.$$

Figure 12-3 provides a graph of the weighted (marginal) cost of capital schedule for Major Foods.

The weighted (marginal) cost of capital schedule can now be used to determine the optimal capital budget for Major Foods. This is illustrated in the next section.

Determining the Optimal Capital Budget

The *optimal capital budget* can be determined by comparing the expected project returns to the company's marginal cost of capital schedule. This is accomplished by first plotting the returns expected from the proposed capital expenditure projects against the cumulative funds required. The resulting graph is called an *investment opportunity curve*. Next, the previously calculated k_a for the three capital "packages" are combined to determine the company's *marginal cost of capital curve*. The optimal capital budget is indicated by the point at which the investment opportunity curve and the marginal cost of capital curve intersect, as shown in Figure 12-4.

Specifically, the Major Foods Corporation's optimal capital budget totals $23 million and includes Projects A, B, C, and D. Projects E and F are excluded, because their returns are expected to be below the 11.35

Figure 12-3   **Weighted (Marginal) Cost of Capital Schedule for Major Foods**

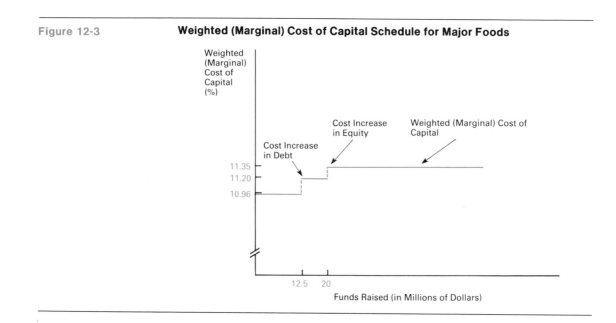

percent cost of funds. Acceptance of Projects E and F would result in a decrease in the firm's value. In principle, the optimal capital budget maximizes the value of the firm.

It should be noted that this procedure assumes that all projects being considered are of equal (average) risk. If this is not the case, one of the capital budgeting under risk techniques discussed in Chapter 11 must be incorporated into the procedure described.

The Cost of Depreciation-Generated Funds

One very large source of funds for many firms is funds generated from depreciation. Also, some firms may generate funds from the sale of assets from time to time. What is the cost of these funds? Since the firm always has the option to either reinvest these funds in the firm or to return them to the stockholders as dividends and to retire outstanding debt, the appropriate opportunity cost of these funds is the firm's weighted (marginal) cost of capital, before considering new stock flotation costs.

With respect to the marginal cost of capital schedule in Figure 12-3, it is generally agreed that these funds have an opportunity cost equal to the first "block" of funds, that is, 10.96 percent. If $10 million in depreciation-generated funds were available, the first block of funds would increase from $12.5 million to $22.5 million, and all other blocks would also be shifted to the right by $10 million.

Figure 12-4   **Determining the Optimal Capital Budget**

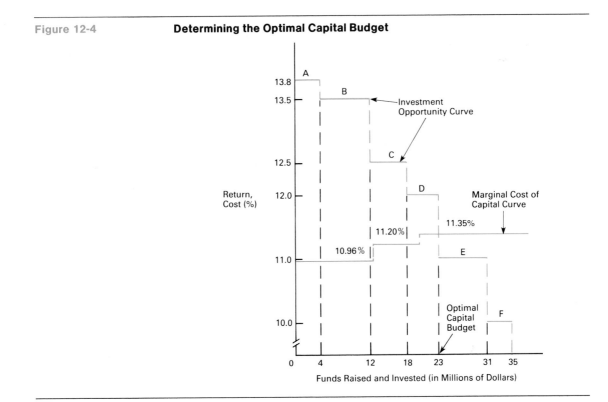

Summary

- A firm's *cost of capital* is defined as the rate the firm has to pay for the debt, preferred stock, common stock, and/or retained earnings it uses to finance its new investments in assets. The cost of capital is the rate of return required by investors in the firm's securities. Cost of capital can also be thought of as the minimum rate of return required on new investments undertaken by the firm.

- The higher the risk of a security, the higher the return required by investors. In general, common stock is more risky than preferred stock, preferred stock is more risky than corporate debt securities, and corporate debt securities are more risky than government debt securities. Investors' required returns generally decrease in the same order.

- A firm's *cost of debt capital,* k_d, is the rate of return required by investors. The after-tax cost of debt, k_i, issued at par is calculated as follows:

$$k_i = k_d(1 - t) = \text{Coupon interest rate}(1 - t),$$

where t is the firm's marginal tax rate.

- A firm's *cost of preferred stock,* k_p, is the rate of return required by the preferred stock investors. It is calculated as follows:

$$k_p = \frac{D_p}{P_{\text{net}}},$$

where D_p is the preferred dividend and P_{net} is the preferred stock price net of flotation costs on new issues. Preferred stock is used relatively infrequently as a source of capital, because its cost is normally about twice that of debt. This is due to the fact that interest on debt is a tax-deductible expense for the firm, whereas dividends on stock are not.

- A firm's *cost of equity capital* is defined as the rate of return required by its common stock investors. Equity capital can be raised *internally* through retained earnings and *externally* through the sale of new common stock.

- A firm's *cost of internal equity* can be determined by either the dividend valuation model or the Capital Asset Pricing Model (CAPM). Using the dividend valuation model and assuming that dividends perpetually grow at a rate of g per year, the following equation for calculating the cost of equity capital, k_e, is obtained:

$$k_e = \frac{D_1}{P_0} + g.$$

More complex calculations are required if the constant growth assumption does not hold. Using the CAPM, the cost of equity capital can be calculated as follows:

$$k_e = r_f + b(k_m - r_f),$$

where r_f is the risk-free rate; b (beta), the relative measure of the stock's return volatility; and k_m, the expected return on the market.

- A firm's *cost of external equity*, k'_e, when dividends are expected to grow perpetually at a constant rate, is as follows:

$$k'_e = \frac{D_1}{P_{net}} + g,$$

where P_{net} is the net proceeds to the firm on a per-share basis.

- Firms normally use an after-tax *weighted cost of capital* to evaluate proposed capital expenditure projects. Each project is presumed to be financed with the same proportion of debt and equity contained in the company's target capital structure. The general formula for calculating the weighted cost of capital, k_a, is as follows:

$$k_a = \begin{pmatrix} \text{Equity} \\ \text{fraction} \\ \text{of} \\ \text{capital} \\ \text{structure} \end{pmatrix} \begin{pmatrix} \text{Cost} \\ \text{of} \\ \text{equity} \end{pmatrix} + \begin{pmatrix} \text{Debt} \\ \text{fraction} \\ \text{of} \\ \text{capital} \\ \text{structure} \end{pmatrix} \begin{pmatrix} \text{Cost} \\ \text{of} \\ \text{debt} \end{pmatrix}.$$

- The *optimal capital budget* maximizes the value of the firm and occurs at the point where the firm's *investment opportunity curve* and *weighted marginal cost of capital curve* intersect. The investment opportunity curve is obtained by plotting the returns expected from proposed capital expenditure projects against the cumulative funds required.

- The cost of depreciation generated funds is equal to the weighted cost of the firm's first "block" of funds.

FOCUS ON CORPORATE PRACTICE

Managing Interest Rate Risk with Options on Eurodollar Futures

Ira G. Kawaller
Vice-President and Director, New York Office,
Chicago Mercantile Exchange

Hedging with interest rate futures contracts is one way of achieving interest rate protection, and this approach is clearly growing in use and gaining increasing acceptance. But recent innovations in financial markets have added yet another tool for the financial manager's arsenal. That is, financial managers now may also use options on interest rate futures to manage this interest rate risk. This article discusses the newest of these contracts: The option on the Eurodollar futures, traded at the Chicago Mercantile Exchange. First, a background on the Eurodollar futures itself.

Eurodollar Deposits and Eurodollar Futures

A Eurodollar deposit is simply a dollar-denominated interest-bearing bank deposit, maintained outside the boundaries of the United States. Two types of deposits are available: *certificates of deposit,* which are traded in a secondary market, and *time deposits,* which are not. In both cases, maturities can be arranged for various lengths, but most typical are those of three months, six months, and one year.

Eurodollar deposits are priced in terms of yield, with bids and offers quoted in sixteenths. The bid side reflects the rate at which banks are willing to lend in the interbank Eurodollar market, and the offered side is the rate that banks are offering to their depositors in this market.

The London Interbank Offered Rate (LIBOR) is somewhat of a benchmark rate for the Eurodollar market. In a sense, it is a fixing in the London market of the offered side of the Eurodollar time deposit market, at a specific time each day. It is important for this discussion, in that the Eurodollar futures contract settles to the three-month LIBOR rate at the expiration of the contract.

The Eurodollar futures *contract* sets rates on Eurodollar time deposits, commencing on a specific forthcoming date—two London business days before the third Wednesday of March, June, September, or December, depending on the contract expiration month. Operationally, futures prices are derived by subtracting an interest rate (in percentage points, carried to two decimal places) from 100. Therefore, as interest rates rise, futures prices will fall, and vice versa. As the face amount of the Eurodollar future is $1 million and its maturity is three months, every basis point move in the futures price (yield) translates to a value of $25. In general, movements in the Eurodollar futures market will be closely correlated to yield movements in the underlying Eurodollar time deposit market, though changes will not be precisely equal over any given period of time.

As long as one maintains the futures position—either long (hoping the market will rise in price, decline in yield) or short (hoping the market will decline in price, rise in yield)—the participant will be obligated to mark the contract to market on a daily basis and make cash settlement for any change in value, daily. This obligation can be terminated at any time by simply "trading out" of the position (that is, making the opposite transaction). Upon the expiration of the contract, any participant still maintaining contracts will have a final mark-to-market adjustment, with the final settlement price based on an average derived from a survey of London bankers who report their perception of the cash market three-month LIBOR rate at the time of the survey.

When using this contract for hedging purposes, the hedger will buy or sell enough futures contracts to provide a dollar-for-dollar offset to an adverse move in interest rates. For example, the funding manager who would suffer under rising interest rates would be a seller of futures contracts. In this case, if rates do rise, the banker will necessarily take in deposits at a higher rate; but the increased cost due to the marginal change in interest rates will be offset by futures profits. Conversely, if rates happen to decline, the lower cost of funds would be offset by futures losses. In some sense, then, the use of futures as a hedging device is a rate-setting mechanism that insulates the hedger from forthcoming interest rate effects—either beneficial or adverse.

Eurodollar Option

Options come in two types: *calls* and *puts*. *Calls* are the right to buy something at a fixed price. *Puts* are the right to sell at a fixed price. Both calls and puts have a limited period for which they are in effect. A June call, for example, expires sometime in June; a September put expires in September, etc. The fixed price referred to above is called the *exercise* or *strike* price. An 89.00-strike June call on a Eurodollar futures contract, for example, gives the buyer of this option the right to purchase a June Eurodollar futures contract at a price of 89.00.[22] This right terminates in June.

Generating Profit with Rising Interest Rates

The manager has three choices for dealing with an expectation of rising interest rates: (1) selling (or shorting) an interest rate futures contract, (2) buying a put option, or (3) selling a call option. All will make money if interest rates do, in fact, rise. Each alternative will have a different outcome, however, depending upon how interest rates actually change—independent of expectations. For the futures contract, for instance, the opportunities and risks are symmetric. That is, the financial manager could realize virtually unlimited profits with this instrument; alternatively, he could realize virtually unlimited losses if interest rates do not move as expected.

Buying the put allows profits to be generated from rising interest rates, but if rates decline the exposure to loss is limited to the price of that option. Put buying may be seen as analogous to purchasing insurance with a deductible clause. A claim can be filed if interest rates rise, and the insurance policy will pay off. Conversely, if interest rates *do not* rise, or if they fall, the put buyer simply lives with the fact that he paid for insurance but does not file a claim.

Finally, the call seller has still another opportunity/risk profile. If interest rates go up as expected, the call will lose value, and thus it can be bought back, cheaper. As a result, the call seller would get to keep some—and perhaps all—of the initial selling price of the option, but no more. On the other hand if interest rates decline, the option price will rise, and the call seller will be forced to buy back his option position at a higher price and therefore at a loss. In other words, by choosing this method of coverage, the manager only achieves profits for a relatively minor interest rate increase, but he is completely exposed to a loss if rates unexpectedly decline. These various opportunities/risk differences are summarized by Table 12-2.

---

[22] In the case of options on Eurodollar futures, the option and the underlying futures contracts have common expiration dates. Put another way, there is never a June option on a September future.

Table 12-2   **Profiting from Rising Interest Rates (Declining Futures Prices)**

Futures at Expiration	Sell Futures @90.00	Buy 90 Put @1.00	Sell 90 Call @1.00
93.00	−3.00	−1.00	−2.00
91.00	−1.00	−1.00	Breakeven
90.00	Breakeven	−1.00	+1.00
89.00	+1.00	Breakeven	+1.00
87.00	+3.00	+2.00	+1.00

Generating Profit with Declining Interest Rates

For those who would suffer under declining interest rates, all the solutions are opposite of those presented above. That is, the choice now becomes buying a futures contract, buying a call option, or selling a put option. The characteristics are analogous: Futures offer symmetric profit opportunity and risk, option buying (calls) offers unbounded profit potential and limited risk, and selling options (puts) offers limited profit potential and unbounded risk. For completeness, Table 12-3 presents possible outcomes that are appropriate for those desiring to generate profit with declining interest rates.

The determination of which hedging strategy is best—that is, whether to use a futures contract, buy an option (a call to protect for declining interest rates or a put to protect for rising interest rates), or sell an option (the opposite of the long option choice)—is unclear at the time the hedge is initiated. In fact, depending on how the underlying interest rate changes, any one of the three choices can be the best. The manager's choice should depend on (1) the certainty that the manager attaches to the associated interest rate forecast and (2) the comfort level associated with the risks among the three choices. Referring to either Table 12-2 or 12-3, one can see that the manager with great confidence in his forecast and an expectation of a sizable interest rate move would be best served by a futures contract. Alternatively, if one expected a large move but had a lesser degree of confidence in the forecast, the long option would be preferred. And finally the short option choice would be best only when relatively small rate moves were anticipated.

From the perspective of a hedger, the choices and trade-offs can be stated in the following way: Hedging with futures insulates the hedger from the effects of subsequent interest rate moves—either adverse or beneficial. Buying options is analogous to purchasing insurance for one-way protection. And, finally, selling options offers a fixed maximum amount of protection and the risk of nonprotection for major adverse interest rate changes. It becomes the manager's responsibility, therefore, to understand these three choices and the risks and opportunities associated with each.

Table 12-3   **Profiting from Declining Interest Rates (Rising Futures Prices)**

Futures at Expiration	Buy Futures @90.00	Buy 90 Call @1.00	Sell 90 Put @1.00
93.00	+3.00	+2.00	+1.00
91.00	+1.00	Breakeven	+1.00
90.00	Breakeven	−1.00	+1.00
89.00	−1.00	−1.00	Breakeven
87.00	−3.00	−1.00	−2.00

Questions and Topics for Discussion

1. How do retained earnings differ from other sources of financing?
2. Does the retained earnings figure shown on a firm's balance sheet necessarily have any relationship to the amount of retained earnings the firm can generate in the coming year? Explain.
3. Why is corporate long-term debt more risky than government long-term debt?
4. Why do investors generally consider common stock to be more risky than preferred stock?
5. Should a firm pay cash dividends in a year in which it raises external common equity?
6. Discuss the meaning of an *optimal* capital budget.
7. Evaluate the statement, Depreciation-generated funds have no explicit cost and therefore should be assigned a zero cost in computing a firm's cost of capital.
8. Describe how to derive the "break points" in the marginal cost of capital schedule.
9. Discuss the pros and cons of various sources of estimates of future earnings and dividend growth rates for a company.

Problems*

1. Calculate the after-tax cost of a $25 million debt issue that Pullman Manufacturing Corporation (40 percent marginal tax rate) is planning to place privately with a large insurance company. This long-term issue will yield 9⅜ percent to the insurance company.
2. Husky Enterprises recently sold an issue of 10-year maturity bonds. The bonds were sold at a deep discount price of $615 each. After flotation costs, Husky received $604.50 each. The bonds have a $1,000 maturity value and pay $50 interest at the end of each year. Compute the after-tax cost of debt for these bonds if Husky's marginal tax rate is 40 percent.
3. Caculate the after-tax cost of preferred stock for Bozeman-Western Airlines, Inc., which is planning to sell $10 million of $6.50 cumulative preferred stock to the public at a price of $50 a share. Flotation costs are estimated to be $2 a share. The company has a marginal tax rate of 40 percent.
4. St. Joe Trucking has sold an issue of $6 cumulative preferred stock to the public at a price of $60 per share. After flotation costs, St. Joe netted $57 per share. The company has a marginal tax rate of 40 percent.
   a. Calculate the after-tax cost of this preferred stock offering assuming this stock is a perpetuity.
   b. If the stock is callable in 5 years at $66 per share, and investors expect it to be called at that time, what is the after-tax cost of this preferred stock offering? (Compute to the nearest whole percent.)
5. The following financial information is available on Fargo Fabrics, Inc.:

Current per-share market price	$20.25
Current per-share dividend	$ 1.12
Current per-share earnings	$ 2.48
Beta	0.90
Expected return on the market	14.0%
Risk-free rate	7.0%

Past 10 years earnings per share:

19X1	$1.39	19X6	$1.95
19X2	1.48	19X7	2.12
19X3	1.60	19X8	2.26
19X4	1.68	19X9	2.40
19X5	1.79	19Y0	2.48

* Color numbers denote problems which have check answers provided at the end of the book.

This past earnings growth trend is expected to continue for the foreseeable future. The dividend payout ratio has remained approximately constant over the past 9 years and is expected to remain at current levels for the foreseeable future.

Calculate the cost of equity capital using the following methods:

a. The dividend capitalization model approach.

b. The Capital Asset Pricing Model approach.

Hint: To estimate g, calculate the average of the first 3 years of earnings and the average of the last 3 years of earnings; then use these averages to estimate the growth rate for the 7-year period of 19X2 to 19X9. This "smooths out" random fluctuations in earnings growth from year to year.

6. The stock of Alpha Tool sells for $10.25 per share. Its current dividend rate, D_0, is $1 per share. Analysts and investors expect Alpha to increase its dividends at a 10 percent rate for each of the next 2 years. This annual dividend growth rate is expected to decline to 8 percent for years 3 and 4, and then to settle down to 4 percent per year forever. Calculate the cost of internal equity for Alpha Tool.

7. The Hartley Hotel Corporation is planning a major expansion. Hartley is financed 100 percent with equity and intends to maintain this capital structure after the expansion. Hartley's beta is 0.9. The expected market return is 16 percent and the risk-free rate is 10 percent. If the expansion is expected to produce an internal rate of return of 17 percent, should Hartley make the investment?

8. Wentworth Industries is 100 percent equity financed. Its current beta is 0.9. The expected market rate of return is 14 percent, and the risk-free rate is 8 percent.

a. Calculate Wentworth's cost of equity.

b. If Wentworth changes its capital structure to 30 percent debt, it estimates that its beta will increase to 1.1. The after-tax cost of debt will be 7 percent. Should Wentworth make the capital structure change?

9. The Ewing Distribution Company is planning a $100 million expansion of its chain of discount service stations to several neighboring states. This expansion will be financed, in part, with debt issued with a coupon interest rate of 15 percent. The bonds have a 10-year maturity and a $1,000 face value, and they will be sold to net Ewing $990 after issue costs. Ewing's marginal tax rate is 40 percent.

Preferred stock will cost Ewing 14 percent after taxes. Ewing's common stock pays a dividend of $2 per share. The current market price per share is $15, and new shares can be sold to net $14 per share. Ewing's dividends are expected to increase at an annual rate of 5 percent for the foreseeable future. Ewing expects to have $20 million of retained earnings available to finance the expansion.

Ewing's target capital structure is as follows:

Debt	20%
Preferred stock	5
Common equity	75

Calculate the weighted cost of capital that is appropriate to use in evaluating this expansion program.

10. Pacific Intermountain Utilities Company has a present capital structure (which the company feels is optimal) of 50 percent long-term debt, 10 percent preferred stock, and 40 percent common equity. For the coming year the

company has determined that its optimal capital budget can be externally financed with $70 million of 10 percent first-mortgage bonds sold at par and $14 million of preferred stock costing the company 11 percent. The remainder of the capital budget will be financed with retained earnings. The company's common stock is presently selling at $25 a share, and next year's common dividend, D_1, is expected to be $2 a share. The company has 25 million common shares outstanding. Next year's net income available to common stock (including net income from next year's capital budget) is expected to be $106 million. The company's past annual growth rate in dividends and earnings has been 6 percent. However, a 5 percent annual growth in earnings and dividends is expected for the foreseeable future. The company's marginal tax rate is 40 percent.

Calculate the company's weighted cost of capital for the coming year.

11. Panhandle Industries, Inc., currently pays an annual common stock dividend of $2.20 per share. The company's dividend has grown steadily over the past 9 years from $1.10 to its present level; this growth trend is expected to continue. The company's present dividend payout ratio, also expected to continue, is 40 percent. In addition, the stock presently sells at 8 times current earnings (that is, its "P/E multiple" is 8).

Panhandle Industries' stock has a beta of 1.15, as computed by a leading investment service. The present risk-free rate is 7.0 percent, and the expected return on the stock market is 13.0 percent.

a. Suppose an individual investor feels that 12 percent is an appropriate required rate of return for the level of risk this investor perceived for Panhandle Industries. Using the dividend capitalization model and the Capital Asset Pricing Model approaches, determine whether this investor should purchase Panhandle Industries' stock.

b. Calculate the company's cost of equity capital using both the dividend capitalization model approach and the Capital Asset Pricing Model approach.

12. Colbyco Industries has a target capital structure of 60 percent common equity, 30 percent debt, and 10 percent preferred stock. The cost of retained earnings is 15 percent, and the cost of new equity (external) is 16 percent. Colbyco anticipates having $20 million of new retained earnings available over the coming year. Colbyco can sell $15 million of first-mortgage bonds with an after-tax cost of 9 percent. Its investment bankers feel the company could sell $10 million of debentures with a 9.5 percent after-tax cost. Additional debt would cost 10 percent after tax and be in the form of subordinated debentures. The after-tax cost of preferred stock financing is estimated to be 14 percent.

Compute the marginal cost of capital schedule for Colbyco, and determine the break points in the schedule.

13. The White Corporation makes small Bozo replicas for sale in the growing Austin market. The firm's capital structure consists of 60 percent common equity, 10 percent preferred stock, and 30 percent long-term debt. This capital structure is believed to be optimal. White is planning to raise funds over the coming year to finance expansion plans. The firm expects to have $40 million of retained earnings available. The cost of retained earnings is 18 percent. Additional common equity can be obtained by selling new common stock at a cost of 19.6 percent. The firm can sell a maximum amount of $20 million of preferred stock at a cost of 15 percent. First mortgage bonds totalling $25 million can be sold at a pre-tax cost of 14 percent. Beyond $25 million, the firm would have to sell debentures at a pre-tax cost of 15 percent. The firm's marginal tax rate is 40 percent.

Identify the size of each block of funds and the cost of the funds in each block. Be sure to identify the *maximum* amount of funds White can acquire.

14. Owens Enterprises is in the process of determining its capital budget for the next fiscal year. The firm's current capital structure, which it considers to be optimal, is contained in the following balance sheet:

Balance Sheet

Current assets	$40,000,000	Accounts payable	$20,000,000
Fixed assets	400,000,000	Other current liabilities	10,000,000
Total assets	$440,000,000	Long-term debt	123,000,000
		Common stock at par	15,500,000
		Paid in capital in excess of par	51,000,000
		Retained earnings	220,500,000
		Total liabilities and stockholders' equity	$440,000,000

Through discussions with the firm's investment bankers, lead bank, and financial officers, the following information has been obtained:

- The firm expects net income from this year to total $80,000,000. The firm intends to maintain its dividend policy of paying 42.25 percent of earnings to stockholders.
- The firm can borrow $18,000,000 from its bank at a 13 percent annual rate.
- Any additional debt can be obtained through the issuance of debentures (at par) which carry a 15 percent coupon rate.
- The firm currently (D_0) pays $4.40 per share in dividends. Dividends have grown at a 5 percent rate in the past. This growth is expected to continue.
- The firm's common stock currently trades at $44 per share. If the firm were to raise any external equity, the newly issued shares would net the company $40 per share.
- The firm is in the 40 percent marginal tax bracket.

Compute Owens' marginal cost of capital schedule.

**An Integrative
Case Problem**

Cost of Capital

The Marietta Corporation, a large manufacturer of mufflers, tail pipes, and shock absorbers, is presently carrying out its financial planning for next year. In about two weeks, at the next meeting of the firm's board of directors, Frank Bosworth, vice-president of finance, is scheduled to present his recommendations for next year's overall financial plan. He has asked Donna Botello, manager of financial planning, to gather the necessary information and perform the calculations for the financial plan.

The company's divisional staffs, together with corporate finance department personnel, have analyzed several proposed capital expenditure projects. The following is a summary schedule of acceptable projects (defined by the company as projects having internal rates of return greater than 8 percent):

Project	Investment Amount (in millions of dollars)	Internal Rate of Return
A	$10.0	25%
B	20.0	21
C	30.0	18
D	35.0	15
E	40.0	14
F	40.0	12
G	40.0	10
H	20.0	9

All projects are expected to have one year of negative cash flow followed by positive cash flows over their remaining years. In addition, next year's projects involve modifications and expansion of the company's existing facilities and products. As a result, these projects are considered to have approximately the same degree of risk as the company's existing assets.

Botello feels that this summary schedule and detailed supporting documents provide her with the necessary information concerning the possible capital expenditure projects for next year. She now can direct her attention to obtaining the data necessary to determine the cost of the capital required to finance next year's proposed projects.

The company's investment bankers indicated to Bosworth in a recent meeting that they feel the company could issue up to $50 million of 9 percent first-mortgage bonds at par next year. The investment bankers also feel that any additional debt would have to be subordinated debentures with a coupon of 10 percent, also to be sold at par. The investment bankers rendered their opinion after Bosworth gave an approximate estimate of the size of next year's capital budget, and after he estimated that approximately $100 million of retained earnings would be available next year.

Both the company's financial management and the investment bankers consider the present capital structure of the company, shown in the following table, to be optimal (assume that book value and market value are equal):

Debt	$ 400,000,000
Shareholders' equity:	
Common stock	150,000,000
Retained earnings	450,000,000
	$1,000,000,000

Botello has assembled additional information, as follows:

- Marietta common stock is presently selling at $21.00 a share.
- The investment bankers also have indicated that an additional $75 million in new common stock could be issued to net the company $19 a share.
- The company's present annual dividend is $1.32 a share. However, Bosworth feels fairly certain that the board will increase it to $1.41 a share next year.
- The company's earnings and dividends have doubled over the past 10 years. Growth has been fairly steady, and this rate is expected to continue for the foreseeable future. The company's marginal tax rate is 40 percent.

Using the information provided, answer the following questions. (Note: Disregard depreciation in this case.)

1. Calculate the cost of each component source of capital.
2. Calculate the marginal cost of capital for the various intervals, or "packages," of capital the company can raise next year. Plot the marginal cost of capital curve.
3. Using the marginal cost of capital curve from Question 2, and plotting the investment opportunity curve, determine the company's optimal capital budget for next year.
4. Should Project G be accepted or rejected? Why?
5. What factors do you feel might cause Bosworth to recommend a different capital budget than the one obtained in Question 3?

Lotus123

**Selected
References**

Arditti, Fred D., and Haim Levy. "The Weighted Average Cost of Capital as a Cutoff Rate: A Critical Analysis of the Classical Textbook Weighted Average." *Financial Management* (Fall 1977): 24–34.

Boudreaux, Kenneth J., Hugh W. Long, John R. Ezzell, R. Burr Porter, Moshe BenHorim, and Alan C. Shapiro. "The Weighted Average Cost of Capital: A Discussion." *Financial Management* (Summer 1979): 7–23.

Copeland, T. E., and J. F. Weston. *Financial Theory and Corporate Policy,* 2nd ed. Reading, MA: Addison-Wesley, 1983.

Fama, E. F. "Risk-Adjusted Discount Rates and Capital Budgeting Under Uncertainty." *Journal of Financial Economics* (August 1977): 3–24.

Gordon, Myron. *The Investment, Financing, and Valuation of the Corporation.* Homewood, Ill.: Irwin, 1962.

INTRODUCTION TO FINANCIAL FUTURES

Glossary of New Terms

Financial futures contract A commitment to receive or deliver a specified dollar amount of a financial instrument at a definite time in the future at a current agreed-upon price.

Hedging A transaction that limits the risk associated with market price fluctuations for a particular investment position.

Long hedge The process of buying a futures contract to protect a current position from a loss due to a decrease in interest rates or an increase in prices.

Margin A required deposit of money to insure that a future commitment will be fulfilled. The deposit amount is usually expressed as a percentage of the future contract's worth.

Margin call The process of requesting additional funds in order to meet the required minimum margin level. These funds may be needed because of an adverse change in market prices or a change in margin requirements.

Short hedge The process of selling a futures contract to protect a current position from a loss due to an increase in interest rates or a decrease in prices.

Speculators Individuals or institutions who assume the risk that hedgers are attempting to avoid.

Introduction

Chapter 12 discusses the relationship between cost of capital and risk, namely, the cost of capital to a firm increases as risk increases. During the 1970s and early 1980s, financial markets in the United States have been characterized by relatively large and rapid interest rate fluctuations. This volatility has increased the level of risk financial market participants must bear. The financial futures markets offer financial managers a method of lowering risk.

The area of financial futures has grown rapidly in recent years. The financial futures contracts actively traded include U.S. Treasury security futures (bills, notes, and bonds), Government National Mortgage Association (GNMA) bond futures, bank certificate of deposit futures, Eurodollar futures, futures based on various stock market indexes, and foreign currency futures.

Futures Market Terminology

Most transactions that individuals enter into take place in the *cash*, or *spot*, market. For example, farmers who sell melons at roadside stands near their farms are dealing in the spot market. Suppose these farmers also grow wheat, and in December they become concerned that the price of wheat may decline from its present level by the time they harvest and sell their wheat next summer. To protect against this possible price decline, they could sell wheat futures contracts. By *selling futures contracts*, the farmers agree to deliver a certain quantity and quality of wheat at a specified time in the future (sometime during July, for example). The prices the farmers will receive for their wheat in July are agreed upon at the time they sell the contracts in December. Therefore, they have "locked in" the future prices they will receive for their wheat; in other words, the farmers have *hedged* their wheat position.

The buyer of a wheat futures contract might be a cereal company that will have to purchase wheat next summer and is concerned about the possibility of a rise in the price of wheat. Alternatively, the buyer of a July wheat futures contract in December might be an individual who simply feels that the price of wheat will increase by July and that he or she can make a profit by trading wheat futures. This individual is referred to as a *speculator* in the parlance of the futures market. Speculators assume the risk that hedgers are attempting to avoid, in return for possible profits.

Basics of Financial Futures

A financial futures contract is a legally binding agreement to receive or deliver a specified dollar amount of a particular financial instrument at a definite future time at a current agreed-upon price. For example, the seller of a ten-year U.S. Treasury Bond futures contract agrees to deliver $100,000 worth of 8 percent coupon (or equivalent), fifteen-year (or equivalent) maturity U.S. Treasury Bonds on a specified business day during the delivery month. The price the seller will receive for the U.S. Treasury Bond in the future is agreed upon at the time the contract is executed. (Actually, less than 1 percent of the sellers of futures contracts make delivery of the commodity or security; usually the sellers buy back the futures contract prior to the end of trading in a contract.)

Participants in the financial futures market can either *buy* or *sell* futures contracts. Buyers of futures contracts are said to be *long* the futures, and sellers are said to be *short* the futures.

Suppose an individual expects interest rates to decrease within the next year. The decrease in interest rates will generally cause bond prices to increase. By *buying* a bond futures contract, the individual can make a profit if interest rates do in fact decrease between the time the contract is bought and the delivery month (or when the contract is sold). Table 12A-1 shows the prices of several U.S. Treasury Bond futures contracts, as of October 7, 1985, and February 21, 1986. Between October 1985 and February 1986, interest rates on U.S. Treasury Bonds dropped from about 10.9 percent to about 9 percent. To illustrate the profit that could have

Table 12A-1   **Prices of U.S. Treasury Bond Futures Contracts***

Maturity Date	Price† October 7, 1985	February 20, 1986
March 1986	73.14	88.12
June 1986	72.12	87.13
September 1986	71.12	86.17
December 1986	70.15	85.24

*The approximate current yield on U.S. Treasury Bonds was 10.9 percent as of October 1985 and 9 percent as of February 1986.
†Prices are quoted in thirty-seconds of 100 percent of par value. A quote of 73.14 equals $73,437.50 (73¹⁴/₃₂ percent of $100,000 par).
Source: *The Wall Street Journal,* October 8, 1985, and February 21, 1986.

been made, consider a person who bought a March 1986 U.S. Treasury Bond futures contract in October 1985 for $73^{14}/_{32}$ percent of par. The price of the $100,000 par value contract was $73,437.50. By February 1986 this contract was selling for $88^{12}/_{32}$ percent of par, or, $88,375.00, and the buyer would have had a profit of $14,937.50. Buyers and sellers of futures contracts are not required to pay the entire contract price when the contract is initially executed. Instead, they are only required to make a partial deposit, or *margin.* Margins are typically less than 10 percent of the contract's price. For example, large institutional traders of Treasury Bond futures contracts can do so for only a 2.5 percent ($2,500) margin, and individuals can trade with $3,000 of margin.

The *seller* of the March 1986 U.S. Treasury Bond futures contract in October 1985 would have *lost* approximately $14,937.50 on the sale by February, 1986. The seller was expecting interest rates to increase, but they declined instead.

Participants in the financial futures markets either *hedge* or *speculate.* In *hedging,* market participants take a futures position approximately equal but opposite to their current commitment in the market. Hedgers protect themselves from market changes by the fact that losses on one side of the position are covered by the gains on the opposite side. Although no hedged position is perfect insurance against risk, hedging does allow investors more protection than does their simply trusting the market to move in their favor.

The following is an example of hedging in the financial futures market. Suppose the manager of a pension fund expects interest rates to increase, causing the pension fund's bond portfolio to decrease in value. To hedge, or protect the value of the fund's assets against this possible interest rate rise, the manager could sell bond futures. Then, if interest rates do in fact rise, the decrease in the value of the fund's bond portfolio will be offset by the profit made on the bond futures. The bond futures that were sold when interest rates were relatively low will decrease in value as interest rates increase. The futures then could be bought back at the lower price, enabling a profit to be made. This example is called a *short hedge,* because the pension fund manager owned the bonds and sold, or *shorted,* the futures contract.

A *long hedge* can be illustrated as follows. Suppose a financial manager anticipates receiving one year from now some funds that are to be invested in long-term bonds. If the financial manager expects interest rates to decline over the next year, causing long-term bond prices to rise, he or she could *buy,* or go long in, U.S. Treasury Bond futures. Then, if interest rates do in fact decline, the profit from the bond futures purchase would offset the increased price of the bonds that have to be purchased. This example is called a *long hedge,* because the financial manager bought, or was *long* in, the futures contract and did not own the bonds.

In both of these hedging examples, financial managers used the futures market to lower their level of risk exposure. In effect, they were able to transfer a portion of their risk to another market participant. If this other party involved in the transaction does not have a position to hedge, he or she is termed a *speculator.*

Fixed-Income Futures and Hedging

The fixed-income futures that are available include U.S. Treasury Bills, U.S. Treasury Notes, U.S. Treasury Bonds, certificates of deposit, and GNMAs. Fixed-income futures are widely used by market participants desiring to hedge against the risk of volatile interest rates.

An actual example of fixed-income futures hedging involves the underwriting of a $1.0 billion note and debenture issue for IBM by an underwriting team lead by Salomon Brothers and Merrill Lynch in October 1979.[23] Apparently, the underwriters were concerned about the possibility of an interest rate rise that would cause the IBM securities to decline in value before being sold by the underwriters.

In this situation, the underwriters would want to sell bond futures contracts. Then, if interest rates did rise, the yield on the bonds for issue would become unattractive, causing their price to fall, and the underwriters would have to absorb this loss. However, the price of the bond futures would also have dropped. Thus, the underwriters' commitment to deliver bonds at a fixed price in the future would earn them a gain, since they would be able to buy back the bonds at a reduced price in the market and then sell them at the higher, fixed price. Alternatively, the underwriters could buy back the bond futures at the lower price.

Although the IBM underwriters did not reveal their hedging technique, it has been suggested that they sold short either U.S. Treasury Bond futures or GNMA futures. Therefore, when interest rates did rise (due to the Federal government's move to tighten credit), these underwriters realized a gain from their short position. This gain helped to almost completely offset the loss they faced as a result of the decreased issuing price of the IBM bonds.

In the IBM example, the underwriters were successful in transferring their capital loss to the futures buyers. However, if interest rates had not changed, the price of the bond futures contract would have remained stable. As a result, neither the futures buyer nor seller would have made a gain or loss. If interest rates had declined, however, the underwriters would have transferred their capital gain to the futures buyers. Therefore, for every hedged transaction in which there is a "winner," there also exists a "loser."

Stock-Index Futures

Futures contracts based on different stock market indexes have been traded since 1982. By the spring of 1983, futures contracts based on the *Standard and Poor's 500 Market Index,* the *New York Stock Exchange Index,* the *Value Line Stock Index,* and the *Standard and Poor's 100 Market Index* were available.

Stock-index futures can be used to protect equity investments. Like other financial futures, stock-index futures are financial instruments contracted for future delivery. However, instead of actually delivering stock shares, stock-index contracts held to maturity simply expire. At the expiration date, the buyers' and sellers' accounts are settled, based on the present level of the particular stock index.

Hedgers can buy stock-index futures contracts based on their expecta-

[23] *Business Week* (Oct. 29, 1979): 50.

tions of future market movements. For example, portfolio managers who expect a temporary downturn in the stock market could sell stock-index futures instead of liquidating large blocks of stock in their portfolios. In this instance, if the stock market index does drop, the gain made from buying back the futures contract at a lower price will help offset the decline in the market value of the stock being held.

Futures transactions also allow financial managers to operate quickly in rapidly changing stock market environments, because a single futures transaction is easier to accomplish than deciding which individual stocks to trade. In addition, futures transactions costs are generally lower than those for comparable security transactions.

Speculators can also participate in the stock-index futures market. For example, if speculators expect the stock market to increase, they can buy a futures contract. If the index does rise, the value of the contract increases, resulting in a profit.

Managing Capital Costs and Investments with Financial Futures Contracts

Financial managers can use financial futures contracts to hedge their positions with respect to planning capital investments and stock and bond offerings. For example, consider the case of the Alaskagas Pipeline Company which plans to sell $50 million in bonds in about six months to partially fund the construction of a new pipeline. The project has been evaluated and found to have a positive, but small, NPV. The senior financial officer of the firm is afraid that interest rates will rise substantially over the next six months and that the project might no longer be desirable at the higher interest rates. The current long-term bond rate is 11 percent. The financial viability of this project can be protected by hedging in the interest rate futures market.

Alaskagas would be harmed if interest rates increase. Thus the firm must sell (take a short position) interest rate futures in order to hedge its position. Because Alaskagas plans to issue fifteen-year bonds to fund the pipeline, it should hedge with the financial instrument most closely related to its own financial plans. This would be a Treasury Bond futures contract. As discussed above, Treasury Bond futures contracts trade in $100,000 increments. Hence, Alaskagas must sell 500 Treasury Bond contracts ($50 million/$100,000 per contract) for delivery in six months. Alaskagas would have to put up margin money or about 3 percent of the par value of the contracts plus pay some brokerage commissions.

Suppose that long-term interest rates do increase over the six-month period from 11 percent to 13 percent. As a result, bonds which could be sold for $1,000 while offering 11 percent interest can now be sold for only $870.75. Alaskagas would lose $129.95 per bond or a total of $6,475,000 ($129.25 per bond times 50,000 bonds). If Alaskagas had sold 500 Treasury Bond contracts at a price of $85,000 each, this loss could be partially, or completely, offset. Because of the rise in interest rates, the Treasury Bond futures contracts decline in value from $42.5 million to $36.025 million. At the end of six months Alaskagas could close out its position by repurchasing 500 futures contracts for $36,025,000 and realizing a profit of $6,475,000—thus offsetting the loss on its own bond issue.

This hedge was set up to be perfect (before considering brokerage commissions and the opportunity cost of the cash tied up to meet margin requirements). A perfect hedge would only occur if the maturities of Alaskagas' bonds were the same as those in the futures contract *and* if interest rates in Treasury Bond futures market exactly paralleled rate movements in the market for Alaskagas' bonds.

It should be observed that if interest rates had actually declined during this six-month period, Alaskagas would not be able to take advantage of this because this transaction hedges against interest rate movement in either direction.

Similar transactions could be undertaken in the equity futures (and options) markets in order to protect against unfavorable market price movements prior to an anticipated common stock offering. The growing number of financial futures and options instruments (discussed in Appendix 17A) have provided financial managers with new tools which can be used to help them manage capital costs.

Questions and Topics for Discussion

1. What is a financial futures contract?
2. What is the difference between a hedger and a speculator?
3. What is the difference between a short hedge and a long hedge?
4. If speculators expect interest rates to decline, would they want to buy or sell bond futures? Explain.
5. How can financial managers use futures contracts to control risk?

13

THE CAPITAL STRUCTURE DECISION

A Financial Dilemma

Coors versus Anheuser-Busch

When a firm has a high level of business risk, it usually seeks to balance this risk with a lower level of financial risk by employing lower levels of debt in its capital structure. The question of determining an optimal capital structure—one that will maximize the value of the firm—is an important one in financial management. Although it is usually not possible to derive a precise answer to this question, it is possible to identify a range of the capital structure over which a firm's cost of capital is likely to be near its minimum, resulting in a value for the firm that is likely to be near its maximum.

Nevertheless, some firms either choose to or are forced to operate outside this range. For example, the brewing industry is characterized by relatively high levels of operating leverage and subsequently high levels of business risk. The industry as a whole has a debt-to-total-assets ratio that averages a modest 40 percent. Coors has the reputation of being very conservative; it seeks to avoid debt financing whenever possible and has a debt-to-total-assets ratio of only 15 percent (with practically no long-term debt). In contrast, Anheuser-Busch (whose stock symbol is BUD) has a debt-to-total-assets ratio of about 35 percent.

On one hand, most analysts would probably conclude that Coors does not use financial leverage as effectively as it could and that this results in lower earnings and stock prices than might otherwise be possible. On the other hand, they would probably compliment BUD for using an appropriate amount of debt, resulting in a reasonable amount of risk and a stock price that is more nearly optimal from a capital structure standpoint. (In early 1986 the price-earnings ratio for Coors was 16 times, whereas it was 18 times for BUD.)

This chapter analyzes the capital structure decision and attempts to identify a firm's optimal capital structure—one consistent with the maximization of shareholder wealth.

Key Chapter Concepts

1. *Capital structure* is defined as the relative amount of permanent short-term debt, long-term debt, preferred stock, and common stock used to finance a firm. The *optimal* capital structure occurs at the point at which the cost of capital is minimized and firm value is maximized.

2. The value of the firm is *independent* of capital structure given perfect capital markets and no corporate income taxes.

3. The optimal capital structure consists entirely of debt if a corporate income tax exists and there are no bankruptcy or agency costs.

4. Given a corporate income tax, bankruptcy costs, and agency costs, an optimal capital structure consisting of both debt and equity is shown to exist.

5. *EBIT-EPS* analysis is an analytical technique that can be used to help determine the circumstances under which a firm should employ financial leverage. The *indifference point* in EBIT-EPS analysis is that level of EBIT where earnings per share are the same, regardless of which of two alternative capital structures is used.

Glossary of New Terms

Agency costs Costs incurred by owners of a firm when the firm is managed by others. Includes monitoring costs, bonding costs, and any losses which cannot be economically eliminated by monitoring and bonding.

Arbitrage The process of simultaneously buying and selling the same or equivalent securities in different markets to take advantage of temporary price differences.

Bankruptcy costs Costs related to financial distress, which are incurred by a firm as it increases its debt level.

Capital structure The amount of permanent short-term debt, long-term debt, preferred stock, and common equity used to finance a firm.

Debt capacity The amount of debt contained in a firm's optimal capital structure.

Financial structure The amount of current liabilities, long-term debt, preferred stock, and common equity used to finance a firm.

Indifference point That level of EBIT where the earnings per share of a firm are the same, regardless of which of two alternative capital structures is employed.

Net income theory A theory of capital structure which states that a firm's value increases as the level of debt in its capital structure increases.

Net operating income theory A theory of capital structure which states that a firm's value is independent of capital structure.

Optimal capital structure The capital structure that minimizes a firm's weighted cost of capital and, therefore, maximizes the value of the firm.

Target capital structure The proportions of permanent short-term debt, long-term debt, preferred stock, and common equity that a firm *desires* to have in its capital structure.

Introduction

This chapter considers how a firm analyzes its capital structure decision. *Capital structure* is defined as the amount of permanent short-term debt,[1] long-term debt, preferred stock, and common stock used to finance a firm. In contrast, *financial structure* refers to the amount of total current liabilities, long-term debt, preferred stock, and common stock used to finance a firm. Thus, capital structure is part of the financial structure, representing the permanent sources of the firm's financing. This chapter deals only with the total permanent sources of a firm's financing; the decision about what proportions of debt should be long-term and short-term is considered in Chapter 18.

To illustrate the capital structure concept, suppose that a company currently has $10 million in permanent short-term debt, $40 million in long-term debt outstanding, $10 million in preferred stock, and $40 million in common stock. In this case the company's current capital structure is said to be "50 percent debt, 10 percent preferred stock, and 40 percent common stock."[2] Thus, capital structure pertains to the permanent debt, preferred stock, and common equity portion of the balance sheet.

This chapter emphasizes the firm's long-range *target capital structure,* that is, the capital structure at which the firm ultimately plans to operate. For most companies the current and target capital structures are virtually identical, and calculating the target structure is a straightforward process. Occasionally, however, companies find it necessary to change from their current capital structure to a different target. The reasons for such a change may involve a change in the company's asset mix (and a resulting change in its risk), or an increase in competition that may imply more risk. For example, in response to increased risk and competition in the electric utility industry, Standard and Poor's, a bond rating agency, increased the desired proportions of equity in the capital structure of utilities associated with various bond rating categories. As a consequence many utilities have moved toward more conservative capital structures.

One reason why firms are concerned about their capital structure is that there appears to exist in practice a capital structure at which the *cost* to the firm *of* its employed *capital* is minimized. At this minimum-cost capital structure, the total value of the firm's securities is maximized; as a result, this minimum-cost capital structure is called the *optimal* capital structure. The amount of debt contained in a firm's optimal capital structure is referred to as its *debt capacity*.

This chapter considers the factors that influence the determination of an optimal capital structure and examines the relationship between capital structure, a firm's cost of capital, and the value of the firm. Capital structure theory is discussed first, and then various aspects of capital structure in practice are considered.

---

[1] *Permanent* short-term debt is contrasted with *seasonal* short-term debt.

[2] Companies normally do not distinguish in their capital structure between whether common equity is obtained by retained earnings or new common stock. In other words, only the *total* common shareholders' equity is considered, not the *relative* amounts in the common stock, contributed capital in excess of par, and retained earnings accounts.

Theoretical Perspectives on Capital Structure and Firm Valuation

This section considers some theoretical perspectives on capital structure and valuation. Two different theories, the *net income theory* and the *net operating income theory,* of capital structure and firm valuation are considered. Then the insightful research work of Franco Modigliani and Merton Miller is discussed. In 1958 these two prominent finance researchers showed that under certain assumptions, a firm's overall cost of capital, and therefore its value, is *independent* of capital structure. Finally, the remaining portions of this section analyze the effect of capital structure on firm valuation, given various assumptions about taxes, bankruptcy costs, and agency costs.

Net Income Theory and Net Operating Income Theory

Two contradictory capital structure theories—the net income theory and the net operating income theory—have existed for many years. Each is described briefly in the following paragraphs.

Net Income Theory   The *net income theory* of capital structure and valuation assumes that the cost of debt and the cost of equity remain constant as the firm's capital structure changes. In addition, the pretax cost of debt, k_d, is lower than the cost of equity, k_e, because debt is less risky than equity. Therefore, as a firm increases its leverage by increasing its level of debt relative to equity, the overall cost of capital, k_a, declines. This is shown in Figure 13-1. The importance of this lowered overall cost of capital is that the value of the firm is calculated by discounting the present value of its expected future cash flows by its overall cost of capital. Therefore, the more debt a firm has in its capital structure, the lower its overall cost of capital and therefore the higher its value.

Net Operating Income Theory   The *net operating income theory* of capital structure and valuation assumes that the cost of debt and the overall cost

Figure 13-1   **Net Income Theory of Capital Structure (No Taxes)**

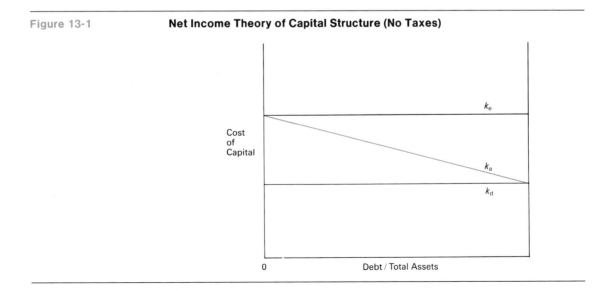

Figure 13-2   **Net Operating Income Theory of Capital Structure (No Taxes)**

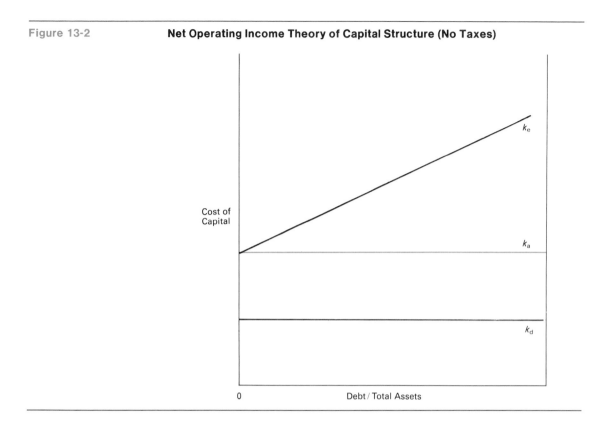

of capital are constant regardless of a firm's leverage position. However, as a firm increases its relative debt level, the cost of equity capital increases. The reason the cost of equity capital increases is that stockholders require a higher return due to the increased risk imposed by the additional debt. The net operating income theory further assumes that the increased cost of equity capital exactly offsets the benefit of the lower cost of debt so that the overall cost of capital does not change with changes in capital structure. This is illustrated in Figure 13-2.

The net operating income theory assumes that a firm's value is calculated by discounting its expected future operating income by its overall cost of capital. Since this theory assumes that the overall cost of capital is independent of capital structure, it follows that the firm's value is independent of capital structure.

Modigliani and Miller's Analysis

The preceding sections describe two different theories of valuation and capital structure. One, the net income theory, states that the value of the firm increases as the level of debt in its capital structure increases. The other, the net operating income theory, says that the value of the firm is independent of capital structure. Obviously, the two theories contradict each other, and both cannot be correct.

In their analysis, Modigliani and Miller (MM) argued that the net income theory of capital structure and valuation is not possible in perfect capital markets in which their assumptions hold.[3] MM use the notion of *arbitrage* to support their claims. *Arbitrage* is the process of simultaneously buying and selling the same or equivalent securities in different markets. For example, suppose that at a given moment, gold is selling at $400 an ounce in New York and $405 an ounce in London. Arbitragers would quickly and simultaneously buy gold in New York and sell it in London, thereby making a profit. In the process, however, they would bid up the New York price and bid down the London price, eliminating the price differential. Interestingly, the existence of arbitragers keeps the prices of the same or equivalent securities approximately equal in different markets.

In their analysis, MM assumed that *perfect* capital markets exist. This implies the following:

- There are no transactions costs for buying and selling securities.
- A sufficient number of buyers and sellers exists in the market, so no single person can have a signficant influence on security prices.
- Relevant information is readily available for individuals and is costless to obtain.
- All investors can borrow or lend at the same rate.

MM made several other assumptions. They assumed all investors are rational and have homogeneous expectations of a firm's earnings. Firms operating under similar conditions will face the same degree of business risk. This assumption is called the *homogeneous risk class assumption*. The final assumption made by MM is that there are no income taxes. In some of their work, MM relax this assumption and consider their analysis in a world in which corporate income taxes exist.

MM state that the net income theory is not possible. Suppose two firms in the same industry differed only in that one was *levered* (that is, it had some debt in its capital structure) and the other was *unlevered* (that is, it had no debt in its capital structure). By simply changing its capital structure, the unlevered firm would require a reward (in the form of an increase in the firm's value) from stockholders for doing so. However, in the perfect capital market without transactions costs, MM argue that stockholders would not reward the firm for increasing its debt. Stockholders could change *their own* financial debt-equity structure without cost to receive an equal return. Therefore, stockholders would not increase their opinion of the value of an unlevered firm just because it took on some debt.

The MM major argument against the net income approach is the arbitrage process. If one of two unlevered firms with identical business risk took on some debt, then according to the net income theory, its value should increase and therefore so would the value of its stock. MM suggest that under these circumstances, investors will sell the overpriced stock of the levered firm. They can then use an arbitrage process of borrowing, buying the unlevered firm's stock and investing the excess funds

---

[3] Franco Modigliani, and Merton Miller. "The Cost of Capital, Corporation Finance, and the Theory of Investment." *American Economic Review* 48 (June 1958): 261–296.

elsewhere. Through these costless transactions, investors can increase their return without increasing their risk. Hence, they have substituted their own personal financial leverage for corporate leverage. MM argue that this arbitrage process will continue until the selling of the levered firm's stock drives down its price to the point where it is equal to the unlevered firm's stock price, which has been driven up due to increased buying.

The arbitrage process occurs so rapidly that the market values of the levered and unlevered firms are equal. Thus, MM conclude that *the value of a firm is independent of its capital structure in perfect capital markets with no income taxes.* This result is illustrated in the following section with an example.

The major criticisms of the MM analysis are based on the assumptions made. First, MM assume costless transactions, which do not exist. Investors pay a cost for their transactions in the market and therefore would want to limit them. Also, MM assume that personal and corporate leverage are equally risky. However, an individual with an investment in a levered company stands to lose only the stock investment. In contrast, if the investor borrows and invests funds, he or she can lose both the stock investment and the borrowed funds, as well as still be held responsible for paying off the debt. The assumption that individuals and corporations can borrow and lend at the same rate is also not necessarily true. And if the borrowing costs are not similar, the arbitrage process may not be possible.

Capital Structure Without a Corporate Income Tax

The following analysis assumes that the net operating income theory holds and that no corporate income tax exists. Table 13-1 contains financial data on two firms, U and L, which have equal levels of operating risk and differ only in their capital structure. Firm U is unlevered and firm L is levered, with a perpetual debt, D, of $2,000 in its capital structure. For simplicity, we assume that the income of both firms which is available for stockholders is paid out as dividends. As a result, the expected growth rate of both firms is zero, since no income is available for the firms to reinvest.

Table 13-1

Capital Structure without a Corporate Income Tax: Financial Data on Firms U and L

	Firm U	Firm L
Equity amount in capital structure	$10,000	$8,000
Cost of equity, k_e	10%	11.25%
Debt amount in capital structure	—	$2,000
Cost of debt, k_d	—	5%
Net operating income	$ 1,000	$1,000
Less: Interest payments to debtholders	—	100
Income available to stockholders, dividend	$ 1,000	$ 900
Total income available to security holders	$ 1,000	$1,000

The present value of both firms is calculated using the following perpetuity valuation equation:

$$\text{Value of firm} = \text{Value of equity} + \text{Value of debt,}$$

$$= \frac{Div}{k_e} + \frac{I}{k_d}, \tag{13.1}$$

where Div is the annual amount of dividends paid to the firm's stockholders, I is the interest paid on the firm's debt, k_e is the return required on common equity, and k_d is the return required on debt. The required return on debt k_d is assumed to equal the coupon rate on the debt, i. For firm U, the present value of the expected future cash flows is $10,000, calculated as follows:

$$\text{Value of firm U} = \frac{\$1,000}{0.10},$$

$$= \$10,000.$$

For firm L, the present value is also $10,000, calculated as follows:

$$\text{Value of firm L} = \frac{\$\ 900}{0.1125} + \frac{\$100}{0.05},$$

$$= \$\ 8,000 + \$2,000,$$

$$= \$10,000.$$

Thus, the values of firms U and L are equal. This example shows that the value of the firm is independent of capital structure, assuming that the net operating income theory holds and no corporate income tax exists.

Capital Structure With a Corporate Income Tax

Next, the relationship between capital structure and firm value is considered, assuming that a corporate income tax exists. Table 13-2 shows financial data for an unlevered firm, U, and a levered firm, L. The total

---

Table 13-2   **Capital Structure with a Corporate Income Tax: Financial Data on Firms U and L**

	Firm U	Firm L
Equity amount in capital structure	$6,000	$4,000
Cost of equity, k_e	10%	11.25%
Debt amount in capital structure, D	—	$2,000
Cost of debt, k_d	—	5%
Net operating income	$1,000	$1,000
Less: Interest payments to debtholders	—	100
Income before taxes	$1,000	$ 900
Corporate tax, $t = 40\%$	400	360
Income available to stockholders, dividend	$ 600	$ 540
Total income available to security holders	$ 600	$ 640

income available to the security holders of firm U is $600, and assuming a cost of equity capital equal to 10 percent, the value of firm U is calculated, using Equation 13.1, to be $6,000.

Because interest paid to debtholders is a tax-deductible expense, the total income available to the debt and equity security holders of firm L, shown in Table 13-2, is $640. This amount is greater than the $600 available to the firm U equity security holders by $40. The $40 amount is the tax shield caused by the tax deductibility of the interest payments. The annual tax shield amount is calculated using the following equation:

$$\text{Tax shield amount} = i \times D \times t, \tag{13.2}$$
$$= (0.05) \times (2000) \times (0.40),$$
$$= \$40.$$

The total value of firm L is obtained using Equation 13.1:

$$\text{Value of firm L} = \frac{Div}{k_e} + \frac{I}{k_d}$$
$$= \frac{\$540}{0.1125} + \frac{\$100}{0.05}$$
$$= \$4800 + \$2000$$
$$= \$6800$$

In this example the value of firm L is greater than firm U's value by an amount equal to $800. This difference in value is caused by the tax shield. In fact, the difference in value between the levered and unlevered firm is equal to the present value of the tax shield from the perpetual debt:

$$\text{Present value of tax shield} = \frac{i \times D \times t}{i}$$
$$= D \times t \tag{13.3}$$

In this equation, the annual tax shield amount, $i\,D\,t$, is discounted at a rate, $i\,(i = k_d)$. In the case of firm L, the present value of the tax shield is $800, calculated as follows:

$$\text{Present value of tax shield} = \$2,000 \times 0.40,$$
$$= \$800.$$

We can now state that the present value of the levered firm is equal to the present value of the unlevered firm plus the present value of the tax shield:

$$\begin{array}{ccc} \text{Value of} & \text{Value of} & \text{Value of} \\ \text{levered firm} = \text{unlevered firm} & + & \text{tax shield.} \end{array} \tag{13.4}$$

From this equation we can conclude, using the net operating income theory with the existence of a corporate income tax, that the value of the

Figure 13-3   **Value of the Firm as a Function of Capital Structure (With Corporate Income Tax)**

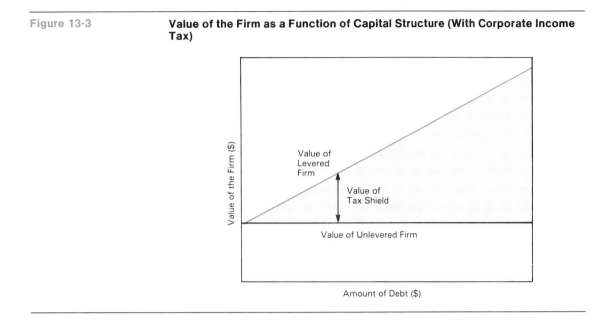

firm increases linearly as the amount of debt in the capital structure increases, as shown in Figure 13-3. This result implies that a firm should increase its level of debt to the point at which the capital structure consists entirely of debt. In other words, the value of the firm is maximized and its optimal capital structure is achieved when capital structure is all debt.[4]

In practice, however, we normally do not observe companies with extremely high levels of debt in their capital structure. Therefore, something must be wrong with our analysis in this section. In terms of the real world, our analysis simply is incomplete; it does not consider bankruptcy and agency costs. These costs are considered in the following section.

Capital Structure With a Corporate Income Tax, Bankruptcy Costs, and Agency Costs

The capital structure analysis in this section assumes a corporate income tax and assumes that bankruptcy and agency costs exist.

Bankruptcy Costs   From a practical viewpoint, a firm cannot expect to gain the benefits associated with the tax deductibility of interest payments without also increasing certain costs. One significant cost category is the costs of financial distress, or bankruptcy. As a firm increases its debt level, lenders may demand very high interest payments to compensate for the increased financial risk taken on by the firm. The high interest payments constitute a cost to the firm. In the extreme, lenders may choose not to lend at all. Under these conditions, the firm may have to forego acceptable projects. Thus, the firm incurs an opportunity cost. In addition, some customers and potential customers may lose confidence in the firm's ability to continue in existence and instead buy from other companies

---

[4] The optimal capital structure consisting entirely of debt sometimes is referred to as the *MM corner solution.*

more likely to remain in business. This loss of customer confidence is another form of bankruptcy cost. As a company experiences cash flow, or insolvency, problems, it may incur legal and accounting costs as it attempts to financially restructure itself. Finally, if the firm is forced to liquidate, assets may have to be sold at less than their market values. These costs are also a form of bankruptcy cost.

The likelihood of bankruptcy is not a linear function of a firm's debt ratio. Rather, there is evidence that it increases at an increasing rate beyond some threshold level. Accordingly, bankruptcy costs also become more important beyond this threshold debt ratio.

Agency Costs In most large firms the security holders (often referred to as the "principals"), both debtholders and common stockholders, are not in a position to actively manage the firm's investment, financing, and daily operational activities. These security holders must employ "agents" to carry out these important activities. Under these circumstances conflicts can develop between the interests of the principal and those of the agent. For example, in the case of the choice of debt versus common equity financing, the debtholders can be viewed as the principal and the common stockholders can be viewed as the agents, since the common stockholders are in a position to direct the investment and financing decisions of the firm through the elected board of directors and the managers hired by the board.[5]

When debt is used in the capital structure of a firm, there are incentives for the common stockholders to undertake actions which may be detrimental to the interests of the debtholders. These actions include investing in projects with a higher risk level and a lower net present value. This is so because in the presence of debt, the stock of a firm can be viewed as if it is a call option on the firm. The value of this option increases with the variance of the underlying assets—in this case the investment projects of the firm. (Chapter 17 contains a detailed discussion of the determinants of the value of an option). Also, the presence of debt may lead a firm to forego otherwise profitable investments under certain circumstances. Finally, in the absence of restraints, stockholders are inclined to increase the proportions of debt in the capital structure continually, thus diminishing the protection afforded to the earlier bondholders.

The agency theory literature in finance and economics indicates that under these circumstances monitoring and bonding expenses will be incurred in order to reduce the incidence of these agency problems. It has been shown that debtholders will anticipate these agency problems and the associated monitoring and bonding costs and charge a higher rate of interest to the firm to account for these costs. Thus the costs of agency relationships between debtholders and stockholders will be borne by the agent, the stockholders in this case. The greater the required monitoring and bonding costs, the greater will be the interest rate charged by debtholders.

In order to fully protect debtholders, extremely detailed protective

---

[5] See A. Barnea, R. Haugen, and L. Senbet, *Agency Problems and Financial Contracting*, Englewood Cliffs, N.J.: Prentice-Hall, 1985, for an excellent overview of the agency problem issue.

convenants would have to be in place and high monitoring costs would be incurred. At the limit, all decisions of the firm would be subject to review by the debtholders. This is obviously not feasible. In addition to its high cost, the firm also would not be able to operate efficiently under these circumstances. Since the stockholders of the firm will bear the costs of the agency relationship between debtholders and stockholders, the stockholders have an incentive to see that monitoring is done efficiently. Without any protective covenants and monitoring, the interest rate charged by debtholders would be very high. Monitoring and bonding activities should be carried out by the firm up to the point that the reduction in the interest rate charged by debtholders is balanced against the cost of additional monitoring and bonding activities. With increasing amounts of debt, the demands by debtholders for increased monitoring of the actions of the firm are also likely to increase.

Thus agency costs can be viewed as an increasing function of the proportion of debt in the capital structure of a firm. Because of this, we have another powerful reason why a firm may choose a value-maximizing capital structure which is less than the 100 percent debt corner solution prescribed by MM.

The Value-Maximizing Capital Structure   When a corporate income tax exists, and when there are positive bankruptcy and agency costs associated with increasing amounts of debt in a capital structure, the value of the firm as a function of its capital structure can be shown as in Figure 13-4. As is indicated in this figure, the present value of the expected bankruptcy costs and the agency costs associated with debt financing offset the present value of the tax shield accruing from debt—resulting in an interior

Figure 13-4   **Value of the Firm as a Function of Capital Structure (With Corporate Income Tax, Bankruptcy Costs, and Agency Costs)**

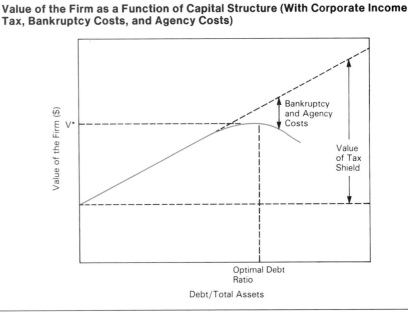

optimal (value-maximizing) capital structure. The value of the firm is equal to V* at the optimal debt ratio.

Capital Structure Decisions Using EBIT-EPS Analysis

One basic issue regarding capital structure involves the question of whether a firm should use debt or equity financing. This question logically should be viewed from the standpoint of the firm's stockholders, and the answer depends essentially on the firm's level of operating income.

Consider the Yuma Corporation with a present capital structure consisting only of common stock (35 million shares). Assume that Yuma is considering an expansion and is evaluating two alternative financing plans.[6] Plan 1, equity financing, would involve the sale of an additional 15 million shares of common stock at $20 each. Plan 2, debt financing, would involve the sale of $300 million of 10 percent long-term debt.

If the firm adopts Plan 1, it remains totally equity financed. If, however, the firm adopts Plan 2, it becomes partially debt financed (leveraged). Because Plan 2 involves the use of financial leverage, this financing issue is basically one of whether it is in the best interests of the firm's existing stockholders to employ financial leverage.

An analytical technique called *EBIT-EPS analysis*[7] can be used to help determine when debt financing is advantageous and when equity financing is advantageous. Table 13-3 illustrates the calculation of EPS at two different assumed levels of EBIT for both financing plans. Since the relationship between EBIT and EPS is linear, the two points calculated in Table 13-3 can be used to graph the relationship for each financing plan; this is shown in Figure 13-5.

In this example, earnings per share at EBIT levels less than $100 million are higher using the equity financing alternative. Correspondingly, at EBIT levels greater than $100 million, earnings per share are higher with debt financing. The $100 million figure is called the *EBIT-EPS indifference point*. By definition, the earnings per share for the debt and equity financing alternatives are equal at the EBIT-EPS indifference point:

$$\text{EPS (debt financing)} = \text{EPS (equity financing)}. \qquad (13.5)$$

This equation may be rewritten as follows:

$$\frac{(\text{EBIT} - \text{Interest for debt alternative}) \times (1 - \text{Tax rate}) - \text{Preferred dividends}}{\text{Number of common shares for debt alternative}}$$

$$= \frac{(\text{EBIT} - \text{Interest for equity alternative}) \times (1 - \text{Tax rate}) - \text{Preferred dividends}}{\text{Number of common shares for equity alternative}} \cdot$$

$$\frac{(\text{EBIT} - I_d)(1 - t) - P}{N_d} = \frac{(\text{EBIT} - I_e)(1 - t) - P}{N_e}, \qquad (13.6)$$

[6] Preferred stock is not included in this example because it merely complicates the matter. Because preferred stock is a fixed income security, it would be treated much like debt in this example.

[7] To review briefly, EBIT is earnings before interest and taxes, or operating income; EPS is earnings per share.

Table 13-3 **EBIT-EPS Analysis—Yuma Corporation (All Figures Except Per-Share Amounts Are in Millions of Dollars)***

	EBIT = $75	EBIT = $125
Equity Financing (Plan 1)		
EBIT	$75	$125
Interest	—	—
EBT	$75	$125
Taxes @ 40%	30	50
EAT	$ 45	$ 75
Shares outstanding	50	50
EPS	$ 0.90	$ 1.50
% change in EBIT		+66.67%
% change in EPS		+66.67%
Debt Financing (Plan 2)		
EBIT	$ 75	$125
Interest	30	30
EBT	$ 45	$ 95
Taxes @ 40%	18	38
EAT	$ 27	$ 57
Shares outstanding	35	35
EPS	$ 0.77	$ 1.63
% change in EBIT		+66.67%
% change in EPS		+112%

*EBIT = earnings before interest and taxes; EBT = earnings before taxes; EAT = earnings after taxes; EPS = earnings per share.

Figure 13-5 **EBIT-EPS Analysis**

where EBIT is earnings before interest and taxes, I_d is the firm's total interest payments if the debt alternative is chosen, I_e is the firm's total interest payments if the equity alternative is chosen, and N_d and N_e represent the number of common shares outstanding for the debt and equity alternatives, respectively. The firm's effective tax rate is indicated as t, and P is the amount of preferred dividends for the firm. This equation may be used to calculate directly the EBIT level at which earnings per share for the two alternatives are equal. The data from the example shown in Table 13-3 yield the EBIT level of $100 million at the indifference point:

$$\frac{(\text{EBIT} - \$30)(1 - 0.4) - 0}{35} = \frac{(\text{EBIT} - \$0)(1 - 0.4) - 0}{50} .$$

$$50(0.6 \text{ EBIT} - \$18) = 35 \times 0.6 \text{ EBIT}.$$

$$30 \text{ EBIT} - \$900 = 21 \text{ EBIT}.$$

$$9 \text{ EBIT} = \$900.$$

$$\text{EBIT} = \$100.$$

Note that in the equity alternative, a 67 percent increase in EBIT (from $75 million to $125 million) results in a 67 percent increase in earnings per share (from $0.90 to $1.50) or a degree of financial leverage of 1.0. In the debt alternative, a 67 percent increase in EBIT results in a 112 percent increase in earnings per share or a degree of financial leverage of 1.67. A similar magnification of earnings per share will occur if EBIT declines. This wider variation in earnings per share, which occurs with the debt financing alternative, is an illustration of *financial risk,* since financial risk is defined as the increased variability in earnings per share due to the firm's use of debt. All other things being equal, an increase in the proportion of debt financing is said to increase the financial risk of the firm.

Financial Leverage and Stock Prices

A more important question involves the impact of financial leverage on the firm's common stock price. Specifically, which financing alternative results in the higher stock price? Suppose the Yuma Corporation is able to operate at the $125 million EBIT level. Then, if the company chooses the debt financing alternative, its EPS will equal $1.63, and if it chooses the equity alternative, its EPS will be $1.50. But the stock price depends on the price-earnings (P/E) ratio that the stock market assigns to each alternative. Suppose the stock market assigns a P/E ratio of 10.0 to the company's common stock if the equity alternative is chosen, and a P/E ratio of 9.8 if the debt alternative is chosen. The common stock price, P_0, can be calculated for both alternatives as follows:

$$P_0 = (\text{P/E ratio})(\text{EPS}).$$

Equity alternative:

$$P_0 = (10.0)(\$1.50) = \$15.$$

Debt alternative:

$$P_0 = (9.8)(\$1.63) = \$15.97, \text{ or approximately } \$16.$$

These calculations show that in this case the stock market places a higher value on the company's stock if the debt alternative is chosen rather than the equity alternative. Notice that the stock market assigned a slightly lower P/E ratio to the debt alternative. The stock market recognized the increased financial risk associated with the debt alternative, but this increased risk was more than offset by the increased EPS possible with the use of debt.

To carry the Yuma Corporation example one important step further, suppose the company, while operating at the $125 million EBIT level, chooses an even higher debt capital structure, which causes its EPS to increase to $2.25. Suppose further that the stock market feels that this high debt capital structure significantly increases the company's financial risk—to the point where bankruptcy could occur if EBIT levels turned downward in a recession. If the stock market assigns a P/E of 6.0, for example, the stock price would be $13.50, or $2.25 × 6.0, and it would be clear that this change in capital structure is not desirable.

It is important to emphasize that the P/E ratios in the above example are simply assumptions. As an analytical technique, EBIT-EPS analysis does not provide a complete solution to the optimal capital structure question.

In summary, the firm can potentially show increased earnings to its stockholders by increasing its level of financial risk. However, since increases in risk tend to increase the cost of capital (which is analogous to a decrease in the P/E ratio), the firm's management has to assess the tradeoff between the higher earnings per share for its stockholders and the higher costs of capital.

Additional Cost of Capital and Capital Structure Considerations

The preceding chapter developed the concept of a weighted cost of capital. This section continues to explore that topic by examining the functional relationship between the cost of capital and the firm's capital structure.

Assuming that the right-hand side of the balance sheet contains only permanent debt and common equity, leverage may be defined as the relative amount of debt in the firm's capital structure and measured by the debt ratio $D/(D + E)$, where D is debt and E is equity.

The first step in the analysis considers the relationship between the cost of debt and capital structure. All other things being equal, investors in debt consider the debt less risky if the firm has a low, rather than high, proportion of debt in its capital structure. As the proportion of debt in the capital structure increases, investors require a higher return on the more risky debt. And since the firm's cost of capital is the investor's required return, the cost of debt increases as the proportion of debt increases.

The precise relationshp between the cost of debt and the debt ratio is difficult to determine. This is due to the fact that it is impossible to observe the cost of debt at two different capital structures (at the same time) for a single firm. Nevertheless, there is good evidence that the cost of debt increases rather slowly for moderate amounts of debt. There is some point at which the capital markets consider any new debt "excessive" and therefore much more risky. The cost of debt curve, k_i, in Figure 13-6 illustrates such a relationship. The actual region where the cost of debt begins to increase more rapidly varies by firm and industry, depending on the firm's level of business risk.

The next step in this analysis focuses on the relationship between the cost of equity capital and capital structure. When a firm has a low debt ratio, any equity employed is less risky than equity used when the firm is financed with a relatively high proportion of debt. Earlier in this chapter it was shown that the greater the fraction of debt used, the greater the variability in earnings per common share. In addition, the greater the fraction of debt used, the greater the risk of bankruptcy. Because the returns expected by stockholders in the form of present and future dividends depend partly on current earnings, it can be concluded that variability in earnings per common share can result in variability of the returns to investors, that is, greater risk. Thus, it can be stated that investors' required returns and the cost of equity capital increase as the relative amount of debt used to finance the firm increases.

Once again, the exact nature of the relationship between the cost of equity and the debt ratio is difficult to determine in practice. However, there is agreement that the cost of equity capital increases at a relatively slow rate as the debt proportion increases up to moderate amounts. Then, in the range where additional debt is viewed as "excessive" and much more risky, the cost of equity increases more rapidly. This is shown in Figure 13-6. As is true in the debt illustration, the region where the cost of equity capital, k_e, begins to increase more rapidly varies by firm and industry.

The relationship between the weighted cost of capital, k_a, and the debt proportion can now be considered. The following equation (Equation 12.18),

$$k_a = \left(\frac{E}{D + E}\right)(k_e) + \left(\frac{D}{D + E}\right)k_i,$$

can be used to calculate k_a for any debt ratio, provided that the values of k_e and k_i at the debt ratio are known. Since the relationships between the debt ratio and k_i and k_e have been developed, the relationship between k_a and the debt ratio follows accordingly. The k_a curve, shown in Figure 13-6, begins at $k_a = k_e$, since by definition the weighted cost of capital for an all-equity firm equals the cost of equity. As even small increments of debt are used, k_a becomes lower; as the debt proportion continues to increase from moderate to excessive, k_a "bottoms out" and then begins to increase. The resulting saucer-shaped curve contains a point at which the firm's overall cost of capital is minimized and its value maximized. This point is the firm's *optimal capital structure*. If the firm is thought of as a cash flow generator, it can be seen that the lower the discount rate (the weighted cost of capital), the higher the firm's value.

Given the importance of an optimal capital structure, it is logical to ask how a firm knows when it is operating at its optimal capital structure. Unfortunately, the answer is that the firm cannot determine this exactly.

Figure 13-6

Overall Cost of Capital as a Function of Capital Structure

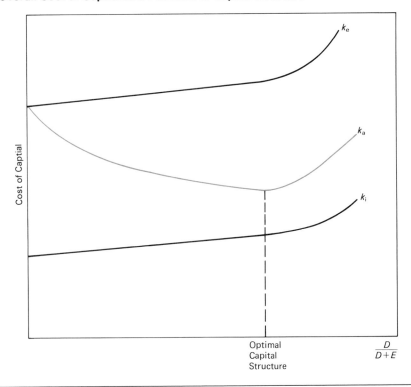

This is not a great problem, however, since the optimal capital structure, in practice, is best depicted as a range of values. Many companies are able to conclude that they are operating near their optimal range by examining how their interest costs behave as their debt proportion is increased. Comparison with other companies in the industry should also help a firm determine whether it can safely increase its proportion of "moderate" debt and reduce its weighted cost of capital.

Determining an Optimal Capital Structure: An Integrative Approach

The tools of EBIT-EPS analysis and the theory of an optimal capital structure can help a firm decide on an appropriate capital structure. This section utilizes an example to develop a five-step procedure designed to assist financial managers in making capital structure decisions.

Balboa Department Stores has been 100 percent financed with equity funds since the firm was founded. While analyzing a major expansion program, the firm has decided to consider alternative capital structures. In particular, it has been suggested that the firm should use this expansion program as an opportunity to increase the long-term debt ratio from the current level of 0 percent to a new level of 30 percent. Interest on the proposed new debt will amount to $100,000 per year.

- **Step 1** Compute the expected level of EBIT after the expansion. Based on Balboa's past operating experience and a projection of the impact of the expansion, it estimates its expected EBIT to be $500,000 per year under normal operating circumstances.

- **Step 2** Estimate the variability of this level of operating income. Based on the past performance of the company over several business cycles, the standard deviation of operating income is estimated to be $200,000 per year. (Operating income is assumed to be normally distributed, or at least approximately so.)

- **Step 3** Compute the indifference point between the two financing alternatives—add new debt or maintain the all-equity capital structure. Using the techniques of EBIT-EPS analysis previously discussed, the indifference point is computed to be $300,000.

- **Step 4** Analyze these estimates in the context of the risk the firm is willing to assume.

  After considerable discussion, it has been decided that the firm is willing to accept a 25 percent chance that operating earnings in any year will be below the indifference point, and a 5 percent chance that the firm will have to report a loss in any year. To complete this analysis, it is necessary to compute the probability that operating earnings will be below the indifference point, that is, the probability that EBIT will be less than $300,000. This is equivalent on the standard normal curve to the following:

$$z = \frac{\$300,000 - \$500,000}{\$200,000}$$

$$= -1.0,$$

or 1.0 standard deviation below the mean. The probability that EBIT will be less than 1.0 standard deviation below the mean is 15.87 percent; this is determined from Table V at the end of the book. Thus on the basis of the indifference point criterion, the proposed new capital structure appears acceptable. The probability of incurring losses must now be analyzed. This is the probability that EBIT will be less than the required interest payments of $100,000. On the standard normal curve, this corresponds to the following:

$$z = \frac{\$100,000 - \$500,000}{\$200,000}$$

$$= -2.0,$$

or 2.0 standard deviations below the mean. The probability that EBIT will be less than 2.0 standard deviations below the mean is 2.28 percent, as shown in Table V. According to this criterion, the proposed capital structure also seems acceptable.

If either or both of these tests had shown the proposed capital structure to have an unacceptable level of risk, the analysis would have been repeated for lower levels of debt than the proposed 30 percent rate. Similarly, since the proposed capital structure has exceeded the standards set by the firm, management might want to consider even higher levels of debt than the proposed 30 percent.

- **Step 5** Examine the market evidence to determine whether the proposed capital structure is too risky in relation to the following: the firm's level of business risk, industry norms for leverage ratios and coverage ratios, and the recommendations of the firm's investment bankers.

  This step is undertaken only after a proposed capital structure has met the "internal" tests for acceptability. Financial leverage is a two-edged sword: it enhances expected returns, but is also increases risk. If the increase in perceived risk is greater than the increase in expected returns, the firm's weighted cost of capital may rise instead of fall, and the firm's value will decline.

  It is important to note that there is no need for a firm to feel constrained by industry standards in setting its own capital structures. If, for example, a firm has traditionally been more profitable than the average firm in the industry, or if a firm's operating income is more stable than the operating income of the average firm, a higher level of financial leverage probably can be tolerated. The final choice of a capital structure involves a careful analysis of expected future returns and risks relative to other firms in the industry.

Summary

- *Capital structure* is defined as the relative amount of permanent short-term debt, long-term debt, preferred stock, and common stock used to finance a firm. The capital structure decision is important to the firm, because there exists in practice a capital structure at which the *cost of capital* is minimized. This minimum-cost capital structure is the *optimal* capital structure, because the value of the firm is maximized at this point.
- The *net income theory* of capital structure states that a firm's value increases as the level of debt in its capital structure increases. The *net operating income theory* states that a firm's value is independent of capital structure.
- Modigliani and Miller show that the value of the firm is *independent* of capital structure given perfect capital markets and no corporate income taxes. MM also show that the optimal capital structure consists entirely of debt if a corporate income tax exists.
- Given a corporate income tax, bankruptcy costs, and agency costs, an optimal capital structure consisting of both debt and equity is shown to exist.
- *EBIT-EPS analysis* is an analytical technique that can be used to help determine the circumstances under which a firm should employ financial leverage. Basically, it involves calculating earnings per share at different levels of EBIT for debt and equity financing plans. This information may then be used to graph earnings per share versus EBIT to determine the EBIT levels at which financial leverage is advantageous to the firm.
- The *indifference point* in EBIT-EPS analysis is that level of EBIT where earnings per share are the same, regardless of which of two alternative capital structures is used. At EBIT levels greater than the indifference level, more financially levered capital structures will pro-

duce higher levels of earnings per share; at EBIT levels less than the indifference point, less financially levered capital structures will produce higher levels of earnings per share.

- A firm can analyze its capital structure decision by performing an EBIT-EPS analysis, computing the risk of unfavorable financial leverage at its expected level of operating income, and analyzing financial leverage ratios and coverage ratios for other firms in the industry. A careful evaluation of these facts, together with an analysis of the firm's business risk, can assist in making the final determination regarding the desirability of a proposed capital structure.

Questions and Topics for Discussion

1. What are the differences between the net income theory and the net operating income theory of capital structure and firm valuation?
2. What is arbitrage?
3. Explain the research results of Modigliani and Miller in the area of capital structure.
4. What is the relationship between the value of a firm and its capital structure without a corporate income tax? With a corporate income tax?
5. What is the relationship between the value of a firm and its capital structure, given the existence of a corporate income tax, bankruptcy costs, and agency costs?
6. What are the major limitations of EBIT-EPS analysis as a technique to determine the optimal capital structure?
7. In practice, how can a firm determine whether or not it is operating at (or near) its optimal capital structure?
8. Under what circumstances should a firm use *more* debt in its capital structure than is used by the "average" firm in the industry? When should it use *less* debt than the "average" firm?
9. Why do public utilities typically have capital structures with about 50 percent debt, whereas major oil companies average about 25 percent debt in their capital structures?

Problems*

1. Referring back to Table 13-1, calculate the value of firm L (without a corporate income tax) if the equity amount in its capital structure decreases to $5,000, and the debt amount increases to $5,000. At this capital structure the cost of equity is 15.0 percent.
2. Referring back to Table 13-2, calculate the value of firm L (with a corporate income tax) if the equity amount in its capital structure decreases to $3,000, and the debt amount increases to $3,000.
3. For firm L in Problem 2 (with equity = $3,000 and debt = $3,000), calculate the income available to the stockholders and the cost of equity.
4. Piedmont Instruments Corporation has estimated the following costs of debt and equity capital for various fractions of debt in its capital structure:

Debt Fraction	k_i	k_e With Bankruptcy Costs and Without Agency Costs	k_e With Bankruptcy and Agency Costs
0.00	—	12.00	12.00
0.10	4.8	12.05	12.05

* Color numbers denote problems which have check answers provided at the end of the book.

Debt Fraction	k_i	k_e With Bankruptcy Costs and Without Agency Costs	k_e With Bankruptcy and Agency Costs
0.30	4.9	12.10	12.20
0.40	5.0	12.20	12.60
0.45	5.2	12.40	13.40
0.50	5.7	12.80	14.80
0.60	7.0	15.00	18.00

  a. Based on these data, determine the company's optimal capital structure, (i) with bankruptcy costs and without agency costs, and (ii) with bankruptcy and agency costs.

b. Suppose the company's actual capital structure is 50 percent debt and 50 percent equity. How much higher is k_a at this capital structure than at the optimal value of k_a, with bankruptcy and agency costs.

c. Is it necessary in practice for the company to know precisely its optimal capital structure? Why?

Lotus123

5. Emco Products has a present capital structure consisting only of common stock (10.0 million shares). The company is planning a major expansion. At this time the company is undecided between the following two financing plans (assume a 40 percent marginal tax rate):

• Equity financing. Under this plan, an additional 5.0 million shares of common stock will be sold at $10 each.

• Debt financing. Under this plan, $50 million of 10 percent long-term debt will be sold.

One piece of information the company desires for its decision analysis is an EBIT-EPS analysis.

  a. Calculate the EBIT-EPS indifference point.

b. Graphically determine the EBIT-EPS indifference point.

Hint: Use EBIT = $10 million and $25 million.

c. What happens to the indifference point if the interest rate on debt increases and the common stock sales price remains constant?

d. What happens to the indifference point if the interest rate on debt remains constant and the common stock sales price increases?

6. Two capital goods manufacturing companies, Rock Island and Davenport, are virtually identical in all aspects of their operations—product lines, amount of sales, total size, and so on. The two companies differ only in their capital structures, as shown here:

	Rock Island	Davenport
Debt (8%)	$400 million	$100 million
Common equity	$600 million	$900 million
Number of common shares outstanding	30 million	45 million

Each company has $1,000 million ($1 billion) in total assets.

    Capital goods manufacturers are typically subject to cyclical trends in the economy. Suppose that the EBIT level for both companies is $100 million during an expansion and $60 million during a recession. (Assume a 40 percent tax rate for both companies.)

  a. Calculate the earnings per share for both companies during expansion and recession.

b. Which stock is riskier? Why?

c. At what EBIT level are the earnings per share of the two companies identical?

d. Calculate the common stock price for both companies during an expansion if the stock market assigns a price-earnings ratio of 10 to Davenport and 9 to Rock Island.

7. Morton Industries is considering opening a new subsidiary in Boston, to be operated as a separate company. The company's financial analysts expect the new facility's average EBIT level to be $6 million per year. At this time the company is considering the following two financing plans (use a 40 percent marginal tax rate in your analysis):

- *Plan 1.* Equity financing. Under this plan, 2 million common shares will be sold at $10 each.
- *Plan 2.* Debt-equity financing. Under this plan, $10 million of 12 percent long-term debt and 1 million common shares at $10 each will be sold.

a. Calculate the EBIT-EPS indifference point.

b. Calculate the expected EPS for both financing plans.

c. What factors should the company consider in deciding which financing plan to adopt?

d. Which plan do you recommend the company adopt?

8. This problem is an extension of Problem 7. Suppose Morton adopts Plan 2, and the Boston facility does initially operate at an annual EBIT level of $6 million.

a. What is the times interest earned ratio?

b. If the lenders require that the new company maintain a times interest earned ratio equal to 3.5 or greater, by how much could the EBIT level drop and the company still be in compliance with the loan agreement?

9. This problem is an extension of Problem 7. Suppose the expected annual EBIT level of $6 million is normally distributed with a standard deviation of $3 million. What is the probability that the EPS will be negative in any given year, if Plan 1 is selected?

10. High Sky, Inc., a hot air balloon manufacturing firm, currently has the following simplified balance sheet:

Assets		Liabilities and Capital	
Total assets	$1,100,000	Bonds (10% interest)	$ 600,000
		Common stock at par ($3), 100,000 shares outstanding	300,000
		Contributed capital in excess of par	100,000
		Retained earnings	100,000
		Total liabilities and capital	$1,100,000

The company is planning an expansion that is expected to cost $600,000. It can be financed with new equity (sold to net the company $4 per share) or with the sale of new bonds at an interest rate of 11 percent. (The firm's marginal tax rate is 40 percent.)

a. Compute the indifference point between the two financing alternatives.

b. If the expected level of EBIT for the firm is $240,000 with a standard deviation of $50,000, what is the probability that the debt financing alternative will produce higher earnings than the equity alternative? (EBIT is normally distributed.)

c. If the debt alternative is chosen, what is the probability that the company will have negative earnings per share in any period?

11. The Anaya Corporation is a leader in artificial intelligence research. Anaya's present capital structure consists of common stock (30 million shares) and debt ($250 million with an interest rate of 15 percent). The company is planning an expansion and wishes to examine alternative financing plans. The firm's marginal tax rate is 40 percent. Two alternatives which are under consideration are:

- Common equity financing. Under this plan an additional 3 million shares of common stock will be sold at $20 each.
- Debt financing. Under this plan the firm would sell $30 million of first mortgage bonds with a pre-tax cost of 14 percent and $30 million of debentures with a pre-tax cost of 15 percent.

  a. Compute the indifference point between these two alternatives.
  b. One of Anaya's artificially intelligent financial managers has suggested that the firm might be better off to finance with preferred stock rather than common stock. He has suggested that the indifference point be computed between the debt financing alternative and a preferred stock financing alternative. Preferred stock ($60 million) will cost 16 percent after tax. Which option should be selected on an EPS basis? (No calculations are necessary if you set the problem up and think about the implications.)

12. The Bullock Cafeteria Corporation has computed the indifference point between a debt and common equity financing option to be $4 million of EBIT. Expected EBIT is $4.5 million with a standard deviation of $600,000

  a. What is the probability that the equity financing option will be superior to the debt option?
  b. Under the debt option, Bullock will incur $3 million in interest expenses. What is the chance of Bullock losing money under the debt option?

13. Jenkins Products has a current capital structure which consists of $50 million in long-term debt at an interest rate of 10 percent and $40 million in common equity (10,000,000 shares). The firm is considering an expansion program which will cost $10 million. This program can be financed with additional long-term debt at a 13 percent rate of interest, or preferred stock at a cost of 14 percent, or the sale of new common stock at $10 per share. The firm's marginal tax rate is 40 percent.

  a. Compute the indifference point level of EBIT between the debt financing option and the common stock option.
  b. Compute the indifference point level of EBIT between the common stock option and the preferred stock option.
  c. Is there an indifference point between the debt and preferred stock options? Why or why not?

14. The Oakland Shirt Company has computed its indifference level of EBIT to be $500,000 between an equity financing option and a debt financing option. Interest expense under the debt option is $200,000 and interest expense under the equity option is $100,000. The expected EBIT for the firm is $620,000, with a standard deviation of $190,000.

  a. What is the probability that the equity financing option will be preferred to the debt financing option?
  b. What is the probability that the firm will incur losses under the debt option?

Selected References   Barnea, A., R. Haugen, and L. Senbet. *Agency Problems and Financial Contracting.* Englewood Cliffs, N.J.: Prentice-Hall, 1985.

Hochman, Shalom, and Oded Palmon. "The Impact of Inflation on the Aggregate Debt-Asset Ratio." *Journal of Finance* 40 (September 1985): 1115–1126.

Lee, Wayne Y., and Henry H. Barker. "Bankruptcy Costs and the Firm's Optimal Debt Capacity: A Positive Theory of Capital Structure." *Southern Economic Journal* 43 (April 1977): 1453–1465.

Miller, M. "Debt and Taxes." *Journal of Finance* 32 (May 1977): 261–275.

Modigliani, F., and M. Miller. "The Cost of Capital, Corporation Finance, and the Theory of Investment." *American Economic Review* (June 1958): 261–297.

Myers, Stewart C. "The Capital Structure Puzzle." *Journal of Finance* (July 1984): 575–592.

14

DIVIDEND POLICY

A Financial Dilemma

Middle South Utilities Suspends Its Dividend*

As a matter of policy, many firms pay out a relatively stable amount of their earnings to shareholders in the form of dividends. In general, a firm will increase dividend payments only when it is confident that it can sustain the higher rate through increased earnings and cash flows. Likewise, there is a reluctance to reduce the dollar amount of dividends from one period to the next unless the firm is faced with severe financial problems.

In August 1985 Middle South Utilities (MSU), which has revenues of $3 billion, suspended its quarterly dividend payment of $0.445 per share, effectively cutting its annual dividend rate from $1.78 per share to zero. This action resulted from a severe cash flow problem that was precipitated in part by the refusal of utility regulators to allow MSU's operating subsidiaries to raise rates sufficiently to recover their investments in the large Grand Gulf I nuclear plant. MSU was asking for rate increases of 50 percent or $1.5 billion. Without rate relief and some financial belt-tightening, such as reducing dividends, renegotiating (that is, stretching out) debt repayment schedules with its lenders, and cutting construction, the company faced the possibility of bankruptcy. According to financial analysts, MSU needed more than $1 billion in new capital during the coming year, but was expected to generate only about $250 million internally. Even with the possibility of $200 million in short-term rate relief, the company would still be faced with a cash shortage of $500 million.

Cutting the company's dividend would generate over $300 million in annual cash savings. Along with other financial measures, this action would go a long way toward solving the firm's short-term cash flow crisis. However, offsetting the savings associated with a dividend cut, there

can be some undesirable effects. As Edwin Lupberger, MSU's chief financial officer, states, "Dividends are the seed corn for all our financing." A dividend cut would put the company in a "Catch 22" situation. The lower dividend payout would make it harder for the company to sell new stock or bonds to finance the estimated $1.5 billion of Grand Gulf costs that would have to be deferred over the next several years. Also, as the company found out, cutting the dividend can have a severe impact on the value of the firm. Over a period of less than one month, MSU's stock price dropped from $14 per share before the dividend suspension announcement to $9 per share after the announcement. This represented a loss of more than $1 billion in market value.

This chapter discusses the elements of a sound dividend policy and how this policy can contribute to the overall firm objective of maximizing shareholder wealth.

* Based on an article in *Business Week* (September 2, 1985).

Key Chapter Concepts

1. Dividend policy determines the ultimate distribution of the firm's earnings between retention (that is, reinvestment) and cash dividend payments to shareholders.
2. Factors influencing the firm's choice of a dividend policy are examined.
3. Theories of the effect of dividend policy on the value of the firm include:
   a. Share values are determined solely by investment decisions and *not* by dividend policy.
   b. Share values are influenced by the division of earnings between dividends and retained earnings.
4. Alternative dividend policies
   a. Passive residual approach
   b. Stable dollar dividend approach
   c. Constant payout ratio approach
   d. Policy of paying a small, regular dividend plus year-end extras
5. Other important topics
   a. How dividends are paid
   b. Stock dividends
   c. Stock splits
   d. Share repurchase as a dividend decision

Glossary of New Terms

Declaration date The day on which the directors of a company declare a dividend.

Ex-dividend date The date on which the right to the most recently declared dividend no longer goes along with the sale of the stock. The ex-dividend date is four business days prior to the *record date*.

Insolvency A situation in which either a firm's liabilities exceed its assets or it is unable to pay its creditors as required.

Passive residual theory A theory of dividend policy that suggests that a company should retain its earnings as long as there are investment opportunities available that promise a rate of return higher than the required rate of return.

Record date The date on which a company makes a list from its stock transfer books of those shareholders who are eligible to receive the declared dividend.

Stock dividend A payment of additional shares of common stock to stockholders.

Treasury stock Common stock that has been reacquired by the issuing company.

Introduction

T he value of a firm is influenced by three types of financial decisions:

- Investment decisions.
- Financing decisions.
- Dividend decisions.

While each is presented as a separate topic in this and most financial management textbooks,[1] it is important to realize that the three are interdependent in a number of ways. For example, the investments made by a firm determine the level of future earnings and future potential dividends; capital structure influences the cost of capital, which in turn determines in part the number of acceptable investment opportunities; and dividend policy influences the amount of equity capital in a firm's capital structure (via the retained earnings account) and, by extension, influences the cost of capital.

There are a number of factors that influence a firm's choice of a dividend policy. Ideally a firm should choose a dividend policy that is most likely to *maximize shareholder wealth*. Thus, dividend policy affects how investors perceive—and value—a firm. However, this is not the only consideration—legal and internal decision-making constraints also play important roles.

This chapter begins by examining the factors that influence a company's choice of dividend policy. Next, it considers the pros and cons of a number of different dividend policies. And, finally, it discusses the mechanics of dividend payments, along with stock dividends and share repurchase plans.

Table 14-1   **Earnings Retention and New Common Stock Issues**

Year	Earnings Retained (in billions of dollars)	New Common Stock Issues (in billions of dollars)
1950	7.2	0.8
1955	13.1	2.2
1960	12.1	1.7
1965	30.0	1.5
1970	14.8	7.0
1975	29.1	7.4
1976	36.9	8.3
1977	53.7	7.9
1978	62.2	7.5
1979	54.5	7.7
1980	32.1	16.1
1981	42.3	23.6
1982	29.2	25.4
1983	76.5	44.4
1984	115.6	18.5

Source: *Federal Reserve Bulletin,* various issues, and *Economic Report of the President,* 1985.

---

[1] In this text investment decisions are dealt with in Chapters 9 through 11 and 19 through 21, and financing decisions are discussed in Chapters 13, 15 through 18, and 22.

Determinants of Dividend Policy

Dividend policy determines how the earnings of a company are distributed. Earnings are either retained and reinvested in the company or they are paid out to shareholders. In recent years the retention of earnings has been a major source of equity financing for private industry. In 1984 corporations retained over $115.6 billion in earnings, while issuing only $18.5 billion in new common stock.

As Table 14-1 shows, this division between new stock issues and retained earnings has tended to vary over time. However, retained earnings (in the aggregate) are more important than new stock issues as a source of equity.

On the one hand, retained earnings can be used to stimulate growth in future earnings and as a result can influence future share values. On the other hand, dividends provide stockholders with tangible current returns. Many factors combine to determine the dividend policy of a firm; these are examined in the following sections.

Legal Constraints

Most states have laws that regulate the dividend payments a firm chartered in that state can make. These laws basically state the following:

- A firm's capital cannot be used to make dividend payments.
- Dividends must be paid out of a firm's present and past *net* earnings.
- Dividends cannot be paid when the firm is insolvent.

The first restriction is termed the *capital impairment restriction.* In some states *capital* is defined as including only the par value of common stock; in others, *capital* is more broadly defined to also include the contributed capital in excess of par account (sometimes called *capital surplus*).

For example, the Johnson Tool and Die Company has the following capital accounts on its balance sheet:

Common stock ($5 par; 100,000 shares)	$ 500,000
Contributed capital in excess of par	400,000
Retained earnings	200,000
Total common stockholders' equity	$1,100,000

If the company is chartered in a state that defines capital as the par value of common stock, then it can pay out a total of $600,000 ($1,100,000 − $500,000 par value) in dividends. If, however, the company's home state restricts dividend payments to retained earnings alone, then Johnson Tool and Die could only pay dividends up to $200,000. Regardless of the dividend laws, however, it should be realized that dividends are paid from a firm's *cash* account with an offsetting entry to the *retained earnings* account.

The second restriction, called the *net earnings restriction,* requires that a firm have generated earnings *before* it is permitted to pay any cash dividends. This prevents the equity owners from withdrawing their initial investment in the firm and impairing the security position of any of the firm's creditors.

The third restriction, termed the *insolvency restriction,* states that an insolvent company may not pay cash dividends. When a company is insolvent, its liabilities exceed its assets. Payment of dividends would interfere with the creditors' prior claims on the firm's assets and thus is prohibited.

These three restrictions affect different types of companies in different ways. New firms, or small firms with a minimum of accumulated retained earnings, are most likely to feel the weight of these legal constraints when determining their dividend policies, whereas well-established companies with histories of profitable performances and large retained earnings accounts are less likely to be influenced by them.

Tax Constraints

Whereas the legal restrictions explained above tend to encourage corporations to retain their earnings, the IRS Code—specifically Sections 531 through 537—has an opposite effect. In essence, the code prohibits corporations from retaining an excessive amount of profits for the purpose of protecting stockholders from paying taxes on dividends received. Dividend payments are considered taxable income. If a corporation decides to retain its earnings in anticipation of providing growth and future capital appreciation for its investors, the investors are not taxed until their shares are sold.

If the IRS rules that a corporation has accumulated excess profits to protect its stockholders from having to pay personal income taxes on dividends, the firm has to pay a heavy penalty tax on those earnings. It is the responsibility of the IRS to prove this allegation, however. Some companies are more likely to raise the suspicions of the IRS than others. For example, small closely held corporations whose shareholders are in high marginal tax brackets, firms that pay consistently low dividends, and those that have large amounts of cash and marketable securities are good candidates for IRS review.

Restrictive Covenants

Restrictive covenants generally have more impact on dividend policy than do the legal constraints just discussed. These covenants are contained in bond indentures, term loans, short-term borrowing agreements, lease contracts, and preferred stock agreements.

These restrictions basically limit the total amount of dividends a firm can pay. Sometimes they may state that dividends cannot be paid at all until a firm's earnings have reached a specified level. For example, the term loan agreement that Atlas Corporation has with the Manufacturers Hanover Trust prohibits the payment of dividends without the prior approval of the bank.

In addition, *sinking fund requirements,* which state that a certain portion of a firm's cash flow must be set aside for the retirement of debt, sometimes limit dividend payments. Also, dividends may be prohibited if a firm's net working capital (current assets − current liabilities) or its current ratio does not exceed a certain predetermined level.

**Liquidity
Considerations**

Dividend payments are cash outflows. Thus, the more liquid a firm is, the more able it is to pay dividends. Even if a firm has a past record of high earnings that have been reinvested, resulting in a large retained earnings balance, it may not be able to pay dividends unless it has sufficient liquid assets, primarily cash.[2] (Middle South Utilities, which was discussed in the Financial Dilemma at the beginning of this chapter, is an example of a company that was faced with a liquidity crisis and was forced to suspend its dividend payments.) Liquidity is likely to be a problem during a business downturn, when both profits and cash flows often decline. Rapidly growing firms with many profitable investment opportunities also often find it difficult to maintain adequate liquidity and pay dividends at the same time.

**Borrowing Capacity
and Access to the
Capital Markets**

Liquidity is desirable for a number of reasons. Specifically, it provides protection in the event of a financial crisis. It also provides the flexibility needed to take advantage of unusual financial and investment opportunities. There are other ways of achieving this flexibility and security, however. For example, companies frequently establish lines of credit and revolving credit agreements with banks, allowing them to borrow on short notice.[3] Large well-established firms are usually able to go directly to credit markets with either a bond issue or a sale of commercial paper. The more access a firm has to these external sources of funds, the better able it will be to make dividend payments.

A small firm whose stock is closely held and infrequently traded often finds it difficult (or undesirable) to sell new equity shares in the markets. As a result, retained earnings are the only source of new equity. When a firm of this type is faced with desirable investment opportunities, the payment of dividends is often inconsistent with the objective of maximizing the value of the firm.

Earnings Stability

Most large widely held firms are reluctant to lower their dividend payments, even in times of financial stress. Thus, a firm with a history of stable earnings is usually more willing to pay a higher dividend than a firm with erratic earnings.

A firm whose cash flows have been more or less constant over the years can be fairly confident about its future and frequently reflects this confidence in higher dividend payments.

Growth Prospects

A rapidly growing firm usually has a substantial need for funds to finance the abundance of attractive investment opportunities. Instead of paying large dividends and then attempting to sell new shares to raise the equity investment capital it needs, this type of firm usually retains larger portions of its earnings and avoids the expense and inconvenience of public stock offerings.

---

[2] For example, John A. Brittain found that corporate dividend payments are positively related to a firm's liquidity. See John A. Brittain, *Corporate Dividend Policy,* Washington, D. C.: Brookings, 1966, pp. 184–187.
[3] See Chapter 22 for a more detailed discussion of this topic.

Inflation

In an inflationary environment, funds generated by depreciation are often not sufficient to replace a firm's assets as they become obsolete. Under these circumstances a firm may be forced to retain a higher percentage of earnings to maintain the earning power of its asset base.

Inflation also has an impact on a firm's working capital needs. In an atmosphere of rising prices, *actual* dollars invested in inventories and accounts receivable tend to increase in order to support the same *physical* volume of business.[4] And, because the dollar amounts of accounts payable and other payables requiring cash outlays are high with rising prices, transaction cash balances normally have to be increased. Thus, inflation can force a firm to retain more earnings as it attempts to maintain its same relative preinflation working capital position.

Shareholder Preferences

In a closely held corporation with relatively few stockholders, management may be able to set dividends according to the preferences of its stockholders. For example, assume that the majority of a firm's stockholders are in high marginal tax brackets. They probably favor a policy of high earnings retention, resulting in eventual price appreciation, over a high payout dividend policy. However, high earnings retention implies that the firm has enough acceptable capital investment opportunities to justify the low payout dividend policy. In addition, recall that the IRS does not permit corporations to retain excessive earnings if they have no legitimate investment opportunities. Also, a policy of high retention when investment opportunities are not available is inconsistent with the objective of maximizing shareholder wealth.

In a large corporation whose shares are widely held, it is nearly impossible for a financial manager to take individual shareholders' preferences into account when setting dividend policy. Some wealthy stockholders prefer retention and capital gains, while other stockholders who are in lower marginal tax brackets, or who depend upon dividends as a source of current income, prefer a higher dividend rate. Therefore, when a firm's ownership is diverse, management should consider investment opportunities, cash flow needs, access to the financial markets, and other related factors when setting dividend policy. Those stockholders who do not find this policy acceptable can sell their shares and buy stock in other firms that are more attractive to them.

It has been argued that firms tend to develop their own "clientele" of investors. This "clientele effect" was originally articulated by Merton Miller and Franco Modigliani[5] and indicated that investors will tend to be attracted to companies which have dividend policies that are consistent with the investors' objectives. Some companies, such as public utilities, which pay out a large percentage (typically 70 percent or more) of their earnings as dividends, have traditionally attracted investors who desire a high dividend yield. In contrast, growth-oriented companies, which pay no (or very low) dividends, have tended to attract investors who prefer

---

[4] The ultimate impact of inflation on a firm's liquidity depends on whether or not the firm is able to pass these higher costs on to its customers in the form of higher prices.

[5] Merton Miller and Franco Modigliani. "Dividend Policy, Growth and the Valuation of Shares." *Journal of Business* 34 (Oct. 1961): 411–433.

earnings retention and greater price appreciation. Empirical studies generally support the existence of a dividend clientele effect.[6]

Protection against Dilution

If a firm adopts a policy of paying out a large percentage of its annual earnings as dividends, it may need to sell new shares of stock from time to time to raise the equity capital needed to invest in potentially profitable projects. If existing investors do not or cannot acquire a proportionate share of the new issue, controlling interest in the firm is *diluted*. Some firms choose to retain more of their earnings and pay out lower dividends rather than risk dilution.

There are alternatives to high earnings retention, however; one of these involves raising external capital in the form of debt. This increases the financial risk of the firm, however, ultimately raising the cost of equity capital and at some point lowering share prices.[7] If the firm feels that it already has an optimal capital structure, a policy of obtaining all external capital in the form of debt is likely to be counterproductive, unless sufficient new equity capital is retained or acquired in the capital markets to offset the increased debt.

Dividend Policy and Firm Value

There are two major schools of thought among finance scholars regarding the effect dividend policy has on a firm's value. While Miller and Modigliani argue that dividend policy does not have a significant effect on a firm's value,[8] Myron Gordon, David Durand, and John Lintner argue that it does.[9] Each of these viewpoints is discussed in the following sections.

Arguments for the Irrelevance of Dividends

The group led by Miller and Modigliani (MM) contends that a firm's value is determined solely by its investment decisions, and that the dividend payout ratio is a mere detail. They maintain that the effect of any particular dividend policy can be exactly offset by other forms of financing, such as the sale of new common equity shares. This argument depends on a number of key assumptions, however, including the following:

- *No taxes.* Under this assumption, investors are indifferent about whether they receive either dividend income or capital gains income.
- *No transaction costs.* This assumption implies that investors in the

---

[6] See Edwin J. Elton and Martin J. Gruber, "Marginal Stockholder Tax Rates and the Clientele Effect," *Review of Economics and Statistics* (February 1970): 68–74; Wilbur C. Lewellen, Kenneth L. Stanley, Ronald C. Lease, and Gary C. Schlarbaum, "Some Direct Evidence on the Dividend Clientele Phenomenon," *Journal of Finance* (December 1970): 1385–1399; and R. Richardson Pettit, "Taxes, Transactions Costs and the Clientele Effect of Dividends," *Journal of Financial Economics* (December 1977): 419–436.

[7] See Chapters 4, 12, and 13.

[8] Miller and Modigliani, *op cit.*

[9] See Myron Gordon, "The Savings, Investment and Valuation of a Corporation," *Review of Economics and Statistics* (Feb. 1962): 37–51; Gordon, *The Investment, Financing and Valuation of the Corporation,* Homewood, Ill.: Irwin, 1962; David Durand, "Bank Stocks and the Analysis of Covariance," *Econometrica* (Jan. 1955): 30–45; and John Lintner, "Dividends, Earnings, Leverage, Stock Prices and the Supply of Capital to Corporations," *Review of Economics and Statistics* (Aug. 1962): 243–269.

securities of firms paying small or no dividends can sell (at no cost) any number of shares they wish in order to convert capital gains into current income.

- *No flotation costs.* If firms did not have to pay flotation costs on the issue of new securities, they could acquire needed equity capital at the same cost, regardless of whether they retained their past earnings or paid them out as dividends. The payment of dividends sometimes results in the need for periodic sales of new stock.
- *Existence of a fixed investment policy.* According to MM, the firm's investment policy is not affected by its dividend policy. Furthermore, MM claim that it is investment policy, *not* dividend policy, that really determines a firm's value.

MM realize that there is considerable empirical evidence that changes in dividend policy do influence stock prices. As discussed later in this chapter, many firms favor a policy of reasonably stable dividends. An increase in dividends conveys a certain type of *information* to the shareholders—namely, that management expects future earnings to be higher. Similarly, a cut in dividends is viewed as conveying unfavorable information about the firm's earnings prospects. MM argue that this *informational content* of dividend policy influences share prices, and *not* the pattern of dividend payments *per se.*

MM also claim that the existence of clienteles of investors favoring a particular firm's dividend policy should have no effect on share value. They recognize that a firm that changes its dividend policy could lose some stockholders to other firms with a more appealing dividend policy. This, in turn, may cause a temporary reduction in the price of the firm's stock. Other investors, however, who prefer the newly adopted dividend policy will view the firm as being undervalued and will purchase more shares. In the MM world, these transactions occur instantaneously and at no cost to the investor, the net result being that a stock's value remains unchanged.

Arguments for the Relevance of Dividends

Scholars belonging to the second school of thought argue that share values are indeed influenced by the division of earnings between dividends and retention. Basically, they contend that the MM propositions are reasonable—given MM's restrictive assumptions—but that dividend policy becomes important once these assumptions are removed.

Specifically, Gordon asserts that shareholders who are risk averse may prefer some dividends over the promise of future capital gains, because dividends are regular, certain returns, while future capital gains are less certain. According to Gordon, dividends reduce investors' uncertainty, causing them to discount a firm's future earnings at a lower rate, thereby increasing the firm's value. In contrast, failure to pay dividends increases investors' uncertainty, which raises the discount rate and lowers share prices. Although there is some empirical evidence in support of this argument, it is difficult to decide which is more valid—the MM informational content of dividends approach or the Gordon uncertainty resolution approach.

Of course, if the assumption of no transaction costs for investors is removed, then investors care whether they are paid cash dividends or receive capital gains. In the MM world, investors who own stock paying low or no dividends could periodically sell a portion of their holdings to satisfy current income requirements. In actuality, however, brokerage charges and odd-lot differentials make such liquidations expensive and imperfect substitutes for regular dividend payments.

Removal of the no-tax assumption also makes a difference to shareholders, since capital gains are not taxed until the stock is sold. In his study of dividend policy from 1920 to 1960, John A. Brittain found evidence in support of this proposition.[10] In general, he found that rising tax rates tend to reduce dividend payout rates.

The existence of flotation costs on new equity sales also tends to make earnings retention more desirable. Given a firm's investment policy, the payout of earnings the firm needs for investments requires it to raise external equity. External equity is more expensive, however, because of flotation costs. Thus, the use of external equity will raise the firm's cost of capital and reduce the value of the firm. In addition, the cost of selling small issues of equity to meet investment needs is likely to be prohibitively high for most firms. Thus, firms that have sufficient investment opportunities to profitably utilize their retained funds tend to favor retention.[11]

The empirical evidence as to whether dividend policy affects firm valuation is mixed. Some studies have found that, because of tax effects, investors require higher pre-tax returns on high dividend payout stocks than on low dividend payout stocks.[12] Other studies have found that share prices are unaffected by dividend payout policy.[13]

Many practitioners believe that dividends are important, both for their informational content and because external equity capital is more expensive than retained equity.[14] Thus, when establishing an optimal dividend policy, a firm should consider shareholder preferences along with investment opportunities and the relative cost of retained equity versus externally raised equity.

Dividend Policies

It has been shown that there are a number of practical considerations that influence a firm's board of directors in determining an "optimal" dividend policy. Next, several alternative dividend strategies are discussed.

---

[10] John A. Brittain, *op. cit.,* especially chap. 4.

[11] This argument provides the basis for the passive residual or marginal theory of dividends discussed later in this chapter.

[12] See Robert H. Litzenberger and Krishna Ramaswamy, "The Effect of Personal Taxes and Dividends on Capital Asset Prices: Theory and Empirical Evidence," *Journal of Financial Economics* (June 1979): 163–196; Litzenberger and Ramaswamy, "Dividends, Short-Selling Restrictions, Tax Induced Investor Clienteles and Market Equilibrium," *Journal of Finance* (May 1980); and Litzenberger and Ramaswamy, "The Effects of Dividends on Common Stock Prices: Tax Effects or Information Effects?" *Journal of Finance* (May 1982): 429–444.

[13] See Fischer Black and Myron Scholes, "The Effects of Dividend Yield and Dividend Policy on Common Stock Prices and Returns," *Journal of Financial Economics* (May 1974): 1–22; and Merton H. Miller and Myron S. Scholes, "Dividends and Taxes: Some Empirical Evidence," *Journal of Political Economy* (December 1983): 1118–1141.

[14] For a survey of chief financial officers' attitudes on dividend policy, see H. Kent Baker, Gail E. Farrelly, and Richard B. Edelman, "A Survey of Management Views on Dividend Policy," *Financial Management* (Autumn 1985): 78–84.

Passive Residual Policy

The passive residual policy suggests that a firm should retain its earnings as long as it has investment opportunities that promise higher rates of return than the required rate. For example, assume a firm's shareholders could invest their dividends in stocks of similar risk with an expected rate of return (dividends plus capital gains) of 18 percent. This 18 percent figure, then, would constitute the required rate of return on the firm's retained earnings.[15] As long as the firm can invest these earnings to earn more than this required rate, it should not pay dividends (according to the passive residual policy), since such payments would require either that the firm forego some acceptable investment opportunities or raise necessary equity capital in the more expensive external capital markets.

Interpreted literally, the residual theory implies that dividend payments will vary from year to year, depending on available investment opportunities. There is, however, strong evidence that most firms try to maintain a rather stable dividend payment record over time. However, this does not mean that firms ignore the principles of the residual theory in making their dividend decisions, because dividends can be smoothed out from year to year in two ways.[16] First, a firm can choose to retain a larger percentage of earnings during years when funding needs are large. If the firm continues to grow, it can manage to do this without reducing the dollar amount of the dividend. Second, a firm can borrow the funds it needs, temporarily raise its debt-to-equity ratio, and avoid a dividend cut in this way. Because issue costs are lower for large offerings of long-term debt, long-term debt capital tends to be raised in large, lumpy sums. If a firm has many good investment opportunities available to it during a particular year, this type of borrowing is preferable to cutting back on dividends. The firm will need to retain earnings in future years to bring its debt-to-equity ratio back in line. A firm that has many good investment opportunities for a number of years may eventually be forced to cut its dividend and/or sell new equity shares to meet financing requirements and maintain an optimal capital structure.

The residual theory also suggests that "growth" firms will normally have lower dividend payout ratios than firms in mature, low-growth industries. For example, many public utilities, such as American Electric Power, Potomac Electric Power, and Public Service Company of New Mexico, tend to have rather high payout ratios. In contrast, growth firms like Digital Equipment, Tandy Corporation, and Marriott Corporation tend to have rather low payout ratios. Table 14-2 summarizes the recent dividend payout ratios and growth rates for these firms.

Stable Dollar Dividend Policy

There is much evidence to indicate that most firms—and stockholders—prefer reasonably stable dividend policies. This stability is characterized by a rather strong reluctance to reduce the dollar amount of dividends

---

[15] This is the rate of return that must be earned on the equity-financed portion of new investments. To earn this return on equity, new investments must earn an overall rate of return equal to the weighted cost of capital—reflecting the fact that all investments are made with a mix of debt and equity funds in the proportions of the target capital structure.

[16] Robert C. Higgins, "The Corporate Dividend-Saving Decision," *Journal of Financial and Quantitative Analysis* (March 1972): 1531–1538, provides empirical support for the view that each period's dividends are a function of longer-term trends.

Table 14-2   **Recent Dividend Payout Ratios and Growth Rates for Six Firms**

Firm	1984 Dividend Payout Ratio (%)	Ten-Year EPS Growth Rate (%)
American Electric Power	88	−1.5
Potomac Electric Power	60	5.5
Public Service Company of New Mexico	92	2.5
Marriott Corporation	9	20.5
Tandy Corporation	0	32
Digital Equipment	0	18

Source: *Value Line Investment Service,* various issues. Reprinted by permission of the publisher. Copyright, Value Line, Inc.

from one period to the next. Similarly, increases in the dollar dividend rate are normally not made until the firm's management is satisfied that future earnings will be high enough to justify the larger dividend. Thus, while dividend rates tend to follow increases in earnings, they also tend to lag behind them to a certain degree.

Figure 14-1 illustrates the relationship between corporate dividends and

Figure 14-1   **Historical Pattern of Profits and Dividends of U.S. Corporations**

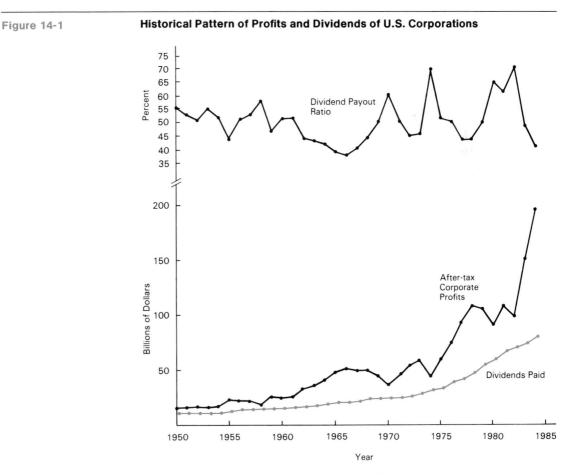

Source: *Economic Report of the President,* 1985.

profits since 1950. It is apparent from this chart that aggregate dividend payments fluctuate much less widely than corporate earnings do. There has been a strong upward trend in the amount of dividends paid, with very few years showing significant reductions. This is in sharp contrast to the more erratic record of corporate earnings.

More specifically, Figure 14-2 shows the dividend and earnings history of the Owens-Corning Company. Once again, it can be seen that there has been an upward trend in dividends over time. It is clear, however, that dividend increases tend to lag earnings increases. Annual dividend payments are also more stable than earnings figures. Note, for instance, the dramatic growth in earnings in 1976, 1977, and 1978, which resulted from the increased demand for fiberglass insulating products, and compare this with the very modest increase in dividends during these years. When earnings declined in 1980, 1981, and 1982, the $1.20 dividend rate was maintained.

There are many reasons why investors prefer stable dividends. For instance, many investors feel that dividend changes possess *informational content*—they equate changes in a firm's dividend levels with profitability. A cut in dividends may be interpreted to indicate that the firm's long-run profit potential has declined. Similarly, a dividend increase is seen as a verification of the expectation that future profits will increase.[17]

Figure 14-2   **Dividends and Earnings for the Owens-Corning Company**

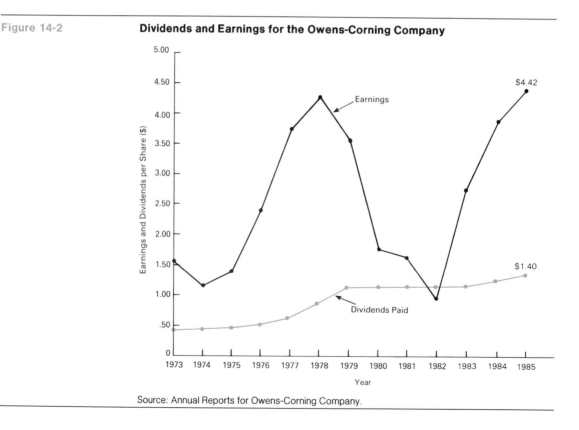

Source: Annual Reports for Owens-Corning Company.

---

[17] Sometimes, however, an increase in a firm's dividend payout ratio may be interpreted to mean the firm no longer has a large number of high-return investment opportunities available to it.

In addition, many shareholders need and depend on a constant stream of dividends for their cash income requirements. While they can sell off some of their shares as an alternative source of current income, associated transaction costs and odd-lot charges make this an imperfect substitute for steady dividend income.

Some managers feel that a stable and growing dividend policy tends to reduce investor uncertainty concerning future dividend streams. They believe investors will pay a higher price for the stock of a firm that pays stable dividends, thereby reducing the firm's cost of equity.

And, finally, stable dividends are legally desirable. Many regulated financial institutions—such as bank trust departments, pension funds, and insurance companies—are limited as to the types of common stock they are allowed to own. To qualify for inclusion in these "legal lists," a firm must have a record of continuous and stable dividends. The failure to pay a dividend or the reduction of a dividend amount can result in removal from these lists. This, in turn, reduces the potential market for the firm's shares and may lead to price declines. For example, in 1982 (a very bad year for farm equipment producers), John Deere experienced a dramatic decline in earnings (97 percent in the second quarter alone). In spite of projected earnings of only $1.00 per share for the year, the company was expected to continue paying at the $2.00 per share yearly rate to preserve its twenty-six-year record of no dividend cuts.

Other Dividend Payment Policies

Some firms have adopted a *constant payout ratio* dividend policy. A firm that uses this approach pays out a certain percentage of each year's earnings—for example, 40 percent—as dividends. If the firm's earnings vary substantially from year to year, dividends also will fluctuate. (The late Penn Central Company had adopted this type of dividend payout policy at one time.)

As shown in Figure 14-1, the aggregate dividend payout ratio for U. S. corporations generally has ranged between 40 and 60 percent, although recent figures (1980–1982) have been in excess of 60 percent. This finding supports the notion that firms try to maintain fairly constant payout ratios over time. On a year-to-year basis, however, these payout ratios have varied substantially. For example, the aggregate payout ratio was about 70 percent during 1982, a recession year, and only 38 percent during 1966, a year of relative prosperity. Because of the reluctance to reduce dividends, payout ratios tend to increase when profits are depressed and decrease as profits increase.

Other firms choose to pay a *small regular quarterly dividend plus year-end extras*. This policy is especially well suited for a firm with a volatile earnings record, volatile year-to-year cash needs, or both. Even when earnings are low, the firm's investors can count on their regular dividend payments. When earnings are high and there is no immediate need for these excess funds, the firm declares a year-end extra dividend. This policy gives management the flexibility to retain funds as needed and still satisfy investors who desire to receive some "guaranteed" level of dividend payments. U.S. Steel, Du Pont, and General Motors have all followed this policy from time to time. Figure 14-3 shows how this policy has affected General Motors. While actual dividend payments have varied

Figure 14-3

Dividends and Earnings for General Motors

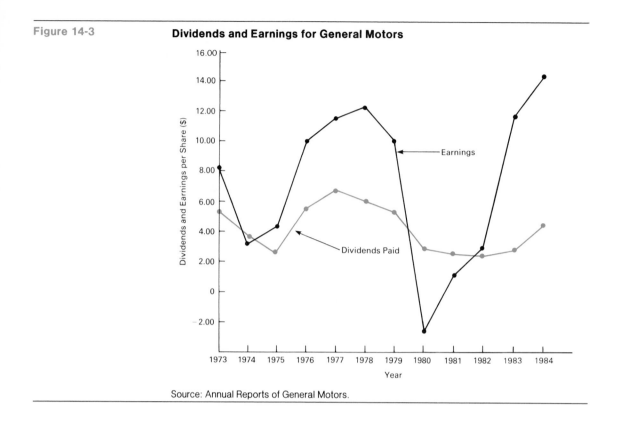

Source: Annual Reports of General Motors.

dramatically from year to year (compare this figure, for example, with Figure 14-2, which shows Owens-Corning's dividends), they have not fallen below $2.40, the "regular" rate in effect in 1975. (This regular rate was temporarily increased in 1979 but subsequently reduced back to $2.40.)

How Dividends are Paid

In most firms, the board of directors holds quarterly or semiannual meetings to evaluate the firm's past performance and decide the level of dividends to be paid during the next period. Changes in the amount of dividends paid have tended to be made rather infrequently—especially in firms that follow a stable dividend policy—and only after there is clear evidence that the firm's future earnings are likely to be either permanently higher or permanently lower than previously reported levels.

Most firms follow a dividend declaration and payment procedure similar to that outlined in the following paragraphs. This procedure usually revolves around a *declaration date,* an *ex-dividend date,* a *record date,* and a *payment date.*

Figure 14-4 is a time line that illustrates the Dickinson Company's dividend payment procedure. The firm's board of directors meets on the *declaration date*—April 15—to consider future dividends. They *declare* a dividend on that date, which will be payable to *shareholders of record* on the *record date* May 15. On that date, the firm makes a list from its stock

Figure 14-4   **Key Dates in the Dickinson Company's Dividend Payment Procedure**

April 15		May 11	May 15		May 29
Declaration Date		Ex-Dividend Date	Record Date		Payment Date

transfer books of those shareholders who are eligible to receive the declared dividend.

The major stock exchanges require four *business days* prior to the record date for recording ownership changes. The day that begins this four-day period is called the *ex-dividend date*—in this case, May 11, as long as May 15 occurs on a Friday. Investors who purchase stock prior to May 11 are eligible for the May 15 dividend; investors who purchase stock on or after May 11 are not entitled to the dividend. On May 11, the ex-dividend date, the stock price can be expected to decline by the amount of the dividend, since this much value has been removed from the firm.

The *payment date* is normally two to four weeks after the record date; in this case, May 29. On this date, Dickinson mails dividend payments to the holders of record.

Figure 14-5 is a typical dividend announcement. It contains information on the company paying the dividend, the payment date, the record date, and the declaration date. It also specifies the amount of the quarterly dividend payment per common share. And, because regular, stable

Figure 14-5   **Sample Public Dividend Announcement**

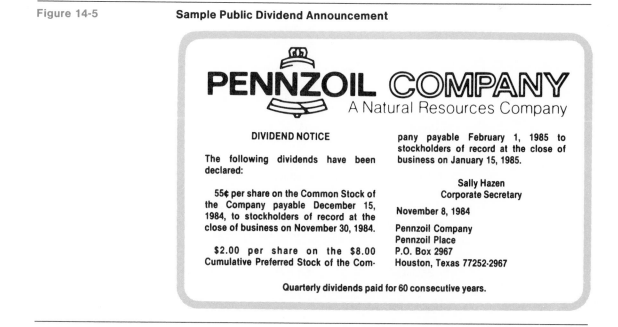

PENNZOIL COMPANY
A Natural Resources Company

DIVIDEND NOTICE

The following dividends have been declared:

55¢ per share on the Common Stock of the Company payable December 15, 1984, to stockholders of record at the close of business on November 30, 1984.

$2.00 per share on the $8.00 Cumulative Preferred Stock of the Com-

pany payable February 1, 1985 to stockholders of record at the close of business on January 15, 1985.

Sally Hazen
Corporate Secretary

November 8, 1984

Pennzoil Company
Pennzoil Place
P.O. Box 2967
Houston, Texas 77252-2967

Quarterly dividends paid for 60 consecutive years.

dividend payments are important to many investors, it notes that the firm has made consecutive quarterly dividend payments for sixty years.

In recent years many firms have established *dividend reinvestment plans.*[18] Under these plans, shareholders can automatically have their dividends reinvested in additional shares of the company's common stock. There are two types of dividend reinvestment plans—one type involves the purchase of *existing* stock and the other type involves the purchase of *newly issued* stock. The first type of plan is done through a bank which, acting as a trustee, purchases the stock on the open market and then allocates it on a pro rata basis to the participating shareholders. In the second type of plan, the cash dividends of the participants are used to purchase, often at a small discount (up to 5 percent) from the market price, newly issued shares of stock.

This second type of plan enables the firm to raise substantial amounts of new equity capital over time as well as reduce the cash outflows required by dividend payments.[19] The advantage of a dividend reinvestment plan to shareholders is that it represents a convenient method for them to purchase additional shares of the company's common stock while at the same time saving on brokerage commissions. The primary disadvantage is that shareholders must pay taxes on the cash dividends reinvested in the company, even though they never receive any cash.[20]

Stock Dividends

A stock dividend is the payment of additional shares of stock to common stockholders. It involves making a transfer from the retained earnings account to the other stockholders' equity accounts.

For example, the Colonial Copies Company has the following common stockholders' equity:

Pre-Stock Dividend Common Stockholders' Equity	
Common stock ($5 par, 100,000 shares)	$ 500,000
Contributed capital in excess of par	1,000,000
Retained earnings	5,000,000
Total common stockholders' equity	$6,500,000

Suppose the firm declares a 10 percent stock dividend and existing shareholders receive 10,000 (10% × 100,000) new shares. Since stock dividend accounting is usually based on the predividend market price, a total of $200,000 (10,000 shares × an assumed market price of $20 per

---

[18] See *Moody's Annual Dividend Record* (December 31, 1985) for a list of the 700 New York and American Stock Exchange companies offering dividend reinvestment plans.

[19] See Richard H. Pettway and R. Phil Malone, "Automatic Dividend Reinvestment Plans of Nonfinancial Corporations," *Financial Management* (Winter 1973): 11–18, for a more detailed discussion of these plans.

[20] The Economic Recovery Tax Act of 1981 permitted shareholders in qualified dividend reinvestment plans of public utility companies to exclude from taxable income up to $750 in reinvested dividends per year ($1,500 for married couples filing joint returns). The shareholders of course have to pay taxes on this income when the stock is sold. This provision of the tax act expired at the end of 1985.

share) is transferred from the firm's retained earnings account to the other stockholders' equity accounts. Of this $200,000, $50,000 ($5 par × 10,000 shares) is added to the common stock account, while the remaining $150,000 is added to the contributed capital in excess of par account. Following the stock dividend, Colonial has the following common stockholders' equity:

Post-Stock Dividend Common Stockholders' Equity	
Common stock ($5 par, 110,000 shares)	$ 550,000
Contributed capital in excess of par	1,150,000
Retained earnings	4,800,000
Total common stockholders' equity	$6,500,000

The net effect of this transaction is to increase the number of outstanding shares and to redistribute funds among the firm's capital accounts. The firm's total stockholders' equity remains unchanged, and each shareholder's proportionate claim to the firm's earnings remains constant. For example, if Colonial Copies Company has 100,000 shares outstanding prior to a 10 percent stock dividend, and its total earnings are $200,000 ($2 per share), a stockholder who owns 100 shares has a claim on $200 of the firm's earnings. Following the 10 percent stock dividend, earnings per share decline to $1.82 ($200,000/110,000 shares). The stockholder who originally owned 100 shares now has 110 shares but continues to have a claim on only $200 (110 shares × $1.82 per share) of the firm's earnings.

Because each shareholder's proportionate claim on a firm's net worth and earnings remains unchanged in a stock dividend, the market price of each share of stock should decline in proportion to the number of new shares issued. In the Colonial Copies example, a $20 pre-stock dividend price should result in a post-stock dividend price decline to $18.18:

$$\text{Post-stock dividend price} = \frac{\text{Original price}}{1 + \dfrac{\text{Percent stock}}{\text{dividend rate}}} = \frac{\$20}{1 + 0.10}$$

$$= \$18.18.$$

If a stockholder's wealth prior to the dividend is $2,000 (100 shares × $20 per share), post-dividend wealth also should remain at $2,000 (110 shares × $18.18 per share).

In essence, all a stock dividend does is increase the number of pieces of paper in the stockholders' hands. Nevertheless, there are a number of reasons why firms declare stock dividends. First, a stock dividend may have the effect of broadening the ownership of a firm's shares, since existing shareholders often sell their stock dividends.[21] Second, in the case

---

[21] See C. Austin Barker, "Evaluation of Stock Dividends," *Harvard Business Review* (July–Aug. 1958): 99–114, for an empirical confirmation of this point.

of a firm that already pays a cash dividend, a stock dividend results in an effective increase in cash dividends, providing that the per-share dividend rate is not reduced. (It is rare for a firm to declare a stock dividend and reduce its cash dividend rate at the same time.) And, finally, the declaration of stock dividends effectively lowers the per-share price of a stock, thereby possibly broadening its investment appeal. Investors seem to prefer stocks selling in approximately the $15 to $70 price range, since more investors will be financially capable of purchasing 100-share round lots.[22] Round lots of 100 shares are more desirable for investors to own because there are lower transactions costs associated with their purchase and sale.

Stock Splits

Stock splits are similar to stock dividends in that they have the effect of increasing the number of shares of stock outstanding and reducing the price of each outstanding share. From an accounting standpoint, stock splits are accomplished by reducing the par value of existing shares of stock and increasing the number of shares outstanding. For example, in a two-for-one stock split, the number of shares would be doubled. Although stock splits have an impact similar to stock dividends, they are normally not considered an element of a firm's dividend policy. They are discussed in more detail in Chapter 16.

Share Repurchases As Dividend Decisions

According to the residual theory of dividend policy, a firm that has more funds than it needs for investments should pay a cash dividend to shareholders. Some firms, however, prefer to repurchase outstanding shares rather than pay cash dividends.

Procedures for Repurchasing Shares

Firms carry out share repurchase programs in a number of ways. For example, a company may buy directly from its stockholders in what is termed a *tender offer,* or it may purchase the stock in the open market, or it may privately negotiate purchases from large holders, such as institutions.

Repurchased shares become known as *treasury stock.* Treasury stock is often used to facilitate mergers and acquisitions; to satisfy the conversion provisions of some preferred stock and debentures, as well as the exercise of warrants; and to meet the need for new shares in executive stock options and employee stock purchase plans. From the stockholders' perspective, share repurchases increase earnings per share for the remaining outstanding shares and also increase stock prices, assuming that investors continue to apply the same *price to earnings (P/E) multiple* to the earnings per share before and after repurchase.[23] The P/E multiple is equal to the price

---

[22] For an empirical view of the effects of stock dividends and splits on share values, see C. Austin Barker, *op. cit.;* Keith B. Johnson, "Stock Splits and Price Change," *Journal of Finance* (Dec. 1966): 675–686; W. H. Hausman, R. R. West, and J. A. Langay, "Stock Splits, Price Changes and Trading Profits: A Synthesis," *Journal of Business* (Jan. 1971): 69–77; and E. Fama, R. Fisher, M. Jensen, and R. Roll, "The Adjustment of Stock Prices to New Information," *International Economic Review* (Feb. 1969): 1–21.

[23] If a stock repurchase results in a substantial increase in the debt-to-equity ratio, the new P/E multiple may be lower because of increased financial risk.

per share divided by the earnings per share. For example, if a stock sells for $40 per share and earns $8 per share, its P/E multiple is 5 times (40/8). The P/E multiple indicates the value placed by investors on a dollar of a firm's earnings. It is influenced by a number of factors, including earnings prospects and investors' perceptions regarding a firm's risk.

For example, the Jetzon Corporation has earnings of $5 million and 1 million shares currently outstanding. The company plans to distribute $2 million—in either the form of cash dividends or share repurchases. The market price of the stock is $30 (after accounting for the impact of the expected $2 dividend distribution).

Assume that the firm decides to repurchase some of its shares by making a tender offer to acquire 62,500 shares at $32 per share ($32 × 62,500 = $2 million). How will this affect the remaining stockholders? If the P/E multiple remains the same before and after the repurchase (P/E = $30/$5, or 6 times), the value of the shares before and after repurchase will be as follows:

	Before Repurchase	After Repurchase
Net earnings	$5,000,000	$5,000,000
Shares outstanding	1,000,000	937,500
Earnings per share	$5.00	$5.33
Price-earnings ratio	6×	6×
Market price (ex-dividend)	$30	$32
Expected dividend	$2	$0

If the firm had chosen to declare a cash dividend instead, shareholder wealth would have been $32 per share ($30 ex-dividend price + $2 dividend). The repurchase of $2 million worth of shares still results in shareholder wealth of $32, but $2 of this total represents price appreciation.

Normally a firm will announce its intent to buy back some of its own shares so that investors will know why there is sudden additional trading in the stock. An announcement of repurchase is also useful to current shareholders, who may not want to sell their shares before they have had an opportunity to receive any price appreciation expected to result from the repurchase program.

Reasons for Share Repurchases

In the context of dividend decisions, the primary reason why a firm may decide to repurchase its own stock in lieu of a cash dividend is tax considerations. Because of the historically lower tax rates on (long-term) capital gains income, most shareholders (who are subject to income taxes) have been better off on an after-tax basis from share repurchases compared with an equivalent amount of dividend income.[24] Although a stock repurchase program seems like a desirable way of distributing a firm's earnings, repurchases are deterred to a large degree by the IRS. Specifically, the IRS will not permit a firm to follow a policy of regular

---

[24] Some other reasons why a firm may engage in a share repurchase program are discussed in Chapter 16.

stock repurchases as an alternative to cash dividends, because repurchase plans convert cash dividends to capital gains.[25] The IRS looks upon regular repurchases as essentially equivalent to cash dividends and requires that they be taxed accordingly. However, the Teledyne Corporation, which pays no cash dividends, has repurchased its common stock *eight* times since 1971 without being subject to IRS penalties. The 1986 tax reform bill will eliminate the distinction between the taxation of ordinary income and capital gains.

Summary

- *Dividend policy* determines the ultimate distribution of a firm's earnings between retention (reinvestment) and cash dividend payments to stockholders. Retained earnings provide investors with a source of potential future earnings growth, whereas dividends provide them with a current distribution.

- A number of factors influence a firm's choice of dividend policy. These include the following:

  1. Legal constraints prohibiting dividends that impair capital.
  2. Tax constraints prohibiting the excess accumulation of profits.
  3. Restrictive covenants in bond indentures and other financing agreements.
  4. The need for liquidity.
  5. Borrowing capacity and access to the capital markets.
  6. Earnings stability.
  7. Capital expansion opportunities.
  8. Inflation.

  Shareholders' preferences also may influence a firm's choice of dividend policy. These are determined by stockholders' tax positions and their desire to maintain control of the firm.

  Some of these factors favor high dividends, while others imply a lower payout policy. The board of directors should weigh these factors in each instance and arrive at the best possible dividend policy.

- Under a restrictive set of assumptions articulated by Miller and Modigliani (MM), the value of a firm is solely dependent on its investment decisions. Under these conditions, dividend policy does not affect the value of the firm. Once the MM assumptions are removed, dividend policy may affect firm value because of the informational content of dividends and because external equity capital is more expensive to acquire than retained earnings.

- There are a number of alternative dividend policies, including the following:

  1. The passive residual approach.
  2. The stable dollar dividend approach.

---

[25] Price appreciation has the benefit of permitting the investor to decide *when* these gains are taken. This permits the investor to postpone any tax from the repurchase transaction until sometime in the future.

3. The constant payout ratio approach.

4. The policy of paying a small, regular dividend plus year-end extras.

There is ample evidence to indicate that many firms favor a stable dividend policy.

- *Stock dividends* are sometimes used in lieu of (and in conjunction with) cash dividends. The net effect of stock dividends is to leave the total value of the firm unchanged while increasing the number of shares outstanding and broadening the ownership base.

- Some firms employ *share repurchase plans* instead of paying cash dividends. Although the purchase of *treasury stock* should not affect before-tax shareholder wealth, repurchases do convert shareholder benefits from ordinary income (dividends) to price appreciation.

FOCUS ON CORPORATE PRACTICE

Stock Splits and Stock Dividends*

Lawrence Ingrassia
Staff Reporter
The Wall Street Journal

Which is the better value—fifty shares of BBDO International, Inc., stock at $68 a share, or 100 shares at $34 a share?

There is no difference, you say? Try telling that to BBDO. On the advice of its investment bankers and of brokers who follow the company closely, BBDO recently declared a 2-for-1 stock split.

The reason is investor psychology. Individuals who play the market prefer stocks that aren't too expensive; and at more than $60 a share, BBDO's stock was getting a bit costly. "We wanted to do what we could to make our stock attractive to investors, and the 'right' trading range is $20 to $40 a share," explains Steve Kahler, executive vice-president of BBDO, an advertising holding company.

A flurry of stock splits and stock dividends is expected this year because the bull market has pushed many stock prices out of the trading range preferred by individual investors. Procter & Gamble Co., Dun & Bradstreet Corp., Dow Jones & Co., Network Systems Corp., Wallace Computer Service, Inc., and Intergraph Corp. are just a few of the companies that have declared or proposed stock splits in the past couple of months.

"By the second half of this year, I expect to see splitting activity start picking up, and it probably will be quite heavy in 1984," predicts Stan West, vice-president of the New York Stock Exchange's business-research division. Historically, he notes, stock splits and stock dividends increase six months to a year after a bull market.

Sign of Bullishness   Stock splits can accomplish a variety of corporate purposes. They generally increase the number of shareholders and the trading volume, as well as signal that management is bullish about a company's prospects.

But mostly, a split caters to the psychology of shareholders. For one thing, it makes them feel as if they're getting something—more shares—for nothing

And, by lowering the per-share price, splits make it easier for individuals to buy round lots of 100 shares. "Small investors don't like to buy 35 shares or 72 shares—they like to buy 100 shares so they feel they're big shots," says Robert Stovall, a senior vice-president at Dean Witter Reynolds, Inc.

Individual investors also firmly believe that stocks that split are good buys, although it is a matter of debate whether a stock split or stock dividend actually improves a stock's price.

In themselves, stock splits or stock dividends don't change the value of the investor's holdings. The owner gets additional shares, but the market price of the shares is reduced so that the total value of the holdings is the same when the split is effected. (The basic difference between a split and dividend is that in a split the par, or stated, value of the stock changes and in a dividend it doesn't.)

Studies of stocks that split disagree on whether splits lead to faster price gains. "The logic of a split is that it should have no effect. All you're doing is taking a piece of paper and tearing it up," says Eugene Fama, a professor of finance at the University of Chicago's Graduate School of Business. A 1970 study by Prof. Fama of New York Stock Exchange stocks that split from 1926 to 1960 showed that "a split per se had no effect on the price of a stock," although the simultaneous announcement of other good news—such as a dividend increase—can help a stock's price.

But in contrast to Prof. Fama's conclusions, a Big Board study found that stocks that split 3 for 2 or more from 1963 to 1980 "increased 2½ times faster (in price) than nonsplitting stocks in the seven years surrounding the split," the exchange's Mr. West says.

The Market Reacts   The price of BBDO International's stock has increased to $68 a share from $61 a share bid in over-the-counter trading on November 30, the day the company's board proposed the 2-for-1 split. "The market seemed to like it . . . but who knows whether (the increase) has to do with the split or not?" says Mr. Kahler, adding that BBDO also announced that it intended to raise its quarterly dividend and that last fall it got Chrysler Corp. as a new advertising account.

Walgreen Co. shareholders also fared well after a 2-for-1 split last February reduced the stock's price to $23 a share; it steadily rose to more than $50 a share. Happy with that performance, Walgreen declared a 100 percent stock dividend, payable February 11.

But the split may be coincidental to the price increase, says Daniel Jorndt, vice-president and treasurer of Walgreen. "There's a significant point that has to be made," Mr. Jorndt says. "Stocks that split are generally of companies that are doing well. So a company's earnings and prospects of future earnings tend to drive a stock toward a split. It's sort of the chicken or the egg deal. . . A split in itself doesn't do anything."

Indeed, a split doesn't help a stock price if the company's economic fortunes take a turn for the worse. Weatherford International, Inc., an oil-field-service concern, had a 3-for-2 split in April 1981, when the oildrilling business still was booming. Weatherford's stock price has since slumped to $13 a share from the

Source: New York Stock Exchange

post-split price of nearly $25, and the main reason is the industrywide recession.

When considering their own portfolio, some corporate executives don't place much importance on stock splits. "As an individual investor, (a split) doesn't mean anything to me. If I want to buy a stock and it's at $50 a share, I will," says Richard Fisher, vice-president for finance and treasurer at Network Systems. Nonetheless, the maker of high-speed computer communications equipment declared a 2-for-1 split, payable April 27, to reduce its stock price from around $40 a share to $20 a share. "Brokers have told us that the best place for stock to sell is the $15 to $25 range," he adds.

Stock splits, perhaps not coincidentally, are good for brokers. Not only do they generate interest and increase trading in a stock, but they also increase commissions in another way. Because of the way most commission schedules are set up in the brokerage business, there is a higher commission on a trade, of, say, seventy-five shares at $10 a share than on a trade of ten shares at $75 a share, even though the dollar value of the trades is the same.

Splits also can serve a purpose for companies that have little stock outstanding or whose management owns a large amount of stock in the company. By splitting its stock, a company can increase the float, or amount of stock in the public's hands. Care Corp., a nursing-home operator, had a 4-for-1 split last week, partly because about 60 percent of the company's 500,000 shares outstanding were controlled by insiders and relatives, leaving only 200,000 shares for trading by others. In addition to lowering the stock price to around $20 a share, the split increased the float to 800,000 shares, notes Charles Bloom, vice-president and treasurer. As a result, he adds, "there has been an increase in trading."

Questions and Topics for Discussion

1. What legal and tax restrictions limit the amount of cash dividends that may be paid by a firm?

2. What other "external" factors limit a firm's ability to pay cash dividends?

3. What is the likely impact of a highly inflationary economy on a firm's ability to pay dividends? Would you expect this impact to be greater or smaller for a rapidly expanding firm? Why?

4. Explain what is meant by the "clientele effect."

5. Explain what is meant by the "informational content" of dividend policy.

6. In the theoretical world of Miller and Modigliani, what role does dividend policy play in the determination of share values?

7. What role do most practitioners think dividend policy plays in determining share values?

8. How can the "passive residual" view of dividend policy be reconciled with the tendency of most firms to maintain a constant or steadily growing dividend payment record?

9. Why do many managers prefer a stable dollar dividend policy to a policy of paying out a constant percentage of each year's earnings as dividends?

10. Under what circumstances would it make sense for a firm to borrow money in order to make its dividend payments?

11. Some people have suggested that it is irrational for a firm to pay dividends and sell new stock in the same year, since the cost of newly issued equity is greater than the cost of retained earnings. Do you agree? Why or why not?

12. What is a "dividend reinvestment plan"? Explain the advantages of a dividend reinvestment plan to the firm and to shareholders.

13. Why do many firms choose to issue stock dividends? What is the value of a stock dividend to a shareholder?

14. What are the tax limitations on the practice of share repurchases as a regular dividend policy?

Problems*

1. Jacobs Corporation earned $2 million after tax. The firm has 1.6 million shares of common stock outstanding.
   a. Compute the earnings per share of Jacobs.
   b. If Jacob's dividend policy calls for a 40 percent payout ratio, what are the dividends per share?

2. Drew Financial Associates currently pays a quarterly dividend of 50 cents per share. This quarter's dividend will be paid to stockholders of record on Friday, February 22, 19X1. Drew has 200,000 common shares outstanding. The retained earnings account has a balance of $15 million before the dividend, and Drew holds $2.5 million in cash.
   a. What is the ex-dividend date for this quarter?
   b. Drew's stock traded for $22 per share the day prior to the ex-dividend date. What would you expect the stock price to open at on the ex-dividend date? Give some reasons why this might not occur.
   c. What is the effect of the dividend payment on Drew's cash, retained earnings, and total assets.?

3. Winkie Baking has just announced a 100 percent stock dividend. The annual cash dividend per share was $2.40 before the stock dividend. Winkie intends to pay $1.40 per share on each of the new shares. Compute the percentage increase in the cash dividend rate that will accompany the stock dividend.

---

* Color numbers denote problems which have check answers provided at the end of the book.

4. Wolverine Corporation plans to pay a $3 dividend per share on each of its 300,000 shares next year. Wolverine anticipates earnings of $6.25 per share over the year. If the company has a capital budget requiring an investment of $4 million over the year and it desires to maintain its present debt to total assets (debt ratio) of 0.40, how much external equity must it raise? Assume Wolverine's capital structure includes only common equity and debt and that debt and equity will be the only sources of funds to finance capital projects over the year.

5. Tulia Dairy pays a $2.50 cash dividend and earns $5 per share. The cash dividend has recently been increased to $2.65 per share, *and* a 3 percent stock dividend has been declared. What is the effective rate of increase in the dividends for Tulia as a result of this action?

6. The Mori Egg Noodle Company has the following equity accounts on its balance sheet:

Common stock ($10 par, 300,000 shares)	$3,000,000
Contributed capital in excess of par	1,500,000
Retained earnings	6,000,000
Total common stockholders' equity	$10,500,000

   a. What is the maximum amount of dividends that may be paid by the Mori Company if the capital impairment provisions of state law are limited to the following?
   i. The par value of common stock.
   ii. The par value and the capital in excess of par accounts.
   b. What other factors may limit Mori's ability to pay dividends?

7. Champoux Hair Factory, Inc., has earnings before interest and taxes of $200,000. Annual interest amounts to $80,000, and annual depreciation is $80,000. Taxes are computed at a 40 percent rate. Existing bond obligations require the payment of $40,000 per year into a sinking fund.

   Champoux wishes to pay a $2 per-share dividend on the existing 20,000 shares. The firm's bond indenture prohibits the payment of dividends unless the cash flow (before dividends and sinking fund payments) is greater than the total of dividends, interest, and sinking fund obligations.
   a. Can Champoux pay the proposed dividend?
   b. What is the maximum dividend per share that may be paid?

8. Lenberg Lens Company believes in the "dividends as a residual" philosophy of dividend policy. This year's earnings are expected to total $10 million. Being a very conservative company, Lenberg is financed solely with common stock. The required rate of return on retained earnings is 12 percent, whereas the cost of newly raised capital is 14 percent because of flotation costs.
   a. If Lenberg has $6 million of investment projects having expected returns greater than 12 percent, what total amount of dividends should Lenberg pay?
   b. If Lenberg has $12 million of investment projects having expected returns greater than 14 percent, what total amount of dividends should Lenberg pay?
   c. What factors, other than its belief in the residual theory of dividends, should Lenberg consider in setting its dividend policy in Part b?

9. Phoenix Tool Company and Denver Tool Company have had a very similar record of earnings performance over the past 8 years. Both firms are in the same industry and, in fact, they compete directly with each other. The two

firms have nearly identical capital structures. Phoenix has a policy of paying a constant 50 percent of each year's earnings as dividends, whereas Denver has sought to maintain a constant dollar dividend policy, with changes in the dollar dividend payment occurring infrequently. The record of the two companies follows:

| | Phoenix | | | Denver | | |
| | | | Average Market | | | Average Market |
Year	EPS	Dividend	Price	EPS	Dividend	Price
19X1	$2.00	$1.00	$20	$2.10	$0.75	$18
19X2	2.50	1.25	24	2.40	0.75	22
19X3	1.50	1.25	15	1.60	0.75	17
19X4	1.00	0.50	10	0.90	0.75	14
19X5	0.50	0.25	8	0.50	0.50	10
19X6	−1.25	nil	8	−1.10	0.50	10
19X7	1.00	0.50	10	1.10	0.75	14
19X8	1.50	0.75	14	1.45	0.75	17

The president of Phoenix wonders what accounts for Denver's current (19X8) higher stock price, in spite of the fact that Phoenix currently earns more per share than Denver and frequently has paid a higher dividend.

a. What factors can you cite that might account for this phenomenon?

b. What do you suggest as an optimal dividend policy for both Phoenix and Denver that might lead to increases in both of their share prices? What are the limitations of your suggestions?

10. The Emco Steel Company has experienced a slow (3 percent per year) but steady increase in earnings per share. The firm has consistently paid out an average of 75 percent of each year's earnings as dividends. The stock market evaluates Emco primarily on the basis of its dividend payout, since growth prospects are modest.

Emco's management presents a proposal to the board of directors that would require the outlay of $50 million to build a new plant in the rapidly expanding Florida market. The expected annual return on the investment in this plant is estimated to be in excess of 30 percent, more than twice the current company average. To finance this investment, a number of alternatives are being considered. They include the following:

a. Finance the expansion with externally raised equity.

b. Finance the expansion with 50 percent externally generated equity and 50 percent internally generated equity. This alternative would necessitate a dividend cut for this year only.

c. Finance the expansion with a mix of debt and equity similar to their current relative proportions in the capital structure. Under this alternative, dividends would not be cut. Rather, any equity needs in excess of that which could be provided internally would be raised through a sale of new common stock.

Evaluate these various financing alternatives with reference to their effects on the dividend policy and common stock values of the company.

11. The Sweet Times Candy Company has the following equity accounts on its balance sheet:

Common stock ($1 par, 500,000 shares)	$ 500,000
Contributed capital in excess of par	2,000,000
Retained earnings	13,000,000
Total common stockholders' equity	$15,500,000

The current market price of the firm's shares is $50.

a. If the firm declares a 10 percent stock dividend, what will be the impact on the firm's equity accounts?

b. If the firm currently pays no cash dividend, what is the impact of a 10 percent stock dividend on the wealth position of the firm's existing stockholders?

c. If the firm currently pays a cash dividend of $1 per share, and this per-share dividend rate does not change after the 10 percent stock dividend, what impact would you expect the stock dividend to have on the wealth position of existing shareholders?

12. Striker's Match Company reports the following financial data:

Net earnings	$3,000,000
Shares outstanding	1,000,000
Earnings per share	$3
Market price per share (ex-dividend)	$40
Expected dividend per share	$2

Striker is considering distributing $2 million to existing stockholders, either as cash dividends or through the repurchase of outstanding shares. The repurchase plan is favored by some of the company's wealthiest and most influential stockholders.

If the shares are repurchased, the company would make a tender offer for 47,619 shares at a price of $42. Alternatively, the firm could pay a $2 dividend, after the payment of which each share would sell for $40.

a. Ignoring taxes, what impact does the choice of a dividend payment or share repurchase plan have on the wealth position of the firm's shareholders?

b. If most shareholders are in a very high marginal tax bracket, which alternative is favored?

c. What are the limitations on the repurchase alternative as an element of the firm's dividend policy?

13. You are the holder of common stock in the G. Lewis Apartment Renovation Company. Historically the firm has paid generous cash dividends. The firm has recently announced that it would replace its cash dividend with a 20 percent annual stock dividend. Is this good news, bad news, or is it impossible to tell from the information provided? Explain the reason for your answer.

Selected References

Aharony, J., and I. Swary. "Quarterly Dividend and Earnings Announcements and Stockholders' Returns: An Empirical Analysis." *Journal of Finance* (March 1980): 1–12.

Asquith, P., and D. W. Mullins, Jr. "The Impact of Initiating Dividend Payments on Shareholders' Wealth." *Journal of Business* (January 1983): 77–96.

Elton, E. J., and M. J. Gruber. "The Effect of Share Repurchase on the Value of the Firm." *Journal of Finance* (March 1980): 135–149.

Hess, P. "The Ex-dividend Behavior of Stock Returns: Further Evidence on the Tax Effect." *Journal of Finance* (May 1982): 445–456.

Higgins, Robert C. "The Corporate Dividend-Savings Decision." *Journal of Financial and Quantitative Analysis* 7 (March 1972): 1527–1541.

Long, J. B., Jr. "The Market Valuation of Cash Dividends: A Case to Consider." *Journal of Financial Economics* (June/September 1983): 235–264.

Millar, James A., and Bruce D. Fielitz. "Stock-Split and Stock-Dividend Decisions." *Financial Management* 2 (Winter 1973): 35–45.

Norgaard, R., and C. Norgaard. "A Critical Examination of Share Repurchase." *Financial Management* (Spring 1974): 44–51.

Steward, Samuel S., Jr. "Should a Corporation Repurchase Its Own Stock?" *Journal of Finance* (June 1976): 911–921.

Vermaelen, T. "Common Stock Repurchases and Market Signalling." *Journal of Financial Economics* (June 1981): 139–183.

PART SIX

SOURCES OF INTERMEDIATE- AND LONG-TERM FUNDS

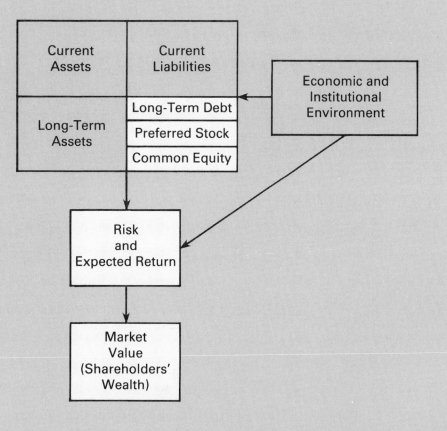

The decision to acquire long-term assets requires that sources of financing be arranged to fund these asset acquisitions. In this part of the book, the major sources of intermediate- and long-term financing are discussed. Chapter 15 deals with term loans and leasing. Chapter 16 looks at long-term debt, preferred stock, and common stock; Chapter 17 considers options, convertible securities, and warrants. Choosing the right mix of financing alternatives can help a firm balance risk, increase returns, and thereby maximize shareholder wealth.

15

TERM LOANS AND LEASES

A Financial Dilemma

Easy Money to a Hoodlum*

In early 1982, Richard Mamarella, a thirty-four-year-old "insurance" man arrived in Burlington, New Jersey, with a record of fraud, perjury, connections to organized crime, and a pad of blank promissory notes that he bought from a printer. Over the next eighteen months Mr. Mamarella filled out one promissory note after another, usually in amounts of six figures or more, totalling $22 million.

For collateral on the loans, he listed nonexistent insurance policies. He listed the borrowers as businessmen he had met or heard of and forged their signatures. These promissory notes were then taken to the First Fidelity Bank of South Jersey, a subsidiary of a holding company with assets of $11.9 billion. The bank advanced him the $22 million and never bothered to check the collateral listed as standing behind the loans. By bribing a junior banking officer with $30,000 and two Atari sets, Mr. Mamarella was able to get the loans approved to Mamarella's bogus insurance premium financing company, IFA, Inc. (Insurance premium financing companies arrange for loans from banks and other lenders which permit business people to buy commercial casualty insurance in monthly installments. The loan proceeds are paid to the insurance company which normally requires its entire payment up front.)

A truly secured loan depends on the character of the borrower and a program to carefully monitor the quality of the security being offered. Through a combination of fraud and negligence, First Fidelity of South Jersey learned a costly lesson in secured lending. This chapter considers a number of intermediate-term sources of financing for a firm, many of which are secured with a specific asset or group of assets.

* Adapted from Jonathan Kwitny, "How a Hoodlum Got $22 Million Bank Loans Without Much Effort," *The Wall Street Journal,* (January 14, 1986), p. 1.

Key Chapter Concepts

1. Term loans are debt obligations having an initial maturity between one and ten years.
   a. The major suppliers of term loans are banks, insurance companies, pension funds, and equipment suppliers.
   b. Term loans are usually amortized over the life of the loan.
   c. The interest rate on term loans obtained from commercial banks is normally greater than the bank's prime rate.
   d. Some term loans from banks require that a compensating balance be maintained at the bank. Other term loans contain a provision which gives the lender an equity participation in the borrowing company.
   e. Most term loans are secured. The loan agreement contains affirmative, negative, and restrictive covenants. In addition the conditions which determine when a default on the loan has occurred are detailed in the loan agreement.
2. Equipment financing loans are commonly made for equipment which is readily marketable. These loans are normally secured with a *conditional sales contract* or a *chattel mortgage*.
3. A *lease* is a contract that allows an individual or a firm to make economic use of an asset for a stated period of time without obtaining an ownership interest in the asset.
4. The major parties to a lease are the *lessor* and the *lessee*.
   a. The lessor is the owner of the asset and the party who receives the lease payments.
   b. The lessee is the user of the asset and the party who makes the lease payments.
5. There are several different classifications of leases.
   a. *Operating leases* are cancelable, period-by-period leases.
   b. *Financial or capital leases* are not cancelable. The lease payments under a financial lease are sufficient to fully amortize the cost of the asset plus provide a return to the lessor.

c. *Leveraged leases* are special financial leases involving three parties: the lessor, the lessee, and a group of lenders. Leveraged leases are especially important to firms which cannot take advantage of the tax benefits of ownership.

6. An asset should be leased rather than owned if the present value cost of leasing is less than the present value cost of owning.

7. Leasing decisions often are influenced by the tax and accounting treatment of the transaction.

Glossary of New Terms

Affirmative loan covenant A portion of a loan agreement that outlines actions a firm's management *agrees to take* as conditions for receiving the loan.

Amortization schedule A schedule of periodic payments of interest and principal owed on a debt obligation.

Balloon loan A loan that requires a large final payment greater than each of the periodic (principal and interest) payments.

Bullet loan A loan that requires only the periodic payment of interest during the term of the loan, with a final single repayment of principal at maturity.

Chattel mortgage A lien on personal property, such as machinery, as security for the repayment of a loan.

Compensating balance A certain percentage of a loan balance that the borrower keeps on deposit with a bank as a requirement of a loan provided by the bank.

Conditional sales contract A financing agreement in which the seller of a piece of equipment retains title until all payments have been made.

Direct lease A lease that is initiated when a firm acquires the use of an asset that it did not previously own.

Financial lease A *noncancelable* agreement that obligates the lessee to make payments to the lessor for a predetermined period of time. These payments are usually sufficient to amortize the full cost of the asset plus provide the lessor with a reasonable rate of return on the investment in the asset.

Lease A contract that allows an individual or a firm to make economic use of an asset for a stated period of time without obtaining an ownership interest in it.

Lessee The user and renter of the property in a lease transaction.

Lessor The property owner who collects rental payments from the lessee in a lease transaction.

Leveraged lease A type of financial lease in which the lessor borrows up to 80 percent of the cost of the leased asset on a nonrecourse basis from a group of lenders. The lessor receives the full tax benefits of ownership. This is also sometimes called a *third-party equity lease* or a *tax lease*.

Negative loan covenant A portion of a loan agreement that outlines actions a firm's management *agrees not to take* during the term of the loan.

Operating lease A *cancelable* lease agreement that provides the lessee with the use of an asset on a period-by-period basis. This is sometimes called a *service* or *maintenance lease*, especially if the lessor provides maintenance services as part of the lease contract.

Restrictive loan covenant A portion of a loan agreement that limits the scope of certain actions a firm may take during the term of the loan.

Sale and leaseback A lease that is initiated when a firm sells an asset it owns to another firm and simultaneously leases the asset back for its own use.

Term loan Any debt obligation having an initial maturity between one and ten years. This is often referred to as *intermediate-term credit*.

Introduction to Term Loans

A *term loan,* or *intermediate-term credit,* is defined as any debt obligation having an initial maturity between one and ten years. It lacks the permanency characteristic of long-term debt.

Term loans constitute the major source of intermediate-term financing. They are made available by a wide variety of financial intermediaries, including commercial banks, insurance companies, pension funds, small business investment companies, government agencies, and equipment suppliers. Since term loans are privately negotiated between the borrowing firm and the lending institution, they are less expensive than public offerings of common stock or bonds. The issuing firm in a public offering pays the registration and issue expenses necessary to sell the securities. For small- to moderate-sized offerings these expenses can be large in relation to the funds raised. For example, one study indicated that the total flotation cost as a percentage of the gross proceeds for a $500,000 debt issue was 8 percent; for a $500,000 common stock issue, it was about 16 percent. These costs dropped to 1.4 percent for a $10 million debt issue and 6.9 percent for a $10 million common stock issue.[1] Because of this potential cost advantage, term loans are well suited for financing small additions to plant facilities and equipment, such as a new piece of machinery, or moderate increases in working capital needs.

Term loans are also preferable to short-term loans, because they provide the borrower with a certain degree of security. Rather than having to be concerned about whether a short-term loan will be renewed, the borrower can have a term loan structured in such a way that the maturity coincides with the economic life of the asset being financed. Thus, the cash flows generated by the asset can service the loan without putting any additional financial strain on the borrower.

Term loans can be used to finance a moderate increase in working capital under these circumstances:

- The cost of a public offering is too high.
- The firm intends to use the term debt only until its earnings are sufficient to amortize the loan.
- The desired increase is relatively long term but not permanent.

Repayment Provisions

A term loan agreement usually requires that the principal be *amortized* over the life of the loan. This means that the firm is required to pay off the loan in installments rather than in one lump sum. This has the effect of reducing the risk to the lender that the borrower will be unable to retire the loan in one lump sum when it comes due. Amortization of principal is also consistent with the idea that term loans are not a permanent part of a firm's capital structure.

The amortization schedule of a term loan might require the firm to make equal quarterly, semiannual, or annual payments of principal and interest. For example, assume a firm borrows $100,000 payable over eight

---

[1] For further information on issue costs, see Securities and Exchange Commission, *Cost of Flotation of Registered Equity Issues,* 1963–1965, Washington, D.C.: USGPO, 1979; and Irwin Friend, *Investment Banking and the New Issues Market,* Cleveland: World Publishing, 1967. See also Chapter 16 of this text.

years, with an interest rate of 9 percent per annum on the unpaid balance. The repayment schedule calls for eight equal annual payments, the first occurring at the end of year 1.

Equation 3.16 from Chapter 3 can be rewritten as follows:

$$PVAN = R(PVIFA_{i,n})$$

$$R = \frac{PVAN}{PVIFA_{i,n}}.$$

Given the present value of the annuity (PVAN) = $100,000, the interest rate (i) = 9 percent, the number of time periods (n) = 8, and the $PVIFA_{0.09,8}$ from Table IV, the annual payment, R, is computed as follows:

$$R = \frac{\$100,000}{5.535}$$

$$= \$18,067.$$

By making eight annual payments of $18,067 to the lender, the borrower will just pay off the loan and provide the lender with a 9 percent return. Table 15-1 shows the principal and interest for each year's annuity payment.

Over the life of this loan the firm will make total payments of $144,536. Of this, $100,000 is the repayment of the principal, and the other $44,536 is interest. It is important to know what proportions of a loan payment are principal and interest, since interest payments are tax deductible.

In this example the repayment schedule calls for equal periodic payments to the lender consisting of both principal and interest. Other

Table 15-1

Sample Loan Amortization Schedule*

End of Year (1)	Annual Annuity Amount (2)	Interest† (3)	Principal Repayment‡ (4)	Remaining Balance (5)
0	$ 0	$ 0	$ 0	$100,000
1	18,067	9,000	9,067	90,933
2	18,067	8,183	9,884	81,049
3	18,067	7,294	10,773	70,276
4	18,067	6,324	11,743	58,533
5	18,067	5,267	12,800	45,733
6	18,067	4,116	13,951	31,782
7	18,067	2,860	15,207	16,575
8	18,067	1,492	16,575	0
	$144,536	$44,536	$100,000	

*Figures in the table have been rounded. Rounding is done to yield a zero ending loan balance. If the table reported payments in terms of both dollars *and* cents, and if fractional cents were permitted, no rounding would be necessary.
†Interest each period is equal to 0.09 times the remaining balance from the previous period; for example, interest in year 1 equals 0.09 × $100,000 = $9,000, and interest in year 2 equals 0.09 × $90,933 = $8,183.
‡The principal repayment each period equals the annual annuity amount ($18,067) minus the per-period interest from Column 3.

types of repayment schedules are also possible, including the following:

- The borrower might be required to make equal reductions in the principal outstanding each period, with the interest being computed on the remaining balance for each period.
- The borrower might be required to make equal periodic payments over the life of the loan that only partially amortize the loan, leaving a lump sum payment that falls due at the termination of the loan period (this is called a *balloon loan*).
- The borrower might be required to make a single principal payment at maturity while making periodic (usually quarterly) interest payments only over the life of the loan (this is called a *bullet loan*).[2]

Interest Costs

The interest rate charged on a term loan depends on a number of factors, including the general level of interest rates in the economy, the size of the loan, the maturity of the loan, and the borrower's credit standing. Generally, interest rates on intermediate-term loans tend to be slightly higher than interest rates on short-term loans because of the higher risk assumed by the lender. Also, large term loans tend to have lower rates than small term loans, because the fixed costs associated with granting and administering a loan do not vary proportionately with the size of the loan. In addition, large borrowers often have better credit standings than small borrowers. An interest rate between 0.25 and 2.5 percent above the prime rate is common for term loans obtained from banks.

The interest rate on a small term loan is sometimes the same throughout the loan's lifetime. In contrast, most larger term loans specify a *variable* interest rate, which depends on the bank's prime lending rate. For example, if a loan is initially made at 0.5 percent above the prime rate, the loan agreement might specify that the interest charged on the remaining balance will continue to be 0.5 percent above the prevailing rate. Thus, whenever the prime rate is increased, the loan rate also increases; if the prime rate declines, so does the interest rate on the loan.

Compensating Balances

It is not uncommon for a bank to require a borrowing firm to keep a percentage of its loan balance—for example, 10 percent—on deposit as a compensating balance. If this balance is greater than the amount the firm would normally keep on deposit with the bank, this requirement effectively increases the firm's cost of the loan. Compensating balance requirements and their effect on the cost of a loan are discussed in detail in Chapter 22.

Equity Participations

The interest rate charged on a term loan also may be influenced by a desire on the part of the lending institution to take an equity position (often called a "kicker") in the company as an additional form of compensation. This is usually accomplished through the issuance of a *warrant* by the

---

[2] These three repayment patterns are illustrated in the "Problems" section at the end of this chapter.

borrower to the lender. A warrant is an option to purchase a stated number of shares of a company's common stock at a specified price sometime in the future. If the company prospers, the lending institution shares in this prosperity on an equity basis. The issuance of warrants in conjunction with a term loan is common when the loan has an above-normal level of risk but the lending institution feels the borrower has promising growth potential. Alternatively, the borrower may issue warrants to secure a more favorable lending rate. Warrants are discussed in detail in Chapter 17.

Security Provisions and Protective Covenants

The security provisions and protective covenants specified by a term loan agreement are often determined by the borrower's credit standing: the weaker the credit standing, the more restrictive the protective covenants.

Security Provisions

In general, security requirements apply more often to intermediate-term loans than to short-term loans. This is due to the fact that longer-term loan contracts tend to have more default risk. Security provisions are also dependent on the size of the borrowing firm. For example, term loans to small firms tend to be secured more often than term loans to large firms, although there is an increasing tendency for all bank-originated term loans to be secured.

The sources of security for a term loan include the following:

- An assignment of payments due under a specific contract.
- An assignment of a portion of the receivables or inventories.
- The use of a floating lien on inventories and receivables.
- A pledge of marketable securities held by the borrower.
- A mortgage on property, plant, or equipment held by the borrower.
- An assignment of the cash surrender value of a life insurance policy held by the borrower for its key executives.

Affirmative Covenants

An affirmative covenant is a portion of a loan agreement that outlines actions the borrowing firm *agrees to take* during the term of the loan. Typical affirmative covenants include the following:

- The borrower agrees to furnish periodic financial statements to the lender, including a balance sheet, income statement, and a sources and uses of funds statement. These may be furnished monthly, quarterly, or annually and are frequently required to be audited. Pro forma cash budgets and projections of the costs needed to complete contracts on hand also may be required.
- The borrower agrees to carry sufficient insurance to cover insurable business risk.
- The borrower agrees to maintain a minimum amount of net working capital (current assets − current liabilities).
- The borrower agrees to maintain management personnel who are acceptable to the financing institution.

Negative Covenants

A negative covenant outlines actions that the borrowing firm's management *agrees not to take* without prior written consent of the lender. Typical negative covenants include the following:

- The borrowing firm agrees not to pledge any of its assets as security to other lenders, as well as not to factor (sell) its receivables. This type of agreement is called a *negative pledge clause* and is found in nearly all unsecured loans. It is designed to keep other lenders from interfering with the immediate lender's claims on the assets of the firm.
- The borrower is prohibited from making mergers or consolidations. In addition, it may not sell or lease a major portion of its assets without written approval of the lender.
- The borrower is prohibited from making or guaranteeing loans to others that would impair the lender's security.

Restrictive Covenants

Rather than requiring or prohibiting certain actions on the part of the borrower, *restrictive covenants* merely *limit their scope*. These are typical restrictive covenants:

- Limitations on the amount of dividends a firm may pay.
- Limitations on the level of salaries, bonuses, and advances a firm may give to employees.

These restrictions, in essence, force the firm to increase its equity capital base, thereby increasing the security for the loan.

Other restrictive covenants might include the following:

- Limitations on the total amount of short- and long-term borrowing the firm may engage in during the period of the term loan.
- Limitations on the amount of funds the firm may invest in new property, plant, and equipment. (This restriction usually applies only to those investments that cannot be financed from internally generated funds.)

And, finally, a firm that has outstanding long-term debt may be restricted as to the amount of debt it can retire without also retiring a portion of the term loan.

These restrictions are quite common, but the list is not all-inclusive. For example, a standard loan agreement checklist published by a large New York City bank lists thirty-four commonly used covenants. In general, covenants included in a loan agreement are determined by the particular conditions surrounding the granting of the term loan, including the credit record of the borrower and the maturity and security provisions of the loan.

Default Provisions

All term loans have *default provisions* that permit the lender to insist that the borrower repay the entire loan immediately under certain conditions. The following are examples:

- The borrower fails to pay interest, principal, or both as specified by the terms of the loan.

- The borrower materially misrepresents any information on the financial statements required under the loan's affirmative covenants.
- The borrower fails to observe any of the affirmative, negative, or restrictive covenants specified within the loan.

A borrower who commits any of these common acts of default will not necessarily be called on to repay a loan immediately, however. Basically, a lender will only use a default provision as a last resort, seeking in the meantime to make some agreement with the borrower, such as working out an acceptable modified lending plan with which the borrower is more able to comply. Normally, a lender will call a loan due only if no reasonable alternative is available or if the borrower is facing near-certain failure.

Suppliers of Term Loans

There are numerous sources of term loans, including commercial banks, insurance companies, pension funds, commercial finance companies, government agencies, and equipment suppliers. Many of these sources are discussed in the following sections.

Commercial Banks and Savings and Loan Associations

Many commercial banks and some savings and loan associations are actively involved in term lending. For example, about one-third of all commercial and industrial loans made by commercial banks are term loans.

In spite of this level of activity, banks generally tend to favor loans having relatively short maturities—that is, less than five years—although some banks will make loans having lifetimes as long as ten years or more. In addition, some banks limit their term lending to existing customers. Often banks will form *syndicates* to share large term loans. This not only limits the risk exposure for any one bank, but also complies with laws that limit the size of *unsecured* loans made to single customers.

Life Insurance Companies and Pension Funds

Whereas commercial banks tend to prefer shorter-term loans, insurance companies and pension funds are most interested in longer-term commitments, for example, ten to twenty years. As a result, it is common for a bank and an insurance company to share a term loan commitment. Under this type of arrangement, the bank might agree to finance the first five years of a loan, with the insurance company financing the loan for the remaining years. This can also be advantageous to the borrower, since banks can generally charge a lower rate of interest for loans having shorter maturities.

From the borrowing firm's perspective, term loan agreements with pension funds and insurance companies have one significant limitation. If a firm decides to retire a term loan with a bank, it may usually do so without penalty. Because insurance companies are interested in having their funds invested for longer periods of time, however, prepayment of an insurance company term loan may involve some penalties.

Term loans from insurance companies and pension funds are usually secured, often with a mortgage on an asset such as a building. These mortgage-secured loans are rarely made for amounts greater than 65 to 75 percent of the value of the collateral, however.

And, finally, term loans from life insurance companies and pension funds tend to have slightly higher stated rates of interest than bank term loans. This is because (1) they are generally made for longer maturities and (2) there are no compensating balance requirements.

Small Business Administration (SBA)

The Small Business Administration (SBA), an agency of the Federal government, was established in 1953 to make credit available to small businesses that cannot reasonably obtain financing from private sources.

Normally an SBA loan is secured by a mortgage on the firm's plant and equipment, third-party guarantees, or an assignment of accounts receivable and/or inventories.

The SBA makes three major types of loans:

- Direct loans.
- Participation loans.
- Economic opportunity loans.

Direct loans are financed by the SBA, and since funds are quite limited, these loans are usually made only when the applicant firm cannot borrow from private sources at reasonable rates.

A *participation loan* is obtained from a local bank, with the SBA guaranteeing up to 90 percent of it. The SBA prefers participation loans over direct loans. Typical SBA loans range between $20,000 and $40,000 and have a maximum ten-year maturity. In addition, they usually carry an interest rate that is considerably below the rate that would be charged for a similar non-SBA loan. A rate about 1 percentage point higher than the U.S. Treasury Bond rate is quite common. Like other term loans, SBA loans must normally be amortized, that is, paid off in periodic (usually monthly) installments.

Economic opportunity loans have been made available since 1970 to assist economically and socially disadvantaged individuals who own their own firms.

Small Business Investment Companies (SBICs)

Small business investment companies (SBICs) are licensed by the government to make both equity and debt investments in small firms. They raise their capital by borrowing from the SBA and other sources.

The SBICs take an equity interest in the small firms they loan funds to, hoping to profit from their growth and prosperity. Unlike SBA loans, which are made to any eligible credit-worthy small business, SBICs specialize in providing funds to firms that have above-average growth potential. Naturally, these firms often have above-average risk as well. Thus, the interest charge on an SBIC loan is generally somewhat higher than that on a normal bank term loan. SBIC loans have maturities as long as ten to twenty years.

Industrial Development Authorities (IDAs)

Many states and municipalities have organized industrial development authorities (IDAs) to encourage new firms to locate in their area or to assist existing firms with expansion plans. In a typical financing plan, a local IDA sells tax-exempt municipal revenue bonds and uses the proceeds to build a firm's new facility. It then leases the plant to the firm, collecting lease payments from the firm that are large enough to pay the principal and interest on the municipal revenue bonds. Because bonds of this nature are tax exempt, the interest on them is generally lower than the interest on bonds issued directly by a private corporation. As a result, an IDA can charge a firm an attractively low lease rate.

The growing need to finance pollution control expenditures has led to the development of *pollution control revenue bonds,* which are issued by municipalities. Proceeds from these bonds are used to acquire pollution control equipment, which is then sold or leased to local industries. Because interest payments on pollution control revenue bonds are tax-free to investors, a firm's cost is much lower than it would be if these investments had to be financed with conventional debt or equity. For example, in February 1986 the Public Service Company of New Hampshire sold $100 million of thirty-year pollution control revenue bonds through the Industrial Development Authority of the State of New Hampshire. The interest cost on these bonds was 10.5 percent compared to a return requirement in excess of 12.0 percent had the bonds not been tax-exempt.

Equipment Loans

When a firm procures a loan to finance new equipment, it may use the equipment itself as collateral for an intermediate-term loan. These loans are called *equipment financing loans.*

Equipment financing loans are commonly made for readily marketable equipment. These loans are normally made for somewhat less than the market value of the equipment, and the difference provides a margin of safety for the lender. This difference may range between 20 and 30 percent for readily marketable and mobile equipment, such as trucks or cars. The amortization schedule for an equipment financing loan is usually tied closely to the asset's economic life.

There are several potential sources of equipment financing, including commercial banks, sales finance companies, equipment sellers, insurance companies, and pension funds. Commercial banks are often the least expensive source of such financing—especially when compared with sales finance companies. The equipment seller may provide financing either directly or through a captive finance subsidiary (that is, the seller's own financing subsidiary). Although at first glance, an equipment seller may appear to charge a very modest interest rate, it is often difficult to make a meaningful comparison between the rates charged by a supplier and other financing sources such as commercial banks. This is because the selling firm might price the equipment in such a way as to conceal part of the cost of carrying its credit customers; that is, noncash customers may pay relatively higher prices than cash customers.

There are two primary security instruments used in connection with equipment financing loans: the *conditional sales contract* and the *chattel mortgage.* Each of these is discussed in the following sections.

Conditional Sales Contract

When a conditional sales contract (sometimes called a *purchase money mortgage*) is used in an equipment financing transaction, the seller retains title until the buyer has made all payments required by the financing contract. Conditional sales contracts are used almost exclusively by equipment sellers. At the time of purchase, the buyer normally makes a down payment to the seller and issues a promissory note for the balance of the purchase price. The buyer then agrees to make a series of periodic payments (usually monthly or quarterly) of principal and interest to the seller until the note has been paid off. When the last payment has been made, the title to the equipment passes to the buyer. In the case of default, the seller may repossess the asset.

Chattel Mortgage

A chattel mortgage is a lien on property other than real estate. Chattel mortgages are most common when a commercial bank or sales finance company makes a direct equipment financing loan. It involves the placement of a lien against the property by the lender. Notification of the lien is filed with a public office in the state where the equipment is located. Given a valid lien, the lender may repossess the equipment and resell it if the borrower defaults on the loan payment.

Introduction to Leasing

A promotional brochure from the Warner and Swasey Financial Corporation states, "The value of a machine is in the use, not its ownership." This is true in the sense that whereas a firm may wish to acquire the *use* of an asset needed in the production of goods and the providing of services, it is not absolutely necessary to acquire legal title to the asset. Leasing is a means of obtaining economic use of an asset for a specific period of time without obtaining an ownership interest in the asset. In the lease contract, the property owner *(lessor)* agrees to permit the property user *(lessee)* to make use of the property for a stated time. In return, the lessee agrees to make a series of periodic payments to the lessor.

Leasing as a source of intermediate- and long-term financing has become increasingly popular since World War II. Prior to that time most lease contracts were written for real estate and farm property. Today there are few major firms that are not involved in leasing. Leased assets range from transportation equipment (such as railroad rolling stock, trucks, automobiles, airplanes, and ships) to computers, medical equipment, specialized industrial equipment, energy transmission equipment, and mining equipment. Some firms lease entire power-generating plants and aluminum reduction mills. In the hotel and motel industry, leases may even include bathroom fixtures, paintings, furniture, and bedding.

The volume of leasing activity has been expanded at about twice the rate of the country's GNP growth since 1970. By the early 1980s, about 20 percent of all capital outlays were financed through leases.

Many types of firms originate leases. These include commercial banks, savings and loan institutions, investment banks, industrial companies, finance companies, and automotive firms.

Because of the growing importance and widespread acceptance of lease financing, the contemporary financial manager should have a good understanding of this financing method. The following sections discuss the characteristics of various types of leases and develop a lease analysis model from the perspective of the lessor. Later sections consider the tax and accounting treatment of leases and the advantages and disadvantages of leases. Finally, a lease analysis model is developed from the perspective of the lessee.

Types of Leases

Leases are classified in a number of ways. "True leases," which are the primary focus of this chapter, are traditional leases in which the lessor is considered to hold the legal title to the leased asset. The asset user, the lessee, has no ownership interest in the asset. *Operating leases* and various types of *financial,* or *capital, leases* are subcategories of true leases.

Operating Leases

An *operating lease,* sometimes called a *service* or *maintenance lease,* is an agreement that provides the lessee with use of an asset on a period-by-period basis. Normally the payments under an operating lease contract are insufficient to recover the full cost of the asset for the lessor. As a result, the contract period in an operating lease tends to be somewhat less than the usable economic life of the asset, and the lessor expects to recover the costs (plus a return) from renewal rental payments, or the sale of the asset at the end of the lease period, or both.

The most important characteristic of an operating lease is that it may be canceled at the option of the lessee as long as the lessor is given sufficient notice. Even though the lessee may be required to pay a penalty to the lessor upon cancelation, this is preferable to being compelled to keep an asset that is expected to become obsolete in the near future. For example, many firms lease their computers under an operating lease arrangement. (Of course, the lessor charges a rental that is consistent with expectations of the asset's economic life.)

Most operating leases require the lessor to maintain the leased asset. In addition, the lessor is normally responsible for any property taxes owed on the asset and for providing appropriate insurance coverage. The costs of these services are built into the lease rate.

Financial, or Capital Leases

A *financial lease,* also termed a *capital lease,* is a noncancelable agreement.[3] The lessee is required to make payments throughout the lease period, whether or not the asset continues to generate economic benefits. Failure to make payments could eventually force the lessee into bankruptcy.

With financial leases, the lessee is generally responsible for maintenance of the asset. The lessee may also have to pay insurance and property taxes. The total payments over the lease period are sufficient to amortize the original cost of the asset and provide a return to the lessor. Some

---

[3] This chapter focuses primarily on financial leases rather than operating leases, because financial leases represent more permanent obligations. The analysis techniques discussed at the end of this chapter, however, are equally applicable to both operating and financial leases.

financial leases provide for a renewal or repurchase option at the end of the lease; these are limited by the IRS.

A financial lease may originate either as a *sale and leaseback* or as a *direct lease.*

Sale and Leaseback   A sale and leaseback occurs when a company sells an asset to another firm and immediately leases it back for its own use. In this transaction the lessor normally pays a price close to the asset's fair market value. The lease payments are set at a level that will return the full purchase price of the asset to the lessor, plus provide a reasonable rate of return. The sale and leaseback is advantageous to the lessee for the following reasons:

- The lessee receives cash from the sale of the asset, which may be reinvested elsewhere in the firm or used to increase the firm's liquidity.
- The lessee can continue using the asset, even though it is owned by someone else.

A good illustration of a sale and leaseback transaction was Pan American World Airways' decision in 1980 to sell and lease back its fifty-nine-story headquarters building to Metropolitan Life Insurance Company for $400 million. The sale was prompted by a continuing stream of losses from its airline operations. In the first half of 1980, Pan Am had losses of over $141 million. The sale was expected to give Pan Am a $340 million cash infusion after deducting selling costs of $10 million and the $50 million outstanding mortgage balance.

Direct Lease   A direct lease is initiated when a firm acquires the use of an asset that it did not previously own. The lease may be with the manufacturer of the asset or a financial institution. In the latter instance, the user-lessee first determines the following:

- What equipment will be leased.
- Which manufacturer will supply the equipment.
- What options, warranties, terms of delivery, installation agreements, and service agreements will have to be made.
- What price will be paid for the asset.

The lessee then contacts a financial institution and works out the terms of the lease, after which the institution (which then becomes the lessor) acquires the asset for the lessee and the lessee starts making the lease payments. Under this arrangement the lessee is usually responsible for taxes, insurance, and maintenance.

Leveraged Leases

Approximately 85 percent of all financial leases currently written in the United States are leveraged leases. Also known as *third-party equity leases* and *tax leases,* leveraged leases are designed to provide financing for assets that require large capital outlays (generally greater than $300,000) and have economic lives of five years or more. Leveraged leases are usually tax motivated because the asset-user (lessee) is not in a tax position where it can make use of the accelerated depreciation tax shields (and, prior to 1986, the Investment Tax Credit [ITC]) if the asset is owned instead of being leased.

A leveraged lease is a three-sided agreement among the lessee, the lessor, and the lenders. The *lessee* selects the leased asset, receives all the income generated from its use, and makes the periodic lease payments. The *lessor* (normally a financial institution, such as a leasing company or a commercial bank) acts either for itself or as a trustee for an individual or a group of individuals to provide the equity funds needed to purchase the asset. The *lenders* (usually banks, insurance companies, trusts, pension funds, or foundations) lend the funds needed to make up the asset's full purchase price. Specifically the lessor normally supplies 20 to 40 percent of the purchase price, and the lenders provide the remaining 60 to 80 percent.

Figure 15-1 is an announcement of a leveraged lease that was arranged by Salomon Brothers for Kansas City Southern Lines. In this case, the Ford Motor Credit Company acted as the lessor and provided equity funds of $4,728,974 to acquire 450 boxcars, which were leased to Kansas City Southern Lines. Debt funds of $10,072,198 were provided by a number of institutional lenders.

Figure 15-1   **Announcement of a Leveraged Lease Financing Arrangement**

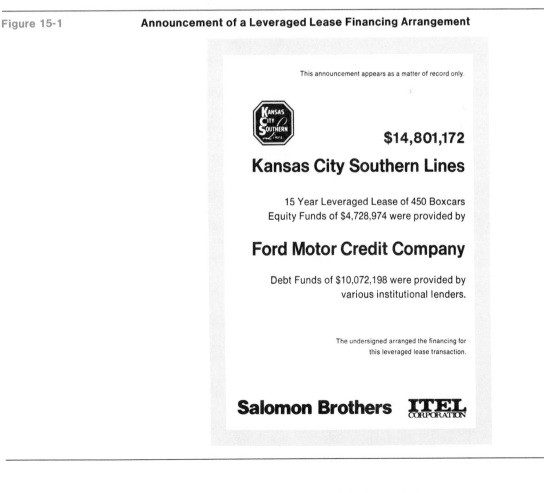

In a leveraged lease the long-term money is supplied to the lessor by the lenders on a nonrecourse basis; that is, the lenders cannot turn to the lessor for repayment of the debt in the event of default. Normally the lender receives mortgage bonds secured by the following:

- A first lien on the asset.
- An assignment of the lease.
- An assignment of the lease rental payments.
- Occasionally, a direct guarantee from the lessee or a third party (such as the government, in the case of merchant vessel financing).

Because the lenders do not have recourse to the lessor in the event of default, the lessor's risk exposure is limited to the 20 to 40 percent equity contribution.

As the owner of the asset, the lessor reports the lease payments as gross income. For tax purposes the lessor is entitled to the full value of any available investment tax credit. The lessor receives additional benefits from the tax-deductible interest and accelerated depreciation. As a result, the lessor incurs large tax losses and receives large cash inflows during the early years of the lease.

Because the lessor receives the entire accelerated depreciation tax shield (and prior to 1986, the ITC) while making a relatively small equity investment, the lessor can provide an attractive lease rate to the lessee. Lease rates of 4 to 6 percent are not uncommon when AAA-rated bonds are yielding from 9 to 10 percent. Figure 15-2 is a diagram of a typical leveraged lease arrangement.

Lessees who anticipate that their taxable income will not be sufficient to allow them to take advantage of the tax benefits of ownership are most likely to use leveraged leases for large transactions. These include firms with low profit levels, large tax loss carryforwards, or large amounts of tax-exempt income. The lessee effectively gives up the tax benefits of ownership in exchange for more favorable lease rates.[4]

Determining the Lease Payments: The Lessor's Perspective

The Wallace Company (lessee) desires to lease a piece of equipment valued at $100,000 from the Gray Company (lessor) for a period of five years. Under the terms of the lease, payments are to be made at the beginning of each of the five years. The Gray Company expects to depreciate the asset on a straight-line basis of $20,000 per year down to a book salvage value of $0. Actual salvage value is expected to be $10,000 at the end of five years. This salvage value will be treated as a recapture of depreciation and taxed at Gray's marginal, ordinary tax rate of 40 percent. Thus the after-tax salvage value will be $6,000 ($10,000 actual salvage less $4,000 tax on depreciation recapture). If Gray requires an 11 percent after-tax rate of return on the lease, what will be the annual lease payments?

- **Step 1** Compute the lessor's amount to be amortized; in this case, the $100,000 initial outlay minus the present value of the after-tax salvage

---

[4] The "Focus on Corporate Practice" example at the end of this chapter discusses a major leveraged lease transaction.

Figure 15-2   **Diagram of a Typical Leveraged Lease**

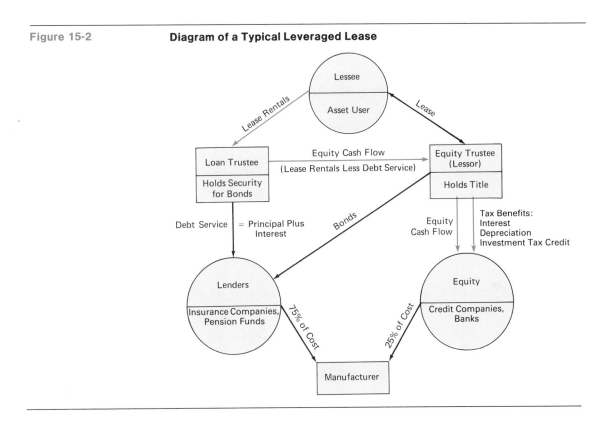

at the end of year 5 minus the present value of the after-tax depreciation tax shield for each year. (Recall that depreciation reduces taxable income by the amount of the depreciation and thus reduces a firm's cash outflow for tax payments by an amount equal to the depreciation times the company's marginal ordinary tax rate.)

Initial Outlay	$100,000
Less: Present value of $6,000 after-tax	
salvage at 11% ($6,000 × 0.593)	3,558
Less: Present value of annual depreciation tax	
shelter ($20,000 × 0.4 × $PVIFA_{0.11,5}$) =	
$8,000 × 3.696	29,568
Amount to be amortized	$ 66,874

(If the asset was eligible for an investment tax credit, the amount to be amortized would be reduced by the amount of the ITC. Also, if an accelerated depreciation method, such as ACRS, was used by the lessor, the present value of the annual depreciation tax shelter would have to be done using a series of Table II PVIF factors, since the annual depreciation tax shelter will normally change most years under accelerated depreciation methods.)

- **Step 2** Compute the annual *after-tax* lease income which the lessor must receive in order to earn the needed 11 percent return. Remember that lease payments received by a lessor are treated as taxable, ordinary income. These payments can be computed using the appropriate interest factor for the present value of an annuity (PVIFA from Table IV). Since lease payments are normally made at the beginning of each year, they constitute an *annuity due*. Thus, the last four payments, which occur at the ends of years 1 through 4, are discounted, whereas the present value of the first payment, made at the *beginning* of year 1, is not discounted. Recall from Chapter 3 that taking the PVIFA for 11 percent and five years and multiplying by $(1 + 0.11)$ gives the required PVIFA for an annuity due. If R is the annual after-tax lease income to the lessor, the present value of the lease income may be set equal to the amount to be amortized to determine the required R, as follows:

$$\text{Amount to be amortized} = R \ (\text{PVIFA}_{0.11,5}) \ (1 + 0.11)$$
$$\$66,874 = R \ (3.696) \ (1.11)$$
$$\$66,874 = R \ (4.103)$$
$$R = \$16,299$$

Thus, the Gray Company needs to receive five beginning-of-the-year, after-tax lease income amounts of $16,299 in order to earn an 11 percent after-tax return on the lease.

• **Step 3** Convert the lease income requirement of the lessor to a lease payment requirement of the lessee. Recalling that lease payments received by the lessor from the lessee are taxed as ordinary income, we can convert the after-tax lease income requirement of the lessor into a lease payment requirement for the lessee as follows:

$$\text{Lease payment required from the lessee} = \frac{\text{Lease income required by lessor (after-tax)}}{1 \text{ minus lessor's marginal ordinary tax rate}}$$
$$= \frac{\$16,299}{1 - 0.4}$$
$$= \$27,165$$

Thus, the Wallace Company will have to make an annual lease payment of $27,165 to the Gray Company at the beginning of each year.

Tax Status of True Leases

Annual lease payments are tax deductible for the lessee if one crucial criterion is met; namely, the IRS must agree that a contract is truly a lease and not just an installment loan being called a lease. Before embarking on a lease transaction, all involved parties should obtain an opinion from the IRS regarding the tax status of the proposed lease. The opinion of the IRS normally revolves primarily around the following general rules:

• The remaining useful life of the equipment at the end of the lease term must be the greater of one year or 20 percent of its originally estimated useful life.

- Leases in excess of thirty years are *not* considered to be leases for tax purposes.
- The lease payments must provide the lessor with a reasonable return on the investment. At this point in time, a range of 8 to 16 percent would probably be viewed as reasonable. This profit potential must exist apart from the transaction's tax benefits.
- Renewal options must be reasonable; that is, the renewal rate must be closely related to the economic value of the asset for the renewal period.
- If the lease agreement specifies a purchase option at the end of the lease period, the purchase price must be based on the asset's fair market value at that time.
- In the case of a leveraged lease, the lessor must provide a minimum of 20 percent equity.
- Limited use property (valuable only to the lessee) may not be leased.

If the IRS does not agree that a contract is truly a lease, taxes are applied as if the property had been sold to the lessee and pledged to the lessor as security for a loan. The reason for the IRS restrictions previously cited is that the IRS wants to prohibit lease transactions that are set up purely to speed up tax deductions. For example, a building would normally be depreciated over eighteen years under ACRS depreciation rules. It would be possible to set up a lease over a three-year period that allowed the lessee to effectively write off the cost of the building for tax purposes over three years. This would increase tax deductions for the lessee at the expense of tax receipts to the U.S. Treasury. These IRS guidelines are designed to prevent this type of abuse.

Finally, it should be noted that under Section 48(d) of the IRS Code, the investment tax credit may be taken by either the lessor or the lessee, or shared between the two. In leveraged leases the investment tax credit is normally taken by the lessor, but this is not required per se by the IRS. In general, the two parties to a lease have considerable latitude in working out a mutually acceptable agreement concerning the investment tax credit. For example, in the leveraged lease transactions discussed in the Focus on Corporate Practice example at the end of this chapter, the Public Service Company of New Mexico retained the ITC in its Palo Verde Unit #1 lease, but the lessors were to receive the ITC in the Unit #2 lease. After 1986 the ITC no longer will exist. Hence, this provision (Sec. 48(d)) of lease analysis will become obsolete.

Leases and Accounting Practices

In recent years firms have tended to disclose more information regarding lease obligations.

In November 1976 the Financial Accounting Standards Board (FASB) issued *Standard No. 13,* which *requires* lessees to capitalize certain types of leases, primarily financial or capital leases. The capitalized value of a lease is determined by computing the present value of all required lease

Table 15-2   **Accounting Treatment of Leases**

Assets		Liabilities	
Lease property under capital leases less accumulated amortization	$1,500	Current: Obligations under capital leases*	$ 150
		Long term: Obligations under capital leases*	1,350
	$1,500		$1,500

*The $150 represents lease payments due during the next year. The $1,350 represents the present value of lease payments due beyond one year in the future.

payments, discounted at a rate equal to the lessee's incremental borrowing rate for a secured loan over a term similar to the lease.[5] Table 15-2 illustrates this procedure.

In addition to making these balance sheet adjustments, a firm must show the following in the footnotes to the financial statements:[6]

• *For financial leases:*

1. The gross amount of assets reported under financial leases as of the date of the balance sheet by major classes according to nature or use.

2. The amount of accumulated lease amortization.

3. Future minimum lease payments as of the date of the latest balance sheet presented, in total and for each of the next five fiscal years.

• *For operating leases:*

1. Future minimum rental payments required as of the date of the latest balance sheet presented, in total and for each of the following five fiscal years.

2. The rental expense for each period for which an income statement is presented.

The lessee also must indicate in the notes to the financial statements the existence and terms of renewal or repurchase options and escalation clauses, any restrictions imposed by leases (such as restrictions on dividends, additional debt, or further leasing), and any contingent rental obligations.

The effect of these new disclosure requirements is to lower a firm's reported return on investment and to increase the reported debt-to-equity ratios of those firms that have acquired portions of their assets through leasing. In the past some analysts argued that one of the advantages of leasing was that it provided "off-balance sheet" financing and tended to increase a firm's capacity to borrow. Whether or not this was true, the new lease-reporting requirements should eliminate this distortion, facilitate

[5] In certain circumstances it is possible for a firm to use a lower rate. See FASB *Standard No. 13* for a more detailed discussion.

[6] The requirements presented here are not inclusive; they merely summarize the most significant disclosures.

clearer analysis of a firm's financial condition, and make it easier to make comparisons among firms.

Advantages and Disadvantages of Leasing

There are a number of potential advantages to leasing. However, the prudent financial manager also should be aware of the disadvantages.

Advantages

Perhaps the major advantage of leasing is that it provides *flexible financing*. Most lease arrangements tend to have fewer restrictive covenants than loan agreements. In addition, leasing is well suited to piecemeal financing. A firm that is acquiring assets over time may find it more convenient to lease them than to negotiate term loans or sell securities each time it makes a new capital outlay.

In the case of real estate leasing, the lessee may *effectively be able to depreciate land*. Since the lease payments will reflect both the lessor's investment in any buildings *and* the cost of the land, the lessee is able to effectively depreciate the land by deducting the full amount of the lease payment for tax purposes. To keep this benefit in perspective, however, it should be noted that the lessee also loses any salvage value associated with the property at the end of the lease.

The lessee also may be able to make *lower payments* because of the tax benefits enjoyed by the lessor. This is especially important in the case of a leveraged lease, when the lessee is a firm with insufficient taxable income to take advantage of the tax benefits of ownership. In fact, the majority of lease transactions which are made are tax motivated.

In addition, it *may* be possible for the lessee to *avoid some of the risks of obsolescence* associated with ownership. The lessor will charge a lease rate intended to provide a specified return on the required net investment. The net investment is equal to the cost of the asset minus the present value of the expected salvage value at the end of the lease. If the actual salvage is less than originally expected, the lessor bears the loss.

For the small or marginally profitable firm, *leasing is often the only available source of financing,* since the title to leased property remains with the lessor and reduces the lessor's risk in the event of failure. If the lessee does fail, the lessor can quickly recover the leased property.

Leasing tends to *smooth out expenses* for the lessee. Since lease payments are a constant annual outlay, whereas ACRS depreciation expenses are large in the early years of ownership and less in later years, earnings tend to appear more stable when assets are leased rather than owned. In addition, reported earnings per share are normally higher in the early years of a lease as compared with ownership because of the use of ACRS depreciation when the asset is owned.

Leasing is said to provide *100 percent financing*, whereas most borrowing requires a down payment. Because lease payments are normally made in advance of each period, this 100 percent financing benefit is diminished by the amount of the first required lease payment.

From the lessee's perspective, leases can *increase a firm's liquidity*. For example, a sale and leaseback transforms some of a firm's fixed assets into cash in exchange for an obligation to make a series of fixed future payments.

And, finally, leasing gives some plant or divisional managers additional *flexibility in acquiring assets* if lease agreements are not subject to internal capital expenditure constraints. In recent years local school districts, municipalities, and the Department of the Navy, among other organizations, have used leasing to circumvent capital outlay restrictions.

Disadvantages

The primary disadvantage of leasing is *cost*. For a firm with a strong earnings record, good access to the credit markets, and the ability to take advantage of the tax benefits of ownership, leasing is often a more expensive alternative. Of course, the actual cost difference between ownership and leasing depends on a number of factors and varies from case to case.

Another disadvantage of leasing is the *loss of the asset's salvage value*. In real estate this loss can be substantial. A lessee may also have *difficulty getting approval to make property improvements* on leased real estate. If the improvements substantially alter the property or reduce its potential range of uses the lessor may be reluctant to permit them.

In addition, if a leased asset (with a financial lease) becomes obsolete or if the capital project financed by the lease becomes uneconomical, *the lessee may not cancel the lease without paying a substantial penalty*.

Lease-Buy Analysis: The Lessee's Perspective

Financial theorists and model builders have devoted a substantial amount of time and effort to developing an analytical framework within which the differential costs associated with leasing versus buying can be compared. At least fifteen different approaches to the problem have been suggested, and there is considerable disagreement as to which one is the best.[7] In spite of this abundance of models, the perplexed financial manager can take some comfort in the fact that the practical effects resulting from the differences in the models tend to be small, since few real-world decisions are changed as a result of which lease-buy model is chosen.[8]

One of the most commonly used approaches to the analysis of a lease versus purchase decision assumes that the appropriate comparison should be between *leasing* and *borrowing to buy*. Advocates of this approach argue that a financial lease is much like a loan in that it requires a series of fixed payments. Failure to make lease payments, like failure to make loan payments, may result in bankruptcy.

The basic approach of the lease-buy analysis model is to compute the *net advantage to leasing* (NAL). The net advantage to leasing compares the present value cost of leasing with the present value cost of owning the asset. If the cost of owning the asset is greater than the cost of leasing the

---

[7] Basically, the various models differ as to which discount rate should be used to evaluate various components of the cash flows and as to which cash flows should be considered.

[8] Evidence of this is presented in a paper by Arthur Gudikunst and Gordon Roberts. "Empirical Analysis of Lease-Buy Decisions," presented at the 1975 Meeting of the Eastern Finance Association.

asset, the NAL is positive and the model indicates that the asset should be leased.

The *net advantage to leasing* calculation is as follows:

Installed cost of the asset
Less: Investment tax credit retained by the lessor
Less: Present value of the after-tax lease payment
Less: Present value of depreciation tax shield
Plus: Present value of after-tax operating costs incurred if owned but not if leased
Less: Present value of the after-tax salvage value
Equals: Net advantage to leasing

The installed cost of the asset equals the purchase price plus installation and shipping charges. The installed cost forms the basis on which depreciation and the investment tax credit (if allowed) are computed. The investment tax credit reduces the cost of ownership and hence reduces the NAL. Sometimes all, or a portion of the ITC is claimed by the lessee. Hence it is important to consider only the amount of the ITC which is claimed by the *lessor* in a transaction when computing the NAL since this is the amount of the ITC which is given up if the asset is leased rather than being owned.

The present value of the after-tax lease payments which are made if the asset is leased reduce the NAL; hence they are subtracted when computing the NAL. These lease payments are discounted at the firm's after-tax marginal cost of borrowing to reflect the fact that lease payments are contractually known in advance and thus are not subject to much uncertainty. The present value of the depreciation tax shield is equal to the depreciation claimed each year if the asset is owned times the firm's marginal tax rate. The depreciation tax shield reduces the cost of ownership and hence is subtracted when computing the NAL. Since the depreciation amounts are also known with relative certainty, they are also discounted at the firm's after-tax marginal cost of borrowing.[9]

Sometimes there are operating costs which are incurred if the asset is owned but not if it is leased. These may include property tax payments, insurance, or some maintenance expenses. If these do exist they represent a benefit of leasing and increase the NAL. Hence the after-tax amount of these costs is added in the NAL calculation. These operating cost savings are also discounted at the after-tax marginal cost of borrowing, reflecting their relative certainty. Finally, if the asset is owned the owner will receive the after-tax salvage value. This is lost if the asset is leased. Hence the after-tax salvage reduces the NAL and must be subtracted when calculating the NAL. Because asset salvage values are generally subject to

---

[9] The depreciation amounts are known with certainty, but the tax shield from depreciation may not be certain. For example, in 1986 Congress was considering a major tax reform plan which could reduce the marginal corporate tax rate, thereby reducing the value of the tax shield. Also, there is always the chance that a company will not have sufficient taxable income to take advantage of the depreciation tax shield.

substantial uncertainty, they are normally discounted at a rate equal to the firm's weighted (marginal) cost of capital.

Consider the following example to illustrate the procedure described above. Copy Products, Inc. (CPI) is trying to decide whether it should purchase or lease a new high-speed laser printing press. (The firm has already computed the net present value of this proposed asset acquisition and found the project to be acceptable.) The laser press can be purchased for $50,000, including delivery and installation. Alternatively, the press can be leased for a six-year period at a beginning-of-the-year lease payment of $10,000. If purchased, CPI could borrow the needed funds at an annual interest rate of 10 percent. If the printing press is purchased, CPI estimates that it will incur $750 per year of expenses to cover insurance and a maintenance contract. These expenses would not be incurred if the press is leased. The printing press will be depreciated under ACRS guidelines as a five-year asset, and the printing press is eligible for the 10 percent investment tax credit (ITC).

If CPI leases the press, the lessor will claim 90 percent of the ITC. CPI expects the actual salvage value to be $20,000 at the end of six years. CPI's marginal tax rate is 40 percent, and its weighted after-tax cost of capital is 15 percent. Which alternative—leasing or buying—should be chosen? In order to answer this question we need to compute the NAL. This is shown in Table 15-3. The calculation in Table 15-3 indicates a net advantage to leasing of −$4,644. Since the NAL is negative, the asset should be owned rather than leased.[10]

This general procedure can be used to evaluate any lease versus buy decision once it has been determined by standard capital budgeting techniques that an asset should be acquired.

Summary

- *Term loans,* or *intermediate-term credit,* include any debt obligation having an initial maturity between one and ten years.

- Term loans, being privately negotiated between the borrower and the lender, tend to be cheaper than public security offerings, since flotation costs on small to medium-sized public offerings are high. Thus, term loans are a good source of funds for financing small and medium-sized increases in working capital or for financing the acquisition of a piece of equipment.

- Term loans are normally amortized by a series of installments. The interest rate ranges between 0.25 and 2.5 percent above the prime rate. Many term loan agreements require that some specific asset be pledged as *security.* In addition, the borrowing firm may have to agree to certain *affirmative, negative,* and *restrictive covenants* governing its actions during the loan period.

---

[10] The lease-buy analysis procedure used above implicitly assumes that the leasing alternative and the borrowing-to-buy alternative have the same impact on the company's debt capacity. This is desirable since leasing and borrowing both represent fixed obligations which are treated by financial analysts as being equivalent to debt.

Table 15-3   **Calculation of the Net Advantage to Leasing for CPI**

End of Year (1)	Installed Asset Cost (2)	ITC Claimed by Lessor[1] (3)	Lease Payment After-tax[2] (4)	Depreciation[3] (5)	Depreciation Tax Shield[4] (6)	Additional Operating Costs if Owned After-tax[5] (7)
0	$50,000	$4,500	$6,000	—	—	—
1	—	—	6,000	$7,125	$2,850	$450
2	—	—	6,000	10,450	4,180	450
3	—	—	6,000	9,975	3,990	450
4	—	—	6,000	9,975	3,990	450
5	—	—	6,000	9,975	3,990	450
6	—	—	—	—	—	450

NAL Cash Flows Except Salvage[6] (8)=(2)−(3)−(4)−(6)+(7)	PVIF @ 6%[7] (9)	Present Value[8] (10)=(8)×(9)	After-Tax Salvage[9] (11)	PVIF @ 15% (12)	Present Value Salvage[10] (13)=(11)×(12)	NAL[11] (14)=(10)−(13)
$39,500	1.000	$39,500	—	—	—	$39,500
−8,400	0.943	−7,921	—	—	—	−7,921
−9,730	0.890	−8,660	—	—	—	−8,660
−9,540	0.840	−8,014	—	—	—	−8,014
−9,540	0.792	−7,556	—	—	—	−7,556
−9,540	0.747	−7,126	—	—	—	−7,126
450	0.705	317	$12,000	0.432	$5,184	−4,867
				Net Advantage to Leasing =		**−$ 4,644**

Notes to table:
1. The ITC claimed by the lessor in this example is equal to 0.90 × 0.10 × $50,000 = $4,500. We assume that the ITC benefit is received at time 0. This is realistic given the payment of quarterly taxes by companies.
2. The after-tax lease payment equals the total lease payment ($10,000) times 1 minus CPI's marginal tax rate (40 percent). The benefit of the tax deductibility of lease payments is assumed to be received at approximately the same time the lease payments are made, reflecting the quarterly payment of taxes.
3. ACRS depreciation is computed using the five-year ACRS rates times the installed cost less one-half of the ITC ($50,000 − 0.5[$5,000] = $47,500). The ACRS rates are 15, 22, 21, 21, and 21 percent respectively over the five years.
4. The depreciation tax shield is equal to the depreciation in column (5) times CPI's marginal tax rate (40 percent).
5. Column (7) is equal to $750 pre-tax cost times 1 minus CPI's marginal tax rate (40 percent).
6. Column (8) is the total of the cash flows needed to compute the NAL which are discounted at the after-tax cost of debt for CPI. It is equal to the installed cost (2), less the ITC claimed by the lessor (3), less the after-tax lease payments (4), less the depreciation tax shield (6), plus the additional after-tax operating costs incurred if the asset is owned.
7. The after-tax cost of debt is 6 percent (10 percent pre-tax cost times 1 minus CPI's marginal tax rate [40 percent]).
8. The present value of column (10) is equal to the cash flows in Column (8) times the PVIF factors in column (9).
9. The after-tax salvage is equal to the pre-tax salvage ($20,000) times 1 minus CPI's marginal ordinary tax rate (40 percent). The ordinary tax rate is used because the salvage value reflects a recapture of depreciation.
10. The present value of the salvage is equal to the after-tax salvage times the PVIF for 15 percent and six years, where the 15 percent represents CPI's weighted cost of capital.
11. The NAL is equal to the sum of the present value cash flows from Column (10) minus the present value of the after-tax salvage from column (13).

- Term loans are supplied by several institutions, including commercial banks (frequently the cheapest supplier of term funds), life insurance companies and pension funds (who prefer making loans having longer maturities), the Small Business Administration, small business investment companies, municipal or state industrial development authorities, and sales finance companies.

- Term loans that are secured by a lien on a piece of equipment are called *equipment financing loans*. They are made by the lending institutions previously named, as well as by equipment sellers or *captive finance subsidiaries.* The two primary security instruments used in equipment financing are the *conditional sales contract* and the *chattel mortgage.*

- A *lease* is a written agreement that permits the *lessee* to use a piece of property owned by the *lessor* in exchange for a series of periodic lease or rental payments.

- An *operating lease* provides the lessee with the use of an asset on a period-by-period basis. An operating lease *may be canceled* at the lessee's option. Most operating leases are written for a relatively short period of time, normally less than five years.

- A *financial lease* is a *noncancelable* agreement that obligates the lessee to make payments to the lessor for a predetermined period of time. There are two major types of financial leases: *sale and leaseback* agreements and *direct leases. Leveraged leases,* also called *tax leases,* have become increasingly common due to the effects of the investment tax credit. Approximately 85 percent of the financial leases written today are leveraged leases.

- Subject to a series of IRS guidelines, firms that lease a portion of their assets may deduct the full amount of the lease payment for tax purposes.

- Recent decisions by the Financial Accounting Standards Board (FASB) require that financial leases be capitalized and shown on the lessee's balance sheet.

- Leasing offers a number of potential advantages, including flexibility, the effective depreciation of land, and tax benefits (in some cases). It also may be the only source of financing available to many marginally profitable firms. It has a number of potential disadvantages, too, however. For example, leasing tends to be more costly than ownership for a firm with a good earnings record and good access to the capital markets.

- A number of analytical models are available to assist the lessor in determining what lease payments to charge. Other models are available to assist the lessee in determining which is the less expensive source of financing—leasing or borrowing to buy.

FOCUS ON CORPORATE PRACTICE

Leveraged Lease Financing of a Portion of a Nuclear Power Plant

Albert J. Robison
Senior Vice-President and Chief Financial Officer
Public Service Company of New Mexico

Public Service Company of New Mexico (PNM) provides electric and natural gas service to areas in north, central, southwestern, and northeastern New Mexico. PNM also provides water service to the City of Santa Fe, New Mexico. Total revenues in 1985 were approximately $800 million with total plant assets exceeding $2.3 billion.

In 1977, PNM was granted a Certificate of Public Convenience and Necessity to participate in the Arizona Nuclear Power Project (also known as Palo Verde Nuclear Generating Station) and to own, operate, and maintain an undivided 10.2 percent interest in each of the three nuclear generating units at Palo Verde, together with all common facilities incident to those units.

In late 1985, PNM refinanced its construction financing for the Palo Verde Unit #1 by entering into a series of sale and leaseback transactions relating to PNM's 10.2 percent undivided ownership interest in that unit and a proportionate share of one-third of PNM's 10.2 percent undivided ownership interest in certain common facilities at the Palo Verde site.

The term of the leases is approximately twenty-eight and one-half years. They provide the option, but not the obligation, for a single renewal at 50 percent of the original rent for a term not less than two years. At the end of the basic term and at the end of the renewal term, PNM has the option to purchase the facilities at their fair market value at that time. The transaction was structured as a leveraged lease with PNM retaining responsibility for operation and maintenance. As is common in leveraged lease transactions, the lessors borrowed approximately 80 percent of the purchase price of the facilities from a "Funding Corporation" formed for that purpose. The funding corporation, in turn, borrowed the debt portion of the purchase price initially from commercial banks but ultimately by issuing public debt that is non-recourse to the lessors and the equity investors. The debt is indirectly secured by the facilities and payable from rentals due from PNM under the leases. The debt is structured to have principal and interest payments that correspond to the receipt of rental payments under the leases. This debt is issued in serial form, that is, obligations with different maturities and principal amounts.

PNM makes lease payments semiannually to the lessors. These payments are sufficient to provide a return on the equity investors' capital investment and to pay the principal and interest on the debt obligations issued for the financing.

The Palo Verde Unit #1 was sold for approximately $450 million, resulting in a pre-tax gain on the sale of approximately $148 million, but was "breakeven" for book purposes.

The sale and leaseback of PNM's share of Palo Verde Unit #1 provides important benefits to PNM's customers. First, the net present value of capital costs are reduced by the transfer of tax benefits to the equity investors and by the recapitalization of the plant financing with greater debt leverage. (Recall that 80 percent of the cost of the plant to the lessors is financed with non-recourse debt, compared to a 50 percent debt ratio for PNM.) Second, the revenue requirements associated with the plant are levelized over the life of the plant, thereby reducing the "rate shock" associated with bringing a nuclear power plant into PNM's rate base.

An economic analysis which compares the cost to customers of lease financing with that of continued ownership, assuming a traditional ratemaking environment, indicates that in the first full year of the lease, revenue requirements are reduced by $40 million. Over the life of Unit # 1, the leasing option reduces the present worth of revenue requirements by at least $140 million. Leasing tends to levelize electric rates over time, providing large savings in early years, which are partially offset in later years when the lease revenue requirements exceed those of ownership. The proceeds from the sale and leaseback of the unit have been used primarily for refunding outstanding debt obligations.

This first ever sale and leaseback of a nuclear power plant is indicative of the potential for leasing in the utility industry. Sale and leaseback arrangements offer a low-cost financing alternative for utilities which can reduce electricity costs significantly for customers and dramatically improve the cash flow position of the utility. In this environment the leasing alternative is rapidly becoming a preferred alternative for financing long-lived assets on a fixed rate basis for terms as long as thirty years.

Questions and Topics for Discussion

1. Under what circumstances might a firm prefer intermediate-term borrowing to either long- or short-term borrowing?

2. Discuss the advantages and disadvantages of the following types of term loans:
   a. Those that require equal periodic payments.
   b. Those that require equal periodic reductions in outstanding principal.
   c. Balloon loans.
   d. Bullet loans.

3. What are the major factors that influence the effective cost of a term loan?

4. Define the following and give an example of each:
   a. Affirmative covenants.
   b. Negative covenants.
   c. Restrictive covenants.

5. What institutions are the primary suppliers of business term loans?

6. Define the following:
   a. A conditional sales contract.
   b. A chattel mortgage.

7. Under what conditions would a firm prefer the following?
   a. A "fixed-rate" term loan from a bank.
   b. A "floating-rate" term loan, with the rate tied to the bank's prime rate?

8. What are the primary differences between operating leases and financial leases?

9. How does a leveraged lease differ from a nonleveraged financial lease? What type of firm or organization is most likely to take advantage of the leveraged lease financing option? What type of individual or financial institution is most likely to act as the lessor in a leveraged lease?

10. From a tax perspective, what are the primary requirements in a lease transaction that must be met in order for the IRS to consider the transaction a genuine lease? Why is a favorable IRS ruling regarding the tax status of a lease important to both the lessor and the lessee?

11. One advantage that has often been claimed of lease financing is that it creates "off-balance sheet" financing. Evaluate this benefit in light of FASB *Opinion No. 13.*

12. How can leasing allow a firm to effectively "depreciate" land?

13. What effect does leasing have on the stability of a firm's reported earnings?

14. It has been argued that leasing is almost always more expensive than borrowing and owning. Do you think this is true? Why or why not? Under what circumstances is leasing likely to be more desirable than direct ownership?

Problems*

Lotus123

1. Lobo Banks normally provides term loans that require repayment in a series of equal annual installments. If a $10 million loan is made, what would be the annual end-of-year payments, assuming the following?
   a. A 10 percent loan for 12 years.
   b. A 10 percent loan for 9 years.
   c. A 6 percent loan for 8 years.

Lotus123

2. Set up the amortization schedule for a 5-year, $1 million, 9 percent term loan that requires equal annual end-of-year payments. Be sure to distinguish between the *interest* and the *principal* portion of each payment. What is the *effective* interest cost of this loan?

* Color numbers denote problems which have check answers provided at the end of the book.

3. Set up the amortization schedule for a 5-year, $1 million, 9 percent loan that requires equal annual end-of-year principal payments each year plus interest on the unamortized loan balance. What is the *effective* interest cost of this loan?

4. Set up the amortization schedule for a 5-year, $1 million, 9 percent bullet loan. How is the principal repaid in this type of loan? What is the *effective* interest cost of this loan?

5. A firm receives a $1 million, 5-year loan at a 10 percent interest rate. The loan requires annual payments of $125,000 per year (at the end of each year) for years 1 to 4.
  a. What payment is required at the end of year 5?
  b. What would you call this type of loan?
  c. How does it differ from the loan in Problem 2?
  d. What is the *effective* interest cost of this loan?

6. A $10 million, 5-year loan bears an interest rate of 7 percent. The loan repayment plan calls for five annual end-of-year payments. Each payment is to include an equal amount of principal repayment ($2 million per year) plus accrued interest. Set up the amortization schedule for this loan. Be sure to distinguish between the *interest* and the *principal* portions of each annual payment. What is the *effective* interest cost of this loan?

7. Huskie Bank has provided the Mucklup Manufacturing Company with a 2-year term loan for $200,000 at a stated annual rate of interest of 10 percent. Interest for the entire 2-year period must be prepaid; that is, the loan's total interest payments must be made at the same time the loan is granted. Mucklup is required to repay the entire $200,000 principal balance at the end of the 2-year period.
    Compute the effective annual percentage cost of the loan.

8. The James Company has been offered a 4-year loan from its bank in the amount of $100,000 at a stated interest rate of 10 percent per year. The loan will require four equal end-of-year payments of principal and interest plus a $30,000 balloon payment at the end of the fourth year.
  a. Compute the amount of each of the end-of-year payments.
  b. Prepare a loan amortization schedule detailing the amount of principal and interest in each year's payment.
  c. What is the effective interest rate on this loan? Prove your answer.

    Hint: Each year's payment may be computed by solving for the annuity payment of a 4-year, 10 percent annuity that has a present value of $70,000—the amount of the loan that is amortized by the four yearly payments—and adding to that amount the interest on the unpaid balloon portion of the loan.

9. A $1 million loan requires 5 end-of-year equal payments of $284,333.
  a. Calculate the *effective* interest rate on this loan.
  b. How much interest (in dollars) is paid over the life of this loan?

10. MacKenzie Corp. is considering leasing a new asset. The lease would run for 8 years and require 8 *beginning-of-year* payments of $100,000 each. If MacKenzie capitalizes this lease for financial reporting purposes at a 10 percent rate, what asset amount will be reported initially on its balance sheet? What liability amount will be reported on its balance sheet? (Remember, lease payments are at the beginning of each year, making them an annuity due.)

11. Ajax Leasing Services has been approached by Gamma Tools to provide lease financing for a new automated screw machine. The machine will cost $220,000 and will be leased by Gamma for 5 years. Lease payments will be made at the *beginning* of each year. Ajax will depreciate the machine on a straight-line basis of $44,000 per year down to a book salvage value of $0. Actual salvage value is estimated to be $30,000 at the end of 5 years. No investment tax credit is permitted under the tax laws prevailing at the time the asset is acquired. Ajax's marginal tax rate is 40 percent. Ajax desires to earn a 12 percent, after-tax rate of return on this lease. What are the required annual beginning-of-year lease payments.

12. The First National Bank of Springer has established a leasing subsidiary. A local firm, Allied Business Machines, has approached the bank to arrange lease financing for $10 million in new machinery. The economic life of the machinery is estimated to be 20 years. The estimated salvage value at the end of the 20-year period is $0. The machinery is eligible for the 10 percent investment tax credit. The tax credit is assumed to be immediately available at the time the asset is acquired. Allied Business Machines has indicated a willingness to pay the bank $1 million per year at the *end* of each year for 20 years under the terms of a financial lease.

    a. If the bank retains the benefit of the investment tax credit, depreciates the machinery on a straight-line basis over 20 years to a $0 estimated salvage value, and has a 40 percent marginal tax rate, what *after-tax* rate of return will the bank earn on the lease?

    b. In general, what effect would the use of ACRS depreciation by the bank have on the rate of return it earns from the lease?

13. Jenkins Corporation wants to acquire a $200,000 computer. Jenkins has a 40 percent marginal tax rate. If owned, the computer would be depreciated on a straight-line basis to a *book* salvage value of $0. The actual cash salvage value is expected to be $20,000 at the end of 10 years. No investment tax credit is available to Jenkins at the time it acquires the computer. If the computer is purchased Jenkins could borrow the needed funds at an annual pre-tax interest rate of 10 percent. If purchased, Jenkins will incur annual maintenance expenses of $1,000. These expenses would not be incurred if the computer is leased. The lease rate would be $28,000 per year, payable at the beginning of each year. Jenkins' weighted after-tax cost of capital is 12 percent.

    a. Compute the *net advantage to leasing*.

    b. In general, what effect would the use of accelerated depreciation, such as ACRS, have on the answer to part a?

    c. Which alternative, leasing or owning, should be chosen?

14. The following stream of after-tax cash flows are available to you as a potential equity investor in a leveraged lease:

End of Year	Cash Flow (After Tax)	End of Year	Cash Flow (After Tax)
0	−50	6	0
1	+30	7	−5
2	+20	8	−10
3	+15	9	−15
4	+10	10	+10
5	+5		

The cash flow in year 0 represents the initial equity investment. The high positive cash flows in years 1 to 5 result from the tax shield benefits from the investment tax credit, accelerated depreciation, and interest deductibility on the nonrecourse debt. The negative cash flows in years 6 to 9 are indicative of the cash flows generated in a leveraged lease after the earlier-period tax shields have been utilized. The positive cash flow occurring in year 10 is the result of the asset's salvage value.

a. What problems would you encounter in computing the equity investor's rate of return on this investment?

b. If, as a potential equity investor, you require an 8 percent after-tax rate of return on investments of this type, should you make this investment?

15. The Jacobs Company desires to lease a numerically controlled milling machine costing $200,000. Jacobs has asked both First Manufacturers Bank Leasing Corp. and Commercial Associates, Inc. (a commercial finance company), to quote an annual lease rate. Both leasing companies now require a 20 percent *pretax* rate of return on this type of lease. Suppose First Manufacturers estimates the machine's salvage value at the end of the lease to be $30,000, and Commercial Associates estimates salvage to be $80,000. Based on this information and disregarding the investment tax credit, what annual (beginning-of-year) lease payments will each leasing company require, if the lease term is 5 years? (Note: Since the required rate of return of both the bank and the finance company is stated on a pre-tax basis, you need not consider depreciation, the investment tax credit, or the tax effects of salvage.)

16. The First National Bank of Great Falls is considering a leveraged lease agreement involving some mining equipment with the Big Sky Mining Corporation. The bank (40 percent tax bracket) will be the lessor; the mining company, the lessee (0 percent tax bracket); and a large California pension fund, the lender. Big Sky is seeking $50 million, and the pension fund has agreed to lend the bank $40 million at 10 percent. The bank has agreed to repay the pension fund $4 million of principal each year plus interest. (The remaining balance will be repaid in a balloon payment at the end of the fifth year.) The equipment will be depreciated on a straight line basis over a five-year estimated useful life with no expected salvage value. Assuming Big Sky has agreed to annual lease payments of $10 million, calculate the bank's initial cash outflow and its first 2 years of cash inflows.

17. As a financial analyst for Muffin Construction you have been asked to recommend the method of financing the acquisition of new equipment needed by the firm. The equipment has a useful life of 6 years. If purchased, the equipment which costs $700,000 will be depreciated under 5-year ACRS rules. The equipment is eligible for a 10 percent investment tax credit (ITC). If leased, the lessor will claim the full ITC. If purchased, the needed funds can be borrowed at a 10 percent pre-tax annual rate. Muffin's weighted after-tax cost of capital is 12 percent. The *actual* salvage value at the end of 6 years is $50,000. Muffin's marginal ordinary tax rate is 40 percent. Annual, beginning-of-year lease payments would be $160,000.

a. Compute the net advantage to leasing.

b. Should Muffin lease or own the equipment?

18. Darling Leasing is considering the lease of a piece of equipment costing $100,000 to Major State University. The period of the lease will be 5 years. The equipment is eligible for a 10 percent investment tax credit. It will be depreciated under ACRS guidelines over 5 years. Darling's marginal tax rate is 40 percent for ordinary income and 28 percent for capital gains. Annual (end-of-year) lease payments will be $24,000. Estimated salvage is $10,000. If Darling requires a 20 percent return on equipment it leases, should the lease be made?

Lotus123

**An Integrative
Case Problem**

Lease and Term Loan Analysis

Bay Products Corporation of North America (BPCNA) currently has no computer facilities. Recent growth in the firm's operations has led management to consider the possibility of adding an in-house mid-size computer to its accounting and financial departments. BPCNA management has called in consultants from a number of computer firms to assist it in designing a useful and cost-effective system. After considering a number of alternatives, BPCNA decided that the DATAMAX 1000 computer, offered by Data Equipment, Inc., best meets its current and projected future needs.

BPCNA evaluated the desirability of the acquisition of the DATAMAX 1000 computer using its normal capital budgeting procedures. It found that the computer has a large positive expected net present value.

Jim Horn, a new management trainee in the financial planning office, has recently been reading about the boom in the leasing industry. He feels that if leasing is growing as rapidly as it seems, there must be some significant advantages to the leasing alternative to ownership.

If purchased, the new computer will cost $100,000 installed. The computer has an estimated economic life of six years and is therefore eligible for the 10 percent investment tax credit. BPCNA would depreciate the computer on a five-year ACRS basis to a $0 estimated salvage value. If purchased, BPCNA could borrow the needed funds at a 10 percent pre-tax annual percentage rate of interest.

If BPCNA decides to lease the computer, it will not receive any of the investment tax credit. Under the terms of the financial lease, BPCNA would be required to make six beginning-of-year lease payments of $22,000 each. BPCNA's weighted cost of capital is 12 percent (after-tax). BPCNA's marginal tax rate is 40 percent.

Under both the lease alternative and the borrow and buy alternative, BPCNA will contract with a computer service company to handle the estimated annual service and maintenance.

1. Compute the net advantage to leasing.
2. Which alternative should BPCNA accept? What other factors might be considered?
3. If the computer is owned and BPCNA borrows the needed funds from a bank in the form of a bullet loan carrying a 10 percent interest rate instead of an equal payment loan at 10 percent, what effect would this have on the decision to lease or buy?
4. What effect would the use of straight-line depreciation have on the lease-buy decision? (Answer verbally; no calculations are needed. Ignore the bullet loan assumption in Question 3.)
5. If, at the end of six years, the computer is expected to have an actual salvage value of $10,000, what would be the impact on the net advantage to leasing?

**Selected
References**

Bower, Richard S, "Issues in Lease Financing." *Financial Management* 2 (Winter 1973): 25–34.

Gordon, Myron J. "A General Solution to the Buy or Lease Decision: A Pedagogical Note." *Journal of Finance* 29 (March 1974): 245–250.

Hochman, S., and R. Rabinovitch. "Financial Leasing Under Inflation." *Financial Management* (Spring 1984): 17–26.

Johnson, Robert W., and Wilbur G. Lewellen. "Analysis of the Lease-or-Buy Decision." *Journal of Finance* 27 (Sept. 1972): 815–823.

McConnell, J.J., and J.S. Schallheim. "Valuation of Asset Leasing Contracts." *Journal of Financial Economics* (August 1983): 237–61.

O'Brien, Thomas J., and B.H. Nunnally, Jr. "A 1982 Survey of Corporate Leasing Analysis." *Financial Management* (Summer 1983): 30–36.

Zinbarg, Edward D. "The Private Placement Loan Agreement." *Financial Analysts Journal* 31 (July–Aug. 1975): 33–35.

16

LONG-TERM DEBT, PREFERRED STOCK, AND COMMON STOCK

A Financial Dilemma

Corporate Restructuring Actions and Bond Ratings*

During 1985 there were $232 billion worth of proposed corporate takeovers, leveraged buyouts, and stock repurchases. This represented 15 percent of the stock market's total value. Such corporate restructurings are usually good news for the stockholders in these companies. In a takeover (either friendly or unfriendly) or leveraged buyout, the stockholders are normally offered a substantial premium over the market price as an inducement to approve the acquisition. Likewise, a stock repurchase normally has the effect of increasing the price of the company's shares.

However, from the bondholder's perspective, these corporate restructurings generally are bad news. Some statistics from the two major agencies that rate the "quality" of corporate securities, Moody's Investors Service and Standard and Poor's Corporation (see Figure 16-1 for a discussion of bond ratings), illustrate the problem. During 1985 Standard & Poor's lowered a record 272 corporate ratings, which was up 57 percent from 1984. At Moody's, one-third of the downgrades in ratings and almost 40 percent of the dollar volume of bond rating cuts in 1985 occurred as a result of what they referred to as "decapitalization" actions, namely leveraged buyouts and the use of debt for stock buy-backs or acquisitions.

Such "decapitalization" actions also have a negative impact on the prices of these debt securities. From a risk-return tradeoff perspective, these types of corporate restructurings increase the company's financial leverage, often beyond what are considered prudent limits, and hence increase the riskiness of the debt issues. Since investors want to be compensated for this additional risk, yields rise and prices fall on these securities.

Management (as well as investors) must be familiar with the characteristics, advantages, and disadvantages of various forms of long-term financing. This chapter examines the alternatives of common stock, preferred stock, and long-term debt in this light.

---

* Based on "Bad Grades: Takeovers Teach a Costly Lesson to Bondholders." *Barron's* (February 24, 1986): 24.

Key Chapter Concepts

1. The characteristics of fixed income (debt and preferred stock) and variable income (common stock) securities are examined, including:
   a. Types of each form of security.
   b. Features.
   c. Users.
   d. Advantages and disadvantages.
2. The process of raising funds in the capital markets (that is, selling securities) and the role of the investment banker are discussed.
3. Methods of selling securities in the primary capital markets include:
   a. Public cash offering.
   b. Direct placement.
   c. Rights offering to shareholders.
4. Other important topics include:
   a. Functioning of the securities markets.
   b. Understanding security price quotations and the financial pages.
   c. Regulation of the securities markets.
   d. Interest rate swaps.
   e. Bond refunding (appendix).
   f. Stockholder voting rights (appendix).
   g. Rights offerings (appendix).

Glossary of New Terms

Bond rating An evaluation of a bond's probability of default. This is performed by an outside rating agency, such as Standard and Poor's or Moody's.

Bond refunding A situation that occurs when a firm redeems a callable bond issue and sells a generally lower interest cost issue to take its place.

Call feature A provision that permits an issuer of bonds (and sometimes preferred stock) to retire the obligation prior to its maturity.

Call premium The difference between a bond's call price and its par value.

Call price The price at which a bond may be retired, or called, prior to its maturity.

Competitive bidding The process of selling a new security offering to the highest bidding underwriting syndicate.

Convertible bond A bond that may be converted into common stock at the holder's option.

Cumulative dividends A typical feature of preferred stock that requires any past-due preferred stock dividends to be paid before any common stock dividends can be paid.

Direct placement The sale of an entire security offering to one or more institutional investors rather than the general public. This is also termed a *private placement.*

Flotation cost The cost of issuing new securities. This includes both underwriting expenses and other issue expenses, such as printing and legal fees.

Income bond A bond that pays interest only if the firm earns sufficient income.

Indenture The contract between the issuing firm and the lenders in a debt obligation.

Interest rate swap An agreement between two companies (and/or financial institutions) whereby one party's floating rate debt obligation is traded for another party's fixed rate obligation.

Investment banker A financial institution that underwrites and sells new securities. In general, investment bankers assist firms in obtaining new financing.

Listed security exchanges Organized secondary security markets that operate at designated places of business. The New York Stock Exchange (NYSE) is an example of a listed security exchange.

Negotiated underwriting A process whereby a firm wishing to sell new securities to the public negotiates the terms of the underwriting with the investment banker or bankers.

Over-the-counter (OTC) securities markets A network of security dealers connected by a communications system of telephones and computer terminals that provides price quotations on individual securities.

Par value An arbitrary value assigned to common stock or preferred stock by the issuing firm. In the case of a bond, the par value is usually $1,000 and represents the amount of principal borrowed and due at maturity.

Preemptive right A provision contained in some corporate charters that gives common stockholders the right to buy on a pro rata basis any new common shares sold by the firm.

Prospectus A document that contains a vast amount of information about a company's legal, operational, and financial position. It is prepared for the benefit of prospective investors in a new security issued by the firm.

Purchasing syndicate A *group* of investment bankers who agree to underwrite a new security issue in order to spread the risk of underwriting.

Right A short-term option issued by a firm that permits an existing stockholder to buy a specified number of shares of common stock at a specified price (the subscription price), which is below the current market price.

Rights offering The sale of new shares of common stock by distributing stock purchase *rights* to a firm's existing shareholders. This is also termed a *privileged subscription.*

Securities and Exchange Commission (SEC) The government regulatory agency responsible for administering Federal securities legislation.

Senior debt Debt that has a higher claim to a firm's earnings and/or assets than junior debt.

Shelf registration A procedure whereby a company is permitted to register all the debt and equity securities it plans to sell over the next two years. The company can then sell these securities whenever it chooses.

Stock split The issuance of a number of new shares in exchange for each old share held by a stockholder.

Subordinated debenture A bond that has a claim on the issuing firm's assets that is junior to other forms of debt in the event of a liquidation. The claims of subordinated debenture holders can be met only *after* all the claims of senior creditors have been met.

Trustee The bondholders' representative in a public debt offering. The trustee is responsible for monitoring the borrower's compliance with the terms of the indenture.

Underwriting A process whereby a group of investment bankers agrees to purchase a new security issue at a set price and then offer it for sale to the general public.

Underwriting spread The difference between the selling price to the public of a new security offering and the proceeds received by the offering firm. This is also termed an *underwriting discount.*

Introduction

Long-term debt, preferred stock, and common stock are the major sources of capital for a firm. Long-term debt and preferred stock are classified as *fixed income securities,* because they involve relatively constant distributions of interest or dividend payments to their holders. For example, Houston Lighting and Power Company sold $50 million of long-term debt in 1971, at which time it agreed to pay its lenders an interest rate of 7.5 percent or $75 a year for each $1,000 of debt outstanding. Since then the company has continued to pay this interest rate, even though market interest rates have fluctuated. Similarly, AT&T issued $1.37 billion of preferred stock in 1971. Its investors paid $50 per share, and the company agreed to pay an annual dividend of $4 per share. Since that time, AT&T has continued to pay this amount, even though common stock dividends have been increased several times.

Common stock, on the other hand, is a *variable income security,* because the dividends paid on common stock tend to fluctuate. For example, in 1975 Tucson Electric Power Company sold new common shares when annual dividends were $0.84 per share. By 1986 the annual rate was $3.30 per share, having been raised several times during the intervening years.

Common stock also differs from long-term debt and preferred stock in that its market price tends to fluctuate more than the price of bonds and preferred stock, thus causing returns on common stock investments to vary more widely over time than returns on preferred stock or long-term debt.

The fixed-income securities—long-term debt and preferred stock—also differ from each other in several ways. For example, the interest paid to long-term lenders is a tax-deductible expense for the borrowing company, whereas dividends paid to preferred stockholders are not. Legally, long-term debtholders are considered creditors, whereas preferred stockholders are considered owners. Thus, a firm is not legally required to pay dividends to its preferred stockholders, and the failure to do so has less serious consequences than does the failure to meet interest obligations on long-term debt. In addition, long-term debt has a specific *maturity,* whereas preferred stock is often *perpetual.*

The next three major sections of this chapter are devoted to detailed discussions of each of these three sources of capital. The remaining two major sections deal with capital markets and the role of investment bankers.

Long-term Debt

Although a company incurs a certain amount of financial risk when it engages in long-term borrowing, it can gain the advantages of positive financial leverage by earning a higher rate of return on its assets than the rate of interest it has to pay for its borrowed funds.[1] Many large U.S. companies operating near their optimal capital structures have up to 40 percent or more long-term debt in their capital structures. As long as a firm does not use an excessive amount of long-term debt, the benefits of favorable financial leverage are likely to outweigh the disadvantages of increased financial risk.

[1] Financial leverage is discussed in Chapter 7.

When a company borrows money in the capital markets, it issues long-term debt securities to investors. These are usually sold in denominations of $1,000 and constitute a promise by the issuing company to repay a certain amount of money (the $1,000 principal) on a particular date (the maturity date) and to pay a specified amount of interest at fixed intervals (usually twice a year). Most debt has a *par value* of $1,000, and debt prices are often expressed as a percentage of that value. For example, a market price listing of "87" indicates that a $1,000 par value bond may be purchased for $870.

There are many different types of long-term debt. The type or types a company chooses to use will depend on its own particular financial situation and the characteristics of the industry as a whole.

Types of Long-term Debt

Long-term debt is generally classified according to whether or not it is secured by specific physical assets of the issuing company. Secured debt issues are usually called *mortgage bonds,* and issues that are not secured by specific assets are called *debentures* or, occasionally, *debenture bonds*. The term *bond* is often used to denote any type of long-term debt security.

At the present time, utility companies are the largest users of mortgage bonds. In recent years the use of mortgage bonds relative to other forms of long-term debt has declined, while the use of debentures has increased. Since debentures are unsecured, their quality depends on the general credit-worthiness of the issuing company. As a result, they are usually issued by large, financially strong firms.

The yield differential between the mortgage bond and debenture alternatives is another example of the risk-return tradeoff that occurs throughout finance. For example, suppose Midstates Oil Company could issue either mortgage bonds or debentures. If the mortgage bonds could be sold with a 10 percent interest rate, the debentures would have to be sold at a higher rate—for example, 10.3 percent—to attract investors. This is due to the fact that investors require a higher return on debentures, which are backed only by the unmortgaged assets of the company and the company's earning power, than they do on mortgage bonds, which are secured by specific physical assets as well as the company's earning power.

Debt issues are also classified according to whether they are *senior* or *junior*.[2] Senior debt has a higher priority claim to a firm's earnings and/or assets than junior debt. Occasionally the actual name of the debt issue will contain a "junior" or "senior" qualifier. In most instances, however, identification of how a particular company's debt issues are ranked requires an analysis of the restrictions placed on the company by the purchasers of the issue.

Unsecured debt also may be classified according to whether it is *subordinated* to other types of debt. In the event of a liquidation or reorganization, the claims of *subordinated debenture holders* are considered only *after* the claims of *unsubordinated debenture holders*. In

---

[2] The senior-junior classification scheme is also used in connection with preferred and common stock. Preferred stock is junior to long-term debt and senior to common stock.

general, subordinated debentures are junior to other types of debt, including bank loans, and may even be junior to *all* of a firm's other debt.

Equipment trust certificates are used largely by railroad and trucking companies. The proceeds from these certificates are used to purchase specific assets, such as railroad rolling stock. The certificate holders own the equipment and lease it to the company. Technically, equipment trust certificates are not true bonds, even though they are guaranteed by the issuing company, because the interest and principal are paid by the *trustee* (the financial institution responsible for looking after the investors' interests). Even so, they are classified as debt because they have all of the characteristics of debt.

Collateral trust bonds are backed by stocks or bonds of other corporations. This type of financing is principally of historical interest; it is used today primarily by holding companies. A holding company may, for example, raise needed funds by pledging the stocks and/or bonds of its subsidiaries as collateral. In this arrangement the holding company serves as the *parent* company. The subsidiary borrows from the parent, and the parent borrows from the capital markets. This makes good sense, because the parent company can generally get more favorable terms for its debt in the capital markets than the subsidiary.

Income bonds are also largely of historical interest, although they are still occasionally used today. Income bonds promise to pay interest only if the issuing firm earns sufficient income; if it does not, no interest obligation exists. These securities are rarely issued directly. Instead, they often are created in reorganizations following bankruptcy and are normally issued in exchange for junior or subordinated issues. Thus, unsecured income bonds are generally considered to be "weak" securities.

Pollution control bonds and *industrial revenue bonds* are issued by local governments rather than corporations. The interest paid to purchasers of municipal bonds is tax exempt, and the interest rate is typically less than what a corporation would have to pay. The interest payments are guaranteed by the corporation for whose benefit the bonds are issued.

Features of Long-term Debt

Long-term debt has a number of unique features. Several of these are discussed in the following paragraphs.

Indenture   An indenture is a contract between a firm that issues long-term debt securities and the lenders. In general, an indenture does the following:

- It thoroughly details the nature of the debt issue.
- It carefully specifies the manner in which the principal must be repaid.
- It lists any restrictions that are placed on the firm by the lenders. These restrictions are called *covenants,* and the firm must satisfy them to keep from defaulting on its obligation.[3] Typical restrictive covenants include

---

[3] A company defaults on its debt when it does not pay interest or required principal on time. When default occurs, the debt is often said to be "triggered," meaning that the entire principal amount comes due immediately. This could result in bankruptcy.

the following:

1. A minimum coverage, or times interest earned ratio, the firm must maintain.

2. A minimum level of working capital the firm must maintain.

3. A maximum amount of dividends the firm can pay on its preferred and common stock.

4. Other restrictions that effectively limit how much leasing and issuing of additional debt the firm may do.

Trustee   Since the holders of a large firm's long-term debt issue are likely to be widely scattered geographically, the Trust Indenture Act of 1939 requires that a trustee represent the debtholders in dealings with the issuing company. A trustee is usually a commercial bank or trust company that is responsible for insuring that all the terms and convenants set forth in the indenture agreement are adhered to by the issuing company. The issuing company must pay the trustee's expenses.

Call Feature   A call feature is an optional retirement provision that permits the issuing company to redeem, or *call,* a debt issue prior to its maturity date at a specified price termed the *redemption,* or *call, price.* Many firms use the call feature because it provides them with the potential flexibility to retire debt prior to maturity if, for example, interest rates decline.

The call price is greater than the par value of the debt, and the difference between the two is the *call premium.* During the early years of an issue the call premium is usually equal to about one year's interest. Some debt issues specify *fixed* call premiums, whereas others specify *declining* call premiums. For example, in 1982 the El Paso Natural Gas Company issued 16.7 percent, twenty-year debentures. During 1982 the company could have retired all or part of this issue at 116.7 percent of par value, and during 1983 the redemption price dropped to 115.77 percent of par. Similar reductions in the redemption price are scheduled for each year up to the year 2000. Many bonds are not callable at all for several years after the initial issue date. This situation is referred to as a *deferred call.*

Details of the call feature are worked out before the debt is sold in the negotiations between the underwriters and the issuing company. Since a call feature gives the company significant flexibility in its financing plans, while at the same time potentially depriving the lenders of the advantages they would gain from holding the debt until maturity, the issuing company has to offer the investors compensation in the form of the call premium in exchange for the call privilege. In addition, the interest rate on a callable debt issue is usually slightly higher than the interest rate on a similar noncallable issue.

Because of the interest savings that can be achieved, a firm is most likely to call a debt issue when prevailing interest rates are appreciably lower than those that existed at the time of the original issue. When a company calls a relatively high interest issue and replaces it with a lower interest issue, the procedure is called *bond refunding.* This topic is discussed in the appendix to this chapter.

Sinking Fund Usually lenders will require that a borrowing company gradually reduce the outstanding balance of a debt issue over its life instead of having the entire principal amount come due on a particular date twenty or thirty years into the future. The usual method of providing for a gradual retirement is a sinking fund, so called because a certain amount of money—for example, 3 percent of the total issue—is put aside annually, or "sunk," into a *sinking fund account.* In practice, however, a company can also satisfy its sinking fund requirements either by purchasing a portion of the debt each year in the open market or, if the debt is callable, by using a lottery technique to determine which actual numbered certificates will be called and retired within a given year. The alternative chosen depends on the current market price of the debt issue. In general, if current interest rates are above the issue's coupon rate, the current market price of the debt will be less than $1,000, and the company should meet its sinking fund obligation by purchasing the debt in the open market. If, on the other hand, market interest rates are lower than the issue's coupon rate, and if the market price of the debt is above the call price, the company should use the call procedure.

Conversion Feature Some debt issues (and some preferred stock issues) have a conversion feature that allows the holder to exchange the security for the company's common stock at the option of the holder. The features of convertible securities are discussed in Chapter 17.

Typical Sizes of Debt Issues Debt issues sold to the public through underwriters are usually in the $25 to $200 million range, although very large firms occasionally borrow up to $500 million or more at one time. Since the use of an underwriting group in a public offering involves considerable expense, it is usually uneconomical for a company to make a public offering of this nature for debt issues less than about $25 million. *Private placements,* however, frequently involve lesser amounts of money—for example, $5 to $10 million—since the entire debt issue is purchased by a single investor, such as an insurance company.

Coupon Rates The coupon rates on new bonds are normally fixed and set equal to market interest rates on bonds of comparable quality so that the bonds sell at or near par value. However, during the inflationary period of the early 1980s when interest rates reached record levels and bond prices were quite volatile, highly-rated companies began issuing bonds with *floating* coupon rates.

An example of a floating rate issue is Baltimore Gas and Electric's floating rate notes due in 1995. Interest is adjusted and paid quarterly at a rate of 112.5 basis points (that is, 1.125 percent) above the applicable ninety-one day Treasury Bill auction rate. The quarterly interest rate is limited to being not greater than 11.90 percent nor less than 7.90 percent. Such a bond protects investors against a rise in interest rates since the market price of the bond does not fluctuate as much as for fixed interest rate bonds.

Another type of bond that was issued in the early 1980s was *original issue deep discount* (OID) bonds. These bonds have coupon rates that are below prevailing market interest rates at the time of issue, and hence sell at a discount from par value. Some OID bond issues pay no interest and are known as *zero coupon* bonds. The Allied Corporation zero coupon money market multiplier note issue, discussed in Chapter 4, is one such example. OID bonds have decreased in popularity in the last few years, due to changes in the tax laws (which eliminated the tax advantages to companies of these issues over debt issued at par) and the issuance by several brokerage firms of lower risk substitutes. One such substitute is Merrill Lynch's "TIGRs"—Treasury Investment Growth Receipts— which are backed by U.S. Treasury Bonds. These securities, which pay no interest, are purchased at a discount from face value and then can be redeemed for the full face value at maturity.

Maturity The typical maturity on long-term debt is about twenty to thirty years. Occasionally companies borrow money for as long as forty years. On the other end of the scale, companies in need of financing often are willing to borrow for only about ten years, especially if they feel that interest rates are temporarily high, as was true in the environment of the late 1970s and until mid-1982—an environment characterized by high rates of inflation and historically high interest rates. By the spring of 1983, many large companies were again issuing fixed-rate debt securities with twenty five- and thirty-year maturities.

Like floating rate bonds described earlier, which protect investors against interest rate risk, firms have also been issuing bonds that are redeemable at par *at the option of the holder*. These are known as extendable notes or put bonds. If interest rates rise and the market price of the bond falls, the holder can redeem them at par and reinvest the proceeds in higher yielding securities. An example of an extendable note is Sears Roebuck's issue of 1999. The notes were issued in January 1984 and are redeemable at the option of the holder after April 15, 1987. (These particular notes were also issued with a floating interest rate.)

From an accounting standpoint, debt obligations maturing in more than one year are usually classified as long-term debt on the balance sheet.

Bond Ratings

Debt issues are rated according to their relative degree of risk by various financial companies, including Moody's Investors Services and Standard and Poor's Corporation (S&P). These agencies consider a variety of factors when rating a firm's securities, including earnings stability, coverage ratios, the relative amount of debt in the firm's capital structure, and the degree of subordination, as well as past experience. According to Moody's rating scale, the highest-quality—lowest-risk issues are rated Aaa, and the scale continues down through Aa, A, Baa, Ba, B, Caa, Ca, and C. On the Standard and Poor's ratings scale, AAA denotes the highest-quality issues, and this rating is followed by AA, A, BBB, BB, B, and so on. S&P also has various C and D classifications for high-risk

| Figure 16-1 | **Moody's and Standard & Poor's Bond-Rating Definitions** |

KEY TO MOODY'S CORPORATE RATINGS*

Aaa   Bonds which are rated Aaa are judged to be of the best quality. They carry the smallest degree of investment risk and are generally referred to as "gilt edge." Interest payments are protected by a large or by an exceptionally stable margin and principal is secure. While the various protective elements are likely to change, such changes as can be visualized are most unlikely to impair the fundamentally strong position of such issues.

Aa   Bonds which are rated Aa are judged to be of high quality by all standards. Together with the Aaa group they comprise what are generally known as high grade bonds. They are rated lower than the best bonds because margins of protection may not be as large as in Aaa securities or fluctuation of protective elements may be of greater amplitude or there may be other elements present which make the long-term risks appear somewhat larger than in Aaa securities.

A   Bonds which are rated A possess many favorable investment attributes and are to be considered as upper medium grade obligations. Factors giving security to principal and interest are considered adequate but elements may be present which suggest a susceptibility to impairment sometime in the future.

Baa   Bonds which are rated Baa are considered as medium grade obligations, that is, they are neither highly protected nor poorly secured. Interest payments and principal security appear adequate for the present but certain protective elements may be lacking or may be characteristically unreliable over any great length of time. Such bonds lack outstanding investment characteristics and in fact have speculative characteristics as well.

Ba   Bonds which are rated Ba are judged to have speculative elements; their future cannot be considered as well assured. Often the protection of interest and principal payments may be very moderate and thereby not well safeguarded during both good and bad times over the future. Uncertainty of position characterizes bonds in this class.

B   Bonds which are rated B generally lack characteristics of the desirable investment. Assurance of interest and principal payments or of maintenance of other terms of the contract over any long period of time may be small.

Caa   Bonds which are rated Caa are of poor standing. Such issues may be in default or there may be present elements of danger with respect to principal or interest.

Ca   Bonds which are rated Ca represent obligations which are speculative in a high degree. Such issues are often in default or have other marked shortcomings.

C   Bonds which are rated C are the lowest rated class of bonds and issues so rated can be regarded as having extremely poor prospects of ever attaining any real investment standing.

*Moody's applies numerical modifiers, 1, 2 and 3 in each generic rating classification from Aa through B in its corporate bond rating system. The modifier 1 indicates that the security ranks in the higher end of its generic rating category; the modifier 2 indicates a mid-range ranking; and the modifier 3 indicates that the issue ranks in the lower end of its generic rating category.
Source: *Moody's Bond Record,* March 1983. Reprinted by permission of Moody's Investors Service, Inc.

Figure 16-1   **(Continued)**

STANDARD & POOR'S CORPORATE AND MUNICIPAL
DEBT-RATING DEFINITIONS

AAA   Debt rated AAA has the highest rating assigned by Standard & Poor's. Capacity to pay interest and repay principal is extremely strong.

AA   Debt rated AA has a very strong capacity to pay interest and repay principal and differs from the higher rated issues only in a small degree.

A   Debt rated A has a strong capacity to pay interest and repay principal although it is somewhat more susceptible to the adverse effects of changes in circumstances and economic conditions than debt in higher rated categories.

BBB   Debt rated BBB is regarded as having an adequate capacity to pay interest and repay principal. Whereas it normally exhibits adequate protection parameters, adverse economic conditions or changing circumstances are more likely to lead to a weakened capacity to pay interest and repay principal for debt in this category than in higher rated categories.

BB, B, CCC, CC   Debt rated BB, B, CCC and CC is regarded, on balance, as predominently speculative with respect to capacity to pay interest and repay principal in accordance with the terms of the obligation. BB indicates the lowest degree of speculation and CC the highest degree of speculation. While such debt will likely have some quality and protective characteristics, these are outweighed by large uncertainties or major risk exposures to adverse conditions.

C   The rating C is reserved for income bonds on which no interest is being paid.

D   Debt rated D is in default, and payment of interest and or repayment of principal is in arrears.

Plus (+) **or Minus** (−)   The ratings from "AA" to "B" may be modified by the addition of a plus or minus sign to show relative standing within the major rating categories.

Source: *Standard & Poor's Bond Guide*, March 1983. Reprinted by permission of Standard and Poor's.

issues; the vast majority of debt issues, however, fall into one of the A or B categories. Figure 16-1 shows Moody's and S&P's bond-rating definitions.

Table 16-1 gives some examples of capital structure and coverage ratios for various companies' debt ratings. In general, as the debt rating decreases from AAA to lower ratings, the percentage of long-term debt in the capital structure increases and the coverage ratio decreases.

As a general rule, "triple A" issues yield the lowest interest rates at any given time. This is another example of the risk—return tradeoff in finance. Since the perceived default risk difference between companies rated A and B is usually less during periods of economic prosperity than during recessionary periods, the interest rate spread between A- and B-rated issues also tends to be smaller during periods of economic prosperity.

Table 16-1   **Selected Examples of Capital Structure and Coverage Ratios
for Various Debt Ratings**

Company	Standard and Poor's Debt Rating*	Long-Term Debt to Total Capitalization†	Times Fixed Charges Earned†
IBM Corp.	AAA	10.97%	17.13
General Electric	AAA	5.60	7.85
Dayton-Hudson	AA	28.97	4.18
Deere & Co.	A	30.41	1.45
Ford Motor	A	16.13	6.42
RCA Corp.	A−	21.66	2.01
Monsanto	A−	16.10	4.61
W.R. Grace	BBB+	37.63	2.00
Ramada Inns	B−	54.70	1.10
Rapid-American Corp.	CCC	46.43	0.46

*Standard & Poor's Bond Guide (January 1986).
†Moody's Industrial Manual, 1985.

Information on Debt Financing Activities

Every business day financial newspapers contain information on debt financing activities. For example, *The Wall Street Journal* devotes at least one page to financing activities in the bond market. This page contains announcements by underwriters concerning the characteristics of the new issues presently being offered.

The Wall Street Journal also contains information on the secondary debt markets, including price quotations for the widely traded corporate debt issues listed on the New York Exchange. The next section is devoted to understanding these price quotations.

Understanding Bond Quotations[4]

The majority of existing debt issues of U.S. corporations are traded over the counter. However, many widely traded issues are listed on the major exchanges. Price quotations for debt issues traded on the New York Exchange are published daily in *The Wall Street Journal*. Table 16-2 shows a selected list from that source on March 3, 1986.

Table 16-2   **Selected Listing of Bond Quotations from the New York Exchange**

					Selected Bond Quotations—March 3, 1986	
Bond	Cur Yld	Vol	High	Low	Close	Net Chg
Alld C zr98	—	37	31¾	30	30⅝	+2⅛
ATT 8.80s05	9.0	657	98	97	97⅞	+ ⅝
duPnt 8.45s04	8.9	10	95	94⅝	95	+ ½
Exxon 6s97	7.2	75	83	81¾	83	+1
RCA 12¼s05	11	7	110	110	110	−1
Tol Ed 9.65s06	10	10	95¼	95¼	95¼	+3⅛
Xerox 6s95	cv	71	98⅜	97½	97½	− ¾

Source: *The Wall Street Journal* (March 4, 1986).

[4] In this discussion the term *bond* includes mortgage bonds, debentures, and notes.

Bond prices are quoted as a percentage of their par value (usually $1,000). For example, the closing price of the Toledo Edison issue on March 3, 1986 was $952.50 per $1,000 bond. The *8.80s05* after the ATT listing (American Telephone & Telegraph) means that the debt issue has a contract, or coupon, interest rate of 8.80 percent. Thus, a holder of the issue receives $44 in interest per bond every six months for a total of $88 (8.8% × $1,000) each year. This debt issue, or series (the *s* stands for "series"), matures in the year 2005, hence, the *05* listing. The current yield is calculated by dividing the annual interest by the day's closing price; for example, $88/$978.75 = 9.0%. However, current yield is only an approximation of the true yield, given by the yield to maturity.[5] A "cv" in the current yield column means that the bond issue is a convertible security, which is discussed in the following chapter.

Users of Long-term Debt

Most large and medium-sized companies finance some portion of their fixed assets with long-term debt. This debt may be in the form of either secured bonds or unsecured debentures. Utilities rely on debt capital to a large degree and, as a group, are the largest users of secured bonds; the *first mortgage bonds* of a utility are typically a safe, low-risk investment. Manufacturing companies, in contrast, rely on debt capital to varying degrees and generally use unsecured debt more often than secured debt.

Many large companies have virtually continuous capital expenditure programs. Usually a company will plan to finance at least partially any new assets with long-term debt. Since it is generally uneconomical to borrow small amounts of long-term capital, however, companies that have ongoing construction programs often gradually "draw down" on their short-term revolving credit agreements. Then, once every couple of years or so, a firm of this type will enter the capital markets and sell long-term debt. At that time a portion of the proceeds is used to repay the short-term borrowings, and the cycle begins again. This procedure is called *funding* short-term debt; as a result, long-term debt is sometimes referred to as *funded debt*.

Most established companies attempt to maintain reasonably constant proportions of long-term debt and common equity in their capital structures. During the course of a company's normal profitable operations, though, long-term debt is gradually retired as it matures, and the retained earnings portion of common equity is increased. This in turn decreases the debt-to-equity ratio. Thus, to maintain their desired capital structures, companies have to raise long-term debt capital periodically. This gradual refunding of debt, along with the tax deductibility of interest, accounts for the fact that about 85 to 90 percent of the external long-term capital raised in the United States is in the form of debt.

Advantages and Disadvantages of Long-term Debt Financing

From the issuing firm's perspective, the major advantages of long-term debt include the following:

- Its relatively low after-tax cost due to the tax deductibility of interest.
- The increased earnings per share possible through financial leverage.

---

[5] Chapter 4 contains a discussion of yield to maturity calculations.

• The ability of the firm's owners to maintain greater control over the firm.

The following are the major disadvantages of long-term debt financing, from the firm's perspective:

• The increased financial risk of the firm resulting from the use of debt.
• The restrictions placed on the firm by the lenders.

From the investors' viewpoint, debt securities in general offer stable returns and thus are considered to be relatively low-risk investments compared with common stock investments. Since debtholders are creditors, however, they do not participate in any increased earnings the firm may experience. In fact, during periods of relatively high inflation, holders of existing debt find that their *real* interest payments decrease, because the nominal interest payments remain constant.

Preferred Stock

As a source of capital for a firm, preferred stock occupies an intermediate position between long-term debt and common stock. Like common stock, preferred stock is part of the stockholders' equity. Like long-term debt, it is considered a fixed-income security, although preferred stockholders receive dividends instead of interest payments. Since the issuing firm often does not promise repayment at a specific date, preferred stock tends to be a more permanent form of financing than long-term debt. Dividends on preferred stock, like interest payments on long-term debt, normally remain constant over time.

The popularity of preferred stock financing has declined in recent decades. Dividends cannot be deducted from income for corporate income tax purposes, whereas interest payments are tax deductible. This means that for a company paying almost half of its income in taxes, the after-tax cost of preferred stock is greater than that of long-term debt, assuming that the pretax preferred stock and long-term debt rates are about the same and that the company makes no change in its capital structure.[6]

Preferred stock bears its name because it usually has preference, or priority, over common stock with regard to the company's dividends and assets. For example, if a company's earnings in a given year are insufficient to pay dividends on preferred stock, the company is not permitted to pay dividends on its common stock. In the event of a liquidation following bankruptcy, the claims on the firm's assets by preferred stockholders are subordinate to those of creditors but have priority over those of common stockholders.

---

[6] For a given company at a particular time, preferred stock will often cost slightly more than long-term debt, even on a pretax basis, because investors require a higher return to compensate them for the greater risk involved with preferred stock. (See Chapter 12 for a further discussion of this topic.) In contrast, preferred dividends received by corporate investors qualify for an 80 percent intercompany dividend exclusion (beginning in 1987), whereas interest income does not. Thus, a preferred stock offering that is largely purchased by other corporations may have a lower yield than similar debt offerings. The 1986 tax reform bill will make preferred stock financing more appealing because of the lower marginal corporate tax rate.

**Features of
Preferred Stock**

Like long-term debt, preferred stock has its own unique distinguishing characteristics. A number of these are discussed here.

Selling Price and Par Value The selling price, or issue price, is the per-share price at which preferred stock shares are sold to the public. At the present time, the most common selling price is $25 per share. In the past, $100 per share was a more common issue price.

The par value is the value assigned to the stock by the issuing company, and it is frequently the same as the initial selling price. No relationship necessarily exists between the two, however. A preferred stock sold at $25 per share may have a $25 par value, $1 par value, or no par value at all. Regardless of what a preferred stock's actual par value is, however, the preferred stockholders are entitled to their issue price plus dividends in the event of liquidation after the claims of creditors have been paid in full.

Preferred stock usually is designated by its dividend amount rather than its dividend percentage. For example, suppose Intermountain Power Company has a series of preferred stock that pays an annual dividend of $2.20, has a $1 par value, and was initially sold to the public at $25 per share. An investor would most likely refer to the stock as "Intermountain Power's $2.20 preferred."

Adjustable Rate Preferred Stock This type of preferred stock became popular in 1982. With these issues, dividends are reset periodically and offer returns that vary with interest rates. For example, Sears Roebuck issued adjustable rate preferred stock on May 2, 1984, with an initial dividend rate of 10.25 percent per annum until June 30, 1984. The quarterly rate thereafter (determined in advance) is to be 2.65 percentage points less than the *highest* of the three-month U.S. Treasury Bill Rate, U.S. Treasury Ten-Year Constant Maturity Rate, and the Twenty-Year Constant Maturity Rate. However, the rate for any dividend period is not to be less than 6.50 percent or greater than 12.50 percent.

Cumulative Feature Most preferred stock is cumulative. This means that if, for some reason, a firm fails to pay its preferred dividend, it cannot pay dividends on its common stock until it has satisfied all preferred dividends in arrears. The principal reason for this feature is that investors are generally unwilling to purchase preferred stock that is not cumulative.

Participation Stock is said to be *participating* if the holders share in any increased earnings the company might experience. Virtually all preferred stock, however, is *nonparticipating;* that is, the preferred dividend remains constant, even if the company's earnings increase. Any dividend increases resulting from higher earnings accrue directly to the common stockholders.

Maturity Preferred stock is technically part of a firm's equity capital. As such, some firms issue preferred stock that is intended to be *perpetual,* that is, a permanent portion of the stockholders' equity having no specific maturity date. Many preferred stock investors, however, desire sinking fund provisions, which guarantee that the issue will be retired over a specified time period.

Call Feature   Like long-term debt, preferred stock can sometimes be redeemed, or *called,* at the issuing firm's option at some specified price. Suppose, for example, that Atlantic Public Service Company issues a $2.10 series of preferred stock that is sold at $25 per share. A typical call provision might allow the company to retire all or part of the issue at $27.10 during the third year, at $26.80 during the fourth year, at $26.50 during the fifth year, and so on until the price reaches $25 during the tenth year. (In this example the stock is not callable during the first two years after issue.)

Whereas the call feature allows the issuing company a measure of flexibility in its financing plans, the call feature is generally not attractive to investors. Thus, a firm usually must also provide investors with a *call premium,* or the difference between the call price and the original selling price, should it decide to attach a call feature to its preferred stock.

The probability that a firm will exercise the call privilege is likely to increase during times when market interest rates have decreased below those that existed at the time of issue. After calling the original issue, the firm can replace it with a lower cost issue.

Voting Rights   As a general rule, preferred stockholders are not entitled to vote for the company's board of directors. However, special voting procedures frequently take effect if the company omits its preferred dividends or incurs losses for a period of time. In such a case, the preferred stockholders often vote as a separate group to elect one or more members of the company's board of directors. This insures that the preferred holders will have direct representation on the board.

Preference Stock   Occasionally, companies that issue preferred stock also issue *preference stock,* which is junior to preferred stock. For example, Tenneco, Inc., has both cumulative preference and cumulative preferred stock in its capital structure. The preference stock is defined by the company as a third class, or order, of preferred stock. Therefore, the preference stock is entitled to dividends after the first preferred and second preferred holders receive their dividends.

Trading of Preferred Shares

Following the initial sale of preferred stock by a firm, investors who purchase the shares may decide to sell them in the secondary markets. Large issues of actively traded preferred stock are listed on the major stock exchanges, such as the New York and the American stock exchanges. However, a majority of preferred stock issues are rather thinly traded, and these are traded over the counter.

Users of Preferred Stock

Utility companies are the most frequent users of preferred stock financing, largely because of the financing constraints placed on them by regulatory agencies. For example, a regulatory agency might require that the utilities under its control limit their use of mortgage bond financing to 60 percent of the amount of new assets. The regulatory agency might also require that these assets be financed with at least 30 percent common equity. Thus, many utilities use preferred stock for about 10 percent of their capitalization. This permits them to satisfy the regulatory agency requirements and to maximize their use of financial leverage by employing a fixed-income security. In addition, utilities are permitted by their regulatory agencies to consider preferred dividends as an expense for rate making purposes.

Within the last twenty five years or so, preferred stock (usually convertible) has been rather widely used in mergers and acquisitions. Frequently, acquiring companies issue preferred stock in exchange for the common stock of acquired companies. This is, in effect, another example of financial leverage, and it can cause an increase in the earnings per common share of the acquiring company.[7]

Other occasional users of preferred stock financing are capital-intensive companies undertaking expansion programs. These companies may choose preferred stock as a means of securing long-term financing for the following reasons:

- Their capital structures and various other restrictions prevent the judicious use of additional long-term debt.
- Depressed common stock prices and the potential dilution of per-share earnings may cause them to decide against external common equity financing.

Often these same companies have relatively low marginal tax rates (because of losses, accelerated depreciation, and investment tax credits) that make the after-tax cost of preferred stock not appreciably different from that of long-term debt. For example, Chrysler, International Harvester (now known as Navistar), and U.S. Steel, as well as a number of airlines, are recent issuers of preferred stock.

In the 1980s large commercial banks were another group of preferred stock users. These banks, including BankAmerica, Chase Manhattan, and Manufacturers Hanover, issued variable-rate preferred stock, partly to get additional equity into their capital structures.

Advantages and Disadvantages of Preferred Stock Financing

From the issuing company's perspective, the principal advantage of preferred stock is that preferred dividend payments are potentially flexible. Omitting a preferred dividend in difficult times usually results in less severe consequences than omitting an interest payment on long-term debt.

In addition, preferred stock financing can increase a firm's degree of financial leverage. However, financial analysts may regard the issuance of preferred stock as equivalent to debt. In this case, the company is viewed as having used up a portion of its "debt capacity." Or, in effect, the company has leveraged with preferred stock rather than long-term debt—at a greater after-tax cost.

From the investors' perspective, companies who purchase the preferred

---

[7] Chapter 23 contains a more detailed discussion of the use of preferred stock in mergers.

stock of other companies accrue certain tax advantages resulting from the 85 percent exclusion of intercompany dividends from Federal income taxes. For example, an insurance company in the 46 percent tax bracket can invest in the preferred stock of another company and pay taxes equal to only about 6.9 percent of the preferred dividend income.[8] In contrast, the same insurance company would be required to include all the interest received in its taxable income.

The principal disadvantage of preferred stock financing is its high after-tax cost as compared with long-term debt, since dividends cannot be deducted for income tax purposes. This means that the after-tax cost to the firm for preferred stock is greater than the after-tax cost of long-term debt, assuming that the firm's capital structure remains constant. As a result, most companies considering long-term financing with fixed-income securities choose long-term debt over preferred stock.

Common Stock

A firm's common stockholders are its true owners. Common stock is a *residual form of ownership* in that the claims of common stockholders on the firm's earnings and assets are considered only *after* the claims of governments, debtholders, and preferred stockholders have been met. Common stock is considered a *permanent* form of long-term financing, since, unlike debt and some preferred stock, common stock has no maturity date.

Unlike long-term debt and preferred stock, which are normally fixed income securities, common stock is a *variable income security*. Common stockholders are said to participate in a firm's earnings, because they may receive a larger dividend if earnings increase in the future, or their dividend may be cut if earnings drop.

Common Stock and Accounting

Common stock appears on the right-hand side of a firm's balance sheet as part of the stockholders' equity. This is shown in Table 16-3.

Table 16-3

Lawrence Company Stockholders' Equity, December 31, 19X5 (in thousands of dollars)

Stockholders' Equity	
Preferred stock; $25 par value; authorized, 2,000,000 shares; issued and outstanding, 1,500,000 shares	$ 37,500
Common stock; $2 par value; authorized, 10,000,000 shares; issued and outstanding, 6,675,000 shares	13,350
Contributed capital in excess of par value*	28,713
Retained earnings	38,257
Total stockholders' equity	$117,820

*The *contributed capital in excess of par* account has several other frequently used names, including *capital surplus* and *additional paid-in capital*. Many accountants feel that the expression *capital surplus* is misleading, because it implies that the firm has excess capital.

[8] This 6.9 percent figure is calculated by multiplying the portion of dividends that is subject to taxes, namely, 15 percent, by 46 percent.

Stockholders' equity includes both preferred stock (if any exists) and common stock. The total equity attributable to the common stock of the Lawrence Company is equal to the total stockholders' equity less the preferred stock:

$$\$117,820,000 - \$37,500,000 = \$80,320,000$$

In other words, the sum of the common stock account, contributed capital in excess of par value account, and retained earnings account equals the total common stockholders' equity.

The *book value* per share of common stock is calculated as follows:

$$\text{Book value per share} = \frac{\text{Total common stockholders' equity}}{\text{Number of shares outstanding}}$$

In the case of the Lawrence Company,

$$\text{Book value per share} = \frac{\$80,320,000}{6,675,000}$$
$$= \$12.03$$

A common stock's book value is calculated on the basis of balance sheet figures and does not necessarily have any relationship to the common stock's *market value*, which is based primarily on expectations concerning general economic conditions and the firm's future earnings.

The balance in the common stock account is calculated by multiplying the number of shares actually outstanding by the *par value*, an arbitrary value assigned to shares of common stock.[9] To continue with this example, the Lawrence Company has 6,675,000 shares outstanding and a $2 par value, resulting in a balance of $13,350,000.

To illustrate the nature of the contributed capital in excess of par value account, suppose Lawrence decides to raise an additional $12 million in external equity capital by selling 600,000 common shares at $20 each.[10] The amount credited to the common stock account is $1,200,000 (600,000 shares times the $2 par value). The remainder of the $12 million is added to the contributed capital in excess of par value account. In other words, this account contains capital that is paid into the firm in excess of the par value when common stock is issued.

Additions to the retained earnings account occur as a result of earnings that are retained in the business, as opposed to earnings that are paid out to the stockholders as dividends. Retained earnings, which are internally generated funds, are the most important source of capital for business.

---

[9] At one time par value was considered important for any possible liquidation proceedings, but today it has little, if any, real signifance. Par value is normally a low figure and tends to be less than $5 per share. Occasionally companies issue stock with no par value. In these instances the balance in the common stock account is a "stated value."

[10] Before sales of the new shares, a reasonable price level might be about $21 or $22 per share. (This example ignores flotation costs.)

Stockholder Rights

Common stockholders have a number of general rights, including the following:

- **Dividend rights.** Stockholders have the right to share equally on a per-share basis in any distribution of corporate earnings in the form of dividends.

- **Asset rights.** In the event of a liquidation, stockholders have the right to assets that remain after the obligations to the government (taxes), employees, and debtholders have been satisfied.

- **Voting rights.** Stockholders have the right to vote on stockholder matters, such as the selection of the board of directors.

- **Preemptive rights.** Stockholders may have the right to share proportionately in any new stock sold. For example, a stockholder who owns 20 percent of a corporation's stock may be entitled to purchase 20 percent of any new issue.

Whereas all stockholders have dividend and liquidation rights, in addition to voting rights (unless the stock is specifically nonvoting), preemptive rights exist in a relatively small minority of firms at the present time. (Voting rights and preemptive rights are discussed in detail in the appendix to this chapter.)

Understanding Stock Quotations

Table 16-4 shows a partial listing of NYSE stocks from the *Wall Street Journal*. Beginning at the left-hand side, the first two columns show the stock's price range during the previous fifty-two weeks. For example, the per-share stock price of Bristol-Myers ranged between $71.25 and $53.625. The column immediately to the right of the stock name shows the current annual dividend rate; for example, the Bristol-Myers annual rate is $1.88 per share. The next column shows the dividend percentage yield; for Bristol-Myers, the figure is 2.7 (calculated as the annual dividend

Table 16-4   Partial Listing of Stock Market Quotations

52 Weeks										
High	Low	Stock	Div.	Yld %	P-E Ratio	Sales 100s	High	Low	Close	Net chg.
$29\frac{3}{8}$	$20\frac{1}{4}$	Bowatr	.72	2.5	13	453	$29\frac{1}{8}$	$28\frac{1}{2}$	29	$+ \frac{1}{4}$
$34\frac{5}{8}$	$25\frac{3}{4}$	BrigSt	1.60	4.8	16	208	$34\frac{1}{2}$	$33\frac{1}{2}$	$33\frac{1}{2}$	$- 1\frac{1}{8}$
$71\frac{1}{4}$	$53\frac{5}{8}$	BristM	1.88	2.7	18	3756	$70\frac{1}{2}$	$68\frac{1}{2}$	$69\frac{1}{8}$	$- 1\frac{3}{8}$
$4\frac{5}{8}$	$3\frac{1}{2}$	BritLnd	—	—	—	9	$3\frac{3}{4}$	$3\frac{5}{8}$	$3\frac{5}{8}$	—
$35\frac{1}{8}$	$22\frac{7}{8}$	BritPt	2.36e	7.5	6	236	32	$31\frac{3}{8}$	$31\frac{1}{2}$	$- \frac{3}{4}$
$30\frac{3}{8}$	22	BrtT2	pp1.17e	4.0	14	33	$29\frac{3}{8}$	29	$29\frac{1}{8}$	$- \frac{1}{8}$
$3\frac{5}{8}$	$\frac{9}{16}$	Brock	—	—	—	179	$\frac{7}{8}$	$\frac{13}{16}$	$\frac{7}{8}$	—
$39\frac{3}{8}$	$18\frac{1}{8}$	Brockwy	1.32	3.6	17	×55	$36\frac{7}{8}$	$36\frac{1}{4}$	$36\frac{1}{4}$	$- \frac{1}{4}$
$46\frac{3}{4}$	$35\frac{1}{4}$	BkyUG	3.24	7.0	9	93	$46\frac{1}{2}$	$46\frac{1}{4}$	$46\frac{1}{4}$	—
$27\frac{1}{4}$	$22\frac{1}{2}$	BkUG	pf2.47	9.2	—	10	$26\frac{7}{8}$	$26\frac{3}{4}$	$26\frac{3}{4}$	$- \frac{1}{4}$
$37\frac{1}{4}$	$30\frac{7}{8}$	BkUG	pf3.95	11	—	13	$35\frac{1}{2}$	$35\frac{1}{4}$	$35\frac{1}{2}$	$+ \frac{1}{4}$
$28\frac{1}{2}$	$19\frac{1}{2}$	BwnSh	.40	1.5	16	44	$27\frac{5}{8}$	$27\frac{1}{8}$	$27\frac{1}{2}$	$+ \frac{3}{8}$

Source: *The Wall Street Journal* March 4, 1986.

divided by the closing price, or $1.88/$69.125 = 2.7%). Then the price-earnings (P/E) ratio (the current price divided by the last twelve months' earnings) is shown. The P/E ratio (18) indicates how much investors are willing to pay for $1 of earnings from the firm. The P/E multiple is influenced by a number of factors, including the risk of the firm and projections of future earnings. The next figure is the sales volume in hundreds of shares; in this case, 375,600 shares of Bristol-Myers common stock were traded on March 3, 1986. The next three columns list the high, low, and closing prices for the day; the final column shows the net change for the day, or the difference between this day's closing price and the closing price on the previous business day (or the last day on which a trade took place). For the day, Bristol-Myers traded between $70.50 and $68.50, closing at $69.125 per share, down $1.375 per share for the day.

Other Features of Common Stock

This section covers other topics related to the ownership of common stock, including *common stock classes, stock splits, stock dividends,* and *stock repurchases.*

Common Stock Classes Occasionally a firm may decide to create more than one class of common stock. The reason for this may be that the firm wishes to raise additional equity capital by selling a portion of the existing owners' stock while at the same time maintaining control of the firm. This can be accomplished by creating a separate class of *nonvoting stock.* Typically so-called Class A common stock is nonvoting, whereas Class B has voting rights; the classes are normally otherwise equal. The Ford Motor Company is an example of a large, widely held company that has more than one class of common stock. Ford's 12.7 million shares of "Class B stock" are entirely held by Ford family interests. This class has 40 percent of the total voting power. Ford's 107.8 million shares of "common stock" are held by the public and have 60 percent of the total voting power. The two classes are otherwise equal. In recent years, General Motors created two new classes of common stock—"E" and "H," which it used in the acquisition of Electronic Data Systems and Hughes Aircraft Company, respectively.

Stock Splits If management feels that the firm's common stock should sell at a lower price to attract more purchasers, it can effect a *stock split.* There seems to be a general feeling in the finance community that the optimum price range for a share of common stock should be very roughly $15 to $70. Consequently, if a stock rises above this range, management may decide on a stock split to get the price back to a more desirable trading level.

For example, the per-share price of Dart & Kraft common stock rose into the $90–$100 range in early 1985. Then in 1985 with the stock trading at about $93, the stock split three for one. Following the split, the stock traded in the $30 range.

Frequently companies choose to raise their dividend levels at the time of a split. Prior to the split, Dart & Kraft's annual dividend was $4.24 per share; after the split, the dividend was raised to $1.56 per share, which amounted to $4.68 per share on the presplit shares.

Many investors believe stock splits are an indication of good financial health. The mere splitting of a stock, however, should not be taken in and of itself as evidence that the stock will necessarily perform well in the future.

From an accounting standpoint, when a stock is split, its par value is changed accordingly. For example, when the split is two for one, the par value is reduced by one-half, and the number of shares is doubled. No changes occur in the firm's account balances or capital structure.

Reverse Stock Splits Reverse stock splits are stock splits in which the number of shares is decreased. They are used to bring low-priced shares up to more desirable trading levels. For example, assume the management of Ajax Steel, whose stock has dropped to about $4 per share, is concerned that potential investors might be unwilling to buy the stock because of the relatively large percentage commission on low-priced stocks, as well as the stigma that is attached to them. One alternative it might choose is a one-for-five reverse stock split, which could bring the stock price back up to about $20 per share. It should be obvious, however, that the reverse stock split itself will not cure any ills Ajax might be experiencing.

Many investors feel reverse stock splits indicate poor corporate health. For this reason they are relatively uncommon.

Stock Dividends A stock dividend is a dividend to stockholders that consists of additional shares of stock instead of cash. Normally stock dividends are in the 2 to 10 percent range—that is, the number of shares outstanding is increased by 2 to 10 percent. From an accounting standpoint, stock dividends involve a transfer from the retained earnings account to the common stock and additional paid-in capital accounts.[11]

Stock Repurchases From time to time companies repurchase some of their own shares (known as *treasury stock*). Figure 16-2 contains an announcement of such a share repurchase by TRW. In addition to tax considerations, which were discussed in Chapter 14, there are a number of other reasons why a firm may decide to repurchase its own stock. These include:

- **Investment.** Management may feel that the common stock is under-valued, based on its assessment of the future earnings potential of the firm. By repurchasing shares, the company hopes to raise its earnings per share and future stock price. Standard Oil Company of Indiana cited this reason when it announced its intention in May 1984 to repurchase as many as 30 million, or 10.3 percent, of the shares outstanding for $1.7 billion, which at the time was believed to be the largest stock repurchase ever undertaken.

- **Financial restructuring.** By issuing debt and using the proceeds to repur-

---

[11] Chapter 14 contains a more detailed discussion of stock dividends.

Figure 16-2 **Share Repurchase Announcement**

Morgan Stanley acted as financial advisor to
TRW, Inc. in this transaction.

TRW Inc.

has repurchased

7,702,471 shares
of Common Stock

as part of a corporate restructuring

chase its common stock, the firm can alter its capital structure to gain the benefits of increased financial leverage.

- **Future corporate needs.** Stock can be repurchased for use in future acquisitions of other companies, stock option plans for executives, conversion of convertible securities, and the exercise of warrants.[12]

- **Disposition of excess cash.** The company may want to dispose of excess cash which it has accumulated from operations or the sale of assets.

[12] Warrants and convertible securities are examined in the following chapter.

These funds are expendable because management may not feel that they can be invested profitably within the company in the forseeable future.

These reasons are not mutually exclusive—a firm may repurchase shares for a combination of reasons.

Advantages and Disadvantages of Common Stock Financing

One of the major advantages of common stock financing is that no fixed dividend obligation exists, at least in principle. In practice, however, dividend cuts are relatively uncommon for companies paying a "regular" dividend, a fact that implies that corporate management generally views a firm's current level of dividends as a minimum for the future. Nevertheless, common stock financing does allow firms a greater degree of flexibility in their financing plans than fixed-income securities do. Thus, common stock is less risky to the firm than fixed income securities. Limits on additional debt and the maintenance of working capital levels are only two of the constraints imposed on a firm when fixed-income security financing is employed.

In addition, common stock financing can be advantageous for a firm whose capital structure contains more than an optimal amount of debt. Under these circumstances, common stock financing can lower the firm's weighted cost of capital.

From the investors' perspective, however, common stock is a riskier investment than debt securities or preferred stock. Because of this, investors in common stock require relatively high rates of return, and this means that the firm's cost for common stock financing is high compared with fixed-income securities.

From another perspective, external common stock financing frequently results in an initial dilution of per-share earnings, particularly if the assets acquired with the proceeds of the financing do not produce earnings immediately. Table 16-5, which contains figures for Desert Electric Power Company for 19X6 and 19X5, illustrates this point.

Notice that whereas the firm's net income increased in 19X6 over 19X5, its earnings per share declined because of the new shares issued. Thus, the additional issue of common shares can dilute the original owners' claims on the firm's earnings. If, on the other hand, the new assets earn a higher rate of return than the existing assets, the original owners will benefit from the increased earnings. Also, the problem of diluted earnings should only

Table 16-5

Example of Diluted Per-Share Earnings as a Result of Common Stock Financing

	Year Ended September 30	
	19X6	19X5
Net income available for common stock	$25,821,000	$20,673,000
Average number of common shares outstanding	15,600,000	12,122,007
Earnings per average share of common stock	$1.66	$1.71

be temporary if the firm is investing wisely and should have no adverse consequences in a well-informed market.

A final disadvantage of external equity financing involves the relatively high flotation costs associated with common stock sold to the public.[13]

Selected Capital Market Topics

This section presents several capital market topics. Capital markets are usually classified as either *primary* or *secondary* markets. New securities are issued in the primary markets, and the firms issuing these securities receive the proceeds from their sale, thus raising new capital. Outstanding securities are traded in the secondary markets, where owners of these securities may sell them to other investors. The corporations whose securities are traded in the secondary markets do not share in the proceeds from these sales.

Although primary and secondary markets are separate, they are closely related. Smoothly functioning secondary markets aid the primary markets, because investors tend to be more willing to purchase new securities when they know they can sell them in the secondary market. In fact, the potential liquidity available in the secondary markets may make investors more willing to accept slightly lower returns on their investments, thereby lowering the cost companies have to pay for their funds.

Listed Security Exchanges and Over-the-Counter Markets

Secondary markets can be further classified as either listed security exchanges or over-the-counter (OTC) markets. Listed security exchanges operate at designated places of business and have requirements governing the types of securities they can list and trade. The OTC security markets do not have centralized places of business, but rather exist as networks of security dealers connected by a communications system of telephones and terminals with price quotations.

Listed Security Exchanges   The New York Stock Exchange (NYSE), sometimes called the *Big Board,* is the oldest and largest stock exchange in the United States. Over 1,900 common and preferred stocks and over 800 bonds are listed on the NYSE. For a company's stock to be listed and traded on the NYSE, the company must meet certain minimum requirements with regard to the number of shares of stock outstanding, the number of shareholders, the geographical distribution of shareholders, the value of assets, the market value of shares, and the net income level. As a result, only the largest U.S. companies tend to be listed on the NYSE.

The NYSE is composed largely of security firms that purchase memberships, or *seats.* The cost of these seats varies, depending on the securities industry outlook. The other organized national exchange is the American Stock Exchange (ASE or AMEX), which, like the NYSE, is located in New York City. The companies listed on the AMEX are smaller on average than those listed on the NYSE.

In addition to the national exchanges, there are a number of *regional* exchanges located around the country. The two largest are the Midwest

---

[13] Flotation costs are discussed in detail later in this chapter.

Stock Exchange in Chicago and the Pacific Stock Exchange in San Francisco and Los Angeles. In general, regional exchanges list stocks of companies located in their geographical areas. Many large companies are listed on both the NYSE and one or more regional exchanges.

Trading activities on the NYSE and several of the regional exchanges—including the Midwest, Pacific, Philadelphia, Boston, and Cincinnati exchanges—are listed together and reported in the financial press as the *NYSE Composite Transactions*. Eventually an electronic communications network called the *Intermarket Trading System* will connect all the major U.S. stock exchanges.

Over-the-Counter Markets   Securities that are not listed on exchanges are said to be traded "over the counter" (OTC). In general, these include stocks of small and relatively unknown companies, although many bank and insurance company stocks, a majority of corporate bonds and preferred stocks, and most U.S. Treasury and municipal bonds are traded in OTC markets. Security firms that deal in OTC stocks and actually carry inventories in certain stocks play an important role in the smooth functioning of OTC markets, and they are said to "make a market" in the securities they inventory.

On each business day *The Wall Street Journal* contains a full page of price quotations on OTC stocks having some national interest. Much of this page is devoted to quotations from the NASDAQ tape, the automated quotation system of the National Association of Security Dealers. This system has helped to more fully integrate the OTC market at the national level.

In addition to the listings contained in *The Wall Street Journal*, the financial pages of newspapers around the country contain price quotations on OTC stocks of companies located in their areas.

Understanding the Financial Pages

The Wall Street Journal and the business sections of daily newspapers in larger cities contain economic and security market news. This subsection discusses *stock market indexes, margin trading,* and *short selling.*

Stock Market Indexes   Stock market indexes give a broad indication of how the stock market, or a segment of the stock market, performed during a particular day. The most frequently quoted stock market index is the Dow Jones Industrial Average (DJIA), which is based on the stock prices of thirty large, well-established industrial corporations.[14] The DJIA is calculated by adding the prices of the thirty stocks and dividing by a number that reflects stock dividends and splits. When a radio announcer says, "The market was up five points today," the announcer means the DJIA was up five points. A one-point movement in the DJIA is equal to about a 7¢ per share movement in the price of an average stock.

---

[14] Dow Jones and Company is a financial company that publishes *The Wall Street Journal.* Every Monday *The Wall Street Journal* lists the companies that make up the Dow Jones averages on the second-to-last page. Every day the values of all the major stock market indexes are listed in *The Wall Street Journal* and in the financial section of most major newspapers.

The Dow Jones Transportation Average is based on twenty major railroad, airline, and trucking stocks, and the Dow Jones Utility Average is derived from fifteen major utility stocks. The DJIA is combined with the transportation and the utility averages to form the Dow Jones Composite Average.

The *Standard and Poor's 500* Stock Price Index (S&P 500) is another frequently quoted stock market index that is significantly broader than the DJIA. It is compiled from the stock prices of 400 leading industrial firms, twenty transportation firms, forty utilities, and forty financial institutions. The S&P 500 is a *market value-weighted index*. This means, for example, that a stock whose total market value is $20 million influences the index twice as much as a stock whose total market value is $10 million.

Margin Trading   Securities purchased with funds borrowed from brokers are said to be *bought on margin*. Investors may have *cash accounts* and *margin accounts* with their brokers. In the case of a cash account, the investor pays the full purchase price of any securities bought; in the case of a margin account, the investor puts up only a portion of the total price (that is, the margin), and the broker lends the investor the remaining portion. Margin trading is designed to increase returns available to investors, but it also increases risk, similar to the impact financial leverage has on corporations. The margin percentage is regulated by the Federal Reserve Board.

Short Selling   Most investors purchase a security (that is, take a *long* position), hope the price will increase during the holding period, and sell it at some future date. However, it is also possible for investors to sell securities they do not own and buy them back later. This is termed *short selling* or taking a *short* position. When making a short sale, the investor borrows the securities to be sold from another investor. When the securities are bought back later by the short seller, they are delivered to the investor that initially loaned them. If the short seller is able to sell a security first at a relatively high price and buy it back later at a lower price, a profit is realized.

Regulation of the Security Markets

Both the individual states and the Federal government regulate the securities business. Beginning with Kansas in 1911, each of the fifty states (with the exception of Delaware) has passed so-called blue sky laws. The term *blue sky* came about when some risky securities were called nothing more than "pieces of blue sky." In spite of these state laws, many investors received incomplete and even fraudulent security information during the 1920s. This fact, combined with the 1929 stock market crash and the general reform spirit of the 1930s, led to the enactment of two principal pieces of security legislation—the Securities Act of 1933 and the Securities Exchange Act of 1934. This Federal legislation has been aimed primarily at insuring full disclosure of security information.

The Securities Act of 1933 requires any firm offering *new* securities to the public to make a complete disclosure of all pertinent facts regarding these securities; the Securities Exchange Act of 1934 expanded the coverage to include trading in *existing* securities. The 1934 act also created the Securities and Exchange Commission (SEC), which is responsible for administering the Federal securities legislation. These Federal laws make no judgments regarding the quality of securities issues; they simply require full disclosure of the facts.[15]

Any company that plans to sell an interstate security issue totaling over $500,000 and having a maturity greater than 270 days is required to register the issue with the SEC.[16] The procedure involves the preparation of a *registration statement* and a *prospectus*. The registration statement contains a vast amount of information about the company's legal, operational, and financial position; the prospectus summarizes the information contained in the registration statement and is intended for the use by potential investors.

After a company has filed a registration statement and prospectus, there is normally a waiting period of twenty days before the SEC approves the issue and the company can begin selling the securities. During the waiting period the company may use a preliminary prospectus in connection with the anticipated sale of securities. This preliminary prospectus is often called a "red herring" because it contains a statement, usually marked in red, saying that the prospectus is "not an offer to sell."

Many capital market participants have complained over the years about the large amount of paperwork and the resulting delays that the SEC rules apparently caused. In 1982 the SEC implemented Rule 415, known as *shelf registration*. This new procedure allows larger companies to register all the debt and equity securities they plan to offer over the following two years. After the shelf registration is completed, the company can then sell securities whenever it chooses. There are a number of advantages to shelf registration. In addition to reducing the amount of SEC paperwork, this procedure allows the firm to time the sale of the securities to its need for the funds. Also, with volatile bond and stock prices, the firm can react quickly and issue securities when market prices are most favorable. Finally, shelf registration can save the company money in terms of underwriting fees. A company no longer has to choose an investment banker before it registers the securities offering. Instead the firm can offer blocks of securities to investment bankers using a competitive bidding ("auction") process. According to one study commissioned by the SEC, raising equity funds through shelf registrations saved companies 1 percent of the funds raised, compared with companies choosing the more traditional underwriting-syndicate method.[17]

The Securities Exchange Act of 1934 also made it possible for the government to regulate "insider" trading. Any time a director, officer, or major stockholder—that is, an "insider"—of a large corporation trades in that corporation's securities, this fact must be reported to the SEC. This

---

[15] In recent years some states have prohibited the sale of certain securities on the grounds of poor quality rather than any problems associated with the disclosure of information.

[16] Security issues of the Federal government and nonprofit organizations do not have to be registered with the SEC. Bank and railroad issues are also exempt, since these industries are regulated by other government agencies.

[17] Bluford H. Putnam and G. Bennett Stewart, "Investment Banking's Changing Face." *The Wall Street Journal* (January 4, 1984).

information is available to the public and is used by some investors in deciding which stocks to buy or sell. This aspect of the 1934 act attempts to prevent insiders from secretly trading securities on the basis of private information.

Interest Rate Swaps

An *interest rate swap* is an agreement between two companies in which one company's floating rate debt repayment obligation is traded for another company's fixed rate obligation. If a company with floating rate debt feels that interest rates are headed higher, it can execute a swap agreement to obtain the equivalent of fixed rate debt. The other party to the swap agrees to pay the interest costs in excess of the specified rate. Both investment banks and commercial banks act as brokers on swaps. Some also act as principals or counterparties in these transactions.

Sears Roebuck engaged in thirty-six interest rate swaps over a three-year period and transformed $2.5 billion of floating rate debt into fixed rate liabilities.[18] As a result of these swaps, Sears was able to reduce the impact on its earnings per share of a one percentage point change in interest rates from 12¢ to 6¢ per share.

Interest rate swaps have experienced tremendous growth since the early 1980s. An estimated $100 billion of interest rate swaps was arranged in 1985.

Role of the Investment Banker

Investment bankers are financial middlemen who bring together suppliers and users of long-term funds in the capital markets. Whenever a large corporation is considering raising funds in the capital markets, it will almost always enlist the services of an investment banker. In fact, most large industrial corporations have ongoing relationships with their investment bankers.

The investment banker is well qualified to advise the corporation on a variety of matters, including the following:

- Long-range financial planning.
- The timing of security issues.
- The purchase of securities.
- The marketing of securities.
- The arrangement of private loans and leases.
- The negotiation of mergers.

In summary, the investment banker is an important source of financial market expertise.

How Securities are Sold

Firms can sell securities in the primary capital markets in one of three ways:

- By selling securities through investment bankers to the public in a *public cash offering.*

[18] *Business Week* (November 5, 1984): 56.

Figure 16-3   **How Securities Are Sold: A Flowchart**

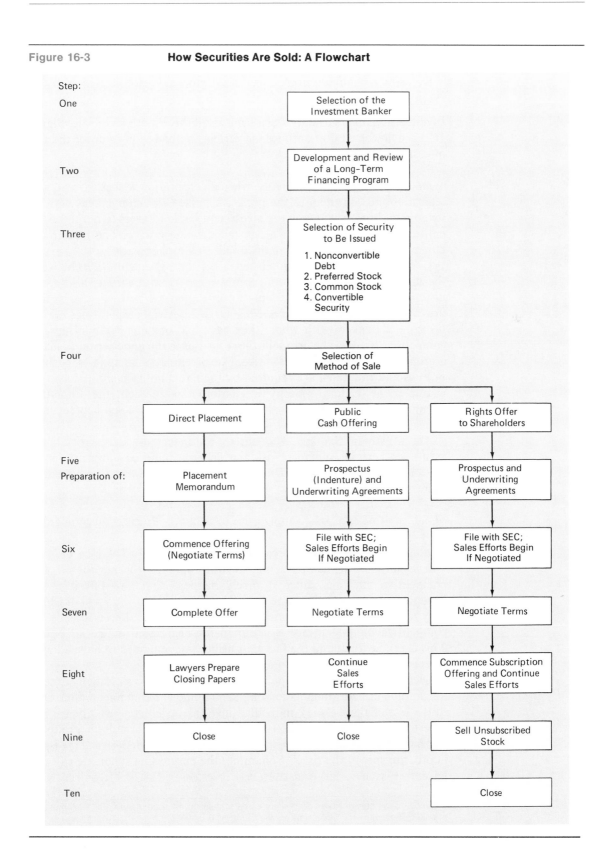

- By placing a debt or stock issue with one or more large investors in a *private,* or *direct, placement.*
- By selling common stock to existing stockholders through a *rights offering.*

Investment bankers usually assist firms in all three methods of sale. Figure 16-3 is a flowchart that outlines the various methods and steps for the sale of corporate securities.

Public Cash Offerings Normally, when a corporation wishes to issue new securities and sell them to the public, it makes an arrangement with an investment banker whereby the investment banker agrees to purchase the entire issue at a set price. This is called *underwriting.* The investment banker then resells the issue to the public at a higher price.

Underwriting can be accomplished either through *negotiations* between the underwriter and the issuing company or by *competitive bidding.* A *negotiated underwriting* is simply an arrangement between the issuing firm and its investment bankers. Most large industrial corporations turn to investment bankers with whom they have had ongoing relationships. In competitive bidding the firm sells the securities to the underwriter (usually a group) that bids the highest price. Many regulated companies, such as utilities and railroads, are required by their regulatory commissions (for example, the Federal Energy Regulatory Commission, the Interstate Commerce Commission, and state regulatory bodies) to sell new security issues in this way.

An investment banker who agrees to underwrite a security issue assumes a certain amount of risk and, in turn, requires compensation in the form of an *underwriting discount* or *underwriting spread,* computed as follows:

$$\text{Underwriting spread} = \text{Selling price to public} - \text{Proceeds to company.}$$

Examples of underwriting spread amounts are shown in Table 16-6.

It is difficult to compare underwriting spreads for negotiated and competitive offerings, since it rarely happens that two offerings are brought to market at the same time that differ only in the ways in which they are underwritten. Generally underwriters receive lower spreads for competitive bidding utility issues than for negotiated industrial offers. This is primarily due to the fact that utilities have tended to have a lower level of risk than industrial companies.

Security issues sold to the public through underwriters normally exceed $25 million in size; amounts totaling $250 million are not uncommon. Due to the size of these issues, individual investment bankers usually are not able to underwrite an entire issue by themselves. Normally a group of underwriters, called a *purchasing syndicate,* agrees to underwrite the issue in order to spread the risk.[19] Sometimes the purchasing syndicate can sell an entire issue to large institutional investors[20]; this is often true with

---

[19] In most cases one to three underwriters agree to manage an issue, handling all legal matters, advertising, and so on. These firms are the *managing underwriters.*

[20] Institutional investors include life insurance companies, pension funds, mutual funds, and commercial banks.

Table 16-6   **Sample Underwriting Spreads for Selected Issues**

Company	Issue Size (in Millions of Dollars)	Underwriting Spread (%)	S&P Rating*
Debt Issues			
First Interstate Bancorp.	$100	0.63	AA
CIGNA Corporation†	100	1.00	AA
Corning Glass Works†	100	1.00	A
U.S. Leasing International†	30	2.00	BBB
Jerrico, Inc.	40	1.88	BB
Petro-Lewis	85	3.35	B
Sunshine Mining Company	30	3.68	B
Common Stock Issues			
El Paso Electric Company	$ 57.5	3.26	
Ryder System, Inc.	83.4	3.88	
Southwest Airlines	34.7	3.89	
Service Corporation International	48.26	4.48	
Adage, Inc.	10.0	6.26	
Atlantic Southeast Airlines	5.2	8.00	

*Standard and Poor's (S&P) bond-rating scale is AAA (for the highest quality issues), AA, A, BBB, BB, B, CCC, CC, C.
†Convertible issues.

high-quality debt issues. On other occasions—particularly with large debt issues or equity issues—the underwriters organize a *selling group* of security firms to market the issue to the public. It is not uncommon for a selling group responsible for marketing a large issue to number over 100 security firms.

An important part of the negotiations between the issuing firm and the investment banker is the determination of the security's selling price. It is in the best interests of both the issuing firm and the underwriter to have the security "fairly priced." If the security is underpriced, the issuing firm will not raise the amount of capital it could have, and the underwriter may lose a customer. If the security is overpriced, the underwriter may have difficulty selling the issue, and investors who discover that they paid too much may choose not to purchase the next issue offered by either the corporation or the underwriter.

Occasionally, with smaller company issues, the investment banker agrees to help market the issue on a "best efforts" basis rather than underwriting it. Under this type of arrangement the investment banker is under no further obligation to the issuing company if some of the securities cannot be sold. The investment banker functions as a *dealer* in an underwriting situation and as a *broker* in a best efforts situation. In a best efforts offering the investment banker does not assume the risk that the securities will not be sold at a favorable price.

Private Placements Many industrial companies choose to *directly,* or *privately, place* debt or preferred stock issues with one or more institutional investors instead of having them underwritten and sold to the public. In these cases, investment bankers who act on behalf of the issuing company receive a "finder's fee" for finding a buyer and negotiating the terms of the agreement. The private market is an important source of long-term debt capital, especially for smaller corporations.

Private security placements have a number of advantages:

- They can save on flotation costs by eliminating underwriting costs.
- They can avoid the time delays associated with the preparation of registration statements and with the waiting period.
- They can offer greater flexibility in the writing of the terms of the contract (called the *indenture*) between the borrower and the lender.

An offsetting disadvantage is that, as a very general rule, interest rates for private placements are about one-eighth of a percentage point *higher* than they are for debt and preferred issues sold through underwriters. For small-sized debt and preferred stock issues—that is, those that are less than about $20 million—the percentage cost of underwriting becomes fairly large. Because of this, these smaller-sized issues are frequently placed privately with institutional investors.

Rights Offerings and Standby Underwritings   Firms may sell their common stock directly to their existing stockholders through the issuance of *rights,* which entitle the stockholders to purchase new shares of the firm's stock at a *subscription price* below the market price. (Rights offerings are also called *privileged subscriptions.*) Each stockholder receives one right for each share owned; in other words, if a firm has 100 million shares outstanding and wishes to sell an additional 10 million shares through a rights offering, each right entitles the holder to purchase 0.1 shares, and it takes ten rights to purchase one share.[21]

When selling stock through a rights offering, firms usually enlist the services of investment bankers, who urge rights holders to purchase the stock. In an arrangement called a *standby underwriting,* the investment banker agrees to purchase—at the subscription price—any shares that are not sold to rights holders. The investment banker then resells the shares. In a standby underwriting the investment banker bears risk and is compensated by an underwriting fee.

Flotation costs   Flotation costs are the costs involved in issuing new securities. The total flotation cost of a security issue sold through underwriters is calculated as follows:

$$\text{Total floation cost} = \text{Underwriting spread} + \text{Company's issue expenses.}$$

The company's issue expenses are usually considerably less than the underwriting spread. For example, when Service Corporation International recently sold 1.35 million shares of common stock, the underwriting spread was $2,160,000, and the issue expenses were $280,564.

Flotation costs can vary widely, depending on the type of the security being offered, the quality of the security, and the size of the issue. Common stock flotation costs range from about 2 percent to as high as 20 percent or more, whereas flotation costs on good quality debt issues fall

---

[21] Rights and rights offerings are discussed in greater detail in the appendix to this chapter.

into roughly the 0.5 to 3 percent range. Table 16-6 shows the underwriting spreads for several issues.

Generally, flotation costs are higher for common stock than for preferred stock issues, and flotation costs of preferred stock are higher than those of debt issues. One reason for this is the amount of risk each type of issue involves. Common stocks usually involve more risk for underwriters than preferred stock, and preferred stock involves more risk than debt. Stock prices are subject to wider price movements than debt prices. Another reason for these differences in flotation costs is that investment bankers usually incur greater marketing expenses for common stock than for preferred stock or debt issues. Common stock is customarily sold to a large number of individual investors, whereas debt securities are frequently purchased by a much smaller number of institutional investors.

Flotation costs also depend on the quality of the issue. Low quality debt issues, for example, tend to have higher percentage flotation costs than high quality issues, since underwriters bear more risk with low quality issues and therefore require greater compensation. And, finally, flotation costs are dependent on the size of the issue—they tend to be higher for small-sized issues, all other things being equal, since underwriters have various fixed expenses (such as advertising expenses, legal fees, registration statement costs, and so on) that are incurred regardless of the issue's size.

Summary

General

- *Long-term debt, preferred stock,* and *common stock* are major sources of capital for a firm.
- Long-term debt and preferred stock are classified as *fixed-income securities,* because interest (on long-term debt) and dividends (on preferred stock) tend to remain constant over time.
- *Capital markets*—the markets for long-term financial assets—can be classified as either *primary* or *secondary.* New securities are issued in the primary markets, whereas existing securities are traded in the secondary markets.

Long-term Debt

- Long-term debt is generally classified according to whether or not it is *secured* by specific physical assets of the issuing company. Secured debt issues are *mortgage bonds,* whereas debt issues backed only by unmortgaged assets and the company's earning power are *debentures.*
- Long-term debt usually has the following features:

  1. The *indenture,* or the contract between the issuing company and the debtholders.

  2. The *trustee,* who represents the debtholders in dealings with the company.

3. The *call feature,* which gives the issuing company the option to retire the debt prior to maturity.

4. The *sinking fund requirement,* which, in practice, means the company must gradually reduce the outstanding balance of the debt issue over its life.

- Bond *refunding* occurs when a company redeems a callable issue and sells a lower cost issue to take its place.

- The major advantages of long-term debt financing include the following:

    1. Its low after-tax cost to the company due to the tax deductibility of the interest paid out.

    2. The increased earnings per share possible through financial leverage.

- The major disadvantage of long-term debt financing is the increased financial risk of the firm.

Preferred Stock

- Preferred stock occupies an intermediate position between long-term debt and common stock as a source of capital. Like common stock, preferred stock is part of the stockholders' equity, and preferred stockholders receive returns in the form of dividends. Preferred stock is also similar to long-term debt in that preferred dividends, like the interest on long-term debt, usually remain constant over time.

- Preferred stock usually has the following features:

    1. The *selling price,* or *issue price,* is the per-share price at which the shares are sold to the public.

    2. The *par value* is an arbitrary value assigned to the stock by the issuing company.

    3. Most preferred stock is *cumulative*—that is, dividends on common stock cannot be paid as long as any past or present preferred dividends remain unpaid.

    4. Virtually all preferred stock is *nonparticipating*—that is, preferred stock does not share in any increased earnings of the firm.

    5. Some preferred stock is *perpetual,* whereas other preferred stock is gradually retired by the firm.

    6. Preferred stock is often *callable.*

- From the issuing company's perspective, preferred stock financing is advantageous due to the potential flexibility of preferred dividend payments.

- The principal disadvantage of preferred stock financing is that dividends are not tax deductible, which causes the after-tax cost of preferred stock to the firm to be higher than the cost of long-term debt, all other things being equal.

Common Stock

- The common stockholders are the true owners of the firm, and, as such, common stock is a permanent form of financing. Common stockholders participate in the firm's earnings, potentially receiving larger dividends if earnings rise or smaller dividends if earnings drop.
- Stockholder rights include the following:

  1. The right to dividends.
  2. The right to any assets remaining after senior claims are satisfied in a liquidation.
  3. Voting rights.
  4. The *preemptive right,* or the right to share proportionately in any new stock sold. This right is available in some firms but not in others.

- If a company's common stock price rises above the price range considered optimal, the company's management can effect a *stock split* to get the price back to a more desirable trading level.
- A firm may decide to repurchase its own shares for various reasons, including investment, financial restructuring, future corporate needs, and disposition of excess cash.
- Common stock permits a firm more flexibility in its financing plans than fixed-income securities do, because, in principle, no fixed-dividend obligation exists.

Capital Markets and Investment Banking

- Listed exchanges, such as the New York and American stock exchanges, have designated places of business, as well as various trading regulations and listing requirements. The over-the-counter markets do not have a centrally designated place of business, but instead exist through a telephone and computer communications network.
- The Securities Act of 1933 and the Securities Exchange Act of 1934 are the principal pieces of securities legislation in the United States. The 1933 act requires complete disclosure of information on *new* securities, and the 1934 act expands this coverage to include *existing* securities. The Securities Exchange Act of 1934 also created the Securities and Exchange Commission (SEC), which is responsible for administering Federal securities legislation.
- *Investment bankers* are financial middlemen that bring together suppliers and users of long-term funds in the capital markets. The principal service provided by investment bankers is the *underwriting* of securities. Underwriting is an insurance function whereby an investment banker agrees to purchase an entire issue at a specific price. The underwriters, usually a group called a *purchasing syndicate,* then resell the issue to the public at a slightly higher price. Since they assume a certain amount of risk when they agree to underwrite a security issue, underwriters earn the difference between the proceeds to the company and the selling price; this is called the *underwriting spread,* or the *underwriting discount.*

- Industrial corporations usually sell their securities through *negotiated underwritings,* whereas utilities and railroads frequently are required by law to sell their new security issues to the highest bidder in *competitive bidding.*

- Some security issues are *privately,* or *directly, placed* with institutional investors instead of being sold to the public through underwriters. The private market is an important source of debt financing for smaller firms.

- Firms may also choose to sell their common stock to their existing stockholders through a *rights offering,* or *privileged subscription.* Rights entitle stockholders to purchase new shares at a *subscription price* that is below the market price. Underwriters usually assist in rights offerings by agreeing to purchase any unsold shares; this is called *standby underwriting.*

- *Flotation costs* are the costs of issuing new securities. They are generally higher for common stock issues than for preferred stock issues, which, in turn, are higher than those for debt issues. Flotation costs tend to be inversely proportional to the issue's quality, since underwriters bear more risk with lower quality issues and therefore require greater compensation.

FOCUS ON CORPORATE PRACTICE

Standard and Poor's Bond-Rating Process

(When the rating agencies, such as Moody's or Standard and Poor's, rate the quality of the securities of a firm, they perform an in-depth analysis of the financial and operating condition of the firm. This "Focus on Corporate Practice" example outlines the key factors considered by Standard and Poor's when rating the securities of industrial companies.)

Industrial Company Rating Methodology Profile

1. **Industry risk:** Defined as the strength of the industry within the economy and relative to economic trends. This also includes the ease or difficulty of entering this industry, the importance of any diversity of the earnings base and the role of regulation and legislation.
   a. Importance in the economic cycle.
   b. Business cyclicality: earnings volatility, lead-lag and duration, diversity of earnings base, predictability and stability of revenues and earnings.
   c. Economic forces impacts; high inflation, energy costs and availability, international competitive position, social-political forces.
   d. Demand factors: real growth projections relative to GNP and basis for projections, maturity of markets.
   e. Basic financial characteristics of the business: fixed or working capital intensive; importance of credit as a sales tool.
   f. Supply factors: raw materials, labor, over/under utilized plant capacity.
   g. Federal, state, foreign regulation.
   h. Potential legislation.
   i. Fragmented or concentrated business.
   j. Barriers to entry/ease of entry.

2. **Issuer's industry position—market position:** The company's sales position in its major fields and its historical protection of its position and projected ability for the future.
   a. Ability to generate sales.
   b. Dominant and stable market shares.
   c. Marketing/distributing requirements of business-strengths, weaknesses, national, international, regional.
   d. R&D: degree of importance, degree of obsolescence; short or long product life.
   e. Support/service organization.
   f. Dependence on major customers/diversity of major customers.
   g. Long-term sales contracts/visibility of revenues/backlogs/prepayments (for example, subscriptions).
   h. Product diversity.

3. **Issuer's industry position—operating efficiency:** This covers the issuer's historical operating margins and assesses its ability to maintain or improve them based upon pricing or cost advantages.
   a. Ability to maintain or improve margins.
   b. Pricing leadership.

    c. Integration of manufacturing operations.

    d. Plant and equipment: modern and efficient or old and obsolete. Low or high cost producer.

    e. Supply of raw material.

    f. Level of capital and employee productivity.

    g. Labor: availability, cost, union relations.

    h. Pollution control requirements and impact on operating costs.

    i. Energy costs.

4. **Management evaluation:**

    a. The record of achievement in operations and financial results.

    b. Planning—extent, integration and relationship to accomplishments. Both strategic and financial. Plan for growth—both internal and external.

    c. Controls—management, financial and internal auditing.

    d. Financing policies and practices.

    e. Commitment, consistency and credibility.

    f. Overall quality of management; line of succession—strength of middle management.

    g. Merger and acquisition considerations.

    h. Performance versus peers.

5. **Accounting quality:** Overall accounting evaluation of the methods employed and the extent to which they overstate or understate financial performance and position.

    a. Auditor's qualifications.

    b. LIFO versus FIFO inventory method.

    c. Goodwill and intangible assets.

    d. Recording of revenues.

    e. Depreciation policies.

    f. Nonconsolidated subsidiaries.

    g. Method of accounting and funding for pension liabilities. Basic posture of the pension plan assumptions.

    h. Undervalued assets such as LIFO reserve.

6. **Earnings protection:** Key measurements indicating the basic long-term earnings power of the company including:

    a. Returns on capital.

    b. Pretax coverage ratios.

    c. Profit margins.

    d. Earnings on assets/business segments.

    e. Sources of future earnings growth.

    f. Pension service coverage.

    g. Ability to finance growth internally.

    h. Inflation-adjusted earning capacity.

7. **Financial leverage and asset protection:** Relative usage of debt, with due allowance for differences in debt usage appropriate to different types of businesses.

    a. Long-term debt and total debt to capital.

    b. Total liabilities to net tangible stockholders' equity.

    c. Preferred stock/capitalization.

    d. Leverage implicit in off-balance sheet financing arrangements, production payments, operating rentals of property, plant and equipment, nonconsolidated subsidiaries, unfunded pension liabilities, etc.

e. Nature of assets.

f. Working capital management—accounts receivable, inventory and accounts payable turnover.

g. Level, nature, and value of intangible assets.

h. Off-balance sheet assets such as undervalued natural resources or LIFO reserve.

8. **Cash flow adequacy:** Relationship of cash flow to leverage and ability to internally meet all business cash needs.

a. Evaluation of size and scope of total capital requirements and capital spending flexibility.

b. Evaluation of variability of future cash flow.

c. Cash flow to fixed and working capital requirements.

d. Cash flow to debt.

e. Free cash flow to short-term debt and total debt.

9. **Financial flexibility:** Evaluation of the company's financing needs, plans, and alternatives and its flexibility to accomplish its financing program under stress without damaging creditworthiness.

a. Relative financing needs.

b. Projected financing plan.

c. Financing alternatives under stress—ability to attract capital.

d. Capital spending flexibility.

e. Asset redeployment potentials—nature of assets and undervalued liabilities.

f. Nature and level of off-balance sheet assets or liabilities. This would include unfunded vested pension benefits and LIFO reserves.

g. High level of short-term debt/high level of floating rate debt.

h. Heavy or unwieldy debt service schedule (bullet maturities in future)—either of debt or sinking fund preferred stock.

i. Heavy percentage of preferred stock as a percentage of total capital.

j. Overall assessment of near-term sources of funds as compared to requirements for funds/internal self-sufficiency/need for external financing.

k. Ownership/affiliation.

Source: *Standard and Poor's Credit Overview: Corporate and International Ratings.* New York: Standard and Poor's, 1982, pp. 90–91. Reprinted by permission of Standard and Poor's, Corporation.

Questions and Topics for Discussion

1. Define the following terms associated with long-term debt:
   a. Mortgage bond
   b. Debenture
   c. Income bond
   d. Indenture
   e. Trustee
   f. Call feature
   g. Sinking fund
   h. Coupon rate
   i. Conversion feature
   j. Extendable notes

2. Suppose a company simultaneously sold two long-term debt issues at par: $9\frac{1}{8}$ percent senior debentures and $9\frac{3}{8}$ percent senior subordinated debentures. What risk-return tradeoff would an investor face who was considering one of these issues?

3. What is the relationship between par value, market value, and book value for the following?
   a. For long-term debt.
   b. For preferred stock.
   c. For common stock.

4. Define the following terms associated with preferred stock:
   a. Cumulative feature
   b. Participation
   c. Call feature
   d. Preference stock

5. In what ways is preferred stock similar to long-term debt? In what ways is it similar to common stock?

6. Define the following terms associated with common stock:
   a. Nonvoting stock
   b. Stock split
   c. Reverse stock split
   d. Stock dividend
   e. Book value
   f. Treasury stock

7. Does the retained earnings figure on a company's balance sheet indicate the amounts of funds the company has available for current dividends or capital expenditures? Explain fully.

8. Discuss the reasons why a firm may repurchase its own common stock.

9. Define the following terms:
   a. Listed security exchanges.
   b. Over-the-counter markets
   c. Stock market index
   d. Margin trading
   e. Short selling

10. Discuss the various stockholder rights.

11. Suppose an associate of yours (who has just lost money in the stock market) comments that the stock exchanges should be shut down because "all people do is lose money in the stock market." What would your response be?

12. What is the general purpose of Federal and state regulation of security markets?

13. What are the basic provisions of the Securities Act of 1933 and the Securities Exchange Act of 1934?

14. What is a *shelf registration?* What are the advantages of this procedure over the traditional method of selling securities?

15. What is an *interest rate swap?* How can swaps be used in raising funds?

16. What are the ways in which firms can sell their securities in the primary capital markets?

17. What factors influence the flotation cost percentage on security issues?

Problems*

1. Consider the British Petroleum common stock listed in Table 16-4 (symbolized as BritPt). Determine the following in regard to British Petroleum:
   a. Current (1986) dividend per share.
   b. Dividend yield.
   c. Price-earnings ratio.
   d. Closing price on March 3, 1986.
   e. Closing price on the previous business day.
   f. Volume of shares traded on March 3, 1986.

2. Consider the Exxon bond listed in Table 16-2. Determine the following in regard to this bond:
   a. Coupon interest rate.
   b. Maturity date (year).
   c. Closing price (dollar amount) on March 3, 1986.

3. Consider the Allied Corporation zero coupon bonds of 1998 (listed in Table 16-2). The bonds were issued in 1982 for $125. Determine the yield-to-maturity (to the nearest whole percent) if the bonds are purchased at the:
   a. Issue price in 1982. (Note: In order to avoid a fractional year holding period, assume that the issue and maturity dates are at the mid-point—July 1—of the respective years).
   b. Market price in 1986.
   c. Explain why the returns calculated in Parts a and b are different.

4. On April 17, 1986, the closing prices of the bonds listed in Table 16-2 were as follows:

Alld C zr 98	33
ATT 8.80s05	99⅜
duPnt 8.45s04	98⅛
Exxon 6s97	86⅝
RCA 12¼s05	110
Tol Ed 9.65s06	97⅛
Xerox 6s95	99

   a. Determine the percentage rate of return on these bonds over the 45-day holding period from March 3rd to April 17th. (Disregard any interest received during the holding period.)
   b. Convert the 45-day holding period rates of return in Part a to annual rates of return. (Hint: Based on 360 days per year, 45 days represents one-eighth of a year. Therefore, multiply the percentage return in Part a by 8 to obtain an annual rate of return.)
   c. What causes the rates of return to vary among the different bonds?

5. Baylor Minerals, Inc., is considering issuing additional long-term debt to finance an expansion. At the present time the company has $50 million in 10 percent debentures outstanding. Its after-tax net income is $10 million, and the company is in the 50 percent tax bracket. The company is required by the debenture holders to maintain its overall coverage ratio at 3.5 or greater.

* Color numbers denote problems which have check answers provided at the end of the book.

    a. What is the present coverage (times interest earned) ratio?

    b. How much additional 10 percent debt can the company issue now and remain "covered"? (Assume for this calculation that earnings before interest and taxes remains at its present level.)

    c. If the interest rate on additional debt is 12 percent, how much unused "debt capacity" does the company have?

6. In 1986 Andrews Oil Corporation sold units at $1,000 each consisting of a 20-year, 10¾ percent, $1,000 principal amount debenture plus 7 shares of the company's stock. At the time of issue the company's stock was selling at $15 a share.

    a. Determine an investor's yield to maturity on the debentures (to the nearest tenth of one percent).

    b. Calculate an investor's expected current interest yield on the debentures.

7. An insurance company in a 40 percent tax bracket is considering an investment in either the bonds or preferred stock of National Telephone and Telegraph. The bonds currently yield 9.0 percent, and the preferred stock yields 9.3 percent.

    a. What after-tax yield can the insurance company expect on the two types of securities?

    b. Should the investment decision be based only on expected return? Discuss.

8. The per-share price range for the common stock of General Motors (GM) for 1985 was 64¼ to 85, whereas the price for GM's $3.75 preferred stock fluctuated between 36 and 43¾. The common stock paid $5.00 in dividends during the year. Assume that you held both the common and the preferred stock for 1 year.

    a. Calculate your percentage returns, assuming that you were lucky enough to have bought both stocks at their lows and sold them at their highs.

    b. Calculate your percentage returns, assuming that you were unlucky enough to have bought both stocks at their highs and sold them at their lows.

    c. What general conclusions can you draw about the relative variability of returns, or *risk,* of the two stocks?

9. The balance sheet and income statement of Eastland Products, Inc., are as follows:

Balance Sheet, December 31, 19X1 (in millions of dollars)

Current assets	$ 40	Current liabilities	$ 20
Fixed assets, net	110	Long-term debt	40
		Preferred stock	10
		Common stock ($1 par)	5
		Contributed capital in excess	
		of par value	20
		Retained earnings	55
Total assets	$150	Total liabilities and equity	$150

Income Statement for Year Ended December 31, 19X1
(in millions of dollars)

Sales	$120
Cost of goods sold	80
EBIT	$ 40
Interest	5
EBT	$ 35
Taxes (40%)	14
Net Income	$ 21

Additional Information:

Total preferred dividends	$ 1 million
Total common dividends	$10 million
Market price of common stock	$32 a share
Number of common shares authorized	10 million

Using these data, calculate the following:

a. Earnings per common share.

b. The common stock price-earnings ratio.

c. The common stock book value (per share).

d. The coverage (times interest earned) ratio.

e. The firm's capital structure.

f. The firm's current dividend yield (common stock).

g. The current dividend payout ratio (common stock).

h. How much of the retained earnings total was added during 19X1?

10. Show the new balance sheet of Eastland Products (Problem 9) after the company sells 1 million new common shares in early 19X2 to net $28 a share. Part of the proceeds, $10 million, is used to reduce current liabilities, and the remainder is temporarily deposited in the company's bank account. Later this remainder (along with additional long-term debt financing) will be invested in new manufacturing facilities.

11. If you purchase a zero-coupon bond today for $225 and it matures at $1,000 in 11 years, what rate of return will you earn on that bond (to the nearest tenth of one percent)?

Selected References

Caks, John. "The Coupon Effect on Yield to Maturity." *Journal of Finance* 32 (March 1977): 103–115.

Ederington, Louis. "Negotiated versus Competitive Underwritings of Corporate Bonds." *Journal of Finance* 31 (March 1976): 17–26.

Hansen, R. S., and J. M. Pinkerton. "Direct Equity Financing: A Resolution of a Paradox." *Journal of Finance* (June 1982): 651–666.

Hayes, S. L., A. M. Spence, and D. V. P. Marks. *Competition in the Investment Banking Industry*. Cambridge, MA: Harvard University Press, 1983.

Ibbotson, R. R. "Price Performance of Common Stock New Issues." *Journal of Financial Economics* 2 (Sept. 1975): 235–272.

Logue, D. E., and R. A. Jarrow. "Negotiation vs. Competitive Bidding in the Sale of Securities by Public Utilities. *Financial Management* (Autumn 1978): 31–39.

Reilly, Frank K., and Michael D. Joehnk. "The Association between Market-Determined Risk Measures for Bonds and Bond Ratings." *Journal of Finance* 31 (Dec. 1976): 1387–1403.

BOND REFUNDING, STOCKHOLDER VOTING RIGHTS, AND RIGHTS OFFERINGS

Glossary of New Terms

Cumulative voting A voting procedure by which stockholders may cast multiple votes for a single board of directors candidate. Cumulative voting makes it easier for stockholders with minority views to elect sympathetic board members.

Ex-rights A stock sells ex-rights when stock purchasers no longer receive the *rights* along with the shares purchased.

Rights-on A stock sells rights-on when purchasers receive the *rights* along with the shares purchased.

Introduction

This appendix considers three additional topics related to bonds and stocks:

- Bond refunding analysis.
- Stockholder voting rights.
- Analysis of rights offerings.

Bond Refunding Analysis

Bond refunding occurs when a company redeems a callable issue and sells a lower cost issue to take its place.[22] The decision of whether or not to refund a particular debt issue is usually based on a capital budgeting (present value) analysis. The principal benefit, or cash inflow, is the present value of the after-tax interest savings over the life of the issue. The principal investment, or cash outflow at the time of refunding, consists primarily of the call premium and the flotation cost of the new debt.

Bond refunding differs from other capital expenditure projects in one very important way: the cash inflows are known with considerably more certainty than the cash flows from a typical capital expenditure project and thus are less risky. As a result, the weighted cost of capital is not used. Instead, the *after-tax cost of the new debt* is believed to be a more appropriate discount rate for bond refunding analysis.

---

[22] Callable preferred stock also can be refunded. The same considerations and analysis apply to both debt and preferred stock.

Bond refunding became an important decision facing many firms in 1986 when interest rates declined substantially from earlier levels. Firms that had issued bonds with coupon rates of 13 percent or more during the period of high inflation and high interest rates in the early 1980s found that they could refund these issues at rates under 10 percent.

As an illustration of bond refunding, consider the following example. The APCO Company issued $100 million of thirty-year, 10 percent debt five years ago. In the meantime, interest rates have declined, and the firm's management feels the decline has bottomed out. The debt issue is now callable at 107 percent of par. The company could refund the old issue with a new twenty-five year, 8 percent, $100 million issue. Flotation costs on the new issue would be 0.5 percent, or $500,000, whereas the unamortized flotation costs on the old issue are $450,000. If APCO decided to call the old issue and refund it, both issues would be outstanding for a three-week period, resulting in overlapping interest payments. The company's marginal tax rate is 50 percent. For purposes of discounting, the after-tax cost of new debt is $0.08 \times (1 - 0.5) = 0.04$.

To determine whether APCO should refund the old issue, a bond refunding analysis is carried out.

- **Step 1** The interest savings (cash inflows) are calculated,[23]

$$\text{Annual interest, after tax} = \text{Issue size} \times \text{Interest rate} \times (1 - \text{Tax rate})$$

Annual interest, old issue = $100 million $\times$ 10% $\times$ 0.5 = $5 million
Annual interest, new issue = $100 million $\times$ 8% $\times$ 0.5 = $\underline{\$4 \text{ million}}$
Annual after-tax interest savings $1 million

$$\text{Present value of interest savings} = \text{Annual after-tax interest} \times \text{PVIFA}_{0.04,25}$$
$$= \$1 \text{ million} \times 15.622$$
$$= \$15.622 \text{ million.}$$

- **Step 2** The net investment (*net cash* outflow at time 0) is calculated. This involves computing the after-tax call premium, the flotation cost of the new issue, the flotation cost of the old issue, and the overlapping interest.

The after-tax call premium is calculated as follows:

$$\text{Call premium, after-tax} = \$7 \text{ million} \times (1 - 0.5)$$
$$= \$3.5 \text{ million.}$$

The call premium is a cash outflow.

The flotation cost on the new issue is 0.5 percent, or $500,000. This amount cannot be deducted from APCO's current period income for tax purposes. Instead, it must be capitalized and amortized over the life of the debt issue, because the benefits that accrue to a firm as a result of a

---

[23] This calculation assumes that interest is received once a year at year-end. Actually, interest is paid every six months. However, the two results are not materially different.

flotation cost expenditure occur over the life of the issue. Thus,

Present value of
flotation cost $=$ Flotation cost $-$ Present value tax effect
of new issue

$$= \text{Flotation cost} - \left(\begin{array}{c} \text{Annual after-tax} \\ \text{savings from} \\ \text{amortization} \end{array} \times \text{PVIFA}_{0.04,25} \right)$$

$$= \text{Flotation cost} - \left(\frac{\text{Flotation cost}}{\text{Number of years}} \times \text{Tax rate} \right.$$

$$\left. \times \text{PVIFA}_{0.04,25} \right)$$

$$= \$500{,}000 - \left(\frac{\$500{,}000}{25} \times 0.5 \times 15.622 \right)$$

$$= \$500{,}000 - \$156{,}220$$

$$= \$343{,}780.$$

The present value of the flotation cost of the *new* issue is a net cash outflow.

APCO has been amortizing the flotation cost of the old issue over its life. If it refunded the issue, the company would no longer receive the benefits from the old issue's flotation cost and could therefore write off the remaining unamortized flotation cost at the time of refunding. Because of the write-off, however, APCO would lose the benefits of the old flotation cost over the remaining life of the issue. Thus,

Present value of   Present value,   Present value,
flotation cost of old $=$ lost benefits, $-$ write-off of old
issue   old flotation cost,   flotation cost,
after tax   after tax

$$= \left(\frac{\text{Old flotation cost}}{\text{Number of years}} \times \text{Tax rate} \times \text{PVIFA}_{0.04,25} \right)$$

$$- (\text{Old flotation cost} \times \text{Tax rate})$$

$$= \left(\frac{\$450{,}000}{25} \times 0.5 \times 15.622 \right) - (\$450{,}000 \times 0.5)$$

$$= \$140{,}598 - \$225{,}000$$

$$= -\$84{,}402.$$

The flotation cost effect of the old issue is a net cash inflow at the time of refunding.

In most bond refundings it is necessary for a firm to sell the new issue and receive the proceeds before paying off the old lenders. Both issues are usually outstanding for less than a month. Thus, the interest expense on the old issue during the overlapping period is considered a cost, or part of the refunding investment. In APCO's case, this expense is calculated as follows:

$$\text{Overlapping interest} = \text{Size of issue} \times \text{Annual interest rate of old issue, after tax} \times \text{Fraction of year both issues outstanding}$$

$$= \$100 \text{ million} \times 0.05 \times \frac{3}{52}$$

$$= \$288,462.$$

The overlapping interest is a cash outflow.

In summary, the net investment is calculated as follows:

Call premium	$3,500,000
Present value of flotation cost, new issue	343,780
Present value of flotation cost, old issue	−84,402
Overlapping interest	288,462
Net investment (cash outflow)	$4,047,840

● **Step 3** Finally, the net present value of refunding is calculated as follows:

$$\text{Net present value of refunding} = \frac{\text{Present value,}}{\text{interest savings}} - \frac{\text{Preset value,}}{\text{net investment}}$$

$$= \$15.622 \text{ million} - \$4.048 \text{ million}$$

$$= \$11.574 \text{ million.}$$

Because the net present value is positive, APCO should call its old issue and refund it with the new one.[24]

Stockholder Voting Rights

A firm's stockholders elect its board of directors by means of either a *majority* or a *cumulative* voting procedure. Majority voting is similar to the voting that takes place in political elections; namely, if two slates of people are running for the board, the one that receives more than 50 percent of the votes wins. With majority voting it is possible that a group of stockholders with a minority viewpoint will have no representation on the board.

Cumulative voting, in contrast, makes it easier for stockholders with minority views to elect sympathetic board members. In spite of this, cumulative voting is rare among major corporations. In cumulative voting, each share of stock represents as many votes as there are directors to be elected. For example, if a firm is electing seven directors, a particular holder of 100 shares would have 700 votes and could cast all of them for *one* candidate, thereby increasing that candidate's chances of being elected to the board. The following formula can be used to determine the

---

[24] Financial analysts can normally determine the *approximate* net present value of refunding by comparing the present value of the interest savings with the after-tax cost of the call premium. However, as is true with any shortcut method, caution should be exercised.

minimum number of shares or votes necessary to elect a certain number of directors:

$$\text{Number of shares} = \frac{\begin{array}{c}\text{Number of}\\\text{directors}\\\text{desired}\end{array} \times \begin{array}{c}\text{Number of}\\\text{shares}\\\text{outstanding}\end{array}}{\begin{array}{c}\text{Number of directors}\\\text{being elected}\end{array} + 1} + 1.$$

Of course, it is possible that not all the shareholders will vote their shares. In this case, the calculation is based on the number of shares actually voting rather than the number of shares outstanding.

Consider the following example. The Markham Company has eleven members on its board and one million shares of common stock outstanding. If seven members were up for reelection in a given year and all the shares were voted, the number of shares necessary to elect one director would be as follows:

$$\frac{1 \times 1,000,000}{7 + 1} + 1 = 125,001.$$

In addition to electing the board of directors, a firm's stockholders may vote from time to time on various other matters, such as whether to retain a particular auditing firm or increase the number of shares authorized.

The election of directors and other voting normally occurs at the annual stockholders' meeting. Since it is usually not possible for all stockholders to attend, management—or anyone else—can solicit votes by *proxy*. Normally, a stockholder can expect to receive a single proxy statement from the firm's management requesting that stockholders follow management's recommendations. In the rather unlikely event that another group of stockholders sends out its own proxy statement, a *proxy fight* is said to occur. Proxy fights are most common when a company is performing poorly.

Analysis of Rights Offerings

In addition to the sale of new common stock through underwriters, new equity capital can be raised through a *rights offering*. In a rights offering the firm's existing stockholders are given an opportunity to purchase a fraction of the new shares equal to the fraction they currently own. For example, if a company has ten million shares outstanding and decides to sell one million additional sales through a rights offering, each shareholder is entitled to purchase 0.1 new share for each share presently owned. (The *rights* themselves are really the documents describing the offer. Each stockholder receives one right for each share currently held.)

In a rights offering, shareholders have the opportunity to maintain their original ownership percentage. Hence, rights offerings are used in equity financing by companies whose charters contain the *preemptive right*. In addition, rights offerings *may* be used as a means of selling common stock in companies in which preemptive rights do not exist. The number of rights offerings has gradually declined over the years.

The following example illustrates what a rights offering involves. The Miller Company has ten million shares outstanding and plans to sell an additional one million shares via a rights offering. In this case, each right entitles the holder to purchase 0.1 share, and it takes ten rights to purchase one share. The company has to decide on a *subscription price*—that is, the price the rightholder will have to pay per new share. The subscription price has to be less than the market price, or rightholders will have no incentive to subscribe to the new issue. As a general rule, subscription prices are 5 to 20 percent below market prices. If the Miller Company's stock is selling at $40 per share, a reasonable subscription price might be $35 per share.

Valuation of Rights

Because a right represents an opportunity to purchase stock below its market value, the right itself has a certain value, which is calculated under two sets of circumstances:

- The *rights-on* case.
- The *ex-rights* case.

A stock is said to "trade with rights-on" when the purchasers receive the rights along with the shares they purchase. In contrast, a stock is said to "trade ex-rights" when the stock purchasers no longer receive the rights.

For example, suppose the Miller Company announced on May 15 that shareholders of record as of Friday, June 20, will receive the rights. This means that anyone who purchased stock on or before Monday, June 16, will receive the rights, and anyone who purchased stock on or later than June 17 will not.[25] The stock trades with rights up to and including June 16 and goes ex-rights on June 17, the *ex-rights date*. On that date the stock's market value falls by the value of the right, all other things being equal.

The theoretical, or formula, value of a right for the rights-on case can be calculated using the following equation:

$$R = \frac{M_0 - S}{N + 1},$$

where R is the theoretical value for the right; M_0, the rights-on market price of the stock; S, the subscription price of the right; and N, the number of rights necessary to purchase one new share. In the Miller Company example, the right's theoretical value is:

$$R = \frac{\$40 - \$35}{10 + 1}$$
$$= \$0.455.$$

The theoretical value of a right when the stock is trading ex-rights can be calculated by using the following equation:

$$R = \frac{M_e - S}{N},$$

---

[25] A stock purchaser becomes a "shareholder of record" four *trading* days after purchase.

Where M_e is the ex-rights market price of the stock; S, the subscription price of the right; and N, the number of rights necessary to purchase 1 new share. If the Miller stock were trading ex-rights, the theoretical value of a right would be as follows:

$$R = \frac{\$39.545 - \$35}{10}$$

$$= \$0.455$$

(Notice that M_e is lower than M_o by the amount of the right—that is, from $40 to $39.545.)

Some shareholders may decide not to use their rights because of lack of funds or for some other reason. These stockholders can sell their rights to other investors who wish to purchase them. Thus, a market exists for the rights, and a market price is established for them. Generally, the market price is higher than the theoretical value, since investors who are optimistic about the stock's short-run performance often "bid up" the price of the right. Investors can earn a higher return by purchasing the rights than by purchasing the stock because of the leverage rights provide. In general, the premium of market value over theoretical value decreases as the rights expiration date approaches. A right is worthless after its expiration date.

One can demonstrate that there is no net gain or loss to shareholders either from exercising the rights or from selling the right at the theoretical formula value.[26] For example, suppose an investor owns 100 shares of the Miller Company common stock discussed earlier. The investor is entitled to purchase 10 (.10 × 100) additional shares at $35 per share. Prior to the rights offering, the 100 shares of Miller Company are valued at $4,000 (100 shares × $40 per share). *Exercise* of the rights will give the investor ten additional shares at at cost of $35 per share or a total of $350. These 110 shares will be valued at $4,350 (110 × $39.545). Deducting the cost of these additional shares ($350) from the total value of the shares ($4,350), one obtains the same value ($4,000) as before the rights offering. *Sale* of the rights will yield $45.50 (100 × $.455) to the investor. Combining this value with the $3,954.50 (100 × $39.545) value of the 100 shares still owned, one also obtains the same value ($4,000) as before the rights offering.

Questions and Topics for Discussion

1. What is *bond refunding?* At what relative level of interest rates is bond refunding most likely to occur? Explain.

2. What is the difference between majority voting and cumulative voting?

3. What is the *preemptive right* of common stockholders? In what type of company is the preemptive right important? Unimportant?

Problems*

1. The Springfield Gas and Electric Company is considering refunding $50 million of 11 percent debt with an 8 percent, 20-year debt issue. The existing, or old, issue also matures in 20 years and is now callable at 108 percent of par.

---

[26] This analysis ignores any brokerage fees incurred in the sale of the rights.
* Color numbers denote problems which have check answers provided at the end of the book.

The unamortized flotation cost on the old issue is $400,000 and the flotation cost of the new issue is 0.875 percent. The company estimates that both issues will be outstanding for 4 weeks, resulting in overlapping interest. The company has a weighted cost of capital of 10.0 percent and a 50 percent marginal tax rate. In addition, the company's financial management feels as though the present interest rate decline has nearly bottomed out. Calculate the net present value of the refunding, and make a recommendation to management on whether or not to refund.

2. Suppose you have accumulated a sizable investment (100,000 common shares) in Alpine Land and Development Company. You are dissatisfied with the performance of the present management and are considering running for the board of directors. The company has a nine-member board and a total of 1,500,000 common shares outstanding. Assume that all shares will be voted in the upcoming election and that four of the nine board members are up for reelection.

   a. If the voting procedure is cumulative, what is the minimum number of shares necessary to insure your election to the board? Is it possible for you to be elected with fewer votes? Explain.

   b. Suppose a close friend of yours also owns a good deal of Alpine and shares your feelings about the present management. If the voting procedure is cumulative, how many shares are necessary to elect both you and your friend to the board?

   c. If the voting procedure is majority, how many votes are necessary for election in Parts a and b of this problem? Explain your answer.

3. Oswego Manufacturing Company has decided to sell additional common stock through a rights offering. The company has 50 million shares outstanding and plans to sell an additional 5.0 million shares through the rights offering. Each shareholder will receive 1 right for each share currently held, and thus each right will entitle shareholders to purchase 0.1 share. Oswego's common stock is currently selling at $50 a share, and the subscription price of the rights will be $45 a share.

   a. Calculate the theoretical value of the right for both the *rights-on* and the *ex-rights* cases.

   b. How much is the market price of the company's stock expected to drop on the *ex-rights* date, all other things being equal? Why?

   c. If the market price of Oswego's common stock increases to $52 a share, what will the theoretical value of the right be (rights-on)?

   d. Discuss the trend of the right's market price over its life, assuming the company's common stock continues to trade in the $50 range. (No numerical calculations are necessary for this part of the problem.)

17

OPTIONS, CONVERTIBLE SECURITIES, AND WARRANTS

A Financial Dilemma

Expanded Use of Options, Convertibles, and Warrants in the 1980s

The 1980s have been characterized by some financial analysts as a period of "creative financings" because of the unusual financing methods employed by some companies. Options, convertibles, and warrants are used as part of some of these creative financings.

During the 1980s some companies (and municipalities) issued bonds containing a *put* option which gave investors the opportunity to *sell* the bonds back to the issuing company at par value prior to maturity. Such an option lessens the bond's interest rate risk and tends to stabilize its price, thus making the bond more attractive to risk-averse investors. For example, in October 1984, Chrysler Financial Corp. issued notes maturing in 1999 which contain a put option exercisable in 1989. Thus, from a maturity standpoint, the notes were actually five-year notes instead of fifteen-year notes at the time they originally were sold. It is estimated that Chrysler Financial saved 0.7 percent a year in interest charges by attaching the put option to the notes.[1] (It should be remembered that virtually all debt securities of major corporations also contain call options which permit issuers to redeem the securities prior to maturity.)

In a somewhat unusual convertible security transaction, IBM issued (January 1986) bonds which are convertible, at the option of the holder, into shares of Intel Corp. common stock which IBM owns. Prior to this convertible bond issuance, IBM owned about 20 percent of Intel, a semiconductor manufacturer. If the bond investors eventually exercise their option to convert the bonds into Intel stock, IBM's percentage ownership would decline to about 13 percent. But the conversion price is $38.50 a share, which repre-

sents a premium over the $30-a-share price at which Intel was selling when the bonds were originally issued.

As a result of difficulties experienced in some sectors of the economy in the mid-1980s, some companies became unable to service their debt. Some of these companies were able to obtain additional working capital loans as well as restructure their existing debt, that is, extend the repayment period. However, the banks, after assessing the high level of risk associated with making the additional loans to troubled companies, wanted higher returns than interest income alone could provide. Accordingly, some banks demanded and received warrants (company-issued options) in return for the restructuring and additional loans. Then, if the company did return to profitability, the banks had an opportunity to earn a high return on the warrants by selling them.

This chapter considers the features and characteristics of options, warrants, and convertible securities. An understanding of these features and characteristics is necessary to evaluate the impact on shareholder wealth of issuing these types of securities.

---

[1] *Forbes* (December 17, 1984): 134.

Key Chapter Concepts

1. An *option* is a security giving the right to buy or sell an asset at a set price during a specified time period.
   a. A *call* option is an option to *buy* an asset at a set price.
   b. A *put* option is an option to *sell* an asset at a set price.
2. The value of a call option is dependent upon four variables:
   a. The relationship between the option's exercise price and the price of the underlying stock.
   b. The time remaining until the option expires.
   c. The level of interest rates.
   d. The expected volatility of the underlying stock's price.
3. A convertible security is a fixed-income security, such as a debenture or a share of preferred stock, that may be exchanged for the company's common stock at the holder's option.
4. A warrant is an option issued by a company to purchase shares of the company's common stock for a particular price during a specified period of time.
5. The owner of either a convertible security or a warrant has a choice of whether or not to obtain the company's common stock.

Glossary of New Terms

Call option An option to *buy* an asset at a set price. Also referred to as a *call*.

Conversion premium The amount by which the market value of a convertible security exceeds the higher of its conversion value or straight-bond (preferred) value.

Conversion price The effective price an investor pays for common stock when the stock is obtained by converting a convertible security.

Conversion ratio The number of common shares an investor obtains by converting a convertible security.

Conversion (stock) value The value of a convertible security, based on the value of the underlying shares of common stock.

Convertible security A fixed-income security that may be exchanged for a firm's common stock at the holder's option. The two most common types of convertible securities are *convertible preferred stock* and *convertible debentures*.

Covered option An option written by an investor who owns the underlying stock. This is in contrast to an *uncovered,* or *naked,* option.

Exercise price The price at which an option holder can purchase or sell a company's stock. This is also termed the *striking price*.

Option A security that gives its holder the right to buy or sell an asset at a set price during a specified time period.

Put option An option to *sell* an asset at a set price. Also referred to as a *put*.

Straight-bond, or investment, value The value a convertible debt security would have if it did not possess the conversion feature.

Warrant A company-issued long-term option to purchase a specified number of shares of the firm's stock at a particular price during a specified time period.

Introduction

I n addition to long-term debt, preferred stock, and common stock, a firm has two other primary forms of long-term financing available to it: convertible securities and *warrants*. Both convertible securities and warrants are forms of options. An option is a security giving the right to buy or sell an asset under specified conditions. Specifically, a convertible security is a fixed-income security, such as a debenture or a share of preferred stock, that may be exchanged for the company's common stock at the holder's option. A warrant is an option issued by a company to purchase shares of the company's common stock at a particular price during a specified period of time. The holder of either a convertible security or a warrant has a choice of whether or not to obtain the company's common stock. Warrants are frequently sold to investors as part of a *unit* that consists of a fixed-income security with a warrant attached. The issuance of convertible securities, warrants, or both often makes it easier for a firm to sell its fixed-income securities.

This chapter describes the variables which influence option values. In addition, this chapter describes the features of convertible securities and warrants and considers the circumstances in which they are used. It also develops and illustrates valuation models for both convertibles and warrants.

Options

An *option* is a security that gives its holder the right, but not the obligation, to buy or sell an asset at a set price during a specified time period. Options are classified as either *call* or *put* options. A call is an option to *buy* a particular asset whereas a put is an option to *sell* it. Examples of options include calls and puts on common stock, warrants, and convertible securities. A call option on a particular common stock is an option to buy shares (usually 100) at a set price during a specified time period, and a put option is an option to sell shares. A *warrant* is a call option issued by a company on its securities, usually stock. A *convertible security* is a fixed income security with a call option on common stock. Another common example of an option is the redemption (call) feature of debt securities which permits a company to call, or redeem, its debt prior to maturity.[2] In addition, as discussed in this chapter's Financial Dilemma, some debt issues also contain a put option which gives investors the right to sell the debt back to the issuing company at par value prior to maturity.

Option Valuation Concepts

Suppose an investor is offered an opportunity to purchase a call option on one share of XYZ stock. Consider the following sets of conditions:

1. The option's exercise price is $25, the XYZ stock price is $30 a share, and the option's expiration date is today. Under these conditions, the investor is willing to pay $5 for the option. In other words, the value of a call option is equal to the stock price minus the exercise price, or

$$\text{Value of a call option at maturity} = \text{Stock price} - \text{Exercise price.} \quad \textbf{(17.1)}$$

---

[2] The redemption, or call feature, of debt securities is discussed in Chapter 16.

2. The option's exercise price is $25, the XYZ stock price is $30 a share, and the option expires in six months. Given these conditions, the investor is willing to pay more than $5 for the option because of the chance that the stock price will increase, thereby causing the option also to increase in value. Therefore,

$$\text{Value of a call option prior to maturity} > \text{Stock price} - \text{Exercise price.} \qquad \textbf{(17.2)}$$

3. The option's exercise price is $0.01, the XYZ stock price is $30, and the option expires in six months. Under these somewhat unusual conditions, the option investor is willing to pay *almost as much as the stock price*. However, under no conditions should the investor be willing to pay more than the stock price. Therefore,

$$\text{Maximum value of a call option} = \text{Stock price.} \qquad \textbf{(17.3)}$$

4. The option's exercise price is $25, the XYZ stock price is $0.01, and the option expires today. The investor most likely is willing to pay nothing for the option given these conditions, but the investor also is not willing to pay someone to take the option "off his hands," since it is an option and can be allowed to expire with no additional cost. Therefore,

$$\text{Minimum value of a call option} = 0. \qquad \textbf{(17.4)}$$

The results of the above sets of conditions are shown in Figure 17-1.[3]

Variables Affecting Call Option Valuation   The examples in the previous section illustrate that the value of a call option is dependent on (1) the relationship between the option's exercise price and the price of the underlying stock and (2) the length of time before the option's expiration date.

   Two other variables influence the value of a call option: the level of interest rates and the expected volatility of the underlying stock's price. These four variables are discussed in the following subsections.

The Relationship Between the Exercise Price and the Stock Price   The effect of the exercise, or strike price, on option value is seen by examining Table 17-1, which lists a number of options quotations for McDonald's. At the time the McDonald's stock was selling at $90.50 a share. For options expiring in June, the call option with an $85 exercise price sold at a higher price than the option with a $90 exercise price. This is due to the fact that buyers have to pay more money to exercise options with higher exercise prices, and thus these options have less value to potential buyers. Therefore, *the higher the exercise price, given the stock price, the lower is the call option value,* all other things being equal.

[3] Figure 17-1 shows a $25 exercise price. Technically Figure 17-1 shows only the results of conditions 1, 2, and 4.

Figure 17-1

Call Option Valuation at Different Stock Prices*

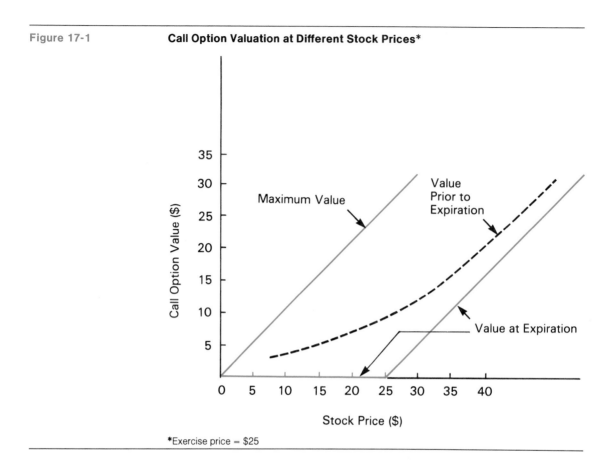

*Exercise price = $25

Time Remaining Until Expiration Date The figures in Table 17-1 show that an option expiring in September has a higher value than an option with a June expiration date. This is due to the fact that investors realize that McDonald's stock has a greater chance to increase in value with three additional months before expiration. Thus, *the longer the time remaining before the option expires, the higher the option value,* all other things being equal.

Interest Rates The buyer of common stock incurs either interest expense (explicit cost) if the purchase funds are borrowed or lost interest income (implicit cost) if existing funds are used for purchase. In either case, an interest cost is incurred.[4]

Buying a call option is an alternative to buying stock, and by buying an option the interest cost associated with stock may appear to be avoided. However, because options are an alternative to ownership, option values are affected by the stock ownership interest costs. As a result, *the higher the level of interest rates* (and, hence, the interest cost of stock ownership) *the higher the call option's value is,* all other things being equal.

---

[4] The interest cost is offset by any dividends received.

Table 17-1   **Selected Options Quotations, Thursday, March 6, 1986***

Option & NY Close	Strike Price	Calls—Last Mar.	June	Sep.	Puts—Last Mar.	June	Sep.
McDonalds	 80	10¾	12½	14	r	⅝	r
90½	 85	5½	8¾	r	3-16	1¾	2⅜
90½	 90	2¼	5¼	r	1⅝	3½	r
90½	 95	s	3¼	4¾	s	r	s
Sears	 40	4¾	5⅝	6⅜	1-16	⅝	1⅛
44¾	 45	⅞	2⅜	3½	1¼	2½	2¾
44¾	 50	s	1	1⅝	s	r	r

r—Not traded. s—No option offered.
Strike price is exercise price.
Last is premium (purchase price).
*Closing prices of all options. Sales unit usually is 100 shares. Security description includes exercise price. Stock close is New York or American exchange final price.
Source: *The Wall Street Journal* (March 7, 1986).

Expected Stock Price Volatility Suppose an investor has a choice of buying a call option on either stock S or stock V. Both stocks currently sell at $50 a share, and the exercise price of both options is $50. Stock S is expected to be the more stable of the two—its value at the time the option expires has a 50 percent chance of being $45 and a 50 percent chance of being $55 a share. In valuing the call option on stock S, the investor considers only the $55 price and its probability, because if the stock goes to $45 a share, the call option with a $50 exercise price becomes worthless.

Stock V is expected to be more volatile—its expected value at the time of option expiration has a 50 percent probability of being $30 and a 50 percent probability of being $70 a share. Similarly, in valuing the call option on stock V, the investor considers only the $70 price and its probability.

The investor now has sufficient information to conclude that the call option on stock V is more valuable than the call option on stock S because a greater return can be earned by investing in an option which has a 50 percent chance of being worth $20 (stock price − exercise price = $70–$50 = $20) at expiration than an option which has a 50 percent probability of being worth $5 (stock price − exercise price = $55–$50 = $5) at expiration. Therefore, the *greater the expected stock price volatility, the higher the call option value is,* all other things being equal.

How Options are Used

Investors who feel that a particular stock's price is likely to increase in the near future might *buy* a call option on that stock (assuming that options on the stock are traded). In contrast, investors who feel that a particular stock's price is likely to decrease might *buy* a put option on that stock.

Instead of buying a put, investors who feel that a particular stock's price is likely to decrease might *sell,* or *write,* a call option on that stock. If the call writer *owns* the underlying stock, the option is said to be *covered;* otherwise it is *uncovered,* or *naked.*[5]

[5] If a put writer is *short* the underlying stock, the option is said to be *covered.*

Investors who buy calls have the potential of making high percentage returns on their investments. In contrast, the maximum possible amount they can lose is the price they paid for the options. To illustrate, suppose an investor pays $250 for an option to purchase 100 shares of RCX Corporation at $30 per share when the stock is selling at that price. If the stock price goes up to $40 per share, for example, the call with an exercise price of $30 will sell at $10 or more per share (for a total of at least $1,000), with the amount over $10 depending partially on how much time remains before the option expires. Thus, the investor in the call will roughly quadruple the investment (that is, $1,000/$250), whereas the stock investor will realize a return of 33 percent (that is, [$4,000 − $3,000]/$3,000). In contrast, if the stock drops from $30 to $20, the call purchaser will lose virtually all of the $250 (that is, a loss of approximately 100 percent) invested, whereas the investor who has purchased 100 shares of the stock will lose $1,000 (that is, a loss of approximately 33 percent).

There are a number of circumstances in which an investor might choose to buy a put. For example, assume Henry Cassel owns a stock that he feels is temporarily overpriced, but he does not want to sell the stock because of its long-term prospects. One alternative (besides selling and buying back later) is to buy a put. At the time Mr. Cassel buys the put, he pays the put price (that is, the premium). If Mr. Cassel is correct and the stock does drop in price, the option premium will increase, and he will make a profit by either selling the put or exercising it. The purchase of a put option provides the investor with perfect protection against a price decline. The cost of this protection is the put premium.

Instead of buying a put, Mr. Cassel could have chosen to *write* (or sell) a call. In this instance, at the time Mr. Cassel writes the call, he receives the proceeds (that is, the premium). If Mr. Cassel is correct and the stock does drop in price, the option premium also will decrease, and he will make a profit by either buying the call back at a lower price or letting it expire.

Another situation in which an investor might choose to buy a put is to protect an unrealized gain. Suppose, for example, Betty Owens has a gain on a stock she owns and would like to sell now at the present price. There are two possible reasons why she would not simply sell the stock now: (1) to defer her taxes on the gain until the next year or (2) to defer selling until her holding period exceeds one year and she is eligible for capital gains treatment on her stock sale. (The 1986 tax reform bill eliminates special capital gains tax treatment.) By buying a put, Ms. Owens can eliminate the risk of a price decline. If the stock goes down between now and when it is sold, the lost revenues from the sale of the stock can be made up from the increase in the put premium. The put is sold at the higher price when the stock is sold.

The writing of *naked options* (that is, when the call option writer does not own the underlying stock) generally is considered quite risky. As a result, investors who desire to write naked options have to meet certain requirements of their brokerage firm with respect to their total portfolio value.

Table 17-1 lists a number of options quotations that can be used to illustrate the mechanics of options trading. For example, the buyer or holder of a Sears 45 call option had the right to purchase 100 shares of Sears common stock at $45 per share prior to the expiration date, which is the Saturday following the third Friday of the month listed (in this case, either March, June, or September 1986). Expiration dates are three months apart, and options are normally not written for time periods longer than nine months. Specifically, the closing price on March 6, 1986, of a Sears September 45 call is listed as $3\frac{1}{2}$. This means that a buyer at that price would have had to pay $350 plus commission for the right to buy 100 shares of Sears common stock at $45 per share prior to the third Saturday in September 1986. In actuality the buyer probably would not have exercised the option, since most options are not exercised. Instead, buyers usually sell their options prior to the expiration date rather than buy the stock at the exercise price.

Convertible Securities

Both debentures and preferred stock can have convertibility or conversion features. When a company issues convertible securities, its usual intention is the future issuance of common stock. To illustrate, suppose the Beloit Corporation issues two million shares of convertible preferred stock at a price of $50 a share. After the sale, the company receives gross proceeds of $100 million. Because of the convertibility feature, the company can expect to issue shares of common stock in exchange for the redemption of the convertible preferred stock over some future time period. In the case of Beloit's convertible preferred, each $50 preferred share can be exchanged for two shares of common stock; that is, the holder has a call option to buy two shares of the company's common stock at an exercise price of $25 a share. Thus, if all the preferred shares are converted, the company in effect will have issued four million new common shares, and the preferred shares no longer will appear on Beloit's balance sheet. No additional funds are raised by the company at the time of conversion.

Features of Convertible Securities

As an introduction to the terminology and features of convertible securities, consider a $100 million, twenty-five year issue of $6\frac{1}{8}$ percent convertible subordinated debentures sold by Cray Research, Inc., a computer manufacturer, in 1986. Convertible securities are exchangeable for common stock at a stated *conversion price*. In the case of the Cray issue, the conversion price is $84. This means that each $1,000 debenture is convertible into common stock at $84 a share.

The number of common shares that can be obtained when a convertible security is exchanged is determined by the conversion ratio, which is calculated as follows:

$$\text{Conversion ratio} = \frac{\text{Par value of security}}{\text{Conversion price}}. \tag{17.5}$$

In the case of Cray Research's convertible subordinated debentures, the conversion ratio is the following:

$$\text{Conversion ratio} = \frac{\$1,000}{\$84}$$

$$= 11.9.$$

Thus, each $1,000 Cray debenture can be exchanged for 11.9 shares of common stock. Although the conversion ratio may change one or more times during the life of the conversion option, it is more common for it to remain constant.

Normally, the conversion price is set about 15 to 30 percent above the common stock's market price prevailing at the time of issue. For example, at the time Cray issued its convertible debentures, the market price of its common stock was about $65 a share. The $19 difference between the conversion price and the market price represents a 29 percent premium.

Holders of convertible securities are protected against dilution by the company. For example, suppose Cray were to split its common stock two for one. The conversion price (and therefore the conversion ratio) would be adjusted so that the holders would not be disadvantaged by the split. Specifically, in the Cray case the new conversion price would be $42, and the new conversion ratio would be 23.8.

Reasons for Issuing Convertible Securities

Three principal and interrelated reasons exist for issuing convertibles:

- To "sweeten" the sale of fixed-income securities, permitting a company to raise funds with a lower interest rate or preferred dividend rate.
- To sell common stock in the future at a higher price than the price prevailing at the time of original issue.
- To acquire and use low cost capital for a period of time until the full benefits of the financing can be reflected in the company's earnings.

Each of these three reasons will be discussed.

Frequently investors prefer fixed-income convertible securities over similar issues that are not convertible. This is because investors are able to combine the relatively secure and stable interest payments or preferred dividends with the appreciation potential of common stock ownership. Hence, the convertibility feature "sweetens" the deal.

Benefits also accrue to the issuing company in the form of lower interest payments or dividends. This occurs because investors are willing to accept the conversion privilege as part of their overall return. As an example, consider again the Cray Research $6\frac{1}{8}$ percent convertible subordinated debentures. At the time Cray sold these convertibles, the company would have had to pay about 9 percent interest on any nonconvertible debt it issued. Thus, the convertibility feature is saving Cray about $2.9 million a year ($[0.09 - 0.06125] \times$ $100 million) in interest expense. Typically, firms can issue convertible securities with interest rates or dividend yields about 3 percent below straight issues, that is, issues without convertibility features.

Another reason firms issue convertible securities is effectively to sell common stock at a higher price than the market price prevailing at the time of issue. Suppose a company needs additional equity financing because of a relatively high proportion of fixed-income securities in its capital structure. If the company's management feels the price of its common stock is temporarily depressed, one alternative is to consider issuing a convertible security. With the conversion price typically set about 15–30 percent above the market price at the time of issue, the use of a convertible security effectively gives the issuing company the potential for selling common stock above the existing market price. However, for the sale to be successful, conditions in the future must be such that investors will want to exercise their conversion option. Also, if the market price rises considerably above the conversion price, it may turn out that the company would have been better off to wait and sell common stock directly rather than sell the convertible issue at all.

The third reason for issuing convertible securities centers around the fact that the earnings resulting from a particular external financing issue may not begin for some time after financing occurs. For example, the construction and start-up period for a major expansion may be several years. During this period the company may desire debt or preferred stock financing. Eventually, once the expansion is fully operational and producing income, the company may want to achieve its original goal of additional common stock financing. The delayed issue of common stock minimizes the dilution in earnings per share that results from the immediate issuance of common stock.

Valuation of Convertible Securities

Because convertible securities possess certain characteristics of both common stock and fixed-income securities, their valuation is more complex than that of ordinary nonconvertible securities. The actual market value of a convertible security is a function of both the *common stock value,* or *conversion value,* and the value as a fixed-income security, or *straight-bond* or *investment value.* Each of these is discussed here.[6]

Conversion Value The conversion value, or stock value, of a convertible bond is defined as the conversion ratio times the common stock's market price:

$$\text{Conversion value} = \text{Conversion ratio} \times \text{Stock price.} \qquad \textbf{(17.6)}$$

To illustrate, assume a firm offers a convertible bond that can be exchanged for forty shares of common stock. If the market price of the firm's common stock is $20 per share, the conversion value is $800. If the market price of the common stock rises to $25 per share, the conversion value becomes $1,000. And if the stock price rises to $30 per share, the conversion value becomes $1,200. In the case of Cray's convertible bonds, the conversion value was 11.9×65, or $774, at the time of issue.

Straight-bond Value The straight-bond value, or investment value, of a convertible debt issue is the value it would have if it did not possess the conversion feature. Thus, it is equal to the sum of the present value of the interest annuity plus the present value of the expected principal repayment:

$$\text{Straight-bond value} = \sum_{t=1}^{m} \frac{\text{Interest}}{(1 + k_d)^t} + \frac{\text{Principal}}{(1 + k_d)^m}, \qquad \textbf{(17.7)}$$

[6] For simplicity, only convertible debt is considered in this discussion, although the principles apply to convertible preferred stock as well.

where k_d is the current yield to maturity for *nonconvertible* debt issues of similar quality and maturity; t, the number of years; and m, the time to maturity.

Considering again Cray Research's $6\frac{1}{8}$ percent, 25-year convertible debentures, the bond value at the time of issue is calculated as follows, assuming that 9 percent is the appropriate discount rate (and that interest is paid annually):

$$\text{Straight-bond value} = \sum_{t=1}^{25} \frac{\$61.25}{(1.09)^t} + \frac{\$1,000}{(1.09)^{25}}$$
$$= \$61.25(\text{PVIFA}_{0.09,25}) + \$1,000(\text{PVIF}_{0.09,25})$$
$$= \$61.25(9.823) + \$1,000(0.116)$$
$$= \$601.66 + \$116$$
$$= \$717.66.$$

Market Value The market value of a convertible debt issue is usually somewhat above the higher of the conversion or the straight-bond value. This is illustrated in Figure 17-2.

Figure 17-2

Convertible Debenture Valuation at Different Stock Prices*

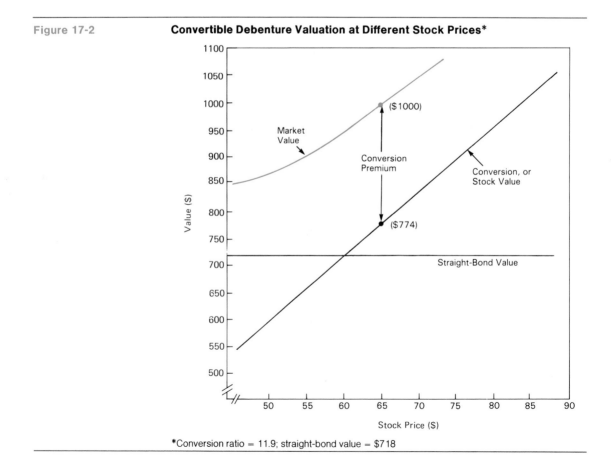

*Conversion ratio = 11.9; straight-bond value = $718

The difference between the market value and the higher of the conversion or the straight-bond value is the *conversion premium* for which the issue sells. This premium tends to be largest when the conversion value and the straight-bond value are nearly identical. This set of circumstances allows investors to participate in any common stock appreciation while at the same time having some degree of downside protection, because the straight-bond value can represent a "floor" below which the market value will not fall.[7] The Cray convertible debentures described in this section were offered to the public at $1,000 per bond and were quickly bought up by investors. In this case, investors were willing to pay $1,000 for an issue having a conversion value of approximately $774 and a bond value of about $718. The $1,000 market value contained a premium of $226 over the conversion value (which was higher than the bond value).

Converting Convertible Securities

Conversion can occur in one of two ways:

- It may be *voluntary* on the part of the investor.
- It can be effectively *forced* by the issuing company.

Whereas voluntary conversions can occur at any time prior to the expiration of a conversion feature, forced conversions occur at specific points in time.

The method most commonly used by companies to force conversion is the exercise of the *call* privilege on the convertible security. For example, consider the Lomas & Nettleton Financial Corp. convertible bonds maturing in 2008, which the company decided to call for redemption in 1986. The bonds had a conversion ratio of 41.24, and the market price of the Lomas & Nettleton common stock at the time of the call was $38.50 per share. Thus, the conversion value was approximately $1,588 per bond. The call price—which was set and agreed upon by both the borrower and the lender at the time of the original issue—was $1,065 per bond.

Holders of the Lomas & Nettleton convertibles had two alternatives under these circumstances:

- Conversion, in which case the holder would receive common stock having a market value of $1,588 per bond.
- Redemption, in which case the holder would receive $1,065 in cash for each bond.

The conversion alternative was the obvious choice, since even those investors who did not wish to hold the common stock could sell it upon conversion for more money than they would receive from redemption. By calling the bonds, Lomas & Nettleton was able to remove $108.7 million in long-term debt from its balance sheet without having to redeem the bonds for cash, and to save $10.6 million a year in interest expense.[8]

Another way in which a company can effectively force conversion is by raising its dividend on common stock to a high enough level that holders of

---

[7] The straight-bond value may fall if long-term interest rates rise, however.
[8] *The Wall Street Journal* (February 6, 1986): 29.

convertible securities are better off converting them and receiving the higher dividend.

Conversion of a significant proportion of a convertible security issue also may take place immediately prior to the time the conversion ratio is scheduled to drop. For example, suppose the conversion ratio on a particular convertible debenture is scheduled to drop from fifty to forty-five as of December 1 of this year. This means that the convertible debenture may be exchanged for fifty common shares before December 1 and forty-five shares after that date (ignoring trading date considerations). To receive the greater number of shares, some investors may choose to convert before December 1. If a conversion ratio is scheduled to decline, the date and the amount of the change in the ratio is specified at the time the original security is issued.

Warrants

As mentioned earlier in this chapter, a warrant is a company-issued option to purchase a specific number of shares of the issuing company's common stock at a particular price during a specified time period. Warrants are frequently issued in conjunction with an offering of debentures or preferred stock. In these instances, like convertibles, warrants serve to "sweeten," or function as an "equity kicker" for, fixed-income security offerings.

However, during the 1980s, the various ways in which warrants were used as a financing device seemed to expand. For example, warrants were used in connection with bond swaps, equity offerings, and debt restructurings. In addition, a small, high risk company in need of additional financing may offer warrants to prospective lenders in order to give the potential for high expected returns to compensate for the loan's high risk.[9]

Features of Warrants

To illustrate some of the features of financing with warrants, consider Federal National Mortgage Association ("Fannie Mae"), which sold 500,000 units, consisting of a $1,000 debenture and 23 five-year warrants, in 1986 to raise approximately $500 million (less flotation costs). Each warrant allowed the purchase of one common share at $44.25.

The *exercise price* of a warrant is the price at which the holder can purchase common stock of the issuing company. The exercise price—which normally remains constant over the life of the warrant—is usually between 10 and 35 percent above the market price of the common stock prevailing at the time of issue. The exercise price of the Fannie Mae warrants is $44.25, approximately 34 percent above the $33 per-share market price of the common stock at the time of issue.

The *expiration date* of the Fannie Mae warrants is February 25, 1991, meaning that the life of these warrants is five years. Typically, the life of a warrant is between five and ten years, although on occasion the life can be longer or even perpetual.

---

[9] The Financial Dilemma at the beginning of this chapter discusses warrants used in connection with debt restructurings.

The management of Fannie Mae hopes that the common share price will rise above the $44.25 level and remain there, especially until after the warrants expire, since this would mean that the company could reasonably expect holders to exercise their warrants. If this happened, Fannie Mae would receive funds totaling approximately $509 million (500,000 units times twenty-three warrants per unit times $44.25 per warrant) at expiration. Thus, the company would realize its goal of raising additional capital at the time of exercise. This is in contrast to a convertible bond or preferred stock, because with convertible securities the company does not receive additional funds at the time of conversion.

If a warrant is issued as part of a unit with a fixed-income security, the warrant is usually *detachable* from the debenture or preferred stock. This means that purchasers of the units have the option of selling the warrants separately and continuing to hold the debenture or preferred stock.[10] As a result, other investors can purchase and trade warrants.

Prior to 1970, warrants were usually not used as a financing vehicle by large, established firms. In April of that year, however, AT&T sold $1.6 billion of thirty-year debentures with warrants to buy 31.4 million common shares at $52 each through May 15, 1975. The use of warrant financing by AT&T undoubtedly caused other large, established firms to consider warrants. Also before 1970, warrants normally were listed either on the American Stock Exchange or traded over the counter, since the New York Stock Exchange would not list them. However, with the AT&T warrants the NYSE changed its policy and began to list warrants of NYSE companies if the warrants met certain requirements, including a life greater than five years. For example, American General, Pan Am, and Mattel, among others, have warrants that are traded on the NYSE.

Holders of warrants do not have the rights of common stockholders, such as the right to vote for directors or receive dividends, until they exercise their warrants.

Reasons for Issuing Warrants

The primary reason for issuing warrants is to sell common stock in the future. Warrants also are used to "sweeten" fixed-income security offerings by giving investors an opportunity to participate in any common stock price appreciation. Just as with convertible securities, warrants also can permit a company to sell common stock at a price above the price prevailing at the time of original issue. In addition, warrants allow a company to sell common stock in the future without incurring underwriting costs at the time of sale.

Valuation of Warrants

In general, a warrant's value is a function of the outlook for the issuing company and the economy as a whole. The warrant's value is also dependent upon the difference between the exercise price and the common stock's market price. In this connection, the formula value of a warrant is

---

[10] It is normally illogical to consider selling the fixed-income security immediately after purchase unless economic conditions change. An investor who desires only the warrant could purchase it separately.

defined by the following equation:

$$\begin{aligned}\text{Formula value} \atop \text{of a warrant} = \text{Max}\left\{0;\left(\begin{array}{c}\text{Common stock} \\ \text{market price} \\ \text{per share}\end{array} - \begin{array}{c}\text{Exercise} \\ \text{price} \\ \text{per share}\end{array}\right)\right. \\ \left. \times \begin{array}{c}\text{Number of shares} \\ \text{obtainable with} \\ \text{each warrant}\end{array}\right\}.\end{aligned} \qquad \textbf{(17.8)}$$

At the time of issue, a warrant's exercise price is greater than the common stock price. Even though the calculated formula value may be negative, it is considered to be zero, since securities cannot sell for negative amounts. For example, the Fannie Mae warrants had an exercise price of $44.25 when the firm's common stock price was $33 per share. Each warrant entitled the holder to 1 share, and the formula value was zero:

$$\text{Formula value} = \text{Max }\{\$0; (\$33 - \$44.25)(1)\}$$
$$= 0.$$

Suppose later, however, that the price of the Fannie Mae common stock reaches $50 per share, and, at the same time, the warrants trade at $12 each. The formula value at this time is calculated as follows:

$$\text{Formula value} = \text{Max }\{\$0;(\$50 - \$44.25)(1)\}$$
$$= \$5.75.$$

Thus, the warrant market price of $12 represents a *premium* of $6.25 over the formula value.

In general, investors consider warrants to be worth more than their formula value. This is due to leverage. The leverage effect of warrants is shown in Table 17-2, which lists actual stock market data for warrants issued by American Express and American Express common stock, as well as Figure 17-3, which graphically plots these values.

Table 17-2   **Market Price Data for American Express Common Stock and Warrants***

Common Stock Market Price Per Share	Warrant Market Price	Warrant Formula Value	Premium Over Formula Value
46	12¾	0	12¾
48⅜	13	0	13
58½	17⅝	3½	14⅛
64⅛	21¾	9⅛	12⅝
70¾	27¼	15¾	11½

*The two market prices occurred simultaneously; for example, when the common stock price was 58½, the warrant price was 17⅝. The warrant exercise price equals $55, and one share of common stock is obtainable with each warrant.

Figure 17-3   **Warrant Valuation at Different Stock Prices***

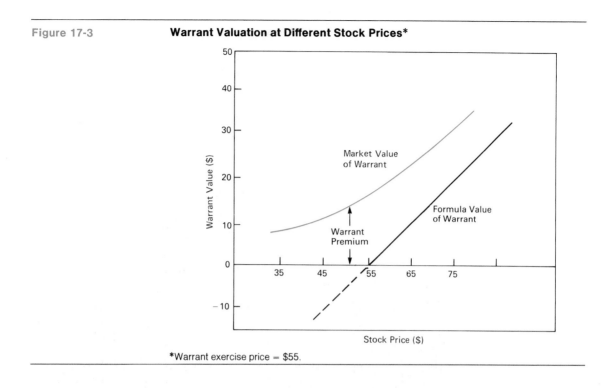

*Warrant exercise price = $55.

As Table 17-2 and Figure 17-3 show, the premium over the formula value reaches a maximum when the warrant exercise price is equal to the common stock price, because, at this point, the opportunities for high percentage returns on investment are greatest. This is not only true for the American Express warrants; it is also true in general. The reason for this is that when the exercise price is equal to the common stock price, warrant investors have the potential for large absolute (and percentage) gains if the stock price increases. At the same time, their potential losses are limited to the price paid for the warrant.

To illustrate the leverage opportunities warrants provide, suppose an investor purchased American Express common stock at $46 per share and sold it at $70.75 per share. The investor's return would be calculated as follows[11]:

$$\text{Rate of return} = \frac{\text{Ending price} - \text{Beginning price}}{\text{Beginning price}} \times 100\%$$

$$= \frac{\$70.75 - \$46}{\$46} \times 100\%$$

$$= 54\%.$$

At the same time, the investor could have purchased the warrants instead, buying them at $12.75 each and selling them at $27.25; the return would

[11] These two returns are not annualized, and the return on the common stock investment does not consider any dividends the investor might have received during the holding period.

have been as follows:

$$\text{Rate of return} = \frac{\$27.25 - \$12.75}{\$12.75} \times 100\%$$
$$= 114\%.$$

As can be seen, an investment in the warrants would have yielded greater returns. This *potential* for high returns encourages investors to pay prices exceeding formula values for warrants. This premium over formula value decreases as the stock price moves beyond the warrant exercise price, because the opportunity for greater returns decreases.

Accounting for Convertible Securities and Warrants

Companies that have convertible securities and warrants outstanding are required by *Accounting Principles Board Opinion 15* to calculate and report to stockholders two earnings-per-share figures—*primary* and *fully diluted.* Primary earnings per share are basically calculated by dividing net income available to common stock by the number of common shares outstanding. The fully diluted figure is a calculation of what earnings per share would have been if convertibles had been converted and warrants had been exercised during the accounting period.[12]

When a company has significant amounts of convertibles and warrants outstanding, the fully diluted figure is usually less than the primary figure and, as such, serves as a better indicator of the company's future earnings per share.

Summary

Options

- An *option* is a security that gives its holder the right to buy or sell an asset at a set *exercise price* until a specified *expiration date.* A *call* is an option to *buy,* and a *put* is an option to *sell.*
- The value of a call option is dependent upon four variables:

  1. The relationship between the exercise price and the stock price.
  2. The time remaining until the option's expiration date.
  3. The level of interest rates.
  4. The expected stock price volatility.

Table 17-3 summarizes the similarities among and differences between convertibles and warrants.

Convertible Securities

- *Convertible* debt or preferred stock securities are exchangeable for a company's common stock at the option of the holder.
- The price at which a convertible security is exchangeable for common stock is the *conversion price.*

[12] These calculations can be relatively complex. For example, warrants are assumed to be exercised only if the market price of the common stock is above the warrant's exercise price.

- The number of common shares that can be obtained when a convertible security is exchanged is the *conversion ratio,* which is calculated by dividing the par value of the security by the conversion price.
- At the time of issue, the conversion price normally exceeds the market price of the common stock by about 15 to 30 percent.
- Convertible securities possess characteristics of both common stock and fixed-income securities. Their market value is a function of both their stock, or conversion, value and their value as a fixed-income security. The *conversion value* is calculated by multiplying the conversion ratio by the current stock price.

Warrants

- A *warrant* is an option issued by a company to purchase shares of the company's common stock at a particular price during a specific time period. Warrants frequently are issued as part of a fixed-income security offering. Warrants also are issued as part of more "creative" financing packages.
- The *exercise price* of a warrant is the price at which the holder can purchase common stock of the issuing company.
- Warrants are issued for the following reasons:

  1. To sell common stock in the future at a higher price than the price at the time of original issue.
  2. To "sweeten" fixed-income security offerings.
  3. To sell common stock in the future without incurring underwriting costs at the time of sale.

- The *formula value* of a warrant depends on the number of common shares each warrant is entitled to and the difference between the common stock market price and the warrant exercise price. Warrants normally sell at a premium over their formula value.

Table 17-3   **Summary Comparison of Convertibles and Warrants (When Warrants Are Issued as Part of a Fixed-Income Security Offering)**

Similarities
1. The intention is the future issuance of common stock at a price higher than that prevailing at the time of the convertible or warrant issue.
2. Both convertibles and warrants can serve to "sweeten" fixed-income security offerings, thereby making the securities easier to sell.
3. Both the convertibility option and the attachment of warrants result in interest expense or preferred dividend savings for the issuing company.

Differences
1. The company receives additional funds at the time warrants are exercised, whereas no additional funds are received at the time convertibles are converted.
2. The fixed-income security remains on the company's books after the exercise of warrants; in the case of convertibles, the fixed-income security is exchanged for common stock and taken off the company's books.
3. Because of the call feature, convertible securities potentially give the company more control over when the common stock is issued.

Questions and Topics for Discussion

1. Define the following terms:
   a. Option.
   b. Call.
   c. Put.
   d. Exercise (striking) price.
   e. Covered option.
   f. Uncovered (naked) option.

2. What are the similarities and differences between options and warrants?

3. What variables are important in determining call option prices?

4. What are the factors investors should consider in deciding whether to buy a put or sell a call on stocks they own?

5. Will option values in general be higher at a time when interest rates are relatively high, compared with a time when interest rates are relatively low, all other things being equal?

6. How does a stock's expected price volatility affect the value of a call option on it?

7. In what ways are convertible securities and warrants similar? Dissimilar?

8. Why do companies issue convertible securities?

9. Why do investors purchase convertible securities?

10. What is the relationship between conversion value, bond value, and market value for a convertible security?

11. How can a company effectively force conversion of a convertible security?

12. What is the relationship between a warrant's formula value and its market value? When is the premium over the formula value usually the greatest?

Problems*

1. The BWS Corporation stock is selling at $50 a share today.
   a. Calculate the value of a BWS call option if its exercise price is $40, and it expires today.
   b. What can you say about the value of a BWS call option if its exercise price is $40, and it expires in 6 months.
   c. Calculate the value of a BWS call option if its exercise price is $60, and it expires today.
   d. What can you say about the value of a BWS call option if its exercise price is $60, and it expires in 6 months.

2. Re-solve Problem 1, substituting the word "put" for "call."

3. The LeMonde Corporation has debentures outstanding (par value = $1,000) that are convertible into the company's common stock at a price of $25 per share. The convertibles have a coupon interest rate of 6 percent and mature 20 years from now. In addition, the convertible debenture is callable at 107 percent of par value. The company has a marginal tax rate of 40 percent.
   a. Calculate the conversion value if LeMonde's common stock is selling at $25 a share.
   b. Calculate the bond value, assuming that straight debt of equivalent risk and maturity is yielding 9 percent.
   c. Using the answers from Parts a and b, what is a realistic estimate of the market value of the convertible debentures? (No calculation is necessary for this part of the problem.)
   d. What is the conversion value if the company's common stock price increases to $35 a share?

---

* Color numbers denote problems which have check answers provided at the end of the book.

    e. Given the situation presented in Part d, what is a realistic estimate of the market value of the convertible debenture? (No calculation is necessary for this part of the problem.)

    f. What is the minimum common stock price that will allow the LeMonde management to use the call feature of the debentures to effectively force conversion?

    g. Suppose that increased expectations concerning inflation cause the yield on straight debt of equivalent risk and maturity to reach 10 percent. How will this affect the bond value of the convertible?

4. In February 1986 Automatic Data Processing issued $150 million of $6\frac{1}{2}$ percent convertible debentures due in 2011. The debentures are convertible into common stock at $83.45 a share. The company's common stock was trading at about $67 a share at the time the convertibles were issued.

    a. How many shares of common stock can be obtained by converting one $1,000 par value debenture; that is, what is the conversion ratio?

    b. What was the conversion value of this issue at the time these debentures were originally issued?

    c. By what percentage was the conversion price above the stock price at the time these debentures were originally issued?

5. The Manchester Corporation has warrants presently outstanding, and each warrant entitles the holder to purchase 1 share of the company's common stock at an exercise price of $20 a share. If the market price of the warrants is $8 and the common stock price is $24 a share, what is the premium over the formula value for the warrants?

6. Horizon Corporation has warrants to purchase common stock outstanding. Each warrant entitles the holder to purchase 1 share of the company's common stock at an exercise price of $20 a share. Suppose the warrants expire on September 1, 1992. One month ago, when the company's common stock was trading at about $21.50 a share, the warrants were trading at $5 each.

    a. What was the formula value of the warrants one month ago?

    b. What was the premium over the formula value one month ago?

    c. What are the reasons investors were willing to pay more than the formula value for these warrants one month ago?

    d. Suppose that in August 1992, the Horizon common stock is still trading at $21.50 a share. What do you think the warrant price would be then? Why?

    e. Horizon paid an annual dividend of $1 a share, as of one month ago, to its common shareholders. Do warrant holders receive dividends?

7. Shaw Products Company, whose present balance sheet is summarized here, is considering issuing $100 million of 6 percent subordinated debentures (par value = $1,000), which are convertible into common stock at a price of $40.

Balance Sheet
(in millions of dollars)

Current assets	$200	Current liabilities	$100
Fixed assets, net	300	Long-term debt	150
Total assets	$500	Common equity	250
		Total liabilities and equity	$500

    a. Show the pro forma balance sheet for the issuance of the convertibles prior to conversion. Assume the proceeds are invested in new plant and equipment, and disregard flotation costs.

b. Show the pro forma balance sheet, assuming conversion of the entire issue.

c. How much additional money will the company raise at the time of conversion?

8. The capital structure of Whitefield Mills, Inc., is as follows:

Long-term debt	$250 million
Common stock, $1 par	25 million
Contributed capital in excess of par value	150 million
Retained earnings	350 million
	$775 million

The company has decided to raise additional capital by selling $75 million of 8 percent debentures with warrants attached. Each $1,000 debenture will have 25 warrants attached, and each warrant will entitle the holder to purchase 1 share of common stock at $30.

a. Show the company's new capital structure after the sale of debentures and the exercise of all the warrants. Assume that no other changes in capital structure occur between now and the time the warrants are exercised.

b. What condition is necessary in order for the warrants to be exercised?

c. How much total money will the company raise as a result of this security issue, if all warrants are exercised?

9. You own 10 Bitterroot Industries, Inc., 8 percent convertible debentures due in 2010. The conversion ratio of the debentures is 30, and the debentures are callable at $1,070 each. You bought the debentures when they originally were issued in 1980 for $1,000 each. At that time, Bitterroot common stock was selling at $28.50 a share, and now it is up to $44 a share. The convertible debentures are now selling at $1,320 each.

Last week you received a notice from Bitterroot Industries stating that the company is calling the debentures.

a. What are your alternatives?

b. Which alternative should you choose?

10. Calculate the percentage return that could have been earned by an investor who purchased American Express common stock at $58\frac{1}{2}$ and sold it at $70\frac{3}{4}$. Compare this return with the return that could have been earned by investing in American Express warrants over the same time period. When the common was at $58\frac{1}{2}$, the warrant was at $17\frac{5}{8}$, and when the common was at $70\frac{3}{4}$, the warrant was at $27\frac{1}{4}$.

11. Calculate the after-tax component cost of capital, k_c, for a 7.5 percent convertible debenture sold at par and due to mature in 25 years. The conversion ratio is 25, and conversion is expected to occur at the end of 10 years, when the common stock price is expected to be $54 a share. The company has a 40 percent marginal tax rate.

Hint: Try $k_c = 7.0\%$.

Selected References

Black, Fischer, and Myron Scholes. "The Pricing of Options and Corporate Liabilities." *Journal of Political Economy* 81 (May-June 1973): 637–654.

Brigham, Eugene F. "An Analysis of Convertible Debentures: Theory and Some Empirical Evidence." *Journal of Finance* 21 (March 1966): 35–54.

Geske, Robert, and Kuldeep Shastri. "Valuation by Approximation: A Comparison of Alternative Option Valuation Techniques." *Journal of Financial and Quantitative Analysis* 20 (March 1985): 45–72.

Harris, Milton, and Arthur Raviv. "A Sequential Signalling Model of Convertible Debt Call Policy." *Journal of Finance* 40 (December 1985): 1263–1282.

Marr, Wayne M., and Rodney G. Thompson. "The Pricing of New Convertible Bond Issues." *Financial Management* 13 (Summer 1984): 31–37.

Schwartz, Eduardo S. "The Valuation of Warrants: Implementing a New Approach." *Journal of Financial Economics* 4 (January 1977): 79–93.

PART SEVEN

THE MANAGEMENT OF WORKING CAPITAL

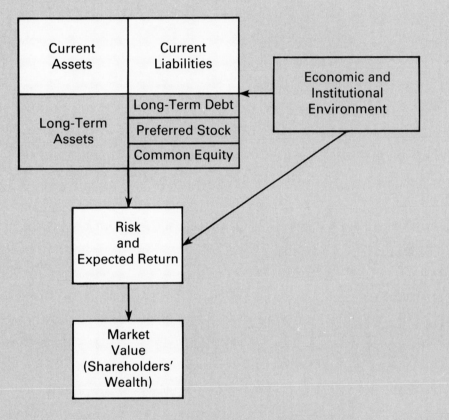

This part of the book considers the financial management of a firm's current assets and current liabilities. This is called *working capital management*. Chapter 18 provides an overview of working capital management, with emphasis on the risk-return tradeoffs that are implied. Chapter 19 deals with the management of cash and marketable securities; Chapter 20, with accounts receivable; and Chapter 21, with inventories. Chapter 22 looks at current liabilities and the sources of short-term credit. Working capital management influences both the risk of a firm and its expected returns. As such, it is an important determinant of firm value.

18

WORKING CAPITAL MANAGEMENT: AN OVERVIEW

A Financial Dilemma

Going Broke While Making a Profit*

At the beginning of the year, John Stickler was in good spirits. He was president of Cactus Creations, a firm that manufactured decorative planters for $6 each and sold them for $8 each, and demand was strong in the growing Sunbelt region. Stickler kept a thirty-day inventory, paid his bills promptly, and billed his customers on terms of net thirty days (that is, payments were due in thirty days). Sales forecasts had been accurate, and a steady increase was anticipated over the next year.

On January 1, the firm's books read as follows:
Cash = $8,000.
Inventory = $6,000.
Receivables = $8,000.
In January Stickler sold 1,000 planters, produced at a cost of $6,000, and collected receivables of $8,000. January's profits totaled $2,000.

On February 1 the firm's books read as follows:
Cash = $10,000.
Inventory = $6,000.
Receivables = $8,000.
February sales increased to an expected 1,500 units. To maintain a thirty-day inventory, production was increased to 2,000 units at a cost of $12,000. All January receivables were collected, and profits through February totaled $5,000.

On March 1 the account balances were as follows:
Cash = $6,000.
Inventory = $9,000.
Receivables = $12,000.
March sales increased to 2,000 units. Collections from February were made on time. Production was increased to 2,500 units to maintain a 2,000-unit inventory. Profits for the month totaled $4,000 ($9,000 year to date).

On April 1 the books read as follows:
Cash = $3,000.
Inventory = $12,000.
Receivables = $16,000.
Sales increased to 2,500 units in April; Stickler was overjoyed. Customers continued to pay on time. Production was increased to 3,000 units to maintain a 2,500-unit inventory. Profits for the month totaled $5,000 ($14,000 year to date). Stickler headed for a long-deserved vacation in the islands.

On May 1 the books read as follows:
Cash = $1,000.
Inventory = $15,000.
Receivables = $20,000.
In May sales exploded to new records—3,000 units—and production was increased to 3,500. Profits for the first five months of the year were $20,000. Then Stickler got an unexpected call from his accountant, telling him to come home as quickly as possible. The firm was out of cash.

On June 1 Cactus Creations' accounts had the following balances:
Cash = $0.
Inventory = $18,000.
Receivables = $24,000.
Stickler came home, confused and perplexed, and immediately arranged a meeting with his banker.

This example illustrates the importance of proper planning and management of a firm's working capital. This chapter is the first of five chapters dealing with this important area.

---

* Adapted from "How to Go Broke. . . While Making a Profit."
Business Week (April 28, 1956): 46-54.

Key Chapter Concepts

1. Working capital management decisions include:
   a. Investment—level of current assets (working capital).
   b. Financing—proportions of short-term and long-term debt.
2. Determination of the optimal level of working capital investment involves profitability versus risk tradeoff analysis:
   a. Higher levels of working capital reduce profitability.
   b. Higher levels of working capital reduce risk (of financial difficulties).
3. Determination of the optimal proportions of short- and long-term debt involves profitability versus risk tradeoff analysis:
   a. Higher proportions of short-term debt increase profitability because of generally lower interest costs.
   b. Higher proportions of short-term debt increase risk of financial difficulties.
4. Other important topics include:
   a. The joint (simultaneous) determination of working capital investment and financing decisions.
   b. Operating cycle and cash conversion cycle.
   c. Term structure of interest rates (Appendix 18A).

Glossary of New Terms

Working capital A firm's total investment in current assets.

Net working capital The difference between a firm's current assets and current liabilities.

Operating cycle For a manufacturing company it consists of three primary activities—purchasing resources, manufacturing the product, and distributing (selling) the product.

Cash conversion cycle This represents the net time interval between the collection of cash receipts from product sales and the cash payments for the company's various resources.

Permanent current assets Current assets that are held to meet the company's long-term minimum needs.

Fluctuating current assets Current assets that are affected by the seasonal or cyclical nature of the company's sales.

Matching approach A financing plan in which the maturity structure of the firm's liabilities is made to correspond exactly to the life of its assets.

Introduction

The management of working capital concerns decisions involving a company's current assets and current liabilities—what they consist of, how they are used, and how their mix affects the risk versus return characteristics of the company. The term *working capital* normally denotes the company's *total* investment in current assets, whereas *net working capital* denotes the *difference* between the company's current assets and current liabilities. From a conceptual standpoint it is useful to view *working capital* as the company's *gross* investment in current assets and *net working capital* as the amount of current assets that is supported, or financed, by noncurrent sources of funds.

Working capital management, through its effect on the firm's expected future returns and the risk associated with these returns, ultimately has an impact on shareholder wealth. Effective working capital management is crucial to a firm's long-run growth and survival. If, for example, a company lacks the working capital needed to expand production and sales, it may lose revenues and profits. A firm that does not have enough working capital may be unable to pay bills on time and will incur the costs associated with a deteriorating credit rating, a potential forced liquidation of assets, and possible bankruptcy.

Working capital management is a continuing process that involves a number of day-to-day operations and decisions that determine the following:

- The firm's level of current asset investment.
- The proportions of short-term and long-term debt the firm will use to finance its assets.
- The level of investment in each type of current asset.
- The specific sources and mix of short-term credit (current liabilities) the firm should employ.

This chapter, which is the first of five dealing with this important area of finance, considers the *aggregate* level of current assets and current liabilities a firm may employ. The following three chapters detail the optimal level of investment in each of the major current asset accounts—specifically, Chapter 19 deals with cash and marketable securities; Chapter 20, with accounts receivable; and Chapter 21, with inventories. Finally, Chapter 22 covers the specific sources and appropriate mixes of short-term credit.

Importance of Working Capital

Working capital differs from *fixed* capital in terms of the time required to recover the investment in a given asset. In the case of fixed capital, or long-term assets (such as land, buildings, and equipment), a company usually needs several years or more to recover the initial investment. In contrast, working capital is turned over, or circulated, at a relatively rapid rate. Investments in inventories and accounts receivable usually are recovered during a firm's normal operating cycle, when inventories are sold and receivables are collected.

A manufacturing company's operating cycle consists of three primary activities—purchasing resources, manufacturing the product, and distributing (selling) the product. These activities create funds flows that are

Figure 18-1   **Operating Cycle of a Typical Manufacturing Company**

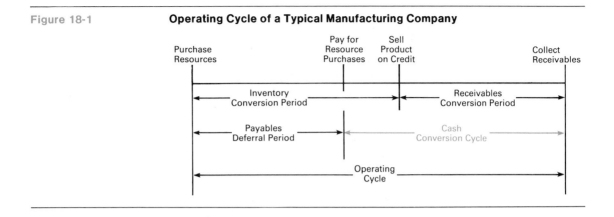

both unsynchronized and uncertain. They are unsynchronized because cash disbursements (for example, payments for resource purchases) usually take place before cash receipts (for example, collection of receivables). They are uncertain because future sales and costs, which generate the respective receipts and disbursements, cannot be forecasted with complete accuracy. If the firm is to function properly, it has to invest funds in various short-term assets (working capital) during this cycle. It has to maintain a *cash balance* to pay the bills as they come due. In addition, the company must invest in *inventories* to fill customer orders promptly and to permit efficient operation of the manufacturing process. And, finally, the company invests in *accounts receivable* to extend credit to its customers.

Figure 18-1 illustrates the operating cycle of a typical manufacturing firm.[1] The length of the operating cycle is equal to the length of the inventory and receivables conversion periods. The inventory conversion period is the length of time required to produce and sell the product. The receivables conversion period represents the length of time required to collect the sales receipts (receivables). The payables deferral period is the length of time the firm is able to defer payment on its various resource purchases (for example, materials, wages, and taxes). Finally, the cash conversion cycle represents the *net time interval* between the collection of cash receipts from product sales and the cash payments for the company's various resource purchases.

The cash conversion cycle shows the time interval over which additional nonspontaneous sources of working capital financing must be obtained in order to carry out the firm's acitivies.[2] An increase in the length of the operating cycle, without a corresponding increase in the payables deferral period, lengthens the cash conversion cycle and creates further working capital financing needs for the company.

A firm's net working capital position is not only important from an internal standpoint; it is also widely used as one measure of the firm's *risk*.

---

[1] The following discussion is based on Verlyn D. Richards and Eugene J. Laughlin, ''A Cash Conversion Cycle Approach to Liquidity Analysis,'' *Financial Management* 9 (Spring 1980): 32–38.

[2] Spontaneous sources of financing (such as trade credit offered by suppliers) automatically expand (contract) as the company's volume of purchases increases (decreases). Nonspontaneous sources of financing (such as bank loans), in contrast, do not automatically expand or contract with the volume of purchases. This concept is discussed further in Chapter 22, which deals with sources of short-term funds.

Risk, as used in this context, deals with the probability that a firm will encounter financial difficulties, such as the inability to pay bills on time. All other things being equal, the more net working capital a firm has, the more likely that it will be able to meet current financial obligations. Since net working capital is one measure of risk, a company's net working capital position affects its ability to obtain debt financing. Many loan agreements with commercial banks and other lending institutions contain a provision requiring the firm to maintain a minimum net working capital position. Likewise, bond indentures also often contain such provisions.

The magnitude and relative importance of working capital investment is shown in Table 18-1, which lists aggregate asset data for various sectors of the economy. In the manufacturing sector, for example, current assets constituted 41.3 percent of the total assets of all U.S. manufacturing corporations. Among the wholesaling and retailing sectors, the percentages were even higher—62.5 and 50.7 percent respectively.

Table 18-2 shows that considerable variation also exists among different industries within the manufacturing sector. For the six industries shown, current assets as a percentage of total assets range from 18.3 to 56.4 percent.

In a survey of large industrial corporations, it was found that about 30 percent of the companies have a formal policy for the management of their working capital and another 60 percent have an informal policy.[3] A significantly greater percentage of the larger companies within the sample

Table 18-1   **Aggregate Assets of U.S. Manufacturing, Wholesaling, and Retailing Corporations**

Assets	Manufacturing, 3rd Quarter 1985*		Wholesale Trade, 3rd Quarter 1985*		Retail Trade, 2nd Quarter 1985*	
	(in millions of dollars)	(%)	(in millions of dollars)	(%)	(in millions of dollars)	(%)
Cash	$ 51,376	2.7%	$ 6,239	3.3%	$ 6,491	3.2%
U.S. government and other securities	51,763	2.7	9,225	4.9	2,442	1.2
Receivables	297,762	15.7	47,557	25.1	30,087	14.8
Inventories	322,218	16.9	47,749	25.2	58,543	28.9
Other current assets	62,625	3.3	7,614	4.0	5,225	2.6
Total current assets†	$ 785,744	41.3%	$118,384	62.5%	$102,788	50.7%
Net property, plant, and equipment	714,467	37.6	42,193	22.3	73,833	36.4
Other assets	401,664	21.1	28,792	15.2	26,091	12.9
Total assets†	$1,901,875	100.0%	$189,369	100.0%	$202,712	100.0%

*Latest period for which data is available.
†In some cases, totals may differ slightly from the sums of individual entries because of rounding.
Source: *Quarterly Financial Report for Manufacturing, Mining, and Trade Corporations.* Federal Trade Commission (4th Quarter 1985).

[3] Keith V. Smith and Shirley B. Sell, "Working Capital Management in Practice," in *Readings in the Management of Working Capital* 2d ed, Keith V. Smith, ed. (St. Paul, MN, West Publishing Company, 1980).

Table 18-2   **Distribution of Aggregate Assets in Various Manufacturing Industries**

	Petroleum and Coal Products	Food and Kindred Products	Printing and Publishing	Motor Vehicles and Equipment	Electrical and Electronic Equipment	Textile Mill Products
Cash	1.1%	3.3%	4.6%	2.5%	2.9%	4.2%
Marketable securities	1.1	2.7	4.3	9.8	2.1	1.7
Receivables—net	7.6	13.1	20.0	13.3	22.2	24.3
Inventories—net	6.1	16.7	9.3	13.5	23.2	23.9
All other current assets	2.4	2.9	4.4	5.3	5.4	2.2
Total current assets*	18.3%	38.8%	42.6%	44.3%	55.7%	56.4%
Fixed assets—net	58.5	35.0	33.4	30.1	26.3	33.3
All other noncurrent assets	23.1	26.2	24.0	25.6	17.9	10.3
Total assets*	100.0%	100.0%	100.0%	100.0%	100.0%	100.0%

*In some cases, totals may differ slightly from the sums of individual entries because of rounding.
Source: *Quarterly Financial Report for Manufacturing, Mining, and Trade Corporations.* Federal Trade Commission (4th Quarter 1985).

have a formal policy than do the smaller companies. In almost one-half of the companies that responded to the survey, the financial vice-president has responsibility for establishing the company's overall working capital policy. The president and treasurer are the next most frequently mentioned positions as having responsibility for working capital policy. There is considerable variation in the frequency with which companies reviewed their working capital policy. Annual, quarterly, and monthly reviews are mentioned with about the same relative frequency (approximately 14 to 18 percent), while approximately one-half of the companies review working capital policy "whenever necessary."

Levels of Working Capital Investment

The size and nature of a firm's investment in current assets is a function of a number of different factors, including the following:

- The type of products manufactured.
- The length of the operating cycle.
- The sales level (since higher sales require more investment in inventories and receivables).
- Inventory policies (for example, the amount of safety stocks maintained, that is, inventories needed to meet higher than expected demand or unanticipated delays in obtaining new inventories).
- Credit policies.
- How efficiently the firm manages current assets. (Obviously, the more effectively management economizes on the amount of cash, marketable securities, inventories, and receivables employed, the smaller the working capital requirements.)

For the purposes of discussion and analysis, these factors are held constant for the remainder of this chapter. Instead of focusing on these factors, this section examines the risk-return tradeoffs associated with alternative levels of working capital investments.

Figure 18-2   **Three Alternative Working Capital Investment Policies**

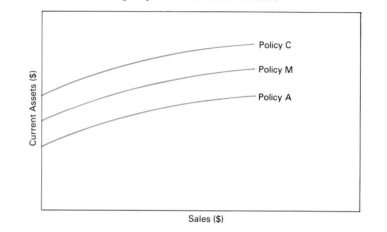

Profitability versus Risk Tradeoff for Alternative Levels of Working Capital Investment

Before deciding on an appropriate level of working capital investment, a firm's management has to evaluate the tradeoff between expected profitability and the risk that it may be unable to meet its financial obligations. Profitability is measured by the rate of return on total assets, that is, EBIT/total assets. As mentioned earlier in this chapter, the risk that the firm will encounter financial difficulties is related to the firm's net working capital position.

Figure 18-2 illustrates three alternative working capital policies.[4] Each curve in the figure demonstrates the relationship between the firm's investment in current assets and sales for that particular policy.

Policy C represents a *conservative* approach to working capital management. Under this policy the company holds a relatively large proportion of its total assets in the form of current assets. Since the rate of return on current assets normally is assumed to be less than the rate of return on fixed assets,[5] this policy results in a *lower expected profitability* as measured by the rate of return on the company's total assets. Assuming that current liabilities remain constant, this type of policy also increases the company's net working capital position, resulting in a *lower risk* that the firm will encounter financial difficulties.

In contrast to Policy C, Policy A represents an *aggressive* approach. Under this policy the company holds a relatively small proportion of its

[4] The relationship between current assets and sales is drawn as a concave, *curvilinear* function, since it is assumed that economies of scale exist in the holding of current assets. In other words, increases in sales normally should require less than proportionate increases in current assets, particularly for cash and inventories. The amount of the company's *fixed* assets is held constant in the following discussion.

[5] This assumption is based on the principle that the lower an asset's risk, the lower its expected return. Current assets are normally less risky than fixed assets, since they can be converted into cash more easily and with less potential loss in value. Therefore, current assets should have lower expected returns.

Table 18-3

Profitability and Risk of Alternative Working Capital Investment Policies for the Ohio Engineering Company (in Millions of Dollars)

	Aggressive	Moderate	Conservative
	Relatively Small Investment in Current Assets	Moderate Investment in Current Assets	Relatively Large Investment in Current Assets
Current assets (C/A)	$ 35	$ 40	$ 45
Fixed assets (F/A)	30	30	30
Total assets (T/A)	$ 65	$ 70	$ 75
Current liabilities (C/L)	$ 20	$ 20	$ 20
Forecasted sales	$100	$100	$100
Expected EBIT	$ 10	$ 10	$ 10
Expected rate of return on total assets (EBIT ÷ T/A)	15.38%	14.29%	13.33%
Net working capital position (C/A − C/L)	$ 15	$ 20	$ 25
Current ratio (C/A ÷ C/L)	1.75	2.0	2.25

total assets in the form of lower yielding current assets and thus has relatively less net working capital. As a result, this policy yields a *higher expected profitability* and a *higher risk* that the company will encounter financial difficulties.

Finally, Policy M represents a *moderate* approach, since expected profitability and risk levels fall between those of Policy C and Policy A.

These three approaches may be illustrated with the following example. The Ohio Engineering Company, a manufacturer of steel-making equipment, has forecasted sales next year to be $100 million and EBIT to be $10 million. The firm has fixed assets of $30 million and current liabilities totaling $20 million.

Ohio Engineering is considering three alternative working capital investment policies:

- An *aggressive* policy consisting of $35 million in current assets.
- A *moderate* policy consisting of $40 million in current assets.
- A *conservative* policy consisting of $45 million in current assets.

Assume that sales and EBIT remain constant under each policy.[6] Table 18-3 contains the results of the three proposed policies.

The aggressive policy would yield the highest expected rate of return on total assets, 15.38 percent, whereas the conservative policy would yield the lowest rate of return, 13.33 percent. The aggressive policy also would

[6] In practice, however, this assumption may not be completely realistic, since a firm's sales are usually a function of its inventory and credit policies. Higher levels of finished goods inventories and a more liberal credit extension policy—both of which increase a firm's investment in current assets—may also lead to higher sales. This effect can be incorporated into the analysis by modifying the sales and EBIT projections under the various alternative working capital policies. Although changing these projections would affect the numerical values contained in Table 18-3, it should not affect the general conclusions concerning the profitability versus risk tradeoffs.

result in a lower net working capital position ($15 million) than would the conservative policy ($25 million).

Using net working capital as a measure of risk, the aggressive policy is most risky, and the conservative policy is the least risky. The current ratio is another measure of a firm's ability to meet financial obligations as they come due. The aggressive policy would yield the lowest current ratio, and the conservative policy would yield the highest current ratio.

Optimal Level of Working Capital Investment

The optimal level of working capital investment is the level that is expected to maximize shareholder wealth. It is a function of several factors, including the variability of sales and cash flows and the degree of operating and financial leverage employed by the firm. Thus, no single working capital investment policy is necessarily optimal for all firms.

Proportions of Short-term and Long-term Financing

Not only does a firm have to be concerned about the *level* of current assets; it also has to determine the *proportions* of short- and long-term debt to use in financing these assets. This decision also involves tradeoffs between profitability and risk.

Sources of debt financing are classified according to their *maturities.* Specifically, they can be categorized as being either *short-term* or *long-term,* with short-term sources having maturities of one year or less and long-term sources having maturities of greater than one year.[7]

Cost of Short-term versus Long-term Debt

Recall from Chapter 2 that the *term structure of interest rates* was defined as the relationship among interest rates of debt securities that differ in their length of time to maturity. This relationship (the *yield curve*) is examined in Appendix 18A. Historically, as illustrated in Appendix 18A, long-term interest rates generally have exceeded short-term rates (see Figure 18A-2).

Also, because of the reduced flexibility of long-term borrowing relative to short-term borrowing, the *effective* cost of long-term debt may be higher than the cost of short-term debt, even when short-term interest rates are equal to or greater than long-term rates. With long-term debt, a firm incurs the interest expense even during times when it has no immediate need for the funds, such as during seasonal or cyclical downturns. With short-term debt, in contrast, the firm can avoid the interest costs on unneeded funds by paying off (or not renewing) the debt. In summary, the cost of long-term debt is generally higher than the cost of short-term debt.

Risk of Long-term versus Short-term Debt

Borrowers (firms) have different attitudes toward the relative risk of long-term versus short-term debt than do lenders. Whereas lenders normally feel that risk increases with maturity, firms feel that there is

---

[7] In this discussion the term *long-term financing* includes any *intermediate-term financing.*

more risk associated with short-term debt. The reasons for this are twofold.

First, there is always the chance that a firm will not be able to refund its short-term debt. When a firm's debt matures, the company either pays off the debt as part of a debt reduction program or arranges new financing. At the time of maturity, however, the firm could be faced with financial problems resulting from such events as strikes, natural disasters, or recessions that cause sales and cash inflows to decline. Under these circumstances the firm may find it very difficult or even impossible to obtain the needed funds. This could lead to operating and financial difficulties. The more frequently a firm must refinance debt, the greater the risk of its not being able to obtain the necessary financing.

Second, short-term interest rates tend to fluctuate more over time than do long-term interest rates (see Figure 18A-2). As a result, a firm's interest expenses and expected earnings after interest and taxes are subject to more variation (risk) over time with short-term debt than with long-term debt.

Profitability versus Risk Tradeoff for Alternative Financing Plans

A company's need for financing is equal to the sum of its fixed and current assets.[8] Current assets can be divided into the following two categories:

- *Permanent* current assets.
- *Fluctuating* current assets.

Fluctuating current assets are those that are affected by the seasonal or cyclical nature of company sales. For example, a firm must make larger investments in inventories and receivables during peak selling periods than during other periods of the year. Permanent current assets are those that are held to meet the company's minimum long-term needs (for example, "safety stocks" of cash and inventories). Figure 18-3 illustrates a typical firm's financing needs over time. The fixed assets and permanent current assets lines are upward sloping, indicating that the investment in these assets and, by extension, financing needs tend to increase over time for a firm whose sales are increasing.

One way in which a firm can meet its financing needs is by using a *matching approach* in which the maturity structure of the firm's liabilities is made to correspond exactly to the life of its assets. This is illustrated in Figure 18-4. As can be seen, fixed and permanent current assets are financed with long-term debt and equity funds, whereas fluctuating current assets are financed with short-term debt.[9] Application of this approach is not as simple as it appears, however. In practice the uncertainty associated with the lives of individual assets makes the matching approach a difficult one to implement.

[8] The following discussion assumes a constant amount of equity financing.

[9] This analysis does not consider "spontaneous" sources of short-term credit, such as accounts payable. Since spontaneous short-term credit is virtually cost-free when used within reasonable limits, a company normally will employ this type of credit to the fullest extent possible before using "negotiated" sources of short-term credit, such as bank loans. Since none of the conclusions concerning the tradeoff between profitability and risk are affected by ignoring spontaneous sources of short-term credit, it need not be considered here.

Figure 18-3   **Financing Needs over Time**

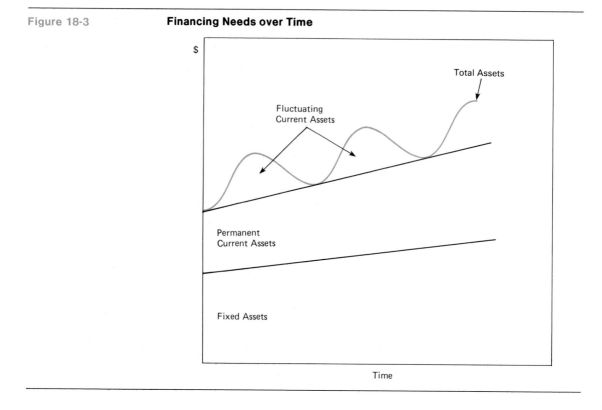

Figures 18-5 and 18-6 illustrate two other financing plans. Figure 18-5 shows a *conservative* approach, which uses a relatively high proportion of long-term debt. The relatively low proportion of short-term debt in this approach reduces the risk that the company will be unable to refund its debt, and it also reduces the risk associated with interest rate fluctuations. At the same time, however, this approach cuts down on the expected returns available to stockholders, since the cost of long-term debt is generally greater than the cost of short-term debt.

Figure 18-6 illustrates an *aggressive* approach, which uses a relatively high proportion of short-term debt. A firm that uses this particular approach must refund debt more frequently, and this increases the risk that it will be unable to obtain new financing as needed. In addition, the greater possible fluctuations in interest expenses associated with this financing plan also add to the firm's risk (variability in earnings). These higher risks are offset by the higher expected after-tax earnings that result from the lower costs of short-term debt.

Consider again the Ohio Engineering Company, which has total assets of $70 million and common shareholders' equity of $28 million on its books. Forecasted sales for next year are $100 million, and expected earnings before interest and taxes (EBIT) are $10 million. Interest rates on the company's short-term and long-term debt are 8 and 10 percent respectively.

Ohio Engineering is considering three different combinations of short-term and long-term debt financing:

Figure 18-4   **Matching Approach to Asset Financing**

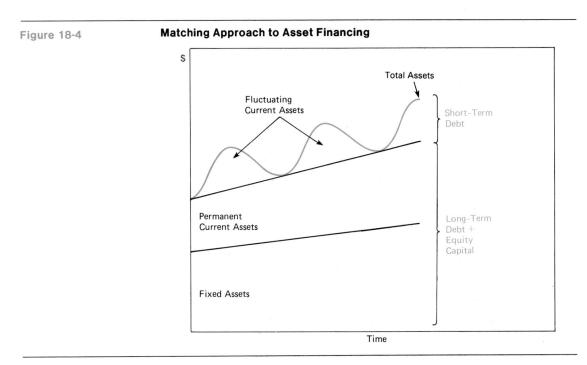

- An *aggressive* plan consisting of $30 million in short-term debt (STD) and $12 million in long-term debt (LTD).
- A *moderate* plan consisting of $20 million in short-term debt and $22 million in long-term debt.
- A *conservative* plan consisting of $10 million in short-term debt and $32 million in long-term debt.

Figure 18-5   **Conservative Approach to Asset Financing**

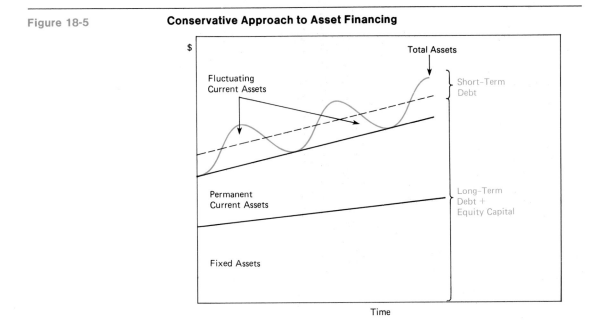

Figure 18-6   **Aggressive Approach to Asset Financing**

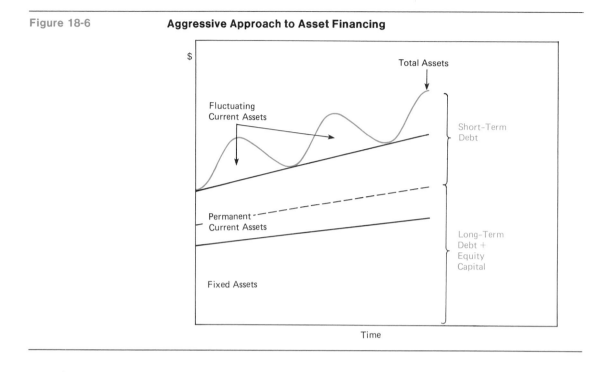

Table 18-4 shows the data for each of these alternative proposed financing plans. From the standpoint of profitability, the aggressive financing plan would yield the highest expected rate of return to the stockholders—11.43 percent—whereas the conservative plan would yield the lowest rate of return—10.71 percent. In contrast, the aggressive plan would involve a greater degree of risk that the company will be unable to refund its debt, since it assumes $30 million in short-term debt and the conservative plan assumes only $10 million in short-term debt. This is further substantiated by the fact that the company's net working capital position and current ratio would be lowest under the aggressive plan and highest under the conservative plan—indicating that the degree of risk that the company will be unable to meet financial obligations would be greater with the aggressive plan. The moderate financing plan represents a middle-of-the-road approach, and the expected rate of return and risk level are between the aggressive and the conservative approaches. In summary, both expected profitability and risk increase as the proportion of short-term debt increases.[10]

---

[10] This example assumes that the costs of short-term and long-term debt would be the same for each of the three financing policies. In practice, however, this would probably not be the case, since lenders generally require higher interest rates before making loans involving higher risks. Thus, a company following an aggressive financing policy probably will have to pay slightly higher interest rates on debt than will a company following a conservative policy. This effect can be incorporated into the analysis by modifying the interest rates on short-term and long-term debt under the various financing policies. This would affect the numerical values in the example, but it should not affect the general conclusions concerning the profitability versus risk tradeoffs.

Table 18-4 **Profitability and Risk of Alternative Financing Policies for the Ohio Engineering Company (in millions of dollars)**

	Aggressive	Moderate	Conservative
	Relatively Large Amount of Short-Term Debt	Moderate Amount of Short-Term Debt	Relatively Small Amount of Short-Term Debt
Current assets (C/A)	$ 40	$ 40	$ 40
Fixed assets (F/A)	30	30	30
Total assets (T/A)	$ 70	$ 70	$ 70
Current liabilities (STD)(C/L) (interest rate, 8%)	$ 30	$ 20	$ 10
Long-term liabilities (LTD) (interest rate, 10%)	12	22	32
Total liabilities (60% of T/A)	$ 42	$ 42	$ 42
Common equity	28	28	28
Total liabilities and common equity	$ 70	$ 70	$ 70
Forecasted sales	$100	$100	$100
Expected EBIT	10	10	10
Less: Interest: STD, 8% / LTD, 10%	2.4 / 1.2 → 3.6	1.6 / 2.2 → 3.8	0.8 / 3.2 → 4.0
Taxable income	$ 6.4	$ 6.2	$ 6.0
Less: Taxes (50%)	3.2	3.1	3.0
Net income after taxes	$3.2	$3.1	$3.0
Expected rate of return on common equity	11.43%	11.07%	10.71%
Net working capital position (C/A − C/L)	$ 10	$ 20	$ 30
Current ratio (C/A ÷ C/L)	1.33	2.0	4.0

Optimal Proportions of Short-term and Long-term Debt

As it is the case with working capital investment policy, no one combination of short- and long-term debt is necessarily optimal for all firms. In choosing a financing policy that maximizes shareholder wealth, a firm's financial manager also must take into account various other factors, such as the variability of sales and cash flows, which affect the valuation of the firm.

Overall Working Capital Management

Until now this chapter has analyzed the working capital investment and financing decisions independently of one another in order to examine the profitability-risk tradeoffs associated with each, assuming that all other factors are held constant. Effective working capital management, however, also requires the consideration of the *joint* impact of these decisions on the firm's profitability and risk.

Referring to the Ohio Engineering Company again, assume that the company is 60 percent debt financed (both short-term and long-term) and 40 percent financed with common stock. Ohio Engineering is evaluating three alternative working capital investment and financing policies. The *aggressive* policy would require a relatively *small* investment in current assets, $35 million, and a relatively *large* amount of short-term debt, $30 million. The *conservative* policy would require a relatively *large* investment in current assets, $45 million, and a relatively *small* amount of short-term debt, $10 million. The firm also is considering a middle-of-the-road approach, which would involve a *moderate* investment in current assets, $40 million, and a *moderate* amount of short-term debt, $20 million.

Table 18-5 shows the data for each approach. The aggressive working capital policy is expected to yield the highest return on shareholders' equity, 12.88 percent, whereas the conservative policy is expected to yield the lowest return, 9.50 percent. The net working capital and current ratio are lowest under the aggressive policy and highest under the conservative policy, indicating that the aggressive policy is the most risky. The moderate policy yields an expected return and risk level that is somewhere between the aggressive and the conservative policies.

Whereas this type of analysis will not directly yield the optimal working capital investment and financing policies a company should choose, it can give the financial manager some insight into the profitability-risk trade-offs of alternative policies. With an understanding of these tradeoffs, the financial manager should be able to make better decisions concerning the

Table 18-5   **Alternative Working Capital Investment and Financing Policies for the Ohio Engineering Company (in millions of dollars)**

		Aggressive	Moderate	Conservative
		Relatively *Small* Investment in Current Assets; Relatively *Large* Amount of Short-Term Debt	Moderate Investment in Current Assets; Moderate Amount of Short-Term Debt	Relatively *Large* Investment in Current Assets; Relatively *Small* Amount of Short-Term Debt
Current assets (C/A)		$ 35	$ 40	$ 45
Fixed assets (F/A)		30	30	30
Total assets (T/A)		$ 65	$ 70	$ 75
Current liabilities (STD)(C/L) (interest rate, 8%)		$ 30	$ 20	$ 10
Long-term liabilities (LTD) (interest rate, 10%)		9	22	35
Total liabilities (60% of T/A)		$ 39	$ 42	$ 45
Common equity		26	28	30
Total liabilities and common equity		$ 65	$ 70	$ 75
Forecasted sales		$100	$100	$100
Expected EBIT		10	10	10
Less: Interest:				
STD, 8%	2.4⎫ 0.9⎭ 3.3	1.6⎫ 2.2⎭ 3.8	0.8⎫ 3.5⎭ 4.3	
LTD, 10%				
Taxable income		$6.7	$6.2	$5.7
Less: Taxes (50%)		3.35	3.1	2.85
Net income after taxes		$3.35	$3.1	$2.85
Expected rate of return on common equity		12.88%	11.07%	9.50%
Net working capital position (C/A − C/L)		$ 5	$ 20	$ 35
Current ratio (C/A ÷ C/L)		1.17	2.0	4.5

working capital policy that will lead to a maximization of shareholder wealth.

Summary

- *Working capital* represents a firm's investment in current assets.
- *Net working capital* is the difference between current assets and current liabilities.
- *Working capital management* is concerned with determining the *aggregate amount* and *composition* of a firm's current assets and current liabilities.
- Working capital decisions affect both the *expected profitability* and the *risk* of a firm. In this context, *risk* refers to the probability that the firm will encounter financial difficulties, such as the inability to meet current financial obligations.
- When the level of working capital is increased, both the expected profitability and the risk are lowered. Similarly, when the level of working capital is decreased, both the expected profitability and the risk are increased.
- When the proportion of short-term debt used is increased, both the expected profitability and the risk are increased. Similarly, when the proportion of short-term debt used is decreased, both the expected profitability and the risk are lowered.
- Effective working capital management requires that the working capital investment and financing decisions be analyzed simultaneously so that their *joint* impact on the firm's expected profitability and risk can be evaluated.
- No single working capital investment and financing policy is necessarily *optimal* for all firms. To select the working capital policy that maximizes shareholder wealth, a financial manager should consider additional factors, including the inherent variability in sales and cash flows and the degree of operating and financial leverage employed.

Questions and Topics for Discussion

1. Describe the difference between working capital and net working capital.
2. Why does the typical firm need to make investments in working capital?
3. Define and describe the difference between the operating cycle and cash conversion cycle for a typical manufacturing company.
4. Discuss the profitability versus risk tradeoffs associated with alternative levels of working capital investment.
5. Describe the difference between permanent current assets and fluctuating current assets.
6. Why is it possible for the cost of long-term debt to exceed the cost of short-term debt, even when short-term interest rates are higher than long-term rates?
7. Describe the matching approach for meeting the financing needs of a company. What is the primary difficulty in implementing this approach?

8. Discuss the profitability versus risk tradeoffs associated with alternative combinations of short-term and long-term debt used in financing a company's assets.

9. As the difference between the costs of short- and long-term debt becomes smaller, which financing plan (that is, aggressive or conservative) becomes more attractive?

10. Why is no single working capital investment and financing policy necessarily optimal for all firms? What additional factors need to be considered in establishing a working capital policy?

11. **a.** Which of the following working capital financing policies subjects the firm to greater risk?
   i. Financing permanent current assets with short-term debt.
   ii. Financing fluctuating current assets with long-term debt.

   b. Which policy will produce the higher expected profitability?

Problems*

1. Consider again the comprehensive example involving the Ohio Engineering Company (Table 18-5). In this example it was assumed that forecasted sales and expected EBIT, as well as the interest rates on short-term and long-term debt, were independent of the firm's working capital investment and financing policies. However, these assumptions are not always completely realistic in practice. Sales and EBIT are generally a function of the firm's inventory and receivables policies. Both of these policies, in turn, affect the firm's level of investment in working capital. Likewise, the interest rates on short-term and long-term debt are normally a function of the riskiness of the firm's debt as perceived by lenders and, hence, are affected by the firm's working capital investment and financing decisions. Recompute Ohio Engineering's rate of return on common stock under the following set of assumptions concerning sales, EBIT, and interest rates for each of the three different working capital investment and financing policies.

Policy	Forecasted Sales (in millions of dollars)	Expected EBIT (in millions of dollars)	Interest Rate STD (%)	Interest Rate LTD (%)
Aggressive	$ 98	$ 9.8	8.5	10.5
Moderate	100	10.0	8.0	10.0
Conservative	102	10.2	7.5	9.5

2. The Fisher Manufacturing Company balance sheet for the year ended 19X6 follows:

December 31, 19X6
(in thousands of dollars)

Assets		
Cash		$ 3,810
Marketable securities		2,700
Accounts receivable		27,480
Inventories		41,295
Plant and equipment	$64,650	
Less: Accumulated depreciation	17,100	
Net plant and equipment		47,550
Total assets		$122,835

* Color numbers denote problems which have check answers provided at the end of the book.

December 31, 19X6
(in thousands of dollars)

Liabilities and Stockholders' Equity

Accounts payable	$ 14,582
Current portion of long-term debt	3,000
Accrued wages	1,200
Accrued taxes	3,600
Other current liabilities	2,200
Long-term debt	33,000
Common stock ($10 par)	19,500
Capital contributed in excess of par	15,000
Retained earnings	30,753
Total liabilities and stockholders' equity	$122,835

   a. Determine Fisher's working capital investment.

   b. Determine Fisher's *net* working capital investment.

   c. Determine Fisher's current ratio.

3. Wilson Electric Company, a manufacturer of various types of electrical equipment, is examining its working capital investment policy for next year. Projected fixed assets and current liabilities for next year are $20 million and $18 million, respectively. Sales and EBIT are partially a function of the company's investment in working capital—particularly its investment in inventories and receivables. Wilson is considering the following three different working capital investment policies:

Working Capital Investment Policy	Investment in Current Assets (in millions of dollars)	Projected Sales (in millions of dollars)	EBIT (in millions of dollars)
Aggressive (small investment in current assets)	$28	$59	$5.9
Moderate (moderate investment in current assets)	30	60	6.0
Conservative (large investment in current assets)	32	61	6.1

   a. Determine the following for each of the working capital investment policies:

      i. Rate of return on total assets (that is, EBIT/total assets).

      ii. *Net* working capital position.

      iii. Current ratio.

   b. Describe the profitability versus risk tradeoffs of these three policies.

4. Wilson Electric Company also is investigating the use of various combinations of short-term and long-term debt in financing its assets. Assume that the company has decided to employ $30 million in current assets, along with $20 million in fixed assets, in its operations next year. Given this level of current assets, anticipated sales and EBIT for next year are $60 million and $6 million, respectively. The company's income tax rate is 50 percent. Stockholders' equity will be used to finance $25 million of its assets, with the remainder being financed by short-term and long-term debt. Wilson is considering implementing one of the following financing policies:

Financing Policy	Amount of Short-Term Debt (in millions of dollars)	Interest Rate LTD (%)	STD (%)
Aggressive (large amount of short-term debt)	$24	8.5	5.5
Moderate (moderate amount of short-term debt)	18	8.0	5.0
Conservative (small amount of short-term debt)	12	7.5	4.5

a. Determine the following for each of the financing policies:
   i. Expected rate of return on shareholders' equity.
   ii. *Net* working capital position.
   iii. Current ratio.
b. Evaluate the profitability versus risk tradeoffs of these three policies.

5. Wilson Electric Company also wishes to analyze the *joint impact* of its working capital investment and financing policies on shareholder return and risk. Again, assume that the company has $20 million in fixed assets. Also, the firm's financial structure consists of short-term and long-term debt and common equity. Wilson wishes to maintain a debt to total assets ratio of 50 percent, where debt consists of both short-term and long-term sources. The following information was developed for the three policies under consideration:

Working Capital Investment and Financing Policy	Investment in Current Assets (in millions of dollars)	Amount of STD (in millions of dollars)	Projected Sales (in millions of dollars)	EBIT (in millions of dollars)	Interest Rate LTD (%)	STD (%)
Aggressive	$28	$24	$59	$5.9	8.5	5.5
Moderate	30	18	60	6.0	8.0	5.0
Conservative	32	12	61	6.1	7.5	4.5

a. Determine the following for each of the three working capital investment and financing policies:
   i. Expected rate of return on shareholders' equity.
   ii. *Net* working capital position.
   iii. Current ratio.
b. Evaluate the profitability versus risk tradeoffs associated with these three policies.

6. Educational Toys, Inc. (ETI), has highly seasonal sales and financing requirements. The company's balance sheet on December 31, 19X0, (*now*) is as follows:

Assets (in millions of dollars)		Liabilities (in millions of dollars)	
Current assets	$20	Short-term debt	$ x
Fixed assets	34	Long-term debt	y
		Net worth (equity)	30
Total assets	$54	Total liabilities and equity	$54

ETI has made the following projections of its asset needs and net additions to retained earnings (that is, equity) for the next 3 years:

Year	Quarter	Fixed Assets (in millions of dollars)	Current Assets (in millions of dollars)	Net Additions to Retained Earnings (in millions of dollars)
19X1	1 (March 31)	$36	$20	$0
	2 (June 30)	36	24	0
	3 (Sept. 30)	36	30	1
	4 (Dec. 31)	36	24	1
19X2	1 (March 31)	38	24	0
	2 (June 30)	38	28	0
	3 (Sept. 30)	38	36	1
	4 (Dec. 31)	38	28	2
19X3	1 (March 31)	40	28	0
	2 (June 30)	40	32	0
	3 (Sept. 30)	40	38	1
	4 (Dec. 31)	40	30	2

Assuming that ETI does not plan to sell any preferred or new common stock over the next 3 years,

a. Determine ETI's quarterly total assets and *total* (short-term and long-term) *debt requirements* for the next 3 years.
b. Plot the firm's *fixed, current,* and *total* assets over time on a graph.

7. Assume that ETI (see Problem 6) follows a *matching* approach in financing its assets. In other words, long-term debt will be used to finance its fixed and permanent current assets, and short-term debt will be used to finance its fluctuating current assets. The costs of short-term and long-term debt to ETI under this plan are 6 and 8 percent per annum (that is, 1.5 and 2 percent per quarter), respectively. Using this information, determine the following:
a. The amount of short-term and long-term debt outstanding each quarter.
b. ETI's total interest costs over the 3-year period under this approach.

8. ETI (see Problem 6) also is considering other financing plans. One plan under consideration is a *conservative* policy. Under this policy the company would determine its *maximum* debt requirements for the coming year and finance this entire amount with long-term debt at an interest rate of 8 percent per annum on December 31 of each year. Any funds in excess of its seasonal (quarterly) needs would be invested in short-term interest-bearing securities to yield a 4 percent per annum rate of return. Using this information, determine the following:
a. The amount of long-term debt ETI would have to borrow each year.
b. ETI's *net* interest costs over the 3-year period under this conservative policy.

9. Finally, ETI (see Problem 6) also is considering an *aggressive* policy. Under this policy the company would determine its *minimum* debt requirements for the coming year on December 31 of each year and finance one-half of this amount with long-term debt, with the remainder being financed by short-term debt. The costs of short-term and long-term debt under this policy are 6 and 8 percent per annum, respectively. Using this information, determine the following:
a. The amount of short-term and long-term debt outstanding each quarter.
b. ETI's total interest costs over the 3-year period under this aggressive policy.

10. Greenwich Industries has forecasted its monthly needs for working capital (net of spontaneous sources such as accounts payable) for 19X3 as follows:

Month	Amount	Month	Amount
January	$7,500,000	July	$6,000,000
February	6,000,000	August	7,500,000
March	3,000,000	September	8,500,000
April	2,500,000	October	9,000,000
May	3,500,000	November	9,500,000
June	4,500,000	December	9,000,000

Short-term borrowing (that is, a bank line of credit) costs the company 10 percent, and long-term borrowing (that is, term loans) costs the company 12 percent. Any funds in excess of its monthly needs can be invested in interest-bearing marketable securities to yield 8 percent per annum.

a. Suppose the company follows a *conservative* policy by financing the *maximum* amount of its working capital requirements for the coming year with long-term borrowing and investing any excess funds in short-term marketable securities. Determine Greenwich's *net* interest costs during 19X3 under this policy.

b. Suppose the company follows an *aggressive* policy by financing *all* its working capital requirements for the coming year with short-term borrowing. Determine Greenwich's interest costs during 19X3 under this policy.

c. Discuss the profitability versus risk tradeoffs associated with these conservative and aggressive working capital financing policies.

11. Gooding Enterprises is considering two alternative working capital investment and financing policies. *Policy A* requires the firm to keep its current assets at 65 percent of forecasted sales and to finance 70 percent of its debt requirements with long-term debt (and 30 percent with short-term debt.) *Policy B,* on the other hand, requires the firm to keep its current assets at 40 percent of forecasted sales and to finance 40 percent of its debt requirements with long-term debt (and 60 percent with short-term debt). Forecasted sales for next year are $20 million. Earnings before interest and taxes are projected to be 15 percent of sales. The firm's corporate income tax rate is 40 percent. Its fixed assets total $10 million. The firm desires to maintain its existing financial structure which consists of 50 percent debt and 50 percent equity. Interest rates on short- and long-term debt are 12 and 15 percent respectively.

a. Determine the expected rate of return on equity next year for Gooding under each of the working capital policies.

b. Which policy is riskier? Cite specific evidence to support this contention.

Selected References

Bierman, H., K. Chopra, and J. Thomas. "Ruin Considerations: Optimal Working Capital and Capital Structure." *Journal of Financial and Quantitative Analysis* 10 (March 1975): 119–128.

Carleton, Willard T., and Ian A. Cooper. "Estimation and Uses of the Term Structure of Interest Rates." *Journal of Finance* 31 (September 1976): 1067–1083.

Kallberg, Jarl G. *Current Asset Management* (New York: Wiley, 1984)

Gilmer, R.H. "The Optimal Level of Liquid Assets: An Empirical Test." *Financial Management* (Winter 1985): 39–43.

Richards, Verlyn, and Eugene J. Laughlin. "A Cash Conversion Cycle Approach to Liquidity Analysis." *Financial Management* 9 (Spring 1980): 32–38.

Smith, Keith V. *Guide to Working Capital Management.* New York: McGraw-Hill, 1979.

Smith, Keith V. *Readings on the Management of Working Capital.* 2d ed. St. Paul, MN West Publishing, 1980.

Vander Weide, James. *Managing Corporate Liquidity.* New York: Wiley, 1985.

APPENDIX 18A

THE TERM STRUCTURE OF INTEREST RATES

Introduction

In the financial markets there is a wide range of interest rates associated with the many different types of credit transactions. Securities[11] are available that offer investors considerably different rates of return[12] depending on such factors as default risk, maturity, marketability, and tax status. The focus of this appendix is on the differential yields of securities with different maturities. The *term structure of interest rates* is defined as the relationship at a given point in time among interest rates of debt securities that differ only in the length of time to maturity. Knowledge of the term structure of interest rates is useful to company treasurers who must make decisions concerning whether to borrow funds by issuing long-term or short-term debt and to investors who must make decisions about whether to purchase long-term or short-term securities.

Plotting interest rates (percent) on the vertical axis and length of time to maturity (years) on the horizontal axis results in a *yield curve.* Two yield curves for U.S. Government securities are shown in Figure 18A-1.[13] Note the different shapes of the two yield curves. The yield curve for August 1981 is *downward sloping,* indicating that the longer the time to maturity, the lower the yield on the security. The yield curve for October 1985, in contrast, is *upward sloping,* meaning that the longer the time to maturity, the higher the yield on the security.[14]

In general, from a historical perspective, the yield curve has been upward sloping much more often than downward sloping. As can be seen in Figure 18A-2, long-term interest rates (as measured by the yields on AAA corporate bonds) have exceeded short-term interest rates (as measured by the yields on prime commercial paper) over much of the last fifty years.

---

[11] The terms *security, debt security, debt, debt instrument, bond, loan, funds, financing,* and so on will be used interchangeably throughout the appendix to refer to a credit obligation between a borrower and lender. A borrower or lender can be an individual, business firm, or financial institution.

[12] The terms *rate of return, interest rate, rate, yield,* and so on will be used interchangeably throughout the appendix to refer to the percentage yield to maturity that is earned on a security when it is held to maturity.

[13] The primary reason for examining U.S. Government securities is that we are able to hold many of the factors affecting yields, such as default risk, constant. Corporate debt security issues, even for the same company, often differ significantly with respect to sinking fund provisions, call features, conversion features, degree of subordination, and whether or not they are secured by specific physical assets. Hence, these bond issues differ with respect to risk. Thus, it is difficult to use them in making yield versus time to maturity comparisons. However, the same general conclusions concerning the term structure of interest rates still apply to these securities.

[14] Upward and downward sloping yield curves are not the only possible shapes. At various times in the past, the yield curve has been relatively flat and also has been "hump" shaped, that is, high intermediate-term yields and low short-term and long-term yields.

Figure 18A-1

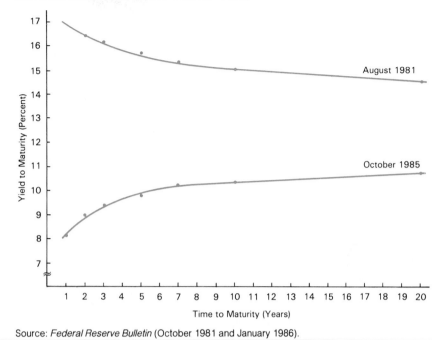

Yield Curves Showing the Term Structure of Interest Rates for U.S. Treasury Securities (August 1981 and October 1985)

Source: *Federal Reserve Bulletin* (October 1981 and January 1986).

Theories of the Term Structure of Interest Rates

Three main theories have been proposed to explain the shape of the yield curve:[15]

● Expectations theory.
● Liquidity premium theory.
● Market segmentation theory.

Expectations Theory

Long-term interest rates, according to the expectations theory, are a function of the expected future (that is, forward) short-term interest rates. Specifically, when interest rates are in equilibrium, the n-period long-term rate is postulated to be equal to the geometric mean[16] of the expected one-period foreward rates for periods 1, 2, 3, ..., n. Only the current period (that is, period 1) short-term rate is known. The other expected short-term forward rates for periods 2, 3, ..., n are for securities that will exist in the future and hence are not observable at the present time (that is, at time 0).

If future short-term interest rates are expected to rise, long-term interest rates must be above the current short-term rate for the geometric mean relationship among interest rates to hold. This would produce an

---

[15] This section draws heavily on Jack Clark Francis, *Investment: Analysis and Management*, 3rd ed., New York: McGraw-Hill, 1980, chap. 10. See also Sergei Dobrovolsky, *The Economics of Corporate Finance*, New York: McGraw-Hill, 1971, chap. 15.

[16] A geometric mean of n rates of return ($X_1, X_2, \ldots, X_n$) is equal to $\bar{X} = [(1 + X_1)(1 + X_2) \ldots (1 + X_n)]^{1/n} - 1$. Geometric means are commonly used when dealing with multiperiod compound interest and growth rates.

Figure 18A-2   **Historical Relationship between Short-Term and Long-Term Interest Rates**

Source: *Historical Chart Book*, Board of Governors of the Federal Reserve System (1985).

upward sloping yield curve. Conversely, if future short-term interest rates were expected to fall, long-term rates would have to be below the current short-term rate, thus producing a downward sloping yield curve.

According to the expectations theory, current and expected future interest rates are dependent on expectations about future rates of inflation. Many economic and political conditions can cause expected future inflation and interest rates to rise or fall. These conditions include expected future government deficits (or surpluses), changes in Federal Reserve monetary policy (that is, the rate of growth of the money supply), and cyclical business conditions. While much empirical data tends to support the expectations theory, other factors in combination with expected future inflation rates are believed to affect interest rates.

Liquidity Premium Theory

The liquidity premium theory holds that the yields on long-term securities should average higher than the yields on short-term securities. In other words, in the absence of other factors, the yield curve should be upward sloping.

This theory is based on the risk preferences of both lenders and borrowers. Lenders, it is argued, prefer short-term over long-term debt because of the higher interest rate risk and default risk associated with long-term debt. This preference is reflected in a willingness by lenders to accept lower yields on short-term debt as compared with long-term debt. Borrowers (primarily business firms), in contrast, prefer to finance their fixed-asset acquisitions (for example, plants and equipment) with long-term funds. Compared with short-term debt, long-term financing reduces the risk that the borrower will be unable to refund the short-term debt when it comes due for renewal periodically and the risk of having to pay uncertain (for example, possibly higher) interest rates at renewal time. Consequently, borrowers are willing to pay higher interest rates for long-term funds as compared with short-term funds.

Market Segmentation Theory

Another theory used to explain the shape of the yield curve is based on market segmentation. According to this theory, the securities markets are segmented by maturity. Furthermore, interest rates within each maturity segment are determined more or less independently by the supply and demand interactions of the segment's borrowers and lenders. If strong borrower demand exists for long-term funds and these funds are in short supply, the yield curve will be upward sloping. Conversely, if strong borrower demand exists for short-term funds and these funds are in short supply, the yield curve will be downward sloping.

Several factors limit the choice of maturities by lenders and borrowers. One such restriction is the legal regulations that limit the types of investments commercial banks, savings and loan associations, insurance companies, and other financial institutions are permitted to make. Another limitation faced by lenders is the desire (or need) to match the maturity structure of their liabilities with assets of equivalent maturity. For example, insurance companies and pension funds, because of the long-term nature of their contractual obligations to clients, primarily are interested in making long-term investments. Commercial banks and money market funds, in contrast, are primarily short-term lenders, because a large proportion of their liabilities are in the form of deposits that can be withdrawn on demand. Similarly, borrowers, such as business firms, limit their choice of debt maturities when they attempt to match the maturity composition of their debt capital with their asset structure. (Recall the matching approach discussed in Chapter 18.)

Summary

At any point in time, the term structure of interest rates is the result of the interaction of the factors previously described. Each of the three theories is descriptive of reality, and each can be supported by empirical data. All three theories are useful in explaining the shape of the yield curve.

Questions and Topics for Discussion

1. Define *yield curve*.
2. What financial variables are held constant when a yield curve is constructed? Why are these variables held constant?
3. What are two reasons why the yield curve might be upward sloping? Downward sloping?
4. Explain how a downward sloping yield curve might affect the financing plans of a firm. Assume the downward sloping curve can be best explained in the context of the expectations theory of interest rates.
5. From the latest issue of the *Federal Reserve Bulletin,* obtain the interest rates on U.S. Treasury Notes and Bonds for 1, 2, 3, 5, 7, 10, and 20 years (see the "INTEREST RATES: Money and Capital Markets" table). Plot these values in a yield curve similar to Figure 18A-1. Is the curve upward sloping or downward sloping (or does it have some other shape)? Based on the expectations theory, what does the shape of this yield curve indicate about future short-term interest rates?

19

THE MANAGEMENT OF CASH AND MARKETABLE SECURITIES

A Financial Dilemma

E.F. Hutton's Interest-Free "Loans"*

E.F. Hutton & Company, a large securities broker-age firm, in May 1985 pleaded guilty to Federal fraud charges involving the operation of a massive check-writing scheme to obtain money from many of its 400 banks without paying interest. The firm pleaded guilty to 2,000 counts of mail and wire fraud and agreed to pay more than $10 million in criminal fines and restitution to the banks. According to the Justice Department, Hutton systematically overdrew hundreds of its own accounts in banks throughout the country and intentionally moved money between banks to artificially delay the collection of funds. The scheme involved checks totaling more than $4 billion written between July 1980 and February 1982. By doing this, Hutton was able to use as much as $250 million in interest-free money on some days.

According to Justice Department documents, Hutton officials frequently misused bank accounts of its branches by writing checks for amounts in excess of the volume of customer funds deposited in these accounts. For example, during 1981 Hutton deposited $33.5 million in valid customer receipts in United Virginia Bank while withdrawing more than $640 million from the same account that year. Hutton also pleaded guilty to extending the "float" time during which checks are cleared by setting up a chain of transfers between branch accounts. These transactions, according to the Justice Department, resembled a check kiting scheme and were carried out illegally without the prior agreement or consent of the banks involved. Indeed, the banks generally didn't realize they were victims until they were told by officials from the government.

While many firms employ techniques to aggressively manage their bank balances and mini-mize their idle cash, Hutton went from being aggressive to actively defrauding the banks. This chapter examines various *legal* methods for controlling the collection and disbursement of cash.

---

* Based on articles from *The Wall Street Journal* (May 3, 1985 and May 6, 1985) and *Business Week* (May 20, 1985).

Key Chapter Concepts

1. Companies hold liquid asset balances for several reasons, including:
   a. To conduct transactions.
   b. For precautionary reasons.
   c. To meet future requirements.
   d. To compensate banks for various services provided to the firm.
2. The optimal liquid assets balance is a function of the following:
   a. Holding costs, which are the opportunity costs the company could earn on these funds in their next best alternative use.
   b. Shortage costs, which include possible lost cash discounts, deterioration of the company's credit rating, higher interest expenses, and financial insolvency.
3. The primary objective in controlling cash collections is to reduce the delay between when the customer mails the payment and when it becomes a collected balance in the firm's bank account.
4. Methods for reducing collection time include:
   a. Decentralized collection centers and concentration banks.
   b. Lock boxes.
   c. Wire transfers and depository transfer checks (DTC).
   d. Special handling of large remittances.
   e. Preauthorized checks (PAC).
5. The primary objective in controlling cash disbursements is to slow payments and keep the firm's funds in the bank as long as possible.
6. Methods of slowing disbursements include:
   a. Scheduling and centralizing payments (zero-balance systems).
   b. Use of drafts rather than checks.
   c. Maximizing check clearing float.
7. The primary criteria the firm should use in selecting marketable securities include:
   a. Default risk.
   b. Marketability (or liquidity).
   c. Maturity date.
   d. Rate of return.

Glossary of New Terms

Bank draft An order to pay that is similar to a check, except that it is not payable on demand. Instead, a bank draft is payable when the issuing firm accepts it.

Banker's acceptance A short-term debt instrument issued by a firm as part of a commercial transaction. Payment is guaranteed by a commercial bank.

Commercial paper Short-term, unsecured promissory notes. Commercial paper is generally issued by large, well-known corporations and finance companies.

Concentration banking The use of decentralized collection centers and local banks to collect customer payments. This speeds up a firm's collections.

Default risk The risk that a borrower will fail to make interest payments, principal payments, or both on a loan.

Depository transfer check (DTC) An unsigned, nonnegotiable check used to transfer funds from a local collection bank to a concentration bank.

Float The difference between an account balance as shown on the bank's books and as shown on the firm's books. Float represents the net effect of the delays in the payment of checks the firm writes and the collection of checks the firm receives.

Lockbox A post office box maintained by a bank to speed up the collection of payments from customers.

Preauthorized check (PAC) Similar to an ordinary check except that it does not require the signature of the person (or firm) on whose account it is being drawn. PACs are useful for firms that receive a large volume of payments of a fixed amount each period.

Repurchase agreement An arrangement with a bank or securities dealer in which an investor acquires certain short-term securities subject to a commitment that the securities will be repurchased by the bank or securities dealer on a specified date.

Wire transfer The process of electronically sending funds from one bank to another through the Federal Reserve System.

Zero-balance system A payment system that uses a master disbursing account that services all other disbursing accounts. A zero balance is maintained in all but the master account until payments must be made.

Introduction

Cash and marketable securities are the most liquid of a company's assets. *Cash* is the sum of the currency a company has on hand and the funds on deposit in a bank checking account or accounts. Cash is the medium of exchange that permits management to carry on the various functions of the business organization. In fact, the survival of a company can depend on the availability of cash to meet financial obligations on time.

Marketable securities consist of short-term investments a firm makes with its temporarily idle cash that can be readily sold and converted into cash when needed. Unlike cash, however, marketable securities provide the firm with interest income.

Referring to Table 18-1 in Chapter 18, it can be seen that cash and marketable securities accounted for only about 2.7 percent each of the total assets of all U.S. manufacturing corporations, ranking well behind inventories and receivables. Even though liquid asset balances tend to be small compared with other categories of current assets, they nevertheless must be managed efficiently if the firm is to operate profitably and minimize the risk of insolvency.

Cash management involves much more than simply paying bills and receiving payments for goods and services. It is a much broader function that is concerned with determining the following:

- The optimal size of the firm's liquid asset balance.
- The most efficient methods of controlling the collection and disbursement of cash.
- The appropriate types and amounts of short-term investments the firm should make.

This chapter examines these decisions in detail.

Liquid Asset Balance

There are a number of reasons why firms hold liquid asset balances, including:

- First, since cash inflows and outflows of the day-to-day operations of the firm are not perfectly synchronized, liquid asset balances are necessary to serve as a buffer between these flows. This reason is the *transactions motive*.[1] Liquid asset balances help the firm handle seasonal fluctuations in cash flows. For example, a firm may wish to hold a large amount of liquid assets during surplus months and "draw down" on them during deficit months.
- Second, since future cash flows and the ability to borrow additional funds on short notice are often uncertain, liquid asset balances are necessary to meet unexpected requirements for cash. This is the *precautionary motive*.
- Third, liquid asset balances are held to meet *future requirements*. These include fixed outlays that are required on specific dates, such as

---

[1] In *The General Theory of Employment, Interest and Money* (New York: Harcourt, Brace, 1935), economist John Maynard Keynes identified three primary reasons why people hold cash—the transactions motive, the precautionary motive, and the speculative motive. Within the *business firm*, the first two motives for holding cash are much more important than the latter one.

quarterly dividend and tax payments, capital expenditures, and repayments of loans or bond issues. The firm may also hold as liquid assets the proceeds from a new debt or equity securities offering prior to using these funds for expansion.

- Finally, a firm generally has to hold cash balances in order to compensate the bank (or banks) for the services provided. These are called *compensating balances*.

The following sections consider the importance of cash from a number of perspectives.

Cash Flows and the Cash Budget

Virtually every activity within a firm generates cash flows. As shown in Figure 19-1, the firm's cash balance is affected by every transaction that involves either a cash inflow or a cash outflow. Cash inflows, or *receipts,* occur when customers pay for their purchases, when the firm obtains bank loans, when it sells new issues of debt and equity securities, and when it sells (or collects interest on) marketable securities. Cash outflows, or disbursements, occur when the firm makes payments to suppliers, when the firm pays wages to employees, taxes to governments, interest and principal to bondholders, and cash dividends to shareholders, and when the firm repays bank loans and purchases marketable securities. Thus, the cash balance at the end of any given period is the result of many interrelated activities.

Cash flows differ with respect to their degree of *certainty*. In general, future outflows are more certain than future inflows. Most expenditures (outflows) are directly controllable by the firm and, as a result, can be forecasted more easily. For example, outflows for such items as raw materials, labor, dividends, debt repayments, and capital equipment are

Figure 19-1   **Cash Flows within a Typical Firm***

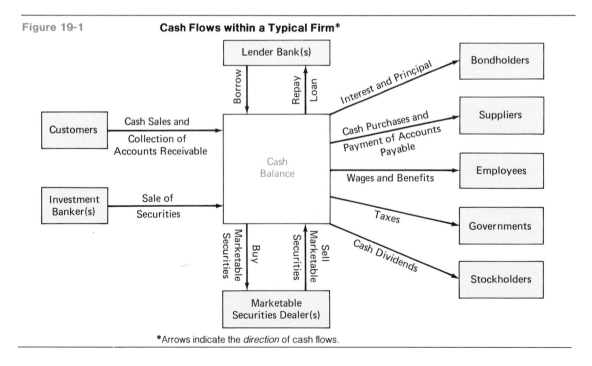

*Arrows indicate the *direction* of cash flows.

determined primarily by management decisions and usually are known in advance of their occurrence. Inflows, in contrast, occur partly as a result of decisions made outside the firm and thus are usually more difficult to control and forecast. For example, cash inflows from sales depend primarily on the buying decisions of customers, as well as on when they make their payments.

The first step in efficient cash management is the development of a *cash budget* showing the forecasted cash receipts and disbursements over the planning horizon of the firm.[2] A complete cash budget also contains a forecast of any cumulative cash shortages or surpluses expected during each of the budgeting subperiods—which is the kind of information needed in making cash management decisions. Many larger firms prepare a series of cash budgets, each one covering a different time period. For example, a firm may prepare daily cash budgets for the next five working days, weekly cash budgets for the next ten weeks, and monthly cash budgets for the next twelve months. The daily and weekly forecasts are used in making short-term decisions, such as determining the amount of marketable securities the firm should purchase or sell. The monthly projections are used in longer range planning, such as determining the amount of bank loans the firm will need. A survey of medium- and large-size companies found that over 80 percent of the respondents relied on cash budgets as a cash forecasting technique.[3]

Knowledge of a potential cash shortage ahead of time gives the financial manager ample opportunity to investigate alternative sources of financing and to choose the least costly one. All other things being equal, lending institutions prefer to make loans to firms that have demonstrated an ability to anticipate their future cash needs. Firms that seem to be faced with frequent cash "emergencies" generally have more difficulty getting loans. Similarly, advance knowledge of a cash surplus allows the financial manager to invest in appropriate marketable securities.

Corporate-Bank Relations

A firm's bank provides it with a variety of both tangible and intangible services. The most significant tangible services include the following:

- Disbursement and payroll checking accounts.
- Collection of deposits.
- Cash management.
- Lines of credit, term loans, or both.
- Handling of dividend payments.
- Registration and transfer of the firm's stock.

The most important intangible banking service is the availability of future credit if and when the need arises. Other intangible services include the following.

---

[2] Chapter 8 contains a discussion of how cash budgets are developed.
[3] R. Kamath, S. Khaksari, H. Meier, and J. Winklepleck. "Management of Excess Cash: Practices and Developments." *Financial Management* (Autumn 1985): 70–77.

- Supplying credit information.
- Providing consulting advice on such matters as economic conditions, mergers, and international business.

A bank is compensated for the services it provides by charging the firm explicit fees and/or requiring the maintenance of a minimum cash balance, or *compensating balance,* in its checking account. The bank can use this compensating balance to make other loans or investments, and the interest income realized is *compensation* for the various services rendered to the firm. Although some banks require firms to maintain *absolute* minimum compensating balances, most stipulate minimum *average* balances.

The monthly account fee that the bank charges a business customer is usually determined by calculating various service charges and then deducting an earnings credit on the account balance. The service charges are computed by multiplying the number of each type of transaction the firm makes per period (such as payroll checks, vendor checks, customer payments, and other deposits) by the bank's charge per item. The earnings credit is computed by multiplying the available balance during the month (which often includes various deductions, such as the bank's reserve requirement) by the earnings credit rate (that is some specified interest rate). When the total service charges exceed the earnings credit, the bank collects a fee from the customer. Due to competition among banks and differences in the methods used to compute account income and costs, service fees and compensating balance requirements for a given level of account activity vary from bank to bank. As a result, a firm should occasionally do some "comparison shopping" to determine whether its present bank is offering the best fee schedule and compensating balance requirement currently available.

Optimal Liquid Asset Balance

When a firm holds liquid asset balances, whether in the form of currency, bank demand deposits, or marketable securities, it is in effect investing these funds. To determine the optimal investment in liquid assets, the firm must weigh the benefits and costs of holding these various balances.

A minumum compensating balance requirement on the part of the bank essentially imposes a *lower limit* on the firm's optimal level of liquid asset balances. When the firm holds liquid assets in excess of this lower limit, it incurs an *opportunity cost*. The opportunity cost of excess liquid assets, held in the form of bank deposits, is the return the firm could earn on these funds in their next best use, such as in the expansion of other current or fixed assets. The opportunity cost of liquid asset balances, held in the form of marketable securities, is the income that could be earned on these funds in their next best alternative use in the firm *less* the interest income received on the marketable securities.

Given the opportunity cost of holding liquid asset balances, why would a firm ever maintain a bank balance exceeding the compensating balance requirements? The answer is that these balances help the firm avoid the "shortage" costs associated with inadequate liquid asset balances.[4]

---

[4] See William Beranek. *Analysis for Financial Decisions.* Homewood, Ill.: Irwin, 1963, chap. 11.

Shortage costs can take many different forms, including the following:

- Forgone cash discounts.
- Deterioration of the firm's credit rating.
- Higher interest expenses.
- Possible financial insolvency.

Many suppliers offer customers a cash discount for prompt payment. Having to forego this cash discount can be quite costly to the firm. In addition, the credit-worthiness of a firm is at least partially determined by the current and quick ratios—both of which can be affected by an inadequate liquid asset balance. This, in turn, can cause the firm's credit rating to deteriorate and make loans on favorable terms more difficult for the firm to secure in the future. The credit rating also can fall if the firm fails to pay bills on time because of inadequate cash. This can make future credit difficult to obtain from suppliers. If the firm has inadequate liquid asset reserves, it may have to meet unforeseen needs for cash by short-term borrowing, and it may be unable to negotiate for the best terms— including the lowest possible interest rate—if its credit rating is questionable. Finally, an inadequate liquid asset balance increases the firm's risk of insolvency, since a serious recession or natural disaster would be more likely to reduce the firm's cash inflows to the point where it could not meet contractual financial obligations.

An inverse relationship exists between a firm's liquid asset balance and these shortage costs: the larger a firm's liquid asset balance, the smaller its associated shortage costs. The opportunity holding costs, in contrast, increase as a firm's liquid asset balance is increased. As shown in Figure 19-2, the optimal liquid asset balance occurs at the point where the sum of the opportunity holding costs and the shortage costs is minimized. Admittedly, many of these shortage costs are difficult to measure. Nevertheless, a firm should at least attempt to evaluate the tradeoffs among these costs in order to economize on cash holdings.

Figure 19-2   **Optimal Liquid Asset Balance**

Controlling the Collection and Disbursement of Cash

The cash collection and disbursement processes provide a firm with two areas to attempt to economize on cash holdings. For example, if sales average $5 million per day and the company can speed up collections by only *one day*, the cash balance will increase by $5 million, and these released funds can be invested in other current assets or in fixed assets. If this additional cash can be invested in projects yielding a 10 percent return, it will generate added income of $500,000 per year (10% × $5 million).

A firm's cash balance as shown on the bank's books generally differs from that shown on the firm's own books. This difference is known as *float* and represents the net effect of the delays in the payment of checks the firm writes and the collection of checks the firm receives. Checks written by the firm result in *disbursement,* or *positive,* float; that is, an excess of bank net collected balances over the balances shown on the firm's books. In contrast, checks received by the firm and deposited in its account result in *deposit,* or *negative,* float; that is, an excess of book balances over bank net collected balances. Often a firm cannot withdraw the deposited funds until the bank *clears* the checks. In other words, the firm's bank must first collect the funds from the other banks upon which the checks are drawn. The amount of time in which a check clears depends on the geographical proximity of the bank that receives the check and the bank on which it is drawn. In general, checks take a maximum of two days to clear through the Federal Reserve System. Checks processed through bank clearing-houses may take longer.[5]

The primary objective of cash collection involves expediting collections and reducing the lag between the time customers pay their bills and the time the checks are collected. In contrast, the primary objective of cash disbursement is to slow payments so that the firm can keep the funds in the bank as long as possible. Expediting collections and slowing disbursements helps increase the firm's cash balance and provide it with funds to use for other profitable investments.

Expediting Collections

Figure 19-3 illustrates the main steps in the cash collection process. The total time involved in this process is a combination of mailing time, company processing time, and check-clearing time, each of which may vary depending on where the firm's customers and their respective banks are located.[6] Some methods available for reducing the collection time are discussed in the following paragraphs.

Decentralized Collection Centers and Concentration Banks Figures 19-4 and 19-5 illustrate two alternative cash collection systems. In the centralized system (Figure 19-4), customers are instructed to send their payments to the firm's headquarters. In the *decentralized* system (Figure

---

[5] Although most banks do not put holds on checks of large corporate clients, they often do on checks of individuals and small business customers. A *Wall Street Journal* article (January 12, 1983, p. 29) cited Citibank's (First National City Bank of New York's) policy as typical: "Its holds range from three business days for a local check to as long as fifteen days for a check drawn on a small-town bank in a distant state."

[6] The particular times shown in Figure 19-3 are merely illustrative. Actual times will vary. (This is also true for Figure 19-7.)

Figure 19-3

Cash Collection Process

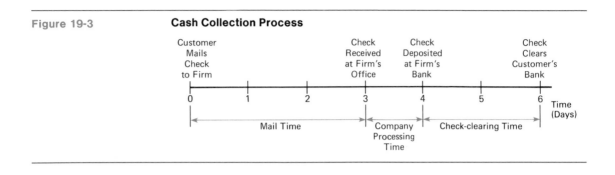

19-5), customers mail their payments to a nearby collection center, which is strategically located to minimize mail delay. The collection center then deposits the checks in a local bank and reports this information to the firm's headquarters. Since most of the checks are drawn on banks that are located in the same geographical area as the collection center, check-clearing time and deposit float are reduced. Each business day, funds in excess of the amount necessary to compensate the local bank for its services are transferred to an account in a *concentration bank,* where the firm maintains a disbursement account upon which checks are written.

A tradeoff exists between the number of collection centers and the potential savings realized. The more collection centers used, the less time required to convert customers' checks into collected balances. However, these savings from faster collections are offset by the direct fees involved, the opportunity costs of the compensating balances the firm must maintain at each local bank, or both. The financial manager must weigh the tradeoffs involved in both savings and costs in deciding on the appropriate number and location of collection centers.

Lockboxes Figure 19-6 illustrates the lockbox collection system. A lockbox is a post office box maintained by a local bank for the purpose of receiving a firm's remittances. Customers mail payments to this post office

Figure 19-4

Centralized Collection System

Figure 19-5   **Decentralized Collection System**

box, which is usually no more than a few hundred miles away.[7] For example, ITT Corporation, a large conglomerate firm, maintains eleven lockboxes around the country.[8] The bank empties the box several times each working day, deposits the payments in the firm's account, puts the checks into the clearing system, and sends the firm a list of the payments received each day. Not only does the lockbox reduce mailing time, it also eliminates company processing time, since the checks are deposited and begin the clearing process *before* the company's accounting department processes the payments received rather than after processing them. The bank normally charges a fee for this service, requires a compensating balance, or both. Funds in excess of the bank's compensating balance requirement are transferred each day to a master collection account in a concentration bank.

The decision to establish a lockbox collection system requires a comparison of the associated benefits and costs. If the earnings on the funds released by the acceleration of collections exceed the foregone returns on the required compensating balances, the service fees charged by the lockbox bank, or both, the establishment of a lockbox collection system is profitable.

If the number of checks being handled is small and the dollar amount of each check is large, a lockbox arrangement is very beneficial to the firm. Under these conditions the bank's work load is light, and the associated service fees, compensating balances, or both, are small. However, when large numbers of checks with small dollar amounts are involved—for example, in the case of oil company credit cards—a lockbox system may not be profitable. Under these conditions the service fees, opportunity costs, or both, on the required compensating balances may exceed the

[7] Determining the optimal location of lockboxes is a complex problem. For some solutions, see Ferdinand K. Levy, "An Application of Heuristic Problem Solving to Accounts Receivable Management," *Management Science* 12 (Feb. 1966): B-236–B-244; and Alan Kraus, et al, "The Lock-Box Location Problem." *Journal of Bank Research* (Autumn 1970): 51–58.

[8] See Ralph E. Jones, "ITT's Cash Management System," *Journal of Cash Management* (May/June 1984): 24–29.

Figure 19-6   **Lockbox Collection System**

U.S. Mail

LETTERS
U S MAIL

Regional
Lockbox
Bank

Automatic
Wire
Transfer

FIRST NATIONAL
BANK

Customers

Post Office Box

Concentration
Bank

earnings the firm realizes from having the funds available a few days earlier.

The lockbox decision can be illustrated with the following example. The Pacific Company, located in Los Angeles, currently receives and processes all customer payments at its corporate headquarters (that is, a *centralized* system). The firm is considering establishing a bank lockbox collection system for seven southeastern states—Florida, North Carolina, South Carolina, Tennessee, Alabama, Georgia, and Mississippi—which would be located in Atlanta. The lockbox would reduce average mailing time for customer payments from three days to one and one-half days, and it would reduce check processing and clearing time from five days to two and one-half days.

Annual collections from the southeastern region are $90,000,000, and the average number of payments received total 550 per day (assume 360 days per year). A bank in Atlanta has agreed to process the payments for an annual fee of $15,000 plus $0.10 per payment received. This bank would not require a compensating balance. Assuming an 8 percent opportunity cost for released funds, should Pacific use the lockbox collection system?

Table 19-1 shows an analysis of this decision. In Step A the amount of funds released ($1,000,000) is found by multiplying average daily collections ($250,000) by the reduction in collection time (four days). The annual (pre-tax) earnings on the released funds ($80,000) are found in Step B by multiplying the amount of funds released ($1,000,000) by the opportunity cost of funds (.08). The annual bank processing fee ($34,800) is computed in Step C as the sum of fixed costs ($15,000) and variable costs ($19,800). Finally, in Step D, the net (pre-tax) benefits of establishing a lockbox system ($45,200) are computed by deducting the annual bank processing fee ($34,800) from the earnings on the released funds ($80,000). Since the net (pre-tax) benefits are positive, Pacific should employ the lock-box collection system.

Table 19-1

Pacific Company's Analysis of the Decision to Establish a Lockbox Collection System for the Southeastern Region

Step A. Reduction in Collection Time = Reduction in Mailing Time + Reduction in Processing & Clearing Time

$$= (3 - 1.5) + (5 - 2.5)$$

$$= 4 \text{ days}$$

Average Daily Collections = Annual Collections ÷ 360

$$= \$90,000,000 \div 360$$

$$= \$250,000$$

Amount of Funds Released = Average Daily Collections × Reduction in Collection Time

$$= \$250,000 \times 4 \text{ days}$$

$$= \$1,000,000$$

Step B. Annual (Pre-tax) Earnings on Released Funds = Amount of Funds Released × Interest Rate

$$= \$1,000,000 \times .08$$

$$= \$80,000$$

Step C. Annual Bank Processing Fee = Fixed Cost + Number of Payments per year × Variable Cost per Payment

$$= \$15,000 + (550 \times 360) \times \$.10$$

$$= \$15,000 + \$19,800$$

$$= \$34,800$$

Step D. Net (Pre-tax) Benefits = Annual (Pre-tax) Earnings on Released Funds − Annual Bank Processing Fee

$$= \$80,000 - \$34,800$$

$$= \$45,200$$

Wire Transfers and Depository Transfer Checks Once deposits enter the firm's banking network, the objective is to transfer surplus funds (that is, funds in excess of any required compensating balances) from its local (collection) bank accounts to its concentration (disbursement) bank account or accounts. Two methods used to perform this task are *wire transfers* and *depository transfer checks.*

With a *wire transfer,* funds are sent from a local bank to a concentration bank electronically through the Federal Reserve System or a private bank wire system. Wire transfers are the fastest way of moving funds between banks, since the transfer takes only a few minutes and the funds become *immediately available* (that is, they can be withdrawn) by the firm upon receipt of the wire notice at the concentration bank. Wire transfers eliminate the mailing and check-clearing times associated with other funds transfer methods. Some firms leave standing instructions with their local (collection) banks to automatically wire surplus funds on a periodic basis (for example, daily, twice a week, and so on) to their concentration bank. Also, some firms specify in their sales contracts that customers must wire their payments on the due dates.

Wire transfer of funds is available to member banks of the Federal Reserve System and to nonmember banks through their correspondent banks. The cost to corporate customers of a wire transfer at most banks ranges from $4 to $20. For a firm with multiple collection centers that use wire transfers on a daily basis, the annual costs can be substantial. Consequently, this method of transferring funds should be used only when the incremental value of having the funds immediately available exceeds the additional cost.

A *mail depository transfer check* (DTC) is an unsigned, nonnegotiable check drawn on the local collection bank and payable to the concentration bank. As it deposits customer checks in the local bank each day, the collection center mails a depository transfer check to the concentration bank authorizing it to withdraw the deposited funds from the local bank. Upon receipt of the depository transfer check, the firm's account at the concentration bank is credited for the designated amount. Depository transfer checks are processed through the usual check-clearing process. While the use of depository transfer checks does not eliminate mailing and check-clearing time, it does insure the movement of funds from the local collection center banks to the concentration bank in a timely manner. Also, the cost of this method of transferring funds is low; often the only cost involved is postage.

An *electronic depository transfer check* (EDTC) can also be used to move funds from a local bank to a concentration bank. The process of transmitting deposit information to a concentration bank is similar to that for mail DTC's described above, except that the information is sent electronically through the Automated Clearing House (ACH) System. This system eliminates the mail float in moving funds from the local bank to a concentration bank. Funds transferred through this automated system are available for use by the firm in one day (or less).

Special Handling of Large Remittances Firms that receive individual remittances in the multimillion-dollar range may find it more profitable to use special courier services to pick up these checks from customers (rather than having their customers mail the checks) and present them for collection to the banks upon which they are drawn.

Use of Preauthorized Checks A *preauthorized check* (PAC) resembles an ordinary check except that it does not require the signature of the person (or firm) on whose account it is being drawn. This system is especially useful for firms that receive a large volume of payments of a fixed amount each period. Insurance companies, savings and loans, charitable institutions, and leasing firms make extensive use of this collection procedure. When preauthorized checks are used, the payer agrees to allow the payee (the firm that is owed the money) to write a check on the payer's account and deposit that check immediately for collection at an agreed-upon time. Preauthorized checks have the advantages of completely eliminating the mail float, reducing billing and collecting expenses, and making the cash flows for both parties highly predictable. Many payers like preauthorized check systems because they do not have to bother to write a check each month.

Slowing Disbursements

Figure 19-7 illustrates the principle steps involved in the cash disbursement process. Several ways in which a firm can slow disbursements and keep funds in the bank for longer periods of time are discussed in the following paragraphs.

Scheduling and Centralizing Payments A firm should pay bills *on time*—not before or after they are due. Payments made ahead of time lower the firm's average cash balance, whereas late payments can impair the firm's credit rating or fail to qualify for a cash discount.

Centralizing payments from disbursement accounts maintained at a concentration bank helps minimize the amount of idle funds a firm must keep in local field offices and divisional bank accounts. A number of firms have set up *zero-balance* systems to use disbursement float more effectively. In a zero-balance system a *master,* or *concentration, account* is set up to receive all deposits coming into the zero-balance system. As checks clear through the zero-balance accounts on which they are issued, funds are transferred to these accounts from the master account. These disbursement accounts are called zero-balance accounts because exactly enough funds are transferred into them daily to cover the checks that have cleared, leaving a zero balance at the end of the day. In general, all disbursements for accounts payable, payroll, and whatever other purposes the firm desires are issued from these zero-balance accounts. For a zero-balance system to operate effectively, the firm must have a well-developed network for reporting deposits and disbursements, as well as a close working relationship with its bank.

Drafts A draft is similar to a check, except it is not payable on demand. Instead, when a draft is transmitted to a firm's bank for collection, the bank must present the draft to the firm for acceptance before making payment. Once the draft has been accepted, the firm can deposit the necessary funds to cover the payment.

The use of drafts rather than checks permits a firm to keep smaller balances in its disbursement accounts, since funds do not have to be deposited in them until the drafts are presented for payment. Normally,

Figure 19-7

Cash Disbursement Process

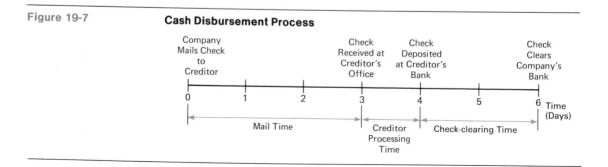

drafts are more expensive to use than checks. However, the lower account balances and higher processing costs cause banks to impose service charges on firms using drafts; this cost must be included in the analysis of the benefits and costs of using drafts to pay bills.

Maximizing Check-clearing Float Some firms make payments to suppliers from checking accounts located a long distance from the supplier. For example, an East Coast supplier might be paid with checks drawn on a West Coast bank. This increases the time required for the check to clear through the banking system.

Investing in Marketable Securities

Rather than let their cash reserves build up in excess of daily cash requirements, many firms invest in interest-bearing short-term marketable securities. Given the higher interest rates (and yields) of recent years, firms have become much more conscious of the sizable opportunity costs (that is, lost income) of idle cash balances. Determining the level of liquid assets that should be invested in marketable securities depends on several factors, including these:

- The interest to be earned over the expected holding period.
- The transaction costs involved in buying and selling the securities.
- The variability of the firm's cash flows.

Various quantitative models have been developed for determining the optimal division of a firm's liquid asset balance between cash and marketable securities.[9] These models vary in complexity, depending partly on the assumptions made about the firm's cash flows. The simpler *deterministic* models assume that cash payments occur at a *uniform certain rate* over time. The more complex *probabilistic* or *stochastic* models assume that cash balances fluctuate from day to day in a *random* or unpredictable manner. While these models provide the financial manager with useful insights into the cost tradeoffs that are involved in effective cash management, they have not been widely implemented in actual decision-making situations.

Choosing Marketable Securities

A firm may choose among many different types of securities when deciding where to invest excess cash reserves. In determining which securities to include in its portfolio, the firm should consider a number of criteria, including the following:

- Default risk.
- Marketability.
- Maturity date.
- Rate of return.

Each of these is discussed in this section.

---

[9] Inventory models were first applied to cash management by William J. Baumol in "The Transactions Demand for Cash: An Inventory Theoretic Approach," *Quarterly Journal of Economics* 66 (Nov. 1952): 545–556. See Dileep R. Mehta, *Working Capital Management,* Englewood Cliffs, N.J.: Prentice-Hall, 1974, chap. 6, for a further discussion of cash management models.

Default Risk   Most firms only invest in marketable securities that have little or no default risk. U.S. Treasury securities have the lowest default risk, followed by securities of other U.S. government agencies and, finally, by corporate and municipal securities. Various financial reporting agencies, including Moody's Investors Service and Standard and Poor's, compile and publish information concerning the safety ratings of the various corporate and municipal securities. Given the positive relationship between a security's expected return and risk and the desire to select marketable securities having minimal default risk, the firm has to be willing to accept relatively low expected yields on its marketable securities investments.

Marketability   A firm usually buys marketable securities that can be sold on short notice for a price that is fairly close to the amount paid for them. Thus, there are two dimensions to a security's marketability, or *liquidity*—namely, the time required to sell the security and the price realized from the sale. If a long period of time, a high transaction cost, or a significant price concession is required to dispose of a security, the security has poor marketability and is generally not considered suitable for inclusion in a marketable securities portfolio. Naturally, there is a tradeoff involved here between risk and return. Generally, a highly marketable security has a smaller degree of risk that the investor will incur a loss, and consequently it usually has a lower expected yield than one with limited marketability.

Maturity Date   Firms usually limit their marketable securities purchases to issues that have relatively short maturities. Recall that prices of debt securities decrease when interest rates rise and increase when interest rates fall. For a given change in interest rates, prices of long-term securities fluctuate more widely than short-term securities with equal default risk. Thus, an investor who holds long-term securities is exposed to a greater risk of loss if the securities have to be sold prior to maturity. This is known as *interest rate risk*. For this reason, most firms generally do not buy marketable securities that have more than 180 to 270 days remaining until maturity, and many firms restrict most of their temporary investments to those maturing in less than ninety days. Since the yields on securities with short maturities often are lower than the yields on securities with longer maturities, a firm has to be willing to sacrifice yield to avoid interest rate risk.

Rate of Return   Although the rate of return, or yield, also is given consideration in selecting securities for inclusion in the firm's portfolio, it is less important than the other three criteria just described. The desire to invest in securities that have minimal default and interest rate risk and that are readily marketable usually limits the selection to those having relatively low yields.

Types of Marketable Securities

Firms normally confine their marketable securities investments to "money market" instruments, that is, those high-grade (low default risk) short-term debt instruments having original maturities of one year or less. Money market instruments that are suitable for inclusion in a firm's marketable securities portfolio include U.S. Treasury issues, other Federal agency issues, municipal securities, negotiable certificates of deposit, commercial paper, repurchase agreements, bankers' acceptances, Eurodollar deposits, money market preferred stocks, money market mutual funds, and bank money market accounts. Each of these will be discussed. (In some cases, firms also will use long-term bonds having one year or less remaining to maturity as "marketable" securities and treat them as money market instruments.)

Table 19-2 lists the characteristics and yields of these various money market instruments. As can be seen in the last three columns of the table, yields on these securities vary considerably over time. Yields are a function of a number of factors, including the state of the economy, the rate of inflation, and government monetary and fiscal policies.

United States Treasury Issues United States Treasury Bills are the most popular marketable securities. They are sold at weekly auctions through Federal Reserve Banks and their branches and have standard maturities of ninety-one days, 182 days, and one year. Treasury Bills are issued at a discount and then redeemed for the full face amount at maturity. Once they are issued, Treasury Bills can be bought and sold in the secondary markets through approximately forty government securities dealers. There is a large and active market for Treasury Bills, which means that a firm can easily dispose of them when it needs cash.

The advantages of Treasury issues include short maturities, a virtually default-free status, and ready marketability. Their primary disadvantage lies in the fact that their yields are normally the lowest of any marketable security.

The Treasury also issues notes that have original maturities of from one to seven years and bonds that have maturities over seven years. As these securities approach their maturity dates, they become, in effect, short-term instruments that are then suitable for inclusion in a firm's marketable securities portfolio.

Other Federal Agency Issues A number of Federal government–sponsored agencies issue their own securities, including the "big five"— the Federal Home Loan Bank, the Federal Land Banks, the Federal Intermediate Credit Bank, the Bank for Cooperatives, and the Federal National Mortgage Association. Although each of these agencies guarantees its own securities, they do not constitute a legal obligation on the part of the U.S. government. Nevertheless, most investors consider them to be very low risk securities, and they sell at yields slightly above U.S. Treasury securities but below other money market instruments. Since these securities are traded in the secondary markets through the same dealers who handle U.S. Treasury securities, they are readily marketable should a firm need to dispose of them before maturity.

Municipal Securities State and local governments and their agencies issue various types of interest-bearing securities. Short-term issues are suitable

Table 19-2 Characteristics and Yields of Money Market Instruments

Instrument	Denominations	Maturities	Marketability		Yields* (%) August 1981	October 1985
U.S. Treasury Bills	Various denominations from $10,000 to $1,000,000	91 days, 182 days, 52 weeks	Highly organized secondary market	(3 months) (6 months) (1 year)	15.51 15.52 14.70	7.16 7.33 7.45
Federal agency issues	Numerous denominations from $1,000 to $1,000,000	Wide variation in maturities from several days to more than 10 years	Well-established secondary market for short-term securities of "big five" agencies		—	
Municipal securities	$5,000 to $5,000,000	1 month to 1 year	Not as good as U.S. Treasury and Federal agency issues		—	
Negotiable certificates of deposit	$100,000 to $1,000,000	1 to 18 months	Fairly good secondary market	(1 month) (3 months) (6 months)	17.91 17.96 17.98	7.85 7.88 7.97
Commercial paper	$5,000 to $5,000,000 or more in multiples of $1,000	2 or 3 days to 270 days	Weak secondary market	(1 month) (3 months) (6 months)	17.58 17.23 16.62	7.81 7.80 7.79
Repurchase agreements	Varying amounts; no standard denominations	1 day to several months	Good, since borrower agrees to repurchase securities at a fixed price			
Bankers' acceptances	Varying amounts, depending on the size of the commercial transaction	30 to 180 days	Good, although less extensive than for most other instruments	(3 months) (6 months)	17.22 16.56	7.76 7.75
Eurodollar deposits	Varying amounts	1 day to 6 months (or more)	Good secondary market for Eurodollar CDs issued by London banks	(3 months)	18.79	8.08
Money market preferred stock	$100,000 to $500,000 depending on issue	—	Saleable at auction every 49 days		—	
Money market mutual funds	Minimum of $1,000 is usually required; no standard denominations	Redeemable at any time	Good, since the fund agrees to redeem shares at any time	Yields vary from fund to fund, but they usually exceed the yield available on Treasury Bills.	—	
Bank money market accounts	Minimum of $2,500 required	Normally redeemable at any time (by law, banks reserve the right to require 7 days' written notice for withdrawals)	Good, except in rare instances when a bank might impose a 7-day written notice requirement		—	

*Source: *Federal Reserve Bulletin*, Table 1:35, various issues.

for inclusion in a firm's marketable securities portfolio. The yields on these securities vary with the credit-worthiness of the issuer. The pre-tax yields on these securities are generally lower than the yields on Treasury Bills because the interest is exempt from Federal (and some state) income taxes. The secondary market for municipal issues is not as strong as for Treasury and other federal agency issues.

Negotiable Certificates of Deposit   Commercial banks are permitted to issue certificates of deposit (CDs), which entitle the holder to receive the amount deposited plus accrued interest on a specified date. At the time of issue, maturities on these instruments range from thirty days to eighteen months. Once issued, CDs become *negotiable,* meaning they can be bought and sold in the secondary markets. Since CDs of the largest banks are handled by government securities dealers, they are readily marketable and thus are suitable for inclusion in a firm's marketable securities portfolio. Yields on CDs are generally above the rates on Federal agency issues having similar maturities.

Commercial Paper   Commercial paper consists of short-term unsecured promissory notes that are issued by large, well-known corporations and finance companies. Some finance companies, such as General Motors Acceptance Corporation (GMAC) and C.I.T. Financial Corporation, which issue large amounts of commercial paper regularly, sell it directly to investors. Industrial, utility, and transportation firms and smaller finance companies, which issue commerical paper less frequently and in smaller amounts, sell their commercial paper through commercial paper dealers. Maturities on commercial paper at the time of issue range from two or three days to 270 days.

The secondary market for commercial paper is weak, although it is sometimes possible to make arrangements with the issuer or commercial paper dealer to repurchase the security prior to maturity. This weak secondary market combined with a somewhat higher default risk results in higher yields on commercial paper than on most other money market instruments.

Repurchase Agreements   A repurchase agreement, or "repo," is an arrangement with a bank or securities dealer in which the investor acquires certain short-term securities subject to a commitment from the bank or dealer to repurchase the securities on a specified date. Securities used in this agreement can be government securities, CDs, or commercial paper. Their maturities tend to be relatively short, ranging from one day to several months, and are designed to meet the needs of the investor.

The yield on a repo is slightly less than the rate that can be obtained from outright purchase of the underlying security. The repo rate approximates the rate on Federal funds, which is the rate used when banks borrow from other banks. While repos are generally considered very safe investments, a number of investors did incur losses when several small government securities dealers (which were active in the repo market) failed.

Bankers' Acceptances A bankers' acceptance is a short-term debt instrument issued by a firm as part of a commercial transaction. Payment is guaranteed by a commercial bank. Bankers' acceptances are commonly used financing instruments in international trade, as well as in certain lines of domestic trade.

These instruments vary in amount, depending on the size of the commercial transactions. A secondary market exists in which these acceptances can be traded should a bank or investor choose not to hold them until maturity, which usually ranges between thirty and 100 days at the time of issue. Bankers' acceptances are relatively safe investments, since both the bank and the borrower are liable for the amount due at maturity. Their yields are comparable to the rate available on CDs.

Eurodollar Deposits Eurodollar deposits are dollar denominated deposits in banks or bank branches located outside the United States. These deposits usually have slightly higher yields than on corresponding deposits in domestic banks because of the additional risks. Eurodollar CDs issued by London banks are negotiable and an active secondary market exists for them.

Money Market Preferred Stocks In 1984, Shearson Lehman (a large brokerage firm) began issuing, on behalf of some of its client companies, a new type of preferred stock, known as money market preferred, which is a suitable short-term investment for excess corporate funds. The dividend yield on this type of security is adjusted every forty-nine days through an auction process, where investors can exchange their stock for cash. As a result, the price of the stock stays near par. Since 85 percent (80 percent beginning in 1987) of the dividends are exempt from corporate income taxes, the after-tax yields are often above the yields on other marketable securities such as CDs or commercial paper. The stock is sold in minimum denominations of $100,000 to $500,000, depending on the issue. Since its original introduction, other investment bankers have also begun offering similar auction rate preferred stock.

Money Market Mutual Funds Many of the higher yielding marketable securities described above are only available in relatively large denominations. For example, negotiable CDs usually come in amounts of $100,000 or more. As a result, a smaller firm that has limited funds to invest at any given time is often unable to obtain the higher yields offered on these securities. An alternative is a *money market mutual fund* that pools the investments of many other small investors and invests in large-denomination money market instruments. By purchasing shares in a money market fund, such as Dreyfus Liquid Assets or Merrill Lynch Ready Assets, a smaller firm can approach the higher yields offered on large-denomination securities. In addition, most of these funds offer limited check-writing privileges, which providers liquidity and enables firms to earn interest on invested funds until their checks clear.

Bank Money Market Accounts Early in 1983 banks were permitted to offer checking accounts with yields comparable to those on money market mutual accounts with limited check-writing privileges. These accounts provide yields that are comparable to those on money market mutual funds.

Summary

- A firm holds liquid asset balances for the following primary reasons:

  1. To conduct transactions.
  2. For precautionary purposes.
  3. To meet future requirements.
  4. To compensate its bank or banks for various services rendered.

- To manage cash effectively, a firm must first develop a *cash budget* showing all of the forecasted cash inflows and outflows over the planning horizon.

- A firm's optimal liquid asset balance depends on both the opportunity cost of holding excess balances and the "shortage" costs associated with not having enough needed cash available.

- The primary objective in controlling cash collections is to reduce the delay between the time when the customer mails the payment and when it becomes a collected balance. Methods for reducing collection time include decentralized collection centers and concentration banks, lockboxes, wire transfers, depository transfer checks, special handling of large remittances, and the use of preauthorized checks.

- The primary objective in controlling cash disbursements is to slow payments and keep the firm's funds in the bank as long as possible. Techniques for slowing disbursements include scheduling and centralizing payments (zero-balance systems), using drafts rather than checks, and maximizing check clearing float.

- The primary criteria a firm should use in selecting *marketable securities* include *default risk, marketability* (or *liquidity*), *maturity date,* and *rate of return.* The most commonly used marketable securities include U.S. Treasury issues, other Federal agency issues, municipal securities, negotiable certificates of deposit, commercial paper, repurchase agreements, bankers' acceptances, Eurodollar deposits, money market preferred stocks, money market funds, and bank money market accounts.

FOCUS ON CORPORATE PRACTICE

Multilateral Netting System

Theodore M. Mertz
Senior Vice President and
Global Cash Management Group Head
Mellon Bank

Mellon Bank has developed a multilateral netting system to streamline the intra-company payment process of a multinational manufacturing company with over 20 subsidiaries in 15 countries, all operating with different currencies. This multilateral netting system is accessible from virtually anywhere in the world and gives the company an efficient and cost-effective method to offset payments between its subsidiaries.

The system is set up with Mellon's London branch as the netting center that clears all intracompany payments. Each month subsidiaries electronically communicate information regarding their intracompany payables via Telecash®, Mellon's proprietary electronic reporting system. Included are the payee numbers, amounts, and any reference which can be used in reconciliation. The netting center also enters the foreign exchange rates into the system. These rates are then used to calculate each subsidiary's net cash position in its local currency.

Subsidiaries can access information on their payables, receivables, and net position via on-line Telecash reports. The parent company and its regional headquarters also can monitor company-wide positions. When positions have been finalized, net payers transfer their funds in local currency to one of Mellon's correspondent banks located in their country. The bank's foreign exchange traders at the netting center then purchase the foreign exchange and transfer the funds to the net payees, also in their local currency. Thus, all subsidiaries maintain their own banking relationships and deal only with their own local currency.

The company's use of multilateral netting has controlled float, lowered fund transfer and foreign exchange costs, and reduced the administration overload. In addition, the company has gained better control over its cash management functions.

Question and Topics for Discussion

1. Define the following terms:
   a. Demand deposits.
   b. Compensating balance.
   c. Disbursement float.
   d. Deposit float.
   e. Lockbox.
   f. Wire transfer.
   g. Depository transfer check.
   h. Zero-balance system.
   i. Draft.

2. What are the primary reasons why a firm holds a liquid asset balance?

3. Describe the cost tradeoffs associated with maintaining the following:
   a. Excessive liquid asset balances.
   b. Inadequate liquid asset balances.

4. Define *float* and describe the difference between *disbursement* float and *deposit* float.

5. Describe the primary services a bank provides to a firm. How is the bank compensated for these services?

6. Describe the methods available to a firm for expediting the collection of cash.

7. Describe the techniques available to a firm for slowing disbursements.

8. Explain the tradeoffs involved in determining the number of collection centers that a firm should use.

9. What factors should the firm consider in deciding whether or not to establish a lockbox collection system?

10. What are the primary criteria in selecting marketable securities for inclusion in a firm's portfolio?

11. What types of marketable securities are most suitable for inclusion in a firm's portfolio? What characteristics of these securities make them desirable investments for temporarily idle cash balances?

Problems*

Note: When converting annual data to daily data or vice versa in these exercises, assume there are 360 days per year.

1. Dexter Instrument Company's sales average $3.0 million per day.
   a. If Dexter could reduce the time between customers' mailing their payments and the funds' becoming collected balances by 2.5 days, determine the increase in firm's average cash balance.
   b. Assuming that these additional funds can be invested in marketable securities to yield 8.5 percent per annum, determine the annual increase in Dexter's (pretax) earnings.

2. Exman Company performed a study of its billing and collection procedures and found that an average of 8 days elapses between the time when a customer's payment is received and when the funds become usable by the firm. The firm's *annual* sales are $540 million.
   a. Assuming that Exman could reduce the time required to process customer payments by 1.5 days, determine the increase in the firm's average cash balance.
   b. Assuming that these additional funds could be used to reduce the firm's outstanding bank loans (current interest rate is 8 percent) by an equivalent amount, determine the annual pretax savings in interest expenses.

---

* Color numbers denote problems which have check answers provided at the end of the book.

3. Great Lakes Oil Company currently processes all its credit card payments at its domestic headquarters in Chicago. The firm is considering establishing a lockbox arrangement with a Los Angeles bank to process its payments from ten western states (California, Nevada, Arizona, Utah, Oregon, Washington, Montana, Wyoming, Colorado, and Idaho). Under the arrangement, the average mailing time for customer payments from the western region would be reduced from 3.0 days to 1.5 days, whereas check-processing and clearing time would be reduced from 6.0 days to 2.5 days. Annual collections from the western region are $180 million. The total number of payments received annually is 4.8 million (an average of 400,000 credit card customers × 12 payments per year). The Los Angeles bank will process the payments for an annual fee of $75,000 plus $0.05 per payment. No compensating balance will be required. Assume that the funds released by the lockbox arrangement can be invested elsewhere in the firm to yield 10 percent before taxes. The establishment of a lockbox system for the western region will reduce payment-processing costs at the Chicago office by $50,000 per year. Using this informtion, determine the following:

   a. The amount of funds released by the lockbox arrangement.
   b. The annual (pretax) earnings on the released funds.
   c. The annual fee Great Lakes Oil must pay to the Los Angeles bank for processing the payments.
   d. The annual *net* (pretax) benefits Great Lakes Oil will receive by establishing this lockbox arrangement with the Los Angeles bank.

4. Great Lakes Oil (see Problem 3) also has received a proposal from a Salt Lake City bank to set up a lockbox system for the firm. Average mailing time for checks in the western region would be reduced to 2 days under the proposal from the Salt Lake City bank, and check-processing and clearing time would also average 2.5 days. The Salt Lake City bank would not charge any fees for processing the payments, but it would require Great Lakes Oil to maintain a $1,500,000 average compensating balance with the bank—funds that normally would be invested elsewhere in the firm (yielding 10 percent) and not kept in a noninterest-bearing checking account.

   a. Determine the annual *net* (pretax) benefits to Great Lakes Oil of establishing a lockbox system with the Salt Lake City bank.
   b. Which of the two lockbox systems (if any) should the firm select?

5. Japanese Motors, a major importer of foreign automobiles, has a subsidiary (Japanese Motor Credit Company, or JMCC) that finances dealer inventories, as well as retail installment purchases of the company's cars. With respect to the financing of retail purchases, JMCC currently employs a centralized billing and collection system. Once a customer's credit has been approved at one of the subsidiary's 50 local branch offices, the information is forwarded to JMCC headquarters (located in Los Angeles), and the customer is issued a book of payment coupons. Each month during the life of the installment contract, the customer mails a coupon stub along with the payment to the Los Angeles office. The average mailing, processing, and check-clearing time with the present collection system is 8 days.

   In an effort to reduce this collection time, JMCC is considering establishing a decentralized collection system. Under this system customers would be instructed to mail their payments to the nearest local branch office, which would then deposit the checks in a local bank and report this information to JMCC headquarters in Los Angeles. As the checks cleared in the local banks, funds would be sent each day to JMCC's central bank in Los Angeles. This decentralized collection system would reduce both mailing time and check-clearing time and reduce the average collection time to 5 days.

JMCC's annual installment collections are $900 million. Implementation of the decentralized collection system is expected to reduce collection costs at the Los Angeles headquarters by $100,000 a year compared with the currently employed centralized collection system. However, branch office collection costs are expected to *rise* by $225,000 if the decentralized system is implemented. JMCC's Los Angeles bank currently requires the firm to maintain a $250,000 balance as compensation for depositing customer payments. Compensating balances at the 50 local banks that JMCC would employ with the decentralized collection system are expected to total $500,000. Any funds released under the decentralized collections system would be used to reduce the firm's debt, which currently carries an interest rate of 7.5 percent.

Using this information, determine the annual *net* pretax benefits JMCC would realize by implementing a decentralized collection system.

6. J-Mart, a nationwide department store chain, processes all its credit sales payments at its suburban Detroit headquarters. The firm is considering the implementation of a lockbox collection system with an Atlanta bank to process monthly payments from its southeastern region. Annual credit sales collections from the region are $60 million. The establishment of the lockbox system would reduce mailing, processing, and check-clearing time from 8 days currently to 3.5 days, reduce company processing costs by $25,000 per year, and reduce the compensating balance of its Detroit bank by $200,000. The Atlanta bank would not charge any fee for the lockbox service but would require J-Mart to maintain a $500,000 compensating balance. Funds released by the lockbox arrangement could be invested elsewhere in the firm to earn 15 percent before taxes. Determine the following:
   a. The amounts of funds released by the lockbox arrangement.
   b. The annual (pretax) earnings on the released funds.
   c. The annual *net* (pretax) benefits to J-Mart of establishing the lockbox system with the Atlanta bank.

7. Peterson Electronics uses a decentralized collection system whereby customers mail their payments to one of six regional collection centers. The checks are deposited each working day in the collection center's local bank, and a depository transfer check for the amount of the deposit is *mailed* to the firm's concentration bank in New York. An average of 5 days elapse between the time the checks are deposited in the local bank and the time the funds become collected funds (and available for disbursements) at the concentration bank. Peterson is considering using wire transfers instead of depository transfer checks in moving funds from the six collection centers to its concentration bank. Wire transfers would reduce the elapsed time *by* 3 days. Depository transfer checks cost $0.50 (including postage), and wire transfers cost $10.00. Assume there are 250 working days per year. Peterson can earn 7 percent before taxes on any funds that are released through more efficient collection techniques. Determine the net (pretax) benefit to Peterson of using wire transfers if annual sales are:
   a. $15 million.
   b. $75 million.

8. Consider problem 7 again. Suppose Peterson is considering using *electronic* depository transfer checks rather than mail depository transfer checks to move funds from its six collection centers to its concentration bank. Electronic depository transfer checks would *reduce* collection time by 2 days and would cost $2.50 each. Determine the net (pretax) benefit to Peterson of using electronic depository transfer checks if annual sales are:
   a. $15 million.
   b. $75 million.

9. Wisconsin Paper Company is considering establishing a zero-balance system for its payroll account. The firm pays its employees every 2 weeks on Friday (that is, 26 pay periods per year). Currently the firm deposits the necessary funds in the payroll account on Friday to cover the total amount of the checks written each pay period, which averages $1 million. However, the firm has found that the majority of the checks did not clear the payroll account until the following week. A typical distribution of when the checks clear the payroll account is as follows:

Day	Amount of Funds Clearing Payroll Account
Friday	$ 300,000
Monday	450,000
Tuesday	150,000
Wednesday	100,000
Total	$1,000,000

Assume that the firm can earn 6 percent on any funds released from its payroll account using a zero-balance system.

a. Determine the annual pretax returns the firm would realize from the use of a zero-balance system for its payroll account.

b. What additional information is necessary to make a decision concerning the desirability of establishing such a system?

10. The High-Rise Construction Company, located in Houston, receives large remittances (that is, progress payments) from customers with whom it has contracts. These checks are frequently drawn on New York City banks. If the checks are deposited in High-Rise's Houston bank, the funds will not become collected balances and usable by the firm until 2 *business* days later. In other words, deposits made on Monday become available for use on Wednesday, and deposits made on Friday become available to the firm on the following Tuesday. However, if High-Rise sends an employee to New York with the check and she presents it for payment at the bank upon which it is drawn, the funds will be available immediately (that is, the same day) to the firm. Assuming that High-Rise can earn 6 percent on short-term investments and that the cost of sending an employee to New York to present the check for payment is $350, determine the following:

a. The net (pretax) benefit to the firm of using this special handling procedure for a $1 million check received on the following days:

    i. Monday.
    ii. Friday.

Why do the answers to Parts i and ii differ?

b. The amount of a check on which the firm just "breaks even" (that is, the net pretax benefit equals zero) using the special handling procedure, assuming that the check is received on the following days:

    i. Monday.
    ii. Friday.

11. Jackson's Thriftway currently processes all of its credit sales at its Seguin, Texas, headquarters. The firm is considering establishing a lock-box arrangement with a Chicago bank to process payments from customers in 12 midwestern states. Average mailing time for customers from this region is currently 4 days. It is expected that the system will reduce this to 2.5 days. Check processing and clearing time would be reduced from 4 days to 1.5 days with the lock-box arrangement. Annual collections from this region are

$200 million. The lock-box arrangement would reduce the compensating balance requirement at the firm's Seguin bank by $400,000 and reduce annual payment processing costs at the Seguin office by $25,000. Funds released by the lock-box arrangement can be invested elsewhere in the firm to earn 14 percent before taxes.

a. The Chicago bank has agreed to process Jackson's customer payments for an annual fee of $130,000. Determine the annual net pre-tax benefits to Jackson's of establishing a lock-box system with the Chicago bank.

b. The Chicago bank has agreed to process Jackson's customer payments "free of charge" if the firm maintains a minimum compensating balance of $2,000,000 in its account at the bank. Determine the annual net pre-tax benefits to Jackson's of establishing the lock-box system under these conditions.

Selected References

Batlin, C. A., and Susan Hinko. "Lockbox Management and Value Maximization." *Financial Management* 10 (Winter 1981): 39–44.

Driscoll, Mary C. *Cash Management: Corporate Strategies for Profit.* New York: Wiley, 1983.

Hartley, W. C. F., and Yale L. Meltzer. *Cash Management.* Englewood Cliffs, NJ: Prentice-Hall, 1979.

Kallberg, Jarl G., and Kenneth Parkinson. *Current Asset Management.* New York: Wiley, 1984.

Maier, Steven F., and James H. Vander Weide. "What Lockbox and Disbursement Models Really Do." *Journal of Finance* (May 1983): 361–371.

Morris, James R. "The Role of Cash Balances in Firm Valuation." *Journal of Financial and Quantitative Analysis* (December 1983): 533–545.

Nauss, Robert M., and Robert E. Markland. "Solving Lockbox Location Problems." *Financial Management* 8 (Spring 1979): 21–31.

Smith, Keith V. *Readings on the Management of Working Capital,* 2d ed. St. Paul, MN: West Publishing Company, 1980.

Stone, Bernell K. "The Design of a Company's Banking System." *Journal of Finance* (May 1983): 373–385.

20

THE MANAGEMENT OF ACCOUNTS RECEIVABLE

A Financial Dilemma

Examples of Credit Management Practices

The *principles* of credit management apply uniformly to virtually all businesses, but actual credit management *practices* vary widely from industry to industry and from company to company.

Consider the credit management policies and practices of Sysco Corporation, the largest distributor of food service products in the United States. Sysco's fiscal 1985 revenues totaled $2.63 billion and its accounts receivable balance at the end of the 1985 fiscal year was $188 million. From these figures, an average collection period of about twenty five days is calculated. This twenty five-day figure is relatively low, but Sysco, which derives 55 percent of its food service revenues from restaurants, requires prompt payment from its customers. Sysco's 1985 Annual Report states that its policy is "to provide its customers with quality products as preferred, delivered in excellent condition and on time, and reflecting the quest for ever-improved efficiencies at reasonable prices." The company does not desire to also serve as a financier for its customers.

Consider also Digital Equipment Corporation (DEC), the second largest computer manufacturer in the United States, with fiscal 1985 operating revenues of $6.69 billion. DEC's average collection period at the end of its 1985 fiscal year was seventy-five days. DEC apparently allows its customers and distributors relatively long time periods in which to make payments. Also, 40 percent of DEC's 1985 operating revenues came from outside the United States. Generally, international accounts receivable have a higher average collection period than domestic receivables, due in part to the increased documentation processing required in international transactions.

This chapter discusses a company's credit-granting decision. It details the principles of a sound credit policy and provides the analytical tools necessary to evaluate proposed changes in this policy.

Key Chapter Concepts

1. *Accounts receivable management* refers to the decisions a business makes regarding its overall credit and collection policies and the evaluation of individual credit applicants.
2. In formulating an optimal credit policy, a company's financial managers must analyze the marginal benefits and costs associated with changes in each of the following variables:
   a. Credit standards.
   b. Credit terms.
   c. Collection efforts.
3. The evaluation of individual credit applicants consists of the following three principal steps:
   a. Gathering relevant information on the credit applicant.
   b. Analyzing the information obtained to determine the applicant's credit-worthiness.
   c. Deciding whether to extend credit to the applicant and, if so, determining the amount of the line of credit.

Glossary of New Terms

Bad-debt loss ratio The proportion of the total receivables volume that is never collected by a business.

Cash discount A discount offered for early payment of an invoice.

Credit period The length of time a credit customer has to pay the account in full.

Discount period The length of time a credit customer has to pay the account and still be eligible to take any cash discount which is offered.

Seasonal datings Credit terms under which the buyer of seasonal merchandise is encouraged to take delivery well before the peak sales period. Payment on the purchase is deferred until after the peak sales period.

Introduction

*A*ccounts receivable consist of the credit a business grants its customers when selling goods or services. They take the form of either *trade* credit, which the company extends to other companies, or *consumer credit,* which the company extends to its ultimate consumers.

Although somewhat less liquid than either cash or marketable securities, accounts receivable constitute a major current asset for most businesses.[1] Table 18-1 in Chapter 18 shows that accounts receivable make up nearly 16 percent of the total assets of manufacturing companies and nearly 25 percent of the total assets of companies engaged in wholesale trade.

For a business to grant credit to its customers, it has to do the following:

- Establish credit and collection policies.
- Evaluate individual credit applicants.

As we will see in this chapter, the success of a company's credit policies can have a significant impact on its total performance. For example, Monsanto's credit manager has estimated that a one-day reduction in the average collection period for the company's receivables increases its cash flow by $10 million and improves profits by $1 million.

Some companies use their accounts receivable to obtain short-term financing. Suppose a company is somewhat weak financially. It is likely that the company cannot borrow short-term funds without putting up collateral for the loan. Frequently the company uses its accounts receivable as the collateral by *pledging* them to the bank. Alternatively the company can consider selling, or *factoring,* its accounts receivable to obtain cash. Because accounts receivable pledging and factoring pertain to short-term financing, they are discussed in detail in Chapter 22.

Establishing Credit and Collection Policies

When a company decides to extend credit to customers, it essentially is making an investment decision, namely, an investment in accounts receivable.[2] Like the decision to invest in any other type of asset, the establishment of an *optimal credit extension policy* requires the company to examine and attempt to measure the *marginal costs* and *marginal returns* (benefits) associated with a number of alternative policies. Also, as in any other investment decision, the primary goal of accounts receivable management should be to maximize shareholder wealth. Therefore, a company should be willing to increase its investment in accounts receivable as long as the expected marginal returns obtained from each additional dollar of receivables investment exceed the associated expected marginal costs of the investment.

---

[1] *Liquidity* refers to the ease and speed with which an asset can be converted into cash—the most liquid of all assets—without a significant price concession.

[2] From the *customer's* perspective, credit represents a form of short-term financing known as *accounts payable*. This is discussed in more detail in Chapter 22. Considering it in yet another way—specifically, in the context of the *sources and uses of funds* statement—credit represents a *use* of funds by the selling company and a *source* of funds to its customers. (See Chapter 8 for a review of this topic.)

What are the marginal returns and costs associated with a more liberal extension of credit to a company's customers? With respect to returns, a more liberal extension presumably stimulates sales and leads to increased gross profits, assuming that all other factors (such as economic conditions, prices, production costs, and advertising expenses) remain constant. Offsetting these increased returns are several types of credit-related marginal costs, including the opportunity costs of the additional capital funds that are employed to support the higher level of receivables. Checking new credit accounts and collecting the higher level of receivables also results in additional costs. And finally, a more liberal credit policy frequently results in increased bad-debt expenses, since a certain number of new accounts are likely to fail to repay the credit that is extended to them.

In determining an optimal credit extension policy, a company's financial managers must consider a number of major controllable variables that can be used to alter the level of receivables, including the following:

- Credit standards.
- Credit terms.
- Collection effort.

Each of these is discussed in the sections that follow.

Credit Standards

Credit standards are the criteria a company uses to screen credit applicants in order to determine which of its customers should be offered credit, and how much. The process of setting credit standards allows the firm to exercise a degree of control over the "quality" of accounts accepted.[3] The quality of credit extended to customers is a multidimensional concept involving the following:

- The time a customer takes to repay the credit obligation, *given that it is repaid.*
- The probability that a customer will fail to repay the credit extended to it.

The *average collection period* serves as one measure of the promptness with which customers repay their credit obligations. It indicates the average number of days a company must wait after making a credit sale before receiving the customer's cash payment. Obviously, the longer the average collection period, the higher a company's receivables investment and, by extension, its cost of extending credit to customers.

The likelihood that a customer will fail to repay the credit extended to it is sometimes referred to as *default risk.* The *bad-debt loss ratio,* which is the proportion of the total receivables volume a company never collects, serves as an overall, or aggregate, measure of this risk. A business can estimate its loss ratio by examining losses on credit that has been extended

---

[3] *Complete* control over the quality of accounts accepted is generally impossible due to uncertainty about future events (for example, a recession or a strike) that could make it difficult or even impossible for a customer to repay its account.

to similar types of customers in the past.[4] The higher a firm's loss ratio, the greater the cost of extending credit.

For example, the Westchester Furniture Company, a furniture manufacturer, is considering making a change in its credit standards. Before reaching any decision, the company must first determine whether such a change would be profitable. The first step in making this decision involves an evaluation of the overall credit-worthiness of the company's existing and potential customers (retailers) using various sources of information.[5] Table 20-1 illustrates the credit sales, average collection period, and loss ratio data for various credit risk groups of the company's customers.

Under its current credit policy, Westchester extends unlimited credit to all customers in Credit Risk Groups 1, 2, and 3 and no credit to customers in Groups 4 and 5, meaning that the customers in these latter two groups must submit payment along with their orders. As a result of this policy, Westchester estimates that is "loses" $300,000 per year in sales from Group 4 customers and $100,000 per year in sales from Group 5 customers.

Westchester also estimates that its *variable* production, administrative, and marketing costs (including credit department costs) are approximately 75 percent of total sales;[6] that is, the *variable cost ratio* is 0.75. Thus, the profit contribution ratio per dollar of sales is as follows:

$$1.00 - 0.75 = 0.25.$$

The company's required pretax rate of return (that is, the opportunity cost) on its receivables investment is 20 percent.

One alternative Westchester is considering is to relax credit standards by extending full credit to Group 4 customers. In evaluating this alterna-

---

Table 20-1   **Credit Evaluation Data Compiled by the Westchester Furniture Company**

Credit Risk Group	Credit Sales ($)	Average Collection Period (Days)	Bad-Debt Loss Ratio (%)
1	900,000	25	—
2	1,100,000	30	0.5
3	400,000	45	3
4	300,000*	60	7
5	100,000*	90	13

*Estimated lost sales due to the fact that no credit is extended to customers in these risk categories.

---

[4] This estimation procedure assumes that the loss ratio does not change significantly over time because of changing economic conditions. Otherwise, the loss ratio should be adjusted to take account of expected future economic changes. This procedure also assumes that credit extension and repayment information is available on a sufficiently large sample of accounts to provide a company with a reliable estimate of its loss ratio. Without this information, the financial manager simply has to make an "educated guess" as to the size of the loss ratio.

[5] Some of these sources of information are described later in this chapter.

[6] This analysis assumes that the collection costs for Credit Risk Group 4 customers are the same as for customers in the other groups and are included in credit department costs.

tive, the financial manager has to analyze how this policy would affect pretax profits. If the marginal returns of this change in credit standards exceed the marginal costs, pretax profits would increase, and the decision to extend full credit to the Group 4 customers would be a good one.

Table 20-2 contains the results of this analysis. In Step A, the marginal profitability of the additional sales is calculated. Next, the cost of the additional investment in receivables is calculated in Step B.[7] In Step C, the additional bad-debt loss is computed. Finally, in Step D, the net change in pretax profits is determined by deducting the marginal costs computed in Steps B and C from the marginal returns found in Step A. Since this net change is a positive $44,000, the analysis indicates that Westchester should relax its credit standards by extending full credit to the Group 4 customers. (However, in actual practice a company should recheck carefully the accuracy of its estimates before implementing a decision of this type.)

This analysis contains a number of both explicit and implicit assumptions of which the financial manager must also be aware. One assumption is that *the company has excess capacity* and thus could produce the additional output at a *constant variable cost ratio* of 0.75. If the company currently is operating at or near full capacity, and additional output could be obtained only by paying more costly overtime rates and/or investing in new facilities, this analysis would have to be modified to take account of these incremental costs. This analysis also assumes that the average collection period of the customers in Groups 1, 2, and 3 would *not increase* once the company began extending credit to Group 4 customers. If it became known that the Group 4 customers had 60 days or more to pay their bills with no penalty involved, the Group 1, 2, and 3 customers, who normally pay their bills promptly, might also start delaying their payments. If this occurred, the analysis would have to be modified to account for such shifts. It was also assumed that the required rate of

---

[7] Note that we have chosen to use sales value in determining the (opportunity) cost of the additional receivables investment. Disagreement exists in the finance literature concerning the measurement of the incremental investment in accounts receivable (and its associated opportunity cost) arising from a change in credit standards. Some authors contend that the relevant measure of investment is the dollar *cost* the firm has tied up in the new accounts receivable rather than the total *sales value*. The rationale for this approach is that the "profit" on the sale—that is, the difference between the amount of the accounts receivable and their associated cost—would be nonexistent without the change in credit standards. Hence, no opportunity cost is incurred on this uncollected "profit." Advocates of this approach use variable cost or total cost as a measure of the amount of funds invested in accounts receivable. Other authors claim that the total sales value of the new accounts receivable is indeed the relevant measure of investment in accounts receivable. The rationale for this approach is that the opportunity cost of the increased level of accounts receivable is the return a company could earn if it reduced accounts receivable back to its original level. In other words, considerations of symmetry require that the opportunity cost of increasing accounts receivable by a given amount should be equal to the returns that could be earned on the funds released from decreasing accounts receivable by the same amount. The interested reader should consult the following references for a more complete discussion of the issues involved: John S. Oh, "Opportunity Cost in the Evaluation of Investment in Accounts Receivable," *Financial Management* 5 (Summer 1976): 32–35; Edward A. Dyl, "Another Look at the Evaluation of Investment in Accounts Receivable," *Financial Management* 6 (Winter 1977): 67–70; Joseph C. Atkins and Yong H. Kim, "Comment and Correction: Opportunity Cost in the Evaluation of Investment in Accounts Receivable," *Financial Management* 6 (Winter 1977): 71–74; Tirlochan S. Walia, "Explicit and Implicit Cost of Changes in the Level of Accounts Receivable and the Credit Policy Decision of the Firm," *Financial Management* 6 (Winter 1977): 75–80; and J. Fred Weston and Pham D. Tuan, "Comment on Analysis of Credit Policy Changes," *Financial Management* 9 (Winter 1980): 59–63.

Table 20-2

Westchester Furniture Company's Analysis of the Decision to Relax Credit Standards by Extending Full Credit to Customers in Credit Risk Group 4

Step A. Additional sales $300,000

Marginal profitability of additional sales
= Profit contribution ratio × Additional sales
= 0.25 × $300,000 $75,000

Step B. Additional investment in receivables
= Additional average daily sales* × Average
   collection period

$$= \frac{\text{Additional annual sales}}{360} \times 60$$

$$= \frac{\$300,000}{360} \times 60$$ $ 50,000

Cost of the additional investment in receivables
= Additional investment in receivables
   × Required pretax rate of return
= 50,000 × 0.20 $10,000

Step C. Additional bad-debt loss
= Bad-debt loss ratio × Additional sales
= 0.07 × $300,000 $21,000

Step D. Net change in pretax profits
= Marginal returns − Marginal costs
= A − (B + C)
= $75,000 − ($10,000 + $21,000)   +$44,000

*Standard practice is to assume that there are 360 days per year.

return on the investment in receivables for Group 4 *does not change* as a result of extending credit to these more risky accounts. A case can be made for increasing the required rate of return to compensate for the increased risk of the new accounts. Finally, this example (and subsequent examples in this chapter) assumes that *no change* in inventory investment takes place as a result of changes in the firm's credit policies. We should recognize that this assumption may not always be correct; that is, the management of accounts receivable and inventories cannot always be considered independently of each other. Often a higher level of sales, which results from more liberal credit standards, only can occur if a company increases its investment in inventories. In summary, for this type of analysis to be valid and to lead to the correct decision, it must include *all* the marginal costs and benefits that result from the decision.

Credit Terms

A company's *credit terms,* or terms of sale, specify the conditions under which the customer is required to pay for the credit extended to it. These conditions include the *length of the credit period* and the *cash discount* (if any) given for prompt payment plus any special terms, such as *seasonal datings.*

Credit Period Table 20-3 contains some examples of "typical" credit terms offered by various industries. For example, credit terms of "net 30" mean that the customer has 30 days from the invoice date within which to pay the bill and that no discount is offered for early payment. A firm's

Table 20-3   **Typical Credit Terms in Various Industries**

Industry/Product	Credit Terms
Canned goods (general)	1½/10, net 60
Cigars (wholesaler)	Net 7
Decorations (interior)	6/10, net 60
Drugs (manufacturer)	2/10, net 60; 1/10, net 30
Fruits and produce (fresh)	Net 7
Furniture (upholstered)	2/30, net 60; 2/10, net 30
Groceries (wholesaler)	Net 7; C.O.D.; 1/10, net 30
Implements (agricultural)	2/10, net 60 with seasonal dating
Jewelry	5/30, net 4 months
Lumber and building materials (wholesaler)	2/10, net 30
Motors (electric, fractional horsepower)	Net 30
Petroleum (gasoline and lubricating oils)	1/10, net 30
Plumbing and heating (wholesaler)	2/10, net 30
Seeds (vegetable and flower)	1½/10, net 60; 2/10, net 60
Silverware	2/30, net 4 months
Stationery	2/10, net 60
Teas (importer)	3/10, net 4 months
Teas (wholesaler)	2/10, net 120
Textiles (velvet)	6/10, 60 days' dating with dating as of April 15 and October 15

Source: Adapted from Theodore Beckman and Robert Bartels, *Credits and Collections: Management and Theory*, 8th ed., New York: McGraw-Hill, 1969, pp. 697–704. Used with permission of McGraw-Hill Book Company.

credit terms are frequently determined by industry customs, and thus they tend to vary among different industries. The credit period may be as short as 7 days or as long as 6 months. Variation appears to be positively related to the length of time the merchandise is in the purchaser's inventory. For example, manufacturers of goods having relatively low inventory turnover periods such as jewelry, tend to offer retailers longer credit periods than distributors of goods having higher inventory turnover periods, such as food products.

A company's credit terms can affect its sales. For example, if the demand for a particular product depends in part on its credit terms, the company may consider lengthening the credit period to stimulate sales. For example, in 1984 IBM apparently tried to stimulate declining sales of its PCjr home computer by extending the length of the credit period in which dealers had to pay for the computers. In making this type of decision, however, a company also must consider its closest competitors. If they lengthen their credit periods, too, every company in the industry may end up having about the same level of sales, a much higher level of receivables investments and costs, and a lower rate of return.

Analyzing the possible effects of an increase in a company's credit period involves comparing the profitability of the increased sales that are expected to occur with the required rate of return on the additional investment in receivables. Additional bad-debt losses also must be considered. If a company continues to accept the same quality of accounts under its lengthened credit terms, no significant change in the bad-debt loss ratio should occur.

For example, Allied Electric Company, a manufacturer of lighting fixtures, is considering changing its credit terms from "net 30" to "net 60." The company expects sales (all on credit) to increase by about 10 percent from a current level of $2,200,000, and it expects its average collection period to increase from 35 days to 65 days. The bad-debt loss ratio should remain at 3 percent of sales. The company's variable cost ratio is 0.75, which means that its profit contribution ratio (per dollar of sales) is $1.00 - 0.75 = 0.25$. Allied's required pretax rate of return on investments in receivables is 20 percent.

Table 20-4 contains an analysis of Allied's decision. Many of the calculations in this table are similar to those in Table 20-2, which analyzed the effects of a change in credit standards. As in Table 20-2, no account has been taken of any increase in inventory that may be necessary to support this increased level of sales. If inventory investment were increased as a result of this decision, it would be necessary to add an additional cost to the analysis of the effects of a change in credit terms. Specifically, the cost of the additional investment in inventory (computed as the additional inventory investment times the required pretax rate of return) would have to be determined.

The marginal returns ($55,000) computed in Step A represent the marginal profitability of the additional sales generated by the longer credit period. The marginal costs (obtained in Steps B and C) consist of

---

Table 20-4   **Allied Electric Company's Analysis of the Decision to Change Its Credit Terms from "Net 30" to "Net 60"**

Step A. Additional sales
   = Percent increase × Present sales
   = 0.10 × $2,200,000 $220,000
   Marginal profitability of additional sales
   = Profit contribution ratio × Additional sales
   = 0.25 × $220,000 $55,000

Step B. Additional investment in receivables
   = New average balance − Present average balance
   $$= \frac{\text{New annual sales}}{360} \times \text{New average collection period}$$
   $$- \frac{\text{Present annual sales}}{360} \times \text{Present average collection period}$$
   $$= \frac{\$2,200,000 + \$220,000}{360} \times 65 - \frac{\$2,200,000}{360} \times 35$$
   = $436,944 − $213,889 $223,055
   Cost of the additional investment in receivables
   = Additional investment in receivables × Required pretax rate of return
   = $223,055 × 0.20 $44,611

Step C. Additional bad-debt loss
   = Bad-debt loss ratio × Additional sales
   = $220,000 × 0.03 $ 6,600

Step D. Net change in pretax profits
   = Marginal returns − Marginal costs
   = A − (B + C)
   = $55,000 − ($44,611 + $6,600)   +$ 3,789

the cost of the additional receivables investment ($44,611) and the additional bad-debt losses ($6,600). The net increase in pretax profits (Step D) that would result from the decision to lengthen the credit period would be +$3,789. Thus, the decision would appear to be worthwhile.

Cash Discounts   A *cash discount* is a discount offered on the condition that the customer will repay the credit extended within a specified period of time. A cash discount normally is expressed as a percentage discount on the net amount of the cost of goods purchased (usually excluding freight and taxes). The length of the discount period also is specified when discount terms are offered. For example, credit terms of "2/10, net 30" mean that the customer can deduct 2 percent of the invoice amount if payment is made within 10 days from the invoice date. If payment is not made by this time, the full invoice amount is due within 30 days from the invoice date. (In some cases the discount period may begin with the date of shipment or the date of receipt by the customer.) Like the length of the credit period, the cash discount varies among different lines of business.

Cash discounts are offered (or increased) in order to speed up the collection of accounts receivable and, by extension, reduce a company's level of receivables investment and associated costs.[8] Offsetting these savings or benefits is the cost of the discounts that are taken, which is equal to the lost dollar revenues from the existing unit sales volume.

For example, the Galaxy Record Company is considering instituting a cash discount. The company currently sells to record distributors on credit terms of "net 30" and wants to determine the effect on pretax profits of offering a 1 percent cash discount on terms of "1/10, net 30." The company's average collection period is now 50 days and is estimated to decrease to 28 days with the adoption of the 1 percent cash discount policy. It also is estimated that approximately 40 percent of the company's customers will take advantage of the new cash discount. Galaxy's annual credit sales are $2,500,000, and the company's required pretax rate of return on receivables investment is 20 percent.

Table 20-5 contains an analysis of Galaxy's proposed cash discount policy. The marginal returns ($30,556) computed in Step A represent the earnings Galaxy expects to realize on the funds released by the decrease in receivables. The marginal costs ($10,000) found in Step B represent the cost of the cash discount. Subtracting the marginal costs from the marginal returns (Step C) yields a net increase in pretax profits of $20,556, indicating that Galaxy should offer the proposed 1 percent cash discount, if it is confident about the accuracy of the estimates used in this analysis.

Seasonal Datings   Seasonal datings are special credit terms that sometimes are offered to retailers when sales are highly concentrated in one or more periods during the year. Under a seasonal dating credit arrange-

---

[8] The offering of a cash discount also may increase demand and sales, since some potential customers may view it as a form of price cut and be willing to purchase the product at this new, "lower" price. Throughout the ensuing analysis it is assumed that the cash discount is *not* perceived as a price cut and that there is no resulting increase in demand. It is also assumed that offering cash discounts will not reduce bad-debt losses by any measurable amount.

Table 20-5 **Galaxy Record Company's Analysis of the Decision to Offer a 1 Percent Cash Discount**

Step A. Decrease in average receivables balance

= Present average balance − New average balance

$$= \frac{\text{Annual sales}}{360} \times \text{Present average collection period}$$

$$- \frac{\text{Annual sales}}{360} \times \text{New average collection period}$$

$$= \frac{\$2,500,000}{360} \times 50 - \frac{\$2,500,000}{360} \times 28$$

= \$347,222 − \$194,444   \$152,778

Earnings on the funds released by the decrease in receivables

= Decrease in receivables × Required pretax rate of return

= \$152,778 × 0.20   \$30,556

Step B. Cost of cash discount

= Annual sales × Percentage taking discount × Percentage discount

= \$2,500,000 × 0.40 × 0.01   \$10,000

Step C. Net change in pretax profits

= Marginal returns − Marginal costs

= A − B

= \$30,556 − \$10,000   +\$20,556

ment, the retailer is encouraged to order and accept delivery of the product well ahead of the peak sales period and then to remit payment shortly after the peak sales period. The primary objective of seasonal dating is to increase sales to retailers who are unable to finance the buildup of inventories in advance of the peak selling period because of a weak working capital position, limited borrowing capacity, or both.

For example, O.M. Scott and Sons, manufacturers of lawn and garden products, has a seasonal dating plan that is tied to the growing season. Payments for winter and early spring shipments are due at the end of April and May, depending on the geographical area, and payments for shipments during the summer months are due in October or November. Payments for purchases made outside the two main selling seasons are due on the 10th of the second month following shipment. A cash discount of 0.6 percent per month is offered to encourage payments in advance of these seasonal dates. The arrangement enables and encourages dealers of lawn and garden products to be fully stocked with Scott products in advance of the peak selling periods.

Seasonal datings also can be used to reduce the manufacturer's inventory storage costs. With a seasonal sales pattern and a uniform production rate throughout the year, large inventory buildups normally occur prior to each selling period. By encouraging retailers to order in advance of these peak periods, a seasonal dating arrangement reduces these inventory buildups and lowers the manufacturer's warehouse storage costs by passing them on to the retailer. A company considering this type of arrangement, however, should note that seasonal datings will probably not appreciably reduce the required investment. Approximately the same amount of working capital is invested in either case—consisting of receivables investment if seasonal datings are offered and inventory investment if seasonal datings are not offered, Thus, the decision to offer a seasonal dating credit plan involves a comparison of the profitability of the expected increased sales plus any savings in inventory investment and warehouse storage costs versus the required return on the additional investment in receivables.

Collection Effort

The collection effort consists of the methods a business employs in attempting to collect payment on past-due accounts. Some commonly used methods include the following:

- Sending notices or letters informing the customer of the past-due status of the account and requesting payment.
- Telephoning and/or visiting the customer in an effort to obtain payment.
- Employing a collection agency.
- Taking legal action against the customer.

Another approach, which is also effective in some cases, is for the firm to refuse to make new shipments to the customer until the past-due bills are paid. While the objectives of the collection effort are to speed up past-due payments and reduce bad-debt losses, a company also must avoid antagonizing normally credit-worthy customers who may be past due for some good reason—for example, because of temporary liquidity problems. A collection effort that is too aggressive may reduce future sales and profits if customers begin buying from other businesses whose collection policies are more lenient.

When determining which methods to use in its collection effort, a company has to consider the amount of funds it has available to spend for this purpose. If the firm has a relatively small amount of money available for collecting past-due accounts, it must confine itself to less costly (and less effective) methods, such as sending letters and making telephone calls. If it has a larger budget, the firm can employ more aggressive (and, it is hoped, more effective) procedures, such as sending out representatives to personally contact past-due customers. In general, the larger a company's collections expenditures, the shorter its average collection period and the lower its level of bad-debt losses. The benefits of additional collection efforts, however, are likely to diminish rapidly at extremely high expenditure levels.

The marginal benefits of the decision to increase collection expenditures consist of the earnings on the funds released from the receivables investment as a result of the shorter average collection period, plus the reduction in bad-debt losses. A business should increase its collection expenditures only if these marginal benefits are expected to exceed the amount of the additional collection expenditures.

Monitoring Accounts Receivable

For a company to effectively control its receivables investment, the credit manager must monitor the status and composition of these accounts. An *aging of accounts* is a useful monitoring technique.[9] In an aging analysis, a company's accounts are classified into different categories based on the number of days they are past due. These classifications show both the aggregate amount of receivables and the percentage of the total receivables outstanding in each category. Aging of accounts receivable provides more information than such summary ratios as, for example, the average collection period. Comparing aging schedules at successive points in time (for example, monthly, quarterly, or semiannually) can help the credit manager monitor any changes in the "quality" of the company's accounts.

Evaluating Individual Credit Applicants

Once a company has established its credit and collection policies, it can use them as a basis for evaluating individual credit applicants.[10] In general, the credit evaluation process consists of these main steps:

- Gathering relevant information on the credit applicant.
- Analyzing the information obtained to determine the applicant's credit-worthiness.
- Deciding whether to extend credit to the applicant and, if so, determining the amount of the line of credit.

The credit evaluation process is limited by both time and cost. Often a business may have only a few days—or, in some cases, only a few hours—in which to evaluate a credit request. Delaying this decision too long may result in the loss of a potential customer's order.

The credit evaluation process also is limited by the amount of resources the credit department has. The amount of time and money a company spends on evaluating a customer's request for credit should depend on the size of the losses the company would experience if it made an incorrect decision. These potential losses stem from either denying credit to a credit-worthy customer or offering credit to a customer who is not credit-worthy. The larger the potential losses, the more time and money a business should spend on evaluating the credit applicant.

Gathering Information on the Credit Applicant

Information for evaluating the credit-worthiness of a customer is available from a variety of sources, including the following:

- Financial statements submitted by the customer.
- Credit reporting organizations.
- Banks.
- The company's own prior experience with the customer.

---

[9] Aging schedules also are discussed in Chapter 6.

[10] Once these policies are established, however, they do not have to remain static over time. The credit manger should review them periodically, making appropriate modifications as dictated by changing economic conditions (for example, rising interest rates) or other circumstances.

These sources differ with respect to their costs and the reliability of the information they provide.

Financial Statements A company can ask a credit applicant to supply various kinds of financial information, such as income statements and balance sheets (preferably audited ones), and possibly even a forecasted budget. This information can be used to evaluate the applicant's financial strength—and the applicant's ability to repay credit obligations. Unwillingness on the part of the applicant to supply financial statements may indicate financial weakness and suggest the need for more detailed checking, the outright refusal to extend credit, or both.

Credit Reporting Organizations A number of national and local organizations collect information on the financial position and credit standing of businesses. Other companies and lending institutions that are considering extending credit to a company may obtain information about it from these organizations, usually for a fee. The most widely known organization of this type is Dun and Bradstreet Credit Services, which provides its subscribers with a credit reference book and written credit reports on individual businesses. D&B's reference book is published bimonthly and contains the names and ratings of over three million businesses located in the United States, including manufacturers, wholesalers, retailers, business services, and other types of businesses.

Figure 20-1 is a sample of the type of listing contained in the D&B reference book. The D&B rating, shown in the far right column, consists of two parts—the firm's estimated financial strength and its composite credit appraisal—and is based on the rating system shown in Figure 20-2.

For example, the FF2P rating shown for Farmers Gin & Grain Co., Inc., in Figure 20-1 indicates that the firm has an estimated financial strength, or net worth, of $10,000 to $19,999 (Category FF in Figure 20-2) and a good composite credit appraisal (Category 2 in Figure 20-2). The letter "P" following the listing indicates that a D&B Payment Analysis Report is also available on that company. The ER3 is an

---

Figure 20-1	Sample Listings from the Dun and Bradstreet Reference Book

> **ABBOTT 312 HILL 71**
> 07 24 Farmers Gin & Grain Co Inc.   FF2P
>   326-7300
> 72 12 S And S Co.   ER3P
>   326-7300
> 58x12 Tufts Gilbert & Sons Inc.   --P
>   326-7300
> **ABERFOYLE (SEE WOLFE CITY)**

Source: Reprinted by permission, Dun and Bradstreet Credit Services, Inc.

Figure 20-2

Dun and Bradstreet Rating System

Estimated Financial Strength			Composite Credit Appraisal			
			High	Good	Fair	Limited
5A	$50,000,000	and over	1	2	3	4
4A	$10,000,000 to	$49,999,999	1	2	3	4
3A	1,000,000 to	9,999,999	1	2	3	4
2A	750,000 to	999,999	1	2	3	4
1A	500,000 to	749,999	1	2	3	4
BA	300,000 to	499,999	1	2	3	4
BB	200,000 to	299,999	1	2	3	4
CB	125,000 to	199,999	1	2	3	4
CC	75,000 to	124,999	1	2	3	4
DC	50,000 to	74,999	1	2	3	4
DD	35,000 to	49,999	1	2	3	4
EE	20,000 to	34,999	1	2	3	4
FF	10,000 to	19,999	1	2	3	4
GG	5,000 to	9,999	1	2	3	4
HH	Up to	4,999	1	2	3	4

General Classification based on Estimated Strength and Composite Credit Appraisal

Estimated Financial Strength	Composite Credit Appraisal		
	Good	Fair	Limited
1R $125,000 and over	2	3	4
2R $50,000 to $124,999	2	3	4

Explanation
When the designation "1R" or "2R" appears, followed by a 2, 3 or 4, it is an indication that the Estimated Financial Strength, while not definitely classified, is presumed to be in the range of the ($) figures in the corresponding bracket, and while the Composite Credit Apprasial cannot be judged precisely, it is believed to fall in the general category indicated.

"INV" shown in place of a rating indicates that Dun & Bradstreet is currently conducting an investigation to gather information for a new report. It has no other significance.

"FB" (Foreign Branch). Indicates that the headquarters of this company is located in a foreign country (including Canada). The written report contains the location of the headquarters.

Absence of a Rating -- The Blank Symbol
A blank symbol (--) should not be interpreted as indicating that credit should be denied. It simply means that the information available to Dun & Bradstreet does not permit us to classify the company within our rating key and that further inquiry should be made before reaching a credit decision.

Absence of a Listing
The absence of a listing in the Dun & Bradstreet Business Information File or in the Reference Book is not to be construed as meaning a concern is non-existent or has discontinued business. Nor does it have any other meaning. The letters "NQ" on any written report mean "not listed in the Reference Book." The letters "FBN" on any written report also mean that the business is not listed in the Reference Book and that the headquarters is located in a foreign country.

Employee Range Designation (ER)	Key to Employee Range Designation		
Certain businesses do not lend themselves to a Dun & Bradstreet rating.	**ER 1**	1000 or more	Employees
Instead, reports on these businesses carry an Employee Range	**ER 2**	500-999	Employees
Designation (ER) which is indicative of size based on number of	**ER 3**	100-499	Employees
employees. No other significance should be attached to this	**ER 4**	50- 99	Employees
classification. The ER listings in the Reference Book represent those	**ER 5**	20- 49	Employees
businesses on which there has been subscriber interest in the past year.	**ER 6**	10- 19	Employees
Additional ER Listings are stored and updated in the D&B Business	**ER 7**	5- 9	Employees
Information File.	**ER 8**	1- 4	Employees
	ER N		Not Available

Source: Reprinted by permission, Dun and Bradstreet Credit Services, Inc.

Employee Range designation and indicates that S and S Co.'s number of employees is in the range of 100-499 employees. (See Key to Employee Range Designations in Figure 20-2).

A D&B credit report provides far more detailed information about a company's financial position than the reference book does. Figure 20-3 shows an example of the first page of a credit report for Gorman Manufacturing Co., Inc. The report contains a summary of trade credit payments to existing suppliers, which can be extremely valuable to companies that are considering extending credit to Gorman Manufactur-

Figure 20-3   **Dun and Bradstreet Credit Report for Gorman Manufacturing Co., Inc.**

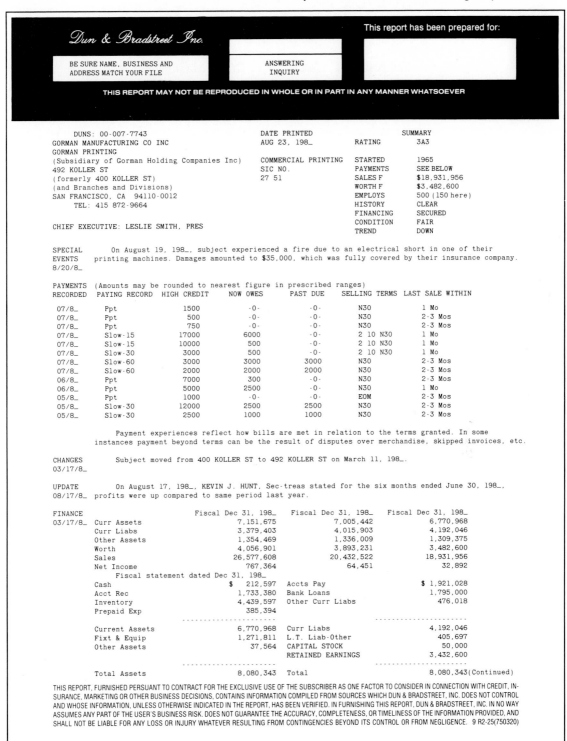

ing Co., Inc. Also included in a typical report are financial data from the firm's balance sheet and income statement, a review of its banking relationships, historical information about the owners, and a description of its operations, including the location of facilities and the kinds of products sold.[11]

The National Association of Credit Management also fills requests for information on the repayment patterns of specific companies. In addition, a number of other organizations collect and disseminate credit information within given industries, such as the toy and furniture industries, as well as within given geographical areas, such as Chicago and New York.

Banks Many banks will assist their business customers in obtaining information on the credit-worthiness of other businesses. Through its contacts with other banks, a customer's bank often can obtain detailed information on the payment patterns and financial status of the company under investigation and pass this information on to a customer.

Prior Experience with the Customer A company's experience with a credit customer can be extremely useful when deciding whether to continue extending credit, increase the amount of credit it currently grants to the customer, or both. If for example the customer tends to remit payments well beyond the due date and/or if the company must employ expensive collection methods in obtaining payments, the credit analyst should weigh this unfavorable information in making the credit extension decision.

Analyzing Credit-worthiness and Making the Credit Decision

Credit analysts ideally should obtain information about an applicant from as many sources as possible, but they also should consider the time and costs involved. Specifically, analysts should weigh the expected returns to be derived from any additional information against the cost involved in obtaining it.

A good way to structure information collection is to proceed *sequentially,* beginning with the least costly and time-consuming sources. If the results of this initial check indicate that more information is needed, the analyst can proceed to additional sources. For example, the analyst may begin by consulting the customer's past credit history with the company. If further information is needed, the analyst then can check the D&B reference book and/or ask the applicant to supply financial statements and a list of companies that have extended trade credit to it in the past. Finally if still more information is needed, the credit analyst can request a D&B credit report on the applicant and/or request credit checks through banks and the applicant's trade creditors.

Because a great deal of information usually is available about a credit applicant, the credit manager must be able to sort through this information and extract the key elements that will enable a reliable overall assessment of the applicant's credit-worthiness to be made. There are no

---

[11] The reliability and comprehensiveness of this type of report depends in part on how willing a business is to supply D&B with pertinent information.

magic formulas for making unerring credit decisions, but there are some traditional guidelines available that can serve as a framework for analysis. These guidelines are called the "five Cs of credit":

- Character.
- Capacity.
- Capital.
- Collateral.
- Conditions.

Character refers to the applicant's willingness or desire to meet credit obligations. Past payment patterns are useful in gauging this aspect of credit-worthiness.

Capacity refers to the applicant's ability to meet financial obligations. A reasonable estimate of an applicant's capacity usually can be obtained by examining its liquidity position and projected cash flows.

Capital constitutes the applicant's financial strength, particularly with respect to net worth. Evidence about a company's capital usually can be obtained by evaluating the balance sheet using financial ratios.

Collateral represents the assets that the applicant may pledge as security for the credit extended to it. However, collateral is seldom a critical consideration, since the primary concern of the company offering trade credit is the timely repayment of the credit, not foreclosing on the pledged assets.

Conditions refer to the general economic climate and its effect on the applicant's ability to pay. A good credit risk in prosperous times might be unable to make payments during a recession.

Many credit analysts feel that the first two Cs, character and capacity, are the most important insofar as they help to insure that the firm considering extending credit will not leave anything important out of the analysis.

Numerical credit scoring systems are another technique that has been found useful, particularly in the area of consumer credit. This technique allows the credit granting business to quantitatively rate various financial and personal characteristics of the applicant, such as the length of the time in business, its D&B credit rating, and its current ratio. The total credit score then can be computed based on the characteristics thought to be related to credit-worthiness. The applicant's credit score next is compared with those of other applicants, or with a minimally acceptable cutoff score. Although numerical credit scoring systems can be beneficial in credit screening, they can be difficult and expensive to install.

Guidelines and techniques such as these can aid in the analysis of an applicant's credit-worthiness; the ability to make sound credit decisions, however, ultimately depends on the decision maker's experience and judgment in evaluating the available information.

Summary

- For a business to extend credit to its customers, it must invest a certain amount of funds in *accounts receivable*.

- A company should change its credit extension policy only if the expected *marginal benefits* of the change will exceed the expected *marginal costs.* A more liberal credit policy normally leads to increased sales and generates marginal benefits in the form of higher gross profits. The marginal costs of this type of policy, however, include the cost of the additional funds invested in accounts receivable, any additional credit checking and collection costs, and increased bad-debt expenses.

- A financial manager can exercise control over the company's level of receivables investment through three credit policy variables: *credit standards, credit terms,* and the *collection effort.* All three variables can be used to control the average collection period and bad-debt loss ratio.

    1. Credit standards are the criteria a business uses to screen its credit applicants.

    2. Credit terms are the conditions under which customers are required to repay the credit extended to them. Credit terms specify the length of the credit period and the cash discount (if any) given for early payment.

    3. The collection effort represents the methods used in attempting to collect payment from past-due accounts.

- Evaluating individual credit applicants involves *gathering information* about the applicant, *analyzing this information* to determine the applicant's credit-worthiness, and then *making the credit decision.*

- The amount of information a business can collect on a credit applicant is limited by both time and cost considerations. In deciding whether to seek more information about an applicant, the credit analyst should weigh the expected returns from more information against the cost of obtaining it.

- Possible sources of relevant information about a credit applicant include financial statements submitted by the applicant, credit reporting organizations (such as Dun and Bradstreet), banks, and the company's own prior experience with the customer.

- The "five Cs of credit," which include *character, capacity, capital, collateral,* and *conditions,* can be used as credit screening guidelines to help insure that a company will consider most of the relevant factors in the analysis and decision-making process.

FOCUS ON CORPORATE PRACTICE

Trade Credit Management at Hiram-Walker

Roy V. Campbell
Corporate Credit Manager
Hiram-Walker

Introduction

Accounts receivable constitutes one of the largest assets on Hiram-Walker's balance sheet. Our receivables represent 15 percent of our total assets. We sell our various brands of liquor and wine to approximately 8,000 customers (wholesalers and distributors) throughout the world,[12] and the quality of this trade credit is most important to our management. Our credit department, which is located in Windsor, Ontario, has overall responsibility for the granting of trade credit, as well as the collection of receivables.

Sources of Credit Information

Hiram-Walker uses various sources of information in evaluating a credit applicant. For example, each applicant is required to complete a Customer Credit Information Form, which requests information concerning the firm's owners and officers, in addition to banking and trade references. The customer also is required to submit financial statements, preferably audited ones. Since we are not always able to get an audited statement from an applicant, in some cases we will settle for one signed by a company officer. We check credit references supplied by the applicant, particularly those from our competitors in the liquor industry. While we also check bank references, banks usually do not provide us with much usable information.

A Dun and Bradstreet report normally is obtained on each credit applicant. Although the *financial* information in these reports is often out of date and not too helpful, the *historical* information on an applicant and its management can be quite useful. Once a company has established credit with us, our sales representatives in the field are an important source of information about any changes in the structure of the company, such as changes in ownership and/or management, that might affect the decision to continue granting credit.

Evaluating the Credit Applicant

Time is of the essence in reaching a decision on whether or not credit should be granted to a customer. Since Hiram-Walker is in a highly competitive industry, lost sales and profits can result if the decision-making process is delayed too long. Much of the checking is done by phone, so we usually can make a decision as soon as we get the customer's financial statements. Typically, the credit granting decision is made within a few days following a request for credit.

One piece of data (from our Customer Credit Information Form) that we consider very important in reaching a decision is the length of time that the customer has been in business. In the past we have found that there is a higher incidence of bankruptcy among more recently established distributors than

[12] In addition to selling to private companies, Hiram-Walker also distributes its product to various government-controlled and/or government-operated enterprises, such as the Pennsylvania State Liquor Control Board, embassies, and military installations.

among older, well-established firms. Standard financial measurements, such as the debt-to-equity ratio and the rate of return on sales, are generally not too useful in evaluating credit applicants. Since many (if not most) liquor distributors are undercapitalized, it is difficult to discriminate among firms with respect to their credit-worthiness on the basis of their debt-to-equity ratios. Also, since more than one-half of liquor distributors' sales represent Federal and state taxes, their rates of return on sales are generally much less than the rates of return earned by firms in other industries. This makes it difficult to determine whether a given credit applicant is earning an "adequate" rate of return on its sales.

In analyzing an applicant's balance sheet, we are primarily concerned with the composition of the firm's debt and the security that has been given for this debt. While banks are the most commonly used source of financing, some distributors obtain financing by factoring their receivables. This indicates to us that the distributor is unable to obtain lower cost bank financing and, by extension, that there may be higher risks involved in extending credit to this customer. Consequently, we are more cautious in extending credit to firms that make extensive use of factoring.

Whenever we find loans payable to the officers of the company on the applicant's balance sheet, it is our policy to require a subordination agreement before extending credit. Such an agreement gives us a priority claim, and hence an added measure of protection, in the event that the distributor is forced into bankruptcy, liquidation, or both. In some instances we may require personal guarantees from the owners and their spouses as a further measure of protection. When a distributor is a subsidiary of a larger company, we often will ask the parent company to guarantee payment of the credit extended to the distributor.

The Uniform Commercial Code limits the extent to which we may use security agreements to protect our receivables. In addition, the Bureau of Alcohol, Tobacco, and Firearms (BATF),[13] whose rules and regulations govern the liquor industry, has ruled informally that security agreements constitute a consignment sale, which is illegal in the industry. Consequently, this credit tool is not available to us in seeking to minimize our risks. In the case of distributors whom we consider high risk, we will give our normal thirty day credit terms provided that they supply us with an irrevocable letter of credit from their bank guaranteeing payment of the account. If they cannot provide such a guarantee, we will only sell to them when their order is accompanied by a certified check.

It is not always possible to judge the credit-worthiness of an applicant based solely on objective factors. Whenever we are planning to grant substantial amounts of credit to a customer, we normally visit their facilities and meet the company's officers, owners, or both. The information obtained from this meeting is used in conjunction with the firm's financial data in making the credit decision.

Evaluating the Performance of the Credit Department

When Hiram-Walker extends credit to customers, we incur costs (that is, interest) on funds invested in receivables, as well as any bad-debt costs that may arise if customers fail to pay for the merchandise shipped to them. In evaluating the performance of our credit department, management is particularly interested in the aging summary of our receivables. The aging summary provides information on the amount of receivables that are delinquent, that is, the amount that has not been paid within the normal thirty-day credit period. This informa-

---

[13]The BATF is part of the Treasury Department of the U.S. government.

tion aids management in determining how good a job our credit department is doing in selecting credit-worthy accounts and collecting the receivables.

Another measure of our credit department's performance is the amount of credit losses (bad debts) incurred. At Hiram-Walker we have been successful in reducing these losses to the point where they are almost insignificant as a percentage of total sales. In a typical year, for example, we might incur losses of $200,000 on sales of over $1 billion.

Questions and Topics for Discussion

1. What are the marginal returns and costs associated with a more liberal extension of credit to a firm's customers?

2. What are the major credit policy variables a firm can use to control its level of receivables investment?

3. Define the following:
   a. Average collection period.
   b. Bad-debt loss ratio.
   c. Aging of accounts.

4. Discuss at least two reasons why a firm might want to offer seasonal datings to its customers.

5. Describe the marginal costs and benefits associated with each of the following changes in a firm's credit and collection policies:
   a. Increasing the credit period from seven to thirty days.
   b. Increasing the cash discount from 1 to 2 percent.
   c. Offering a seasonal dating credit plan.
   d. Increasing collection expenditures (and effort).

6. Describe the three steps involved in evaluating credit applicants.

7. What are the primary sources of information about the credit-worthiness of credit applicants?

8. Describe the "five Cs of credit" used in evaluating the credit-worthiness of a credit applicant.

9. How does a firm's required rate of return on investment enter into the analysis of changes in its credit and collection policies?

10. A firm is currently selling on credit terms of "net 30," and its accounts receivable average 30 days past due (that is, the firm's average collection period is 60 days). What credit policy variables might the firm consider changing to reduce its average collection period?

11. "The objective of the firm's credit and collection policies should be to minimize its bad-debt losses." Do you agree or disagree with this statement? Explain.

12. Discuss how each of the following factors would tend to affect a firm's credit extension policies:
    a. A shortage of working capital.
    b. An increase in output to the point where the firm is operating at full production capacity.
    c. An increase in the firm's profit margin (that is, its profit contribution ratio).
    d. An increase in interest rates (that is, borrowing costs).

Problems*

Note: Assume 360 days per year when converting from annual to daily amounts or vice versa.

1. Miranda Tool Company sells to retail hardware stores on credit terms of "net 30." Annual credit sales are $18 million and are spread evenly throughout the year. The company's variable cost ratio is 0.70, and its accounts receivable average $1.9 million. Using this information determine the following for the company:
   a. Average daily credit sales.

* Color numbers denote problems which have check answers provided at the end of the book.

    b. Average collection period.

    c. Average investment in receivables.

2. Drake Paper Company sells on terms of "net 30." The firm's variable cost ratio is 0.80.

    a. If annual credit sales are $20 million and its accounts receivable average 15 days *overdue,* what is Drake's investment in receivables?

    b. Suppose that, as the result of a recession, annual credit sales decline by 10 percent to $18 million, and customers delay their payments to an average of 25 days *past the due date.* What will be Drake's new level of receivables investment?

3. Looking back at Tables 20-1 and 20-2, evaluate the impact on the Westchester Furniture Company's pretax profits of extending full credit to the customers in Credit Risk Group 5.

4. Once again, consider the Westchester Furniture Company example. Assume that rising labor and interest costs have increased Westchester's variable cost ratio from 0.75 to 0.80 and its required pretax rate of return on receivables investment from 20 to 25 percent. Reevaluate the effect on Westchester's pretax profits of extending full credit to the customers in Credit Risk Group 4.

5. In evaluating the extension of credit to customers in Credit Risk Group 4 in the chapter (Tables 20-1 and 20-2), it was assumed that no increase in inventory investment was required to support the additional $300,000 in annual sales. Suppose instead that an additional inventory investment (that is, raw materials, work-in-process, and finished goods) of $120,000 is required to expand sales by $300,000. Furthermore, assume that Westchester's required (pretax) rate of return on inventory investment is 20 percent. Reevaluate the decision to extend credit to Group 4 customers under these new conditions.

Lotus123

6. Baker Company, a wholesale distributor of jewelry, sells to retail jewelry stores on terms of "net 120." Its average collection period is 150 days. The company is considering the introduction of a 4 percent cash discount if customers pay within 30 days. Such a change in credit terms is expected to reduce the average collection period to 108 days. Baker expects 30 percent of its customers to take the cash discount. Annual credit sales are $6 million. Baker's variable cost ratio is 0.667, and its required pretax return on receivables investment is 15 percent. Determine the following:

    a. The funds released by the change in credit terms.

    b. The net effect on Baker's pretax profits.

Lotus123

7. In an effort to speed up the collection of receivables, Hill Publishing Company is considering increasing the size of its cash discount by changing its credit terms from "1/10, net 30" to "2/10, net 30." Currently, the company's collection period averages 43 days. Under the new credit terms it is expected to decline to 28 days. Also, the percentage of customers who will take advantage of the cash discount is expected to increase from the current 50 percent to 70 percent with the new credit terms. Bad-debt losses currently average 4 percent of sales and are not expected to change significantly if Hill changes its credit policy. Annual credit sales are $3.5 million, the variable cost ratio is 60 percent and the required pretax rate of return (that is, the opportunity cost) on receivables investment is 14 percent. Assuming that Hill does decide to increase the size of its cash discount, determine the following:

    a. The earnings on the funds released by the change in credit terms.

    b. The cost of the additional cash discounts taken.

    c. The net effect on Hill's pretax profits.

8. The North Carolina Furniture Company (NCFC) manufactures upholstered furniture, which it sells to various small retailers in the Northeast and Midwest on credit terms of "2/10, net 60." The company currently does not grant credit to retailers with a 3 (fair) or 4 (limited) Dun and Bradstreet Composite Credit Appraisal. If NCFC were to extend credit to retailers in the "fair" category, an additional $1.2 million per year in sales could be generated. The estimated average collection period for these customers is 90 days, and the expected bad-debt loss ratio is 6 percent. Approximately 20 percent of these customers are expected to take the cash discount. NCFC's variable cost ratio is 0.70, and its required pretax rate of return on receivables investment is 20 percent. Determine the net change in NCFC's pretax profits from extending credit to retailers in the "fair" category.

9. Michigan Pharmaceuticals, Inc., a wholesale distributor of ethical drugs to local pharmacies, has been experiencing a relatively long average collection period, since many of its customers face liquidity problems and delay their payments well beyond the due date. In addition, its bad-debt loss ratio is high, since a number of pharmacies have closed because of financial difficulties. To avoid these problems in the future, Michigan Pharmaceuticals is considering a plan to *institute more stringent credit standards* to keep the average collection period and bad-debt losses from rising beyond acceptable limits. Specifically, the firm plans to refuse to grant additional credit to any current customers that are more than 15 days past due on their payments. Such a change in credit policy is expected to reduce current annual sales of $6.5 million by 20 percent, *reduce* the average collection period from 110 days to 75 days, and lower bad-debt losses from 8 to 4 percent. The firm's variable cost ratio is 0.75, and its required pretax return on receivables investment in 15 percent. Determine the net effect of this plan on the pretax profits of Michigan Pharmaceuticals.

10. Madison Electric Company sells on terms of "net 30." Given the following information on its receivables, construct an aging of accounts schedule as of September 1, showing the percentage of accounts that are current, 1 to 30 days past due, 31 to 60 days past due, 61 to 90 days past due, and over 90 days past due. (Assume 30 days in each month.)

Account Number	Invoice Date	Amount Due
1311	August 15	$1,315
1773	July 14	721
1217	July 25	677
1319	August 14	1,711
1814	April 10	325
1713	August 5	917
1443	May 8	493
1144	June 28	211
1972	May 5	755
1011	April 21	377
1619	August 28	1,550
1322	August 13	275
1173	March 5	675
1856	August 12	695
1317	June 10	720

11. Creole Industries, Inc. estimates that if it spent an additional $20,000 to hire another collection agent in its credit department, it could lower its bad-debt

loss ratio to 3.5 percent from a current rate of 4 percent and also reduce its average collection period from 50 to 45 days. (Assume that sales remain unchanged if the agent is hired.) Creole's annual credit sales are $5 million, and its variable cost ratio is 0.75. The firm's required pretax rate of return on receivables investment (that is, the opportunity cost) is 18 percent. Determine the net effect on Creole's pretax profits of hiring the additional collection agent.

Lotus123

12. Jenkins Supply Corp. sells $120 million of its products to wholesalers on terms of "net 50." Currently, the firm's average collection period is 65 days. In order to speed up the collection of receivables, Jenkins is considering offering a 1 percent cash discount if customers pay their bills within 15 days. The firm expects 40 percent of its customers to take the discount and its average collection period to decline to 40 days. The firm's required pre-tax return on receivables investments is 20 percent.

Determine the net effect on Jenkins' pre-tax profits of offering a 1 percent cash discount.

Lotus123

13. The Bimbo Corporation has been experiencing a decline in sales relative to its major competitors. Since Bimbo is confident about the quality of its products, it suspects that this sales loss may reflect its relatively stringent credit standards and terms. The firm currently has credit sales of $50 million annually. With current credit terms of "net 20," its average collection period is now 25 days. Bad debt losses are 2 percent of credit sales. The firm's variable cost ratio is 0.80, and its required pre-tax return on receivables investments is 20 percent.

Bimbo plans to change its credit terms to "2/10, net 30." It expects 20 percent of its customers to take advantage of the cash discount. Bimbo also plans to relax credit standards and take on more risky accounts. This action is expected to increase credit sales by 30 percent. Bad-debt losses are expected to increase to 3 percent of credit sales, and the average collection period is expected to become 30 days.

Determine the net effect of this plan on the pre-tax profits of Bimbo.

14. Allied Apparel Company received a large order from Websters Department Stores, which operates a chain of approximately 300 popular-priced department stores located primarily in the New England-Middle Atlantic states area. Allied is considering extending trade credit to Websters. As part of its credit check, Allied obtained Websters' balance sheets and income statements (shown below) for the last 3 years. Websters' Dun and Bradstreet rating is 5A3. A check of several of Websters' trade creditors has revealed that the firm generally takes any cash discounts when they are offered but averages about 30 days overdue on its payments to two suppliers whose credit terms are "net 30."

A Dun and Bradstreet publication entitled *Key Business Ratios* yielded the following information concerning the "average" financial ratios for firms in the same line of business as Websters:

Current assets to current liabilities	2.82
Net income after taxes to sales	1.89%
Net income after taxes to net worth	5.65%
Total liabilities to net worth	1.48

Websters Department Stores, Balance Sheet (in thousands of dollars)

	19X1	19X2	19X3
Assets			
Current assets:			
Cash and marketable securities	$ 9,283	$ 13,785	$ 23,893
Accounts receivable (net)	162,825	179,640	140,543
Inventories	119,860	135,191	129,707
Other	1,994	2,190	1,956
Total current assets	$293,962	$330,806	$296,099
Long-term assets:			
Buildings and equipment (net)	$ 27,426	$ 30,295	$ 30,580
Other	11,821	14,794	16,687
Total long-term assets	$ 39,247	$ 45,089	$ 47,267
Total assets	$333,209	$375,895	$343,366
Liabilities and net worth			
Current liabilities:			
Accounts payable	$ 23,637	$ 21,861	$ 15,020
Notes payable	117,010	135,929	165,299
Other	49,273	49,229	29,653
Total current liabilities	$189,920	$207,019	$209,972
Long-term liabilities:			
Debentures	$ 38,001	$ 36,101	$ 35,201
Term loan	—	28,440	29,701
Other	4,986	853	655
Total long-term liabilities	$ 42,987	$ 65,394	$ 65,557
Net worth:			
Common stock	$ 5,576	$ 5,576	$ 5,576
Preferred stock	2,580	2,580	2,580
Retained earnings	92,146	95,326	59,681
Total net worth	100,302	103,482	67,837
Total liabilities and net worth	$333,209	$375,895	$343,366

Websters Department Stores, Income Statement (in thousands of dollars)

	19X1	19X2	19X3
Sales	$494,550	$556,132	$529,857
Cost of sales	337,580	384,899	390,980
Gross profit	$156,970	$171,233	$138,877
Selling, general and administrative expenses	133,330	155,494	187,926
Net profit before taxes	$ 23,640	$ 15,739	$−49,049
Income taxes	7,715	6,222	−14,741
Net income after taxes	$ 15,925	$ 9,517	$−34,308
Dividends	6,343	6,337	1,337
Additions to retained earnings	$ 9,582	$ 3,180	$−35,645

In evaluating Websters' application for trade credit, answer the following questions:

a. What positive financial factors would lead Allied to decide to extend credit to Websters?

b. What negative financial factors would lead Allied to decide *not* to extend credit to Websters?

c. What additional information about Websters would be useful in performing the analysis?

Selected References

Ben-Horim, Moshe, and Haim Levy. "Management of Accounts Receivable Under Inflation." *Financial Management* 12 (Spring 1983): 42–48.

Brick, Ivan E., and W. K. H. Fung. "The Effect of Taxes on the Trade Credit Decision." *Financial Management* 13 (Summer 1984): 24–30.

Dyl, Edward A. "Another Look at the Evaluation of Investments in Accounts Receivable." *Financial Management* 6 (Winter 1977): 67–70.

Gentry, James A., and Jesus M. De La Garza. "A Generalized Model for Monitoring Accounts Receivable." *Financial Management* 14 (Winter 1985): 28–38.

Sartoris, William, and Ned C. Hill. "A Generalized Cash Flow Approach to Short-term Financial Decisions." *Journal of Finance* 38 (May 1983): 349–360.

Stowe, John D. "An Integer Programming Solution for the Optimal Credit Investigation/Credit Granting Sequence." *Financial Management* 14 (Summer 1985): 66–76.

21

INVENTORY MANAGEMENT

A Financial Dilemma

Apple Computer's Inventory Decisions

The U.S. computer industry in 1985 suffered a slowdown in sales. As a result, Apple Computer (and other computer manufacturers) was faced with the problem of how to cope with rising inventories and the costs of carrying them. As orders from dealers slowed, Apple closed four plants for a week each to keep inventory levels and costs under control.[1] In addition, the company lowered its price on some products and finally decided to discontinue its top-of-the-line Macintosh XL.

The sales decline not only affected the computer manufacturers and their inventory policies, but the sales downturn also caused inventory problems for the semiconductor industy. As computer sales began to decline and computer inventories began to rise, computer manufacturers, including Apple, cut back on their microchip orders, thereby leaving semiconductor manufacturers with rising quantities of unsold inventories. Thus, the semiconductor companies were faced with the same inventory management questions as their customers in the computer industry. And, as the semiconductor companies offered price discounts to the computer manufacturers, the computer manufacturers had to reexamine their ordering policies.

This chapter discusses the principles of inventory management and develops a number of models which managers can use in making inventory decisions.

[1] *The Wall Street Journal* (May 2, 1985):2.

Key Chapter Concepts

1. The determination of the optimal level of inventory investment requires that the benefits and costs associated with alternative levels be measured and compared.
2. The types of inventory-related costs include:
   a. Ordering costs.
   b. Carrying costs.
   c. Stockout costs.
3. The use of inventory control models can aid in efficiently managing a company's level of inventory investment.
4. The economic order quantity model permits determination of the quantity of an inventory item that should be ordered so that total inventory costs are minimized.

Glossary of New Terms

ABC inventory classification A method of dividing inventory items into three groups—those with a relatively large dollar value but a small percentage of the total items, those with a small dollar value but a large percentage of the total items, and those items in between.

Carrying costs All costs associated with holding items in inventory for a period of time.

Economic order quantity The quantity of an inventory item that should be ordered so that total inventory costs are minimized.

Inventory cycle The time between placement of successive orders of an item.

Just-in-time inventory and production concept An approach to inventory and production management in which required inventory items are supplied exactly as needed by production.

Lead time The time between when an order is placed for an item and when the item actually is received in inventory.

Ordering costs All costs associated with placing and receiving an order.

Reorder point The inventory level at which an order should be placed for replenishment of an item.

Stockout costs The cost of lost sales associated with the inability to fill orders from inventory.

Introduction

T
he final category of current assets examined in this text is *inventories*. In a manufacturing firm, inventories serve as a *buffer* between the various phases of the procurement-production-sales cycle. They *uncouple* the various phases by giving the firm flexibility with respect to timing the purchase of raw materials, scheduling production facilities and employees, and meeting fluctuating and uncertain demand for the finished product. Inventories also serve similar purposes in the procurement-sales cycle of a wholesaling or retailing firm.

Table 18-1 in Chapter 18 indicates the size and relative importance of inventories. The total value of inventories represented about 17 and 29 percent of the total assets of companies in the manufacturing and retailing sectors, respectively. Inventories also constituted about 41 percent of the total current assets in manufacturing and about 57 percent of the current assets in the retailing sector.

This chapter explores the various types of inventories and their functions, along with the different categories of inventory-related costs. It also develops some models and procedures that can be used in efficiently managing a firm's level of inventory investment. Although financial managers do not have primary responsibility for managing a company's inventories, they are responsible for seeing that funds are invested wisely within the firm. To perform this function, financial managers must have a good working knowledge of inventory control techniques.

Inventories frequently are used as collateral for short-term loans. Because inventory loans are a source of short-term financing, this topic is discussed in Chapter 22.

Types and Functions of Inventories

Manufacturing firms generally hold three types of inventories:

- Raw materials inventories.
- Work-in-process inventories.
- Finished goods inventories.

Like any other asset, the holding of inventories constitutes an investment of funds. Determining the optimal level of inventory investment requires that the benefits and costs associated with alternative levels be measured and compared. To do this, it is necessary to determine the specific benefits associated with holding the various types of inventories.

Raw Materials Inventories

Raw materials inventory consists of items a business purchases for use in its production process. It may consist of basic materials (for example, iron ore for a steel-making operation), manufactured goods (for example, jet engines for an airplane assembly operation), or both. Maintaining adequate raw materials inventories provides a company with advantages in both purchasing and production. Specifically, the purchasing department benefits by being able to buy needed items in large quantities and take advantage of *quantity discounts* offered by suppliers. In addition, if rising prices, shortages of specific items, or both are forecasted for the future, maintaining a large stock of raw materials insures that the company will have adequate supplies at reasonable costs.

Knowing that there will be adequate stocks of raw materials available when needed permits the production department to meet production schedules and make the most efficient use of its personnel and facilities. Thus, there are a number of valid reasons why a company's purchasing and production departments will want to maintain large inventories of raw materials.

Work-in-Process Inventories

Work-in-process inventory consists of all items that are presently in the production cycle at some intermediate stage of completion. For example, they may be currently undergoing some type of operation (such as assembly or painting); they may be in transit between operations; or they may be stored somewhere, awaiting the next step in the production cycle.

Work-in-process inventories are a necessary part of modern industrial production systems, since they give each operation in the production cycle a certain degree of independence. This, in turn, aids in the efficient scheduling of the various operations and helps minimize costly delays and idle time. For these reasons a company's production department will want to maintain reasonable work-in-process inventories. In general, the longer a firm's production cycle, the larger its work-in-process inventory.

Finished Goods Inventories

Finished goods inventory consists of those items that they have completed the production cycle and are available for sale. With the exception of large-scale, specialized types of equipment—such as industrial machinery, military armaments, jet airplanes, and nuclear reactors, which normally are contracted for *before* they are produced—most consumer and industrial products are manufactured and stored in inventory to meet forecasted future sales.

Keeping enough finished goods inventories on hand provides significant benefits for both the marketing and the production departments. From marketing's perspective, large finished goods inventories enable it to fill orders promptly, minimize lost sales, and avoid shipment delays due to stockouts. From production's standpoint, maintaining a large finished goods inventory permits items to be manufactured in large production runs, which helps keep unit production costs low by spreading fixed set-up expenses over large volumes of output.

Inventory-related Costs

At the same time that there are a number of benefits to be realized from holding inventories, there are also a number of costs that must be considered, including the following:

- Ordering costs.
- Carrying costs.
- Stockout costs.

Ordering Costs

Ordering costs represent all the costs of placing and receiving an order. They are stated in dollars per order. When a company is ordering from an external source, these include the costs of preparing the purchase requisition, expediting the order (for example, long distance calls and follow-up letters), receiving and inspecting the shipment, and handling payment. Factors such as an item's price and engineering complexity also affect its ordering costs. When an order is placed for an item that is manufactured *internally* within a company, ordering costs consist primarily of *production set-up* costs, which are the expenses incurred in getting the plant and equipment ready for a production run.

In practice, the cost per order generally contains both fixed and variable components, since a portion of the cost—such as that of receiving and inspecting the order—normally varies with the quantity ordered. However, many simple inventory control models, such as the EOQ model (which is described later in this chapter), treat cost per order as fixed by assuming that these costs are independent of the number of units ordered.

Carrying Costs

Carrying costs constitute all the costs of holding items in inventory for a given period of time. They are expressed either in dollars per unit per period or as a percentage of the inventory value per period. Components of this cost include the following:

- Storage and handling costs.
- Obsolescence and deterioration costs.
- Insurance.
- Taxes.
- The cost of the funds invested in inventories.

Storage and handling costs include the cost of warehouse space. If a company leases warehouse space, this cost is equal to the rent paid. If a company owns the warehouse, this cost is equal to the value of the space in its next-best alternative use (that is, the opportunity cost). These costs also include depreciation on the inventory handling equipment, such as conveyors and forklift trucks, and the wages and salaries paid to warehouse workers and supervisors.

Inventories are valuable only if they can be sold. *Obsolescence costs* represent the decline in inventory value caused by technological or style changes that make the existing product less salable. *Deterioration costs* represent the decline in value caused by changes in the physical quality of the inventory, such as spoilage and breakage.

Another element of carrying cost is the *cost of insuring* the inventory against losses due to theft, fire, and natural disaster. In addition, a company must pay any *personal property taxes* and *business taxes* required by local and state governments on the value of its inventories.

The *cost of funds invested in inventories* is measured by the *required rate of return* on these funds. Since inventory investments are likely to be of "average risk," the overall weighted cost of capital should be used to measure the cost of these funds. If it is felt that inventories constitute an investment with either above-average or below-average risk, some adjustment in the weighted cost of capital may be necessary to account for this difference in risk. Chapters 5 and 11 discuss the determination of risk-adjusted discount rates. Some firms incorrectly use the rate of interest on borrowed funds as a measure of this cost. This tends to understate the true cost, since a given amount of lower cost debt must be balanced with additional higher cost equity financing. Inventory investment cost constitutes an opportunity cost in that it represents the return a firm foregoes as a result of deciding to invest its limited funds in inventories rather than in some other asset. Thus, for most inventory decisions, the appropriate opportunity cost is the firm's weighted cost of capital.

The cost of carrying inventories can represent a significant cost of doing business. Table 21-1 contains some ranges on annual inventory carrying costs, expressed as a percentage of inventory value. This study found that *total* annual carrying costs were in the range of 20 to 45 percent for most of the businesses surveyed.

Like ordering costs, inventory carrying costs contain both fixed and variable components. Most carrying costs vary with the inventory level, but a certain portion of them—such as warehouse rent and depreciation on inventory handling equipment—are relatively fixed over the short run. Most of the simple inventory control models, such as the EOQ model, treat the entire carrying cost as variable.

Stockout Costs

Stockout costs are incurred whenever a business is unable to fill orders because the demand for an item is greater than the amount currently available in inventory. When a stockout in raw materials occurs, for example, stockout costs include the expenses of placing special orders (backordering) and expediting incoming orders, in addition to the costs of any resulting production delays. A stockout in work-in-process inventory results in additional costs of rescheduling and speeding production within the plant, and it also may result in lost production costs if work stoppages occur. Finally, a stockout in finished goods inventory may result in the immediate loss of profits if customers decide to purchase the product from a competitor, and in potential long-term losses if customers decide to order from other companies in the future.

Inventory Control Models

Given the significance of the benefits and costs associated with holding inventories, it is important that the firm efficiently control the level of inventory investments. There are a number of inventory control models

Table 21-1

Inventory Carrying Costs (as a Percentage of Inventory Value)

Cost Category	Low	High
Storage costs	1.0%	4.0%
Obsolescence and physical loss	5.0	10.0
Insurance costs	1.0	3.0
Property taxes	1.0	3.0
Cost of money	12.0	25.0

Source: W.E. Dollar, *Effective Purchasing and Inventory Control for Small Business.* Boston, Mass.: Inc./CBI Publications, 1983, p. 71.

available that can help in determining the optimal inventory level of each item. These models range from the relatively simple to the extremely complex. Their degree of complexity depends primarily on the assumptions made about the demand or usage for the particular item and the lead time required to secure additional stock.

A related question involves the extent of control and the type of inventory model which should be applied to different inventory items. A technique called *ABC inventory classification* can be helpful in this regard. The ABC method divides a company's inventory items into three groups. Group A consists of those items with a relatively large dollar value but a relatively small percentage of the total items, whereas group C contains those items with a small dollar value but a large percentage of the total items. Group B contains the items which are in between groups A and C. A typical result of an ABC analysis is that group A contains roughly 1 to 10 percent of the total number of items carried in inventory, but these items may represent as high as 80 to 90 percent of the total dollar value of the inventory. On the other hand, group C may contain about 50 percent of the total number of items, but these items may constitute less than 10 percent of the inventory's total dollar value. Group B contains the remaining items. Even though the actual cutoff between the groups is somewhat arbitrary, the ABC method provides management with information which can be used to determine how closely different inventory items should be controlled.

As an example, consider the Greenbelt Co., which manufactures lawn mowers. It purchases gasoline motors from another company, and, because of their cost, the motors are classified as group A items. As a result, the Greenbelt management has determined the inventory costs associated with the motors and uses a detailed model to calculate the economic order quantity. On the other hand, Greenbelt classifies all nuts and bolts it uses as a group C item. As a result, the company's policy on nuts and bolts consists of little more than simply keeping an ample supply on hand.

In the "classical" inventory models, which include both the simpler *deterministic* models and the more complex *probabilistic* models, it is assumed that demand is either uniform or dispersed and *independent* over time.[2] In other words, demand is assumed either to be *constant* or to fluctuate over time due to *random* elements. These types of demand situations are common in retailing and some service operations.

The simpler deterministic inventory control models, such as the *economic order quantity* (EOQ) *model,* assume that both demand and lead times are *constant* and known with *certainty*. Thus, deterministic models

---

[2] *Dependent* demand models, in contrast, assume that demand tends to be "lumpy," or to occur at specific points in time. Dependent demand tends to occur when products are manufactured in lots, since all the items required to produce the lot are usually withdrawn from inventory at the same time rather than unit by unit. Dependent demand is a direct result of the demand for a "higher level" item. Material requirements planning (MRP) models have been developed to deal with the case of dependent demand. See J. Evans, D. Anderson, D. Sweeney, and T. Williams, *Applied Production and Operations Management,* St. Paul, Minn.: West Publishing Co., 1984, chap. 14, for a discussion of MRP.

Figure 21-1

Certainty Case of the Inventory Cycle

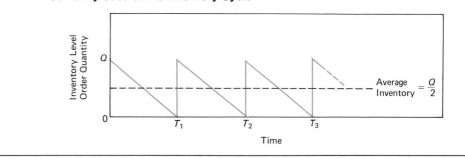

eliminate the need to consider stockouts. The more complex probabilistic inventory control models assume that demand, lead time, or both are *random variables with known probability distributions.*[3]

Basic EOQ Model

In its simplest form, the EOQ model assumes the annual demand or usage for a particular item is known with certainty. It also assumes that this demand is stationary or uniform throughout the year. In other words, seasonal fluctuations in the rate of demand are ruled out. Finally, the model assumes that orders to replenish the inventory of an item are filled instantaneously. Given a known demand and a zero lead time for replenishing inventories, there is no need for a company to maintain additional inventories, or safety stocks, to protect itself against stockouts.

The assumptions of the EOQ model yield the saw-toothed inventory pattern shown in Figure 21-1. The vertical lines at the 0, T_1, T_2, and T_3 points in time represent the instantaneous replenishment of the item by the amount of the order quantity, Q, and the negatively sloped lines between the replenishment points represent the use of the item. Since the inventory level varies between 0 and the order quantity, average inventory is equal to one-half of the order quantity, or $Q/2$.

This model assumes that the costs of placing and receiving an order are the same for each order and independent of the number of units ordered. It also assumes that the annual cost of carrying 1 unit of the item in inventory is constant regardless of the inventory level. Total annual inventory costs, then, are the sum of ordering costs and carrying costs.[4] The primary objective of the EOQ model is to find the order quantity, Q, that minimizes total annual inventory costs.

---

[3] Rather than survey all the various inventory control models in depth, this chapter develops the deterministic EOQ model to illustrate the cost tradeoffs involved in determining the optimal inventory level. It then examines the factors that must be considered and the cost tradeoffs involved in developing a probabilistic model, without using mathematical analysis or formal solution techniques.

[4] The *actual cost* of the item (that is, either the price paid for items purchased externally or the production cost for items manufactured internally) is excluded from this analysis, since it is assumed to be constant regardless of the order quantity. This assumption is relaxed later when quantity discounts are considered.

Algebraic Solution In developing the algebraic form of the EOQ model, the following variables are defined:

Q = The order *quantity*, in units.

D = The annual *demand* for the item, in units.

S = The cost of placing and receiving an order, or *set-up* cost.

C = The annual cost of *carrying* 1 unit of the item in inventory.

Ordering costs are equal to the number of orders per year multiplied by the cost per order, S. The number of orders per year is equal to annual demand, D, divided by the order quantity, Q. Carrying costs are equal to average inventory, $Q/2$, multiplied by the annual carrying cost per unit, C.

The total annual cost equation is as follows:

$$\text{Total costs} = \text{Ordering costs} + \text{Carrying costs.} \tag{21.1}$$

By substituting the variables just defined into Equation 21.1, the following expression is obtained:

$$\text{Total costs} = (\text{Number of orders per year} \times \text{Cost per order}) + (\text{Average inventory} \times \text{Annual carrying cost per unit}), \tag{21.2}$$

or, in algebraic terms,

$$\text{Total costs} = \left(\frac{D}{Q} \times S\right) + \left(\frac{Q}{2} \times C\right). \tag{21.3}$$

The EOQ is the value of Q that minimizes the total costs given in Equation 21.3. The standard procedure for finding this value of Q involves calculus.[5] The optimal solution, or EOQ, is equal to the following:

$$Q^* = \sqrt{\frac{2SD}{C}} \tag{21.4}$$

Another item of information that sometimes is useful for planning purposes is the optimal length of one inventory cycle, that is, the time between placements of orders for the item. The optimal length of one inventory cycle, T^*, measured in days, is equal to the economic order quantity, Q^*, divided by the average daily demand, $D/360$ (assuming 360 days per year), as follows:

$$T^* = \frac{Q^*}{D/360} \tag{21.5}$$

---

[5] Specifically, the first derivative of Equation 21.3 with respect to Q is set equal to 0, and the equation is solved for Q.

This equation can be rewritten as follows:

$$T^* = \frac{360 \times Q^*}{D} \tag{21.6}$$

The following example illustrates the use of the EOQ model. Midwest Department Stores sells Simmons mattresses through its retail outlets located in the Detroit metropolitan area. All inventories are maintained at the firm's centrally located warehouse. Annual demand for the Simmons standard-sized mattress is 3,600 units and is spread evenly throughout the year. The cost of placing and receiving an order is $31.25.

Midwest's annual carrying costs are 20 percent of the inventory value. Based on a wholesale cost of $50 per mattress, the annual carrying cost per mattress is $0.20 \times \$50 = \$10$. Because Simmons maintains a large regional distribution center in Detroit, Midwest can replenish its inventory virtually instantaneously. The company wishes to determine the number of standard-sized mattresses it should periodically order from Simmons in order to minimize the total annual inventory costs. Substituting $D = 3,600$, $S = \$31.25$, and $C = \$10$ into Equation 21.4 yields the following EOQ:

$$Q^* = \sqrt{\frac{2 \times \$31.25 \times 3,600}{\$10}}$$

$$= 150 \text{ mattresses.}$$

Using Equation 21.3, we can calculate the total annual inventory costs of this policy:

$$\text{Total costs}^* = \frac{3,600}{150} \times \$31.25 + \frac{150}{2} \times \$10$$

$$= \$1,500.$$

Finally, Equation 21.6 can be used to determine Midwest's optimal inventory cycle for these matresses:

$$T^* = \frac{360 \times 150}{3,600}$$

$$= 15 \text{ days.}$$

Thus, the EOQ of 150 mattresses and the optimal inventory cycle of 15 days for this item indicate that Midwest should place an order for 150 mattresses every 15 days.

Graphic Solution   The order quantity that minimizes total annual inventory costs can be determined graphically by plotting inventory costs (vertical axis) as a function of the order quantity (horizontal axis). As can be seen in Figure 21-2, annual ordering costs, DS/Q, vary *inversely* with

Figure 21-2

Graphic Solution of the EOQ Model

the order quantity, Q, since the number of orders placed per year, D/Q, decreases as the size of the order quantity increases. Carrying costs, $CQ/2$, vary *directly* with the order quantity, Q, since the average inventory, $Q/2$, increases as the size of the order quantity increases.

The total inventory cost curve is found by vertically summing the heights of the ordering cost and carrying cost functions. The order quantity corresponding to the lowest point on the total cost curve is the optimal solution—that is, the economic order quantity, Q^*.

Extensions of the Basic EOQ Model

The basic EOQ model just described makes a number of simplifying assumptions, including those pertaining to the demand for the item, replenishment lead time, the behavior of ordering and carrying costs, and quantity discounts. In practical applications of inventory control models, however, some of these assumptions may not be valid. Thus, it is important to understand how different assumptions affect the analysis and the optimal order quantity. The following sections examine what occurs when some of these assumptions are altered.

Nonzero Lead Time The basic EOQ model assumes that orders to replenish the inventory of an item are filled instantaneously; that is, the lead time is zero. In practice, however, some time usually elapses between when a purchase order is placed and when the item actually is received in inventory. This lead time consists of the time it takes to manufacture the item, the time it takes to package and ship the item, or both.

If the lead time is *constant* and *known with certainty,* the optimal order quantity, Q^*, is not affected, although the time when an order should be placed is. Specifically, a company should not wait to reorder until the end of the inventory cycle, when the inventory level reaches zero—such as at points T_1, T_2, and T_3 in Figure 21-3. Instead, it should place an order *n days prior* to the end of each cycle, *n* being equal to the replenishment lead time measured in days. The *reorder point* is defined as the inventory level at which an order should be placed for replenishment of an item. Assuming that demand is constant over time, the reorder point, Q_r, is equal to the lead time, *n* (measured in days), multiplied by daily demand:

$$Q_r = n \times \frac{D}{360},$$ (21.7)

where $D/360$ is daily demand (based on 360 days per year).

For example, if the lead time for standard-sized mattresses ordered by Midwest Department Stores (see the previous section) is 5 days, and annual demand is 3,600 mattresses, an order for 150 mattresses (that is, the economic order quantity) should be placed when the inventory level reaches the following:

$$Q_r = 5 \times \frac{3,600}{360}$$

$$= 50 \text{ mattresses,}$$

which occurs on the 10th day of each inventory cycle. Five days later, on the 15th day of the inventory cycle—when the inventory level falls to zero—Midwest will receive the order, and the inventory level will again rise to 150.

Quantity Discounts Large orders often permit a company to realize substantial per-unit savings (that is, economies of scale) in manufacturing, order processing, and shipping. Many companies encourage their customers to place large orders by passing on to them a portion of these savings in

---

Figure 21-3 **Nonzero Replenishment Lead Time Case of an Inventory Cycle**

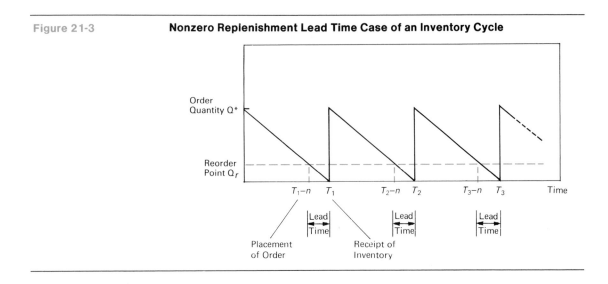

the form of *quantity discounts*. With a quantity discount, the cost per unit to the customer is variable and depends on the quantity ordered. The following approach can be used to determine the effect of a quantity discount on the optimal order quantity.

First, the EOQ is determined, using Equation 21.4. Next, the annual *net* returns when the order quantity is increased from the EOQ level up to the order size necessary to receive the discount are calculated.[6] The annual net returns are equal to the discount savings on the annual demand less any increase in annual inventory costs, as defined in Equation 21.3. If the annual net returns are *positive,* the optimal order quantity is the order size necessary to receive the discount; if they are not, the optimal order quantity is the smaller EOQ value.

For example, suppose Simmons offers a 2 percent, or $1, quantity discount per mattress on orders of 600 or more standard-sized mattresses. Midwest wishes to determine the optimal order quantity under these conditions. Midwest's EOQ is 150 mattresses. Thus, the annual net returns of increasing the order quantity from 150 to 600 need to be calculated.

The discount savings on annual demand are defined as follows:

$$\text{Discount savings} = \text{Discount per unit} \times \text{Annual demand}. \quad \textbf{(21.8)}$$

In Midwest's case, this is calculated as follows:

$$\text{Discount savings} = \$1 \times 3,600$$
$$= \$3,600.$$

If Midwest were to order the discount order quantity, Q', of 600 mattresses, the carrying cost per unit, C', would be reduced to $9.80 ($49 \times 0.20$). Substituting the appropriate quantities into Equation 21.3 yields the following total annual inventory costs:

$$\text{Total costs}' = \frac{3,600}{600} \times \$31.25 + \frac{600}{2} \times \$9.80$$
$$= \$187.50 + \$2,940$$
$$= \$3,127.50.$$

As calculated earlier, the total annual inventory costs at the EOQ of 150 are $1,500. The *change* in annual inventory costs, Δ Total costs, resulting from the increased order quantity, is calculated as follows:

$$\Delta \text{ Total costs} = \text{Total costs}' - \text{Total costs}^*$$
$$= \$3,127.50 - \$1,500$$
$$= +\$1,627.50.$$

---

[6] It is assumed that the order quantity necessary to receive a discount is *above* the EOQ level. If this were not the case, the firm would receive the discount automatically when placing an order for the amount of the EOQ.

The annual net returns are equal to the discount savings less the increased inventory costs, or $3,600 - $1,627.50 = $1,972.50. Because the annual net returns in this analysis are positive, Midwest should increase its order quantity from 150 to 600 mattresses and take advantage of the quantity discount.

Probabilistic Inventory Control Models

Thus far the analysis has assumed that demand or usage is uniform throughout time and known with certainty, as well as that the lead time necessary to procure additional inventory is also a fixed, known value. However, in most practical inventory management problems either (or both) of these assumptions may not be strictly correct. Typically, demand fluctuates over time due to seasonal, cyclical, and "random" influences, and imprecise forecasts of future demands are often all that can be made. Similarly, lead times are subject to uncertainty because of such factors as transportation delays, strikes, and natural disasters. Under these conditions, the possibility of stockouts exists. To minimize the possibility of stockouts and the associated stockout costs, most companies use a standard approach of adding a *safety stock* to their inventory. A safety stock is maintained to meet unexpectedly high demand during the lead time, unanticipated delays in the lead time, or both.

Figure 21-4 shows the inventory pattern characterized by these more realistic assumptions. During the first inventory cycle ($0 - T_2$), an order to replenish the inventory is placed at T_1, when the inventory level reaches the predetermined order point. The order then is received at T_2. The second cycle ($T_2 - T_4$) is similar to the first, except for the fact that demand exceeds the normal inventory of the item, and part of the safety stock is consumed during the lead time prior to receipt of the order at T_4. During cycle 3 ($T_4 - T_6$), demand exceeds the normal inventory plus the safety stock and, as a result, a stockout occurs during the lead time prior to receipt of the order at T_6.

Determining the optimal safety stock and order quantities under these more realistic conditions is a fairly complex process that lies beyond the

Figure 21-4   **Uncertainty Case of the Inventory Cycle**

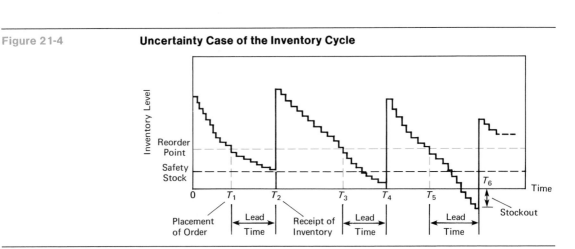

scope of this text.[7] However, the factors that have to be considered in this type of analysis can be briefly identified. All other things being equal, the optimal safety stock increases as the uncertainty associated with the demand forecasts and lead times increases. Likewise, all other things being equal, the optimal safety stock increases as the cost of stockouts increases. Determining the optimal safety stock involves balancing the *expected* costs of stockouts against the cost of carrying the additional inventory.

Just-in-Time Inventory Models

Inventory models used in the U.S. which rely on safety stocks sometimes are referred to as "just-in-case" models. In contrast, the Japanese have developed *just-in-time inventory models*. This approach, first developed at Toyota Motor Company in the 1950s, is based on the idea that all required inventory items are supplied to production at exactly the right time and in exactly the right quantities. Just-in-time inventory models are being used at U.S. auto and tractor manufacturers. The just-in-time approach works best for companies engaged in repetitive manufacturing operations, and it requires careful coordination in order for implementation to be successful. But U.S. companies have reported reductions in inventory investment using the just-in-time approach.

Summary

- Inventories serve as a *buffer* between the various stages of the manufacturing firm's procurement-production-sales cycle. By uncoupling the various phases of the firm's operations, inventories provide the firm with *flexibility* in timing purchases, scheduling production, and meeting fluctuating, uncertain demand for the finished product.

- Inventory-related costs include *ordering costs, carrying costs,* and *stockout costs.* Ordering costs include all the costs of placing and receiving an order. Carrying costs include the various costs of holding items in inventory, including the cost of funds invested in inventory. Stockout costs are the costs incurred when demand exceeds available inventory, such as lost profits.

- ABC inventory classification is a method of dividing inventory items into three groups—those with a relatively large dollar value but a small percentage of the total items (A), those with a small dollar value but a large percentage of the total items (C), and items in between (B). Group A items should be more closely controlled than group B or C items.

- Inventory control models usually are classified into two types: *deterministic,* if demand and lead time are known with *certainty,* and *probabilistic,* if demand and/or lead time are *random variables* with known probability distributions.

- The objective of the deterministic *economic order quantity* (EOQ) *model* is to find the order quantity that minimizes total inventory costs.

---

[7] See any of the following books for a discussion of these more complex models: H. M. Wagner, *Principles of Operations Research: With Applications to Managerial Decisions,* 2nd ed., Englewood Cliffs, N.J.: Prentice-Hall, 1975; J. Evans, D. Anderson, D. Sweeney, and T. Williams, *Applied Production and Operations Management,* St. Paul, MN: West Publishing Co., 1984; and Richard I. Levin and Charles A. Kirkpatrick, *Quantitative Approaches to Management,* 4th ed., New York: McGraw-Hill, 1978.

- The economic order quantity is equal to $\sqrt{2SD/C}$, where D is the annual demand; S, the fixed cost per order; and C, the annual carrying cost per unit.
- Some of the assumptions made in the basic EOQ model do not necessarily apply in practice. In the event of a nonzero lead time or quantity discounts, for example, the model must be modified.
- Probabilistic inventory control models require consideration of the possibility of *stockouts*. One approach used to handle this problem is to add a *safety stock* to the inventory.
- *Just-in-time inventory models* are based on the concept that required inventory items are supplied exactly as needed by production. Successful implementation of just-in-time models can reduce inventory investment.

Questions and Topics for Discussion

1. Define the following terms:
    a. Stockout.
    b. Deterministic inventory control models.
    c. Probabilistic inventory control models.
    d. Safety stock.
    e. Lead time.
    f. Quantity discount.
2. Describe the benefits of holding the following:
    a. Raw materials inventories.
    b. Work-in-process inventories.
    c. Finished goods inventories.
3. Describe the components of carrying costs.
4. How do ordering costs for items purchased externally differ from ordering costs for items manufactured internally within the firm?
5. Describe the nature of stockout costs associated with a stockout in the following:
    a. Raw materials inventories.
    b. Work-in-process inventories.
    c. Finished goods inventories.
6. What is ABC inventory classification? How can this method be useful to a business?
7. Describe the assumptions underlying the basic EOQ model.
8. In general terms, describe how to deal with each of the following conditions when determining the optimal inventory level:
    a. Constant (nonzero) replenishment lead time known with certainty.
    b. Quantity discounts.
    c. Demand and replenishment lead time subject to uncertainty.
9. How does the firm's required rate of return on investment enter into inventory decisions?
10. What are just-in-time inventory models?

Problems*

Note: Assume that there are 360 days per year when converting annual data to daily data or vice versa.)

1. Allstar Shoe Company produces a wide variety of athletic-type shoes for tennis, basketball, and running. Although sales are somewhat seasonal, production is uniform throughout the year. Allstar's production and sales average

* Color numbers denote problems which have check answers provided at the end of the book.

1.92 million pairs of shoes per year. The company purchases shoelaces for its entire product line. Shoelaces are bought in lots of 10,000 pairs at a price of $800 per lot. Ordering costs are $20, including the cost of preparing the purchase order and inspecting the shipment when it arrives at the company's warehouse. Annual inventory carrying costs average 15 percent of the inventory value. Assuming that the shoelace manufacturer is located nearby and that orders are filled on the same day they are placed (that is, virtually instantaneously), determine the following:

a. The EOQ for shoelaces.

b. The total annual inventory costs of this policy.

c. The frequency with which Allstar should place its orders for shoelaces.

2. Quick-Copy Duplicating Company uses 110,000 reams of standard-sized paper a year at its various duplicating centers. Its current paper supplier charges $2.00 per ream. Annual inventory carrying costs are 15 percent of inventory value. The costs of placing and receiving an order of paper are $41.25. Assuming that inventory replenishment occurs virtually instantaneously, determine the following:

a. The firm's EOQ.

b. The total annual inventory costs of this policy.

c. The optimal ordering frequency.

3. Looking again at the information in Problem 2, compute and plot ordering costs, carrying costs, and total inventory costs for order quantities of 2,000, 4,000, 5,000, 5,500, 6,000, 7,000, and 9,000 reams. Connect the points on each function with a smooth curve, and determine the EOQ from the graph (and the table used in constructing the graph).

4. Suppose Quick-Copy's paper supplier (see Problem 2) offers a 1 percent discount on orders of 10,000 or more reams. Determine the net annual pretax returns to Quick-Copy of taking the discount.

5. Suppose another paper supplier offers Quick-Copy (see Problem 2) the following price discount schedule:

Quantity (Reams)	Price per Ream
0–9,999	$2.000
10,000–19,999	1.985
20,000 and up	1.975

Assuming that Quick-Copy places its order with this other supplier, determine its optimal order quantity.

6. East Publishing Company employs a high-speed printing press in its operations. A typical production run of 5,000 to 50,000 copies of a textbook can be produced in less than 1 day. The manager of the business textbook division is attempting to determine the optimal number of copies of the second editions of its financial management and managerial economics textbooks to produce. Expected annual demand for the two books are 50,000 and 22,500 copies, respectively. Furthermore, the manager does not want to produce more than a 3-year supply of either book, since these textbooks normally are revised after the 3rd year. Setup costs of getting the printing press (and bindery) ready for a production run of a given textbook are $2,500 and $2,000, respectively, for the two books. Annual carrying costs are $0.80 per copy (16 percent annual carrying charge times the $5.00 production cost per copy). For each textbook, determine the following:

a. The economic order quantity.

b. The total annual inventory costs.

c. The optimal ordering frequency.

7. Arizona Instruments uses integrated circuits (ICs) in its business calculators. Its annual demand for ICs is 120,000 units. The ICs cost Arizona Instruments $10 each. The company has determined that the EOQ is 20,000 units. It takes 18 days between when an order is placed and when the delivery is received. Carrying costs are 20 percent of the inventory value. Determine the following:
   a. The optimal ordering the frequency.
   b. The average inventory and annual carrying costs.
   c. The reorder point.

8. Suppose Arizona Instruments (see Problem 7) decides to maintain a 3-month safety stock of ICs to meet unexpected demand and possible shipment delays (due to strikes, shortages, and so on) from its supplier. Determine the following:
   a. The amount of safety stock, in units.
   b. The average inventory and annual carrying costs.
   c. The reorder point.

9. *Sensitivity of EOQ Model to Estimation Errors.* The calculation of the EOQ using Equation 21.4 assumes that the values of the parameters of the model (S, C, and D) are known or can be determined precisely. In actual applications of the model, these parameter values must be estimated and are therefore subject to possible error.

   This problem examines the effects of possible estimation errors on the EOQ. Refer again to Problem 2. Determine the *estimated* EOQ and the percentage error between the *estimated* EOQ and the *actual* EOQ, as determined in Problem 2; that is, $[(Q^*_{est} - Q^*_{act}) \div Q^*_{act}] \times 100$ under each of the following conditions:
   a. *Estimated* carrying costs are 13.5 percent of inventory value (10 percent less than the *actual* value of 15 percent).
   b. *Estimated* ordering costs are $33 per order (20 percent less than the actual value of $41.25).
   c. *Estimated* carrying costs and ordering costs are both 20 percent higher than the *actual* costs (18.0 percent and $49.50, respectively).

   What conclusions can be drawn from this example concerning the size of the errors in the EOQ value relative to possible errors in estimating the parameters of the model?

10. *Variable Ordering Costs.* The basic EOQ model assumes that ordering costs are fixed and independent of the order quantity. In practice, however, ordering costs can consist of both fixed and variable components. For example, a portion of the costs of receiving and inspecting an order normally will vary with the order quantity.

    This problem examines the effects of variable ordering costs on the EOQ. Assume that ordering costs consist of a fixed component, S', and a variable component, $V' \times Q$, where V' is the variable ordering cost per unit. Under this assumption, the total inventory cost equation becomes the following:

$$\text{Total costs}' = \text{Number of orders per year} \times \text{cost per order}$$
$$+ \text{Average inventory}$$
$$\times \text{Annual carrying cost per unit}$$

$$= \frac{D}{Q} \times (S' + V'Q) + \frac{Q}{2} \times C$$

$$= \frac{DS'}{Q} + DV' + \frac{QC}{2}.$$

Refer again to Problem 2. Assume that the fixed cost of placing an order, S', is $41.25, and that variable ordering cost per unit, V', is $0.01.

a. Compute and plot ordering costs, carrying costs, and total costs for order quantities of 2,000, 4,000, 5,000, 5,500, 6,000, 7,000, and 9,000 reams. Connect the points on each function with a smooth curve, and determine the EOQ from the graph (and the table used in constructing the graph).

b. How does the answer to Part a compare with the EOQ values determined in Problem 2a? What conclusions can be drawn from this example concerning the effects of variable ordering costs on the EOQ?

Selected References

Evans, J., D. Anderson, D. Sweeney, and T. Williams. *Applied Production and Operations Management.* St. Paul, MN: West Publishing, 1984.

Levin, Richard I., and Charles A. Kirkpatrick. *Quantitative Approaches to Management,* 4th ed. New York: McGraw-Hill, 1978.

Wagner, H. M. *Principles of Operations Research: With Applications to Managerial Decisions,* 2nd ed. Englewood Cliffs, N.J.: Prentice-Hall, 1975.

Walleigh, Richard C. "What's Your Excuse for Not Using JIT?" *Harvard Business Review* 64 (March-April 1986): 38–54.

22

OBTAINING SHORT-TERM FUNDS

A Financial Dilemma

Texaco's Financial Difficulties*

Texaco, like many other large well-known companies, issues commercial paper (short-term unsecured borrowings) as a means of acquiring some of its funds. However, one characteristic of the commercial paper market is its impersonal nature. If a company encounters financial difficulties, its commercial paper owners demand payment when the commercial paper matures, thereby preventing the company from reissuing more commercial paper.

In December 1985, Texaco experienced liquidity problems because of the market's unwillingness to allow Texaco to roll over its maturing commercial paper. Texaco's problems resulted from a 1985 court decision entering an $11.1 billion judgment against Texaco in connection with its acquisition of Getty Oil Co. after Pennzoil Co. had agreed in 1984 to buy Getty.

Texaco was faced with the dilemma of how to raise sufficient funds to meet its liquidity needs. On the other hand, the banking community also had the dilemma that even if it provided Texaco with the needed funds, Texaco might declare bankruptcy and default on the loans before they were repaid. The solution to the dilemma involved a group of major banks agreeing to lend Texaco $1.7 billion. Because of Texaco's financial problems, the banks required Texaco to sell them about $2.0 billion of its receivables to cover the loan and provide an additional cushion. The loan was certain to be repaid as Texaco's customers made their payments directly to the banks involved.

This chapter considers the characteristics, advantages, and disadvantages of various sources of short-term credit. As this example illustrates, short-term borrowing exposes a company to the constant risk that this credit may not be renewed. As a result, most companies seek a balance between long-term and short-term sources of financing.

Key Chapter Concepts

1. *Trade credit*, or *accounts payable*, is the principal source of *spontaneous* short-term credit.
2. *Bank loans, commercial paper, accounts receivable loans*, and *inventory loans* are the major sources of negotiated short-term credit.
3. The cost of trade credit is dependent on the size of any cash discount offered and the lengths of the credit and discount periods.
4. The types of short-term bank credit include *single loans, lines of credit*, and *revolving credit agreements*.
5. Commercial paper is a short-term unsecured credit instrument issued by major corporations with good credit ratings.
6. A company can use its accounts receivable to obtain short-term financing. It can either *pledge* the accounts receivable as collateral for a loan or sell (*factor*) the receivables to obtain cash.
7. A company also can use its inventory as collateral for a short-term loan.

Glossary of New Terms

Annual percentage rate (APR) The effective, or true, annual interest rate paid on a loan.

Commercial paper Short-term unsecured promissory notes issued by major corporations with good credit ratings.

Discount loan A loan in which the bank deducts the interest in advance at the time the loan is made.

Factoring The sale of a firm's accounts receivable to a financial institution known as a *factor*.

Field warehouse financing agreement A loan agreement in which the inventory that is being pledged as collateral is segregated from the company's other inventories and stored on its premises under the control of a field warehouse company.

Floating lien An inventory loan in which the lender receives a security interest or general claim on all of a company's inventory.

Line of credit An agreement that permits a firm to borrow funds up to a predetermined limit at any time during the life of the agreement.

Pledging of accounts receivable A short-term borrowing arrangement with a financial institution in which a loan is secured by the borrower's accounts receivable.

Prime rate The lowest rate normally charged by banks on loans made to their most credit-worthy business customers.

Promissory note A formal short-term credit obligation that states the amount to be paid and the due date.

Revolving credit agreement A binding agreement that commits a bank to make loans to a company up to a predetermined credit limit. To obtain this type of commitment from a bank, a company usually pays a *commitment fee* based on the unused portion of the pledged funds.

Terminal warehouse financing agreement A loan agreement in which the inventory that is being pledged as collateral is stored in a bonded warehouse operated by a public warehousing company.

Trust receipt A security agreement under which the borrower holds the inventory and proceeds from the sale of the inventory in trust for the lender. This is also known as *floor planning*.

Introduction

A company normally employs a combination of short-term credit and long-term debt and equity in financing its current and fixed assets. The various sources of long-term financing already have been discussed. The focus of this chapter is on the major sources of short-term credit.

Short-term credit includes all of a company's debt obligations that originally were scheduled for repayment within one year.[1] Short-term credit may be either *unsecured* or *secured*.[2] In the case of unsecured short-term debt, a firm obtains credit from the lender without having to pledge any specific assets as collateral, and the lender depends primarily on the cash-generating ability of the firm to repay the debt. If the firm becomes insolvent and declares bankruptcy, the unsecured lender usually stands little chance of recovering all or even a significant portion of the amount owed.

In the case of secured short-term debt, the borrower pledges certain specified assets—such as accounts receivable, inventory, or fixed assets—as collateral.[3] The Uniform Commercial Code, which was adopted by all states during the 1960s, outlines the procedures that must be followed in order for a lender to establish a valid claim on a firm's collateral.

The first step in this process involves the execution of a *security agreement*, which is a contract between the lender and the firm specifying the collateral held against the loan. The security agreement then is filed at the appropriate public office within the state where the collateral is located. Future potential lenders can check with this office to determine which assets the firm has pledged and which are still free to be used as collateral. Filing this security agreement legally establishes the lender's security interest in the collateral. If the borrower defaults on the loan or otherwise fails to honor the terms of the agreement, the lender can seize and sell the collateral to recover the amount owed. Thus, the lender in a secured short-term debt agreement has *two* potential sources of loan repayment: the firm's cash-generating ability and the collateral value of the pledged assets.

In general, companies prefer to borrow funds on an unsecured basis, since the added administrative costs involved in pledging assets as security raise the cost of the loan to the borrower. In addition, secured borrowing agreements can restrict a company's future borrowing. Many companies are not able to obtain unsecured credit, however. For example, a company may be financially weak or too new to justify an unsecured loan, or it may want more credit than the lender is willing to give on an unsecured basis. In any of these circumstances, the company either must provide collateral or it will not receive the loan.

The short-term credit sources available to a company can be either *spontaneous* or *negotiated*. Spontaneous sources, which include *trade credit, accrued expenses,* and *deferred income,* are discussed in the

---

[1] Short-term credit does *not* always correspond exactly to the current liabilities shown on the firm's balance sheet. Current liabilities also include that portion of long-term debt (such as term loans and mortgages) that is scheduled for repayment during the next year.

[2] Long-term debt also may be either unsecured or secured.

[3] As an alternative to pledging specific assets as collateral for a loan, a company may get a third party to *cosign,* or *guarantee,* the loan. If the borrower defaults, the third party becomes responsible for repayment. Lenders usually will accept only financially sound third parties, such as a stockholder, supplier, or customer who has a vested interest in the company's success.

following sections. Later sections of this chapter consider the various negotiated sources, such as *bank credit, commercial paper, receivables loans,* and *inventory loans.*

Trade Credit

Whenever a business receives merchandise ordered from a supplier and then is permitted to wait a specified period of time before having to pay, it is receiving *trade credit.*[4] In the aggregate, trade credit is the most important source of short-term financing for business firms. Smaller businesses in particular usually rely heavily on trade credit to finance their operations, because they are often unable to obtain funds from banks or other lenders in the financial markets.

Most trade credit is extended on an *open account* basis. A firm sends a purchase order to a supplier, who then evaluates the firm's credit-worthiness using various information sources and decision criteria.[5] If the supplier decides to extend the firm credit, it ships the ordered merchandise to the firm, along with an invoice describing the contents of the shipment, the total amount due, and the terms of sale. When the firm accepts the merchandise shipped by the supplier, it in effect agrees to pay the amount due as specified by the terms of sale on the invoice. Once it has been established, trade credit becomes almost automatic and is subject to only periodic reviews by the supplier. Open account trade credit appears on the balance sheet as *accounts payable.*

Promissory notes sometimes are used as an alternative to the open account arrangement. When a company signs a promissory note, which specifies the amount to be paid and the due date, it is formally recognizing an obligation to repay the credit. A supplier may require a company to sign a promissory note if it questions the company's credit-worthiness. Promissory notes usually appear on the balance sheet as *notes payable.*

Credit Terms

Credit terms, or terms of sale, specify the conditions under which a business is required to repay the credit that a supplier has extended to it. These conditions include the *length* and the *beginning date* of the credit period, the *cash discount* (if any) given for prompt repayment, and any *special terms,* such as *seasonal datings.*[6]

Cost of Trade Credit

Trade credit is considered a *spontaneous* source of financing, since it normally expands as the volume of a company's purchases increases. For example, suppose a company experiences increased demand for its products. As a result, the company increases purchases from suppliers by 20 percent from an average of $10,000 per day to an average of $12,000 per day. Assuming that these purchases are made on credit terms of "net 30" and that the company waits until the last day of the credit period to make payment, its average accounts payable outstanding (trade credit) auto-

---

[4] If the supplier does not feel the firm is credit-worthy, it can require that payment be made either before the goods are shipped (cash before delivery, or CBD) or upon delivery of the merchandise (cash on delivery, or COD). These are cash sales and do not involve an extension of credit.

[5] These sources and criteria are discussed in Chapter 20.

[6] This topic is discussed in Chapter 20.

matically will increase by 20 percent from $300,000 ($10,000 × 30) to $360,000 ($12,000 × 30).

Because the use of trade credit is flexible, informal, and relatively easy to obtain, it is an attractive source of financing for virtually all firms, especially new and smaller firms. To make intelligent use of trade credit, however, a firm should consider the associated costs. Unlike other sources of financing, such as bank loans and bonds, which include explicit interest charges, the cost of trade credit is not always readily apparent. It may appear to be "cost-free" because of the lack of interest charges, but this reasoning can lead to incorrect financing decisions.

Obviously, someone has to bear the cost of trade credit. In extending trade credit, the supplier incurs the cost of the funds invested in accounts receivable, plus the cost of any cash discounts that are taken. Normally, the supplier passes on all or part of these costs to its customers implicitly as part of the purchase price of the merchandise, depending on market supply and demand conditions. If a company is in a position to pay cash for purchases, it may consider trying to avoid these implicit costs by negotiating lower prices with suppliers.

If the terms of sale include a cash discount, the firm must decide whether or not to take it. If the firm *takes the cash discount,* it forgoes the credit offered by the supplier beyond the end of the discount period. Assuming that the firm takes the cash discount and wants to make maximum use of the credit offered by suppliers, it should pay its bills on the last day of the discount period. Under these conditions trade credit does represent a "cost-free" source of financing to the firm (assuming that no additional discounts are available if the firm pays cash on delivery or cash before delivery).

If a company *forgoes the cash discount* and pays bills after the end of the discount period, a definite opportunity cost of trade credit is incurred. In calculating the cost of not taking the cash discount, it is assumed that the company will make maximum use of extended trade credit by paying on the last day of the credit period. Paying after the end of the credit period, or *stretching accounts payable,* subjects the company to certain other costs; these are considered in the following section.

The effective annual percentage cost of forgoing a cash discount is equal to the discount rate per period times the number of periods per year:

$$\begin{array}{l} \text{Effective annual} \\ \text{percentage cost} \end{array} = \frac{\text{Percentage discount}}{100 - \text{Percentage discount}} \times \frac{360}{\text{Credit period} - \text{Discount period}} . \tag{22.1}$$

For example, suppose the Benson Company has extended $150 of trade credit on terms of "2/10, net 30." As shown in Figure 22-1, the company can either pay the discounted amount ($147) by the end of the discount period (day 10) or the full amount of the invoice ($150) by the end of the credit period (day 30).

By *not* paying on the tenth day—that is, by forgoing the cash discount—the company has the use of $147 (98 percent of the invoice

Figure 22-1

Benson Company's Cost of Forgoing the Cash Discount

Credit Terms "2/10, net 30"

amount) for an additional twenty days and effectively pays $3 in interest. Substituting this information into Equation 22.1 yields the following:

$$\text{Effective annual percentage cost} = \frac{2}{100 - 2} \times \frac{360}{30 - 10}$$

$$= \frac{2}{98} \times \frac{360}{20}$$

$$= 36.7\%.$$

As this example shows, the annual cost of forgoing cash discounts can be quite high. Therefore, when making financing decisions, a company should compare this cost to the costs of other sources of credit.

Also, the company which offers credit terms of "2/10, net 30" should consider the annual percentage cost of having the use of funds for an additional twenty days. As the above calculation illustrates, the annual percentage cost of offering cash discounts when the credit terms are "2/10, net 30" is about 37 percent. Accordingly, a company may want to consider other less expensive methods of encouraging prompt payment of trade credit. However, other benefits may accrue to a company which offers cash discounts. For example, a company actually may increase its sales by offering cash discounts. Or, a company may find that its bad-debt loss ratio is lowered if it offers a discount.

Abuses of cash discounts also exist; for example, a purchaser may deduct the discount amount even when payment is made after the discount period has passed. As a result, the seller has to decide whether to simply accept the lower payment or attempt to collect the unearned cash discount amount. With either alternative the seller incurs costs.

Stretching Accounts Payable

Rather than pay suppliers within the credit period specified in the terms of sale, a firm can postpone payment of the amount due to beyond the end of the credit period. *Stretching* payments in this manner generates additional short-term financing for the firm, but this credit is not cost-free. Not only does the firm incur the costs of forgoing any cash discounts, but its credit rating may also deteriorate, along with its ability to obtain future credit. Late payment penalties or interest charges also may be added to these costs, depending on specific industry practices. Although occasional stretching of payables—for example, to meet a seasonal need for funds—might be tolerated by suppliers and involve little or no cost to the firm, a firm that persistently stretches accounts payable well beyond their due dates may find its trade credit cut off by suppliers, who may adopt a cash before delivery (CBD) or a cash on delivery (COD) policy when dealing with the firm in the future. Finally, when a firm develops a reputation for being consistently slow in meeting financial obligations, banks and other lenders may refuse to loan funds on reasonable terms.

Accrued Expenses and Deferred Income

Accrued expenses and deferred income are additional spontaneous sources of unsecured short-term credit.

Accrued Expenses

Accrued expenses—such as *accrued wages, taxes,* and *interest*—represent liabilities for services rendered to the firm that have not yet been paid for by the firm. As such, they constitute an interest-free source of financing.

Accrued wages represent the money a business owes to its employees. Accrued wages build up between paydays and fall to zero again at the end of the pay period, when the employees receive their paychecks. A company can increase the average amount of accrued wages by lengthening the period between paydays. For example, changing from a two-week pay cycle to a four-week pay cycle would effectively double a firm's average level of accrued wages. Also, a company can increase accrued expenses by delaying the payment of sales commissions and bonuses. Legal and practical considerations, however, limit the extent to which a company can increase accrued wages in this manner.

The amounts of *accrued taxes and interest* a firm may accumulate also is determined by the frequency with which these expenses must be paid. For example, corporate income tax payments are normally due quarterly, and a firm can use accrued taxes as a source of funds between these payment dates. Similarly, accrued interest on a bond issue requiring semiannual interest payments can be used as a source of financing for periods as long as six months. Of course, a firm has no control over the frequency of these tax and interest payments, so the amount of financing provided by these sources depends solely on the amounts of the payments themselves.

Deferred Income

Deferred income consists of payments received for goods and services that the firm has agreed to deliver at some future date. Since these payments increase the firm's liquidity and assets—namely, cash—they constitute a source of funds.

Advance payments made by customers are the primary sources of deferred income. These payments are common on large, expensive products, such as jet aircraft. Since these payments are not "earned" by the firm until delivery of the goods or services to the customers, they are recognized on the balance sheet as a liability called *deferred income.*

Short-term Bank Credit

Commercial banks are an important source of both secured and unsecured short-term credit. In terms of the aggregate amount of short-term financing they provide to business firms, they rank second behind trade credit. While trade credit is a primary source of *spontaneous* short-term financing, bank loans represent the major source of *negotiated* short-term funds.

A major purpose of short-term bank loans is to meet the firm's seasonal needs for funds—such as financing the buildup of inventories and receivables. Bank loans used for this purpose are regarded as self-liquidating, since sale of the inventories and collection of the receivables are expected to generate sufficient cash flows to permit the firm to repay the loan prior to the next seasonal buildup.

When a firm obtains a short-term bank loan, it normally signs a promissory note specifying the amount of the loan, the interest rate being charged, and the due date. The loan agreement also may contain various protective covenants.[7] Short-term bank loans appear on the balance sheet under *notes payable.* The effective, or true, annual interest rate on a loan is called the *annual percentage rate,* or *APR.* It is also the internal rate of return between the funds received and the funds paid back.

Short-term bank financing is available under three different arrangements:

- Single loans (notes).
- Lines of credit.
- Revolving credit agreements.

Single Loans (Notes)

Businesses often need funds for short time periods to finance a particular undertaking. In such a case they may request a bank loan. This type of loan is sometimes referred to as a *note.* The length of this type of loan can range from thirty days to one year, with most being for thirty to ninety days.

The interest rate charged on a bank loan usually is related to the *prime rate,* which is the lowest rate banks normally charge on loans made to their most credit-worthy, or *prime,* business customers. The prime rate fluctuates over time with changes in the supply of and demand for loanable funds. During the 1970s and 1980s, for instance, the prime rate ranged from as low as 4$\frac{1}{2}$ percent to as high as 21.5 percent.

The interest rate a bank charges on an individual loan at a given point in time depends on a number of factors, including the borrower's credit-worthiness relative to prime (lowest) credit risks. The interest rate often includes a premium of 1 to 2 or more percentage points higher than the prime rate, depending on how the bank officer perceives the borrower's

---

[7] The section on term loans in Chapter 15 discusses these protective covenants.

overall business and financial risk. If the borrower is in a weak financial position and has overall risk that is thought to be too high, the bank may refuse to make an unsecured loan, regardless of the interest rate. When making the loan decision, the loan officer also considers the size of the checking account balance the company maintains at the bank, the amount of other business it does with the bank, and the rates that competitive banks are charging on similar loans.

The effective annual percentage cost of a bank loan is also a function of when the borrower must pay the interest and whether the bank requires the borrower to maintain a compensating balance.[8]

Interest Payments If the interest on a loan is paid at *maturity,* the effective annual percentage cost is equal to the stated interest rate. In the case of a *discounted loan,* however, the bank deducts the interest at the time the loan is made, and thus the borrower does not receive the full loan amount. In other words, the borrower pays interest on funds it does not receive, and the effective annual percentage cost of the loan is greater than the stated interest rate. It can be calculated as follows:

$$\frac{\text{Effective annual}}{\text{percentage cost}} = \frac{\text{Annual interest charges}}{\text{Funds received}} \times 100. \qquad \textbf{(22.2)}$$

For example, suppose the Wixom Company receives a one-year, $5,000 discounted loan at an interest rate of 8 percent. The firm pays $400 interest in advance ($0.08 \times \$5,000$) and receives only $4,600 ($5,000 − $400). According to Equation 22.2, the effective annual percentage cost of the loan Wixom receives is as follows:

$$\text{Effective annual percentage cost} = \frac{\$400}{\$4,600} \times 100$$
$$= 8.7\%.$$

Discounted bank loans today are relatively uncommon; however, other securities—commercial paper and Treasury Bills, for example—are sold on a discount basis.

Compensating Balances A compensating balance is a certain percentage, usually 5 to 20 percent, of a loan balance that the borrower keeps on deposit with a bank as a requirement of a loan made by the bank. The compensating balance requirement is stated either in terms of an *absolute minimum* balance or an *average* balance over some stipulated period; borrowers prefer average balances to minimum balances. A compensating balance increases the return the bank earns on the loan and also provides

---

[8] The effective annual percentage cost of a bank loan also can depend on the loan payment schedule. Throughout this analysis it is assumed that the firm repays the entire amount of the loan on the maturity date. Some loan agreements, however, call for repayment of the loan in monthly or quarterly *installments* over the year. Calculating the effective annual percentage cost of this type of loan requires the use of slightly different formulas from the ones described here.

the bank with a small measure of protection ("right or offset") in the event that the borrower defaults. Compensating balances tend to diminish in importance during periods of slack loan demand.

If the required compensating balance is *in excess* of the amount of funds that normally would be maintained in the company's checking account, the effective annual percentage cost of the loan is greater than the stated interest rate. It can be calculated as follows:

$$\frac{\text{Effective annual}}{\text{percentage cost}} = \frac{\text{Annual interest charges}}{\text{Usable funds}} \times 100, \qquad \textbf{(22.3)}$$

where *usable funds* represent the net amount of the loan that the company can spend after taking into account the amount borrowed, any required compensating balance, and the balance normally maintained in the bank account.

For example, suppose the Cutler Company obtains a $200,000 bank loan at 9 percent interest but is required to maintain a 20 percent average compensating balance. In other words, the company must maintain a $40,000 (0.20 × $200,000) average compensating balance to obtain the loan. If Cutler currently maintains a $30,000 average balance that can be used to meet the compensating balance requirement, it needs to keep an additional $10,000 in the account, and thus the loan generates $190,000 in usable funds. The interest charges on the loan are $18,000 ($200,000 × 0.09). Substituting these values into Equation 22.3 yields the following:

$$\text{Effective annual percentage cost} = \frac{\$18,000}{\$190,000} \times 100$$
$$= 9.5\%.$$

However, if Cutler currently has no balances in its bank account that can be used to meet the average compensating balance requirement, it has to keep $40,000 of the $200,000 loan in the checking account, and the amount of usable funds is reduced to $160,000. In this case, the effective annual percentage cost becomes significantly higher:

$$\text{Effective annual percentage cost} = \frac{\$18,000}{\$160,000} \times 100$$
$$= 11.3\%.$$

Lines of Credit

A firm that needs funds periodically throughout the year for a variety of purposes may find it useful to negotiate a line of credit with its bank. A line of credit is an agreement that permits the firm to borrow funds up to a predetermined limit at any time during the life of the agreement. The major advantage of this type of borrowing agreement, as compared with single loans, is that the firm does not have to renegotiate with the bank every time funds are required. Instead, it can obtain funds on short notice with little or no additional justification. Another advantage to establishing a line of credit is that the firm can plan for its future short-term financing requirements without having to anticipate exactly how much it will have to borrow each month.

A line of credit usually is negotiated for a 1-year period, with renewals being subject to renegotiation each year. In determining the size of a credit line, a bank will consider a company's credit-worthiness, along with its projected financing needs. As part of the application for a line of credit, the company is normally required to provide the bank with a cash budget for the next year, along with current and projected income statements and balance sheets. The interest rate on a line of credit usually is determined by adding to the prime rate a premium based on the borrower's credit-worthiness. Since the prime rate normally fluctuates over time, the interest rate charged varies during the life of the agreement.

A line of credit agreement normally includes certain protective covenants. In addition to possibly including a compensating balance requirement, the loan agreement usually contains an annual "clean-up" provision requiring that the company have no loans outstanding under the line of credit for a certain period of time each year, usually 30 to 90 days. This type of policy helps reassure the bank that the firm is using the line of credit to finance seasonal needs for funds, and not to finance permanent capital requirements. Finally, a line of credit agreement may also contain provisions (similar to those in a term loan agreement) that require the firm to maintain a minimum working capital position, limit total debt and lease financing, and restrict dividend payments.

Revolving Credit Agreements

Although a line of credit agreement does not legally commit the bank to making loans to the firm under any and all conditions, the bank normally will feel morally obligated to honor the line of credit. Some banks, however, have chosen not to provide financing to a firm when the firm's financial position has deteriorated significantly or when the bank lacks sufficient loanable funds to satisfy all its commitments. If the firm desires a guaranteed line of credit, it must negotiate a revolving credit agreement.

Under a revolving credit agreement, or "revolver," the bank is *legally committed* to making loans to a company up to the predetermined credit limit specified in the agreement. Revolving credit agreements differ from line of credit agreements in that they require the borrower to pay a commitment fee on the unused portion of the funds. This fee is typically in the range of 0.25 to 0.50 percent. Revolving credit agreements are frequently made for a period of 2 to 3 years.

Calculating the effective annual percentage cost of funds borrowed under a revolving credit agreement is slightly more complex than with either a single loan or a line of credit. In addition to the interest rate, commitment fee, compensating balance, and the firm's normal account balance, the effective cost of a revolving credit loan also depends on the amount borrowed and the credit limit of the agreement. The effective annual percentage cost can be calculated using the following equation:

$$\begin{array}{c}\text{Effective}\\\text{annual}\\\text{percentage}\\\text{cost}\end{array}=\dfrac{\begin{array}{c}\text{Annual}\quad\text{Annual}\\\text{interest}+\text{commitment}\\\text{charges}\quad\quad\text{fee}\end{array}}{\text{Usable funds}}\times 100. \qquad \textbf{(22.4)}$$

For example, suppose the Kalamazoo Company has a $4 million revolving credit agreement with its bank. The agreement requires the company to maintain a 20 percent average compensating balance on any funds borrowed under the agreement, as well as to pay a 0.5 percent commitment fee on the unused portion of the credit line. The interest rate on borrowed funds is 8 percent. Kalamazoo's average borrowing under the agreement during the current year is expected to be $2 million. The company maintains an average of $100,000 in its account at the bank, which can be used to meet the compensating balance requirement.

To calculate the effective annual percentage cost of the revolving credit agreement, Kalamazoo must determine the amount of usable funds generated by the loan, the total interest charges, and the commitment fees. Given average borrowing of $2 million during the year, Kalamazoo is required to maintain an average compensating balance of $400,000 (0.20 × $2 million). Since the company currently maintains an average balance of $100,000, $300,000 of the loan is needed to meet the compensating balance requirement. Therefore, the amount of usable funds is $1.7 million. Interest charges on the average amount borrowed are $160,000 (0.08 × $2 million), and the commitment fee on the unused portion of the credit line is $10,000 (0.005 × [$4 million − $2 million]). Substituting these figures into Equation 22.4 yields the following effective annual percentage cost of the loan:

$$\begin{aligned}\begin{array}{c}\text{Effective annual}\\\text{percentage cost}\end{array}&=\dfrac{\$160{,}000+\$10{,}000}{\$1{,}700{,}000}\times 100\\[2mm]&=\dfrac{\$170{,}000}{\$1{,}700{,}000}\times 100\\[2mm]&=10\%.\end{aligned}$$

Thus, the effective cost of the revolving credit agreement can be significantly higher than the stated interest rate.

Many financially sound companies view revolving credit agreements as a form of financial insurance, and, as a result, these companies frequently have no borrowings outstanding against the agreements. For example, at the end of fiscal 1985 Digital Equipment Corporation had revolving credit agreements totaling $480 million, but they were unused at the time.[9]

---

[9] *Annual Report.* Digital Equipment Corporation, 1985, p. 51.

Commercial Paper   Commercial paper consists of short-term unsecured promissory notes issued by major corporations. Only companies with good credit ratings are able to borrow funds through the sale of commercial paper. Purchasers of commercial paper include corporations with excess funds to invest, banks, insurance companies, pension funds, money market mutual funds, and other types of financial insitutions.

Large finance companies, such as General Motors Acceptance Corporation (GMAC) and CIT Financial Corporation, issue sizable amounts of commercial paper on a regular basis, selling it directly to investors like those just mentioned. Large industrial, utility, and transportation firms, as well as smaller finance companies, issue commercial paper less frequently and in smaller amounts; they sell it to dealers who, in turn, sell the commercial paper to investors.

Maturities on commercial paper at the time of issue range from several days to a maximum of 9 months. Companies usually do not issue commercial paper with maturities beyond 9 months, since these issues must be registered with the Securities and Exchange Commission. The size of an issue of commercial paper can range up to several million dollars. It is usually sold to investors in multiples of $100,000 or more. Large issuers of commercial paper normally attempt to tailor the maturity and amounts of an issue to the needs of investors.

Commercial paper represents an attractive financing source for large, financially sound firms, since interest rates on commercial paper issues tend to be below the prime lending rate. To successfully market commercial paper (and get an acceptable rating from Moody's, Standard and Poor's, or both), however, the company must normally have unused bank lines of credit equal to the amount of the issue.

The primary disadvantage of this type of financing is that it is not always a reliable source of funds. The commercial paper market is impersonal. A firm that is suddenly faced with temporary financial difficulties may find that investors are unwilling to purchase new issues of commercial paper to replace maturing issues. (This happened to Penn Central just prior to its bankruptcy.) In addition, the amount of loanable funds available in the commercial paper market is limited to the amount of excess liquidity of the various purchasers of commercial paper. During tight money periods there may not be enough funds available to meet the aggregate needs of corporate issuers of commercial paper at reasonable rates. As a result, a company should maintain adequate lines of bank credit and recognize the risks of relying too heavily on commercial paper. Finally, a commercial paper issue usually cannot be paid off until maturity. Even if a company no longer needs the funds from a commercial paper issue, it still must pay the interest costs.

Commercial paper is sold on a discount basis. This means that the firm receives less than the stated amount of the note at issue and then pays the investor the full face amount of maturity. The effective annual percentage cost of commercial paper depends on the maturity date of the issue and the prevailing short-term interest rates. In addition to the interest charges, borrowers also must pay a *placement fee* to the commercial paper dealer for arranging the sale of the issue. The effective annual percentage cost can be computed as follows:

$$\text{Effective annual percentage cost} = \frac{\text{Interest charges} + \text{Placement fee}}{\text{Funds received}}$$
$$\times \frac{360}{\text{Maturity length (days)}} \times 100. \quad \textbf{(22.5)}$$

The funds received are equal to the face amount of the issue less the interest charges and placement fee. The second term on the right-hand side of Equation 22.5—360/maturity length (days)—is used to convert the stated interest charges and placement fee to an annual rate.

For example, suppose Mammouth Steel Company is considering issuing $10 million in commercial paper. A commercial paper dealer has indicated that Mammouth could sell a 90-day issue at an interest rate of 9.5 percent. The placement fee would be $25,000. Using Equation 22.5, the effective annual percentage cost of this commercial paper issue is as follows:

$$\begin{aligned}
\text{Effective annual percentage cost} &= \frac{(0.095/4)\$10,000,000 + \$25,000}{\$10,000,000 - (0.095/4)\$10,000,000 - \$25,000} \\
&\quad \times \frac{360}{90} \times 100 \\
&= \frac{\$262,500}{\$9,737,500} \times 4 \times 100 \\
&= 10.78\%.
\end{aligned}$$

The interest rate (9.5 percent, or 0.095) in this calculation is divided by 4, since the interest is to be paid for only one-fourth (90 days) of the year.

Accounts Receivable Loans

Accounts receivable are one of the most commonly used forms of collateral for *secured* short-term borrowing. From the lender's standpoint, accounts receivable represent a desirable form of collateral, since they are relatively liquid and their value is relatively easy to recover if the borrower becomes insolvent. In addition, accounts receivable involve documents representing customer obligations rather than cumbersome physical assets. Offsetting these advantages, however, are potential difficulties. One disadvantage is that the borrower may attempt to defraud the lender by pledging nonexistent accounts. Also, the recovery process in the event of insolvency may be hampered if the customer who owes the receivables returns the merchandise or files a claim alleging that the merchandise is defective. Finally, the administrative costs of processing the receivables can be high, particularly when there is a large number of invoices involving small dollar amounts.

Nevertheless, many companies use accounts receivable as collateral for short-term financing by either *pledging* their receivables or *factoring* them.

Pledging Accounts Receivable

The pledging process begins with a loan agreement specifying the procedures and terms under which the lender will advance funds to the firm. When accounts receivable are pledged, the firm retains title to the receivables and continues to carry them on its balance sheet. However, the pledged status of the firm's receivables should be disclosed in a footnote to the financial statements. (Pledging is an accepted business practice, particularly with smaller businesses.) A firm that has pledged receivables as collateral is required to repay the loan, even if it is unable to collect the pledged receivables. In other words, the borrower assumes the default risk, and the lender has *recourse* back to the borrower. Both commercial banks and finance companies make loans secured by accounts receivable.

Once the pledging agreement has been established, the firm periodically sends the lender a group of invoices along with the loan request. Upon receipt of the customer invoices, the lender investigates the creditworthiness of the accounts to determine which are acceptable as collateral. The percentage of funds that the lender will advance against the collateral depends on the quality of the receivables and the company's financial position. The percentage normally ranges from 50 to 80 percent of the face amount of the receivables pledged. The company then is required to sign a promissory note and a security agreement, after which it receives the funds from the lender.

Most receivables loans are made on a *nonnotification basis,* which means the customer is not notified that the receivable has been pledged by the firm. The customer continues to make payments directly to the firm. To protect itself against possible fraud, the lender usually requires the firm to forward all customer payments in the form in which they are received. In addition, the borrower is usually subject to a periodic audit to insure the integrity of its receivables and payments. Receivables that remain unpaid for 60 days or so usually must be replaced by the borrower.

The customer payments are used to reduce the loan balance and eventually repay the loan. Receivables loans can be a continuous source of financing for a company, however, provided that new receivables are pledged to the lender as existing accounts are collected. By periodically sending the lender new receivables, the company can maintain its collateral base and obtain a relatively constant amount of financing.

Receivables loans can be an attractive source of financing for a company that does not have access to unsecured credit. As the company grows and its level of receivables increases, it can normally obtain larger receivables loans fairly easily. And, unlike line of credit agreements, receivables loans usually do not have compensating balance or "clean-up" provisions.

The effective annual percentage cost of a loan in which receivables are pledged as collateral includes both the interest expense on the unpaid balance of the loan and the service fees charged for processing the receivables. Typically, the interest rate ranges from 2 to 5 percent over the prime rate, and service fees are approximately 1 to 2 percent of the amount of the pledged receivables. The services performed by the lender under a pledging agreement can include credit checking, keeping records of the pledged accounts and collections, and monitoring the agreement. This type of financing can be quite expensive for the firm.

Factoring Accounts Receivable

Factoring receivables involves the outright sale of the firm's receivables to a financial institution known as a *factor*. A number of so-called old-line factors, in addition to some commercial banks and finance companies, are engaged in factoring receivables. When receivables are factored, title to them is transferred to the factor, and the receivables no longer appear on the firm's balance sheet.

Traditionally, the use of factoring was confined primarily to the apparel, furniture, and textile industries. In other industries the factoring of receivables was considered an indication of poor financial health. Today, factoring seems to be gaining increased acceptance in other industries.

The factoring process begins with an agreement that specifies the procedures for factoring the receivables and the terms under which the factor will advance funds to the firm. Under the normal factoring arrangement, the firm sends the customer order to the factor for credit checking and approval *before* filling it. The factor maintains a credit department to perform the credit checking and collection functions. Once the factor decides that the customer is an acceptable risk and agrees to purchase the receivable, the firm ships the order to the customer. The customer usually is notified that its account has been sold and is instructed to make payments directly to the factor.

Most factoring of receivables is done on a *nonrecourse* basis; in other words, the factor assumes the risk of default.[10] If the factor refuses to purchase a given receivable, the firm still can ship the order to the customer and assume the default risk itself, but this receivable does not provide any collateral for additional credit.

In the typical factoring agreement, the firm receives payment from the factor at the normal collection or due date of the factored accounts. This is called *maturity factoring*. If the firm wants to receive the funds prior to this date, it usually can obtain an advance from the factor; this is referred to as *advance factoring*. Therefore, in addition to credit checking, collecting receivables, and bearing default risk, the factor also performs a lending function and assesses specific charges for each service provided. The maximum advance the firm can obtain from the factor is limited to the amount of factored receivables *less* the factoring commission, interest expense, and reserve that the factor withholds to cover any returns or allowances by customers. The reserve is usually 5 to 10 percent of the factored receivables and is paid to the firm after the factor collects the receivables.

The factor charges a factoring commission, or service fee, of 1 to 3 percent of the factored receivables to cover the costs of credit checking, collection, and bad-debt losses. The rate charged depends on the total volume of the receivables, the size of the individual receivables, and the default risk involved. The factor normally charges an interest rate of 2 to 5 percent over the prime rate on advances to the firm. These costs are somewhat offset by a number of internal savings that a business can realize through factoring its receivables. A company that factors all its receivables does not need a credit department and does not have to incur

---

[10] If the receivables are sold to the factor on a *recourse* basis, the firm is liable for losses on any receivables that are not collected by the factor.

the administrative and clerical costs of credit investigation and collection
or the losses on uncollected accounts. In addition, the factor may be better
able to control losses than a credit department in a small or medium-sized
company due to its greater experience in credit evaluation. Thus, although
factoring receivables may be a more costly form of credit than unsecured
borrowing, the net cost usually will be below the stated factoring commission and interest rates because of credit department and bad-debt loss
savings.

For example, the Masterson Apparel Company is considering factoring
its receivables because of the large degree of credit risk inherent in its
business. The company primarily sells large quantities of apparel to a
relatively small number of retailers, and if even one retailer does not pay,
the company could experience severe cash flow problems. By factoring,
Masterson transfers the credit risk to the factor. The factor requires a 5
percent reserve for returns and allowances, charges a 2 percent factoring
commission, and will advance Masterson funds at an annual interest rate
of 12 percent. Factoring receivables will allow the company to eliminate its
credit department and save $50,000 per year in administrative and clerical
costs. Factoring also will eliminate bad-debt losses, which average 0.5
percent of credit sales of $6 million per year. The company's receivables
turn over 6 times per year.

Table 22-1 calculates the amount of funds Masterson can borrow from
the factor and the effective annual percentage cost of these funds.[11] As can
be seen in the table, Masterson can obtain an advance of $911,400 from
the factor. *Net* annual costs of these funds are $151,600 for an effective
annual percentage cost of 16.6 percent. Masterson can compare the cost of
this factoring arrangement with the cost of other sources of funds in
deciding whether or not to factor its receivables.

Inventory Loans

Inventories are another commonly used form of collateral for secured
short-term loans. Like receivables, many types of inventories are fairly
liquid. Thus, lenders consider them to be a desirable form of collateral.
When judging whether a firm's inventory would be suitable collateral for a
loan, the primary considerations of the lender are the type, physical
characteristics, identifiability, liquidity, and marketability of the inventory.

Firms hold three types of inventories—*raw materials, work-in-process,*
and *finished goods*. Normally, only raw materials and finished goods are
considered acceptable as security for a loan. The physical characteristic
with which lenders are most concerned is the item's *perishability*. Inventory that is subject to significant physical deterioration over time is usually
not suitable as collateral.

Inventory items also should be *readily identifiable* by means of serial
numbers or inventory control numbers. This helps protect the lender
against possible fraud and also aids the lender in establishing a valid title
claim to the collateral if the borrower becomes insolvent and defaults on

---

[11] Although the reserve for returns is deducted when figuring the amount of funds advanced by the
factor, it is not part of the cost of factoring, since the factor will return it to Masterson provided that
the company's customers make no returns or adjustments.

Table 22-1   **Cost of Factoring Receivables for the Masterson Apparel Company**

Annual credit sales	$6,000,000	
Receivables turnover	6 times (every 60 days)	
Average level of receivables	$6,000,000 ÷ 6	$1,000,000
Less: Factoring commission	0.02 × $1,000,000	−20,000
Less: Reserve for returns	0.05 × $1,000,000	−50,000
Amount available for advance before interest is deducted		$ 930,000
Less: Interest on advance	(0.12 × 60/360) × $930,000	− 18,600
Amount of funds advanced by factor		$ 911,400
Factoring commission per 60 days	$20,000	
Interest expense per 60 days	18,600	
Gross factoring cost per 60 days	$38,600	
Gross factoring cost per year ($38,600 × 6)		$ 231,600
Less: Annual credit department savings		−50,000
Less: Annual bad-debt losses (0.005 × $6,000,000)		−30,000
Net annual cost of factoring receivables		$ 151,600

$$\text{Effective annual percentage cost} = \frac{\text{Net annual cost of factoring receivables}}{\text{Amount of funds advanced by factor}} \times 100$$

$$= \frac{\$151{,}600}{\$911{,}400} \times 100$$

$$= 16.6\%$$

the loan. The ease with which the inventory can be *liquidated* and the stability of its *market price* are other important considerations. In the event that the borrower defaults, the lender wants to be able to take possession, sell the collateral, and recover the full amount owed with minimal expense and difficulty.

Both commercial banks and finance companies make inventory loans. The percentage of funds that the lender will advance against the inventory's book value ranges from about 50 to 80 percent and depends on the inventory's characteristics. Advances near the upper end of this range normally are made only for inventories that are standardized, nonperishable, easily identified, and readily marketable. To receive an inventory loan, the borrower must sign both a promissory note and a security agreement describing the inventory that will serve as collateral.

In making a loan secured with inventories, the lender can either allow the borrower to hold the collateral or require that it be held by a third party. If the borrower holds the collateral, the loan may be made under a *floating lien* or *trust receipt* arrangement. If a third party is employed to hold the collateral, either a *terminal warehouse* or a *field warehouse* financing arrangement can be used.

Floating Liens

Under a floating lien arrangement, the lender receives a security interest or general claim on *all* of the firm's inventory; this may include both present and future inventory. This type of agreement often is employed when the average value of the inventory items is small, the inventory turns over frequently, or both. Specific items are not identified. Thus, a floating lien does not offer the lender much protection against losses from fraud or bankruptcy. As a result, most lenders will not advance a very high percentage of funds against the book value of the borrower's inventory.

Trust Receipts

A trust receipt is a security agreement under which the firm holds the inventory and proceeds from the sale in trust for the lender. Whenever a portion of the inventory is sold, the firm is required to immediately forward the proceeds to the lender; these then are used to reduce the loan balance.

Some companies engage in inventory financing on a continuing basis. In these cases, a new security agreement is drawn up periodically, and the lender advances the company additional funds using recently purchased inventories as collateral.

All inventory items under a trust receipt arrangement must be readily identified by serial number or inventory code number. The lender makes periodic, unannounced inspections of the inventory to make sure that the firm has the collateral and has not withheld payment for inventory that has been sold.

Businesses which must have their inventories available for sale on their premises, such as automobile and appliance dealers, frequently engage in trust receipt financing. This is also known as *floor planning*. Many "captive" finance companies that are subsidiaries of manufacturers, such as General Motors Acceptance Corporation (GMAC), engage in floor planning for their dealers.

Terminal Warehouse and Field Warehouse Financing Arrangements

Under a *terminal warehouse* financing arrangement, the inventory being used as loan collateral is stored in a bonded warehouse operated by a public warehousing company. When the inventory is delivered to the warehouse, the warehouse company issues a warehouse receipt listing the specific items received by serial or lot number. The warehouse receipt is forwarded to the lender, who then advances funds to the borrower.

Holding the warehouse receipt gives the lender a security interest in the inventory. Since the warehouse company will release the stored inventory to the firm only when authorized to do so by the holder of the warehouse receipt, the lender is able to exercise control over the collateral. As the firm repays the loan, the lender authorizes the warehouse company to release appropriate amounts of the inventory to the firm.

Under a *field warehouse* financing agreement, the inventory that serves as collateral for a loan is segregated from the firm's other inventory and stored on its premises under the control of a field warehouse company. The field warehouse company issues a warehouse receipt, and the lender advances funds to the firm. The field warehouse releases inventory to the firm only when authorized to do so by the lender.

Although terminal warehouse and field warehouse financing arrangements provide the lender with more control over the collateral than it has when the borrower holds the inventory, fraud and/or negligence on the part of the warehouse company can result in losses for the lender. The fees charged by the warehouse company make this type of financing more expensive than floating lien or trust receipt loans. In a terminal warehouse arrangement, the firm incurs storage charges, in addition to fees for transporting the inventory to and from the public warehouse. In a field warehouse arrangement, the firm normally has to pay an installation charge, a fixed operating charge based on the overall size of the warehousing operation, and a monthly storage charge based on the value of the inventory in the field warehouse.

Overall warehousing fees are generally 1 to 3 percent of the inventory value. The total cost of an inventory loan includes the service fee charged by the lender and the warehousing fee charged by the warehousing company, plus the interest on the funds advanced by the lender. Any internal savings in inventory handling and storage costs that result when the inventory is held by a warehouse company are deducted in computing the cost of the loan.

Summary

- Short-term credit may be either *secured* or *unsecured*. In the case of secured credit, the borrower pledges certain assets (such as inventory, receivables, or fixed assets) as collateral for the loan. In general, firms prefer to borrow on an unsecured basis, since pledging assets as security generally raises the overall cost of the loan and also can reduce the firm's flexibility by restricting future borrowing.

- *Trade credit, accrued expenses,* and *deferred income* are the primary sources of spontaneous short-term credit. *Bank loans, commercial paper, accounts receivable loans,* and *inventory loans* represent the major sources of *negotiated* short-term credit.

- Trade credit is extended to a firm when it makes purchases from a supplier and is permitted to wait a specified period of time before paying for them. It is normally extended on an *open-account* basis, which means that once a firm accepts merchandise from a supplier, it agrees to pay the amount due as specified by the terms of sale on the invoice.

- *Stretching accounts payable,* or postponing payment beyond the end of the credit period, can be used to obtain additional short-term financing. The costs of stretching accounts payable include forgone cash discounts, penalties, and interest, as well as possible deterioration of the firm's credit rating and ability to obtain future credit.

- *Accrued expenses,* such as accrued wages, taxes, and interest, are liabilities for services provided to the firm that have not yet been paid for by the firm.

- *Deferred income* consists of payments received for goods and services a company will deliver at a future date.

- Short-term *bank credit* can be extended to the firm under a *single loan,* a *line of credit,* or a *revolving credit agreement.* A line of credit permits the firm to borrow funds up to a predetermined limit at any time during the life of the agreement. A revolving credit agreement legally commits the bank to provide the funds when the firm requests them.

- *Commercial paper* consists of short-term unsecured promissory notes issued by major corporations with good credit ratings.

- *Accounts receivable loans* can be obtained by either *pledging* or *factoring* receivables. In the case of a pledging arrangement, the firm retains title to the receivables, and the lender advances funds to the firm based on the amount and quality of the receivables. With factoring, receivables are sold to a factor, who takes the responsibility for credit checking and collection of the accounts. With pledging, the lender does not assume credit risk and has *recourse* back to the borrower if payment is not made, whereas factoring is normally a nonrecourse form of financing.

- Several types of *inventory loans* are available. In a *floating lien* or *trust receipt* arrangement, the borrower holds the collateral. In a floating lien arrangement, the lender has a general claim on all of the firm's inventory. In a trust receipt arrangement, the inventory being used as collateral is specifically identified by serial or inventory code numbers. In a *terminal warehouse* and a *field warehouse* arrangement, a third party holds the collateral; in the case of a terminal warehouse arrangement, collateral is stored in a public warehouse, whereas in a field warehouse arrangement, collateral is stored in a field warehouse located on the borrower's premises.

- No one source (or combination of sources) of short-term financing is necessarily optimal for all firms. Many other factors, in addition to effective annual percentage cost, need to be considered when choosing the optimal source or sources of short-term financing. Some of these factors include the availability of funds during periods of financial crisis or tight money, restrictive covenants imposed on the firm, and the nature of the firm's operations and funds requirements.

FOCUS ON CORPORATE PRACTICE

Corporate Credit Analysis

Richard H. Brock
Senior Vice-President
InterFirst Bank Dallas, N.A.

The purpose of corporate credit analysis is to identify risks inherent in a loan transaction through assessing complete and accurate financial and business information about the prospective borrower. Whether a lender is extending credit to a privately held middle market company or one ranked in the Fortune 500, fundamental factors of sound credit analysis remain principally the same. Emphasis is on the borrower's ability to meet the terms of repayment as agreed upon with the lender. Key areas of focus in the credit process include an evaluation of (1) the loan purpose; (2) company background and management review; (3) growth and profitability; (4) financial, ratio, and cash flow analysis; and (5) industry analysis.

Underlying these factors is an assessment of the borrower's integrity, reliability, and character. Technical or analytical analysis is only complete when viewed in the context of past track record and performance. The verification of information obtained from the customer through credit investigations; audited financial statements (three years' minimum); on-site plant or office visits; industry sources; and data from Standard and Poor's, Moody's or SEC reports (if the firm is publicly held) represents an important step in the analysis.

Furthermore, a credible analysis relies heavily on the bank officer's ability to judge various credit strengths and weaknesses. The importance of judgment cannot be overemphasized, as few lending decisions are considered absolutely risk-free. Properly assessing critical factors and structuring the credit to address these risks facilitate many transactions that otherwise would be considered unbankable. For example, during the early years of exploration and production, the oil and gas industry found obtaining credit based on oil reserves in the ground to be extremely difficult. Today, bankers (and other institutional and equity partners) use petroleum engineering expertise to evaluate the net present value of future net income of the producing properties used as collateral. This method, referred to as *production payment financing,* is now commonplace and represents an important vehicle for providing capital to the energy industry.

Loan Purpose Analysis

A primary consideration in credit analysis is the specific purpose for which the loan proceeds are to be used. It is also important to identify the source of funds to liquidate the credit (that is, working capital, cash flow, debt refinancing, or equity placement). The use of funds generally falls into two broad categories: working capital (short term) and capital/asset financing (long term). A fertilizer manufacturer's seasonal credit needs (primarily receivables and inventory financing) stand in stark contrast to a forest products firm's capital expansion need to increase paper mill capacity. The sale of the current assets serves as the primary repayment source in the case of the fertilizer manufacturer. In contrast, the profitable operation of the new paper mill over a prolonged period of time is the primary repayment source in the case of the forest products firm. Other special financing requirements include acquisitions, recapitalization, project financing, and off balance sheet activities, all of which can require unique and innovative structures. Conformity with bank policy and regulatory statutes (such as usury laws) must be considered in the initial stages of the loan, in addition to evaluating sources of collateral or other credit support.

Company Background and Management Review

Obtaining a detailed knowledge of the borrower's business is absolutely essential to a comprehensive analysis. Ownership and corporate structure, production and distribution facilities, raw material supply, major trade creditors, major customers, customer concentration, and product/service quality are major elements. Determining the scope of operations, such as domestic and/or international activities, facilitates the assessment of political, economic, and social risks. In recent years, employee and labor relations have increased in importance and must be considered. In industries such as high technology, product obsolescence represents a major risk, whereas in other companies, price, quality, and service may be of primary importance.

A complete review of management depth, reputation, stability, and experience is a critical element of the analysis. Quality management can be considered one of the most important advantages in operating a business during economic declines or in capitalizing on an opportunity in the marketplace. Information outlining management history and employment generally is required to be submitted with the credit request.

Growth and Profitability

Sales and profit growth over a period of years reflects consistency, a highly desirable factor in the extension of credit. Of primary interest is performance during adverse economic conditions. Ability to repay debts generally is agreed to be a function of the quality and consistency of earnings and cash flow. The source of earnings and sales growth (that is, by line of business and by price or volume), as well as profit margin and income statement trend analysis, are of primary interest. Much of this information can be obtained based on a review of the most recent fiscal and quarterly (or monthly) financial statements. Return on sales, assets and equity, and ratios reflecting efficiency are useful analytical tools. Revenue recognition methods also must be examined to determine the quality of sales and earnings. Other accounting policies affecting the income statement (such as amortization of investment tax credits and inventory valuation) require complete review. Actual debt service ability can be determined only after examining the method of financial presentation.

Financial, Ratio, and Cash Flow Analysis

An analysis of the balance sheet indicates the quality and liquidity of the assets, the nature of the liabilities, and the relationship between assets and liabilities. A complete dissection of each major category must be accompanied by analytical information—such as an analysis of the working capital cycle, accounts receivable aging and credit policies, inventory controls, and valuation method (LIFO or FIFO). Fixed assets that have *actually* depreciated faster than represented on the financial statements can overstate net worth. Conversely, assets whose market value exceeds cost or book value can be sources of hidden equity or possibly values for collateral. Capitalization of the firm reflects the relative level of debt (senior or subordinated) and equity (common or preferred stock and retained earnings) used to finance the entity and reflects the additional borrowing capacity of the firm. Access to long-term debt and equity capital markets provides sources of additional financial flexibility.

Accounting policies also must be analyzed in light of a conservative or liberal presentation. This can have a considerable impact on the quality of reported earnings and net worth. Items such as contingent liabilities, unfunded pension liabilities or pending litigation represent additional risk factors. Measures of various balance sheet items include the current and quick ratio (liquidity), total debt to tangible worth (leverage), and debt as a percentage of total capital (capitalization). Many other analytical ratios also are used, depending on the specific firm or industry being evaluated.

The generation of cash flow sufficient to meet demands for the repayment of current maturities of term debt, capital expenditures, dividends, and growing working capital requirements is required. A strong and stable cash flow that provides excellent coverage for both debt service and internal financing of growth generally characterizes high quality credits. In certain instances, such as for a radio or cable television operation, leverage could be fairly high, but excellent cash flows may reduce risk significantly.

Considering that loan repayments are scheduled for future periods, cash flow projections should be provided for at least the term of the credit. These projections, combined with various assumptions for factors such as sales growth, operating and gross profit margins, and interest rate levels, typically are presented under a worst case, best case, and most likely scenario. Cash flow projections also are useful in analyzing the proposed amortization of the loan and in structuring financial covenants in the loan agreement in order to maintain a degree of control over this source of repayment.

Industry Analysis

In addition to analyzing the company seeking credit, the credit analyst also must make a thorough and long-range analysis of the industry in which the borrower operates. Factors unique to each industry must be viewed in the context of the impact on the credit applicant. Comparisons with other companies are useful in determining relative strength. The overall industry condition also must be viewed from an economic perspective. For example, is the industry in the growth or mature phase of development? Not only must the lender feel assured that the borrower will remain in business, but also that the overall industry outlook itself is fundamentally sound.

Summary

This "Focus on Corporate Practice" example has discussed the factors a commercial loan officer considers when evaluating a credit applicant. A good financial manager will be equally aware of the lender's decision process, so it will be possible to present a strong loan application to the lending institution.

**Questions and
Topics for
Discussion**

1. Define and discuss the function of *collateral* in short-term credit arrangements.

2. Explain the difference between *spontaneous* and *negotiated* sources of short-term credit.

3. Under what condition or conditions is trade credit *not* a "cost-free" source of funds to the firm?

4. Define the following:
   a. Accrued expenses.
   b. Deferred income.

5. Explain the differences between a line of credit and a revolving credit agreement.

6. What are some of the disadvantages of relying too heavily on commercial paper as a source of short-term credit?

7. Explain the differences between pledging and factoring receivables.

8. Explain the difference between a floating lien and a trust receipts arrangement.

9. Explain why the effective annual percentage cost of secured credit is frequently higher than that of unsecured credit.

10. Explain why banks normally include a "clean-up" provision in a line of credit agreement.

11. Define the following terms:
    a. Prime rate.
    b. Compensating balance.
    c. Discounted loan.
    d. Commitment fee.

12. What savings are realized when accounts receivable are factored rather than pledged?

13. Determine the effect of each of the following conditions on the costs of borrowing under a line of credit arrangement (assuming that all other factors remain constant):
    a. The bank raises the prime rate.
    b. The bank lowers its compensating balance requirements.
    c. The firm's average bank balance increases as the result of its instituting more stringent credit and collection policies.

14. Under what condition or condtions, if any, might a firm find it desirable to borrow funds from a bank or other lending institution in order to take a cash discount?

Problems*

Note: Assume that there are 360 days per year when converting from annual to daily amounts or vice versa.

1. The Milton Company currently purchases an average of $20,000 per day in raw materials on credit terms of "net 30." The company expects sales to increase substantially next year and anticipates that its raw material purchases will increase to an average of $22,000 per day. Milton feels that it may need to finance part of this sales expansion by *stretching* accounts payable.
   a. Assuming that Milton currently waits until the end of the credit period to pay its raw material suppliers, what is its current level of trade credit?
   b. If Milton stretches its accounts payable an extra 10 days beyond the due date next year, how much *additional* short-term funds (that is, trade credit) will be generated?

* Color numbers denote problems which have check answers provided at the end of the book.

2. Determine the annual percentage cost of forgoing the cash discount under each of the following credit terms:

a. 2/10, net 60.

b. 1½/10, net 60.

c. 2/30, net 60.

d. 5/30, net 4 months (assume 30 days per month).

e. 1/10, net 30.

f. 3/10, net 4 months.

3. Determine the annual percentage cost of forgoing the cash discount if the credit terms are "1/10, net 30," and the invoice is not paid until it is 20 days past due.

4. Determine the effective annual percentage cost of a 1-year, $10,000 discounted bank loan at an interest rate of 9.5 percent. Assume that no compensating balance is required.

5. The Pulaski Company has a line of credit with a bank under which it can borrow funds at an 8 percent interest rate. The company plans to borrow $100,000 and is required by the bank to maintain a 15 percent compensating balance. Determine the effective annual percentage cost of the loan under each of the following conditions:

a. The company currently maintains $7,000 in its account at the bank that can be used to meet the compensating balance requirement.

b. The company currently has no funds in its account at the bank that can be used to meet the compensating balance requirement.

6. Pyramid Products Company has a revolving credit agreement with its bank. The company can borrow up to $1.0 million under the agreement at an annual interest rate of 9 percent. Pyramid is required to maintain a 10 percent compensating balance on any funds borrowed under the agreement and to pay a 0.5 percent commitment fee on the unused portion of the credit line. Determine the effective annual percentage cost of borrowing each of the following amounts under the credit agreement:

a. $250,000

b. $500,000

c. $1,000,000

7. Wellsley Manufacturing Company has been approached by a commercial paper dealer offering to sell an issue of commercial paper for the firm. The dealer indicates that Wellsley could sell a $5 million issue maturing in 180 days at an interest rate of 7.5 percent per annum (deducted in advance). The fee to the dealer for selling the issue would be $7,500. Determine Wellsley's effective annual percentage cost of this commercial paper financing.

8. The Brandt Company has been approached by two different commercial paper dealers offering to sell an issue of commercial paper for the company. Dealer A offered to market an $8 million issue maturing in 90 days at an interest cost of 8.50 percent per annum (deducted in advance). The fee to Dealer A would be $12,000. Dealer B has offered to sell a $10 million issue maturing in 120 days at an interest rate of 8.75 percent per annum (deducted in advance). The fee to Dealer B would be $15,000. Assuming that Brandt wishes to minimize the effective annual percentage cost of issuing commercial paper, which dealer should it choose?

9. Gibson Sporting Goods Company needs to raise $1,500,000 during the next year. One option under consideration is to pledge a portion of its receivables as collateral for a loan from the Business Finance Corporation (BFC). BFC has agreed to advance Gibson 75 percent of the face value of the receivables at 3 percent above the prime lending rate, which is currently 8 percent. The

service fee will be 1.5 percent of the amount of the pledged receivables. Gibson's average collection period for receivables is 45 days. Assume that the interest and service fees are *not* deducted in advance. Determine the following:

   a. The amount of receivables Gibson must pledge during the coming year to obtain the needed funds.

   b. The *annual* cost of pledging its receivables and borrowing under this arrangement.

   c. The effective annual percentage cost of this source of financing.

10. Rework Problem 9 assuming Gibson's average collection period is 60 days.

11. Stein Textile Company is considering factoring its receivables. The company has annual credit sales of $2,400,000, with a 90-day average collection period. Bad-debt losses average 2 percent of sales, and credit department costs are $2,000 per month. Both of these costs will be eliminated if Stein factors its receivables. The factor charges a fee of 3 percent on all receivables and requires a 10 percent reserve for returns and allowances. It will advance funds to Stein at an annual interest rate of 12 percent (interest is deducted from the amount of the advance). Determine the following:

   a. The amount of funds Stein can obtain by factoring its receivables.

   b. The *net* annual cost of factoring its receivables and borrowing under this arrangement.

   c. The effective annual percentage cost of this factoring arrangement.

12. Rework Problem 11 assuming that Stein has a 60-day average collection period.

13. The Eaton Company needs to raise $250,000 to expand its working capital and has been unsuccessful in attempting to obtain an unsecured line of credit with its bank. The firm is considering *stretching* its accounts payable. Eaton's suppliers extend credit on terms of "2/10, net 30." Payments beyond the credit period are subject to a $1\frac{1}{2}$ percent per month penalty. Eaton purchases $100,000 per month from its suppliers and currently takes cash discounts. Assuming that Eaton is able to raise the $250,000 it needs by stretching its accounts payable, determine the following:

   a. The firm's annual lost cash discounts.

   b. Annual penalties.

   c. The effective annual percentage cost of this source of financing.

14. The Eaton Company (see Problem 13) decides that the cost of stretching accounts payable is too high and is considering obtaining a loan from a sales finance company secured by inventories under a field warehousing arrangement. Eaton would be permitted to borrow up to $300,000 under such an arrangement at an annual interest rate of 12 percent. The additional cost of maintaining a field warehouse is $15,000 per year. Determine the effective annual percentage cost of a loan under this arrangement if Eaton borrows the following amounts:

   a. $300,000.

   b. $250,000.

15. Which of the following credit terms would you prefer as a customer?

   a. 2/10 net 30.

   b. 1/10 net 40.

   c. 2/10 net 40.

   d. 1/10 net 25.

   e. Indifferent between all options.

   Explain your choice.

16. Harpo's Music Mart needs to raise $300,000 to increase its working capital. The bank, mindful of Harpo's strained financial condition, has refused to loan the firm the needed funds. Mr. Harpo is considering *stretching* its accounts payable in order to raise the funds. Current credit terms are "3/10, net 30." Payments beyond the credit period are subject to a 1 percent per month penalty. Harpo purchases $125,000 per month from its suppliers and currently takes cash discounts. If Harpo is able to raise the $300,000 it needs by stretching its accounts payable, determine the effective annual percentage cost of this source of financing.

An Integrative Case Problem

Working Capital Management

Anderson Furniture Company manufactures furniture and sells its products to department stores, retail furniture stores, hotels, and motels throughout the United States and Canada. The firm has nine manufacturing plants located in Virginia, North Carolina, and Georgia. The company was founded by Edward G. Anderson in 1906 and has been managed by members of the Anderson family since that time. E. G. Anderson III is currently chairman and president of the company. The treasurer and controller of the company is Claire White, who was hired away from a competing furniture company a few years ago. Anderson owns 35 percent of the common stock of the company and (along with the shares of the firm owned by relatives and employees) has effective control over all of the firm's decisions.

Financial data relating to last year's (19X1) operations, along with relevant industry comparisons, are shown in Table 1. The firm's overall rates of return on equity and total assets have been around the industry average over the past several years—sometimes slightly above average and sometimes slightly below average. The company currently is operating its plants near full capacity and would like to build a new plant in Georgia at a cost of approximately $7.5 million. White has been exploring various alternative methods of financing this expansion and has been unsuccessful thus far in developing an acceptable plan. The sale of new common stock is not feasible at this time because of depressed stock market prices. Likewise, Anderson's banker has advised the firm that the use of additional long-term debt or lease financing is not possible at this time, given the firm's large amount of long-term debt currently outstanding and its relatively low times interest earned ratio. Anderson has ruled out a cut in the firm's dividend as a means of accumulating the required financing. The only other possible sources of financing available to the firm at this time, according to White, appear to be a reduction in working capital (current assets), an increase in short-term liabilities, or both.

Upon learning of these proposed financing methods, Anderson expressed concern about the effect these plans might have on the liquidity and risk of the firm. White replied that the firm currently follows a very conservative working capital policy and that these financing methods would not increase shareholder risk significantly. As evidence, she cited the firm's relatively high current and quick ratios. Anderson was unconvinced and asked White to provide additional information on the effects of these financing plans on the firm's financial status.

1. Anderson's bank requires a compensating balance of $3 million. How much additional funds can be freed up for investment in fixed assets if the firm reduces its cash balance to the minimum required by the bank?
2. How much additional financing can be obtained from receivables if Anderson institutes more stringent credit and collection policies and is able to reduce its average collection period to the industry average? (Assume that credit sales remain constant at $75 million.)
3. How much additional financing can be obtained for fixed-asset expansion if Anderson is able to increase its inventory turnover ratio to the industry average through tighter control of its raw materials, work-in-process, and finished goods inventories? (Assume that the cost of goods sold remains constant at $60.75 million.)
4. Anderson's suppliers extend credit to the firm on terms of "net 30." Anderson normally pays its bills on the last day of the credit period. How much additional financing could be generated if Anderson were to *stretch* its payables 10 days beyond the due date?

Table 1

Anderson Furniture Company's Financial Data (in Thousands of Dollars)

December 31, 19X1			
Balance Sheet			Industry Average
Assets			
Cash	$ 3,690	6.5%	5.0%
Receivables, net	15,000	26.3	21.6
Inventories	20,250	35.5	33.4
Total current assets	$38,940	68.3%	60.0%
Net fixed assets	18,060	31.7	40.0
Total assets	$57,000	100.0%	100.0%
Liabilities and stockholders' equity			
Accounts payable	$ 3,000	5.3%	7.0%
Notes payable (8%)	3,750	6.6	10.0
Total current liabilities	$ 6,750	11.8%	17.0%
Long-term debt (10%)	18,000	31.6	28.0
Stockholders' equity	32,250	56.6	55.0
Total liabilities and equity	$57,000	100.0%	100.0%

Income Statement for the Year Ended December 31, 19X1		
Net sales (all on credit)	$75,000	100.0%
Cost of goods sold	60,750	81.0
Gross profit	$14,250	19.0
Selling and administrative expenses	7,500	10.0
Earnings before interest and taxes	$ 6,750	9.0
Interest expense	2,100	2.8
Net income before taxes	$ 4,650	6.2
Income taxes (45.16%)	2,100	2.8
Net income after taxes	$ 2,550	3.4%

Significant Ratios	Anderson	Industry Average
Current	5.76	3.5
Quick	2.77	1.6
Average collection period (days)	72	58
Inventory turnover (Cost of goods sold/inventory)	3.0	3.5
Sales to total assets	1.3	1.6
Debt to equity	0.8	0.9
Times interest earned	3.2	4.7
Net income after tax/sales	3.4%	2.4%
Net income after tax/equity	7.9%	7.9%

5. Prepare a pro forma balance sheet (dollars and percentages) as of December 31, 19X2, assuming that Anderson has instituted *all* actions described in Questions 1, 2, 3, and 4, and that the funds generated have been used to build a new plant. (Assume that long-term debt and stockholders' equity at the end of 19X2 remain the same as at the end of 19X1. In other words, no new long-term debt is issued or old long-term debt is retired, and all net income after taxes is paid out in common stock dividends. Also assume that net fixed assets, *except for the new plant,* remain unchanged during 19X2. Finally assume that notes payable remain unchanged during 19X2). Hint:

The *total* amount of funds generated from the reduction of current assets and the increase in current liabilities determined in Questions 1, 2, 3, and 4 is $7.5 million (rounded to the nearest $1,000). Round all figures to the nearest $1,000.

6. Prepare a pro forma income statement for 19X2. Assume that sales increase to $87 million as a result of the plant expansion. Also assume that the cost of goods sold and selling and administrative expense ratios (as a percentage of sales) remain constant. Finally, assume that interest expense and the firm's tax rate remain the same in 19X2.

7. Calculate the firm's current, quick, times interest earned, and rate of return on equity ratios based on the pro forma statements determined in Questions 5 and 6. How do these ratios compare with the actual values for 19X1 and the industry averages?

8. What considerations might lead Anderson and White to disagree about the desirability of using short-term sources of funds to finance the plant expansion?

9. What other sources of short-term funds might the firm consider using to finance the plant expansion?

**Selected
References**

Bartter, Brit J., and Richard J. Rendleman, Jr. "Fee-Based Pricing of Fixed
Rate Bank Loan Commitments." *Financial Management* 8 (Spring 1979):
13–20.

MacPhee, William A. *Short-Term Business Borrowing: Sources, Terms, and
Techniques.* Homewood, Ill.: Dow Jones-Irwin, 1984.

Moskowtiz, Louis A. *Modern Factoring and Commercial Finance.* New York:
Thomas Y. Crowell Company, 1977.

Stone, Bernell K. "Allocating Credit Lines, Planned Borrowing and Tangible
Services Over a Company's Banking System." *Financial Management* (Summer 1975): 65–83.

Stone, Bernell K. "The Cost of Bank Loans." *Journal of Financial and Quantitative Analysis* 7 (Dec. 1972): 2077–2086.

PART EIGHT

SELECTED TOPICS IN CONTEMPORARY FINANCIAL MANAGEMENT

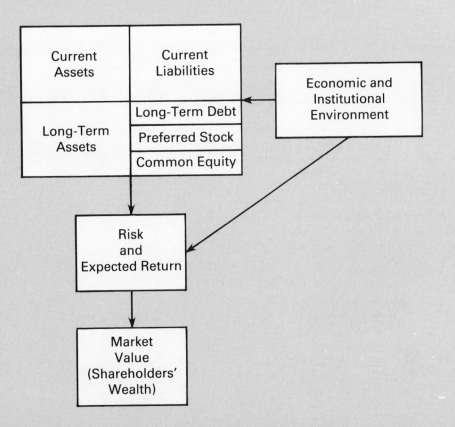

Part Eight looks at a number of additional topics that are important for the financial manager. Chapter 23 considers the merger and acquisition alternative to internal investment growth. Chapter 24 discusses alternatives that are open to the failing firm. Finally, Chapter 25 discusses some key aspects of international financial management. The financial manager who wishes to maximize the value of the firm for its investors needs to have a solid working knowledge of decision-making techniques in each of these areas.

23

MERGERS AND ACQUISITIONS

A Financial Dilemma

The Union Carbide-GAF Affair*

In December 1985, GAF Corp., a specialty chemicals and building materials producer, offered to buy Union Carbide for $68 a share, all in cash, in an unfriendly takeover attempt. Just prior to the attempt, Union Carbide stock was trading at $63 a share. Then, about a week later, Union Carbide made an exchange offer of $85 a share, in cash and debt securities, to buy 35 percent of its stock.

The second round of bidding began about 10 days later when GAF raised its cash offering price to $74 a share. A week later, Union Carbide expanded its $85-a-share offer to include 55 percent of its stock. At about the same time, GAF said that it would be willing to pay $78 a share, if the Union Carbide board of directors would consider the $78 offer a friendly takeover attempt and accept it. The Union Carbide board rejected the $78 offer, and finally on January 8, 1986, GAF ended its pursuit of Union Carbide.

By buying back its shares and preventing the GAF takeover, Union Carbide approximately doubled its long-term debt and lowered the book value of its equity by about 75 percent. Union Carbide also raised its common stock dividend from $3.60 to $4.50 a share in an apparent attempt to increase the value of its stock.

One reason why GAF was interested in acquiring Union Carbide may have been that GAF considered Union Carbide's stock to be undervalued. A possible reason for the undervaluation was the uncertainty related to the outcome of lawsuits resulting from the Union Carbide plant disaster in December 1984 at Bhopal, India, in which over 2,000 deaths occurred.

In examining this merger it is apparent that a number of valuation determinations had to be made by both GAF and Union Carbide. This chapter presents an overview of mergers and discusses the methods used to value merger candidates.

* Adapted from "Landmark Victory: Outside Directors Led the Carbide Defense That Fended Off GAF," *The Wall Street Journal* (January 13, 1986): 1.

Key Chapter Concepts

1. Reasons why a company may choose external growth by merger over internal growth can include the following:
   a. The availability of lower cost assets.
   b. Greater economies of scale.
   c. The availability of more secure raw material supplies and additional end-product markets.
   d. The possibility of more rapid growth.
   e. Greater diversification.
   f. Tax considerations.
2. The valuation of merger candidates involves application of capital budgeting principles. A merger is an acceptable project if the present value of its expected cash inflows exceeds the acquisition cost.
3. The acquisition of a company with a higher P/E ratio causes the earnings per share figure of the acquiring company to decrease if the exchange ratio is based on current stock market prices and no synergy exists. Similarly the acquisition of a company with a lower P/E ratio causes the earnings per share figure of the acquiring company to increase.
4. In the pooling of interests method of accounting for mergers, the acquired assets are recorded at their cost when acquired. In the purchase method, acquired assets are recorded at their fair market values, and any additional amount paid is listed as goodwill, which then must be amortized.

Glossary of New Terms

Conglomerate merger A combination of two or more companies in which neither competes directly with the other and no buyer-seller relationship exists.

Exchange ratio The number of shares an acquiring company must give, or *exchange*, for each share of an acquired company in a merger.

Goodwill An intangible asset equal to the premium over fair market value of the acquired assets that is paid for a company in a merger.

Holding company A corporation that controls the voting power of one or more other companies.

Horizontal merger A combination of two or more companies that compete directly with each other.

Leveraged buyout A transaction in which the buyer of a company borrows a large portion of the purchase price, using the purchased assets as partial collateral for the loans.

Merger A combination of two or more companies into one surviving company. Mergers are also called *acquisitions* or *consolidations*.

Pooling of interests method A method of accounting for mergers in which the acquired company's assets are recorded on the acquiring company's books at their cost when originally acquired. No goodwill account is created under the pooling method.

Purchase method A method of accounting for mergers in which the total value paid or exchanged for the acquired firm's assets is recorded on the acquiring firm's books. Any difference between the acquired assets' fair market value and their purchase price is recorded as goodwill.

Tender offer A public announcement by a company or individual indicating that it will pay a price above the current market price for the shares "tendered" of a company it wishes to acquire.

Vertical merger A combination of two or more companies that have a buyer-seller relationship with one another.

Introduction

Whereas mergers and acquisitions encompass a wider area of a firm's activities than the financial area alone, they nevertheless have significant implications for the financial management function. This chapter discusses various features of mergers and acquisitions, emphasizing their financial aspects.

Merger Terminology

Businesses grow *externally* by acquiring, or combining with, other ongoing businesses. This is in contrast to *internal* growth, which is achieved by purchasing individual assets, such as those evaluated in the discussion of capital expenditures in Chapters 9 through 11. When two companies combine, generally the acquiring company pays for the acquired business either with cash or with its own securities, and the acquired company's liabilities and assets are transferred to the acquiring company.

A *merger* is technically a combination of two or more companies in which all but one of the combining companies legally cease to exist and the surviving company continues in operation under its original name. A *consolidation* is a combination in which all of the combining companies are dissolved and a new firm is formed. The term *merger* generally is used to describe both of these types of business combinations. *Acquisition* also is used interchangeably with *merger* to describe a business combination. In the following discussion, the term *merger* is used, and it is assumed that only two companies are involved—the acquiring company and the merger candidate.[1]

Tender Offers

Although many mergers are the result of a friendly agreement between the two companies, a company may wish to acquire another company even when the combination is opposed by the management (or board of directors) of the merger candidate company. In such a case, the acquiring company makes a *tender offer* for common shares of the merger candidate. In a tender offer, the acquiring company effectively announces that it will pay a certain price above the then existing market price for any of the merger candidate's shares that are "tendered" (that is, offered to it) before a particular date.

After an unfriendly takeover attempt has been initiated, the merger candidate's management frequently tries to find another, more friendly acquiring company (called a "white knight") that would be willing to enter into a bidding war with the first acquiring company. On some occasions, either if the takeover candidate cannot find a white knight, or if it simply does not want to be taken over, the takeover candidate can attempt to buy back its shares from the company or investor who initiated the unfriendly takeover attempt.[2]

In recent years many companies have taken various measures designed to discourage unfriendly takeover attempts.[3] One such measure involves

---

[1] In some instances, merger candidates may be referred to as *takeover candidates, to-be-acquired companies, acquired companies,* or *target companies.*

[2] If the shares are bought back at a premium over the shares' market price, the amount of the premium is referred to as "greenmail."

[3] The financial press has described these antitakeover measures as "shark repellents."

staggering the terms of the board of directors over several years instead of having the entire board come up for election at one time. Thus, the acquiring firm will have difficulty electing its own board of directors in order to gain control. Another measure is to give key executives "golden parachute" contracts, under which the executives would receive large benefits if they were terminated without sufficient cause after a merger. Still another measure used by some companies to discourage takeover attempts involves the issuing of bonds which contain a put option (called a "poison put") that can be exercised only if an unfriendly takeover occurs. The issuing company hopes that the cashing in by bondholders of a portion of its debt will make the takeover unattractive.

Holding Companies

Another form of business combination is the *holding company*, in which the acquiring company simply purchases all or a controlling block of another company's common shares. The two companies then become *affiliated*, and the acquiring company becomes the holding company in this *parent-subsidiary* relationship. For example, Central and South West Corporation is an electric utility holding company. Its principal subsidiaries are Central Power and Light Company, Public Service Company of Oklahoma, Southwestern Electric Power Company, and West Texas Utilities Company.

Stock Purchases and Asset Purchases

A merger transaction may be a stock purchase or an asset purchase. In a *stock purchase,* the acquiring company buys the stock of the to-be-acquired company and assumes its liabilities. In an *asset purchase,* the acquiring company buys only the assets (some or all) of the to-be-acquired company and does not assume any of its liabilities.

Normally, the buyer of a business prefers an asset purchase rather than a stock purchase, because unknown liabilities, such as any future lawsuits against the company, are not incurred. In addition, an asset purchase frequently allows the acquiring company to depreciate its new assets from a higher basis than is possible in a stock purchase. As a result of the unknown liability question, many large companies that acquire small companies refuse to negotiate on any terms other than an asset purchase.

Divestitures and Restructurings

Divestitures and *restructurings* can be an important part of a company's merger and acquisition strategy. After an acquiring company completes an acquisition, it frequently examines the various assets and divisions of the recently acquired company to determine whether or not all the acquired company's pieces "fit" into the acquiring company's future plans. If not, the acquiring company may sell off, or *divest,* a portion of the acquired company. In so doing, the acquiring company is said to be *restructuring* itself.

Divestitures and restructurings, however, frequently are not associated directly with a company's acquisitions. A company may divest itself of certain assets because of a change in overall corporate strategy. For example, in 1985 Warner-Lambert, a drug and consumer products manufacturer, decided to get out of the hospital supply business. The company used the proceeds from the sale of its hospital supply assets to buy back some of its stock. As a result, Warner-Lambert changed, or restructured, the asset side of its balance sheet; this is called an *operational restructuring*. In addition, the company changed its capital structure and thereby carried out a *financial restructuring*.

Types of Mergers

Mergers generally are classified according to whether they are *horizontal, vertical,* or *conglomerate*. A *horizontal merger* is a combination of two or more companies that compete directly with one another; the acquisition in 1985 of American Hospital Supply by Baxter Travenol Laboratories, both large health care products companies, for example, was a horizontal merger. The U.S. government has vigorously enforced antitrust legislation in an attempt to stop large horizontal combinations, and this effort has been effective. However, horizontal combinations in which one of the firms is failing often are viewed more favorably. Also, mergers which allow the companies to compete effectively in world markets are viewed more favorably—the acquisition of RCA by General Electric is an example.

A *vertical merger* is a combination of companies that may have a buyer-seller relationship with one another. For example, if Sears were to acquire one of its appliance suppliers, this would constitute a vertical merger. This type of business combination has gradually declined in importance in recent years.

A *conglomerate merger* is a combination of two or more companies in which neither competes directly with the other and no buyer-seller relationship exists. For example, the Phillip Morris acquisition of General Foods in 1985 for $5.6 billion in cash was a conglomerate merger.

Reasons for Mergers

The following are some of the reasons why a firm might consider acquiring another firm rather than choosing to grow internally:

- A firm may be able to acquire certain desirable assets at a lower cost by combining with another firm than it could if it purchased the assets directly.[4]

- A firm may be able to achieve greater economies of scale by merging with another firm; this is particularly true in the case of a horizontal merger. When the net income for the combined companies after merger exceeds the sum of the net incomes prior to the merger, *synergy* is said to exist.

- A firm that is concerned about its sources of raw materials or end-product markets might acquire other firms at different stages of its production or distribution processes. These are vertical mergers. For example, in 1984 Mobil Corp., a major international oil company considered strong in refining and marketing but somewhat "crude poor," acquired Superior Oil Company which owned large oil and gas

---

[4] In this context, when the *market* value of a company's common stock is below its *book* value (or, more importantly, below the replacement value of the firm's net assets), this company frequently is referred to as a possible "takeover candidate."

reserves and had no refining and marketing operations. The acquisition resulted in Mobil becoming a better balanced oil company.

- A firm may wish to grow more rapidly than is possible through internal expansion. Acquiring another company may allow a growing firm to move more rapidly into a geographic or product area in which the acquired firm already has established markets, sales personnel, management capability, warehouse facilities, and so on, than would be possible by starting from scratch. For example, Schlumberger, in an attempt to partially diversify out of the oil field services business into electronics and computer technology, acquired Fairchild (a semiconductor producer) and Applicon (a manufacturer of computer-related systems), among other companies. These companies had established products and markets.

- A firm may desire to diversify its product lines and businesses in an attempt to reduce its business risk by smoothing out cyclical movements in its earnings. For example, a capital equipment manufacturer might achieve steadier earnings by expanding into the replacement parts business. During a recession, expenditures for capital equipment may slow down, but expenditures on maintenance and replacement parts may increase.

- A firm which has suffered losses and has a tax-loss carryforward may desire to merge with a company that is generating taxable income in order to use the tax-loss carryforwards.

This list, while not exhaustive, does indicate the principal reasons why a firm may choose external expansion over internal growth.

Valuation of Merger Candidates

In principle, the valuation of merger candidates is an application of the capital budgeting techniques described in Chapters 9 through 11. The purchase price of a proposed acquisition is compared to the present value of the expected future cash inflows from the merger candidate. If the present value of the cash inflows exceeds the purchase price, the merger project has a positive net present value and is acceptable.

In the case of an acquisition candidate whose common stock is actively traded, the market value of the stock is a key factor in the valuation process. To induce the stockholders of the acquisition candidate to give up their shares for the cash and/or securities of the acquiring firm, they have to be offered a premium over the market value of the stock (prior to the merger announcement). Generally, a 10 to 20 percent premium is considered a minimum offer. Even then, in many situations, stockholders may hold out for much better offers—either from the company making the initial offer or from other interested companies.

Three major methods typically are used to value merger candidates: the comparative price-earnings ratio method, the adjusted book value method, and the discounted cash flow method.

The *comparative price-earnings ratio method* examines the recent prices and price-earnings (P/E) ratios paid for other merger candidates that are comparable to the company being valued. For example, if two companies in a specific industry recently were acquired at P/E ratios of

10, the comparative P/E ratio method suggests that a P/E ratio of 10 may be reasonable for other, similar companies. Financial analysts who use this method should exercise caution and determine whether the companies being compared are really similar. This method, which focuses on the current income statement, may not be useful if the P/E ratios of recent, similar mergers vary widely.

The *adjusted book value method* involves determining the market value of the company's underlying assets. For example, suppose a company has equipment on its books that is fully depreciated but still in use. The market value of this equipment is determined, and the company's shareholders' equity (book value) is adjusted by the difference between the asset's book value and its market value. Financial analysts who use this method should exercise caution, because the determination of the market value of the merger candidate's assets may be difficult.

The *discounted cash flow method* for valuing merger candidates calculates the present value of the company's expected future cash flows and compares this figure to the proposed purchase price to determine the proposed acquisition's net present value. Consider the following example. Suppose the annual after-tax cash flow from a merger is calculated to be $2 million and is expected to continue for fifteen years. If the appropriate risk-adjusted discount rate is 14 percent, for example, the present value of the expected cash inflows is as follows:

Present value of an annuity of $2 million for 15 years at 14%

$$= \$2,000,000 \ (PVIFA_{0.14, 15})$$
$$= \$2,000,000 \ (6.142)$$
$$= \$12,284.000.$$

Therefore, if the merger candidate's purchase price is less than $12,284,000, the proposed merger has a positive net present value and is an acceptable "project."

In principle, the discounted cash flow method is the most correct of the three methods discussed in this section, because this method compares the present value of the cash flow benefits from the merger with the present value of the merger costs. However, in practice, the future cash inflows from a merger can be quite difficult to estimate.

Most financial analysts who work on proposed mergers use all of these methods to attempt to value merger candidates. In addition, they consider a large number of other factors in valuing merger candidates. These factors include the merger candidate's management, products, markets, distribution channels, production costs, expected growth rate, debt capacity, and reputation.

Analysis of a Merger

The following merger examples illustrate some of the steps and considerations involved in typical mergers. Diversified Industries, Inc., is considering acquiring either High-Tech Products, Inc., or Stable Products, Inc. High-Tech Products has a high expected growth rate and sells at a higher P/E ratio than Diversified. Stable Products, on the other hand, has a low expected growth rate and sells at a lower P/E ratio than Diversified. Table

Table 23-1   **Selected Financial Data: Diversified Industries and Two Merger Candidates**

	Diversified Industries	Stable Products	High-Tech Products
Sales	$1,200 million	$130 million	$100 million
Net earnings, E	$ 120 million	$ 12 million	$ 16 million
Number of shares outstanding, NS	40 million	4 million	4 million
Earnings per share, EPS	$3.00	$3.00	$4.00
Dividends per share, D_0	$1.65	$1.50	$0.80
Common stock market price	$30.00	$21.00	$52.00
Price-earnings ratio	10.0	7.0	13.0
Expected annual growth rate, g	7%	5%	14%

23-1 contains financial statistics on Diversified and the two merger candidates.

The possible merger of Diversified with Stable Products is considered first. To entice Stable Products' present stockholders to tender their shares, Diversified probably would have to offer them a premium of at least 10 to 20 percent above Stable Products' present stock price. Suppose Diversified decides to offer a price of $24 per share, and Stable Products accepts. The exchange is on a stock-for-stock basis. As a result, because Diversified's stock price is $30 a share, Stable Products' shareholders receive 0.8 shares of Diversified common stock for every 1.0 share of Stable Products stock they hold; in other words, the *exchange ratio* is 0.8. The exchange ratio, ER, is the number of acquiring company shares received per share of acquired company stock owned.

Next, the possible merger of Diversified with High-Tech Products is considered. If Diversified decides to offer $60 a share and High-Tech Products accepts, the High-Tech Products' shareholders would receive two shares of Diversified common stock for every share of High-Tech Products stock they hold; in other words, the exchange ratio would be 2.0.

The pro forma financial statement summary is shown in Table 23-2 for Diversified, assuming separate mergers with each of the merger candi-

Table 23-2   **Diversified Industries: Pro Forma Financial Statement Summary Assuming Separate Mergers***

	Before Merger	After Merger with Stable Products	After Merger with High-Tech Products
Sales	$1,200 million	$1,330 million	$1,300 million
Net income	$ 120 million	$ 132 million	$ 136 million
Common shares outstanding	40 million	43.2 million	48 million
Earnings per share	$ 3.00	$ 3.06	$ 2.83

*The exchange ratio is 0.8 shares of Diversified common stock for each 1.0 share of Stable Products and 2.0 shares of Diversified for each 1.0 share of High-Tech Products. The net income figure for Diversified Industries (after merger) assumes that no economies of scale or synergistic benefits are realized as a result of either proposed merger.

dates. The following equation is used to calculate the postmerger earnings per share for the combined companies, EPS_c:

$$EPS_c = \frac{E_1 + E_2 + E_{12}}{NS_1 + NS_2\,(ER)} \tag{23.1}$$

where E_1 and E_2 are the net earnings of the acquiring and acquired companies respectively, E_{12} is the immediate synergistic earnings from the merger, and NS_1 and NS_2 are the number of shares outstanding of the acquiring and acquired companies respectively. For the acquisition of Stable Products by Diversified, $EPS_c = \$3.06$, calculated as follows:

$$EPS_c = \frac{\$120 \text{ million} + \$12 \text{ million} + 0}{40 \text{ million} + [(4 \text{ million})\,(0.8)]}$$
$$= \$3.06.$$

As a result of a merger with Stable Products, Diversified has earnings per share of $3.06, as compared with $3.00 without the merger. In other words, the merger transaction can cause Diversified's earnings to change, due to P/E differences between merging companies. Specifically, if the exchange ratio is based on current stock market prices and no synergy exists, *the acquisition of a company with a lower P/E ratio causes the earnings per share figure of the acquiring company to increase.* Similarly, *the acquisition of a company with a higher P/E ratio causes the earnings per share figure to decrease.* This short-term earnings per share change is caused solely by the merger transaction, and a rational stock market does not perceive this change to be *real* growth or *real* decline.

A more important question remains: What will happen to the price and the P/E ratio of Diversified's stock after a merger has been accomplished? Obviously, it can either go up, stay the same, or go down. Normally the stock market seems to view mergers rationally, recognizing that the post-merger P/E ratio is a weighted average of the two premerger P/E ratios. As a result, the postmerger share price of the acquiring company is usually in the same range as it was prior to the merger, unless significant economies of scale or synergistic benefits are achieved in the merger.

With regard to a possible merger with Stable Products, suppose Diversified's management is not willing to incur an initial dilution in its earnings per share. What is the maximum price and exchange ratio Diversified should agree to under this criterion? The maximum price is calculated using the following equation:

$$P_{max} = (P/E)_1\,(EPS)_2, \tag{23.2}$$

where P_{max} is the maximum offering price without incurring an initial EPS dilution $(P/E)_1$ is the price to earnings ratio of the acquiring company, and EPS_2 is the earnings per share for the to-be-acquired company. Diversified can offer up to $30 a share for Stable Products without diluting its EPS:

$$P_{max} = (10)\ (\$3.00)$$
$$= \$30.$$

A price of $30 a share in this example results in an exchange ratio of 1.0, because Diversified's stock also is selling at $30 a share.

Suppose Diversified Industries merges with High-Tech Products and initially dilutes its EPS to $2.83 from its present $3.00 level, assuming no immediate synergy. Diversified's managers may want to know how long it will take the expected EPS of the combined companies to equal the expected EPS of Diversified without the acquisition. To answer this question, we have to consider the expected growth rates of the individual companies given in Table 23-1. Without a merger, Diversified's earnings, dividends, and assets are expected to grow at an annual rate of 7 percent, and High-Tech Products' are expected to grow at 14 percent a year. Assume that the combined companies grow at 9 percent a year. The expected EPS growth for Diversified with and without the merger is shown in Figure 23-1. Based on the expected growth rates, the EPS of Diversified with the merger will be equal to its EPS without the merger in about three years.[5] This information will be used by the Diversified management in its decision whether or not to acquire High-Tech products.

Leveraged Buyouts   One frequently used method to buy a company or a division of a large company is a leveraged buyout, or LBO. In a typical leveraged buyout, the buyer borrows a large amount of the purchase price, using the purchased assets as collateral for a large portion of the borrowings. The buyers are frequently the managers of the division or company that is being sold. It is anticipated that the earnings of the new company will be sufficient to service the debt and permit the new owners to earn a reasonable return on their investment.

The majority of LBOs involve relatively small companies. However, a number of LBOs involving large companies have occurred. One widely publicized LBO involved the purchase of Gibson Greetings, Inc., a card manufacturer, from RCA for $80 million in 1982.[6] Less than two years later, Gibson's stock was valued at about $290 million in an initial public stock offering. Examples of large NYSE companies that have gone private in LBOs include Jack Eckerd Corp. (1986) and Beatrice Companies (1985).

The following LBO example illustrates some of the steps and considerations involved in typical LBOs. As a part of a corporate restructuring, Universal Industries, Inc., recently has decided to sell its Gray Manufac-

---

[5] The number of years, n, for the two alternatives to produce equal EPS levels is calculated using the following equation:
$$EPS_1(1 + g_1)^n = EPS_2(1 + g_2)^n,$$
where EPS_1 and EPS_2 are the initial EPS values for each alternative, and g_1 and g_2 are the expected annual growth rates for each alternative.

[6] The investor group, which included former U. S. Treasury Secretary William E. Simon, actually put up approximately $1 million in cash.

Figure 23-1   **Diversified Industries' Expected EPS Growth With and Without the High-Tech
                           Products Acquisition**

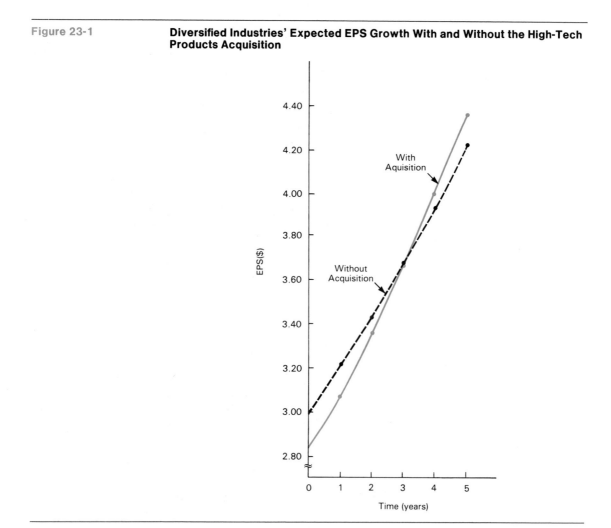

turing Division, a manufacturer of industrial products. The Gray division's top management, together with several private investors, are
considering buying Gray and operating it as a separate company. As is
fairly typical of LBO candidates, Gray is in a mature industry and its
products have a low probability of becoming obsolete. In addition, Gray's
fixed assets have a present market value greater than their book value.

The Gray financial statements listed in Table 23-3 show that Gray
presently has an annual pre-tax loss of $1,000,000, and therefore its return
on stockholders' equity is negative. The Gray management group intends
to return Gray to profitability by various cost-cutting and other measures.
Gray's parent company, Universal Industries, also could have initiated
cost-cutting measures to attempt to return Gray to profitability. However,
partly because of Universal's new corporate strategy to get out of the
industrial products business, it has chosen instead to sell Gray.

Following negotiations between the Gray management group and
Universal Industries, the management group agreed to purchase all of the
assets of the Gray division for $30 million.

Table 23-3   **Leveraged Buyout of Gray Manufacturing Co.**

Balance Sheet
($ million)

	Before LBO	Pro Forma After LBO
Current assets	$22	$22
Fixed assets, net	8	16
Total assets	$30	$38
Current liabilities	$15	$15
Long-term debt	—	18
Stockholders' equity	15	5
Total liabilities and equity	$30	$38

Annual Income Statement
($ million)

	Before LBO	Pro Forma After LBO
Revenues	$30	$30
Cash operating expenses	29	21
Interest expense	1	5
Depreciation	1	3
Earnings before tax	$(1)	$ 1

The Gray management group plans to take the following steps to complete the LBO transaction.

1. The management group has put together equity totaling $5 million. Some of these funds will come from liquidated Universal Industries retirement and employee benefit plans. In LBO terminology, equity is sometimes referred to as "ground floor financing."

2. The management group has arranged for short-term commercial bank financing, agreeing to pledge Gray's accounts receivable and inventory as collateral. This level of financing is called either "second floor" or "top floor" financing.

3. The management group also has arranged to finance the remaining portion of the buyout with subordinated long-term debt financing from an investment banking firm specializing in providing financing for LBOs. This subordinated debt is called "mezzanine" financing because of its position between the ground floor and the second floor financing. Mezzanine financing is high-risk capital because the company's fixed assets do not provide sufficient collateral for the debt. In addition, Gray's cash flow forecast for its early years as a separate entity indicates that it may experience some difficulty in servicing its debt obligations. As a result, the investment bankers providing the mezzanine financing have insisted that the debentures include attached warrants to provide additional opportunities for return other than the debt's interest payments. Because these debentures are highly risky, they are referred to as "junk bonds." *Junk bond* is a term frequently

applied to a debt issue rated Ba or lower by Moody's or BB or lower by Standard & Poor's.[7]

4. The management group intends to initiate a major cost-cutting program as soon as Gray becomes a separate company. They plan to cut unnecessary personnel at all levels, and for the remaining employees they plan to cut salaries and employee benefits. In return, however, they do plan to offer key employees stock options, and all employees will participate in a bonus plan.

In addition, Gray personnel will no longer have to provide reports to Universal which in turn reports to its stockholders and the Securities & Exchange Commission. Also, the Gray managers themselves will no longer be spending time talking to security analysts.

5. The management group has determined that Gray's fixed assets (real estate and equipment) have a market value of approximately $16 million, or about twice their present book value. As a result of the LBO, the fixed assets will be written up to their market value and depreciated on the basis of the higher value. The increased depreciation charge will shelter a greater portion of Gray's cash flow from Federal income taxes, all other things being equal.

This example illustrates many of the steps a buyer usually takes in a leveraged buyout.

Accounting Aspects of Mergers

Two basic methods can be used to account for mergers: the *purchase method* or the *pooling of interests method*. In the purchase method, the total value paid or exchanged for the acquired firm's assets is recorded on the acquiring company's books. The tangible assets acquired are recorded at their fair market values, which may or may not be more than the amount at which they were carried on the acquired firm's balance sheet prior to the merger. Any difference between the total value paid and the fair market value of the acquired assets is termed *goodwill*.[8]

In the pooling of interests method, the acquired company's assets are recorded on the acquiring company's books at their cost (net of depreciation) when originally acquired. Thus, any difference between the purchase price and the book value is not recorded on the acquiring company's books, and no goodwill account is created.

The pooling of interests method has certain advantages over the purchase method. All other things being equal, reported earnings will be higher under the pooling method, primarily because depreciation will not be more than the sum of the depreciation charges prior to the merger. In addition, since goodwill is not created on the balance sheet in a pooling, it cannot appear as an amortization charge on the acquiring firm's income statement. Finally, since goodwill is not recognized as a deduction for income tax purposes, it has to be deducted from net income *after taxes*.

---

[7] In the case of privately placed debt, a *junk bond* is a debt issue whose characteristics would cause it to be rated Ba, BB, or lower if it were rated.

[8] The expression *goodwill* rarely appears on the balance sheet; instead, we often find "investment in consolidated subsidiaries in excess of net assets at date of acquisition, less amortization."

Table 23-4

Comparison of the Purchase and the Pooling of Interests Methods of Accounting for Mergers*

| | Before Acquisition | | Company B (After Acquisition of Company A) | |
	Company A	Company B	Purchase Method	Pooling of Interests Method
Total assets, book value	$10	$50	$63	$60
Liabilities, book value	3	15	18	18
Stockholders' equity, book value	7	35	45	42

*Terms of merger: Company B acquires common stock of Company A for $10 million.

For example, suppose that Company B acquires Company A's outstanding common stock for $10 million. The book value of the acquired shares is $7 million. Table 23-4 shows the results of this merger, according to both the purchase and pooling of interests methods.

In the pooling of interests method, the two balance sheets are combined, and the $3 million difference between the purchase price and the book value of Company A's stock is not considered. In the purchase method, in contrast, the $3 million difference between the purchase price and the book value is recorded on both sides of Company B's postmerger balance sheet as an increase in total assets and as stockholders' equity.

The book value of Company A's *assets* is $10 million. Suppose that the market value of Company A's assets at the date of acquisition is $11 million. Company B paid $3 million above the book value of *stockholders' equity*. Of this $3 million, the $1 million difference between the assets' market value and book value is recorded on the balance sheet in the appropriate tangible assets accounts. The other $2 million is recorded as goodwill.

The present accounting rules pertaining to mergers limit use of the pooling of interests method to mergers which essentially combine the entire existing interests of *common* stockholders in independent companies. Otherwise, the purchase method must be used. As a result, most mergers are accounted for using the purchase method.

Tax Aspects of Mergers

Taxes can play an important role in determining how an acquired company's shareholders receive compensation for their shares. Merger transactions that are effected through the use of voting equity securities (either common stock or *voting* preferred stock) are tax-free. For example, if an acquired company's stockholders have a gain on the value of their shares at the time of the merger, the gain is not recognized for tax purposes if these shareholders receive voting equity securities of the acquiring company; any gains are not recognized until the newly acquired shares are sold.

In contrast, if the acquired company's shareholders receive cash or *nonvoting* securities (such as debt securities, *nonvoting* preferred stock, or warrants) in exchange for their shares, any gains are taxable at the time of the merger. When a partial cash down payment is made, however, the exchange can be treated as an installment purchase, and the seller can spread the tax liability which is created over the payment period.

Summary

- Business combinations include *mergers, consolidations,* and *holding companies.* Technically, a merger is a business combination in which all but one of the companies legally cease to exist, and the surviving company continues in operation under its original name. A consolidation is a business combination in which all the combining companies are dissolved and a new company is formed. A holding company owns controlling interest in another legally separate company, and the relationship between these *affiliated* companies is called a *parent-subsidiary relationship.*

- *Mergers are classified according to whether they are horizontal, vertical,* or *conglomerate.* In a horizontal merger, the combining companies are direct competitors. In a vertical merger, the companies have a buyer-seller relationship. In a conglomerate merger, neither company competes directly with the other, and no buyer-seller relationship exists.

- There are a number of reasons why companies choose external growth over internal growth, including the following:

  1. The availability of lower cost assets.
  2. Greater economies of scale.
  3. The availability of more secure raw material supplies and additional end-product markets.
  4. The possibility of more rapid growth.
  5. Greater diversification.
  6. Tax considerations.

- Three major methods are used to value merger candidates: the *comparative price-earnings ratio method, the adjusted book value method, and the discounted cash flow method.* The discounted cash flow method, which is an application of capital budgeting techniques, is the most theoretically correct valuation method.

- The acquisition of a company with a higher P/E ratio causes the earnings per share figure of the acquiring company to decrease if the exchange ratio is based on current stock market prices and no synergy exists. Similarly the acquisition of a company with a lower P/E ratio causes the earnings per share figure of the acquiring company to increase.

- In a *leveraged buyout* the buyer of a company borrows a large portion of the purchase price, using the purchased assets as partial collateral for the loans.

- In the *pooling of interests* method of accounting for mergers, the acquired assets are recorded at their cost when acquired. In the *purchase* method, acquired assets are recorded at their fair market values, and any additional amount paid is listed as *goodwill,* which then must be amortized.

Questions and Topics for Discussion

1. Define the following terms:
   a. Merger.
   b. Consolidation.
   c. Holding company.
2. Describe some of the measures used by companies to discourage unfriendly takeover attempts.
3. What is the difference between an asset purchase and a stock purchase?
4. What is the difference between an operational restructuring and a financial restructuring?
5. Discuss the differences between the following types of mergers:
   a. Horizontal mergers.
   b. Vertical mergers.
   c. Conglomerate mergers.
6. What are some of the reasons why firms merge with other firms?
7. What methods do financial analysts use to value merger candidates? What are the limitations of each method?
8. Explain what happens to the post merger earnings per share figure when a company with a relatively high P/E ratio acquires a company with a lower P/E ratio, assuming the exchange ratio is based on current stock market prices and no synergy exists.
9. What are the differences between the *purchase* method and the *pooling of interests* method of accounting for mergers?
10. What is a leveraged buyout? What is mezzanine financing?
11. What is a "tax-free merger"?

Problems*

1. The Blue Oil Corporation and the Grey Plastics Company have agreed to a merger. The Grey Plastics stockholders will receive 0.75 shares of Blue for each share of Grey held. Assume that no synergistic benefits are expected.
   a. Complete the following table:

	Blue Oil	Grey Plastics	Combined Companies
Sales (millions)	$500	$125	___
Net income (millions)	$60	$13	___
Common shares outstanding (millions)	16	4	___
Earnings per share	$3.75	$3.25	___
Common stock (price per share)	$41.25	$26	___
Price-earnings ratio	___	___	10.0

   b. Calculate the premium percentage received by the Grey stockholders.

2. Redo the table in Problem 1 assuming *both* that immediate synergistic earnings of $3 million per year will occur as a result of the merger and the P/E ratio of the combined companies is 10.5.

* Color numbers denote problems which have check answers provided at the end of the book.

3. The McPherson Company is considering acquiring the McAlester Company. Selected financial data for the two companies are shown here:

	McPherson	McAlester
Sales (millions)	$250	$30
Net income (millions)	$20	$2.25
Common shares outstanding (millions)	5	1
Earning per share	$4.00	$2.25
Dividends per share	$1.20	$0.40
Common stock (price per share)	$40.00	$18.00

Both companies have 40 percent marginal tax rates. Assume that no synergistic benefits are expected.

a. Calculate the McPherson Company's postmerger earnings per share if the McAlester stockholders accept an offer of $20 a share in a stock-for-stock exchange. (The expression *stock-for-stock exchange* means that the common stock of one company is exchanged for the common stock of another company.)

b. Recalculate Part a, assuming that the McPherson common stock price is $42 a share. (All other figures remain constant.)

c. Calculate McPherson's earnings per share if the McAlester stockholders accept one $6 convertible preferred share (stated value, $100) for each 5 shares of McAlester stock held.

d. Calculate McPherson's earnings per share if each group of 50 shares of McAlester stock is exchanged for one 8 percent, $1,000 debenture.

e. Compare the premerger expected dividend return on the McAlester stock with the expected postmerger dividends or interest available with the exchanges described in Parts a, c, and d. (Undoubtedly, at the time of acquisition, McPherson would have pointed out these expected increases in yield to the McAlester stockholders.) Assume that an investor initially holds 100 shares of McAlester stock.

f. What can be said about comparing the expected total premerger return (dividends plus price appreciation) on the McAlester stock versus the expected total postmerger return on the McPherson securities?

4. Ball Industries is considering acquiring the Keyes Corporation in a stock-for-stock exchange. Selected financial data on the two companies follow:

	Ball	Keyes
Sales (millions)	$600	$75
Net income (millions)	$30	$10
Common shares outstanding (millions)	6	4
Earnings per share	$5.00	$2.50
Common stock (price per share)	$50	$20

Assume that no synergistic benefits are expected.

a. What is the maximum exchange ratio Ball should agree to if one of its acquisition criteria is no initial dilution in earnings per share?

b. Suppose an investor had purchased 100 shares of Keyes common stock 5 years ago at $12 a share. If the Keyes stockholders accept an offer of $24 a share in a stock-for-stock exchange, how much capital gains tax would this investor have to pay at the time the Keyes shares are exchanged for the Ball shares? (Assume a capital gains tax rate of 20 percent for this investor.)

5. Referring to Problem 4, calculate the post merger earnings per share if the Keyes stockholders accept an offer by Ball of $24 a share in a stock-for-stock exchange. Assume that immediate synergistic earnings of $4 million will occur as a result of the acquisition.

6. Looking back at Tables 23-1 and 23-2, assume that Diversified Industries acquires High Tech Products in a stock-for-stock transaction and no immediate synergistic benefits are expected. How long will it take the expected EPS of the combined companies to equal the expected EPS of Diversified without the merger if Diversified is expected to grow at an annual rate of 7 percent without the merger and the combined companies are expected to grow at 8 percent a year?

**An Integrative
Case Problem**

Mergers and Acquisitions

Admiral Foods Corporation is a diversified food processing and distributing company that has shown excellent growth over the past ten years as a result of a balanced program of acquisitions and internal growth.

One segment of the food business in which Admiral has only recently begun to compete, however, is the fast-food business. The present top management of Admiral Foods feels that good future growth in the fast-food business is still possible, regardless of the rapid expansion of the 1980s. During the past year, members of the Admiral staff have examined and analyzed a number of independent fast-food firms.[9] One company that the analysis indicated as potentially suitable for acquisition by Admiral is Favorite Food Systems, Inc.

Favorite Food Systems, Inc., which was founded by John Favorite in 1964, is a West Coast chain with current annual sales of approximately $75 million. Favorite's history can best be described as up and down, with the general trend up. The company survived several brief shaky periods during the late 1960s. In 1973 the company went public. (The Favorite family now controls about 57 percent of the common stock.) By 1976 Favorite Foods was recommended by two brokerage firms and was touted by one investment service as "another potential McDonald's." This and other predictions never came true. In fact, Favorite Food Systems' growth rate has slowed appreciably during the past five years. One reason frequently given in the trade for Favorite's growth slowdown is Mr. Favorite's apparent indecision regarding expansion. As a result, the competition has increasingly gotten the jump on Favorite with the best locations in new residential growth areas.

The following table shows last year's balance sheets and income statements for both Admiral and Favorite.

**Admiral Foods Corporation Balance Sheet
(in millions of dollars)**

Current assets	$225.0	Current liabilities	$101.0
Fixed assets, net	307.0	Long-term debt	106.0
		Common equity	
		(10,000,000 shares)	325.0
		Total liabilities	
Total assets	$532.0	and equity	$532.0

**Admiral Foods Corporation Income Statement
(in millions of dollars)**

Sales	$1261.0
Expenses, excluding depreciation	1118.2
Depreciation	36.0
Earnings before interest and taxes	$ 106.8
Interest	12.8
Earnings before taxes	$ 94.0
Taxes (40%)	37.6
Net income	$ 56.4

[9] Many of the fast-food and restaurant chains are divisions of larger firms. For example, Burger King and Steak and Ale are part of Pillsbury, and Red Lobster is part of General Mills.

**Favorite Food Systems, Inc., Balance Sheet
(in millions of dollars)**

Current assets	$10.6	Current liabilities	$ 6.5
Fixed assets, net	12.1	Long-term debt	2.2
		Common equity	
		(2,000,000 shares)	14.0
		Total liabilities	
Total assets	$22.7	and equity	$22.7

**Favorite Food Systems, Inc., Income Statement
(in millions of dollars)**

Sales	$75.2
Expenses, excluding depreciation	65.4
Depreciation	1.4
Earnings before interest and taxes	$ 8.4
Interest	0.4
Earnings before taxes	$ 8.0
Taxes (40%)	3.2
Net income	$ 4.8

Additional Information

	Admiral Foods Corporation	Favorite Food Systems
Dividends per share	$ 2.50	$ 0.60
Common stock (price per share)	$50.00	$15.00

Marie Harrington received her B.B.A. degree in finance three years ago and went to work for Admiral Foods as a financial analyst in the corporate budget department. Recently she became a senior financial analyst responsible for analyzing mergers and major capital expenditures. One of her first assignments is to prepare a financial analysis of the proposed Favorite acquisition. It is the conservative policy of Admiral Foods to analyze acquisitions assuming that no synergistic benefits will occur. Admiral Foods has found that the amount of synergy in a merger is relatively difficult to forecast. During Ms. Harrington's discussions with her supervisor, the following questions came up.

1. Calculate the exchange ratios, based on the common stock market value and earnings per share.

2. Mr. Favorite has suggested an exchange ratio based on a 25 percent increase over Favorite's current market price. Calculate this exchange ratio.

3. What is the maximum exchange ratio Admiral Foods should agree to if one of its acquisition criteria specifies no initial dilution in earnings per share? What per-share price for Favorite Food Systems does this exchange ratio represent?

4. Even though Ms. Harrington's assignment is primarily financial in nature, what other considerations are important in a merger such as this?

5. Calculate the Admiral Foods postmerger earnings per share assuming each share of Favorite stock is exchanged for 0.40 shares of Admiral stock.

6. In discussions with Admiral, Mr. Favorite has stated that he would prefer to exchange his Favorite shares for either Admiral common stock or a convertible preferred rather than cash or debentures. Why?

7. If Admiral Foods is concerned about the possibility that Mr. Favorite will sell his new Admiral shares relatively soon after the merger (and thereby put downward pressure on the price of Admiral's stock), what can Admiral do to effectively prevent such a sale?

8. If Mr. Favorite is unsuccessful in his negotiations with Admiral, two of his key managers, together with a group of private investors, have expressed a willingness to take the company private in a leveraged buyout transaction. How do you think such a transaction would be structured?

9. Based on the information given in the case and your analysis, what do you feel is a fair exchange ratio?

Selected References

Bierman, Harold, Jr. "A Neglected Tax Incentive for Mergers." *Financial Management* 14 (Summer 1985) 29–32.

Desmond, Glenn M., and Richard E. Kelley. *Business Valuation Handbook.* Llano, Calif.: Valuation Press, 1977.

Jemison, David B., and Sam B. Sitkin. "Acquisitions: The Process Can Be a Problem." *Harvard Business Review* 64 (March–April 1986): 107–116.

Lewellen, Wilbur G., and Michael G. Ferri. "Strategies for the Merger Game: Management and the Market." *Financial Management* 12 (Winter 1983): 25–35.

Malatesta, Paul H., and Rex Thompson. "Partially Anticipated Events: A Model of Stock Price Reactions with an Application to Corporate Acquisitions." *Journal of Financial Economics* 14 (June 1985): 237–250.

24

BUSINESS FAILURE

A Financial Dilemma

Continental Airlines and the Bankruptcy Laws*

In September 1983 Continental Airlines, a loss-plagued subsidiary of Texas Air Corporation, filed for bankruptcy. This move was designed to eliminate its high-cost labor contracts. The company reduced its route structure, laid off almost two-thirds of its 12,000 employees, and reduced the wages of its remaining workers by more than 50 percent in many cases. It then began building a "new" low-cost airline.

Continental was quite successful in using the bankruptcy laws in reducing labor costs. Two years later in 1985, while still in bankruptcy and operating under court protection, the company earned a record $62.2 million profit. Continental also filed a reorganization plan in which it promised to fully repay creditors, who are owed nearly $900 million.

This action taken by Continental (and other companies) to reduce labor costs was subsequently curtailed by Congress, partly as a result of an intensive lobbying campaign by organized labor. In 1984, after the Supreme Court ruled (in a similar case involving Wilson Foods) that companies could abrogate existing labor contracts as soon as they filed for bankruptcy, a bankruptcy reform law was enacted which makes it more difficult for companies to void labor contracts. The new rules for trying to reduce labor costs in a reorganization bid require the company to attempt to work out an agreement with the union before it asks for help from the bankruptcy court. The bankruptcy judge then has to weigh the fairness to all parties of the company's offer.

This chapter discusses the alternatives available to companies facing financial difficulties, such as Continental Airlines.

* Based on articles in *The Wall Street Journal* (January 22, 1986): 32 and (March 14, 1986): 1, and *Business Week* (July 16, 1984): 27.

Key Chapter Concepts

1. In a financial context, a firm is:
   a. *Technically insolvent* when it is unable to meet its current obligations as they come due, even though the value of its assets exceeds its liabilities.
   b. *Legally insolvent* if the recorded value of its assets is less than the recorded value of its liabilities.
   c. *Bankrupt* if it is unable to pay its debts and it files a bankruptcy petition in accordance with the Federal bankruptcy laws.
2. The primary causes of business failures are generally considered to be incompetent and inexperienced management.
3. A failing company can either:
   a. Attempt to resolve its difficulties with its creditors on a voluntary, or informal, basis, or
   b. Petition the courts for assistance and formally declare bankruptcy.
4. In a bankruptcy proceeding, if the going-concern value of the firm is greater than its liquidation value, it is reorganized; otherwise it is liquidated.
   a. A reorganization plan is carried out under Chapter 11 of the Bankruptcy Reform Act.
   b. A liquidation is carried out under Chapter 7 of the Bankruptcy Reform Act.

Glossary of New Terms

Assignment The process of informally liquidating a business. Assignment occurs outside the jurisdiction of the bankruptcy courts.

Bankruptcy A situation in which a firm is unable to pay its debts, and its assets are turned over to the court for administration.

Bankruptcy Reform Act of 1978 A new U.S. bankruptcy act that significantly changed certain aspects of the Federal bankruptcy laws.

Chapter 11 The reorganization chapter of the Bankruptcy Reform Act. Under Chapter 11, a company continues to operate while it attempts to work out a reorganization plan.

Chapter 7 The liquidation chapter of the Bankruptcy Reform Act. Under Chapter 7, a compa-ny's assets are sold off, and the proceeds are distributed to creditors.

Composition A situation in which a failing business is permitted to discharge its debt obligations by paying less than the full amounts owed to creditors.

Extension A situation in which a failing business is permitted to lengthen the amount of time it has to meet its obligations with creditors.

Legal insolvency A situation in which the recorded value of a firm's assets is less than its liabilities.

Technical insolvency A situation in which a firm is unable to meet its current obligations as they come due, even though the value of its assets may exceed its liabilities.

Introduction

This chapter considers what happens when businesses experience severe and extended problems that might cause failure. The purpose is to present an overview of business failure and the alternatives available to the failing firm. The chapter first defines business failure and then discusses its frequency and causes. Next, the various alternatives available to failing firms are discussed, including the procedures involving the Federal bankruptcy laws.

Definitions of Business Failure

Business failure can be considered from both an *economic* and a *financial* viewpoint. In an economic sense, *business success* is associated with firms that earn an adequate return (equal to or greater than the cost of capital) on their investments. Similarly, *business failure* is associated with firms that earn an inadequate return on their investments. An important aspect of business failure involves the question of whether the failure is *permanent* or *temporary*. For example, suppose a company has $1,000,000 invested in assets and only generates operating earnings of $10,000. Obviously, this 1 percent return on investment is inadequate. However, the appropriate course of action depends to some extent on whether this business failure is judged to be permanent or temporary. If it is permanent, the company probably should be liquidated. If failure is temporary, the company probably should attempt "to ride out the storm," especially if steps can be taken to speed the company's return to business success. From an economic standpoint, business failure also is said to exist when a firm's revenues are not sufficient to cover the costs of doing business.

It is more common, however, for business failure to be viewed in a *financial context,* either as a *technical insolvency,* a *legal insolvency,* or a *bankruptcy*. A firm is said to be *technically insolvent* if it is unable to meet its current obligations as they come due, even though the value of its assets exceeds its liabilities.[1] A firm is *legally insolvent* if the recorded value of its assets is less than the recorded value of its liabilities. A firm is *bankrupt* if it is unable to pay its debts and it files a bankruptcy petition in accordance with the Federal bankruptcy laws.

Business Failure Trends

Table 24-1 shows several kinds of statistics dealing with business failures over time. Between 1968 and 1979, the number of failures in the United States averaged about 10,000 per year. However, beginning with the severe 1981–82 recession, the failure figures increased significantly. The number of failures, as well as the failure rate continued increasing even after the recession ended. This was attributed to a number of factors, including:[2]

1. Continued high interest rates put pressure on company balance sheets.

2. Low levels of inflation forced firms to operate more efficiently, that is, it was harder to pass price increases on to customers.

3. The recovery was characterized by a high degree of high-technology

---

[1] A firm that is *technically insolvent* can also be said to be *illiquid.*
[2] *Dun & Bradstreet Looks at Business* (March/April 1985): 2.

Table 24-1   **Failure Trends since 1925**

Year	Number of Failures*	Total Failure Liabilities	Failure Rate per 10,000 Listed Concerns	Average Liability per Failure
1925	21,214	$ 443,744,000	100	$ 20,918
1930	26,355	668,282,000	122	25,357
1935	12,244	310,580,000	62	25,366
1940	13,619	166,684,000	63	12,239
1945	809	30,225,000	4	37,361
1950	9,162	248,283,000	34	27,099
1955	10,969	449,380,000	42	40,968
1960	15,445	938,630,000	57	60,772
1965	13,514	1,321,666,000	53	97,800
1966	13,061	1,385,659,000	52	106,091
1967	12,364	1,265,227,000	49	102,332
1968	9,636	940,996,000	39	97,654
1969	9,154	1,142,113,000	37	124,767
1970	10,748	1,887,754,000	44	175,638
1971	10,326	1,916,929,000	42	185,641
1972	9,566	2,000,244,000	38	209,099
1973	9,345	2,298,606,000	36	245,972
1974	9,915	3,053,137,000	38	307,931
1975	11,432	4,380,170,000	43	383,150
1976	9,628	3,011,271,000	35	312,762
1977	7,919	3,095,317,000	28	390,872
1978	6,619	2,656,006,000	24	401,270
1979	7,564	2,667,362,000	28	352,639
1980	11,742	4,635,080,000	42	394,744
1981	16,794	6,955,180,000	61	414,147
1982	24,906	15,611,000,000	88	627,000
1983	31,334	16,073,000,000	110	513,000
1984	52,078†	—	—	—
1985	57,067†	—	—	—

Sources: 1925–1981. *The Business Failure Record.* New York: Dun and Bradstreet, 1983. Reprinted by permission. 1982–1983. *Statistical Abstract of the United States 1986* 106th Edition. Washington D.C.: U.S. Department of Commerce, 1985. 1984–1985. *Dun & Bradstreet Looks at Business* (March/April 1986):1.
*A business failure is defined by Dun and Bradstreet as a firm that ceases operations without paying all of its outstanding debts. This includes firms which have entered Chapter 11, Chapter 7, and Chapter 13 bankruptcy proceedings, plus firms which have reached out-of-court agreements with their creditors.
†These figures are not strictly comparable to the earlier years because Dun and Bradstreet added more than twenty-five business categories (mainly services) to the failure coverage.

investment, which is inherently high risk because of rapid innovation and new product development.

4. A reduced stigma associated with bankruptcy—entering bankruptcy is viewed as an acceptable business strategy for avoiding total liquidation.

Typically, less than 5 percent of the business failures involve companies with liabilities over $1 million. However, the 1981–1985 period claimed an unusually high number of very large companies, as is shown in Table 24-2. Some of these companies may successfully reorganize while in bankruptcy

Table 24-2   **Large Nonfinancial Companies Filing Bankruptcy Petitions during the 1981–1985 Period**

Company	Date	Liabilities
Itel	January 1981	$1.7 billion
Seatrain Lines	February 1981	785 million
Wickes	April 1982	2.0 billion
AM International	April 1982	510 million
Braniff	May 1982	1.1 billion
Manville	August 1982	1.1 billion
GHR Energy	January 1983	1.2 billion
Continental Airlines	September 1983	1.1 billion
Wheeling-Pittsburgh	April 1985	865 million

Sources: Edward I. Altman, *Corporate Financial Distress,* New York: Wiley, 1983; and various issues of *Business Week* and *The Wall Street Journal.*

and emerge to become profitable companies again. Some of them, however, may be liquidated and cease to exist.

Another interesting business failure trend involves the ages of failed businesses. Of the 16,794 businesses that failed in 1981, approximately 23 percent had been in business 3 years or less, and approximately 49 percent had been in business 5 years or less. Only 20 percent had been in business more than 10 years.[3]

Causes of Business Failure

Although there are a number of reasons why businesses fail, most failures seem to be due at least in part to incompetent and inexperienced management. Dun and Bradstreet compiles a large amount of bankruptcy data, including causes of business failure. Table 24-3 shows the *underlying* causes of recent business failures. The results show that almost 90 percent of these businesses failed because of management inexperience or incompetence. The Dun and Bradstreet analysis includes a classification of *apparent* causes, as well as *underlying* causes. Of the businesses that failed due to inexperience and incompetence (that is, the first four items shown in Table 24-3), about two-thirds were "evidenced by the inability to avoid conditions which resulted in inadequate sales." The next most frequent apparent cause was heavy operating expenses.[4]

When businesses experience problems such as inadequate sales and heavy operating expenses, they frequently encounter cash flow problems as well. As a result of the cash flow problems, these businesses often increase their short-term borrowings. If the problems persist, the cash flow difficulties can become more acute, and the business may not be able to meet its obligations to its creditors on a timely basis. At this point, the firm's owners and management have to ask about the alternatives that are available to failing businesses.

[3] *The Business Failure Record,* New York: Dun and Bradstreet, 1983, p. 10.
[4] *The Business Failure Record,* p. 13.

Table 24-3   **Causes of 16,794 Business Failures (Classification of Failures Based on Opinion of Informed Creditors and Information in Dun and Bradstreet Reports)**

Underlying Causes	Percentage
Lack of experience in the line	11.1
Lack of managerial experience	12.5
Unbalanced experience*	19.2
Incompetence	45.6
Neglect	0.7
Fraud	0.3
Disaster	0.5
Reason unknown	10.1
Total	100.0
Number of failures	16,794
Average liabilities per failure	$414,147

*Experience not well rounded in sales, finance, purchasing, and production on the part of the individual in the case of a proprietorship, on the part of two or more partners or officers constituting a management unit.
Source: *The Business Failure Record.* New York: Dun and Bradstreet, 1983, p. 12. Adapted by permission.

Alternatives for Failing Businesses

In general, a failing company has two alternatives:

- It can attempt to resolve its difficulties with its creditors on a *voluntary,* or *informal,* basis.
- It can petition the courts for assistance and *formally* declare *bankruptcy.*

A company's creditors also may petition the courts, and this may result in the company's being involuntarily declared bankrupt.

Regardless of whether a business chooses informal or formal methods to deal with its difficulties, eventually the decision has to be made whether to *reorganize* or *liquidate* the business. Before this decision can be made, both the business's liquidation value and its going-concern value have to be determined. *Liquidation value* equals the proceeds that would be received from the sale of the business assets minus its liabilities. *Going-concern value* equals the capitalized value of the company's operating earnings minus its liabilities. Basically, if the going-concern value exceeds the liquidation value, the business should be reorganized; otherwise, it should be liquidated. However, in practice, the determination of the going-concern and liquidation values is not an easy matter. For example, problems may exist in estimating the price the company's assets will bring at auction. In addition, the company's future operating earnings and the appropriate discount rate at which to capitalize the earnings may be difficult to determine. Also, management is understandably not in a position to be completely objective about these values.

Informal Alternatives for Failing Businesses

Regardless of the exact reasons why a business begins to experience difficulties, the result is often the same—namely, cash flow problems.

Frequently, the first steps taken by the troubled company involve stretching its payables. In some cases, this action can buy the troubled company up to several weeks of needed time before creditors take action.

If the difficulties are more than just minor and very temporary, the company may next turn to its bankers and request additional working capital loans. In some situations, the bankers may make the additional loans, especially if they perceive the situation to be temporary. Another possible action the company's bankers and creditors may take is to restructure the company's debt.

Debt restructuring by bankers and other creditors can be quite complex. However, debt restructuring basically involves either *extension, composition,* or a combination of the two. In an *extension,* the failing company tries to reach an agreement with its creditors that will permit it to lengthen the time it has to meet its obligations. In a *composition,* the firm's creditors accept some percentage amount less than their actual original claims, and the company is permitted to discharge its debt obligations by paying less than the full amounts owed. The percentage a company's creditors will agree to in the event of a composition is usually greater than the percentage they could net if the company had to sell its assets to satisfy their claims. If a company's creditors feel that the company can overcome its financial difficulties and become a valuable customer over the long run, they may be willing to accept some form of composition.

Debt restructuring by lenders can involve deferment of both interest and principal payments for a time. Before lenders will agree to these deferments, they often require the troubled company's suppliers to also make various concessions. In addition, the lenders frequently demand and receive *warrants* in return for making their deferment concessions.

Large companies that experience cash flow difficulties often sell off real estate, various operating divisions, or both to raise needed cash. For example, Chrysler, in the midst of its 1980–1982 problems, sold its profitable tank-manufacturing division, as well as certain real estate assets. Also, International Harvester sold its construction equipment division in 1982 to raise the cash needed to stay in business.

Another method often used by failing companies to raise needed cash involves the sale and leaseback of its land and buildings. Some companies also resort to more unusual methods of conserving cash, such as offering preferred stock to certain employees in exchange for a portion of their salary.

Frequently, failing companies voluntarily form a *creditors' committee,* which meets regularly and attempts to help the company out of its predicament. The creditors usually are requested to accept deferred payments, and in return the creditors usually request that the company cut various expenditures. If the company and its creditors are able to reach an agreement on the appropriate actions to take, the legal and administrative expenses associated with formal bankruptcy procedures are not incurred. Accordingly, both the company and creditors may be better off as a result.

Liquidation also can occur outside the bankruptcy courts. The process is called an *assignment*. Usually a trustee, who is probably one of the major creditors, is assigned the assets. The trustee then has the responsibility of selling the assets and distributing the proceeds in the best interests of the creditors.

Formal Alternatives for Failing Businesses under the Bankruptcy Laws

If a failing company is unable to reach a voluntary agreement with its creditors, it can seek assistance and protection in the bankruptcy courts. The Bankruptcy Reform Act of 1978 states the basic mechanics of the bankruptcy procedure.[5]

Either the debtor company or its unsecured creditors may initiate bankruptcy procedures. After the initial *bankruptcy petition* has been filed, both the failing company and its creditors receive protection from the courts. The company itself is protected from any further actions on the part of the creditors while it attempts to work out a *plan of reorganization.*[6] Normally, the troubled company is allowed to continue operations. If there is reason to believe that continuing operations will result in further deterioration of the creditors' position, however, the court can order the firm to cease operating.

An important aspect of the bankruptcy procedures involves what to do with the failing firm. Just as in the case of the informal alternatives, a decision has to be made about whether a firm's value as a *going concern* is greater than its *liquidation* value. Generally, if this is the case and a suitable plan of reorganization can be formulated, the firm is reorganized; otherwise, it is liquidated.

Reorganization Chapter 11 of the Bankruptcy Reform Act outlines different bankruptcy procedures. In a Chapter 11 proceeding, the failing company basically seeks court protection from its creditors while it attempts to work out a *plan of reorganization.*

During Chapter 11 proceedings, the failing company presents its current financial status and its proposed plan of reorganization. This plan of reorganization is normally similar to either composition or extension. The reorganization plan then must be approved by a majority of each class of creditors (who are classified by number and the dollar amount owed them). If the plan is approved, any dissenters are bound to it under the law. The court has considerable latitude in a Chapter 11 bankruptcy. For example, depending on the nature of the case, it may decide to appoint a *trustee,* who will be responsible for running the business and protecting the creditors' interests.

Chapter 11 bankruptcy proceedings may be initiated either voluntarily by the failing company or by a group of three or more of its unsecured creditors that have aggregate claims of at least $500. The only requirement the three or more unsecured creditors have for filing the bankruptcy petition is to assert that the debtor company is not paying its present debts as they come due.

---

[5] The Bankruptcy Reform Act of 1978, in general, streamlined the U.S. bankruptcy procedures and increased the number of bankruptcy courts. The Reform Act contains eight odd-numbered chapters, 1 through 15, which are labeled with arabic numerals instead of the roman numerals used in the old Bankruptcy Act.

[6] The debtor company has 120 days to work out a plan of reorganization. After that, the creditors may file a plan of their own.

After the plan of reorganization has been worked out and submitted to the bankruptcy court for its approval, it is also presented to the creditors for their approval. If the bankrupt company is able to obtain approval from the bankruptcy court and its creditors, it can leave Chapter 11. As an example of a reorganization plan, consider Lionel Corporation, which filed for bankruptcy under Chapter 11 in February 1982.[7] Lionel had unsecured creditors whose claims totaled $139 million. The company proposed paying the creditors $70 million in cash initially and another $45.5 million in cash over eleven years, beginning in 1984. In addition, the creditors would receive $10 million par value of a new 8 percent convertible preferred stock and about 3.8 million newly issued common shares. The creditors would then own 35 percent of the company's outstanding common shares.

The bankruptcy court and the Securities and Exchange Commission (SEC) review the plan of reorganization for *fairness* and *feasibility*. The term *fairness* means that the claims are to be settled in the order of their priority. The priority of claims is discussed in detail in the next section on liquidation. A *feasible* plan of reorganization is one that gives the business a good chance of reestablishing successful operations. For example, the plan must provide an adequate level of working capital, a reasonable capital structure and debt-to-equity ratio, and an earning power sufficient to reasonably cover interest and dividend requirements.

The following example illustrates the procedures involved in formulating a reorganization plan. Suppose that the capital structure listed on the books of Troubled Times, Inc., a company undergoing reorganization, is as follows:

Mortgage bonds	$ 6,000,000
Debentures	5,000,000
Preferred stock	1,000,000
Common stock	8,000,000
	$20,000,000

The trustee estimates the company's liquidation value to be $10 million and its going-concern value to be $12 million. Thus, the company is "worth more alive than dead," and a reorganization rather than a liquidation is attempted. The following is one possible recapitalization that the trustee might submit to the bankruptcy court:

Debentures	$ 3,000,000
Income bonds	2,000,000
Preferred stock	1,000,000
Common stock	6,000,000
	$12,000,000

This recapitalization would result in fewer fixed charges for the reorganized company and thereby afford it a better chance of succeeding. The reorganization also might involve an extension of the debt maturities,

---

[7] *The Wall Street Journal* (March 23, 1983):1.

which would help the company's funds flow by causing the debt's principal retirement to occur at later dates.

The trustee's next task is to allocate these new securities to the old security holders according to the priority of claims. The claims of senior security holders must be settled before those of junior security holders. In this example, the original mortgage bonds are exchanged for the new debentures, income bonds, and new preferred stock. The original debenture holders receive five-sixths of the new common stock, and the original preferred stockholders receive one-sixth of the new common stock. The original common stockholders receive nothing.

Following the SEC review for fairness and feasibility, the bankruptcy court approves the plan for submission to the firm's security holders. The holders who are affected by the reorganization plan then vote by group. Before the court can finally approve the plan, a two-thirds majority of each group of affected debtholders and a simple majority of the firm's stockholders must vote in its favor. Dissenters may appeal the decision to a higher court.

For example, Penn Central, the largest U.S. railroad, declared bankruptcy in 1970. Following eight years of bankruptcy proceedings, a court-approved plan of reorganization became effective in October 1978. Under the terms of this plan, the holders of Penn Central's secured bonds received 10 percent of their claims in cash (generated from the sale of various assets), 30 pecent in new mortgage bonds, 30 percent in new preference (preferred) stock, and 30 percent in new common stock. Thus, the reorganization plan effectively established a *new* capital structure for the firm that consists of less debt and more equity. Penn Central's common stockholders also participated in the reorganization, although they received only $1/25$ share of the new common stock for each Penn Central share they held at that time.

Liquidation If for some reason reorganization is judged unfeasible, a legally declared bankrupt company may be liquidated. The liquidation procedures are described in Chapter 7 of the Bankruptcy Reform Act. In the liquidation procedure, a *referee* normally is appointed to handle the administrative aspects of the bankruptcy procedure. The referee then arranges for a meeting of the creditors, and they in turn select a *trustee,* who liquidates the business and pays the creditors' claims according to the priority of claims set forth in Chapter 7.

The priority of claims states that, in general, secured debts are satisfied first from the sale of the secured assets. The following list specifies the order of priority in which unsecured debts must be paid:

1. The expenses involved in the administration of the bankruptcy.

2. Business expenses incurred after an involuntary petition has been filed, but before a trustee has been appointed.

3. Wages owed for services performed during the 3 months prior to the bankruptcy proceedings, not to exceed $2,000 per employee.

4. Certain unpaid contributions to employee benefit plans (limited to $2,000 per employee).

Table 24-4   **Balance Sheet, Failures Galore, Inc.***

Assets		Liabilities and Capital	
Current assets	$ 6,000,000	Accounts payable	$ 2,000,000
Fixed assets, net	6,500,000	Bank notes payable	2,000,000
		Accrued wages	200,000
		Accrued taxes	300,000
		Mortgage bonds	2,000,000
		Debentures	2,000,000
		Subordinated debentures	2,000,000
		Preferred stock	1,000,000
		Common equity	1,000,000
Total assets	$12,500,000	Liabilities and equity	$12,500,000

*The subordinated debentures are subordinate to the bank notes payable. Assume that all the accrued wages can be paid out of the liquidation proceeds.

5. Certain customer layaway deposits, not to exceed $900 per individual.

6. Taxes owned to Federal, state, and local governments.

7. Claims of general and unsecured creditors.

8. Preferred stockholders—they receive an amount up to the par value or stated value of the preferred stock.

9. Common stockholders—they share any remaining funds equally on a per-share basis.

To illustrate the priority of claims in a liquidation, consider the balance sheet prior to liquidation of Failures Galore, Inc., shown in Table 24-4.[8]

Suppose that the total proceeds of the liquidation are $6.8 million. The distribution of these proceeds is shown in Table 24–5. The proceeds have been distributed in accordance with the priority of claims. Each general and unsecured creditor receives a settlement percentage of the funds owed after priority claims have been settled. As shown in Table 24–5, these priority claims are bankruptcy administration expenses, wages, and taxes owed. In addition, mortgage bondholders receive $1.5 million from the sale of secured assets; this leaves the mortgage bondholders as general creditors for the balance of their claim ($500,000). After these priority claims have been met, there is $4.25 million in assets remaining to meet the remaining creditor claims of $8.5 million. Each general creditor receives 50 percent of the claim, except bank notes. Because the subordinated debentures are subordinate to bank notes, the bank notes receive the proportionate claim of the subordinated holders ($1 million in this case) in addition to the $1 million directly due the bank notes. Hence, because of the subordination provision in the debentures, the bank notes are paid off in full.

---

[8] Assume that this liquidation is a voluntary petition, that no unpaid contributions to employee benefit plans exist, and that no customer layaway deposits are involved. In other words, items 2, 4, and 5 in the priority of claims do not apply to this example.

Table 24-5   **Distribution of the Proceeds from the Liquidation of Failures Galore, Inc.**

Total liquidation proceeds	$6,800,000
1. Bankruptcy administration expenses	$ 550,000
2. Wages owed to employees	200,000
3. Taxes owed to governments	300,000
Total priority claims	$1,050,000
Funds available for claims of creditors	$5,750,000
4. Payment to mortgage bondholders (proceeds from sale of secured assets)	1,500,000
Funds available for claims of general and unsecured creditors	$4,250,000

$$\text{Settlement percentage for general and unsecured creditors} = \frac{\text{Funds available for general and unsecured creditors}}{\text{Total claims of general and unsecured creditors}}$$

$$= \frac{\$4,250,000}{\$8,500,000}$$

$$= 50\%$$

	Total Claim	Settlement, 50% of Claim (Before Subordination Adjustment)	Settlement, 50% of Claim (After Subordination Adjustment)
Accounts payable	$2,000,000	$1,000,000	$1,000,000
Bank notes payable	2,000,000	1,000,000	2,000,000
Mortgage bonds	500,000	250,000	250,000
Debentures	2,000,000	1,000,000	1,000,000
Subordinated debentures	2,000,000	1,000,000	0
	$8,500,000	$4,250,000	$4,250,000

Funds available for preferred and common stockholders $0

Summary

- A firm is *bankrupt* if its total liabilities exceed the value of its total assets. A firm is *technically insolvent* if it cannot meet its current obligations as they come due, even though the value of its assets exceeds its liabilities.

- *Incompetent and inexperienced management* are generally considered to be the primary causes of most business failures.

- Failing firms have two basic alternatives:

  1. They can attempt to resolve the difficulties with their creditors on an *informal*, voluntary basis.

  2. They can petition the courts for assistance and *formally* declare *bankruptcy*.

  In addition, the creditors may petition the courts, and the firm may involuntarily be declared bankrupt.

- Legal bankruptcy proceedings focus on the decision of whether the failing firm should be *reorganized* or *liquidated*. If its going-concern value is greater than its liquidation value, the business will usually be reorganized; otherwise, it will be liquidated.

- The Bankruptcy Reform Act contains two chapters that outline different bankruptcy procedures. In a Chapter 11 proceeding, the troubled company seeks court protection from its creditors while it works out a *reorganization plan.* If reorganization is judged not feasible, the bankrupt company is liquidated. The liquidation procedures are set forth in Chapter 7 of the Bankruptcy Reform Act.

FOCUS ON CORPORATE PRACTICE

Bankers Who Step in If Loans Go Bad
Reveal Lenders' Other Face*

Julie Salamon
Staff Reporter
The Wall Street Journal

They are variously known as undertakers, morticians, black hats, or goons. But members of this banking fraternity prefer to think of themselves as surgeons.

They are workout specialists, the bankers who take over when a business loan goes bad. Most companies don't know these specialists exist. Those companies that do wish they didn't.

"You come to dread them," says the treasurer of a Midwestern leisure-products maker. Back when its prospects were bright, this company had been wooed and won by an eager loan officer from Continental Illinois Bank & Trust Co. "He brought me to Chicago to meet the president of the bank, to eat lunch in the executive dining room," the treasurer recalls. "He knocked himself out coming to the company and telling me what the bank could do for us. It was nice."

But when business soured, the solicitous loan officer disappeared. Then "this new banker shows up. And he keeps coming back every day, wanting to know why this or that employee is needed, why we had to have those airline tickets," says the treasurer. "Suddenly you've lost control. The bank has become your boss."

Plenty To Do

Such trauma is becoming more common. Business failures rose nearly 50 percent in 1981, and what bankers refer to as "nonperforming loans" doubled and tripled at many institutions. Banks' intensive-care wards, or workout areas (literally, where problems are "worked out"), are already crowded and likely to become more so if the economy doesn't improve.

Neither companies nor banks trumpet the arrival of the special forces, but an announcement of "debt restructuring" is a signal that the work-out crew has taken charge. Other signs: news reports that "lenders" forced a "troubled company" to dismiss its president, sell a division, or forgo new products. Those mysterious and pushy "lenders" are usually workout people.

Thus, when the chairman and six other officers or directors of Wickes Co. quit this week, holders of the company's heavy debt insisted they were just bystanders. But the chief workout officer at one bank, Richard Daniel of Security Pacific, did comment that "we've long been dissatisfied with what is going on at Wickes and let our feelings be known."

Despite these suggestions of omnipotence, a bank can't actually take control of a customer's business when a loan looks shaky. By law, if a bank starts running a business, the lender risks losing its status as a creditor should the company go bankrupt. So workout officers don't tell a company what to do. They simply say no to so many things that only one course of action is left.

Big Stick

Or, they hint. Strongly. "We don't say you've got to hire Joe Smith to be your top financial guy or we're finished with you," says Paul T. Walker, Chase Manhattan Bank's chief workout officer. "We can say, 'You have a void in your present management.' Then we may offer some suggestions, give them a list of ten people." Continental Illinois' workout man rejected the Midwestern leisure-products company's plans to expand its business and then told the company a 15 percent sales-force reduction would be "prudent."

Companies listen for one reason: Knuckling under beats bankruptcy, the likely consequence of a loan default. When asked about his worst times since International Harvester began rescheduling its $4.7 billion debt last year, Archie R. McCardell, its chairman, recalls "the many nights when several of us would go home knowing we'd have to get up at 2 A.M. or 3 A.M." to answer a phone call from an anxious European banker. He never knew, he adds, "whether someone would take that final step" and force the company into bankruptcy.

Big workouts, such as Chrysler and International Harvester, attract lots of attention. But mostly workout units move quietly, much to the relief of their patients. Like people who undergo radical surgery, companies often find workout so painful and embarrassing they don't want to discuss it, even after they are back on their feet. Says Harris Levin, a New York bankruptcy lawyer: "It's a humiliation and a nightmare."

A bank, too, usually is content to keep the spotlight off its workout people; after all, the busier they are, the more mistakes the loan department has made. Thus, workout people operate in relative obscurity in less glorious parts of banks. Plush carpets and original paintings may be needed to attract new customers, but potential deadbeats don't require such niceties. At Security Pacific Bank in Los Angeles, the workout department is on the 13th floor. A long, bleak corridor leads to Citibank's workout staff in New York. Visitors to Chase's problem loan section in New York step off the elevator onto linoleum.

Workout departments aren't usually listed in bank directories. But a company can guess it has troubles if it is asked to report to Institutional Recovery Management (Citibank), to Special Assets (Security Pacific in Los Angeles), to Central Loan Department (Irving Turst Co. in New York), or to other departments beginning with "special."

The euphemisms serve a practical purpose. Sometimes ailing companies extricate themselves from workout at one bank by borrowing from another institution. If the new banker, unaware of the customer's less-than-perfect status, calls the old one for information and hears "workout," he will run the other way.

A company's change in status from master to slave often comes abruptly. At Citibank, customers are simply told one day to arrive at the 19th floor of the bank's Park Avenue office. "It's always interesting to watch them walk down that corridor, look at that sign (Institutional Recovery Management) and watch their faces change as it dawns on them they might be in trouble," chuckles Peter Fitts, Citibank's top workout officer.

Some banks make the transfer more gently. At Chase, workout officers start showing up at meetings along with the company's regular banker. After a couple of meetings, the account officer disappears.

Workouts usually last at least a year, sometimes much longer. The Midwestern leisure-products company was in workout for five years before it could get loans again. International Harvester has been struggling with its lenders for more than a year and is far from free of them.

The process is tedious. Bankers negotiate fine points in meeting after meeting with companies and, in big workouts, with other bankers. Sometimes they have to go to great lengths to win allies among other bankers whose stake in a company might not be as great but who can still veto decisions. To keep other lenders informed of the progress of Chrysler's K-cars, Scott Taylor, a former Chase workout officer, produced a film on how the cars were assembled. "If you keep people out in the cold, they're likely to say no," he explains.

In dealing with borrowers, however, workout specialists can be a bit more forceful. Citibank's Mr. Fitts, a big, tall man, has his own technique: He states his views, then puffs quietly on his cigar until everyone else agrees.

What It Takes

The list of qualities distinguishing a good workout officer varies with who is asked. Practitioners assess themselves as analytical, patient, perceptive, decisive, and humorous. Other bankers offer such adjectives as churlish, sadistic, thick-skinned, single-minded, obnoxious, and insensitive.

The S.W.A.T. teams naturally have developed their own lingo. Troubled companies are rarely called customers; workout people refer to them as clients" or "turkeys" or, most frequently, simply as "names." As Mr. Taylor, who dealt with Chrysler, explains, "When you spend two weeks locked in a hotel and at the Treasury in Washington and you don't get to see your family because of some company, you don't think of that company as a customer anymore."

Linked by work that is often grueling and sometimes thankless, the specialists tend to stick together. An example came at International Harvester's first meeting with creditors to discuss delaying debt repayment. Workout officers weren't invited. But those from three banks, who knew one another from the Chrysler case, conspired to get themselves invited, figuring they would end up handling the matter anyway. Each told his superiors the other workout people were going, and soon all had invitations from their own banks.

Need for Specialists

There once was a time when workout was a banking backwater, where bankruptcy specialists kicked the bones of dead customers. It was thought easier to let sick companies go under and bear the loss than to try to find a way to keep them alive. But the bankruptcy actions arose at such giants as Penn Central and W.T. Grant; their debts were scattered among many banks, which had to squabble over the remains. There were huge, embarrassing write-offs.

Next, Chrysler and other big borrowers got in trouble with the changing markets and difficult economy. Banks realized they would have to start restructuring debts en masse or face numerous multimillion-dollar write-offs. Most chose to create squads of officers who did nothing but work with customers to change business habits and try to restore profitability. Even smaller banks began adding full-time trouble-shooters.

But not all troubled companies are ready to accept a bank as Big Brother. William F. (Willie) Farah recently took some lenders to court on a complaint that they brought his company close to bankruptcy. He had quit as president of Farah Manufacturing Co. when it went through hard times in the mid-1970s. As a condition of a loan from State National Bank of El Paso, Continental Illinos, and Republic Bank of Dallas, Mr. Farah had to stay on the sidelines while a turn-around specialist the banks brought in sold millions of dollars of the Texas clothing company's assets to repay loans. In a judgment the banks plan to appeal, a Texas court awarded Mr. Farah $19 million in damages.

Bankers say they have only one concern in these spats: getting their money back. "We have the right to get paid and they have an obligation to pay us," says Mr. Walker, the chief workout officer at Chase. "The bank didn't cause the company to make bad investments or whatever it was that caused them to lose money."

Playing Cleanup

Workout specialists often feel they are looking at the error of others' ways: unwillingness by companies to admit that their projections were off, or bad judgment by a bank loan officer who acted out of friendship, pressure to make loans, or simply ineptitude. "Loan officers are supposed to get a detailed forecast or where a company's going before they make a loan," says Richard Daniel, the head of Security Pacific's Special Assets division. "But most officers don't watch whether sales are what were projected or whether receivables are turning over like they were supposed to."

Such remarks don't endear workout people to their banker colleagues, who resent being depicted as financial Santa Clauses. Winning a single big account, loan officers note, can take two or three years of work. First, they must come up with a financial package somehow distinguishable from competitors. Then there are the endless lunches, dinners, and other mandatory social contacts. "Your personal relationship with the treasurer can make or break a deal," says a Citibank loan officer. "He isn't just looking at the institution—the big banks look alike to him. He's wondering, 'Is this guy like me?' "

Once the deal is made, the loan officer has to turn to new conquests and thus is often juggling twenty-five or more big accounts at once. So when one of those loans looks shaky (most banks have regular reviews), the special team is called for what may be a seven-day-a-week job working out the company's problems in repaying.

Getting the News

This can be a dreadful moment for the officer who arranged the loan. The workout people "just march in and say to the company, 'Your business plan looks crummy; this and this will have to go,' " says the Citibank loan officer. "You say to yourself, 'My God, I don't want to give my company up to these goons.' "

The dread is also more personal, he adds: "You also start agonizing about your own reputation. You feel like you've totally lost face." In fact, losing an account to workout usually doesn't mean the end of a promising career, unless the loan officer essentially hoodwinked superiors into accepting the loan—or unless it is the officer's second or third loser.

Partly to keep such officers on their toes, some banks shun the workout system. Explains John Greathouse, the top credit oficer at Chicago's Amalgamated Bank & Trust Co., "If a loan officer knows he's going to have to live with those loans, day and night, good or bad, he'll learn to stay away from problems."

Most workout specialists once were loan officers themselves. They didn't necessarily bring in the most business—they often lacked the slap and tickle a good salesman needs—but they were quickest to spot trouble and fix it. They understand balance sheets and business plans. What they don't understand is why anyone should be so eager for new business as to skim over such details.

"It doesn't take a whole lot of skill to lend people money," says one workout officer. "Getting money back—that makes you feel like a banker."

Questions and Topics for Discussion

1. Explain the difference between the economic and financial definitons of business failure.

2. Explain the differences among the following terms related to financial failure:
   a. Technical insolvency.
   b. Legal insolvency.
   c. Bankruptcy.

3. What are the alternatives available to the failing firm?

4. Basically, what determines whether a bankrupt company is reorganized or liquidated?

5. In a debt reorganization, explain the difference between a *composition* and an *extension*.

6. Explain why an informal settlement may be preferable to declaring bankruptcy for both the failing firm and its creditors.

7. What are the differences between Chapter 7 and Chapter 11 of the Bankruptcy Reform Act?

8. In connection with reorganization plans, what do *fairness* and *feasibility* mean?

9. Explain how a firm that has failed can be reorganized to operate successfully.

10. Rank in order of priority (highest to lowest) the following claims on the proceeds from the liquidation of a bankrupt firm:
    - Taxes owed to Federal, state, and local governments.
    - Preferred stockholders.
    - Common stockholders.
    - Expenses of administering the bankruptcy.
    - Secured creditors.
    - Unsecured creditors.
    - Wages in three months before bankruptcy (up to $2,000 per employee).
    - Customer deposits (up to $900 each).
    - Expenses incurred after the bankruptcy petition is filed and before a trustee is appointed.
    - Contributions to employee benefit plans (up to $2,000 per employee).

Problems*

1. Consider Failures Galore, Inc. (Tables 24-4 and 24-5), discussed in this chapter. If total liquidation proceeds are $5,950,000, determine the distribution of these proceeds among the various creditors of Failures Galore.

2. Rework Problem 1 given total liquidation proceeds of $7,650,000 for Failures Galore, Inc.

* Color numbers denote problems which have check answers provided at the end of the book.

3. Go-For-Broke Company is being liquidated under Chapter 7 of the bankruptcy code. When it filed for bankruptcy, its balance sheet was as follows:

Assets		Liabilities & Capital	
Current Assets	$14,500,000	Accounts Payable	$12,145,000
Fixed Assets		Accrued Wages*	2,030,000
Land & Buildings		Accrued Taxes	1,160,000
(net)	6,525,000	Notes Payable (Bank)†	1,350,000
Equipment	7,975,000	Total Current Liabilities	$16,685,000
Total Assets	$29,000,000	Mortgage Bonds‡	4,775,000
		Debentures	2,450,000
		Stockholders' Equity	5,090,000
		Total Liabilities & Equity	$29,000,000

*All accrued wages must be paid out of the liquidation proceeds. †The bank loan is unsecured.
‡Mortgage bonds are secured by land and buildings.

Assume that the liquidation is a voluntary petition, that no unpaid contributions to employee benefit plans exist, and that no customer layaway deposits are involved. The proceeds from the liquidation of the company's assets are as follows:

Current Assets	$ 9,425,000
Land & Buildings	3,045,000
Equipment	4,130,000
Total	$16,600,000

Bankruptcy administration charges are $643,750. Determine the distribution (dollar amount and percentage) of these proceeds among the various creditors of Go-For-Broke.

4. Rework Problem 3 assuming that the debentures ($2,450,000) are subordinated to (bank) notes payable.

Selected References

Altman, Edward I. *Corporate Financial Distress*. New York: Wiley, 1983.

Altman, Edward I. and Joseph Spivak. "Predicting Bankruptcy: The Value Line Relative Financial Strength System vs. the Zeta Bankruptcy Classification Approach." *Financial Analysts Journal* (November/December 1983): 60–67.

Baldwin, Carliss Y., and Scott P. Mason. "The Resolution of Claims in Financial Distress: The Case of Massey-Ferguson." *Journal of Finance* (May 1983): 505–516.

Castagna, A. D., and Z. P. Matolcsy. "The Market Characteristics of Failed Companies: Extensions and Further Evidence." *Journal of Business Finance and Accounting* (Winter 1981): 467–483.

Clark, Truman A., and Mark I. Weinstein. "The Behavior of Common Stock of Bankrupt Firms." *Journal of Finance* (May 1983): 489–504.

Collins, Robert A. "An Empirical Comparison of Bankruptcy Prediction Models." *Financial Management* (Summer 1980): 52–57.

Warner, J. B. "Bankruptcy, Absolute Priority, and the Pricing of Risky Debt Claims." *Journal of Financial Economics* (May 1977): 239–276.

White, Michelle J. "Bankruptcy Costs and the New Bankruptcy Code. "*Journal of Finance* (May 1983): 477–488.

25

INTERNATIONAL FINANCIAL MANAGEMENT

A Financial Dilemma

Hercules' Issuance of Notes Denominated in European Currency Units*

In March, 1985, Hercules Incorporated, a Wilmington, Delaware-based chemicals and plastics manufacturer, issued 10.125 percent seven-year notes. Instead of being denominated in U.S. dollars, as is usual for securities of U.S. companies, these notes are denominated in European Currency Units (ECU). The ECU is a composite currency whose value is based on the weighted value of ten European currencies.

The Hercules debt issue totaled ECU 50,000,000 or about $33,000,000, based on the exchange rate between the U.S. dollars and the ECU at the time of issuance.

The Hercules financial managers apparently had a choice between whether to issue ECU-denominated or U.S. dollar-denominated debt. They chose the ECU-denominated debt in order to hedge the company's European assets. For example, if the value of the ECU drops compared to the U.S. dollar value, presumably the U.S. dollar value of Hercules' European assets also decreases. However, if this happens the U.S. dollar amount of both the interest and principal which Hercules has to pay also decreases. The Hercules management stated that while the weight of the various currencies in the ECU did not match exactly the relationship of Hercules' European assets, the ECU-denominated debt issue did make a reasonably good hedge overall.

The Hercules ECU-denominated issue marked the first time that an ECU debt issue was offered domestically by a U.S. industrial company. As a result, U.S. investors who have liabilities denominated in European currencies can buy such an is-

sue as a hedge. Also, U.S. buyers who believe that the ECU will strengthen versus the U.S. dollar can speculate with ECU-denominated debt issues.

The increased amount of international trade and the internationalization of money and capital markets make it essential for financial managers to understand the basic elements of international financial management. This is the topic of this chapter.

---

* Adapted from "Hercules Issues Notes Denominated in ECUs to Domestic Investors," *The Wall Street Journal* (March 18, 1985): 53.

Key Chapter Concepts

1. Companies engaged in international financial transactions face such problems as political and exchange rate risk in addition to those encountered in domestic transactions.
2. The exchange rate is the rate at which a currency can be converted into another currency.
   a. The spot rate is the present exchange rate for immediate delivery.
   b. The forward rate is the present exchange rate for deliveries of currencies in the future.
3. The theory of *interest rate parity* states that the annual percentage differential in the forward market for a currency quoted in terms of another currency is equal to the approximate difference in interest rates in the two countries.
4. A hedge is an offsetting transaction designed to reduce or prevent risk. Forward exchange hedges and money market hedges are used to reduce transaction exposure. Financing with debt denominated in the same currency as foreign assets is a means of hedging against translation exposure.
5. International financing sources include:
   a. Letters of credit
   b. Eurocurrency markets
   c. Eurobonds
   d. National and international development bonds.

Glossary of New Terms

Eurodollars U.S. dollars that have been deposited in European banks or European branches of U.S. banks.

Eurobond An international bond which is issued outside the country in whose currency the bonds are denominated.

European currency unit (ECU) A composite currency whose value is based on the weighted value of ten European currencies.

Exchange rate The rate at which a currency can be converted into another currency.

Foreign bond An international bond which is denominated in the currency of the country in which it is issued.

Forward rate The rate of exchange between two currencies being bought and sold for delivery at a *future* date.

Interest rate parity The theory that the annual percentage differential in the forward market for a currency quoted in terms of another currency is equal to the approximate difference in interest rates in the two countries.

International bond A bond which is issued outside the country of the borrower.

Letter of credit A document issued by a bank guaranteeing payment for a particular shipment of goods.

London interbank offered rate (LIBOR) Interest rate at which banks in the Eurodollar market lend to each other.

Multinational corporation A firm that has direct investments in more than one country.

Spot rate The rate of exchange between two currencies that are being bought and sold for *immediate* delivery.

Introduction

A growing number of companies engage in various types of international financial transactions. These transactions can take many different forms. At one end of the spectrum are companies that *export* finished goods for sale in a foreign country and/or *import* raw materials or products from abroad for use in a domestic operation. In 1985 U.S. exports and imports totaled over $214 billion and $338 billion, respectively. The difference between exports and imports is the merchandise trade balance. In 1985, the U.S. had a trade deficit of $124 billion (imports of $338 billion minus exports of $214 billion), a record deficit up to that time.

At the other end of the spectrum are the *multinational corporations,* which have direct investments in manufacturing and/or distribution facilities in more than one country. Between these extremes are various other degrees of involvement in international financial transactions, including foreign branch sales offices, licensing arrangements, and joint ventures with foreign firms.

Firms that are engaged in international financial transactions face unique problems and risks not encountered by firms that operate in only one country. First, there are difficulties associated with doing business in different currencies. Financial transactions between U.S. firms and firms (or individuals) in foreign countries normally involve foreign currency, which has to be converted into U.S. dollars at some stage. Thus, firms that do business on an international basis are concerned with the *exchange rate* between U.S. dollars and foreign currencies. Second, there are problems associated with the different governmental regulations, tax laws, business practices, and political environments in foreign countries. Some of the more important aspects of these problems are considered in this chapter.[1]

Foreign Currencies and Exchange Rates

Whenever a U.S. firm purchases goods or services from a firm in another country, two currencies normally are involved. For example, when a U.S. company purchases materials from a British supplier, the British firm usually prefers payment in British pounds, whereas the U.S. company prefers to make payment in U.S. dollars. If the sales agreement requires that payment be made in pounds, the U.S. company will have to exchange (that is, *sell*) dollars to obtain the required number of pounds. The exact amount of dollars the U.S. company will have to sell depends on the *exchange rate* between the two currencies.

Suppose, for example, that the exchange rate at the time of the transaction is $1.45 per pound.[2] Furthermore, assume that the British supplier and the U.S. firm have agreed on a price of £2,000,000 for the materials. Therefore, the U.S. firm will have to exchange $2,900,000 (that

---

[1] Space limitations make it impossible to consider the entire scope of these problems in this text. For a more complete discussion of these issues, see the following references: David K. Eiteman and Arthur T. Stonehill, *Multinational Business Finance,* 3rd ed., Reading, Mass.: Addison-Wesley, 1982; Rita M. Rodriguez and E. Eugene Carter, *International Financial Management,* 3rd ed., Englewood Cliffs, N.J.: Prentice-Hall, 1984; Alan C. Shapiro, *International Corporate Finance: Survey & Synthesis,* Tampa, Fla.: Financial Management Association, 1985; and Gerald D. Gay and Robert W. Kolb, *International Finance: Concepts and Issues,* Reston, Va.: Reston Publishing Co., 1984

[2] This was the approximate exchange rate on March 3, 1986.

is, £2,000,000 × $1.45/pound) to obtain the British currency to pay for the purchase.

The exchange rate can be expressed either in terms of dollars per pound or in terms of pounds per dollar. If the exchange rate from dollars to pounds is $1.45/pound, the exchange rate from pounds to dollars is £0.6897/dollar (that is, 1 ÷ $1.45/pound). Thus, a *reciprocal* relationship exists between the two exchange rates.

Foreign currency that is needed for international financial transactions usually can be exchanged for domestic currency in most countries either at large commercial banks or at a central bank operated by the government. Banks normally charge a small fee for this service. Exchange rates between U.S. dollars and the currencies of most countries are reported daily in *The Wall Street Journal*. Table 25-1 lists the exchange rates between U.S. dollars and various currencies as of March 3, 1986, and July 3, 1985. These are known as *spot rates*. Spot rates represent the rate of exchange for currencies being bought and sold for *immediate delivery* today.

Currencies also can be bought and sold today for delivery at some *future time,* usually 30, 90, or 180 days from today. In these cases, *forward rates* are used rather than spot rates. Forward exchange rates between U.S. dollars and the currencies of several of the major industrial countries also are reported daily in *The Wall Street Journal*. Table 25-2 lists some forward exchange rates as of March 3, 1986.

Forward exchange rates can be either higher or lower than the spot rates; higher rates are termed *premiums,* and lower rates are termed *discounts*. A comparison of the spot and forward rates in Table 25-1 and 25-2 shows that the forward exchange rates of British pounds, Canadian dollars, and French francs are below their respective spot exchange rates, whereas the forward exchange rates of Japanese yen, Swiss francs, and West German marks are above their respective spot rates.

Table 25-1   **Sampling of Spot Foreign Exchange Rates**

| Country | Currency | Exchange Rate (U.S. Dollars) | |
		March 3, 1986	July 3, 1985
Australia	Dollar	0.6955	0.6695
Brazil	Cruzeiro	0.000073	0.000170
Britain	Pound	1.4465	1.3160
Canada	Dollar	0.7015	0.7371
China	Yuan	0.3125	0.3483
France	Franc	0.1467	0.1085
India	Rupee	0.0810	0.0810
Italy	Lira	0.000664	0.000518
Japan	Yen	0.005571	0.004034
Netherlands	Guilder	0.3987	0.2924
South Africa	Rand	0.5020	0.5060
Sweden	Krona	0.1395	0.1144
Switzerland	Franc	0.5330	0.3946
West Germany	Mark	0.4517	0.3301
—	ECU	0.9667	0.7402

Source: *The Wall Street Journal* (March 4, 1986 and July 5, 1985).

Table 25-2   **Sampling of Forward Foreign Exchange Rates**

	Exchange Rate (U.S. Dollars)—March 3, 1986		
Currency	30-Day Forward	90-Day Forward	180-Day Forward
Pound	1.4405	1.4305	1.4170
Canadian dollar	0.6998	0.6943	0.6898
French franc	0.1458	0.1443	0.1433
Yen	0.005579	0.005600	0.005632
Swiss franc	0.5350	0.5384	0.5436
Mark	0.4531	0.4556	0.4596

Source: *The Wall Street Journal* (March 4, 1986).

The premium between the spot rate, S, and the forward rate, F, can be expressed on an annual percentage basis using the following equation:

$$\text{Premium} = \left(\frac{F - S}{S}\right)\left(\frac{12}{n}\right)(100\%), \tag{25.1}$$

where n is the number of months forward. If the result calculated using Equation 25.1 is negative, an annual percentage discount instead of a premium exists.

Using the exchange rates listed in Tables 25-1 and 25-2, the following premium involving the West German mark is calculated:

$$\text{Premium} = \left(\frac{0.4596 - 0.4517}{0.4517}\right)\left(\frac{12}{6}\right)(100\%)$$

$$= 3.50\%.$$

Similarly, the following British pound calculation is performed:

$$\text{Premium} = \left(\frac{1.4170 - 1.4465}{1.4465}\right)\left(\frac{12}{6}\right)(100\%)$$

$$= -4.08\%.$$

These calculations show that the 180-day forward West Germany mark (quoted in U.S. dollars) is trading at a 3.5 percent annual premium compared to the spot rate, whereas the 180-day forward British pound is trading at about a 4 percent discount. This means that the spot rate for West German marks is expected to increase in the future, whereas the spot rate for British pounds is expected to decrease in the future.

As will be shown later in this chapter, firms engaged in international transactions can use the forward foreign exchange market to hedge against adverse fluctuations in exchange rates.

Interest Rate Parity   The theory of *interest rate parity* states that the annual percentage forward premium for a currency quoted in terms of another currency, calculated in Equation 25.1, is equal to the approximate difference in interest rates prevailing in the two countries. For example, interest rate parity between Britain (U.K.) and the U.S. is said to exist if the following equation holds:

$$\left(\frac{F - S}{S}\right)\left(\frac{12}{n}\right) = \frac{i_{US} - i_{UK}}{1 + i_{UK}},\qquad (25.2)$$

where i_{US} in the U.S. interest rate and i_{UK} is the comparable U.K. rate.[3]

When interest rate parity does not hold, arbitrage opportunities exist.[4] Suppose a particular British interest rate is 14 percent and the comparable U.S. rate is 8 percent when the annual discount on forward pounds is 4 percent. Suppose also that a U.S. trader using the foreign exchange market sells U.S. dollars and buys spot British pounds and invests the pounds to earn 14 percent. Simultaneously, the trader sells forward pounds at the prevailing 4 percent annual discount. At the end of the forward period, the trader converts pounds back to dollars. The overall result is that the U.S. trader earns 10 percent instead of the 8 percent available in the U.S. domestic money markets. Because the overall transaction in this example is riskless, the trader is said to be perfectly hedged, or covered. As a result, the procedure carried out in this example by the U.S. trader is referred to as *covered interest arbitrage*. Interestingly, the existence of foreign exchange traders and the opportunities to gain profits by covered interest arbitrage transactions causes approximate interest rate parity to exist between countries. We calculated earlier in this chapter that the forward British pound, quoted in U.S. dollars, was trading at an annual discount of about 4 percent compared to the spot pound as of March, 1986. At that time, British interest rates were about 4 percent higher than comparable U.S. rates. Thus, approximate interest rate parity existed at that time between the U.S. and Britain.[5]

Factors that Affect Exchange Rates

Exchange rates between currencies change over time, reflecting supply and demand considerations for each currency. For example, the demand for British pounds comes from a number of sources, including foreign buyers of British exports who must pay for their purchases in pounds, foreign investors who desire to make investments in physical or financial assets in Britain, and speculators who expect British pounds to increase in value relative to other currencies. The British government also may be a source of demand if it attempts to keep the value of the pound (relative to other currencies) from falling by using its supply of foreign currencies or gold to purchase pounds in the market.

Sources of supply include British importers who need to convert their pounds into foreign currency to pay for purchases, British investors who desire to make investments in foreign countries, and speculators who expect British pounds to decrease in value relative to other currencies.

---

[3] When interest rates are relatively low, the Equation 25.2 denominator approaches 1.0 and the interest rate difference in the numerator is a good approximation of the fractions's value.

[4] Arbitrage is discussed in Chapter 13. It is a simultaneous buying and selling of equivalent goods in different markets.

[5] This discussion disregards transaction costs such as commissions charged by foreign exchange dealers.

Exchange rates also are affected by economic and political conditions that influence the supply or demand for a country's currency. Some of these conditions include differential inflation and interest rates among countries, the government's trade policies, and the government's political stability. A high rate of inflation within a country tends to lower the value of its currency with respect to the currencies of other countries that are experiencing lower rates of inflation. The exchange rate will tend to decline as holders sell or exchange the country's currency for other currencies whose purchasing power is not declining at as high a rate. In contrast, relatively high interest rates within a country tend to increase the exchange rate as foreign investors seek to convert their currencies and purchase these higher yielding securities.

Government trade policies that limit imports—such as the imposition of tariffs, import quotas, and restrictions on foreign exchange transactions—reduce the supply of the country's currency in the foreign exchange market. This, in turn, tends to increase the value of the country's currency with respect to other currencies and thus increase exchange rates.

Finally, the political stability of the government will affect the risks perceived by foreign investors and companies doing business in the country. These risks include the possible expropriation of investments or restrictions on the amount of funds (such as returns from investments) that may be taken out of the country.

Effects of Exchange Rate Levels on Business Conditions and Practices

The exchange rate between two currencies can affect the way competing companies in the two countries do business and can have an impact on business conditions in the two countries. Consider the exchange rate data in Table 25-1 between the Japanese yen (JY) and the U.S. dollar. In March 1986 $1 equaled about JY180 (1 ÷ 0.005571), and in July 1985 $1 equaled about JY248 (1 ÷ 0.004034). In relative terms, the dollar was "weak" and the yen was "strong" in March 1986, whereas in July 1985 the dollar was "strong" and the yen was "weak."

Suppose the U.S. Camera Company makes a camera in the U.S. for $20 and sells it both in the U.S. for $25 and in Japan, and the Japan Camera Company makes essentially the same camera in Japan for JY4000 and sells it both in Japan for JY5000 and in the U.S.[6] When the dollar is relatively strong, that is, $1 equals JY250, the following will occur:

1. Japan Camera can sell its camera in the U.S. at $20 each and maintain the same profit margin it earns in Japan, or it can improve its margin by raising the price.

2. In order to compete with the Japanese import, U.S. Camera must consider cutting its price in the U.S. market. It also has to control its costs rigidly, thereby helping to keep the U.S. inflation rate low.

3. U.S. Camera cannot compete effectively in Japan. If it tries to maintain the yen equivalent of the $25 U.S. price, U.S. Camera has to price its camera at JY6250, compared to the JY5000 price charged by Japan Camera.

---

[6] This example disregards transportation costs between the U.S. and Japan.

Table 25-3   **Example of Transaction Exchange Rate Risk**

Date	Exchange Rate	Amount of Transaction	
		U.S. Dollars	British Pounds
Purchase date	$1.45/pound	$2,900,000	£2,000,000
Payment date	$1.50/pound	$3,000,000	£2,000,000

4. For every JY1000 that U.S. Camera is able to earn in Japan when the exchange rate is JY250 = $1, it reports $4.00 in earnings to its stockholders.

When the dollar is relatively weak, that is, $1 = JY180, the following occur:

1. U.S. Camera can sell its camera in Japan at a price of JY4500 and maintain the same profit margin it earns in the U.S. It should be able to compete effectively with Japan Camera's JY5000 price.

2. Japan Camera cannot compete effectively in the U.S. If it tries to maintain the dollar equivalent of a JY5000 price, Japan Camera must price its cameras at $27.78, compared to the $25 price charged by U.S. Camera.

3. For every JY1000 that U.S. Camera earns in Japan when the exchange rate is JY180 = $1, it reports $5.55 in earnings to its stockholders.

This example shows that a relatively weak U.S. dollar tends to help U.S. exports and can improve the dollar earnings of U.S. companies doing business outside the U.S., both by lowering the prices quoted in foreign currencies and by translating the foreign earnings into more U.S. dollars.

Managing Exchange Rate Risk

Since exchange rates between currencies can and do fluctuate over time, companies engaged in international business are exposed to *exchange rate risk*. International companies can lower exchange rate risk exposure by *hedging*. In general, a hedge is an offsetting transaction designed to reduce or prevent risk. Examples of hedging techniques are illustrated in the following sections for both *transaction* and *translation* exposure.

Foreign Trade   Consider again the situation described earlier in which a U.S. company purchases materials from a British supplier. Since the amount of the transaction (£2,000,000) is stated in pounds, the U.S. company bears the exchange risk. This example of transaction exposure is illustrated in Table 25-3. Assume that the British supplier extends 90-day trade credit to the U.S. company and that the value of the pound increases from $1.45/pound on the purchase date to $1.50/pound on the payment date. If the U.S. firm takes the trade credit extended to it, the cost of the purchase effectively increases from $2,900,000 to $3,000,000 (that is, £2,000,000 × $1.50/pound).[7]

---

[7] In this and the following discussion of exchange rate risk, we are ignoring the brokerage fees involved in executing foreign exchange contracts. Due to these costs, some firms choose not to protect themselves against exchange rate risk.

There are two basic hedging techniques that the U.S. company can use to protect itself against transaction exchange risk:

- Execute a contract in the forward exchange market.
- Borrow U.S. funds and invest in interest-bearing British securities.

Both of these methods are examined in the paragraphs that follow.

First, the U.S. firm could execute a contract in the forward exchange market to buy £2,000,000 at the *known* ninety-day forward rate rather than at the *uncertain* spot rate prevailing on the payment date. This is referred to as a *forward market hedge*. Assume, for example, that the 90-day forward rate is $1.455/pound. Based on this rate, the U.S. firm would be able to exchange $2,910,000 (that is, £2,000,000 × $1.455/pound) 90 days later on the payment date when it is required to pay for the materials. Thus, the U.S. firm would be able to take advantage of the trade credit and, at the same time, hedge against foreign exchange risk.

A second hedging technique, called a *money market hedge,* involves the U.S. firm borrowing the funds from its bank, exchanging them for pounds at the spot rate, and investing them in interest-bearing British securities. By investing in securities that mature on the same date as the payment is due to the British supplier (that is, 90 days after the purchase date), the U.S. firm will have the necessary amount of pounds available to pay for the materials. The net cost of this money market hedge to the U.S. firm will depend on the interest rate on the funds it borrows from its bank relative to the interest rate on the funds it invests in securities. For example, if the bank charges 10 percent per annum and the securities yield 8 percent per annum, the net cost to the U.S. firm would be approximately $14,500, that is, $(0.10 - 0.08) \times (90/360) \times \$2,900,000$.

Foreign Investment   Firms with direct investments in foreign subsidiaries also face exchange rate risk in the form of translation exposure. Changes in the exchange rate affect the value of the subsidiary's assets and liabilities and, ultimately, the income of the multinational parent company. Under current accounting procedures, the following general rules apply when the balance sheets of foreign subsidiaries are translated into the parent company's balance sheet:[8]

- Current assets, unless covered by forward exchange contracts, and fixed assets are translated into dollars at the rate of exchange prevailing on the date of the balance sheet.
- Current and long-term liabilities payable in foreign currency are translated into dollars at the rate of exchange prevailing on the date of the balance sheet.

A decline in the value of a foreign currency relative to the U.S. dollar reduces the conversion value of the foreign subsidiary's liabilities, as well as its assets. Therefore, the parent company's risk exposure depends on the foreign subsidiary's net equity position (that is, assets minus liabilities). Thus, on the books of the parent company, the subsidiary's creditors in

---

[8] The present U.S. accounting rules for foreign currency translation are set forth in *Statement of Financial Accounting Standards Number 52,* issued by the Financial Accounting Standards Board.

Table 25-4

Effect of a Decrease in the Exchange Rate on American Products' Balance Sheet

	Exchange Rate			
	$0.80 (Canadian) = $1.00 (U.S.)		$0.75 (Canadian) = $1.00 (U.S.)	
	$(Canadian)	$(U.S.)	$(Canadian)	$(U.S.)
Assets	$12,000,000	$9,600,000	$12,000,000	$9,000,000
Liabilities	8,000,000	6,400,000	8,000,000	6,000,000
Net equity position	$ 4,000,000	$3,200,000	$ 4,000,000	$3,000,000

effect bear part of the decline in the value of the subsidiary's assets. Present accounting rules require that these translation losses (as well as gains) be reported on the balance sheet as a separate adjustment to stockholders' equity and not on the income statement of the parent company. Revenue and expense items are translated at existing exchange rates and are reported on the parent company's income statement.

The impact of a decrease in the exchange rate on the firm's balance sheet can be illustrated with the following example. American Products has a subsidiary, Canadian Products, with total assets of $12,000,000 (Canadian) and total liabilities of $8,000,000 (Canadian). Based on an exchange rate of $0.80 (Canadian) per dollar (U.S.), the net equity position of the Canadian subsidiary on American Products' balance sheet as shown in Table 25-4 is $3,200,000 (U.S.). Suppose now that the exchange rate declines to $0.75 (Canadian) per dollar (U.S.) and all other things remain the same. As can be seen in the table, the net equity position of the Canadian subsidiary on American Products' balance sheet declines to $3,000,000 (U.S.), resulting in a $200,000 currency exchange loss.

In general, when a foreign subsidiary's assets are greater than (less than) its liabilities, currency exchange losses (gains) will occur when the exchange rate decreases. The opposite effects are true for increases in the exchange rate. A company can hedge against translation exposure by financing its foreign assets with debt denominated in the same currency.[9]

The multinational company can also minimize its exchange rate risk, as well as the risk of expropriation and/or nationalization of its assets by a foreign government, by developing a *portfolio* of foreign investments. Rather than making all its direct investments in foreign subsidiaries that are located in one particular country, the firm can spread its foreign investments among a number of different countries, thus limiting the risk of incurring large losses within any one country.

Financing Foreign Trade and Investments

Firms engaged in foreign trade and investment have a variety of sources of financing that may not be available to domestic firms. This section examines some of these sources.

Foreign Trade

Firms that import goods into their countries often can arrange an import *letter of credit* to finance the transaction. Basically, a letter of credit is a document issued by a bank guaranteeing payment for a particular

---

[9] The Financial Dilemma at the beginning of this chapter gives an example of this type of hedge.

shipment of goods. A letter of credit substitutes the credit-worthiness of the bank for that of the importer, thereby greatly reducing the credit risk to the seller.

To illustrate the use of a letter of credit, consider again the example discussed earlier in the chapter of the U.S. company that is purchasing materials from a British supplier. Suppose the British supplier agrees to ship the materials upon receipt of an irrevocable letter of credit from the U.S. firm's bank, with payment to be made in 90 days. The U.S. firm then would arrange with its bank for the letter of credit. By issuing a letter of credit, the bank agrees to pay drafts drawn on the firm's account when they are presented by the British supplier's bank. Upon shipment of the materials, the British firm presents a draft to its bank for payment in 90 days. The draft then is sent to the U.S. firm's bank for acceptance. Once the draft has been accepted by the U.S. bank, it becomes a *bankers' acceptance*—a form of marketable security. If the British firm does not wish to wait 90 days for payment, it can sell the draft at a discount from the face amount to the bank or another investor.

Foreign Investment

For a number of reasons, U.S. firms frequently find it desirable to finance a substantial portion of their foreign investments with funds raised abroad. First, the U.S. government has at various times imposed restrictions, or *quotas,* on the amount of funds U.S. firms can invest abroad. As a result, non-U.S. sources of financing must be used in part to finance foreign investments. Second, firms often find it desirable to obtain part of their financing in the foreign countries in which they are making their investments. This helps minimize any losses the firms might incur if the foreign currencies were devalued or if the foreign governments imposed restrictions on the outflow of funds from their countries. Finally, by borrowing funds abroad, U.S. firms can avoid the disclosure requirements (and associated costs) imposed by the SEC on debt securities that are issued in the United States.

As an alternative to borrowing funds in the United States, large, well-established multinational corporations can borrow funds either in the international financial markets or in the domestic financial markets of countries where subsidiaries are located. Within the international financial markets are the Eurodollar market and the international bond market. *Eurodollars* are U.S. dollars that have been deposited in foreign (primarily "European") banks or foreign branches of U.S. banks. They are created, for example, when a U.S. firm transfers funds (that is, dollars) from its U.S. bank to a foreign bank where it has an account. The foreign bank then can lend these dollar deposits in the form of *Eurodollar loans* to other companies (such as foreign subsidiaries of U.S. multinational corporations). The interest rate in the Eurodollar market usually is related to the *London interbank offered rate,* or *LIBOR.* LIBOR is the interest rate at which banks in the Eurodollar market lend to each other. For example, large well-established multinational corporations usually can borrow at about 0.5 percent over LIBOR. Since LIBOR frequently is about 1.5 percent below U.S. bank prime rates, large companies can often borrow in the Eurodollar market at sub-prime rates.

An international bond is a bond issued outside the country of the borrower. Bonds issued in the international bond markets are either *Eurobonds* or *foreign bonds.* A Eurobond is a bond which is issued outside the country in whose currency the bonds are denominated, and a foreign bond is denominated in the currency of the country in which it is issued. For example, in 1986 Chrysler Financial Corporation issued 10-year bonds in London denominated in West German marks. This issue is a Eurobond issue or, more specifically, a Euromark bond issue. Had Chrysler Financial issued the bonds in West Germany, they would have been classified as foreign bonds.

The Eurobond market has grown rapidly in recent years. In 1985, for example, a record $133 billion of Eurobonds were offered, while foreign bond issues in that year totaled $32 billion.[10] The Eurobond market is characterized by relatively low capital costs for borrowers. For example, in 1986 when Amoco Corp. issued $200 million of 9¾ percent Eurodollar bonds, it was estimated that the company saved about 25 to 30 basis points over what it would have cost to raise the capital in the U.S.[11] At the same time, investors were attracted to the Amoco bonds because the yield was 83 basis points over U.S. Treasury issues.[12]

In addition to Eurobonds denominated in a single currency, the number of Eurobond offerings denominated in *European currency units,* or ECUs, is growing rapidly. An ECU is a composite currency whose value is based on the weighted value of 10 European currencies. For multinational companies with direct investments in several major European countries, ECU-denominated debt provides a convenient means of hedging against translation exposure.[13]

A foreign subsidiary also may be able to obtain loans from international agencies, such as the World Bank and the Inter-American Development Bank. In addition, a number of governments have established national banks that provide financing for projects that promote economic development within their countries.

Thus, a wide variety of sources of funds is available for financing foreign investments. In determining the most appropriate mix of financing for a given overseas investment, the firm should consider many other factors besides interest rates.

Summary

- Firms engaged in international financial transactions face risks and problems that are not faced in domestic transactions, including difficulties encountered in doing business in different currencies and problems associated with different governmental regulations, tax laws, business practices, and political environments.

- The *exchange rate* is the rate at which one currency can be converted into another. The *spot rate* is the rate of exchange for currencies being bought and sold for *immediate delivery today.* The *forward rate* is the

---

[10] *The Wall Street Journal* (January 6, 1986):27.
[11] A *basis* point is 0.01 percent. Therefore, 100 basis points equals 1 percent.
[12] *The Wall Street Journal* (February 19, 1986):54.
[13] The Financial Dilemma at the beginning of this chapter describes an ECU-denominated financing.

rate of exchange between currencies to be delivered at a future point in time—usually 30, 90, and 180 days from today.

- The theory of *interest rate parity* states that the annual percentage differential in the forward market for a currency quoted in terms of another currency is equal to the approximate difference in interest rates in the two countries.

- Firms engaged in international transactions incur *exchange rate risk* because of fluctuations over time in the exchange rates between currencies. *Forward exchange* hedges and *money market* hedges can be used to minimize some of the effects of unfavorable changes in exchange rates.

- A wide variety of sources of funds is available for financing foreign trade and investments, including letters of credit, the Eurodollar market, the international bond market, and both national and international development banks.

Questions and Topics for Discussion

1. Define the following terms:
   a. Multinational corporation.
   b. Spot exchange rate.
   c. Forward exchange rate.
   d. Letter of credit.
   e. LIBOR.
   f. ECU.
2. What is the theory of interest rate parity?
3. What is covered interest arbitrage?
4. Describe two techniques that a company can use to hedge against transaction exchange risk.
5. Describe the factors that cause exchange rates to change over time.
6. How can a firm with direct investments in foreign subsidiaries hedge against translation exposure?
7. What are the advantages to a U.S. firm of financing its foreign investments with funds raised abroad?
8. What is the difference between the Eurodollar market and the Eurobond market?
9. What is the difference between a Eurobond and a foreign bond?

Problems*

1. Japanese Motors exports cars and trucks to the U.S. market. On July 3, 1985, its most popular model was selling (wholesale) to U.S. dealers for $7,500. What price must Japanese Motors charge for the same model on March 3, 1986, to realize the same amount (of Japanese yen) as it did a year earlier? Refer to Table 25-1.

2. Valley Stores, a U.S. department store chain, annually negotiates a contract with Alpine Watch Company, located in Switzerland, to purchase a large shipment of watches, On July 3, 1985, Valley purchased 10,000 watches for a total of 1,260,000 Swiss francs. Refer to Table 25-1 and determine the following:

* Color numbers denote problems which have check answers at the end of the book.

a. The total cost and cost per watch in U.S. dollars.

b. The total cost and cost per watch in U.S. dollars of 12,000 watches on March 3, 1986, assuming that Alpine's price per watch (in Swiss francs) remains unchanged.

3. Determine the percentage change in the value of the U.S. dollar between July 3, 1985, and March 3, 1986, relative to the value of the following currencies (refer to Table 25-1):

a. Brazil.

b. Britain.

c. Japan.

d. ECU.

e. West Germany.

4. If the U.S. Treasury Bill rate is 7.0 percent, the spot rate between U.S. dollars and British pounds is 1£ = $1.50, and the 90-day forward rate is 1£ = $1.49, what rate of interest is expected on British Treasury bills, assuming interest rate parity between the dollar and pound exists?

5. Suppose that British short-term interest rates are 13 percent, and the corresponding U.S. rate is 8 percent. Suppose at the same time that the discount on forward pounds is 3 percent per year. Do these conditions present an opportunity for covered interest arbitrage? If so, what steps should a trader in New York take? What annual rate will the trader earn?

6. Mammouth Mutual Fund of New York has $5 million to invest in certificates of deposit (CDs) for the next 6 months (180 days). It can buy either a Philadelphia National Bank (PNB) CD with an annual yield of 10 percent or a Cologne (West Germany) Bank CD with a yield of 12.5 percent. Assume that the CDs are of comparable default risk. The analysts of the mutual fund are concerned about exchange rate risk. They were quoted the following exchange rates by the international department of a New York City bank:

West Germany (Deutsche Marks)	
Spot	$0.4200
30-day futures	0.4190
90-day futures	0.4170
180-day futures	0.4155

a. If the Cologne Bank CD is purchased and held to maturity, determine the net gain (loss) in U.S. dollars relative to the PNB CD assuming that the exchange rate in 180 days equals today's spot rate.

b. Suppose the West German mark declines in value by 5 percent relative to the U.S. dollar over the next 180 days. Determine the net gain (loss) of the Cologne Bank CD in U.S. dollars relative to the PNB CD for an uncovered position.

c. Determine the net gain (loss) from a covered position.

d. What other factor or factors should be considered in the decision to purchase the Cologne Bank CD?

7. Last year, the French marketing subsidiary of International Pharmaceuticals Corp. (IPC), a New Jersey-based drug manufacturer, earned 700,000 French francs. This year, partly due to a weaker U.S. dollar, the French subsidiary will earn 900,000 French francs. Last year, the exchange rate was 10 francs per dollar, and this year it is 7 francs per dollar. Calculate how many U.S. dollars the French subsidiary contributes to IPC's earnings in each year.

**Selected
References**

Eiteman, David K., and Arthur T. Stonehill. *Multinational Business Finance,* 3rd ed. Reading, Mass: Addison-Wesley, 1982.

Gay, Gerald D., and Robert W. Kolb, *International Finance: Concepts and Issues.* Reston, Va.: Reston Publishing Co., 1984

Kidwell, David S., M. Wayne Marr, and G. Rodney Thompson. "Eurodollar Bonds: Alternative Financing for U.S. Companies." *Financial Management* 14 (Winter 1985): 18–27.

Madura, Jeff. *International Financial Management.* St. Paul, MN: West Publishing, 1986.

Rodriquez, Rita M., and E. Eugene Carter. *International Financial Management,* 3rd ed. Englewood Cliffs, N.J.: Prentice-Hall, 1984.

Shapiro, Alan C. *International Corporate Finance: Survey and Synthesis.* Tampa, Fla.: Financial Management Association, 1986.

MAJOR 1986 FEDERAL INCOME TAX REFORM PROVISIONS[1]

Introduction

In October, 1986 Congress passed the Tax Reform Act of 1986. The tax bill represents the most comprehensive tax reform measure since the passage of the 1954 Tax Code. Generally, the Tax Reform Act lowers tax rates on income for both individuals and corporations and also decreases the deductions which may be taken. In this appendix we provide a detailed summary of the key provisions of the Act.

Corporate Income Taxes

For tax years beginning on or after July 1, 1987, the tax rates imposed on corporations are as follows:

Taxable Income	Rate
$1–$50,000	15%
$50,001–$75,000	25%
Over $75,000	34%

An additional 5 percent tax up to $11,750 is imposed on taxable corporate income over $100,000, up to $335,000. Thus, any corporation with taxable income of $335,000 or greater will pay a flat rate of 34 percent on all income.

For a tax year that begins before and includes July 1, 1987 (*e.g.,* calendar year 1987 tax returns) a blend of old and new tax rates is used. For example, a calendar year corporation will have a maximum 40 percent tax rate in 1987.

Capital Gains and Losses

Effective January 1, 1987, the preferential tax rate for capital gains is repealed. Thus, corporate net capital gains will be taxed at the regular corporate rate, or a maximum of 34 percent. Capital losses continue to be deductible only against capital gains.

Dividend Income

The percentage exclusion applicable to intercompany dividends is reduced from 85 percent to 80 percent. As a result, for corporations having a marginal tax rate of 34 percent, intercompany dividends are taxed at an effective rate of 6.8 percent (that is, $[(1 - 0.80) \times 34\%]$).

Investment Tax Credit (ITC)

The Investment Tax Credit (ITC) is repealed for property placed in service after December 31, 1985, except in the case of certain long-lived property contracted for before December 31, 1985. In addition, the Tax Reform Act reduces the value of unused credits carried over from previous years.

---

[1] Source: Ernst and Whinney, *Tax Reform — 1986* (September 23, 1986).

Tax Loss Carrybacks and Carryforwards

Net operating losses can be carried back three years and forward 15 years, just as under the pre-1986 Tax Reform Act tax laws. The Act substantially limits the use of net operating loss carryforwards in the case where the loss corporation is acquired by another firm.

Depreciation

The Tax Reform Act of 1986 generally reduces the annual depreciation expense for an asset by somewhat increasing the write-off period. Under the new, modified ACRS system, assets are grouped into six classes for personal property and two classes for real estate. Each class is assigned a recovery period and a depreciation rate. The six classes for personal property are:

3-Year 200 Percent Class Includes property with an Asset Depreciation Range (ADR) midpoint life of 4 years or less, except for automobiles and light, general purpose trucks. The Asset Depreciation Range system of guideline economic lives for assets was enacted in 1971. Generally, ADR rules are extremely complex.

5-Year 200 Percent Class Includes property with an ADR midpoint of more than 4 and less than 10 years. It also includes automobiles and light trucks, certain technological equipment, research and experimentation property, and semiconductor manufacturing equipment.

7-Year 200 Percent Class Includes property with an ADR midpoint of at least 10 years and less than 16 years. This class includes most manufacturing equipment, railroad track, and property having no ADR midpoint and not classified elsewhere. Includes nearly all 5-year ACRS assets under the previous ACRS tax provisions.

10-Year 200 Percent Class Includes property with an ADR midpoint of at least 16 years and less than 20 years.

15-Year 150 Percent Class Includes property with an ADR midpoint of at least 20 years and less than 25 years.

20-Year 150 Percent Class Includes property (other than real property) with an ADR midpoint life of 25 years or more.

27.5-Year Straight-Line Class Includes residential rental property. Recovery is based upon straight-line depreciation.

31.5-Year Straight-Line Class Includes all non-residential real property. Recovery is based upon straight-line depreciation.

Unlike the old ACRS system, the modified ACRS system requires taxpayers to compute the applicable recovery percentages for each year. These percentages consider the recovery method, period of recovery, and applicable conventions. Expected salvage value of the asset *does not* enter into the calculation. The full installed cost of the asset is depreciated under the modified ACRS system.

The half-year convention is normally used for personal property placed into service or disposed of during a year. Under the half-year convention, property placed in service or disposed of during a taxable year is treated as if it were placed in service at the midpoint of that year.

For example, assume that the ABC Corporation purchases for $200,000 and places into service an asset which is assigned to the 5-year, 200 percent class. Considering the half-year convention, the depreciation deductions allowed are as follows:

Year	Depreciation Allowed	Effective Depreciation Rates[2]
1	$40,000	20.00%
2	64,000	32.00
3	38,400	19.20
4	23,040	11.52
5	23,040	11.52
6	11,520	5.76
Total	$200,000	

As discussed in Appendix 9A following Chapter 9, under the declining balance method the annual depreciation amount for an asset is calculated by multiplying the straight-line rate by the declining balance percentage figure to get an accelerated rate. In the case above, the straight line rate is 20 percent (based on a 5-year class life). Thus the declining balance rate is 40 percent. This rate is multiplied by the asset's book value at the end of each previous year. A switch is made to straight-line depreciation during the first year when the straight-line depreciation exceeds the declining balance depreciation. In this example, that occurs in year 4.

For residential rental and nonresidential real property, depreciation is based on the number of months the property is in service during the taxable year. A mid-month convention is used for real property, *i.e.,* it is assumed that real property is placed into service at the middle of the first in-service month, and depreciation during that month is equal to one-half of the normal one month rate.

Firms may elect to expense, rather than depreciate, up to $10,000 of property a year. The $10,000 limit is reduced on a dollar-for-dollar basis when the cost of qualified property placed in service during a year exceeds $200,000. The amount is also limited to the amount of taxable income derived from an active trade or business.

Leasing

Finance lease provisions of the old tax law which were designed to replace safe-harbor leasing are repealed. Only true leases as defined in the tax code will be accorded a leasing tax treatment.

Individual Income Taxes

Beginning in 1988, two rates apply to individuals: 15 percent and 28 percent. For married couples filing jointly, taxable income is taxed at 15

---

[2] Effective depreciation rates (applied to the installed cost of assets) for 7-year 200 percent assets are 14.2857%, 24.4898%, 17.4927%, 12.4948%, 8.9249%, 8.9249%, 8.9249%, and 4.4623% for each of the eight respective years.

percent up to $29,750 and at 28 percent for annual income amounts over $29,750. For single filers, taxable income is taxed at 15 percent up to $17,850 and at 28 percent for amounts over $17,850. For high income filers, the 15 percent rate is phased out. This is accomplished by applying a 33 percent tax rate to taxable income levels between $71,900 and $149,250 for joint returns. For 1987, the individual tax rates are lower than the 1986 rates and higher than the 1988 rates.

The long-term capital gains rate for individuals, beginning in 1988, is the same as the individual's marginal tax rate. For 1987, the maximum capital gains rate for individuals is 28 percent.

The $100 dividend exclusion is eliminated also. Dividend income received by individuals now is fully taxable.

Reference Materials

Tables R-2

Index to Glossary Terms R-11

Subject Index R-15

Check Answers to Selected Problems R-23

Table I

Compound Value Interest Factor (CVIF)
($1 at i% for n years)
$$CVIF = (1 + i)^n$$
$$FV_n = PV_0(CVIF_{i,n})$$

Period, n	1%	2%	3%	4%	5%	6%	7%	8%	9%	10%	11%	12%	13%
0	1.000	1.000	1.000	1.000	1.000	1.000	1.000	1.000	1.000	1.000	1.000	1.000	1.000
1	1.010	1.020	1.030	1.040	1.050	1.060	1.070	1.080	1.090	1.100	1.110	1.120	1.130
2	1.020	1.040	1.061	1.082	1.102	1.124	1.145	1.166	1.186	1.210	1.232	1.254	1.277
3	1.030	1.061	1.093	1.125	1.158	1.191	1.225	1.260	1.295	1.331	1.368	1.405	1.443
4	1.041	1.082	1.126	1.170	1.216	1.262	1.311	1.360	1.412	1.464	1.518	1.574	1.630
5	1.051	1.104	1.159	1.217	1.276	1.338	1.403	1.469	1.539	1.611	1.685	1.762	1.842
6	1.062	1.126	1.194	1.265	1.340	1.419	1.501	1.587	1.677	1.772	1.870	1.974	2.082
7	1.072	1.149	1.230	1.316	1.407	1.504	1.606	1.714	1.828	1.949	2.076	2.211	2.353
8	1.083	1.172	1.267	1.369	1.477	1.594	1.718	1.851	1.993	2.144	2.305	2.476	2.658
9	1.094	1.195	1.305	1.423	1.551	1.689	1.838	1.999	2.172	2.358	2.558	2.773	3.004
10	1.105	1.219	1.344	1.480	1.629	1.791	1.967	2.159	2.367	2.594	2.839	3.106	3.395
11	1.116	1.243	1.384	1.539	1.710	1.898	2.105	2.332	2.580	2.853	3.152	3.479	3.836
12	1.127	1.268	1.426	1.601	1.796	2.012	2.252	2.518	2.813	3.138	3.498	3.896	4.335
13	1.138	1.294	1.469	1.665	1.886	2.133	2.410	2.720	3.066	3.452	3.883	4.363	4.898
14	1.149	1.319	1.513	1.732	1.980	2.261	2.579	2.937	3.342	3.797	4.310	4.887	5.535
15	1.161	1.346	1.558	1.801	2.079	2.397	2.759	3.172	3.642	4.177	4.785	5.474	6.254
16	1.173	1.373	1.605	1.873	2.183	2.540	2.952	3.426	3.970	4.595	5.311	6.130	7.067
17	1.184	1.400	1.653	1.948	2.292	2.693	3.159	3.700	4.328	5.054	5.895	6.866	7.986
18	1.196	1.428	1.702	2.026	2.407	2.854	3.380	3.996	4.717	5.560	6.544	7.690	9.024
19	1.208	1.457	1.754	2.107	2.527	3.026	3.617	4.316	5.142	6.116	7.263	8.613	10.197
20	1.220	1.486	1.806	2.191	2.653	3.207	3.870	4.661	5.604	6.728	8.062	9.646	11.523
24	1.270	1.608	2.033	2.563	3.225	4.049	5.072	6.341	7.911	9.850	12.239	15.179	18.790
25	1.282	1.641	2.094	2.666	3.386	4.292	5.427	6.848	8.623	10.835	13.585	17.000	21.231
30	1.348	1.811	2.427	3.243	4.322	5.743	7.612	10.063	13.268	17.449	22.892	29.960	39.116
40	1.489	2.208	3.262	4.801	7.040	10.286	14.974	21.725	31.409	45.259	65.001	93.051	132.782
50	1.645	2.692	4.384	7.107	11.467	18.420	29.457	46.902	74.358	117.391	184.565	289.002	450.736
60	1.817	3.281	5.892	10.520	18.679	32.988	57.946	101.257	176.031	304.482	524.057	897.597	1,530.05

Period, n	14%	15%	16%	17%	18%	19%	20%	24%	28%	32%	36%	40%
0	1.000	1.000	1.000	1.000	1.000	1.000	1.000	1.000	1.000	1.000	1.000	1.000
1	1.140	1.150	1.160	1.170	1.180	1.190	1.200	1.240	1.280	1.320	1.360	1.400
2	1.300	1.322	1.346	1.369	1.392	1.416	1.440	1.538	1.638	1.742	1.850	1.960
3	1.482	1.521	1.561	1.602	1.643	1.685	1.728	1.907	2.067	2.300	2.515	2.744
4	1.689	1.749	1.811	1.874	1.939	2.005	2.074	2.364	2.684	3.036	3.421	3.842
5	1.925	2.011	2.100	2.192	2.288	2.386	2.488	2.932	3.436	4.007	4.653	5.378
6	2.195	2.313	2.436	2.565	2.700	2.840	2.986	3.635	4.398	5.290	6.328	7.530
7	2.502	2.660	2.826	3.001	3.185	3.379	3.583	4.508	5.629	6.983	8.605	10.541
8	2.853	3.059	3.278	3.511	3.759	4.021	4.300	5.590	7.206	9.217	11.703	14.758
9	3.252	3.518	3.803	4.108	4.435	4.785	5.160	6.931	9.223	12.166	15.917	20.661
10	3.707	4.046	4.411	4.807	5.234	5.695	6.192	8.594	11.806	16.060	21.647	28.925
11	4.226	4.652	5.117	5.624	6.176	6.777	7.430	10.657	15.112	21.199	29.439	40.496
12	4.818	5.350	5.926	6.580	7.288	8.064	8.916	13.215	19.343	27.983	40.037	56.694
13	5.492	6.153	6.886	7.699	8.599	9.596	10.699	16.386	24.759	36.937	54.451	79.372
14	6.261	7.076	7.988	9.007	10.147	11.420	12.839	20.319	31.961	48.757	74.053	111.120
15	7.138	8.137	9.266	10.539	11.974	13.590	15.407	25.196	40.565	64.359	100.712	155.568
16	8.137	9.358	10.748	12.330	14.129	16.172	18.488	31.243	51.923	84.954	136.969	217.795
17	9.276	10.761	12.468	14.426	16.672	19.244	22.186	38.741	66.461	112.139	186.278	304.914
18	10.575	12.375	14.463	16.879	19.673	22.901	26.623	48.039	85.071	148.023	253.338	426.879
19	12.056	14.232	16.777	19.748	23.214	27.252	31.948	59.568	108.890	195.391	344.540	597.630
20	13.743	16.367	19.461	23.106	27.393	32.429	38.338	73.864	139.380	257.916	468.574	836.683
24	23.212	28.625	35.236	43.297	53.109	65.032	79.497	174.631	374.144	783.023	1,603.00	3,214.20
25	26.462	32.919	40.874	50.658	62.669	77.388	95.396	216.542	478.905	1,033.59	2,180.08	4,499.88
30	50.950	66.212	85.850	111.065	143.371	184.675	237.376	634.820	1,645.50	4,142.07	10,143.0	24,201.4
40	188.884	267.864	378.721	533.869	750.378	1,051.67	1,469.77	5,455.91	19,426.7	66,520.8	219,562	700,038
50	700.233	1,083.66	1,670.70	2,566.22	3,927.36	5,988.91	9,100.44	46,890.4	229,350	*	*	*
60	2,595.92	4,384.00	7,370.20	12,335.4	20,555.1	34,105.0	56,347.5	402,996	*	*	*	*

*These interest factors exceed 1,000,000.

Table II

Present Value Interest Factor (PVIF)
($1 at i% for n years)

$$PVIF = \frac{1}{(1 + i)^n}$$

$$PV_0 = FV_n(PVIF_{i,n})$$

Period, n	1%	2%	3%	4%	5%	6%	7%	8%	9%	10%	11%	12%	13%
0	1.000	1.000	1.000	1.000	1.000	1.000	1.000	1.000	1.000	1.000	1.000	1.000	1.000
1	0.990	0.980	0.971	0.962	0.952	0.943	0.935	0.926	0.917	0.909	0.901	0.893	0.885
2	0.980	0.961	0.943	0.925	0.907	0.890	0.873	0.857	0.842	0.826	0.812	0.797	0.783
3	0.971	0.942	0.915	0.889	0.864	0.840	0.816	0.794	0.772	0.751	0.731	0.712	0.693
4	0.961	0.924	0.889	0.855	0.823	0.792	0.763	0.735	0.708	0.683	0.659	0.636	0.613
5	0.951	0.906	0.863	0.822	0.784	0.747	0.713	0.681	0.650	0.621	0.593	0.567	0.543
6	0.942	0.888	0.838	0.790	0.746	0.705	0.666	0.630	0.596	0.564	0.535	0.507	0.480
7	0.933	0.871	0.813	0.760	0.711	0.665	0.623	0.583	0.547	0.513	0.482	0.452	0.425
8	0.923	0.853	0.789	0.731	0.677	0.627	0.582	0.540	0.502	0.467	0.434	0.404	0.376
9	0.914	0.837	0.766	0.703	0.645	0.592	0.544	0.500	0.460	0.424	0.391	0.361	0.333
10	0.905	0.820	0.744	0.676	0.614	0.558	0.508	0.463	0.422	0.386	0.352	0.322	0.295
11	0.896	0.804	0.722	0.650	0.585	0.527	0.475	0.429	0.388	0.350	0.317	0.287	0.261
12	0.887	0.788	0.701	0.625	0.557	0.497	0.444	0.397	0.356	0.319	0.286	0.257	0.231
13	0.879	0.773	0.681	0.601	0.530	0.469	0.415	0.368	0.326	0.290	0.258	0.229	0.204
14	0.870	0.758	0.661	0.577	0.505	0.442	0.388	0.340	0.299	0.263	0.232	0.205	0.181
15	0.861	0.743	0.642	0.555	0.481	0.417	0.362	0.315	0.275	0.239	0.209	0.183	0.160
16	0.853	0.728	0.623	0.534	0.458	0.394	0.339	0.292	0.252	0.218	0.188	0.163	0.141
17	0.844	0.714	0.605	0.513	0.436	0.371	0.317	0.270	0.231	0.198	0.170	0.146	0.125
18	0.836	0.700	0.587	0.494	0.416	0.350	0.296	0.250	0.212	0.180	0.153	0.130	0.111
19	0.828	0.686	0.570	0.475	0.396	0.331	0.276	0.232	0.194	0.164	0.138	0.116	0.098
20	0.820	0.673	0.554	0.456	0.377	0.312	0.258	0.215	0.178	0.149	0.124	0.104	0.087
24	0.788	0.622	0.492	0.390	0.310	0.247	0.197	0.158	0.126	0.102	0.082	0.066	0.053
25	0.780	0.610	0.478	0.375	0.295	0.233	0.184	0.146	0.116	0.092	0.074	0.059	0.047
30	0.742	0.552	0.412	0.308	0.231	0.174	0.131	0.099	0.075	0.057	0.044	0.033	0.026
40	0.672	0.453	0.307	0.208	0.142	0.097	0.067	0.046	0.032	0.022	0.015	0.011	0.008
50	0.608	0.372	0.228	0.141	0.087	0.054	0.034	0.021	0.013	0.009	0.005	0.003	0.002
60	0.550	0.305	0.170	0.095	0.054	0.030	0.017	0.010	0.006	0.003	0.002	0.001	0.001

Period, n	14%	15%	16%	17%	18%	19%	20%	24%	28%	32%	36%	40%
0	1.000	1.000	1.000	1.000	1.000	1.000	1.000	1.000	1.000	1.000	1.000	1.000
1	0.877	0.870	0.862	0.855	0.847	0.840	0.833	0.806	0.781	0.758	0.735	0.714
2	0.769	0.756	0.743	0.731	0.718	0.706	0.694	0.650	0.610	0.574	0.541	0.510
3	0.675	0.658	0.641	0.624	0.609	0.593	0.579	0.524	0.477	0.435	0.398	0.364
4	0.592	0.572	0.552	0.534	0.516	0.499	0.482	0.423	0.373	0.329	0.292	0.260
5	0.519	0.497	0.476	0.456	0.437	0.419	0.402	0.341	0.291	0.250	0.215	0.186
6	0.456	0.432	0.410	0.390	0.370	0.352	0.335	0.275	0.227	0.189	0.158	0.133
7	0.400	0.376	0.354	0.333	0.314	0.296	0.279	0.222	0.178	0.143	0.116	0.095
8	0.351	0.327	0.305	0.285	0.266	0.249	0.233	0.179	0.139	0.108	0.085	0.068
9	0.308	0.284	0.263	0.243	0.225	0.209	0.194	0.144	0.108	0.082	0.063	0.048
10	0.270	0.247	0.227	0.208	0.191	0.176	0.162	0.116	0.085	0.062	0.046	0.035
11	0.237	0.215	0.195	0.178	0.162	0.148	0.135	0.094	0.066	0.047	0.034	0.025
12	0.208	0.187	0.168	0.152	0.137	0.124	0.112	0.076	0.052	0.036	0.025	0.018
13	0.182	0.163	0.145	0.130	0.116	0.104	0.093	0.061	0.040	0.027	0.018	0.013
14	0.160	0.141	0.125	0.111	0.099	0.088	0.078	0.049	0.032	0.021	0.014	0.009
15	0.140	0.123	0.108	0.095	0.084	0.074	0.065	0.040	0.025	0.016	0.010	0.006
16	0.123	0.107	0.093	0.081	0.071	0.062	0.054	0.032	0.019	0.012	0.007	0.005
17	0.108	0.093	0.080	0.069	0.060	0.052	0.045	0.026	0.015	0.009	0.005	0.003
18	0.095	0.081	0.069	0.059	0.051	0.044	0.038	0.021	0.012	0.007	0.004	0.002
19	0.083	0.070	0.060	0.051	0.043	0.037	0.031	0.017	0.009	0.005	0.003	0.002
20	0.073	0.061	0.051	0.043	0.037	0.031	0.026	0.014	0.007	0.004	0.002	0.001
24	0.043	0.035	0.028	0.023	0.019	0.015	0.013	0.006	0.003	0.001	0.001	0.000
25	0.038	0.030	0.024	0.020	0.016	0.013	0.010	0.005	0.002	0.001	0.000	0.000
30	0.020	0.015	0.012	0.009	0.007	0.005	0.004	0.002	0.001	0.000	0.000	0.000
40	0.005	0.004	0.003	0.002	0.001	0.001	0.001	0.000	0.000	0.000	0.000	0.000
50	0.001	0.001	0.001	0.000	0.000	0.000	0.000	0.000	0.000	0.000	0.000	0.000
60	0.000	0.000	0.000	0.000	0.000	0.000	0.000	0.000	0.000	0.000	0.000	0.000

Table III

Compound Sum of an Annuity Interest Factor (CVIFA)
($1 per year at i% for n years)

$$CVIFA = \frac{(1 + i)^n - 1}{i}$$

$$CSAN = R(CVIFA_{i,n})$$

Period, n	1%	2%	3%	4%	5%	6%	7%	8%	9%	10%	11%	12%	13%
1	1.000	1.000	1.000	1.000	1.000	1.000	1.000	1.000	1.000	1.000	1.000	1.000	1.000
2	2.010	2.020	2.030	2.040	2.050	2.060	2.070	2.080	2.090	2.100	2.110	2.120	2.130
3	3.030	3.060	3.091	3.122	3.152	3.184	3.215	3.246	3.278	3.310	3.342	3.374	3.407
4	4.060	4.122	4.184	4.246	4.310	4.375	4.440	4.506	4.573	4.641	4.710	4.779	4.850
5	5.101	5.204	5.309	5.416	5.526	5.637	5.751	5.867	5.985	6.105	6.228	6.353	6.480
6	6.152	6.308	6.468	6.633	6.802	6.975	7.153	7.336	7.523	7.716	7.913	8.115	8.323
7	7.214	7.434	7.662	7.898	8.142	8.394	8.654	8.923	9.200	9.487	9.783	10.089	10.405
8	8.286	8.583	8.892	9.214	9.549	9.897	10.260	10.637	11.028	11.436	11.859	12.300	12.757
9	9.369	9.755	10.159	10.583	11.027	11.491	11.978	12.488	13.021	13.579	14.164	14.776	15.416
10	10.462	10.950	11.464	12.006	12.578	13.181	13.816	14.487	15.193	15.937	16.722	17.549	18.420
11	11.567	12.169	12.808	13.486	14.207	14.972	15.784	16.645	17.560	18.531	19.561	20.655	21.814
12	12.683	13.412	14.192	15.026	15.917	16.870	17.888	18.977	20.141	21.384	22.713	24.133	25.650
13	13.809	14.680	15.618	16.627	17.713	18.882	20.141	21.495	22.953	24.523	26.212	28.029	29.985
14	14.947	15.974	17.086	18.292	19.599	21.051	22.550	24.215	26.019	27.975	30.095	32.393	34.883
15	16.097	17.293	18.599	20.024	21.579	23.276	25.129	27.152	29.361	31.772	34.405	37.280	40.417
16	17.258	18.639	20.157	21.825	23.657	25.673	27.888	30.324	33.003	35.950	39.190	42.753	46.672
17	18.430	20.012	21.762	23.698	25.840	28.213	30.840	33.750	36.974	40.545	44.501	48.884	53.739
18	19.615	21.412	23.414	25.645	28.132	30.906	33.999	37.450	41.301	45.599	50.396	55.750	61.725
19	20.811	22.841	25.117	27.671	30.539	33.760	37.379	41.446	46.018	51.159	56.939	63.440	70.749
20	22.019	24.297	26.870	29.778	33.066	36.786	40.995	45.762	51.160	57.275	64.203	72.052	80.947
24	26.973	30.422	34.426	39.083	44.502	50.816	58.117	66.765	76.790	88.497	102.174	118.155	136.831
25	28.243	32.030	36.459	41.646	47.727	54.865	63.249	73.106	84.701	98.347	114.413	133.334	155.620
30	34.785	40.568	47.575	56.085	66.439	79.058	94.461	113.283	136.308	164.494	199.021	241.333	293.199
40	48.886	60.402	75.401	95.026	120.080	154.762	199.635	259.057	337.882	442.593	581.826	767.091	1,013.70
50	64.463	84.572	112.797	152.667	209.348	290.336	406.529	573.770	815.084	1,163.91	1,668.77	2,400.02	3,459.51
60	81.670	114.052	163.053	237.991	353.584	533.128	813.520	1,253.21	1,944.79	3,034.82	4,755.07	7,471.64	11,761.9

Period, n	14%	15%	16%	17%	18%	19%	20%	24%	28%	32%	36%	40%
1	1.000	1.000	1.000	1.000	1.000	1.000	1.000	1.000	1.000	1.000	1.000	1.000
2	2.140	2.150	2.160	2.170	2.180	2.190	2.200	2.240	2.280	2.320	2.360	2.400
3	3.440	3.473	3.506	3.539	3.572	3.606	3.640	3.778	3.918	4.062	4.210	4.360
4	4.921	4.993	5.066	5.141	5.215	5.291	5.368	5.684	6.016	6.362	6.725	7.104
5	6.610	6.742	6.877	7.014	7.154	7.297	7.442	8.048	8.700	9.398	10.146	10.846
6	8.536	8.754	8.977	9.207	9.442	9.683	9.930	10.980	12.136	13.406	14.799	16.324
7	10.730	11.067	11.414	11.772	12.142	12.523	12.916	14.615	16.534	18.696	21.126	23.853
8	13.233	13.727	14.240	14.773	15.327	15.902	16.499	19.123	22.163	25.678	29.732	34.395
9	16.085	16.786	17.518	18.285	19.086	19.923	20.799	24.712	29.369	34.895	41.435	49.153
10	19.337	20.304	21.321	22.393	23.521	24.709	25.959	31.643	38.592	47.062	57.352	69.814
11	23.044	24.349	25.733	27.200	28.755	30.404	32.150	40.238	50.399	63.122	78.998	98.739
12	27.271	29.002	30.850	32.824	34.931	37.180	39.580	50.985	65.510	84.320	108.437	139.235
13	32.089	34.352	36.786	39.404	42.219	45.244	48.497	64.110	84.853	112.303	148.475	195.929
14	37.581	40.505	43.672	47.103	50.818	54.841	59.196	80.496	109.612	149.240	202.926	275.300
15	43.842	47.580	51.660	56.110	60.965	66.261	72.035	100.815	141.303	197.997	276.979	386.420
16	50.980	55.717	60.925	66.649	72.939	79.850	87.442	126.011	181.868	262.356	377.692	541.988
17	59.118	65.075	71.673	78.979	87.068	96.022	105.931	157.253	233.791	347.310	514.661	759.784
18	68.394	75.836	84.141	93.406	103.740	115.266	128.117	195.994	300.252	459.449	700.939	1,064.70
19	78.969	88.212	98.603	110.285	123.414	138.166	154.740	244.033	385.323	607.472	954.277	1,491.58
20	91.025	102.444	115.380	130.033	146.628	165.418	186.688	303.601	494.213	802.863	1,298.82	2,089.21
24	158.659	184.168	213.978	248.808	289.494	337.010	392.484	723.461	1,322.66	2,443.82	4,450.00	8,033.00
25	181.871	212.793	249.214	292.105	342.603	402.042	471.981	898.092	1,706.80	3,226.84	6,053.00	11,247.2
30	356.787	434.745	530.321	647.439	790.948	966.712	1,181.88	2,640.92	5,873.23	12,940.9	28,172.3	60,501.1
40	1,342.03	1,779.09	2,360.76	3,134.52	4,163.21	5,529.83	7,343.86	22,728.8	69,377.5	207,874	609,890	*
50	4,994.52	7,217.72	10,435.6	15,089.5	21,813.1	31,515.3	45,497.2	195,373	819,103	*	*	*
60	18,535.1	29,220.0	46,057.5	72,555.0	114,190	179,495	281,733	*	*	*	*	*

*These interest factors exceed 1,000,000.

Table IV

Present Value of an Annuity Interest Factor (PVIFA)
($1 per year at *i*% for *n* years)

$$PVIFA = \frac{1 - \dfrac{1}{(1 + i)^n}}{i}$$

$$PVAN = R(PVIFA_{i,n})$$

Period, n	1%	2%	3%	4%	5%	6%	7%	8%	9%	10%	11%	12%	13%
1	0.990	0.980	0.971	0.962	0.952	0.943	0.935	0.926	0.917	0.909	0.901	0.893	0.885
2	1.970	1.942	1.913	1.886	1.859	1.833	1.808	1.783	1.759	1.736	1.713	1.690	1.668
3	2.941	2.884	2.829	2.775	2.723	2.673	2.624	2.577	2.531	2.487	2.444	2.402	2.361
4	3.902	3.808	3.717	3.630	3.546	3.465	3.387	3.312	3.240	3.170	3.102	3.037	2.974
5	4.853	4.713	4.580	4.452	4.329	4.212	4.100	3.993	3.890	3.791	3.696	3.605	3.517
6	5.795	5.601	5.417	5.242	5.076	4.917	4.766	4.623	4.486	4.355	4.231	4.111	3.998
7	6.728	6.472	6.230	6.002	5.786	5.582	5.389	5.206	5.033	4.868	4.712	4.564	4.423
8	7.652	7.325	7.020	6.733	6.463	6.210	5.971	5.747	5.535	5.335	5.146	4.968	4.799
9	8.566	8.162	7.786	7.435	7.108	6.802	6.515	6.247	5.995	5.759	5.537	5.328	5.132
10	9.471	8.983	8.530	8.111	7.722	7.360	7.024	6.710	6.418	6.145	5.889	5.650	5.426
11	10.368	9.787	9.253	8.760	8.306	7.887	7.499	7.139	6.805	6.495	6.207	5.938	5.687
12	11.255	10.575	9.954	9.385	8.863	8.384	7.943	7.536	7.161	6.814	6.492	6.194	5.918
13	12.134	11.348	10.635	9.986	9.394	8.853	8.358	7.904	7.487	7.103	6.750	6.424	6.122
14	13.004	12.106	11.296	10.563	9.899	9.295	8.745	8.244	7.786	7.367	6.982	6.628	6.302
15	13.865	12.849	11.938	11.118	10.380	9.712	9.108	8.559	8.060	7.606	7.191	6.811	6.462
16	14.718	13.578	12.561	11.652	10.838	10.106	9.447	8.851	8.312	7.824	7.379	6.974	6.604
17	15.562	14.292	13.166	12.166	11.274	10.477	9.763	9.122	8.544	8.022	7.549	7.120	6.729
18	16.398	14.992	13.754	12.659	11.690	10.828	10.059	9.372	8.756	8.201	7.702	7.250	6.840
19	17.226	15.678	14.324	13.134	12.085	11.158	10.336	9.604	8.950	8.365	7.839	7.366	6.938
20	18.046	16.351	14.877	13.590	12.462	11.470	10.594	9.818	9.128	8.514	7.963	7.469	7.025
24	21.243	18.914	16.936	15.247	13.799	12.550	11.469	10.529	9.707	8.985	8.348	7.784	7.283
25	22.023	19.523	17.413	15.622	14.094	12.783	11.654	10.675	9.823	9.077	8.422	7.843	7.330
30	25.808	22.397	19.600	17.292	15.373	13.765	12.409	11.258	10.274	9.427	8.694	8.055	7.496
40	32.835	27.355	23.115	19.793	17.159	15.046	13.332	11.925	10.757	9.779	8.951	8.244	7.634
50	39.196	31.424	25.730	21.482	18.256	15.762	13.801	12.233	10.962	9.915	9.042	8.304	7.675
60	44.955	34.761	27.676	22.623	18.929	16.161	14.039	12.377	11.048	9.967	9.074	8.324	7.687

Period, n	14%	15%	16%	17%	18%	19%	20%	24%	28%	32%	36%	40%
1	0.877	0.870	0.862	0.855	0.847	0.840	0.833	0.806	0.781	0.758	0.735	0.714
2	1.647	1.626	1.605	1.585	1.566	1.547	1.528	1.457	1.392	1.332	1.276	1.224
3	2.322	2.283	2.246	2.210	2.174	2.140	2.106	1.981	1.868	1.766	1.674	1.589
4	2.914	2.855	2.798	2.743	2.690	2.639	2.589	2.404	2.241	2.096	1.966	1.849
5	3.433	3.352	3.274	3.199	3.127	3.058	2.991	2.745	2.532	2.345	2.181	2.035
6	3.889	3.784	3.685	3.589	3.498	3.410	3.326	3.020	2.759	2.534	2.399	2.168
7	4.288	4.160	4.039	3.922	3.812	3.706	3.605	3.242	2.937	2.678	2.455	2.263
8	4.639	4.487	4.344	4.207	4.078	3.954	3.837	3.421	3.076	2.786	2.540	2.331
9	4.946	4.772	4.607	4.451	4.303	4.163	4.031	3.566	3.184	2.868	2.603	2.379
10	5.216	5.019	4.833	4.659	4.494	4.339	4.193	3.682	3.269	2.930	2.650	2.414
11	5.453	5.234	5.029	4.836	4.656	4.486	4.327	3.776	3.335	2.978	2.683	2.438
12	5.660	5.421	5.197	4.988	4.793	4.611	4.439	3.851	3.387	3.013	2.708	2.456
13	5.842	5.583	5.342	5.118	4.910	4.715	4.533	3.912	3.427	3.040	2.727	2.469
14	6.002	5.724	5.468	5.229	5.008	4.802	4.611	3.962	3.459	3.061	2.740	2.478
15	6.142	5.847	5.575	5.324	5.092	4.876	4.675	4.001	3.483	3.076	2.750	2.484
16	6.265	5.954	5.669	5.405	5.162	4.938	4.730	4.033	3.503	3.088	2.758	2.489
17	5.373	6.047	5.749	5.475	5.222	4.990	4.775	4.059	3.518	3.097	2.763	2.492
18	6.467	6.128	5.818	5.534	5.273	5.033	4.812	4.080	3.529	3.104	2.767	2.494
19	6.550	6.198	5.877	5.584	5.316	5.070	4.844	4.097	3.539	3.109	2.770	2.496
20	6.623	6.259	5.929	5.628	5.353	5.101	4.870	4.110	3.546	3.113	2.772	2.497
24	6.835	6.434	6.073	5.746	5.451	5.182	4.937	4.143	3.562	3.121	2.776	2.499
25	6.873	6.464	6.097	5.766	5.467	5.195	4.948	4.147	3.564	3.122	2.776	2.499
30	7.003	6.566	6.177	5.829	5.517	5.235	4.979	4.160	3.569	3.124	2.778	2.500
40	7.105	6.642	6.233	5.871	5.548	5.258	4.997	4.166	3.571	3.125	2.778	2.500
50	7.133	6.661	6.246	5.880	5.554	5.262	4.999	4.167	3.571	3.125	2.778	2.500
60	7.140	6.665	6.249	5.882	5.555	5.263	5.000	4.167	3.571	3.125	2.778	2.500

Table V   **Normal Distribution (Area of the Normal Distribution that is to the right *or* left of z Standard Deviations from the Mean)**

Number of Standard Deviations From Mean (z)	Area to the Left or Right (One Tail)	Number of Standard Deviations From Mean (z)	Area to the Left or Right (One Tail)
0.00	0.5000	1.55	0.0606
0.05	0.4801	1.60	0.0548
0.10	0.4602	1.65	0.0495
0.15	0.4404	1.70	0.0446
0.20	0.4207	1.75	0.0401
0.25	0.4013	1.80	0.0359
0.30	0.3821	1.85	0.0322
0.35	0.3632	1.90	0.0287
0.40	0.3446	1.95	0.0256
0.45	0.3264	2.00	0.0228
0.50	0.3085	2.05	0.0202
0.55	0.2912	2.10	0.0179
0.60	0.2743	2.15	0.0158
0.65	0.2578	2.20	0.0139
0.70	0.2420	2.25	0.0122
0.75	0.2264	2.30	0.0107
0.80	0.2119	2.35	0.0094
0.85	0.1977	2.40	0.0082
0.90	0.1841	2.45	0.0071
0.95	0.1711	2.50	0.0062
1.00	0.1587	2.55	0.0054
1.05	0.1469	2.60	0.0047
1.10	0.1357	2.65	0.0040
1.15	0.1251	2.70	0.0035
1.20	0.1151	2.75	0.0030
1.25	0.1056	2.80	0.0026
1.30	0.0968	2.85	0.0022
1.35	0.0885	2.90	0.0019
1.40	0.0808	2.95	0.0016
1.45	0.0735	3.00	0.0013
1.50	0.0668	3.05	0.0011
		3.10	0.0010
		3.25	0.0006
		3.50	0.00023
		4.00	0.00003
		4.99	0.0000003

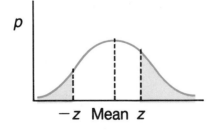

Index to Glossary Terms*

ABC inventory classification (21), p. 675
ACRS depreciation (9), p. 278
Activity ratios (6), p. 168
Affirmative loan covenant (15), p. 483
Agency costs (13), p. 425
Agency relationships (1), p. 3
Amortization schedule (15), p. 483
Annual percentage rate (APR) (22), p. 695
Annuity (3), p. 57
Arbitrage (13), p. 425
Assignment (24), p. 751

Bad-debt loss ratio (20), p. 647
Balance sheet (6), p. 168
Balloon loan (15), p. 483
Bank draft (19), p. 619
Banker's acceptance (19), p. 619
Bankruptcy (24), p. 751
Bankruptcy costs (13), p. 425
Bankruptcy Reform Act of 1978 (24), p. 751
Beta (5), p. 132 and (12), p. 383
Bond (4), p. 101
Bond rating (16), p. 517
Bond refunding (16), p. 517
Book value (4), p. 101
Breakeven analysis (7), p. 216
Bullet loan (15), p. 483
Business risk (7), p. 216

Call feature (16), p. 517
Call option (17), p. 569
Call premium (16), p. 517
Call price (16), p. 517
Capital Asset Pricing Model (CAPM) (12), p. 383
Capital gains (long term) (2A), p. 48
Capital gains yield (4), p. 101
Capitalization of income (4), p. 101

Capital budget (8), p. 247
Capital budgeting (9), p. 278
Capital expenditure (9), p. 278
Capital losses (long term) (2A), p. 48
Capital markets (2), p. 32
Capital rationing (9), p. 278
Capital recovery problem (3), p. 57
Capital structure (13), p. 425
Carrying costs (21), p. 675
Cash budget (8), p. 247
Cash conversion cycle (18), p. 593
Cash discount (20), p. 647
Certainty equivalent (11), p. 355
Chapter 11 (24), p. 751
Chapter 7 (24), p. 751
Characteristic line (5), p. 132
Chattel mortgage (15), p. 483
Coefficient of variation (5), p. 132
Commercial paper (19), p. 619 and (22), p. 695
Common stock (2), p. 32
Comparative analysis (6), p. 168
Compensating balance (15), p. 483
Competitive bidding (16), p. 517
Composition (24), p. 751
Compound interest (3), p. 57
Concentration banking (19), p. 619
Conditional sales contract (15), p. 483
Conglomerate merger (23), p. 729
Contingent project (9), p. 278
Contribution margin (7), p. 216
Conversion premium (17), p. 569
Conversion price (17), p. 569
Conversion ratio (17), p. 569
Conversion (stock) value (17), p. 569
Convertible bond (16), p. 517
Convertible security (17), p. 569
Corporation (2), p. 32
Correlation (5), p. 132
Coupon rate of interest (4), p. 101
Covariance (5), p. 132

*The number in parentheses indicates the chapter or appendix in which the term is discussed.

Covered option (17), p. 569
Credit period (20), p. 647
Cumulative dividends (16), p. 517
Cumulative voting (16A), p. 560

Debenture (4), p. 101
Debt capacity (13), p. 425
Declaration date (14), p. 451
Default risk (19), p. 619
Degree of combined leverage (DCL) (7), p. 216
Degree of financial leverage (DFL) (7), p. 216
Degree of operating leverage (DOL) (7), p. 216
Depository transfer check (DTC) (19), p. 619
Depreciation (9), p. 278
Deterministic model (8), p. 247
Direct lease (15), p. 483
Direct placement (16), p. 517
Discount loan (22), p. 695
Discount period (20), p. 647
Discount rate (3), p. 57
Discriminant analysis (6), p. 168
Diversification (5), p. 132
Dividend yield (4), p. 101

EAT (6), p. 168
EBIT (6), p. 168
Economic order quantity (21), p. 675
Effective interest rate (3), p. 57
EPS (6), p. 168
Eurodollars (25), p. 771
Eurobond (25), p. 771
European currency unit (ECU) (25), p. 771
Exchange rate (25), p. 771
Exchange ratio (23), p. 729
Ex-dividend date (14), p. 451
Exercise price (17), p. 569
Expected value (2), p. 32
Ex-rights (16A), p. 560
Extension (24), p. 751

Factoring (22), p. 695
Field warehouse financing agreement (22), p. 695
FIFO (6), p. 168
Financial analysis (6), p. 168
Financial forecasting (8), p. 247
Financial futures contract (12A), p. 418
Financial lease (15), p. 483
Financial leverage (7), p. 216
Financial leverage ratios (6), p. 168
Financial planning model (8), p. 247
Financial ratio (6), p. 168
Financial risk (7), p. 216
Financial structure (13), p. 425
Fixed costs (7), p. 216

Float (19), p. 619
Floating lien (22), p. 695
Flotation cost (16), p. 517
Fluctuating current assets (18), p. 593
Foreign bond (25), p. 771
Forward rate (25), p. 771
Future value (or terminal value) (3), p. 57

Going-concern value (4), p. 101
Goodwill (23), p. 729

Hedging (12A), p. 418
Holding company (23), p. 729
Horizontal merger (23), p. 729
Hurdle rate (11), p. 355

Income bond (16), p. 517
Income statement (6), p. 168
Indenture (16), p. 517
Independent project (9), p. 278
Indifference point (13), p. 425
Insolvency (14), p. 451
Interest (3), p. 57
Interest rate parity (25), p. 771
Interest rate risk (4), p. 101
Interest rate swap (16), p. 517
Internal rate of return (IRR) (10), p. 317
International bond (25), p. 771
Inventory cycle (21), p. 675
Investment banker (2), p. 32 and (16), p. 517
Investment opportunity curve (12), p. 383
Investment tax credit (ITC) (2A), p. 48

Just-in-time inventory and production concept (21),
    p. 675

Lead time (21), p. 675
Lease (15), p. 483
Legal insolvency (24), p. 751
Lessee (15), p. 483
Lessor (15), p. 483
Letter of credit (25), p. 771
Leveraged buyout (23), p. 729
Leveraged lease (15), p. 483
LIFO (6), p. 168
Line of credit (22), p. 695
Liquidation value (4), p. 101
Liquidity ratios (6), p. 168
Listed security exchanges (16), p. 518
Lockbox (19), p. 619
London interbank offered rate (LIBOR) (25), p. 771
Long hedge (12A), p. 418

Margin (12A), p. 418
Margin call (12A), p. 418
Marginal cost of capital (12), p. 383
Marginal tax rate (2A), p. 48
Market-based ratios (6), p. 168
Matching approach (18), p. 593
Merger (23), p. 729
Money markets (2), p. 32
Mortgage bond (4), p. 101
Multinational corporation (25), p. 771
Multiple rates of return (10), p. 317
Mutually exclusive project (9), p. 278

Negative loan covenant (15), p. 483
Negotiated underwriting (16), p. 518
Net cash flow (9), p. 278
Net income theory (13), p. 425
Net investment (9), p. 278
Net operating income theory (13), p. 425
Net present value (NPV) (10), p. 317
Net working capital (18), p. 593
Nominal interest rate (3), p. 57
Normal project (9), p. 278

Operating budget (8), p. 247
Operating cycle (18), p. 593
Operating lease (15), p. 483
Operating leverage (7), p. 216
Opportunity cost (10), p. 317
Optimal capital budget (12), p. 383
Optimal capital structure (13), p. 425
Optimization model (8), p. 247
Option (17), p. 569
Ordering costs (21), p. 675
Over-the-counter (OTC) securities markets (16), p. 518

Partnership (2), p. 32
Par value (16), p. 518
Passive residual theory (14), p. 451
Payback (PB) period (10), p. 317
Percentage of sales forecasting method (8), p. 247
Permanent current assets (18), p. 593
Perpetual bond (4), p. 101
Perpetuity (3), p. 57
Pledging of accounts receivable (22), p. 695
Pooling of interests method (23), p. 729
Portfolio (5), p. 132
Preauthorized check (19), p. 619
Preemptive right (16), p. 518
Preferred stock (2), p. 32
Present value (1), p. 3 and (3), p. 57
Primary markets (2), p. 32
Prime rate (22), p. 695

Principal (3), p. 57
Probabilistic model (8), p. 247
Profitability index (PI) (10), p. 317
Profitability ratios (6), p. 168
Pro forma financial statements (8), p. 247
Project postaudit (10), p. 317
Promissory note (22), p. 695
Prospectus (16), p. 518
Purchase method (23), p. 729
Purchasing syndicate (16), p. 518
Put option (17), p. 569

Record date (14), p. 451
Reinvestment rate (10), p. 317
Reorder point (21), p. 675
Repurchase agreement (19), p. 619
Required rate of return (4), p. 101
Restrictive loan covenant (15), p. 483
Revolving credit agreement (22), p. 695
Right (16), p. 518
Rights offering (16), p. 518
Rights-on (16A), p. 560
Risk (2), p. 32
Risk-adjusted discount rate (11), p. 355
Risk premium (2), p. 32

Sale and leaseback (15), p. 483
S corporation (2A), p. 48
Seasonal datings (20), p. 647
Secondary markets (2), p. 32
Securities and Exchange Commission (SEC) (16), p. 518
Security market line (SML), p. 132
Senior debt (16), p. 518
Sensitivity analysis (8), p. 247
Shareholder wealth (1), p. 3
Shelf registration (16), p. 518
Short hedge (12A), p. 418
Simulation (11), p. 355
Sinking fund problem (3), p. 57
Sole proprietorship (2), p. 32
Speculators (12A), p. 418
Spot rate (25), p. 771
Standard deviation (5), p. 132
Stock dividend (14), p. 451
Stockholders' equity (6), p. 168
Stockout costs (21), p. 675
Stock split (16), p. 518
Straight-bond, or investment, value (17), p. 569
Subordinated debenture (16), p. 518
Systematic risk (5), p. 132

Target capital structure (13), p. 425
Tax credit (2A), p. 48

Tax deduction (2A), p. 48
Technical insolvency (24), p. 751
Tender offer (23), p. 729
Terminal warehouse financing agreement (22), p. 695
Term loan (15), p. 483
Term structure of interest rates (2), p. 32
Total risk (7), p. 216
Treasury stock (14), p. 451
Trend analysis (6), p. 168 and (8), p. 247
Trustee (16), p. 518
Trust receipt (22), p. 695

Underwriting (2), p. 32 and (16), p. 518

Underwriting spread (16), p. 518
Unsystematic risk (5), p. 132

Variable cost (7), p. 216
Vertical merger (23), p. 729

Warrant (17), p. 569
Wire transfer (19), p. 620
Working capital (18), p. 593

Yield to maturity (4), p. 101

Zero-balance system (19), p. 620

Index

A

ABC inventory classification, 680
Above normal growth dividend valuation model, 120-122, 393-394
Accelerated cost recovery system (ACRS) depreciation, 292, 295-298, 312-313, 786-787
Accelerated depreciation, 294-295, 313-314, 496
   declining balance method, 313-314
   sum-of-years' digits method, 313-314
Accounting Principles Board (APB), 584
Accounts receivable, 595, 648, 665, 707-710
Accounts receivable loans, 707-710
Accrued expenses, 700
Acid-test ratio, 174
ACRS depreciation, 292, 295-298, 312-313, 497, 501
Activity ratios, 171, 175-178
Acquisition, 730
Adjustable rate preferred stock, 530
Adjusted book value method, 734
Advance factoring, 709
Affirmative covenants, (term loans) 487
Agency problems, 7-8, 434-435
   costs, 7-8, 434-435
   relationships, 7
Aging schedule, 174-175, 658
American Stock Exchange (ASE or AMEX), 38, 531, 540
Amortization, 484-486
Annuities,
   annuity due, 69, 72-73, 76, 498
   equivalent annual annuities, 352-353
   ordinary annuity, 69-75
Arbitrage, 429-430
Asset expansion projects, 290-292
Asset replacement decision, 292-301
Assignment, 756

Average collection period, 175-176, 649

B

Bad-debt expense, 649, 666, 710
Bad-debt loss ratio, 649, 653
Balance sheet, 171, 248
Balance sheet quality, 196-197
Balloon loan, 486
Bankers acceptances, 638, 780
Bankruptcy, 158, 197-198, 752, 755
Bankruptcy costs, 433-434
Bankruptcy Reform Act of 1978, 757, 759
Bank loans, 701-705, 715-717, 763-766
   line of credit, 701, 703-704
   revolving credit agreement, 701, 704-705
   single loan, 701-702
Bank money market accounts, 638-639
Beta, 151-156, 356, 367-370, 396-397
"Blue sky" laws, 542
Bond quotations, 527-528
Bond ratings, 524-526, 553-555
Bond refunding, 523, 561-563
Bonds, 105-112, 519-529
   advantages and disadvantages, 519-529
   types, 520-521
   users, 528
   valuation, 105-112
      finite maturity, 105-108
      perpetual bonds, 108-109
   yield to maturity, 109-112
Book value, 104-105, 534, 741-742
Breakeven analysis, 219-227
   algebraic method, 221-222
   cash breakeven analysis, 225-226
   degree of operating leverage, 230-231
   examples, 222-224
   graphic method, 220-221
   limitations, 226-227
   risk assessment, 224-225

Broker (securities), 36, 547
Budgets, 254-259
   capital, 254, 259
   cash, 254-259
   operating, 254-255
   production, 255
   sales, 254
Bullet loan, 486
Business combinations, 730
Business failure, 752-761
   alternatives for failing businesses, 755-761
   causes, 754
   definitions, 752
   trends, 752-754
Business risk, 231, 385

C

Call feature,
   bonds, 522-523
   convertible securities, 579
   preferred stock, 531
Call option, 570-575
Call premium,
   bonds, 522
   preferred stock, 531
Call price,
   bonds, 522
   preferred stock, 531
Capital asset pricing model, 140-159, 367-370, 372-373, 395-397
   assumptions and limitations, 157-158
   cost of equity, 395-397
   uses of 156-157
Capital budget, 254, 259, 404-405
   optimal, 404-405
Capital budgeting, 279-302, 318-339
   decision criteria, 318-330, 336-338
      internal rate of return, 318, 323-327, 337
      net present value, 318, 321-323, 336-337
      payback period, 318-321, 336, 358

Capital budgeting (continued)
  profitability index, 318, 327–329, 338
  decision-making process, 283–285, 318–339
  multinational firms, 341–342
  risk, 356–370
Capital expenditure, 279–280
Capital expenditure projects,
  classification, 280–281, 283–285
  contingent projects, 281
  estimating cash flows, 285–302
  independent projects, 280, 326, 328
  mutually exclusive projects, 280–281, 326, 328, 350–353
  postaudit, 333–334
Capital impairment restriction, 453
Capital lease, 493–497
Capital markets, 37–38
Capital rationing, 281, 328–333
Capital recovery problem, 75
Capital stock, 34
Capital structure, 426–443
  optimal, 426, 435–436, 439–443
  target, 426
Capitalization-of-income method of valuation, 102–103, 114–117
Careers in finance, 19–28
Carrying cost, 677–679, 681–682
Cash, 621
Cash balance, 595
Cash breakeven analysts, 225–226
Cash budget, 255–259, 622–623, 704
Cash collection, 626–632
Cash conversion cycle, 595
Cash disbursement, 626, 632–633
Cash discount, 625, 652, 655, 697–700
Cash flows, 285–302, 622–623, 716–717
Cash management models, 633
Certainty equivalent, 360–361
Chapter 7 (Bankruptcy Act), 759–760
Chapter 11 (Bankruptcy Act), 757–758
Characteristic line, 152–153
Chattel mortgage, 491–492
Chief financial officer, 8
"Clean-up" provision, 704
"Clientele effect," 456–457
Coefficient of variation, 138–139
Collateral, 696, 708, 710, 707–713, 739

Collateral trust bonds, 521
Collection effort, 649, 657
Combined leverage, 236–239
Commercial bank, 38–39, 194, 489, 662, 709, 711, 739
Commercial paper, 637, 706–707
Commitment fee, 704
Common stock, 35, 113–122, 533–540, 740
  accounting, 533–534
  advantages and disadvantages, 539–540
  classes, 536
  stock dividends, 464–468
  stock repurchases, 468–470, 537–539
  stock splits, 468, 472–474, 536–537
  stockholder rights, 535
  valuation, 113–122
Comparative price-earnings ratio method, 733–734
Compensating balances, 486, 622, 624, 702–705, 708
Competitive bidding, 543–547
Composition, 756
Compound interest, 61–65
Compound sum of an annuity,
  annuity due, 72–73
  ordinary annuity, 69–72
Compound sum of an annuity interest factor (CVIFA), 71
Compound value interest factor (CVIF), 63–65
Compounding periods, 77–79
Computerized financial planning models, 263–264
Concentration bank, 626–627
Conditional sales contract, 491–492
Conglomerate merger, 733
Consolidation, 730
Constant growth dividend valuation model, 118–120, 392–393
Constant payout ratio dividend policy, 463
Contingent projects, 281
Continuous compounding and discounting, 96–98
Contribution margin, 221–222
Controller, 8
Conversion feature, 523,
Conversion premium, 576
Conversion price, 575
Conversion ratio, 575–576
Conversion value, 577
Convertible securities, 570, 575–580
  conversion, 579–580
  features, 575–576

reasons for issuing, 576–577
  valuation, 577–579
Corporate income taxes, 48–53,
  capital gains income, 50
  deferred Federal income taxes, 52,
  dividend income, 50,
  Investment Tax Credit (ITC), 50–51, 292–293,
  loss carrybacks and carryforwards, 51–52,
  ordinary income, 48–50,
  S corporations, 52–53
Corporate organization, 34
Corporate securities, 34–35
Corporate-bank relations, 623–624
Corporation, 34–35
Correlation, 142–143
  coefficient, 142–143
Cost of capital, 280, 384–405
  divisional, 369–370, 372–373
  marginal, 281–283, 401–404
  relationship to capital structure, 427–428, 439–441
  weighted, 399–404
Cost of debt, 388–390
  relationship to capital structure, 427–428, 439–440
Cost of depreciation-generated funds, 405
Cost of equity, 391–399, 427–428, 440–441
  internal (retained earnings), 391–398
  external, 391, 398–399
  relationship to capital structure, 427–428, 440–441
Cost of preferred stock, 390–391
Cost of trade credit, 697–699
Covariance, 152
Coupon interest rate, 107, 389, 523–524
Covenants (term loans), 487–488
Covered interest arbitrage, 775
Covered option, 573
Credit period, 652–655, 697
Credit policy, 648–658
  credit standards, 649–652
  credit terms, 649, 652–657
  collection effort, 649, 657
Credit rating, 625
Credit scoring systems, 663
Credit standards, 649–652
Credit terms, 649, 652–657, 697
Creditors' committee, 756
Cumulative feature (preferred stock), 530
Cumulative voting, 563–564
Current ratio, 172–174

D

Dealer (securities), 36, 547
Debentures, 106, 520, 760
Debt capacity, 426
Debt ratio, 179
Debt restructuring, 756
Debt securities, 35, 105–112, 388–390, 741
   cost, 388–390
Debt-to-equity ratio, 179–180, 500
Decentralized collection centers, 626–627
Declaration date (dividend), 464–466
Declining balance depreciation method, 313–314
Deep discount bonds, 389–390
Default provisions (term loans), 488–489
Deferred Federal income taxes, 52, 260–261
Deferred annuitites, 81–82
Deferred income, 700–701
Degree of combined leverage, 236–239
Degree of financial leverage, 219, 233–235, 600
Degree of operating leverage, 219, 228–231, 600
Depreciation, 294–298, 312–314, 405, 496, 740, 786–787
Deposit float, 626
Depository transfer check, 630–631
Detachable warrants, 581
Deterministic inventory control models, 680–687
Direct lease, 494
Disbursement float, 626
Discounted cash flow (capital budgeting), 304
Discounted cash flow method (merger), 734
Discounted loan, 702
Discounting, 65
Discriminant analysis, 197–198
Diversification, 141–149
Divestitures, 731–732
Dividend policy, 452–470
   constant payout ratio policy, 463–464
   effect on value of firm, 457–459
   inflation, 456
   legal constraints, 453–454
   passive residual policy, 460
   restrictive covenants, 454
   share repurchases, 468–470
   stable dollar policy, 460–463
   stock dividends, 466–468, 472–474

   tax constraints, 454
   theoretical perspectives, 457–459
Dividend valuaton models, 113–122, 124–125
   above normal growth model, 120–122, 393–394
   constant growth model, 118–120, 392–393
   cost of equity, 391–395
   general model, 116–118, 391–392
   Gordon model, 119
   growth models, 118–122, 392–394
   n-period model, 115–116
   one-period model, 114
   two-period model, 115
   zero growth model, 120, 392–393
Dividend yield, 535–536
Dividend payout ratio, 463–464
Divisional costs of capital, 369–370, 372–373
Dow Jones Industrial Average, 541–542
Draft (bank), 632–633
Dun and Bradstreet, 191, 659–662, 665, 754
Du Pont chart, 188–190

E

Earnings per share, 436–438, 584
   primary, 584
   fully diluted, 584
Earnings quality, 195–196
EBIT-EPS analysis, 436–438
   indifference point, 436–438
Econometric techniques, 253–254
Economic order quantity model, 680–687
   basic model, 681–684
   extensions, 684–687
Economies of scale, 252
Economic Recovery Tax Act (ERTA) of 1981, 292, 295, 312
Effective rate of interest, 79–80, 96–98
Electronic spreadsheets (worksheets), 85–86, 366–367
EOQ model, 680–687
Equipment financing loans, 491–492
   conditional sales contract, 491–492
   chattel mortgage, 491–492
Equipment trust certificates, 521
Equity multiplier ratio, 190
Equity participations, 486–487

Equity securities, 35, 529–540
   cost, 391–399
Equivalent annual annuities, 352–353
Estimating cash flows (capital expenditures), 285–302
   bias, 302
   net cash flows, 287–290, 335–336, 362–363
   net investment, 287, 335
   uncertainty, 301–302
Eurobonds, 781
Eurodollar deposits, 408–410, 638, 780
European currency units, 781
Exchange rate (currencies), 772–779
   forward rate, 773–774
   risk, 777–779
   spot rate, 773–774
Exchange ratio (securities), 735
Exercise price,
   option, 570–571
   warrant, 580
Expectations theory, 615–616
Expected return, 44–45, 134–135, 143
Expected value, 134–135
Expiration date,
   option, 572
   warrant, 580
Extension, 756
Ex ante return, 44
Ex post return, 44
Ex-dividend date, 464–466
Ex-rights, 565–566
Extendable notes, 524

F

Factor, 709
Factoring receivables, 488, 648, 709–710
Federal agency issues, 635
Federal income taxes, 48–54, 785–788
Field warehouse, 712–713
FIFO, 199
Finance companies, 40, 709, 711
Financial Accounting Standards Board (FASB), 199–202, 499–501
Financial analysis, 169–202, 716–717
Financial asset, 37, 102
Financial deregulation, 40
Financial forecasting, 248–254
   econometric techniques, 253–254
   future performance, 197–198

Financial forecasting (continued)
    percentage of sales method,
        248-252
    trend analysis, 186-188, 252-
        253
Financial futures, 408-423
Financial intermediaries, 36-40
Financial lease, 493-494
    direct, 494
    sale and leaseback, 494
Financial leverage, 217, 231-236,
    438-439
Financial leverage ratios, 171,
    178-181
Financial management,
    history of field, 10-11
    organization of function, 8-10
Financial markets, 37-38
Financial middlemen, 36
Financial planning models, 263-
    264
Financial ratios, 169-198
    activity, 171, 175-178
    financial leverage, 171, 178-
        181
    liquidity, 171-175
    market-based, 171, 183-186
    profitability, 171, 181-183
Financial risk, 235-236, 385
Financial statements, 171, 217,
    259-263, 658-659, 665
    pro forma, 248, 261-263
Financial structure, 426
First-in-first-out (FIFO) inventory
    valuation, 199
"Five C's of credit," 663
Fixed asset turnover ratio, 177-
    178
Fixed charge coverage ratio, 180-
    181
Fixed costs, 217-219
Fixed income futures, 421
Fixed income securities, 519, 570
Float, 626
Floating lien, 712
Floor planning, 712
Flotation costs, 389-390, 398-
    399, 459, 484, 510, 548-549,
    561
    debt, 389
    external equity, 398-399
    preferred stock, 390
Fluctuating current assets, 601
Forced conversion, 579-580
Foreign currency, 772-779
Foreign investment, 778-781
Foreign trade 777-780
Forward (exchange) rate, 773-774
Forward market hedge, 778

Forms of business organization,
    33-35
    corporation, 34-35
    partnership, 33-34
    sole proprietorship, 33
Formula value (warrant), 581-584
Fully diluted earnings per share,
    584
Funded debt, 528
Funds, 259
Funds flow analysis, 171, 259-263
    funds flow statement, 171, 259-
        263
    sources and uses of funds
        statement, 171, 259-263
    sources of funds, 259-261
    uses of funds, 259-261
Futures, 408-410, 418-423
Future (terminal) value, 61-65

G
General dividend valuation model,
    116-118, 391-392
Goals of the firm, 4-7
    profit maximization, 5
    shareholder wealth maximiza-
        tion, 5-6, 117-118
    other goals, 6-7
    social responsibility, 6
Going concern value, 102, 755,
    757
Golden parachute, 731
Goodwill, 740
Gordon (common stock) valuation
    model, 119
Gross profit margin ratio, 182
Growth models, 118-122, 392-
    394
    constant growth, 118-120, 392

H
Hedging, 408-410, 420, 777-779
History of financial management,
    10-11
Holding company, 731
Homogeneous risk class assump-
    tion, 429
Horizontal merger, 733
Hurdle rate, 358-359

I
Income bonds, 521
Income statement, 171, 217
Income taxes, 48-54, 785-788
Indenture, 521-522
Independent projects, 280, 326,
    328
Individual income taxes, 53-54

Industrial Development Authorities
    (IDA), 491
Industrial revenue bonds, 521
Inflation,
    capital expenditures, 338-339
    dividend policy, 456
    financial statement analysis,
        198-202
    real interest rates, 150-151
    required rate of return, 384
    security market line, 150-151
Information content (of dividends),
    458-459, 462
"Insider," 543-544
Insolvency, 625
Insolvency restriction, 454
Institutional Brokers' Estimate Ser-
    vice (IBES), 394-395
Insurance companies, 39-40, 489,
    711
Intercompany dividends, 50
Interest, 58-65
    simple interest, 59-61
    compound interest, 61-65
Interest rate parity, 774-775
Interest rate risk, 108, 385, 408-
    410, 616, 634
Interest rate swaps, 544
Intermediate term credit, 484
Internal rate of return, 318, 323-
    327, 337
    advantages and disadvantages,
        326-327
    decision rule, 326
    reinvestment rate assumption,
        329-330
    trial-and-error computation, 325
International bond, 781
International financial manage-
    ment, 772-781
Interpolation, 111, 325
Inventories, 595
Inventory, 676-688
    control models, 679-688
    costs, 677-679
    types, 676-677
Inventory loans, 710-713
    field warehouse, 712-713
    floating lien, 712
    terminal warehouse, 712-713
    trust receipt, 712
Inventory profits, 198-199
Inventory turnover ratio, 176-177
Investment banker, 36-37, 544-
    549
Investment companies, 39
Investment opportunity curve,
    281-283, 404-405
Investment Tax Credit (ITC), 50-

51, 292-293, 496-497, 499-
503
Irrelevance of dividends theory,
457-458

J

Junior debt, 520
Junk bond, 739-740
Just-in-time inventory models, 688

L

Last-in-first-out (LIFO) inventory
valuation, 199
Lead time, 680-681, 684-685
Leases, 492-504,
accounting practices, 499-501
advantages, 501-502
determining the lease payments, 496-498
disadvantages, 502
financial (or capital) lease, 493-
494
lease-buy analysis, 502-504
leveraged leases, 494-496,
507-508
operating (or service or maintenance) lease, 493
tax status, 498-499
types of, 493-496
Lease-buy analysis, 502-504
Legal insolvency, 752
Letter of credit, 779
Leverage, 217-239, 583
Leveraged buyouts, 737-740
Leveraged leases, 494-496, 507-
508
LIBOR, 780
LIFO, 199
Line of credit, 623, 701, 703-704,
706
Liquid asset balance, 621-625
optimal, 624-625
Liquid assets, 259
Liquidation, 755, 759-761
Liquidation value, 102, 755, 757
Liquidity premium theory, 615-617
Liquidity ratios, 171-175
Listed security exchanges, 540-
541
Loan amortization, 75
Lock-box, 627-630
London interbank offered rate
(LIBOR), 780
Long hedge, 420
Long position, 542
Long-range financial planning, 266
Long-term capital gain (or loss),
50, 290, 785

Long-term debt (bonds), 105-112,
519-529
advantages and disadvantages,
528-529
features, 521-524
types, 520-521
users of, 528
valuation, 105-109
yield to maturity, 109-112, 389
Loss carrybacks and carryforwards, 51-52, 733, 786
Lotus 1-2-3, 85-86, 366-367

M

Margin, 420, 542
Margin trading, 542
Marginal cost of capital, 281-283,
401-405
Marginal tax rate, 49
Market equilibrium, 104
Market-based ratios, 171, 183-
186
Market-book (price) ratio, 185-
186
Market segmentation theory, 615,
617
Market value,
assets, 103-104, 741
common stock, 534
convertible debt issue, 578-579
Market value weights, 400
Marketability risk, 385
Marketable securities, 621, 633-
639
default risk, 633-634
marketability (or liquidity), 633-
634
maturity date, 633-634
rate of return, 633-634
types, 634-639
Matching approach, 601-602
Maturity factoring, 709
Maximization of shareholder
wealth, 5-6, 117-118, 452,
600, 606-607
Mergers, 730-742
accounting for aspects of, 740-
741
leveraged buyouts, 737-740
reasons for, 732-733
tax aspects of, 741-742
terminology, 730-732
types, 732
valuation, 733-737
Mezzanine financing, 739
Microcomputers, 84-86
Modigliani and Miller (MM) analysis, 427-430, 456-459

Money market hedge, 778
Money market mutual funds, 638
Money market preferred stocks,
638
Monitoring accounts receivable,
658
Money markets, 37-38
Moody's 191, 524-526, 706, 715
bond ratings, 524-526
Investor Services, 524
manuals, 191
Mortgage bonds, 520, 528
Multinational company, 640, 772,
779
Multiple internal rates of return,
327
Municipal securities, 635-636
Mutually exclusive projects, 280-
281, 326, 328, 350-353

N

Naked option, 573-574
Negative covenants (term loans),
488
Negotiable certificates of deposits, 637
Negotiated underwriting, 546-547
Net advantage to leasing, 502-
504
Net cash flows, 288-290, 335-
336, 362-363
Net earnings restriction, 453-454
Net income theory of valuation,
427-430
Net investment, 287, 335
Net operating income theory of
valuation, 427-430
Net present value, 321-323, 336-
337, 362-363
advantages and disadvantages,
323
decision rule, 322-323
reinvestment rate assumption,
329-330
unequal lives, 350-353
Net profit margin ratio, 182
Net working capital, 287, 290,
454, 487, 594-596
New York Stock Exchange
(NYSE), 38, 531, 535, 540
Nominal rate of interest, 79, 96-98
Nondiversifiable (or systematic)
risk, 148
Nonnormal (or nonconventional) investment project, 285, 327
Nonrecourse factoring, 709
Normal (or conventional) investment project, 285, 327

Normal probability distribution, 136–138, 225, 236, 363–364
Notes payable, 697

O

Open account, 697
Operating budgets, 254–255
Operating cycle, 594–595
Operating lease, 493
Operating leverage, 217, 219, 228–231
Opportunity cost, 332, 624, 678, 698
Optimal capital budget, 404–405
Optimal capital structure, 426, 435–436, 439–443
Options, 570–575
   how used, 573–575
   valuation concepts, 570–573
Ordering costs, 677–678, 681–682
Organization of financial management function, 8–10
Original issue deep discount bonds, 524
"Over-the-counter" market, 38, 531, 540–541

P

Par value,
   common stock, 534
   long-term debt, 107, 520, 523
   preferred stock, 530
Partnership, 33–34
Passive residual dividend policy, 460
Payback period, 318–321, 336
   advantages and disadvantages, 319–321
   decision rule, 319
Payment date (dividend), 464–466
Percentage of sales forecasting method, 248–252
Pension funds, 39, 489
Perfect capital markets, 429
Permanent current assets, 601
Perpetual bonds, 108–109
Perpetuities, 77, 108–109, 113
Physical asset, 102
Plan of reorganization, 757–759
Pledging accounts receivables, 648, 708
Pollution control bonds, 521
Pooling of interests method, 740–741
Portfolio (investment), 140, 779
Portfolio risk, 140–159
Preauthorized checks, 631–632
Precautionary motive, 621
Preemptive right, 35, 535, 564

Preference stock, 531
Preferred stock, 35, 112–113, 390–391, 529–533, 741
   advantages and disadvantages, 532–533
   cost, 390–391
   features, 530–531
   users of, 531–532
   valuation, 112–113
Present value, 5, 65–69, 73–76, 80–82
Present value of an annuity due, 76
Present value of an annuity interest factors (PVIFA), 73–75
Present value of an ordinary annuity, 73–75
Present value interest factors (PVIF), 67–69
Price-earnings (P/E) ratio, 183–185, 438–439, 468–469, 536, 733–737
Primary claims, 37
Primary earnings per share, 584
Primary markets, 38
Prime rate, 486, 701, 704, 706, 709, 780
Principal, 59, 105, 520
Priority of claims, 759–760
Private (or direct) placement, 546–548
Privileged subscription, 548
Pro forma financial statements, 248, 487
Probabilistic inventory control models, 680, 687–688
Probability distributions, 134–138
Profit contribution ratio, 650
Profit maximization, 5, 281
Profitability index, 327–329, 338
   decision rule, 328–329
Profitability ratios, 171, 181–183
Promissory note, 492, 697, 701, 711
Prospectus, 543
Protective covenants (term loans), 487–488, 701, 704
Public cash offering, 544–547
Purchase method, 740–741
Purchase money mortgage, 492
Purchasing syndicate, 546–547
Put bonds, 524
Put option, 570, 731

Q

Quantity discounts, 676, 685–687
Quick ratio, 174

R

Record date (dividend), 464–466
Referee, 759

Regional security exchanges, 38, 540–541
Registration statement, 543
Regulation of the securities markets, 542–544
   "blue sky" laws, 542
   Securities Act of 1933, 542
   Securities and Exchange Act of 1934, 542–543
   shelf registration, 543
Reinvestment rate assumption, 329–330
Reorganization, 755, 757–759
Replacement chain, 350–351
Repurchase agreements, 637
Required rate of return, 102–103, 107, 114–116, 149–150, 280, 368, 384, 678
Residual form of ownership, 533
Restrictive covenants (term loans), 488
Restructuring, 731–732
Return on investment, 182–183, 188–190, 500
Return on stockholders' equity ratio, 183, 190
Return on total assets ratio, 182–183, 188–190
Reverse stock splits, 537
Revolving credit agreement, 701, 704–705
Rights, 535, 564–566
   valuation, 565–566
Rights offering, 546, 548, 564–566
Rights-on, 565–566
Risk, 44–45, 133–159, 356–370, 595–596, 600–601
   adjusting for, 357–367
      certainty equivalent approach, 360–361
      hurdle rate approach, 359–360
      NPV/payback approach, 358
      risk-adjusted discount rate approach, 358–359, 367–368
      sensitivity analysis, 365–367
      simulation approach, 362–365
      subjective approach, 357–358
   beta risk, 356, 367–370
   business risk, 228–231, 385
   capital asset pricing model, 140–159, 395–397
   exchange rate risk, 777–779
   financial risk, 231–236, 385
   interest rate risk, 108, 385, 634
   measurement of, 135–139
   overall risk, 236–239

portfolio risk, 140–159, 356,
  project risk, 356–367
  systematic risk, 148, 151–154
  unsystematic risk, 148–149
Risk premium, 44, 358–359, 367–
  369, 384–386, 395
Risk structure of interest rates, 41
Risk-adjusted discount rate, 358–
  359, 367–368, 372–373,
  678–679
Risk-free,
  investment, 44
  interest rate, 133, 150–151,
  358–359, 360–361, 372,
  384–385, 395–397
Risk-return tradeoff, 43–45, 151–
  157, 217, 384–386, 520, 526,
  598–607
Robert Morris Associates, 191
"Rule of 72," 64

S

S corporations, 52–53
Safety stock, 601, 687–688
Sale and leaseback, 494
Salvage value, 289–290, 496,
  502–503
Savings and loan associations, 39,
Saving-investment cycle, 35–36
Seasonal dating, 652, 655–657,
  697
Secondary claims, 37
Seconday markets, 38, 540
Securities Act of 1933, 542
Securities and Exchange Commis-
  sion (SEC), 542–543, 706,
  715, 758
Securities Exchange Act of 1934,
  542–543
Security agreement, 666, 696,
  711–712
Security market line, 149–151,
  154–156, 395–397
Security provisions (term loans),
  487–489
Semivariable costs, 218–219
Senior debt, 520
Sensitivity analysis, 264, 365–367
Share repurchases, 468–470
Shareholder (or stockholder)
  wealth maximization, 5–6,
  117–118, 452
Shelf registration, 543
Short hedge, 420
Short selling, 542
Shortage costs, 624–625
Short-term capital gain (or loss),
  50

Short-term credit, 696–713
  negotiated, 696–697
  secured, 696
  spontaneous, 696–697
  types, 696–697
  unsecured, 696
Simple interest, 59–61
Simulation, 362–365
Single loan (note), 701–702
Sinking fund, 523
Sinking fund problem, 71–73
Small Business Administration
  (SBA), 490
Small Business Investment Com-
  panies (SBIC), 490
Social responsibility goals, 6
Sole proprietorship, 33
Sources and uses of funds state-
  ment, 171, 259–263
Sources of comparative financial
  data, 191–194
Sources of funds, 259–261
Speculator, 419–420
Spot (exchange) rate, 773–774
Stable dollar dividend policy, 460–
  463
Standard and Poor's, 191, 524–
  526, 553–555, 706, 715, 740
  bond ratings, 524–526, 553–
  555
  500-stock Index, 542
  manuals, 191
Standard deviation, 135–138
Standard normal probability func-
  tion, 136–138, 225, 236, 363–
  364
Standby underwriting, 548
Stock dividends, 464–468, 472–
  474, 537
Stock-index futures, 421–422
Stock market indexes, 541–542
  Dow Jones Industrial Average,
  541
  Standard and Poor's 500-stock
  Index, 542
Stock quotations, 535–536
Stock repurchases, 468–470,
  537–539
Stock splits, 468, 472–474, 536–
  537
Stockholder rights, 35, 535
Stockholders (or shareholders),
  34, 533
Stockout costs, 677, 679
Straight-bond (or investment) val-
  ue, 577–578
Straight-line depreciation, 294,
  312
Stretching accounts payable,
  698–700

Subordinated debt, 520–521, 760,
  739
Subscription price, 565
Sum-of-years' digits depreciation
  method, 313–314
Suppliers of term loans, 489–491
Synergy, 732, 736
Systematic (or nondiversifiable)
  risk, 148, 151–154

T

Target capital structure, 426
Taxes (income), 48–54, 785–788
Tax aspects of mergers, 741–742
Tax constraints (on dividend poli-
  cy), 454
Tax credits, 50–51, 204–206
Tax Equity and Fiscal Responsibil-
  ity Act (TEFRA) of 1982, 292,
  295, 312
Tax lease, 494–496
Tax Reform Act of 1986, 785–788
Tax status of leases, 498–499
Technical insolvency, 752
Tender offer, 468, 730
10K reports, 194
Term loans, 484–491, 623
  compensating balances, 486
  equity participations, 486–487
  interest costs, 486
  repayment provisions, 484–487
  security provisions and protec-
  tive covenants, 487–489
  suppliers of, 489–491
Term structure of interest rates,
  41, 600, 614–617
Terminal warehouse, 712–713
Third-party equity lease, 494–496
Thrift institutions, 39
TIGR's (Treasury Investment
  Growth Receipts), 524
Times interest earned ratio, 180
Total asset turnover ratio, 178
Trade credit, 648–649, 665–667,
  697–700
  cost, 697–700
  credit terms, 649, 652–657, 697
Transactions costs, 429
Transactions motive, 621
Treasurer, 8–10, 34
Treasury bills, 635
Treasury stock, 468, 537
Trend analysis,
  forecasting, 252–253
  ratios, 186–188
Trustee,
  bankruptcy, 756–757, 759
  bond, 522
Trust receipt, 712

U

Uncertainty, 301-302
Underwriting, 546-549
  flotation costs, 548-549
  negotiated, 546
  purchasing syndicate, 546-547
  spread (or discount), 546-547
  standby, 548
Uniform Commercial Code, 666,
  696
U.S. financial system, 35-38
Unsystematic risk, 148-149
Usable funds, 703, 705
Uses of funds, 259-261, 703, 705

V

Valuation, 102-125, 427-430,
  577-579, 565-566, 581-584,
  733-737
  assets, 102-105
  bonds, 105-112,
  common stocks, 113-122, 124-
  125, 391-394

  convertible securities, 577-579
  merger candidates, 733-737
  net income theory, 427-430
  net operating income theory,
  427-430
  preferred stocks, 112-113
  rights, 565-566
  warrants, 581-584
Variable cost ratio, 222, 650-651
Variable costs, 217-219
Variable income securities, 519-
  533
Vertical merger, 732
Voluntary conversion, 579-580
Voting rights,
  common stockholders, 535,
  563-564
  preferred stock, 531

W

Warrants, 486-487, 570, 580-
  584, 739, 742, 756
  features, 580-581

  reasons for issuing, 581
  valuation, 581-584
Weighted cost of capital, 368,
  399-404, 678
White knight, 730
Wire transfer, 630-631
Working capital management,
  594-607
  levels of investment, 597-600
  proportions of short-term and
  long-term financing, 600-605

Y

Yield curve, 41, 614
Yield to maturity, 109-112, 389

Z

Zero-balance systems, 632
Zero coupon bonds, 111, 524
Zero growth dividend valuation
  model, 120, 393-394

Check Answers To Selected Problems

Chapter 2

1. Rate of return = 14%
3.b. Rate of return = 9.74%
4.a. Expected rate of return = 15.0%

Appendix 2A

1. Tax due = $1,063,450

Chapter 3

1.a. FV_3 = $1,191
3. CSAN = $240,410.40
5. R = $302.43
6. i = 13%
7.a. 9 years
9.a. PV = $584.80
11. i = 20%
14.a. PV = $1,281.58
15. R = $5,907.83
17. R = $13,018.71
20.a. PV = $29,806
22. FV_{25} = $3,386
24. PVAN = $51,354
26. R = $30,807
27. R = $690,274
29. R = $3,890
31.a. PV = $31,401
34. R = $51,980.44
36. FV = $94,337
38. i_m = 3.6% per quarter
41. R = $21,879
45. R = $111,031

Appendix 3A

2. PV = $2,744
4. i = 8.62%

Chapter 4

1.b. P = $800
3.a. P = $1,159
4. P = $964
5. r = 11.5%
9.a. P = $22.22
10.a. P = $88.33
13. P = $21.34
15. P = $57.36
18. P = $16.21

Chapter 5

1.a. $E(R_X)$ = 15%; $E(R_Y)$ = 10%
1.b. σ_X = 11.62%; σ_Y = 4.94%
2. Probability of returns greater than 33% = 15.87%
4.a. P = $27.65
5.a. $E(R)$ = 11.6%
6.a. (i) $E(R)$ = 8.2%; (ii) σ_p = 4.87%
7.b. $E(R)$ = 13.05%
7.c. σ_p = 3.64%
11.a. $E(\text{beta})$ = 1.4
12.a. P = $11.11
16.a. W_A = 61.54%; W_B = 38.46%
17. $E(R_p)$ = 14.93%; σ_p = 2.07%
18.b. σ_p = 7.8% when ρ = 1.0; σ_p = 6.18% when ρ = −0.2
20. β_p = 1.17

Chapter 6

1.a. $222,222
2.a. Firm A: Sales/TA = 1.33; NI/Sales = .15; TA/Equity = 1.50; ROE = .30
3.a. 15%
11. Total Assets = $5,000,000; Cash = $222,000
13.b. Current ratio = 2.2; Quick ratio = 1.4
14. $4,666,680
16. New return on equity = 14.29%
22.a. Return on equity = 25%
23.a. Return on equity = 28.57%

Chapter 7

1. EPS at sales of $6.6 million = $6.90
4.a. DCL = 2.778
7.a. (i) 5,000 copies
10.b. DOL = 1.875; DFL = 1.67; DCL = 3.13
11.a. $3,000,000
14.a. DOL = 10.67
14.b. DFL = 1.765
18. EPS = $1.74
20. 9.2%

Chapter 8

1.b. Additional financing needed = $500,000
3. Additional financing needed = $500,000
6. Loans needed in January = $40,000
9. Additional financing required = $85 million

Chapter 9

1.a. $2,850; $4,180; $3,990; $3,990; $3,990
2. ITC recapture = $6,000; Tax on depreciation recapture = $6,860
4. Year 1 = $400,000; Year 2 = $900,000
6. NCF = $12,333
9. NCF_1 = $188.4; NCF_2 = $220.32
10. NINV = $340,500
14. NCF_1 = $4,194; NCF_2 = $5,311
16. $130,150

Chapter 10

1.b. NPV = $158
2. IRR = 11.58%
4. PV = $364.53
8. NPV = $16,077
9. NPV = $20,264
10. IRR ≈ 8%
12. NPV = $5,431
14.a. NPV = $24,266
17. n ≈ 19 years

Appendix 10A

1.a. NPV_A = $1,888.5; NPV_B = $2,292

Chapter 11

1.a. $117.50
1.b. $47.10
3.a. 3.8%
7.a. NPV = $503,600
8.a. NPV = $158,061
9.b. NPV = −$0.1795 million

11.a. NPV = $255,250
14.c. NPV = $18,705

Chapter 12

2. k_i = 7.2%
4.b. k_p ≈ 13%
5.a. k_e = 12.9%
8.a. k_e = 13.4%
9. k_a = 17.3%
12. First break point = $33,333,333; k_a for first block = 13.10%
14. First break point = $60,000,000; k_a for first block = 13.19%

Chapter 13

1. $10,000
4.a. 45% debt and 55% equity— with bankruptcy and without agency costs
5.a. EBIT* = $15 million
7.a. EBIT* = $2.4 million
10.a. EBIT* = $170,000
11.a. EBIT* = $133.2 million
14.a. 26%

Chapter 14

1.b. $0.50
3. 16.7%
4. $1,425,000
7.b. $1.60

Chapter 15

1.a. R = $1,467,567
5.a. $972,373
7. i ≈ 11.8%
8.a. Year 1 payment = $25,083; Year 4 payment = $55,083
9.a. i = 13%
12.a. i = 6.24%
13.a. NAL = $10,624
16. Initial outflow = $10 million; Cash inflow$_1$ = $3.6 million

Chapter 16

1.b. 7.5%
2.c. $830
3.a. r = 14%

5.b. $21.4 million
8.a. Common stock = 40.1%; Preferred stock = 31.9%
10. Current assets = $58; Common stock at par = $6; Contributed capital in excess of par = $47; Retained earnings = $55
11. r = 14.5%

Appendix 16A

1. NPV refunding = $7,756,203
3.a. $0.455 in both cases

Chapter 17

1.c. $0
3.a. $1,000
3.b. $726
4.a. 11.98 shares
6.a. $1.50
6.b. $3.50
7.c. $0
8.c. $131.25 million

Chapter 18

1. ROE: Aggressive = 12.13%; Moderate = 11.07%; Conservative = 10.21%
3.a.(i) Aggressive = 12.29%; Moderate = 12.0%; Conservative = 11.73%
4.a.(iii) Aggressive = 1.25; Moderate = 1.67; Conservative = 2.50
5.a.(i) Aggressive = 9.54%; Moderate = 9.08%; Conservative = 8.67%
7.b. $7.79 million
10.a. Net cost = $886,667

Chapter 19

1.a. $7,500,000
3.d. −$15,000
5. $418,750
6.c. $92,500
9.a. $10,617.10
11.a. $262,111

Chapter 20

1.b. 38 days
3. $7,000
5. $20,000
7.c. −$11,083
9. $122,417
11. $17,500
12. $1,186,667

Chapter 21

1.a. 80,000
3. 5,500
4. $1,911.25
6.a. Finance book: 17,678; Economics book: 10,607
8.a. 30,000
10.a. 5,500

Chapter 22

1.b. $280,000
2.a. 14.69%
5.a. 8.70%
6.a. 11.67%
9.a. $16,000,000
11.c. 12.4%
13.c. 20.4%
16. 22%

Chapter 23

1.b. 19.0%
3.a. $4.045
3.d. $4.258
4.a. 0.50 shares Ball for each Keyes share
6. 6 years

Chapter 24

1. Funds available for creditors = $3,400,000; Bank notes receive $1,600,000

Chapter 25

1. $10,358
2.a. Cost per watch = $49.72
3.a. +57.1%
6.a. $62,500